世界交通运输工程技术论坛（WTC2021）论文集

（下册）

世界交通运输大会执委会 编

人民交通出版社股份有限公司

北京

内 容 提 要

本书为世界交通运输工程技术论坛(WTC2021)论文集,是由中国公路学会、世界交通运输大会执委会精选的378篇论文汇编而成。此论文集重点收录了交通运输工程领域的前沿研究及创新成果,分为公路工程、桥梁工程、隧道工程、交通工程、运输规划、水上运输、轨道交通、航空运输、交叉学科9个方向。

本书可供从事交通运输工程等领域的人员参考,也可供院校相关师生学习。

图书在版编目(CIP)数据

世界交通运输工程技术论坛(WTC2021)论文集:上中下册/世界交通运输大会执委会编. — 北京:人民交通出版社股份有限公司,2021.6

ISBN 978-7-114-17355-4

Ⅰ.①世… Ⅱ.①世… Ⅲ.①交通工程—文集 Ⅳ.①U491-53

中国版本图书馆 CIP 数据核字(2021)第 095758 号

Shijie Jiaotong Yunshu Gongcheng Jishu Luntan(WTC2021)Lunwenji(Xiace)

书　名:	世界交通运输工程技术论坛(WTC2021)论文集(下册)
著 作 者:	世界交通运输大会执委会
责任编辑:	韩亚楠　郭晓旭
责任校对:	赵媛媛　卢 弦
责任印制:	张 凯
出版发行:	人民交通出版社股份有限公司
地　　址:	(100011)北京市朝阳区安定门外外馆斜街3号
网　　址:	http://www.ccpcl.com.cn
销售电话:	(010)59757973
总 经 销:	人民交通出版社股份有限公司发行部
经　　销:	各地新华书店
印　　刷:	北京交通印务有限公司
开　　本:	880×1230　1/16
印　　张:	163
字　　数:	4900 千
版　　次:	2021年6月　第1版
印　　次:	2021年6月　第1次印刷
书　　号:	ISBN 978-7-114-17355-4
定　　价:	600.00元(含上、中、下册)

(有印刷、装订质量问题的图书由本公司负责调换)

世界交通运输大会执委会学部委员会

编 委 会

主　　席　　沙爱民　　张占民

副主席　　龙奋杰　　陈春阳　　安　实　　顾祥林
　　　　　　王云鹏　　刘　攀　　赵　鹏　　何　川
　　　　　　杜修力　　严　伟　　王小勇　　谈传生
　　　　　　吴超仲　　周建庭　　巨荣云

编辑委员会

主　　任　　刘文杰

委　　员　　汪海年　　陈艾荣　　陈建勋　　陈　峻
　　　　　　姚恩建　　葛颖恩　　张卫华　　曹先彬
　　　　　　王兴举　　等

本 册 目 录

第五篇 运 输 规 划

道路停车电子化收费背景下的居住停车综合治理研究
………………………………… 赵禄成 姚广铮 秦逸飞 蔡传慈 刘 洋(1809)
建设京港台高铁(阜阳—黄冈段)的必要性——基于沿线旅客出行意愿特征分析
………………………………… 武方涛 孙斯嘉 李禹志 郝鑫桐 史伟伟(1813)
基于多源数据的出租车出行需求特征影响研究 ……… 严 海 刘珂彤 伍速锋 刘润坤(1820)
基于改进Ga-LM-BP神经网络的城市轨道交通短时客流预测研究 ………………… 姚 帆(1826)
大型活动期间非常态应急接驳车辆调度研究综述 …………………… 张啸林 熊志华(1832)
基于GM-RBF组合模型的地铁进站短时客流预测
………………………………… 陈亚鑫 徐永能 何 流 程 慧 张 晨(1842)
考虑出行成本及个人属性的出行方式选择模型 ……… 曾明哲 南彦洲 付泽坤 刘林建(1850)
RRM应用于城际高铁出行的研究分析 ………………………… 刘 林 孙小慧 左 志(1856)
基于问卷调查的上海自贸区临港新片区综合交通体系优化策略研究 ………… 刘 梅 顾 煜(1859)
基于节能减排的交通运输规划研究 ………………………………………………… 樊宏哲(1867)
交通基础设施网络综合立体高质量发展研究——以浙江省为例
………………………………………… 李 乐 丁 剑 程亚杰 何佳玮(1870)
基于Tropos-SWOT模型的道路客运发展战略分析
………………………………………… 左博睿 帅 斌 吴贞瑶 赏珂祺 李 尧(1872)
西部陆海新通道的水运战略构想 ………………………………………… 王 斌 杨秋平(1879)
基于SWOT的产业路发展情况分析——以陕西省为例 …………………… 马 欣 马 帆(1884)
Study on the Efficiency Evaluation and Influencing Factors of Transportation Infrastructure
in Jiangsu Province ……………………………………………… Xinxin Hu Hong Chen(1889)
国家道条修订与上海道路运输管理转型 ………………………………………… 陈俊彦(1897)
考虑旅客出行选择行为的高速铁路票价定价策略的研究综述 …… 刘 琼 孙小慧 左 志(1905)
北京CBD区域共享单车使用规律研究 ………………………… 潘 龙 姚恩建 陈艳艳(1911)
韧性视角下城市群交通网络评估 ………………………………… 陈明玉 陆化普 徐佳君(1916)
基于文本挖掘与关联规则相结合的天窗未兑现原因诊断分析
………………………………………… 徐长安 李晟东 李斯涵 倪少权(1921)
基于VISSIM仿真隧道出口与平面交叉小净距路段交通适应性研究
………………………………………… 李芷倩 张 驰 胡瑞来(1925)
京津冀区域道路运输燃料清洁化策略研究 ……… 宋媛媛 黄全胜 肖 杨 王人洁 姜文汐(1933)
基于PK-means算法的菜鸟驿站JDC选址研究 ……… 杜 渐 刘宇畅 戴 明 邢宏伟(1940)
基于改进TOPSIS法的省际物流发展能力评价 ……… 胡刘康 王来军 王 宁 楼国良 任 哲(1946)
基于专用车道的危险品道路运输路径研究 ………………………… 陈海燕 常连玉 麦 乐(1957)
Research on Location Problem of Express Distribution Center based on Barycenter Method

...... Yiwei Zheng(1963)

基于博弈分析的电子产品逆向物流研究 ...... 王雪韵　胡大伟　张世鹏(1969)

A Research to Assess the Logistics Solutions for Pharmaceutical Companies in Outbreak Situations Based on Fuzzy TOPSIS ...... Shuaiqi Wang(1974)

基于 Floyd 及 KL-means 聚类算法的交通运输网络设计 ...... 林　琰　孙　笑　杨　硕(1984)

Unmanned Aerial Vehicle Route Planning with the Error-Correction-Point-Based Navigation: Model and Solution Algorithm ...... Ziyu Zhang　Wei Zhang　Zhaoyao Bao　Chi Xie(1989)

On the Minimum Required Driving Ranges of Electric Vehicles to Overcome Some Travel Restriction Barriers ...... Jiapei Li　Chi Xie(1997)

具有充电窗口和分时电价的电动公交车辆时空充电策略优化
...... 鲍照耀　李昕妍　傅寒珺　李佳佩　丁稼轩　谢　驰(2005)

基于第三方物流服务模式的生鲜产品企业合作博弈研究 ...... 张世鹏　胡大伟　王雪韵(2009)

Integrated Operator-Based and User-Based Vehicle Relocation for One-Way Carsharing Systems ...... Linzhi Jiang　Chi Xie(2016)

中心城市周边中小城市的交通发展路径 ...... 李子木(2023)

城市中心区快速路布局与用地关系协调的思考 ...... 毛建民　彭　挺　张　序(2029)

基于地铁站点客流规律的城市功能布局探析 ...... 姚　帆　王静嫒(2035)

Optimization Strategy of County Public Service Facilities Based On the Analysis of Residents' Travel Behavior ——A Case Study of Typical Counties
...... Yueyan Zhang　Qian Chen　Xiaoyu Wang(2044)

交通强国背景下中小城市综合交通规划的探讨与实践 ...... 任彦铭　张　旭(2058)

响应预约需求的定制公交线路动态规划模型与求解算法 ... 郑　好　王　云　闫学东　李云伟(2063)

基于熵值法与 DEA 的城市公交线路组合评价方法 ...... 王　瑄　齐　超　陈学武(2071)

大型高铁枢纽布局及交通组织特征研究 ...... 蔡燕飞　刘安迪　戴继锋　罗　彦(2080)

中小城市公交免费政策下居民出行行为研究——以济源市为例 ...... 李　帅　朱成明　肖新梁(2085)

Exploring the Impacts of Accessibility Measures to Public Transport Equity with Decomposition of Zenga index ...... Zhigang Yao　Yuhao Fu　Jie Yang(2089)

基于 POI 数据的公共服务设施步行可达性分析——以上海市为例 ...... 余　淼　王　洋(2098)

新能源汽车推广政策对消费者购买汽车的效果研究 ...... 高　蕾　王碧玲　柳靖钰(2101)

保障高速公路畅通问题的研究 ...... 刘德雄(2106)

浙江省高速公路网合理规模研究 ...... 程亚杰　何佳玮　李　乐　戴美伟　陈坤杰(2109)

Applicability of Immersive Virtual Reality Platform in Pedestrian Crossing Experiments
...... Dingyi Ye　Yuliang Hong　Junfeng Li　Guanghua Zhao　Wenbo Huang(2113)

国内外机动车驾驶人安全考核与培训分析及比对 ...... 徐　鑫　刘传攀　袁天宇　马兰婕(2124)

窗口服务人数配置标准的研究 ...... 刘德雄(2131)

The Role of 5G Enabling Rail Innovations and Applications
...... Rui Xue　Zhiqiang Ma　Xiaoning Ma　Siqi Sun　Dongsheng Yang(2134)

智慧出行服务新模式的解析和场景应用 ...... 殷　韬　廖璟埸(2142)

基于影响非对称分析的旅客空巴联程服务满意度研究 ...... 张霁扬　季钧一　杨　敏(2149)

浅析非现场执法在公路治超领域的应用 ...... 韩国兴　阿米娜·玉努斯　陈　晖　张柱庭(2157)

A Customized Passenger Transport Service Mix Pricing Study Based on CVP Analysis Method and Dynamic Pricing Strategy ...... Jiawei Gui　Qunqi Wu　Yahong Jiang(2162)

公私合营模式下环境可持续的道路收费与养护策略优化方法 ...... 赵　宇　陈　笑(2170)

第六篇 水上运输

三峡河段智能通航框架与评价体系构建 ……………………………………… 谭志荣　王　洋　王海滨(2185)
世界一流港口集疏运网络建设 …………………………………………………………… 刘万锋　周嘉男(2192)
垃圾重量不确定环境下船舶收集海洋垃圾路径优化
………………………………………… 陈晓惠　段　刚　范　涛　魏越娇　陶　玲(2195)
Risk Evolution Simulation on Process Safety of LNG-Fueled Vessel Traffic with STAMP
　　Model and Genetic Algorithm ……… Wenjing Li　Shenping Hu　Shaoyong Xuan　Jinxian Weng(2200)
珠江口水域航标灯塔桩设计与施工刍议 ……………………………………………… 袁靖周　岳志伟(2212)
基于无线自组网的多媒体应急通信保障系统 ………………… 谭志荣　陈　维　冒　欣　王海滨(2219)
模袋混凝土在码头前沿护底工程中的应用 ……………………………… 封有德　陶　然　黄睿奕(2222)
LNG 码头前沿冲突水域风险可视化研究 …………………… 谭志荣　屈文鹏　王　洋　叶晓庆(2228)
船舶号灯可见度评价模型 ……………………………………… 阎际驰　朱金善　李春男　李志荣(2233)
基于 MNL 模型的中国邮轮消费选择行为研究 ………………………… 吴鋆杰　余　尧　肖军华(2239)
海洋强国建设背景下我国船员流失问题与对策 ………………………………………… 刘嘉琪　葛颖恩(2243)
Liner Shipping Route and Schedule Optimization with Uncertain Sailing Time: Application to
　　the Northern Sea Route ……………………………………………………… Jiaxuan Ding　Chi Xie(2246)
Research and Application of Multifunctional Light Buoy in Guangdong-Hong Kong-Macao
　　Greater Bay Area ………………………………………………………… Hong Chen　Jingzhou Yuan(2257)

第七篇 轨道交通

基于社会力模型的地铁站行人流组织优化研究 ……………………………………… 詹　郡　李昕光(2269)
既有线运用 27t 轴重货车经济效益研究 …………………………………………………………… 宋文波(2273)
对东北地区高铁运输组织管理的观察与思考 ……………………………………………………… 程显平(2279)
地铁短期客流预测模型研究综述 …………………… 张　源　郝亚睿　张　鹏　李佳晨　温　岩(2285)
列车网络控制系统 CCU 安全冗余设计 ………………………………… 张　凯　梁海泉　胡景泰(2289)
基于改进决策树 SVM 多分类算法的 GSM-R 系统干扰识别研究 ……………………… 张志满　马　征(2293)
基于车—车通信的新型 CBTC 系统运力分析 …………………………… 张启鹤　王海峰　叶晨雨(2299)
基于 PSO-RF-SVR 组合模型的城市轨道短时客流预测研究 ………………………… 徐金华　鲁文博(2308)
基于 SVDD 的滚动轴承健康状态评估 ………………… 巫忠书　杜红梅　杨　阳　李夫忠　李凤林(2313)
铁路电务大数据平台框架体系研究 ……………………………………………………………… 陈建译(2318)
基于多目标跟踪的地铁车厢客流检测方法 ……………………………… 郭　宁　胡小晨　董德存(2323)
季节性冻土挡墙综合检测与安全风险评估 ……………………………… 张　棋　牛乐乐　苏　谦(2329)
Statistical Analysis and Prediction Model for Maintenance Management in Urban Railway System
………………………………………………………… Yixin Shen　Chi Kwong Wong　Siu Ming Lo(2337)
四轮转向车辆转向中心位置后移研究 …………………………………… 杨更生　杨蔡进　张卫华(2350)
城市轨道交通车辆内置消毒装置的设计及应用研究
………………………………………… 涂　杰　吴　娟　梁同天　黄小庆　袁　满(2358)
Study on Wheel Flat-Induced Impact Force Considering the Flexibility of Wheelset
………………………………………………………………………… Wei Wang　Qiyuan Peng(2366)
基于最优航向索引算法的门式虚拟轨道列车循迹控制策略 …………………………… 孙泽良　冷　涵(2376)

磁悬浮列车基础梁的柔性对悬浮稳定性的影响 ………………………… 李 钦 沈 钢(2383)
轨道交通用直线电机的电磁力对比分析 ………………… 张树鑫 黄苏丹 曹广忠 吴 超(2387)
时速400公里高速铁路接触网弹性吊索结构优化研究 ………… 陈 可 鲁小兵 杨 洋 杨成吉(2395)

第八篇 航空运输

基于时空图卷积网络的机场流量和航线流量预测
  ……………………………………………… 姚 远 卞 磊 刘 宇 唐红武 王殿胜(2405)
飞行态势—管制相依网络的脆弱性分析 ………… 林福根 温祥西 吴明功 王泽坤 杨文达(2414)
基于航迹预测的随机化飞行冲突探测方法 ………… 徐鑫宇 万路军 蔡 明 高志周(2422)
世界繁忙机场空管运行分析框架研究 ………… 许健武 许超前 唐奇志 和 平 李文峰(2428)
不同温度和湍流强度下尾涡演化规律的大涡模拟研究 ……… 潘卫军 罗玉明 韩 帅 王靖开(2435)
A New Metric for the Psychomotor Vigilance Test Based on Standard Deviation
  ……………………………………………… Sun Ruishan Han Shaohua Zhang Yao(2440)
基于改进STAMP模型的应急响应系统设计与情报体系构建分析——以航空器特情事件为例
  …………………………………………………………………………… 岳仁田 李君尉(2450)
未来空域下无人机通信性能指标研究 ………………… 周 强 卫永安 刘广才 王龙杰(2459)
基于人工势场法的无人机路径规划 ………………………………… 梁卜文 张晋通(2462)
无人机运行风险分析研究 ………………………………… 周 强 张杰玮 刘广才(2468)
多目标决策下快速出口滑行道位置的计算方法 … 黄学林 王观虎 耿 昊 雷继超 王 伟(2472)
航空器推出翼尖运动学轨迹模型分析研究 ………………… 潘卫军 张启阳 朱新平(2477)
昆明长水国际机场到达层出租车上客区改善研究 ………… 马书欣 李晓东 陈 兴(2484)
城市群背景下面向机场群协同发展的交通韧性评价研究 ………… 徐佳君 陆化普 陈明玉(2488)

第九篇 交叉学科

基于图注意力卷积网络的短时交通流预测 ………… 潘卫鹏 郭唐仪 唐 坤 何 流(2495)
基于BiGRU-LAN的航空器适航命名实体识别方法 ……………………… 衡红军 胡 刚(2500)
我国智慧交通应用体验和未来建设 …………………………………… 盛一凡 陈宽民(2506)
柴油车油耗测量方法及测量不确定度的对比 ………… 蔡盼盼 景 峥 李向红 张春化(2511)
Optimised Decision Making of Transportation Infrastructure Asset Management ……… Jiarong Li(2519)
基于收费数据的高速公路可达性特征分析 ………………… 李起辉 胡爱辉 向宏杨(2527)
Analysis of Factors Affecting Passenger Boarding Comfort Based on a Cabin Environmental
  Stress Model ……………………………………………… Lina Ma Yong Tian Can Xu(2533)
Design of a New Cooperative Vehicle-Infrastructure System Based on Multi-Access Edge
  Computing Devices ………… Jinjue Li Ziliang He Yuxuan Sun Ruochen Hao Wanjing Ma(2544)
Analysis on the Relationship between the Coordinated Development of Transportation and
  Tourism ……………………… Juan Wu Jie Tu Yajun Yu Simeng Guo Jia Peng(2554)
基于累积前景理论的旅游交通方式研究综述 ……………… 路社非 孙小慧 左 志(2561)
铁路路堑区域风吹雪作用下防雪栅对积雪重分布影响及相关因素分析 ……… 李鹏翔 白明洲(2566)
Deformation and Monitoring Analysis of Soil Rock Composite Foundation Pit under Moving Load
  ……………………………………… Tengfei Jiang Annan Jiang Mengfei xu Xingshong Li(2571)

第五篇 运输规划

道路停车电子化收费背景下的居住停车综合治理研究

赵禄成　姚广铮　秦逸飞　蔡传慈　刘洋

（南京市城市与交通规划设计研究院股份有限公司北京分公司）

摘　要　机动车保有量与停车位增速的不匹配发展，使得停车供需矛盾日益凸显。道路停车电子化收费发挥了价格调控资源的作用，并通过居住认证等方式为缓解居住小区"停车难"提供了有效抓手，但由于存在小区配建不足、居民缴费意愿不强、局部停车秩序差、局部存量资源待优化等现实情况，居住停车仍存在一些问题和较大改善空间。本文以北京市某区为例，对居住停车的居民意愿、道路停车电子化收费的实施效果和现状居住停车仍存问题进行全面调查与分析，并从政府层面、小区层面和社会层面提出了改善措施建议，包括优化改善原则、完善体制机制、增容停车设施、精细调度治理、宣传执法加强等方面。

关键词　运输规划　停车治理　交通调查与分析　居住停车　综合治理

0　引　言

机动车保有量的持续增长，而车位供应总量及增速的不足，导致居住小区停车问题日益凸显，部分学者对居住小区的停车治理开展了调研与分析工作。根据北京市普查及预测初步结果显示，北京市仍有较大车位缺口。道路停车位使用便捷，停车免费也引发了部分百姓对于"免费车位"的诉求，在总体供需仍有缺口的情况下，不利于有偿车位的高效利用。

《北京市机动车停车条例》要求"本市机动车停车坚持有偿使用、共享利用、严格执法、社会共治。"北京市各区均已开展道路停车电子化收费改革工作，营造了更好的停车环境，但居民投诉停车问题常常发生。在此背景下，通过交通调查方式获取原始数据，以居民意愿为切入点，分析道路停车电子化收费后的实施效果和实施后居住停车仍存的问题，并提出针对性的建议措施，对于切实改善居住停车具有一定研究意义。

1　民意调查与分析

停车治理特别是居住停车治理应坚持"以人为本"。为更好地了解当地百姓对居住停车的看法与建议，开展问卷调查，为停车调研及居住停车改善策略研究提供依据。

民意调查以问卷形式向某区的居民发放，共发放问卷151份，有效问卷135份（非研究范围内的常住居民和问卷信息填写不全的均视为无效问卷）。有效问卷的群体中，年龄介于26~61岁之间，男女比例为58∶77。其中，认为停车最严重的问题为"停车难"的108份，占比80%，认为"停车乱"的23份，占比17%，其他4份，占比3%，占比情况如图1所示。对问卷反馈的问题所在位置进行分析，停车难问题点位空间集聚性凸显，主要分布在几个居住小区抱团的片区；停车秩序乱的道路主要集中在居住小区周边的低等级道路。

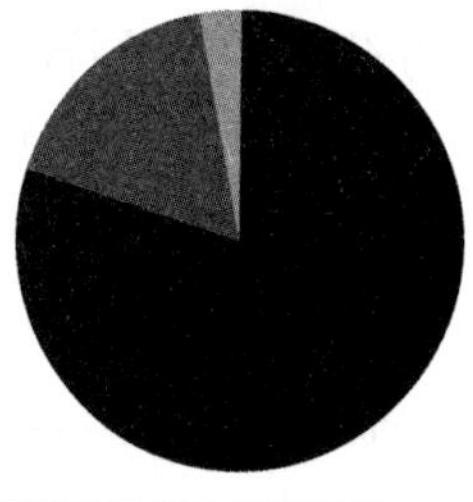

图1　停车问题民意调查结果

2　停车调查与分析

2.1　电子化收费道路停车特征分析

实施电子收费对避免停车收费"政策失灵"具有较强重要性。本文研究所在区的部分道路停车位实施电子化收费一段时间后,道路秩序明显改善,热点区域价格调控作用初显。

2.1.1 电子收费后道路停车位利用率降低

2019年该区正式实施道路停车电子化收费,电子化收费实现了道路停车从免费到收费的过渡。经调研,电子化收费实施前后道路停车位的使用情况见表1。实施电子化收费前,道路停车位基本呈饱和状态,整体利用率超过90%,日间和夜间的车位几乎均被占用。实施电子化收费后车位利用率整体大幅下降,停车位利用率仅为38%。

电子收费前后停车位利用率　　　　表1

道路序号	收费前日间利用率	收费前夜间利用率	收费后日间利用率	收费后夜间利用率
1	100%	100%	81%	53%
2	97%	95%	22%	11%
3	100%	100%	21%	5%
4	83%	99%	32%	40%
5	81%	95%	10%	3%
6	83%	84%	18%	17%
7	100%	93%	24%	2%
8	91%	96%	60%	7%
9	100%	100%	89%	16%
10	86%	83%	17%	8%
11	92%	93%	57%	11%
12	95%	98%	20%	9%

注:调研日期为电子收费前工作日日间和夜间(时间跨度3个月,共开展4轮调查)。

由于较多老百姓对价格有一定的敏感度,收费后的车位整体利用率较低,价格调控需求的作用明显起效。对于热点区域周边(3号路和12号路),未实施电子化收费时道路停车位使用率很高,现状由"一位难求"变为了"一位可求",即价格挤走了一部分非必要需求。

2.1.2 电子化收费后不同道路停放次数差异性明显

不同道路的停车总次数见图2,每条路的车位总停车次数差异明显。一方面,不同道路的车位总数存在差异;另一方面,不同道路使用率确实存在差异,1号路和3号路的车位数相差小于5个,而总停车次数的差值超过9000次。进一步分析车位周转率可知,不同道路的车位使用频率差异较大,如图3所示,1号路和2号路的差值高达172,较低的周转率表明车位周转的活跃程度低,1号路、9号路和11号路周边商业、办公较多,月周转率较高,表明该3条路存在相对旺盛的出行停车需求。

注:月周转率为某条道路月停放总数/车位数。

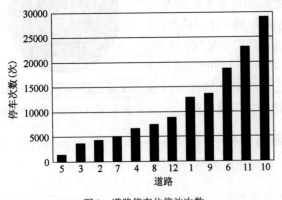

图2　道路停车位停放次数

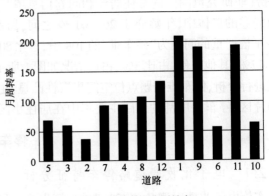

图3　道路停车位周转率

2.1.3 电子化收费后道路停车位的使用集中于日间

电子化收费后，老百姓使用停车位的单次停放时长较短。单次停放时长分布如图 4 所示，停放时长绝大多数小于 2h，占比达到 82.2%。可见，电子收费实施后，价格发挥了明显的调控需求的作用，也是实施前后利用率降低的重要原因。

不同道路停车位的出、入停车位时间分布如图 5 和图 6 所示，驶入停车位的时间从 7 时后呈现快速增加趋势，9 时～15 时为高峰停车时间，即电子化收费实施后白天的车位利用率较夜间高很多。

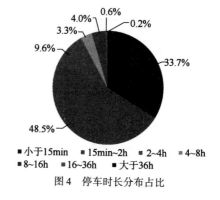

图 4　停车时长分布占比

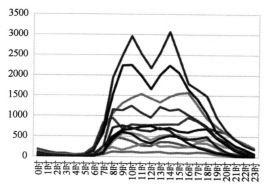

图 5　不同道路停车位车辆驶入车位时间分布

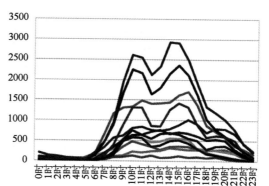

图 6　不同道路停车位车辆驶离车位时间分布

道路停车电子化收费改革之初考虑到居住停车问题，夜间（19 点～次日 7 点）停车费率优惠，而实施电子化收费后，19 点后停入、次日 6 点～9 点间驶出的次数占全部总停放次数的比例不足 2%，表明跨夜停放的车辆较少，夜间道路停车位的服务能力不高，结合调研，问卷调查中部分"停车难"小区周边的道路停车位也存在闲置。

2.2　居住停车供需情况

随着人民生活水平的提高，户均家庭用车数显著增加，2015 年北京市交通大调查数据表明北京市户均拥车数量约 0.5 辆/户；2020 年对该区的部分居住小区开展供需调查，户均拥车数达到 0.85 辆/户，接近 1 户 1 车。由于规划建设滞后于发展需求，经统计，该区域户均配建车位数仅为 0.6 个/户，而老旧小区的配建较低，停车供需矛盾更加突出。经统计分析，约 78% 的居住小区存在配建车位不满足停车需求的情况，户均车位缺口高达 0.4 个/户，如图 7 所示。

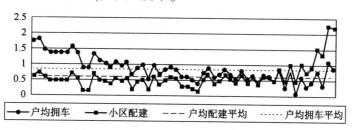

图 7　居住小区拥车和配建停车位数量分布图

2.3　道路停车秩序调查

道路停车电子化采用"高位视频 + 停车管理员"的模式，每个路段配置了停车管理员，引导车辆入位，进一步保障了设置停车位路段的停车秩序，电子化收费道路停车秩序明显改善。

通过对道路实地调查发现，道路违停而临近小区内确存在闲置车位，见表 2。个别小区在问卷调查中被提及"停车难"的小区，表明部分居民认为"停车难"并非无位可停，而是无免费车位可停。

小区内闲置车位与周边道路车辆违停对比　　　　　　　　　　表2

序　号	小区内部闲置车位数(辆)	周边违停数量(辆)
1	100	50
2	142	131
3	143	95
4	150	60
5	199	65
6	220	100
7	256	130
8	270	110
9	300	70

电子收费实施后,出现了电子化收费车位闲置而周边道路及步道违停严重的现象。部分电子化收费道路停车位闲置,而相交道路的人行道和自行车道均存在较多违停,干扰交通秩序,影响城市形象。

3　居住停车治理实施对策建议

居住停车治理关乎民生,治理工作的有效开展涉及政府、小区及社会企业等多方面,需相关单位协同共治,牢牢把握以"人民为中心,实事求是"的原则,以改革道路停车电子化收费为着力点,治理工作延伸至居住停车层面,通过完善工作机制、优化资源利用、新建设施增容、科学调控需求、落实执法宣传保障等措施,有效缓解居住停车难题。

3.1　小区层面:明确实施主体,内外充分挖潜

(1)开展问题自诊,内部充分利用。小区停车问题的实施主体应为全体业主(或业委会)。现状一些小区"停车难"并非真的无车位,而是"无免费车位"或"收费与服务不匹配,内部车位闲置",所以在其他资源接入小区停车治理前,应由全体业主(或业委会)完成初步"问题自诊",将"内部停车资源已实现充分利用"作为利用外部资源的前置条件。

(2)内部挖潜增容,明确管理策略。完成问题自诊的居住小区,一方面,进一步内部挖潜,即小区内腾退空地、平改立等方式增加停车位;另一方面,需求规划,以家庭为单位制定停车位的分配规则和分配方案。

(3)外部积极拓展,错时认证补充。进一步挖掘小区周边的停车资源,如公共建筑的停车资源、道路停车资源等,通过"错时共享、居住认证"等方式,满足居住小区停车需求的同时也提升了周边停车资源的利用率。

3.2　政府层面:完善体制机制,加强部门配合

(1)完善体制机制,压实属地责任。属地政府应作为居住停车综治的"吹哨人",发挥"街乡吹哨,部门报道"制度优势,通过压实属地责任,发挥主观能动性,盘活用活区域资源,并协调调动相关委办局支持,相关单位各司其职,衔接配合。

(2)布局产业发展,停车设施增容。通过政策引导推动停车产业化发展,引导社会资本投资规划建设停车场,包括闲置地块改造临时停车场、停车场用地新建扩建停车场等。

(3)建设智慧停车平台,赋能精细治理。建设智慧平台,统筹区域停车资源,实现道路停车位、路外停车位的信息联动,充分发挥既有停车资源的效能,实现停车资源优化配置,提升行业管理水平。

(4)加强宣传执法,改善停车秩序。通过宣传有助于激发更好的治理效果,加大停车执法力度,加大热点区域巡查及非现场执法设备的投入力度。

3.3　社会层面:引入专业团队,促进产业发展

(1)停车系统信息化程度不高是制约停车管理精细化、百姓出行便捷化、停车运营高效化的阻碍。

虽然道路停车管理已实现数据化、动态化和可视化,但现状路外停车场存在着独自管理、手段落后的现象,且停车场信息不互通,缺失一个统一的停车信息平台来统筹利用资源。

(2)充分吸收优秀规划、设计等咨询单位的实践经验,使停车发展战略、停车规划等顶层设计科学、合理和可落地。此外,开展项目时应兼顾区域整体性,停车相关的单体项目与区域关联性极强,应注意二者协同性。

(3)专业的停车建设运营管理企业具备业务能力强、涉足产业链全、资金充足等优势,专业团队在提供优质服务的同时成本控制相对较低。若统筹区域停车资源,可充分发挥资源集中的改善效果,如服务统一性(一个信息平台、一套支付系统)和车位高效利用(错时共享、动态调价)。

4 结　语

长远来看,居住停车综合治理体系应从需求出发,打造"智慧赋能溯源需求,价格杠杆调控需求,产业发展满足需求"的模式,近期应积极推动相关措施促进停车体系优质发展:第一,深入扩大道路停车电子化收费改革,取消"有位失管"道路停车位,并严格执法;第二,引导社会资本投资建设运营公共停车场,并依托信息管理平台建立动调控体系,促进产业发展平衡,实现区域动态供需平衡。

参考文献

[1] 刘娜,陈莹. 扬州市居民住宅区停车位现状调查和治理策略研究[J]. 经济研究导刊,2013(04):179-181.

[2] 单伟娜,宁超. 天津城镇化进程中老旧小区停车治理研究[C]// 2019城市发展与规划论文集. 2019.

[3] 郭劲松,徐婷,寇美玲,等. 老旧小区停车综合治理研究-以长沙市为例[J]. 城乡规划:城市地理学术版(3期):65-71.

[4] 关宏志,严海,王兆荣,等. 停车产业化政策分析及建议——以北京市为例[J]. 城市交通,2009(02):7-12.

[5] 北京市第十五届人民代表大会常务委员会. 北京市机动车停车条例[J]. 北京市人大常委会公报,2018(2).

[6] 容军. 北京路侧停车收费政策完善及对"政策失灵"的思考[J]. 道路交通与安全,2018,018(004):1-5.

[7] 王晓明. 关于北京市停车问题的思考[J]. 城市交通,2005(03):32-35.

建设京港台高铁(阜阳—黄冈段)的必要性
——基于沿线旅客出行意愿特征分析

武方涛　孙斯嘉　李禹志　郝鑫桐　史伟伟

(长安大学)

摘　要　阜阳—黄冈高铁项目是国家铁路网"八纵八横"京港台高速铁路的重要组成部分,其北段商丘至阜阳段与商合杭高铁共线,现已建成通车,南段黄州至黄梅段已在建设中,而本路段高铁线路的建设将弥补整段京港台高铁的覆盖空白区。本文通过分析沿线旅客出行意愿特征,具体为分析沿线旅客出行基本特征、出行基本情况和出行选择意愿等特征,来阐述新建阜阳—黄冈高铁的必要性,为决策者提供依据,为项目投资者提供参考。

关键词　阜阳—黄冈高铁　建设必要性　出行意愿特征

0 引言

本路线起于阜阳枢纽,跨越安徽、河南、湖北,西连中原城市群支撑城市,西北和北部连接中原城市群及皖北中心城市,东面通往长三角,往南通向以武汉为中心的长江中游城市群,线路全长约328km。

目前的研究和文献中鲜有论述京九高铁阜阳—黄冈段的建设必要性。常占奎从路网功能定位及运输需求预测方面阐述了新建温武吉铁路的建设必要性;李志鹏、张博等从地区社会经济方面来研究建设甬台温高铁的必要性;江佳璐通过对桂林至湛江铁路的运量预测结果及与相关路线进行对比来验证项目建设的必要性;任峥峥以沿江通道的区位特征、产业布局、经济特征为依据分析了沿江铁路通道的发展现状、存在问题及不同时期铁路运输需求,从而提出沿江铁路通道规划建设的必要性。

综上可知,目前论证铁路建设必要性的研究多从社会经济特征、交通运输结构、在路网中的功能和定位、运输需求预测的角度来阐述,而本文通过对线路沿线区域旅客出行现状及出行意愿进行分析,以不同的角度来阐述建设京港台高铁(阜阳—黄冈段)的必要性。

1 区域旅客出行特征调查

1.1 调查时间

调查工作从2020年9月16日开始,于2020年9月30日结束,共历时15d。

1.2 调查内容

本次调查内容分为两大类。
(1)旅客基本信息:旅客职业、旅行目的、旅费来源、月均收入等;
(2)旅行基本情况:旅行起迄点、乘降车站、车次号、车类型及型号、乘坐等级、旅程票价、乘降区间运行时间、进出乘车点时间等。

1.3 调查样本容量的确定

由于阜阳—黄冈影响区域内交通流动性及流量较大,所以在进行样本抽样时采用简单随机抽样的方法,由有关数理统计和误差理论可知:

$$n = \frac{(u_a S/d)^2}{1+(u_a S/d)^2/N} \tag{1}$$

式中,n 为样本容量;S 为标准差,一般取1.10;d 为随机变量在 $1-\alpha$ 的置信水平下的绝对误差限;N 为运输通道的总客流量。

由此可确定抽样率为:

$$f = \frac{n}{N} = \frac{(u_a S)^2}{d^2 N + (u_a S)^2} \tag{2}$$

由历年统计资料,阜阳—黄冈交通走廊的旅客对外出行流量日均为100万人次左右,因此在绝对误差3%和85%的置信水平时 $U\alpha = 1.04$,抽样率为:

$$f = 0.1452\%$$

相应的 $n=1452$,即至少取1452份,才能满足抽样误差不超过3%,置信水平为85%的要求。

考虑到 n 过大,会使调查费用显著增加;n 过小又会使样本对总体的代表性降低,增大抽样误差。另外又由于此条城际线路较长,涉及区域较广,确定 $n=1750$。

1.4 调查方式

1.4.1 交通小区的划分

根据阜阳—黄冈高铁线路走向将本研究的调查范围以现有的行政区划为基础划分为13个交通小区,从而进行后续对具体调查点的选取及调查实施。

1.4.2 调查点的选取

本次交通调查选择沿线重要的公路汽车站和火车站进行,对 15 个铁路客运站点、12 个城市客运站点进行旅客出行意愿调查;对于各个车站问卷调查数量则根据 1.4 中计算得出所需样本总量平均分配,同时根据火车站站点等级(表 1)高低适当增减不同车站问卷数量,最终得出客运站旅客出行意愿调查点(问卷)一览表见表 2。

项目影响区铁路客运站统计表 表 1

序 号	行政区划	站点名称	等级	序 号	行政区划	站点名称	等级
1	阜阳市	阜阳站	一等站	7	阜南县	阜南站	四等站
		阜阳西站	一等站	8	淮滨县	淮滨站	三等站
				9	潢川县	潢川站	二等站
2	麻城市	麻城站	二等站	10	黄州区	黄州站	二等站
		麻城北站	二等站			黄冈站	二等站
3	新洲区	新洲站	三等站	11	团风县	团风站	四等站
4	固始县	固始站	三等站	12	新县	新县站	三等站
5	光山县	光山站	三等站	13	红安县	红安西站	—
6	商城县	商城站	三等站				

客运站旅客出行意愿调查点(问卷)一览表 表 2

调查地点	问卷数(份)	调查地点	问卷数(份)
阜阳市火车站	100	阜阳市长途汽车中心站	100
阜阳市火车西站	100		
阜南县火车站	50	阜南县汽车站	50
潢川县火车站	100	潢川县汽车站	50
淮滨县火车站	50	淮滨县汽车站	50
固始县火车站	50	固始县顺达客运站	50
商城县火车站	50	商城县汽车站	50
光山县火车站	50	光山县汽车站	50
新县火车站	50	新县汽车站	50
红安县火车西站	50	红安县汽车站	50
麻城火车站	100	麻城市汽车客运中心	100
麻城火车北站	100		
团风县火车站	50	团风县汽车站	50
黄冈市火车站	100	黄冈市汽车站	100

1.4.3 调查实施

具体的调查实施采取电子问卷(图 1)快速录入结合纸质问卷填写后录入的方式。

(1)在调查地点(城市客运站、铁路客运站)分发出行意愿问卷(电子及纸质)给旅客,由旅客本人填写完毕后收回,发放 1400 份。

(2)通过调查员询问出行者,由调查员填写问卷相关内容,发放 700 份。

1.5 问卷的发放与回收

本次调查累计发放问卷 1750 份,回收有效问卷约 1725 份(收回率约为 98.6%),见表 3。

图 1　电子问卷

旅客出行意愿调查问卷统计　　　　表 3

类　别	实地调查		合　计
	汽车站	火车站	
计划调查旅客	750	1000	1750
实际调查旅客	736	989	1725

2　调查数据分析

2.1　出行者的社会经济特性

2.1.1　旅客职业分布

本次调查依据统计资料及劳动人事部门对职业的划分标准,结合阜阳—黄冈沿线地区的具体情况,将出行者的职业划分为 7 类。此次调查中受访者不同职业分布及旅行方式选择如图 2 所示。

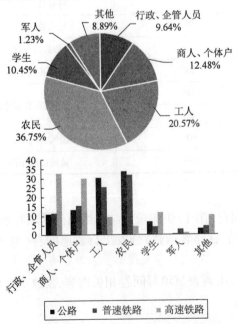

图 2　受访者职业分布及出行方式选择构成统计图

工人、农民选择铁路出行方式的比例最大,这与他们的经济收入水平相符;而工人选择公路出行的比例也比较大,因为该地区乡镇人口较多,多数工人需乘坐班车到市、县换乘。

比较乘坐火车、汽车的旅客职业构成比例我们发现,行政、企管人员选择高铁出行的比例最大,且明显高于其他职业,可能与行政、企管人员经常性公差有关。

2.1.2 旅客收入情况

此次调查中受访者收入分布情况如图3所示。

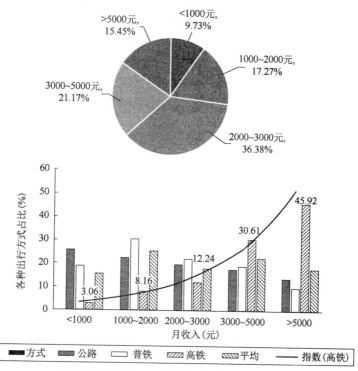

图3 受访者月收入分布及出行方式选择构成统计图

随着收入水平的提高,月收入在3000元以上的旅客出行时选择高速铁路出行的比例明显上升,并具有很大的稳定性。旅客对出行速度与出行环境的要求提高。

2.2 出行者出行特性

2.2.1 出行者出行目的

本次调查将出行者的出行目的分为公差、经商、外出务工、旅游、探亲访友、就医疗养及其他7种类型,具体如图4所示。

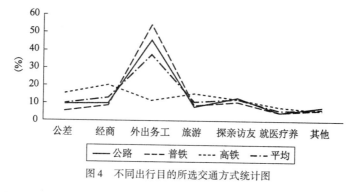

图4 不同出行目的所选交通方式统计图

2.2.2 出行到站耗时(接驳时间)

本次调查统计了旅客从出发地到车站所耗费的时间,即旅客到达车站前接驳过程所需要的时间,接驳时间统计结果如图5、图6所示。

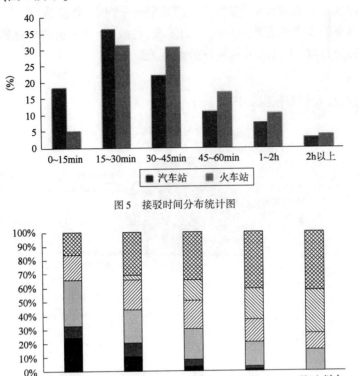

图5 接驳时间分布统计图

图6 车站集散交通方式及其时间分布

该地区接驳时间大多分布在 15~45min, 45min 以上的接驳时间占了 20%~30%, 而接驳时间越短则说明旅客出行的"途外可达性"越好, 接驳时间越长则说明旅客出行的"途外可达性"越差。该统计结果说明了阜阳—黄冈高铁项目影响区范围内可达性较低。

2.2.3 出行换乘

调查统计得到的旅客出行换乘情况, 如图7所示。

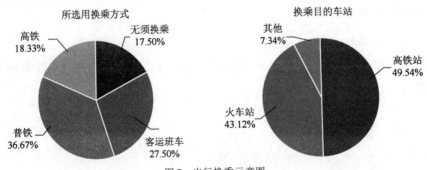

图7 出行换乘示意图

旅客出行大多须通过客运班车普铁等进行换乘, 分析认为该地区乡镇人口较多, 多数工人需乘坐班车到市、县换乘, 且域内交通网络欠发达, 需换乘至其他等级较高的火车站或高铁站到达目的地。

2.3 出行者对交通方式的选择意愿

针对沿线居民每次出行(出行距离 50km 以上或出行时间 2h 以上), 询问其在本客专开通后是否愿意转变乘坐。经调查, 约有 84.59% 的出行中, 居民愿意改变原有出行方式, 改乘本客专。约有 15.41% 的出行居民不愿意改变原有出行方式, 其原因主要为站点设置较远, 不在本市, 需进行换乘, 如图8所示。

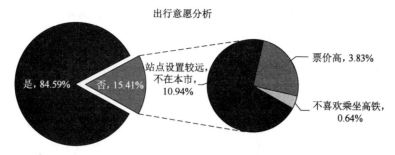

图 8　出行意愿分析

由表 4 及图 9 可知短距离内选择高速铁路的比例较高,占 38.45%,可以认为这与高速铁路具有速度快、环境舒适等优势及人们经济收入与生活水平的提高有很大关系。

最愿意选择的旅行方式比例(%)　　表 4

交通方式	200km 以内	200～500km	500～800km	800km 以上
公路	47.22	26.82	8.19	2.77
普速铁路	14.33	33.63	34.45	35.59
高速铁路	38.45	39.55	39.19	20.80
飞机	—	—	18.17	40.84
合计	100	100	100	100

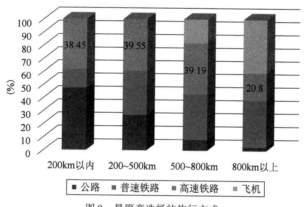

图 9　最愿意选择的旅行方式

中长距离出行主要由火车和飞机承担。随着距离的增加,旅客选择高速公路出行的比例逐渐减少,选择铁路出行的比例先增后减,选择飞机出行的比例逐渐增大。

3　结　语

区域内人口流动性大,客运需求旺盛,形成了以外出务工为主的出行。

从旅客收入分析,区域内经济欠发达,但随着收入的提高,旅客选择高铁的比例越来越高,月收入大于 5000 元的旅客选择高铁出行的比例达 45.92%。可见随着经济水平日益的提高,这一比例将稳定的增长。

从出行特性分析,目前域内并未规划建设为域内出行服务的高铁客运专线,交通运输网络欠发达,大多需通过换乘至等级较高的车站出行,其中换乘至高铁站比例高达 49.54%。

从出行意愿分析,受访者中约有 84.59% 的旅客愿意改乘京九客专。而在出行距离方面,短距离内,区域内旅客愿意乘坐高铁的比例高达 38.45%,而 200～800km 旅客愿意选择铁路的比例为 73.41%,选择高铁的比例为 39.37%。

从出行现状及意愿说明铁路尤其是高铁为当地居民欢迎的交通方式。而当地客运需求日益旺盛,人们经济收入与生活水平也日渐提高,该区域迫切需要一条具有高运力的高速铁路线路。新建阜阳—黄冈高铁变得至关重要,这将使得公路客流向铁路客流转移,产生增量客流,为项目影响区旅客的中、长距离出行提供便捷的服务。

参考文献

[1] 常占奎.新建温武吉铁路建设必要性研究[J].高速铁路技术,2020,11(04):13-16.
[2] 李志鹏,张博.建设甬台温高铁的必要性研究[J].铁道建筑技术,2020(08):60-63.
[3] 江佳璐.浅析桂林至湛江铁路建设的必要性[J].交通与运输,2018,34(01):49-51.
[4] 任峥峥.长江经济带沿江铁路通道规划建设必要性分析[J].铁道标准设计,2017,61(06):49-52.
[5] 冯建栋,王昊.郑州市公交乘客特性及出行意愿调查分析[J].交通科技与经济,2015,17(04):64-70.

基于多源数据的出租车出行需求特征影响研究

严海[1] 刘珂彤[1] 伍速锋[2] 刘润坤[3]

(1.北京工业大学交通运输部城市公共交通智能化交通运输行业重点实验室;
2.中国城市规划设计研究院;3.北京航空航天大学交通科学与工程学院)

摘 要 挖掘及分析出租车出行特征和规律特点对平衡出租车供需关系具有重要参考价值。基于此,将各类POI(Points of Interest)数、公交车需求量定义为影响栅格内出租车需求的空间属性,利用自然断点法对出租车订单数和各空间属性数据进行量化分级;然后利用Apriori算法挖掘栅格内出租车需求量和空间属性之间的关联性。通过分析挖掘结果可得如下结论:公交车和出租车需求在不同时间段有所差异,工作日通勤时间段居民更偏向于选择公交出行;各类POI在不同时间段对出租车需求的影响也具有差异性。

关键词 交通数据挖掘 需求特征影响 自然断点法 关联规则 出租车需求

0 引 言

出租车作为一种传统的定制化交通出行方式,由于其快捷、灵活的特点,已成为居民出行不可或缺的选择之一。居民对出租车的需求在每日特定时间或区域会呈现出周期性的规律,因此,掌握不同时空状态下的出租车需求规律,实现出租车供需关系的平衡正在成为相关行业和研究部门关注的重点。

随着互联网与交通产业结合的不断升级,有更多的关于地理和交通的数据被记录,其中用于出租车需求规律分析的主要有出租车卫星定位数据、公共交通刷卡数据、POI数据。付鑫等基于出租汽车运行卫星定位轨迹数据,构建了一类城市出行复杂网络,揭示了城市居民活动的空间特征、活动规律及其与城市功能空间布局之间的相互影响作用。孙阳等利用从浮动车数据及百度地图数据中提取出的出租车和公交出行特征数据进行了分析,比较了出租车与公共交通的出行差异。周海波利用滴滴打车数据和POI数据中分析了人们的打车需求的规律,得出了打车时间特性和POI具有关联性的结论。上述文献均是利用单一类型的数据对出租车需求规律进行分析研究,也都取得了显著成果。但是利用单一的数据源得出的结论可能会有一定的局限性,忽视了事物之间的相互影响机制。目前在出租车需求特征方面的研究中,采用多源数据融合的研究仍较少,利用多源数据融合来挖掘出租车需求特性,不仅可以得到出租车的需求规律,而且可以进一步得到出租车产生需求的影响因素。

针对上述的研究现状,本文利用多源数据来探究公交车需求量、各类POI在不同时空下和出租车需求量之间的关联性以及量化分析对出租车需求的影响程度,首先将研究区域——苏州中心城区进行等面

基金项目:国家重点研发计划项目(2018YFB1601300)。

积的栅格划分,根据时空属性把出租车需求量、公交车需求特征、POI大数据匹配入每一个栅格内;然后,将各类POI数、公交车需求量定义为影响栅格内出租车需求的空间属性,利用自然断点法对出租车订单数和各空间属性数据进行量化分级,从而得到出租车需求及其空间属性的等级特性;最后利用Aprior算法在不同时间段下挖掘各空间属性和出租车需求量之间的关联性及量化分析空间属性对出租车需求的影响,从而为出租车出行热点区域的识别以及公交线路规划合理性提供判断依据。

1 数据预处理

1.1 时间阈值处理及时段划分

对出租车订单数据和公交IC卡刷卡数据按阈值和间隔进行异常数据剔除。将出租车订单和IC卡的阈值设置如下:

(1) 出租车订单数据中单次出行时间的阈值:$2\min \leqslant t \leqslant 4h$。
(2) 出租车每个订单中的平均速度的阈值:$10\text{km/h} \leqslant v \leqslant 90\text{km/h}$。
(3) IC卡刷卡时间间隔:$t \geqslant 3\min$。

为了研究不同时间段出租车需求特征,将一天的时间段分为早晚高峰期(通勤时间段)、平峰期、夜间,其中早高峰时间段为7:00~9:00,晚高峰时间段为17:00~19:00;平峰时间段为5:00~7:00、9:00~17:00、19:00~21:00;夜间时间段为21:00~5:00。将出租车订单数据和公交IC卡数据按发生日期和时刻进行提取,并进行统计。

1.2 空间地理信息匹配

本文研究范围为苏州市中心城区,WGS-84坐标系下的经纬度范围为[120.548017,31.250371]至[120.687739,31.350309]。从段宗涛研究中发现,乘客打车出行频率最高的距离在1~3km,占到了42.35%。因此,利用ArcGIS软件将研究区域划分为大小为1km×1km的栅格,栅格总数为140个,并空间连接出租车订单数据、公交IC卡刷卡数据、POI数据与划分的栅格。最后分别统计每个栅格内三类数据的数量,结果如图1~图3所示。

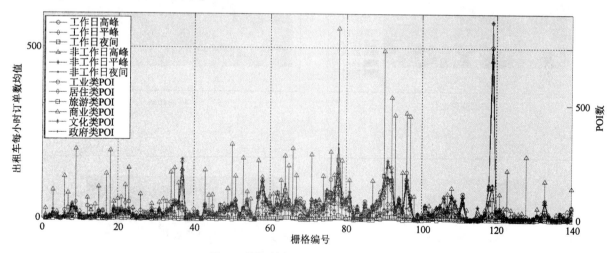

图1 不同区域各时间段出租车订单需求量

2 研究方法

2.1 基于自然断点法的栅格空间属性分级

自然断点法分级是按照数据中固有的自然分组,通过对分级间隔加以识别,在数据不连续空缺处设置边界,对相似值进行恰当分组,使各级之间差异最大化。这种方法较好保持了数据的统计特性且完全根据数据的分布情况,避免了人为的干扰。本文利用自然断点法将数据中不连续的地方作为分级的依据对数据进行分级,将各栅格的出租车每小时订单数、公交车每小时乘客数、各类 POI 数分为三个等级,等级 1、等级 2、等级 3 的对应数量范围依次增大。三个等级定义如下:

等级 1:数值小,即出租车、公交车需求小,POI 分布少。

等级 2:数值居中,即出租车、公交车需求居中,POI 分布中等。

等级 3:数值大,即出租车、公交车需求大,POI 分布多。

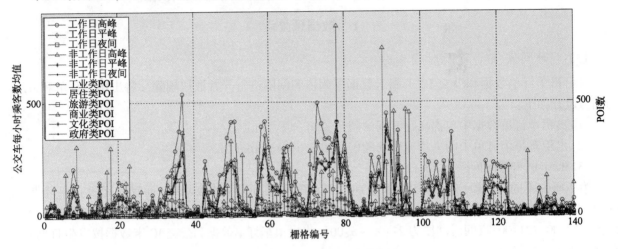

图 2 不同区域各时间段公交车需求量

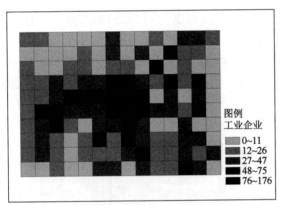

a) 工业企业类

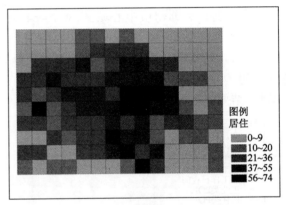

b) 居住类

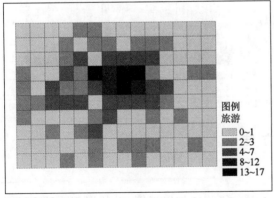

c) 旅游类

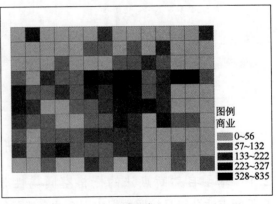

d) 商业类

图 3

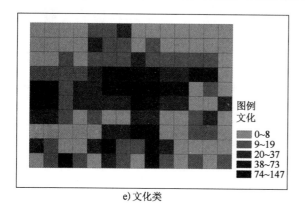
e) 文化类

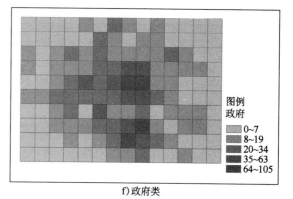
f) 政府类

图3 六类POI空间分布特征

栅格内出租车需求及其空间属性等级标号用表示标号加等级数来表示,具体见表1。

出租车需求及空间属性等级标号示例(工作日高峰时段) 表1

栅格编号	出租车	公交车	工业企业	居住	旅游	商业	文化	政府
116	Taxi1	TR2	I1	L1	T1	B1	C2	G1
117	Taxi2	TR2	I1	L2	T2	B1	C1	G2
118	Taxi3	TR2	I2	L2	T2	B1	C1	G1
119	Taxi1	TR2	I1	L2	T1	B1	C1	G1

2.2 基于关联规则的出租车需求影响因素分析

关联规则是寻找同一个事件中出现的不同项之间的相关性,即找出事件中频繁发生的项或属性的所有子集,以及它们之间的相互关联性。按照关联规则的相关概念定义,在本文中事务数据库 D、事务表 X、项集 A 和 B 定义为:

D:出租车需求和7类空间属性;

X:栅格分级数据;

A:某类空间属性的某一等级;

B:出租车需求的某一等级。

本文通过Apriori算法挖掘各栅格空间属性的等级和出租车需求等级的关联规则,利用置信度指标和提升度lift指标考量关联规则的相关性。为全面对比各空间属性在所有等级下对出租车需求的影响程度,将最小支持度和置信度均设置为1%,最终挖掘出90%以上各空间属性不同等级为前项,出租车需求等级为后项的关联规则。用关联规则中的置信度来量化不同等级的空间属性对出租车需求的影响程度,置信度越高则表示某一等级空间属性与某一等级出租车需求量之间的相关性越强。

3 结果与分析

工作日内不同时间段出租车需求量的关联规则结果,如表5所示。为了更清晰直观地显示表2中在工作日不同时间段的关联结果对比,图4~图6分别以柱状图的形式展示了高峰、平峰、夜间时间段中不同属性和出租车需求量的置信度。由于本文篇幅有限,对工作日高峰时段的关联规则结果进行详细分析,其他时段分析过程略去。

工作日高峰平峰夜间关联结果对比 表2

	Taxi1						Taxi2						Taxi3					
	高峰		平峰		夜间		高峰		平峰		夜间		高峰		平峰		夜间	
	con	lift	con	lift	con	lift	con	lift	con	lift	con	lift	con	lift	con	lift	con	lift
TR1	0.85	1.42	0.84	1.34	0.76	1.00	0.15	0.42	0.14	0.47	0.19	1.00	0	0	0.02	0.31	0.05	1.00
TR2	0.53	0.89	0.25	0.40	0	0	0.40	1.16	0.66	2.15	0	0	0.06	1.28	0.09	1.27	0	0

续上表

	Taxi1						Taxi2						Taxi3					
	高峰		平峰		夜间		高峰		平峰		夜间		高峰		平峰		夜间	
	con	lift	con	lift	con	lift	con	lift	con	lift	con	lift	con	lift	con	lift	con	lift
TR3	0	0	0	0	0	0	0.80	2.29	0	0	0	0	0.16	3.20	0.8	11.2	0	0
I1	0.72	1.19	0.75	1.21	0.89	1.16	0.26	0.75	0.23	0.74	0.10	0.55	0.02	0	0.02	0.32	0	0
I2	0.47	0.78	0.47	0.75	0.64	0.84	0.42	1.21	0.40	1.30	0.27	1.44	0.11	2.22	0.13	1.87	0.09	1.78
I3	0	0	0	0	0	0	1	2.86	0.71	2.33	0.71	3.85	0	0	0.29	4.0	0.29	5.71
L1	0.83	1.38	0.86	1.38	0.92	1.20	0.16	0.45	0.13	0.41	0.06	0.34	0	0.83	0	0	0	0
L2	0.5	0.83	0.5	0.80	0.79	1.04	0.46	1.31	0.42	1.36	0.17	0.90	0.04	0	0.08	1.17	0.04	0.83
L3	0.28	0.46	0.31	0.50	0.38	0.50	0.59	1.67	0.52	1.68	0.48	2.60	0.14	2.76	0.17	2.41	0.14	2.76
T1	0.74	1.23	0.76	1.23	0.88	1.14	0.24	0.67	0.21	0.69	0.11	0.61	0.025	0.5	0.03	0.35	0	0
T2	0.47	0.78	0.49	0.79	0.71	0.92	0.47	1.34	0.45	1.47	0.27	1.48	0.06	1.18	0.06	0.82	0	0
T3	0	0	0	0	0	0	0.66	1.90	0.33	1.09	0.33	1.79	0.22	4.44	0.55	7.78	0.56	11.11
B1	0.73	1.22	0.74	1.19	0.88	1.14	0.25	0.71	0.24	0.78	0.11	0.62	0.02	0.42	0.02	0.29	0	0
B2	0.35	0.59	0.41	0.65	0.59	0.78	0.57	1.62	0.49	1.58	0.35	1.89	0	1.62	0.11	1.51	0.05	1.08
B3	0	0	0	0	0	0	0.57	1.63	0.29	0.93	0.29	1.54	0.29	5.71	0.57	8.00	0.57	11.43
C1	0.75	1.25	0.78	1.25	0.92	1.20	0.23	0.66	0.20	0.65	0.07	0.40	0.02	0	0.02	0.29	0	0
C2	0.34	0.57	0.34	0.55	0.5	0.65	0.55	1.58	0.5	1.63	0.39	2.13	0.10	2.11	0.16	2.21	0.11	2.11
C3	0	0	0	0	0	0	0.86	2.45	0.71	2.33	0.57	3.08	0	0	0.29	4.00	0.29	5.71
G1	0.74	1.22	0.74	1.19	0.89	1.16	0.24	0.69	0.24	0.79	0.09	0.49	0.02	0.40	0.02	0.28	0.02	0.40
G2	0.28	0.47	0.38	0.60	0.53	0.70	0.63	1.79	0.5	1.63	0.40	2.19	0.09	1.88	0.13	1.75	0.06	1.25
G3	0.22	0.37	0.22	0.36	0.22	0.29	0.56	1.59	0.33	1.09	0.44	2.39	0.22	4.44	0.44	6.22	0.33	6.67

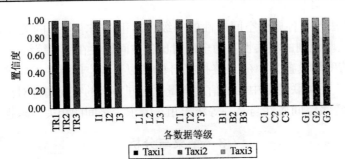

图4 工作日高峰时间段关联规则结果

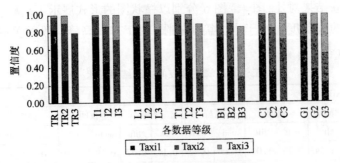

图5 工作日平峰时间段关联规则结果

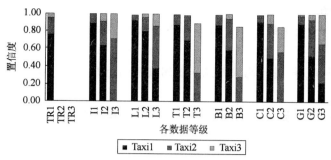

图6 工作日夜间时间段关联规则

从表5以及图4的置信度对比中可以看出,在工作日高峰时间段时,以 Taxi3 为后项的关联规则的置信度都较小,均值为0.08,公交乘客数为前项的关联规则中 TR1-Taxi1、TR2-Taxi1、TR3-Taxi2 的置信度比较大,分别为0.85、0.53、0.80,其 lift 指标分别为1.42、1.16、3.20,均大于1,此关联规则为强关联结果。工业企业 POI 为前项的关联规则中 I1-Taxi1、I2-Taxi1、I3-Taxi2 的置信度比较大,分别为0.72、0.47、1。其 lift 指标。在居住 POI 类等级 L3 为前项的关联规则中,L3-Taxi2 的置信度为0.59,比 L3-Taxi1、L3-Taxi3 的置信度都大,且其 lift 指标大于1。商业和旅游 POI 为首项的关联规则中,T3-Taxi2、B3-Taxi2 的置信度0.67和0.57远大于 T3-Taxi3(0.22)和 B3-Taxi3(0.29),且 lift 指标都大于1。文化 POI 为首项的关联规则中,C3-Taxi2、C2-Taxi2 的置信度较大,分别为0.55、0.86,且 lift 指标大于1。政府 POI 为首项的关联规则中:G3-Taxi1、G3-Taxi2、G3-Taxi3 的置信度相差不大,在0.2~0.6之间浮动。

从上述的数据强关联结果可以看出:

(1)工作日高峰时段,出租车的需求较小,乘坐出租车并不是居民主要通勤方式。

(2)从单个因素对出租车需求的影响来看,每个因素对出租车需求的影响有类似的特征。随着各类因素的等级提高,其对应的出租车高等级为后项的关联规则置信度整体呈上升趋势。这是因为公交车乘客数和POI数都反映且影响了栅格中的人流量,人流量越多的区域打车需求也越多。但是,由于各类影响因素的性质不一样,因此对出租车的影响也有所差异。

对平峰时段和夜间时段的分析过程与高峰时段类似,由于本文篇幅限制,在此不再赘述。综合来看,对比工作日高峰、平峰、夜间时间段公交车数、各类 POI 数对出租车订单数的影响,可得出在工作日不同时间段中各类 POI 数对出租车需求的影响是有所差异的。公交车乘客数和出租车需求量在高峰时间段时无正相关性,而在平峰和夜间时间段具有明显正相关。此外,从整体来看,在工作日整天中,平峰时间段内对出租车的需求最大,夜间时间段内出租车的需求量最小。

4 结　语

为探究出租车需求特征规律,本文以苏州市中心城区为研究区域进行了研究,主要得出以下两方面结论:

(1)公交车和出租车需求量的关系在不同时间特征下具有差异性。在工作日通勤时间段公交车更具有吸引力,居民对出租车的需求较小;非通勤时间段,公交车和出租车没有明显的竞争性。非工作日出租车的吸引力有所上升,出租车的需求量相比公交出行需求量有所增加。

(2)各类 POI 对出租车需求的影响具有差异性。商业类 POI 集中的区域,打车需求较大;居住、文化类 POI 的集中程度和打车需求量的正相关性较低,可见打车不是该类区域居民的主要出行方式;工业企业类 POI 的集中程度和出租车需求量的正相关性较低,但在夜间打车需求量会有所增加;旅游类 POI 集中的区域,整体打车需求较大,但工作日以及高峰时间段和打车需求量的正相关性降低。

参考文献

[1] 陆建,王炜.城市出租车拥有量确定方法[J].交通运输工程学报,2004(01):92-95.

[2] 付鑫,杨宇,孙皓.出租汽车出行轨迹网络结构复杂性与空间分异特征[J].交通运输工程学报,

[3] 孙阳,林航飞.基于GPS数据的上海出租车与公交出行特征比较分析[J].交通与运输(学术版), 2018(02):77-80.

[4] 周海波,魏延生,罗洪军,等.基于感兴趣点和滴滴数据的打车需求分析[J].地理信息世界,2019,26(2):60-66.

[5] 段宗涛,陈志明,陈柘,等.基于Spark平台城市出租车乘客出行特征分析[J].计算机系统应用,2017,26(3):37-43.

[6] REY S J, STEPHEN P, Laura J. An evaluation of sampling and full enumeration strategies for Fisher Jenks classification in big data set-tings[J]. Transactions in GIS, 2017, 21(4): 796-810.

[7] XU Xin. Cultural communication in double-layer coupling social network based on association rules in big data[J]. Personal and Ubiquitous Computing, 2020, 24(1): 57-74.

基于改进Ga-LM-BP神经网络的城市轨道交通短时客流预测研究

姚 帆

(长安大学运输工程学院)

摘 要 针对传统BP神经网络收敛速度慢、易收敛到局部极小值等缺点,利用引进位置参数的双极S形函数对激活函数进行改进,采用LM算法对训练算法进行改进,利用遗传算法对初始权值和阈值进行优化,得到改进Ga-LM-BP神经网络。将改进后的模型用于城市轨道交通短时客流预测,结果表明相比传统BP神经网络,改进模型大大提高了预测的效率和精度,更适用于城市轨道交通短时客流预测。

关键词 交通行为与出行需求预测 短时客流预测 BP神经网络 城市轨道交通 遗传算法 LM算法

0 引 言

为了准确描述城市轨道交通客流的时变性,保证运营组织的合理和高效,进行精确的短时客流预测是十分重要的。目前常用的短时客流预测方法主要包括线性模型、非线性模型和组合模型。其中传统BP神经网络收敛速度慢、易收敛到局部极小值,预测速度和精度差。本文通过改进激活函数,引入LM算法和遗传算法对传统BP神经网络进行改进,将改进后的模型用于城市轨道交通短时客流预测,取得了较好的效果。

1 BP神经网络概述

1.1 BP神经网络的原理

BP神经网络是一种由输入层、输出层及一个或多个隐含层组成的多层前馈形神经网络。BP神经网络的结构形式如图1所示。

BP神经网络的训练过程如下:

(1) 给定初始权值,误差函数E,精度要求和最大迭代次数。

(2) 输入一对样本(X,Y),样本对包含输入和期望得到的输出。

(3) 计算每一层神经元的输出值,计算公式如下:

$$y_j = f(\sum w_{ij} y_i)$$

式中,$f(x)$为激活函数。

(4)误差计算,在得到神经网络的输出值 Y_m 后,通过给定的误差函数 E 计算输出值与真实值的误差。

(5)权值修正,使用误差反向传播原则,按如下公式对权值进行修正:

$$w'_{jm} = w_{jm} + \eta \Delta w_{jm}$$

$$\Delta w_{jm} = -\mu \frac{\partial E}{\partial w_{jm}}$$

式中,μ、η 表示学习率。

(6)不断进行迭代,直到全局误差满足相应的误差要求或达到给定的迭代次数为止。

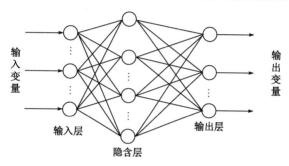

图1 BP神经网络结构形式

1.2 传统BP神经网络的不足

首先,传统BP神经网络的激活函数为$f(x)=1/(1+e^{-x})$,其输出范围为$(0,1)$,当通过梯度计算调整权值和阈值时,会导致调整量过小,影响神经网络的收敛速度。其次,传统BP神经网络采用梯度下降法修正权值和阈值,将产生一个全局最优和多个局部最优的位置,易陷入局部最优,使结果精度低。同时梯度下降法在曲面曲率不同的位置对权值和阈值的调整程度不同,会导致误差的减小速度不稳定。最后,传统BP神经网络的初始权值和阈值随机生成,导致神经网络的精确性和收敛速度波动较大。

2 改进 Ga-LM-BP 神经网络

2.1 对激活函数的改进

改进方法:使用形如$f(x)=2/(1+e^{-2x})-1$双极S形函数,输出范围为$(-1,1)$,导数为$f'(x)=4e^{-2x}/(1+e^{-2x})^2$。再对激活函数引入位置参数 α,得到改进的激活函数$f(x)=2/[1+e^{-2(x-\alpha)}]-1$,记$\beta=e^{2\alpha}$,此时导数为$f'(x)=4\beta e^{-2x}/(1+\beta e^{-2x})^2$,通过调整位置参数 α,可控制神经网络的收敛速度。

2.2 对训练算法的改进

LM算法的基本原理如下:设 w_k 代表进行第 K 次迭代时权值及阈值构成的列向量,由牛顿法可得

$$w_{k+1} = w_k - H_k^{-1} g_k$$

式中,H_k 为 Hessian 矩阵,g_k 为误差和函数的梯度。

设 $E(w)$ 为误差和函数,列向量 $e(w)$ 表示神经网络权值输出值与真实值之间的误差,则有:

$$E(w) = \frac{1}{2} \sum_i e_i^2(w) = \frac{1}{2} e^T(w) e(w)$$

误差和函数的梯度为：

$$\nabla E(w) = J^{\mathrm{T}}(w) e(w)$$

式中，$J(w)$ 为 Jacobian 矩阵。

此时的 Hessian 矩阵为：

$$\nabla^2 E(w) = J^{\mathrm{T}}(w) J(w) + S(w)$$

式中，$S(w)$ 为误差，通常可忽略不计。

据此，LM 算法改进后的表达式为：

$$w_{k+1} = w_k - [J^{\mathrm{T}}(w_k) J(w_k) + \mu I]^{-1} J^{\mathrm{T}}(w) e(w)$$

式中，$\mu > 0$ 为比例因子；I 为单位阵，确保 $J^{\mathrm{T}}(w) J(w)$ 的可逆。

LM-BP 神经网络通过如下过程实现：对于(输入，输出)样本对计算误差和函数 $E(w)$，并算出雅可比矩阵 $j(w)$，计算新的权值并保留旧值。给定初始 μ 值，$E(w_m)$ 被求出后，若其值减小，则 $\mu = \mu/\theta (\theta > 1)$，对权值进行调整，并重算 $E(w)$；否则，使 $\mu = \mu\theta(\theta > 1)$，对权值不做调整，再计算新的权值。

2.3 初始权值及阈值的优化

2.3.1 遗传算法的原理

本文通过遗传算法优化 LM-BP 神经网络的初始权值及阈值，根据具体的适应度函数值筛选初始种群中的优良个体，再通过选择、交叉及变异产生新的个体，不断地搜索寻找最优解。

2.3.2 Ga-LM-BP 神经网络的实现步骤

Ga-LM-BP 神经网络的实现步骤如下：

(1) 设输入层、输出层及隐含层的神经元数目分别为 l, m, n，得到初始权值及阈值的结构。

(2) 对初始权值及阈值进行实数编码，得到染色体

$$X_i = (w_{11}, w_{12}, \cdots, w_{lm}, u_{11}, u_{12}, \cdots, u_{mn}, b_1, b_2, \cdots, b_m, c_1, c_2, \cdots, c_n)$$

其中 w 为输入层-隐含层连接权值，u 为隐含层-输出层连接权值，b 和 c 分别为隐含层和输出层的阈值。据此随机地生成规模为 N 的初始种群。

(3) 选择误差函数作为适应度函数，即 $F(X) = E$，计算初始种群中每个染色体的适应度函数值。

(4) 采用轮盘赌法进行选择，染色体 X_i 被选择的概率为 $P(X_i)$，其计算公式为：

$$f(X_i) = \frac{1}{F(X_i)}$$

$$P(X_i) = \frac{f(X_i)}{\sum_{i=1}^{N} f(X_i)}$$

(5) 任选两条染色体进行交叉，产生子代染色体，保留父代与子代中适应度更高的染色体。

(6) 在种群中任选染色体改变其在某些基因座上的基因，通过变异操作来获取更加优良的个体。

(7) 达到迭代次数要求或给定的误差要求后，停止遗传算法，获得 LM-BP 神经网络的初始权值和阈值。

(8) 多次训练得到预测结果。

2.4 改进 Ga-LM-BP 神经网络的实现流程

改进 Ga-LM-BP 神经网络的实现流程如图 2 所示。

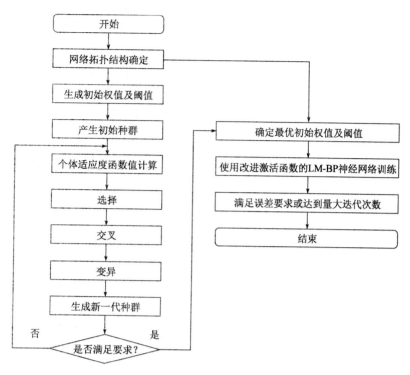

图 2 改进 Ga-LM-BP 神经网络的实现流程

3 案例分析

3.1 数据处理与分析

本文选取西安地铁小寨站 2018 年 9 月 3 日—9 月 14 每日 6:00~23:30 时间粒度为 15min 的进站客流量数据。本文选取工作日进站客流量进行预测。预测前首先对预测时段客流量与前几个工作日同一时段客流量进行相关性分析,使用斯皮尔曼相关系数。定义 $Q_i(n)$ 为小寨站第 i 个工作日第 n 个时段的进站客流量,相关系数见表1。

各工作日同一时段进站客流量相关系数　　表1

相关系数	$Q_i(n)$	$Q_{i-1}(n)$	$Q_{i-2}(n)$	$Q_{i-3}(n)$	$Q_{i-4}(n)$
$Q_i(n)$	1	0.992	0.989	0.983	0.986
$Q_{i-1}(n)$	0.992	1	0.993	0.985	0.984
$Q_{i-2}(n)$	0.989	0.993	1	0.99	0.985
$Q_{i-3}(n)$	0.983	0.985	0.99	1	0.989
$Q_{i-4}(n)$	0.986	0.984	0.985	0.989	1

由分析结果知,预测时段客流量与前四个工作日同一时段客流量的具有较强的相关性,故使用前四个工作日的客流来预测最后一个工作日的客流量是合理的。

最终确定神经网络的输入变量为 $Q_{i-4}(n)$、$Q_{i-3}(n)$、$Q_{i-2}(n)$、$Q_{i-1}(n)$,输出变量为 $Q_i(n)$,模型为4维输入,1维输出。

3.2 基于传统 BP 神经网络的预测

本文采用三层 BP 神经网络,采用试凑法经过大量试验得到不同隐含层神经元个数下的预测均方误差见表2,故取隐含层神经元个数为10。

表2 隐含层神经元个数不同取值对应的预测均方误差

隐含层神经元个数	3	4	5	6	7	8	9	10
mse	0.003006	0.002339	0.001979	0.001783	0.001688	0.001616	0.001411	0.001382

本文学习速率取0.01。使用80%的数据进行训练,20%的数据用于验证,构建BP神经网络预测西安地铁小寨站9月13日及14日的进站客流量,预测结果及相对误差如图3和图4所示。

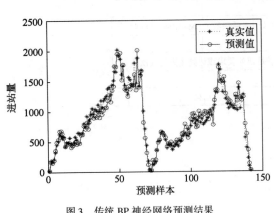

图3 传统BP神经网络预测结果

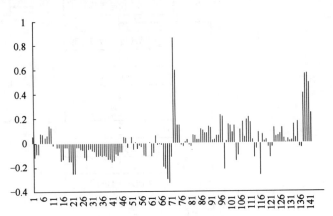

图4 传统BP神经网络预测相对误差

3.3 基于改进Ga-LM-BP神经网络的预测

通过改变位置参数可以得到不同的激活函数,不同位置参数对神经网络性能的影响见表3。

表3 不同位置参数取值下的预测均方误差及迭代次数

位置参数	-3	-2	-1	0	1	2	3	4	5
mse	0.00233	0.00192	0.00211	0.00200	0.00177	0.00195	0.00157	0.00168	0.00202
迭代次数	37	35	34	32	34	31	28	31	35

由表3可知,取 $\alpha=3$ 时预测速度和精度最好,得激活函数为 $f(x)=2/[1+e^{-2(x-3)}]-1$。

使用三层4-10-1型神经网络,学习速率取0.01,训练算法为LM算法。

取遗传算法的编码长度为66,取种群大小为40,终止进化代数为100,采用轮盘赌法进行选择。优化后的初始权值及阈值见表4。

表4 遗传算法优化后的初始权值及阈值

权值及阈值	取值									
w	-0.8889	0.947892	0.666295	-0.33733	-0.68223	-0.81203	0.676542	-0.54107	0.35312	0.198166
	0.282504	0.086591	0.373104	-0.10555	0.551034	-0.47531	-0.75958	0.758186	0.25269	0.293146
	0.433702	0.066417	0.284383	-0.24098	0.337984	0.053802	0.772338	0.687174	-0.00264	0.382705
	0.947715	0.892495	0.333663	-0.24338	0.776513	0.405121	0.264145	0.204429	0.26223	0.764553
u	-0.51898	0.616265	-0.27479	-0.51265	-0.14473	0.850994	0.227704	-0.45059	0.739042	-0.91794
b	0.999373	0.997451	0.987902	-0.99996	0.999289	-0.9995	0.999639	0.997245	0.997732	0.999926
c	-0.10642									

利用改进的Ga-LM-BP神经网络进行多次训练并预测,预测结果与相对误差如图5和图6所示。

传统BP神经网络与改进Ga-LM-BP神经网络预测效果对比见表5。

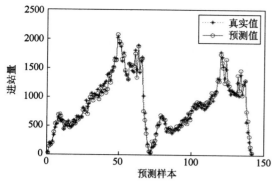

图 5 改进 Ga-LM-BP 神经网络预测结果

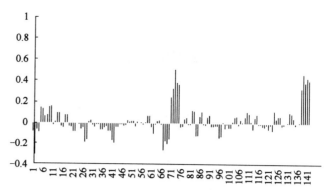

图 6 改进 Ga-LM-BP 神经网络预测相对误差

传统模型与改进模型预测效果对比　　表 5

指　　标	传统 BP 神经网络	改进 BP 神经网络
mse	0.00153	0.000963
mae	0.0288	0.0256
迭代次数	35	12

由表 5 可以看出,相比传统 BP 神经网络,改进 Ga-LM-BP 神经网络的预测及过 mse 值减小了 0.000567,mae 值减小了 0.0032,同时迭代次数由 35 次减少为 12 次。

4　结　　语

本文通过改进传统 BP 神经网络的激活函数和训练算法并优化初始权值和阈值得到改进 Ga-LM-BP 神经网络,分别使用传统 BP 神经网络和改进 Ga-LM-BP 神经网络对西安地铁小寨站两个工作日的进站客流量进行了预测。主要研究成果及结论如下:

(1)将单极 S 形函数改进为引入位置参数 α 的双极 S 形函数,通过调整位置参数可以实现对神经网络收敛速度的控制。

(2)通过引入 LM 算法对传统 BP 神经网络的训练算法进行改进,提高了梯度下降的速度。

(3)使用遗传算法对传统 BP 神经网络的初始权值和阈值进行优化,提高了神经网络的精确性和收敛速度。

(4)分别使用传统模型和改进模型对西安地铁小寨站两个工作日的进站客流量进行了预测。表明改进 Ga-LM-BP 神经网络比传统 BP 神经网络相对误差降低,迭代次数大大减少。

参考文献

[1] 陈深进,薛洋.基于改进卷积神经网络的短时公交客流预测[J].计算机科学,2019,46(05):175-184.

[2] 赵鹏,李璐.基于 ARIMA 模型的城市轨道交通进站量预测研究[J].重庆交通大学学报(自然科学版),2020,39(01):40-44.

[3] 马超群,李培坤,朱才华,等.基于不同时间粒度的城市轨道交通短时客流预测[J].长安大学学报(自然科学版),2020,40(03):75-83.

[4] Li Q, Qin Y, Wang Z Y, et al. Prediction of Urban Rail Transit Sectional Passenger Flow Based on Elman Neural Network[J]. Applied Mechanics & Materials, 2014, 505-506:1023-1027.

[5] Li M T, Ji X F, Zhang J, et al. FA-BP Neural Network-Based Forecast for Railway Passenger Volume[J]. Applied Mechanics and Materials, 2014, 641-642:673-677.

[6] 杨静,朱经纬,刘博,等.基于组合模型的城市轨道交通短时客流预测[J].交通运输系统工程与信息,2019,19(03):119-125.

[7] 马飞虎,金依辰,孙翠羽.基于 EMD 优化 NAR 动态神经网络的地铁客流量短时预测模型[J].应用科学学报,2020,38(06):936-943.

大型活动期间非常态应急接驳车辆调度研究综述

张啸林　熊志华

（北京交通大学综合交通运输大数据应用技术交通运输行业重点实验室）

摘　要　因外界恶意破坏、恶劣天气、系统设备故障等非常态因素干扰，体育赛事、文艺演出、商业活动等大型活动会引发交通系统客流集中、拥挤，甚至会威胁乘客的生命安全。为保障大型活动交通安全、顺畅、高效，研究大型活动期间交通网络面对非常态情景，如何进行应急接驳车辆调度问题，对提高轨道交通网络的安全性与应急能力十分迫切和必要。因此，本文梳理大型活动交通特征以及非常态事件的交通影响，以北京冬奥会为时空约束，分析冬奥期间交通网络可能发生的非常态事件，以及为应对非常态应急车辆调度问题，旨在为冬奥会非常态综合交通协同优化调度提供支撑。结合大型赛事以及突发事件特征，从应急接驳车辆调度的情景、理论基础、目标和约束条件方面进行剖析，提出以乘客总延误最小为目标，给出在大型活动期间突发事件下应急接驳车辆的调度模型。

关键词　大型活动　突发事件　应急接驳　车辆调度模型　启发式算法

0　引　言

安全是重大赛事必须坚守的底线。2022年北京冬季奥运会交通系统由铁路、城市轨道交通、道路交通等综合交通网络构成，涉及城际、城市、赛事点等多层级交通网络空间范围，交通安全、畅通是重点关注的领域之一。尤其是针对冬奥会异常场景下跨交通方式运力资源协同调度，是有效防控交通风险，强化交通应急救援能力的基础。

由于突发事件的突发性、公共性和危害性，常会造成人员滞留、聚集、拥挤等。为最大程度减小损失，在某交通方式发生紧急状况时，需确定多方式综合交通协同组织方法来疏解滞留的乘客。因此建立一个安全、高效、便捷的非常态接驳车辆调度方案，保证每一个赛事的参与者能准时、安全地到达赛场，是大型赛事顺利举办的前提与保障。

目前，大型活动研究主要聚焦在活动分类与性质、客流特点与影响因素以及客流疏解方面。郑云霄分析了不同类型活动客流的时空分布规律；Lu Zhao等研究体育赛事结束后，乘客对站点的选择行为，并建立Logit模型；钱慧敏等分析了大型活动期间乘客出行与平日的差异及影响因素；付宇等发现大型活动期间客流短时间内突变，并建立短期流量预测模型；孟昊宇对大型活动的交通组织、交通保障、交通管理等方面进行广泛的研究。

有关交通领域中突发事件研究主要聚焦在时间序列与事故致因、紧急情况下乘客特点以及紧急救援与预控措施三方面。针对突发事件处置的交通系统突发事件预案，如《公路交通突发事件应急预案》《国家城市轨道交通运营突发事件应急预案》等表明交通系统非常态事件已经得到重视。尤其轨道交通系统因环境封闭、客流量大、网络化运营制约，一旦遭受到外界恶意破坏、设备故障等非常态，轻则造成列车晚点、停运、乘客滞留难以疏散，重则造成设备毁坏、人员伤亡，对国家造成经济损失和负面影响。

有关应急调度研究主要借助公交调度的思想解决应急接驳问题。非常态时，调用公交车辆或专用车辆进行接驳，并及时调整列车运行方案。如以总接驳时间最小或总经济损失最小为目标、以企业效益最大为目标、以车辆间隔均方差最小为目标、总配送成本最低为目标、疏散耗能最小等为目标建立应急接驳调度模型，并涉及相应的求解算法。

基金项目：国家重点研发计划资助，中央高校基本科研业务费专项资金。

综上所述,目前单独针对大型活动交通特征、突发事件客流特点及车辆调度方面的研究已有很多,但同时考虑大型活动影响、非常态下乘客行为、接驳启动条件以及经济损失多方面因素在内的研究较少,如知网中以"轨道交通、调度"为检索字段的文章数量为2302篇,以"轨道交通、突发事件"为检索字段的文章数量为1116篇,以"轨道交通、大型活动"为检索字段的文章数量为134篇,而以"轨道交通、突发事件、大型活动、调度"为检索字段的文章数量仅有14篇。

因此本文立足于大型活动期间非常态应急接驳车辆调度问题展开分析,以掌握大型活动期间非常态交通特征以及构建应急调度预案要素。

1 大型活动场及非常态交通特征分析

1.1 大型活动交通特性

目前大型活动的界定并没有统一标准,《北京市大型社会活动安全管理条例》中有如下定义:主办方租用、借用或以其他形式临时占用场所、场地,面向社会公众举办的文艺演出、体育比赛、展览展销、招聘会、庙会、灯会、游园会等群体性活动。根据等级规模可分为一般等级活动,大规模活动及超大规模活动。曾红艳根据活动地点将大型活动分为单一地点活动与多地点活动。郑云霄根据人员到离情况分为集中爆发型与持续集散型。根据上述分类,2022年北京冬奥会属于国际超大规模体育赛事,属于多地点的持续集散型活动。

大型活动一般有固定的举办时间、地点,客流往往在活动过程中及前后出现高峰特征,即客流在时间与空间维度的分布集中。因此,大型活动对的交通影响范围和持续时间有限,但举办地点附近站点客流量陡增,且具有高峰性质。不同类型活动的客流特征也不同,如集中爆发型活动,在开场、散场时间前后会造成客流的明显高峰特点,即集散过程持续时间短、峰值高;而持续集散型活动,会在活动期间产生客流的高原特征,即集散时间长、峰值低。不同类型活动客流特点如图1所示。这一现象会导致活动地点临近站点客流量、线路断面不均衡性以及临近站点车厢满载率增加,给交通系统带来更大压力。

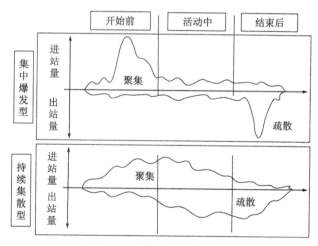

图 1 不同类型活动客流特点示意图

大型活动客流还具有时空波动性、出行方式多样性、集中性、外部性、连续性、可预知性及差异性等。客流量受到活动自身因素外,如交通因素、固定常规客流因素、天气、节假日等其他因素影响,在管理上具有紧迫性与复杂性。Lu Zhao等认为客流影响主要来自乘客对站点的选择行为,并运用Logit模型,考虑乘客的出行距离、方向、时间等因素,从而选择自己认为最方便的方式出行。Chen Li等分析了活动的影响范围与持续时间。许秀峰等、付宇等分别提出了基于层次分析法、Xgboost方法的大型活动轨道交通客流量预测方法及站内客流情况评价方法。

1.2 交通系统突发事件及其影响

根据《中华人民共和国突发事件应对法》,突发事件定义为突然发生,造成或可能造成严重社会危害,需要采取应急处置措施,以应对的自然灾害、事故灾难、公共卫生事件、社会安全事件。交通系统中,高速公路突发事件可定义为:在某一时刻突然发生,使交通中断,妨碍高速公路正常运营,并可能对群众的生命财产安全造成损失,需要各应急救援部门采取措施进行处置的事件。诱因包括自然因素、人为因素、道路因素及车辆因素,且人为因素占比最大。轨道交通突发事件可定义为:城市轨道交通系统正常运营时段,由设备故障、自然灾害等不可预知因素导致,在一定范围内发生的,影响轨道交通系统正常运转,对城市交通系统及社会经济带来一定负面影响的事件。根据《国家城市轨道交通运营突发事件应急预案》,按人员伤亡、经济损失和运营状况可分为特别重大、重大、较大与一般四个等级。诱因包括技术扰动、自然扰动和人为扰动,且可能发生在各类站点或站间的任一位置。因此,交通系统中突发事件包括车辆故障、道路损坏、信号故障、自然灾害、交通事故、消防治安问题及公共事件等在内的一切可能影响交通系统正常运行的事件。

道路系统中突发事件的影响包括由大风、大雪等恶劣天气导致道路通行能力下降或出行需求改变;因地震、滑坡等地质灾害造成道路中断;因交通事故导致出行延误、人员伤亡等。据统计,我国每年发生道路交通事故超过50万起,超过90%的事故由驾驶员操作不当引起。由于道路交通异常的随机性、危害性与频发性,需要交通部门、急救、消防等多个部门共同处理。为量化突发事件对道路交通的影响,彭路强从影响持续时间、通行能力变化、车辆构成变化、延误几个方面分析影响程度;马庚华计算了非常态下的时空容量损耗,利用Van Aerde模型计算突发事件的影响范围与排队长度。

轨道交通事故中排除施工事故,我国近十年共发生近2000起。对轨道交通系统的影响包括突发电力故障、车辆故障、信号设备故障和车门故障造成线路区间运营中断;恶劣天气导致地铁系统倒灌;恐怖袭击导致地铁全线网疏散并停运。据统计,运营延误时间在30min之内的因素中75.5%是车辆故障、车门和信号故障;自然灾害,如暴雨、台风等恶劣天气造成的影响时间长,甚至造成运营中断。由于突发事件的公共性、危害性、紧迫性、破坏性、救援难度大、容易产生二次事故等特点,乘客会出现恐慌、冲动、侥幸、从众等心里,并影响其行为。

为量化突发事件的影响,Lu Zhao等、茹小磊利用实测数据,通过建立模型描述乘客选择行为。王言中提出大型活动应急疏散需求计算方法,并认为应急疏散目的地可用恩格尔系数法与重力模型法进行预测。但由于异常事件的不确定性,且发生概率较低,大部分研究采用仿真分析方式来研究乘客行为与紧急疏散方法。如赖艺欢、田郝青应用社会力模型(连续行人仿真模型)进行仿真;姚加林、李伟、萨木哈尔·波拉提应用元胞自动机模型(离散仿真模型)进行仿真;代宝乾应用流体力学模型进行仿真。应用软件包括legion、Sim walk、Anylogic、vissim、mass motion、STEPS等多款仿真软件。各模型特点对比见表1。

常用仿真模型对比 表1

建模方法	特征	软件
元胞自动机模型	微观角度下将时间、空间和速度散化,其径路被划分为等距离的格子,每个元胞或为空或被占据,并按一定规则更新	Legion STEPS
社会力模型	微观角度下分析,假设行人在主观驱动力、行人间相互作用力以及行人与建筑间作用力的共同作用下运动	Anylogic Vissim mass motion
改进的社会力模型	在社会力模型基础上加以改进,加入出口选择机制、可变步速机制等	Anylogic
流体力学模型	以人员守恒为基础,将人流视为流体进行宏观分析	STEPS

2 应急接驳车辆调度模型

2.1 冬奥交通网络及非常态情景构建

北京冬奥分为北京、延庆和张家口三个赛区,其综合交通网络包括京张高铁、京藏、京新、京礼高速、城市轨道交通以及常规公交等。由于比赛时间为冬季,不可避免会出现恶劣天气、设备故障或其他事故的可能性。据以往数据显示,高铁网络(如商杭高铁、沪昆高铁、京沪高铁)曾多次因大风天气使异物触碰供电网或设备故障,导致运行中断;高速公路网络曾多次因恶劣天气、交通事故导致线路中断,如2019年2月6日,因大雪天气导致京藏高速昌平至延庆区段与京新高速沙城至涿鹿区段封闭、京礼高速临时管制,同年4月3日,京藏高速发生16车相撞的大型交通事故,导致京藏高速暂时中断;地铁系统也多次因设备故障、人为干扰等原因中断运行,威胁乘客安全,造成损失。据统计,北京地铁2012年5月—2019年5月期间共发生547起突发事件,年平均70起。

冬奥会交通网络涉及城际、城市、交通网络、赛事点等多层级交通网络空间范围,非常态下应急车辆调度研究对于保障交通网络安全高效运行意义重大,对现有应急车辆调度研究梳理,有助于把握非常态下应急车辆调度目标、约束和求解方法,为开展实际应用提供理论基础。因此,本文围绕轨道交通(含高铁)系统在非常态下的应急车辆接驳问题开展。

轨道交通系统受多因素干扰,如设备故障、紧急运输任务、突发性灾难、人身伤亡事故等,造成某个(某些)车站和线路中断运行。为避免客流拥堵在线网内快速传播,并最大限度地降低损失,需建立安全、完善、可靠、反应快速的应急车辆调度系统,为快速有效的预警预控、事中紧急救援以及事后妥善安置的应急管理系统服务。西直门是京张高铁起点,也是北京城市轨道交通的重要换乘站点。京张高铁承担着联通三大赛区的重任,提高对接、接驳京张高铁的安全保障,对保障冬奥会期间交通安全高效运行十分必要。

假设西直门站受影响,场景如图2所示。图中中断点表示轨道交通运行中断,此时需要由派车点派接驳车辆前往各中断点,并输送滞留乘客到指定接驳目的地,派车数量、发车频率和接驳的线路等需根据优化确定最佳。

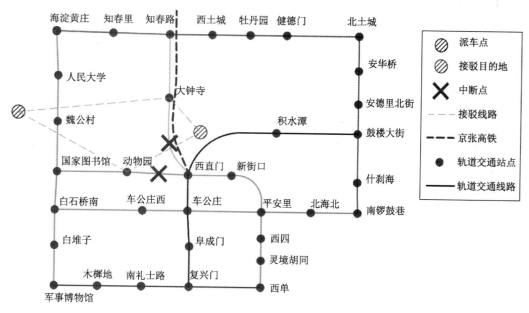

图2 突发事件下应急公交车辆接驳示意图

2.2 应急接驳模型基础

2.2.1 应急接驳启动条件

面对轨道交通系统非常态情景,需要做好应急调度预案,但并不一定要启动应急接驳。潘义强提出周边公交车剩余运力计算方法,旨在当中断区间小、时间短,造成影响较小且剩余运力满足需求时,只需借助周边公交进行接驳。同时考虑乘客延误与经济损失给出应急接驳启动阈值。刘静根据车站的换乘客流量、车站所在区位以及站点等级分别量化了车站换乘强度、区位强度与等级强度,定义应急强度 = 车站换乘强度 + 区位强度 + 等级强度,应急强度越高越需要应急接驳。徐亚楠将滞留的乘客看作排队系统中等待服务的顾客,并根据站台面积计算最大排队长度限制,进而提出了基于排队论的应急接驳车辆启动阈值确定方法。张聪聪总结各城市轨道交通应急预案,最终给出了根据预估中断时间判断是否需要启动应急接驳方法。

2.2.2 接驳客流需求

现有非常态情景下受客流影响规模获取有两类。一类是来源于历史数据,通过大数据分析,拟合不同情景下的统计模型,对突发事件发生和持续影响时间段内受影响的进站量与日常日平均进站量比值作为参数,估计突发事件下的客流量。据李臣统计,事发时段约62%的OD对误差在20%以下,在持续影响时段,约51%的OD对预测误差在20%以下。第二类就是通过构建静态、动态推演、仿真模型,根据实际的突发事件以及交通网络的实际环境进行客流分配获取。吴丽娟认为如果某时刻发生了突发事件,乘客的选择行为主要有:继续等待轨道交通出行、选择其他方式出行、出站乘车到相邻轨道交通站点再次进站。根据改变后的路网结构,构建虚拟轨道交通网络(包括各换乘方式和路径)及列车时刻表,对进站量平均值进行调整,得到在不同仿真周期中各种选择方式的比例,从而得到非常态下的接驳客流需求。据徐亚楠调查,以休闲娱乐为目的的出行者选择继续等待的概率较高,以通勤为目的的出行者则更倾向于改变交通方式。张聪聪提出当某些路径阻抗过大时,往往不会被采用,可用Dijkstra或Dial算法计算出有效路径,将有效径路的流量转化为应急接驳需求量。

2.2.3 乘客延误分析

轨道交通中断导致乘客滞留,使大量乘客出行延误进而产生经济损失。受影响客流主要包括中断时处于轨道交通系统内的乘客、中断开始未进入系统并受影响客流、由于不能到达目的地改变路径的客流等。潘义强假设乘客继续选择轨道交通出行且进站量不发生变化,给出受影响乘客数与乘客总延误计算公式,并计算站台乘客密度计算方法,用于评价突发事件下站点的服务水平。此时受影响乘客数为 $P_{总} = \frac{qT_e}{60} + P_0 + P_1$,延误大小为 $T_m = \frac{(P_0 + P_1 + P_{总}) \times T_e}{2 \times 60}$,符号意义见表3。由于乘客出行延误会造成社会经济损失,损失值大小可通过劳动力价值刻画,若派出应急接驳车辆,减小延误的同时会产生成本,该成本与派车数量、发车频率、行车线路有关。

按照潘义强的思路,若考虑出行方式改变,并假设其概率为 $P_{改}$,且达率不变,则累计乘客数随时间的变化关系如图3所示,阴影部分为站内乘客总延误: $T_m = \frac{(P + P_{总} - P_{离}) \times T_e}{2 \times 60}$。

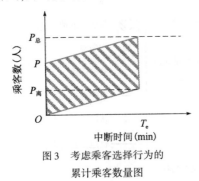

图3 考虑乘客选择行为的累计乘客数量图

2.2.4 派车点选址模型

为保证接驳系统的应急作用,要求应急接驳车辆需短时间内到达需求站点。因此,需要选定能够确保车辆可以快速响应的蓄车点地址。主要应用的模型有集合覆盖模型、最大覆盖模型、p-中值选址模型以及反向覆盖模型等,以最大限度覆盖中断点,尽可能提升效率,确定最佳蓄车点场地,并在此基础上继续寻找最优调度方案,此类方法枢纽选址中较为常见。各选址模型对比见表2。

选址模型对比 表2

建模方法	思 想
集合覆盖机模型	满足所有需求点(中断点)都在服务范围内的前提下使供给点(蓄车点)数量尽可能少
最大覆盖模型	假设供给点数量有限,不一定满足全覆盖,确定供给点位置使其尽可能多的覆盖需求点
p-中心模型	假设有p个供给点,确定各中断点客流需求作为权值,使加权后平均距离最短
p-中值模型	将p-中心模型中的加权后平均距离最短改为加权后总接驳时间最短,以提升效率
反向覆盖模型	以需求点为圆心,以接驳时间为半径,使乘客等待时间尽可能短

2.2.5 模型参数解释

上文以及后文中涉及目标函数、约束条件，有众多参数，其符号意义见表3。

模型中符号意义 表3

符号	意义
S_h	应急车辆派车点集合
M_q	乘客目的地集合
E_i	轨道交通中断站点集合
N	可用车辆数（辆）
Q_B	额定载客量（人）
δ_B	车辆最大满载率
δ_{Bj}	第 j 辆车的实际满载率
T_e	应急疏散时间（min）
f	应急接驳车辆的发车频率（辆/h）
λ_B	应急接驳车辆单位运营成本[元/(km·车)]
D_B	应急接驳车辆行驶距离（km）
P_0	中断前存于该站点内的乘客数量（人）
P_1	中断时列车内人数（人）
$P_离$	选乘其他方式出行的人数（人）
q	站点进站客流量（人/h）
$d_{i,j}^{on}$	疏运目的地为 G_i 的旅客在中断站 E_i 的上车人数
$d_{i,j}^{off}$	疏运目的地为 G_i 的旅客在中断站 E_i 的下车人数
ψ	全线车辆车头时距方差
$h_{k,j}^{(t)}$	第 k 辆车与第 $k-1$ 辆车在 j 站点的车头时距
$t_{i,k}$	车辆 B_k 在蓄车点到中断站 E_i 的行驶时间
$x_{i,k}$	若 $x_{i,k}=1$ 表示公交车辆 B_k 被调配至中断站 E_i
$t_{i,j}^1$	车辆由中断站 E_i 到目的地 G_i 的行驶时间
$t_{i,j}^2$	车辆由中断站 E_i 到目的地 G_i 的返程时间
M	车辆在中断站与目的地之间的循环次数
$t'_{i,j,k}$	车辆执行最后一次疏运任务的单程行驶时间
θ	正数权重，保证尽量采取车辆数少的方案
f_1	接驳公交总开行成本（元）
f_2	乘客总经济损失（元）
$\Delta T_{i,i-1}$	第 i 辆车与前车的发车间隔
r	接驳公交线路个数（条）
F	总经济损失（万元）
γ	人均劳动力价值[元/(人·h)]
σ	发车间隔之差限制阈值
ω	权重

2.3 接驳调度模型

2.3.1 目标函数

车辆调度包括常态与非常态两种情况，面向管理者与出行者两个群体，不同情况下优化方向不同，常态下从管理者角度出发,可以总载客量最大或总成本最小为目标,以使公交公司利益最大化;为使车辆到达稳定,可以车头时距方差最小为目标,旨在使整个系统运行更稳定,减小乘客延误。非常态下从管理者角度出发,考虑乘客损失与车辆开行成本,可以总经济损失最小为目标;但非常态更多考虑出行者受影响情况,可选择总接驳服务时间最小为目标,旨在满足需求的前提下,使所有接驳车辆总运行时间最小,或以乘客总延误时间最小为目标,尽可能减小损失,迅速疏解滞留乘客,目标函数整理见表4。

目标函数整理 表4

目标函数	具体模型	参考文献
总载客量最大	$\max S = T_e f \sum_i \sum_j (d_{i,j}^{on} - d_{i,j}^{off})$	[18]
总运输成本最小	$\min F = \sum_{i \in E_i} \lambda_B x_{i,k} D_{B,i}$	[20-22]
疏散耗能最小	$\min E = \sum_{i \in E_i} x_{i,k} D_{B,i}$	[7,23]
车头时距方差最小	$\min \psi = \sum_{j \in E_i} \omega_j^{(t)} \left\{ \frac{1}{m-1} \cdot \sum_k^N [h_{k,j}^{(t)} - h_{标准}]^2 \right\}$	[19]
总接驳服务时间最小	$\min T = T_1 + T_2 + \theta \sum_{i=1}^{\alpha} \sum_{k=1}^{\gamma} x_{i,k}$ $T_1 = \sum_{i=1}^{\alpha} \sum_{k=1}^{\gamma} t_{i,k} x_{i,k}$ $T_2 = \sum_{k=1}^{\gamma} \left[\sum_{i=1}^{\alpha} \sum_{j=1}^{\beta+2} (t_{i,j}^1 + t_{i,j}^2) M - t'_{i,j,k} \right]$	[14-15]
总经济损失最小	$\min F = f_1 + f_2$ $f_1 = \lambda_B \sum_{i=1}^{n} D_B \cdot T_e \cdot f$ $f_2 = \gamma \cdot T_m$	[14,16-17]

2.3.2 约束条件

约束条件给定求解范围,在车辆应急调度模型中,需要满足以下约束:

(1)车辆数约束:为保证经济性,认为可用车辆有限,保证派车数不超上限。

$$\sum_i x_{k,i} \leq N \tag{1}$$

(2)客流需求约束:根据前文所述,认为接驳客流需求已知,为保证接驳能力满足需求,可疏解掉所有滞留乘客。

$$N \cdot Q_B \cdot \delta_B \cdot M \geq \sum_{i \in E_i} \sum_{j \in G_i} (d_{i,j}^{on} - d_{i,j}^{off}) \tag{2}$$

(3)时间约束:线网恢复运行后,应急接驳就失去了必要性,需保证应急接驳时间不超过中断时间。

$$\sum_{i=1}^{\alpha} \sum_{j=1}^{\beta+2} [t_{i,k} x_{i,k} + (t_{i+j}^1 + t_{i+j}^2) M - t'_{i,j,k}] \leq T_e, \forall k = 1,2,\cdots,\gamma \tag{3}$$

(4)频率约束:提高发车频率可提升接驳的效果,但会出现所有车辆都被派出而无法循环。为保证应急接驳的持续性,车辆的发车频率须在最大与最小发车频率之间。

$$f_{\min} \leq f \leq f_{\max} \tag{4}$$

(5) 往返次数约束：最小往返次数为0，且不超最大次数限制。

$$M \leq M_{\max} = \frac{T_e - t_{i,k} - (t_{i,j}^1 + t_{i,j}^2) + t'_{i,j,k}}{t_{i,j}^1 + t_{i,j}^2} \tag{5}$$

(6) 满载率约束：为保证安全，车辆实际满载率不得超最大满载率限制。

$$\delta_{Bj} \leq \delta_B, \forall j \in N \tag{6}$$

(7) 发车间隔约束：为保证车辆到达连续且稳定，要求发车间隔波动不超过一定限制。

$$|\Delta T_{i,i-1} - \Delta T_{i-1,i-2}| \leq \sigma, \forall i \in [3, N] \tag{7}$$

(8) 其他物理约束：如车辆数只能为自然数，某车辆只能前往某个中断点等。

$$M \in N, x_{i,k} \in \{0, 1\} \tag{8}$$

2.3.3 模型求解

现有求解接驳车辆调度模型算法大致有：转化为运输问题或利用二次规划求解；采用遗传算法(GA)求解；采用粒子群算法(PSO)进行求解或采用修改后的粒子群算法求解。

遗传算法广泛应用于工程搜索最优解，编码形式一般选用二进制编码形式，适应度函数一般要求非负，极大问题可直接使用目标函数，极小问题可取倒数或取反后加个常数，在算子操作过程中，为避免过早或过慢收敛，交叉概率一般取 0.4~0.9，变异概率取 0.001~0.1。粒子群算法由于存在信息交互，所有粒子同时寻找到值相等的局部最优解的概率极低，解决了遗传算法等过可能早陷入局部最优解的弊端。李宁研究结果表明在此类问题上PSO方法效果远好于GA方法，粒子数量要依据任务数确定，一般为任务数的6-8倍，为避免过早局部收敛，重叠粒子数一般为1~2，当粒子数足够大时，粒子数的增加对算法效果无太大影响。王铁君通过判断粒子是否早熟，对PSO方法进行了改进。

2.4 非常态车辆调度模型整合

聚焦于北京冬奥非常态应急接驳车辆调度，为最大程度保障活动正常开展，以所有乘客总等待时间最短为目标建立模型，如式(9)所示。

$$\min T = T_m + \frac{P_{\text{总}} P_{\text{改}}}{2f} = \left[P + \left(P + \frac{qT_e}{60}\right)(1 - P_{\text{改}})\right]\frac{T_e}{2} + \left[P + \frac{qT_e}{60}\right]\frac{P_{\text{改}}}{2f}$$

$$\text{s.t.} \begin{cases} \sum_i x_{k,i} \leq N \\ N \cdot Q_B \cdot \delta_B \cdot M \geq P_{\text{总}} \cdot P_{\text{改}} \\ \delta_{Bj} \leq \delta_B, \forall j \in N \\ f_{\min} \leq f \leq f_{\max} \\ x_{i,k} \in \{0, 1\} \end{cases} \tag{9}$$

目标函数包含两部分，其中第一项为所有继续等待乘坐轨道交通出行的乘客总延误，第二项为选择应急接驳公交出行的乘客总延误。约束条件初步考虑车辆数约束、客流需求约束、发车频率约束、满载率约束及物理约束。式中 $P_{\text{改}}$ 初步考虑用logit模型计算，考虑各方式的出行时间，此时 T_m 为关于 f 的函数，若设 $P_{\text{改}}$ 为常数，则 T_m 为常数，根据已有研究，可使用PSO算法求解。

假设西直门站部分线路发生中断且中断时间较短，场景如图4a)所示，此时乘客既可以通过轨道交通换乘到达西直门站，也可通过含应急接驳公交在内多种方式到达目的地。此时模型中 $P_{\text{改}}$ 的值在 0~1 之间。假设西直门站完全中断且中断时间较长，场景如图4b)所示，此时乘客无法通过轨道交通内部换乘到达，所有乘客均需要换成接驳公交，此时 $P_{\text{改}} = 1$，轨道交通系统乘客延误 $T_m = 0$，延误值将全部转移至接驳公交系统,此时总延误只与发车频率负相关。

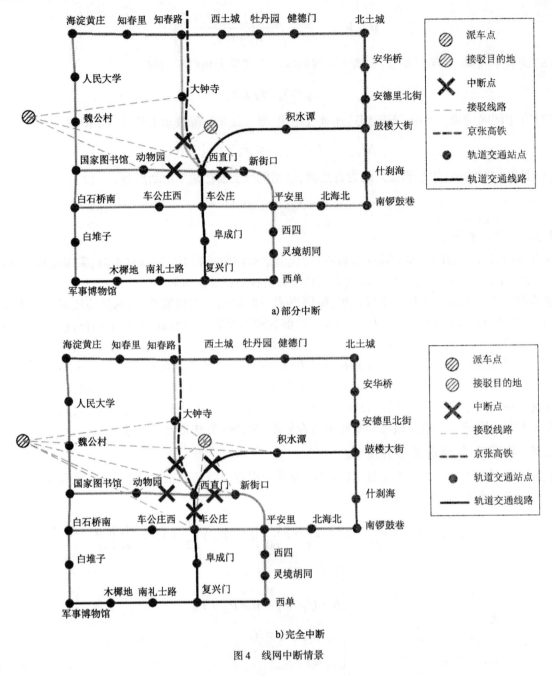

图4 线网中断情景

3 结 语

本文通过对大型活动期间非常态下车辆应急接驳研究的梳理,分析了大型活动期间的交通特征及非常态对交通的影响,剖析了冬奥会交通网络非常态情景设计的合理性。在此基础上,构建非常态的接驳车辆调度场景,精细化分析应急接驳调度模型的目标函数、约束条件,提出以乘客总延误最小为目标的大型赛事期间非常态应急接驳车辆调度模型。应急调度模型针对性强,后续将展开案例研究,为冬奥会非常态综合交通协同优化调度提供支撑。

参考文献

[1] 郑云霄.大型活动下城市轨道交通进出站客流短时预测研究[D].北京:北京交通大学,2018.
[2] Lu Zhao, En-jian Yao, Sha-sha Liu. Passenger Flow Analysis for the Surrounding Subway Stations of Large

Special Event Site during Dissipation[J]. Advances in Engineering Research, 2017(129):274-277.
[3] 钱慧敏,李静,张琳,等. 持续型大型活动影响因素及客流分布特征分析[J].交通工程,2020,20(1): 61-65.
[4] 付宇,翁剑成,钱慧敏. 基于XGBoost算法的大型活动期间轨道进出站量预测[J].武汉理工大学学报,2020, 44(5):832-836.
[5] 孟昊宇.北京2022年冬奥会道路交通安保对策及工作机制研究[J].北京警察学院学报.2019,(1): 29-34.
[6] 茹小磊.城市轨道交通应急接驳设计[D].西安:长安大学,2016.
[7] 胡华磊.大型活动突发事件公交应急调度的研究[D].北京:北京交通大学,2008.
[8] 徐亚楠.城市轨道交通应急接驳公交疏散预案研究[D].南京:东南大学,2018.
[9] 杜云飘.城市轨道交通突发事件应急管理研究[D].西安:长安大学, 2018.
[10] Renming Liu, Shukai Li. Collaborative optimization for metro train scheduling and train connections combined with passenger flow control strategy [J]. omega,2020(90):1-18.
[11] Jungang Shia, Lixing Yang. Cooperative passenger flow control in an over-saturated metro network with operational risk thresholds[J]. omega,2020(90):1-18.
[12] 潘义强.城市轨道交通突发中断下的应急公交接驳研究[D].哈尔滨:哈尔滨工业大学,2019.
[13] 陈治亚,谭斐,冯芬玲.地铁突发运营中断下应急公交调度研究[J].铁道科学与工程学报,2019,16 (9):2360-2367.
[14] 曾红艳.大型体育赛事专用车辆调度模型研究[D].广州:华南理工大学,2012.
[15] 张聪聪.轨道交通突发中断下的应急公交接驳模型研究[D].吉林:吉林大学,2019.
[16] 崔玲玲,陈涛,张玉萍.针对突发事件的公交车辆动态调度[J].交通信息与安全,2009,27(1):62-66.
[17] 龙琼,胡列格,张谨帆.突发事件下公交车辆快速动态滞站调度算法[J].中国公路学报,2013,26 (2):154-159.
[18] 李宁,邹彤,孙德宝.车辆路径问题的粒子群算法研究[J].系统工程学报,2004,19(6):596-600.
[19] 王铁君,邬月春.基于混沌粒子群算法的物流配送路径优化[J].计算机工程与应用,2011,47(29): 218-221.
[20] 马帅.城市生鲜食品冷链物流配送中心选址及路径优化问题研究[D].北京:北京交通大学,2018.
[21] 胡华,刘志钢,朱海燕.城市轨道交通突发事件下的公共汽车应急调配方法[R].城市轨道交通,2012(12):67-73.
[22] 北京市人大常委会. 北京市大型社会活动安全管理条例[S].2005.
[23] 冯诚.大型活动散场时段地铁车站客流分布预测与控制[D].北京:北京建筑大学,2020.
[24] Chen Li, Yanyan Chen. Analysis Method for Passenger Flow Characteristics of Urban Rail Transit under Emergent Events Based on AFC Data[J]. Beijing University of Technology,2019:2051-2063.
[25] 许秀峰,杜文.层次分析法在轨道交通站点客流吸引率计算中的应用[J].世界轨道交通,2004,0 (12):36-38.
[26] 张奕.高速公路突发事件应急决策支持系统的研究[D].北京:中国人民公安大学,2020.
[27] 迟昊.地面公共交通突发事件的应急管理与信息上报研究[J].真知灼见,2020,15-20.
[28] 刘晓虎.高速公路交通安全突发事件应急方法探讨[J].工程技术,2020(21):57-59.
[29] 夏泽郁,汤育春,李启明.基于韧性理论的中国城市轨道交通事故统计分析[J].都市快轨交通. 2020,33(3):148-156.
[30] 彭路强.高速公路突发事件交通影响与处置措施研究[D].北京:中国人民公安大学,2020.
[31] 刘晓闽.北京市交通事故数据研究与分析研判[D].北京:北京工业大学,2014.

[32] 胡鑫.高速公路突发事件应急救援存在问题与对策研究[J].广东公路交通,2020(6):39-41.
[33] 马庚华,郑长江,付文进.突发事件下城市交通影响范围研究[J].武汉理工大学学报,2019,43(4):627-630.
[34] 尹洪英,徐丽群.道路交通网络脆弱性评估研究现状与展望[J].交通运输系统工程与信息,2010,3:7-13.
[35] 邢莹莹.城市轨道交通复杂网络特性及脆弱性研究[D].上海:上海交通大学,2017.
[36] 裴彦.暴雨灾害条件下轨道交通网=网络脆弱性与抗毁性研究[D].西安:长安大学,2019.
[37] 赖艺欢.基于仿真技术的城市轨道交通突发大客流应急组织方案研究[D].北京:北京交通大学,2017.
[38] 朱小马.地铁车站突发性大客流应急疏散研究[D].兰州:兰州交通大学,2017.
[39] 王言中.大型活动分层多模式公交应急疏散模型及策略研究[D].哈尔滨:哈尔滨工业大学,2020.
[40] 田郝青,张喜.基于Anylogic仿真技术的地铁换乘站客流组织优化评价研究[J].电子工程设计,2018,26(19):84-88.
[41] 姚加林,龙舜.基于元胞自动机的地铁车站行人疏散仿真[J].铁道科学与工程学报,2019,16(11):2897-2902.
[42] 李伟,张鑫龙.考虑个体行为的改进CA模型人员疏散研究[J].计算机工程与应用,2020:1-11.
[43] 萨木哈尔·波拉提,邹馨捷,郝明,等.基于元胞自动机的人员疏散模型探讨[J].安全与环境工程,2020,27(5):122-127.
[44] 代宝乾.公共聚集场所出口应急疏散能力研究[D].北京:中国矿业大学,2009.
[45] 钱蕾,周玮腾,韩宝明.城市轨道交通运营突发事件数据可视化分析[J].铁道科学与工程学报,2020,17(4):1025-1035.
[46] 刘静.城市轨道交通突发事件下的公交车辆应急调度方法研究[D].北京:北京交通大学,2016.
[47] 李臣,汪波,白云云,等.基于AFC数据的城市轨道交通突发事件客流影响分析[J].铁道科学与工程学报,2019,16(10):2620-2627.
[48] 吴丽娟.基于AFC数据的城市轨道交通网络乘客出行路径匹配及突发事件影响研究[D].北京:北京交通大学,2016.
[49] 王佳冬,袁振洲,宁尚彬.城轨运营中断下应急公交车辆调度模型[J].交通运输系统工程与信息,2019.19(4):149-154.
[50] 邱振龙.公交智能调度算法研究与优化[J].中国科技信息,2006(23):82-85.
[51] 李眸寒.基于客流需求及交通状况的公交调度优化方法研究[D].南京:东南大学,2015.

基于GM-RBF组合模型的地铁进站短时客流预测

陈亚鑫[1] 徐永能[1] 何流[1] 程慧[1] 张晨[2]
(1.南京理工大学自动化学院;2.国家电网泰州供电公司)

摘 要 当前,我国城市轨道交通正处在加速发展的阶段,其承担着城市大运量、快速化的运输责任。影响轨道交通客流量的变动有诸多的因素,如社会因素、自然因素等都与其变化有着些许联系。为使地铁客流预测的准确度有明显的提升,本文提出一种基于GM-RBF组合模型的地铁进站客流预测方法。首先构建GM(1,1)预测模型来预测出多个序列;其次对GM模型和RBF神经网络进行应用上的组合,利用RBF模型建立残差反馈,从而可以解决灰色模型在客流预测上低精度的问题;最后通过分析IC卡数据,将一天内客流数据按每5min为一个时间片段,同时考虑地铁站天气变化因素对客流的影响,对相应的天气数据实现量化处理,从而可以对地铁站进站进行短时客流预测。实验表明,GM-RBF 预测模型 MAPE 为 9.8891%,MAE 为 3.2439,RMSE 为 5.5818。GM-RBF 组合模型的误差评价指标与 GM 模型和 RBF 预测模型对比,精度方面有了显著的提高,所以该组合模型在地铁进站短时客流预测方面有良好的适用性。

关键词 灰度预测 神经网络 组合预测模型 轨道交通 客流预测

0 引　言

随着城市规模的不断扩张,城市生活水平的不断进步,城市轨道交通建设不断加快,国内外众多地铁运营系统已经实现了网络化运营,对于出行者、运营商和管理机构而言,客流预测结果会对城市公交各个方面造成一系列的影响,所以精确而又可靠的城市轨道交通短时客流预测就变得尤为重要。IC 卡记录包括乘客站点信息、刷卡时间、闸机号等丰富有用的数据,在客流预测方面有重大意义。因此,选择合适的客流预测方法,以多源数据为基础来提高城轨客流需求预测的准确性尤为关键。

高精确率、实时性强的短时客流预测对城轨交通系统的组织与控制有着至关重要的影响。然而,影响城市地铁客流的因素有多方面,如站点的布置、乘车时间、外部交通路况、天气变化、国家政策、城市大型活动等,预测误差减小会对城市整体公共交通系统的调度起着非常重要的作用。地铁客流预测是站在当前时刻对未来某一时刻,甚至若干个时刻的客流做出实时准确的预测。当前,国内外有两大类算法模型来预测客流:一类是线性评估模型,其主要模型有 ARIMA 模型、MLR 模型、Kalman Filtering 模型等;另一类则为机器学习方法,如 SVM、Neural Network、Deep Learning 等。Mo Y 等把时空信息、历史客流量、天气变化数据作为输入变量,利用 Neural Network 解决了公交客流实时预测的问题;Ma X 等采用并行的 CNN 和 LSTM 分别对轨道客流在时间和空间的特征方面进行提取,且对 20min 客流进行预测;王秋雯等提出一种考虑时空特征的基于卷积长短时记忆神经网络和自适应 k-means 聚类算法对轨道客流预测的方法;金聪等对各个站点进行多元线性回归分析收集客流数据、天气数据以及周边业态分布数据对地铁客流预测;杜恒等分析了各天气因素对客流的影响,并基于此影响提出了预测模型,提高了预测的精度;邹巍等分析了导致轨道交通客流组织不确定性、非线性和变化大的原因,并提出了基于 WNN 与 GA 算法的城市轨道交通短时客流预测方法;付洁研究不同因素对铁路客运量产生的影响大小,提出了一种基于灰色 Verhulst 和 RBF 混合模型的客运量预测;陆百川等通过多源数据分析,结合 GA 和 WNN 混合模型提高了短时交通流预测精度。

灰色理论(GM)预测的优点主要体现在样本数据需求少、计算简单、工作量不大、短时预测精确度高的优点,但在处理复杂线性问题能力方面表现得还较差。人工神经网络拥有很强大的计算能力,同时它的容错性强、自适应性也很好,然而对样本的需求数量较大。本文利用地铁进站刷卡数据,考虑天气变化因素对客流的影响,提出一种地铁进站短时客流预测模型算法,把灰色(GM)模型与 RBF 径向基神经网络相结合。该组合模型不仅融合灰色模型需求量少、短时预测精度高等优势,还具备了 RBF 神经网络的处理能力强、自适应性好等优点,实现了地铁进站短时客流预测精度的提高。

1 GM-RBF 神经网络预测模型

1.1 GM 灰色模型

目前,最为广泛使用的灰色预测模型为 GM(1,1)模型。该模型的基本思想是把原始数据进行不断累加,然后构建出一阶线性微分方程模型,将模型计算值再进行累减后算出预测的值。具体步骤如下。

假设原有非负数据列为:

$$X^{(0)} = \{x^{(0)}(1), x^{(0)}(2), \cdots, x^{(0)}(n)\} \tag{1}$$

基金项目:中央高校自主科研基金(XJ2020004701);国家自然科学基金(52072214)。

式中,$X^{(0)}$ 为原始数据序列。对原始的数据列处理,累加后得到数据列为:

$$X^{(1)} = \{x^{(1)}(1), x^{(1)}(2), \cdots, x^{(1)}(n)\} \tag{2}$$

其中,$X^{(1)}k = \sum_{i=1}^{k} x^{(0)}(i), k = 1, 2, \cdots, n$。

灰色 GM(1,1) 模型的白化微分方程为:

$$\frac{dX^{(1)}}{dt} + aX^{(1)} = b \tag{3}$$

式中:a、b——参数;
a——发展系数;
b——灰色系数。

通过进行离散化来处理方程,得到的灰色 GM(1,1) 模型为:

$$X^{(0)}(k) + aZ^{(1)}k = b \tag{4}$$

$$Z^{(1)}(k) = \frac{[x^{(0)}(k-1) + x^{(0)}(k)]}{2} \tag{5}$$

其中,a、b 用最小二乘法确定,即

$$\hat{a} = [a \quad b]^T = (B^T B)^{-1} B^T Y \tag{6}$$

$$Y = [x^{(0)}(2) \quad x^{(0)}(3) \quad \cdots \quad x^{(0)}(n)] \tag{7}$$

$$B = \begin{bmatrix} -Z^{(1)}(2) & 1 \\ -Z^{(1)}(3) & 1 \\ \vdots & \vdots \\ -Z^{(1)}(n) & 1 \end{bmatrix} \tag{8}$$

将式(6)求得的参数 a、b 代入式(4)中得到模型的时间的响应函数为:

$$\hat{x}^{(1)}(k+1) = \left[x^{(1)}(k) - \frac{b}{a}\right] e^{-ak} + \frac{b}{a} \tag{9}$$

利用 1-IAGO 对预测序列进行累减,从而得到的 GM(1,1) 模型的表达式为:

$$\hat{x}^{(0)}(k+1) = \hat{x}^{(1)}(k+1) - \hat{x}^{(1)}(k), k = 1, 2, \cdots, n \tag{10}$$

原始数据均值为:

$$\bar{x} = \frac{1}{n} \sum_{k=1}^{n} x^{(0)}(k) \tag{11}$$

原始数据方差为:

$$S_1^2 = \frac{1}{n} \sum_{k=1}^{n} (x^{(0)}(k) - \bar{x})^2 \tag{12}$$

记残差为:

$$e^{(0)}(k) = x^{(0)}(k) - \hat{x}^{(0)}(k) \tag{13}$$

残差均值为:

$$\bar{e} = \frac{1}{n-1} \sum_{k=2}^{n} e^{(0)}(k) \tag{14}$$

残差方差为:

$$S_2^2 = \frac{1}{n-1} \sum_{k=2}^{n} [e^{(0)}(k) - e]^2 \tag{15}$$

1.2 RBF 神经网络

RBF(Radial Basis Function)径向基神经网络的结构简单、学习速度比其他同类快,且具有良好的逼近能力,在非线性函数逼近、模式识别等众多领域里得到广泛的运用。RBF 神经网络 n-p-m 三层网络结构:第一层为输入层,其主要为数据源节点,起到信号传输的作用;第二层为隐含层,包含 RBF 神经网络

的激活函数;第三层为输出层,实现把隐含层所得到的结果进行线性加权求和。其结构如图1所示。

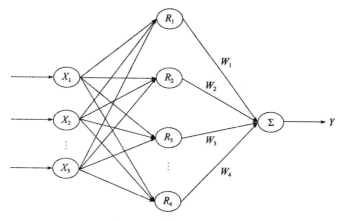

图1 RBF 神经网络结构

高斯函数 $H_j(x)$ 通常被作为激活函数被应用在隐含层:

$$H_j(x) = \exp\left(-\frac{\|X_i - c_j\|^2}{2\sigma_j^2}\right), j = 1,2,\cdots,n \tag{16}$$

式中:X_i——输入变量;

c_j——第 j 个基函数得中心;

σ_j——第 j 个隐节点得宽度;

n——隐含层的节点个数。

输出层节点的输出值为

$$y_i = \sum_{k=1}^{p} w_{ki} H_i(x), i = 1,2,\cdots,n \tag{17}$$

式中:y_i——输出层第 i 个节点的输出值;

n——输出层节点个数;

w_{ki}——隐含层第 i 个单元和输出层第 k 个单元和输出层第 i 个单元之间的连接权值。

1.3 GM-RBF 组合模型

为了提高城轨交通客流预测的准确性,本文把 GM 模型和 RBF 神经网络各自的优点相结合,采用 GM-RBF 混合预测模型的方法对客流进行预测。本文预测值定为模型的输入样本,实际的值定为输出样本,采用了神经网络模型,利用一定结构,对神经网络进行预测,就可以得出众多有关节点的权值与阈值,用来模拟预测值和实际值之间的残差,以及序列之间的相互关系。GM-RBF 神经网络结构如图2所示。

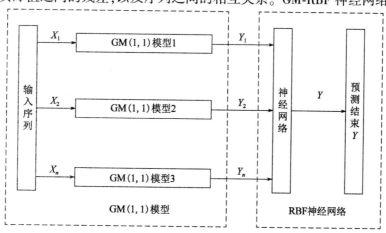

图2 GM-RBF 神经网络结构

根据 GM-RBF 组合预测模型的原理,具体建模实施方法如下:

(1)获取样本地铁进站的数据,构建 GM(1,1)模型,从而获得累加序列。

(2)为提高 GM-RBF 的预测精度,对输入和输出的数据使用式(18)来进行归一化处理。

$$T = T_{min} + \frac{T_{max} - T_{min}}{X_{max} - X_{min}}(X - X_{min}) \tag{18}$$

式中:X——原始数据;

X_{max}——原始数据的最大值;

X_{min}——原始数据的最小值;

T——目标数据;

T_{max}——目标数据的最大值;

T_{min}——目标数据的最小值。

(3)通过 RBF 神经网络学习确定相应参数与权值以构建预测模型。

(4)把新的客流数据输入 RBF 神经网络来进行预测而能够输出预测值。

(5)对结果利用式(19)来进行反归一化的处理。

$$X = X_{min} + \frac{X_{max} - X_{min}}{T_{max} - T_{min}}(T - T_{min}) \tag{19}$$

(6)对反归一化结果再进行白化处理,最后得到预测值。

2 实例分析

本文采集的样本数据为无锡地铁一号线和二号线 2015 年 5 月 14 日至 2015 年 5 月 20 日内一个星期的地铁进出站数据,经过预处理拥有两条线所有站点进出站数据约 310 万条。地铁 IC 卡刷卡数据内容见表1,其中包括 ID 号、票卡类型、线路编号、线路名称、站点编号、站点名称、刷卡终端号、交易日期、交易时间以及交易类型等数据信息。

地铁 IC 卡刷卡数据 表1

字 段 名	字段类型	字段说明
ID	int	交易编号
Card_ID	int	卡号
Card_Type	str	票卡类型
Route_ID	int	线路编号
Route_Name	str	线路名称
Station_ID	int	站点编号
Station_Name	str	站点名称
Terminal_ID	int	刷卡终端(闸机)编号
Transaction_Date	int	交易日期
Transaction_Time	int	交易时间
Transaction_Type	int	交易类型:1 上车、2 下车

利用 python 在网上选取,采集到 2018 年 5 月 14 日至 2018 年 5 月 20 日该市地铁一号线与二号线换乘站三洋广场站距离最近的气象观测站数据作为该站点的天气数据,并汇总为天气信息表。为了方便计算,将天气类型进行量化处理,见表2。

天气类型量化处理关系 表2

天 气 类 型	量化系数	天 气 类 型	量化系数
晴	12	雷阵雨	6
多云	10	中雨	4
小雨	8	大雨	2

通过数据处理,筛选出无锡地铁 2018 年 5 月 14 日至 2018 年 5 月 20 日三阳广场站的数据,选取 5min 粒度下每日有效时段为 5:35~23:35,共计 1512 组进站 IC 客流数据,选用前 1296 组进站数据来对 GM-RBF 预测模型进行训练,选取剩余 216 组数据用来作为对神经网络预测的测试样本。为了评价 GM-RBF 组合模型的预测效果,预测结果与灰色 GM(1,1)模型、RBF 径向基神经网络模型进行对比分析。预测结果和误差曲线如图 3~图 8 所示。

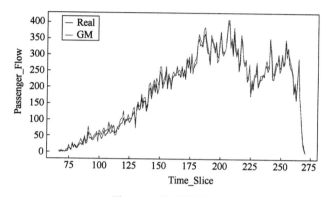

图 3　GM 模型预测结果

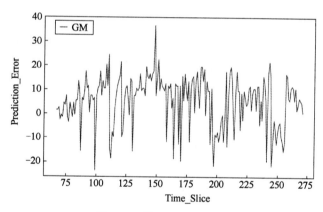

图 4　GM 模型预测误差曲线

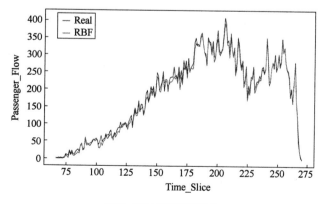

图 5　RBF 模型预测结果

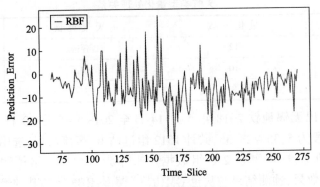

图6 RBF模型预测误差曲线

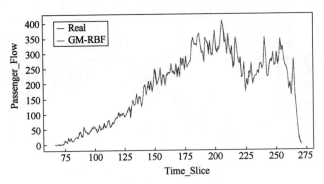

图7 GM-RBF组合模型预测结果

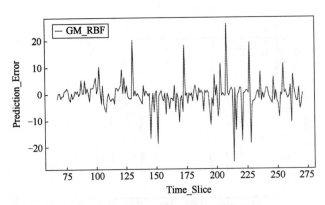

图8 GM-RBF组合模型预测误差曲线

由图3~图8可以看出,GM模型、RBF预测模型两者预测结果曲线与实际客流曲线吻合度较低,且误差得绝对值大多数在(10,20)之间,而GM-RBF组模型得到的预测结果都与实际值高度吻合,极少部分误差绝对值大于25,绝大多数是误差绝对值在(0,5)之间,效果总体保持平稳,波动小于其他两种预测模型。

在科学研究过程中,MAPE、RMSE、MAE这三个指标是用来评价预测方法的性能和预测结果的有效性。三种模型预测指标对比见表3。

三种模型预测结果指标分析 表3

	MAPE*	MAE	RMSE
GM	25.86149%	10.38537	11.9231
RBF	20.1979%	7.678048	9.5064
GM-RBF	9.889063%	3.243902	5.5818

注:* 由于实际客流中有时间段为0人,为避免MAPE计算时无意义,该指标忽略0人的时间段。

由表3可看出,GM-RBF网络的三个误差评价指标明显小于GM和RBF预测所得到的指标,有更高的预测准确度,因此GM-RBF组合模型能够实现对地铁客流精准、有效的预测。

3 结 语

本文通过对GM和RBF分析,综合两种预测模型的优点,且对两种预测模型的不足进行互相补充,提出一种GM-RBF神经网络预测模型。通过IC卡数据的分析以及天气数据对客流的影响因素,该模型实现了对地铁进站客流的短时预测。结果表示,GM-RBF预测模型MAPE为9.8891%,MAE为3.2439,RMSE为5.5818,三种评价指标的结果都小于单一的GM模型和RBF预测模型,证明该模型能够有效提高预测精度。但由于本文只考虑的天气影响因素对地铁进站客流的影响,实际上,进站客流还受到用地性质、节假日等因素影响,未来可将这些因素考虑到模型中以提高模型精度,且本文只考虑进站客流,未来可以将模型应用于出站客流上。

参考文献

[1] XUE R, JIAN, CHEN S K. Short-term bus passenger demand prediction based on time series model and interactive multiple model approach[J]. Discrete Dynamics in Nature and Society, 2015,66(1):61-78.

[2] 李小胜,王申令.带线性约束的多元线性回归模型参数估计[J].统计研究,2016,33(11):86-92.

[3] RASYIDI M A, KIM J, RYU K R. Short-Term Prediction of Vehicle Speed on Main City Roads using the k-Nearest Neighbor Algorithm[J]. Journal of Intelligence and Information Systems(S095-9902), 2014,20(1):121-131.

[4] 张春辉,宋瑞,孙杨.基于卡尔曼滤波的公交站点短时客流预测[J].交通运输系统工程与信息,2011,11(4):154-159.

[5] 杨信丰,刘兰芬.基于AP聚类的支持向量机公交站点短时客流预测[J].武汉理工大学学报(交通科学与工程版),2016,40(1):36-40.

[6] COSTARELLI D, VINTI G. Pointwise and uniform approximation by multivariate neural network operators of the max-pro-duct type[J]. Neural Network, 2016,81(9):81-90.

[7] VIEIRA S, PINAYA W H L, MECHELLI A. Using deep learning to investigate the neuroimaging correlates of psychiatric and neurological disorders: methods and applications[J]. Neuroscience and Biobehavioral Reviews, 2017,74:58-75.

[8] 焦李成,赵进,杨淑媛,等.深度学习、优化与识别[M].北京:清华大学出版社,2017:100-120.

[9] MO Y, SU Y Y. Neural networks based real-time transit passenger volume prediction[C]//SU Y Y. Power Electronics and Intelligent Transportation System(PEITS), 2009 2nd International Conference on. Shenzhen: IEEE, 2009: 303-306.

[10] Ma X, Zhang J, Du B, et al. Parallel Architecture of Convolutional Bi-Directional LSTM Neural Networks for Network-Wide Metro Ridership Prediction[J]. IEEE Transactions on Intelligent Transportation Systems, 2018, PP(99):1-11.

[11] 王秋雯,陈彦如,刘媛春.基于卷积长短时记忆神经网络的城市轨道交通短时客流预测[J].控制与决策,2020:1-10.

[12] 金聪,周健勇.基于天气对地铁的短时客流预测[J].物流科技,2020,43(03):99-104.

[13] 杜恒.天气因素对轨道交通客流的影响[C].2017年中国城市交通规划年会论文集,2017.

[14] 邹巍,陆百川,邓捷,等.基于遗传算法与小波神经网络的客流预测研究[J].武汉理工大学学报(交通科学与工程版),2014,38(05):1148-1151.

[15] 付洁,黄洪.基于Verhulst-RBF的铁路客运量预测[J].铁路计算机应用,2019,28(11):1-4-17.

[16] 陆百川,舒芹,马广露.基于多源交通数据融合的短时交通流预测[J].重庆交通大学学报:自然科学版,2019,38(5):13-19,56.

[17] 李洪嘉,姚红光,李思睿,等.基于灰色-神经网络的虹桥综合交通枢纽客流预测[J].科学技术创新,2020(36):121-122.

[18] 赵超,林思铭,许巧玲.基于GM-RBF神经网络的高校建筑能耗预测[J].南京理工大学学报,2014,38(01):48-53.

[19] 李斌,郝涛,史明华.基于支持向量机的交通流组合预测模型[J].天津工业大学学报,2008,27(2):73-76.

[20] 李晓俊,吕晓艳,刘军.基于径向基神经网络的铁路短期客流预测[J].铁道运输与经济,2011,33(6):86-89.

[21] 卫敏,余安乐.具有最优学习率的RBF神经网络及其应用[J].管理科学学报,2012,15(4):50-57.

[22] 谢振东,李之明,徐锋,等.城市交通一卡通大数据应用[M].北京:人民交通出版社股份有限公司,2016:171-188.

[23] 吕何,孔政敏,张成刚.基于混合优化随机森林回归的短期电力负荷预测[J].武汉大学学报(工学版),2020,53(08):704-711.

考虑出行成本及个人属性的出行方式选择模型

曾明哲　南彦洲　付泽坤　刘林建

(长安大学运输工程学院)

摘要　本文旨在进行城市日常交通出行行为决策建模。以荷兰奈梅亨市实际调查中收集的数据为基础,以小汽车、公交和铁路三种交通方式为因变量,进行皮尔逊相关性分析,筛选对交通方式选择有显著影响的因素作为自变量,建立了多项logit(MNL)模型、嵌套logit(NL)模型和混合logit(ML)模型,后进行模型检验和评估分析,得出最优的出行方式选择模型,并对该模型进行敏感性评估,分析策略更改对交通方式分担率的影响。结果表明,对交通方式选择有显著影响的因素包括小汽车和公交的出行时间、小汽车和公交的出行成本、轨道交通的进出时间和出行者性别等;其中NL模型在R方检验和似然比检验中表现最优,个人选择小汽车和公交的概率预测准确度均大于70%;最终估计的交通方式划分比为:汽车54.66%,地铁29.35%,公交15.99%。本文建立的模型对预测城市交通分担率及分析居民出行行为特点具有参考价值。

关键词　出行方式选择　多项logit模型　嵌套logit模型　混合logit模型　敏感性分析

0　引　言

当面对多种选择时,人们倾向于一种效用最大化的选择是合理的。这个概念被广泛地称为随机效用最大化(RUM),统计模型允许存在感知差异。在交通研究中,实现这一点的最著名模型之一是多项logit(MNL)模型。

出行方式预测的非集计模型是基于最大随机效用理论的一种较为完善的模型。与集计模型相比,非集计模型误差较小,能充分利用样本数据,且只需要少量样本。在非集计模型中,logit模型具有物理意义明确、计算简单等优点。它是目前最成熟、应用最广泛的非集计模型。对于交通方式选择,目前已发现了多个影响因素,例如出行特点、出行时间、车内时间和成本、旅行时间价值、工作时停车设施的可用性、交通安全和其他家庭成员非机动车方式出行的次数。在空间原因中,将居住位置和城市形态也认为是重要因素。此外,出行者本身的态度、感知、行为规范、信仰和习惯也被认为是方式选择的决定因素。

综合了解到,出行者在选择交通方式时主要受三大类因素影响,即费用、时间以及个人属性,因此本研究综合考虑该三类因素来建立出行者交通方式选择模型,能较大程度地贴近实际。目前多以出行方式的影响因素为研究重点,多只以单一 logit 模型进行分析,因此本文综合分析 MNL 模型、NL 模型、ML 模型三大 logit 模型,来达到考虑出行成本及个人属性的出行方式行为决策建模的目的。

1 数据收集与分析

1.1 数据描述

在这项研究中,我们将使用在荷兰奈梅亨市进行的实际调查收集的数据,估计从奈梅亨到该国西部主要城市,即阿姆斯特丹、鹿特丹和海牙的人们在铁路、公交和汽车之间选择方式的 logit 模型。在一次随机电话调查中确定了符合条件的奈梅亨居民,并要求他们参加家庭访谈。进行了 235 次访谈得到 235 条受访者数据。受访者被要求报告上述旅行的特点,以及前往同一目的地但使用其他(未选择)方式的旅行的特点。

1.2 数据统计分析

从图 1 可以看出,年龄、目的和性别对人们出行方式的选择有不同的影响。在图 1a)中,60 岁以上人群选择乘坐公交车出行的比例明显低于其他年龄段人群,仅为 5.56%。在图 1b)中,显而易见,当出行目的为办公时,乘坐地铁出行的比例明显大于其他目的,达到 50%;除办公外,其他出行目的在交通方式的选择上没有明显差异。图 1c)中,59.54% 的男性选择小汽车出行,50% 的女性选择小汽车出行;26.72% 的男性选择地铁出行,34.62% 的女性选择地铁出行;可以得出结论,该地区男性比女性更喜欢开车出行,而女性更喜欢乘地铁出行。

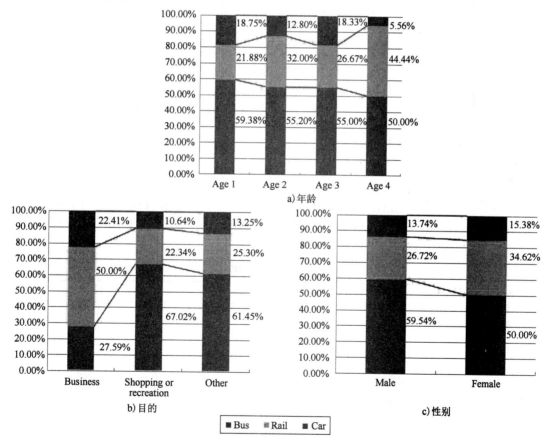

图 1 不同年龄、目的、性别分类下交通方式划分

为了进一步探讨方式划分与各因素之间的关系,在原始调查数据的基础上进行了相关分析。可以知道 OVTRAIL、PURPOSE、TCCAR、TCBUS、TTCAR 和 TTBUS 变量的 Sig(double tail)值均小于 0.01,说明当置信度为 0.01 时,这些变量与交通方式的选择相关性显著。

2 建模结果分析

2.1 变量定义

三种出行方式分别是汽车(0)、铁路(1)和公交(2)。通过组合不同的特征变量得到不同的效用函数,建立不同的 logit 模型。表 1 显示了下一部分建模中需要用到变量的基本信息。

原始变量设置　　　　表1

变量类型	变量名	参数符号	变量符号	数据类型
常量	小汽车常量	ASC1		
	地铁常量	ASC2		
	公交常量	ASC3		
出行属性	小汽车出行时间	BETA_TTCAR	TTCAR	连续变量
	小汽车出行费用	BETA_TCCAR	TCCAR	
	小汽车步行时间	BETA_OVTCAR	OVTCAR	
	地铁出行时间	BETA_TTRAIL	TTRAIL	
	地铁票价	BETA_TCRAIL	TCRAIL	
	地铁步行时间	BETA_OVTRAIL	OVTRAIL	
	地铁换乘次数	BETA_CHANGERAIL	CHANGESR	
	公交出行时间	BETA_TTBUS	TTBUS	
	公交票价	BETA_TCBUS	TCBUS	
	公交步行时间	BETA_OVTBUS	OVTBUS	
	公交换乘次数	BETA_CHANGEBUS	CHANGEB	
出行者属性	年龄 = 4	BETA_AGE	dum0	Yes:1; No:0
	性别	BETA_GENDER	GENDER	Female:1; Male:0
	目的 = 1	BETA_PURPOSE1	dum1	Yes:1; No:0
		BETA_PURPOSE2	dum2	Yes:1; No:0

2.2 MNL 模型

根据相关性分析,选择 OVTRAIL、PUPROSE、TCCAR、TCBUS、TTCAR、TTBUS 作为主要影响变量;且考虑图 1 的分析,另增加了性别变量,加入后表现良好。利用 BIOGEME 软件对模型进行参数估计,最终得到模型变量的参数见表 2,模型检验结果见表 3。

MNL 模型标定结果　　　　表2

Name	Value	Std err	t-test	p-value	Robust Std err	Robust t-test	p-value
ASC1	0.00	fixed					
ASC2	−26.4	5.41	−4.88	0.00	6.19	−4.26	0.00
ASC3	63.4	15.4	4.13	0.00	15.5	4.10	0.00
BETA_GENDER	1.18	0.370	3.18	0.00	0.392	3.00	0.00
BETA_OVTRAIL	−1.48	0.383	−3.87	0.00	0.423	−3.50	0.00
BETA_PURPOSE	−0.910	0.230	−3.97	0.00	0.218	−4.18	0.00
BETA_TCBUS	−24.6	4.17	−5.92	0.00	4.33	−5.69	0.00
BETA_TCCAR	−4.87	1.18	−4.13	0.00	1.41	−3.45	0.00
BETA_TTBUS	−16.0	2.98	−5.35	0.00	3.15	−5.07	0.00
BETA_TTCAR	−7.81	1.72	−4.53	0.00	1.68	−4.66	0.00

MNL 模型检验结果 表3

似然比检验值	236.505
调整后 R^2	0.423

根据非集计模型的检验方法:

(1)实践中优度比大于 0.2 便可以接受,在表 3 中可知,$R^2=0.423$,说明本模型拟合良好,模型精度基本满足要求。

(2)在表 2 中,所有参数标定结果的 t 检验值的绝对值均大于 1.96,即在 95% 置信水平下,所有变量对出行方式的选择都有显著影响。

(3)模型的似然比检验值为 $236.505>\chi_{0.05}(9)$,即模型参数等于 0 的假设被拒绝,因此模型中的变量对出行方式选择有显著影响。

2.3 NL 模型

这是一个两层的 NL 模型,第一层分为轨道和公路两种交通方式,其中选择肢 B(轨道)不继续分层,选择肢 A(公路交通方式)有两个下层的选择肢:小汽车和公交(图 2)。利用 BIOGEME 软件对模型进行参数估计,最终得到模型变量的参数见表 4,模型检验结果见表 5。

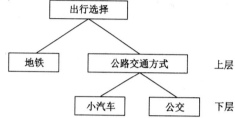

图 2 嵌套 logit 模型出行方式选择示意图

NL 模型标定结果 表4

Name	Value	Std err	t-test	p-value	Robust Std err	Robust t-test	p-value
ASC1	0.00	fixed					
ASC2	-22.1	5.22	-4.23	0.00	6.11	-3.61	0.00
ASC3	41.6	12.0	3.46	0.00	11.3	3.68	0.00
BETA_GENDER	1.04	0.358	2.91	0.00	0.367	2.84	0.00
BETA_OVTRAIL	-1.41	0.371	-3.80	0.00	0.395	-3.57	0.00
BETA_PURPOSE	-0.803	0.215	-3.74	0.00	0.201	-4.00	0.00
BETA_TCBUS	-17.8	3.80	-4.70	0.00	3.81	-4.68	0.00
BETA_TCCAR	-3.98	1.08	-3.70	0.00	1.32	-3.03	0.00
BETA_TTBUS	-11.3	2.63	-4.31	0.00	2.70	-4.20	0.00
BETA_TTCAR	-6.78	1.56	-4.35	0.00	1.55	-4.37	0.00

MNL 模型检验结果 表5

似然比检验值	260.853	λ_A	1.91
调整后 R^2	0.483	λ_B	1

根据非集计模型的检验方法:

(1)在表 4 中,所有参数的 t 检验值均大于 1.96,即在 95% 置信水平下,所有变量对出行方式的选择都有显著影响。

(2)在表 5 中,$R^2=0.483$,模型拟合良好,表明模型的精度基本满足要求。

(3)在表 5 中,模型的似然比检验值为 $260.853>\chi_{0.05}(9)$,即模型参数等于 0 的假设被拒绝,因此模型中的变量对出行方式选择有显著影响。

(4)$\mu=1$。由表 5 可知,$\lambda_A=1.91$,$\lambda_B=1$,可以得出:$0\leqslant\mu/\lambda_A\leqslant1$,$0\leqslant\mu/\lambda_B\leqslant1$,说明在公路交通选择肢下,公交和小汽车之间存在一定的相关性,本 NL 模型的层次划分是合理的。

2.4 ML 模型

在 MNL 模型的基础上,将步行时间看作存在一个随机效用,且假设它的随机参数 $\beta(\theta)$ 是正态分布。

得到模型变量的参数见表6,模型检验结果见表7。

ML 模型标定结果 表6

Name	Value	Std err	t-test	p-value	Robust Std err	Robust t-test	p-value
ASC1	0.00	fixed					
ASC2	−28.6	6.45	−4.43	0.00	8.11	−3.52	0.00
ASC3	64.2	15.5	4.13	0.00	15.9	4.03	0.00
BETA1	−1.69	0.488	−3.46	0.00	0.642	−2.63	0.01
BETA_GENDER	1.22	0.410	2.98	0.00	0.453	2.70	0.01
BETA_PURPOSE	−1.01	0.272	−3.71	0.00	0.300	−3.37	0.00
BETA_TCBUS	−25.6	4.51	−5.68	0.00	5.20	−4.93	0.00
BETA_TCCAR	−5.25	1.34	−3.91	0.00	1.82	−2.89	0.00
BETA_TTBUS	−16.5	3.13	−5.29	0.00	3.43	−4.82	0.00
BETA_TTCAR	−8.60	2.11	−4.07	0.00	2.33	−3.69	0.00
SIGMA1	0.243	0.185	1.31	0.19	0.285	0.85	0.40

ML 模型检验结果 表7

似然比检验值	240.031
调整后 R^2	0.432

(1)在表6中,大部分参数的 t 检验值绝对值均大于1.96,即在95%置信水平下,这些变量对出行方式的选择有显著影响。但从表中可以看出,参数'SIGMA1'的 t 检验值为1.31,1.2816<1.31<1.96,即在80%的显著性水平,拒绝了零假设,没有通过 t 检验的一般标准。

(2)在表7中,模型的似然比检验值为240.031 $>\chi_{0.05}(10)$,即模型参数等于0的假设被拒绝,因此模型中的变量对出行方式选择有显著影响。

(3)在表7中,$R^2=0.432$,模型拟合良好,说明模型的精度基本满足要求。

3 模型比较及方式划分

从表8可以明显看出,NL 模型最优,对方式选择问题的描述效果明显更好。根据 NL 模型公式,得到小汽车、公交和地铁的方式划分率见表9。

模 型 检 验 表 表8

模型	MNL model	NL model	ML model
似然比检验值	236.505	260.853	240.031
调整后 R^2	0.423	0.483	0.432

城市整体交通方式划分率 表9

		小汽车	地铁	公交
方式划分率	预测	54.66%	29.35%	15.99%
	实际	55.32%	30.21%	14.47%
	误差	0.66%	0.86%	1.52%

利用调查样本数据对 NL 模型的准确度进行验证,结果见表10。

个人交通方式选择概率预测准确度 表10

方式	实际值	预测值			预测准确度	平均准确度
		小汽车	地铁	公交		
小汽车	130	95	12	23	73.08%	
地铁	71	23	40	8	56.34%	66.67%
公交	34	4	6	24	70.59%	

（1）由表9可以看出，对三类交通方式的划分率预测精度整体较高，误差均小于2%，表明本研究建立的出行方式选择模型在对城市整体交通方式换分率的计算中具有极高的应用价值。

（2）从表10可以看出，对个人交通方式选择预测概率检测中，可以发现小汽车和公交的预测精度较高，分别达到73.08%和70.59%，而地铁的预测精度较低，为56.34%。考虑到居民个体在选择交通方式时，除固定的影响因素外，本就存在一定的随机主观性，因此本模型70%左右的预测精度可以被接受，具有实际应用价值，能有效反映当地居民出行选择交通方式时的考量。

（3）模型对个人交通方式选择的平均预测精度为66.67%，可以看出仍有极大的优化空间。可能是模型中考虑的因素不够全面，除随机影响外，还有一些对居民出行影响较大的因素没有考虑进去。

4 结 语

（1）本文比较了交通方式选择问题中不同的logit模型。结果表明，NL模型明显优于其他logit模型。小汽车和公交存在较强相关性，因此考虑了这一因素的NL模型能更好地描述出行者选择交通方式时的考量。

（2）从NL模型中可以看出，出行时间和出行成本主要影响小汽车和公交的选择，而步行时间和性别是选择地铁的主要影响因素。建立的NL模型在对城市整体交通方式划分率的预测中极具应用价值。

（3）该模型的预测精度有待进一步提高，主要受数据采集不完全的限制，不能满足分析的精度要求。下一步的研究工作是考量更多的影响因素、更多的交通方式，进一步优化出行方式选择模型。

参考文献

[1] Mcfadden D. Econometric models of probabilistic choice[M]// Structural Analysis of Discrete Data with Econometric Applications, 1981.

[2] Murthy A S N, Ashtakala B. Modal Split Analysis Using Logit Models[J]. Journal of Transportation Engineering, 1987, 113(5):502-519.

[3] 刘彤,巩丽媛,郑建,等. Logit模型的推导方法研究[J]. 科学技术与工程,2009,9(02):357-359.

[4] Racca D P, Ratledge E. Factors That Affect And/or Can Alter Mode Choice[J]. Consumer Preferences, 2003.

[5] Bhat C R, Sardesai R. The impact of stop-making and travel time reliability on commute mode choice[J]. Transportation Research Part B Methodological, 2014, 40(9):709-730.

[6] Algers S, Bergstrom P, Dahlberg M, et al. Mixed Logit Estimation of the Value of Travel Time[J]. Papers, 1998.

[7] Koppelman F S, Bhat C. A self instructing course in mode choice modeling: multinomial and nested logit models[J]. Logits, 2006.

[8] Hamre A, Buehler R. Commuter Mode Choice and Free Car Parking, Public Transportation Benefits, Showers/Lockers, and Bike Parking at Work: Evidence from the Washington, DC Region[J]. Journal of Public Transportation, 2014, 17(2):67-91.

[9] Aziz H M A, Nagle N N, Morton A M, et al. Exploring the impact of walk-bike infrastructure, safety perception, and built-environment on active transportation mode choice: a random parameter model using

New York City commuter data[J]. Transportation, 2017.

[10] Ding C, Wang D, Liu C, et al. Exploring the influence of built environment on travel mode choice considering the mediating effects of car ownership and travel distance[J]. Transportation Research Part A Policy & Practice, 2017, 100(Jun.):65-80.

[11] Chen C F, Chao W H. Habitual or reasoned? Using the theory of planned behavior, technology acceptance model, and habit to examine switching intentions toward public transit[J]. Transportation Research Part F Traffic Psychology & Behaviour, 2011, 14(2):128-137.

RRM应用于城际高铁出行的研究分析

刘 林 孙小慧 左 志

(新疆大学建筑工程学院)

摘 要 相对于广泛应用的随机效用理论,后悔理论能够从外部出行环境条件不确定的视角下反映出行者的出行行为,在实际交通出行中能够更加准确把握决策者的决策过程。在后悔理论发展相对成熟以及在交通领域有一定理论研究应用的背景下,本研究首先对后悔理论的产生、发展及改进过程进行简述;其次,对城际高铁研究及后悔最小化理论在交通领域的相关研究文献进行分析和总结;最后,讨论后悔理论在城际高铁客流预测领域的应用趋势,后悔理论的模型改进方向以及应用理论模型进行多方面探索的可能。期待本研究能够为未来的相关研究提供一定的理论参考。

关键词 随机后悔最小化理论 城际高铁 出行行为 客流分担

1 RRM的产生

随机效用最大化理论(Random Utility Maximization,RUM)是指所有的出行者都会以效用为选择标准,选择效用最大化的方案,在该理论中,决策者是完全理性的。然而研究表明决策者很难做到完全理性。因此,随机效用最大化理论对出行者的实际出行行为预测就出现了较大偏差。Bell认为既然单因素效用函数不能很好地解释人们的非理性决策行为,就尝试着把后悔和欣喜因素纳入效用函数,提出了后悔理论。Chorus等在后悔理论的基础上,提出了基于随机后悔最小化理论(Random Regret Minimization,RRM),随机后悔最小化理论指当一个已经放弃的选择比所选择的选择更好时,你就会感受到后悔,后悔的选择理论和模型是围绕后悔最小化建立起来的,即个人在选择时会将预期的后悔最小化,而不是将预期的效用最大化。

2 RRM的发展及完善

Chorus的随机后悔最小化理论指决策者在决策时期望预期后悔最小化。故假设有以下的选择情况,决策者面临着一组J个备择方案,每个备择方案以M个属性X_m来表示,这些属性在备择方案之间具有可比性。那么该集合预测备择i的选择概率为:

$$P_i = \exp(V_i) / \sum_{j=1\cdots J} \exp(V_i) \tag{1}$$

备择方案j在属性m的表现比i差时,后悔为零,当i在属性m上的表现比j差时,它作为属性值差的线性增长函数。那么,可估参数β_m是属性m的后悔函数的斜率。由此可得随机后悔效用函数表达(系统后悔值)为:

$$R_i = \max_{j \neq i} \{ \sum_{M=1\cdots m} \max\{0, (x_{jm} - x_{im})\} \} \tag{2}$$

因此,可以得到RMM模型的选择概率公式:

$$P_i = \exp(-R_i) \Big/ \sum_{j=1\cdots J} \exp(-R_j) \tag{3}$$

该式中 R_i 为方案 i 的系统后悔值，R_j 为方案 j 的系统后悔值。

由于 RRM 模型的似然函数是不平滑的，无法用现有的离散选择软件进行计算，阻碍了模型的普遍适用性。所以 Chorus 等对上面的随机最小化模型做了进一步的改进，提出了新的具有普遍适用的 RRM 模型。新的 RRM 模型效用函数表达式为：

$$R_i = \sum_{j \neq i} \sum_{m=1\cdots M} \ln\{1 + \exp[\beta_m \cdot (x_{jm} - x_{im})]\} \tag{4}$$

因此，可以得到新的 RRM 模型的选择概率公式：

$$P_i = \exp(-R_i) \Big/ \sum_{j=1\cdots J} \exp(-R_j) \tag{5}$$

3 城际高铁研究现状分析

3.1 出行行为分析

城际高铁开通以后，不仅给旅客带了交通方式的改变，也在出行目的、出行频率等方面极大地改变了旅客的出行习惯。在交通方式方面，城际高铁开通前，由主流交通方式是普通火车和大巴，现在高铁以其高速和公交式的运行模式在所有交通工具中占据优势，成为城际出行的最主要交通方式。在出行频率上，城际高铁的建设促使城市之间优势互补，合理分工，带来了人口的高速流动。例如北京和天津两地，在高铁开通前，人均往来于京津的出行频率强度指数 2.46，开通后，频率前度指数增加到 3.24。在出行目的上，以访友为目的的出行在较少，而以休闲娱乐为目的的出行在增加。因此，高铁的开通，在出行方式、出行目的、出行频率方面，极大地改变了旅客的出行方式。

3.2 客流分担

高铁开通对高速公路旅客运输的影响，最近几年高速铁路的客运量增速越来越大，相反高速公路的客运量不增反降。从 2015 年开始出现了负增长的趋势，这是由于近年来我国经济的快速发展，居民收入水平的提高，人们的消费水平也在不断提升，越来越多的旅客在中长途出行时更愿意选择运输速度快、服务质量好、安全性高、旅行体验舒适、正点率高的高铁出行。

高铁开通对民航客流影响，根据胡清华研究得出的民航和高铁在客运方面所存在的分担率关系：当运距小于 750km 的时候，高铁在两者的竞争中比较占有优势；当运距大于 750km 而小于 1050km 的时候，两者之间的竞争最为激烈，尤其是当两者之间的运输距离大于 800km 而小于 900km 的时候，各自所占的市场比列几乎均为 50%。

在高铁开通后，更多高速公路的旅客更愿意转移至高铁，航空的旅客根据距离的不同在二者之间有不同的选择。

3.3 经济效益分析

石林等研究发现，高铁修建有助于形成区域经济一体化，同时也有利于经济发展的梯度效应，助推区域经济的平衡；吴锦顺研究结果表明，高铁对城市 GDP 和人口增长有正影响，高铁发展引起沿线周边地区投资增加，推动城市间的合作和交流，促进了经济增长。不仅如此，高铁的开通对优化城市产业结构、改善就业水平的作用明显，并且通过拓展城市土地开发优化了城市空间结构。

通过研究者的研究成果可以得出，高铁修建可以促进经济的发展，给高铁沿线城市带来更多的物质条件。

3.4 "时空压缩"效益分析

高铁修建对地区间空间联系的"时空压缩"效益显著，以北京与天津为例，在高速铁路的作用下，北京与天津之间的城际出行模式，越来越像城内出行的模式，便捷的城际高铁使得人们可以在 1d 之内顺利实现多种出行需求并实现当日往返于两个城市之间。在山东半岛城市群与长江三角城市群开通高铁后，二者之间的累计节省时间在 2~4h 区间范围内，累计节约时间随距离增加而增加。从研究者的研究成果知道,高铁的开通在时间与空间上大大缩短了旅客的距离。

4 RRM应用于交通出行的研究现状分析

以上对城际高铁研究现状进行了总结,现在对随机后悔最小化理论在交通出行的应用现状进行分析。

4.1 RMM应用于轨道交通分析

江妍妮等以自由出行的群体在面对多重因素的不同选择时,容易对某一个优势因素所引导,做出令旅客后悔的决定。因此,引入后悔理论,以随机后悔最小化理论建立模型。分析了自由出行者乘车时间和换乘次数两个属性,计算出三条路径的理论后悔值。结果表明当一条路径的表现平平,即整体性较好时,该路径的后悔值越小,出行者更倾向于选择。李得伟用随机后悔最小化模型为基础建立模型,以北京市的轨道交通网为例进行案例分析,得到基于后悔的路径选择规则更全面的考虑旅客在进行路径选择时的负面情绪,为客流分配提供了一个新的视角。

4.2 RMM应用于出行选择行为分析

鲜于建川等应用随机后悔最小化理论与随机效用最大化理论,分别建立RRM-MNL模型和RUM-MNL模型研究了出行方式选择行为。研究结果表明RRM-MNL模型能够描述在多属性方案选择过程中的部分补偿性决策行为和折中效应,能更真实地反映实际出行选择过程。李梦等使用随机后悔理论研究出行者的路径选择行为,引入后悔厌恶水平,构建了多项logit的随机均衡模型,克服了随机后悔最小化模型不能刻画后悔程度的缺陷。结果表明后悔厌恶水平是出行者路径选择行为的重要参数,后悔厌恶水平越高,选择最短路径的出行者越多。

在以上研究者的研究中,可以知道随机后悔最小化理论在实际的出行行为预测中更符合实际的情况,为随机后悔最小化理论的推广应用提供了实证。

4.4 RMM应用于出行时间信息感知价值研究分析

闫祯祯等为了衡量出行者在比较交通信息行为和规避风险决策模式下的交通信息感知价值,基于后悔理论构建了交通信息感知价值模型。结果表明,当交通信息可靠度较高时,随着两条路径出行时间信息预测值的同时增大,通勤者会倾向于选择感知不确定性小的路径;获取信息后两条路径期望出行时间更新均值越接近,通勤者对信息的感知价值越小。

出行时间信息感知价值的量化为我们提供了一个参考方向,在以后的研究过程中可以通过相应的方法把舒适、满意等主观的体验感量化,形成可以看得见的数值模型。

5 结 语

随机后悔最小化理论在轨道交通中的应用、在出行行为的分析上可以得到很好的借鉴。但是在实际应用中,随着高铁的迅速发展,随机后悔最小化理论应用于高铁的客流预测研究比较少见,相对于其他理论的形成与发展,随机后悔最小化理论在模型结构、模型参数以及模型解释方面有待完善。例如,通过调整参数和变量来改善模型的适用性,增强模型对于现实世界的表达能力;或者通过优化模型结构,使模型更加简单,更易使用;或者从广泛适用的角度,重新对模型进行解释,使模型在更多的领域得到应用。在高铁的发展中,随机后悔最小化理论不仅可以应用到出行行为分析,还可以应用到出行时间信息感知价值研究分析,因此可以借鉴的是,可以通过模型设置及问卷设计的方法,尝试应用分析出行者的主观感受,把主观感受具体量化,从心理及价值感知等角度更为详细的分析出行者的出行行为。

参考文献

[1] Chorus C G. A new model of random regret minimization[J]. Ejtior,2010,10(2):181-196.

[2] Chorus C G. Random regret minimization:an overview of model properties and empirical evidence[J]. Transport reviews,2012:75-92.

[3] 栾琨,隽志才,倪安宁.出行路径选择的随机后悔最小化模型[J].交通信息与安全,2012,30(6):77-80.
[4] 王晓玉,王立晓,左志.后悔理论及其在出行中的应用研究综述[J].武汉理工大学学报,2018:231-237.
[5] 张顺明,叶军.后悔理论述评[J].系统工程,2009:45-50.
[6] 王晓玉.基于广义随机后悔最小化的通勤出行方式选择行为研究[D].乌鲁木齐:新疆大学,2018.
[7] 赵凯华.交通出行选择行为理论与模型应用分析[J].中国铁路,2017:55-61.
[8] 江妍妮,杨聚芬.基于后悔理论的城市轨道交通乘客路径选择[J].交通运输,2019:108-110.
[9] 鲜于建川,隽志才,朱泰英.后悔理论视角下的出行选择行为[J].交通运输工程学报,2012:67-73.
[10] 刘林.随机后悔最小化模型研究应用综述.2020.
[11] 侯雪,刘苏,张文新,胡志丁.高铁影响下的京津城际出行行为研究[J].经济地理,2011:1573-1580.
[12] 张琳.城际旅客出行方式选择行为研究[D].西安:长安大学,2019.
[13] 李强.高速铁路开行对区域高速公路旅客运输的影响研究[D].兰州:兰州交通大学,2018.
[14] 樊俐君.厦门航空应对高铁竞争的策略研究:基于4p分析框架[D].厦门:厦门大学,2019.
[15] 王璐.我国高铁对经济发展与居民福利的影响研究[J].经济理论与实践,2019:149-150.
[16] 田光辉.高速铁路背景下山东半岛城市群与长三角城市群经济联系空间格局变化[D].烟台:鲁东大学,2019.
[17] 高玉芳.基于后悔理论的城市轨道交通动态配流模型研究[D].北京:北京交通大学,2018.
[18] 李梦,黄海军.基于后悔理论的出行路径选择行为研究[J].管理科学学报,2017:1-9.
[19] 闫祯祯,刘楷,王晓光.基于后悔理论的交通信息感知价值[J].交通运输系统工程与信息,2013:76-84.

基于问卷调查的上海自贸区临港新片区综合交通体系优化策略研究

刘 梅 顾 煜

(上海市城乡建设和交通发展研究院)

摘 要 设立中国(上海)自由贸易试验区临港新片区是国家赋予上海的重大战略任务,面向"十四五",临港新片区综合交通围绕节点型和枢纽型城市交通体系的建设为主旨,为了准确了解市民在交通出行中感受和改善意愿,本文通过线上问卷调查,分析了市民对综合交通的关注热点和意见,并在此基础上提出了优化意见,为"十四五"时期综合交通规划编制提供技术支撑。

关键词 综合交通 临港新片区 问卷调查 "十四五"

0 引 言

设立中国(上海)自由贸易试验区临港新片区(以下简称"临港新片区")是国家赋予上海的重大战略任务,"十四五"规划是临港新片区综合交通高质量发展、全面开启建设节点型和枢纽型城市交通体系的第一个五年规划,为了找准交通发展短板,坚持问计于民,新片区及时组织开展综合交通"十四五"规划网络问卷意见征询,为新片区综合交通"十四五"的发展找准方向。

1 临港新片区现状

临港新片区位于上海东南角,距离人民广场约75km,总面积为873km²。地处长江口和杭州湾交汇处,北临浦东国际航空枢纽,南接洋山国际枢纽港,是上海沿海大通道的重要节点区域,也是长江经济带和海上丝绸之路经济带两大国家重点发展区域。经过十余年的发展建设,临港新片区已经初步具备了海运、空运、铁路、内河、轨道、公路、常规公交等交通条件,综合交通体系在不断完善和优化之中。

2 调查的范围和内容

本次网络意见征询围绕公共交通、道路交通、对外交通三个方面,聚焦临港新片区重点发展区域如滴水湖周边、产业园区等,深入了解公共交通、停车系统、慢行交通等方面的存在的问题以及发展需求。共收集到有效问卷2675份,调查具有一定的样本量(参与网络问卷调查的市民,以下简称市民),调查样本年龄分布近似正态分布(图1),从年龄构成来看,参与调查的市民年龄以20~50岁的为主,占90%。市民的职业类型涵盖各行各业,其中,企事业员工占76%,个体经营者占9.6%(图2)。

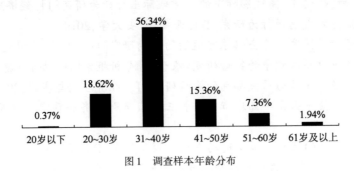

图1 调查样本年龄分布

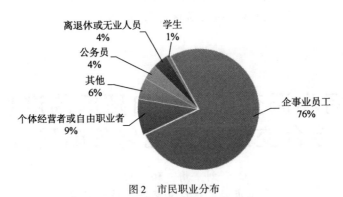

图2 市民职业分布

3 调查的主要结论

3.1 居住和工作地

超过60%的市民住在临港新片区、工作在临港新片区之外。62%的市民住在临港新片区、在临港新片区外工作,23.7%的市民工作、生活均在临港新片区,7.5%的调查参与者工作生活均在临港新片区之外,但是到过临港新片区。居住在临港新片区之外,在临港新片区内工作的占5.4%(图3)。

图3 市民居住和工作地分布

居住在临港新片区的市民,以南汇新城镇、泥城镇、万祥镇为主,工作地以南汇新城镇和泥城镇为主,工作在临港新片区之外,工作地以浦东、闵行、普陀区为主(图4~图6)。

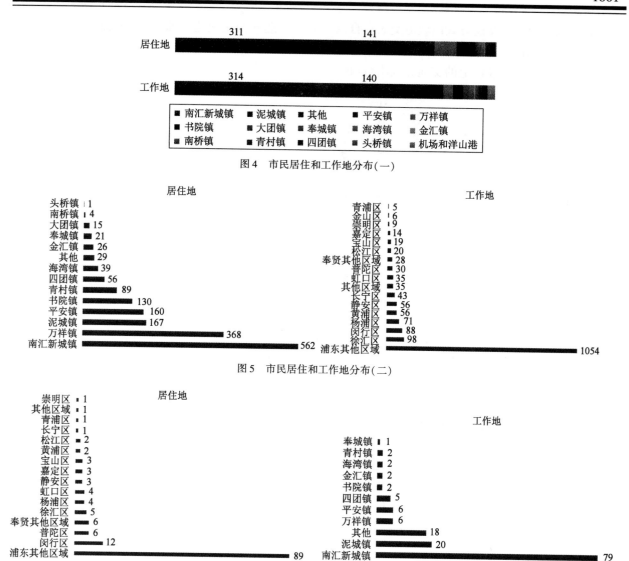

图 4　市民居住和工作地分布(一)

图 5　市民居住和工作地分布(二)

图 6　市民居住地和工作地分布(三)

3.2　通勤时间和交通方式

通勤时耗普遍较长。从市民通勤出行时耗来看(图7)，出行时耗(单程)超过60min的占62%，通勤时耗普遍较长。其中，居住在临港新片区，工作在临港新片区外的居民81%的通勤时间(单程)超过60min(图8)；在临港新片区工作，住在临港新片区之外的63%的居民通勤时耗(单程)超过60min。目前，上海市大于60min通勤比重约为19%（指标计算样本：中心城区通勤人口，居住、就业至少一端位于中心城区），超长时间的极端通勤，将不易于市民身心健康，容易引发一系列环境与社会问题。

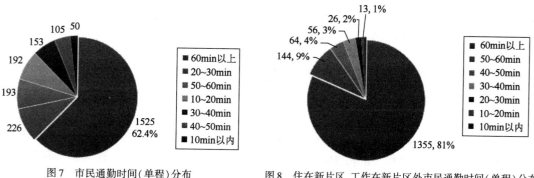

图 7　市民通勤时间(单程)分布　　　图 8　住在新片区，工作在新片区外市民通勤时间(单程)分布

通勤出行使用的交通方式以轨道交通和自驾车为主。选择使用轨道交通、自驾车、公交车作为通勤方式的居民分别占52%、51%、37%。其中,约27%的居民只采用自驾车的方式通勤出行,60%以上的居民日常通勤选择两种及以上的交通方式出行(图9)。

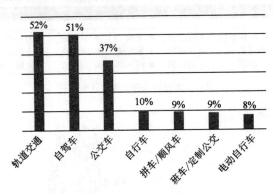

图9 通勤出行使用交通方式

3.3 公共交通出行

3.3.1 地面公交

公交站点可达性不足、线路绕行较远是市民认为最应解决的问题。50%左右的市民从居住地/工作地步行至最近公交站点的时间在10min以上。67%的居民认为等车时间较长,41%的居民认为线路绕行较远(图10)。同时,换乘次数多、换乘距离远、车站没有公交电子站牌等问题应引起重视。

高峰期间增加班次,优化调整线路和站点等是居民最期待改进的主要方向。由于轨道交通服务范围受限,高峰期间地面公交出行的需求较高,分别有70%、70%、46%的居民选择"增加高峰发车班次""调整线路站点""延长运营时间"作为改善地面公交服务品质的建议和要求。同时,随着出行多样化、个性化的需求增加,21%的居民希望发展网约化的公交,14%的居民希望提高到站的准点率,8%的居民希望提高站点的信息化水平、丰富信息发布方式(图11)。

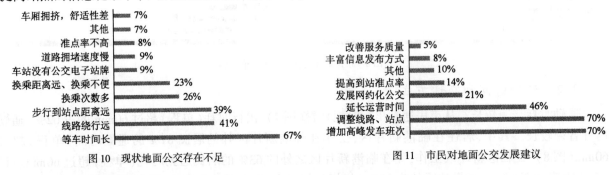

图10 现状地面公交存在不足　　图11 市民对地面公交发展建议

3.3.2 轨道交通

轨道交通高峰期间直达班车发车能力、车站可达性不足是市民认为是最为突出的问题。目前新片区联系上海市中心区的快速公共交通方式只有轨道交通16号线,高峰期间车厢拥挤情况严重,有50%的居民认为"高峰直达班次不足""到达站点不方便",44%的居民认为站站停车速度较慢、37%的居民认为高峰等车时间长(图12)。

增加高峰直达车发车班次、提高站站停列车运行速度是居民最期待的改进方向,占比分别为62%、46%,有45%和37%的居民认为"优化地面接驳公交""延长运营时间"作为改善地轨道交通服务品质的建议和要求(图13)。

新片区网约车吸引力明显大于巡游出租车。从总体上看,选择使用网约车(包括专车、快车、顺风车)的市民占50%,选择使用出租车的占8%,网约车的吸引力明显大于出租车,这与新片区区域出租车运营数量较少有关。从年龄分布来看,青壮年(20~40岁)网约车使用率占比80%,出租车使用率占比

71%。从职业构成来看,企事业员工、个体经营者或自由职业者更倾向于使用网约车(图14)。

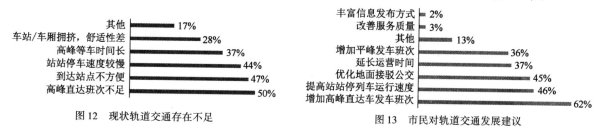

图12　现状轨道交通存在不足　　　　　图13　市民对轨道交通发展建议

方便、快捷是市民选择网约车的主要原因。76%的市民认为网约车更容易打到车,39%认为价格更便宜,选择使用巡游出租车的市民,70%认为更安全、规范。

"缩短约车响应时间""提高扬招出租车比例""增加出租车上下车候客点"是居民对传统出租车的主要改善建议,占比分别为57%、46%、37%,同时,增加出租车上下车候客点、改善出租车驾驶员文明驾驶习惯、改善车内环境等也是市民期待改善的方面(图15)。

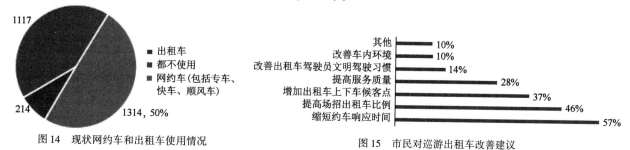

图14　现状网约车和出租车使用情况　　　　　图15　市民对巡游出租车改善建议

3.4　道路交通出行

3.4.1　道路交通

与上海市区联系的通道偏少,客车和货车互相干扰严重,各镇、产业区之间互相联系通道不够,是居民认为道路交通存在的主要问题,占比分别为82%、49%、35%。有27%、25%、23%的居民认为存在道路损坏情况较为严重、断头路较多、道路间隔距离较远的问题(图16)。

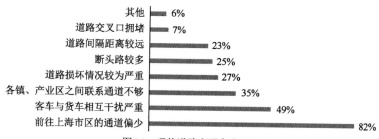

图16　现状道路交通存在不足

加快高等级干线公路建设、主城区内加密路网、减少客货干扰是居民最期待的改善道路交通的方向,占比分别为63%、54%、40%。同时,有34%、27%、24%的居民认为应该提升道路交通管理水平,加快建设乡道、村道,高速公路收费政策优化(图17)。

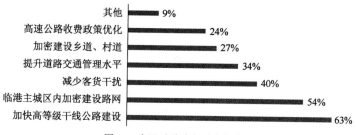

图17　市民对道路交通改善建议

3.4.2 慢行交通

舒适性、安全性不足是市民认为慢行交通存在的主要问题。分别有 67%、65%、64% 的居民认为缺少板凳等休憩设施、行人和非机动车混行、过街不方便。另有 54%、48%、40% 的居民认为存在宽度不足、绿化环境有待提升、非机动车停车位不足等问题（图18）。

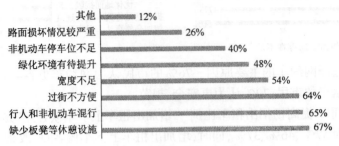

图18　现状慢行交通存在不足

加强滨水步道的休憩功能、完善非机动车道和人行道连续性、增加人性化过街设施是市民认为慢行交通主要改善方向。此外，分别有 26%、21%、16% 的居民建议增设非机动车停放空间、提升慢行通道绿化景观环境、提升慢行道路面平整性（图19）。

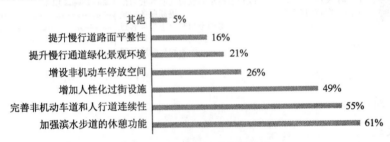

图19　市民对慢行交通改善建议

共享单车数量不足、地铁站区域数量短缺是市民认为最为突出的问题。96% 的市民认为企业整体投放量不足，82% 的市民认为地铁站区域车子数量短缺。增加共享单车停放点、优化并增加自行车道是市民最期待新区政府提供共享单车的配套设施（图20、图21）。

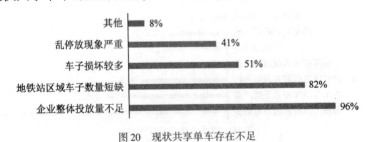

图20　现状共享单车存在不足

图21　市民对共享单车改善建议

3.4.3 停车系统

轨道交通站点、热门旅游景点区域停车问题最为突出。分别有 70%、38% 的居民认为轨道交通 16 号线,海昌、航海博物馆等旅游景点停车矛盾最为突出,部分住宅小区和产业园区也存在停车问题(图22)。

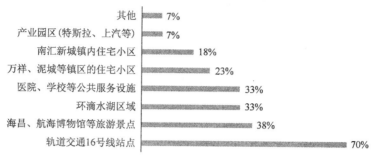

图22 现状停车系统存在问题

挖掘潜在停车资源、提升公共交通服务水平、加强周边停车资源错峰共享是市民认为改善停车问题的主要方向。分别有51%、38%、37%的市民认为通过住宅、公共建筑内增设机械车位、提升公共交通服务水平、加强周边停车资源错峰共享作为改善停车问题的建议和要求(图23)。

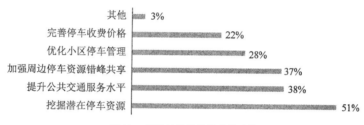

图23 市民对停车系统改善建议

3.5 对外交通出行

虹桥火车站、浦东国际机场是新片区市民进出上海最经常使用的对外交通枢纽。37%的市民进出上海选择虹桥火车站,27%的市民进出上海选择浦东机场、14%的市民选择通过个体机动化的出行方式进出上海,10%的市民选择上海南站(图24)。

到达枢纽的时间普遍较长。到达虹桥枢纽的市民80%以上时耗在80min以上,到达浦东机场的市民72%以上时耗在40min以上。到达上海南站的市民68%以上时耗在80min以上,到达上海站的市民80%以上时耗在80min以上(图25)。

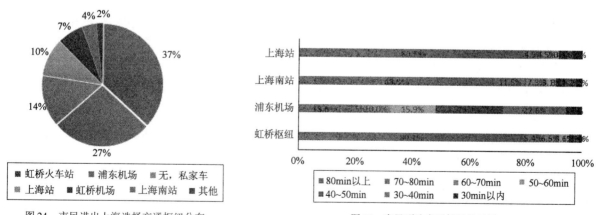

图24 市民进出上海选择交通枢纽分布　　　图25 市民到达交通枢纽的时间

到达不同枢纽的交通方式有差异。到达虹桥枢纽的市民48%以上选择轨道交通;到达浦东机场的市民34%以上选择私家车,另有25%的市民选择通过轨道交通与公交车、私家车、网约车接驳的方式到达浦东机场;到达上海南站的市民45%以上选择轨道交通,到达上海站的市民50%以上选择轨道交通(图26)。

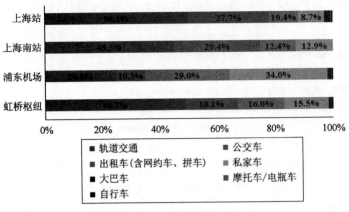

图 26 市民到达交通枢纽的交通方式

4 相关思考与建议

4.1 对外交通

(1) 加快配合推进铁路通道及枢纽建设。依托上海东站,加强新片区与上海铁路枢纽的快速联系,通过沪通二期、沪乍杭铁路项目的研究和建设,增强新片区杭州方向、苏中、苏北、皖赣方向及以远的辐射能力,提升区域运输服务能力。

(2) 规划建设市域轨道交通。提升既有轨道交通 16 号线的运输能力,优化列车运营组织,推动联系临港新片区与浦东枢纽的市域轨道两港快线建设,加快市域轨道南枫线的研究和建设,加强与周边区域的联系。

(3) 完善高快速路和干线公路整体布局。规划建设形成 G1503、S2 和两港快速路 3 条高快速路格局,加强新片区与上海中心城、浦东、奉贤等地区的快速联系;推进新沪杭公路、大川公路等新建工程的建设,促进区域协同发展。

4.2 公共交通

(1) 优化和完善轨道交通线网。通过加快轨道交通研究和建设,包括提高既有轨道交通 16 号线运输能力,加快联系临港新片区和浦东枢纽的市域轨道两港快线建设,优化完善轨道交通接驳服务,扩大轨道交通服务范围。

(2) 完善多层次的地面公交系统。结合城镇和产业布局,构筑与出行需求相匹配的中运量示范走廊,填补轨道交通与常规公交之间的服务空挡;优化调整地面公交线网,结合道路建设、城市开发时序对公交线路进行优化。加强与轨道交通 16 号线、中运量站点接驳换乘的功能,满足通勤、上学和就医等需求,兼顾生活休闲功能,积极完善共享班车等辅助公交服务。

4.3 道路交通

(1) 提高路网密度,优化路网级配。加快骨干道路建设,为组团之间的快速联系提供通道保障,推进重点片区次支路建设,强化产业配套,打通区内断头路工程,破除道路节点瓶颈。

(2) 打造高品质慢行交通网络,营造高品质出行环境。构建安全顺畅的通勤生活网络,结合丰富滨水资源,构建高品质滨水慢行空间环境,完善货运和配送网络体系。

5 结语

上海临港新片区作为上海"十四五"期间重点发展的"两翼"之一和"五大新城"之一,需要构建符合新片区特点的高质量综合交通体系来支撑新片区面向全球、服务全国、融入长三角。同时,在进一步完善临港新片区综合交通体系时,需要充分吸纳公众意见和建议,打造让人民满意的城市交通。

参考文献

[1] 顾煜,薛美根,许俊康,等.高标准谋划上海自贸区临港新片区综合交通体系[C]//交通治理与空间重塑——2020年中国城市交通规划年会论文集.北京:中国建筑工业出版社,2020:601-608.

基于节能减排的交通运输规划研究

樊宏哲

(昆明市政工程设计科学研究院有限公司)

摘 要 文章分析了低碳交通运输规划的考虑因素,对我国低碳交通运输规划存在的问题进行了剖析,并针对性地提出了解决策略。希望相关研究能为低碳交通运输体系的发展提供帮助。

关键词 低碳交通 节能减排 运输 规划

0 引 言

社会经济的快速发展,使得交通运输能耗及碳排放也迅速增长,发展低碳交通运输受到全世界的关注。低碳交通运输是将低碳节约理念应用到交通运输规划、建设、运营的各个环节,通过开展技术创新、政策引导、社会呼吁等方式,对运输装备、结构、需求等进行调整,从而尽可能提高能源使用效率,减少碳排放总量。发展低碳交通运输,能够有效降低交通运输的单位碳排放量,提高社会经济的发展效益。目前,我国已出台了一系列关于交通运输节能减排的政策,有利于推动全社会形成低碳交通运输新格局,但是在低碳交通运输规划方面,仍然暴露出了一些明显的问题。

1 低碳交通运输规划的考虑因素

1.1 宏观因素

(1)社会经济的发展。社会经济的发展直接影响到公众的生产与生活行为,进而影响交通运输的需求,因此社会经济的变革将导致交通需求与供给的相应变化,影响交通运输的方式。同时社会经济的发展决定了交通运输的基础设施及网络完善,对形成低碳交通新格局具有决定性的影响。

(2)环境质量要求。交通运输行业对自然环境的影响主要是噪声和尾气污染,而环境的可持续性是社会长远发展的根本。交通运输结构不合理、载具碳排放量过大,都会造成环境的超负荷,导致社会发展的不可持续,环保及资源节约的要求也为发展低碳交通提供了更为具体的指标。

(3)国家产业结构。交通运输能够为经济发展和产业升级提供巨大保障,因此低碳交通运输规划需要在满足各级结构交通需求的前提下,降低单位运输的能耗及碳排放,满足更大的社会需求。同时国家产业结构的升级涉及各行各业的经济行为调整,也与交通运输的需求及节能要求相联系。此外,近年来,我国各交通节能行业也处于快速发展的时期,图1为我国近五年来交通节能行业产值规模。

图1 2015—2019年我国交通节能行业产值规模

1.2 微观因素

(1) 交通基础设施建设。低碳交通运输规划涉及不同交通方式的衔接,而相关的基础设施如公路、机场、城市道路、港口、交通枢纽站场、广场等的建设和接驳策略,对于客运、货运的便捷性和周转率都有较大影响,进而影响交通运输的结构调整和能源节约。不合理的换乘方式和站场设置,会对运输时效造成不利影响,增大整个运输环节的能源消耗,增大碳排放污染。

(2) 交通运输结构。不同的交通运输方式、速度、运能、人均耗能及碳排放均有差异,因此交通运输结构的不同将导致综合交通运输的能源消耗不同。而在具体的某一类交通运输方式中,运力结构的不同也会影响到此种交通方式的节能减排效果。如城市私家车数量急剧增加,据国家统计局数据显示,1989年中国私家车的保有量在73万辆左右,而截至2019年,全国私家车保有量已经高达4575万辆。这导致道路运力结构不合理引发的交通拥堵,不但增大了车辆等待时碳排放,更对人们的出行、城市的发展产生不利影响,因此在进行低碳交通运输规划时必须充分考虑当前交通运输结构的组成。

(3) 交通运输组织。运输组织结构分为集约型、分散型两种。目前我国交通运输组织仍以分散型组织为主,尤其在道路交通运输行业,运输企业主要为个体经营,在企业管理、运输装备等方面未能形成信息化、集约化,难以发挥规模效应,从而导致交通运输效益较低、能源浪费较多。

(4) 能源消费结构。不同的能源消费结构的碳排放量和环境污染差别巨大,相比汽油、柴油,天然气对大气的友好程度较高,且具有明显的价格优势。数据显示,2019年,我国交通运输业能源消耗约48.6亿吨标准煤,占去年能源消耗总量的9.24%。而同年我国的天然气等清洁能源占能源消费总量的23.4%,比上年上升1.3%。而近年兴起的电能、生物柴油、甲醛燃料等也能使得我国的能源消费结构不断优化,这有利于提升能源利用率、降低污染排放。因此能源消费结构也是低碳交通运输规划的重要考虑因素。

2 我国低碳交通运输规划存在的问题

2.1 缺乏完善的规划理论

目前国内虽然已出台了一些法律规章对低碳交通运输规划作出了明确要求(截至2020年6月,我国总共颁布法律法规358条,其中交通法律为8部,交通行政法规为58部,规章319条),但其中并未涉及低碳交通运输规划应当采用的具体理论、方法、模型等,低碳交通规划理论的缺乏,导致在实际编制规划时标准不一、科学性不足。同时与规划相关的基础性数据如碳排放清单、监测统计资料等并不全面,难以进行系统、有效的统计和分析。在实际操作过程中,各个地方部门与企业编制的低碳发展规划、节能减排规划,未能充分纳入低碳交通运输总规划,导致各单位的规划间缺乏联动性,且难以监督落实情况。各地基于自身经验编制的低碳规划,在编制依据、编制方法、审批流程等方面均具备明显的随意性、经验性,其规划的合理性、科学性与实际可操作性也难以评价。

2.2 缺少低碳交通顶层设计

近年来,虽然国务院通过部门职能调整,将不同交通运输方式的管理职能和部门进行了整合,但是体制性障碍仍然存在,公路、铁路、民航、水运等不同交通运输方式仍然难以形成统一的、整体的综合协调发展,各家仍然在各自的领域内开展提高能效、节能减排的研究,构建单一运输方式下的低碳交通运输发展体系。因此,从发展综合交通运输的低碳节能方向来看,需要提升各方眼界,基于综合交通运输体系的绿色低碳发展,制定顶层战略规划,明确各类交通运输方式的低碳发展目标和方式。

2.3 缺乏适应的配套技术支撑

目前,我国缺乏适应的低碳交通运输配套技术主要表现在两个方面:一是交通运输节能减排技术的发展不足,二是低碳交通运输的政策性工具缺乏。虽然国内近年来较为重视交通运载工具节能减排技术的研发,如电动汽车的发展、生物燃料的研制等,但是相关研究成果难以大规模转化为实际生产力,人们还是普遍依赖化石燃料运输工具。从政策工具层面来看,法律法规、部门规章等虽然明确提出发展低碳交通运输,但是具体的行政监督方法、标准规范等工具仍显不足,同时对合同能源管理、节能减排自愿协议等机制的研究相对滞后,难以充分调动民众和市场的力量,合力建设低碳交通运输体系。

2.4 与其他各类规划的协调性不足

当前国内综合、专项交通发展规划普遍先于土地利用规划、环境功能规划、城市规划等编制完成,因此难以与相关规划形成协调配合。相比较西方发达国家,我国虽然在法律法规、行政规章层面明确提出了发展低碳交通运输体系,也制定了一系列节能减排、资源与环境保护的管理办法,但是具体的实施方案、执行标准、后期评估方法等均没有形成明确的意见,对环境的保护、资源的利用效果无法形成有效评价。而且在交通运输系统内部,各个交通专项发展规划也是独立开展,尤其是交通枢纽及场站的规划更是难以形成统筹,制约了综合低碳交通发展。

3 低碳交通运输规划的策略

3.1 加强低碳交通理论及方法研究

全球气候变化的严峻形势不容忽视,在西方发达国家,发展低碳交通运输的相关研究已经与社会学、政治学、经济学、环境学等学科形成广泛交叉,并取得了更为系统的科研成果。就发展低碳交通运输而言,交通运输对资源消耗和碳排放的影响十分明显,其高流动性、高能源依赖性及其他派生性能,都使交通运输成为低碳研究的重难点,国内应集中科研力量进行低碳交通运输理论及方法的研究,吸收国内外研究及相关交叉学科的研究成果进行再创新,分析影响低碳交通运输规划的关键因素,为规划提供科学的、切实可行的理论支撑和方法。

3.2 开展低碳交通运输规划顶层设计

交通运输主管部门应充分理解低碳综合交通规划的战略发展意义,关注社会经济发展及交通预期的变化,加强对各类交通运输方式的特点和发展趋势把握,及时制定整个交通系统的低碳发展规划,从影响因素识别、体系构建、方法创新、模型建立、管理制度等各方面明确各交通运输方式的阶段目标,以科学的、可操作的顶层设计为后续各交通方式开展专项低碳规划,提供明确的边界和要求。

3.3 加强技术创新及制度建设

低碳交通运输技术是实现交通运输行业绿色低碳发展的重要抓手。一方面应强化低碳交通技术创新,通过清洁能源、新型载具、系统整合工具等先进技术的研发和应用,提高单位交通运输的效能,降低碳排放和能源污染。另一方面,通过低碳交通的管理制度建设,优化交通运输结构和组织方式,通过优先发展公共交通、结构优化、扶持低碳运输方式、提升转运效率等途径,加快建设现代化低碳综合交通运输体系,并以此降低交通运输整体对能源的消耗。在此基础上,及时开展多城市、多批次的低碳交通运输试点建设,总结相关经验并积极优化建设流程和方法,以更经济的能源消耗满足社会发展的交通需求。与此同时,还应注重加强对公众出行方式的引导,鼓励公众采取更为低碳环保的交通工具,优化运输结构和组织,调动社会公众的力量,实现对全行业的低碳发展的长效监管。

3.4 促进各类规划的协调

在交通运输规划的早期阶段,应充分考虑与国土、环境、能源等相关规划的协调,尤其在低碳交通发展规划制定前,应根据未来环境要求及交通运输需求变化的预测,从环境功能、环境影响、能源消耗等角度,审查各交通基础设施的规模、功能定位等,必要时应作出适当调整和让步,以形成低碳交通运输规划与其他各项规划的协调。避免各交通方式出现重复建设、产能过剩、无序竞争、高耗能、低效率等问题,影响低碳交通运输体系的可持续性。

4 结 语

低碳综合运输体系是今后我国的交通发展方向,相关部门应当重视对低碳交通运输规划的理论及方法研究,从因素分析、顶层设计、技术创新、模型方法、管理制度等各方面,提高低碳交通运输规划的科学性、整体性,加快低碳交通运输体系的建设,实现综合交通运输系统的经济目标与节能减排目标,实现交通体系的可持续性发展。

参考文献

[1] 毛建民.疫情期间的交通管理措施及其对交通规划工作的启示[J].《规划师》论丛,2020(00):489-495.

[2] 高进军,陆礼.低碳交通运输的政策设计与实践进展[J].交通企业管理,2018(5):8-11.

[3] 哪雪,徐萍,陆键等.基于LCA的低碳公路的实现途径[J].公路,2019(3):133-139.

[4] 郭杰,伊文婧.中国低碳交通发展的几点思考[J].中国能源,2018(10):40-44.

[5] 于晓妹.城市局部道路网的分类与规划指标研究[D].南京:南京林业大学,2020.

交通基础设施网络综合立体高质量发展研究
——以浙江省为例

李 乐 丁 剑 程亚杰 何佳玮

(浙江数智交院科技股份有限公司)

摘 要 新时代交通基础设施网络的发展要求是建设现代化高质量综合立体交通网络,本文以浙江省为例,聚焦综合立体、高质量,在分析发展成就与发展瓶颈的基础上,结合浙江自身特征,提出了高质量发展策略与发展路径,旨在为浙江和全国其他地区交通基础设施网络发展提供参考。

关键词 交通 基础设施 综合立体 高质量

0 引 言

党的十九大提出了建设交通强国,为统筹推进这一重大战略,中共中央、国务院制定了《交通强国建设纲要》(简称《纲要》),对交通强国建设进行了顶层设计和系统谋划。《纲要》强调要推动交通发展由追求速度规模向更加注重质量效益转变,由各种交通方式相对独立发展向更加注重一体化融合发展转变,由依靠传统要素驱动向更加注重创新驱动转变,简言之即推动高质量发展、推动一体化发展、推动创新发展。同时,更是将"基础设施布局完善、立体互联"作为首要任务,提出"建设现代化高质量综合立体交通网络",为新时代交通基础设施建设指明了方向。

浙江作为东部沿海发达省份,综合交通发展水平整体处于全国前列,已成为名副其实的交通大省,但面对新时代交通强国战略实施要求和土地环境等要素日益趋紧的复杂形势,探索新时代交通基础设施网络更高效率、更高质量、更可持续的发展路径,对于浙江交通更好落实国家战略部署、为全省现代化建设当好先行意义重大。

1 基础设施网络发展现状

浙江综合交通基础设施投资建设一直走在全国前列,"十三五"更是以全国第一的投资总量,实现里程碑式发展,到2020年底,线网规模达14.2万km,高铁和高速公路面积密度分别位居全国第五和第三,宁波舟山港货物吞吐量连续12年稳居世界第一、集装箱吞吐量连续3年全球前三,内河航道实现市市"通江达海",成为全国第二个拥有三大千万级机场的省份,为全省经济社会发展提供了坚实保障。但对照高质量发展要求,跨区域外联通道不足,骨干路网拥堵较为突出,山区、海岛交通发展相对滞后;综合枢纽能级不高,港口综合服务能力有待提升,机场全球链接能力不足,融合发展有待拓展和深化;绿色发展体系尚不健全,内河航运瓶颈依然突出;科技创新动能还需增强等已成为当前制约综合效益发挥、高质量发展关键瓶颈。

2 发展策略

聚焦更好发挥交通基础性、先导性和战略性作用,以打造现代化高质量综合立体交通网络为目标,重点做好"四个更加注重":一是更加注重融入重大战略。紧密结合国家、区域和全省重大战略实施,瞄准世界前列目标,加快构建海陆空立体开放国际运输大通道,依托高能级港口机场群及综合枢纽,打造高影响力的国际开放门户。二是更加注重综合立体。强化系统思维,注重"铁轨公水空管邮枢廊"九要素一体融合,加强战略、规划、设施、标准、信息等各层面衔接,提升综合运输整体效能。三是更加注重质量效益。坚持做大规模与做强实力并重、拓展增量与盘活存量并重、普惠均衡与个性品质并重、设施提升与治理提效并重。四是更加注重创新驱动。更加注重动力转变,强化数字赋能,推动前沿技术应用,加快培育新业态新模式,提升现代化水平。

3 发展路径

聚焦高质量竞争力现代化,着力完善通道、枢纽、网络综合立体交通布局,优化存量,做优增量,统筹推进综合交通基础设施高质量融合发展。

一是构建立体多元的综合交通运输通道。综合运输通道是现代化综合交通运输体系的重要组成部分,是发挥大国规模经济优势的重要支撑力和战略性资产,是综合立体交通网的主骨架,由两种或两种以上交通方式线路组成,承担全省主要客货运输需求,也是集约节约利用空间资源、各种运输方式从独立竞争发展转向统筹协同发展的根本体现。布局原则一是与国家、国际运输网络充分衔接,连通周边主要经济区及周边省份省会城市、中心城市,切实提升全省对外开放格局;二是连通全省所有20万人口以上城市、地级行政中心、主要陆路、海上和航空口岸,其中国家级综合运输通道覆盖所有地级行政中心;三是连接全省重点经济区、重要工业和能源生产基地;四是为全省四大都市区及市域间的沟通提供多条走廊,满足国土开发和国防功能的需要;五是构建通道的铁路干线、公路干线、内河高等级航道、航空主航线以及油气主管道有机衔接和相互协调,体现全省交通多样性和集约型,促进形成以优势互补为基础的一体化交通体系。最终构建形成"六纵六横"水陆空立体多元的综合立体交通通道,构建畅联国家重大战略空间的主轴线,强化与京津冀、粤港澳、成渝等城市群互联,加快构建串联区域性重大战略空间的主廊道,强化对长江中游地区、海西等地区的辐射拓展。

二是统筹建立开放多级的城市枢纽体系。综合交通枢纽为整合铁路、公路、航空、内河航运、海港和运输管道为一体的海陆空协同枢纽体系,是衔接多种运输方式、辐射一定区域的客、货转运中心,是提升网络综合效益的核心与关键。同时随着新型城镇化背景下都市经济的快速发展,以四大都市区为重点,联动其他高度城镇化地区,建设多中心、多层级、分工协调的城市枢纽体系将是实现全省空间集约化、高质量的必然选择。因此,本次突破以往具体枢纽站场布局,将城市作为一个综合交通枢纽,在全省范围内统筹布局,优化资源配置,提高整体效率,避免资源浪费。具体原则一是以全局视野、系统观念,在区域维度将城市整体作为一个综合交通枢纽进行研究,探寻一份适配城市发展格局、提升城市发展能级的交通枢纽规划方案。二是立足适配新经济发展格局,通过扩大城市双向流通总量、提升流通效率,激发流通活力,强化城市区域竞争力。三是聚焦综合交通运输体系的"顺畅高效",根据国土空间规划和未来发展模式要求,确定面向都市圈、城市群的综合交通总格局,做好内畅外联与集疏运这篇文章。四是更加注重对经济社会的支撑,探寻城市更高质量公平、宜居、低碳、韧性、可持续的城市发展模式,实现城市综合效益最大化。最终,共建长三角国际性综合交通枢纽集群,基本建成以国际性综合交通枢纽城市、国际铁路枢纽、国际枢纽海港为核心,以全国性综合交通枢纽城市为节点的全省综合交通枢纽体系,全面打造"枢纽上的浙江"。

三是打造多网融合的综合交通基础设施网络。构建由优质发达的快速骨干网、高效完善的普通干线网、普惠广泛的基础服务网组成的综合交通基础设施网络。其中,高速铁路、高速公路、民用航空共同构成全省快速骨干交通网,提供高品质、快速交通运输服务,是现代化综合立体交通网的骨干网络;普速铁路、普通国省道、港口、航道、油气管道等共同构成了运行效率高、服务能力强的综合交通普通干线网络;以农村公路、支线铁路、支线航道等为主体,通用航空为补充,构成广覆盖、深通达、惠及广的综合交通基础服务网络。

四是努力做优互联互通的交通基础设施增量。高水平开启"轨道上的浙江"建设任务,优先保障"市市通高铁",全面补齐"省域1小时交通圈"短板,加快完善货运铁路干线和港口后方通道布局,积极推动城际铁路、市域铁路建设,打造更快速、更便捷的"市域、城区1小时交通圈"。完善现代公路网络,加快推进高速公路跨省跨区域重要通道建设、繁忙通道扩容改造和普通国省道干线待贯通、低等级路段攻坚行动。全面建设世界一流强港,打造"重要窗口"的硬核力量。重点培育杭州机场国际枢纽功能,增强宁波、温州机场辐射能级,加快提升浙江连接全球能力,补齐国际航空货运等短板。加快构建多级综合客货运枢纽体系,通过组织优化设计,尽可能实现地上、地下、水上、空中各交通网络的立体互联和无缝流转,发挥好各方式的比较优势和组合效率,提升联程联运和多式联运水平,充分释放多网融合后的整体效能。

五是充分挖掘蕴含潜能的交通基础设施存量。一是积极采用既有铁路补强、局部改造、站房站台改造,优先利用既有资源开行城际列车。加大高速公路互通的合理化改造,在城市化密集区域适度加密高速公路互通,推进政府购买服务差异化收费政策实施,加快实施一批高速公路服务区改扩建工程。继续推进普通国道"三提",鼓励都市区走廊快速路建设、沿线综合整治、节点平改立等建设。提高农村路网通畅能力,着力实施行政村通双车道提升工程。二是加强交通设施管理养护。加强公路养护资金保障,加大养护大中修工程和日常小修保养资金投入力度。推进联网收费系统优化升级,进一步提高ETC通行效率。有序规范、更换交通标志标线,增强交通设施诱导功能。加强航道养护,实施通航关键节点改造,建设美丽航道。三是加强智慧化赋能,依靠互联网、大数据、云计算、人工智能等现代信息技术,加快推进"新基建"建设,推动交通基础设施数字转型、智能升级;全面推进"数字交通"建设,创新政府服务模式;深化新科技革命下的未来交通发展研究,推动交通出行、无车承运物流等领域发展模式向共享经济转型;谋划打造以浙江省大湾区全域智能交通服务体系为代表的智慧交通服务体系。

4 结　语

新时代交通运输行业已进入综合交通高质量发展的新阶段,本文在分析浙江交通基础设施网络发展现状的基础上,坚持问题导向和目标导向,提出服务重大战略、建设综合立体高质量交通基础设施网络的发展策略,以及从加强通道资源综合统筹、优化资源配置,加强枢纽空间集约共享、强化衔接转换,优化供给结构、提升优质增量、挖掘既有存量等方面,提出高质量发展路径,期望为全国其他地区提供一定的借鉴。

参考文献

[1] 傅志寰. 推动高质量发展　推动一体化发展　推动创新发展[J]. 中国水运, 2019, (12).
[2] 乌兰娜仁, 吴迪, 奚宽武. 浙江省综合交通发展国际对标研究[J]. 综合运输, 2019, 7(42):44-48.

基于Tropos-SWOT模型的道路客运发展战略分析

左博睿[1,2,3]　帅　斌[1,2,3]　吴贞瑶[1,2,3]　赏珂祺[1,2,3]　李　尧[1,2,3]

(1. 西南交通大学交通运输与物流学院;2. 西南交通大学综合交通运输智能化国家地方联合工程实验室;
3. 西南交通大学综合交通大数据应用技术国家工程实验室)

摘　要　为寻求综合交通体系革新下的道路客运发展策略,构建Tropos-SWOT战略分析模型对道路客运业进行战略分析。Tropos-SWOT 模型结合 Tropos 建模手段,将 SWOT 法分析过程拓展为目标层、外因层、内因层及决策层四个层次,通过逐层分析,层次化展现战略决策过程以明确决策与分析之间的相互关系,进而获得有效战略决策。模型对道路客运业的分析结果显示:现阶段道路客运监管不当与运营体系效率低下是受外部环境影响最集中的关键内因,在信息平台的支撑下完成跨区域部门的建立可有效支持行业改革。此外,通过实例验证了 Tropos-SWOT 模型能有效应用于战略分析中,可为管理者进行战略决策提供一定的技术支持。

关键词 道路客运 Tropos-SWOT 分析 SWOT 法 战略分析 Tropos 模型

0 引 言

客运是我国交通运输事业重要组成部分之一,一直以来灵活、高效地承担着最广泛地域内的国民出行重任。然而在历经多年的发展后,由于自身管理弊端、外部交通方式冲击等内外因素共同作用,道路客运发展呈现"断崖式"走低,运营指数屡创新低。随着交通强国纲要的提出,道路客运业如何扭转困境,进而协同其他交通方式共同建立综合一体化交通运输体系是道路客运管理者关注的焦点问题。

深化道路客运改革,及时调整战略方向需选用有效的战略分析方法。SWOT 法是目前应用范围最广的战略分析方法之一,方法通过分析产业在运营过程中存在的内部优势(Strength)、劣势(Weakness),外部的机遇(Opportunity)、威胁(Threats)及互相交叉结合情况(SO 分析、ST 分析、WO 分析、WT 分析),获得有效战略措施以指导产业生产发展。An 等基于 SWOT 法对北京旅游咨询公司进行了分析,提出了提高旅游企业竞争力的相关战略。黄文成等基于 SWOT 法分析了自驾游汽车专列,提出了改善运输组织方式、构建信息化平台等建议。于波等将 PEST 法嵌入 SWOT 法中,构建了 PEST-SWOT 分析方法,在政治、经济、社会、技术等领域分析了先进制造业现阶段存在的优势与劣势及外部的机会与威胁,同时提出了进攻型、偏重防守型、防守型和适度进攻型四种战略类型。唐热情等基于 SWOT 法分析了成渝公路客运在高铁竞争条件下的发展战略,提出及时战略转移等防御性对策。

既有研究基于 SWOT 法一定程度探讨了目标产业现阶段外部条件与内在能力的可能结合途径,以此提出的各类型的发展战略可为产业生存发展提供对策。然而 SWOT 法在应用过程中仍存在以下缺陷:①并无更详细的决策过程,对应的交互分析中外因、内因具体交互分析过程展现不清晰;②未能意识到分析对象的系统特征,外因、内因交互后或决策提出后,未能就其对系统产生影响的路径进一步分析并展现,也未能明确受影响的细分子系统;③决策提出具有孤立性,对于决策与对策之间存在的互相关系缺乏合理探讨。

鉴于此,为更形象展现 SWOT 分析过程及拓展 SWOT 分析决策思路,本文结合 Tropos 模型提出了 Tropos-SWOT 战略分析模型。模型基于 Tropos 层次化建模手段直观展现了战略分析过程中的外因、内因作用途径及对应子系统影响关系,其后进一步拓展决策分析过程,明确决策施加对象关联关系并讨论决策间相互支持关系。以道路客运产业为分析对象进行案例探究,在分析过程中明确道路客运行业现状、提出具体对策建议、并根据对策关系提出具有实践意义的战略实施方针,以期为道路客运行业发展提供一定的借鉴参考。

1 Tropos-SWOT 分析模型

Tropos 模型是应用于面向对象的软件需求开发阶段的模型方法。模型以目标为导向,基于依赖、缓和、任务描述等方法层次化的完成系统建模工作。Tropos-SWOT 模型借鉴 Tropos 模型的层次化建模理念,依据战略分析思路将分析结构划分为目标层、对策层、内部因素层、外部因素层四个层次。目标层中基于 Tropos 模型目标架构设立形式建立,并通过目标逐步迭代完成子系统识别。对策层中探讨不同的内外因素结合后可能对不同子系统施加的影响,其后提出针对性战略对策进而分析对策间的互相支持关系。

基金项目:西南交通大学"双一流"建设项目(JDSYLYB2018029)。

内、外因素层则在传统 SWOT 法指导下进行产业优势、劣势、机遇、威胁的梳理,并在此基础上基于 SWOT 法完成内外因素的交叉分析。Tropos-SWOT 模型示意图如图 1 所示。

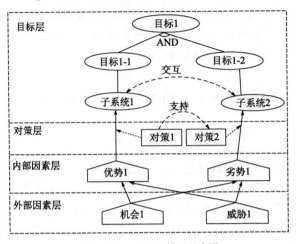

图 1　Tropos-SWOT 模型示意图

具体建模步骤如下:①基于目标导向的完成分析对象的系统整体运行框架的建立,明确划分子系统及辨析各子系统的交互关系;②依据各子系统的构建完成对应的优势(S)、劣势(W)分析,构建内部因素层;依据目前外部环境完成机会(O)、威胁(T)分析,构建外部因素层;③内外因素层交互分析。明确内外因素可能的结合途径,进行 SO 分析、ST 分析、WO 分析、WT 分析,因素作用关系由外因层指向内因层,分析完成后由内因层指向影响关系所对应子系统;④在对策层中,针对具备战略实施空间的分析结论采取对策,对策作用途径以箭头指向对应的分析路径;⑤对策层构建完成后分析对策互相之间可能存在的互相联系,进而提出合理的决策实施方针。

Tropos-SWOT 模型可在 SWOT 法基础上更为直观地展现对象系统运行方式、决策、因素作用路径及决策依赖关系,较好弥补传统 SWOT 法分析粗略、对策探讨缺失的不足,具体模型实施过程将在道路客运战略分析中展现。

2　道路客运 Tropos-SWOT 分析

2.1　系统框架建立

本文将道路客运系统粗粒化至要素层面分析,在进一步的研究中可依据 Tropos 目标导向的将各子系统更为详细地分解建模。在要素层面上,道路客运系统划分为运营主体(客运公司)、车站、道路、乘客(表1),其中运营主体、车站构成了道路客运的核心。此外,由于在我国政府部门对于道路客运有较强的影响及监管作用,故将地方政府监管部门也纳入系统内部考虑。子系统划分完成后,分析各子系统相互联系,完成目标层构建,如图 2 中目标层所示。其后依据既有文献及资料收集整理,基于 SWOT 法梳理道路客运业现阶段发展形式。

基于目标导向的道路客运系统划分　　表1

(子)系统	(子)系统目标	(子)系统	(子)系统目标
道路客运系统	可持续发展的道路运输系统 M1	车站	车站接发、组织有序(M1.3)
地方政府监管部门	政府对客运服务流程有效监管(M1.1)	乘客	获得最具效用的出行服务(M1.4)
运营主体	运营主体营收良好(M1.2)	道路	良好的道路状况(M1.5)

2.2　内部因素分析

2.2.1　优势分析

S1 道路客运运营市场化,运营主体拥有自主的定价权。

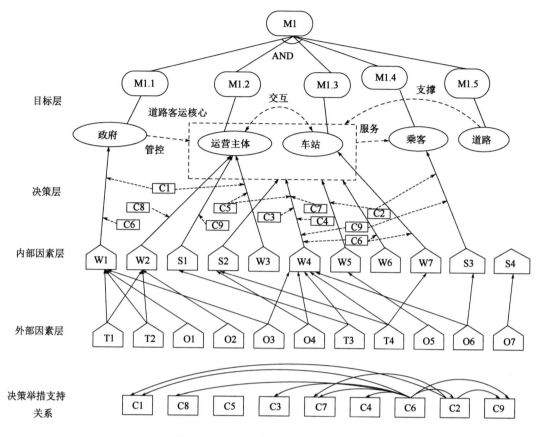

图 2　Tropos-SWOT 道路客运系统战略分析

S2 客运班列设置相对灵活,基础建设投入较小,运营成本低。道路客运运营过程中仅考虑车辆、人员、站场建设,基础投资小,即投即用,资金周转快速;汽车调度方便,班列调整灵活,客观限制较小,可有效替代、衔接、转运其他运输方式。

S3 与其他运输方式比较,道路客运价格相对低廉。

S4 道路基础设施建设完善。我国道路发展迅速,路网密度大,覆盖范围广,可通达性极强,全面覆盖的道路网络为道路客运服务提供了有效支撑。

2.2.2　劣势分析

W1 行政干预企业,行政许可程序复杂,政府影响程度大。政府部门对道路客运的管理着重依赖于线路资源的核实与审批,然而过多的审批流程及事前管控导致了道路客运行业脱离市场、滞后于市场及道路运输主体地位不明确等现象。此外,由于线路资源由地方政府管控,导致企业竞争关系集中于线路资源竞争,由此为适应地方管理与获取线路资源,大型运输企业多实行子公司制度,以线路资源获取为公司盈利最大依凭,对乘客出行的主观感受并不重视。

W2 环境污染严重,能耗高,易造成拥堵。道路运输客观条件不佳,在同等运输距离条件下,道路运输能耗远大于铁路运输,环境污染也大于铁路运输,且易造成拥堵现象。

W3 道路客运安全性较差,事故率、伤亡人数等指标远高于同期其他运输方式。

W4 产业结构单一,管理散乱,效益不佳。在呈现地域化、区域性的道路客运运营中,运营主体混杂、分散运营、独立运营、私营车主加盟等情况散乱存在,加之车站也缺乏合理的监督管控,道路客运核心总体呈"弱小散乱"的态势。此态势下道路客运客流来源也仅依赖线路资源分配,整体生产效率、经营效益不佳,以致班次缩减、人员裁撤、服务下降与营收亏损成为不断恶性循环的常态现象。

W5 企业整体信息化水平不佳。目前部分车站已有网络查票、购票服务,然而仍然存在较大的局限性与零散性,总体信息资源的整合程度、大数据的应用程度、信息化作业程度均不高。此外,产业整体未能有效对已有出行数据进行整理以分析旅客出行的需求和趋势,存在较为严重的信息孤岛现象,乘客综合性信息查询与购票服务也存在较大困难。

W6 无整体性机构,集约化程度低下。由于缺乏统一的组织管理,道路运输企业机构臃肿,每一个运营主体都有相对独立的企业配套建设。此外,由于各主体呈竞争关系,企业之间的资源、信息整合程度低下,以此造成运输线路的供需不平衡,运输资源的分配与优化难度大,更难以形成规模效益。此外,由于无统一机构管理,缺乏塑造核心价值认同,道路客运人员在缺乏统一服务培训的同时人员流动性也较大。

W7 车站收取站务费,抑制客运盈利。道路运输企业中,车站与运营主体为合作关系,车站主要收入来源为车辆站务费、旅客站务费及附属业务收入。然而随着客运收益降低,车站基于盈利导向,收费标准却随着市场化进程不断提高,主体运营成本进一步攀升。

2.3 外部因素分析

2.3.1 机会分析

O1 国家层面的"精准扶贫""乡村振兴"等一系列强农惠农战略实施,为农村客运科学、精准发展提供有力保障,为道路客运优势区间的进一步发展提供了政策支持。

O2 新能源汽车市场兴起。新能源汽车具有能耗低、污染小、舒适度高等特性,受到政府与大众的广泛关注。

O3 主要城市群客流潜力。我国主力建设京津冀、长三角、粤港澳大湾区等世界级现代化城市群,城市群内部有巨大的出行潜力,交通强国发展纲要也指出未来我国将大力推广城际道路客运的公交化运行模式。

O4 高铁及枢纽场站运营带来了新的诱增客流和集散客流。高铁站及机场一般建于城市边缘地带,诱增大量城市中心与站场的接驳客运量。

O5 网络平台成熟,互联网技术高速发展。目前,铁路,航空票务服务皆可在网络平台上进行,信息透明,操作简易;互联网平台相继推出网络约车、租车等服务,信息平台与交通运输行业的深入交互取得极大成效。同时我国交通强国纲要也指出要大力发展智慧交通,推动大数据、互联网、人工智能、区块链、超级计算等新技术与交通行业深度融合。

O6 经济稳定增长,人员在不同地域流动明显。随着经济的发展,人们多样化、快速化、个体化的出行需求不断增长,旅游业的快速繁荣,城乡人员交互的密集也为道路客运产业的发展提供了新的活力。

O7 道路基础建设未来进一步发展。我国交通强国建设纲要特别提出在2035年之前,我国将建成发达的快速网、完善的干线网、广泛的基础网,城乡区域交通协调发展达到新高度。交通基础设施的不断完善,为道路客运发展提供基础保障。

2.3.2 威胁分析

T1 部门区域公路客运补贴政策缩减。由于道路客运在资源消耗、环境污染等方面较铁路处于劣势,政府对行业的支撑远小于对高铁的支持力度,公路客运补贴政策大体处于缩减、维持原状或缓慢增长的状态,行业发展情况不容乐观。

T2 为有效促进城市发展,缓解市区拥堵,多个城市同时期出台主城区内部的汽车客货运站场搬迁方案,部分车站搬离城市中心。

T3 其他交通方式冲击。随着综合交通运输体系的发展,高铁、线上平台对道路客运传统优势区间造成了强烈的冲击,传统道路旅客运输客流被大量分流。此外由于道路客运服务具有一定的滞后性,对乘客需求不敏感,伴生出诸多依托人流聚集区域的站外客运服务,此类服务灵活高效,但非法运营情况同样突出且难以监管,对道路客运服务也造成了强有力的冲击。

T4 运输成本增长。为同步其他交通方式发展以形成有效竞争力,运营主体需购置服务特性较好的运输车辆、增加人员培训费用、车站需要提升基础设施服务质量,于此同时燃油费等消耗性资源的费用也在不断增长,运输成本的增加对营收普遍下降的道路客运行业有着较大的威胁。

2.4 对策提出

梳理产业现阶段 SWOT 因素后,基于 SWOT 法中 SO 分析、ST 分析、WO 分析、WT 分析详细分析外部因素、内部因素互相之间可能的结合途径,如图 2 外部因素层与内部因素层链接空间中指针所示。其后进一步分析内外因素作用下具体受到影响的目标子系统,影响关系由指针表现,在决策层中由内因层指向目标层,如图 2 决策层所示。

由图 2 内外因素交互分析可知,目前外因与内因关系集中对应于内部因素层中的 W1、W4,即以交通强国等国家战略的提出与潜在客流的变化为代表的外部环境变动将具体影响到道路客运监管现状及运营体系为代表的现存内部劣势,并由此对道路客运业提出了更高的发展挑战。此外,W2 也是决策考虑要点之一,改变道路客运高能耗、高污染的现状是目前行业亟待解决的关键问题。进一步分析交互结果与目标层子系统对应关系,道路客运的运营主体是现阶段受到最广泛影响的参与实体而与运营公司同处于道路客运核心地位的车站也将同期面临较为深刻的发展变动。针对现有形式邀请专家集中讨论,此处共选用三位专家,领域涵盖运输经济、运输安全、产业经济等相关领域,依据具备战略实施空间的分析结果,提出了九条具有建设性的对策建议。

C1 道路客运管理部门推进经营许可、线路审批、运输变更等方面的改革工作。其中,安全监管变事前控制为运输中监管,包含推进企业自主经营权、对于违规现象从重处罚、通过法律、经济和行政手段对汽车运输市场实行严格的管理和积极的引导。此外,促进运输企业"以乘客为中心"的服务观念的形成,面向市场,积极服务,为乘客提供更灵活、人本化的道路客运服务。

C2 依托网络平台和大数据处理技术,建立全国性的乘客信息化平台及客运业务处理平台。乘客通过平台便捷地选择车次与车站,其后平台依据乘客出行数据,科学布局车站选址,合理推算客流及其分布规律,最终达到供需合理,运力配置相宜。此外,工作人员依托网络平台进行业务办理,有利于简化流程并规范操作。

C3 积极拓展其他业务,增强自身盈利能力。具有战略规划与开拓性思维,综合运用运力,与学校机构、旅游公司、大型企业达成定时定点的运输协议,在降低合作企业成本的同时增加自身盈利。

C4 自主开拓旅游市场。为抓紧并吸收庞大的旅游群体带来了大量的运输需求,道路客运业需统筹规划,整体性推出高品质的旅游运输服务,其中包含积极推行短线旅游、市内接送一日游、景区班列等业务。

C5 优化衔接工作。通过衔接关系发挥道路客运的技术经济特性以引导竞争方向,实现转化竞争关系为协作关系,积极争取城际铁路辐射区域外的客源、中间客源并吸引末端、支线客流。此外积极探索高铁接驳服务,通过协调高铁发车时间,积极发挥替代作用,真正推动综合交通体系的系统效应。

C6 整合现有政府资源与企业资源,建立跨区域、统一的部门机构。机构依托现代化技术更为合理地配置资源和协调合作各方,推动道路客运业由"弱小散乱"现状向集约化、信息化发展,提升客运服务效率并实现成本控制,最终形成规模效益。此外,统一管理有助于良好品牌效益的形成,并可由此推动规范化的员工培训机制形成,通过统一服务标准、服装配饰等增强员工凝聚力的同时也增强乘客的旅行服务体验。

C7 响应交通强国号召,在我国主要城市群积极探索城际公交车,推动城市群内部人员互通,促进区域性经济发展。

C8 根据具体情况综合考虑合理配置新能源车辆。举措有助于改善政府部门与公众对道路客运能耗高、污染大的固有观感,进而提升品牌价值及乘客体验,且可潜在吸引政府政策支持。

C9 面对不同的地区、时段及消费人群提供多样化与差异化服务。建立票价差异化服务体系,如推出浮动票价机制、特价车票抢购机制、团购优惠车票机制、往返折扣车票机制等。此外,可进一步建立班车车型差异化服务机制,通过具体客流推测、现有购票信息、线路属性以选用不同规格、客员的具体对应车型。

对策提出后,区别于传统 SWOT 对策简单罗列,建立对策层通过指针指向直观明确对策对应的具体内外因交互分析及作用的细分子系统,对应影响路径如图 2 中决策层所示。

2.5 决策支持关系分析

上述举措建议一定程度上均能促进道路客运业发展。然而区别于传统 SWOT 法提出举措即终止分析,Tropos-SWOT 中举措的实施过程往往并非孤立,互相之间存在一定支持联系。由此进一步分析所提出决策间支持关系,进而建立其相互间支持路径以明确战略实施具体方案。经分析,C6 建立跨区域的统一部门对诸多举措都有支持作用,应是道路客运系统组织改革的核心,也是应首先实行的重点基础工作。C2 信息平台的建立受到了 C6 的支持,同时也对 C1、C7、C9 决策起到了一定支持作用,是需要优先发展的举措之一。由此,在统一部门及信息平台支持下,诸多举措并进的实施策略应是道路客运业的重要发展方向。

基于上述分析,本文提出构建新型道路客运系统的综合性对策实施方针,如图 3 所示。在国家宏观调整下,运营主体、车站、审批管理等监管部门集合为统一的大型跨区域部门,在信息化平台支撑下完成资源分配,运力调度,手续办理等业务流程,引导竞争为分工,变控制为指导;此外,基于平台完成乘客全国性票务服务,方便乘客的同时有效收集数据进行客流预测与统计,为运输生产的生产排班、差异化票价等业务提供技术支持。在统一机构建立的基础上,巩固与调整主营业务,契合客流变化、对接国家战略、统筹性优化与其他交通方式衔接工作;综合拓展多元业务,与公司、学校等达成战略合作协议;强化附属业务,积极探索车站商业化服务及物流集散服务;建立统一服务标准,员工培训、服务流程、设施配置标准化以提高服务质量,最终达到行业的良性发展。

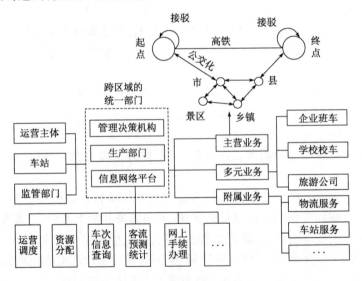

图 3　新型道路客运系统概念图

3　结　语

(1)Tropos-SWOT 模型一定程度上弥补传统 SWOT 法分析过程模糊,决策思路针对性不强的缺陷,可层次化展现详细的产业战略分析过程,是对 SWOT 方法的有效拓展。

(2)基于 Tropos-SWOT 的战略分析结果显示,交通强国等政策的提出与潜在客流的变化等外因与道路客运监管不当及运营体系效率低下等内因结合后将对道路客运业现阶段发展提出较大挑战,基于此提出了管理改革、建立信息平台等九条具有实践意义的对策建议。其后,剖析对策相互关系,进一步提出了在跨区域的部门统一领导下、依托信息化平台建立新型道路客运系统的综合性战略实施方针。该方针可推动道路客运业战略变革,为道路客运业发展提供一定的参考建议。

参考文献

[1] 道路客运屡创新低[EB/OL]. [2019-05-15]. http://www.crtm.cn/ezine/25334.html.
[2] AnY, Ma X, Chen W. Research on the development strategy of tourism consulting companies based on SWOT model[C]// 2014 IEEE Workshop on Advanced Research and Technology in Industry Applications (WARTIA). IEEE, 2014.
[3] 黄文成,帅斌,李林卿. 我国开行自驾游汽车运输专列的SWOT分析[J]. 铁道经济研究,2017(06):38-42.
[4] 于波,范从来. 我国先进制造业发展战略的PEST嵌入式SWOT分析[J]. 南京社会科学,2011(07):34-40.
[5] 唐热情,黄伟宏,郭良久. 成渝两地高速公路客运经营策略研究[J]. 重庆交通大学学报(自然科学版),2007(06):148-152.
[6] DENG Xiuquan, et al. Risk propagation mechanisms and risk management strategies for a sustainable perishable products supply chain. Computers & Industrial Engineering, 2019.
[7] 王思桥. 重庆市道路客运管理优化研究[D]. 重庆:重庆大学,2018.
[8] 韩佳琦. 公路客运班线运营安全风险耦合分析及管理策略[D]. 吉林:吉林大学,2017.
[9] 周新军. 高速铁路助推中国低碳经济效应[J]. 中国科学院院刊,2011,26(04):452-461.

西部陆海新通道的水运战略构想

王 斌 杨秋平

(交通运输部水运科学研究院)

摘 要 本研究从需求方面分析了我国西南省份与东南亚地区贸易情况,西南省份与东南亚地区、中亚地区与东盟之间的贸易额不断增加,"西南陆海新通道"的开通为其节省了时间和成本。"西南陆海新通道"经过东南亚、南亚及中东欧等国家,其文化、经济、宗教信仰等方面的差异和冲突带来运输安全风险。地区政局动荡、领土纷争,将会影响新通道的顺利运行。然而,西南地区的出海通道并非一条,如何充分发挥水路运输的比较优势,构建出"西南陆海新通道"建设的"第二通道",是本文需要探讨的问题。

关键词 水运 新通道 战略构想 中缅陆水联运

0 引 言

二十多年西南出海大通道建设中,解决了一系列发展中的矛盾,如有效整合北部湾港口群、建立北部湾经济区、打通内陆地区、发展东盟多边合作等,为西部陆海新通道奠定了一定的基础。如今,"一带一路"倡议的提出再次让广西开始重新挖掘通道建设中的战略价值。中新(重庆)战略性互联互动示范项目虽然落户重庆,但凭借与新加坡多年合作的积淀,广西政府和港航企业共同推动"陆海新通道"的建设。西南出海大通道徘徊了二十余年,终于完成了"陆海新通道"的战略变局。

2017年9月,陆海新通道在重庆诞生。两年间,陆海新通道实现了丝绸之路经济带与21世纪海上丝绸之路的无缝衔接,改写了我国对外开放版图。广西与重庆、贵州、甘肃、青海、新疆、云南、宁夏、陕西8省区市签署了合作共建"陆海新通道"协议。广西相继开通了5条班列线路,至重庆、成都、昆明、兰州、贵阳、青海西部6省区市,并实现"渝新欧""蓉欧"等中欧班列与"一带一路"的无缝对接。2019年8月,国家发展改革委印发了《西部陆海新通道总体规划》,标志着陆海新通道上升为国家战略。

"西部陆海新通道"途径东南亚、南亚及中东欧等国家,"西部陆海新通道"的常态化运营会因为各国和地区的文化、民族、经济、宗教信仰等方面的差异与冲突而存在潜在的运输安全风险。局部地区的领土纷争、内部分裂、国内动乱或者边界局部战争,将会影响新通道的顺利运行。然而,西南地区的出海通道并非一条,如何充分发挥水路运输的比较优势,构建出"西南陆海新通道"建设的"第二通道",是本文需要探讨的问题。我国与中南半岛国家已形成包括澜沧江-湄公河合作机制、"中缅经济走廊"、"中老经济走廊"等一系列合作机制框架,在各个战略合作框架下,目前物流运输通道、基础设施互联互通等领域下若干重大工程、重点项目已经初具规模,本文通过比选分析各通道的优劣势,最终提出"第二通道"的方案,为西南出海新通道提供了技术方案储备。

1 东南亚、中亚共享西南出海大通道成果

西部陆海新通道北接丝绸之路经济带,南连21世纪海上丝绸之路。成渝地区和北部湾地区是西部陆海新通道建设的重点,该区域向北连接亚欧大陆桥,与丝绸之路经济带连通;向南通过北部湾与海上丝绸之路衔接;在重庆与长江黄金水道衔接。辐射区域包括了我国西南、西北地区,东盟、中亚、中东和欧洲地区。

西南出海大通道周边国家一般是指东南亚地区国家,共有18个,包括:新加坡、菲律宾、老挝、尼泊尔、马来西亚、文莱、印度、不丹、泰国、印度尼西亚、巴基斯坦、越南、缅甸、孟加拉国、斯里兰卡、柬埔寨、马尔代夫、东帝汶。我国与东南亚进出口贸易中,西南地区与东南亚贸易额占比最高,很大一部分经北部湾地区进行中转。

1.1 我国西南省份与东南亚地区贸易情况

越南是东南亚对我国西南地区第一大出口国,因广西、云南与越南的沿边优势,南向通道要重点关注东南亚地区对西南地区进出口发展情况。2019年我国西南地区对越南出口额为151.2亿美元,占比46.8%。越南增长最为明显,2019年相比于2016年增长了6倍,我国西南地区向其他东南亚国家出口总贸易额较为平稳。第二为马来西亚,出口额为40.9亿美元,占比12.6%;其次为泰国、缅甸、新加坡、印度尼西亚等国家。我国西南地区从东南亚进口贸易总体呈上升趋势,越南、缅甸、泰国和马来西亚是我国西南地区主要进口贸易国。其中,越南增长较为明显,2019年贸易额相比于2018年增长了将近2倍,其他东南亚国家进口情况总体较为平稳。西南地区对东南亚国家主要出口产品为工业制成品,以电机、机器、机械器具及零件为主;主要进口产品是矿物燃料、橡胶、水果等产品。

1.2 大宗散货贸易情况

大宗散货出口方面,我国向东南亚地区石油气出口量最多,达到100.5万t,其中西南省份向东南亚通过水路出口石油气26.7万t(图1),其中26.5万t都是广西向越南出口的。

我国从东南亚地区进口煤炭方面,主要通过水路运输,进口量最多的国家是印度尼西亚,达到13751.1万t。其中,我国西南地区中,广西从印度尼西亚水路进口煤炭最多,达到了1165.7万t(图2)。

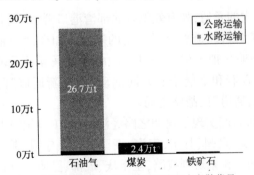

图1 我国西南地区向东南亚地区出口大宗散货量(分运输方式)

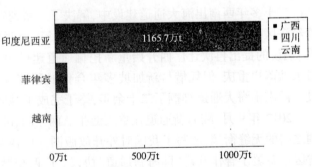

图2 我国西南地区从东南亚地区进口煤炭量(水运)

我国从东南亚地区进口石油气主要通过水路和管道。从马来西亚、印度尼西亚、缅甸等国家进口石油气，分别为801.7万t、492.7万t和341.9万t，其中从马来西亚和印度尼西亚主要通过水路进口（图3），从缅甸通过管道进口。其中我国西南地区中主要是广西通过水路运输进口石油气。

我国从东南亚地区进口铁矿石，主要进口国为马来西亚、缅甸、越南、印度尼西亚、老挝、泰国和菲律宾进口。从马来西亚进口主要是水路运输，进口量达到317.9万t。缅甸主要通过公路进口，达到276.8万t。越南大部分通过公路进口，只有8.5万t铁矿石通过水路进口。印度尼西亚主要通过水路进口，达到133.4万t。

其中，我国西南地区中，云南通过水路运输从马来西亚进口铁矿石达到7.8万t，接下来是广西从越南进口5.8万t，从马来西亚进口1.2万t以及从老挝进口不足1万t，如图4所示。

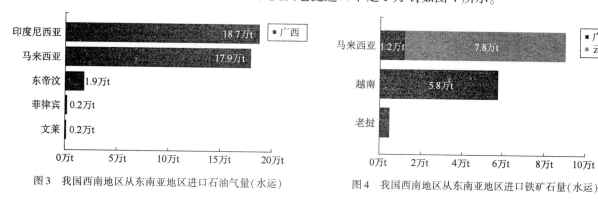

图3 我国西南地区从东南亚地区进口石油气量（水运）　　图4 我国西南地区从东南亚地区进口铁矿石量（水运）

1.3 适箱货贸易情况

据中国海关2019年统计，适箱货（包括过境及一般货物）由广西出发，经西部陆海通道至中欧班列出口到欧洲、中南亚地区的，共计金额2972.5万美元。其中，出口到俄罗斯的最多，达到一千多万美元，其次是德国和哈萨克斯坦，分别达到了487.4万美元和471.7万美元。适箱货（包括过境及一般货物）由欧洲、中南亚地区通过中欧班列进口再经西部陆海通道运至广西的，共计金额1501.7万美元。其中，从英国、德国和哈萨克斯坦进口的最多，分别为440.9万美元、424.5万美元和410.9万美元。

近些年，中亚地区与东南亚地区贸易额逐年增长，东南亚地区从中亚地区进口额增长显著，从2015年的2亿美元增长到2019年超过14亿美元，其中以哈萨克斯坦增长最为显著，2019年较2015年增长了将近10倍，其他中亚地区的国家也均有不同幅度的增长。出口额同样增长明显，从2015年的10亿美元增长到2019年将近20亿美元，哈萨克斯坦增长最为显著，2019年较2015年增长了5亿美元，蒙古国也从2015年1.55亿美元增长到2019年的3.05亿美元，增长了几乎一倍，其他中亚地区的国家也均有不同幅度的增长。2019年东南亚从中亚主要进口货类为矿物燃料、矿物油及其蒸馏产品，沥青物质，矿物蜡，金额达到了4.31亿美元，占到总贸易额的59%，其次是钢铁，金额达到了1.39亿美元，占到了19%（图5）。出口的主要货类为电机、电气设备及其零件；录音机及放声机、电视图像、声音的录制和重放设备及其零件、附件，金额达到了4.7亿美元，占总贸易额的48%；核反应堆、锅炉、机器、机械器具及零件金额达到了1.46亿美元，占总贸易额的15%（图6）。

随着"一带一路"倡议的不断推进，中亚五国进出口额增速明显，中亚地区与东南亚地区贸易不断增长。贸易路径的改变大大节省了运输时间，提升运输效率。例如哈萨克斯坦向东盟国家出口货物，从我国北方港口出海运至东盟国家，但通过兰渝铁路，哈萨克斯坦货物可以从我国西部向南通过铁路运输至北部湾港口出海。

2 云南以其特有的区位优势，谋划新的出海通道

2.1 中缅陆水联运新通道

云南长期以来一直把广西北部湾港作为首选的出海通道，通过北部湾港运送了大量的资源类货物。

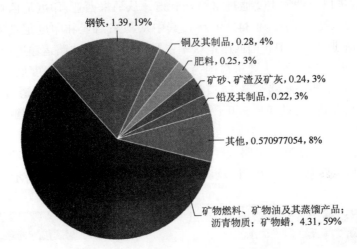

图 5 2019 年东南亚从中亚进口货类情况

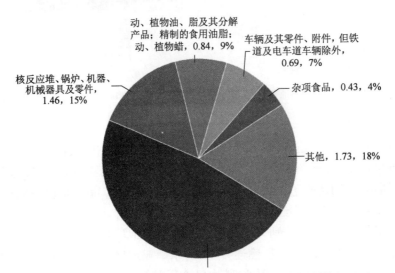

图 6 2019 年东南亚从中亚出口货类情况

随着南向通道的中老铁路的开通,大量货物可通过泛亚铁路从我国西部运至东南亚地区,形成国际铁路联运。泛亚铁路从昆明市出发,分为东中西三线曼谷汇合后,经过吉隆坡最终到达新加坡。云南在西部陆海新通道中的地位将由通道参与方变成通道建设主体之一。

除上述铁路通道建设之外,云南具备构建中缅陆水联运新通道的基础。中缅陆水联运新通道,从昆明经昆瑞高速公路,从瑞丽口岸出境,到达缅甸伊洛瓦底江八莫港,顺江而下到达缅甸海港,由仰光港或皎漂港出海进入印度洋。可以将中缅陆水联运新通道作为"西南陆海新通道"建设的"第二通道"。

2.2 可行性分析

中缅陆水联运新通道的构建处在最佳的历史时期。近年来,在两国领导人的战略引领下,中缅关系处于历史上的最好时期。两国相继签署共建"一带一路"倡议、"中缅经济走廊"等战略合作备忘录,缅甸国务资政昂山素季连续参加中国"一带一路"国际合作论坛,两国关系从胞波情谊上升为"中缅命运共同体"。缅甸具有天然的地理位置优势,并具有特别重要的战略意义。目前印度洋是世界上最繁忙和最具战略价值的贸易通道,同时缅甸的战略地位逐渐上升。

中缅陆水联运新通道的建设有利于推动两国"通道经济"建设。缅甸伊洛瓦底江优越的通航条件、皎漂、仰光深水港和较为便利的陆上交通网络,为我国尤其是西南地区进入南亚、东南亚市场创造有利的交通条件,也为缅甸及第三国进入我国市场提供便捷的通道,推动中国、南亚、东南亚三大经济增长区、三大市场连为一体,推动我国与南亚地区国家区域经济一体化、贸易便利化。从社会影响方面来看,中缅伊洛瓦底江陆水联运国际新通道的建设将提高缅甸居民的生活水平,使得船舶水运成本能够降低,促进缅甸城市可持续发展。

中缅陆水联运新通道可以节约物流成本。我国西南地区以水陆联运方式向西进入南亚、西亚、非洲和欧洲最便捷的通道,无须绕道我国东部港口和马六甲海峡,大大节约了资金与时间成本。云南大宗货物由八莫中转,经伊洛瓦底江水运进出仰光港或沿岸各港口、城镇,运费只及公路经曼德勒转水运的1/3,或汽车直达仰光港的1/8。由昆明经伊洛瓦底江陆水联运国际新通道从仰光到南亚、西亚、非洲、欧洲各国,较昆明至中国沿海各港口到上述地区都减少3000多公里运距,运时也缩短5~6d。

中缅陆水联运新通道已具备一定的前期基础。该通道建设于20世纪90年代开始开展过大量前期工作,1997年我国和缅甸双方签署过"新通道"的会议纪要,后由于缅方国内政治的原因,中缅陆水联运运输协定计划停滞不前。2017年云南省政府层面积极开展工作,推进重启"新通道"。在中缅经济走廊交通领域方面,中缅两国成立合作专项工作组,建立了良好的部级层面对话联络机制。

2.3 遇到的困难

由于通道建设涉及两国的各个方面,中缅陆水联运新通道建设需要两国的共同努力来实现。在我国,该通道目前以地方政府推动为主,缺乏国家层面统筹谋划。由于缺乏国家层面统筹推进机制支持,虽然云南方面一直积极努力,但目前中缅只能以民间合作方式进行,难以取得实质性的进展,中缅通道经济性、民生性效果不能体现和发挥。缅方方面,中缅陆水联运新通道涉及缅国内复杂政治局势,政府内部意见不统一。缅国内民族矛盾激烈,中央政府与少数民族武装之间的纷争从未停止过。中缅陆水联运新通道涉及的缅方境内70km公路段处于缅北民族地方武装控制范围,属于政府军和克钦独立军犬牙交错的控制区,情况复杂。缅甸政府、民众、企业希望加强与我方政府、企业合作,但牵涉国家主权问题等政治外交事务,缅甸中央政府对缅北地区复杂形势实际管控能力有限,缅方外交部门持谨慎沉默态度。2019年中缅经济走廊交通合作领域专项工作组会议期间,中方已提议关于重启中缅陆水联运新通道方案的相关讨论,缅方选择回避。

3 建设"新通道"措施建议

(1)开展相关的研究工作,出台新通道实施方案。

建议将"中缅陆水联运新通道"的建设项目纳入交通领域重点国际合作储备项目,联合有关部门开展前期的论证工作。开展项目的前期论证工作,建议从政治、经济、技术等方面进行实施方案论证工作。建立邀请国内专家参与到项目研究中,对研究工作推进技术指导。

(2)建立常态化对话机制,凝结共识。

充分利用民间平台来拓展合作渠道与人员交流,推进两国知名专家、社会团体、民间企业等,为"新通道"建设提供智力支持,就装备与技术标准、生态环境、经济、产业合作等话题开展广泛的交流互动,全方位推进中缅两国政府间的合作,为推动新通道建设达成广泛共识凝聚力量。在外交方面,就新通道的建设方案、合作安全、合作机制等方面建立常态化对话机制。

(3)签署中缅陆水联运新通道建设及运输协定。

待条件成熟,把握共建"一带一路"倡议、中缅经济走廊建设有利时机,积极推进将"新通道"建设列入中缅双方交通合作领域专项工作,共同推进起草中缅伊洛瓦底江陆水联运新通道建设及客货运输协定,为"新通道"建设提供有效制度保障,同时,将该通道建设作为中缅经济走廊建设互联互通重点项目之一正式提出。

(4)启动通道关键数据信息的监测分析工作。

根据以构建的西南出海大通道监测跟踪指标体系,充分利用互联网、卫星遥感信息技术等辅助摸清各通道现有航运、经济、社会等基础情况,利用国内外便利宏观数据来源及实地港口码头、航运市场数据采集来源，实时跟踪监测跟踪掌握该区域水运基础设施情况，跟踪港口布局和主要港口功能、跟踪沿线运输法规政策情况、跟踪该区域国际国内航线及发展态势等信息。

4 结语

近年来，我国西南省份与东南亚地区、中亚地区与东盟之间的贸易额不断增加，由广西北部湾港口出海至东南亚地区与传统出海路径相比，既节省了时间也节省了费用，这一通道的开通促进了西南省份与东南亚地区的贸易，为西部大开发战略提供了有力的支撑。但是目前西南出海通道较为单一，途径国家或地区存在政局动荡和领土纷争的风险，本文分析了云南特有的区位优势，谋划出新的出海通道来作为技术储备。在分析中缅陆水联运新通道的可行性之后，也提出了开通这一通道将会遇到的困难，并给出相应的措施建议。未来，还应在新通道建设方面继续探索，对比不同通道的优劣势，找出一条相对科学可行的新通道。

参考文献

[1] 西部陆海新通道总体规划.
[2] 牧原,郝攀峰,许伟.试看南向通道的战略布局[J].中国远洋海运,2018.
[3] 沿海沿边开放建设西南出海大通道扶贫攻坚战[J].传承,2013.
[4] 何智娟.新互联互通南向通道建设背景下广西国际物流发展SWOT分析[J].发展改革,2019.
[5] 王晓明.道建设背景下深入推动"广西货"走"广西港"面临的难题及对策[J].经济师,2020.
[6] 郑锐.西南港口与越南港形成跨国界港口群可行性研究[J].港口物流,2014.
[7] 郝洁,李大伟.将南向通道建设为西部地区全面开放战略大通道的思考[J].智库论坛,2019.

基于SWOT的产业路发展情况分析
——以陕西省为例

马 欣 马 帆

(陕西省交通运输发展研究中心)

摘 要 近年来，随着脱贫攻坚、乡村振兴等政策的深入实施，我国基础设施建设有了飞速发展，公路深入农村腹地，涌现了一批公路带动乡村发展的生动案例，初步实现了"产业绕路建,路通产业兴"的美好画面。产业路的建设与发展在带动地方经济中的重要作用不言而喻，然而当前产业路发展中还存在一定的问题和制约，究竟该如何更好地发展产业路，笔者以陕西省为例，在深入陕西各地调研的基础上，应用SWOT方法对当地产业发展的优势、劣势、机会与威胁进行深入分析，并提出可行性措施，以期对我国产业路建设与发展提供借鉴。

关键词 交通运输 发展措施 SWOT方法 产业路

0 引 言

2016年杨传堂部长在全国两会"部长通道"上明确提出要重点打造"产业路"，我国多个省市也启动产业路建设相关探索。究竟何为产业路，目前学术领域及政府部门等对于其没有明确的定义，从交通运输部及部分省份相关文件及举措来看，多将产业路、资源路、旅游路一起提出，作为扶贫路的一个重要方向，多以农村公路为主。笔者认为，产业路是服务产业发展尤其是产业园区发展的重要基础设施，产业园区主要包括农业园区和工业园区，所以产业路的建设应当主要服务工农业发展，在本文的研究中主要围绕公路服务工农业产业发展,尤其是产业园区发展进行展开。

SWOT分析方法在行业研究、区域研究及企业研究中有着广泛的应用。由著名管理学家K.J.安德鲁斯1971年首次提出,何得桂、李丽莉等在其文章中应用SWOT方法对具体问题进行深入分析并提出对策建议。这些文献给了笔者以启示,进而在深入调查研究的基础上,通过SWOT方法对陕西省产业路建设与发展情况进行深入分析,并结合其优势、劣势、机会与威胁,制定了基于AHP评价指标体系等一系列可行性措施,助力陕西省产业路建设与发展。

1 陕西省产业路发展环境SWOT分析

1.1 优势分析

1.1.1 自然条件优势

陕西省地势呈南北高,中部低,由西向东倾斜,北山和秦岭把陕西分为三大自然区域:北部是陕北高原,中部是关中平原,南部是秦巴山区。陕北黄土高原北部为风沙区,南部是丘陵沟壑区,畜牧业较为发达,煤、石油、天然气储量丰富;关中平原地势平坦,交通便利,气候温和,物产丰富,经济发达;陕南秦巴山地包括秦岭、巴山和汉江谷地秦巴山区是林特产的宝库,汉江谷地土质肥美,物产丰富。

1.1.2 交通发展优势

近年来,陕西省交通基础设施建设稳步推进,已实现县县通高速、乡乡通油路、村村通硬化路的目标,基本形成了以高速公路为骨架、干线公路为支撑、农村公路为经络的公路交通网络,为陕西省产业园区发展打通基础动脉。

1.1.3 政策支持优势

从国家层面到省级再到市县,逐层推进农村及产业园区发展,并颁布了一系列利好政策。从国家层面看,为应对产业发展需求,交通部印发了《关于进一步发挥交通扶贫攻坚基础支撑作用的实施意见》等文件,提出要重点打造产业路,从顶层明确了交通+的发展模式。从陕西省来看,陆续出台了《关于印发加快县域工业集中区和产业园区建设行动计划的通知》等文件,为建设与园区布局、产业发展相匹配的交通基础设施提供了参考依据。从市县层面来看,各市县也积极利用利好政策,加快产业园区建设,推动产业路发展。

1.1.4 产业园区基础优势

近年来,陕西省持续加强产业园建设,农业园区建设方面,陕西省目前建成省级现代农业园区近400个,全省农民合作社总数达到6.13万家。工业园区建设方面,预计"十三五"末期增建国家级重点园区至16家、省级重点园区至38家。工农业园区的发展对全省产业路的建设提出了更高的要求,同时也为产业路的发展奠定了良好的基础。

1.2 劣势分析

1.2.1 公路基础设施不能充分满足产业发展需求

对标陕西省产业发展需求,公路基础设施仍存在很大的短板和不足。一是通达程度不足,网络布局还需优化。二是道路技术等级偏低,提级改造需求旺盛。受陕西省地形地貌和各地经济水平发展影响,关中地区道路修建标准相对较高,陕北陕南地区还存在路面状况较差等问题。三是公路损坏严重,养护压力与日俱增。

1.2.2 交通+产业融合深度不够

产业路建设发展涉及交通、农业、工信等多个部门,但是就目前来看,各部门间有效合作机制尚未形成,尤其是在县一级,在承接产业转移对接、重点项目推进、交通基础设施规划等方面,各部门还存在各管一家的情况。同时,交通与产业融合发展还没有顶层性、整体性、系统性的规划设计,农业、林业、水利、住建、交通等各类规划差异矛盾比较突出,各市县长远规划谋划不足。

1.3 机会分析

1.3.1 国家战略机遇

近年来,国家提出了乡村振兴、脱贫攻坚、交通强国战略、黄河流域生态保护和高质量发展战略等一系列战略部署,出台了《实施乡村振兴战略的意见》《交通强国建设纲要》等纲领性文件,为陕西省产业路建设与发展带来了前所未有的机遇。

1.3.2 产业发展机遇

近年来陕西省产业园区迎来了大发展。农业上持续加强产业园区创建工作,全省涉农的102个区县中,均有省级现代农业园区,全省已基本形成国家、省、市、县梯次推进的现代农业园区发展格局。工业园区建设方面,陕西省着重构建国家级重点园区、省级重点园区以及特色产业园区协调发展的工业园区布局体系,并结合地区特征,着重打造"一轴两翼"工业空间布局。

1.3.3 经济发展机遇

处于西部地区的陕西省近几年来始终保持较高速发展的趋势,2016—2019年GDP增长速度均在6%以上,截至2019年,GDP总值已达到2.58万亿,人均GDP为66649元,全省经济持续健康发展,为加强全省基础设施建设促进产业路发展提供充足保障。

1.4 威胁分析

1.4.1 土地要素制约

受国家宏观调控政策影响,用地审批门槛提高,土地供应趋紧,国土空间"三区三线"划定对交通建设发展提出新的要求,产业路规划建设用地保障压力加大,现有规划建设用地空间布局不能支撑产业路发展;而且,随着土地建设和征迁成本的提升,对产业路路建设和提级改造也带来了重大影响。

1.4.2 资金要素制约

资金问题是长期制约公路交通发展的"瓶颈"。国家系统性金融风险防控要求不断提高,市县筹资渠道收窄,地方政府普通公路建设融资难问题未能得到有效化解,建设资金短缺问题依然突出。同时,农村公路建设需求不断增加,受经济下行等因素制约,作为责任主体的很多市县财政配套压力大,建设产业路积极性不是很高。此外,公路养护任务日趋繁重,养护资金需求逐年增加,养护资金补助标准与养护管理工作形势不相适应,缺口较大。

1.4.3 环保安全要素制约

公路建设和生态保护的矛盾日益突出。生态、资源环境刚性约束不断增强,环保要求逐年提高,公路与环境保护协同发展仍需进一步规范和加强。同时,陕南、陕北山区地质条件差,生态环境承载能力弱,水毁、泥石流、滑坡等公路病害频繁发生,公路灾害治理工作与环保工作要求还有一定差距,不能有效保障公路运输服务需求,需要倍加注重生态和环境保护。

2 陕西省产业路发展策略分析

基于上述陕西省产业路发展内外部环境的深入分析,通过采用SWOT矩阵对陕西省产业路发展的四个方面策略进行分析(表1)。

陕西省产业路发展SWOT矩阵分析　　　　表1

外部因素 \ 内部因素	机会(O)	威胁(T)
	国家战略机遇 产业发展机遇 经济发展机遇	土地要素制约 资金要素制约 环保安全要素制约

续上表

优势(S)	发展型策略(O-S)	拓展型策略(T-S)
自然条件优势 交通发展优势 政策支持优势 产业园区基础优势	(1)强化顶层设计,做好战略规划 (2)加强产业路发展的宣传,争取多方支持 (3)加强政策支持 (4)积极融入国家发展战略	(1)提升产业路发展层次,争取更多外部支持 (2)规范产业路建设标准,建立评价指标体系 (3)建立产业路发展项目库
劣势(W)	弥补型策略(O-W)	防御型策略(T-W)
公路基础设施不能充分满足产业发展需求 交通+产业融合深度不够	(1)补齐公路建设短板 (2)加强部门合作,推动融合发展	(1)拓宽资金筹措渠道 (2)强化土地、环保要素保障,优化发展环境

2.1 结合优势和机会,拟定 O-S 增长型发展策略

2.1.1 强化顶层设计,做好战略规划

加强产业路建设顶层设计,统筹各方资源,加强交通规划与城镇体系规划、区域发展规划的规划对接,实现交通与资源流动、产业发展良好互动。结合陕西省城镇布局、现有路网结构、产业结构调整、产业园区未来发展需求等,加强与各部门规划的衔接。

2.1.2 加强产业路发展的宣传,争取多方支持

产业路建设服务产业发展,造福当地百姓,要加大对产业路建设发展的宣传力度,通过微视频等多种途径,宣传产业路对脱贫致富的带动作用,加大人民群众对"产业绕路建,路通产业兴"的认识,增加企业与群众对产业路建设与发展的支持,加强交通+产业融合发展,促进陕西省产业路发展与产业兴旺。

2.1.3 加强政策支持

结合陕西省产业发展需求,贯彻落实《十三五交通扶贫规划》《关于推动"四好农村路"高质量发展实施意见》等要求,研究制定适应产业路发展的政策措施,鼓励出台交通促进产业发展的相关政策文件,重点对支撑产业发展的道路给予政策和资金上的优惠和支持,优化产业发展的基础条件,加快形成交通运输与产业融合发展的新格局。

2.1.4 积极融入国家发展战略

陕西省产业路建设要深度融入共建"一带一路",新时代推进西部大开发形成新格局、黄河流域生态保护和高质量发展等战略实施,积极适应国家生态文明建设和绿色发展,在产业路建设过程中推行实施绿色公路建养,让产业路不仅成为带动一方产业发展的致富路,更是成为展现当地风土特色的风景线。

2.2 剖析优势和威胁,构建 T-S 拓展型发展策略

2.2.1 提升产业路发展层次,争取更多外部支持

充分将产业路发展与交通强国战略、脱贫攻坚战略、高质量发展战略等有机结合,建议将产业路建设与发展上升为国家层面的工程,国家加大对产业路建设的资金支持和政策支持力度,省级层面加大推进力度,与陕西省交通运输"十四五"发展规划相结合,提高产业路发展层次。同时,产路发展服务于民,助力当地经济发展,可以广泛争取地方政府与各企事业单位的支持,推动产业路发展。

2.2.2 规范产业路建设标准,建立评价指标体系

目前,产业路建设存在评价标准不统一,立项困难等问题,可针对产业路建设中的实际问题,建立产业路建设评价指标体系,规范产业路建设标准。从调研实际来看,目前产业路建设主要服务产业园区,利

用 AHP 方法,构建评价指标体系,如图 1 所示。

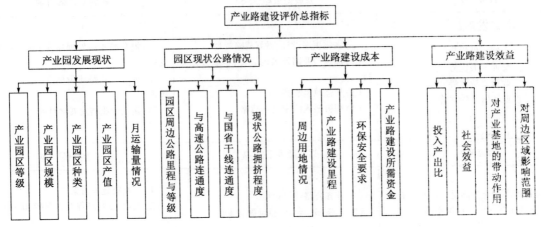

图 1 产业路建设评价指标体系

2.2.3 建立产业路发展项目库

按照符合国家、省交通运输发展战略、规划布局及相关政策,满足区域、行业发展要求的原则,对照全省产业发展规划、产业园区布局,系统梳理陕西省产业园区道路通畅、提级改造、养护维修等方面的交通需求,建立专项项目库,并纳入"十四五"项目库统一管理,可借鉴广西、福建相关经验,明确项目建设范围、补助金额、项目建设顺序等,有序推进项目实施,不断增强经济社会发展的后续力和动力源。

2.3 对比劣势与机会,制定 O-W 弥补型发展策略

2.3.1 补齐公路建设短板

统筹推进公路网络建设,增大公路辐射范围,形成交通经济环路网络,带动区域经济协调发展;同时,推进资源产地、农业示范区、产业园区等主要经济节点的对外连接公路建设,促进资源优势转化为发展优势;三是提高农村公路通达度,优先重点道路的提及改造,并采取多种措施保障对外运输快速化、便利化,促进带动相关产业发展。

2.3.2 加强部门合作,推动融合发展

充分发挥地方政府在推进产业园区和产业路建设中的作用,加强部门间交流融合,建立起由政府统一领导,交通、农业、工业等多部门共同参与的产业园区和产业路建设协调机制。探索实施各部门联席会议制度,协调解决工程方案、资金筹措、征地拆迁等重点难点问题。

2.4 面对劣势与威胁,规划 T-W 防御型发展策略

2.4.1 拓宽资金筹措渠道

陕西省要统筹用好财政、金融等各种手段,调动政府、企业等多方面积极性,多渠道筹措建设资金。一是要充分利用政策,积极向中央申请资金,同时充分利用各部门对产业园区发展的资金支持,设立产业路建设专项补助办法,保障资金到位;二是积极拓展社会资本注入,通过成立县级交通投资有限公司、鼓励园区增加配套资金等方式加大对周边道路建设和养护的资金投入,通过发放债券、鼓励村民捐助等方式,大力吸纳社会资本进入交通建设领域,助力产业路建设。

2.4.2 强化土地、环保要素保障,优化发展环境

陕西省要聚焦项目落地和经济发展,优化土地要素保障机制。加强规划管控,统筹路线走向和三区三线界定范围,预留交通基础设施建设用地;优化交通规划设计理念,加强交通项目线形和技术方案比选,提高土地综合利用效率。同时,加强公路建设重点项目用地、环保等要素的供给和服务保障,实现交通、产业和空间的协调发展。

3 结语

对于产业路发展而言,应当充分把握政策优势与时代机遇,结合地方实际,充分发挥自身优势,制定完善的发展规划,加强资金等要素保障,促进产业路建设与发展,进而带动当地产业发展,为我国经济发展贡献力量。

参考文献

[1] 何得桂,廖白平. 机遇与挑战:西部地区开展避灾移民的SWOT态势分析——以陕南为例[J]. 灾害学,2014,29(2):95-101.

[2] 李丽莉,肖洪浪,邹松兵,等. 甘肃建设生态省的SWOT分析[J]. 冰川冻土,2015,37(1):258-265.

[3] 陕西省交通运输厅. 陕西2019数字交通[EB/OL](2020-06).

[4] 陕西省农业农村厅. 专业数据、新型经营主体统计[EB/OL]. http://222.90.83.241:9001/agriresources/? source = management.

[5] 陕西省工业和信息化厅. 陕西省"十三五"工业经济发展规划. 2016.

[6] 陕西省统计局. 陕西现代农业园区发展研究. 2014.

[7] 刘鹏,马永青,韩艳,等. 基于AHP-模糊综合评价法的河北省桃产业效益综合评价研究[J]. 广东农业科学,2015(17):178-183.

Study on the Efficiency Evaluation and Influencing Factors of Transportation Infrastructure in Jiangsu Province

Xinxin Hu Hong Chen

(School of Highway, Chang'an University)

Abstract This paper uses the data of transportation infrastructure and national economy of Jiangsu Province from 2014 to 2018, Data envelopment analysis(DEA) is used for empirical analysis. From static and dynamic aspects, the DEA-Malmquist index is used to evaluate the transportation infrastructure efficiency of Jiangsu Province from 2014 to 2018, and DEA-Tobit two-stage method is used to analyze the factors affecting the efficiency change of the transportation system. The results show that:(1)From 2014 to 2018, it is shown that the comprehensive efficiency index and pure efficiency index of each city are low, and the scale efficiency index is at the medium level. The development of the transportation infrastructure of each city in Jiangsu Province is unbalanced. (2)From 2014 to 2018, the total factor productivity index of each city fluctuated greatly. Technological progress and application problems are the main causes of fluctuations. (3) Using the DEA-Tobit two-stage method to analyze the basic data, industrial structure, and dependence on foreign investment have a positive impact on the efficiency of transportation infrastructure, while government behavior and government investment in education have a negative impact.

Keywords Transportation infrastructure DEA Malmquist index Tobit model

0 Introductidn

In recent years, China's transportation industry has developed rapidly. In 2019, the operating mileage of the railway is 139000 km, the total mileage of the highway is 5012500 km, and the navigable mileage of the inland waterway is 127300 km. Transportation infrastructure is an important aspect of urban infrastructure, has a significant role in supporting social and economic development and urban construction. At present, the main problem restricting the development of China's transportation industry is the lack of total investment and waste caused by the unreasonable allocation of transportation resources. Therefore, it is necessary to evaluate the efficiency of China's transportation system and study its influencing factors.

Based on the annual data of public transport operation of 35 central cities in China from 2010 to 2013, the Three-stage DEA method is used to evaluates the cost efficiency and service efficiency of public transport (Zhanghuang et al., 2016). Based on the data of 2015, this paper constructs a data envelopment analysis (DEA) model to analyze the transport efficiency of 20 urban rail transit in China and evaluates the correlation between transport efficiency and various factors by using the Tobit regression model (Zhang and You, 2018).

The construction of transportation infrastructure can greatly improve China's transportation network connection. But blindly investing in transportation infrastructure may not bring corresponding economic benefits. Transportation infrastructure construction should adapt to regional economic development and regional urban system structure, so it is necessary to evaluate the utilization of transportation infrastructure from the perspective of efficiency. Based on the relevant basic data of Jiangsu Province from 2014 to 2018, this paper uses DEA-BBC and Malmquist index model to analyze the efficiency of transportation infrastructure in Jiangsu Province. On this basis, it uses the Tobit model to study its influencing factors and master the efficiency characteristics of transportation infrastructure construction.

1 Research Methods

1.1 Data Envelopment Analysis

To evaluate and analyze the efficiency of the industry, data envelopment analysis (DEA) is the most widely used and mature measurement method among the nonparametric methods. According to the hypothesis of variable returns to scale, the DEA model can be divided into the CCR model and the BCC model. BCC model can decompose the comprehensive technical efficiency of the CCR model into pure technical efficiency and scale efficiency.

This paper mainly uses the DEA-BBC model based on input orientation to get the comprehensive efficiency, pure technical efficiency, and scale efficiency of transportation infrastructure in Jiangsu Province. When the comprehensive efficiency, pure technical efficiency or scale efficiency is less than 1, to obtain the maximum output, under the premise of technical stability, it is necessary to adjust the input factors or production scale to improve the efficiency of transportation infrastructure and improve the situation of redundant input or insufficient output. Therefore, the closer the efficiency values are to 1, the better.

1.2 Malmquist Index Model

The results of the DEA model reflect the static efficiency, but can not reflect the dynamic change of efficiency with time. When the data of the evaluated DMU is panel data with multiple time point observations, we can further analyze the change of productivity and the effect of technical efficiency and technological progress on productivity change, which is Malmquist's total factor productivity index analysis. Malmquist index can be calculated by DEA method and decomposed into technical efficiency change (EC) and production technology change (TC).

DEA Malmquist index method is suitable for the evaluation of TFP with multiple evaluation objects, multiple inputs, and multiple outputs. When the efficiency index is greater than 1, it means growth or progress, otherwise, it means decline or recession. Based on the BBC model with variable returns to scale and the Malmquist productivity index model, this paper further explores the dynamic trend of transportation infrastructure construction efficiency from 2014 to 2018.

1.3 Tobit Regression Model

To measure the influencing factors and their influence degree of system efficiency, coelli developed a two-step method based on DEA Analysis in 1998. In the first step, DEA analysis is used to evaluate the efficiency value of decision-making units. In the second step, the efficiency value obtained in the above step is used as the dependent variable, and the influencing factors are used as the independent variables to establish the regression model, and the influence is judged by the coefficient of the independent variable the influence direction and intensity of environmental factors on environmental efficiency.

The efficiency value calculated by the DEA model is restricted, discrete, and truncated, which is between 0-1 and meets the demands of the Tobit model. Therefore, the paper chooses the DEA Tobit model to study and analyze the influencing factors of urban public transport system efficiency.

2 Empirical Research

2.1 Transport Infrastructure Efficiency Analysis

2.1.1 Index Selection

This paper intends to select the highway mileage (km), railway mileage (km), inland waterway mileage (km), and the number of employees (person) of relevant transportation units in 13 cities of Jiangsu Province from 2014 to 2018 as the input indicators. Furthermore, the corresponding output indicators are the total passenger volume (10000 people) and the total freight volume (10000 tons). The data comes from the statistical yearbook of 13 cities in Jiangsu Province.

2.1.2 Static Measurement and Analysis of Transport Infrastructure Efficiency

According to deap 2.1 software, the efficiency values of 13 cities in Jiangsu Province from 2014 to 2018 are calculated, including comprehensive efficiency value, pure technical efficiency value, and scale efficiency value (Tab. 1).

Efficiency of Transportation Infrastructure in Jiangsu Province in 2014-2018 Tab. 1

Firm	Crste	Vrste	Scale	Return to scale
Suzhou	1.000	1.000	1.000	—
Nanjin	1.000	1.000	1.000	—
Wuxi	1.000	1.000	1.000	—
Nantong	0.787	0.886	0.888	drs
Xuzhou	1.000	1.000	1.000	—
Changzhou	0.918	1.000	0.918	Irs
Yanchen	0.627	0.744	0.844	drs
Yangzhou	0.750	0.741	0.986	Irs
Taizhou	1.000	1.000	1.000	—
Zhenjiang	0.821	1.000	0.821	Irs

continue

Firm	Crste	Vrste	Scale	Return to scale
Huanan	0.663	0.665	0.998	drs
Lianyungang	0.540	0.566	0.954	Irs
Suqian	1.000	1.000	1.000	
Mean	0.854	0.894	0.954	Irs

From the efficiency value in the table, it can be seen that from 2014 to 2018, the pure technical efficiency and scale efficiency of Suzhou, Nanjing, Wuxi, Xuzhou, Taizhou, and Suqian in Jiangsu Province are equal to 1, which is effective; the pure technical efficiency and scale efficiency of Nantong, Yancheng, Yangzhou, Huai'an, and Lianyungang are less than 1, among which Nantong, Yancheng, and Huai'an are in the stage of diminishing returns to scale, and Lianyungang and Lianyungang are in the stage of decreasing returns to scale Yangzhou's return to scale is increasing. The pure technical efficiency reflects the level of financial expenditure management and the reasonable degree of transportation resource planning under the existing technical level. Therefore, the management and technology of Nantong, Yancheng, Yangzhou, Huai'an, and Lianyungang can not keep up with the pace of the times. For Nantong, Yancheng, and Huai'an, only by reducing the scale of transport infrastructure investment can we improve their scale efficiency and comprehensive efficiency. Lianyungang and Yangzhou promote the comprehensive efficiency of transportation by reasonably increasing the input of production factors. Although the pure technical efficiency of Changzhou and Zhenjiang is 1, the scale efficiency is less than 1, the return to scale is increasing, and the comprehensive technical efficiency is less than 1. It can be seen that the transportation efficiency of Changzhou and Zhenjiang needs to be improved. From the perspective of scale efficiency index, only Nantong, Changzhou, Yancheng, and Zhenjiang are lower than the average value of scale efficiency index, so more investment is needed to guide the correct use of investment funds. From the perspective of the scale efficiency index, the scale efficiency index of cities in the front rank of urban development is larger, while the scale efficiency index of cities in the later rank is smaller. Therefore, the development level of cities affects the external transportation investment to a certain extent. The development of transportation infrastructure in Jiangsu Province is unbalanced. Some regions need to pay attention to the development of transportation infrastructure. According to their technology or capital, they can improve the efficiency of transportation infrastructure and enhance their competitiveness.

2.1.3 Dynamic Measurement and Analysis of Transport Infrastructure Efficiency

Malmquist index can dynamically reflect the changing trend of transportation infrastructure efficiency of each city. The original data of the selected index from 2014 to 2018 is brought into the Malmquist model, and deap 2.1 software is used to calculate the change and decomposition of the Mlamquist index of 13 cities in Jiangsu Province from 2014 to 2018, and then the change and decomposition of the Mlamquist index of Jiangsu Province as a whole are obtained Tab. 2.

Malmquist Index and Decomposition of Transportation Infrastructure in Each City Tab. 2

firm	effch	techch	pech	sech	tfpch
Suzhou	1.000	0.852	1.000	1.000	0.852
Nanjin	1.000	1.048	1.000	1.000	1.048
Wuxi	1.000	1.051	1.000	1.000	1.051
Nantong	1.032	1.046	1.038	0.994	1.080
Xuzhou	1.000	0.983	1.000	1.000	0.983

continue

firm	effch	techch	pech	sech	tfpch
Changzhou	1.006	1.046	1.000	1.006	1.052
Yanchen	1.038	1.016	1.038	0.999	1.054
Yangzhou	1.007	1.056	1.019	0.988	1.064
Taizhou	1.000	1.068	1.000	1.000	1.068
Zhenjiang	1.000	1.036	1.000	1.000	1.036
Huanan	1.017	1.001	1.019	0.998	1.018
Lianyungang	1.004	1.039	1.013	0.991	1.043
Suqian	0.990	0.929	1.000	0.990	0.920
Mean	1.007	1.011	1.010	0.997	1.019

From 2014 to 2018, the average total factor productivity index of each city was 1.019, showing a slight upward trend. The overall efficiency of transportation infrastructure in Jiangsu Province was further improved, and the efficiency of transportation infrastructure in some areas was significantly improved. Of course, there are also some cities, such as Suzhou, Xuzhou, Suqian, and so on, whose TFP index is lower than 1 and whose transportation infrastructure is inefficient. This is mainly due to the low technological progress index of these cities. This shows that the promotion and application of new transportation technology are insufficient at this stage, and the promotion of new technology has a lag effect on the improvement of technical efficiency. We should pay attention to the application of advanced technology, improve the level of operation and management, and correctly use investment funds. We need to pay attention to the improvement of the technical level to ensure the demand of transportation infrastructure in the economic competition.

2.2 Analysis of Influencing Factors of Transportation Infrastructure Efficiency

To better put forward policy suggestions for improving output efficiency, this chapter analyzes the influencing factors of transportation infrastructure efficiency. The efficiency value based on DEA empirical analysis is between (0,1), which belongs to truncated data, Tobit model can carry out truncated regression. Tobit model is constructed to analyze the factors that affect the efficiency of the transportation system in Jiangsu Province. The pure technical efficiency obtained from DEA empirical analysis is taken as the dependent variable, and other factors that may affect the efficiency of the urban transportation systems are taken as the independent variable. The independent variable comes from the statistical yearbook and the statistical bulletin of the national economic and social development of cities in each year.

2.2.1 Index Selection

This paper holds that the efficiency of urban transportation industry is affected by many factors. From the macro-economic and economic aspects, the efficiency of urban public transport system is the result of the comprehensive effect of social and economic development, urban development, traffic investment, traffic infrastructure and other factors.

(1) Industrial structure

Considering that the optimization and adjustment of industrial structure can improve the total factor productivity, it is of great significance to introduce the proportion of non-agricultural industries to analyze the efficiency of transportation infrastructure.

Noagri = the added value of the secondary and tertiary industries/GDP.

(2) Dependence on foreign investment

The proportion of regional foreign capital reflects its ability to utilize and digest foreign capital, and also reflects its dependence on foreign capital and its own development level.

Forei = actual foreign investment/total social fixed investment.

(3) Government investment in Education

The emphasis on education has an indirect impact on the status of regional human capital. As a factor of total factor productivity, human capital has a certain impact on the efficiency of transportation infrastructure.

Edu = education expenditure/local financial expenditure.

(4) Government investment

As a part of public infrastructure investment, the development of transportation infrastructure is obviously inseparable from the support and guidance of the government. This paper uses the proportion of government expenditure in GDP as the indicator of government behavior.

gov = education expenditure/local financial expenditure.

2.2.2 Tobit Empirical Analysis

(1) Descriptive statistics of variable data

This paper analyzes the four possible influencing factors of nonagri, forei, edu and gov respectively (Tab. 3).

Descriptive Statistics of Variables   Tab. 3

Variable	noagri	forei	edu	gov
Observed	65	65	65	65
Mean	0.917865	0.016799	0.165424	0.141668
Standard Deviation	0.070062	0.020971	0.052940	0.047749
Maximum	0.989065	0.096153	0.314797	0.253734
Minimum	0.635469	0.000820	0.061026	0.083666

(2) Unit root test

Because the unit root process in the time series will make the series unstable, leading to the failure of regression analysis and pseudo regression phenomenon, in order to verify the stability of the panel data series, this paper uses LLC Methods unit root test was conducted on the data, and Eviews 11.0 software was used for the operation. If the original hypothesis of the unit root was rejected in the test, we said that the sequence was stable, otherwise, it was not stable. The unit root test was used to test the three explanatory variables of noagt, forei, edu and gov, and LLC test was used. The results are shown in Tab. 4.

Unit Root Text of Explanatory Variables   Tab. 4

Variable	noagri	forei	edu	gov
P	0.000	0.000	0.000	0.001

Since P-value is less than 0.01, it means that each variable is significant at 1%, and all variables reject the hypothesis of the existence of unit root, which indicates that the panel data is stable and there is no unit root, so regression analysis can be carried out.

(3) Regression analysis

Eviews 11.0 software is used for regression analysis of the Tobit model, and the calculation results are shown in the table below (Tab. 5).

regression results of influencing factors model of infrastructure efficiency Tab. 5

Variable	Coefficient	Std. Error	Z-Statistic	Prob
Noagri	0.081718	0.092041	0.887848	0.0374*
Forei	0.996249	0.325248	3.063048	0.0022***
Edu	-0.092589	0.152823	-0.605859	0.0542*
gov	-0.6793193	0.162259	-4.888433	0.0000***
C	1.159588	0.106368	10.90162	0.0000***

Note: *, **, and *** indicate significant stress at the levels of 10%, 5%, and 1%, respectively.

From the model regression results, the Tobit regression fitting effect is better, reflecting the rationality of the selected variables to a certain extent.

Among them, the proportion coefficient of the non-agricultural industry is positive, and it passes the t-test at a 10% significance level. It shows that the increase of the proportion of non-agricultural industry has a significant role in promoting the transportation efficiency of transportation infrastructure. Industrial structure and transportation complement each other. The change of industrial structure affects the development of transportation. Transportation itself belongs to the tertiary industry. From the previous research, the freight volume and the secondary industry have the largest correlation, and the passenger volume and the tertiary industry have the largest correlation. We should increase the proportion of the secondary and tertiary industries, to optimize the industrial structure and promote economic development.

The correlation coefficient of foreign capital dependence is 0.996249, P-value is 0.0022, which shows that foreign capital dependence has a significant positive correlation with the pure technical efficiency of transportation infrastructure at the level of 1%, indicating that improving foreign capital dependence can promote the efficiency of transportation resource allocation. In recent years, increasing foreign investment has played a role in promoting the efficiency of the transportation industry. We should continue to introduce foreign investment, diversify financing, broaden financing channels, actively encourage and use foreign investment, and improve the transportation efficiency of transportation infrastructure.

The coefficient of government investment in education is negative, and it passes the t-test at the 10% significance level. This shows that although the increase of education investment can improve the education level of Jiangsu Province, in recent years a large number of talents outflow, which greatly offset the improvement of the quality of personnel education brought by education investment. Besides, the increase of education sharing rate also reduces the financial expenditure of other projects to a certain extent. Because the impact of education investment on economic development needs a long period, the improvement of the proportion of education investment in the short term will not have a great impact on the efficiency of infrastructure. However, because it takes up the financial expenditure and reduces the financial expenditure of other projects, it will also have a negative impact on the efficiency of transportation infrastructure.

The ratio coefficient of government investment is also negative. At the 1% significance level, the t-test shows that government investment hurts the efficiency of transportation infrastructure. In recent years, although government investment has been increasing, it has not played a significant role. This shows that the government's investment has not been implemented and has not been well utilized. The government needs to find a good investment direction and make the best use of every investment. To increase the investment in transportation infrastructure, we need to pay attention to the scientific planning of investment. Accurate investment can avoid repeated investment and construction, and reduce the degree of resource waste as much as possible.

3 Conclusion

This paper uses DEA and Malmquist index method to measure the efficiency and total factor productivity of transportation infrastructure in Jiangsu Province, and uses Tobit model to analyze the influencing factors of transportation infrastructure efficiency in Jiangsu Province. Finally, the paper puts forward some policy suggestions to improve the efficiency of urban transportation system.

3.1 Analysis Results

(1) The results of DEA analysis show that under the background of accelerating urbanization, the efficiency of transportation infrastructure in Jiangsu Province is in the upper-middle level. From 2014 to 2018, the pure technical efficiency and scale efficiency of Suzhou, Nanjing, Wuxi, Xuzhou, Taizhou, and Suqian in Jiangsu Province are equal to 1, reaching the effective level; Nantong, Yancheng, Yangzhou, Huai'an, and Lianyungang have reached the effective level The pure technical efficiency and scale efficiency of Yungang are less than 1, and the management and technology can not keep up with the pace of the times. It is necessary to strengthen the management level, design the incentive mechanism, and improve the pure technical efficiency by improving the transportation infrastructure and reasonably planning the infrastructure construction. From the perspective of scale efficiency index, only Nantong, Changzhou, Yancheng, and Zhenjiang are lower than the average value of scale efficiency index, so more investment is needed to guide the correct use of investment funds. The development of transportation infrastructure in Jiangsu Province is unbalanced. Some regions need to pay attention to the development of transportation infrastructure. According to their own technology or capital, they can improve the efficiency of transportation infrastructure and enhance their competitiveness.

(2) Malmquist total factor productivity index analysis results show that from 2014 to 2018, the average value of the total factor productivity index in Jiangsu Province is 1.019, showing a slight upward trend, but the development of urban transportation infrastructure is obviously unbalanced. The total factor productivity index (Tfpc) of most cities is greater than 1. Of course, there are also some cities, such as Suzhou, Xuzhou, and Suqian, where the total factor productivity index is less than 1 and the transportation infrastructure is inefficient. This is mainly due to the low technological progress index of these cities. This shows that the promotion and application of new transportation technology are insufficient at this stage, and the promotion of new technology has a lag effect on the improvement of technical efficiency. We should pay attention to the application of advanced technology, improve the level of operation and management, correctly use investment funds, and improve the efficiency of transportation infrastructure and enhance competitiveness according to our own technical or financial problems.

(3) By verifying the influencing factors of transportation infrastructure efficiency, this paper further analyzes the influence of the proportion of the non-agricultural industry, the proportion of foreign capital dependence, the proportion of education investment, and the proportion of government investment on transportation efficiency. From the regression results, it is found that the proportion of non-agricultural industry and the increase of foreign investment will improve the output efficiency of urban transportation infrastructure. At the same time, it is found that due to the serious brain drain, the increase of education investment crowns out other public financial expenditure, which affects the necessary efficiency of transportation in Jiangsu Province, and the output efficiency value does not rise but falls. In recent years, although government investment has been increasing, it has not played a significant role. This shows that the government's investment has not been implemented and has not been well utilized.

3.2 Policy Recommendations

Based on the estimation results of Jiangsu transportation infrastructure efficiency, the following policy recommendations are given

(1) We should pay attention to the allocation of resources in the process of transportation facilities construction, and increase support for less developed areas.

The development of transportation infrastructure in cities of the province is unbalanced, and the stock of some transportation infrastructure is still insufficient, resulting in a greater contradiction between supply and demand. Therefore, the government should relax the original investment restrictions, actively guide the investment direction, continue to introduce foreign capital, diversify financing, broaden financing channels, actively encourage and use foreign investment, and improve the transportation efficiency of transportation infrastructure.

(2) In infrastructure construction, both quality and quantity should be guaranteed.

While promoting the construction of transportation infrastructure stock, we should reasonably consider the construction layout and planning, guard against blind investment and follow-up investment, and scientifically plan the investment intensity. At the same time, the layout of transportation infrastructure should be overall. In the choice of region, space, and various facilities, we should leave room for future social development.

(3) Promote the efficiency of transportation infrastructure in accordance with the characteristics of different regions.

The DEA Malmquist index method is used to estimate the efficiency trend and efficiency level of 13 cities in the province. Therefore, we should comprehensively consider the regional characteristics, cultural characteristics, and economic development, and invest in the construction of transportation infrastructure according to local conditions.

Reference

[1] Zhang H, J You. An Empirical Study of Transport Efficiency of Urban Rail Transit Based on Data Envelopment Analysis and Tobit Model[J]. Tongji Daxue Xuebao/Journal of Tongji University,2018,46(9): 1306-1311.

[2] Zhang Y, et al. Efficiency research of urban public transport in china based on the analysis of threestage DEA model [J]. Jiaotong Yunshu Xitong Gongcheng Yu Xinxi/Journal of Transportation Systems Engineering and Information Technology,2016,16(1): 32-37.

国家道条修订与上海道路运输管理转型

陈俊彦

(上海市城乡建设和交通发展研究院)

摘　要　交通强国和依法治国对道路运输管理提出现代化转型要求,本研究支撑地方道路运输管理转型和立法工作,研究分析国家层面对道路运输优化管理和转型发展的总纲,结合地方道路运输发展现状,提出管理转型思路。本文以上海道路运输管理为例,通过法律条款解读、行业管理调研、行业发展分析等研究方法,以符合运输现代化治理的要求,提出转型总体思路。研究认为,国家法规的修订,构建了道路运输行业新体系,在业态和管理机制上都有所拓展。上海道路运输管理转型过程中,客运行业应当根据运输需求的新特征变化,鼓励运营模式创新和灵活发展,并减少制度性阻碍;货运行业应当调整应当充分利用技术创新和模式变革,提高运输服务智慧化水平,并着力解决中心城通行权问题。

关键词　道路运输条例　管理转型　条款解读　地方性法规　上海

0 引言

建立和完善综合交通法规体系,是加快建设交通强国的重要内容,也是实现交通运输治理体系和治理能力现代化的重要举措。"十四五"时期是构建现代化综合交通法规体系的重要启动阶段,在建设交通强国和构建现代化综合交通体系的总体要求下,将全面地梳理、整合既有的综合交通法规资源,首先建立综合交通法规体系架构,然后逐步修订完善相关法律法规,以期在2035年基本形成系统完备、架构科学、布局合理、分工明确、相互衔接的综合交通法规体系,基本完成龙头法和重点配套行政法规的修订工作。

《中华人民共和国道路运输条例》(以下简称《国家道条》)是公路法规系统中的重要的行政条例,自2004年颁布实施后未经大幅修订,和公共交通条例等其他行政条例相比,修订必要性更为紧迫,修订条件也更为成熟。因此,国家层面和地方层面修订道路运输条例,既始于行业治理工作的需要,也是对修订《中华人民共和国道路运输法》和构建综合交通法规体系的重要支撑。上海道路运输需求大、市场活跃度高,尤其是在技术创新和商业模式多元化发展的背景下,对运输管理提出了更高的要求,也需要更加符合治理要求的地方条例来提供依法治理保障。目前国家层面的运输条例进入了意见征求阶段,对道路运输的管理对象、关键制度都基本完成了修订工作,总体上结合了当前的管理需要从面上对道路运输行业管理完成了闭环制度设计。国家层面道路运输条例的修订和即将出台,将加速《上海市道路运输管理条例》(以下简称《上海道条》)的修订工作。

1 国家道条的修订解读

1.1 立法定位

2020年,交通运输部发布了法制工作要点,其中首当其冲地提出加快完善综合交通法规制度体系,首要工作是调整完善综合交通运输立法制度设计,印发关于完善综合交通法规体系的意见,促进不同运输方式法律制度的有效衔接,推动建立与交通强国相适应的综合交通法规体系。在建立综合交通立法制度后,下步将逐步推动行业立法和部门规章的制定工作。综合交通法规体系将由若干版块组成,其中公路板块的法规体系将有《中华人民共和国道路运输法》和包括道条在内的5个基础性行政法规和若干规章组成。《国家道条》是相关行政法规中最具修订条件的一部,并已开展修订工作并完成了修订的征求意见稿。

在构建综合交通法规体系的背景下,本次《国家道条》的修订进行了较大篇幅的改动,道路运输管理业态构成发生了较大变化,将出租汽车、租车等业态纳入了道路运输管理行业体系中,并针对行业发展的新特点和新要求进行了更新。

1.2 框架结构

根据《国家道条》意见征求稿,道路运输管理总体分为7章,包含道路运输经营、道路运输相关业务、国际道路运输、安全管理、执法监督等内容,其中安全管理和执法监督章节中条款更新的比例较高,足见本次条例的修订,对依法治国和以人为本的重视程度。

第一章为总则,主要对立法目标、管理对象、管理原则、管理部门等内容进行界定。值得注意的是,本次修订着重强调了道路运输行业中对多式联运的支持。

第二章为道路运输经营,是道路运输管理条例的核心章节,也是由本章构成了道路运输管理法规体系的主体,集中了最主要的管理制度。该章包含了客运、货运、出租汽车、共同规定等四个部分。其中出租汽车是三定方案明确其管理职责划归交通部以后,根据其行业特点和管理要求,将其纳入道路运输管理;共同规定是新增章节,对客货运和出租汽车在经营过程中,在公平竞争、投诉监督、无障碍服务、服务规范、运输价格、网约服务安全制度等各方面提出的新的要求,也是建设交通强国和建设现代化运输服务体系对行业管理新要求的体现。

第三章为道路运输相关业务,在传统的运输站场、机动车维修、驾驶员培训的行业基础上,增加了汽车租赁行业,进一步理顺了汽车租赁和出租车的关系。在本章,道路运输相关业务整体上市场调节机制比较成熟,相关业务基本上在"十三五"期间完成准入改革,不再实施准入许可而采用备案,在本次修订稿中也回应了采取备案制度以后,配套实施的相关管理制度,如电子化管理、从业人员培训制度,等等。

第四章为国际道路运输,本章节在上一版道条中就已经存在,目前国际道路运输实施备案制,并且进一步体现深化开放的要求,在本次修订中明确了国家道路运输便利化工作的要求。

第五章为安全管理,现行道条有安全管理的相关内容,在修订稿中对安全管理进行了更丰富的补充,在本章节中,新设立的条款共7条,占章节的44%,足见新形势和新发展阶段下,道路运输对安全管理工作的重视程度。

第六章为执法监督,也是在本次修订中大篇幅扩充的版块,本章节中新设立的条款共9条,占章节的60%,在依法治国和推进治理能力现代化建设的新要求下,规范执法、科学执法、高效管理、机制创新成为了建设新时代现代化运输治理能力的内容之一,本次修订稿就创设性地提出了开放信息查询系统、实施电子证照、安全背景联动核查、考核公示机制、违法记分制度、网络定制杜甫信息报送要求等新的管理制度。

第七章为法律责任和附则。

1.3 创新内容

本次《国家道条》修订的意见征求稿,是建设现代化综合交通法规体系走出的第一步,也体现了依法治国和治理创新的总体要求。主要表现在四个方面:

一是理顺行业体系,构建现代化道路运输行业的系统架构。道路运输条例是道路运输行业依法治理的最基本依据,条例对道路运输行为和管理范畴的界定是道路运输行业体系的基本解释。本次《国家道条》的修订,决定将出租汽车、汽车租赁等行业纳入道路运输管理范畴,并形成了"3+4+X"的道路运输行业体系。3指道路运输的三个基本业态:旅客运输、货物运输、出租汽车;4指道路运输的四个相关业态:场站、汽修、驾培、租赁;X指道路运输管理的若干综合性要求,目前包括了:国际运输、安全管理、执法监督。未来,将以该行业体系为框架,以《国家道条》为基本管理依据,以相关配套行政规章为细化补充,构建各相关利益方参与共治的现代化道路运输行业系统。

二是激发行业活力,探索充分发挥市场调节作用的新型治理模式。以往道路运输行政管理部门扮演的是管理角色,以行业规范和门槛准入为特征,但在新时代下道路运输行业的发展需要依靠市场自己培育和规范,减少行政管理部门对市场的过度干预。"十三五"期间,交通运输部已经下放多项有关道路运输行业行政审批项目,包括货运站场、汽修、驾培、4.5t以下货车经营等,行政权力的弱化体现了党中央深化服务型政府理念的决心,进一步放开运输市场也有利于培育市场的自我调控能力。本次《国家道条》的修订,将"十三五"期间的深化改革成果一并纳入了草案中,同时也根据行业特点和管理需要,制定了一系列的配套管理措施,但总体上是围绕服务型政府的主线,以优化道路运输经营环境、提高道路运输服务质量为出发点。如货运行业取消了4.5t以下货运车辆的许可,但还是明确了货运行业经营的资质条件和人员要求,并且对网络定制货运的备案要求、网络定制货运的信息管理、运输计划、电子运单管理等都提出了明确要求。

三是加强技术赋能,逐步建立以信息技术为支撑的新型行业治理模式。法律赋权和技术赋能是建设交通强国和构建现代化综合交通治理体系最重要的两个方面,本次《国家道条》的修订,尤其重视信息技术的运用,几乎在每个业态中都制定了加强管理中新技术支撑的条款。在客货运经营中,都要求逐步实施电子证照和服务动态监管,通过信息技术的采集和平台管理,提高管理效能。针对货运业、出租汽车行业中的网络定制模式,明确了互联网信息公开、实时监测等要求,借助网络平台经济体的技术优势实现管理的信息化升级。在汽修、驾培等运输相关行业中,也明确了电子档案、数据平台管理、开放信息查询系统等要求。

四是推进新旧业态互济。随着互联网新业态的快速发展,在资本和技术创新的助力下,新业态对传统业态形成了较大的冲击。另一方面,新业态借助网络化、信息化和平台化的管理方式,突破了传统的行业管理固有模式,虽然管理制度还有待完善,但是创新的管理方式也为传统行业管理提供了转型借鉴。本次《国家道条》的修订,非常大的一个亮点就是全面地削弱新旧业态之间的管理制度差异,特别是对互联网新业态,强调其本质运输属性和互联网附加属性,对于本质运输属性仍然应当按照运输行业管理的基本要求进行管理,如营业准入制度、从业人员管理制度等,而对于互联网附加服务,则通过备案的形式加强事中事后监管。

2 上海道路运输行业体系

2.1 行业管理体系

从《国家道条》和《上海道条》的篇章架构和传统的运输管理工作架构来看,道路运输业主要分为道路客运、道路货运和相关业态,其中相关业态主要是机动车维修、机动车驾驶人培训、运输场站等典型业态。但随着运输行业内部细分不断丰富,相关新业态也在快速发展,亟须对道路运输行业的业态分类进行更优的分类。上海道路运输行业体系见表1。

上海道路运输行业体系　　　　　　表1

	传统业态	现存业态
旅客运输经营	省际班线客运	省际班线客运
	旅游客运	省际包车(含旅游包车、通勤车、点对点包车)
	包车客运	市内包车(含定制班线)
	—	专用客运(不属于运输行业)
货物运输经营	普通货运	普通货运
	集装箱专用货运	专用货运
	罐式容器专用货运	
	冷链专用货运	
	大件运输	
	危险品运输	危险品运输
	市内小型货运	市内小型货运
运输相关业务	客运站经营	客运站经营
	货运站经营	货运站经营
		分拣站和前置仓经营
	机动车维修经营	传统汽修
		互联网汽修(车生活服务、上门汽修)
	机动车驾驶人培训	驾校培训
		汽车陪练

2.2 管理转型要求

《国家道条》是国务院令,属于行政立法范畴,其立法目标是规范道路运输市场行为。《上海道条》与之不同,作为地方性人大立法,不仅要关注行业管理的基本需求,还应当体现地方人大授权道路运输管理部门管理和引导行业健康发展,支撑城市发展总体战略的作用。道路运输经营活动和一般市场经营活动不同,本质上是利用道路等公共基础设施开展相关经营,因此,道路运输具有公共性和基础性的本质。对于这一类经营公共资源行为,地方政府应当发挥两个方面的作用:一是政府依法发挥监管作用,对于利用公共基础设施开展的经营活动,政府应当实施监管,也需要权力机关通过地方性条例赋予政府部门相应的管理权限;二是政府依法发挥引导作用,道路运输服务直接影响经济产业发展、社会文明进步和市民生活,其本身亦是优化营商环境和城市现代化发展的重要内容,在立法工作中应当体现发展导向和引导作用。

3 上海道路运输管理转型方向

3.1 客运管理转型

道路客运是综合运输体系中运输量最大、通达度最深、服务面最广的一种运输方式。长期以来,道路客运的快速发展有效满足了人民群众出行需求和社会经济发展需要,发挥了基础性、保障性作用。

3.1.1 发展现状

截至2020年6月,上海共有班线客运企业34家,省际班车营运车辆1386辆、沪籍省际线路1007条,以及涉及本市运营的外省市班线车辆3000辆。疫情冲击行业以后,当前省际班线的复运率仅67%,客运量仅25%。日均发送人次1.74万人次,到达人次1.6万人次。

截至2020年6月,上海共有省际包车企业104户(不含班线兼营),营运车辆7758两,省际包车的主要业务为省际旅游包车、省际通勤车、点对点包车等。当前受疫情影响,旅游业尚未开放的背景下,旅游包车业务暂未开放,在2019年5月本市省际包车标志牌申请量为3.3万余条,当前同比降低了80%。

截至2020年6月,本市的市内包车企业246户,营运车辆5216辆,其中新能源大客车占比较高,纯电动车辆3827辆、氢能源车300辆。从体量来看,市内包车企业数远高于省际客运(班线和包车),但车辆数低于省际客运,主要呈现分散的特点,且大部分车辆是在鼓励新能源汽车发展和定制班车业态发展触动下加快发展的业态。互联网预约出行的信息化汇集匹配技术和市场培育情况都已经得到了很快的发展,结合新能源大客车的产业推动效应,本市已经有了驿动、顺祥、飞路等多家定制班线企业,成为市内包车的主要运营模式。

3.1.2 转型发展方向

道路客运具有过程参与的特点,客运服务的全程化、多元化、高端化是旅客在接受客运服务的过程中能切身感受到,从治理优化的方向来看,需要注重其体验性,包括一站式服务、智能化多元供给、全程管家模式创新等。根据"部客规"的定位,目前道路旅客运输总体上为省际班线、省际包车、市内包车三大类。从大的发展趋势来看,省际班线的市场正在萎缩,市内包车因定制班车的模式创新而壮大发展,未来旅客运输的发展方向是鼓励省际班线灵活发展、维持省际包车规范管理、适度引导市内包车智能网约化发展。

省际班线是不同城市之间定点、定班的基础性公共出行服务,其受高速铁路和未来城际快线、市域铁路的冲击影响最大,预计未来行业规模将进一步收缩。未来发展主要引导其灵活管理、多元发展。在新的"部客规"中,明确允许其通过网约定制的方式灵活安排上下客点,为其适应新的技术和需求松绑。同时,鼓励交游融合,简化管理制度,通过结合客运站建设旅游集散中心,拓展班线旅游服务新模式。

省际包车是服务于临时集合的团体出行需求,即使在城际铁路网络完善的情况下,也因其便利性和私密性具有市场需求。特别是在长三角一体化高质量发展的背景下,未来行业发展趋势依然看多。未来发展主要引导其规范经营、高效管理。在新的"部客规"中对包车经营企业不再作客位数的要求,但对于企业规模化和专业化经营仍然有要求,要求经营者自有营运客车数量20辆以上,并实施备案制度,发放包车标志牌。

市内包车原先是省际包车内部的一部分业务,旅游包车的功能和省际包车有所重叠之外,市内包车还比省际包车多了通勤班车、定点班车的功能。而正是信息技术的扩张和成熟,使得通勤和定点出行的团体需求越来越容易汇聚和达成,使得网约化的定制班车成为市内包车行业新的增长点。未来发展主要引导其发挥智能化和信息化的优势,作为公共交通覆盖水平相对较低的市内区域集约化出行的重要方式。在完善治理工作方面,也需要注重通过制度建设引导其智能网约化发展,吸引供给端和需求端共同培育这一新业态。

客运管理转型方向如图1所示。

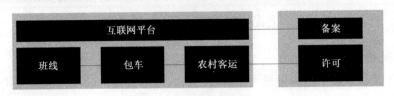

图1 客运管理转型方向

3.2 货运管理转型

3.2.1 发展现状

截至2020年6月,上海的道路货运企业共计2.7万户,货运车辆22.2万辆(含各类普货和专用货车),其中具有动力的车辆15万辆、挂车7万辆,在岗从业人员共计19万人。专用货运主要包括集装箱运输、罐式容器车、冷链运输、大件运输,截至2020年6月,上海集装箱经营业户3804户,集装箱车辆8.7万辆,其中无动力的挂车为4.6万辆;罐式容器经营业户864户,罐式容器车辆0.7万辆;冷链运输经营业户2089户,冷藏车辆0.9万辆;大件运输经营业户717户,大件运输车辆0.7万辆。总体来看,上海货运行业的市场结构以普通货运和集装箱货运为主,两者占整体市场中车辆结构的82.4%(图2)。

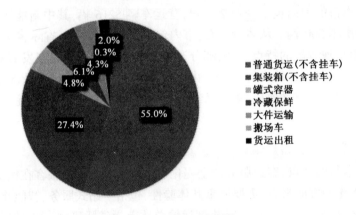

图2 上海货运车辆结构

具体的行业细分中,危险品运输和市内小型货运是两个重要的管理行业。

截至2020年6月,上海危险货物道路运输企业共计299户,其中经营性的286户,非经营性的13户,其中三类高危(剧毒、放射、爆炸)企业16户。危险货运专用车辆11331辆,其中具有动力的(整车和牵引车)6817辆,挂车4514辆。危险货运运输从业人员共计18350人,其中道路客货管理人员79人,危险货运驾驶员8644人,押运员9175人,装卸管理人员447人。

市内小型货运车辆具有轻、灵、快的特点,和传统的道路货运特征不同,2019年开始交通部出台新规对4.5t以下的小型货运不再实施许可制度,对于小型货运行业而言,行业管理倾向于发挥其灵活的特性,促进市内小型货运行业灵活性,为城市配送、市内配送等市民需要的、危险性有限的业务开展保障更大的灵活度。截至2020年6月,上海小型货运车辆6.86万辆,其中包含纯电动货运车辆1.2万余辆、历史遗留下来的沪BH号牌3000多辆。本市的市内运输主要对象是商品运输,也包括部分的工业品、市民搬场、冷链、邮政快递等。

3.2.2 转型发展方向

货运具有和客运不同的特点和发展内涵,其兼具生产性服务和生活性服务。在满足生产需要的货运服务中,重点是标准化、低成本、高可达,需要科学的基础设施规划布局和数字化无缝的运输组织,并且具有很强的国际开放需求。在满足生活需要的货运服务中,重点是智慧物流、稳定可靠,并且需要在后台进行得井井有条而尽量减少和其他生活服务的干扰影响。在未来现代化货运转型发展下,需要重点关注以下几方面的特点:

一是货运服务具有较大的附加价值增长空间。在传统货运发展的基础上,已经衍生出了专业货运、同城速达、冷链运输、搬场服务、清障牵引、货运出租车等新业态和货运新需求。从行业定位和实际发展来看，衍生服务的优劣好坏，比起运输功能本身，更加决定了这些含增值服务的货运行业服务水平。比如搬场运输车辆门槛低，但是搬运专业性强，而且已经开始出现特定人群、特定物品的搬场细分市场；道路牵引更是专业化运输，快速响应、专业处理是其业务工作的重点需求；新货运出租业本身的业内竞争因市民需求过于分散而竞争激烈，吸引资本进入的原因也是背后的调度平台和供需匹配模式创新，而非运输需求本身。因此，增值服务成为货运转型发展的重要特色之一，需要进一步深耕大数据管理、智能化服务、差异化经营。在行业管理上，一方面对其道路货运行为做好基本的管理，另一方面也要适度引导这些业态智慧化转型发展。

二是货运发展对配套设施的功能需求在不断演化。道路货运未来发展多元价值的趋势，无论是传统货运还是含增值服务的货运，仅仅依靠传统的粗放发展和成本逐底竞争无法支撑整个货运业的健康可持续发展。上海市道运局提出了以新能源车整合平台为基础整合资源，建立"车、桩、货、路"一体化的公共信息服务平台，将车辆、充电设施、城配数据、维修服务平台、公共交通信息数据等功能进行集成，为政府部门、行业用户提供公共服务，为车辆使用提供上线服务支持。同时，根据交通运输部绿色城市配送的要求，实现城市绿色货运配送全程管理可视化，实现信息查询、线路追踪、驾驶员监控、整合交通、商务、邮政、公安、工商、税务、海关等部门可公开的电子政务信息，向社会公开，实现便民利企的物流政务资源共享的开放式城市配送综合服务平台。

三是中心城通行管理是现代化货运面临的新挑战之一。随着城市道路拥堵加剧，不少城市在中心城采取禁货管理措施，上海已经实施了多年的货车夜运政策。一方面，公安部门对进入城市核心区域的货运车辆配发通行证，在通行权上货运车辆有一定的限制，这尤其体现在 4.5t 以下货车取消两证以后，基本上已经关闭了小型货运车辆的增量空间。另一方面，自营配送行为在法律界定上很难以货运经营行为来定性，也是由于城市货运资源十分有限，许多新兴商业模式很难依靠基础货运设施和城市货运服务来完成运输，而是通过自营的方式解决，如商业网点配补货、送货上门、家电家具售后服务、商超配送服务、外卖和带购平台等。但是在立法的角度上，虽然这部分自营行为不是道路货运经营行为，不受行业经营管理，但是自营行为仍然在使用城市道路资源达成货物运输目的，应当接受安全管理、秩序管理、环境影响管理，建议在下一步优化治理的过程中明确所涉及的相关政府管理部门职责，实现跨部门的协同治理。

货运管理转型方向如图 3 所示。

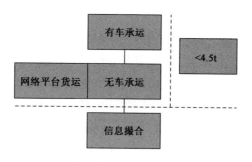

图 3　货运管理转型方向

3.3　道路运输服务业管理转型

3.3.1　发展现状

上海已经形成"中心城以五大站点为主，远郊区一区一主站及简易配客站"的总体布局。全市共有 26 个客运站，其中一级站 7 个，二级站 3 个，三级站 11 个，四级站 4 个，尚未评级的客运站 2 个。全市的客运班线主要集中在一级站，7 个一级站班线数量打全市的 72%，旅客发送量占全市的 83.7%，其中以客运总站和客运南站为主，这两个站在班线数量和旅客发送量都超过了全市的一半。

截至 2020 年 6 月，上海道路货物运输站实际经营业户 49 户。根据综合交通调查，全市道路货运场站 848 个，其中集装箱货运站 152 个，综合货运站 595 个，混合货运站 101 个。全市道路货运场站占地面积超过1900万 m²，其中集装箱堆场面积为526.8万 m²、零担配载134.3万 m²。

本市实有机动车年均增长量约为30万辆，机动车维修行业也处于持续壮大的过程中。从行业协会的相关介绍中看，汽修行业呈现维修辆次下降、维修产值增加的趋势。从行业特征来看，汽车维修市场以4S店、综合性维修企业为主。4S店数量占维修企业的3%~12%，占据77.3%的维修产值，但分布比较分散，存在路途遥远、排队时间长、价格高、维修不透明等不足之处。

根据综合交通调查，本市从事驾培的机构203户，教练车1.78万辆，其中小型客车教练车1.77万辆，教练员2.45万人。城市小客车保有量持续的增长带动了驾培市场的繁荣，20世纪六七十年代的驾培主要由客货汽车运输场和专业公司相继开办的培训班和技工学校来完成，到了80年代才开始采取分行政区、分规模等级的驾培管理。到90年代中后期在市郊相继建立了封闭式的教考场地，此后逐步形成遵循市场规律、合理配置资源、教考分离、社会办学的公共服务型行业。

3.3.2 转型发展要求

随着市民道路运输行业需求的日益多样化和各种个性化服务的蓬勃发展，道路运输相关业态得到了快速发展，这些相关业态的治理要求也和上一轮道条编制时大不相同。从行业发展的特点来看，大部分运输相关业态在20世纪90年代刚刚开始市场化经营，各项标准和管理规范还不健全，大部分业态采取许可管理是符合当时的背景和管理要求的。但随着互联网和信息技术的快速发展，互联网平台企业快速渗透到运输的各行各业中，不仅是道路运输相关业态，客运和货运经营也出现了大量的平台型互联网企业，倒逼客货运场站、停车管理进行信息化和智能化转型。在新的背景下，道路运输相关业态实施许可管理不仅无法满足加强行业事中事后监管的需要，而且增加了行业经营的制度成本。"十三五"期间，交通部陆续对汽修、驾培、货运场站调整为备案管理，减轻企业经营负担，优化运输市场营商环境。

从相关业态的行业定位来看，其主要发挥对道路运输经营的服务功能，尤其是在网络化智能化发展的时代背景下，客货运站、货运代理等业态将在道路运输一体化服务中更多地发挥信息汇聚和运力优化配置的功能，而非原来意义上的流程节点。因此，在将来道路运输相关业务版块的治理目标中，应当进一步发挥相关业态的现代化服务属性，借助信息技术和人工智能技术，转变业态发展定位，提高运输资源配置能力，发展成为现代化道路运输一体化服务的重要组成部分。

4 结　语

现代化的交通治理体系建设，法规体系为其基础，2020年交通部对《国家道条》进行了重大修订，拉开了交通运输治理转型的序幕。本文针对2020年11月发布的《国家道条》（公众意见征求稿）开展及时的梳理分析，并提出了新道条将理顺行业体系、激发行业活力、加强科技赋能和推进（新旧）业态互济四个主要条例功能。当然，囿于篇幅和研究时间的限制，对于国家道条已经明确的出租汽车纳入道路运输管理，以及众多道路运输衍生行业，如汽车租赁、清障牵引、路内停车、共享停车等未在本文作深入研究，但这些行业发展也是未来道路运输业重要构成。本文谨对道路客运、道路货运、客货场站及汽修驾培等传统道路运输业开展了研究分析，特别是在各细分市场中都同时面临着行业规范和鼓励创新的多重要求，本文初步地对上海的道路运输行业发展现状和转型方向提出了初步的思考和研究建议，以期为行业发展和管理优化提供思路。

参考文献

[1] 邵丹,陈俊彦,李薇,等.管理创新背景下的上海交通综合法规体系评估[C]// 中国城市规划学会城市交通规划学术委员会.2016年中国城市交通规划年会论文集.2016:8.

[2] 云观.上海道路运输业发展现状和展望[J].交通与运输,2004(01):18-19.

[3] 毛惠明.上海市道路运输管理条例出台[J].武汉交通管理干部学院学报,1996(Z1):101.

[4] 余伯镛,张京怀.《上海市道路运输管理条例》的立法构想[J].上海公路,1995(03):4-6.

[5] 葛明明.关于上海交通运输管理立法工作中的若干思考[J].上海公路,1995(01):6-8.

考虑旅客出行选择行为的高速铁路票价定价策略的研究综述

刘 琼 孙小慧 左 志

(新疆大学建筑工程学院)

摘 要 随着我国铁路运输行业的迅猛发展,高铁逐渐成为人们重要的交通出行方式,而其合理的票价定价是居民选择高铁作为出行方式的重要前提,并能为铁路的运营收益提供有效保障。本文回顾了我国铁路票价定价的历史沿革,对国内外学者在旅客出行选择行为和票价定价策略两方面的研究成果进行了梳理和总结。通过总结研究成果发现:国内对高速铁路的研究案例多集中在东部高铁密集的发达地区,较少关注西部欠发达地区或中小尺度的高铁线路。本研究基于国内现有的票价定价策略,并借鉴国外的票价优惠政策,提出了建立高速铁路市场化定价机制、采取差异化的定价体系、实施丰富的优惠政策、建立预售期和折扣率关联的多元化定价策略,以期为铁路票价制定研究提供一定的参考。

关键词 高速铁路 出行选择行为 票价 定价策略

0 引 言

20 世纪 60 年代至 70 年代后期,以 1964 年 10 月日本东海道新干线铁路的正式建成和投入使用为标志,全球范围内正式开启了首条以商业化规模运营的高速铁路。1998 年 8 月,广深铁路开通了最高运行速度为 200km/h 的营运列车,成为中国首条实现列车高速运行指标的客运铁路。中国国家铁路局发布的《高速铁路设计规范》(TB 10621—2014)把高速铁路 High-Speed Railway(HSR)的概念定义为新建设计时速范围为 250km(含)到 350km(含),运行动车组列车的标准轨距的客运专线铁路。国务院发展和改革委员会把中国高铁定义为设计时速 250km 及以上标准的新线路或者既有线铁路,并且颁布了与之相应的《中长期铁路网规划(2016 年)》政策文件,将部分设计时速 200km 轨道交通线路纳入中国高速铁路网范畴。自 2008 年 8 月 1 日中国第一条时速 350km 的高速铁路——京津城际铁路开通运营以来,高速铁路在整个中国大陆地区取得了新的迅猛发展。根据统计,截至 2020 年底,铁路营业里程已经达到 14.38 万 km,其中,高速铁路的营业里程已经达到 3.9 万 km。随着我国高速铁路的不断推进,高速铁路在运行车辆时速、客票售价等方面的问题已经受到了越来越多的重视。因此,对高速铁路车票价格制定的合理性进行研究就显得至关重要,既有利于推动铁路交通运输企业服务品质的改善,又能够引导广大消费者更加科学、理性的选择自己所需要的出行方式。

本研究回顾了我国铁路票价定价的发展历程及应用现状,以及近十年,国内外学者在旅客出行选择行为及定价策略方面的文献,从研究内容和模型方法方面对票价制定策略进行了总结和梳理,以期为未来的铁路票价制定研究提供一定参考。后续章节安排如下:第一节对我国的铁路票价定价发展过程进行回顾和总结,继而整理了国内外学者在旅客出行选择行为及定价策略方面的文献,最后对未来的票价定价研究提出相应研究建议。

1 我国铁路票价发展历程及现状

1.1 我国铁路票价制定发展历程

我国铁路客票定价机制经历了从票价严格管制阶段、集中管理下的放松管制阶段、价格听证的多元化调整阶段、到市场化运价推行阶段。

1949年后，中国的铁路逐渐地整合形成了统一的体系，并且开始采用了国家统一的定价机制。1955年，全国铁路公司实行了统一的货物运输价格和旅客运输价格，降低了中国铁路的运价，达到了抑制通货膨胀，支持其他产品和行业发展的目的。

1982年以后，中国政府就开始建立起相对多元化的定价方式。将铁路货运票价划分为九种类别，根据客运服务质量水平进行调整，定价方式根据客运服务质量水平差异而不同，以高等级服务质量标准出行时可以收取更高的售票费用。1991年，实施了新的《铁路法》，价格体系制定的职责平衡也就发生了改变。1998年颁布《价格法》，全国范围内推广了公共服务类产品的定价及公众听证会制度，提高了铁路价格定价的公允性和透明度。

2002年国家计委组织举行了铁路价格听证会，促使产生了一系列铁路相关优惠政策：铁道部门有在特定的时间段(节假日、春节)适当地调整铁路的运价，针对某些列车的类型也制定了专门的铁路定价优惠政策。

2013年中国铁路总公司正式成立，虽然铁路的运价和交通方式并没有发生什么改变，铁路的票价也不会因此而出现大幅度的上浮，同时对于票价的下浮也没有任何限制，但是可以看出我国的铁路运输企业正在努力加快铁路市场化的进程。2016年为推动铁路运价市场化，发展和改革委员会发布放开高铁动车组票价的通知，由铁路公司自行定价。

1.2 我国铁路票价制定现状

高速铁路具有速度快、能耗低、运量大等多方面优势，其票价制定依据运价里程、遵循递远递减的原则。客票价格与其运价里程息息相关，运价里程以国务院铁路主管部门发布的《铁路客运运价里程表》为准。按照《国家纪委关于高等级软座快速列车票价问题的复函》(计价管〔1997〕1068号)的规定，旅行速度达到每小时110km以上的动车组列车软座票价基准价：每人公里特等座车位0.4208元，每人公里一等座车位0.3366元，二等座车位0.2805元，可上下浮动10%。

高速铁路线路上的车次等级主要为G字头与D字头列车，对于二等座票价：G字头时速350km约为0.48元每人公里，D字头时速250km约为0.32元每人公里。后来高铁实施了两次降价后：G字头票价下跌5%，时速降到300km，约为0.46元每人公里；D字头时速降到200km，票价下跌5%，售价约为0.30元每人公里。对于一等座的票价：G字时速300km票价约为0.74元每人公里，D字头时速200km票价约为0.37元每人公里。

自2016年对于设计时速为200公里以上的动车组列车的客运票价均由铁路运输企业依法自主进行制定后，铁路总公司和中国铁路局经过了综合考量市场需要、铁路工程建设运营成本和旅客车票购买消费倾向等多种影响因素，对一些不同线路不同站台的票价进行了优化和调整。调整了席别比价的关系，并根据旅客量和需要，进行了分季节、分时段、分席别、分区段等实行不同层次、灵活升降的售票体系，总体呈现出有升有降的特征，为广大旅客的出行提供了更多的选择。

2 国内外旅客出行选择行为及铁路票价定价策略研究综述

2.1 国内外旅客出行选择行为的研究内容分析

对于旅客交通出行方式的选择行为进行研究，是对交通出行需求量预测的重要组成部分，也是实施交通运输规划和管理政策制定的基础。国内外已经有不少学者针对城镇居民出行方式的选择行为进行了许多深入系统的研究。对于出行方式的选择行为主要是研究个人在作出出行决策时的偏好。非集计模型主要是用于研究旅客出行选择方式的行为的惯用研究方法，非集计模型以各类出行者个体作为研究对象，能够充分利用调查中获取到的数据综合地考虑各类出行者的心理活动和经验习惯，使得非集计模型更加准确地反映各类出行者的身份及出行特征，其实际应用越来越广泛。非集计模型又可称之为离散选择模型(Discrete Choice Model)，离散选择模型通常大致可以分为probit模型和logit模型，logit模型对于出行方式的选择行为相关方面运用比较广泛。

20世纪70年代以来,以Mcfadden等为研究代表的一些专家学者将经济学中的效用理论引入到交通规划模型中来,以概率论作为主要理论研究基础,从非集计的理论视野和数学角度针对各种出行方式选择问题进行了深入研究,将该模型推入深化到了实用阶段。

从出行交通方式出行的特性因素方面研究的出行选择行为。Hensher等(1985)以进出站的时间、候车的时间、车上时间、总费用作为诸多特性变量,运用MNL(Multinomial Nested Logit)模型对通道内各种交通运输方式的乘客分担比例进行估计。国内学者王慧晶等(2011)通过修正Logit模型的MNL形式,提出了武广铁路客运专线客流量转移的估算模型。Kouwenhoven等(2014)以旅行时间、旅行成本和旅行时间可靠性描述备选方案,建立了新的时间值(VOTs)和旅行时间可靠性(VORs)值,用于荷兰交通项目的成本效益分析(CBA)。Tsai(2016)针对机票可能附加的属性,如起飞时间、预订时间、机票有效期、变更费、退票费和票价等,探讨旅客在机票选择上的偏好,以研究票价与购买意愿之间的关系。

考虑了旅客的个人特征因素的出行选择行为研究。Abane(1993)在研究中利用多项Logit模型分析研究通勤出行,结果表明出行者的年龄、性别和月收入都对其通勤出行交通方式的选择结果具有重要的影响。国内学者李亚(2018)以随机效用最大化理论为依据,选取不同的出行时段及乘车方式作为备选项(选择肢),以各类旅客主体、列车服务特性及出行特性指标作为函数的效用变量,构建一个上层为出行时段,下层为乘车方式的Nested Logit模型,能够较为准确地表明各类铁路旅客的出行选择行为。李文霞等(2019)从如何有效提高运输通道内多种运输效益协同发展的角度考虑,调查分析不同经济收入水平的旅客在运输属性方面主观偏好,运用修正熵权法将不同运输方式的指标权重计算修正以赋值,建立广义出行费用函数,运用logit模型的改进形式以兰渝运输路线为例,对其不同运输方式的客流分担率问题进行了计算研究和预测分析。

探讨旅客对于同一线路不同出行交通方式的选择偏好。例如高速铁路、航空飞机、普速铁路等,结合不同的市场选择一些影响变量,以评估乘客的出行选择行为。Claudia Capozza(2016)量化了铁路出行时间对飞机客票价格的影响。Lee等(2016)探讨当航空运输与高铁竞争时旅客对运输方式的选择,研究除了考虑传统的交通选择变量,如旅行时间、旅行成本和服务频率,还引入两个新的特征变量,即"交通安全"和"免税购物的可用性",以充分反映市场的特殊性质。Ma等(2019)分析了中国最繁忙、最赚钱的京沪高铁(HSR)对与这条高铁平行的航空市场的影响。Bergantino等(2020)发现改变高铁模式选择的概率随着年龄、收入和教育程度以及出行目的(商务)而增加,但后者仅适用于长途连接(500公里以上);需求的潜在转变更有可能来自航空运输(航空到高铁)和传统铁路服务(铁路到高铁),以反映市场的特殊特征。刘春济等(2020)探讨了感知价格对旅客乘坐高速铁路出行意向的影响机制。Ren(2020)等探讨了高铁对中国社会公平的影响。

还有关于城市内的交通出行方式选择的行为研究。任倩(2019)对出行者在地铁和常规公交两种不同交通方式之间的选择行为进行研究时,加入了出行者在交通工具使用方面的特性要求和主观评价的6项潜变量,如下:对交通工具的舒适度要求、可靠度要求,对常规公交的舒适度评估、可靠度评估,对地铁的舒适度评价、可靠度评价,并根据随机参数logit模型分析研究旅客出行方式的选择行为。

目前,也有越来越多的理论发展试图摆脱离散选择理论,随着机器学习及量子理论在许多领域的广泛应用,人们对其在个体选择行为建模中的应用越来越感兴趣。Zhao等(2020)将机器学习模型中得到的行为输出(如边际效应和弹性)结果与logit模型的结果进行了全面的比较和实证评估。Hancock等(2020)研究量子概念的模型,通过其适应性和对上下文变化的有效建模,发现它在改进最先进的旅行选择模型范型方面具有重要的前景。

综上所述,国内外的学者基于大量的研究分析,从不同角度用各种多元化的方法对旅客出行方式选择行为做了详细的研究和探索,并取得了丰富的研究成果,对旅客出行选择行为的研究产生了深远影响。

2.2 国内外交通票价定价策略的研究内容分析

国内外专家学者对交通运输的票价问题研究较为广泛,在票价的制定过程中,涉及旅客、交通运输企业和其他竞争对手等多方经济主体,切入角度多从旅客群体和交通运输企业两个方面出发。研究多基于旅客行为分析、运输企业收益、供求关系不同侧重点定价。

Nuzzolo等(2000)提出了乘客出行方式Nested-Logit选择模型,同时,研究了意大利铁路运输服务属性的变化对于票价制定的影响。刘立荣(2010)构建了基于旅客实践价值的客运专线的客票定价模型。Zhao等(2013)综合分析考虑了我国城市轨道交通运营企业和旅客各自的利益,构建了双层规划模型,并利用粒子群优化算法对该模型进行求解。WU等(2013)利用功效系数法,提出了城际铁路客运合理定价决策的多准则建模方法。马新超(2013)通过借鉴国外的高速铁路、国内民航的定价制度体系及策略,对兰新第二双线的定价机制提出相关的建议。刘玉敬(2015)以实现高铁运输企业的收益最大化及出行旅客的广义费用最小化为研究目标,构建高铁旅客票价制定的双层规划模型,并以京沪高铁为例进行论证。赵慧(2016)建立了城市轨道交通定价拉姆齐模型,并应用于长白城际轨道交通进行验证。李楠煜(2017)以兰州轨道交通为背景进行了三种旅客票价制定方案的情景设计,根据其客流量的预测和成本费用测算的情况开展经济效益评估,比选出了票价推荐方案,并提出在开通运营初期可采取的票价优惠政策。孔令华(2017)通过构造一个与运营企业利润相关的票价函数,引入了运输市场和其竞争对手的影响变量,并对北京至长沙段的高速列车票价问题进行了相应的案例研究。Yan等(2019)利用价格信号来调整资源容量分配,并建立高速列车在不同运营路线下的资源容量分配与票价率的协同优化模型。陈阳(2019)通过分析旅客在城际铁路出行时选择的行为,构建了基于累计前景理论的双层规划定价模型,通过眉山至成都城际铁路的案例分析进行论证。宋文波(2019)以高速铁路票额的分配作为研究对象,考虑了旅客的动态购票需求的高速铁路票额的分配和考虑了制定动态票价的高速铁路票额分配关系,并构建了相关模型提出了优化方法。张琦(2019)研究了高铁与民航间的客流竞争行为,通过双层规划模型的建立来确定高铁在与民航竞争下以座席细分为前提的定价方法,并对北京至武汉的客运线路进行了实例分析。景云(2019)等以京沪线路的高铁和动车组为研究对象,基于第三代前景理论、Logit模型效用函数、随机动态规划作为理论依据,建立基于乘客出行选择行为的动态定价模型。

综上,国外专家对于基于旅客行为进行分析的铁路票价策略制定问题研究较为广泛,对于不同经济主体的考虑也比较多,深入分析了旅客的出行行为,不但研究了旅客出行选择行为对票价定价的影响,还进一步探索了票价政策对于旅客提前订票行为的相应影响等。国内学者对基于供求关系的铁路定价策略问题研究得比较多,对其供求关系问题的研究更为深入,将期望效用理论、随机效用最大化理论、系统动力学等理论引入到票价定价的研究中,构建了票价与客流量之间的相互联系,从而进一步探索最优票价的制定。由既有的研究我们可以看出,目前我国的铁路票价机制比较偏向于铁路运输的特殊属性,即公益性和社会性,同时应尽可能地兼顾铁路企业的运营收入。

2.3 小结

本章首先结合国内外交通方式选择研究现状,分别从交通出行选择行为研究和交通票价定价策略的研究两方面入手,对国内外的研究现状进行论述。为了探析交通出行选择行为的机理,国内外研究人员对影响出行选择行为的因素进行了大量广泛而深入的研究。同时,国内外学者基于效用理论对人们出行选择行为开展了许多研究,取得了许多重要的研究成果。目前研究存在的问题主要是:虽然高速铁路已经被广泛研究,但多为集中在东部地区的研究。中国不同地区对高铁的偏好是不同的,交通基础设施对于不同地理位置的个人、群体或地区的影响是不同的。

3 结 语

本文是在我国铁路票价经济市场化和运营体制改革与发展的背景下,结合铁路票价制定的历史沿革即目前的票价制定方案,对以旅客的出行选择行为为导向的高速铁路票价制定策略问题展开研究。本文的结论与高速铁路在票价制定过程中的建议如下:

(1)建立高速铁路市场化定价机制。虽然铁路运输商品具有公益性和社会性,但是随着我国社会经济的进步与发展,铁路的单一票价制定方案日趋落后,使其在激烈的交通运输市场竞争中处于劣势。高速铁路和普速铁路不同,它不仅在基础建设上投资庞大,而且在运营成本上也要远远超过普速铁路,不能过多地强调铁路运输的公益性,从而极大地降低了我国高速铁路的竞争力。目前,国内部分高速铁路线路也正在开始尝试浮动售票,从而进一步探索新的票价定价策略。因此,以普速铁路制定的单一票价体系作为基础,可满足居民最基本的交通出行需求,从而体现铁路交通运输企业的公益性和社会性;通过建立高速铁路市场化的定价体系,引导各类旅客选择各自偏好的出行方式,实现高速铁路交通运输企业盈利的目标,是目前相对合理的方案。

(2)采取差异化的定价体系。差异化主要表现在三个方面。最显著的是地域差异,我国地域辽阔而人口分布不均,导致东西部地区客运需求分布不均运量差异大、人均 GDP 不同,且同一地区的不同城市之的运量也可能存在较大的差异;同时客运需求不平衡还会造成运输费用和成本的差异化。其次,相同的客运产品也可能存在较大的差异性,例如城际列车中速度最快和速度最慢的,在相同票价下的出行时间就会有所差异;所以,应该针对服务属性有较大差别的列车产品进行差异化定价。最后,出行旅客群体之间也存在着很大的差异。不同种类的旅客对票价、时间和舒适程度的感知不同,制订多层次的票价,既有助于引导旅客选择个人偏好的客运产品,同时实现资源最优配置,还可以推动铁路运营的收入增长,达成双方的利益最大化。

(3)实施丰富的优惠政策。合理的定价体系并非简单地针对不同的客运产品制定某个相对的最佳票价,还应该延伸宽度使其多样化。对冷门路线,合理推出优惠票价或一定折扣,吸引对价格敏感的旅客以提升其客运市场占有率。例如,新疆维吾尔自治区、西藏自治区的部分铁路线路呈现明显的旅游淡旺季,故在其淡季可推行折扣售票吸引客流,这对提高收益也是一种有效的方式。或者借鉴民航交通运输公司的定价策略,诸如采取里程奖励、建立 vip 旅客个性化服务等手段留住商务乘客,建立常旅客计划,以提高旅客的满意度,促进旅客对高速铁路出行方式信任度的建立。以上措施从单张车票盈利来看是不利的,但起到了吸引旅客、刺激人们出行、提升市场占有率的作用,从而提高了铁路运营收入。

(4)建立预售期和折扣率关联的策略。考虑退票和改签等行为,可能会对铁路运输公司造成额外的损失,并且随着不同交通客运方式的竞争,高速铁路可采用预售期和折扣率联动定价策略。通过较早时间段的客票预售,引导运输企业有计划地合理安排服务和运力,对于折扣率高的预售客票在改签或退票时,收取较高的手续费。据此,在旅客退票或改签方面对票价方案制定的影响,也是有待进一步深入地研究的。

参考文献

[1] 黄武军. 我国高速铁路客票定价管理与策略研究[D]. 北京:中国铁道科学研究院,2017.
[2] 刘玉敬. 基于旅客出行选择行为的高铁客票定价方法研究[D]. 北京:北京交通大学, 2015.
[3] Ben-Akiva M, Lerman SR. Discrete choice analysis: theory and application to travel demand. MIT[M]. Cambridge, Massachusetts, 1985.
[4] Hensher D A, Bradley M. Using stated response data to enrich revealed preference discrete choice models[J]. Marketing Letter,1993,4(2):139-152.
[5] 王慧晶,李夏苗. 基于 Logit 模型的武广客运专线转移客流量计算研究[J]. 湖南铁路科技职业技术学院学报,2011,11(2):23-78.
[6] Marco Kouwenhoven, Gerard C de Jong, Paul Koster, et al. New values of time and reliability in passenger transport in The Netherlands [J]. Resacrch in Transportation Economics, 2014,47:37-49.
[7] Tsung-Hsien Tsai. Homogeneous service with heterogeneous products: Relationships among airline ticket fares and purchase fences[J]. Journal of Air Transport Management ,2016(55):164-175.
[8] Abane A. Mode Choice for the Journey to Work among Formal Sector Employees in Accra, Ghana[J]. Journal of Transport Geography,1993,1(4):219-229.
[9] 李亚. 铁路旅客出行时段与乘车方式的联合选择行为研究[J]. 铁道运输与经济,2018,40(9):86-91.
[10] 李文霞,张春民,李卓,等. 兰渝运输通道内多种运输方式客流分担率研究[J]. 武汉理工大学学报

(交通科学与工程版),2019,43(2):321-326.

[11] Claudia Capozza. The effect of rail travel time on airline fares: First evidence from the Italian passenger market[J]. 2016(6):18-24.

[12] Joon-Kyu Lee, Kwang-Eui Yoo, Ki-Han Song. A study on travelers' transport mode choice behavior using the mixed logit model: A case study of the Seoul-Jeju route[J]. Journal of Air Transport Management, 2016,56:131-137.

[13] Wenliang Ma, Qiang Wang, Hangjun Yang, et al. Effects of Beijing-Shanghai high-speed rail on air travel: Passenger types, airline groups and tacit collusion[J]. Research in Transportation Economics, 2019(74):64-76.

[14] Angela Stefania Bergantino, Leonardo Madio. Intermodal competition and substitution. HSR versus air transport: Understanding the socio-economic determinants of modal choice[J]. Research in Transportation Economics,2020,79.

[15] 刘春济,高静. 感知价格影响公众乘坐高铁出行意向的机制研究[J]. 上海对外经贸大学学报,2020,27(1):111-123.

[16] Xiaohong Ren, Zhenhua Chen, Fang Wang, et al. Impact of high-speed rail on social equity in China: Evidence from a mode choice survey[J]. Transportation Research Part A, 2020, 138: 422-441.

[17] 任倩. 基于随机参数 logit 模型的公共交通出行方式选择行为研究[D]. 广州:华南理工大学,2019.

[18] Xilei Zhao, Xiang Yan, Alan Yu, et al. Prediction and behavioral analysis of travel mode choice: A comparison of machine learning and logit models[J]. Trtavel Behaviour and Society,2020(20):22-35.

[19] Thomas O Hancock, Jan Broekaert, Stephane Hess, et al. Quantum probability: A new method for modelling travel behaviour[J]. Transportation Research Part B, 2020, 139: 165-198.

[20] Agostino Nuzzolo, Umberto Crisalli, Francesca Gangemi. A behavioural choice model for the evaluation of railway supply and pricing policies[J]. Transportation Research Part A,2000(34):395-404.

[21] 刘立荣. 基于旅客实践价值的客运专线客票定价理论与实证研究[D]. 北京:北京交通大学,2010.

[22] Zhao Xueyu, Yang Jiaqi. Research on the Bi-level Programming Model for Ticket fare pricing of Urban Rail Transit Based on Particle Swarm Optimization Algorithm[J]. Procedia-Social and Behavioral Sciences,2013(96):633-642.

[23] WU Keqi, MAO Baohua, WANG Yongliang, et al. Intercity Rail Transport Pricing Strategy Based on Efficacy Coefficient Method[J]. Journal of Transportation Systems Engineering and Information Technology, 2013,13(3), 105-110.

[24] 马海超. 兰新第二双线客运票价定价策略研究[J]. 铁道运输与经济,2013,35(7):1-5.

[25] 赵慧. 基于拉姆齐模型的城际轨道交通定价方法研究[D]. 吉林:吉林大学. 2016.

[26] 李楠煜. 兰州轨道交通票价制定研究[D]. 兰州:兰州交通大学, 2017.

[27] 孔令华. 高速客运市场的分担率和高铁定价[D]. 大连:东北财经大学,2017.

[28] Zhen-ying Yan, Xiao-juan Li, Bao-ming Han. Collaborative optimisation of resource capacity allocation and fare rate for high-speed railway passenger transport[J]. Journal of Rail Transport Planning & Management, 2019,10: 23-33.

[29] 陈阳. 基于旅客行为分析的城际铁路票价制定策略研究[D]. 成都:西南交通大学,2019.

[30] 宋文波. 以旅客需求为导向的高速铁路票额分配理论和方法研究[D]. 北京:北京交通大学,2019.

[31] 张琦. 竞争视角下高铁定价方法研究[D]. 北京:北京交通大学, 2019.

[32] 景云,刘应科,郭思冶. 基于乘客选择行为的高速铁路动态联合定价策略研究[J]. 铁道学报,2019,41(9):28-33.

北京CBD区域共享单车使用规律研究

潘 龙[1] 姚恩建[2] 陈艳艳[1]

(1.北京市交通工程重点实验室,北京工业大学;
2.综合交通运输大数据应用技术交通运输行业重点实验室,北京交通大学)

摘 要 共享单车以其灵活的使用特性成为最后一公里的有效解决方案,尤其是在日常通勤出行强度很高的北京CBD区域。相比于以往针对城市级别的共享单车使用规律研究,本文聚焦CBD区域,基于共享单车出行起讫点数据,通过数据清洗,获取研究区域出行数据。在对比CBD区域和北京市整体共享单车使用规律的基础上,结合公共交通站点、地标性建筑等信息,分别从时间和空间维度剖析了CBD区域共享单车的使用规律。本文的研究结果可以为交通管理部门和共享单车企业掌握共享单车使用规律、提升使用效率提供相应的理论和数据支持。

关键词 共享单车 使用规律 聚类热图

0 引 言

近十年来,共享单车在世界范围内迅猛发展。特别是无桩共享单车,以其自由停取的特点,成为广受出行者欢迎的新兴出行方式。我国无桩共享单车的用户数量由2016年的2800万飞速增长为2017年的2.05亿,并且在2018年持续增长为2.35亿。其中小黄车和摩拜单车两大共享单车企业主导了共享单车市场,据2018年5月的统计数据,两大企业分别拥有2800万和2100万活跃用户。

与有桩共享单车不同,无桩共享单车(下文共享单车均指无桩共享单车)灵活停取的特点使其成为最后一公里问题的有效解决方案,特别适用于与其他公共交通方式进行无缝衔接,以拓展公共交通可达性。以北京CBD区域为例,该区域是众多金融、媒体、商业聚集地,日常通勤需求量很大。由于该区域包含的7个地铁站和60余个公交站点主要集中在快速路和主干路上,最后一公里接驳难题尤为突出,所以共享单车在CBD区域公共交通体系中的作用显得尤为重要。

学者们通常从城市视角针对共享单车使用规律进行了较多研究。汤秋庆等利用深圳市共享单车的使用数据,分析其骑行时空特征,并对共享单车停放设施规划提出了相关建议。林青雅等基于深圳市共享单车出行数据分析居民骑行出行需求、骑行走廊特征、站点接驳需求和单车调度特征等出行特征。周超等基于共享单车数据对南京市出行时空特征进行了研究。刘冰等基于公共自行车出行数据,分析了杭州市出行特征时空分布情况。针对学校区域,汤旸等分析校园共享单车出行数据,分析其出行特征,并提出相关措施建议。

以往相关研究通常以城市为单位分析共享单车使用规律,研究结果较为粗略,难以匹配城市功能性区域的细致分析需求。因此,深入剖析CBD区域共享单车的使用规律,对于日常通勤和公共交通体系的有效运行都具有重要意义。本文针对上述问题,利用共享单车出行起讫点数据,获取进出CBD和CBD内部的共享单车时空出行分布,分析其使用规律,并与北京市共享单车出行规律进行对比分析。

本文的结构安排包括:第一节介绍研究区域、共享单车数据及其数据处理和清洗方法;第二节将CBD区域共享单车使用规律与北京市整体使用规律进行对比分析;第三节通过聚类热力图分析CBD区域共享单车出行时空分布规律;第四节提出本文研究结论和下一步研究展望。

1 研究区域和数据

本节首先介绍了研究区域和数据情况,并详细描述了数据处理和数据清洗工作。

1.1 研究区域和数据

本文的研究区域为北京CBD(图1),是国内最为重要的国际商业中心之一,在2020年的《2020全球商务区吸引力报告》中,北京CBD排名世界第七,国内第一。该区域涵盖了众多金融、传媒和商业龙头企业,是北京国际商务和现代服务中心,也是国际化和现代化的集中展现区域。如引言部分所介绍,北京CBD区域的办公、商业区密度高,日常通勤需求量很大;与此同时,该区域的地铁站点和公交站点主要集中于快速路和主干路上,相关管理部门也将推动绿色出行、改善非机动车出行环境作为重要的发展任务,因此共享单车是解决最后一公里接驳的重要衔接手段,也将在CBD区域的通勤出行中持续扮演重要的角色。

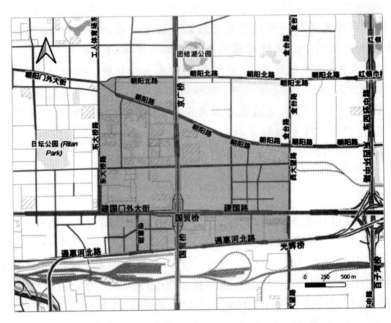

图1 北京CBD区域

研究数据来源于小黄车和摩拜两大共享单车公司,为了研究日常通勤特征,本文选取2018年4月11日一天的工作日数据作为研究数据。该数据记录了出行起讫点的坐标、出行起始时间、出行结束时间等信息。

为了研究区域内的共享单车使用规律,本文提取了起讫点位于区域内的出行,并同时通过百度地图提取了区域内的POI信息数据,包括重要写字楼、地铁出入口和公交站点等信息。

1.2 数据处理

通过数据处理过程,将原始数据中的错误数据和异常数据予以剔除,保证研究数据的准确性。

本文首先剔除距离异常的出行数据。如果出行距离过短,可能出现车辆损坏、出行者改变意愿而放弃共享单车、或绕行导致的起终点接近(如骑车出发取快递而后又返回出发地点,该类出行很难通过本文的数据判断得出)等。与之相反,GPS出现错误或车锁损坏导致无法锁车等情况则可能导致异常长距离出行。上述异常出行均不在本文考虑的出行范围内,通过起讫点的坐标信息可以计算起讫点间的距离,可以用该距离作为标准筛选异常出行。根据北京市疫情期间共享单车骑行特征报告,出行距离通常分布于50m~8km之间,因此超出上述范围的出行并剔除。

同时,共享单车骑行速度过快的出行也被认为是异常出行予以剔除。当骑行速度过快时,可能出现GPS点漂移的情况,因此当骑行速度大于25km/h的出行被剔除。另外,出行总时长异常的出行也予以剔除。出行时长过长,可能是因为车锁损坏或出行者忘记锁车等原因,因此当出行时长小于30s或大于1h的出行予以剔除。

通过上述筛选过程,共获得54613条出行数据。

2 共享单车使用规律对比分析

对 CBD 区域的共享单车出行进行统计分析,获取平均出行时长、出行距离、出行速度等统计指标,分析 CBD 区域整体使用规律,并将上述指标与北京市出行统计结果进行对比,获得 CBD 区域和北京市的出行描述性统计结果,见表 1。

共享单车出行统计分析　　　　表 1

	出行时长(min)		出行距离(m)		出行速度(km/h)	
	CBD	北京整体	CBD	北京整体	CBD	北京整体
平均值	12.2	10.5	1434	1156	7.3	7.1
中位数	9.5	7.8	1064	856	7.3	7.1
标准差	9.3	8.7	1187	1028	2.7	2.9
数据量	54613	1920231	54613	1920231	54613	1920231

表 1 表明,CBD 区域共享单车出行的平均时长为 12.2min,平均距离为 1434m,平均速度为 7.3km/h。与北京市共享单车出行数据相比,CBD 区域的出行时长和距离均高于北京市相关数据 20% 左右,表明在 CBD 区域内,相比于北京市,共享单车满足了更长距离的出行需求和接驳需求。

3 CBD 区域共享单车使用规律分析

本节将基于出行数据,从时间和空间层面分析 CBD 区域共享单车的使用规律。

3.1 时间分布

CBD 区域共享单车出行按小时统计的时间分布情况如图 2 所示。图 2a)展示了整体 CBD 区域共享单车出行时间分布情况,在早高峰(7 点~9 点)和晚高峰(17 点~19 点),共享单车出行次数明显高于其他时段。

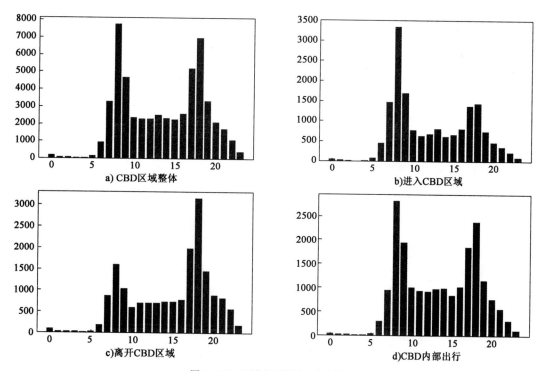

图 2　CBD 区域出行随时间分布情况

进一步地,将 CBD 区域出行按照起讫点情况分别划分为进入 CBD 出行(起点位于 CBD 外,终点位于 CBD 内)、离开 CBD 出行(起点位于 CBD 内,终点位于 CBD 外)和 CBD 内部出行(起终点均位于 CBD

内)。在上述三类出行中,CBD 内部出行占总出行的 40.7%,是最为主要的出行类型;进入 CBD 出行和离开 CBD 出行占比分别为 28.6% 和 30.7%,均低于 CBD 内部出行。

统计各类出行的时间分布情况如图 2b)~d)所示。可以看出,尽管三类出行都具有早高峰和晚高峰,其高峰期的具体特征呈现显著的不同。进入 CBD 出行中,早高峰的出行量明显高于其他时段的出行,晚高峰的出行量略微高于平峰时段。与之相比,离开 CBD 的出行呈现出相反的特征,其晚高峰出行量明显高于早高峰和平峰时段。这表明进出 CBD 的共享单车出行可能主要为通勤出行,又由于 CBD 主要为商业办公用地,因此早高峰多为上班出行,晚高峰多为下班出行,故而呈现出上述特征。CBD 内部出行时间分布则呈现出早高峰和晚高峰相似的出行量,需要进一步从空间分布剖析其使用规律。

3.2 空间分布

为了体现 CBD 区域共享单车出行空间分布特征,将研究区域内早高峰时段(7 点~9 点)、平峰时段(11 点~13 点)和晚高峰时段(17 点~19 点)的出行起点和出行终点分别统计,并利用热力图制作起点和终点分布情况如图 3~图 5 所示。

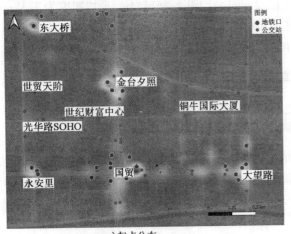 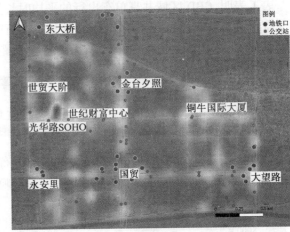

a) 起点分布　　　　　　　　　　　　　　b) 终点分布

图 3　早高峰时段热力图

早高峰时段(图 3),出行起点主要聚集在地铁站口周边,包括东大桥、金台夕照、国贸等地铁站口起点聚集明显,永安里、大望路地铁站口也有较多出行起点聚集。出行终点则重点集中于光华路 SOHO 等写字楼区域附近,世纪财富中心、铜牛国际大厦等办公区也有较为明显的出行终点聚集。说明早高峰时段共享单车主要承担了由地铁周边至工作地点的接驳作用。

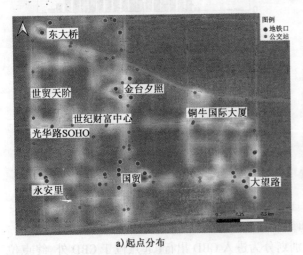 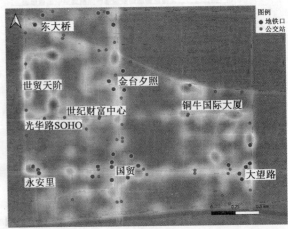

a) 起点分布　　　　　　　　　　　　　　b) 终点分布

图 4　平峰时段热力图

平峰时段(图4),由于此时的出行并非为通勤出行,出行起点和终点的分布相对高峰时段更加分散。在平峰时段,出行起点可以看出较为集中于东大桥、金台夕照和国贸地铁站,同时在区域内主要道路上均有一定数量的分布。出行终点则重点分布于世贸天阶周边的道路,可能是由于该区域周边拥有较为密集的餐馆,方便工作人员在附近就餐。

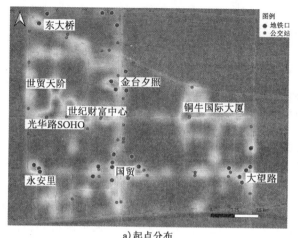 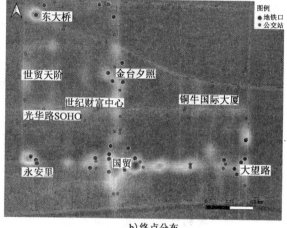

a) 起点分布　　　　　　　　　　　　　　　b) 终点分布

图5　晚高峰时段热力图

晚高峰时段(图5),与早高峰时段的使用规律相反,出行起点主要集中在办公区域,如光华路SOHO、世纪财富中心、世贸天阶、铜牛国际大厦等区域,出行终点则主要分布在地铁站附近,如国贸、东大桥、永安里地铁站等。整体上,晚高峰时段的共享单车出行主要承担了工作地点和地铁站之间的接驳作用。

4　结　语

本文针对以往研究通常以城市为单位分析共享单车使用规律、较为缺乏城市功能性区域细致分析需求的问题,针对通勤出行强度高、共享单车使用频繁的CBD区域,从时间和空间维度剖析CBD区域共享单车使用规律。研究结果表明,CBD区域的共享单车使用规律与北京市整体规律存在较为显著的差异,体现在出行时间、出行距离更长。从时间维度,CBD区域共享单车使用呈现出明显的早高峰和晚高峰特征,尤其是早高峰多为进入CBD出行、晚高峰为离开CBD出行;从空间维度,早高峰的共享单车出行多为由地铁站出发、前往工作地点的出行,晚高峰则转变为由工作地点前往地铁站的出行,在平峰时段,出行终点集中在世贸天阶周边餐饮较为集中的区域。本文的研究结果可以为交通管理部门和共享单车企业掌握共享单车使用规律、提升使用效率提供相应的理论和数据支持。

结合建成环境数据,下一步可以构建空间回归模型,研究区域内的空间异质性,以分析共享单车出行产生、到达与周边建成环境之间的关系。

5　致　谢

本研究受到"北京市朝阳区博士后工作经费资助项目"的资助。

参考文献

[1] 汤秋庆,蒋静辉.基于摩拜存取数据的深圳市自行车停放设施规划研究[J].交通与运输,2020,33(S2):215-218.

[2] 林青雅,丘建栋,谢开强.深圳市共享单车出行时空特征及需求分析[C]//中国城市规划学会城市交通规划学术委员会.品质交通与协同共治——2019年中国城市交通规划年会论文集.2019:10.

[3] 周超,周亚男,李振世,等.基于大数据的南京市共享单车时空特征研究[J].西南师范大学学报

(自然科学版),2018,43(10):66-73.
[4] 刘冰,曹娟娟,周于杰,等.城市公共自行车使用活动的时空间特征研究——以杭州为例[J].城市规划学刊,2016(03).
[5] 汤谞,何祎豪,纪宁,等.大学校园共享单车出行行为特征分析[J].交通与运输,2019,32(S1):203-206,211.
[6] 北京市疫情期间共享单车骑行特征报告[R].北京:北京交通发展研究院,2020.

韧性视角下城市群交通网络评估

陈明玉 陆化普 徐佳君

(清华大学土木工程系交通研究所)

摘 要 为了交通网络稳定运行、保障生命安全、减少财产损失,进行韧性视角下城市群交通网络的评估具有十分重要的意义,也是我国交通强国建设征途上迫切需要解决的难题之一。本文运用复杂网络理论,设置三种不同攻击场景以及恢复策略,提出了网络效率变化值和加权最大连通子图两个指标,给出韧性的定量评估,并以粤港澳大湾区铁路网为实例进行仿真。研究结果表明:在对应的每一种攻击方式中,韧性值最小的是随机恢复策略,按度排序和按介数排序的恢复策略较为有效;在同种攻击方式和恢复策略下,韧性值随着开始恢复时间的延后而变小。研究结果能够为科学制定城市群交通发展规划及相关政策奠定基础。

关键词 交通安全 韧性 复杂网络 城市群

0 引 言

交通网络是经济与人类生活的重要载体,自然灾害、恐怖袭击等干扰情景的发生都会对交通网络的运行造成损伤,甚至造成大面积瘫痪。伴随着交通网络规模的不断增加,结构及其功能日趋复杂,交通网络韧性逐渐引起学者的重视。

韧性的概念来自生态学家Holling,用来表征系统吸收各类变化的能力。如今的韧性逐步演化涵盖更广阔的概念范畴,但较多学者认为韧性表现为系统抵抗(预防和承受)任何可能的危害、吸收初始损害并恢复正常运行的综合能力。Bruneau等开创了"4R"框架:健壮性、冗余性、资源性和快速性来表示系统的韧性损失。基于网络拓扑的模型方法更加微观,可以表示出与时间相关的更多细节,而且有利于模拟多种攻击方式以反映系统韧性。Zhang等利用网络效率衡量地铁网络的恢复能力,以上海地铁为例分别检验了2010年和2015年地铁网在随机失效和最大连接度攻击下的韧性。Yonca等利用网络中平均最终恢复时间、恢复过程的效率,以及不确定性评估因地震及其引发的滑坡造成的堵塞后的道路韧性。李兆隆等针对货运道路网络,分别从网络性能恢复速度和累计损失两方面度量弹复性,有效求解大规模交通网络应急恢复阶段的最优恢复策略。

以往研究主要集中于影响效果上,缺乏对恢复交通网络的探讨,并且目前针对韧性的研究大多集中在国家或地区层面,中小区域如城市群的研究较少。鉴于以往研究的不足,本文通过构建交通网络拓扑结构探究城市群交通网络的韧性,提出韧性测度方法。以粤港澳大湾区城市群为实例进行仿真,分析不同干扰事件以及恢复策略下对交通网络韧性影响差异情况。

基金项目:中国工程院重大咨询项目,交通强国战略研究(二期)(2019-ZD-22);交通运输部项目,《国家综合立体交通网规划纲要(2020—2050)》咨询评估(LTW-39)。

1 交通网络韧性定义

面临干扰情景,交通网络性能会经历平衡、吸收、恢复和新的平衡阶段,韧性在其中体现。如图 1 所示,交通网络性能 $P(t)$ 以一条实线表示。P_0 代表 t_0 时的网络性能,t_a 为干扰发生时刻,$P(t)$ 开始下降,进入到吸收干扰阶段。限于干扰规模以及网络自身具备一定承载能力,网络性能在 t_r 时达到最低点。通过一些有效措施,使 $P(t)$ 逐渐恢复,在 t_n 恢复到一个新的稳定阶段。在此过程中,从 t_a 到 t_n,$P(t)$ 函数与 P_0 的面积比例定义为交通网络的韧性,如式(1)所示,$P(t)$ 为交通网络性能,t_n 表示进入新平衡阶段的时刻,t_a 表示干扰时刻。

$$R = \frac{\int_{t_a}^{t_n} P(t) \, dt}{P_0 \cdot (t_n - t_a)} \tag{1}$$

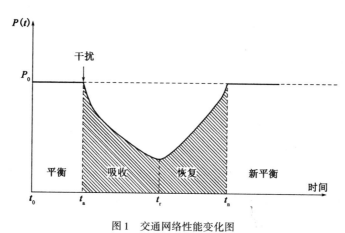

图 1 交通网络性能变化图

2 交通网络韧性测度方法

2.1 拓扑结构抽取

将交通网络抽取成无向图 $G(V,L,W)$,其中 V 表示节点,即交通枢纽;L 表示为节点之间的交通服务连接关系,用邻接矩阵表示,即邻接连通为 1,非邻接连通为 0;W 表示权重,以交通枢纽能够提供服务的人数作为节点的权重。

2.2 干扰情景设置

在模拟交通网络所遭受的打击时,通常采用随机攻击和恶意攻击两种策略。随机攻击策略模拟的是广泛存在的故障情景,常用随机选择被攻击的节点来进行。相比之下,恶意攻击策略需要识别网络中的关键元素。学者常常考虑按照度和介数排序,对交通网络节点进行删除。因此,本文的干扰情景设置为:依据度排序攻击、依据介数排序攻击和随机攻击。

2.3 恢复策略设置

政府及相关部门会采用不同的恢复策略来提高网络性能。一般考虑选择先攻击先恢复的顺序排序,也有可能由于重要节点在国民经济和国家安全中的重要作用,按照重要程度进行恢复。同时,由于工程技术、施工难度不同,最终可能导致恢复序列以随机顺序呈现。因此本文恢复策略设置为:依据度排序恢复、依据介数排序恢复以及随机恢复。其中随机恢复采用 5 次随机排序得到结果的平均值。

2.4 交通网络韧性测度

采用网络效率变化值 P_{ie} 与加权最大连通子图 LCS_W 作为上文提到的交通网络性能 $P(t)$ 指标,具体如下：

$$P_{ie} = \frac{E}{E_0} \quad (2)$$

$$E = \frac{1}{N(N-1)} \sum_{i<j} \frac{1}{d_{ij}} \quad (3)$$

$$LCS = \frac{N_{\max}}{N_0} \quad (4)$$

$$LCS_W = \frac{\sum_{i \in \sigma_{N_{\max}}} W_i}{\sum_i W_i} \quad (5)$$

式中，网络效率 E 定义为最短路径距离倒数的平均值，E_0 表示初始状态的效率，N 为节点数，d_{ij} 为节点 i 与节点 j 的最短路径距离，P_{ie} 表示维持原始状态网络效率的能力。$N_{\max}$ 为最大连通子图的节点数，N_0 为初始网络节点数，$i \in \sigma_{N_{\max}}$ 表示节点 i 属于最大连通子图 $\sigma_{N_{\max}}$，W_i 为节点 i 的权重，即交通枢纽能够提供服务的人数。

攻击的过程中，原连通图生成若干子图。其中，连通节点最多的被定义为最大连通子图。如式(4)所示，最大连通子图 LCS 是由最大连通子图中的节点数与原始网络中的节点数之比来度量的。在本文中，考虑交通枢纽能够服务的人群数，采用加权的最大连通子图大小 LCS_W 衡量交通网络性能。

3 粤港澳大湾区算例

3.1 大湾区交通网络拓扑

本文以粤港澳大湾区铁路网为例，进行模型验证。首先抽取铁路网的拓扑关系 $G(V, L, W)$。采用 12306 网站查询各火车站到发车次，作为权重 W。根据高德地图得到的大湾区火车站分布图，图 2 为其拓扑结构。

图 2 大湾区铁路网拓扑结构

3.2 大湾区交通韧性测度

为比较恢复策略的效果差异，分别预设网络中攻击节点数达到总节点数的 10%、20%、30% 时开始恢复。干扰情景设置为：依据度排序攻击、依据介数排序攻击和随机攻击；恢复策略设置为：依据度排序恢复、依据介数排序恢复以及随机恢复。

图 3 和图 4 分别显示了以网络效率变化值 P_{ie} 和以加权最大连通子图 LCS_W 为测度的韧性值。在两种测量方式下，韧性值不同，但基本趋势相似。在三种攻击方式中，当 10% 失效开始恢复时，依据度排序攻击的韧性值最小；当 20% 和 30% 失效开始恢复时，依据度排序和依据介数排序攻击的韧性值较小，说明大湾区铁路网在遭受恶意袭击时，表现出较弱的承担能力。在对应的每一种攻击方式中，随机恢复所对应的韧性值最小，表明合理恢复顺序的必要性。在同种攻击方式和恢复策略下，选择开始恢复的时间越晚，韧性值越小，以依据度排序的攻击情景和恢复策略为例，20% 和 30% 失效开始恢复的韧性值为 10% 失效开始恢复的 0.81 和 0.73，表明尽早恢复的必要性。

在依据度排序的攻击中，介数恢复策略的效果较好，相比度恢复策略对应的韧性值提高约 10%。在依据介数排序的攻击中，度恢复策略的效果较好，类似地相比介数恢复策略对应的韧性值提高约 10%。在随机攻击中，度恢复策略的效果表现出较强优越性，相比随机恢复策略对应的韧性值提高约 30%，相比介数恢复策略对应的韧性值提高约 10%。

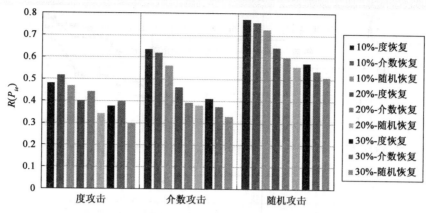

图 3 大湾区交通网络韧性值（网络效率变化值 P_{ie}）

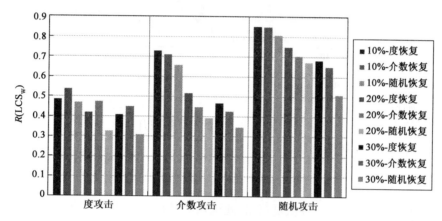

图 4 大湾区交通网络韧性值（加权最大连通子图 LCS_W）

图 5 和图 6 分别表示依据度排序攻击在 30% 节点失效下恢复的网络效率变化值 P_{ie} 和加权最大连通子图 LCS_W 的变化，以此为例进行详细分析。深圳北站、广州南站、广州站是度数最大的前三个火车站，在这三个节点遭受攻击后，网络效率变化值 P_{ie} 和加权最大连通子图 LCS_W 分别下降到原来的 44% 和 51%。依据度排序的第六个节点东莞西失效后，网络效率变化值 P_{ie} 下降了 2.1%，然而加权最大连通子图 LCS_W 下降了 24.8%，体现出能够服务的人群数的剧烈变化。这两个指标值分别侧重于网络整体连通性和服务能力，在韧性评价中必不可少。

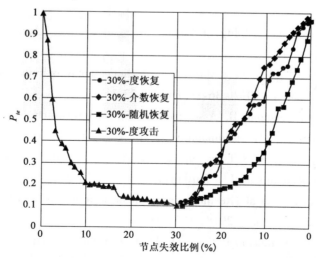

图 5 依据度排序攻击在 30% 节点失效下恢复的网络效率变化值 P_{ie}

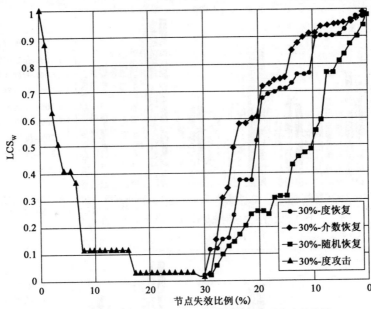

图6 依据度排序攻击在30%节点失效下恢复的加权最大连通子图 LCS$_W$

在恢复过程中,随机恢复的表现效果最差。而介数恢复效果较好,主要由于恢复的节点能够尽快保证整个网络的连接,第六个节点顺德站的恢复为整个网络效率提升了8.9%,第五个节点广州东站的恢复使加权最大连通子图提升了16%,贡献最大。

4 结 语

本文通过构建三种干扰场景和三种恢复策略:随机顺序、依据度排序和依据介数排序,用网络效率变化值 P_{ie} 与加权最大连通子图 LCS$_W$ 作指标,提出了交通网络韧性测度方法,并探索了粤港澳大湾区的铁路网韧性特征。在 P_{ie} 和 LCS$_W$ 的测度下,韧性值的变化趋势相似。在对应的每一种攻击方式中,随机恢复策略的效果最差;在同种攻击方式和恢复策略下,较早的恢复时间节点选择可以使韧性值升高。这些结果表明,韧性可以通过尽快开始灾后恢复并选择对应情景下的恢复策略来提高。

广州、深圳是大湾区的中心城市,在面临干扰情景时,深圳北站、广州南站、广州站的失效会造成网络性能的较大幅度下降,相关规划部门可以推动多种交通方式配合衔接,弥补失效所带来的影响,运营管理部门对于失效枢纽应尽快进行修复,以保证运输能力的恢复。

参考文献

[1] Holling C S. Resilience and Stability of Ecological Systems [J]. Annual Review of Ecology and Systematics, 1973, 4(1): 1-23.

[2] Ouyang M, Dueñas-Osorio L, Min X. A three-stage resilience analysis framework for urban infrastructure systems [J]. Structural Safety, 2012, 36-37(none): 23-31.

[3] Murdock H, de Bruijn K, Gersonius B. Assessment of Critical Infrastructure Resilience to Flooding Using a Response Curve Approach [J]. Sustainability, 2018, 10(10).

[4] Bruneau M, Chang S E, Eguchi R T, et al. A Framework to Quantitatively Assess and Enhance the Seismic Resilience of Communities [J]. Earthquake Spectra, 2003, 19(4): 733-52.

[5] Zhang D-m, Du F, Huang H, et al. Resiliency assessment of urban rail transit networks: Shanghai metro as an example [J]. Safety Science, 2018, 106: 230-43.

[6] Aydin N Y, Duzgun H S, Heinimann H R, et al. Framework for improving the resilience and recovery of transportation networks under geohazard risks [J]. International Journal of Disaster Risk Reduction, 2018, 31: 832-43.

[7] 李兆隆,金淳,胡畔,等. 基于弹复性的交通网络应急恢复阶段策略优化[J]. 系统工程理论与实践, 2019, 39(11): 2828-41.
[8] Guo Q, Amin S, Hao Q, et al. Resilience assessment of safety system at subway construction sites applying analytic network process and extension cloud models—Science Direct [J]. Reliability Engineering & System Safety, 2020, 201.
[9] Duan Y, Lu F. Robustness of city road networks at different granularities [J]. Physica A Statistical Mechanics and Its Applications, 2014, 411: 21-34.

基于文本挖掘与关联规则相结合的天窗未兑现原因诊断分析

徐长安　李晟东　李斯涵　倪少权
(西南交通大学交通运输与物流学院)

摘　要　本文以天窗未兑现文本信息为依据,提出基于文本挖掘与关联规则相结合的天窗未兑现原因诊断分析方法。首先,针对天窗未兑现原因记录的不规范性和随意性,采用向量空间模型对天窗未兑现记录表进行分析和特征提取,在此基础上,运用关联规则技术对天窗未兑现原因进行诊断分析,挖掘天窗未兑现原因与其他特征变量之间的潜在关系,并得到相应的强关联规则。最后,以某铁路局集团公司2018年的天窗未兑现文本数据为例,进行实验分析,结果表明,该方法能够得到传统方法无法获取的天窗未兑现原因与其他特征变量之间的共现规律,这些规律可用于天窗设置的反馈优化。

关键词　铁路运输　文本挖掘　关联规则　天窗未兑现　向量空间模型

0　引　言

　　天窗是列车运行图中不铺画列车运行线或调整、抽减列车运行,为营业线施工和维修作业预留的时间。它是铁路行车安全的技术保障,对保证铁路各种运输设备处在良好状态起着十分重要的作用。在实际运营过程中,由于车流变化,列车晚点,雨雪天气,自然灾害等许多不确定因素的影响,导致部分线路天窗的兑现率不高,这给铁路运输组织工作带来了很大的安全隐患。因此,进一步完善天窗未兑现原因诊断分析,并在天窗设置阶段就考虑到影响天窗兑现的因素,加强天窗设置的计划性,对保障铁路安全有序运营具有重要意义。

　　我国铁路天窗兑现情况由现场人员以非结构化文本形式记录。由于记录缺乏统一的术语与概念,以及现场人员素质参差不齐,导致天窗兑现记录表呈现一定的不规范性,给天窗兑现相关的理论研究带来了很大挑战。目前,关于天窗兑现方面的研究依然很少,现有研究多是采用定性手段分析天窗兑现影响因素以及提出相应的改进措施,少有文献进行天窗兑现方面定量分析。而铁路现场生产部门仍然采用人工经验进行天窗未兑现原因的诊断分析,已无法满足铁路生产对安全性和快速性的要求。

　　由于天窗兑现情况数据中既包含数值数据,又包含文本数据,传统的数据分析方法无法对天窗兑现数据进行有效分析,近年来兴起的文本挖掘,关联规则分析等数据挖掘方法为天窗兑现分析提供了一种新的解决思路。文本挖掘是一种专门针对文本类数据的数据挖掘方法,它能够实现文本的信息提取和文

基金项目:国家重点研发计划资助(2017YFB1200702,2016YFC0802208);国家自然基金项目(61703351);中国铁路总公司科技研究计划项目(P2018T001,K2018X012,N2018X006-01)。

本分类,将文本数据转化为计算机易于处理的结构化形式。目前已在安全隐患文本分类,铁路信号设备故障诊断等领域成功应用。关联规则是一种数据驱动的无监督机器学习方法,主要用于知识发现。它能够从历史数据中挖掘潜在规律,为计划制定提供决策反馈支持,目前已成功运用于安全管理,事故预防等领域。

考虑天窗兑现情况记录文本数据特点,本文提出了文本挖掘与关联规则相结合的铁路天窗未兑现原因诊断分析框架。针对天窗未兑现原因记录的不规范性问题,利用文本挖掘中的向量空间模型来进行天窗未兑现文本数据的结构化处理,并实现天窗未兑现文本数据的特征提取。同时,本文选取关联规则技术作为天窗未兑现原因诊断分析方法。关联规则分析是揭示复杂数据内在结构特征的一种数据挖掘方法,主要用于从数据集中发现数据项之间的联系。为验证本文提出方法的有效性,以某铁路局集团公司2018年某月份天窗兑现情况记录数据进行试验分析。

1 天窗使用情况概述

天窗兑现是天窗实际时间(或次数)与天窗计划时间(或次数)的比值,它是铁路部门考核天窗利用情况的重要指标,对强化天窗资源管理,完善天窗考核分析制度具有重要作用。然而,天窗兑现受到列车运行及调整,自然灾害,不同部门间配合协调等多重因素的影响,任何一个环节出现问题都会影响天窗利用,导致天窗无法兑现。图1和图2分别给出了某铁路局公司2018年维修天窗兑现情况以及天窗未兑现原因统计情况。

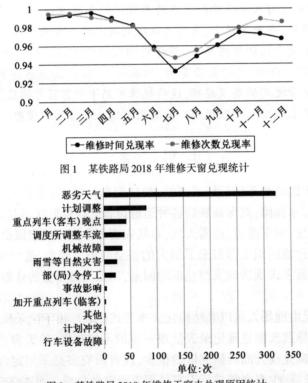

图1 某铁路局2018年维修天窗兑现统计

图2 某铁路局2018年维修天窗未兑现原因统计

天窗未兑现不仅会浪费本已紧张的铁路运力资源,也会影响铁路设施设备的检修,对铁路运输安全造成很大的潜在威胁。因此,基于铁路部门累积的天窗未兑现文本数据,利用数据挖掘手段对这些历史数据进行分析,找出天窗设置和天窗利用过程中的一些关联关系和潜在规律,既能够指导工务,电务等维修部门更好地利用天窗,提高天窗兑现率。

2 天窗未兑现原因诊断分析方法

天窗未兑现原因诊断分析需要解决两个方面的问题:天窗未兑现数据的分析和特征提取;天窗未兑

现原因的诊断分析。天窗未兑现数据的分析和特征提取是天窗未兑现原因诊断分析的前提与基础。天窗未兑现原因的诊断分析是天窗未兑现数据分析和特征提取的目标。本文选取文本挖掘技术进行天窗未兑现数据的分析和特征提取，运用关联规则方法进行天窗未兑现原因的诊断分析。

2.1 文本挖掘

文本挖掘作为数据挖掘的一种方法，可以将文本里包含的信息进行结构化处理，有效实现文本信息抽取。文本挖掘实现信息抽取的主要步骤如图 3 所示。

文本特征提取是实现文本挖掘的关键步骤，它把从文本中抽取出的特征词进行量化来表示文本信息。本文采用理论基础比较成熟的向量空间模型来描述文本向量，将文本数据转换为计算机可以处理的结构化数据。另外，考虑到天窗未兑现文本提取涉及众多领域知识，本文采用基于语境框架的文本特征提取方法，该方法的基本思路仍然是"统计—抽取"模型，但将语义分析融入统计算法，表现出较好的特征提取能力。

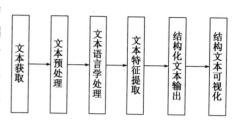

图 3 文本挖掘实现信息抽取的主要步骤

2.2 关联规则

关联规则分析是研究大型复杂数据变量间关系的一种有效方法，它是一种基于数据驱动的数据挖掘方法，不需要变量之间存在特定的函数关系。关联规则分析中的关键指标包括：支持度（Support）、置信度（Confidence）与提升度（Lift）。其中支持度和置信度用来描述关联规则的强度，提升度用来描述关联规则的可用性。

本文采用最常用也是最经典的 Apriori 算法进行关联规则分析，其核心思想是找出存在于事务数据集中最大的频繁项集，在利用得到的最大频繁项集与预先设定的最小置信度阈值生成强关联规则。

2.3 文本挖掘与关联规则相结合的天窗未兑现原因诊断分析框架

基于文本挖掘与关联规则相结合的天窗未兑现原因诊断分析框架如图 4 所示，整个框架主要包括两个部分：文本数据处理和关联规则提取。

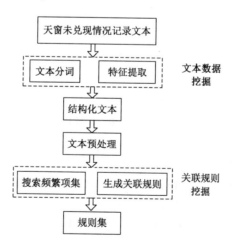

图 4 天窗未兑现原因诊断分析框架

3 实例分析

3.1 数据来源及预处理

本文数据来源于某铁路局集团公司 2018 年某月份共 36 条天窗施工维修兑现情况统计数据，该数据集以天为单位记录了所辖站段的工务、电务、供电等部门的施工与维修计划兑现情况，并以文本形式给出了天窗未兑现的原因记录。运用数据分析的开源软件 R 语言作为工具，编程实现本文数据的文本挖掘与关联规则分析过程,在文本挖掘中使用的程序包有 jieba、tm 和 wordcloud。在关联规则分析中使用的程序包为 arules。

3.2 基于关联规则的天窗未兑现原因诊断分析

根据 2.2 节介绍的方法,设定最小支持度阈值15%,最小置信度阈值50%。则可从所有频繁项集中得到相应事件的强关联规则,以右项为"车站取消"的事件为例,说明其对应的关联规则。表1给出了该事件支撑排名前5的规则集。其中,规则1表明,工务段是天窗未兑现发生主体单位,这是由于工务部门承担了较大比例的检修任务。规则2、3表明,天气影响和运输调整是天窗未兑现的主要影响因素,因此,加强天窗设置的可调整性是未来可行的方向。规则4、5表明,车站天窗较难兑现,尤其在一些枢纽车站,涉及多方向,多线别,天窗兑现难度较大。

天窗未兑现诊断分析关联规则(支撑排名前10)　　表1

编号	左 项	右 项	支撑	置信度	提升
1	{作业单位=工务段}	{结果=车站取消}	0.3244	0.6855	1.2123
2	{作业单位=工务段,原因=天气影响}	{结果=车站取消}	0.3214	0.6835	1.2088
3	{作业单位=工务段,原因=运输调整}	{结果=车站取消}	0.3154	0.6838	1.2093
4	{作业单位=工务段,作业地点=车站}	{结果=车站取消}	0.3125	0.6818	1.2057
5	{作业单位=工务段,作业地点=车站,原因=运输调整}	{结果=车站取消}	0.3095	0.6797	1.2021

4 结 语

针对天窗兑现情况记录文本的特点,提出了基于文本挖掘与关联规则相结合的天窗未兑现原因诊断分析方法。该方法既能实现天窗未兑现文本数据的结构化处理,又能挖掘文本数据中潜藏的共现规律,是分析天窗未兑现情况的一种新的思路和解决方案。随着天窗兑现情况记录文本的累积,未来将可能面对数据量过大导致模型运行速度不足的问题,如何提高海量数据下数据驱动模型的训练速度,值得进一步研究。

参考文献

[1] 徐长安,倪少权,陈钉均,等.天窗设置理论与优化技术研究综述[J].交通运输工程与信息学报, 2017, 15(4):24-31.

[2] 田宜洛.影响综合天窗兑现的因素分析及对策[J].铁道运输与经济,2000,22(9):20-22.

[3] 王胜.浅谈维修天窗作业集约化的相关建议[J].西铁科技,2019(3):35-38.

[4] 杨连报,李平,薛蕊,等.基于不平衡文本数据挖掘的铁路信号设备故障智能分类[J].铁道学报,2018.

[5] 赵阳,等.基于文本挖掘的高铁信号系统车载设备故障诊断[J].铁道学报,2015(8):53-59.

[6] Agrawal R, Imielinski T, Swami A, Mining association rules between sets of items in large databases[J]. In ACM SIGMOD Record, 1993,22(2):207-216.

[7] 许未,何世伟,刘朝辉,等.基于关联规则的铁路事故致因网络构建与分析[J].铁道运输与经济, 2020, 493(11):76-83.

[8] 陈孝慈,谭章禄,单斐,等.基于Bigram的安全隐患文本分类研究[J].中国安全科学学报,2017, 27(8):156-161.

[9] 晋耀红,苗传江.一个基于语境框架的文本特征提取算法[J].计算机研究与发展,2004(4):582-586.

[10] CHENG C W, LIN C C, LEU S S. Use of association rules to explore cause—effect relationships in occupational accidents in the Taiwan construction industry[J]. Safety science,2010,48(4):436-444.

基于 VISSIM 仿真隧道出口与平面交叉小净距路段交通适应性研究

李芷倩　张　驰　胡瑞来

(长安大学)

摘　要　隧道和平面交叉作为道路中的重要组成部分,其合理的净距将直接影响道路交通的运行质量和安全性。通过对道路平面交叉口与隧道净距定义的界定,分析了各种交通条件的影响因素,对隧道出口与平面交叉口路段的净距长度与交通适应性进行了研究。以交通冲突率作为评价指标,分析隧道出口与平面交叉口小净距路段对安全性的主要影响因素,建立相应的计算模型,结果表明:交通量、大型车比例、转向交通量比例、净距长度均可作为隧道与平面交叉小净距路段交通适应性的主要影响因素指标。

关键词　隧道　平面交叉口　净距　交通适应性

0　引　言

近年来随着我国经济的快速发展,我国公路里程也日益增加,各级公路的修建为我国的物资运输和人员来往提供了巨大方便。但在山区地区,隧道和平面交叉作为道路中的重要组成部分,在公路运营阶段,隧道与平面交叉的净距中的交通安全事故愈来愈多,如何考虑隧道与平面交叉的净距是目前的重点问题之一。隧道与平面交叉的净距段作为连接隧道与主要公路的关键部分,考虑到交通流量、车速、车辆组成、是否设置信号灯、车道设置情况等因素,车辆在此路段行驶状况往往更为复杂,与行车安全紧密联系,因此设计时合理地考虑隧道与平面交叉的净距尤为重要。

目前国内外关于隧道与平面交叉净距的交通适应性研究较少,各学者主要是从平面交叉口的交通特性和安全性进行研究。Apostoleris Konstantinos 等人建立了平面交叉口风险关键影响参数的层次结构,提出了碰撞减少系数(CRF)的数学方程;Reid J D 分析了各类交叉口形式的安全特性及改善方法,并强调交叉口的渠化方式及视距的重要性;我国目前关于隧道与平面交叉的净距规范标准主要参考日本规范来制定;《城市地下道路工程设计规范》从行车安全角度规定了城市地下道路出口接地点与地面交叉口的距离:对于信号控制交叉口,最小安全距离不宜小于 1.5 倍停车视距,条件受限时不得小于 1 倍停车视距,但采用理论计算的方法,忽略了左转交通流比例等交通特性对最小安全距离的影响。董爱妹等通过对不同流量下四路环形交叉口现状分析,分别对其进行单、双重信号控制及感应控制,并利用 VISSIM 仿真得出交通量较小时无信号控制优于信号控制,较大时双重信号控制下环形交叉口运行效果最优;刘斌等借助 VISSIM 交通仿真软件,提出了 T 形交叉口的优化信号设计方案,有效地减少了 T 形交叉口车辆延误时间和车辆排队长度;张丽等通过对平面交叉口存在的主要问题进行分析,结合 VISSIM 软件仿真,提出了在交叉口渠化中以信号控制为重点的优化设计方案;谢秋荣针等以单点定时交通控制交叉口为对象,研究了 VISSIM 软件在交通配时优化的应用,证明了 VISSIM 软件在优化交通配时方面的可行性;郑发东等分析了山地城市道路平面交叉口的交通安全状况以及交叉口处的机动车与行人的交通特性,对交叉口处混合交通流的交通冲突特性进行了研究;杨少伟、张弛等人分别从驾驶员在隧道出口处的"明适应"距离、驾驶员识认交通标志距离、车辆变道的行驶距离和安全驶入平面交叉口的距离等方面,分析了各种影响因素,建立了城市道路平面交叉口与隧道合理净距的计算模型,并给出了不同运行速度下城市道路平面交叉口与隧道合理净距的参考值;刘继军以宿松县将军山隧道西侧出洞口与龙湖路交叉口的方案设计为依托,对城市山岭隧道洞口临近交叉口的方案设计进行了具体分析,提出了相应方案;魏澜分析了城市道路平交口与隧道出口安全间距的各种影响因素,提出了不同设计速度道路平交口与隧道出口的最小安全间距值。

目前国内外研究主要都是针对平面交叉口的交通特性和交通安全,少有研究从城市道路隧道与平面交叉口的净距进行研究。其次,在城市道路隧道与平面交叉口的净距研究中,多是考虑隧道与平面交叉口之间的净距长度是否符合规范,而对于隧道与平面交叉口之间的交通特性和交通适应性的考虑有所欠缺。由于隧道交通环境的特殊性,导致隧道安全问题突出,易成为事故多发路段。隧道及其过渡连接段处在两种不同的行车环境下,当驾驶员驾车驶入或驶出隧道时,会因为隧道照明、线形等原因产生各种视觉问题,致使驾驶员对周围环境及道路条件等的判断出现偏差,易造成操作失误。尤其在山岭重丘地区,隧道的线形指标条件受限,交通事故发生的概率更大。现有调查表明:隧道路段事故多发生在进出隧道路段,所以对隧道出口路段的安全状况研究十分重要。因此,为研究隧道出口与平面交叉小净距路段的交通适应性,本文以沿江高速A、B匝道隧道与临海大道的平面交叉口作为依托工程,利用VISSIM仿真软件,选取交通量、大型车比例、转向交通比例、净距长度值作为变量进行正交试验,并进行理论分析,以对隧道出口与平面交叉口小净距路段的交通适应性进行研究。

1 影响因素分析

隧道与平面交叉口净距可定义为隧道洞口至平面交叉口进口道停车线之间的距离。小净距路段为满足驾驶员出隧道后的"明适应距离"、停车视距和红灯期间的车辆排队长度的最小距离的路段。

影响隧道洞口到平面交叉口的距离长短的主要考量依据还是交通安全问题,而分析交通安全事故的原因主要是从分析人、车、路与环境对交通安全事故的影响出发,因此,本文将影响隧道与平面交叉口净距设置的因素总结为以下几点:交通流量、车辆速度、车辆组成、交通流特性、驾驶员视觉特性、驾驶员反应特性、交通指示标志的设置、平交口信号灯相位、车道设置情况等。

本文主要从交通流特性的角度出发,研究不同影响因素下隧道出口与平面交叉口小净距路段的交通适应性。其中,交通量大小直接影响道路上的车辆密度,进而影响道路拥挤程度、行车效率和安全;当交通流中大型车占比大时,干扰增加,行车延误也会随之增大;无论是左转还是右转,在通过交叉路口时,其车速都远低于直行车,势必会造成行车延误,而且转向时交叉口造成的冲突也会影响安全性;车辆驶出隧道后进入平面交叉口前需要对大量道路信息做出判断,如识别交通标志标线、变换车道等,若净距长度设置不当极易引起较大延误和安全问题。

(1)交通量:隧道与平面交叉口之间路段的设计长度会受到交通流量大小的影响,这是由于交通流量与道路长度的比值(即交通密度)可以作为反映一条道路拥挤程度和车辆行驶自由度的一项指标。若设计路段过短则会造成交通密度过大,交通变得拥挤,合理地根据交通流量大小设计隧道与平面交叉之间路段长度,可使路段交通流量均匀分布,同时也能有效地提高安全性。

(2)大型车比例:当交通流中小型车比例较大时,车流的平均速度会相对较高且车速差较小,车辆间互相干扰也较小,通行效率较高。同样当交通流中以大型车为主时,车流平均速度虽低于小型车车流,但其车速差同样较低,车辆间相互干扰较小,通行效率较高。但对于混合行驶的车流,混合行驶的车辆越多,车辆间互相干扰就越大,通行效率也随之降低,所需净距也相对增长。因此车辆组成结构中,小型车和大型车的比例也是影响隧道与平面交叉净距设置的重要因素。

(3)转向交通比例:当平面交叉区域范围转向交通量较大时,在隧道出口与平面交叉口净距段范围内,车辆的换道次数随需要在平面交叉口转向交通量的增大而增大。换道次数的增加,极大地增加了行车风险。

(4)净距长度:当平面交叉与隧道之间的距离过小时,一方面,车辆驶出隧道后进入平面交叉口前驾驶员需要对大量道路信息做出判断,受隧道压抑环境和"黑洞""白洞"的影响,容易产生紧张和急躁情绪,极易在平面交叉口产生意外情况,如在交叉口处犹豫、突然变换车道、紧急制动等,影响了正常行车,严重时会引发追尾等交通事故,影响隧道的正常运营;另一方面,当隧道洞口位于平面交叉口影响范围内时,道路环境更为复杂,驾驶行为与常规路段有较大差异,驾驶员驾驶负荷和心理压力大幅度增加,不利于行车安全。

综合上述分析,本文选取交通量、大型车比例、转向交通比例、净距长度值作为变量进行试验设计,进一步分析各影响因素与隧道出口与平交口交通安全的关系。

1.1 单因素试验设计

目前最常用的统计学方法是先单因素、再多因素的分析方法,即筛选有意义的变量纳入多因素回归模型,形成简洁的分析模型。基于上述影响因素,为清楚地了解到各个交通流特性因素对小净距路段的交通适应性影响程度,进行单因素试验设计。仿真采用的道路设计速度设置为40km/h,双向四车道,车道宽度为3.5m。

预试验是小范围的可行性试验,用于初步探索方向,为试验方案的设计提供依据。通过预试验,对选取的各个影响因素进行合理的分析。通过 VISSIM 仿真,分别获取不同半径圆曲线路段以及不同隧道长度时小净距路段上的延误与交通冲突率,结果见表1。分析可知,隧道长度、道路线形对各评价指标基本不影响。分别在有无信号灯控制两种情况下进行试验,以大型车比例作为变量时为例,交通延误对比如图1所示。通过分析可知,是否有信号控制对各指标的影响趋势均呈线性关系,基本相同。

不同半径圆曲线路段直行延误对比 表1

交通量(veh/h)	大型车比例(%)	速度(km/h)	半径(m)	交通延误(s)
1500	20	50	直线	1.50
1500	20	50	700	1.29

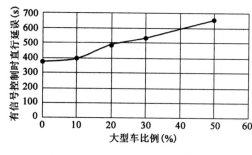 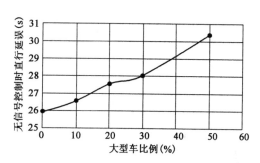

图1 有无信号控制时直行延误对比

基于上述预试验,道路线性对本仿真试验结果不产生影响,故简化设计,采用直线路段,且采用无信号控制的平面交叉口。隧道长度对交通适应性的影响在可忽略的范围内,故隧道长度取1500m。由于转向交通量比例涉及左转、直行和右行,组合较多,为利于试验与统计的进行,本研究将右转向交通量比例定为20%,调整左转与直行交通量的比例进行单变量控制。

其他仿真参数设置如下:洞口明适应长度取50m,即洞口50m外不准变道;主车道为双向四车道,进口道为3车道,渐变段长度取值40m,拓宽段为83m;并设置期望速度分布与减速区。单因素试验设计的仿真策略见表2。

考虑不同参数条件下行车安全分析仿真策略 表2

仿真编号	交通量(veh/h)	大型车比例(%)	左转向交通量比例(%)	净距长度(m)
1	500、800、1200、1500、1800	10	10	260
2	800	0、10、20、30、50	10	260
3	800	10	0、10、20、30、50	260
4	800	10	10	150、260、500、800、1200

1.2 评价指标

在道路安全评价方面,通常采用交通冲突率来表征。交通冲突是指两个或两个以上的交通参与者在时间和空间上相互接近,导致至少一方采取必要避险措施才能保证不发生交通事故的现象。根据现有研究,交通冲突与交通安全成正比关系,道路发生交通事故的可能性越大,道路的交通事故率越高。因此,冲突率可以作为交通安全评价指标,并且能客观准确地反映平面交叉口与隧道区段的安全水平。交通冲突率的计算公式如下:

$$f = \frac{TC}{Q \cdot L} \quad (1)$$

式中:f——冲突率[次/(veh·km)];

TC——小时均冲突次数(次/h);

Q——车辆通过量(veh/h);

L——隧道出口与平面交叉口的净距长度(km)。

而在道路交通流拥挤量化方面,交通延误是较为常用的评价指标。交通延误是指车辆在行驶中,由于受到驾驶员无法控制的或意外的其他车辆的干扰或交通控制设施等的阻碍所损失的时间。不仅反映了道路的通行效率和服务水平,也反映了道路使用者的受阻程度和感受的服务质量,故选用交通延误作为指标进行分析评价。交通延误的计算公式如下:

$$总延误 = 总停驶车辆数 \times 抽样时间间隔(辆 \cdot s) \quad (2)$$

故使用交通延误和交通冲突率两个指标分别表征隧道出口与平面交叉小净距路段的行车效率和行车安全性。

1.3 结果分析

将前文设定的参数代入试验,如图2所示。每一个影响因素对应一组试验,以相关性分析为检验指标,完成各个因素单独变化时的交通适应性评价,选取相关性高的变量纳入模型。

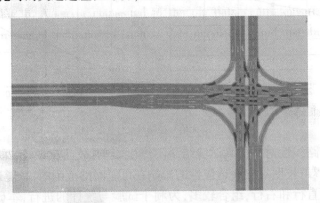

图2 单因素试验仿真运行

1)交通延误分析

通过VISSIM数据分析系统软件对导出的数据进行分析,分别计算各个转向的平均延误。通过仿真数据分析,得到左转、直行和右转的转向延误分别与交通量、大型车比例、转向交通量比例以及净距长度的关系,具体分析结果如图3所示。

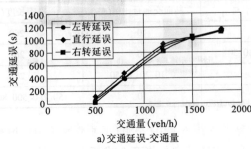

a)交通延误-交通量

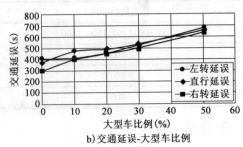

b)交通延误-大型车比例

图 3

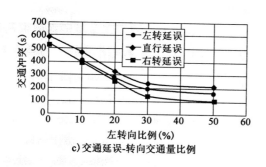
c) 交通延误-转向交通量比例

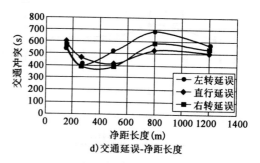
d) 交通延误-净距长度

图3 不同影响因素单独作用下交通延误的变化情况

在图3中,纵坐标为各转向延误时间(s),横坐标分别为交通量、大型车比例、转向交通量比例和净距长度值。上述坐标图分别体现了在不同交通量、大型车比例、转向交通量比例和净距长度值下各转向延误的变化情况。为进一步得到各影响因素与评价指标间的相关性大小,分析各影响因素与交通延误的相关性强度,具体分析结果见表3。

各因素与交通延误的相关性强度　　表3

相关系数		交通量	大型车比例	转向交通量比例	净距长度
延误	左转	0.9745	0.9707	-0.8982	0.5466
	直行	0.9696	0.9849	-0.9309	-0.1212
	右转	0.9785	0.9948	-0.9423	0.3427

对图3a)进行具体分析,随着交通量的逐渐增加,交通延误先是逐渐增加,然后增长速率变缓。两者的相关系数值在0.97~0.98,相关性强度高。对图3b)进行具体分析,大型车比例对于路段各转向交通延误线性相关系数值高达0.99,交通冲突率随交通量的增大呈直线上升的趋势。对图3c)进行具体分析,当驶入平面交叉口后左转交通量比例小于30%时,交通延误的降低速率较快;当该左转交通量比例大于30%时,交通延误的降低速率减小,相对平缓。对图3d)分析可知,随着净距长度的增加,交通延误先是逐渐减小到一定值后增加,再达到峰值后减小。

综合上述分析,交通延误与交通量、大型车比例成正比,与左转向交通量比例成反比,与净距长度值无显著线性关系;结合交通量各因素与交通延误的相关性强度,因此交通量、大型车比例、转向交通量比例可作为隧道与平面交叉小净距路段的主要影响因素指标。

2) 交通冲突率分析

通过SSAM软件对导出的数据进行分析,筛选得出隧道出口与平面交叉小净距路段的交通冲突数据。通过仿真数据分析,得到交通冲突率与交通量、大型车比例、转向交通量比例以及净距长度的关系,具体分析结果如图4所示。

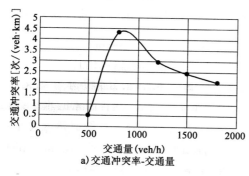
a) 交通冲突率-交通量

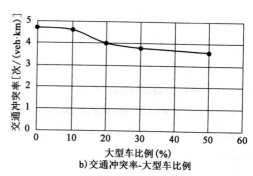
b) 交通冲突率-大型车比例

图 4

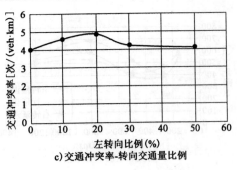
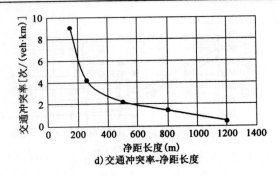

c) 交通冲突率-转向交通量比例　　d) 交通冲突率-净距长度

图4　不同影响因素单独作用下交通冲突率的变化情况

在图4中,纵坐标为交通冲突率[次/(veh.km)],横坐标分别为交通量、大型车比例、转向交通量比例和净距长度值。上述4张坐标图分别体现了在不同交通量、大型车比例、转向交通量比例和净距长度值下,交通冲突率的变化情况。为进一步得到各影响因素与评价指标间的相关性大小,分析各影响因素与交通冲突率的相关性强度,具体分析结果见表4。

各因素与交通延误的相关性强度　　　　　　　　　　表4

相关系数	交通量	大型车比例	转向交通量比例	净距长度
交通冲突率	0.1289	-0.9420	-0.1592	-0.8502

对图4a)进行具体分析,交通量小于800veh/h时,随着交通量的逐渐增加,交通冲突率迅速增加,且增长速率快;当交通量大于800veh/h时,交通冲突率随交通量增长而减小,两者的相关性强度低。对图4b)进行具体分析,大型车比例对于小净距路段的交通冲突率线性相关系数值高达-0.94,交通冲突率随大型车比例的增大呈下降的趋势。对图4c)进行具体分析,当驶入平面交叉口后左转交通量比例在0~20%时,交通冲突率逐渐增长;当该比例大于20%时,交通冲突率反而降低。对于交通冲突,一般而言,随着净距长度的增加,交通冲突数逐渐增加,主要原因在于随着净距长度的增加,车辆换道的次数增加,进而交通冲突数增加。进一步分析图4d)交通冲突率可知,随净距长度的增加,交通冲突率呈逐渐下降的趋势。净距长度小于500m时,交通冲突率较高,且降低速度较快;大于500m时,降低速度则变缓。

综合上述分析,交通冲突率与大型车比例、净距长度值成反比,与交通量、左转向交通量比例无显著线性关系;结合交通量各因素与交通冲突率的相关性强度,因此大型车比例、净距长度可作为隧道与平面交叉小净距路段的主要影响因素指标。

2　评价模型构建

各影响因素在影响小净距路段行车安全性时,并不是完全孤立、没有关联的,且不同因素对车辆行驶的影响程度不会完全相同,必定存在强弱之分。因此,需要进行多因素分析并得到各种因素的影响强弱。而正交试验是最常用的试验设计方法之一,利用它可以科学地安排与分析多因素试验。它能从较多的样本点中,挑选出适量的具有代表性的点,再根据相应的正交表来合理安排试验并进行数据分析。本文选用正交试验法进行多因素分析。

2.1　正交试验设计

正交表则是一种特殊的表格,是安排试验和分析试验结果的基本工具,分为等水平正交表和混合水平正交表(因素的水平数是指因素的取值个数)。本文采用等水平正交表,其各因素的水平数相等,可以记为$L_n(r^m)$,其中L、n、r、m分别表示正交表代号、正交表横行数(需做的试验次数)、因素水平数、正交表纵列数(最多能安排的因素个数)。在设计时,应当根据因素数和水平数来挑选恰当的正交试验表,并保证因素水平数与正交试验表对应的水平数相同,在得到结果后分析并进行显著性检验。

本文对于隧道出口与平面交叉口小净距路段交通适应性研究,拟采用$L_{16}(4^5)$正交表,设计四因素四水平正交试验,因素集为交通量、大型车比例、驶出车辆比例、净距长度,因素水平划分表见表5。

因素水平划分表

表5

因素水平	交通量(veh/h)	大型车比例(%)	转向交通量比例(%)	净距长度(m)
1	250	10	10	100
2	500	20	20	150
3	750	30	30	200
4	1000	50	50	250

仿真参数如下：长隧道中禁止变道、无限速；匝道设计速度为40km/h；隧道出口明适应距离控制为50m，禁止换道，进入隧道前设置50m减速区；期望速度分布调整，按正态分布设置；设置3处检测点，分别位于外侧车道、中间车道、内侧车道，以隧道入口作为起点，完成转向后的车道作为终点采集数据。

正交试验设计表见表6。

正交试验设计表

表6

因素分类		净距长度(m)	交通量(veh/h)	空 列	大型车比例(%)	左转向交通量比例(%)
试验号	1	100	250	1	10	10
	2	100	500	2	20	20
	3	100	750	3	30	30
	4	100	1000	4	50	50
	5	150	250	2	30	50
	6	150	500	1	50	30
	7	150	750	4	10	20
	8	150	1000	3	20	10
	9	200	250	3	50	20
	10	200	500	4	30	10
	11	200	750	1	20	50
	12	200	1000	2	10	30
	13	250	250	4	20	30
	14	250	500	3	10	50
	15	250	750	2	50	10
	16	250	1000	1	30	20

2.2 结果分析

通过SSAM软件对导出的数据进行分析，筛选得出隧道出口与平面交叉小净距路段的交通冲突数据。计算各试验组的交通冲突见表7。

多影响因素作用下交通冲突率的变化情况

表7

试验组	净距长度(m)	交通量(veh/h)	空列	大型车比例(%)	左转向交通量比例(%)	交通冲突率[次/(veh·km)]
1	100	250	1	10	10	0.200
2	100	500	2	20	20	0.480
3	100	750	3	30	30	2.947
4	100	1000	4	50	50	5.680
5	150	250	2	30	50	0.187
6	150	500	1	50	30	0.720
7	150	750	4	10	20	2.471
8	150	1000	3	20	10	4.453
9	200	250	3	50	20	0.300
10	200	500	4	30	10	0.710
11	200	750	1	20	50	0.873

续上表

试验组	净距长度(m)	交通量(veh/h)	空列	大型车比例(%)	左转向交通量比例(%)	交通冲突率[次/(veh·km)]
12	200	1000	2	10	30	1.160
13	250	250	4	20	30	0.208
14	250	500	3	10	50	0.272
15	250	750	2	50	10	0.896
16	250	1000	1	30	20	1.472
K_1	9.3067	0.8947	3.2653	4.1031	6.2593	
K_2	7.8311	2.1820	2.7227	6.0147	4.7231	
K_3	3.0433	7.1871	7.9720	5.3153	5.0347	
K_4	2.8480	12.7653	9.0691	7.5960	7.0120	

将正交试验的结果进行显著性检验,见表 8。由此可得,四个因素对于交通冲突率的影响作用显著性强。其中交通冲突率与交通量和净距长度之间有非常显著的相关性。

显著性检验 表8

因素	离差平方和 SS	自由度	F 值	显著性	临界值
净距长度	0.8182	3	10.46	显著	$F_{0.01}(3,15)=5.42$
交通量	1.8962	3	12.71	显著	$F_{0.01}(3,15)=5.42$
大型车比例	0.0997	3	7.24	显著	$F_{0.01}(3,15)=5.42$
转向交通量比例	0.0695	3	5.85	显著	$F_{0.01}(3,15)=5.42$
误差	0.0782	15		显著	

建立多元线性回归模型,运用试验数据标定模型系数,得到如下表达式:

$$y = -0.0114x_1 + 0.0042x_2 + 0.0208x_3 + 0.0088x_4 \quad (3)$$

式中,x_1 表示净距长度,x_2 表示交通量,x_3 表示大型车比例,x_4 表示左转向交通量比例,各变量的单位与表中一致。

模型的拟合度可以通过主要特征指标与理想值进行比较,结果见表 9,相关系数为 0.85,说明模型中因变量可以被自变量良好解释,该多元线性回归模型的预测准确性良好。

模型拟合优度检验 表9

评价指标	RMSE	SSE	R	R^2	DC
多元线性回归模型	0.83	11.01	0.85	0.73	0.73

3 结 语

随着城市规模的不断扩大,为了提高通行效率,以隧道作为城市道路的情况越来越多。但由于城市路网密集,道路交叉口多,城市隧道出口通常紧邻道路交叉口,存在明显的安全隐患,需要限制隧道出口至道路平交口的最小安全距离。

本文主要以满足车辆行驶的需要为基础,确定了以隧道出口的明适应距离、完整认读标志并完成换道操作的距离、停车视距以及平面交叉口进口道排队长度为隧道出口与平面交叉口净距的组成部分,分析隧道出口与平面交叉口最小净距长度的主要影响因素,建立相应的计算模型,结果表明:交通量、大型车比例、转向交通量比例、净距长度均可作为隧道与平面交叉小净距路段交通适应性的主要影响因素指标,其中交通量、大型车比例、转向交通量比例与交通冲突率呈正比,而净距长度则呈反比。研究结论有助于理解道路的交通流特性影响隧道与平面交叉小净距路段交通适应性的决策机理,在被交路与隧道洞口距离过近时,参考上述研究可确定隧道出口与平面交叉口的合理净距,对于工程设计具有指导意义。本文对隧道出口与平面交叉口的最小净距只从安全性的角度进行了评价,未来还需要进一步从能否满足平面交叉口服务水平进行评价,且在不同运行速度和不同交通适应性等级下,平面交叉口与隧道间合理净距的参考值还有待研究。

参考文献

[1] Apostoleris Konstantinos, Matragos Vassilios, Psarianos Basil, Mavromatis Stergios. Methodology for Risk Ranking of At-Grade Intersections on Existing Rural Two-Lane Highways[J]. Journal of Transportation Engineering, Part A: Systems, 2021, 147(2).

[2] Reid J D, Hummer J E. Travel time comparisons between seven unconventional arterial intersection designs[C/CD]. Washington D. C., 2001.

[3] 中交第一勘察设计研究院. 公路路线设计规范: JTG D20—2017[S]. 北京: 人民交通出版社股份有限公司, 2017.

[4] 上海市政工程设计研究总院有限公司. 城市地下道路工程设计规范: CJJ 221—2015[S]. 北京: 中国建筑工业出版社, 2015.

[5] 董爱妹. 环形交叉口的信号控制及仿真研究[D]. 大连: 大连交通大学, 2012.

[6] 刘斌, 王建蓉. 基于VISSIM的城市道路平面交叉口仿真研究[J]. 甘肃科学学报, 2012, 24(04): 131-134.

[7] 张丽. 基于VISSIM仿真的城市道路交叉口优化设计[J]. 交通标准化, 2012(08): 135-138.

[8] 谢秋荣. 基于VISSIM平台应用技术研究[D]. 西安: 长安大学, 2016.

[9] 郑发东. 山地城市道路平面交叉口交通冲突特性研究[D]. 重庆: 重庆交通大学, 2011.

[10] 张弛, 杨少伟, 潘兵宏. 城市道路平面交叉口与隧道净距研究[J]. 公路交通科技, 2016, 33(10): 137-141.

[11] 刘继军. 城市山岭隧道出口与交叉口距离分析[J]. 科技创新与应用, 2020(12): 57-59.

[12] 魏澜. 城市道路平面交叉口与隧道出口最小安全间距探讨[J]. 福建建筑, 2012(06): 63-64, 62.

[13] 王露. 山地城市隧道出口路段驾驶适宜性技术研究[D]. 重庆: 重庆交通大学, 2017.

[14] 陈长坤, 辛梦阳, 王建军, 等. 高速公路隧道群交通安全影响因素辨识[J]. 黑龙江交通科技, 2015, 38(11): 146-148.

[15] 吴德华. 双车道公路车速标准差与交通冲突相关性研究[J]. 公路工程, 2013, 38(3): 61-63, 82.

[16] 范超. 基于可变指标的城市路网交通状态分析[D]. 南京: 东南大学, 2014.

京津冀区域道路运输燃料清洁化策略研究

宋媛媛　黄全胜　肖杨　王人洁　姜文汐

(交通运输部规划研究院交通排放控制监测技术实验室)

摘　要　京津冀区域是我国人口聚集、经济密集、货运集中的区域, 也是我国大气污染防治的重点区域。本文在总结分析京津冀区域道路运输发展和能源消耗现状的基础上, 结合京津冀区域道路运输的发展需求, 识别了京津冀区域道路运输燃料清洁化面临的瓶颈, 研究了京津冀区域道路运输燃料清洁化的适用技术路线和政策清单, 提出了京津冀区域道路运输燃料清洁化行动建议, 为提高京津冀区域道路运输燃料清洁化水平提供技术支撑和决策参考。

关键词　道路运输　清洁燃料　策略研究　京津冀

基金项目: 2018年度交通运输战略规划政策研究项目; 大气重污染成因与治理攻关项目(No. DQGG0207-03); 国家重点研发计划重点专项(No. 2017YFC0212103)。

0 引言

京津冀区位优势得天独厚，政治文化地位突出，科研力量、产业实力雄厚，是我国交通网络最为密集的地区之一。京津冀区域以全国2.3%的地域面积承载了8.2%的人口，实现了6.5%的货物运输量，单位国土面积完成货运量1.5万t，约是全国平均水平的3倍，是我国最具发展活力的三大经济增长极之一，同时也是我国重要的能源消费中心和大气污染防治的重点区域。京津冀区域产业以重化工为主，货运强度较高，煤炭、矿石、建材等大宗货物公路中短距离运输需求较旺盛。公路运输是京津冀区域的主要运输方式，占比达84.4%，显著高于全国平均水平，其能源消耗量和排放占比一直处于高位，同时清洁化能源使用占比较低。本文结合京津冀区域道路运输发展的现状和需求，梳理京津冀区域道路燃料清洁化适用技术和政策清单，提出京津冀区域道路运输燃料清洁化行动建议，旨在通过提高道路运输车辆清洁化程度，降低道路运输单位能耗和排放强度，促进京津冀区域道路运输行业转型升级，支持京津冀区域打赢蓝天保卫战。

1 京津冀区域道路运输燃料清洁化发展现状

1.1 京津冀道路运输装备清洁化发展现状

京津冀地区是我国经济发展水平较高的地区，经济活动丰富，因此产生较丰富的运输活动。京津冀地区的旅客运输和货物运输均以公路运输为主。2017年京津冀区域的公路货物运输周转量为8454亿吨公里，占全国的13%；公路旅客运输周转量为412亿人公里，占全国的4%。近年来，京津冀区域主要通过在道路运输领域推广应用新能源及清洁燃料运输装备，推进区域道路运输清洁化进程。如北京在2020年8月底已累计推广纯电动车超过35万辆，其中公共领域7.06万辆，约占全国的10%。天津在2018年底，新能源汽车推广规模已经达到11.78万辆，位居全国单一城市前五位。河北省在2019年底新能源汽车保有量超13万辆，居全国第11位。

京津冀区域新能源和清洁燃料汽车在公共交通领域有较快发展。如表1和图1所示，京津冀区域的天然气、电动车等清洁能源公共交通车辆有近5万辆，占整个公共交通车队的73%。

2017年京津冀公共汽电车分燃料类型数量   表1

类别	合计	北京	天津	河北
合计	69567	24076	13813	31678
汽油车	1078	—	180	898
乙醇汽油车	20	—	—	20
柴油车	17591	7982	6678	2931
液化石油气车	2	—	—	2
天然气车	19137	8583	719	9835
双燃料车	971	—	—	971
无轨电车	1326	1326	—	—
纯电动车	24351	5318	3678	15355
混合动力车	2012	862	2558	1592
其他	79	5	—	74

1.2 京津冀道路运输能源消耗现状

根据统计年鉴，京津冀区域的交通运输与仓储、邮政业的能源消耗情况见表2。2017年北京市交通运输、仓储和邮政业的能源消费总量为1386.78万吨标准煤，占全市能耗消费的19.4%；天津市交通运输、仓储和邮政业的能源消费总量为549.46万吨标准煤，占全市能耗消费的7.03%；河北省交通运输、仓储和邮政业的能源消费总量为1215万吨标准煤，占全市能耗消费的4.00%。从能源结构来看，柴油、汽油、燃料油等化石能源是交通部门主要的能源品种，近年来消耗明显攀升。京津冀区域交通运输与仓储、邮政业汽油、煤油、柴油消费量约占全省（市）能源消费总量的11.7%、99.9%、49.1%。近年来交通部门天然气、电力等清洁能源消费量有所增加，如液化天然气消费占比达76.6%，电力占比约3.7%。

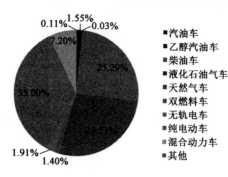

图1　2017年京津冀公共汽电车分燃料类型占比

2017年京津冀交通运输部门能源消费量及占比　表2

能源类别	合　　计	交通运输、仓储和邮政业	占全市总能耗的比重(%)
能源消费总量(万吨标准煤)	45337.57	3151.24	7.0
煤(万t)	9089.83	14.41	0.2
汽油(万t)	1254.34	147.25	11.7
煤油(万t)	773.03	771.97	99.9
柴油(万t)	1248.22	612.72	49.1
燃料油(万t)	84.11	47.91	57.0
液化石油气(万t)	145.22	1.8	1.2
液化天然气(万t)	43.25	33.12	76.6
天然气(亿m³)	301.79	8.76	2.9
热力(万百万千焦)	77937.4	1424.7	1.8
电力(亿千瓦时)	5247.57	196.31	3.7

　　京津冀区域的道路运输分能源品种的消耗现状较难计算，但该区域的公共汽电车数据相对翔实。因此，以京津冀区域的公共汽电车为例进行不同燃料类型车辆消耗能源的核算。采用以保有量和行驶里程为活动水平的能耗计算方法，计算得到京津冀区域的公共汽电车能耗量，结果见表3。总体来看，京津冀区域的公共交通能源消耗以柴油、天然气和电力为主，基本各占1/3。北京和天津的公共汽电车中柴油消耗量最大，占比分别为44%和72%；河北的公共汽电车中天然气和电力占比较大，分别为35%和42%。

2017年京津冀公共汽电车能源消耗量(万吨标准煤)　表3

燃料类别	北　京	天　津	河　北	京津冀区域合计
汽油	0.0	0.5	2.3	2.8
柴油	25.0	24.2	14.0	63.2
乙醇	0.0	0.0	0.1	0.1
天然气	21.9	1.8	25.1	48.8
电力	10.3	7.1	29.8	47.2
合计	57.2	33.6	71.1	161.9

　　根据前文分析，目前京津冀道路运输领域采用清洁能源的比重仍较低。分析原因主要有以下方面：一是道路运输车辆核心技术有待突破。尽管近年来新能源小型乘用车和轻型物流车技术逐步成熟，但在重型货车领域，短期内仍缺乏成熟的清洁燃料解决方案。二是政策针对性有效性有待加强。目前京津冀

区域新能源和清洁燃料车辆的推广政策主要集中在原则性的规划使用政策,个别城市出台了补贴政策,这些政策的针对性不强,无法有效保障新能源和清洁燃料车辆的大力推广。三是配套产业链条有待完善。目前整个新能源和清洁燃料汽车产业链条仍存在短板,如京津冀区域的电动车充电基础设施供不应求,无法满足日益增长的充电需求,后续专业化的维修保养能力仍需进一步提升等。

2 京津冀区域道路运输燃料清洁化适用技术研究

推广应用新能源和清洁燃料车辆是道路运输燃料清洁化最重要的手段,考虑到不同燃料类型车辆技术的成熟度、推广应用潜力等,本文重点选取天然气、纯电动、插电式混合动力以及氢燃料电池汽车进行分析。

2.1 道路运输燃料清洁化主要技术比较

通过分析天然气车辆、纯电动车辆以及氢燃料车辆的技术现状、政策现状、应用现状以及发展趋势,可以判断,不同燃料类型的车辆在交通运输各子领域的适用性不同,运用的时间早晚与规模大小会存在差异。例如,天然气汽车应用时间较长,技术较为成熟,续驶里程长,但会存在改装车辆尾气排放不达标问题;混合动力汽车能够大幅降低油耗,不需要大规模的充电基础设施;纯电动汽车实现了不烧油、零污染,缺点是续驶里程短,充电时间长,适用于市区短途轻载运输。氢燃料电池汽车续驶里程长、载重能力强、加注时间短,更适用于长途中重载运输。

从技术成熟度来看,目前天然气车辆的技术较为成熟,但符合最新排放标准的天然气车辆尾气后处理装置较为复杂,后期维修保养成本较高;纯电动和混合动力汽车随着近年来的规模化应用,技术成熟度逐步提升,但动力电池的稳定性、可靠性、安全性仍需要进一步提升;氢燃料电池汽车的示范应用有力地推动了燃料电池动力系统、关键零部件的技术进步,但仍需进一步提升燃料电池电堆性能与比功率、提高寿命、降低成本。

从燃料供给保障来看,目前天然气加气站基本能满足城市、城际客货运输需求,但在冬季天然气供应紧张时局部地区难以保障;电动汽车的充、换电站近年来大规模建设,但在部分地区仍难以满足充换电需求;氢燃料电池汽车在氢的制取、储运、加氢等方面刚刚起步,目前尚不具备规模化应用的条件。

从当前动力系统成本来看,燃料电池汽车适合长里程、高负荷的车型。在当前补贴的情境下,燃料电池汽车的总成本明显高于传统燃油车、天然气车和新能源车;随着新能源汽车购置补贴的下降、燃料电池汽车技术进步带来成本的下降,燃料电池汽车与传统燃油车和纯电动汽车的成本差距逐步缩小。天然气汽车使用的经济性主要取决于油气价格比。

不同燃料类型车辆特点及适用性比较见表4。

不同燃料类型车辆特点及适用性比较 表4

车辆燃料类型	成本情况	尾气排放情况	优缺点	适用领域
天然气汽车	使用经济性取决于油气价格比	存在改装车辆尾气排放不达标问题	技术成熟、续驶里程长、加注方便	适用领域广泛,城市公交、出租。城际客运、货运
纯电动汽车	补贴退坡直至取消,成本不具备优势	终端零排	续驶里程短,充电时间长	出租车、城市配送等市区短途轻载运输
混合动力汽车	补贴退坡直至取消,成本不具备优势	尾气排放相较于燃油汽车有所降低	不需要大规模的充电基础设施	过渡性产品,主要在公路客运等领域应用
氢燃料电池汽车	目前购置成本、燃料成本较高,不具备商业化发展条件	终端零排	续驶里程长、载重能力强、加注时间短	长途中重载运输

2.2 京津冀区域道路运输燃料清洁化技术路径

统筹考虑国家发展战略和汽车技术变革趋势,结合京津冀地区能源供给、机动车保有量结构、社会发

展实际情况和需求,研究设定以下技术路线:

(1)新能源汽车作为近期和中长期、全领域重点应用产品。其中,纯电动汽车作为主流产品,主要覆盖城市公交车、出租车、物流配送等领域;插电式/增程式混合动力汽车作为近中期可选方案,主要在公路客运等领域应用。

(2)天然气汽车作为近中期可选方案,在当前相关领域新能源汽车产品尚未完全满足市场化应用需求情况下,主要应用于城乡客运车、长途中重卡车等中大型车辆和中长距离的客货运输等车辆。

(3)燃料电池汽车作为未来发展的重要技术路线,近期重点针对公交车、商用车、中重型货车等领域开展示范运营,待技术更加成熟、成本进一步降低、燃料供应更加充足后再全面推广应用,并逐步扩大至其他车用领域。

基于上述研究,综合考虑到不同燃料类型车辆技术的成熟度、优缺点、燃料供应、成本情况、推广应用潜力等,经过专家咨询和综合研判,重点选取天然气、纯电动、插电式混合动力以及氢燃料电池汽车等作为京津冀区域道路运输燃料清洁化的主要车辆技术,提出其在"十四五"期的技术路线图(图2)。

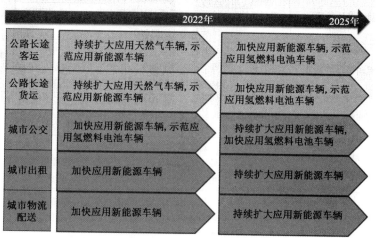

图2 京津冀区域道路运输燃料清洁化技术路线图

3 京津冀区域道路运输燃料清洁化政策清单

道路运输燃料清洁化完全依靠市场行为近期内无法实现,必须依托一套多样化的政策手段来推动,本文对现有政策进行梳理,从现有政策延续、现有政策优化、创新探索政策等层面,提出京津冀区域道路运输清洁化的政策清单和执行建议。

3.1 道路运输燃料清洁化现行政策

3.1.1 制定战略规划

国务院在2012年发布了《节能与新能源汽车产业发展规划(2012—2020年)》,国务院办公厅在2020年又印发了《新能源汽车产业发展规划(2021—2035年)》,从国家层面上为新能源汽车产业的发展指明了方向。在地方层面上,各省市陆续出台了新能源汽车发展的中长期规划以及配套基础设施建设专项规划。京津冀区域的多个省市也相继颁布了或启动了新能源和清洁能源汽车发展规划,有力推动了新能源和清洁能源汽车的推广和应用。

3.1.2 完善财政补贴

从2010年开始,国家层面出台了一系列的政策,从整体指导性和方向性对新能源汽车的发展和推广应用进行了定位。国家层面和有关部委先后出台了30余项支持和激励政策,有关新能源和清洁能源车辆的发展规划、充电站基础设施建设和相关指导意见,对社会投资也起到了积极的引导作用。与此同时,各省市也相继出台了地方的补贴支持政策。

3.1.3 创新路权优惠

在应用方面,各省市也相继出台了地方配套支持政策,主要是从落实新能源车辆号牌管理,给予新能源车辆通行权优惠政策等方面。自2016年12月1日起,深圳已率先试点启用了新能源汽车专用号牌,2017年11月起,北京、上海等10个城市陆续启用新能源车辆专用号牌。为推动新能源车辆在城市物流配送领域的应用,北京、深圳、成都、武汉等地均制定了一系列政策措施落实新能源物流配送车的通行权。

3.2 京津冀区域道路运输清洁化适用政策

区域道路运输清洁化过程中,需要技术和政策的双向作用,目前从国家到地方已相继出台了部分政策措施,推动各地的运输装备清洁化转变。但从政策的针对性、区域的联动性等方面来看,目前京津冀区域道路运输燃料清洁化的政策体系还有待完善。根据前文分析,初步提出道路运输领域清洁化各项政策的主要内容及推广建议等,见表5。

道路运输清洁化政策建议清单　　表5

政策清单		政策属性	执行建议
燃油经济性和排放性能改进政策	渐次提升燃油品质	现行延续	实时开展燃油供应的技术经济性研究,并根据京津冀区域大气污染防控要求和社会经济发展水平,分区域、分层次渐次提升京津冀区域车用汽柴油标准
	提升机动车排放标准	现行延续	对现有政策进行推广和加强。以北京、天津及石家庄等通道城市为重点,分区域分阶段逐步推广、渐次推进,逐步在京津冀全区域执行更为严格的机动车排放标准
	柴油货车治理措施	现行延续	在《柴油货车污染治理攻坚战行动计划》框架下,细化现有政策要求。京津冀各区域分别按实际情况和要求制定和落实柴油货车治理措施
	交通领域"能效领跑者"制度	创新探索	对既有政策在交通领域创新使用。针对北京、天津和河北省的交通领域重点用能企业开展实施能效领跑者制度试点,开展能效考核,支持交通用能单位开展节能降碳过程改造,逐步推动汽柴油车辆的能效提升
	基于油耗的税收优惠政策	创新探索	逐步取消现有新能源汽车车辆购置税免税政策,研究实施基于油耗的税收优惠政策,并根据油耗调整建立优惠政策动态调整机制
	碳市场政策	创新探索	根据北京等碳交易试点城市的交通运输领域碳交易进展,积极开展交通运输领域碳排放核算方法与标准及配额分配方法的修订工作,逐步完善交通运输碳交易顶层设计方案。鼓励交通企业通过市场交易促进节能减排成本最优化
新能源及清洁燃料汽车	完善区域清洁燃料汽车发展规划	现有延续	建议结合京津冀一体化发展背景下,产业结构和人口布局在空间上的发展预测,从京津冀区域尺度制定新能源和清洁能源车辆的中长期发展规划
	清洁能源和新能源汽车的财政补贴政策	现有政策优化	优化补贴目标,制定可操作的财政补贴政策;加大对氢燃料为主的燃料电池乘用车关键技术开发的财政补贴;制定和完善对新能源公交车、物流车的运营补贴;支持充换电等基础设施建设补贴;完善新能源汽车的保险服务体系
	完善车辆分类通行管控政策	现有政策优化	在京津冀重点区域制定和完善新能源和清洁能源车的通行管控政策;以雄安新区、张家口市域和2022冬奥会北京赛区或特定通道划定低排放交通示范区;选择特定货运通道开展绿色货运通道试点等
	差异化收费政策	创新探索	利用价格机制促进道路运输领域清洁化转型,对区域内新能源和清洁能源车辆实行高速公路差异化收费、停车差异化收费政策
	低排放区政策	创新探索	以雄安新区、张家口市域和2022冬奥会北京赛区或特定通道划定低排放交通示范区,针对运输装备设定污染物和温室气体排放限值
	交通运输天然气大用户直供政策	创新探索	建议京津冀区域道路运输企业成立天然气道路运输企业联盟,协调天然气供应企业签订量价互保协议,成为天然气供应企业的大用户,享受天然气直供的便利与低价

4 京津冀区域道路运输燃料清洁化行动建议

本文按照"中心城市引领、南北两极带动、区域协同发展"的思路,统筹考虑区域发展不平衡的实际情况和差异化的现实需求,提出在京津冀区域开展道路运输燃料清洁化的专项行动。综合运用政策、技术手段,提升区域环境本底优良城市道路运输燃料清洁化水平、降低区域大气污染严重城市道路运输装备排放、优化区域综合实力领先城市道路运输燃料消费结构。

一是在重点区域先行先试。综合考虑不同地区的发展基础、资源禀赋特征,鼓励探索差异化发展路径。遴选出北京、天津、张家口、石家庄、邯郸等典型城市作为重点发展的试点城市,在新能源和清洁燃料汽车推广、充电加气基础设施布局建设、电力资源配置、租赁运营管理、政府治理措施等方面,创新建立成体系的标准规范导则,打造区域内样板,形成典型案例和可复制模式。

二是在北京、天津着力打造"城市生产物资绿色运输示范区"。采用清洁的运输方式运送砂石集料等矿建物资,打造大型城市生产物资绿色运输示范区。推动砂石集料等矿建物资在市内通过"铁路市内远距离运输+新能源重卡接驳"的全过程零排放绿色运输,鼓励砂石集料等矿建物资市内短途运输及接驳使用结构多元的新能源和清洁燃料车辆,包括纯电动、混合动力、氢燃料电池车辆以及国六排放标准的天然气和柴油车辆。制定资金激励政策鼓励采用公铁联运模式和新能源货车,在重污染天气对采用绿色运输的矿山企业实施限产豁免。

三是在张家口着力打造"氢燃料电池汽车运营示范区"。充分发挥张北地区可再生能源优势,建设氢燃料电池汽车运营示范区。重点在公交车、城市物流车、中重型货车等领域开展氢燃料电池汽车示范运营,创建零排放公交车队、零排放货运车队。在氢气供给、储运和加氢站建设运营,以及燃料电池汽车示范运营等方面制定相应的管理和政策保障措施,在加氢设施建设、示范运营、测试开发、应用评价等细分领域走在全国前列。

四是在石家庄、邯郸着力打造"清洁货运特色示范区"。加快推动新能源车辆在货运领域的应用。推进工业、物流、城市配送等企业车辆结构升级,提高物流园区、工业园区、机场、铁路货场等新能源作业车辆比例。加快完善充电基础设施,在物流集散地建设集中式充电桩和快速充电桩,为承担物流配送的新能源车辆在城市通行提供便利。在中心城区开展城市纯电动轻型物流配送车辆示范工程。在矿山、钢铁、煤炭等短途运输领域开展电动重卡示范,实现场内运输电动化。鼓励开展车电分离、电池租赁、整车租赁等新型商业模式探索,通过运营补贴、优惠电价、专项购置补贴等方式,对运营企业给予支持。

5 结　语

本文系统梳理了道路运输燃料清洁化的适用技术,分析了各类技术的优缺点和适用领域,并在京津冀区域现有政策的基础上,从现有政策延续、现有政策优化、创新探索政策等层面提出了区域道路运输燃料清洁化政策清单。通过适用技术和政策清单的研究,形成技术+政策的矩阵式组合行动方案。综合考虑不同地区的发展基础、资源禀赋特征,研究提出了鼓励京津冀区域城市探索差异化的道路运输燃料清洁化发展路径,并针对京津冀区域不同的城市,分类提出开展道路运输燃料清洁化的行动建议。

参考文献

[1] 国务院. 国务院关于印发打赢蓝天保卫战三年行动计划的通知(国发[2018]22号)[EB/OL]. http://www.gov.cn/zhengce/content/2018-07/03/content_5303158.htm.

[2] 生态环境部. 关于印发《柴油货车污染治理攻坚战行动计划》的通知(环大气[2018]179号)[EB/OL]. http://www.mee.gov.cn/xxgk2018/xxgk/xxgk03/201901/t20190104_688587.html.

[3] 国务院. 中共中央 国务院印发《交通强国建设纲要》(2019)[EB/OL]. http://www.gov.cn/zhengce/2019-09/19/content_5431432.htm.

[4] 国务院. 国务院办公厅关于印发推进运输结构调整三年行动计划(2018—2020年)的通知(国办发[2018]91号)[EB/OL]. http://www.gov.cn/gongbao/content/2018/content_5335366.htm.

[5] 王军方,丁焰,尹航,等. 京津冀及周边柴油货车污染防治路径研究[J]. 环境保护,2019,47(20):12-15.

[6] 丁焰,王军方,尹航. 京津冀地区机动车污染防治重点及建议[J]. 环境保护,2018,46(19):20-24.

[7] 谭晓雨,王人洁,闫琰,等. 京津冀地区货运车辆能源环境影响分析[J]. 环境影响评价,2019,240(03):44-49.

[8] 刘莹. 实施"公转铁"结构转型:北京探索3种砂石骨料绿色运输模式[J]. 商用汽车,2020,352(04):84-86.

[9] 杨春雷,马冰. 关于砂石骨料绿色供应链的调研与思考[J]. 铁路采购与物流,2019,149(02):53-55.

基于PK-means算法的菜鸟驿站JDC选址研究

杜渐 刘宇畅 戴明 邢宏伟

(交通运输信息安全中心有限公司)

摘要 JDC的选址在终端配送过程中占有极为重要的地位,通过合理规划JDC的覆盖范围,可以使总成本(包括固定成本、运输成本和罚款成本)最小化。以重庆大学城终端配送实际场景为例,提出一种结合局部搜索和惩罚的改进的PK-means算法,解决JDC位置问题。研究成果可以用于帮助减少公路货运车辆的数量,降低物流业的终端配送成本,促进终端配送系统中的联合配送模式效率提升。

关键词 终端配送 JDC 位置选址 PK-means算法

0 引言

随着电子商务的发展,快递业对终端配送业务的需求急剧增长,形如菜鸟驿站的共配网点应运而生。终端配送是物流行业涉及的仓、储、转、运四个过程中花销最高、效率提升最为困难的环节,其涉及的大量货运需求对配送效率提出了极高的要求。为解决终端配送问题,联合配送中心(JDC, Joint Delivery Center)的概念应运而生,JDC可以提供物流活动,例如分拣、仓储和定制包装等服务,合理的JDC选址可以使得货运车辆更加集中地配送邻近区域的几家驿站,从而有效减少货运车辆数量及运送时间,降低道路运输成本,整体提升末端配送效率。

本文主要贡献如下:①定义菜鸟驿站覆盖范围的JDC的半径;②根据固定成本、运输成本和罚款成本建立选址模型;③设计了结合局部搜索和惩罚的改进PK-means算法以确定JDC的最佳位置。

1 联合配送与成本研究

1.1 传统JDC简介

当前,从分中心运送到各个驿站的配送路线多采用直接分配的形式,要求大量装载部分车辆,在占用更多道路资源的同时还会造成更大的环境污染,直接分配的模式如图1a)所示。JDC通过一定算法进行规划,将大范围的驿站划分为多个以驿站组合起来的小型区域,配送车辆在配送时只需配送邻近的几个驿站即可。图1b)展示了联合配送的概念。

在传统的JDC定位问题的研究中,大多仅客观地考虑路线距离、运输成本等因素,很少将各驿站的自身情况,包括收发件数量、以往信用问题等纳入考虑范围。通过引进惩罚机制,将"惩罚"标记作为评价选址合理性的要素之一解决上述问题。假设每个JDC都有一个覆盖半径,该半径由各驿站与JDC之间的地理空间距离决定。有一些驿站由于过去的信用问题诸如派件延迟、服务态度恶劣等因素会被标记为

"惩罚",被惩罚的驿站将由自己负责配送及返回。

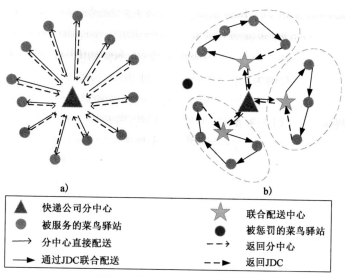

图1 直接配送与联合配送示例

1.2 成本关系

物流系统总成本主要包括固定成本和运输成本,这与JDC的数量和位置有关。固定成本与JDC的数量呈线性关系,增加JDC的数量以提高分配效率,还是减少JDC的数量以实现规模经济,是设施选址问题中的关键问题。

为确保联合分配策略的获利能力,每个JDC都有一个覆盖半径。覆盖半径影响JDC的利润率。利润率是联合配送服务产生的营业收入与成本之比,由式(1)表示。营业收入与JDC的产能利用率成正比,运输成本与JDC的覆盖半径成正比,在式(2)中定义。如果利润率大于1,则覆盖半径范围在(R_1,R_2)之内。覆盖半径$R*$表示JDC的利润率达到最大值,当JDC达到收支平衡时,覆盖半径用式(3)表示。罚款成本是指因信用等问题需要自行支付的配送费用,它与驿站的货运需求成比例,在式(4)中定义。

$$E = \frac{Q \times \theta \times b}{f + c} \tag{1}$$

$$c = \delta R \tag{2}$$

$$R = \frac{Q \times \theta \times b - f}{\delta} \tag{3}$$

$$p = \lambda q \tag{4}$$

式中,Q为JDC的容量,θ为产能利用率,b为产能的单位利润,f为开设JDC的固定成本,c为运输成本,δ为单位运输成本,R为JDC的覆盖半径,p为罚款成本,q为驿站的快件需求。

2 选址模型构建

2.1 模型条件

在此模型中,有m个潜在的JDC和n个驿站,联合配送由第三方物流公司提供,总成本包括开设JDC的固定成本,向驿站提供联合配送服务的运输成本,以及因信用问题产生的自行运输罚款。

为了便于建模,做出了以下几种假设:
(1)JDC向驿站提供一种通用产品;
(2)给出驿站位置、货运需求和以往信用评价;
(3)JDC在不同位置的固定成本相同;
(4)信用不良的驿站将被罚款;
(5)JDC向多个驿站提供通用产品,驿站只能从一个JDC接收通用产品;

(6) JDC 和驿站之间的路况和单位运输成本相同;
(7) JDC 的容量满足驿站的货运需求;
(8) JDC 的辐射范围具有约束半径。

(1)~(4)用于简化模型,(5)~(6)用于确保从 JDC 运送到驿站的货物的单一来源,(7)~(8)用于限制 JDC 的服务能力。

2.2 定义和符号描述

表1给出了指标,集合,参数和决策变量。

模型中使用的符号 表1

类型	符号	解释
标识	i	驿站标识,$i=1,2,\cdots,n$
	j	JDC 标识,$j=1,2,\cdots,n$
设定	I	驿站,$|I|=n, i\in I$
	I_j	被 JDC 配送的驿站
	I_p	被惩罚驿站
	J	JDC
参数	c_{ij}	驿站 i 到 JDC j 的交通成本
	f_j	运营一个 JDC 的固定成本
	X_i	驿站 i 选址
	Y_j	JDC j 选址
	l_{ij}	驿站 i 和 JDC j 之间的路径长度 $l_{ij}=(1.5-\varepsilon_{ij})\|X_i-Y_j\|$
	p_i	未配送驿站产生的罚款,$p_i=\lambda q_i$
	q_i	驿站 i 的货物需求
	Q_j	JDC j 的供给能力
	γ_j	JDC j 的辐射覆盖范围 $\gamma_j=\dfrac{Q_j\times\theta_j\times b-f_j}{\delta}$
	λ	单位罚款成本
	δ	单位运输成本
决策变量	x_{ij}	二进制变量,当 JDC j 服务驿站 i 为1,否则为0
	y_j	二进制变量,当 JDC j 开放时为1,否则为0
	z_i	二进制变量,当驿站被惩罚时为1,否则为0

2.3 目标功能和约束

模型的目标是:应该将哪些位置设置为 JDC;JDC 服务哪些驿站、不提供哪些驿站使总成本最小化,如式(5)所示。

$$\min C = \min \sum_{j=1}^{m} f_j y_j + \sum_{i=1}^{n}\sum_{j=1}^{m} c_{ij} x_{ij} + \sum_{j=1}^{n} p_i z_i \tag{5}$$

模型限制如下:

$$\sum_{i=1}^{n} x_{ij} + \sum_{i=1}^{n} z_i = 1, \forall j \in J \tag{6}$$

$$x_{ij} \leq y_j, \forall i\in I, j\in J \tag{7}$$

$$\sum_{j=1}^{m} y_j \leq k \tag{8}$$

$$\sum_{i=1}^{n} q_i x_{ij} \leq Q_j y_j, \forall j\in J \tag{9}$$

$$l_{ij}x_{ij} \leq \gamma_j, \forall i \in I, j \in J \quad (10)$$

$$x_{ij}=1, i \in I_j; x_{ij}=0, i \notin I_j, \forall j \in J \quad (11)$$

$$y_j=1, j \in \overline{J}; y_j=0, j \notin \overline{J}, \forall j \in J \quad (12)$$

$$z_i=1, i \in I_p; z_i=0, i \notin I_p \quad (13)$$

$$I_j \cup I_p = I, \forall i \in I, j \in J \quad (14)$$

式(5)为包括运输成本、固定成本和罚款成本在内的总成本,运输成本和固定成本是终端配送的既有支出,罚款成本是筛选 JDC 的指标之一;式(6)确保驿站得到服务或受到惩罚;式(7)保证已存在的 JDC 可以为它提供驿站;式(8)限制了 JDC 的数量,式(9)限制了 JDC 的容量,约束(10)限制了 JDC 的覆盖范围,式(11)~(13)表示决策变量的0-1属性,式(14)代表驿站之间的关系。

3 PK-means 算法介绍

3.1 算法说明

PK-means 算法是在传统 K-means 算法的基础上,结合了局部搜索和惩罚指数改进得到的算法。式(15)中的函数用作 PK-means 算法的簇准则。

$$\min \sum_{i \in J} \sum_{j \in J} (1.5 - \varepsilon_{ij}) ||X_i - Y_j|| \quad (15)$$

PK-means 算法具有有效的迭代性能和快速的收敛速度,PK-means 算法和带惩罚的局部搜索的过程如图2所示。

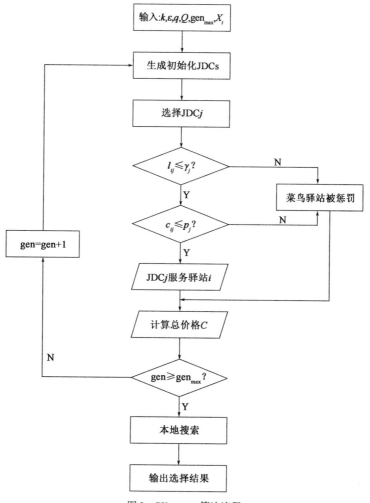

图2 PK-means 算法流程

3.2 选择初始集群中心

PK-means 算法中两个最重要的事项是 k 值的确定和初始聚类中心的选择。k 值表示位于研究范围内的 JDC 数量。它由驿站的食品材料总需求和式(16)中 JDC 的供应能力决定。

$$k = \sum_{i=1}^{n} \frac{q_i}{Q \times \varphi} \tag{16}$$

式中,φ 是用于将 k 的值调整为整数的参数,范围为 0~1。

为了获得散乱的初始聚类中心并避免算法的局部优化,使用联合分布距离来限制初始聚类中心之间的距离,该距离由式(17)计算。

$$\gamma = \sqrt{\frac{S}{k\pi}} \tag{17}$$

式中,S 代表研究区域的面积。

选择初始聚类中心的步骤如下:

步骤1:在研究区域中随机选择一个点作为第一个聚类中心,以加入初始 JDC 集合。

步骤2:随机选择另一个点,并计算从该点到最后一个聚类中心的欧几里得距离。如果该距离大于 γ,则将该点视为第二个 JDC;否则,该点为第二个 JDC。否则,请选择另一个点,直到初始 JDC 的数量达到 k。

3.3 集群和迭代

集群和迭代算法步骤如下。

步骤1:计算罚款成本 p_i,从驿站 i 到最近的 JDC j 的阻抗距离 l_{ij} 以及运输成本 c_{ij}。如果 l_{ij} 小于 j 并且 c_{ij} 小于 p_i,则 JDC j 将为驿站 i 提供服务。否则,驿站将受到惩罚。

步骤2:依据式(5)计算总价格;

步骤3:确定迭代次数是否达到最大值。如果不是,返回步骤1继续进行迭代。

3.4 本地搜索

最快的下降策略用于在局部搜索操作的邻域中选择最佳解。解 P 的邻域定义 Neighbour(P)。该策略旨在找到满足 P 的解 P',$P' = \arg \max(C(P) - C(P'))$。这就意味着在任何属于 $P' \in \text{Neighbor}(P)$ 的情况下 $C(P) < C(P')$。本地搜索的一次交换操作用于交换集群中心的进出。

4 案例实践

以重庆大学城的菜鸟驿站为例,大学城区域共有菜鸟驿站83家,每日派件量4万件左右,揽件量1千件左右,在学生开学、毕业等特殊时期快递件数更会成倍增长。JDC 接下来将在重庆大学城驿站的实验场景下开展对 PK-means 算法的应用。

首先确定迭代次数取值,预设参数如下:$f = 15000$,$Q = 5000$,$b = 0.2$,$\delta = 0.1$,$\lambda = 0.05$,$k = 4$,迭代次数最大值设为 100。图 3a)显示了不同迭代次数下的总成本,可以看到当迭代次数大于 80 次时,总成本的值是稳定的。结合局部搜索的 PK-means 算法具有较快的收敛速度和最优解,可以避免分类错误,保证聚类结果的准确性。

图 3b)显示了不同 k 值下的总成本,当 k 为 4 时总成本达到最小值。

通过传统 K-means 算法和 PK-means 算法对重庆大学城部分网点模拟,在图 4 中展示了 JDC 的位置与各驿站的聚类结果,经过模拟定位了 4 个 JDC 同时又划分了 5 类驿站。其中黄色星形为 JDC 选址,红色的定位标识被惩罚的驿站,另外四类颜色的点代表被 4 个 JDC 服务的驿站。

通过实验比较,PK-means 算法在平均聚类内距离的指标以及平均集群间距离等方面都有一定提升,详细信息见表 2。可以看出 PK-means 算法的聚类结果可以使同一聚类内的相似度最大,而不同聚类之间的相似度最小。

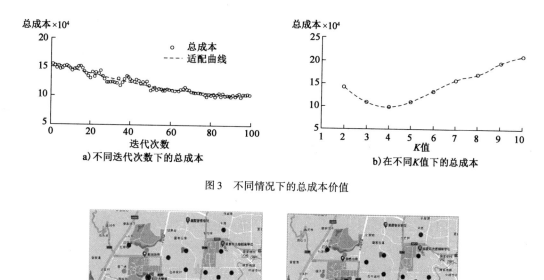

图 3　不同情况下的总成本价值

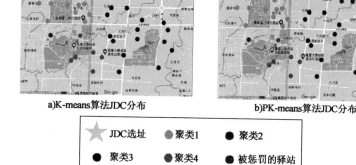

图 4　K-means 算法与 PK-means 算法下 JDC 的分布

两种算法的评价指标比较　　　　　　　　　　　　　　　　　　　　　表 2

	平均集群间距离	平均聚类内距离
K-means 算法	0.784	0.615
PK-means 算法	0.923	0.528
变化率	15.1%	14.1%

5　结　语

本文提出一种新的选址问题模型以及 PK-means 算法,可以降低终端配送的总成本,提高物流效率,增加联合配送模式的潜在市场,降低物流业的运输成本,为其他行业的 JDC 选址问题提供指导。

在实际应用中,JDC 的位置问题比本文构建的模型要更复杂。后续可以在不确定的环境中结合快件需求,在模型中引入诸如驾驶员的付款和路线规划等其他可变制约条件,为 JDC 选址模型的构建增加新的维度,使该模型更加贴近现实业务结构。

参考文献

[1] Yuyang Zhou, Ruxin Xie, Tianhui Zhang, et al. Joint Distribution Center Location Problem for Restaurant Industry Based on Improved K-Means Algorithm With Penalty[J]. IEEE Access, 2020, 8:37746-37751.

[2] Z Wang. Delivering meals for multiple suppliers: Exclusive or sharing logistics service, [J]. Logistics

[3] Y He, X Wang, Y Lin, et al. Sustainable decision making for joint distribution center location choice[J]. Transp Environ, 2017, 55: 202-216.

[4] M Musavi, A Bozorgi-Amiri. A multi-objective sustainable hub location-scheduling problem for perishable food supply chain[J]. Comput, 2017, 113: 766-778.

[5] X Wu, L Nie, M Xu. Aperishable food supply chain problem considering demand uncertainty and time deadline constraints: Modeling and application to a high-speed railway catering service[J]. Logistics Transp, 2018, 111: 186-209.

[6] J-F Audy, S D'Amours, L-M Rousseau. Erratum: Cost allocation in the establishment of a collaborative transportation agreement-An application in the furniture industry[J]. Oper. Res. Soc., 2017, 61(10): 1559.

[7] Y Wang, X Ma, M Liu, et al. Cooperation and profit allocation in two-echelon logistics joint distribution network optimization[J]. Appl. Soft Comput., 2017, 56: 143-157.

[8] M Janjevic, A Ndiaye. Investigating the theoretical cost-relationships of urban consolidation centres for their users[J]. Transp. Res. A, Policy Pract., 2017, 102: 98-118.

[9] F A Konuk. Price fairness, satisfaction, and trust as antecedents of purchase intentions towards organic food[J]. Consum. Behav., 2017, 17(2): 141-148.

[10] S Li, Z Wei, A Huang. Location selection of urban distribution center with a mathematical modeling approach based on the total cost[J]. IEEE Access, 2018, 6: 61833-61842.

基于改进TOPSIS法的省际物流发展能力评价

胡刘康[1] 王来军[2] 王宁[2] 楼国良[2] 任哲[1]

(1. 长安大学汽车学院; 2. 长安大学运输工程学院)

摘要 为研究各省际单位物流发展能力的演化差异，构建了物流发展能力评价指标体系，基于优势关系粗糙集属性约简及Shapley值法建立了改进TOPSIS评价模型。首先，整理16个省际单位的各项统计面板数据，采用优势关系粗糙集属性约简方法对评价属性集进行约简；然后引入Shapley值法以数学公理和公式推导为基础，客观地分配了约简集的属性权重。在此基础上，构建了改进TOPSIS法评价模型并编写MATLAB求解程序，对16个省际单位的物流发展能力进行评价分析。将评价结果与熵权-TOPSIS法及CRITIC-TOPSIS法研究结果进行对比，利用聚类分析法验证了改进Shapley-TOPSIS法的有效性；运用Spearman相关系数法证明了改进Shapley-TOPSIS法的稳定性。最后，运用评价模型测度了2014-2018年各省际单位物流发展能力排名的演化差异，并分析了其物流发展能力排名差异性演变的原因。研究表明：统计面板数据的变化符合评价模型反映的省际单位物流发展能力的演化差异。研究结果有助于理清各评价属性指标对省际单位排名差异性演化的作用方向，对于提升物流发展能力具有理论指导意义和实际参考价值。

关键词 物流发展能力评价 属性约简 权重分配 Shapley值法 改进TOPSIS法

0 引言

随着经济社会的迅猛发展，中国各省际单位的物流能力也有了长足的进步。省际物流能力与省际经济发展互为支撑，省际物流发展能力的强弱是衡量省际经济发展水平的重要因素。因此，提升省际物流发展能力是推动省际经济发展的重要途径。受诸多因素的影响,各省市物流发展能力存在较大的差距,对省际物流发展能力进行客观的评价将有利于各级政府科学决策,具有一定的理论与现实意义。

1 文献综述

对省际单位的物流能力评估是近年来物流经济领域研究的一个热点问题,相关论文很丰富。从评价方法角度划分,当前的研究成果可分为两类:一是运用单一定性或定量评价方法;二是将其中两种或两种以上方法相结合。王小丽基于灰色关联分析法建立灰色关联度模型,选取影响区域物流能力的主要指标,得出了河南省各市区域物流能力的强弱次序;Feng 等采用层次分析法,以山东青岛、日照等6个港口为研究对象,建立港口物流运输效率评价指标体系和评价模型,实现了对几个港口效率值的排序,并提出了改进建议。刘鹏为评价我国物流企业的低碳物流能力,选取模糊综合评价法创建低碳物流能力评判模型,结合实际案例加以应用,并通过结果分析给出了具体的低碳发展能力提升建议。Zhang 基于 TOPSIS 法构建了电子商务消费者满意度评价指标体系,设计了农产品电子商务的评价模型,通过实证分析,发现了京东生鲜平台的满意度最高,淘宝网的满意度最低。翟小可等以农村电商物流服务能力为评价研究对象,选取了23个影响农村电商物流服务质量的指标组成评价体系,采用层次分析法和模糊综合评价法构建评价模型,评价得出珠海市农村电商物流服务质量结果良好。Ramazan Eyüp Gergin 等采用层次分析法和 TOPSIS 法对土耳其各地区物流绩效进行评价,通过对影响因素指标数据的处理分析,得出了各地区的物流绩效排序并提出了绩效改进的建议。

从属性权重分配方法角度划分,可分为主观赋权法和客观赋权法两大类。主观赋权法主要包括采用专家打分法或 G1 法对定性指标进行评价打分,具体如下:Kuo Gao 等采用专家打分法对区域经济发展水平、物流系统规划、物流需求规模、物流供应规模以及信息化水平等影响运输和物流系统建设的五个指标进行评分,比较分析每个指数在中国中部六省的数据表现,结果表明:河南省排名最高,其经济发展水平、物流系统规划、物流需求规模、信息化水平都高于其他五省。郭子雪等为有效评价城市物流业的竞争力,构建了城市物流业竞争力评价指标体系,采用 G1 法确定了指标权重,以河北省11个城市为研究对象进行实证分析。研究发现:唐山和石家庄的物流业竞争力远大于其余城市。但主观赋权法,主要依赖专家主观经验进行打分,需要很强的先验经验,主观性较大。现有的研究成果中,使用较多的是熵权法、变异系数法及 CRITIC 法等客观权重法,其中熵权法的运用最为广泛。例如:M. A. Rahman 等采用熵权系数法最大限度地减少了数学权重选择的主观性以改进货运运输选择决策模型。通过数值仿真,实现了决策模型对卡车、铁路以及多式联运(铁路/卡车和航空/卡车)等运输方式的排序选择。鄢飞为全面分析区域物流发展的差异性,采用变异系数法对区域物流发展差异情况进行测度,研究发现西北五省的区域物流规模差异有所减小,为促进区域物流专业化发展以及加强区域物流的协调提供了参考与借鉴。贺玉德等基于 DEA 协同发展模型,采用 CRITIC 法进行属性权重分配,对2002—2012年四川省区域物流和区域经济发展数据进行实证分析,结果发现四川省区域物流与区域经济协同发展效度在2008年及以前较为平稳,2009年及以后逐渐下降。客观权重法的原理是通过建立数学模型对各属性指标进行赋权,能在一定程度上考虑权重的客观性。这些方法从不同的角度对权重赋值问题进行了研究,但也都有一定的适用范围和局限性。

Shapley 值法是合作博弈领域进行利益分配的常用方法。其一大优势就是计算过程以严格的数学公理以及公式推导为基础,充分考虑属性间的相互关系,按照成员对联盟的边际贡献率客观公正地分配利益,能够避免分配上的平均主义,具有合理性和公平性。因此,本研究基于优势关系粗糙集属性约简的基础上引入 Shapley 值法对属性权重进行分配。以期能够最大限度地减少属性权重分配时对先验知识和经验的依赖,客观公正地分配属性权重。基于此,本文将基于优势关系粗糙集属性约简以及 Shapley 值法的属性权重分配方法与 TOPSIS 法相结合。构建改进 TOPSIS 法的省际物流发展能力评价模型,以北京、天津、河北等16个省际单位的相关统计数据为样本,对省际物流发展能力进行客观评价,并与现有方法的研究结果进行对比,为物流发展能力评价研究提供新的方法和理论指导。

2 构建评价指标体系

省际物流发展能力评价是对以省市为单位的物流产业竞争力水平进行评价,构建评价指标体系是定性与定量相结合的过程。通过分析与物流发展能力密切相关的统计数据指标可以有效反映一个省市的物流产业竞争力。在借鉴相关学者研究成果的基础上,通过对指标的初选和筛选过程,选取了经济发展水平、物流服务能力、物流行业现状、物流基础设施四个维度作为一级指标。经济发展水平指一级指标包括省际区域GDP、目的地及货源地进出口总额、交通运输及仓储邮政业全社会固定资产投资等三项二级指标。物流服务能力一级指标包含物流服务能力等级、货运总量、物流业务总量等三项二级指标。物流行业现状一级指标包含交通运输及仓储和邮政业就业人员平均工资、增加值及企业单位数等三项二级指标。物流基础设施一级指标包括了物流网络密度、交通运输、仓储及邮政业从业人员数量、物流网点数量等三项二级指标。构建的省际物流发展能力评价指标体系如图1所示。

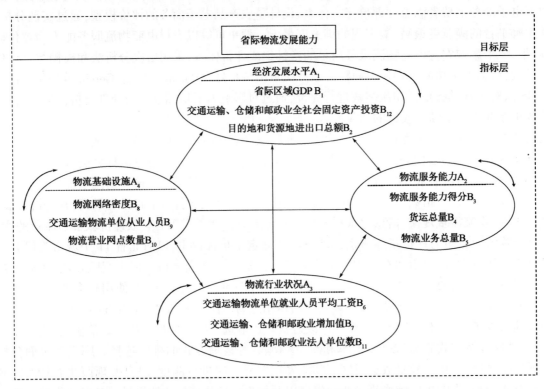

图1 省际物流发展能力评价指标体系及指标间相互关系

3 基于改进TOPSIS法的省际物流发展能力评价

3.1 属性约简以及基于Shapley值法的权重分配

基于Shapley值法的属性权重分配首先要利用优势关系粗糙集属性约简方法对评价属性集进行属性约简,仅留下对评价结果影响较大的决策属性集,以减少复杂性。然后,采用基于Shapley值法的属性权重分配方法确定约简集各属性的权重值大小,以Shapley值法严格的数学公理和公式推导为基础,客观公正地分配约简集的属性权重。

3.1.1 基于优势关系的属性约简

由优势关系信息系统及其属性约简的相关性质定理可知,信息量不仅可以用于度量优势关系信息系统中的不确定性,同时也可以用于分类的模糊性度量,并且信息量可以理解为属性集为区分元素间优劣关系所做贡献。利用相关定理即可求取优势关系信息系统的保持信息量不变的属性约简集,可有效缩减评价所需的工作量,减少复杂性。

定义1 信息系统(U,D,f)中,$U=\{x_1,x_2,\cdots,x_m\}$为对象集,$D=\{d_1,d_2,\cdots,d_m\}$为属性集,$f:U\to D$为U到D的关系集。

定义2 信息系统(U,D,f)中,属性集$V\subseteq D$。若$\forall d_k\in V$,有$f_{dk}(x_i)\leqslant f_{dk}(x_j)$,称$x_j$在属性集$V$上优于$x_i$。称$T_V\leqslant(x_i)=\{x_j|f_{dk}(x_i)\leqslant f_{dk}(x_j),\forall d_k\in V\}$为$x_i$的优势集。

定义3 信息系统(U,D,f)中,属性集V的信息量为:

$$H(V)=\sum_{i=1}^{|U|}\frac{1}{|U|}\left(1-\frac{|Z_V\leqslant(x_i)|}{|U|}\right) \tag{1}$$

式中,$|U|$表示集合U中元素的个数。信息量不仅具备表征优势集不确定性的能力,还能作为衡量属性重要程度的标准。

定义4 信息系统(U,D,f)中,$V\subseteq D$。当$H(V)=H(D)$且$H(V-\{d\})<H(D)$($\forall d\in D$)时,称V为D的约简集。由公式可得,$H(V)=H(D)$时,有$T_V\leqslant(x_i)=T_D\leqslant(x_i)$。记$\{S<(x_i,x_j)|S<(x_i,x_j)\neq\emptyset, x_i,x_j\in U\}$为辨识矩阵。约简集$V$具有如下性质:$\forall S\in T$,$V$满足$V\cap S\neq\emptyset$。

利用以上性质,可在信息量不变的情况下,对属性集D进行约简,得到约简集V。

3.1.2 基于Shapley值法的属性权重分配

采用基于Shapley值法的属性权重分配方法确定约简集各属性的权重值大小,以Shapley值法严格的数学公理和公式推导为基础,可以有效地减少对先验知识的依赖以及赋权的主观性,能客观公正地分配约简集的属性权重。

定义5 对集合$H=\{h_1,h_2,\cdots,h_n\}$,若任一子集$G\subseteq H$都对应一个函数:

$$c(G)=\sum_{g_i}H(\{g_i\})-H(G) \tag{2}$$

式中,满足$c(\emptyset)=0$,$c(G_1\cup G_2)\geqslant c(G_1)+c(G_2)$($G_1\cap G_2=\emptyset$),则称$c(G)$为子集$G$的效益函数,其中$c_{hi}$为$H$的元素$h_i$对效益所做的贡献。记Shapley值为:

$$\varphi_{hi}(c)=\sum_{G\in H_i}\frac{(n-|G|)!(|G|-1)!}{n!}[c(G)-c(G\backslash h_i)] \tag{3}$$

式中,$i=1,2,\cdots,n$;H_i是H所有包含h_i元素的子集;$G\backslash h_i$表示子集G中剔除了元素h_i。

3.2 基于改进TOPSIS法的省际物流发展能力评价模型

本文对TOPSIS法进行改进,在利用粗糙集进行优势关系属性约简得到保持信息量不变的属性约简集的基础上,引入Shapley值法对属性权重进行分配,建立改进TOPSIS法的省际物流发展能力评价模型,改进TOPSIS算法的评价流程如图2所示。具体步骤如下。

步骤1: 构建初始数据矩阵。根据省际物流发展能力评价指标体系选取集合为$B=\{B_1,B_2,\cdots,B_n\}$的12项二级指标为评价属性集,以北京、天津、河北等集合为$X=\{X_1,X_2,\cdots,X_n\}$的16个省际单位为评价对象集,构建初始数据矩阵。

步骤2: 初始矩阵规范化。通过评价矩阵属性集与省际物流发展能力的系统动力关系,将10项属性集指标划分为收益型和成本型指标。收益型指标,即属性值越大,省际物流发展能力越强;对于成本型指标,即属性越大,省际物流发展能力越弱。初始矩阵无量纲化计算公式如下。

(1)收益型指标p_{ij}:

$$p_{ij}=\frac{x_{ij}-\min_i x_{ij}}{\max_i x_{ij}-\min_i x_{ij}} \tag{4}$$

(2)成本型指标p_{ij}:

$$p_{ij}=\frac{\max_i x_{ij}-x_{ij}}{\max_i x_{ij}-\min_i x_{ij}} \tag{5}$$

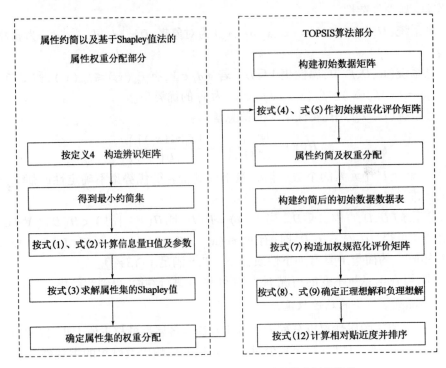

图2 基于改进TOPSIS法的省际物流发展能力评价模型

式中,$i = 1,2,\cdots,m;j = 1,2,\cdots,n$。得到无量纲化评价矩阵 P:

$$P = (p_{ij})_{m*n} = \begin{bmatrix} p_{11} & p_{12} & \cdots & p_{1n} \\ p_{21} & p_{22} & \cdots & p_{2n} \\ \vdots & \vdots & \vdots & \vdots \\ p_{m1} & p_{m2} & \cdots & p_{mn} \end{bmatrix} \quad (6)$$

步骤3:进行属性约简及属性权重分配。根据属性约简的定义对评价矩阵属性集进行约简,选取出最终参与属性权重分配的约简属性集。由定义4及约简集的性质求取出最小约简集,并得到约简后的无量纲化评判矩阵 P'。基于Shapley值法对最小约简集 V 中的属性集进行权重分配。

步骤4:构造加权规范化评价矩阵。根据属性约简过程的求解数据以及基于Shapley值法得到的属性权重分配结果,得到更新的评价矩阵 P'':

$$P'' = (p'_{ij})_{m*n} = (p_{ij} * \omega_j) = \begin{bmatrix} p'_{11} & p'_{12} & \cdots & p'_{1n} \\ p'_{21} & p'_{22} & \cdots & p'_{2n} \\ \vdots & \vdots & \vdots & \vdots \\ p'_{m1} & p'_{m2} & \cdots & p'_{mn} \end{bmatrix} \quad (7)$$

步骤5:确定正理想解和负理想解。根据更新后的评价矩阵 P'',确定正理想解 V^+ 和负理想解 V^- 分别为:

$$V^+ = \{(\max p'_{ij}|j\in P^+),(\min p'_{ij}|j\in P^-)|i=1,2,\cdots,m\} = (V_1^+, V_2^+, \cdots, V_m^+) \quad (8)$$

$$V^- = \{(\max p'_{ij}|j\in P^-),(\min p'_{ij}|j\in P^+)|i=1,2,\cdots,m\} = (V_1^-, V_2^-, \cdots, V_m^-) \quad (9)$$

式中,P^+ 为效益型指标集,P^- 为成本型指标集。

步骤6:计算评价矩阵对象集与正负理想解的相对距离 D_i^+、D_i^- 以及相对贴近度 D_i'。相对贴近度 D_i' 表示评价对象集与理想解的接近程度,D_i' 取值越大表明该评价对象越优,按贴近度从大到小的顺序就可以对各省际物流发展能力进行排序。计算公式如下:

$$D_i^+ = \sqrt{\sum_{j=1}^{n}(p'_{ij} - V_i^+)^2}, i = 1,2,3,\cdots,m \quad (10)$$

$$D_i^- = \sqrt{\sum_{j=1}^{n}(p'_{ij} - V_i^-)^2} \quad (i=1,2,3,\cdots,m) \tag{11}$$

$$D'_i = \frac{D_i^-}{D_i^+ + D_i^-} \quad (i=1,2,3,\cdots,m) \tag{12}$$

4 实证分析

本文选取了北京、天津、河北、山西、内蒙古、辽宁、黑龙江、上海、浙江、安徽、福建、江西、河南、湖北、湖南、四川16个省际单位为研究对象,进行横向和纵向的对比分析。二级评价指标来源于国家统计局分省年度数据(2014—2018年)。12项属性集指标中,物流服务能力得分指标B_3为参考文献[7]专家打分法得到的主观权重指标。交通运输、仓储和邮政业城镇单位就业人员平均工资指标B_6为成本型指标,其余11项均为效益型指标。

4.1 构建初始数据矩阵及归一化处理

利用式(4)、式(5)可对原始数据进行无量纲化处理,以2014年为例,对16个省市物流发展能力初始评价矩阵进行归一化处理得到的初始规范化评价数据矩阵,具体参数见表1。

初始规范化评价数据矩阵表 表1

省份	B_1	B_2	B_3	B_4	B_5	B_6	B_7	B_8	B_9	B_{10}	B_{11}	B_{12}
X_1	0.3126	0.2923	0.0000	0.0000	0.4417	0.2720	0.1547	0.5253	1.0000	0.3185	0.6246	0.1225
X_2	0.1082	0.2953	0.6000	0.0569	0.0327	0.1061	0.0219	0.5888	0.0000	0.0000	0.5465	0.1156
X_3	0.6078	0.1806	0.0667	0.4498	0.1242	0.9241	1.0000	0.3587	0.3186	0.3067	0.4327	0.6297
X_4	0.0000	0.0074	0.2000	0.3393	0.0200	0.7276	0.0665	0.3350	0.2234	0.2855	0.1193	0.1573
X_5	0.1827	0.0000	0.8667	0.4054	0.0000	0.6783	0.3680	0.0000	0.1519	0.1569	0.0466	0.3504
X_6	0.5788	0.2518	0.6667	0.4797	0.0519	0.7336	0.4703	0.2898	0.5062	0.2869	0.6247	0.5353
X_7	0.0831	0.0323	0.2667	0.0826	0.0113	0.8233	0.0000	0.0972	0.2922	0.1921	0.0000	0.1086
X_8	0.3942	1.0000	0.7333	0.1556	0.5132	0.0000	0.2109	1.0000	0.8069	0.3600	0.6983	0.0000
X_9	1.0000	0.8300	1.0000	0.4113	1.0000	0.4752	0.4919	0.4757	0.3999	0.6927	1.0000	0.5068
X_{10}	0.2950	0.0638	0.3333	1.0000	0.0815	0.9786	0.0591	0.4988	0.1608	0.2927	0.5024	0.2688
X_{11}	0.4120	0.3412	0.9333	0.2090	0.2537	0.7041	0.3719	0.3136	0.2114	0.3372	0.5583	0.5255
X_{12}	0.1077	0.0545	0.1333	0.3074	0.0484	0.7799	0.0157	0.3580	0.1403	0.2591	0.3640	0.0969
X_{13}	0.8090	0.1216	0.5333	0.4273	0.1063	1.0000	0.5798	0.5945	0.6570	0.5940	0.4114	0.3842
X_{14}	0.5333	0.0584	0.4667	0.3046	0.1201	0.8685	0.2909	0.5109	0.4378	0.4874	0.6095	0.5635
X_{15}	0.5208	0.0297	0.4000	0.4329	0.0773	0.8889	0.3353	0.4463	0.2364	0.4192	0.1110	0.3872
X_{16}	0.5755	0.1051	0.8000	0.3249	0.1412	0.7164	0.2246	0.2231	0.5881	1.0000	0.3080	1.0000

4.2 属性约简及属性权重分配

由定义4及约简集的性质构建辨识矩阵T,可列举出辨识矩阵T中指标数较少的非空元素:$\{B_3\}$、$\{B_4\}$、$\{B_6\}$、$\{B_8\}$、$\{B_9\}$、$\{B_{11}\}$、$\{B_2, B_8\}$、$\{B_7, B_9\}$、$\{B_3, B_6, B_7\}$……

由约简集的性质($\forall S \in T, V \cap S \neq \emptyset$),可求得最小约简集$V = \{B_3, B_4, B_6, B_8, B_9, B_{11}\}$。基于Shapley值法可对最小约简集$V$中的6个属性集进行属性权重分配。由式(1)可得。

$$H(V) = \sum_{i=1}^{|U|} \frac{1}{|U|}\left(1 - \frac{[x_i]_V \leq}{|U|}\right) = \frac{235}{16*16} \tag{13}$$

同时,$H(B_3), H(B_4), H(B_6), H(B_8), H(B_9), H(B_{11}), \cdots, H(B_3, B_4, B_6, B_8, B_8, B_{11})$的信息量$H$值均

可求得。由式(2)、式(3)可得到计算 Shapley 值解所需要的多方参数值解,所需的所有参数值解见表2。

求解 Shapley 值所需的多方参数值解 表2

$c(\emptyset)=0$	$c(B_6,B_8)=59/256$	$c(B_4,B_6,B_8)=159/256$	$c(B_3,B_6,B_8,B_9)=254/256$
$c(B_3)=0$	$c(B_6,B_9)=59/256$	$c(B_4,B_6,B_8)=161/256$	$c(B_3,B_6,B_8,B_{11})=253/256$
$c(B_4)=0$	$c(B_6,B_{11})=45/256$	$c(B_4,B_6,B_{11})=153/256$	$c(B_3,B_6,B_9,B_{11})=253/256$
$c(B_6)=0$	$c(B_8,B_9)=74/256$	$c(B_4,B_8,B_9)=153/256$	$c(B_3,B_8,B_9,B_{11})=271/256$
$c(B_8)=0$	$c(B_8,B_{11})=84/256$	$c(B_4,B_8,B_{11})=157/256$	$c(B_4,B_6,B_8,B_9)=264/256$
$c(B_9)=0$	$c(B_9,B_{11})=76/256$	$c(B_4,B_9,B_{11})=155/256$	$c(B_4,B_6,B_8,B_{11})=263/256$
$c(B_{10})=0$	$c(B_3,B_4,B_6)=155/256$	$c(B_6,B_8,B_9)=156/256$	$c(B_4,B_6,B_9,B_{11})=262/256$
$c(B_3,B_4)=62/256$	$c(B_3,B_4,B_8)=146/256$	$c(B_6,B_8,B_{11})=154/256$	$c(B_4,B_8,B_9,B_{11})=264/256$
$c(B_3,B_6)=43/256$	$c(B_3,B_4,B_9)=151/256$	$c(B_6,B_9,B_{11})=150/256$	$c(B_6,B_8,B_9,B_{11})=262/256$
$c(B_3,B_8)=56/256$	$c(B_3,B_4,B_{11})=155/256$	$c(B_8,B_9,B_{11})=177/256$	$c(B_3,B_4,B_6,B_8,B_9)=368/256$
$c(B_3,B_9)=62/256$	$c(B_3,B_6,B_8)=139/256$	$c(B_3,B_4,B_6,B_8)=253/256$	$c(B_3,B_4,B_6,B_8,B_{11})=369/256$
$c(B_3,B_{11})=72/256$	$c(B_3,B_6,B_9)=142/256$	$c(B_3,B_4,B_6,B_9)=254/256$	$c(B_3,B_4,B_6,B_9,B_{11})=369/256$
$c(B_4,B_6)=85/256$	$c(B_3,B_6,B_{11})=140/256$	$c(B_3,B_4,B_6,B_{11})=256/256$	$c(B_3,B_4,B_8,B_9,B_{11})=374/256$
$c(B_4,B_8)=54/256$	$c(B_3,B_8,B_9)=156/256$	$c(B_3,B_4,B_8,B_9)=257/256$	$c(B_3,B_6,B_8,B_9,B_{11})=369/256$
$c(B_4,B_9)=58/256$	$c(B_3,B_8,B_{11})=166/256$	$c(B_3,B_4,B_8,B_{11})=261/256$	$c(B_4,B_6,B_8,B_9,B_{11})=375/256$
$c(B_4,B_{11})=62/256$	$c(B_3,B_9,B_{11})=165/256$	$c(B_3,B_4,B_9,B_{11})=262/256$	

根据定义5及式(3)编写求解 Shapley 值的 MATLAB 脚本文件,将以上求解得到的多方参数值解编入程序,在 MATLAB 命令窗口输入命令语句"F = Shapley(@eigen,6)",并运行程序,即可得到各属性分配的 Shapley 值解。然后,根据式(2)可求解出结果,并将结果归一化可得到6个属性指标对应的权重分配大小 ω_i,属性集的 Shapley 值及权重分配结果见表3。

属性集的 Shapley 值解及权重分配 表3

属性集	B_3	B_4	B_6	B_8	B_9	B_{11}
Shapley 值解	0.3009	0.3177	0.3001	0.3236	0.3245	0.3277
ω_i	0.1828	0.1645	0.1837	0.1581	0.1571	0.1536

根据属性约简得到的最小约简集 V,可对初始评价矩阵进行约简。通过编写改进 TOPSIS 算法的 MATLAB 脚本文件,将约简后的属性集指标类型编码、初始数据矩阵、属性权重值 ω_i 写入"data-TOPSIS.xlsx"文件,并保存在 MATLAB 的当前工作目录下供程序调用,具体数据见表4。在 MATLAB 命令窗口输入命令语句"TOPSIS",并运行程序,即可得到约简后的无量纲化评判矩阵 P'。

约简后的改进 TOPSIS 算法初始数据矩阵表 表4

属性集	B_3	B_4	B_6	B_8	B_9	B_{11}
指示值*	1	1	0	1	1	1
初始数据						
X_1	1	26551	78183	1.3750	60.2300	14437
X_2	10	49753	84736	1.5221	14.3400	13246
X_3	2	209946	52425	0.9883	28.9600	11511
X_4	4	164918	60187	0.9335	24.5900	6731
X_5	14	191869	62134	0.1562	21.3100	5622
X_6	11	222138	59951	0.8286	37.5700	14438
X_7	5	60213	56406	0.3817	27.7500	4912

续上表

属 性 集	B_3	B_4	B_6	B_8	B_9	B_{11}
X_8	12	89980	88929	2.4762	51.3700	15560
X_9	16	194250	70156	1.2598	32.6900	20161
X_{10}	6	434298	50271	1.3135	21.7200	12573
X_{11}	15	111757	61115	0.8838	24.0400	13425
X_{12}	3	151878	58120	0.9868	20.7800	10462
X_{13}	9	200801	49426	1.5353	44.4900	11185
X_{14}	8	150762	54620	1.3416	34.4300	14207
X_{15}	7	203053	53816	1.1917	25.1900	6605
X_{16}	13	159034	60631	0.6739	41.3300	9609
属性权重	0.1828	0.1645	0.1837	0.1581	0.1571	0.1536

4.3 构造加权规范化评价矩阵

由约简后的无量纲化评判矩阵 P' 以及利用 Shapley 值法求解得到的属性权重。利用公式 $P''_{ij} = P'_{ij} \times \omega_i$，将新的评判矩阵 P' 和权重数值 ω_i 结合。将以上算法过程编入改进 TOPSIS 算法程序并运行，即可得到加权规范化评价矩阵 P''。

$$P'' = \begin{bmatrix} 0 & 0 & 0.0500 & 0.0831 & 0.1571 & 0.0959 \\ 0.1097 & 0.0094 & 0.0195 & 0.0931 & 0 & 0.0839 \\ 0.0122 & 0.0740 & 0.1698 & 0.2567 & 0.0501 & 0.0665 \\ 0.0366 & 0.0558 & 0.1337 & 0.0530 & 0.0351 & 0.0183 \\ 0.1584 & 0.0667 & 0.1246 & 0 & 0.0239 & 0.0072 \\ 0.1219 & 0.0789 & 0.1348 & 0.0458 & 0.0795 & 0.0960 \\ 0.0487 & 0.0136 & 0.1512 & 0.0154 & 0.0459 & 0 \\ 0.1341 & 0.0256 & 0 & 0.1581 & 0.1268 & 0.1073 \\ 0.1828 & 0.0677 & 0.0873 & 0.0752 & 0.0628 & 0.1536 \\ 0.0609 & 0.1645 & 0.1798 & 0.0789 & 0.0253 & 0.0772 \\ 0.1706 & 0.0344 & 0.1293 & 0.0496 & 0.0332 & 0.0857 \\ 0.0244 & 0.0506 & 0.1433 & 0.0566 & 0.0220 & 0.0559 \\ 0.0975 & 0.0703 & 0.1837 & 0.0940 & 0.1032 & 0.0632 \\ 0.0853 & 0.0501 & 0.1595 & 0.0808 & 0.0688 & 0.0936 \\ 0.0731 & 0.712 & 0.1633 & 0.0706 & 0.0371 & 0.0171 \\ 0.1462 & 0.0534 & 0.1316 & 0.0353 & 0.0924 & 0.473 \end{bmatrix} \quad (14)$$

4.4 确定正理想解和负理想解

根据式(8)、式(9)可计算得到正理想解 V^+ 和负理想解 V^-，求得的结果如下：

$$V^+ = (V_1^+, V_2^+, \cdots, V_m^+) = (0.1828, 0.1645, 0, 0.1581, 0.1571, 0.1536) \quad (15)$$

$$V^- = (V_1^-, V_2^-, \cdots, V_m^-) = (0, 0, 0.1837, 0, 0, 0) \quad (16)$$

4.5 计算对象集与正负理想解的相对距离 D_i^+、D_i^- 以及相对贴近度 D_i'

利用式(7)、式(9)计算待评价地区到正理想解、负理想解的相对距离 D_i^+、D_i^- 以及相对贴近度 D_i'，求得的具体结果见表5。

各省市相对贴近度排序 表5

序号	省际单位	Shapley-TOPSIS法				熵权-TOPSIS法		CRITIC-TOPSIS法	
		D_i^+	D_i^-	D_i'	排序	D_i'	排序	D_i'	排序
X_1	北京	0.2682	0.2422	0.4745	4	0.4351	9	0.4860	4
X_2	天津	0.2521	0.2341	0.4815	3	0.4596	5	0.4898	3
X_3	河北	0.3089	0.1263	0.2902	13	0.2921	13	0.2805	13
X_4	山西	0.3087	0.1064	0.2564	15	0.2623	14	0.2457	15
X_5	内蒙古	0.2998	0.1835	0.3796	11	0.4097	10	0.3904	11
X_6	辽宁	0.2262	0.2027	0.4727	5	0.4818	3	0.4855	5
X_7	黑龙江	0.3463	0.0772	0.1823	16	0.1844	16	0.1894	16
X_8	上海	0.1573	0.3239	0.6732	1	0.6340	1	0.6937	1
X_9	浙江	0.181	0.2837	0.6105	2	0.6056	2	0.6297	2
X_{10}	安徽	0.2769	0.2088	0.4299	9	0.4612	4	0.4038	10
X_{11}	福建	0.256	0.2101	0.4508	6	0.4572	6	0.4705	6
X_{12}	江西	0.311	0.1077	0.2573	14	0.2526	15	0.2500	14
X_{13}	河南	0.2551	0.1947	0.4329	8	0.4382	8	0.4329	8
X_{14}	湖北	0.2558	0.1743	0.4053	10	0.3972	11	0.4115	9
X_{15}	湖南	0.2968	0.1322	0.3082	12	0.3254	12	0.2962	12
X_{16}	四川	0.2481	0.1974	0.4431	7	0.4571	7	0.4604	7

为验证本文方法的合理性与有效性,此处将本文的省际物流发展能力评价模型求解结果与基于熵权法及CRITIC法的TOPSIS模型进行对比。通过编写熵权-TOPSIS法及CRITIC-TOPSIS法的MATLAB程序,求解得到的省际物流发展能力评价排序结果对比见表5。以相对贴近度为聚类依据,运用SPSS软件对16个省市物流发展能力进行聚类分析,可根据分析结果将16个省际单位分为三个等级,分类结果见表6。由三种评价方法贴近度计算结果的聚类分析等级排序表及贴近度雷达分布(图3)可知,三种方法得出的TOPSIS法贴近度聚类分级差异很小且雷达图重合度很高,16个省际单位中只有安徽的聚类等级不同,且省际物流发展能力排序贴近度很高,由此可以证明Shapley-TOPSIS法的合理性与有效性。

聚类分析等级排序表 表6

等级	等级标准	方法	省际单位
一	[0.50,1)	Shapley-TOPSIS法	上海、浙江
		熵权-TOPSIS法	上海、浙江
		CRITIC-TOPSIS法	上海、浙江
二	[0.42,0.50)	Shapley-TOPSIS法	天津、北京、辽宁、福建、四川、河南、安徽
		熵权-TOPSIS法	辽宁、安徽、天津、福建、四川、河南、北京
		CRITIC-TOPSIS法	天津、北京、辽宁、福建、四川、河南
三	[0,0.42)	Shapley-TOPSIS法	湖北、内蒙古、湖南、河北、江西、山西、黑龙江
		熵权-TOPSIS法	内蒙古、湖北、湖南、河北、山西、江西、黑龙江
		CRITIC-TOPSIS法	湖北、安徽、内蒙古、湖南、河北、江西、山西、黑龙江

为验证本文评价模型算法的稳健性,引入Spearman相关系数法判断该种方法相对于其他方法一致性程度的整体水平。即对于不同评价方法得到的排序结果计算两两之间的Spearman相关系数,如某种方法的结果与其他方法结果之间的相关系数值都较大,则可认为该方法较优。

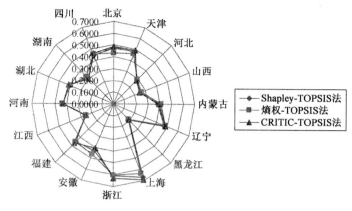

图3 贴近度雷达图

Spearman 相关系数：

$$r = 1 - \frac{6\sum_{i=1}^{n}d_i^2}{n(n^2-1)} \quad (17)$$

将表5中三种方法的贴近度排序结果代入模型中计算可得到表7的$\bar{r}$。对比可知，Shapley-TOPSIS 法 > CRITIC-TOPSIS 法 > 熵权-TOPSIS 法。说明 Shapley-TOPSIS 法要优于 CRITIC-TOPSIS 法和熵权-TOPSIS法，所求结果具有更好的稳健性。

聚类分析等级排序表　　　　表7

r	Shapley-TOPSIS 法	熵权-TOPSIS 法	CRITIC-TOPSIS 法	$\bar{r}$
Shapley-TOPSIS 法	1.0000	0.8893	0.9964	0.9619
熵权-TOPSIS 法	0.8893	1.0000	0.8643	0.9179
CRITIC-TOPSIS 法	0.9964	0.8643	1.0000	0.9536

5 结 语

针对原有主客观赋权法先验经验依赖性强、适用范围小且有局限性的不足。为评价各省际单位的物流发展能力状况，本文基于相关学者的研究成果，构建了物流发展能力评价指标体系，运用优势关系粗糙集属性约简方法并引入合作博弈领域的 Shapley 值法对约简后的属性集进行权重分配以改进 TOPSIS 评价模型。运用评价模型测度了各省际单位物流发展能力排名的演化差异，并举例详细分析了各省际单位的物流发展能力排名差异性演变的原因。主要研究结论如下：

（1）利用优势关系粗糙集属性约简方法，以各省际单位的面板统计数据为基础，对物流发展能力评价指标体系进行约简，求取优势关系信息系统的保持信息量不变的属性约简集，有效地缩减了评价所需的工作量，减少了复杂性。通过相关计算，结果保留了物流服务能力等级 B_3、货运量 B_4、物流从业人员平均工资 B_6、物流网络密度 B_8、物流从业人员数量 B_9、物流企业数量 B_{11} 6 项属性指标。

（2）通过引入合作博弈领域的 Shapley 值法，依据其严格的数学公理和公式推导客观公正地分配约简后的属性集权重，以减少决策者对先验知识和经验的依赖。为求解方便准确，依据 Shapley 值法的相关公式及公理性约束编写了求解 Shapley 值的 MATLAB 程序，首先求解出属性集的多方参数值解，将其编入程序即可求解出各属性集分配的权重。结果发现，权重占比最大的指标为物流从业人员平均工资 B_6，占比最小的指标为物流企业数量 B_{11}。

（3）基于优势关系粗糙集属性约简及 Shapley 值法实现了对 TOPSIS 评价模型的改进。通过编写改进 TOPSIS 算法的 MATLAB 程序，实现了对各省际单位物流发展能力的评价排序。利用聚类分析及 Spearman 相关系数法与基于熵权法和 CRITIC 法的改进 TOPSIS 评价模型研究结果进行对比，论证了本文研究模型的合理性与稳健性。研究发现三种方法聚类分级差异很小，聚类分析结果为：上海、浙江 2 个省际单位物流发展能力最强为第一等级；天津、北京、辽宁、福建、四川、河南、安徽7个省际单位为第二等级；湖北、内蒙古、湖南、河北、江西、山西、黑龙江7个省际单位物流发展能力最弱为第三等级。

（4）利用本文评价模型测度了各省际单位物流发展能力排名的演化差异，并举例分析了各省际单位排名差异性演变的原因。研究发现，14个省际单位的物流发展能力聚类分级排序均未发生变化，结果表现稳定。以天津和湖北为例分析其等级排序出现波动的原因，结果表明：统计面板数据的变化符合评价模型反映的两个省际单位物流发展能力的反向性演化差异。

6 结 语

结合前述研究结果，本文主要介绍了一种基于粗糙集属性约简及利用Shapley值法进行属性权重分配的改进TOPSIS模型对省际物流发展能力进行评价。通过与其他两种常用评价模型研究结果的对比分析，验证了本文模型的合理性与稳健性。利用模型测度了2014—2018年各省际单位物流发展能力排名的演化差异，并结合面板统计数据分析了各省际单位排名差异性演变的原因，结果显示评价模型表现稳定。本文的改进TOPSIS模型可为评价优选研究提供新的方法选择。

参考文献

[1] 王小丽.基于灰关联理想方案决策的区域物流能力评价[J].统计与决策,2013(16):42-44.

[2] Feng Hao, Ye Chong, Gao Rongwei. AHP-Based Evaluation of Port Logistics Transportation Efficiency[J]. Journal of Coastal Research,2020,106(Special):477-480.

[3] 刘鹏.我国物流企业的低碳物流能力评价[J].商业经济研究,2017(10):87-89.

[4] Xiaheng Zhang; Doudou Li. Research on E-commerce Logistic Satisfaction Based on TOPSIS Method[J]. International Journal of Frontiers in Sociology,2019,1(1):12-22.

[5] 翟小可,吴祈宗.基于AHP-模糊综合评价的农村电商物流服务质量评价研究[J].数学的实践与认识,2019,49(05):121-127.

[6] Ramazan Eyüp Gergin, Birdo an Baki. Evaluation by Integrated AHP and TOPSIS Method of Logistics Performance in Turkey's Regions[J]. Business and Economics Research Journal,2015,6(4):115-135.

[7] Kuo Gao, Xinxin Shao. A Comparative Study on the Construction of Transportation and Logistics System in Central China[J]. Journal of Coastal Research,2019:665-667.

[8] 郭子雪,齐美然,李杨.基于G1法的河北省城市物流业竞争力评价研究[J].数学的实践与认识,2017,47(18):39-48.

[9] M A Rahman, V A Pereda. Freight transport and logistics evaluation using entropy technique integrated to TOPSIS algorithm[J]. Intelligent Transportation and Planning,2018:66-686.

[10] 鄢飞.区域物流发展的差异性分析[J].科技管理研究,2015,35(17):82-88.

[11] 贺玉德,马祖军.基于CRITIC-DEA的区域物流与区域经济协同发展模型及评价——以四川省为例[J].软科学,2015,29(03):102-106.

[12] Gladysz B, Mercik J. The Shapley Value in Fuzzy Simple Cooperative Games[J]. Intelligent Information And Database Systems, Aciids 2018, PT I Lecture Notes in Artificial Intelligence,2018:410-418.

[13] 索中英,程嗣怡,韩小妹.基于Shapley值的优势关系粗糙集客观权重分配方法及应用[J].空军工程大学学报(自然科学版),2016,17(05):100-105.

[14] 徐宇恒,程嗣怡,周一鹏,等.基于Shapley-TOPSIS的辐射源威胁评估[J].空军工程大学学报(自然科学版),2020,21(02):91-96.

[15] 李婵娟.我国省际物流业发展差异的演变与解释——基于Shapley值法的实证分析[J].价格月刊,2017(11):62-67.

[16] 张旭,袁旭梅,王亚娜,等.基于云PDR的区域物流能力评价研究[J].北京交通大学学报(社会科学版),2020,19(02):108-117.

[17] 张建军,赵启兰,刘桂艳.区域物流能力与区域经济发展耦合互动机理研究[J].数学的实践与认识,2019,49(12):50-60.

[18] 魏国辰,冀雪华.我国区域物流发展能力综合评价研究——基于ANP-TOPSIS模型对京津冀地区物流业分析[J].价格理论与实践,2019(05):134-137.

[19] Pawlak Z. Rough sets[J]. International Journal of Computer & Information ences, 1982, 11(5): 341-356.

[20] Greco S, Matarazzo B, Slowinski R. Rough approximation by dominance relations[J]. International Journal of Intelligent Systems, 2010, 17(2):153-171.

[21] 王一华.中国大陆图书情报专业期刊的综合评价——基于熵权法、主成分分析法和简单线性加权法的比较研究[J].情报科学,2011,29(06):943-947.

基于专用车道的危险品道路运输路径研究

陈海燕[1]　常连玉[1]　麦　乐[2]

(1. 交通运输部管理干部学院; 2. 长安大学)

摘　要　根据危险品运输过程中涉及的安全、成本等主要影响因素,构建考虑运输风险、运输成本和车道保留影响的多目标整数规划模型。设计Dijkstra算法和目标集成法相结合的混合算法求解模型。结果表明,采用专用车道进行危险品运输可使危险品运输整体网络的风险降低70%~80%,使运输时间减少40%左右,使普通车辆运行时间增加12%左右。

关键词　专用车道　危险品运输路线　多目标整数规划模型　混合算法

0　引　言

截至2019年底,危险货物道路运输经营业户约1.29万家,危险货物道路运输从业人员达165.6万人。危险货物的生产和运输规模正以每年约10%的速度增加。危险品一旦在运输途中发生事故,往往会对周边地区的经济、公共卫生和环境造成长期的灾难性后果。

国内外学者围绕危险品运输问题展开大量研究。针对危险品道路运输路线选择,早期的学者主要致力于单一目标的优化,包括最小化风险成本、人口暴露、事故后果等,后来有学者开始研究多目标优化,相较于单目标更复杂,更实用。Zero考虑成本和风险作为优化目标进行研究;Yingying Kang考虑风险价值和风险公平性;Diego考虑了风险和设施成本;陆键等人针对运输路段交通事故概率未知的情况,构建考虑运输成本和风险的危险品运输网络选线模型,并设计启发式算法求解。现阶段的研究多基于路段进行考虑,对整体运输成本考虑较少。有关运输选线问题的研究多采用复杂算法,其对于决策过程中的实用性有待考证。

针对以往研究的不足,本文确立了如下研究点:①基于整体运输网络进行研究,考虑危险品运输过程中涉及的多个因素,包括运输成本、网络风险、车道保留的影响;②考虑决策者不同风险偏好,基于目标集成方法和Dijkstra法设计求解算法。

1　数学模型

1.1　问题描述

假设$G=(V,A)$是危险品运输网络,其中V是节点集,A为节点相互连接的路段集。(i,j)表示从节

基金项目:交通运输部应用基础研究项目(2014319226270),荣获中国物流与采购联合会科技进步三等奖(证书号CFLP2018-02-03-17-02)。

点 i 到节点 j 的路段。O 为起点集,D 为终点集,K 类型的危险品必须从起点 o 运送至目的地 d 点,且 o, $d \in V$。

1.2 风险评估

在定量化风险评估中,通常将风险定义为危险品运输事故发生的概率乘以事故后果,如式(1)所示:

$$R = p * c \tag{1}$$

式中,R 为风险值;p 为危险品运输途中事故概率;c 为影响的人口数量。

1.3 专用车道设置的影响评估

将影响值量化为对运行时间的影响,其与原始通行 (i,j) 路段的时间成正比,车道数成反比,如式(2)所示:

$$E_{ij} = \frac{T_{ij}}{M_{ij} - 1} \tag{2}$$

式中,E_{ij} 为影响;T_{ij} 为车辆通过 (i,j) 路段的原始时间;M_{ij} 为 (i,j) 路段的车道数量。

1.4 数学模型

构建基于专用车道的危险品运输路线选择模型中,作如下假设:①危险品运输途中事故发生的概率恒定;②运输网络上各个路段有两条车道;③危险品的运输只经由专用车道运输。

参数说明表见表1。

参数说明表　　　　表1

参　数	参　数　说　明
$G = (V, A)$	无向运输网络
$O\{o_1, o_2, o_3, \cdots, o_w\} \in V$	运输起点
$D\{d_1, d_2, d_3, \cdots, d_w\} \in V$	运输终点
$W\{w_1, w_2, w_3, \cdots, w_n\}$	货物类型
C_{ij}	运输成本
E_{ij}	影响值
R_{ij}	危险货物运输车辆在专用路段 (i,j) 的风险值
S_w	运输成本阈值
Q_{ij}	路段 (i,j) 的风险阈值
P_{ij}	事故发生概率
H_{ij}	事故受影响人数
T_{ij}	车辆通过 (i,j) 路段所用的时间
M_{ij}	车道数量
V_{ij}	平均行驶车速
L_{ij}	节点 i 到节点 j 之间的欧式距离

假设危险品的运输只可经由专用车道运输。由此存在两个 0-1 决策变量:决策变量 y_{ij} 表示 (i,j) 路段是否设置专用车道;决策变量 x_{ij}^w 表示运输危险品 W 的车辆是否经过 (i,j) 路段。决策变量如下:

$$x_{ij}^w = \begin{cases} 1, \text{路段}(i,j) \in A \text{之间有危险品运输专用车道且运输危险品} W \text{的车辆通过该路段} \\ 0, \text{其他} \end{cases}$$

$$y_{ij} = \begin{cases} 1, \text{路段}(i,j) \in A \text{之间有危险品运输专用车道} \\ 0, \text{其他} \end{cases}$$

所建立的模型如下:

$$\min f_1 = \sum_{(i,j) \in A, w \in W} c_{ij} * x_{ij}^w \tag{3}$$

$$\min f_2 = \sum_w \sum_{(i,j) \in A} R_{ij}^w * x_{ij}^w \tag{4}$$

$$\min f_3 = \sum_{(i,j) \in A} E_{ij} * y_{ij} \tag{5}$$

$$\text{s.t.} \quad \sum_j x_{o_w j}^w = 1, \forall w \in W, o_w \in O, \forall (o_w, j) \in A \tag{6}$$

$$\sum_i x_{i d_w}^w = 1, \forall w \in W, o_w \in O, \forall (o_w, j) \in A \tag{7}$$

$$\sum_j x_{ij}^w = \sum_j x_{ji}^w, \forall w \in W, \forall i \neq o_w, d_w \forall (o_w, j) \in A \tag{8}$$

$$x_{ij}^w \leq y_{ij}, \forall w \in W, \forall (i,j) \in A \tag{9}$$

$$\sum_{(i,j) \in A, w \in W} c_{ij} * x_{ij}^w \leq Sw, \forall (i,j) \in A \tag{10}$$

$$\sum_w \sum_{(i,j) \in A} R_{ij}^w * x_{ij}^w = \sum_w \sum_{(i,j) \in A} P_{ij} * H_{ij} * x_{ij}^w \leq Q_{ij}, \forall (i,j) \in A \tag{11}$$

$$x_{ij}^w \in \{0,1\}, \forall w \in W, \forall (i,j) \in A \tag{12}$$

$$y_{ij} \in \{0,1\}, \forall w \in W, \forall (i,j) \in A \tag{13}$$

目标函数(3)表示运输危险货物 w 的成本。目标函数(4)表示运输网络风险。目标函数(5)表示车道保留对普通道路使用者的影响。若路段 (i,j) 之间不保留车道，则 E_{ij} 为 0。约束(6)和约束(7)表示运输车辆从起点 o 到终点 d 之间仅保留一条车道。约束(8)保证节点流量守恒。约束(9)保证危险货物运输车辆仅由专用车道运输。约束(10)为运输总成本。约束(11)为运输总风险。约束(12)和约束(13)为决策变量的 0-1 整数约束。

2 求解算法

上述模型是一个多目标 0-1 混合整数线性规划问题。解决多目标问题常采用的方法有加权法、迭代法、ε-constraint 方法等。一般来说计算较复杂且不考虑决策者风险偏好，不适用于现实中的动态决策。本文基于目标集成方法和 Dijkstra 算法设计模型求解。该方法可根据决策者的风险偏好，将多目标转化为单目标，求解步骤如下：

(1) 以式(6)~式(12)为约束，采用 Dijkstra 求解算法分别求得三个目标函数的最优路径解 k_1、k_2、k_3。

(2) 确定每个目标函数的下边界 $\delta_{\min}$，即该目标函数的理想点，公式如下：

$$\delta_{\min} = \min \delta(o,j) \tag{14}$$

式中，o 为始发点，j 为与 o 相邻的节点。

(3) 以 k_i 为路径，求得另外两个目标函数的值 r_i^{ki}，确定每个目标函数的上边界 $\delta_{\max}$，即该目标函数的非理想点，公式如下：

$$\delta_{\max} = \max_{1 \leq i \leq 3} \{r_i^{ki}\} \tag{15}$$

(4) 确定每个目标的隶属度函数或评价函数，公式如下：

$$\varphi_i = \begin{cases} 1, \delta < \delta_{\min} \\ \dfrac{\delta_{\max} - \delta}{\delta_{\max} - \delta_{\min}}, \delta_{\min} \leq \delta \leq \delta_{\max} \\ 0, \delta > \delta\max \end{cases} \tag{16}$$

(5) 依据决策者偏好确定各个目标占的权重 $\omega = \{\omega_1, \omega_2, \cdots, \omega_n\}$ 且 $\sum_{i=1}^{n} \omega_i = 1$。选择合适的集成算子 M_w^β 将多目标集成为单目标来表达决策者偏好。

$$M_w^\beta = (\sum_{i=1}^{3} w_i * f_i^\beta)^{1/\beta} (0 < |\beta| < \infty) \tag{17}$$

式中，f_i 表示集成目标，ω_i 表示该目标所占的权重，权重越大，该目标越重要。在实际中，一般将 β 设为 1、2 和 $-\infty$。当 β 为 1 时，其为加权平均模型即 $M_w^1 = \sum_{i=1}^{n} w_i * f_i$；当 β 为 2 时，其为加权平方平均模型即

$M_w^2 = (\sum_{i=1}^{n} w_i * f_i^2)^{1/2}$；当 β 为 $-\infty$ 时，其为 $M_w^{-\infty} = \min f_i$。选择了集成算子后，可将该多目标规划问题表示成如下形式：

$$\text{maximize} u(x) = F_w(\varphi_i(x)) \tag{18}$$

（6）上述问题（18）是一个单目标最短路径问题，可采用 Dijkstra 算法求得上述目标函数的最优路径解。

（7）结束。

3 实例求解

为简化模型求解过程，假设 $w = 1$。选取西安市某部分道路运输网络以运输石油为例进行验证，网络包含 8 个节点和 13 条边，其中节点 1 为运输起点，节点 8 为运输终点。

收集相关参数数据，包括 c_{ij}、p'_{ij}、H_{ij}、M_{ij}、v_{ij} 和 L_{ij}，其中 p'_{ij} 为不设置专用车道时运输事故概率。S_w 依概率 $L_{ij} * U(1, \sqrt{2})$ 随机生成，其中根据 L_{ij} 为节点间的欧氏距离，$U(a, b)$ 为均匀分布。Q_{ij} 定义为 $Q_{ij} = \sum_{w=1}^{W} P_{ij}^w * U(0.4, 0.6)$，$T_{ij}$ 定义为 L_{ij}/v_{ij}，其中 v_{ij} 为车辆通过 (i,j) 路段的平均行驶车速。R'_{ij} 被定义为 $p'_{ij} * H_{ij}$，因此定义 R_{ij} 为 $a * R'_{ij}$。E_{ij} 定义为 $T_{ij}/(M_{ij} - 1)$。其中参数 a 随机产生于区间 $[0.4, 0.8]$。

计算路段特征 C_{ij}、E_{ij} 和 R_{ij}。采用 z-score 标准化方法进行数据标准化处理。如式（19）所示：

$$x' = \frac{x - \min}{\max - \min} \tag{19}$$

式中，u 为样本均值，σ 为样本标准差。表 2 为标准化后的数据。

标准化后的数据表（成本 C_{ij}，风险 R_{ij}，影响 E_{ij}） 表 2

	1	2	3	4	5	6	7	8
1	0	(0.03, 0.053, 0)	(0.1, 0.023, 0.08)	(0.065, 0, 0.20)	0	0	0	0
2	(0.03, 0.053, 0)	0	(0.21, 0.129, 0.24)	0	(0.9, 0.635, 0.64)	0	0	0
3	(0.1, 0.023, 0.08)	(0.21, 0.129, 0.24)	0	(0.192, 0.167, 0.12)	0	(0.45, 0.783, 0.72)	0	0
4	(0.065, 0, 0.2)	0	(0.192, 0.167, 0.12)	0	0	0	(1, 1, 0.92)	0
5	0	(0.9, 0.635, 0.64)	0	0	0	(0.135, 0.095, 0.32)	0	(0.35, 0.28, 1)
6	0	0	(0.45, 0.783, 0.72)	0	(0.135, 0.095, 0.32)	0	(0.35, 0.242, 0.12)	(0.3, 0.697, 0.979)
7	0	0	0	(1, 1, 0.92)	0	(0.35, 0.242, 0.12)	0	(0, 0.432, 0.76)
8	0	0	0	0	(0.35, 0.28, 1)	(0.3, 0.697, 0.979)	(0, 0.432, 0.76)	0

以式（6）~ 式（12）为约束，采用 Dijkstra 算法求得三个目标函数的最优路径解，分别为 ①-③-⑥-⑧、①-②-⑤-⑧ 和 ①-②-⑤-⑧。由于三个路径并非完全相同，继续求解。计算上述每条路径的另外两个目标函数值，求解结果见表 3。

最短路径三维矩阵 表 3

目标函数值	成本最小运输线路 ①-③-⑥-⑧	风险最小运输线路 ①-②-⑤-⑧	影响最小运输线路 ①-②-⑤-⑧
f_1	0.850	1.930	1.930
f_2	1.503	0.968	0.968
f_3	1.779	1.641	1.641

由上述三维矩阵确定每个目标函数的上下边界，得到各个目标的隶属度函数如下：

$$\varphi_1 = \begin{cases} 1, \delta < 0.03 \\ \dfrac{1.93-\delta}{1.93-0.03}, 0.030 \leqslant \delta \leqslant 1.930 \\ 0, \delta > 1.93 \end{cases}$$

$$\varphi_2 = \begin{cases} 1, \delta < 0 \\ \dfrac{1.503-\delta}{1.503}, 0 \leqslant \delta \leqslant 1.503 \\ 0, \delta > 1.503 \end{cases}$$

$$\varphi_3 = \begin{cases} 1, \delta < 0 \\ \dfrac{1.779-\delta}{1.779}, 0 \leqslant \delta \leqslant 1.779 \\ 0, \delta > 1.779 \end{cases}$$

确定各个目标占的权重 $\omega = \{\omega_1, \omega_2, \omega_3\}$,选择合适的加权开方乘方平均数 M_w^β 将多目标决策模型中的目标函数转化成单目标函数。在本文中,将 β 设为 1、2 和 $-\infty$。求得的路径见表4。

不同权重下的最优运输路径计算结果 表4

权重(w_1,w_2,w_3)	β	最优运输路径	目标函数值(成本,风险,影响)
(0.8,0.1,0.1)	$\beta=1$	①-③-⑥-⑧	(0.850,1.503,1.779)
	$\beta=2$	①-③-⑥-⑧	(0.850,1.503,1.779)
	$\beta=-\infty$	①-③-⑥-⑦-⑧	(0.900,1.480,1.680)
(0.5,0.1,0.4)	$\beta=1$	①-③-⑥-⑧	(0.850,1.503,1.779)
	$\beta=2$	①-③-⑥-⑧	(0.850,1.503,1.779)
	$\beta=-\infty$	①-③-⑥-⑦-⑧	(0.900,1.480,1.680)
(0.2,0.6,0.2)	$\beta=1$	①-②-⑤-⑧	(1.280,0.968,1.640)
	$\beta=2$	①-②-⑤-⑧	(1.280,0.968,1.640)
	$\beta=-\infty$	①-③-⑥-⑦-⑧	(0.900,1.480,1.680)
(0.2,0.3,0.5)	$\beta=1$	①-②-⑤-⑧	(1.280,0.968,1.640)
	$\beta=2$	①-②-⑤-⑧	(1.280,0.968,1.640)
	$\beta=-\infty$	①-③-⑥-⑦-⑧	(0.900,1.480,1.680)
(0.15,0.7,0.15)	$\beta=1$	①-②-⑤-⑧	(1.280,0.968,1.640)
	$\beta=2$	①-②-⑤-⑧	(1.280,0.968,1.640)
	$\beta=-\infty$	①-③-⑥-⑦-⑧	(0.900,1.4800,1.68)

为验证专用车道对危险品运输的影响,设 Risk_r 和 Time_r 分别为运输路径的总运输风险和运输时间。设 Risk_{nr} 为未使用预留车道时的总运输风险,Time_{nr} 为其对应的总运输时间。计算 $\text{Risk}_r/\text{Risk}_{nr}$ 和 $\text{Time}_r/\text{Time}_{nr}$ 说明预留车道前后的运输风险和运输时间的变化。为研究专用车道对普通车辆的影响。设 GR 为出行时间增长率,定义为运输时间增加量除以实施专用车道前的运行时间,如式(20)所示:

$$GR = \sum_W \sum_{(i,j) \in A} E_{ij} x_{ij}^w \Big/ \sum_W \sum_{(i,j) \in A} T_{ij} x_{ij}^w \tag{20}$$

计算结果见表5。

实施专用车道前后对比 表5

路径	$\text{Risk}_r/\text{Risk}_{nr}$	$\text{Time}_r/\text{Time}_{nr}$	GR
①-②-⑤-⑧	0.286	0.645	0.126
①-③-⑥-⑧	0.254	0.612	0.131
①-③-⑥-⑦-⑧	0.267	0.589	0.122

结果表明,实施专用车道可使危险品运输风险降低70%~80%;使运输时间减少40%左右;会使普通车辆运行时间增加12%左右。

4 结 语

本研究从运输成本、运输风险和车道保留的影响三个角度出发,构建了确定环境下的危险品运输多目标决策模型,设计Dijkstra算法和目标集成法相结合的混合算法求解模型。

本研究的贡献在于:①基于整体运输网络进行研究,考虑危险品运输过程中涉及的多个目标,包括运输成本、整体风险和车道保留的影响;②提出了求解多目标函数最优路径的折中解方法;③将专用车道引入危险品运输网络选线问题中。

参考文献

[1] 孙一帆.基于区域范围的重大危险源风险评估及应急场所布局研究[D].西安:长安大学,2019.

[2] 滕玥,孙丽君,周雅娴.考虑危险品运输风险的多车型车辆路径优化方法[J].系统工程,2020(01):1-11.

[3] Yunfei Fang, Xiaoyuan Wang, Peng Wu, et al. Model and solution for lane reservation problem with optimally grouping tasks[J]. IEEE,2018.

[4] Smith N, Hensher D. The future of exclusive busways: the Brazilian experience[J]. Transport Reviews, 1998, 18(2):131-152.

[5] John Black. Strategic transport planning, demand analysis of transport infrastructure and transport services for the 27th Summer Olympiad held in Sydney, Australia, 2000[J]. Journal of Transportation Engineering and Information,2004(02):14-30+40.

[6] Efthymis Zagorianakos. Athens 2004 olympic games transportation plan: a missed opportunity for Strategic Environmental Assessment (SEA) integration[J]. Journal of Transport Geography,2003,12(2):115-125.

[7] Judith Princeton, Simon Cohen. Impact of a Dedicated Lane on the Capacity and the Level of Service of an Urban Motorway[J]. Procedia-Social and Behavioral Sciences, 2011, 16:196-206.

[8] Yunfei Fang, Feng Chu, Saïd Mammar, et al. An optimal algorithm for automated truck freight transportation via lane reservation strategy[J]. Transportation Research Part C,2013(26):170-183.

[9] Zhou Z, Chu F, Che A, et al. epsilon-Constraint and Fuzzy Logic-Based Optimization of Hazardous Material Transportation via Lane Reservation[J]. IEEE Transactions on Intelligent Transportation Systems, 2013, 14(2):847-857.

[10] Bai Xue, Zhou Zhili, et al. Evaluating lane reservation problems by carbon emission approach[J]. Transport Research Part D, 2017:178-192.

[11] 陆键,刘禹杰,马晓丽.基于博弈论的危险品运输网络选线[J].中国公路学报,2018,31(04):322-329.

[12] Zero L, Bersani C, Sacile R, et al. Bi-objective shortest path problem with one fuzzy cost function applied to dangerous goods transportation on a road network[J]. System of Systems Engineering Conference, IEEE, 2016:1-5.

[13] Yingying Kang, Rajan Batta, Changhyun Kwon. Generalized route planning model for hazardous material transportation with VaR and equity considerations[J]. Computers and Operations Research,2014(43):237-247.

[14] Diego Beneventti G, Andrés Bronfman, Germán Paredes-Belmar, et al. A multi-product maximin hazmat routing-location problem with multiple origin-destination pairs[J]. Journal of Cleaner Production,2019(240).

[15] Erkut E, Verter V. Modeling of Transport Risk for Hazardous Materials[J]. Operations Research, 1998,

[16] Yingfeng Wu, Chengbin Chu, Feng Chu, et al. Heuristic for lane reservation problem in time constrained transportation[C]// Automation Science and Engineering, 2009. CASE 2009. IEEE International Conference 2009:543-548.

[17] T'Kindt V, Billaut J C. Multicriteria scheduling problems: a survey[J]. RAIRO-Operations Research, 2001, 35(2):143-163.

[18] 韩世莲,刘新旺.物流运输网络多目标最短路问题的模糊满意解[J].运筹与管理,2014: 23(05): 55-61.

[19] Che A, Wu P, Chu F, et al. Improved Quantum-Inspired Evolutionary Algorithm for Large-Size Lane Reservation[J]. IEEE Transactions on Systems, Man, and Cybernetics: Systems, 2015, 45(12).

Research on Location Problem of Express Distribution Center based on Barycenter Method

Yiwei Zheng

(Kharkov National Automobile highway University)

Abstract When logistics enterprises plan and design distribution centers, reasonable selection of distribution centers can greatly reduce their operating costs and speed up the flow of goods. In view of the location problem of express distribution center, based on the average daily receiving and sending volume of each existing distribution point of SF express inSaihan district and Xincheng District of Hohhot, the optimized coordinates of distribution center in the region are obtained by gravity method, which provides the basis for SF express to choose a reasonable distribution center and reduce transportation costs.

Keywords Logistics Distribution Centre Site selection Barycenter method

0 Introduction

Distribution center is an important part of modern logistics system. The location of distribution center not only needs to consider a series of common problems of all enterprises, such as workload, transportation cost, human resources, but also needs to consider the local specific geographical location, population density distribution, traffic conditions, economic and social factors factor.

As shown by Baohua W. et al., robust optimization model is used in logistics optimization, and enumeration method and genetic algorithm are proposed. Iyigun Cem. et al. proposed an iterative method for logistics location. By using distance and probability, the multi facility location problem is transformed into a single facility location problem. Wang Zimin adopted the least square method to establish a linear regression equation to analyze the relationship between economic growth, Internet development and the trend of express industry.

There are many factors affecting the site selection, and the evaluation and analysis methods can be divided into fixed and quantitative methods. The qualitative method considers the influencing factors comprehensively and selects the best from them, while the quantitative method focuses on some single key factors and uses data calculation to determine the accurate evaluation scheme. For example, advantages and disadvantages comparison method, expert survey method, weighted factor comparison method and other qualitative methods;

volume cost profit analysis method and gravity method are mainly used for quantitative methods. Both have their own advantages, but in the actual location decision, qualitative method should be used as far as possible, and quantitative method as a supplement.

Taking Saihan district and Xincheng District of Hohhot as examples, this paper investigates the actual value of the average daily delivery volume of each existing distribution point of SF express within the area, adopts the single facility location method and gravity method to optimize the location problem, and obtains the optimized location coordinates.

1 Gravity Center Location Method

Barycenter method, also known as grid method or precise barycenter method, can solve the problem of facility location by using the principle of solving barycenter for a group of discrete particles in physics. In the case that the transportation cost accounts for a large proportion of the production cost, the center of gravity method is suitable for delivery from one factory to multiple distribution centers or warehouses, or from one distribution center or warehouse to multiple sales points. It can be very effective to solve the optimal location coordinates, the minimum transportation cost and the number of iterations of the algorithm. Barycenter method is suitable for single distribution center or factory location. It is assumed that in the model (Fig.1), the freight volume of a region is regarded as the freight volume of a centralized point. The transportation cost is only related to the linear distance between the distribution center and the distribution point.

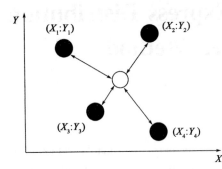

Fig.1 Gravity Center Model

Let the coordinates of each store be (x_n, y_n), the objective function of Q_i is as follows:

$$C_x = \frac{\sum D_{ix} Q_i}{\sum Q_i} \quad (1)$$

$$C_y = \frac{\sum D_{iy} Q_i}{\sum Q_i} \quad (2)$$

where

C_x——the coordinate of the center of gravity point x;

D_{ix}——the x coordinate of i location;

C_y——the coordinate of the center of gravity point y;

D_{iy}——the y coordinate of i location.

2 Case Analysis

Hohhot is divided into four districts: Saihan District, Xincheng District, Yuquan District and Huimin district. Saihan district mainly includes inner Mongolia University, Inner Mongolia Agricultural University and Inner Mongolia Normal University. The new urban area mainly includes inner Mongolia University of technology, Art College of Inner Mongolia University and Inner Mongolia Vocational College of Finance and taxation.

2.1 Site Selection of Saihan District Distribution Center

2.1.1 Average daily Freight Volume of Saihan District

According to the actual survey and statistics, the daily freight volume of each distribution point of SF express in Saihan district is shown in Tab. 1.

Average daily Freight Volume of Saihan District   Tab. 1

Business Outlets	Freight Volume (Diece/Day)
SF express Business Point, Hulunbeier South Road	325
SF Express Jinyu Diamond Store	300
SF Express (Golden Garden)	300
SF Express (Qiushi Store)	150
SF Express (Wanda Store)	800
SF Express (Greenland Cezanne)	1200
SF Express (Dingxiang Road)	300

2.1.2 Center of Gravity Location Process

Shunfeng Qiushi store, Wanda store, Greenland Saishang store, Dingxiang Road store, Jinyu diamond store, jinhuayuan store and Hulunbeier South Road store are numbered in turn, as shown in Fig. 2.

Saihan District SF Express Distribution Point Number   Tab. 2

Distribution Point	Number
SF Express (Qiushi Store)	A
SF Express (Wanda Store)	B
SF Express (Greenland Cezanne)	C
SF Express (Dingxiang Road)	D
SF Express Jinyu Diamond Store	E
SF Express (Golden Garden)	F
SF Express Business Point, Hulunbeier South Road	G

As shown in Fig. 2, the intersection of south 2nd Ring Road and Zhaojun road is selected as the coordinate origin, the horizontal axis is the horizontal axis, and the vertical axis is the vertical axis to establish the coordinate system.

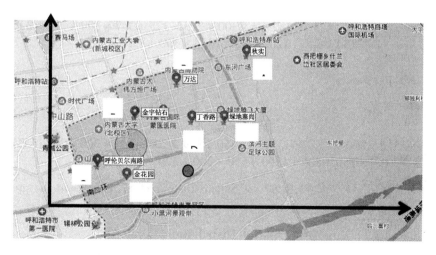

Fig. 2 Coordinates of Distribution Points in Saihan District

The coordinates of each point on the map are determined according to a certain proportion, as shown in

Fig. 3. The coordinates of each distribution point are obtained from the map, as shown in Tab. 3.

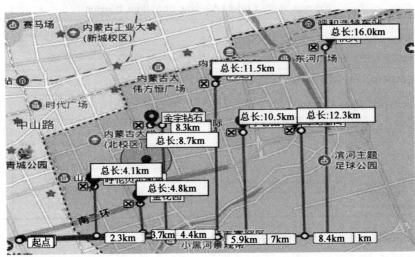

Fig. 3 Distribution Point Coordinates

Coordinates of Distribution Points in Saihan District   Tab. 3

Distribution Point	Coordinate
SF Express (Qiushi Store)	$P_A(9.1, 6.9)$
SF Express (Wanda Store)	$P_B(5.9, 5.6)$
SF Express (Greenland Cezanne)	$P_C(8.3, 4.0)$
SF Express (Dingxiang Road)	$P_D(6.7, 3.8)$
SF Express Jinyu Diamond Store	$P_E(4.0, 3.9)$
SF Express (Golden Garden)	$P_F(3.7, 1.1)$
SF Express Business Point, Hulunbeier South Road	$P_G(2.3, 1.8)$

Substituting X and Y of each distribution point into (1) and (2) respectively, the following results are obtained:

$$C_x = \frac{\sum D_{ix} Q_i}{\sum Q_i}$$

$$= \frac{9.1 \times 150 + 5.9 \times 800 + 8.3 \times 1200 + 4 \times 300 + 2.3 \times 325 + 3.7 \times 300 + 2.3 \times 325}{150 + 800 + 1200 + 300 + 325 + 300 + 325}$$

$$= 5.03$$

$$C_y = \frac{\sum D_{ix} Q_i}{\sum Q_i}$$

$$= \frac{6.9 \times 150 + 5.6 \times 800 + 4 \times 1200 + 3.8 \times 550 + 3.9 \times 300 + 1.1 \times 300 + 1.8 \times 325}{150 + 800 + 1200 + 550 + 300 + 300 + 325} = 3.67$$

Mark the center of gravity $P_1(5.03, 3.67)$ of Saihan District of SF express in the green mark in Fig. 2 according to the coordinate system.

2.2 Site Selection of Xincheng District Distribution Center

2.2.1 Average daily Freight Volume of Xincheng District

According to the actual survey and statistics, the daily freight volume of each distribution point of SF express in Xincheng district is shown in Tab. 4.

Average daily Freight Volume of Xincheng District Tab. 4

Business Outlets	Freight Volume (Diece/Day)
SF Express (Longyu Recreation Park North)	475
SF Express (North Asia motor)	600
SF Express (Victoria)	550
SF Express (University of Technology)	300
SF Express (racetrack)	500

2.2.2 Center of Gravity Location Process

The North store of Shunfeng Longyu Recreation Park, North Asia Auto Store, Victoria Store, University of Technology Store and Racecourse Store are numbered in turn, as shown in Fig. 5.

Xincheng District SF Express Distribution Point Number Tab. 5

Distribution Point	Number
SF Longyu Recreation Park	H
North Asia Auto Store	I
Victoria Store	J
University of Technology Store	K
Racecourse Store	L

As shown in Fig. 4, the coordinate system is established with the intersection of Zhongshan Road and Tongdao South Road as the coordinate origin, the horizontal axis as the horizontal axis and the vertical axis as the vertical axis.

Fig. 4　Coordinates of Distribution Points in Xincheng District

The coordinates of each point on the map are determined according to a certain proportion, as shown in Fig. 5. The coordinates of each distribution point are obtained from the map, as shown in Tab. 6.

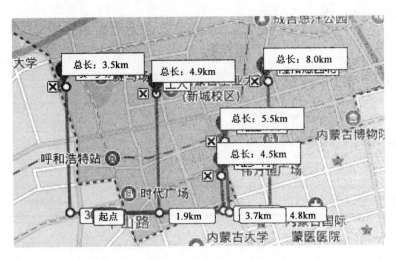

Fig. 5 Distribution Point Coordinates

Coordinates of Distribution Points in Xincheng District   Tab. 6

Distribution Point	Coordinate
SF Longyu Recreation Park	$P_H(4.8, 3.2)$
North Asia Auto Store	$P_I(3.7, 1.8)$
Victoria Store	$P_J(3.6, 0.9)$
University of Technology Store	$P_K(1.9, 3.0)$
Racecourse Store	$P_L(-0.36, 3.14)$

Substituting X and Y of each distribution point into (1) and (2) respectively, the following results are obtained:

$$C_x = \frac{\sum D_{ix} Q_i}{\sum Q_i} = \frac{4.8 \times 475 + 3.7 \times 600 + 3.6 \times 550 + 1.9 \times 300 - 0.36 \times 500}{457 + 600 + 550 + 300 + 500} = 2.29$$

$$C_y = \frac{\sum D_{ix} Q_i}{\sum Q_i} = \frac{3.2 \times 475 + 1.8 \times 600 + 0.9 \times 550 + 3.0 \times 300 + 3.1 \times 500}{475 + 600 + 550 + 300 + 500} = 2.66$$

Mark the center of gravity $P_2(2.83, 2.66)$ of Xincheng District of SF express in the green mark in Fig. 4 according to the coordinate system.

3 Conclusions

A single distribution center is the simplest distribution center. For many distribution points, only one distribution center is set up to organize goods distribution. In this paper, we take Saihan district and Xincheng District as the research object, investigate the actual value of the average daily delivery volume of each existing distribution point of SF express within the regional scope, and use the gravity method to optimize the location problem. The optimized location coordinates are obtained as the coordinates of the gravity point of Saihan District, $P_1(5.03, 3.67)$, and the coordinates of the center of gravity in the new urban area are the center of gravity $P_2(2.83, 2.66)$, which can realize the reasonable distribution of distribution centers.

Of course, this paper only considers the transportation cost, in the later research process, we can properly consider the impact of other factors on the distribution center, and further improve the theoretical research.

Reference

[1] Baohua W, Shiwei He. Robust Optimization Model and Algorithm for Logistics Center Location and

[1] Allocation under Uncertain Environment [J]. Journal of Transportation Systems Engineering and Information Technology,2009,9:69-74.
[2] Cem Iyiguna, Adi Ben-Israel. A generalized Weiszfeld Method for the Multi-facility Location Problem. Operations Research Letters,2010,38: 207-214.
[3] Wang Zimin. Research on the Relationship between Economic Growth, Internet Development and Express Delivery Industry [J]. Journal of Beijing Jiaotong University,2012,11,63-67,73.
[4] Yi Junmin. Logistics Engineering[M]. Electronic Industry Press,2009.
[5] Kong Jili,Feng Ailian. Design and Implementation of Experimental Teaching Single Facility Gravity Method Location System[J]. Logistics Engineering and Management,2010,32:139-142.

基于博弈分析的电子产品逆向物流研究

王雪韵　胡大伟　张世鹏

（长安大学）

摘　要　科技的进步使电子产品更新换代的速度越来越快，与此同时，废弃电子产品的大量产生也带来了许多问题，如何回收处理这些电子废弃物十分关键。为分析这个问题，本文基于博弈理论和逆向物流的思想，建立以政府、消费者、企业三者利益为主体的博弈模型，分析使三者之间达到稳定的影响因素，结果发现，政府参与管控的力度一定程度上决定着消费者参与逆向物流的积极程度，而消费者对逆向物流的重视较大程度上影响着生产商对逆向物流的投入，三者有着相互制约的关系，最后提出对电子废弃物逆向回收建议。

关键词　博弈论　逆向物流　电子废弃物

0　引　言

联合国大学在对全球电子垃圾研究的报告中显示，2016 年，全球电子垃圾的总量约为4470 万 t，其中有近40.7% 出现在部分东南亚国家及中国。电子产品往往包含许多对人体有害的物质，随意丢弃会对环境和人体健康造成极大的危害。除了这个原因之外，许多电子设备都含有黄金等贵金属，回收电子废弃物能带来巨大的经济效益。

我国学者周垂日总结了国外学者的研究成果，对逆向物流进行定义。刘小运等研究了竞争环境下零售商逆向物流的定价策略，何捷娴等从制造商的角度建立 LED 照明行业逆向物流模式选择决策模型。部峪佼等调查分析了 B2C 模式下中小型跨境企业逆向物流成本的影响。马建龙等构建了以总成本为目标的固体废弃物逆向物流动态选址模型，并用仿真实验验证了模型的有效性。周珍等针对有无政府引导设计了两种废旧汽车逆向物流网络。李伯棠等考虑碳交易收支建立了再制造物流网络鲁棒混合线性规划模型，为低碳逆向物流网络设计提供思路。

我国电子行业发展迅猛，电子废弃物处理逐渐成为隐患。王子薇提出利用物联网、大数据等技术进行网络构建，雏骏通过调查构建兰州市废旧手机回收网络体系。林雅菲等利用预测模型构建北京市废旧家电逆向物流体系。汪嘉琪提出了一个多目标优化模型，有效降低了回收成本。

许多学者也开始将博弈论应用在逆向物流的研究上，易霄翔研究了逆向物流正规回收商和非正规回收商分别和政府之间的博弈关系。原逸超等应用演化博弈理论研究政府和企业之间的博弈关系。通过分析发现，在关于逆向物流博弈的研究中二者博弈研究的较多，但同时考虑企业、消费者、政府的研究较少，本文采用完全信息静态博弈的理论，以递进的方式分别研究了政府与生产商二者之间，政府、生产商和消费者三者之间的博弈关系,得到三者混合策略的纳什均衡解并进行分析,最后给出建议。

1 政府、生产商和消费者之间的博弈模型的构建

1.1 博弈三方的关系分析

政府、生产商和消费者之间存在的博弈关系分析如下：

(1)政府。在博弈过程中,政府起着很重要的作用,政府拥有命令企业执行的能力和给予奖励的措施,政府的态度对消费者有着巨大的影响,政府的鼓励可以使更多的消费者参与回收过程。

(2)生产商。本文中讨论的是电子产品的原始生产商,由这些企业生产也由这些企业回收,不讨论外包。企业进行回收可以再次收获其中的价值,获得消费者的青睐,不进行回收则会受到政府方面的处罚,也会因为不良的企业形象失去众多潜在客户。

(3)消费者。消费者的收益主要是政府的奖励补贴等。消费者群体的意见和倾向对生产商具有一定影响力,企业长时间进行良好的逆向回收工作能够加速环境美化的过程,生存环境的优化也算是消费者得到的一份间接收益。

1.2 模型假设和主要参数

假设1:消费者、政府、生产商均为理性人,三者追求的目标均是达到利益最大化。

假设2:二者进行的是完全信息静态博弈。

假设3:政府在博弈中的身份为管理者,可采取的决策:"管理"和"不管理"。生产商是执行者,可采取的决策:"执行"和"不执行"。

假设4:消费者是三方博弈中的参与者,消费者的策略分别是"参与"和"不参与",消费者选择策略"参与"的概率为z。

相关参数如下。

G:政府管理生产商所获得的环境收益。

P:政府管理生产商支出的管理成本。

T:政府对不合格的生产商进行罚款获得的收益。

A:政府给配合回收的生产商的补贴。

B:生产商未执行逆向回收时的基本收入。

C:政府管理前的额定管理成本。

R:生产商执行逆向回收从电子废弃物中额外取得的经济收益。

W:生产商执行逆向回收付出的全部成本。

Q:消费者参与逆向回收时获得的政府补贴。

J_1:生产商执行逆向回收时消费者参与回收获得的收益。

J_2:生产商执行逆向回收时消费者不参与回收获得的收益。

D:消费者参与逆向回收付出的人力、物力和时间等成本。

e:生产商执行逆向回收时,消费者所获得的环境效益。

f:生产商不执行逆向回收时废物堆积对消费者生活造成的空间、环境等间接损害。

2 政府、生产商和消费者之间的博弈模型的构建

2.1 混合策略下政府和生产商之间的博弈

首先考虑政府和生产商之间的博弈,这时假设政府对生产商管理的概率为x,生产商执行逆向回收的概率为y。可以得到如表1所示的收益矩阵。

政府和生产商之间的混合策论博弈			表1
	生产商		
政府	执行(y)	不执行($1-y$)	
管理(x)	$G+C-P-A, B-W+A+R$	$C-P+T, B-T$	
不管理($1-x$)	$G+C, B-W+R$	C, B	

政府管理的收益:$H_1 = y(G+C-P-A) + (1-y)(C-P+T)$
政府不管理的收益:$H_2 = y(C+G) + (1-y)C$
政府的总体收益:
$$H_3 = x[y(G+C-P-A) + (1-y)(C-P+T)] + (1-x)[y(C+G) + (1-y)C]$$
对总收益 H_3 关于管理概率 x 求导得到解:$y^* = \dfrac{T-P}{A+T}$
生产商执行的收益:$F_1 = x(B-W+A+R) + (1-x)(B-W+R)$
生产商不执行的收益:$F_2 = x(B-T) + (1-x)B$
生产商的总收益:
$$F_3 = y[x(B-W+A+R) + (1-x)(B-W+R)] + (1-y)[x(B-T) + (1-x)B]$$
对总收益 F_3 关于执行概率 y 求导得到解:$x^* = \dfrac{W-R}{A+T}$

对上述博弈结果进行分析。

（1）政府为了达到效益最大化应该将取"管理"的概率取为$\dfrac{W-R}{A+T}$，概率 x 与 A、T 存在明显的减函数关系，即加大对生产商的补贴和惩罚力度，都会促使政府倾向于管理生产商，因此国家出台更严格的补贴和惩罚政策，可以规范企业、也可以提高地方政府的重视程度和参与度。x 与 R 也有着明显的减函数关系，当企业获得的经济利益越高时，政府越倾向于管理。这个结果表明企业的逆向回收应该重视回收后的再利用过程，在废弃物中获取更多的价值才更能调动企业的积极性和政府的关注，因此建议大力发展回收再利用相关技术。

（2）生产商为了达到利益最大化应该将"执行"概率取为$\dfrac{T-P}{A+T}$，概率 y 与 A 存在明显的减函数关系，即加大对生产商的补贴力度会促进生产商参与逆向回收。y 与 P 有着明显的减函数关系，即当政府管理投入的成本越高，生产商越倾向于执行逆向回收，政府对企业的帮扶越大，企业参与逆向物流的积极性越高。

2.2 混合策略下政府、生产商和消费者之间的博弈

现引入消费者，通过分析得出三者博弈所得收益，其中表2中自上而下分别是政府、生产商、消费者的收益。

政府、生产商、消费者之间的混合策论博弈					表2
	消费者参与(z)		消费者不参与($1-z$)		
政府	生产商执行(y)	生产商不执行($1-y$)	生产商执行(y)	生产商不执行($1-y$)	
管理(x)	$G+C-P-A-Q$ $B-W+A+R$ $Q-D+e+J_1$	$C-P-Q+T$ $B-T-S$ $Q-D-f$	$G+C-P-A$ $B-W+A+R$ $e+J_2$	$C-P-T$ $B-T$ $-f$	
不管理($1-x$)	$C+G$ $C-W+R$ $e+J_1+D$	C $B-S$ $-D-f$	$C+G$ $C-W+R$ $e+J_2$	C B $-f$	

政府采取"管理"策略的收益：

$\text{Profit}_x = z[y(G+C-P-A-Q)+(1-y)(C-P+T-Q)] + (1-z)[y(G+C-P-A)+(1-y)(C-P+T)] = yG - yA + C + T - P - yT - zQ$

政府采取"不管理"策略的收益：

$\text{Profit}_{1-x} = z[y(G+C)+(1-y)C] + (1-z)[y(C+G)+(1-y)C] = yG + C$

生产商采取"执行"策略的收益：

$\text{Profit}_y = x[z(B-W+A+R)+(1-z)(B-W+A+R)] + (1-x)[z(B-W+R)+(1-z)(B-W+R)] = xA + B + R - W$

生产商采取"不执行"策略的收益：

$\text{Profit}_{1-y} = x[z(B-T-S)+(1-z)(B-T)] + (1-x)[z(B-S)+(1-z)B] = B - zS - xT$

消费者采取"参与"策略的收益：

$\text{Profit}_z = y[x(Q-D+e+J_1)+(1-x)(e+J_1-D)] + (1-y)[x(Q-f-D)+(1-x)(-D-f)] = xQ + ye + yJ_1 - D - f + yf$

消费者采取"不参与"策略的收益：

$\text{Profit}_{1-z} = y[x(J_2+e)+(1-x)(J_2+e)] + (1-y)[-fx-f(1-x)] = yJ_2 + yf - f + ye$

根据混合策略的概念，对三组数据进行求解。

令 $\text{Profit}_x = \text{Profit}_{1-x}$，即 $yG - yA + C + T - yT - zQ = yG + C$，得到政府达到博弈均衡时，生产商采取"执行"策略的概率：

$$y = \frac{T-P-zQ}{A+T}$$

令 $\text{Profit}_y = \text{Profit}_{1-y}$，即 $xA + B + R - W = B - zS - xT$，得到生产商达到博弈均衡时，消费者采取"参与"策略的概率：

$$z = \frac{W-xA-xT-R}{S}$$

令 $\text{Profit}_z = \text{Profit}_{1-z}$，即 $ye + yJ_1 + xQ - D - f + yf = yJ_2 + ye - f + yf$，得到消费者达到博弈均衡时，政府采取"管理"策略的概率：

$$x = \frac{yJ_2 - yJ_1 + D}{Q}$$

对上述博弈进行分析。

(1) 当政府"管理"策略的概率 $x = \frac{yJ_2 - yJ_1 + D}{Q}$，$x$ 跟参数 J_2、D 有着明显的递增函数关系，即加大消费者参与的成本和企业执行时消费者不参与回收获得的收益会打击消费者参与的积极性。同时，x 与 J_1、Q 是减函数关系，当政府对参与的消费者的补贴增多、消费者参与回收获得的环境收益越多时，消费者也更倾向于参与回收。

(2) 当生产商"执行"策略的概率 $y = \frac{T-P-zQ}{A+T}$，y 与 A、P、Q 有着明显的递减函数关系，随着 A、P、Q 的增大，y 在不断变小，政府倾向于不管理的可能性越大，因为想要达到较好的管理效果，政府需要投入极高的成本，此时加大对生产商的罚款 T，随着 T 的增大，y 的增大速度较快，政府倾向于"管理"。

(3) 当消费者"参与"的概率 $z = \frac{W-xA-xT-R}{S}$ 时，z 与 A、T、R 有着明显的递减函数关系，随着 A、T、R 的增大，z 逐渐减小，生产商倾向于选择执行，即增加政府对生产商的补贴，加大对违规生产商的罚款和利用技术手段加大回收的电子废弃物的剩余价值有利于推动生产商执行回收。同时，z 与 S 有着明显的反比关系，当 S 增大时，z 减小的速度较快，即消费者对企业形象的看法对促进企业进行逆向回收的有着较大的影响。

3 结　　语

根据博弈结果提出几点建议：

(1)政府加大管理力度、提高补贴水平。在对博弈三方分析中,对生产商的补贴在大部分均衡解中都有着很大的影响,提高对生产商的补贴水平来呼吁和吸引更多生产商进行电子废弃物的逆向回收这一措施将会起到立竿见影的效果。同时,研究政府和生产商关系时发现,政府倾向于管理的态度对生产商的影响也很大,政府越认真管理,生产商越会感到压力而愿意执行。

(2)加大惩罚力度、发展回收技术。在政府的能够投入管理的成本有限时,对生产商的惩罚能够很大程度的影响生产商执不执行的意愿,我国的电子废弃物回收还没有形成完善的体系,这时加大惩罚力度,能在管理初期就得到良好的效果。同时,在对生产商分析时发现增加电子废弃物的回收价值能够促使企业对其进行逆向回收,所以建议积极发展再利用新技术,这样既可以获得电子废弃物直接的价值,也在无形中得到间接的环境收益。

(3)重视引导消费者。消费者积极参与就会带动生产商积极执行,所以政府应该利用好这一优势,通过补贴奖励,来引导消费者积极参与企业逆向回收。同时,当企业执行逆向回收时消费者无需参与就能获得的环境收益越多,消费者的主动性就越不强,所以建议实际生活中政府可以考虑出台政策和规定等促使消费者参与逆向回收,采取鼓励和惩罚并行的模式,比起单独补贴更能增加消费者的参与度。

参考文献

[1] 国外CSR动态[J].WTO经济导刊,2018(01):17-19.

[2] 张馨艺.全球电子废弃物增长迅速[J].生态经济,2020,36(10):1-4.

[3] 叶智毅.关于电子废弃物循环再利用的分析与探究[J].中国资源综合利用,2019,37(07):63-65.

[4] 周垂日,梁樑,许传永,等.逆向物流研究的新进展:文献综述[J].科研管理,2007(03):123-132.

[5] 刘小运,王艳杰.竞争环境下逆向物流的定价决策研究[J].渤海大学学报(自然科学版),2016,37(01):11-14,18.

[6] 何捷娴,樊宏,尹荔松.LED照明行业逆向物流模式选择决策分析[J].科技管理研究,2015,35(02):214-218.

[7] 部峪佼,贾嘉,王晓歌.基于B2C模式中小跨境电商企业逆向物流成本优化研究[J].对外经贸,2019(08):90-91,98.

[8] 马建龙,蒋婧秋.城市固体废弃物逆向物流与节约环境治理成本研究——基于多周期与多目标的动态选址分析[J].价格理论与实践,2020(07):77-80.

[9] 周珍,杨斌,许波桅,等.政府引导下的报废汽车逆向物流网络优化设计[J].现代制造工程,2015(12):113-120,125.

[10] 李伯棠,赵刚.基于鲁棒优化的低碳再制造物流网络模型[J].山东大学学报(理学版),2017,52(01):43-55.

[11] 程宇林.试论电子产品行业发展现状[J].科技展望,2016,26(10):296.

[12] 王子薇."互联网+"背景下电子废弃物逆向物流网络构建研究[J].福建茶叶,2019,41(05):32.

[13] 雒骏.兰州市废旧手机回收处理体系研究[D].兰州:兰州交通大学,2017.

[14] 林雅菲,杨鎣铭.基于报废量预测的北京市废旧家电逆向物流研究[J].中国市场,2017(05):159-163,173.

[15] 汪嘉琪.电子废弃物逆向物流网络的多目标优化模型[J].科技与创新,2019(24):32-34.

[16] 易霄翔.电子废弃物逆向物流回收商与政府之间的演化博弈研究[J].物流工程与管理,2015,37(11):20-24,49.

[17] 原逸超,石岿然.基于演化博弈理论的WEEE方面政府环境规制策略研究[J].数学的实践与认识,2018,48(16):55-63.

A Research to Assess the Logistics Solutions for Pharmaceutical Companies in Outbreak Situations Based on Fuzzy TOPSIS

Shuaiqi Wang

(Cardiff University)

Abstract With the outbreak of the COVID-19 in early 2020, logistics research has gradually become a major issue for material protection during the pandemic. This article focuses on the importance of medical logistics risk response under the pandemic. It proposes a risk evaluation method for the risk control plan of medical enterprise logistics transportation in a fuzzy and uncertain environment.

Firstly, a combination of fuzzy decision-making theory, group decision-making, and TOPSIS methods were used to propose an evaluation method framework for pharmaceutical companies' response to the epidemic logistics plan. Secondly, consideration and establishment of a risk evaluation index system for pharmaceutical companies from the perspective of emergencies such as the pandemic was considered. Finally, the method verification was carried out on a pharmaceutical company's three logistics solutions in Linyi City as an example.

Keywords Fuzzy TOPSIS Risk assessment Epidemic risk Medical logistics

0 Introduction

(1) Research Background

The pharmaceutical logistics industry actively promotes the construction of logistics information by developing pharmaceutical cold chain logistics. It is more and more adapted to the trend of rapid economic development and technological progress in the world today.

At the beginning of 2020, the sudden new crown epidemic brought as ignificant impact to all walks of life. During the epidemic, medical logistics' development determines whether medical supplies can be supplied to the disaster-stricken areas in time, which has become the logistical support for the nation's fight against the epidemic. Firstly, the awareness of information communication is weak, and the flow of information is slow. The lack of a unified and standardized material management information platform for emergency medical supplies has led to the inability to effectively share and match the demand for medical supplies and logistics services such as production, storage, procurement, supply, and donation with supply information promptly. Secondly, the advantages of modern logistics are not prominent, and logistics costs are high. During the epidemic, the medical logistics supply chain monitoring and response plan lacked lower-level transparency. This is because digital platforms' application is not widespread in the entire supply chain, which brings difficulties to the timely response and dispatch of medical supplies. The logistics information network coverage is not comprehensive enough, which affects the effectiveness and efficiency of transportation.

(2) Domestic and foreign research

Based on the existing literature review, there are relatively few studies on supply chain risk management locally and abroad. This narrative mainly focuses on extending the theory and technology of risk management to supply chain management. Therefore, supply chain risk management is a relatively new concept. The source of supply chain risk is due to the existence of various uncertain factors. Since the enterprises on the supply chain network are interconnected, problems in any one enterprise will cause other enterprises on the supply chain network to be affected. The problems would lead to the rupture of the supply chain. Therefore, supply chain risks can also be referred to as supply chain vulnerability. As early as 2000, some scholars researched supply chain risk management. For example, Christopher and Towill (2000) pointed out that many economic development trends have made the supply chain's fragility more and more evident in year after year. In 2003, Svensson also believed that there are many interference factors in the supply chain. For a stable development of the supply chain, it is necessary to deal with these interference factors. This requires supply chain companies to understand the existing interference and the source of the interference to understand themselves and their competitors and achieve victory in all battles. Zimon (2019) research shows that no matter what role it plays in the supply chain, a standardized management system is useful in supply chain risk management. According to the general evaluation, few respondents among logistics operators have a low assessment of the legality of implementing a standardized management system. Thus, logistics companies should consider implementing standardized management systems to improve supply chain management, enhance supply chain risk management, and achieve sustainable development of supply chains.

Based on existing literature and studies, an enterprise's strategic and tactical decisions determine the extent to which it can reduce or aggravate the impact of enterprise risk events. However, public health emergencies are inevitable, and their influence can be reduced by building an efficient emergency logistics system.

Various scholars have studied the impact of major public health emergencies on the industry and the corresponding countermeasures. However, there are few systematic studies from the perspective of logistics enterprises. The research on supply chain risk management is presently mainly concentrated on qualitative aspects, with few quantitative research results. Therefore, this article is based on logistics companies' research across the country during the COVID-19 pandemic. First, it analyzes the impact of the construction of the epidemic, such as a public health event, on logistics companies. Secondly, it analyzes and proposes three logistics risk management plans under the epidemic. Lastly, it uses the TOPSIS method to evaluate and rank the three projects to get the best strategy.

(3) Thinking about risk management under the epidemic

Since medicines are not generally stored like ordinary commodities, they need to meet certain storage conditions, and they can be transported promptly when required. However, the current storage equipment is not developed enough, such as simple refrigeration equipment. The shortage of equipment makes it more challenging to store medicines, and it is impossible to transport medicines to areas where they are needed quickly. Besides, the logistics operation process is not formal enough. When a crisis occurs, the logistics and transportation that are not formal will become more chaotic, the cost will increase significantly, and the work efficiency will decrease. With the rapid development of big data, artificial intelligence can also be used to realize the informatization of emergency logistics of pharmaceutical storage. Big data to discover drug storage supervision ensures the quality of drug storage and carries out large-scale scientific and reasonable storage. In a public health emergency such as an epidemic, the required medical supplies can be quickly dispatched. Secondly, improve and optimize the pharmaceutical logistics center's functions, connect pharmaceutical companies, hospitals, and pharmacies, share information promptly, accurately and flexibly respond to requirements, and control the supply chain in advance. Finally, a better network storage plan can be improved, enabling the scientific design of drug storage in the area to be covered.

1 Evaluation framework and index system of pharmaceutical companies under the epidemic situation based on fuzzy TOPSIS

1.1 Evaluation methods based on fuzzy decision theory, group decision-making, and TOPSIS study decision-makers' priority in a fuzzy environment

For example, given a fuzzy order (reflexive, transitive binary fuzzy relation), or a non-transitive ordinary binary link, how to arrange a total order approximately; for the problem of multi-index and multi-utility function, how to use the method of fuzzy set theory synthesizes an optimal charge and how to order multi-level decision problems. These questions have been initially answered. Group process is a discipline with a long research history and modern application value in decision science. It studies how to combine the preferences of each member of a group of individuals for certain things into group preferences so that the group can sort or select all items in this category. As a means of selection, group decision-making is a powerful tool for dealing with major qualitative decision-making problems. C. L. Hwang and K. Yoon in 1981 first proposed the TOPSIS method. It is a sorting method according to the proximity of a limited number of evaluation objects to the idealized target. It is based on existing objects—evaluation of pros and cons. Among these decision-making methods, TOPSIS has become one of the most commonly used multi-objective evaluation methods because of its simplicity and intuitiveness. However, the general TOPSIS method has many shortcomings, especially in the calculation formula of closeness. If there are some unique sample points in the TOPSIS method, it may cause an unreasonable ranking. The virtual worst-case end is introduced, and the closeness calculation formula is improved. There are some problems in the calculation formula of the TOPSIS method, which leads to sorting errors. Based on two reference points close to the ideal point and far from the ideal negative point, a new formula for calculating the relative closeness is defined. The fuzzy TOPSIS method can competently deal with the quantitative, qualitative, and fuzzy uncertain factors that affect the evaluation of the pharmaceutical enterprise's logistics plan and objectively evaluate the choice of the pharmaceutical enterprise's logistics plan.

A fuzzy TOPSIS-based evaluation framework for pharmaceutical enterprise management programs is shown in Fig. 1.

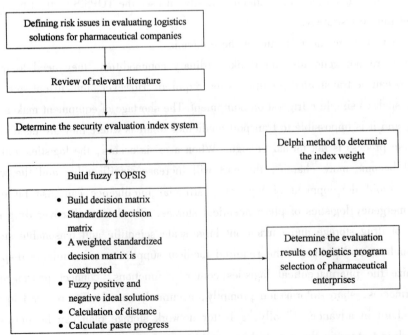

Fig. 1 A fuzzy TOPSIS-based evaluation framework for pharmaceutical enterprise management programs

1.2 Constructing an evaluation index system

The aging risk lies in the fact that there are particularly many uncertain factors in logistics transportation, which lead to long periods and low efficiency of logistics transportation, and delays in order processing, transportation, and distribution.

Information risk is embodied in two aspects: real-time tracking capability and information security. Information errors or difficulties in real-time tracking during logistics information delivery and medicines may be damaged or lost. Nowadays, logistics is gradually relying on network technology to develop. The network itself has certain security risks and even suffers from malicious attacks, which may cause information and data leakage.

Logistics losses are expected and challenging to solve in both domestic and foreign industries. The causes are mainly divided into force majeure factors such as natural disasters and customer satisfaction.

Pharmaceutical logistics involves a variety of transportation methods and logistics nodes. It has high requirements on the packaging technology, storage conditions, and return and exchange procedures of the goods, which increases the logistics costs of packaging, inventory, and transportation in the logistics process.

According to existing literature, logistics management investment refers to the funds invested in the supply chain transportation management process. The amount of funds is closely related to the standardization of supply chain management, which also impacts logistics transportation efficiency.

The environmental risk of pharmaceutical logistics refers to the risk of cross-border e-commerce logistics caused by the external environment's uncertainty, including force majeure, economic environment, policy environment, and industry environment.

Based on the above literature data, the evaluation index system shown in Tab. 1 was proposed. All the indicators will have a particular impact on the performance of logistics transportation of pharmaceutical companies.

Evaluation of index system Tab. 1

Assessment level	Indicators	Index significance
Risk limitation	Order processing efficiency	Refers to the speed and efficiency with which orders are processed
	Transport efficiency	Speed and efficiency in transportation
Information risk	Real-time information tracking capability	Refers to the real-time tracking of logistics information in the process of transmission
	Logistics information security degree	Refers to the security degree of logistics information relying on the network
Risk of loss	Cargo damage	Damage caused in the course of transportation of goods
	Customer returns and exchanges	Refers to the quality of goods and customer satisfaction
The cost of risk	The cost of transportation	The cost of transporting goods
	Inventory cost	The cost of keeping goods in stock
Logistics management input	Logistics management input	Refers to the funds invested in the transportation management of the supply chain
Environmental risk	Risk of Force Majeure	Risks arising from natural disasters and war
	Political risk	Refers to whether the policies formulated by the country in the field of pharmaceutical logistics are favorable

1.3 Decision-making process

The TOPSIS method has seven main steps, which are as follows:

Step 1: Construct language variables and their corresponding trigonometric functions.

This paper uses fuzzy semantic words to characterize the fuzzy description of decision-making members' evaluation index weights and index values. It defines two sets of fuzzy semantic words: very unimportant, unimportant, medium important, important (first set), and very important, very dissatisfied, dissatisfied, Average, satisfied, and very satisfied (second set). These fuzzy semantic words have their corresponding triangular fuzzy numbers, as shown in Tab. 2.

Triangular fuzzy comparison table Tab. 2

Index weight fuzzy semantic words	Indicator value fuzzy semantic words	Triangular fuzzy number
Very unimportant	Very dissatisfied	(0, 0, 0.25)
unimportant	Dissatisfied	(0, 0.25, 0.5)
Medium important	General	(0.25, 0.5, 0.75)
Important	Satisfied	(0.5, 0.75, 1)
Very important	Very satisfied	(0.75, 1, 1)

Step 2: Construct a decision matrix.

There are m risk control plans if P decision-makers make group decisions, and there are n risk evaluation indicators. Here, the group decision method is used to determine the evaluation index value. The triangular fuzzy number is used to represent the quantitative index. The fuzzy semantic word is used to describe the qualitative index. Therefore, the safety evaluation index values in decision-making $i(i=1,2,\cdots,n)$ can be expressed by $\tilde{x}_{ij} = (x_{ij1}, x_{ij2}, x_{ij3})$. I suppose $\tilde{x}_{ij}^p = (x_{ij1}^p, x_{ij2}^p, x_{ij3}^p)$ represents the fuzzy evaluation of the i index of the $j(j=1,2,\cdots,m)$ risk control plan by the $p(p=1,2\cdots,P)$ decision-maker. It $\tilde{x}_{ij} = (x_{ij1}, x_{ij2}, x_{ij3})$ can be calculated by formulas (1) and (2).

$$\tilde{x}_{ij} = \frac{1}{P} \otimes \sum_{p=1}^{P} \tilde{x}_{ij}^{i'} \tag{1}$$

Among them, $x_{ij1} = \frac{1}{P}\sum_{p=1}^{P} x_{ij1}^p; x_{ij2} = \frac{1}{P}\sum_{p=1}^{P} x_{ij2}^{i'}; x_{ij3} = \frac{1}{P}\sum_{p=1}^{P} x_{ij3}^p \tag{2}$

Fuzzy semantic words also determine the weight of the index. $\tilde{w}_i^p = (w_{i1}^p, w_{i2}^p, w_{i3}^p)$ is assumed that represents the $i(i=1,2,\cdots,n)$ fuzzy evaluation value of the $p(p=1,2,\cdots,p)$ decision-maker on the index's weight. Equations (3) and (4) are used to integrate the weight evaluation value $\tilde{w}_i = (w_{i1}, w_{i2}, w_{i3})$ of each decision-maker.

$$\tilde{w}_i = \frac{1}{m} \otimes \sum_{p=1}^{m} \tilde{w}_i^p = (w_{i1}, w_{i2}, w_{i3}) \tag{3}$$

Among them,

$$w_{i1} = \frac{1}{P}\sum_{p=1}^{P} w_{i1}^p; w_{i2} = \frac{1}{P}\sum_{p=1}^{P} w_{i2}^p; w_{i3} = \frac{1}{P}\sum_{p=1}^{P} w_{i3}^p \tag{4}$$

Step 3: Standardize the decision matrix.

If $\tilde{x}_{ij} = (x_{ij1}, x_{ij2}, x_{ij3})$ is a fuzzy number, then the normalized value is $\tilde{y}_{ij} = (y_{ij1}, y_{ij2}, y_{ij3})$, then the calculation formula is:

$$\tilde{y}_{ij} = \left(\frac{x_{ij1}}{x_{i3}^+}, \frac{x_{ij2}}{x_{i3}^+}, \frac{x_{ij3}}{x_{i3}^-}\right), x_{i3}^+ = \max x_{ij3} \tag{5}$$

is the maximum endpoint value of the fuzzy number in the efficiency criterion:

$$\tilde{y}_{ij} = \left(\frac{x_{i1}^-}{x_{ij3}}, \frac{x_{i1}^-}{x_{ij2}}, \frac{x_{i1}^-}{x_{ij1}} \right), x_{i1}^- = \min x_{ij1} \tag{6}$$

represents the minimum endpoint value of the fuzzy number in the cost-type criterion.

Step 4: Calculate the weighted normalization matrix.

$$\tilde{z}_{ij} = \tilde{y}_{ij} \otimes \tilde{w}_i = (z_{ij1}, z_{ij2}, z_{ij3}) = (y_{ij1} \times w_{i1}, y_{ij2} \times w_{i2}, y_{ij3} \times w_{i3}) \tag{7}$$

Step 5: Determine the fuzzy ideal solution and fuzzy negative ideal solution.

$$\tilde{z}^+ = (\tilde{z}_1^+, \tilde{z}_2^+, \cdots, \tilde{z}_i^-, \cdots, \tilde{z}_n^+) \tag{8}$$

$$\tilde{z}^- = (\tilde{z}_1^-, \tilde{z}_2^-, \cdots, \tilde{z}_j^-, \cdots, \tilde{z}_n^-) \tag{9}$$

The fuzzy ideal solution and fuzzy negative ideal solution are determined by sorting the barycenter method's fuzzy number. The fuzzy solution is fuzzy according to the following formula $\tilde{z}_{ij} = (z_{ij1}, z_{ij2}, z_{ij3})$. The fuzzy positive and negative ideal solution is determined according to the magnitude of z_{ij}.

$$z_{ij} = \frac{z_{ij1} + z_{ij2} + z_{ij3}}{3}, \forall i, j \tag{10}$$

Step 6: Calculate the distance between each candidate solution and the fuzzy positive and negative ideal solution.

Definition 1: The distance between the triangular fuzzy number $\tilde{B} = (b_1, b_2, b_3)$ and fuzzy number $\tilde{U} = (u_1, u_2, u_3)$ is:

$$d(\tilde{B}, \tilde{U}) = \sqrt{\frac{1}{3}[(b_1 - u_1)^2 + (b_2 - u_2)^2 + (b_3 - u_3)^2]} \tag{11}$$

According to Definition 1, the distance from the $\tilde{z}_{ij}$ to positive ideal solution $\tilde{z}^+$ is $d_{ij}^1 = d(\tilde{z}_{ij}, z_i^1)$, and the distance from the negative ideal solution $\tilde{z}_i^-$ is $d_{ij} = d(\tilde{z}_{ij}, z)$. Then, the distance from the $j(j = 1, 2, \cdots, m)$ risk control scheme to $\tilde{z}^+$ is $D_i^1 = \sum_{i=1}^n d_{ij}^1$, and the distance to $\tilde{z}^-$ is $D_i = \sum_{i=1}^n d_{ij}$.

Step 7: Calculate the relative sticking progress with the fuzzy positive ideal solution, and sort it

$$T_j^+ = \frac{D_j}{D_j^+ + D_j^-} \tag{12}$$

Where T_j^1 represents the relative closeness degree between the $j(j = 1, 2, \cdots, m)$ risk control scheme and the fuzzy positive ideal solution, and the greater the T_j^1 value, the higher the evaluation of the system.

2 Case Analysis

At the beginning of the epidemic, a charity's logistics operation in Wuhan was repeatedly criticized, mainly because of the opaque information, unbalanced distribution of materials, and unclear cargo information; hence, public opinion pushed it to the forefront. The problem reflected in this incident is that China's logistics has not fully utilized its advantages at this stage.

It can be seen tha timproving the logistics supply chain platform, improving the logistics warehousing system, and improving logistics efficiency has become a major issue that the academic industry needs to solve.

This paper will take a pharmaceutical company in Linyi City as an example to analyze the choice of logistics solutions for pharmaceutical enterprises under the epidemic, which still belongs to the growth trend in the general environment of the pharmaceutical industry development. 2019 pharmaceutical manufacturing business income will reach 263.27 billion yuan, an increase of about 8.5% over last year; 2020 pharmaceutical manufacturing business income will reach 2817 billion yuan, an increase of about 7% over last year. In terms of sales, the pharmaceutical market sales will reach 178.16 billion yuan in 2019, up 4% from last year; the pharmaceutical market sales will reach 1,835.1 billion yuan in 2020, up 3% from last year. 2019 China's pharmaceutical market size has reached about 1.64 trillion yuan. China's pharmaceutical market will continue to maintain a growth rate comparable to previous years and reach about 2.13 trillion yuan in 2023. And a company in Linyi suffered from the epidemic in 2020, but the annual sales growth of 3% over the same period last year.

Among the industry dynamics, the outbreak of the Spring Festival in 2020 boosted the short-term demand for Internet healthcare in China, accelerating the development of the industry, and the pharmaceutical industry spurted. A pharmaceutical company in Linyi City uses a traditional logistics model to send drug sales agents to communicate with hospitals or pharmacies about the demand for medical supplies and further transport medical supplies to the hospital or pharmacy. Nowadays, the company insists on consolidating advantageous products, promoting potential products, implementing market development strategy, showing solid, sustainable and healthy development trend of product marketing, and further sales management by establishing drug supply chain management platform. Although a pharmaceutical supply chain management platform has been initially established, pharmaceutical transportation efficiency is still low due to imperfect platform construction, untimely, accurate, and flexible information transmission. Also, since the company has its headquarter in Linyi City, Shandong Province, medical supplies are mainly stored in Linyi City. The delivery of medicines in other areas cannot be done promptly, especially in remote areas outside the province. For its enterprises, a more scientific and reasonable network storage plan should be proposed.

To solve the risk problem of medical logistics under the epidemic situation, three options are provided. The first plan is to build a drug supply chain management platform. This will connect the modern logistics information system of drug circulation with hospitals or pharmacies' business management system through interface programs. The plan will use advanced logistics information methods to integrate the medical Logistics into a new management mode under a unified platform, thereby optimizing the entire drug supply chain and reducing circulation costs.

Drug supply chain management platform is shown in Fig. 2.

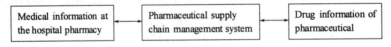

Fig. 2　Drug supply chain management platform

The second plan considers that it is difficult for pharmaceutical companies to directly build a supply chain management platform with hospitals, so third-party logistics is used for distribution. According to the supplier management inventory concept, the third-party logistics company combines the hospital's actual situation. It uses modern logistics analysis methods to ensure the hospital's drug logistics' safety, accuracy, and efficiency. It mainly includes the construction of modern drug warehouses, automated logistics equipment, and the combination of logistics and information flow.

Third-party logistics supply chain management platform is shown in Fig. 3.

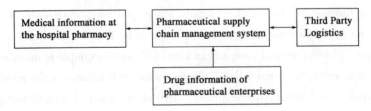

Fig. 3　Third-party logistics supply chain management platform

The third plan is to design a networked storage plan. The networked warehousing plan essentially adopts a decentralized inventory strategy, placing a certain amount of inventory in a regional warehouse that can cover a certain distribution area based on regional sales and distribution frequency, forming a nationwide warehousing network (Fig. 4), centralized management, and overall optimization. Thus, set up safety stocks according to the actual situation to ensure medical transportation response speed in emergencies. On the one hand, the networked warehousing solution can improve emergency warehousing efficiency in response to China's new crown virus epidemic prevention and control. Besides, it can provide feasible ideas for the research on logistics warehousing theory.

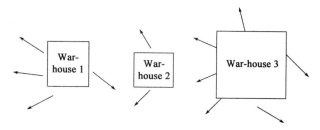

Fig. 4 Networker warehousing

Take Linyi, a pharmaceutical company, for example. The company's pharmaceutical logistics business face the epidemic's challenge. It will now use the method proposed in this article to evaluate the three programs. Considering that choosing the most suitable solution is a difficult problem, to make the evaluation more scientific, the corresponding experts were selected to form a three-person decision-making group. The specific evaluation process was as follows:

Step 1: According to the content of Tab. 1, the group decision method was used to obtain each evaluation index value, and equations (1) and (2) was used to process the fuzzy numbers, as shown in Tab. 3.

Risk assessment indicators for pharmaceutical transport schemes Tab. 3

Plans and decision-makers		Risk limitation	Information risk	Risk of loss	The cost of risk	Management input	Environmental risk
Plan1	Decision maker 1	General	Satisfied	Very unsatisfied	Very satisfied	(45,67,98)	Unsatisfied
	Decision maker 2	Satisfied	Very satisfied	Satisfied	Satisfied		General
	Decision maker 3	General	Very satisfied	Satisfied	General		General
Plan2	Decision maker 1	Very satisfied	Satisfied	Unsatisfied	Very unsatisfied	(87,98,100)	General
	Decision maker 2	Satisfied	Satisfied	General	General		Satisfied
	Decision maker 3	Satisfied	Unsatisfied	Very satisfied	Unsatisfied		Very satisfied
Plan3	Decision maker 1	Unsatisfied	Satisfied	Very unsatisfied	General	(60,65,70)	Very satisfied
	Decision maker 2	General	Satisfied	Satisfied	Unsatisfied		Satisfied
	Decision maker 3	Very satisfied	General	Unsatisfied	Unsatisfied		Satisfied

Step 2: Integration process of risk evaluation index weight.

Equations (3) and (4) was used to process the fuzzy numbers shown in Tab. 4 to obtain the evaluation indicators' integrated weights, respectively.

Fuzzy evaluation and integration of evaluation index weight Tab. 4

Decision-makers	Risk limitation	Information risk	Risk of loss	The cost of risk	Management input	Environmental risk
Decision maker 1	Medium important	Important	Medium important	Very important	Medium important	Important
Decision maker 2	Medium important	Very important	Medium important	Important	Important	Important
Decision maker 3	Very important	Important	Unimportant	Very important	Important	Medium important
Integrated weight	(0.42,0.67,0.83)	(0.58,0.83,1)	(0.17,0.42,0.67)	(0.67,0.92,1)	(0.43,0.68,0.9)	(0.42,0.67,0.92)

Step 3: Weighted decision matrix.

According to formulas (5), (6), and (7), the weighted decision matrix, as shown in Tab. 5 was calculated.

Weighted decision matrix Tab. 5

The evaluation index/Plan	Plan 1	Plan 2	Plan 3
Risk limitation	(0.14, 0.39, 0.69)	(0.29, 0.56, 0.83)	(0.14, 0.46, 0.62)
Information risk	(0.39, 0.76, 1)	(0.19, 0.48, 0.83)	(0.24, 0.56, 0.92)
Risk of loss	(0.06, 0.21, 0.50)	(0.06, 0.24, 0.50)	(0.03, 0.14, 0.39)
The cost of risk	(0.34, 0.69, 0.92)	(0.05, 0.23, 0.50)	(0.05, 0.30, 0.58)
Management input	(0.18, 0.44, 0.84)	(0.36, 0.63, 0.86)	(0.25, 0.42, 0.60)
Environmental risk	(0.07, 0.28, 0.62)	(0.21, 0.50, 0.85)	(0.24, 0.56, 0.92)

Step 4: Fuzzy positive and negative ideal solutions.

According to equations (7), (8), and (9), the following fuzzy positive and negative ideal solutions were obtained:

$\tilde{z}^+ = \{(0.29,0.56,0.83),(0.39,0.76,1),(0.06,0.24,0.50),(0.34,0.69,0.92),(0.36,0.63,0.86),(0.24,0.56,0.92)\}$

$\tilde{z}^- = \{(0.14,0.39,0.69),(0.19,0.48,0.83),(0.03,0.14,0.39),(0.05,0.23,0.50),(0.18,0.42,0.60),(0.07,0.28,0.62)\}$

Step 5: Post the progress calculation result.

According to formulas (10) and (11), the post's progress between each evaluated plan and the positive and negative ideal solution was calculated.

Judging from the calculation results in Tab. 6, the decision-maker determined the three risk control options' pros and cons: Plan 1 > Plan 2 > Plan 3.

The progress of each evaluation scheme and the positive and negative ideal solutions Tab. 6

Evaluation scheme	D_j^+	D_j^-	$D_j^+ + D_j^-$	T_j^+
Plan 1	0.579	0.835	1.414	0.590
Plan 2	0.674	0.661	1.336	0.495
Plan 3	0.940	0.494	1.434	0.345

Therefore, establishing a supply chain management service platform for the medical industry is the most appropriate logistics solution under the epidemic. A supply chain management platform can unify logistics, capital flow, information flow and service flow, and can generate relevant real-time transaction data, thus solving five problems faced by the current healthcare logistics supply chain.

Firstly, many health systems, if not independently operating departments, use different materials management information systems and agencies and departments with different processes. There would be multiple systems and multiple processes that lack cohesiveness and uniformity.

Next one, there will be high distributor fees. Most healthcare organizations spend hundreds of thousands of dollars a year on supply distribution with outside parties.

Besides, there will be a wholesaler-led pharmacy process that will obtain medications primarily from outside distributors and wholesalers, controlling the systems and processes for purchasing, ordering, receiving, and distributing medications

In addition, there is limited data available. In many health care organizations, the same products are known by different names depending on the facility or department. This reality limits the ability to aggregate data for decision making, volume purchasing, and volume ordering, thereby impacting profits.

Finally, many intermediaries or most distributors serve many customers and stock the products that are best for them to sell, but not necessarily what people need or want. This means that most healthcare organizations obtain supplies or purchase from many different distribution facilities to meet their needs.

3 Conclusions

This paper evaluates edical logistics' risk control programs under the epidemic and studies the risk evaluation index system. The paper also establishes a fuzzy TOPSIS evaluation method to solve multi-objective decision-making problems. Taking a pharmaceutical company in Linyi City as an example, the index selection was carried out, and three solutions were put forward according to the current logistics situation. The best solutions were evaluated and sorted out by TOPSIS method. Besides, the drug supply chain management platform was constructed. Although the matching process was carried out based on a limited number of solutions, it can still be seen from the optimization results that TOPSIS is a useful tool and has great potential in actual operations.

Compared with the existing research literature, this article has determined certain innovations based on two aspects: establishing evaluation indicators based on the possible risks caused by emergencies such as epidemics and using a pharmaceutical company as the research background. The examples show that this method has strong applicability and can provide effective decision-making support for industry authorities and enterprises' logistics management. Future research directions and development prospects: The relationship between enterprises and logistics suppliers has also risen from a simple transaction related to a strategic partnership, which can be regarded as a "shock absorber" for the entire supply chain. This can reduce the uncertainty of the supply chain and reduce the whole system's cost, thus helping increase the market's response speed and enhance the market's competitive position. How to scientifically evaluate and select third-party logistics providers that suit their own needs is an important topic for enterprises to strengthen their supply chain construction. It is also a hot and challenging research topic.

References

[1] Arno M, et al. An exploration of supply chain risk management in the South African third-party logistics industry, 2019, 19(1), 1-13.

[2] Chen S H, Hwang C L. Fuzzy multiple attribute decision making: methods and applications [C]. New York: Springer Verlag Berlin Heidelberg, 1992:465-486.

[3] Christopher M, Towill D. Supply Chain Migration from lean and functional to Agile and Customised[J]. An International Journal, 2000, 5(4): 206-213.

[4] Dominik Z, Peter M. Standardized management systems and risk management in the supply chain, 2019, 37(2): 305-327.

[5] Fangfu S, Zhimeng L. The impact of major public health emergencies on the economy, transmission, and response: A case study of Covid-19 epidemic [J]. Business Economics, 2020 (3): 12-20.

[6] Gerhard U, et al. Taxonomies of trust in supply chain risk management in the South African third party logistics industry, 2019, 19(1): 1-14.

[7] HE Y, LIU N. Methodology of emergency medical logistics for public health emergencies [J]. Transportation research, 2015, 79(4): 178-200.

[8] Jia L. The epidemic situation of express logistics "new bureau" [N]. China Post News, 2020.
[9] Lingmin J. Ideal Solution Method and Its Application in the Comprehensive Evaluation of Commercial Bank's Operation Performance [J]. Systems Engineering Theory and Method Application, 2002, 11(3): 227-230.
[10] Shuyuan L, et al. Influences of Coronavirus epidemic on the recent development and direction of logistics industry [J]. Logistics Engineering and Management, 2020, 42(4): 36-37.
[11] Svensson G. A Conceptual Framework for the Analysis of Vulnerability in Supply Chains [J]. International Journal of Physical Distribution and Logistics Management, 2000, 30(9): 731-750.
[12] The Bullwhip Effect in Supply Chain [J]. Sloan Management Review, 1997, 38(4): 93-102.
[13] Tianjin maritime. Challenges and opportunities of logistics industry under epidemic situation [J]. 2020, (1), 64.
[14] Xin M, Yiqian H. Analysis on the status quo of pharmaceutical supply chain in China [J]. Logistics Science and Technology, 2010(06): 22-25.
[15] Yang C. Construction of pharmaceutical logistics supply chain [J]. China Logistics & Purchasing, 2003, (23): 54-55.

基于Floyd及KL-means聚类算法的交通运输网络设计

林琰 孙笑 杨硕

(安徽建筑大学土木工程学院)

摘 要 随着经济发展和社会进步，交通运输网络日趋大型化、复杂化；同时在环境友好、资源集约的理念下，用深挖现存道路网络承载能力存量，来代替盲目新建运输通道增量已成为普遍共识和发展趋势。本文基于Floyd交通最短路径算法，并充分考虑现实交通网络环境和条件，提出了一套以"先聚集后运输"为基本思路的交通运输网络最短路径设计模型。结合实际案例，利用Matlab软件对其进行编程求解，给出具体的运输网络路径方案，再通过多层次检验、比对，最终实现优化资源配置和高质高效运输的目的。

关键词 交通运输网络 运筹学 最短路径算法 聚类算法

0 引 言

自新中国成立以来，随着我国交通事业的不断发展，以及运输设施和技术的革新，我国的交通运输效率已显著提高，但由于存在客货运量巨大、地域广阔复杂等限制因素，我国在完善交通运输网络方面仍有极大的上升空间。另外，在补足交通基础设施短板的同时，在现如今环境友好、资源节约等理念下，加快推动交通运输高质量发展，从增量扩能向存量优化转变已成为普遍共识和趋势，充分利用现有的交通网络条件，深挖承载潜力，以满足人民群众日益增长的美好生活对交通的需求。

在满足路网承载力的假设下，解决当前交通运输问题，其根本在于优化交通运输网络，形成经济、高效、便捷的运输通道。这类问题一般被称为最短路径分析问题，对于该类问题，目前大多数解决方案都是基于Dijkastra算法或Floyd算法。然而，面对现状交通网络大型化、复合化，路权因素多样化、复杂化的发

基金项目：安徽建筑大学科研项目(项目号：2020QDZ37)。

展趋势,单一地采用路径寻优算法已无法满足运输最优化的需求,亟须运用多种方法的组合模式。基于此,本研究运用将复杂问题逐步简化的降维分析思想,拟采用 K-Means 聚类算法对大量的交通节点进行分析,形成少量的聚类中心点;同时考虑实际情况,为充分利用现有道路和运输中转节点,对 K-Means 聚类算法进行优化,形成结合现状的优化聚类中心,以此作为下一步最短路径分析的基础。基于改进的 K-Means 算法结合 Floyd 算法建立交通运输网络路径设计模型,并运用到交通运输网络设计问题中,得出模型的可行性和适用性。

1 模型建立

1.1 设计思路

交通运输网络设计问题的目标是要设计一个合理的公路运输网络。对此,本研究主要以经济效益为主要目标,而以管理、运输、时间等效益为次要目标,提供一种设计运输网络路径方案的统一思路,解决一般性的运输网络设计问题。鉴于运输网络错综复杂的原因,确定本研究的模型设计思路是设置一些中转点,通过中转点来逐步汇总相应运输物资,最终形成最优化的公路运输网络。模型整体分为以下 4 个步骤:

(1)改进常规 K-Means 聚类算法,将规定区域地点聚类成若干子区域,每个子区域的中心与现状运输物资点重合,并将这些运输物资点作为区域运输的中转点,即子区域所有运输物资点的物资均运输到该中转点。

(2)运用 Floyd 算法建立最短路径邻接矩阵,将所有属于同一聚类的运输物资点的物资运输至临近的、(1)中生成的中转点。

(3)通过统筹考虑中转点所在交通网络位置以及其携带物资量等属性,给出物资运输基本方案。

(4)根据修路和运输成本,对原有物资运输方案总耗费进行分析,在原有物资运输基本方案上进一步检验、比对和优化,给出最优的物资运输方案。

1.2 K-Means 聚类算法基本概念

K-Means 算法,是典型的无监督聚类算法,按照样本集之间距离的大小,通过反复迭代,将样本集划分为 K 簇,相同簇内的样本尽量紧密的聚集在一起,而不同簇间的距离则尽可能的大。通常用簇的中心位置的样本或样本统计平均来描述该簇的特性。对于物资运输问题进行聚类,实际上就是根据位置和相互距离关系,将整个规定区域划分成若干个子区域,每个子区域中采油点距离该物资运输区域中心点的距离都最近。K-Means 聚类算法伪代码表示如下:

获取输入数据的维度 Dim 和个数 N
 随机生成 K 个 Dim 维的点
 While(算法未收敛)
  对 N 个点:计算每个点属于哪一类
  对于 K 个中心点:
   找出所有属于自己这一类的所有数据点
   把自己的坐标修改为这些数据点的中心点坐标
 End
输出结果:原始聚类中心

1.3 KL-Means 聚类算法

尽管 K-Means 聚类法能将空间上大范围的物资运输区域,聚类为若干子区域,但值得注意的是,这些子区域的中心点并没有与现状的物资运输点重合,可能只是空间上虚拟的点(可以用对比图来表示出来)。考虑到如果以这些空间上虚拟的中心点作为物资中转点,还需要新建道路将物资运输点与该中心点进行连接,徒增费用消耗。为了充分利用现状道路资源,将现有物资运输点作为聚类子区域的中心点,本研究对常规的 K-Means 聚类算法进行改进,即对常规 K-Means 聚类算法得到的聚类中心点与子区域内的现状物资运输点进行相关分析,取相关度最高的物资运输点作为新聚类中心,即为中转点。

改进后的伪代码表示:
获取输入数据的维度 Dim 和个数 N
  随机生成 K 个 Dim 维的点
  While(算法未收敛)
    对 N 个点:计算每个点属于哪一类
    对于 K 个中心点:
      找出所有属于自己这一类的所有数据点
      把自己的坐标修改为这些数据点的中心点坐标
  End
获得 K 个原始聚类中心

  For 依次对 K 个原始聚类中心进行遍历
    计算 K 个原始聚类中心与该类中其他各点的相关系数
    取相关系数较大的点作为该簇的优化聚类中心点
  End
输出结果:K 个优化聚类中心

对于该步骤中相关系数的计算方法采用欧式距离的倒数,数值越高说明相关性越大,反之则越小,具体如式(1)所示:

$$k = 1/\sqrt[2]{(x_i - x_j)^2 + (y_i - y_j)^2} \tag{1}$$

式中:i——第 i 类的聚类中心;
  j——所有点中的第 j 号点;
  x、y——横纵坐标值。

我们将这种经过深度优化的 K-means 算法称为 KL-means 聚类算法,L 为英文 Least 的首位字母,取最小、最短距离(least distance or nearest)之意。

1.4 基于 Floyd 和 KL-Means 组合算法的最短路径设计方法

Floyd 算法,是一种利用动态规划的思想寻找给定的加权图中多源点之间最短路径的算法。

针对本题求最短路径问题,本研究选用 Floyd 算法求解,算法思想如下:对于赋权图 $G = (V, E, A_0)$,其中顶点集 $V = \{v_1, v_2, \cdots\cdots, v_n\}$,邻阶矩阵:

$$A_0 = \begin{bmatrix} a_{11} & \cdots & a_{1n} \\ \vdots & \ddots & \vdots \\ a_{n1} & \cdots & a_{nn} \end{bmatrix} \tag{2}$$

$$a_{ij} = \begin{cases} 权值, 当 v_i 和 v_j 有边的时候 \\ \infty, 当 v_i 和 v_j 无边的时候 \end{cases}, i \neq j;$$

Floyd 算法的基本思想是递推产生一个矩阵序列 $A_1, \cdots, A_k, \cdots, A_n$,其中矩阵 A_k 的第 i 行第 j 列元素 A_k

$(i,j) = \min(A_{k-1}(i,j), A_{k-1}(i,j) + A_{k-1}(k,j))$,$k$ 是迭代次数,$k = 1,2,\cdots,n$。最后,当 $k = n$ 时,A_n 中各项即是各顶点间的最短通路值,称 A_n 为最短路径邻接矩阵。

通过最短路径邻接矩阵 A_n,可以获得各簇中的点至各个中转点的最短运输路径。于是,以 KL-means 聚类算法选择的各优化聚类中心作为各簇的转运点,再利用最短路径邻接矩阵 A_n 确定转运的具体路径,最终可以设计出同时兼顾经济效益、时间效益、管理效益的最优化的整体运输网络路径方案。

2 算 例

本文建立了基于 Floyd 和 KL-means 聚类算法的交通运输网络设计模型,并且通过对模型进行求解,得到了较好的运输效益。在该部分中,就将利用本研究中构建的模型,对"如何在疫情条件下,将全国物资调度至武汉"这一具体运输问题展开研究,并具体设计物资的运输方案,并给出具体的运输方案及运输线路。

我们以全国范围内的道路运输网络为基础网络,经过调研和数据收集,获得全国范围内的交通重要节点和运输重要干路。首先利用 KL-Means 聚类算法对节点及道路数据进行分析,获得聚类中心作为最佳中转点;然后,运用 Floyd 算法,将每类中各节点物资分别转运至其相应的中转点;最后,根据运输需要和实际目的地要求,形成总体运输方案。

利用 KL-means 聚类算法,对原始的 178 个点进行聚类,结果如图 1 和表 1 所示,共形成 6 个中转点。

聚类中心汇总表　　　　　表1

中转点编号	X 坐标	Y 坐标	对应实际节点编号
1	747	221	162
2	690	493	82
3	478	450	30
4	219	194	5
5	624	357	128
6	560	579	52

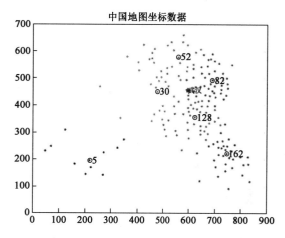

图 1　KL-Means 聚类效果图

通过最短路径邻接矩阵建立交通网络,将所有物资转运至中转点(即 KL-Means 算法结果中各聚类中心点)。在不对最终结果造成过多影响的同时,将零碎、复杂的问题整体化、集约化,以便后续形成更优化的调度方案。每个聚类中的节点物资调度至中转点路径如图 2 所示。

生成整个运输方案的步骤可以分为两个阶段,阶段 I 即将同一类采集点的物资运输至中转点(聚类中心),再对各中转点位置、现有道路网络及运输目的进行分析,最终获得运输方案(阶段 II),各阶段具体计划见表 2。

最佳运输方案策划　　　　　表2

方案进展	具体计划
阶段 I	将物资运输至 6 个中转点
阶段 II	将 6 个中转点汇集的物资统一运至武汉

阶段 II 中,由于各转点皆具有较大的物资承载权值,因此,直接选择将各中转点的物资转运至目标点,利用 Floyd 算法对各节点及现有道路网络数据进行分析,即可得其具体运输路径如图 3 所示。

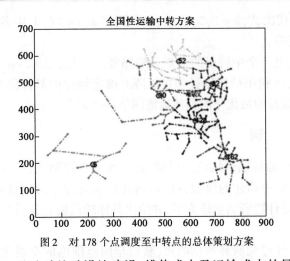
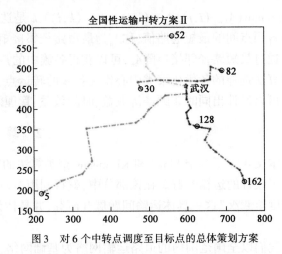

图 2 对 178 个点调度至中转点的总体策划方案　　　　图 3 对 6 个中转点调度至目标点的总体策划方案

通过对基础设施建设、维修成本及运输成本的量化计算,对方案总体效益进行精确评估。于此,主要根据对其道路升级、建设里程及与运输里程的统计,并将其具体数值作为建设成本及运输成本的相对指标,进一步对运输网络效益展开评估。

为进一步对本方案开展相对优度评估,查询了众多国内外对该类问题的类似研究,总结出另一种对解决该类问题应用比较广泛的方法,即仅基于 Floyd 算法建立的交通运输网络设计模型。经过计算,基于 Floyd 算法模型计算的理论建设相对成本达 21357 元,运输相对成本达 142181 元,而本研究基于 KL-Means 和 Floyd 组合算法形成的方案最终计算得出的理论建设相对成本达 21143 元,运输相对成本达 60780 元(表3),比较可得后者所设计的交通运输路径,能实现更少的建设以及运输成本。

各方案比较及汇总　　　　　　　　　　　　　　　表 3

方　案	建设相对成本(元)	运输相对成本(元)
基于 Floyd 模型	21357	142181
基于 KL-Means 和 Floyd 组合模型	21143	60780

本研究还对于"基于 KL-Means 和 Floyd 组合模型"评估结果所产生的原因展开了分析:①建设成本方面,利用本模型制定的总方案,通过对物资统一化的运输,提高了道路使用率的同时也减少了对于长距离道路的建设,从而大大降低了基础设施建设成本。充分利用了现存道路网络、提高了道路建设的"性价比";②运输成本方面,通过"先聚集,后运输"的运输方式,将零碎的运输化为统一运输,提高了单位运输效率,大大降低了运输里程总和。所以,在两大方面原因的综合作用下,较之于其他方案而言,最终利用本模型所制定的运输网络路径方案能实现经济效益最优化的主要目标。

3　结　语

本文以全国物资运输为例,建立了基于 Floyd 和 KL-means 聚类算法的交通运输网络设计模型,通过对模型进行求解,得到了较好的运输效益。事实上,不仅仅局限于一般物资运输,只要运输网络满足双向运输以及运输对象为非紧急类物资,皆可以利用本模型进行求解,如:西气东输、西电东送、南水北调等。

利用本研究中构建的模型,可对于该类物资的运输方案展开统一的设计,并能给出具体的运输方案及运输线路。首先利用 KL-Means 聚类算法对节点及道路数据进行分析,获得聚类中心作为最佳中转点;然后,运用 Floyd 算法,将每类中各节点物资分别转运至其相应的中转点,最后根据运输需要和实际目的地要求,形成总体运输方案。设计思路以及其形成的方案,通过深挖现存道路网络承载能力存量、提高单位运输效率,实现经济效益最优化的同时,也实现了良好的运输、管理效益,最终实现了系统总体效益的最优化。

综上所述,对于一般性问题,本模型可以针对大量且复杂的节点数据进行良好的降维处理,将其概括为少量但极具代表性的节点,这对总体运输方案制定具有重要意义。同时,也可以通过本研究设计的模型方法,分析所选定的聚类中心,作为未来全国交通重要枢纽,为国家对地区交通建设重点的选择提供了方向,也为国家规划发展战略的制定提供参考。

参考文献

[1] 姜启源,谢金星,叶俊.数学模型[M].3 版.北京:高等教育出版社,2003.
[2] 司守奎,孙兆亮,等.数学建模算法与应用[M].2 版.北京:国防工业出版社,2019.
[3] 王炜,过秀成,等.交通工程学[M].2 版.南京:东南大学出版社,2011.
[4] 程琳.城市交通网络流理论[M].南京:东南大学出版社,2010.

Unmanned Aerial Vehicle Route Planning with the Error-Correction-Point-Based Navigation: Model and Solution Algorithm

Ziyu Zhang[1]　Wei Zhang[1]　Zhaoyao Bao[2]　Chi Xie[1]

(1. Tongji University, School of Transportation Engineering;
2. Shanghai Jiao Tong University, School of Naval Architecture, Ocean and Civil Engineering)

Abstract　Unmanned aerial vehicles (UAVs) are widely used to provide civilian services such as ground surveillance, cargo delivery, air quality measurement, disaster and emergency management, and so on. However, the position of a UAV may not be precisely obtained since errors of position are generated inevitably due to varying flight environments and stochastic external interferences. To correct the flight position errors, this paper introduces a UAV route planning problem considering error-correction points in the three-dimensional space. An integer programming model is formulated to characterize the problem mathematically and a multi-criteria label correcting algorithm is developed to obtain the optimal flight route with real-time error correction requirements. Two error-correction-point data sets are used for the validation of the proposed model and solution algorithm, as well as for the presentation of the optimal flight routes. Numerical result shows it takes only 850 ms to obtain the optimal path with 103.5 km in the data set 1 and 423 ms to obtain the optimal path with 108.1 km in the data set 2.

Keywords　Unmanned aerial vehicles　Routing planning　Error correction　Multi-criteria label-correcting algorithm

0　Introduction

Anunmanned aerial vehicle (UAV) is generally known as an aircraft without a human pilot onboard, which is originally used for some dull, dirty, or dangerous missions for humans. The applications of UAV have penetrated numerous aspects of both civil and military scenarios, like aerial photography, product deliveries, agriculture, traffic monitoring, law enforcement, disaster and emergency management, wildfire suppressions, and so on.

To ensure UAV completes target missions like product deliveries precisely, the primary requirement is to navigate UAV move exactly along the route that is planned dynamically or in advance. This requirement needs to be satisfied in terms of two aspects: ① performing navigation accurately; ② solving the UAV route planning problem. Under normal circumstances, accurate navigation can be easily achieved by locating the position of a UAV through the Global Positioning System (GPS) or other positioning systems. However, the GPS signal is not always accessible and might be inaccurate in some situations, for instance, in an indoor environment (Courbon et al., 2010). Taking the complex and various usage of the UAV into account, the autonomous navigation system has received attention. It can be applied to program an optimal route for the UAVs in an environment without available GPS (Han et al., 2019). One of the autonomous navigation systems, the Inertial Navigation System (INS), possesses a strong anti-interference ability and is usually adopted to some special conditions. Navigation devices in INS include motion sensors and rotation sensors that can continuously calculate the positions, orientations, and velocities of a moving object by dead reckoning without the need for external references. To reach a higher route accuracy, auxiliary techniques, such as Terrain Contour Matching (TECOM), Geomagnetic Navigation System, Gravity Navigation System, etc., are usually combined with the INS to form a comprehensive navigation system (Min and Yuan, 1998). Courbon et al. (2010) did a good survey about the application of visual techniques in the combined INS system. During the operation of INS, the position of a UAV may not be precisely obtained and flight errors are generated inevitably due to INS internal biases, varying flight environment, and external stochastic interferences. The UAV has to check and correct these flight position errors to avoid being lost during the flight. As a result, INS based navigation methods mentioned above can perform when the UAV reaches some auxiliary points in the three-dimensional space. At these points, it manages to recognize correction points by matching stored characteristic information of correction points and then correct its accumulated flight position errors, which indicates a joint consideration of the flight error correction and the UAV route planning.

A great deal of researches concentrating on the UAV route planning problem has been done with various planning objectives and associated solution algorithms. Objectives, for instance, minimizing travel distance, fuel consumption, flight duration, detection threat, and so on, are the main concerns (Dasdemir et al., 2020). Numerous studies treat the route planning problem for a UAV as a multi-objective problem, which considers the trade-off between minimizing the travel distance and detouring to avoid terrible terrain conditions and external threats. As for algorithms for solving the UAV route planning problem, most of the previous studies focused on graphic-based algorithms and evolutionary algorithms. Graphic-based algorithms, like using the Voronoi diagram to divide the battle area (Beard et al., 2002) or applying Eppstein's k-best paths algorithm to find the optimal path with the origin and destination known previously (Eppstein, 1999), ignore the motion constraints of UAVs. Therefore, some dynamic algorithms are applied later to address it. With the scale and complexity of the UAV routing problem increasing, evolutionary algorithms draw extensive attention. The genetic algorithm (GA) was used in solving the task point assignment and path planning problems for multiple UAVs (Eun and Bang, 2009). A line-segments method was applied to solve a bi-objective problem, which minimizes flight cost and risk generally associated with a three-dimensional vehicle routing problem (Lamont et al., 2007).

In this paper, a route planning problem is proposed aiming to program the shortest path for UAVs equipped with INS. A set of auxiliary points are predetermined in the space for correcting UAV flight errors by scouting in advance. Thus, since the UAVs apply the combined INS system to navigate itself under the circumstance without GPS signal, the relay requirements are imposed on them and they should reach some relay points to check and correct their flight errors to avoid being lost. Due to the inaccessibility of electrocommunication, relevant geographic or visual information of these points is collected and sent to UAVs before the autonomously real-time route determination. What matters most for the UAVs is that their navigation systems should figure out the shortest path instantly and support the UAVs arriving at their destination successfully. The Shortest Path

Problem with Relays (SPPR) was proposed as a mathematical programming problem that aims to minimize total travel time or cost with relay requirements. These relay requirements might be caused by refueling, recharging, reloading, error recorrecting, etc. The purpose of the proposed UAV routing problem is to minimize UAV's travel distance between the origin and destination where the correction requirement must be met, therefore the SPPR framework will apply to it.

For the remainder of this paper, in Section 1, we present the problem statement in detail and an integer linear programming model is generated for this problem; in Section 2, the multi-label correcting algorithm used in this paper is specified; in Section 3, case studies and sensitivity analysis based on this model are presented; and we conclude this paper in Section 4.

1 Problem Formulation

1.1 Problem Statement

There are several aspects that the position errors derived from when applying INS i.e., the approximate mathematical model, initial alignment, computer algorithm, and inertial elements. Specifically, the errors caused by inertial elements are the major errors that account for nearly 90% of the total errors. During the flight, the inertial element bias will accumulate as time goes by, probably resulting in excessive position errors in the end (Xu and Fang, 2008). In order to correct them, the combination of the visual navigation system or geographic navigation system and INS is usually applied, and it enables to provide graphic information or geographic information for UAV to determine the feasibility of correction. In this problem, the spatial areas that are suited for error correction are abstracted as error-correction-points for the sake of simplification and divided into vertical or horizontal error-correction-points. As the name suggests, there is only one type of errors can be corrected at each point. If the UAV reaches the correction points, the cumulative errors in the corresponding direction will be cleared. On the contrary, it will lead to a failed correction if the cumulative errors exceed the correction ability of a certain error-correction-point. In general, the UAV will arrive at the destination through several error-correction-points. Frequent corrections might assist the UAV to arrive at the destination successfully with higher probability, but the total flight distance is usually longer. In this paper, we devote to finding a route for the UAV between specified origin and destination with minimum flight distance and times of correction, and the cumulative position errors are less than the limitation that guarantees the achievement of flight missions.

1.2 Definition of The Subpath

Xie and Jiang (2016) first introduced the concept of subpath in the field of electric vehicle (EV) charging decision problem. A subpath is part of path k if this part consists of several consecutive arcs that all belong to path k and if the charging stations are located at the head and tail nodes of this part. Labeled the head and tail nodes of this subpath of path k by p and q, this subpath is denoted by k^{pq}. Applied the concept of subpath in the UAV route planning problem, subpaths denote parts of a path that is started and ended by the used error-correction-points.

1.3 Model Formulation

To formulate the problem intuitively, given a directed network (N, A), where N is the set of error-correction-points denoted by nodes in the network, and A is the set of arcs representing virtual links between error-correction-points. There are two subsets of N named N_h and N_v, which include horizontal and vertical error-correction-points respectively. The UAV route planning problem is formulated as an integer programming model.

The objective function is as follows:

$$\min Z(x) = \sum_{(i,j)} x_{ij} d_{ij} \quad (1)$$

The objective function $Z(x)$ is to minimize the total distance from the origin to the destination, which is the sum of the distances of the successively used arcs.

$$\sum_{k \in K} y_k = 1 \quad (2)$$

Equations (2) are the constraint that guarantees that in the space with numerous error-correction-points, there must be one and only one route to be chosen for the UAV.

$$y_k \delta_{ij,k} = \sum_{(p^v,q^v) \in V_k} y_k^{vv,pq} \delta_{ij,k}^{vv,pq} + \sum_{(p^h,q^h) \in H_k} y_k^{hh,pq} \delta_{ij,k}^{hh,pq} + \sum_{(p^v,q^h) \in E_k} y_k^{vh,pq} \delta_{ij,k}^{vh,pq} + \sum_{(p^h,q^v) \in F_k} y_k^{hv,pq} \delta_{ij,k}^{hv,pq} \quad \forall k \in K \quad (3)$$

Equations (3) are the constraints that specify the relationship between the activation indicators of a path and its subpath and make sure that any link on an active path is covered by one and only one active subpath of this path, that is, there is no overlap between different active subpaths of a path.

$$y_k^{vv,pq} d_k^{vv,pq} \varepsilon \leq \alpha_1, \ y_k^{vh,pq} d_k^{vh,pq} \varepsilon \leq \beta_1, \ y_k^{hv,pq} d_k^{hv,pq} \varepsilon \leq \alpha_2, \ y_k^{hh,pq} d_k^{hh,pq} \varepsilon \leq \beta_2 \quad \begin{aligned} &\forall k \in K, \\ &(p^v,q^v) \in V_k, \\ &(p^v,q^h) \in E_k, \\ &(p^h,q^v) \in F_k, \\ &(p^h,q^h) \in H_k \\ &q^v \neq s \end{aligned} \quad (4)$$

The set of inequalities (4) are the constraints that ensure the accumulated flight error at each used error-correction-point of each direction is not greater than the maximum error, less than which the flight error of a certain direction can be corrected.

$$y_k^{vv,pq} d_k^{vv,pq} \varepsilon \leq \theta, \ y_k^{vh,pq} d_k^{vh,pq} \varepsilon \leq \theta, \ y_k^{hv,pq} d_k^{hv,pq} \varepsilon \leq \theta, \ y_k^{hh,pq} d_k^{hh,pq} \varepsilon \leq \theta \quad \begin{aligned} &\forall k \in K, \\ &(p^v,q^v) \in V_k, \\ &(p^v,q^h) \in E_k, \\ &(p^h,q^v) \in F_k, \\ &(p^h,q^h) \in H_k \\ &q^v = s \end{aligned} \quad (5)$$

The set of inequalities (5) are the constraints that ensure both vertical and horizontal flight errors at the destination point are not greater than θ units, which represents the achievement of flight missions.

$$y_k, y_k^{vv,pq}, y_k^{vh,pq}, y_k^{hv,pq}, y_k^{hh,pq} \in \{0,1\} \quad \begin{aligned} &\forall k \in K, \\ &(p^v,q^v) \in V_k, \\ &(p^v,q^h) \in E_k, \\ &(p^h,q^v) \in F_k, \\ &(p^h,q^h) \in H_k \end{aligned} \quad (6)$$

Above are binary constraints for the path and subpath variables.

Besides, several notations in the model need extra explanations as below.

$$x_{ij} = \sum_{k \in K} y_k \delta_{ij,k} \quad \forall (i,j) \in A \quad (7)$$

$$d_k^{vv,pq} = \sum_{(i,j) \in A} d_{ij} \delta_{ij,k}^{vv,pq}, \quad d_k^{vh,pq} = \sum_{(i,j) \in A} d_{ij} \delta_{ij,k}^{vh,pq},$$
$$d_k^{hv,pq} = \sum_{(i,j) \in A} d_{ij} \delta_{ij,k}^{hv,pq}, \quad d_k^{hh,pq} = \sum_{(i,j) \in A} d_{ij} \delta_{ij,k}^{hh,pq}$$
$$\begin{aligned}&\forall k \in K, \\ &(p^v, q^v) \in V_k, \\ &(p^v, q^h) \in E_k, \\ &(p^h, q^v) \in F_k, \\ &(p^h, q^h) \in H_k\end{aligned} \quad (8)$$

2 Solution Algorithms

Amulti-label correcting algorithm is developed to find the optimal Pareto UAV routing path. Although there is only one object in the model formulated above, the accumulated errors in both directions are needed to be considered since they determined whether the flight mission can achieve successfully. The multi-label correcting algorithm is applied to achieve a trade-off among various conflicting or consistent objects that have to be considered simultaneously (Figueira et al., 2010). In previous studies, the multi-label correcting algorithm has been proven to be extremely efficient in numerous fields, for example, transportation, mechanical, telecommunications, and supply chain (Liang et al., 2013). In the UAV routing problem, the developed algorithm searches for a non-dominated route that has the smallest cumulative vertical error, the smallest cumulative horizontal error, or the fewest times of corrections while minimizing the total travel length. When the algorithm terminates a Pareto path that has either the smallest travel distance or the fewest times of correction or has both will be obtained. In the process of finding the Pareto-optimal paths, some labels are attached to the nodes to record the current Pareto-optimal solutions.

When all of the new labels of node i are strictly less than those of the old labels, the new labels will be accepted and attach to node i. On the contrary, if all of the new labels are greater than or equal to the old labels, the new labels will be abandoned. As for the old labels, if all of the old labels are greater than or equal to the new labels, the old ones should be abandoned, and they will be held if otherwise.

The algorithmic procedure of the developed multi-label correcting algorithm can be summarized as follows:

Step 0: Initialization. Set the four labels of the origin node as 0 and the four labels of other nodes as $+\infty$.

Step 1: Node searching. Take a node i from node set N and search all nodes which are linked from node i. All neighboring nodes are stored in the set $\{j\}$.

Step 2: Label updating. If node i is the vertical error-correction point, and the current vertical error is not greater than α_1 as well as the horizontal error is not greater than α_2, then update the label of node j and set the vertical error to be zero. If node i is the horizontal error-correction point, and the current vertical error is not greater than β_1 as well as the horizontal error is not greater than β_2, then update the label of node j and set the horizontal error to be zero. If vertical error and horizontal error from node i to node j are greater than the tolerant value, turn to step 1. Then update the node set N by adding node j into N.

Step 3: Termination. Check the set of node N. If N is empty, then this algorithm terminates. Otherwise, go to step 1.

3 Case Study

In this section, two sets of vertical and horizontal error-correction-points are used to test the developed solution algorithm and find the optimal route for a UAV in INS. The first set contains 613 error-correction-points and the second set contains 317 error-correction-points. Each error-correction-point is identified by its spatial coordinate position and error correction type (vertical or horizontal). The parameters in data set 1 are set as follows: $\alpha_1 = 25$, $\alpha_2 = 15$, $\beta_1 = 20$, $\beta_2 = 25$, $\theta = 30$, $\delta = 0.001$. The parameters in data set 2 are set as follows: $\alpha_1 = 20$, $\alpha_2 = 10$, $\beta_1 = 15$, $\beta_2 = 20$, $\theta = 25$, $\delta = 0.001$.

The optimal paths for a UAV with INS in data set 1 and data set 2 are shown in Tab. 1. For data set 1 with 850 ms computing time, the optimal path is 103.5 km and has 9 times of corrections. For data set 2 with 423 ms computing time, the optimal path is 108.1 km and has 11 times of corrections. For the convenience of visual observation, the optimal paths obtained are displayed in Fig. 1.

Optimal path of two data sets Tab. 1

Data set	The ID of correction nodes	Accumulative times of corrections	Accumulative flight distance (km)	Vertical error before the correction (m)	Horizontal error before the correction (m)	Type of error-correction point
1	0	0	0	0	0	origin A
	503	1	13.4	13.4	13.4	11
	200	2	14.3	0.9	14.3	01
	80	3	30.0	16.6	15.7	01
	237	4	34.6	21.2	4.6	11
	170	5	42.3	7.7	12.3	11
	278	6	52.8	10.4	22.7	01
	369	7	64.2	21.9	11.4	11
	214	8	77.5	13.3	24.7	01
	397	9	86.5	22.3	9.0	11
	612	9	103.5	17.0	26.0	destination B
2	0	0	0	0	0	origin A
	163	1	13.3	13.3	13.3	01
	114	2	18.6	18.6	5.3	11
	8	3	32.5	13.9	19.3	01
	309	4	38.1	19.4	5.5	11
	305	5	44.0	6.0	11.5	01
	123	6	53.2	15.1	9.2	11
	45	7	63.2	10.0	19.2	01
	160	8	70.7	17.5	7.5	11
	92	9	76.5	5.8	13.3	01
	93	10	86.0	15.3	9.5	11
	61	11	95.9	9.8	19.3	01
	326	11	108.1	22.2	12.3	destination B

Note: in the column of "type of error-correction point", 11 and 01 present the vertical error is corrected successfully, and the horizontal error is corrected successfully respectively.

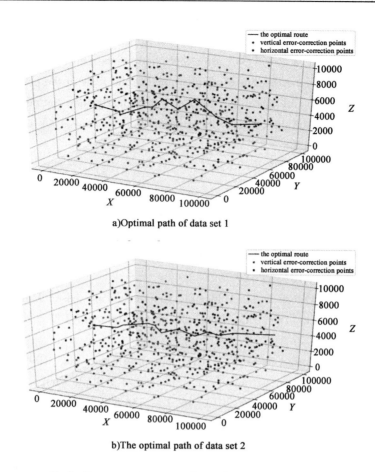

Fig. 1 Error-correction points and optimal path for data set 1 and 2

Compared the error-correction-points in the space of the two data sets as shown in Tab. 2, the number of error-correction points in data set 2 is less than that in data set 1 and consequently, the computing time of data set 2 is half of that of data set 1 due to the less workload of searching in the algorithm. Meanwhile, the origins in the two data sets are the same while the destination in data set 2 is further than that in data set 1, which leads to the contraction of the feasible region when applying the algorithm to data set 2. As a result, the length of the optimal route is 4632 meters further than that of data set 1, and there are more corrections needed in data set 2.

Comparison of solution results between data set 1 and 2   Tab. 2

Data set	The number of error-correction points	Computing time (ms)	Length of optimal route (km)	Times of corrections
1	613	850	103.5	9
2	317	423	108.1	11

4 Conclusion

In this paper, a UAV route planning problem is proposed and formulated into an integer programming model aiming to correct position errors in real-time when the GPS signal is inaccessible or when the UAV performs flights based on the INS. The introduced concept of subpaths connecting two error correction points is the key to describe the route planning problem mathematically. To guarantee that the UAV reaches its destination node as soon as possible, the objective function is to minimize the flight distance while considering various kinds of error correction constraints. A multi-criteria label correcting algorithm is developed for obtaining the optimal flight routes dynamically with the requirements of real-time position error correction. Two data sets are used for testing and validating the solution algorithm. Data set 1 with 613 error correction points requires a computing time of 850 ms and data set 2 with 317 error correction points requires only a computing time of 423 ms, which means the computing time grows linearly proportional to the scale of the problem. The optimal flight routes derived from the two data sets are more than 100 km which clearly show the applicability of our solution algorithms. One of the future research directions of this study is to extend this UAV route planning problem by considering the turning radius constraint of UAVs.

Reference

[1] Beard R W, Mclain T W, Goodrich M A, et al. Coordinated Target Assignment and Intercept for Unmanned Air Vehicles[J]. IEEE Transactions on Robotics and Automation, 2003, 18(6): 911-922.

[2] Courbon J, Mezouar Y, Guénard N, et al. Vision-based Navigation of Unmanned Aerial Vehicles[J]. Control Engineering Practice, 18(7): 789-799.

[3] Dasdemir E, Köksalan M, Öztürk D T. A Flexible Reference Point-based Multi-objective Evolutionary Algorithm: An Application to The UAV Route Planning Problem[J]. Computers and Operations Research, 2020, 114, 104811.

[4] Eppstein D. Finding the k shortest paths[J]. SIAM Journal of Computing, 1999, 28(2): 652-673.

[5] Eun Y, Bang H. Cooperative Task Assignment/path Planning of Multiple Unmanned Aerial Vehicles Using Genetic Algorithm[J]. Journal of Aircraft, 2012, 46(1): 338-343.

[6] Figueira J R, Liefooghe A, Talbi E G, et al. A Parallel Multiple Reference Point Approach for Multi-objective Optimization[J]. European Journal of Operational Research, 2010, 205(2): 390-400.

[7] Han T, Almeida J S, Silva S P P D, et al. An Effective Approach to Unmanned Aerial Vehicle Navigation using Visual Topological Map in Outdoor and Indoor Environments[J]. Computer Communications, 2020, 150, 696-702.

[8] Konak A. Network Design Problem with Relays: A Genetic Algorithm with A Path-based Crossover and A Set Covering Formulation[J]. European Journal of Operational Research, 2012, 218(3): 829-837.

[9] Lamont G B, Slear J N, Melendez K. UAV Swarm Mission Planning and Routing Using Multi-objective Evolutionary Algorithms[C]// IEEE Symposium on Computational Intelligence in Multi-Criteria Decision-Making, Honolulu, HI. IEEE, 2007:10-20.

[10] Liang W Y, Huang C C, Lin Y C, et al. The Multi-objective Label Correcting Algorithm for Supply Chain Modeling[J]. International Journal of Production Economics, 2013, 142(1): 172-178.

[11] Min C, Yuan J. Introduction of Military Aircraft Route Planning[J]. Flight Dynamics, 1998, 4: 14-19.

[12] Xu F, Fang J. Velocity and Position Error Compensation Using Strapdown Inertial Navigation System/celestial Navigation System Integration Based on Ensemble Neural Network[J]. Aerospace Science and Technology, 2008, 12(4): 302-307.

[13] Xie C, Jiang N. Relay Requirement and Traffic Assignment of Electric Vehicles[J]. Computer-Aided Civil and Infrastructure Engineering, 2016, 31(8), 580-598.

[14] Zhang X, Duan H. An Improved Constrained Differential Evolution Algorithm for Unmanned Aerial Vehicle Global Route Planning[J]. Applied Soft Computing Journal, 2015, 26, 270-284.

On the Minimum Required Driving Ranges of Electric Vehicles to Overcome Some Travel Restriction Barriers

Jiapei Li   Chi Xie

(Tongji University, College of Transportation Engineering)

Abstract   Due to scarce charging infrastructure, inadequate driving ranges and overlong charging time, range anxiety has prevailed in the driving population of electric vehicles (EVs), which presents as the fear or stress of EV drivers stranding with an empty onboard battery in the course of their driving trips. Increasing the driving range can effectively alleviate the range anxiety, but the driving range of EVs is heavily dependent on battery and energy management technologies and it may take a long time and require vast investments to improve or upgrade the existing technologies to a significantly higher level. In the path of technology enhancement and development, it is important to understand the relationship of the product acceptance rate and technology performance and maturity, at least approximately. Partially for satisfying this requirement, this paper presents a systematic approach to identify the minimum required driving ranges of EVs that overcome two critical travel restrictions. From the perspective of travel behaviors, the first restriction can be described as that travellers may not make their trips because no path with sufficient charging opportunities can be found in the network; the second one is that although travellers can make their trips relying on EVs, they may have to make necessary detours from their desired minimal-cost or minimal-time paths to reach the destinations. Obviously, either finding no path or making detours would greatly lower down the adoption and utilization willingness of potential EV consumers. Whenever either of travel restrictions in a market can be overcome, it is anticipated that the local EV acceptance and usage rates will make a great leap. In this text, we name the system goals or travel conditions achieved from breaking through the above two restrictions the feasibly optimal routing condition and the ideally optimal routing condition, respectively. In accordance, we constructed two mixed linear integer programming models for finding the minimum required driving ranges to reach these two travel conditions networkwide, and further designed two dynamic programming algorithms, written in the label-correcting and label-setting forms, respectively, for solving the two driving range minimization problems. Numerical results obtained from synthetic and real transportation networks demonstrate the effectiveness of the modeling and solution methods and provide a number of insightful suggestions. The research outcome presented in this paper may be used to provide important vehicle design criteria or performance indicators for EV manufacturers.

Keywords   Electric vehicles   Driving ranges   Travel restrictions   Dynamic programming

0 Introduction

As an emerging alternative-fuel transportation mode, EVs have been gradually accepted by the public in recent years. Thanks to the electricity-driven power, EVs have the advantages of reducing the energy consumption, improving the air quality, preventing the global warming and so on (Khan and Kushler, 2013).

It is acknowledged that one of the major barriers that hamper a large-scale adoption of EVs is range anxiety, which is often described as the fear or stress of EV drivers stranding with an empty onboard battery in the course of their driving trips (Marrow et al., 2008; Mock et al., 2010; Franke and Krems, 2013). Range anxiety, occurring more often in long-distance travels than in daily commuting trips, reflects the gap between the mileage drivers expect to complete for reaching their productivity and leisure activity sites and the mileage their vehicles and charging infrastructure may support. It is commonly believed that improving the driving range of EVs plays an important role for effectively alleviating the range anxiety. But the driving range of EVs is heavily dependent on battery and energy management technologies and it may take a long time and requires vast investments to improve the existing or develop new related technologies to a significantly higher level. In the course of battery technology enhancement and development, the extra investments on improving driving ranges will definitely result in the already expensive manufacturing costs becoming more unaffordable. Consequently, it is important for EV manufacturers to understand the relationship of the product acceptance rate and technology performance and maturity, at least approximately. Partially for satisfying this requirement, this research aims to find the utmost effective, i.e., the minimum required driving range that could relieve or even overcome the range anxiety concern for EV drivers as well as provide a most cost-effective strategic decision for EV manufacturers.

Previous studies concerning the driving range problems of EVs can be classified into two categories from two sides of demand analysis and supply design. The focus of the first type of studies (Weiss et al., 2016; Li et al., 2016) from the perspective of EV suppliers aimed to find a tradeoff between the financial investments and returns from improving the EV driving ranges. The second type of studies (Pearre et al., 2011; Stark et al., 2015; Wu et al., 2015; Shi et al., 2019; Zhou et al., 2020) was estimating the accurate required driving range for users' daily driving demand usually based on empirical daily driving databases, such as gasoline vehicle driving patterns, massive trip records of taxis, longitudinal GPS surveys and so on. This research belonging to the second type aims to develop a systematic optimization approach at the network topology level. In fact, we have identified two critical travel restrictions by range anxiety. From the perspective of travel behaviors, the first restriction as an extremely negative travel status can be described as that travellers may not find any path in the network to finish their trips due to no sufficient charging stations to support battery recharges, under which the trip must be canceled or be made by another travel mode; the second one is that although travellers can make their trips relying on EVs, they may have to take extra travel time or cost for taking detours other than on their minimal-cost or minimal-time paths to reach the destinations since the charging stations for EVs are not as ubiquitous as the gas stations. The two restrictions are of particular interest to EV manufacturers, representing the two most critical levels of travel restriction barriers, which negatively affect the convenience and preference of driving EVs for trip making, the vehicle driving experience and the vehicle purchase willingness and usage behaviors of potential consumers on some degree. In terms of travel choice decisions and travel cost saving, it is anticipated that the experience of using EVs will give a significant promotion and the local EV acceptance and usage rates will make a great leap, when either of travel restrictions in a market is overcome. We name the system goals or travel conditions achieved from breaking through the above two restrictions the *feasibly optimal routing condition* and the *ideally optimal routing condition*, respectively. The former travel condition represents the turning point at which trips can be made, while the latter indicates the turning point at which trips can be made and without any detour. In accordance, this paper aims to identify the two travel conditions and find the minimum required driving ranges of EVs to achieve the two travel conditions for relieving range anxiety.

The remainder of this paper is organized in the following order. Section 1 formulates the optimization problems in mathematical forms. Section 2 proposes the solution methods for the optimization problems and further gives the Pseudo-code in detail. Section 3 illustrates the numerical results by testing on two different example network. In the end, Section 4 elaborates a few remarkable conclusions and research tasks in further.

1 Problem Formulations

This section presents an optimization framework of the minimum required driving range problems for EVs. In this section, two mathematical programming models corresponding to the two optimization problems proposed in this research are developed, respectively. For describing the distance limit constraint concisely, we refer to the definition of subpath that is proposed by Xie and Jiang (2016).

Some modeling assumptions are commonly specified underlying all the problems, such as: ① all EVs are of the same type and have the same driving range; ② all charging stations have a sufficiently large capacity and no vehicle needs to wait for recharging; ③ all EV drivers aim to route on a minimum-cost path subject to the driving range of their vehicles; ④ charging cost and time are not taken into account in travel cost; ⑤ electricity consumption of any electric vehicle is linear to its driving distance; ⑥ all networks of interest in this study are intercity highway networks, where their geographical scale makes range anxiety arising as a prominent concern in intercity trip makings and traffic congestion could be ignored mostly.

The notation used in our models, including sets, variables and parameters, are presented as Tab. 1.

Notation Tab. 1

	Notation	explanation
Sets	N	Set of nodes, $N = \{n\}$
	A	Set of links, $A = \{(i,j)\}$
	W	Set of O-D pairs, $W = \{r\text{-}s\}$. We typically use "$r\text{-}s$" to represent an O-D pair, where r is the origin node and s is the destination node
	K_{rs}	Set of paths between O-D pair $r\text{-}s$, $K_{rs} = \{k\}$
	V_k^{rs}	Set of charging station pairs on path k between O-D pair $r\text{-}s$, $V_k^{rs} = \{v = p\text{-}q\}$
Variables	d	The maximum driving range of an electric vehicle after a full charging
	y_k^{rs}	Activation indicator of path k between O-D pair $r\text{-}s$, where path k can be used to carry traffic flow if $y_k^{rs} = 1$, and otherwise if $y_k^{rs} = 0$
	$y_k^{rs,pq}$	Activation indicator of the subpath connecting charging station pair $p\text{-}q$, which is part of path k between O-D pair $r\text{-}s$, where this subpath can be used to carry traffic flow if $y_k^{rs,pq} = 1$, and otherwise if $y_k^{rs,pq} = 0$
Parameters	d_{ij}	Travel distance of link (i,j)
	$d_k^{rs,pq}$	Travel distance of subpath $k^{rs,pq}$ on path k connecting O-D pair $r\text{-}s$
	$\delta_{ij,k}^{rs}$	Link-path incidence indicator, where $\delta_{ij,k}^{rs} = 1$ if (i,j) is part of path k connecting O-D pair $r\text{-}s$, and otherwise if $\delta_{ij,k}^{rs} = 0$
	$\delta_{ij,k}^{rs,pq}$	Link-subpath incidence indicator, where $\delta_{ij,k}^{rs,pq} = 1$ if (i,j) is part of subpath connecting charging station location pair $p\text{-}q$ on path k between O-D pair $r\text{-}s$, and otherwise if $\delta_{ij,k}^{rs,pq} = 0$
	k^*	The shortest path connecting O-D pair $r\text{-}s$

1.1 The Minimum Required Driving Range in the Feasibly Optimal Condition

$$\min d \quad (1)$$

s. t.

$$\sum_{k \in K_{rs}} y_k^{rs} = 1 \quad \forall (r,s) \in W \quad (2)$$

$$y_k^{rs}\delta_{ij,k}^{rs} = \sum_{(p,q)\in V_k^{rs}} y_k^{rs,pq}\delta_{ij,k}^{rs,pq} \quad \forall (r,s)\in W, k\in K_{rs}, (i,j)\in A \tag{3}$$

$$d_k^{rs,pq} y_k^{rs,pq} \leq d \quad \forall (r,s)\in W, k\in K_{rs}, (p,q)\in V_k^{rs} \tag{4}$$

$$d \geq 0 \tag{5}$$

$$y_k^{rs} \in \{0,1\} \quad \forall (r,s)\in W, k\in K_{rs} \tag{6}$$

$$y_k^{rs,pq} \in \{0,1\} \quad \forall (r,s)\in W, k\in K_{rs}, (p,q)\in V_k^{rs} \tag{7}$$

where

$$d_k^{rs,pq} = \sum_{(i,j)\in A} d_{ij}\delta_{ij,k}^{rs,pq} \quad \forall (r,s)\in W, k\in K_{rs}, (p,q)\in V_k^{rs} \tag{8}$$

The minimum required driving range problem in the feasibly optimal condition is formulated as a mixed linear integer programming model. The objective function ① is to minimize the driving range of EVs. Constraint ② describes the feasible routing condition, which ensures at least one feasible path for each O-D pair. Constraint ③ depicts the relationship between an active path and its active subpaths, which stipulates any link on an active path should be covered by one and only one active subpath of this path. Constraint ④ characterizes the driving range limit of EVs. This constraint regulates the driving range of EVs must be greater than or equal to the distance of any active subpath that is a part of an active path connecting a pair of charging stations. Constraint ⑤ is the driving range variable nonnegative constraint. Constraint ⑥ and ⑦ are activation indicator of path and subpath binary constraints, respectively. Constraint ⑧ is the definitional constraint of subpath distance, which defines the distance relationship between links and subpaths.

1.2 The Minimum Required Driving Range in the Ideally Optimal Condition

$$\min d \tag{9}$$

s.t.

$$y_{k^*}^{rs} = 1 \quad \forall (r,s)\in W \tag{10}$$

$$y_{k^*}^{rs}\delta_{ij,k^*}^{rs} = \sum_{(p,q)\in V_{k^*}^{rs}} y_{k^*}^{rs,pq}\delta_{ij,k^*}^{rs,pq} \quad \forall (r,s)\in W, (i,j)\in A \tag{11}$$

$$d_{k^*}^{rs,pq} y_{k^*}^{rs,pq} \leq d \quad \forall (r,s)\in W, (p,q)\in V_{k^*}^{rs} \tag{12}$$

$$d \geq 0 \tag{13}$$

$$y_{k^*}^{rs,pq} \in \{0,1\} \quad \forall (r,s)\in W, (p,q)\in V_{k^*}^{rs} \tag{14}$$

where

$$d_{k^*}^{rs,pq} = \sum_{(i,j)\in A} d_{ij}\delta_{ij,k^*}^{rs,pq} \quad \forall (r,s)\in W, (p,q)\in V_{k^*}^{rs} \tag{15}$$

The minimum required driving range problem in the ideally optimal condition is also formulated as a mixed linear integer programming model, where k^* is the shortest path between O-D pair r-s. The difference between the two problem formulations is the description of path parameter due to the different individual route choices in different optimal routing conditions. To be specific, in the feasibly optimal condition, the optimal path can be chosen from a set of any feasible path between each O-D pair, indicating that the individual is free to choose any path between his or her O-D pair. While for the ideally optimal condition, the optimal path only come from the shortest path between each O-D pair, implying that the individual is confined to choose the shortest path between his or her O-D pair.

2 Solution Methods

The above discrete optimization problems actually can be converted to network routing problems for their solutions. For the former network optimization problem, the minimum driving range over a network with a set of given charging stations is simply the maximum of the minimum driving ranges of all O-D pairs. For each O-D pair, its minimum driving range can be found by searching for all possible paths to identify a path that provides a minimum value, where this minimum value is the minimax driving range among all feasible sets of active subpaths on this path. The minimax driving range is the minimum one among the maximum subpath distance of all feasible paths between an O-D pair. It is intuitive that, to find the minimum required driving range over a network, we could first find the maximum subpath distances on each path between an O-D pair, and further identify the minimum one among all the maximum subpath distances, which is the minimum required driving range between the O-D pair. The final procedure is to compare all the minimum required driving ranges between all O-D pairs and obtain the maximum one. For the latter network optimization problem, the minimum required driving range over a network with a set of given charging stations is the maximum of the minimum required driving ranges of all O-D pairs. For each O-D pair, its minimum required driving range, which is the maximum active subpath distance on the shortest path, should be identified by searching for the shortest path between each O-D pair. Since a single prespecified path between each O-D pair is taken into account, when finding the shortest path between each O-D pair, the search process on the specific paths becomes simpler.

However, when facing a large size network, enumerating all feasible solutions for both optimization problems seems to result in a serious computational difficulty. It motivated us to develop more effective and efficient algorithms to solve these problems.

2.1 The Minimum Driving Range Problem in the Feasibly Optimal Condition

This search process for each O-D pair can be effectively conducted by a dynamic programming process similar to the bi-criteria label-correcting algorithm. During the search process, the optimal solutions may come into being a Pareto-optimal solution set, in which each solution is a two-dimensional vector including the minimum driving range of all previously checked partial paths from origin node r to the current node j, denoting $d_p^{rs}(j)$, and the current driving range between the last charging station node to this node, denoting $d_c^{rs}(j)$. The Pseudo-code of bi-criteria label-correcting algorithm for solving the minimum driving range problem in the feasibly optimal condition is shown as follows.

Pseudo-code of the bi-criteria label-correcting algorithm (in the feasibly optimal condition)
begin
    $d := 0$;
    for each origin node r do
    begin
        $d_p(r):0$; $d_c(r):0$; $pred(r) := 0$;
        for each node $i \in \dfrac{N}{\{r\}}$ do $d_p(i) := 0$; $d_c(i) := \infty$; $pred(i) := r$;
        $Q := \{r\}$;
        while $Q \neq \emptyset$ do
        begin
        take node i from Q;
        for each $(i,j) \in A(i)$ do
            for each label of node i do
            begin
                $\bar{d}_p(j) = d_p(i)$; $\bar{d}_c(j) = d_c(i) + d_{ij}$;
                if $(\bar{d}_p(j), \bar{d}_c(j)) \prec (d_p(j), d_c(j))$ then update $d_p(j) := \bar{d}_p(j)$; $d_c(j) := \bar{d}_c(j)$;
                $pred(j) := i$; And if $j \notin Q$, add j into Q;
                else if $(\bar{d}_p(j), \bar{d}_c(j)) \not\prec (d_p(j), d_c(j))$ and $(d_p(j), d_c(j)) \not\prec (\bar{d}_p(j), \bar{d}_c(j))$

then add $(\bar{d}_p(j), \bar{d}_c(j))$ into label set of node j; And if $j \notin Q$, add j into Q;
   end;
  end;
 for each destination node s do
  $d_\xi(s) = \max\{d_c(s), d_p(s)\}$;
  $d = \max\{d, d_\xi(s)\}$;
 end;
end;

2.2 The Minimum Driving Range Problem in the Ideally Optimal Condition

As discussed, in the ideally optimal condition, the minimum required driving range can be found by searching on the shortest path between each O-D pair. In this paper, we propose a dynamic programming process similar to the label-setting algorithm without the pregeneration procedure for finding the shortest path between each O-D pair, in which each solution is a 3-dimensional vector including the total travel cost $c^{rs}(j)$ from origin node r to the current node j, $d_p^{rs}(j)$ and $d_c^{rs}(j)$. The label-setting search process is to find the minimum-cost path meanwhile identifying the minimum required driving range by recording each active subpath distance on this path. The Pseudo-code of label-correcting algorithm for solving the minimum driving range problem in the ideally optimal condition is presented as follows.

Pseudo-code of the label-setting algorithm (in the ideally optimal condition)
begin
 $d := 0$;
 for each origin node r do
 begin
  $S := \emptyset$; $\bar{S} := N$; //S is the permanently labeled set; $\bar{S}$ is the temporarily labeled set
  $c(r) := 0$; $d_p(r) := 0$; $d_c(r) := 0$; $pred(r) := 0$;
  for each node $i \in \frac{N}{\{r\}}$ do $c(i) := \infty$; $d_p(i) := 0$; $d_c(i) := 0$; $pred(i) := r$;
  while $|S| < |N|$ do
  begin
   let $i \in \bar{S}$ be a node for which $c(i) = \min\{c(j): j \in \bar{S}\}$;
   if i is a charging station node, then $d_p(i) := \max\{d_c(i), d_p(i)\}$; $d_c(i) := 0$;
   $S := S \cup \{i\}$;
   $\bar{S} := \bar{S} - \{i\}$;
   for each $(i,j) \in A(i)$ do
    if $c(j) > c(i) + c_{ij}$ then $c(j) := c(i) + c_{ij}$; $d_p(j) := d_p(i)$; $d_c(j) := d_c(i) + d_{ij}$;
    $pred(j) := i$;
  end;
  for each destination node s do
   $d_\xi(s) = \max\{d_c(s), d_p(s)\}$;
   $d = \max\{d, d_\xi(s)\}$;
 end;
end;

3 Numerical Analysis

In this section, we provide a numerical evaluation to present the effectiveness of the solution methods developed in the last section. To be specific, we illustrate the optimal driving range solution from applying the two algorithms by testing various scenarios on a real-world transportation network, namely, the Yangtze River Delta network, which consists of 38 nodes, 138 directed links, and 306 O-D pairs. The information including the network topology, link attributes and charging station nodes are presented in Fig. 1.

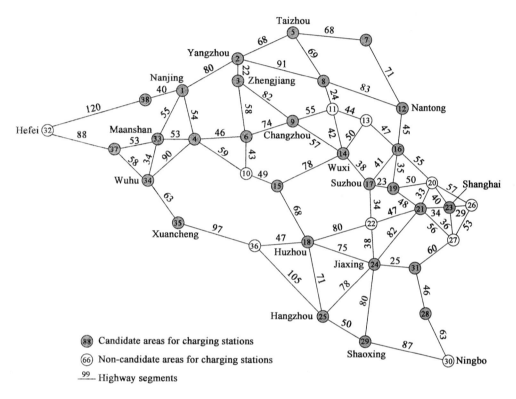

Fig. 1 Yangtze River Delta Network

Given twelve different charging station scenarios as parallel experiments with different budget limits by setting to 4, 6, 8 and 10, we solve the minimum required driving range problem in the feasibly and ideally optimal condition, respectively. Tab. 2 illustrates the optimal driving range solutions in the two kinds of optimal conditions. From the result, the minimum required driving range in the feasibly optimal condition is approximately within the range from 120 to 210, which can be met by most of the existing EVs on the market. While the minimum required driving range in the ideally optimal condition is approximately within the range from 280 to 550, which may be a challenge for EV manufacturers. And we can find that the minimum required driving range in the ideally optimal condition is always larger than that in the feasibly optimal condition given the same charging station scenario, which is consistent with the three satisfaction levels we identified in this text.

Optimal Driving Range Solution in the Yangtze River Delta Network Tab. 2

The given charging stations	The minimum required driving range	
	feasibly optimal condition	ideally optimal condition
the number of charging stations = 10		
2,4,8,9,15,17,18,24,33,38	134	548
1,6,8,15,17,18,29,31,35,37	121	279

		continue
The given charging stations	The minimum required driving range	
	feasibly optimal condition	ideally optimal condition
8,14,18,23,25,31,33,34,35,37	144	375
the number of charging stations = 8		
2,4,8,15,17,18,24,33	141	548
1,4,6,8,17,18,31,35	160	339
4,8,15,16,21,29,33,35	162	383
the number of charging stations = 6		
4,8,15,17,24,33	141	548
2,15,17,18,31,34	172	409
2,6,17,18,25,35	209	281
the number of charging stations = 4		
6,14,24,33	141	548
4,14,18,37	208	460
2,4,17,29	195	514

4 Conclusions

The minimum required driving range problem arise from the requirement that EV manufacturers attempt to understand the relationship between EV acceptance rate and battery technology performance. Generally, a larger driving range can better relieve the range anxiety, but it requires a larger battery capacity or a battery of higher electricity storage density, which requires EV manufactures to invest more time and efforts to improve or upgrade the existing technologies to a significantly higher level. From the perspective of travel behaviours, two critical travel restriction barriers due to insufficient driving range or insufficient charging opportunities may greatly impede the adoption and utilization of EVs on the individual level: ① trips cannot be finished; ② trips can be finished with detours. It is acknowledged that whenever either of travel restrictions in a regional market can be overcome, it is anticipated that the local EV acceptance and usage rates will make a great leap.

This study develops a systematic approach to identify the minimum required driving ranges of EVs that overcome these two travel restrictions and defines two system goals or travel conditions achieved from breaking through the above two restrictions. To identify the minimum required driving ranges for achieving these two travel conditions networkwide, we constructed two mixed linear integer programming models and further designed two dynamic programming algorithms, written in the label-correcting and label-setting forms, respectively, for solving the two problems. Numerical results obtained from synthetic and real transportation networks demonstrate the effectiveness of these modeling and solution methods.

Finding the optimal driving range of EVs in this research relies on a given charging station distribution scenario in a transportation network. Both extending the driving range of EVs and constructing more charging infrastructures are two technical approaches to tame the range anxiety concern and encourage the adoption and utilization of EVs. It would be interesting to further study a joint optimization problem that simultaneously takes into account both the driving range upgrading plan made by EV manufacturers and the charging infrastructure development plan made by charging infrastructure investors in the same modeling framework. Obviously, such a framework requires the participation of a government authority that will coordinate the behaviors of the two parties and decide how the relevant government resources and policies are implemented.

References

[1] Franke T, Krems J F. What Drivers Range Preferences in Electric Vehicle Users[J]. Transportation Policy,2013, 30(1), 56-62.

[2] Khan S,Kushler M. Plug-in Electric Vehicles: Challenges and Opportunities. American Council for an Energy-Efficient Economy[EB/OL]. (2013-06-12)[2021-07-06]. https://www.aceee.org/research-report/t133.

[3] Li Z, Jiang S, Dong J, et al. Battery Capacity Design for Electric Vehicles Considering the Diversity of Daily Vehicles Miles Traveled[J]. Transportation Research Part C, 72, 272-282.

[4] Marrow K,Karner D, Francfort J. Plug-in Hybrid Electric Vehicle Charging Infrastructure Review. U.S. Department of Energy[C]. Washington D C: Report INL/EXT-08-150582008.

[5] Mock P,Schmid S A, Friedrich H E. Market Prospects of Electric Passenger Vehicles. In: Pistoia, G. (Ed.), Electric and Hybrid Vehicles: Power Sources, Models, Sustainability, Infrastructure and the Market[J]. Elsevier, Amsterdam, The Netherlands,2010, 545-577.

[6] Pearre N S, Kempton W, Guensler R L, et al. Electric Vehicles: How Much Range is Required for a Day's Driving[J]. Transportation Research Part C, 2011,19, 1171-1184.

[7] Shi X, Pan J, Wang H, et al. Battery Electric Vehicles: What Is the Minimum Range Required[J]. Energy, 2019,166, 352-358.

[8] Stark J, Link C,Simic D, et al. Required Range of Electric Vehicles-An Analysis of Longitudinal Mobility Data[J]. IET Intelligent Transport Systems, 2015,9(2),119-127.

[9] Weiss C, Mallig N, Heilig M, et al. How Much Range is Required[C]. A Model Based Analysis of Potential Battery Electric Vehicle Usage. (Hrsg.), 95th Annual Meeting of Transportation Research Board,2016.

[10] Wu X,Freese D, Cabrera A,et al. Electric Vehicles' Energy Consumption Measurement and Estimation [J]. Transportation Research Part D, 2015,34, 52-67.

[11] Xie C, Jiang N. Relay Requirement and Traffic Assignment of Electric Vehicles[J]. Computer-Aided Civil and Infrastructure Engineering,2016, 31, 580-598.

[12] Zhou Y, Wen R, Wang H et al. OPtimal Battery Electric Vehicles Range: A Study Considering Heterogeneous Travel Patterns, Charging Behaviors, and Access to Charging Infrastructure[J]. Energy, 2020, 197, 116945.

具有充电窗口和分时电价的电动公交车辆时空充电策略优化

鲍照耀[1] 李昕妍[2] 傅寒珺[2] 李佳佩[2] 丁稼轩[2] 谢驰[2]

(1.上海交通大学;2.同济大学)

摘 要 本研究提出一个具有充电时间窗口、并考虑分时电价的电动公交车辆充电策略优化整数线性规划模型。在时间和电量离散化的基础上,通过开发多准则标号法,确定公交车队中的每一辆公交车每天最优的充电的时间片段及地点。本研究通过一个示例电动公交系统(12辆电动公交车、108次环线服务次数、2个充电站),对所提出的模型和开发的算法进行了验证。我们发现在考虑分时电价下最优的充电策略可为公交系统节省40%以上的充电成本。

关键词 电动公交 充电规划 时间窗口 分时电价

0 引言

公交系统作为城市交通的重要组成部分,为人们提供了一种绿色经济可持续的出行方式,在缓解城市交通拥堵和降低车辆尾气排放方面都发挥了重要作用。相较于传统柴油公交车,电动公交具有如更低的或零的尾气排放、运行及维护成本更低、行驶噪声低以及乘用更舒适等优点[1]。

虽然纯电动公交具有许多优点,但还存在许多制约其发展的问题,充电需求即其中之一。本研究中电动公交使用整车充电的方式进行补电,因此公交需要足够的充电时间窗口来进行补电。电动公交充电时间的选择不仅要考虑对正常线路运营的影响,在很多城市施行分时电价政策的情况下,还需考虑不同时区电价情况。为降低电动公交运营成本,在安排电动公交充电时,应尽可能选择平段或低谷时段充电,避免在峰段充电[2]。

近年来,为了能够有效地使用电动公交车替代传统燃油公交车来满足城市中人们通勤,部分学者针对电动公交充电基础设施规划、电动公交运营调度做了深入的研究[4-7]。但是无论是在电动公交充电基础设施规划研究中,还是在电动公交运营调度问题中,电动公交的充电策略都是被简单的考虑,针对电动公交充电规划的研究还相对较少。

本文结构安排如下:第一部分为电动公交充电线性规划模型构建;第二部分为本文开发的用于求解最优充电策略的多准则标号法工作原理简述;第四部分为算例结果分析;最后为总结展望部分。

1 模型

1.1 问题描述

本研究再给定车辆运营时刻表情况下,考虑离散化的时间片段。通过决策电动公交车在某一个充电窗口内的某一个充电时间片段是否充电,我们能够动态的选择公交车在非运营时段的充电起止时刻。在考虑分时电价的影响下,建立了具有充电时间窗口的电动公交车辆充电策略优化模型。

1.2 充电策略优化模型

本文提出的具有充电时间窗口和分时电价的电动公交系统充电策略优化问题,用以下整数模型来描述:

$$\min Z(x) = \sum_{i \in I} \sum_{k^i \in K} \sum_{n_{ki} \in N_k} \sum_{y_m \in Y_m} \sum_{m \in M} x_{n_{ki}} E_{n_{ki}} c_m \delta m, y_{n_{ki}} \quad (1)$$

s.t.

$$B_{k^{i}+1} = B_{k^i} + \sum_{n_{ki} \in N_{ki}} x_{n_{ki}} E_{n_{ki}} - P_{k^i, k^i+1}, \forall (r,s) \in W, k \in K_{rs} \quad (2)$$

$$B_{k^i} + \sum_{n_{ki} \in N_{ki}} x_{n_{ki}} E_{n_{ki}} \leq Mu_i, \forall i \in I, k^i \in K^i \quad (3)$$

$$B_{k^i} \geq Ml_i, \forall i \in I, k^i \in K^i \quad (4)$$

$$x_{n_{ki}} \in \{0,1\}, \forall i \in I, k^i \in K^i, n_{ki} \in N_{ki} \quad (5)$$

此模型的目标函数为最小化公交系统充电成本总和。约束(2)是公交车的电量守恒约束。约束(3)是电池充电容量限制约束。约束(4)是公交车的行驶里程限制约束。约束(5)为充电决策变量$x_{n_{ki}}$的二元取值约束。

下面一个章节我们将针对上述整数线性规划模型所描述的公交车对充电策略优化问题,开发一个基于动态规划思想的多准则标号法进行精确求解。

2 求解算法设计

对于车队中的每一辆电动公交车,均使用多准则标号法求得最优充电计划。某一辆车的某一个充电窗口由若干个充电时间片段组成。以时间窗口 k^i-1 为例,它由充电时间片段 $1_{k_{i-1}}, 2_{k_{i-1}}, \cdots, n_{k_{i-1}}$ 组成。对于每一个充电时间片段,公交车 i 可以选择充电或者选择不充电。以充电时间片段 $1_{k_{i-1}}$ 为例,如果公交车在这个片段选择充电,那么变量 $x_{1_{k_{i-1}}}=1$;否则 $x_{1_{k_{i-1}}}=0$。当前充电窗口的每一个充电片段的决策变量值确定后,会得到一个跟决策变量值相对应的充电窗口充电方案。对于时间窗口 k^i-1,使用 $\{x(p)_{1_{k_{i-1}}}, \cdots, x(p)_{n_{k_{i-1}}}\}$ 来代表可能的充电方案中的一种,记作 pk^i-1。使用标号 $e(k^i-1)_p$ 和标号 $c(k^i-1)_p$ 来记录公交车在 k^i-1 窗口采用充电方案 $\{x(p)_{1_{k_{i-1}}}, \cdots, x(p)_{n_{k_{i-1}}}\}$ 后电池的电量和充电费用的累计值,记作一对标号 (e_pk^i-1, c_pk^i-1)。假设公交车 i 的最后一个充电窗口为 k^i+t,我们通过找到查找所有充电方案对应的所有标号对集合的所有标号对中具的有最小值标号 $c_sk^i+t_{min}$,在通过标号逆溯的方法得到要产生最小标号 c_sk^i+t 对应的公交车 i 每一个充电窗口的充电方案。

$$c_sk^i+t_{min} = \min\{c_sk^i+t \mid \forall (e_qk^i+t, c_qk^i+t) \in \{(e_qk^i, c_qk^i)\}, sk^i+t \in Sk^i+t\} \quad (6)$$

动态规划算法的步骤总结见表1。

动态规划框架下的多准则标号法　　　　表1

步骤	内　容
Step 0	初始化: 初始化第0个窗口费用标号 $c(k^i)=0$;窗口起始电量标号 $e(k^i)=B_0$;时间窗口 $k^i=0$
Step 1	计算第 k^i 个充电时间窗口的可行充电方案: 令 $k^i=k^i+1$,对于充电时间窗口 k^i-1 电量标号集合 $\{e(k^i-1)\}$ 中每一个标号,找到当前充电窗口 ki 中可行的充电电量数值集合 $\{b(k^i)\}$。对于每一个可行充电电量,计算其相对应的最小充电成本,得到在窗口 k^i 完成充电后的电量标号集合 $\{e(k^i)\}$ 和相对应的费用标号集合 $\{c(k^i)\}$
Step 2	标号更新与帕累托(Pareto)优劣判别: 对于任意一组标号 $(e(k^i), c(k^i))$,以双目标准则判断其有无保留的必要
Step 3	终止判别: 如果 ki 是车辆 i 最后一个充电时间窗口,算法终止;否则,执行 Step 1

3 算例验证与分析

以下通过一个示例来展示本文所提出的电动公交车辆充电策略优化模型和求解算法的有效性。这个简单的公交系统拥有12辆电池容量均为300kW·h的电动公交车来运营。每辆公交车从公交场站出发前的初始电池充电状态(State of Charge,SOC)均为55%。从早上6:00钟开始,第一辆公交车从场站调度至环线终点站开始运营(时刻表见表2)。每辆公交车的充电速率设置为108 kW;每辆公交车的耗电量设置为2.1kW·h/km。

公交系统的发车时刻表　　　　表2

发车时间	达到停靠站 A 时间	达到停靠站 B 时间	到达停靠站 C 时间
06:00	06:15	06:35	06:45
06:10	06:25	06:40	06:55
06:20	06:35	06:50	07:05
.	.	.	.
.	.	.	.
.	.	.	.
23:40	23:55	24:10	24:25
23:50	24:05	24:20	24:35
24:00	24:15	24:30	24:45

公交线路信息				表3
线路类型	车队车辆总数	长　度	发车间隔	线路服务次数(一天)
环线	12辆	20 km	10 min	108次

将上述参数输入到模型后,应用所开发算法得到此车队在考虑分时电价后的一天内充电计划如图1所示。

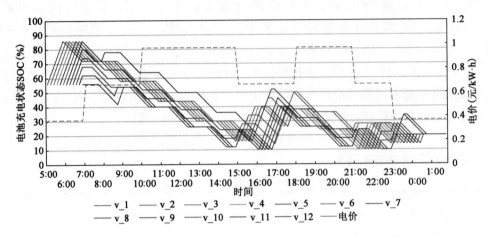

图1　公交车充电安排(考虑分时电价)

图1中每条实线代表一辆公交车的充电计划。结果显示车辆会在早间5:00~7:00间在公交场站进行补电,随后调度到公交车终点站开始环线运营。这是由于在早上7:00前属于谷时电价。因此对于考虑分时电价的场景,公交车队在开始营运前会在公交场站补电,减少运营期间在服务环线终点站的充电需求。对于7:00~24:00这个时段,我们发现公交车会避免在电价峰时充电。同时由于公交车在7:00~14:00这个时段电池电量比较充足,能够满足其运营里程的需求,因此在这个时段大部分公交车也不会进行补电。

作为对比,我们计算了在不考虑分时电价的情况下,车队的充电计划结果如图2所示。

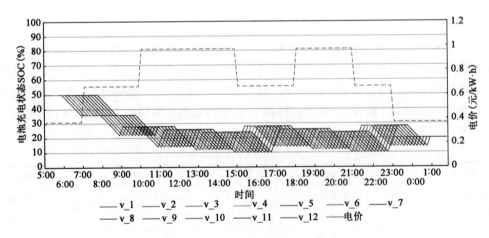

图2　公交车充电安排(不考虑分时电价)

对于此示例公交系统一天的运营需求,在考虑分时电价下的充电策略花费1873元,相比于不考虑分时电价下的充电策略花费(2714.4元)节约了44.9%的充电费用。

4　结　　语

本研究考虑动态变化电价、行驶里程限制,允许电动公交车在非运营时段动态选择充电起止时刻和地点,以及引入公交运营公司根据实际情况设置电池电量的上下界以同时考虑了保护电池使用寿命和公交运营的可靠性,以最小化公交系统中公交车队电力补给成本,最终实现开发可以广泛地应用于电动公交车队时空充电策略的系统优化方法。此研究建立基于时间和充电电量离散化的整数规划模型,并开发基于动态规划框架的多准则标号法以高效精确地求得问题全局最优解。

参考文献

[1] 王岱,李盼,包宇喆,等. 基于分时电价的纯电动公交的充电优化[J]. 长安大学学报(自然科学版),2013,33(03):81-87.

[2] 高佳宁. 考虑分时电价的纯电动公交行车计划编制方法研究[D]. 北京:北京交通大学,2018.

[3] 李世春,王扬,钟浩,等. 深化调峰的电动私家车/出租车群组合优化充放电策略[J]. 可再生能源,2020,38(06):824-830.

[4] LI Jing quan. Battery-Electric Transit Bus Developments and Operations: A Review[J]. International Journal of Sustainable Transportation, 2016, 10 (3): 157-169.

[5] Ibapra-Rojas O J, Delgado F, Giesen R, et al. Planning, Operation, and Control of Bus Transport Systems: A Literature Review[J]. Transportation Research Part B: Methodological, 2015, 77: 38-75.

[6] An Kun. Battery Electric Bus Infrastructure Planning Under Demand Uncertainty[J]. Transportation Research Part C: Emerging Technologies, 2020, 111: 572-587.

[7] AN Kun, Jing Wen tao, Kim I. Battery-Swapping Facility Planning for Electric Buses With Local Charging Systems[J]. International Journal of Sustainable Transportation 2020, 14 (7): 489-502.

基于第三方物流服务模式的生鲜产品企业合作博弈研究

张世鹏　胡大伟　王雪韵

(长安大学)

摘　要　生鲜产品生产企业生产出的产品由于运输不及时以及生鲜产品销售企业销售能力不够或者客户对产品需求太多,会造成产品堆积以及货源不足等问题,不能实现整体利益最大化。本文以合作博弈为基础,基于Shapley值法构建了第三方物流企业、生鲜产品生产企业和生鲜产品销售企业三方合作联盟,并对合作联盟进行收益分配。为了使收益分配更加合理,本文考虑了影响联盟的资本投入、风险承担、贡献程度因素,构建了引入影响因子的修正收益分配模型。通过采集数据和分析计算对两种收益分配模型进行比较,结果表明,修正后的收益分配模型更加科学、公平、合理,与实际情况更加贴合。

关键词　合作博弈　修正收益分配模型　Shapley值法　第三方物流服务模式　生鲜产品企业

0　引　言

在收益分配相关研究中,大多数人都是基于Shapley值法对利益分配问题进行研究[1]。张力研究了Shapley值法在我国航空物流服务供应链中的收益分配问题[2]。武士超等以终端物流为基础,结合各个物流企业自身优势,研究了各个物流企业共同配送的情况下的利益分配问题[3]。杨倩倩等在Shapley值法的基础,考虑企业整体实力和承担风险能力,构建改进的Shapley值分配模型[4]。王莺等在Shapley值法的基础上用一致许可值法优化了收益分配[5]。安鑫山等在Shapley值法的基础上,加入了一致许可值法,通过比较得出一致许可值法可以弥补由于 Shapley 值法没有考虑外部因素影响,可以使收益分配更加合理化[6]。蔡蓉等对合作博弈的快递终端服务联盟构建及利益分配进行研究,通过 Shapley 值与 Owen 值进行比较两种情况下的收益分配,得出合理分配向量[7]。李昌文在合作博弈供应链的基础上,对其稳定性展开了研究[8]。吕会军等以 Shapley 值法为基础,分析了对收益分配的影响因素,构建了改进后的 Shapley 值模型[9-11]。湘萌等提出了6个能够影响利益分配的影响因素,进而建立了修正的 Shapley 值模型[12]。朱清研究了基于供应链视角下的生鲜电商主题合作机制[13]。付志强研究了基于多方博弈的生鲜产品共同配送模式[14]。李锑在 Shapley 值法的基础上引入了综合修正因子,构建了修正后的 Shapley 值法模型,从而使各个联盟的收益分配更加合理[15]。

然而,对于第三方物流企业以及生鲜产品企业之间联盟的合作博弈研究基本处于空白。本文首先构建了 Shapley 值法的三方合作博弈模型,在此基础上,又综合考虑了影响联盟收益分配因素,构建了引入影响因子收益分配模型并给出算例,从而为三方合作提供了理论性的参考。

1 合作博弈模型

1.1 Shapley 值法模型

Shapley 值法是通过各个参与人在联盟中付出的多少对收益进行合理分配[16],定义如下:

设联盟集合 $N = \{1,2,\ldots,n\}$,N 表示整个联盟参与人的集合,对于集合 N 中任何一个子集记为 S,每一个子集 S 对应着一个新的收益函数 $V(S)$,满足以下条件:

$$V(\phi) = 0 \tag{1}$$

$$V(S_1 \cup S_2) \geq V(S_1) + V(S_2), S_1 \cap S_2 = \varphi, S_1, S_2 \in N \tag{2}$$

$$X_i \geq V(i), i = 1,2,\cdots,n \tag{3}$$

$$\sum_{1}^{n} X_i = V(N) \tag{4}$$

式(1)表示联盟不合作收益为0;式(2)表示联盟 N 中,任意子集都不相交,任意组合的合作收益分配都会大于单个个体收益;式(3)表示参与人收益大于其不参与时的收益;式(4)表示所有参与人联盟时的收益之和等于其最大收益。

若所有参与人都参与了联盟,那么在集合 N 下每个参与人所分配到的收益就是 Shapley 值,$\phi_i(V)$ 表示第 i 个参与人在联盟 N 下所得的分配收益,则 Shapley 值对大联盟收益分配公式为:

$$\phi_i(V) = \sum_{S \subset N} \frac{(|S|-1)!(n-|S|)!}{n!} \times [V(S) - V(S/\{i\})] \tag{5}$$

式(5)中,$|S|$ 表示联盟 S 参与人个数;n 表示合作博弈中参与人个数;$V(S)$ 表示联盟收益;$V(S/\{i\})$ 表示联盟除去 i 所获得的收益;$[V(S) - V(S/i)]$ 表示参与方 i 在联盟 S 中所做贡献;$\frac{(|S|-1)!(n-|S|)!}{n!}$ 表示每种排序出现的概率。

1.2 影响因素对联盟收益分配的影响

1.2.1 资本投入因素

假设参与人分别投入了 n 个项目,其中 n 是项目种数。以 p_{ij}(i 表示不同参与人;j 表示投入不同资本)表示不同参与人在第 j 项的成本价值。用 C_j 表示第 j 项资本在整个项目中的重要程度。价值权重 C_j 的判断可以采用层次分析法[17]进行测算。利用 C_j 修正三方企业所投入的第 j 种项目的成本价值 p_{ij},从而形成新成本价值 V_j 为:

$$V_j = \frac{p_{ij}}{\sum_{i=1}^{n} p_{ij}} \tag{6}$$

$$\alpha_i = \sum_{j=1}^{n} (V_{ij} \times C_j) \tag{7}$$

式中，V_{ij}为参与方i投入的成本价值；α_i为参与方i的资本投入比例。

1.2.2 风险承担因素

各参与企业在风险承担中的成本价值F_{ik}（i表示参与人，k表示风险指标）。用W_k表示第k项风险指标权重在联盟中的重要程度。然后对F_{ik}进行调整，形成新风险承担因子为：

$$R_i = F_{ik} \times W_k \tag{8}$$

$$\beta_i = \frac{R_i}{\sum_{i=1}^{n} R_i} \tag{9}$$

式中，R_i为参与方i的风险分担成本价值；β_i为参与方i的风险分担比例。

1.2.3 贡献程度因素

首先确定在突发情况下所发生的事件对联盟所造成的损失，再了解各企业在此事件上所作出的投入，这些投入包括处理此事件所花费的所有成本Q_{ij}（i表示参与人，j表示投入的不同成本）。通过计算得各参与联盟的贡献度因子为：

$$\gamma_i = \frac{Q_{ij}}{\sum_{i=1}^{n} Q_{ij}} \tag{10}$$

1.3 构建修正收益分配模型

本文将上述三个影响收益分配的因素作为修正指标，然后采用层次分析法（AHP）[20]进行赋权以定量确定其相对重要程度，从而修正Shapley值分配法。

1.3.1 修正指标权重计算

由评价小组就上述三个因素的相对重要程度进行标度值打分（1-9分制），并构造$n=3$阶判断矩阵为：

$$A = \begin{bmatrix} a_{11} & a_{12} & a_{13} \\ a_{21} & a_{22} & a_{23} \\ a_{31} & a_{32} & a_{33} \end{bmatrix} \tag{11}$$

式中，a_{ij}为第i个因素与第j个因素相比的重要程度。对矩阵进行一致性检验并将矩阵归一化处理后得到各修正指标的权重λ_i。

1.3.2 构建引入影响因子的修正收益分配模型

本文在Shapley值法的基础上，考虑了资本投入因子α_i，风险承担因子β_i，联盟贡献程度因子γ_i。他们的修正因素矩阵$M = [\alpha_i \ \beta_i \ \gamma_i]$，然后对收益矩阵$M$进行归一化处理得到矩阵$\hat{M} = [\hat{\alpha}_i \ \hat{\beta}_i \ \hat{\gamma}_i]$，根据修正指标的权重，利用公式：

$$R_i = \lambda_i \times M' \tag{12}$$

得到修正后的参与人的收益分配为：

$$V_i = \phi_i + \left(R_i - \frac{1}{n}\right) \times V(S) \tag{13}$$

2 算例分析

假设三方企业不合作时，第三方物流企业A的收益是500万元，生鲜产品生产企业B的收益是400万元，生鲜产品销售企业C的收益是300万元。并且，当A、B进行合作时的收益1500万元，A、C进行合作时的收益1300万元，B、C合作时的收益是1100万元。当A、B、C共同合作的收益是2500万元。

2.1 Shapley值法求解

通过式(5)可以计算出联盟中A、B、C的收益分配，如表1~表3所示。

表1 第三方物流企业的收益分配(单位:百万元)

S	A	A∪B	A∪C	A∪B∪C
V(S)	10/3	15	13	25
|S|	1	2	2	3
(|S|−1)!(n−|S|)!/n!	1/3	1/6	1/6	1/3
V(S/i)	0	4	3	11
$\varphi_A(V)$	5/3	11/6	5/3	14/3

因此,A 的收益分配为:

$$\phi_A(V) = \sum_{S \subseteq N \setminus i} \frac{(|S|-1)!(n-|S|)!}{n!} \times [V(S) - V(S \setminus i)] = 59/6 = 9.8(百万元)$$

表2 生鲜产品生产企业的收益分配(单位:百万元)

S	B	A∪B	B∪C	A∪B∪C
V(S)	4	15	11	25
|S|	1	2	2	3
(|S|−1)!(n−|S|)!/n!	1/3	1/6	1/6	1/3
V(S/i)	0	5	3	13
$\phi_B(V)$	4/3	5/3	4/3	4

因此,B 的收益为:

$$\varphi_B(V) = \sum_{S \subseteq N \setminus i} \frac{(|S|-1)!(n-|S|)!}{n!} \times [V(S) - V(S \setminus i)] = 25/3 = 8.4(百万元)$$

表3 生鲜产品销售企业的收益分配(单位:百万元)

S	C	A∪C	B∪C	A∪B∪C
V(S)	3	13	11	25
|S|	1	2	2	2
(|S|−1)!(n−|S|)!/n!	1/3	1/6	1/6	1/3
V(S/i)	0	5	4	15
$\phi_C(V)$	1	4/3	7/6	10/3

因此,C 的收益为:

$$\phi_C(V) = \sum_{S \subseteq N \setminus i} \frac{(|S|-1)!(n-|S|)!}{n!} \times [V(S) - V(S \setminus i)] = 41/6 = 6.8(百万元)$$

并且,可以看出:

$$\phi_A(V) > 5(百万元)$$
$$\phi_B(V) > 4(百万元)$$
$$\phi_C(V) > 3(百万元)$$
$$\phi_A(V) + \phi_B(V) = \frac{109}{6} > 15(百万元)$$
$$\phi_A(V) + \phi_C(V) = \frac{50}{3} > 13(百万元)$$
$$\phi_B(V) + \phi_C(V) = \frac{91}{6} > 11(百万元)$$
$$\phi_A(V) + \phi_B(V) + \phi_C(V) = 25(百万元)$$

因此 Shapley 值法得到的收益分配方案是:在 A、B、C 合作的基础上,A 的分配收益为 980 万元;B 的分配收益 840 万元;C 的分配收益为 680 万元。

2.2 引入影响因子修正收益分配模型求解

2.2.1 各影响因子计算

(1) 资本投入

首先根据专家评价法得到资本价值权重,如表4所示。

资本价值权重　　　　　　　　　　　　　　　表4

资本种类	投资资本	设备资本	人力资本	C_j
投资资本	1	3	2	0.554
设备资本	1/3	1	1	0.215
人力资本	1/2	1	1	0.231

资本投入影响因子测算可根据参与人的实际投入计算,如表5所示。

资本投入影响因子测算　　　　　　　　　　　表5

影响指标	第三方物流企业	生产企业	销售企业
资本投入 P_1	0.5	0.3	0.2
设备投入 P_2	0.3	0.7	0
人力投入 P_3	0.4	0.3	0.3

根据式(6)、式(7)得:

$$\alpha_1 = P_{1j} \times C_j = 0.434$$
$$\alpha_2 = P_{2j} \times C_j = 0.386$$
$$\alpha_3 = P_{3j} \times C_j = 0.180$$

A 的资本投入因子 α_1 为 0.434,B 的资本投入因子 α_2 为 0.386,C 的资本投入因子 α_3 为 0.18。

(2) 风险承担

根据上文提到的层次分析法得到风险指标权重表,如表6所示。

风险指标权重　　　　　　　　　　　　　　　表6

风险指标	技术	建设	市场	自然	F_{ik}
技术	1	8	5	3	0.567
建设	1/8	1	1/2	1/6	0.056
市场	1/5	2	1	1/3	0.104
自然	1/3	6	3	1	0.273

按照风险承担调整方法和风险指标权重,可求得下面风险承担影响因子测算,如表7所示。

风险承担影响因子测算　　　　　　　　　　　表7

影响指标	第三方物流企业	生产企业	销售企业
技术	1	0	0
建设	0	1	0
市场	0	0	1
自然	1/3	1/3	1/3
风险指标权重		W = [0.567　0.056　0.104　0.273]	

$$\beta_1 = F_{1k} \times W_j = 0.658$$
$$\beta_2 = F_{2k} \times W_j = 0.147$$
$$\beta_3 = F_{3k} \times W_j = 0.195$$

A 的资本投入因子 β_1 为 0.658，B 的资本投入因子 β_2 为 0.147，C 的资本投入因子 β_3 为 0.195。

(3) 贡献程度

由于在联盟过程中经常遇到突发情况的问题，因此有些时候需要三方企业能够快速解决问题，设三方企业在解决问题中所作出的贡献相同，投入的成本相同。因此，可以设 A、B、C 的贡献程度因子为 $\gamma_1 = \gamma_2 = \gamma_3 = 1/3$。

2.2.2 各收益分配计算

通过专家评价法可得修正后的各影响因子权重，如表 8 所示。

修正影响因子权重　　　　　　　　　表 8

修正因子	资本投入	风险承担	贡献程度	λ
资本投入	1	2	1/4	0.368
风险承担	2	1	5	0.535
贡献程度	1/4	1/5	1	0.097

因此修正后的矩阵 M 为：

$$M = \begin{bmatrix} 0.434 & 0.386 & 0.180 \\ 0.658 & 0.147 & 0.195 \\ 1/3 & 1/3 & 1/3 \end{bmatrix}$$

根据表 8 得 $\lambda = [0.368 \quad 0.535 \quad 0.097]$

然后根据式(12)得：

$$R = \lambda \cdot M = [0.368 \quad 0.535 \quad 0.097] \times \begin{bmatrix} 0.434 & 0.386 & 0.180 \\ 0.658 & 0.147 & 0.195 \\ 1/3 & 1/3 & 1/3 \end{bmatrix} = [0.544 \quad 0.253 \quad 0.203]$$

因此，根据公式(14)可得修正后的联盟收益分配为：

(1) A 修正后的收益分配：

$$V_1 = \varphi_1 + \left(R_1 - \frac{1}{3}\right) \cdot V(S) = \frac{59}{6} + \left(0.544 - \frac{1}{3}\right) \cdot 25 = 15.1 \text{（百万元）}$$

(2) B 修正后的收益分配：

$$V_2 = \varphi_2 + \left(R_2 - \frac{1}{3}\right) \cdot V(S) = \frac{25}{3} + \left(0.253 - \frac{1}{3}\right) \cdot 25 = 6.3 \text{（百万元）}$$

(3) C 修正后的收益分配：

$$V_3 = \varphi_3 + \left(R_3 - \frac{1}{3}\right) \cdot V(S) = \frac{41}{6} + \left(0.203 - \frac{1}{3}\right) \cdot 25 = 3.6 \text{（百万元）}$$

2.3 结果分析

如表 9 所示，A 在修正后的联盟收益分配中比 Shapley 值法所求出的收益增加了 530 万元，而 B 和 C 在修正后的联盟收益分配中比 Shapley 值法所求出的收益分别减少了 200 万元、320 万元。

两种分配方案收益的比较（单位：百万元）　　　　　　　　　表 9

分配方法	A	B	C
Shapley 值法	9.8	8.4	6.8
修正后的 Shapley 值法	15.1	6.3	3.6

对 Shapley 值法进行影响因子修正，其实就是对收益分配进行了一次权重的分配。在联盟企业不断增多的情况下，加入影响因子的修正收益分配模型也同样适用于联盟。所以，加入影响因子的修正收益分配模型更公平合理。

3 结 语

本文基于第三方物流的发展状况,构建了第三方物流企业、生鲜产品生产企业以及生鲜产品销售企业联盟,先通过 Shapley 值法得出各参与企业的收益分配。同时,又引入了影响收益分配的影响因素,重新建立修正后的收益分配模型,并且通过算例进行求解验证。数值计算分析表明,在进行收益分配时,考虑联盟的资本投入、风险承担以及贡献程度因素,加入影响收益分配的影响因子对收益分配进行修正后,更具有公平性、科学性、合理性,符合实际情况。对于第三方物流企业,收益分配的增加,可以调动物流企业加入联盟的积极性,加大物流企业资本的投入,早日建成全国物流网络联盟。从而使运输效率更加高效,运输路线更加合理,降低物流运输成本,完善城市以及全国物流运输系统,在互联网、智能化的作用下使现代物流实现智能化。

本文只给出三方合作的企业联盟,其实在实际过程中,可能会有对方参与下的联盟,使联盟更加复杂化,因此还需要结合实际进行更加精细化的分析。对收益分配的计算过程中,也没有选取更具有说服力的具体企业数据。虽然有不足之处,但是也验证了该方法的可行性,可以为企业合作收益分配提供一个可行性的参考。

参考文献

[1] Shapley L S, Shubik M. A Method for Evalue Valuating the Distribution of Power in A Committee System [J]. American Political Science Review, 1954, 48(48): 787-792.
[2] 张力. 基于 Shapley 值在我国航空物流服务供应链收益分配研究[D]. 天津:中国民航大学, 2017.
[3] 武士超, 王梅月, 马欣. 基于改进的 Shapley 值法的物流联盟利益分配问题研究[J]. 项目管理技术, 2018(10):73-77.
[4] 杨倩倩, 胡大伟, 褚宏帆. 共享汽车和共享单车的合作博弈研究[J]. 交通信息与安全, 2018, 4(36): 126-132.
[5] 王莺, 李军. 基于一致许可值的供应链合作收益分配研究[J]. 科技和产业, 2013, 13(10):141-165.
[6] 安鑫山, 许佳莹. 共享单车参与的城市公租单车合作博弈[J]. 交通运输研究, 2020, 6(2):60-67.
[7] 蔡蓉, 胡大伟. 基于合作博弈的快递终端服务联盟构建及利益分配研究[J]. 2019, 10(9):9-14.
[8] 李昌文. 基于合作博弈理论的供应链联盟稳定性研究[D]. 广州:华南理工大学, 2018.
[9] 吕会军, 李锦飞. 基于 Shapley 值法新模型的动态联盟利润分配研究[J]. 商业研究, 2007, 7(2):64-66.
[10] 蔡继荣. 考虑风险因素 Shapley 值法的联盟收益分配策略[J]. 商业经济, 2018, 9(505):122-124.
[11] 张英, 徐伊平, 周兴建. 基于改进 Shapley 值法的供应链制造联盟利益分配研究[J]. 武汉理工大学学报(信息与管理工程版), 2019, 10(45):503-508.
[12] 黄湘萌, 杨帅. 绿色供应链协同利益分配策略研究——基于区块链技术的 Shapley 值修正模型[J]. 技术经济与管理研究, 2020(08):14-19.
[13] 朱清. 基于供应链视角下的生鲜电商主体合作机制[D]. 长沙:湖南大学, 2017.
[14] 付志强. 基于多方博弈的生鲜产品共同配送模式研究[D]. 北京:北京交通大学, 2017.
[15] 李锑. 基于改进 Shapley 值法的动态物流联盟利益分配[J]. 物流技术, 2020, 39(03):106-110.
[16] 陈思源. 合作博弈 Shapley 值的扩展与应用[D]. 西安:西安电子科技大学, 2011.
[17] 赵焕臣, 许树柏, 金生. 层次分析法——一种简易的新决策方法[M]. 北京:科学出版社, 1986.
[18] 汪国懋. 基于层次分析法的水利 PPP 项目风险评价[J]. 重庆理工大学学报, 2016, 30(9):156-160.
[19] 罗石钧, 龚仁燕. 层次分析法(AHP)在项目风险管理中的运用[J]. 工程建设与设计, 2011(S1): 195-198.
[20] 盛松涛, 安怡蒙. 基于 AHP-Shapley 值法的水利工程 PPP 项目收益分配研究[J]. 水利水电技术, 2019, 50(2):16-167.

Integrated Operator-Based and User-Based Vehicle Relocation for One-Way Carsharing Systems

Linzhi Jiang　Chi Xie

(Tongji University, School of Transportation Engineering)

Abstract　Carsharing has gained growing popularity due to its geographically wide accessibility to vehicles for users without owning them. In a one-way carsharing system, the fluctuating and asymmetric vehicle usage, however, often causes the problem of vehicle stock imbalance across different stations. Two strategies, vehicle relocation based on professional operators and trip pricing imposed on vehicle users, are adopted in this study to relieve this imbalance problem by intervening the demand pattern and supply distribution. A nonlinear programming model is accordingly proposed to determine the optimal trip price, vehicle relocation and operator assignment schemes with the system profit maximized. A case study based on a large one-way carsharing system in Shanghai is conducted to test the modeling and solution methods and explore the potential of improving the carsharing service performance. A sensitivity analysis on the demand elasticity is conducted, and the revenue-cost structure with different relocation resource provisions is further assessed.

Keywords　One-way carsharing system　Vehicle relocation　Trip pricing　Operator assignment

0　Introduction

Carsharing has received much attention in the urban transportation service industry in recent years due to its economic and environmental benefits as an alternative to private cars and many public transportation modes. As carsharing systems, which date back to Sefage service of Zurich, Switzerland in 1948 (Shaheen et al. 1999), give users access to a fleet of vehicles without owning them, it has gained growing popularity for its convenience, flexibility, and relatively lower cost.

Traditional car rental systems are generally round-trip systems, in which users need to pick up and return shared vehicles to the same stations (Nourinejad and Roorda 2014). As the system has gradually evolved to provide users with more convenience, some carsharing companies have offered users one-way carsharing services. Users are allowed to return their shared vehicles to any stations in the general station-based one-way systems (Kek et al. 2009), or any legal parking place in predetermined operational areas in a special type of one-way systems called free-floating systems (Weikl and Bogenberger 2015). In these systems, demand fluctuation due to a variety of socio-economic factors and vehicle usage by users causes the vehicle-user imbalance problem. So the user demand cannot be well matched by the vehicle supply (Kek et al. 2009, Di Febbraro et al. 2012).

Several strategies have been studied to relieve the vehicle-user imbalance issue for the one-way carsharing systems. From the perspective of time horizon in the decision-makings, those strategies can be classified into three levels (Ferrero et al. 2018): operational, tactical, and strategic. The strategic level decisions which focus on long-term issues refer to the policies which need to be considered when designing the carsharing systems, including the locations and capacities of stations (Correia and Antunes 2012, Boyacı et al. 2015, Huang et al. 2018). The tactical dimension concentrates on planning decisions that may include the fleet size and initial distribution of vehicles at stations (Boyacı et al. 2015, Xu et al. 2018). The last type called operational strategies considers the daily management of the system, involving the operation of vehicles and operators and dynamic trip pricing (Kek et al. 2009, Weikl and Bogenberger 2015, Gambella et al. 2017, Jian et al. 2018, Barth et al. 2004, Di Febbraro et al. 2012, Waserhole et al. 2013, Jorge et al. 2015). However, as decisions of different levels are not independent of each other, several research topics cannot be strictly limited to one single level and some articles are described as finding a decision-making system from integrated design and operational dimensions (Illgen and Höck 2019).

As operational-level strategies, vehicle relocation by operators is considered to be the most widely used method, and trip pricing is another promising approach to solve the vehicle-user imbalance problem for one-way carsharing systems. Under the vehicle relocation strategy (Kek et al. 2009, Zakaria et al. 2014, Weikl and Bogenberger 2015, Zhao et al. 2018), a group of professional drivers (namely, operators) are assigned to drive vehicles from the stations with redundant vehicles to the stations with a shortage, which will affect the supply distribution. But this method has certain restrictions, including the limited number of operators and the rebalancing difficulty of operators. So trip pricing is also adopted to address the imbalance problem by intervening the demand pattern when the demand is cost-sensitive. Under the trip pricing strategy (Barth et al. 2004, Di Febbraro et al. 2012, Jorge et al. 2015, Xu et al. 2018), trips to specific undersupplied stations can be offered at a lower price or even for free while a higher price will be charged for trips to stations with an oversupply of vehicles, which will change the demand pattern and accordingly affect the supply distribution.

Existing studies rarely consider the elastic demand of the one-way carsharing system, while the user demand is a crucial factor in the decision makings of carsharing systems. So this research focuses on the integration of vehicle relocation and trip pricing of one-way station-based carsharing systems with the consideration of elastic demand to maximize the profit for system managers by determining optimal dynamic trip pricing, vehicle relocation and operator assignment schemes.

In conclusion, those contributions are made by this research. Firstly, we integrate vehicle relocation and trip pricing strategies to address the supply-demand imbalance problem, while just a few studies are focusing on user-based techniques, and articles with the consideration of operators and users for relocation issues simultaneously are even much less. Secondly, to consider system dynamics, the network is extended to a space-time network and all the movements of vehicles, operators, and users are represented as network flows to avoid the limitation of solution efficiency of integer programming (Fu et al. 2020). Then a nonlinear programming model with elastic demand is developed for this operational-level problem, while demand elasticity is only considered by limited literature.

The remainder of this study is structured as follows. We present the problem statement in the next section. A nonlinear programming model to generate optimal dynamic trip pricing, vehicle relocation and operator assignment schemes for vehicle-user imbalance problems is formulated in section 3. And a case study based on a one-way carsharing system in Shanghai is presented in section 4.

1 Problem Statement

This paper considers a one-way carsharing system with the predetermined number and locations of stations, which have a limited number of vehicle parking spots. The fleet size and personnel size are given, resulting in some fixed costs, such as the capital and maintenance costs of vehicles and human resource costs. A user can reserve the shared vehicle for a specific O-D station pair in the system to complete his or her trip. While making trip decisions affected by many factors, users will choose whether to travel and which transportation mode to use, including carsharing and other transportation modes. In this paper, the user demand for the carsharing system is considered to be elastic to trip price. Users can choose if they will take shared vehicles to meet their needs according to the trip price, if not, they may give up the trip or use other modes of transportation.

Importantly, trip pricing strategy is developed based on elastic demand. It is commonly known that the travel costs consisting of monetary cost and time cost are crucial factors affecting travel demand (Litman 2019). For the one-way carsharing system, users are aggregated according to their departure stations, destination stations, and rental starting time. The demand of each group with the same O-D station pair and starting time is assumed to be elastic with regard to the trip price for that O-D station pair. It is commonly known that users may switch to other transportation modes, shift their travel time or give up the trip with high trip price of that O-D station pair in the carsharing system, while low trip price attracts users to choose shared vehicles from other modes of transportation, and new demand may also be generated as a result. We consider a power function to express the dependence of user demand on travel costs and adopt the form of linear expression to improve the solve efficiency.

Specifically, user demand from station i to station j with the starting time interval k is a continuous function of the trip price $e^k l_{ij}$, and the function is first assumed to be written as follows:

$$d^k l_{ij} = a^k_{ij} - b^k_{ij} e^k_{ij} - c^k_{ij} t^k_{ij}$$

where a^k_{ij}, b^k_{ij}, and c^k_{ij} are all positive parameters, e^k_{ij} denotes trip price, and t^k_{ij} represents travel time. As the factor t^k_{ij} is a known parameter, user demand $d^k l_{ij}$ is a function of trip price e^k_{ij}. Besides, the demand function can be explained that the higher the trip price, the less users are willing to use shared vehicles.

2 Problem Formulation

2.1 Modeling assumptions

Based on the concepts mentioned above, first, we make some assumptions to facilitate modeling and describe some system elements as follows:

Assumption 1: To consider system dynamics, the daily operation period is divided into several time intervals with the same time duration, so the network is extended into a time-expanded space-time network.

Assumption 2: The demand of each O-D station pair with the same starting time is assumed to be elastic with regard to the trip price for that O-D station pair. And the elastic demand function is expressed as a linear Tab. 1.

Notations used to formulate the model are summarized as Tab. 1:

Notation of model   Tab. 1

Index	
i, j	Indices for parking station
k, l	Indices for time interval
Set	
N	Set of parking stations
A	Set of arcs connecting any two stations, where $A = \{(i,j)\}$
K	Set of time intervals, where $K = \{0, 1, 2, \cdots, k, \cdots\}$
Parameter	
$c^{u,k}_{ij}$	Cost of driving a shared vehicle by users from station i to station j at time interval k
$c^{v,k}_{ij}$	Cost of relocating a shared vehicle from station i to station j at time interval k
$c^{p,k}_{ij}$	Cost of an operator moving from station i to station j at time interval k
c^s_i	Cost of a shared vehicle parking at station i for one time duration

continue

Parameter	
c_i	Parking capacity of station i
v^0_i	The initial number of vehicles in station i at the start of the total operation period
p^0_i	The initial number of operators in station i at the start of the total operation period
Decision variable	
ek_{ij}	The system's revenue from a user using a shared vehicle from station i to station j departing at time interval k
vkl_{ij}	Vehicle relocation flow from station i to station j starting at time interval k and ending at time interval l
ukl_{ij}	User flow from station i to station j starting at time interval k and ending at time interval l
pkl_{ij}	Operator movement flow from station i to station j starting at time interval k and ending at time interval l
vk_i	Number of vehicles parking at station i at time interval k
pk_i	Number of operators staying at station i at time interval k

2.2 A nonlinear programming model

Based on the assumptions and notation above, the optimization model considering elastic demand is formulated as the following:

$$\max \sum_k \sum_i \sum_j (ek_{ij} - c^{u,k}_{ij}) u^{kl}_{ij} - \sum_k \sum_i \sum_j c^{v,k}_{ij} v^{kl}_{ij} - \sum_k \sum_i \sum_j c^{p,k}_{ij} p^{kl}_{ij} - \sum_k \sum_i c^s_i v^k_i \tag{1}$$

subject to

$$v^{k+1}_i = v^k_i - \sum_j v^{kl}_{ij} - \sum_j u^{kl}_{ij} + \sum_j v^{lk}_{ji} + \sum_j u^{lk}_{ji} \quad \forall i \in N, k, l \in K \backslash k_{last} \tag{2}$$

$$p^{k+1}_i = p^k_i - \sum_j v^{kl}_{ij} - \sum_j p^{kl}_{ij} + \sum_j v^{lk}_{ji} + \sum_j p^{lk}_{ji} \quad \forall i \in N, k, l \in K \backslash k_{last} \tag{3}$$

$$v^k_i \leq c_i \quad \forall i \in N, k \in K \tag{4}$$

$$u^{kl}_{ij} \leq d^{kl}_{ij} \quad \forall i, j \in N, k, l \in K \tag{5}$$

$$u^{kl}_{ij}, v^{kl}_{ij}, p^{kl}_{ij}, p^k_i, v^k_i, e^k_{ij} \geq 0 \tag{6}$$

where

$$d^{kl}_{ij} = f(e^k_{ij}) = a^k_{ij} - b^k_{ij} e^k_{ij} - c^k_{ij} t^k_{ij} \tag{7}$$

The objective function (1) is to maximize the profit of the carsharing system during the whole operation period, which is the difference between the revenue earned from user trips and the total operational costs. The costs consider vehicle relocation cost, vehicle usage cost by users, operator movement cost by other transportation modes, and the cost of vehicle parking at the station.

Constraints (2) represent the conservation of vehicle flows, which update the number of vehicles parking at each station and each time interval. These constraints indicate that the number of vehicles coming out of the station is equal to the number of vehicles coming into the station, which consider the vehicle parking flows as inflows and outflows.

Constraints (3) are the operator conservation constraints, which update the number of operators at each station and each time interval. Similarly, those constraints guarantee that the number of operators coming out of the station equals the number of operators coming into the station, which consider the operator parking flows as inflows and outflows.

Constraints (4) ensure that the number of vehicles parking at each station at each time interval cannot exceed the station's capacity.

Constraints (5) guarantee that the user flow which is the served demand should be less than or equal to the demand resulting from a specific trip price for each O-D station pair. The elastic demand function, denoted by $f(ek_{ij})$ (Expression (7)), has been described in detail above.

Constraints (6) specify the domain of variables, which must be non-negative.

3 Numerical Analysis

In this section, a case study focusing on the data from one of the largest carsharing companies in Shanghai is presented to evaluate the performance of the proposed model. The method is coded in Python 3.7 calling Gurobi on a personal computer with 1.8 GHz CPU and 8GB RAM.

The morning operation period (6:30 to 11:30 am) of the one-way carsharing system in Shanghai is studied here. The information we get about the one-way carsharing company includes station names, locations, and capacities. A total of 1,411 vehicle parking spots are located in 25 stations in Shanghai with predetermined locations. The size of each dot indicates the number of vehicle parking spots of the corresponding station, and the capacities of these 25 stations are between 45 and 78. Additionally, the whole morning operation period is divided into 20 time intervals and each time interval covers 15 minutes. The travel time of each O-D station pair at each time interval is obtained by Baidu map API, and the difference of travel time for different time intervals of the whole operation period is considered. The vehicle usage cost by users and relocation cost per time interval is set as ¥7.5/(15min). The cost of operator movement between stations for one time interval is set as ¥10/(15min). And the cost of vehicle parking at the station for one time interval is set as ¥3/(15min).

3.1 Impact of demand elasticity

As the elastic demand function determines how user demand changes with regard to the variation of trip price, demand elasticity, which can be measured by b_{ij}^k, has a great influence on the system performance. As the number of vehicles represents the resource supply of the system and has a great impact on the system, while elastic demand function determines user demand. This analysis aims to explore how the elasticity and the interaction between demand and supply affect the system performance. As shown in Fig. 1, four scenarios with 200, 600, 1000 and 1400 vehicles are tested to evaluate the changing pattern of system profit over different values of b_{ij}^k.

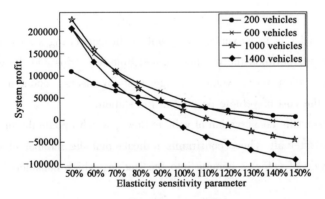

Fig. 1 System profit over elasticity in different scenarios

Fig. 1 implies that a smaller value of elasticity leads to higher system profit, which may be explained by some economics knowledge. As the value of b_{ij}^k represents the sensitivity of demand to trip price, so in scenarios with small values of b_{ij}^k, a big change in trip price will cause a small change in user demand, so the carsharing companies are able to raise the trip price without decreasing the demand to obtain more system profit. Moreover, it can be seen from Figure 1 that the optimal vehicle number for profit maximization is different in systems with different values of elasticity. It indicates that elasticity is a crucial factor while suggesting the optimal fleet size of the system. Accordingly, this demonstrates the significance of considering the demand elasticity in the decision-makings of the carsharing systems.

3.2 Revenue-cost structure analysis

In this subsection, an analysis on the revenue-cost structure is conducted to assist the improvement of system profit by increasing the revenue or reducing the cost. As the system resources has a great impact on it, cost structures under various vehicle numbers and operator numbers are presented in Fig. 2.

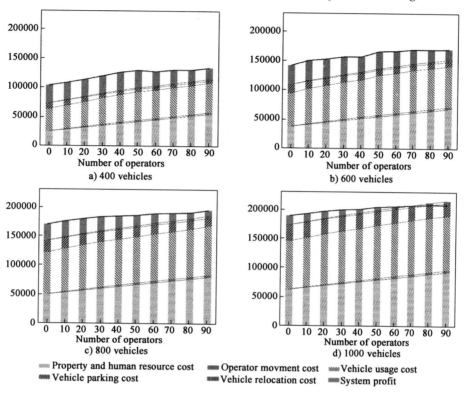

Fig. 2 Cost structure under scenarios with different vehicle and operator numbers

The height of each stacked bar represents the value of system revenue, consisting of system profit and the total costs. So the changing trend of the top line denotes the variation of system revenue, and it can be seen from those figures that it keeps increasing with the rising number of operators and vehicles, as more user demand can be served by the system. And the changing trend of demand can be observed from the changing trend of vehicle usage cost by users, since this part of cost is proportional to the amount of served demand. And it can also be found that this part of cost accounts for a large proportion of the total costs.

In addition to the vehicle usage cost and property and human resource cost that have a significant impact on the system profit, the parking cost is also an important part that cannot be ignored. It implies that with more vehicles, the idle time of the vehicles increases, resulting in an obvious increase in vehicle parking cost, especially in the downtown area.

Besides, it can also be observed that the number of operators has a positive impact on the reduction of parking cost. Therefore, it may be profitable for carsharing companies to improve the utilization of vehicles and provide more services to users by employing an appropriate number of operators. Moreover, it can be found from the last figure that too many vehicles and operators can make the system unprofitable. This phenomenon combined with the previous analysis indicates that the fleet size and personnel size are quite significant for the carsharing systems.

4 Conclusions

In this paper, the integrated operator-based and user-based vehicle relocation strategy has been investigated to relieve the imbalance problem one-way station-based carsharing systems. Specifically, vehicle relocation based on professional operators and trip pricing imposed on vehicle users are adopted to maximize the system profit. All the movements of users, vehicles, and operators are constructed as network flows in a time-expanded space-time network. Under the assumption that the user demand is elastic with regard to the trip price, a nonlinear programming model is proposed to maximize system profit by determining the optimal dynamic trip price, vehicle relocation and operator assignment schemes. Then the model is applied to a large one-way carsharing system in Shanghai to explore the carsharing service performance under various scenarios. First, we make a sensitivity analysis on the demand elasticity, which indicates its great impact on system profit and demonstrates the significance of this research to consider the demand elasticity in the decision-makings. Moreover, the cost structure under various vehicle numbers and operator numbers is also assessed for assisting the improvement of system profit. It implies that improving the utilization of vehicles by employing an appropriate number of operators is profitable for carsharing companies. While electricity consumption is not considered in this research, introducing electric shared vehicle into this operator-based and user-based vehicle relocation optimization problem can be done in the future work.

5 Acknowiedgements

This research is sponsored by the National Natural Science Foundation of China (Grant No. 71771150, 71471111, 71890970, 72021002) and National Key Research and Development Program of China (Grant No. 2018YFB1600900).

References

[1] Barth M., M. Todd, L. Xue. (2004). User-Based Vehicle Relocation Techniques for Multiple-Station Shared-Use Vehicle Systems. Transportation Research Record, 1887: 137-144.

[2] Boyaci B., K. G. Zografos, N. Geroliminis. (2015). An Optimization Framework for the Development of Efficient One-Way Car-Sharing Systems. European Journal of Operational Research, 240(3): 718-733.

[3] Correia G. H., A. P. Antunes. (2012). Optimizationapproach to Depot Location and Trip Selection in One-Way Carsharing Systems. Transportation Research Part E, 48(1): 233-247.

[4] Di Febbraro A., N. Sacco, M. Saeednia. (2012). One-Way Carsharing: Solving the Relocation problem. Transportation Research Record, 2319(1), 113-120.

[5] Ferrero F., G. Perboli, M. Rosano, et al. (2018). Car-Sharing Services: An Annotated Review. Sustainable Cities and Society, 37: 501-518.

[6] Fu H., C. Xie. (2020). Dynamic Vehicle Relocation by Professional Operators and Designated Drivers for One-Way Carsharing Systems. Working Paper, School of Transportation Engineering, Tongji University, Shanghai, China.

[7] Gambella C., E. Malaguti, F. Masini, et al. (2017). Optimizing Relocation Operations in Electric Car-Sharing. Omega, 81: 234-245.

[8] Huang K., G. H. Correia, K. An. (2018). Solving the Station-Based One-Way Carsharing Network Planning Problem with Relocations and Non-Linear Demand. Transportation Research Part C, 90: 1-17.

[9] Illgen S., M. and Hock. (2019). Literature Review of the Vehicle Relocation Problem in One-Way Car Sharing Networks. Transportation Research Part B, 120: 193-204.

[10] Jian S., D. Rey, and V. Dixit. (2019). An Integrated Supply-Demand Approach to Solving Optimal Relocations in Station-Based Carsharing Systems. Networks and Spatial Economics, 19(2): 611-632.

[11] Jorge D., G. Molnar, and G. H. Correia. (2015). Trip Pricing of One-Way Station-Based Carsharing Networks With Zone and Time of Day Price Variations. Transportation Research Part B, 81: 461-482.

[12] Kek A. G., R. L. Cheu, Q. Meng, et al. (2009). A Decision Support System for Vehicle Relocation Operations in Carsharing Systems. Transportation Research Part E, 45(1): 149-158.

[13] Litman T. (2019). Understanding Transport Demands and Elasticities: How Prices and Other Factors Affect Travel Behavior. Victoria Transport Policy Institute, BC, Canada.

[14] Nourinejad M., and M. J. Roorda. (2014). A Dynamic Carsharing Decision Support System[J]. Transportation Research Part E, 66: 36-50.

[15] Shaheen, S., D. Sperling, C. Wagner. (1999). A Short History of Carsharing in the 90's. Journal of World Transport Policy and Practice, 5(3), 16-37.

[16] Weikl S., and K. Bogenberger. (2015). A Practice-Ready Relocation Model for Free-Floating Carsharing Systems With Electric Vehicles: Mesoscopic Approach and Field Trial Results. Transportation Research Part C, 57: 206-223.

[17] Xu M., Q. Meng, Z. Liu. (2018). Electric Vehicle Fleet Size and Trip Pricing for One-Way Carsharing Services Considering Vehicle Relocation and Personnel Assignment. Transportation Research Part B, 111: 60-82.

[18] Zakaria R., M. Dib, L. Moalic, A. Caminada. (2014). Car Relocation for Carsharing Service: Comparison of CPLEX and Greedy Search. IEEE Symposium on Computational Intelligence in Vehicles and Transportation Systems (CIVTS). IEEE, 2014: 51-58.

[19] Zhao M., X. P. Li, J. T. Yin, J. X. Cui, L. X. Yang, and S. An. (2018). An Integrated Framework for Electric Vehicle Rebalancing and Staff Relocation in One-Way Carsharing Systems: Model Formulation and Lagrangian Relaxation-Based Solution Approach. Transportation Research Part B, 117: 542-572.

中心城市周边中小城市的交通发展路径

李子木

(江苏省规划设计集团有限公司交通规划与工程设计院)

摘　要　在新的时代背景和城镇化战略形势下,中心城市提升首位度的需求,不仅对其周边的中小城市起到带动作用,同时也提出了更为高质量的发展要求。中心城市周边中小城市的交通系统不再是其自身的交通系统,而是要与中心城市的发展统筹重构。本文以南京市及其周边城市句容市为例,通过发展背景及战略形式分析,建立了需求分析模型,测试了协同发展的交通模式。通过调整研究视角,从中心城市的角度重新审视中小城市的交通发展战略,并从依托中心城市高速铁路、高快速路、公共交通等角度,提出了中小城市的一体化交通发展路径。

关键词　交通规划　交通发展　中小城市　中心城市

0　引　言

随着时代的发展、新型城镇化进程的推进,区域中心城市切实的发挥出其强大的集聚能力,城市群、都市圈等已经不仅仅停留在概念程度。中心城市周边中小城市开始"临近"中心城市发展,甚至连为一体,承接城市功能的转移,参与更为紧密的分工协作[1]。中小城市作为城市群塑造城市体系不可或缺的重要环节,其可持续发展是我国现阶段城市健康稳定发展和城市群质量提升的关键[2]。交通系统作为中小城市与中心城市联系的最重要、最直接通道,其服务品质和发展战略关系不仅关系到自身的可持续发展,更加关系到城市群、都市圈的功能实现与服务共享。中小城市有其自身独特的交通特征[3],同时,在中心城市提升首位度、扩张腹地的背景下,其交通问题愈发凸显。本文以南京市及其周边城市句容市为例,解析中心城市周边中小城市的交通发展路径。

1 发展背景

1.1 新时代提出的新要求

(1)南京周边城市句容面临的问题,是大城市与小城市缺乏协同发展的不平衡,是城市与乡村发展中的不平衡和不充分,是人与环境缺乏协调发展的不平衡。应充分发展同城化一体化的交通体系,统筹发展城乡交通网络,构建生态休闲的交通系统。

(2)满足句容人民对"句容交通"的美好向往,交通系统是句容美好生活的重要组成部分。构筑以百姓为本的交通系统,是满足句容人民美好生活需要的重要一环。

(3)为实施乡村振兴战略,充分调动句容的特色资源,以生态农业和全域旅游为重要支点,打造乡村振兴的"句容名片"。

1.2 江苏省委省政府"六个高质量"发展任务

推动高质量发展,是江苏作为东部发达省份必须扛起的重大责任。要围绕"六个高质量"发展任务。加快推动城市群建设、乡村振兴和综合交通体系建设,推动城乡融合发展。

新时代的句容,应紧紧围绕高质量发展任务,尤其是针对城乡建设高质量、人民生活高质量、生态环境高质量的相关要求,构建城乡统筹、以人为本、绿色生态的高质量综合交通体系。

2 战略形势

2.1 城市群层面

城市群是带动区域若干城市协同发展的重要范畴,中心城市是其核心,周边的中小城市既要融入其中,又要凸显自身特色。

(1)长三角城市群,是"一带一路"与长江经济带的重要交汇地带,是中国参与全球竞争的重要平台、经济社会发展的重要引擎。句容是长三角城市群的节点之一,更好的融入将提供十足的发展潜力。

(2)扬子江城市群,是中国经济发展基础最好,综合竞争力最强的地区之一,是江苏省的核心发展区域。句容隶属镇江,更紧邻省会南京,可以依托扬子江城市群的战略核心,融入核心发展轴线。

2.2 都市圈层面

南京都市圈正式获批,句容将被纳入到南京的50km半径的核心腹地范围内,以南京为跳板,融入全国网络。

(1)南京都市圈,是以南京为中心的经济区域带,地跨苏皖两省,是长三角带动中西部地区发展的重要传导区域,具有重要地位。句容是南京都市圈中,距离南京主城区最近的节点城市,更在50km的核心腹地内,必将起到承启门户的枢纽作用,交通地位尤为重要。

(2)宁镇扬同城化是江苏省首个区域同城化发展规划,定位为"一带一路"节点城市、长江经济带门户城市,致力于打造扬子江城市群龙头城市。从国家战略高度的层面而言,宁镇扬板块处于长三角一体化、长江经济带、沿海地区开发和国家级南京江北新区等多个国家战略的交汇点上。句容位于镇江与南京之间,是多条发展轴带的必经之路,是同城化施行的前沿阵地。

2.3 交通新格局

(1)高铁时代的机遇。高速铁路已经成为实现区域一体化的重要推手,能够极大地带动城市潜力的提升。高速铁路对不同层级的城市有着不同的作用:对大城市来说,对资源的争夺更加激烈;对中等城市及其周边小城市来说,生产要素面临流失;对特大城市来说,周边小城市承接外溢,高铁会促进城市协同发展。句容作为特大城市南京的周边城市,将可能承接南京产业与人口的疏解和迁移,与南京协同发展,更快实现区域一体化发展。

(2)轨道上的江苏。江苏加快推进高铁网建设,加强各层次轨道交通规划建设有机衔接,形成以轨道交通为客运主骨架的综合交通运输网络。在此背景下,与句容相关的重大交通设施的落实将是交通跨越发展的重要前置条件。

3 战略及模式测试

3.1 城市定位及交通应对

句容的城市定位是"江南特色文化休闲基地、宁镇绿色创新协同发展区、南京都市圈生态宜居城市",致力于打造"一福地四名城"。句容的城市发展需要跳出行政桎梏,以区域一体化发展眼光打造"同城化先行区"。针对城市定位,从交通的角度进行解读:

(1)宁镇扬一体化先导区。采用"以宁为核、全域融入"的策略,全面对接南京。

(2)南京东郊花园副城。统筹空间展现风貌,发挥句容资源特色。

(3)美好生活示范之城。致力于打造安全通畅智慧绿色的城市交通系统。

3.2 交通发展模式测试

基于句容与南京交通出行总量,通过对双城联系的不同发展模式的测试,分析句容作为中心城市的周边城市较为适宜的交通模式结构,测试不同发展情景下的交通运行状况(表1及图1)。

联系强度情景模式相关测试参数 表1

情景模式	句容各区域	与南京联系强度	联系道路饱和度
情景一	中心城区	30%~35%	0.82
	宝华、郭庄	40%~45%	
情景二	中心城区	20%~25%	0.71
	宝华、郭庄	30%~35%	
情景三	中心城区	10%~15%	0.64
	宝华、郭庄	20%~25%	

 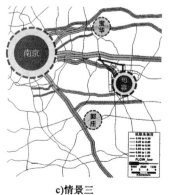

a)情景一　　　　b)情景二　　　　c)情景三

图1 联系强度多情景模型测试结果

(1)情景一:句容融入南京都市圈模式。句容和南京有较大的交通联系,具有一定比例的通勤交通出行,公共交通出行便利。

(2)情景二:句容作为南京卫星城发展模式。句容和南京联系较为密切,弹性交通出行占比较大,通勤出行较少。

(3)情景三:句容和南京相对独立发展模式。句容和南京联系强度较低,两个城市更加独立,只有少量的弹性出行存在。

3.3 城市交通战略测试

(1)总体出行预测

结合城市总体规划及相关规划,预测城市人口及岗位,并利用原单位法进行交通产生量和吸引量的预测。考虑各种交通方式的特点,步行采用转移曲线模型确定,对于自行车、公共交通和其他机动车则采用竞争模型法确定。结合句容实际出行特征,出行距离小于1公里的占5%,出行距离小于5公里的占75%,大多数出行为慢行交通方式的优势距离(图2)。

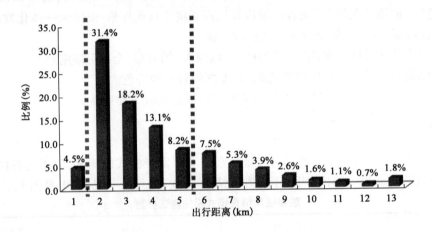

图2 句容市城市交通出行距离分布图

(2)方式选择测试

通过对中心城区不同出行方式组合方案的测试,分析句容市较为适宜的交通模式结构,测试机动车自由发展和绿色交通主导发展情景下的交通运行状况(表2及图3)。

情景一:机动车自由发展模式。公共交通常规发展,尽量满足小汽车出行要求的交通发展模式。

情景二:各种交通方式平衡发展模式。小汽车受到一定调控;优先发展公共交通和慢行交通。

情景三:绿色交通主导发展模式。加强交通需求管理,小汽车的使用受到调控;交通政策向绿色交通倾斜。

交通方式情景模式相关测试参数　　　　表2

情景模式	交通方式	结构比例	干路交通饱和度
情景一	小汽车交通	30%~35%	0.75
	绿色交通	60%~65%	
情景二	小汽车交通	20%~25%	0.61
	绿色交通	70%~75%	
情景三	小汽车交通	10%~15%	0.52
	绿色交通	80%~85%	

a) 情景一　　　　　　　b) 情景二　　　　　　　c) 情景三

图3　交通方式多情景模型测试结果

4　发展路径

4.1　突破传统视角,从中心城市都市圈角度审视周边城市

(1)传统的自我为中心向双核心转变

传统视角下的城市综合交通规划,一般以本市为中心,在市域范围内分析研究其交通发展背景和发展趋势,提出交通发展目标,继而对城市交通和对外交通进行规划布局。

句容地处南京都市圈核心圈层,与南京同城化趋势明显,仅从句容自身角度难以准确把握句容市的现状交通特征和发展趋势。需要突破传统视角的局限性,以南京句容为双核心,将对外交通放大到南京都市圈层面综合考虑,城市交通在满足句容自身发展以外,还需重点兼顾服务南京的需求。

(2)从中心城市视角分析周边城市优势

城的优势:南京副城。句容素有"南京新东郊、金陵御花园"之美誉,其中,宝华、开发区、郭庄镇等更是句容对接南京,接受南京辐射的前沿地带,与南京联系便捷。随着南京市域轨道S6线的建设,使得句容市的交通区位优势越加明显,足以支撑成为南京副城。

乡的优势:南京东郊后花园。句容南倚茅山,北濒大江,赤山湖横陈城西,宁镇山脉透迤境内,境内生态旅游资源丰富,拥有茅山风景名胜区、宝华山、茅山新四军纪念馆、赤山湖国家湿地公园等著名景点。随着带薪休假等制度的完善,句容的生态旅游资源对南京及周边地区的吸引力也将持续上升,足以支撑成为南京东郊后花园(图4)。

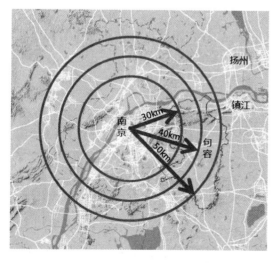 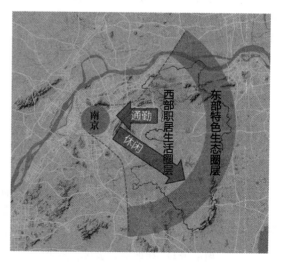

图4　南京都市圈及句容城乡优势分析示意图

4.2 全面纳入中心城市的战略路径

(1) 借高铁建设契机,放大强化枢纽效应

南京致力于打造国家高铁枢纽,其目标是打通大沿海、大沿江通道,成为"一带一路"出口节点,构建1.5小时的高速铁路交通圈。句容应充分利用南沿江铁路及扬马城际规划建设的机遇。通过高铁网络,句容可以快速连接南京南站枢纽以及空港枢纽。一方面,可以南京为跳板,将自身纳入国家铁路通道,实现更广阔的区域联系,缩短时空距离。另一方面,新的交通模式也将带来通勤模式的改变,利用高铁通道及机场可以通达全国,句容将跃入区域节点网络中(图5)。

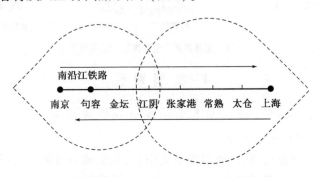

图5 南沿江铁路在区域层面对句容的影响示意图

(2) 通过区域一体化高快速路重构路网体系

依托南京内外双环+放射线的高快速路系统,建设中心径向线快速连接南京与句容。在北侧进行S122快速化改造,连接句容中心城区北部区域与南京城东区域。在南侧进行G104快速化改造,连接句容中心城区南部区域及城南综合交通枢纽与南京江宁区。在句容城区的北、东、南形成U形的快速路结构。

总体形成"中心径向线+U形快速路"的同城化快速路结构(图6)。在南京城区快速路"大环"的结构中,加入同城化快速路"小环"。通过这种结构,更好地将句容中心城区纳入南京的环路体系,强化同城化联系,加强城际交流。构建同城化快速路网体系,强化宁句联络,更便于发掘句容有别于南京的优势资源,与南京形成强互补。

在连片地区形成一体化的城市道路网络体系,加速连片地区的无缝衔接。对接连片地区的道路线位,针对道路断面、等级等技术标准不匹配情况,提升道路等级和技术指标。协调连片地区的道路建设时序,未建道路协调时序确保同步竣工;已建道路确保未建路段尽早通车。

(3) 依托都市圈轨道带动公交优先发展

南京构建多层级的城市轨道交通网络,包括城市轨道交通线路、市域市郊铁路为主的都市圈轨道等(图7)。南京都市圈通过市域快线来进一步支撑都市圈活动,保证都市圈活力。

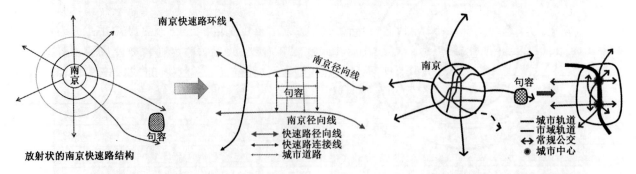

图6 区域一体化高快速路体系示意图 　　　图7 一体化公共交通布局示意图

句容应重点加强三个方向上的都市圈轨道连接,衔接主要跨界联动发展地区。首先,建设宁句城际轨道,连接南京地铁2号线,连接句容城区。其次,建设宁镇轨道,连接南京、宝华、龙潭及镇江。最后,新

增宁熟快线/1号线南延线路,加强南部江宁、湖熟、郭庄等区域的联系。

5 结语

中心城市周边的中小城市,究竟是与中心城市竞争中败下阵来,还是被中心城市吸走资源成为灯下黑区域,抑或是通过各系统尤其是交通系统的一体化发展实现合作共赢,是其发展过程中不得不考虑的问题。中心城市有扩张发展的需求,周边城市有承载利用中心城市资源及红利的迫切需要。在构建中小城市交通体系的时候,一定不能故步自封,要将规划视角提升到更高的层面,与中心城市统筹考虑,才能构建切实可行、顺应时代发展的交通系统。

参考文献

[1] 吴才锐,徐海贤,王剑. 大城市郊县城市综合交通规划策略研究——以银川市永宁县为例[C]. 城乡治理与规划改革——2014中国城市规划年会论文集. 海口,2014,709-720.

[2] 武勇杰. 新型城镇化背景下中小城市发展的关键问题研究[D]. 北京:北京交通大学,2018.

[3] 刘晓庆,李子木. 中小型城市公交便捷准时的服务模式探讨[J]. 交通节能与环保,2018(5):42-44.

城市中心区快速路布局与用地关系协调的思考

毛建民[1] 彭挺[1] 张序[2]

(1. 重庆市交通规划研究院;2. 重庆市沙坪坝区住房和城乡发展委员会)

摘要 快速路主要承担城市对外及城市组团间长距离交通联系功能,不宜穿越城市核心区。本文以重庆两江新区快速路一横线为例,从用地的重大调整导致快速路穿越中心区的问题出发,由此而引发的快速路道路功能定位的重新研究和道路建设模式的反复论证,以及后续规划管理过程中的控制方式和区域路网结构的被动调整,最后通过综合交通规划评估及优化纳入新一轮国土空间规划中,旨在为快速路与用地的协调处理方面提供经验借鉴。

关键词 快速路 城市中心区 功能定位 用地协调

0 引言

城市交通规划和城市总体规划具有共生性[1],然而在实践中常分开编制,城市规划师认为交通规划师的任务就是如何最大限度地在城市交通设施上配合城市规划,交通规划往往处于被动和从属的地位,二者缺乏良好地互动反馈,易导致城市用地与道路关系不协调的问题。本文以重庆市两江新区龙盛核心区快速路一横线为例,回顾二者的互动演变过程,探讨如何妥善处理快速路穿越城市核心区的问题。

1 问题分析

1.1 用地情况

根据《重庆两江新区总体规划(2010—2020)》[2],龙盛片区东西宽8km,南北长约20km,规划范围面积约178km²,规划人口80万人,如图1所示。定位为国家战略新兴产业和先进制造业基地,用地布局以生产性用地(包括工业、创新产业、仓储)为主。

1.2 路网布局

在《两江新区总体规划（2010—2020）》中规划一横线为快速路，在龙盛片区沿渝万铁路北侧布局，沿线用地以工业用地为主。项目西接渝遂高速，东接三环高速，线路全长80.7km，道路红线54m。功能定位为主城北部片区重要的客运快速通道，承担快速、大容量、长距离的交通服务，相关成果亦纳入《重庆市城乡总体规划(2007—2020)(2011年修订)》中，如图2所示。

图1 重庆两江新区总体规划用地布局图

图2 重庆市快速路一横线位置示意图

1.3 存在问题

快速路因其快速、高效等特点[3]，在保证中长距离交通供给等方面具有明显优势。快速路一横线龙盛段南侧规划引入渝万高铁复盛站，在分区规划和控制性详细规划编制时对复盛站周边用地进行了较大调整，用地由工业用地调整为以商业、商务为主，拟结合高铁站打造城市副中心，如图3所示。

受制于快速路部分已建成和控规编制原因，对快速路网结构没有进行相应调整，致使快速路穿越城市中心区，如图4所示。然而，平面式快速路对沿线两侧用地分隔较大，且易将过境交通引入核心区，对中心区品质产生不利影响。同时，快速路两侧的用地开发强度应适当控制，尤其是商业地块在快速路两侧的开发应更为慎重。

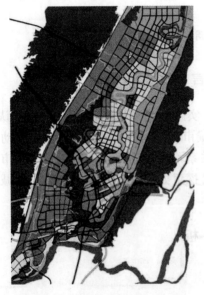
图3 龙盛组团用地调整示意图

图4 重庆快速路一横线建设示意图

因此，在道路设计方案研究阶段时，对道路功能定位提出反思，需要统筹兼顾中心区城市功能，避免对城市分割和景观影响，同时要保证过境交通快速通过和中心区交通便捷进出。

2 城市中心区快速路布局考虑因素

快速路是城市道路系统的骨架,是诱导和制约城市结构功能和土地利用发展的重要因素。在线网布局时需考虑如下因素,并根据城市规模、用地发展和交通需求的增长适时建设。

(1)城市空间布局。快速路的技术标准决定了快速路对用地布局具有极强的阻隔性[4-7],应布局于组团边缘,不宜穿越商业性、生活性用地,以实现城市交通与土地利用的协调发展。

(2)区域交通网络。快速路作为高速公路与城市道路之间的衔接与过渡,一般与城市主干道及以上等级道路连接,要考虑其与衔接道路能否实现集散协调,实现道路资源的有效整合。

(3)交通主流向分布。快速路布局应与城市交通流主流向相一致,实现长短交通、快慢交通的合理分离,提高路网整体效率。

(4)工程可行性与经济性。在快速路布局时应合理选择布置形式,充分考虑工程实施的可行性和经济性,为工程实施创造条件。

3 道路功能定位与调整程序

3.1 功能定位

根据土地利用规划和综合交通规划,建立交通需求模型,进行交通需求预测分析。预测表明,龙盛中心区早高峰机动化交通发生量约0.68万人次,吸引量约5.6万人次,早晚高峰呈现较强的方向不均衡性。路段交通量在5800~7500 pcu/h之间,由西向东呈逐渐减小趋势,由于通勤客流的叠加,最大交通量集中在绕城高速至龙复路段,如图5所示。通过模型预测显示,一横线承担过境功能和沿线服务双重功能,从二者流量比例来看,过境约占60%,沿线服务约占40%,图6中绿色线条为过境交通量。

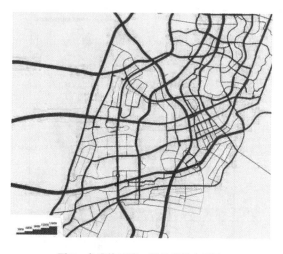 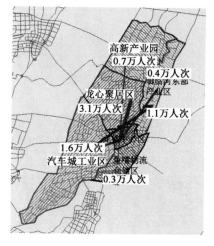

图5 龙盛快速路一横线背景交通量　　图6 龙盛中心区对外发生吸引量

因此,一横线是必须有的重要规划快速通道,在快速路穿越中心区时,结构上宜从中心区边缘通过,若不可避免地穿越中心区时,应采用合理的敷设形式和交通组织方式处理好二者关系,将过境交通从中心区分离出去,起到保护核心区的作用,并严格控制出入口,确保通行效率。

3.2 外部通道衔接优化

快速路作为高速公路与城市道路之间的缓冲与过渡,受区域高速公路布局及衔接方式影响较大,外部路网结构的重大变化会影响通道的功能,需对区域路网结构进行优化,如图7所示。①规划在外围新建三环高速组织对外交通。②利用三环高速线路在龙盛"U"字形布局及东环铁路桥建设的契机,新增与绕城高速的联络线组织对外交通,避免对外交通进入核心区。③优化渝长高速扩能通道在外围转换节点,优化一横线与外围通道的衔接方式,减少过境交通对城市中心区的冲击。

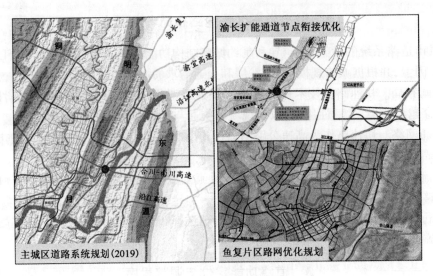

图 7 快速路一横线区域路网优化方案

3.3 快速路调整程序

根据区域路网结构和对外衔接节点优化后,极大地改变了一横线的道路流量组成,过境交通量大为减少,并将原规划一横线衔接沿山快速路通道调整为衔接内部主干路,加强沿线服务功能,其过境交通功能极大弱化,通过《主城区快速路网评估》将原快速路一横线绕城高速以东段调整为主干路(图8),成果纳入新一轮国土空间规划中,如图9所示。

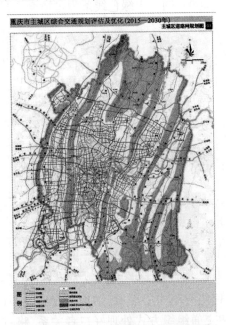
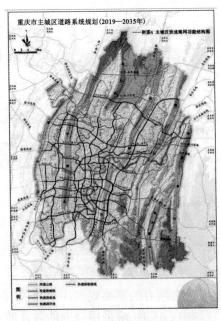

图 8 主城区综合交通评估与优化路网规划图　　图 9 重庆市国土空间规划快速路布局图

4 道路建设模式

城市快速路网规划是保证城市道路建设科学性、合理性、经济性以及可操作性的关键环节,而快速路建设模式论证则是这一环节中的重要组成部分,特别是交通衔接组织对快速路功能发挥起着至关重要的作用[8-9]。

快速路有地面、路堑式、高架、隧道等多种形式,应分别从道路功能、区域影响、环境景观、占地规模、远期拓展、总投资等诸多角度综合分析,根据此道路功能及中心区城市功能要求以及与现状地形的结合形式,共形成3个方案(图10~图14),优缺点比较见表1。

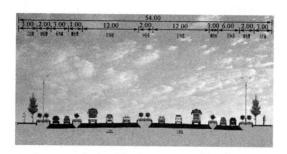

图10 方案一横断面布局图

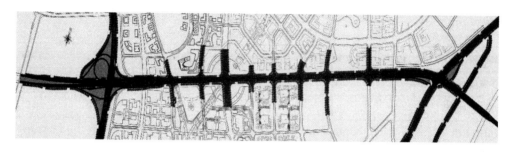

图11 方案一平面布局图

方案一采用过境交通与到达交通分离的交通组织方式。主线设计时速80km/h,辅道设计时速40km/h,主线双向六车道通行过境交通,两侧各设单向两车道辅道通行到达交通。近期实施双向六车道、平交方案,远期增设辅道。

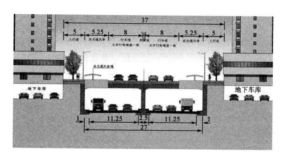

图12 方案二横断面布局图

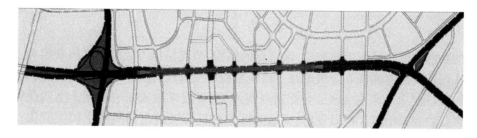

图13 方案二平面布局图

方案二采用过境交通与到达交通分流的交通组织方式。过境交通明挖六车道主线通道通过,到达交通通过现状地面层双向四车道辅路进入中心区,辅路与南北向道路平交将一横线南北两侧地块连成整体,减小快速路对城市发展的影响,加强南北联系,增强商业氛围。

方案三为推荐方案,其平面布置与方案二相同,主线完全利用已建道路,尽量贴近现状地面,双向四车道辅路在此基础上抬高7m与平场标高齐平,同时在辅道两侧建筑地下空间设置车库及地下商业街。

主线道路近期实施,采用与周边道路平交方式,两侧建筑平街为商业区。后期实施上层辅路,辅路与周边道路平交,辅路平街层为商业区,辅路标高以下各层建筑,调整为地下商业街或车库。

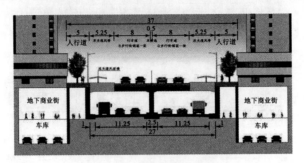

图14 方案三横断面布局图

三个方案优缺点比较 表1

方案比较	方案一	方案二	方案三
用地红线宽度(m)	54	37	37
与交通需求适应情况	好	好	好
生态城市适应性	好	较差	好
与地形结合情况	较差	较差	好
现状道路利用	好	差	好
近远期结合情况	好	差	好
建安费估算	3.2亿元 (近期2.1亿元)	6.22亿元	6.08亿元 (近期2.1亿元)
优缺点	1. 对景观影响小; 2. 对交通组织不利; 3. 投资较低; 4. 占地大	1. 对景观影响小; 2. 满足远期交通需求,过境交通从主线通过,对核心区无干扰,辅路与南北向道路平交,利于核心区商业氛围形成; 3. 现状道路无法利用; 4. 投资大	1. 对景观影响小; 2. 满足远期交通需求,过境交通从主线通过,对核心区无干扰,辅路与南北向道路平交,利于核心区商业氛围形成; 3. 与城市整体地势结合好,减少对现状地貌的破坏; 4. 分期投资较大

5 结　语

城市道路的功能定位与城市用地布局、区域路网结构、节点衔接方式等诸多因素相关,本文从时间轴角度回顾了重庆两江新区龙盛核心区快速路一横线功能演变过程,探讨如何妥善处理快速路穿越城市核心区的问题,最终通过《重庆市主城区综合交通规划评估》将成果纳入新一轮国土空间规划中,皆在为快速路穿越中心区提供经验借鉴。可以看出,用地的重大调整会对道路功能产生较大变化,在道路功能定位、建设模式、交通组织等方面会有较大不同,贯穿性快速通道对沿线两侧组团的分隔影响较大,且将过境交通引入核心区,对周边道路产生不利的冲击,建议在新区快速路网规划布局时慎重进入城市核心区。

参考文献

[1] 佚名.城市交通建设与城市用地协调发展[J].城市交通,2006,4(1):78.
[2] 重庆两江新区龙盛片区总体规划(2010-2020)[R].中国城市规划设计研究院,2010.
[3] 权宏伟.宁波市中心城区快速路网布局及建设形式分析[J].城市道桥与防洪,2015(12):15-20.

[4] 高奖.大城市快速路规划与设计关键问题研究[D].南京:东南大学,2006.
[5] 徐斌.浅谈城市快速路建设中的难点特点[J].城市道路与防洪,2011(11):93-97.
[6] 黄文健,杨涛.城市快速道路规划建设若干技术问题初探[J].现代交通技术,2008,5(2):63-66.
[7] 黄俊,曹林涛.快速路穿越城市中心城区探讨[J].城市道路与防洪2018(10):13-14.
[8] 朱军功,高志刚,王晶,等.浅析大城市快速路系统规划控制要求:以重庆市主城区为例[J].交通与运输,2013(7):19-22.
[9] 张海军,杨晓光,赵建新.城市快速路交通衔接组织研究[J].城市交通,2005,1:51-54.

基于地铁站点客流规律的城市功能布局探析

姚　帆　王静媛

(长安大学运输工程学院)

摘　要　考虑多源非通勤客流影响,基于数据筛选和数据处理技术对西安地铁车站客流数据进行特征提取,采用主成分分析法提取客流特征,依据客流特征采用二分K-means聚类在工作日、周末及节假日分别将站点聚类为4类、6类和7类;其次,以站点周边土地利用为导向识别站点类型,探讨城市功能布局特征。研究结果表明:二分K-means聚类能够很好地避免初始质心随机创建带来的缺陷;地铁站点的客流规律存在时空差异,站点类型体现了不同时空下由客流规律表征的站点属性的不同侧面;西安市城市功能布局在传统九宫格局基础上呈现以明城墙内为中心按"文化商贸—居住—生产"排列的圈层式分布。

关键词　交通与土地利用　地铁客流　主成分分析　二分K-means聚类　城市功能布局

0　引　言

车站类型识别可明确站点在轨道交通网络中的功能、布局及站点周边土地使用性质[1]。

国内外学者在城市交通与土地利用及城市空间结构的互动关系方面进行了一些探索。Polzin等[1]从直接影响、间接影响及次要影响3个方面分析了公共交通与土地使用的关系;Srinivasan[2]在区域和局部两种规模下建立了土地使用变化和交通运输的关系模型。Roth等[3]利用伦敦地铁刷卡数据揭示了城市区域多中心结构及其演变。尹芹等[4]利用北京地铁客流数据采用时间序列聚类对站点分类并分析了车站分布与城市空间格局;曹瑞[5]等利用智能卡数据和层次聚类识别验证了地铁车站周边的职住用地分布。

本文采用主成分分析法和二分K-means聚类对传统方法进行改进;根据客流特征对工作日、周末和节假日分别进行站点聚类,比较站点功能及其空间分布变化,挖掘城市功能空间布局特点,以期为探究城市发展规律,促进城市轨道交通网络合理布局提供依据。

1　数据来源及预处理

本文选取西安地铁1、2、3号线2018年4月29日至5月1日与2018年5月14日至20日1周各站点6:00—24:00的30min进出站客流数据。再对5个工作日、周末及3个节假日的客流数据做均值滤波,以消除单日突发事件影响。最后,采用Z-Score标准化使各站点数据具有可比性且量级统一。

2　客流特征提取

本文选取各站点6:00—24:00的30min进出站客流量标准化值共72个初始变量,高维数据下变量间可能存在相关,故引入主成分分析法将存在线性相关的初始变量转化为少量无关的主成分并最大化保留原始数据信息。以贡献度累计值高于 85% 及特征值大于 1 为标准,对工作日、周末和节假日分别提取 11 个、14 个和 12 个主成分作为聚类变量。

3 聚类模型确定

3.1 二分 K-means 聚类模型

二分 K-means 聚类过程如下:

步骤 1 设定聚类数目 k,将所有点作为 1 个簇,放入簇表 S 中。

步骤 2 从 S 中取出样本点与质心误差平方和(Sum of Squared Error,SSE)最大的簇 C_i,利用经典 K-means 算法对 C_i 进行多次二分聚类,将聚类结果中总 SSE 最小的两个簇放入 S。

步骤 3 重复这一过程,直至得到 k 个簇,这 k 个簇的质心即为 K-means 聚类初始质心。

3.2 聚类数目的确定

本文采取手肘法获得聚类数目,SSE 与聚类数 k 关系图肘部对应的 k 值即为最优聚类个数,据此将工作日、周末和节假日的聚类数设为 4 类、6 类和 7 类。

4 城市轨道交通站点聚类分析

4.1 工作日聚类结果

4.1.1 居住型

该类站点客流分布如图 1 所示,进站早高峰和出站晚高峰明显,高峰时段主要为 7:00—8:00 和 18:00—19:00,客流分布曲线为单峰型,客流分布不均衡。车站周围主要为居住用地。

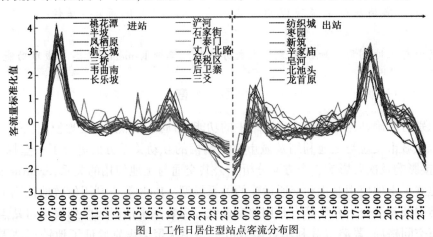

图 1 工作日居住型站点客流分布图

4.1.2 办公型

该类站点客流分布如图 2 所示,客流分布为单峰型,进站晚高峰和出站早高峰显著,高峰主要集中在 8:00—9:00 及 18:00—19:00,客流分布不均衡,周围主要分布就业用地。

4.1.3 职住错位型

该类站点客流分布如图 3 所示,客流分布曲线为双峰型,同时存在进出站早晚高峰,进站高峰时段主要集中在 7:00—8:00 和 18:00—19:00,出站高峰时段主要集中在 8:00—9:00 和 18:00—19:00。表明该类站点周围同时存在居住和就业两种用地,属于职住错位型。

4.1.4 商业及交通枢纽型

该类站点客流分布如图 4 所示。进站客流从 6:00 逐渐增加,在 18:00 达到高峰,随后下降,21:00 后再次增加,高峰小时客流占比为 0.125;出站客流存在早晚高峰,高峰时段主要为 8:00—9:00 及 18:00—19:00。出站晚高峰反映了晚上到达的休闲娱乐客流,21:00 后的进站小高峰反映了夜晚休闲娱乐及出行返程客流。

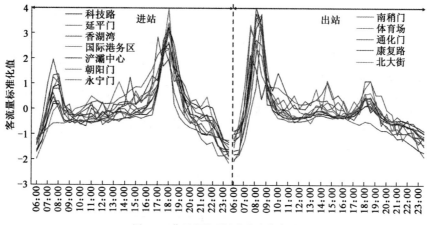

图 2　工作日办公型站点客流分布图

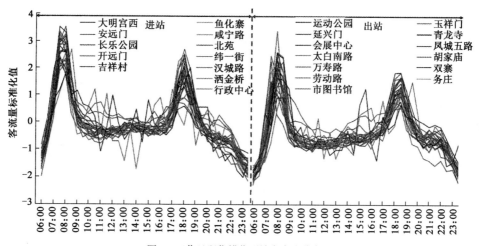

图 3　工作日职住错位型站点客流分布图

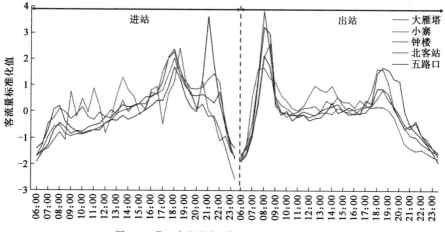

图 4　工作日商业及交通枢纽型站点客流分布图

4.2　周末聚类结果

4.2.1　居住型

该类站点客流分布如图 5 所示，客流存在进站早高峰和出站晚高峰，高峰主要集中在 7∶00—8∶00 和 18∶00—19∶00，其他时段客流曲线也存在波峰，但峰值远小于进站早高峰和出站晚高峰，平峰时段客流量较工作日有所增大。

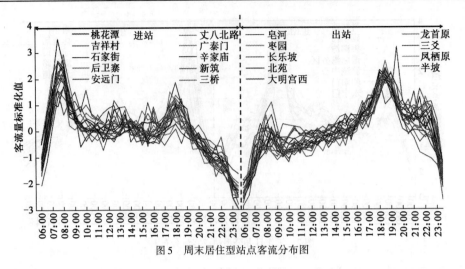

图 5 周末居住型站点客流分布图

4.2.2 办公型

该类站点客流分布如图 6 所示,进站晚高峰和出站早高峰明显,高峰主要集中在 8:00—9:00 和 17:00—19:00,平峰时段客流量高于工作日,客流分布更均衡。

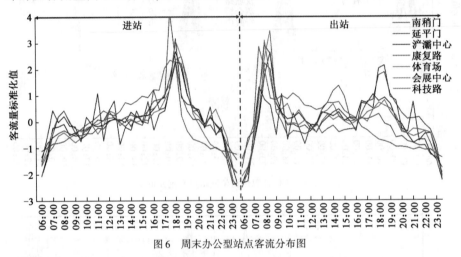

图 6 周末办公型站点客流分布图

4.2.3 商业及交通枢纽型

聚类第 3 类和第 4 类为商业及交通枢纽型站点。与工作日相比,类型 3 客流各波峰峰值更加接近,平峰时段客流量更大。与第 3 类相比,类型 4 站点进出站高峰不显著(图 7)。

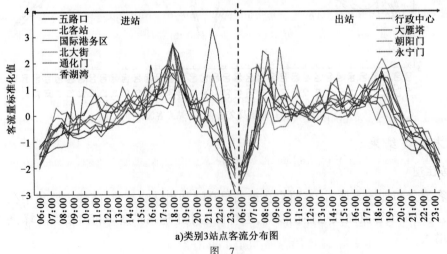

a)类别3站点客流分布图

图 7

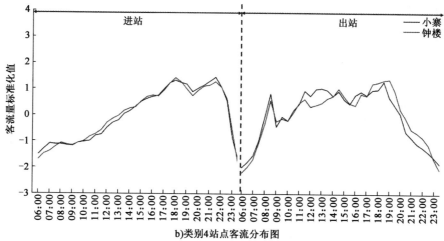

b) 类别4站点客流分布图

图7 周末商业及交通枢纽型站点客流分布图

4.2.4 综合型

此类站点客流分布如图8所示,客流分布曲线不规律,有进出站早晚高峰,其他时段也存在小高峰,表明此类站点周边除居住和就业用地外,还有商业、景区等其他类型用地。此类站点客流规律较复杂,部分站点客流规律较工作日不同。

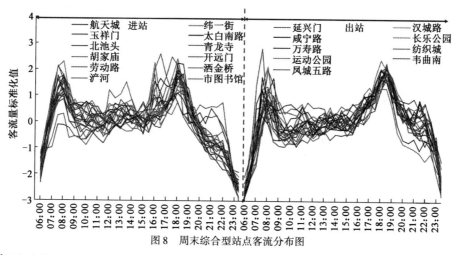

图8 周末综合型站点客流分布图

4.2.5 郊区站点

此类站点客流分布如图9所示,站点客流较小,进出站客流规律差异大,客流分布曲线无规律,此类站点处于城市功能尚不完善的外围区域,客流为郊区客流。

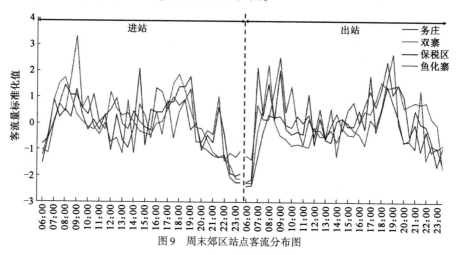

图9 周末郊区站点客流分布图

4.3 节假日聚类结果

4.3.1 居住型

聚类类型1及类型2为居住型站点。相较工作日和周末,节假日此类站点客流潮汐特征减弱。类型1站点进站客流在7:00—9:00达最大值,9:00后客流稳定,18:00后开始下降;出站客流从6:00—18:00缓慢增加,18:00—21:00为最大值,21:00后开始下降。与类型1相比,类型2站点客流分布更均衡(图10)。

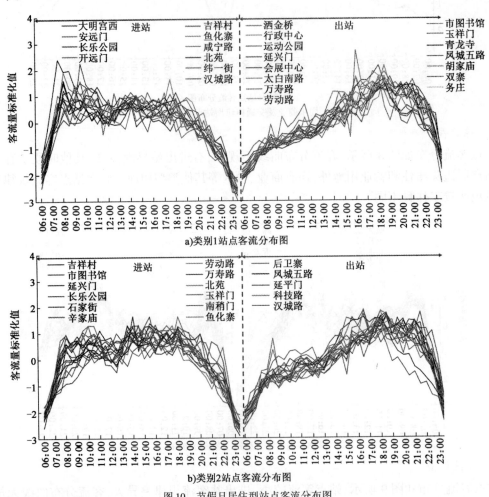

a)类别1站点客流分布图

b)类别2站点客流分布图

图10 节假日居住型站点客流分布图

4.3.2 商业及景区型

聚类类型3及类型4为商业及景区型站点,客流分布如图11所示。类型3全天出站客流较大,客流稳定且峰值不明显,进站客流从6:00至16:00逐渐增加,20:00后开始下降,部分站点21:00再次出现进站高峰。第4类站点存在进站晚高峰及出站早高峰,进站晚高峰集中在18:00,出站早高峰集中在8:00—10:00。

4.3.3 交通枢纽型

聚类类别5为交通枢纽型站点,客流分布如图12所示。客流分布均衡且波动较为规律,9:00—20:00客流量稳定,全天运营时段进出站客流量较大。

4.3.4 综合型

此类站点客流分布如图13所示,站点客流分布均衡,客流波动无规律,相较工作日,全日运营时段客流量较大。

4.3.5 郊区站点

此类站点客流分布如图14所示,客流分布与周末同类型站点类似,无特定规律。

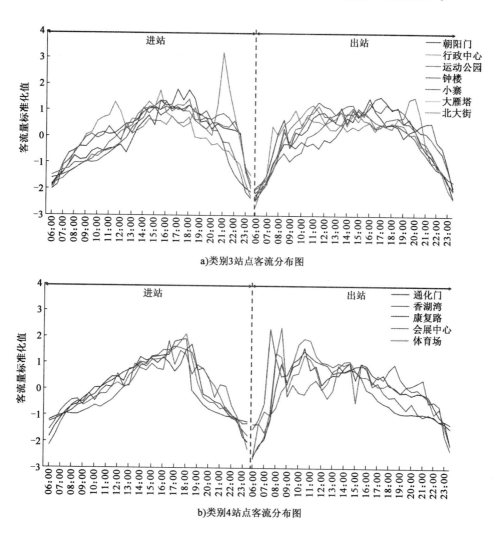

a) 类别3站点客流分布图

b) 类别4站点客流分布图

图11 节假日商业及景区型站点客流分布图

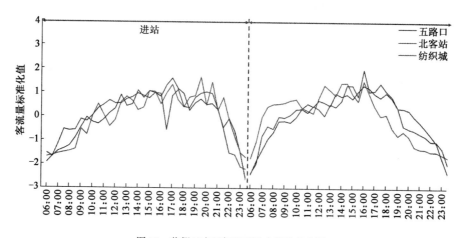

图12 节假日交通枢纽型站点客流分布图

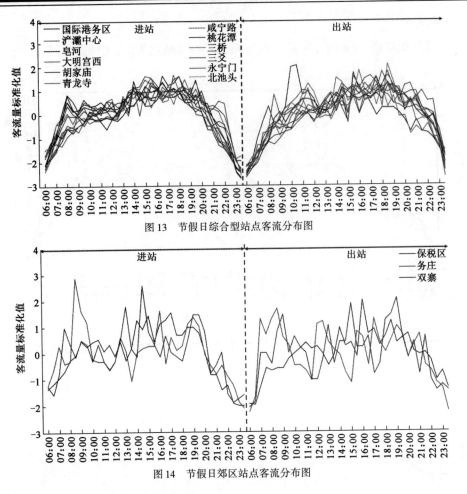

图 13 节假日综合型站点客流分布图

图 14 节假日郊区站点客流分布图

4.4 站点分布特点与城市功能布局

4.4.1 站点分布特点

工作日站点空间分布如图 15 所示,居住型站点多分布于西部、南部、东部及东北部。办公型站点多分布在二环内;职住错位型站点西部和北部城区数量多于东部及南部城区;商业及交通枢纽型站点数量最少。

周末办公型站点数量减少,商业型站点数量增多,出现部分综合性站点。二环区域内商业型及居住型站点增加,东部和南部部分居住型站点转变为综合型站点,郊区站点的客流方向差异性及时间不规律性开始显现。周末站点空间分布如图 16 所示。

图 15 工作日站点空间分布图

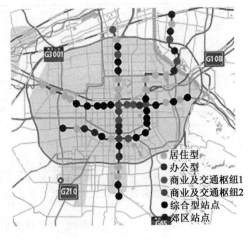

图 16 周末站点空间分布图

节假日居住型及商业景区型站点增加,办公型站点减少,就业用地对站点类型识别的影响减弱。商业及景区型站点部分分布于二环内,其余分散在北部、东北部及东南部;居住型站点多分布在西部、南部和东北部,少量分布在北部;综合型站点分布在西部、东北部和东南部。节假日站点空间分布如图17所示。

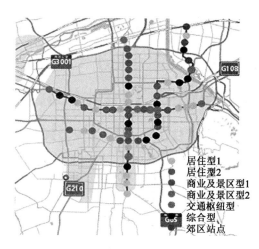

图17 节假日站点空间分布图

4.4.2 城市功能布局特征

以西安主城区各区域为基本单元进行分析,二环内工作日多分布办公、职住错位型站点,周末及节假日多分布商业景区型站点;东北部工作日多分布居住型站点,周末及节假日综合型和商业景区型站点交错分布;北部工作日多分布职住错位型站点,周末和节假日多分布综合型及居住型站点;西部工作日及周末多分布居住及办公型站点,节假日多分布居住型及综合型站点;南部多分布居住型和综合型站点,与目前研究认为的西安城市功能九宫格局是一致的。

以主城区各圈层为基本单元进行分析,明城墙内主要分布办公和商业型站点;第三圈层办公相关站点分布最多;外围区域城市功能尚不完善,分布有居住型、综合型和郊区站点,没有确定的功能特征;反映了西安城市功能以明城墙内为中心,按"文化商贸-居住-生产"呈圈层式布局的特点。

5 结 语

(1)基于客流数据分析,对工作日、周末和节假日分别提取客流特征并建立站点聚类模型,表明了所用模型的有效性及相较于传统聚类方法在结果准确性和迭代速度上的优势。

(2)客流规律及站点类型存在时空差异,表明不同时段的客流规律体现出站点属性的不同侧面,更为全面地体现了站点周边的土地利用情况。

(3)西安市城市功能布局在九宫格局基础上呈现以明城墙内为中心,按"文化商贸-居住-生产"呈圈层式分布的特征,不同类型车站客流集散与城市空间功能布局有对应的耦合效应。

参考文献

[1] Polzin P E, Steven E. Transportation Land-use Relationship: Public Transit's Impact on Land Use[J]. Journal of Urban Planning and Development, 1999, 125(4):135-151.

[2] Srinivasan S. Linking Land Use and Transportation in A Rapidly Urbanizing Context: A Study in Delhi, India[J]. Transportation, 2005, 32(1):87-104.

[3] Roth C, Kang S M, Batty M, et al. Structure of Urban Movements: Polycentric Activity and Entangled Hierarchical Flows[J]. Plos one, 2011, 6(1):e15923.

[4] 尹芹,孟斌,张丽英. 基于客流特征的北京地铁站点类型识别[J]. 地理科学进展, 2016, 35(1):128-136.

[5] 曹瑞,涂伟,巢佰崇,等. 基于智能卡数据的地铁周边职住用地识别与分析[J]. 测绘地理信息,2016,41(3):74-78.

Optimization Strategy of County Public Service Facilities Based On the Analysis of Residents' Travel Behavior
——A Case Study of Typical Counties

Yueyan Zhang[1]　Qian Chen[2]　Xiaoyu Wang[1]

(1. Jiangsu Key Laboratory of Urban ITS, Department of Transportation, Southeast University;
2. Jiangsu Province Collaborative Innovation Center of Modern Urban Traffic Technologies
Department of Transportation, Southeast University)

Abstract　The concept of "People-Oriented" is the mainstream trend of the development of public facilities environment construction and transportation planning at home and abroad. The degree of public facilities environment construction affects residents' travel demand, and residents' travel demand also provides guidance support for public facilities planning. This paper selects four representative counties in China, selects education and medical facilities as the research objects of public service facilities, and conducts a questionnaire survey on residents' travel behavior to public service facilities. Secondly, the spatial basic data and public facilities distribution of each county are calculated based on ArcGIS. And the Logit regression model is established to analyze the influencing factors of residents' travel behavior and its correlation with facility layout. Finally, this paper summarizes the behavior rules of residents' facilities selection, and put forward the optimization strategy of public facilities allocation for different types of counties.

Keywords　People oriented　Public service facilities allocation　ArcGIS　Logit regression　Travel behavior

0　Introduction

In order to further steadily promote the process of urbanization, the National New Urbanization Plan (2014—2020) puts forward various requirements for the improvement of urban sustainable development capacity, mainly including accelerating the transformation of urban development mode and enhancing the carrying capacity of urban public service. Urban public service facilities are the space carrier of modern urban public services, which provide residents with basic public services closely related to life, such as education, medical treatment, transportation, leisure and entertainment. The development level of county towns, population, traffic conditions, facilities layout conditions, socio-economic attributes and other factors determine the differences of public service facilities planning. Due to the improvement of urbanization level, the type and quality of public service facilities of urban residents have changed. At present, the current situation of public service facilities in most counties of China is far from the actual demand of residents for public service facilities. From the perspective of people-oriented, combined with the travel behavior of residents visiting public service facilities, this paper discusses the correlation and influencing factors between residents' travel and urban public service facilities. Taking different types of counties as examples, this paper aims to optimize the allocation of public facilities resources from the spatial level combined with residents' needs. Integrating the concept of human settlement governance into planning and realizing sustainable development is conducive to improving the utilization efficiency of resources and further improving the quality of life of urban residents.

1 Literature Review

Domestic and foreign scholars have done a lot of research on the influencing factors of travel behavior. Through the field interview and online travel questionnaire data survey method, Jiang Huipeng et al (2017) scholars use SP survey to get the travel characteristics and influencing factors of College Students' bike sharing travel; Dorien Simons et al (2017) concluded that income, travel time, safety and other factors are the factors for students and young office workers to choose travel mode. Under the synergistic effect of multiple factors, Jiang Wei et al (2019) used the results of multiple logistic regression model to quantitatively point out the influence degree of each influencing factor on travel mode choice behavior and the change rate of choice intention of all kinds of travelers.

In the daily travel destinations of residents, public service facilities account for a large proportion. Domestic and foreign scholars have summarized more research results on the allocation and layout of public facilities at the city or county level. By using the method of geographic analysis and spatial multi-objective analysis (SMCA) based on land scale, M. Taleai et al (2014) put forward the comprehensive evaluation framework of spatial fairness (ISEE) based on multi criteria spatial analysis to measure the fairness of a variety of public service facilities or the same facilities in different spatial scales under the same scale. Gao Junbo et al (2017) built a comprehensive equity index model of spatial facilities, considered the scale and grade of facilities, traffic network configuration and other factors, and took Guangzhou as an example to explore the measurement method of spatial distribution equity. In view of the contradiction between supply and demand of urban spatial land, Duan Yaqiong (2019) proposed the optimization mechanism of intensive land use and low-carbon by mining the spatial-temporal behavior and land-use characteristics of residents in Xi'an built-up area from the two dimensions of "residents' travel time-space behavior" and "land use" through multi-source data.

Domestic and foreign research on the characteristics of residents' travel behavior, demand analysis, influencing factors research is substantial. However, there are few studies on the spatial layout of public facilities and the rationality of facilities layout. Combined the travel rules of visiting public service facilities with the layout characteristics of public service facilities, based on four typical counties in China, this paper quantitatively calculates the significant factors influencing residents' travel choice behavior. And the development of more targeted traffic management measures combined with the traffic environment is conducive to improving the relationship between supply and demand and ensuring the service level of facilities.

2 Data Sources

2.1 Questionnaire Design and Data Collection

Educational facilities and medical facilities are selected as the interviewees of public facilities, and a questionnaire is designed to obtain the characteristics and willingness of residents' travel behavior. The questionnaire is divided into three parts:

(1) The first part is the personal attribute information of residents, including gender, age, occupation status, longitude and latitude distribution of residence, residential area.

(2) The second part is the travel information of residents, mainly for visiting educational facilities and medical facilities. First of all, there are differences in the levels of public facilities represented by education and

medical care, as shown in Tab. 1.

Classification of Public Service Facilities　　　　　　　　　　　Tab. 1

Level	Educational Facilities	Medical Facilities
Junior	primary school	Clinic / Township clinic / infirmary
intermediate	Junior high school / Senior High School / secondary vocational school	Township HealthCenter / Community Health Service Center
Senior	Universities / colleges / higher vocational schools / special education schools, etc	County General Hospital / traditional Chinese medicine hospital

The questionnaire information mainly includes the type of educational / medical facilities visit (primary, intermediate or advanced), visit frequency (number of days per week and number of visits per day), travel mode (car, bus, non motor vehicle and walking), and travel distance of residents visiting public facilities.

(3) The third part investigates the residents' satisfaction or suggestions on the visits to educational and medical facilities:

①Educational facilities: the most concerned factors when choosing schools, the factors when choosing travel modes, the reasons for not choosing public transportation, the acceptable travel time or cost

②Medical facilities: the principle of medical treatment (small hospital for minor diseases or large hospital for minor diseases), the degree of satisfaction with different levels of medical facilities, the acceptable travel time and travel distance.

Four representative counties are selected: Qingcheng County (Gansu Province), Jintang County (Sichuan Province), Wu'an County (Hebei Province) and Changxing County (Zhejiang Province). In the four counties, questionnaires on the using characteristics of public service facilities are carried out. The residential areas in the counties are fully covered as far as possible. The number of returned questionnaires is shown in Tab. 2. The basic socio-economic attributes (age distribution, gender distribution, education level distribution, occupation distribution, etc.) and residents' travel characteristics of the four counties were obtained by questionnaire survey.

Number of Questionnaires Collected in Counties　　　　　　　　　Tab. 2

County	Chang xing	Jin tang	Wu an	Qing cheng
Number of returned questionnaires	2431	1673	1287	1914

2.2 County Spatial Geographic Data

In order to complete the research on the correlation between spatial facilities and residents' travel behavior, the travel distance and travel mode of residents visiting educational facilities and medical and health facilities are modeled. Based on the national fund project, four counties in China are obtained: Qingcheng (northwest region), Jintang (southwest region), Wu'an (North China) and Changxing (southeast region) The content of basic spatial data is shown in Tab. 3.

Basic Data Requirements of County Planning　　　　　　　　　　Tab. 3

Data requirements	Data content
Vector map	It includes the overall planning map, land use planning map and regulatory detailed planning map of central urban area provided by the County Construction Bureau, includes the information of road boundary line and community partition
Population	The grid image of population distribution provided by Landscan, and the population distribution of residential area provided by the local public security department of the county.
POI	The index feature data is used to calculate the information of interest points of facilities, such as bus stops, hotels and commercial facilities captured from Gaud map

The attribute characteristics of travel residents, age, gender, income and other factors affect residents' travel mode choice behavior (Yuan, et al, 2018). And the distribution of public service facilities, road network density, public transport development degree and other factors are related to the behavior of visiting public facilities (Chai, Yet al, 2015, Suzuki, et al 2012). In order to analyze the correlation between travel behavior and spatial facilities and provide data basis for subsequent logit models, it is necessary to obtain corresponding quantitative indicators from basic information, This paper establishes a database based on ArcGIS platform, uses built-in analysis tools arctool box, spatial connection, kernel density analysis, and combines the resident travel data (age, travel distance, residential location information, etc.) in the questionnaire survey to calculate the relevant characteristic indicators of public facilities allocation in four counties, as shown in Tab. 4.

Indicators of County Public Facilities Allocation Tab. 4

Serial number	Index	Definition
①	Age	Age of residents visiting public facilities
②	Facility scale level	Scale and grade of medical / educational facilities
③	Travel distance	Travel distance of residents visiting public facilities
④	Population density of residential areas	Relative population density in the grid where the facility visitors live
⑤	Road length around residential area (m)	The total length of roads in the grid where the visitors live
⑥	Number of residential bus stops	Total number of grid bus stops where facility visitors live
⑦	Length of urban roads around facilities (m)	Total length of urban roads in the grid of the visited facilities
⑧	Road length around facilities (m)	Total length of county and township roads within the grid of the visited facilities
⑨	Number of bus stops around facilities	The number of bus stops in the grid of the visited facilities
⑩	Population density around facilities	Relative population density in the grid of the visited facilities

2.3 County Development Overview

Relying on key R & D projects, considering human geography, economic level, transportation development and other factors, four counties are selected to carry out data collection and analysis. The information is shown in Tab. 5.

Comparison of County Characteristics Tab. 5

County	Changxing	Jintang	Wu'an	Qingcheng
Area Characteristic	Central hinterland of Yangtze River Delta	Northeast of Chengdu Plain	The border of Shanxi and Hebei Provinces	It belongs to Longdong Loess Plateau
Economic Level (GDP/)	60.978 billion yuan	44.04 billion yuan	66.05 billion yuan	6.901 billion yuan
Area Covered	1430km², under the jurisdiction of 9 towns and 2 townships	1156km², 19 towns, 2 townships and 1 provincial Development Zone	1806km², under the jurisdiction of 9 towns and 13 townships	2690.04km², under the jurisdiction of 7 towns and 8 townships
Total Population	632400	903000	846000	292000
Traffic Scale	① With developed external transportation, it has a 2-hour traffic circle with Jiangsu and Zhejiang cities. ② within the territory, there are 1051 national roads, provincial roads, county roads, etc., with a total mileage of 2165.069 km.	The total mileage of roads to Chengdu City reaches 4579.8 km	1482.6km of open road	① At present, all the transportation in the county is undertaken by highway, and there is no railway and navigation confluence. ② The county has 102 National, provincial, county, township and village roads, with a total length of 971.969 km

continue

County	Changxing	Jintang	Wu'an	Qingcheng
Road Network Facilities	It has initially formed a multi-level hub system of railway, highway and public transportation	The road network framework of "three express ways and three expressways" is basically formed externally; and the county road network structure of "crossing, connecting trunk and branch" is basically formed internally	The "ring road network" is composed of the "nine vertical expressway" and the "nine vertical expressway"	There are only a few main roads in the urban area, which lack the support of branch road system for road traffic
Vehicle Ownership	162000 vehicles	226900 vehicles	65500 vehicles	64500 vehicles
Public transportation	There are 22 County buses, 65 urban and rural buses and 4 town buses	There are 39 bus lines in the county, 22 inter county bus lines, 8 inter city bus lines and 17 rural bus lines	There are 33 bus lines, 17 lines in the county and 16 lines in urban and rural areas	There are 2 County buses and 8 urban and rural buses

Note: the above data are from the statistical data at the end of 2018.

In this paper, the economic level, total population, traffic status, road network facilities, public transport development status and other elements of the county sample data, referring to the classification method of small town development (Wang Daixia et al, 2018) and the City Scale Standards[①], the four counties are respectively positioned as:

Counties I are Changxing County and Jintang County: high level of economic development, large population scale, high degree of urbanization, road network with a certain scale, large total highway mileage, and public transport construction taking shape.

Counties II is Wu'an County: the scale of economic development is inferior to that of the first type, and the scale of traffic and the degree of public transport development are general.

Counties III is Qingcheng County, with small population, weak economic level, imperfect road facilities, less total highway mileage and less bus lines.

It provides a reference for the comparison of travel behavior influencing factors and public facilities allocation in different levels (types) of counties.

2.4 General Situation of Public Service Facilities in Counties-taking Medical and Educational Facilities As an Example

1) Distribution of medical and educational facilities

Based on the survey of county public service facilities, the distribution of medical facilities and educational facilities in four counties is shown in Tab. 6.

---

① http://www.gov.cn/zhengce/content/2014-11/20/content_9225.htm.

County	Medical facilities				Educational facilities			
	Junior	Intermediate	Senior	total	Junior	Intermediate	Senior	total
Changxing	148	16	7	171	36	15	10	61
Jintang	179	23	7	209	79	28	0	107
Wuan	78	33	10	121	143	15	1	159
Qingcheng	86	5	2	93	195	23	2	220

Number of medical and educational facilities Tab. 6

The number of medical facilities in Changxing County and Jintang county is large, and the county medical resources are rich, but the number of general hospitals at or above the county level is relatively small. Qingcheng county is short of medical resources, and the number of general hospitals, clinics and other facilities is the least compared with the other three counties.

In terms of educational facilities, Wu'an county and Qingcheng county have the largest number of educational facilities, but the proportion of higher education resources (Vocational Colleges and above) is very small, which is basically primary facilities. The total number of educational facilities in Changxing County lags behind the other three counties, but its higher education resources are the most abundant.

2) Spatial distribution of county public facilities

From the perspective of spatial distribution, the educational facilities in Jintang county (Fig. 1a)) are distributed along the provincial highway skeleton, concentrated in the northwest area of the county, the central urban area, and the density in the south is uniform, and each area is scattered. Fig. 1b) shows that the concentration of medical facilities in Jintang county is obvious, mainly concentrated in the northwest region, which is also the area where village roads and county roads are concentrated. However, the coverage of medical facilities in the middle and south of the county is very low, and there are obvious vacancies in the East, resulting in the overall lack of medical facilities.

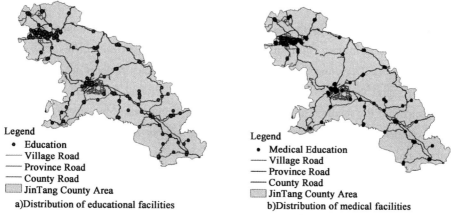

Fig. 1 distribution of public facilities in Jintang County

Fig. 2a) shows that the number of educational facilities in Wu'an county is evenly distributed, the central urban area of the county is relatively concentrated, from the central urban area outward to other directions, the density of educational facilities is balanced, and there is no shortage of educational facilities in the county. Fig. 2b) shows that the medical facilities in Wu'an county are concentrated in the central urban area, while the medical facilities in other areas are scarce. A small number of medical facilities are distributed in the surrounding towns, showing a trend of sporadic distribution. The total amount of medical facilities is insufficient, and the scope of service is relatively limited.

Compared with the other three counties, Qingcheng county has a lower degree of development and a smaller total population. The distribution of public facilities is concentrated in the middle and east of the county.

According to Fig. 3a) and b), there is no significant difference between the distribution of educational facilities and medical facilities, showing the phenomenon of excessive concentration. Medical and educational facilities are very scarce in the west, South and north of the county.

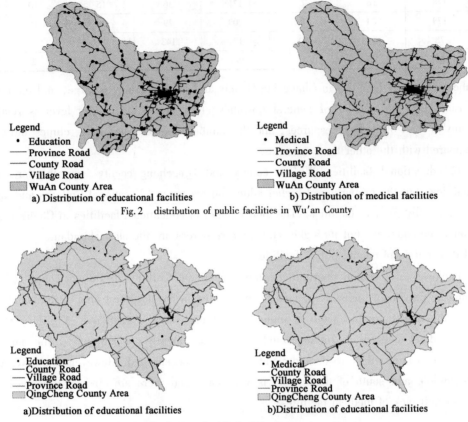

Fig. 2 distribution of public facilities in Wu'an County

Fig. 3 distribution of public facilities in Qingcheng County

From the perspective of spatial distribution, Fig. 4a) shows that the educational facilities in Changxing County are mainly concentrated in the central urban area, and they are distributed from the central urban area to the boundary of Changxing County, and the density is relatively uniform, so there is no excessive concentration of educational resources, and there is a slight vacancy in the educational facilities in the central and western regions. Fig. 4b) shows that the medical facilities of Changxing County are relatively concentrated in the central urban area and the western region, the overall coverage of the county is low, and the overall lack of medical facilities in the north and South distribution areas.

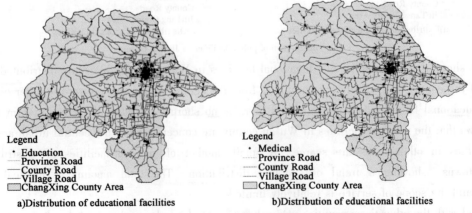

Fig. 4 distribution of public facilities in Changxing County

3 Model Establishment

3.1 Index Extraction of County Spatial Facilities

Through ArcGIS platform, after gridding each county, the spatial facilities indicators shown in Table 4 are sorted out and calculated, and the spatial basic data indicators of road network in different counties in China are obtained, as shown in Tab. 7.

Index Values of County Spatial Facilities Tab. 7

County	Wu'an		Qingcheng		Jintang		Changxing	
Index	Mean	Median	Mean	Median	Mean	Median	Mean	Median
①	29.30	32.00	28.78	32.00	26.62	16.00	26.19	17.00
②	1.50	1.00	2.49	3.00	2.34	3.00	2.43	3.00
③	11111.24	5000.00	7273.96	2000.00	6515.39	4000.00	5262.18	3135.31
④	689.36	541	110.43	112.00	739.81	627.00	656.22	535.91
⑤	3408.02	1316.23	10719.13	1548.1	4800.18	473.56	3259.04	3301.57
⑥	2.34	2.12	—		3.89	1	2.70	2.00
⑦	57955.7	56075.1	11712.0	3172.8	47837.5	47871.7	38190.50	44590.9
⑧	6367.80	5323.43	1539.35	1256.43	9617.86	3495.24	4632.61	3121.25
⑨	2.16	1	—		6.53	2	15.01	12.00
⑩	688.28	578	111.54	114	756.05	659	2892.63	2665.12

3.2 Data Standardization

The MNL model of travel choice for residents visiting public service facilities in different counties is established. Firstly, the spatial facilities index data of each county are dimensionless. Dimensionless is a representative method of multi evaluation index assignment. Due to the different nature and meaning of each index, it usually has different dimensions and orders of magnitude [12]. In order to ensure the reliability of the research results, this paper uses the extreme value method of linear dimensionless to dimensionless the statistical data of land use characteristic index, and the calculation process is shown in the following:

$$x_i = \frac{X_i - \min X_i}{\max X_i - \min X_i} \tag{1}$$

where, x_i——Index standard value of class i public facilities;

X_i——Actual value of class i public facilities index;

$\max X_i$——Maximum index of class i public facilities;

$\min X_i$——Minimum index of class i public facilities.

3.3 Multinomial Logit Model of Influencing Factors of Travel Mode Choice

Travel choice behavior includes the choice of travel time, route, means of transportation, etc., that is, the choice of travel mode, the mode of transportation selected in the specified situation, and the factors and mechanism influencing the choice of travel mode [14]. The part of personal attributes refers to the unique characteristics of an individual, including age, gender and so on. Relevant studies [15-17] show that high-income groups tend to travel with high comfort, and families pay more attention to safety and comfort. Residents' choice of travel mode is a complex decision-making process for residents to complete specific activities under certain time and space constraints. It is not only restricted by land use and other built environment, but also related to residents' own attributes and subjective will.

Multinomial logit (MNL) model is a commonly used traffic analysis model, which can more accurately reflect the individual characteristics and differences, and better explain and reflect the traffic behavior characteristics of travelers (Han Zhiling et al 2018). Assuming that the residents in the county as a whole are taken as the behavior decision-making unit, in a set of travel modes that can be selected and the choice modes are independent of each other, the people in the sample will choose the most effective travel mode. The multinomial logit model is based on the theory that travelers choose the way of maximum utility under certain selection conditions. (Ran, et al 2017). The utility function is composed of fixed term and random term, which can be expressed as:

$$U_{i,n} = V_{i,n} + \varepsilon_{i,n} \tag{2}$$

Where $U_{i,n}$ is the utility function of the i-th scheme for traveler n; $V_{i,n}$ is the fixed term of utility function for resident n when choosing the i-th scheme; $\varepsilon_{i,n}$ is the random term of utility function when choosing the i-th scheme for resident n. Suppose the random term in the utility function $\varepsilon_{i,n}$ obeys double exponential distribution, And each variable is independent of each other, the probability of resident n choosing the i-th scheme is obtained as follows:

$$P_{i,n} = \frac{\exp V_{i,n}}{\sum_{i=1}^{N} \exp V_{i,n}} = \frac{\exp(\sum_{k=1}^{K} \theta_k x_{ink})}{\sum_{i=1}^{N} \exp(\sum_{k=1}^{K} \theta_k x_{ink})} \tag{3}$$

Where, $P_{i,n}$ is Probability of choosing scheme i for the n-th traveler; N is the total number of schemes selected by the provider; x_{ink} is the k-th characteristic variable of the i-th scheme is selected for the n-th traveler; Then we can solve the parameter estimation of (2) by using the maximum likelihood method $\theta_1, \theta_2, \theta_3, \cdots, \theta_k$.

3.4 Selection of Limbs and Determination of Characteristic Variables

In the selected counties (Changxing County, Wu'an County, Qingcheng county and Jintang County), rail transit has not yet been built. This paper selects walking, bus, car (including self driving, carpooling, taxi and online car), non-motor vehicles (including bicycles and electric vehicles) Compared with motorcycle, the four common modes of transportation were analyzed as the choice.

If walking is selected as the reference class, the model expression of traveler's choice of the i-th travel mode is as follows:

$$\ln\left[\frac{p(\text{mode}=i)}{p(\text{mode}=1)}\right] = \alpha_i + \sum_{k=1}^{K} \theta_{ik} x_{ik} \tag{4}$$

Where, α_i Is the intercept term; θ_{ik} Is the regression coefficient; k is the label dummy variables, the value is $1, 2, \cdots, K$.

Taking "walking" as the reference mode, the influence degree of the choice behavior and influencing factors of the remaining modes can be expressed by the following formula:

$$logit \frac{p_2}{p_1} = a_{11}x_1 + \cdots + a_{1k}x_k + b_1 \tag{5}$$

$$logit \frac{p_3}{p_1} = a_{21}x_1 + \cdots + a_{2k}x_k + b_2 \tag{6}$$

$$logit \frac{p_4}{p_1} = a_{31}x_1 + \cdots + a_{3k}x_k + b_3 \tag{7}$$

$$p_1 + p_2 + p_3 + p_4 = 1 \tag{8}$$

Before establishing the model, the influencing factors need to be screened, and the factors that have a significant impact on Residents' choice behavior should be brought into the model as characteristic variables. In this paper, two types of public service facilities, medical facilities and educational facilities, are represented. The influencing factors of residents' travel mode choice when visiting public service facilities are mainly divided into two categories. ① The socio-economic factors of residents: age, travel distance and travel time. ② the spatial facilities allocation factors of county: the length of urban road network, the length of county and township roads, and the number of bus stops around the residential and facility points.

In this paper, Pearson correlation coefficient is used to test the correlation between various factors and the results of residents' travel mode choice when visiting public facilities, and to determine the factors significantly related to residents' travel mode choice. According to the results of Pearson correlation test, the influencing factors with significance level greater than 0.05 were excluded.

4 Analysis of Case Results And Discussion

4.1 Analysis on Layout Characteristics and Travel Behavior of Changxing County

As shown in the Tab. 8, For walking, the main positive factor is the length of the road network around the facilities, and the negative factor is the number of bus stops, which can be explained as the dense, long and continuous urban roads facilitate walking. The number of bus stops around the target public service facilities has a negative impact on walking, which is caused by passengers switching from walking to public transportation. Compared with walking, there is a negative correlation between E-bike travel and the length of road network, block size and average road section around the facility. The results show that there is a complementary relationship between the two modes.

Characteristic coefficients of logit regression in Changxing County　　Tab. 8

Characteristic variable		Correlation Coefficient			
	Travel mode	Walk	Non-Motor Vehicle	Bus	Car
	Intercept	-2.373	-0.949	-2.236	-0.133
Characteristics of facility configuration	Length of urban road network	0.194	-0.170	-0.644	0.203
	Length of county and township roads	-0.034	0.035	-0.141	-0.018
	Number of bus stops	-0.370	-0.064	0.376	0.104
Attribute characteristics	Age	0.132	0.095	-0.074	-0.130
	Facility level	-0.83	-0.133	0.286	0.267
	Access distance	-0.548	-0.057	0.452	0.153
	Number of bus stops in residential areas	0.065	0.128	0.219	-0.241

For bus trips, except for the number of bus stops, the estimated coefficients of all characteristic variables are negative. This means that good road conditions do not promote bus travel, but more bus stops can play a positive role in the choice of this mode. For private car travel, there is no significant negative coefficient in the model estimation results, but dense road network and large blocks have a positive impact on private car travel.

Older visitors are more likely to travel on foot and by E-bike; the higher the scale of facilities and the longer the distance, the higher the proportion of motorized travel, and the lower the proportion of walking and E-bike travel. In this example, distance is the most important feature, especially for walking and bus trips. Facility size also has a significant impact on all four travel modes, while the impact of visitor age is relatively small.

4.2 Analysis of Facility Layout and Travel Behavior in Jintang County

As shown in the Tab. 9, the absolute value of the correlation coefficient of the county and township highway length index to the choice of four travel modes is the largest. For walking, the main positive impact factor is the length of road network around the facilities, and the negative impact factor is the length of county and township roads and the number of bus stops. When the roads in the county are long and continuous, the walking convenience increases. When the number of bus stops in the grid is large, residents will tend to choose other modes of transportation, and the probability of choosing walking is reduced.

Characteristic coefficients of logit regression for residents visiting facility counties in Jintang County Tab. 9

Characteristic variable		Correlation Coefficient			
	Travel mode	Walk	Non-Motor Vehicle	Bus	Car
	Intercept	12.755	22.239	12.346	52.320
Characteristics of facility configuration	Length of urban road network	0.035	−0.580	0.420	0.196
	Length of county and township roads	−0.012	−0.503	0.005	0.497
	Number of bus stops	−0.197	−0.638	0.362	0.078
Attribute characteristics	Age	0.035	0.031	0.020	−0.096
	Facility level	0.146	0.308	0.237	−0.691
	Access distance	−0.066	−0.001	−0.014	−0.173
	Number of bus stops in residential areas	0.100	0.090	0.405	−0.595

Compared with walking, the length of road network around the facilities, the length of county and township roads and the number of bus stops have a negative impact on non motor vehicle travel behavior, which indicates that in Jintang County, non motor vehicle travel is less attractive to bus travel, and people do not tend to choose electric self driving as a substitute for bus travel.

For bus travel, the length of urban road network and the number of bus stops can promote public transport travel, which indicates that good road conditions and bus stops can promote residents to choose bus travel. For private car travel, only the number of bus stops has a significant negative coefficient, while dense and good road network conditions have a positive impact on private car travel, which indicates that with the increase of the number of bus stops, residents are more likely to choose bus instead of car travel.

4.3 Influencing Factors of Residents Visiting Public Facilities in Wu'an County

As shown in Tab. 10, among these characteristics, the length of urban road network and the number of bus stops around facilities in Wu'an county have the greatest correlation with the choice of travel mode, while the length of county and township roads has less correlation with the choice of travel mode. For walking, the positive impact index is the length of urban road network around public facilities, and the negative impact factor is the number of bus stops. The longer the public facilities network is, the more likely the residents in the county choose to visit. The more bus stops in the grid where the facilities are located, the more likely the residents will choose bus instead of walking, and the travel mode will change from walking to bus. Compared with walking, there is a positive correlation between the length of county road network, the number of bus stops and non motorized vehicles. Under the condition of more bus stops, the probability of residents choosing electric vehicles to replace walking is higher, and the substitution of non motorized vehicles and buses is not strong. It can promote the choice of bus stops.

Characteristic coefficients of logit regression for residents visiting facilities in Wu'an County Tab. 10

Characteristic variable		Correlation Coefficient			
Travel mode		Walk	Non-Motor Vehicle	Bus	Car
Intercept		21.810	-16.905	-19.385	33.243
Characteristics of facility configuration	Length of urban road network	-0.444	0.175	-0.286	0.556
	Length of county and township roads	0.006	0.392	0.012	0.747
	Number of bus stops	-0.297	0.358	0.141	0.657
Attribute characteristics	Age	0.012	0.02	0.028	-0.049
	Facility level	-0.195	-0.075	0.515	-0.245
	Access distance	-0.03	-0.085	0.057	0.131
	Number of bus stops in residential areas	0.196	0.391	-0.452	-0.374

For private car travel, dense and long urban road length index has a positive impact on Residents' choice of car travel, and the factor coefficient is relatively largest. However, the number of bus stop facilities is less attractive to the residents who choose to travel by car, and the possibility of replacing car is low.

4.4 Influencing Factors of Travel Mode Choice for Visiting Public Facilities in Qingcheng County

There are only two bus lines in Qingcheng county. The residents who choose bus to visit public facilities are fixed and relatively few, and the bus station facilities index has not passed the significance test. As shown in the table, among these characteristics, the length of the road network around the facilities has the greatest correlation with the choice of the four travel modes. When the length of the urban road network is dense and long, the vast majority of residents choose to travel by car. Due to the fixed bus lines, it is less likely for residents to visit public service facilities and choose the other three travel modes to replace cars. The public transport in the county has a low passenger flow rate, and the choice of travel is more inclined to car mode Tab. 11.

Characteristic coefficients of logit regression for residents visiting facilities in Qingcheng County Tab. 11

Characteristic variable		Correlation Coefficient			
Travel mode		Walk	Non-Motor Vehicle	Bus	Car
Intercept		-12.313	-12.67	-13.917	13.249
Characteristics of facility configuration	Length of urban road network	-0.297	-0.240	-0.166	0.703
	Length of county and township roads	0.052	-0.271	-0.390	0.610
Attribute characteristics Length of county and township roads	Age	0.011	0.01	0.026	-0.014
	Facility level	-0.151	-0.398	-0.047	0.004
	Access distance	-0.001	0.034	-0.001	0.05

4.5 Comparative Analysis of Four Typical Counties

4.5.1 Common law

Compared with the four counties, the influencing factors of residents' travel mode choice to visit public facilities have the following common rules:

(1) There is a significant correlation between walking mode and travel distance, and the trend of walking and proximity is obvious. For the county facilities with higher road density, the residents tend to walk more. There is a close relationship between the layout of public facilities and the distance between residential areas. Residents also tend to choose the nearest facilities for similar facilities with higher facilities.

(2) County and township road construction has a positive impact on car travel. The above shows that when the length of county and township roads is long, residents will probably choose cars to visit public facilities.

(3) When the bus route is perfect, residents choose the way of bus to visit educational or medical facilities.

It is possible to replace other modes of travel. There are great differences in the development level of public transport in the four counties. The travel mode selection coefficients of Changxing, Wu'an and Jintang show that when the bus lines are perfect, they are more likely to replace walking or car travel, and residents tend to choose the bus mode. Among them, Qingcheng county has the least bus lines, and there are only two in the county, but the line stations in the county, including the main public facilities, bear part of the passenger flow.

4.5.2 Difference analysis

The direction of optimization strategy the layout and perfection of public facilities in the three types of counties is different.

From the perspective of residents' personal attributes and land planning and construction factors, this paper analyzes the in fluencing factors of urban residents' using low-carbon travel mode when visiting public service facilities.

(1) Class I counties: Changxing and Jintang are taken as examples. The economy is developed, the road construction is perfect, the county has a road network scale extending in all directions, and the public facilities are complete. According to the travel characteristics and influencing factors analysis, the corresponding people-oriented and sustainable planning concept is proposed to further enhance the sustainable development of county traffic. It is suggested that residents should be encouraged to take appropriate low-carbon travel mode to complete different travel purposes in the built-up area of the county It has the advantages of low energy consumption, low pollution and high energy efficiency, optimizes the public transport network and improves the related infrastructure construction, enhances people's low-carbon awareness, and improves the public's initiative to participate in low-carbon travel.

(2) Class II counties: Taking Wu'an County as an example, there are imbalanced distribution of public facilities and excessive concentration of medical facilities in these counties. It is suggested that in the future planning and development, we should gradually realize the balanced development of public facilities and strengthen the layout coverage. At the same time, the proportion of non motor vehicle travel residents in the county is high. Improving the bicycle travel road environment and storage environment, building a good travel road traffic environment and ensuring residents' travel comfort are people-oriented.

(3) Three types of counties: the degree of economic development, strengthening the scale of road network construction, public transport construction. The development of public transport in the county is relatively small, and the construction of road network in the county is not perfect. The government should strengthen the construction of public transport, improve residents' satisfaction with public transport, and strengthen travel convenience and guidance. Due to the small number of public facilities, the investment in public facilities can be increased according to the population size and residents' needs, and the service radius and coverage can be reasonably planned.

5 Conclusions

Through the reasonable allocation of public service facilities to achieve "people-oriented" sustainable development, this paper selects four typical areas (Changxing County, Zhejiang Province, Qingcheng County, Gansu Province, Jintang County, Sichuan Province, Wu'an County, Hebei Province) to carry out the residents' travel survey and public service facilities survey from the perspective of residents' travel behavior, and uses ArcGIS to integrate a variety of basic data, according to the "data processing" ——Based on the logic of "characteristic analysis model construction configuration optimization", this paper uses SPSS to extract the travel behavior data from the questionnaire, establishes a logit model, verifies the correlation between the facility layout and residents' travel mode choice, and further summarizes the characteristics and problems of facility layout in four counties based on "behavior" analysis, which provides reference for the layout of community public service facilities" Finally, some suggestions are put forward. The conclusions are as follows: there are differences in the correlation between the travel mode choice behavior of county residents visiting public facilities and the facility layout factors under different development degrees.

Through the analysis of the typical county questionnaire, we can see that in terms of individual attribute characteristics, the age composition, gender composition, occupation type of the four urban residentshave a strong correlation with their travel behavior. At the same time, due to the influence of living standards and travel distance of public facilities, travelers also have certain requirements on the characteristics of vehicles, and the travel behavior characteristics of residents of different ages also have certain differences.

The improvement of the layout of public service facilities can promote individuals to travel by walking, non motor vehicles and public transport. Through the comparative analysis of four facilities layout, traffic road density and public transport construction degree of residents visiting public facilities, it is found that with the improvement of facilities layout, residents' daily activity space tends to be concentrated in the community walking scale space, and their willingness to walk is enhanced.

In this study, four specific County cases are discussed, and the universal conclusion is limited. In the future, it is necessary to further clarify the research object, focus on a kind of community or specific population, find out the community facilities configuration needs and the existing common problems, and further explore the optimization direction, such as quantitative analysis of facilities optimization strategies from the perspective of carbon emissions, and take targeted planning and updating measures.

6 Acknowledgements

This work is supported by the National Key R&D Program of China under Grant No. 2020YFB1600501.

References

[1] JiangHuipeng, Zhou Xizhao. The change of College Students' travel under the influence of bike sharing: a case study of Shanghai University of technology[J]. Logistics engineering and management, 2017, 39.07: 143-145.

[2] Dorien Simons, Ilse De Bourdeaudhuij, Peter Clarys, et al. Choice of transport mode in emerging adulthood: Differences between secondary school students, studying young adults and working young adults and relations with gender, SES and living environment[J]. Transportation Research Part A, 2017.

[3] Jiang Wei, ZhangDongjun, Chen Hang. The impact of online car Hailing policy on urban residents' travel behavior[J]. Journal of Management Cadre College, Ministry of transport, 2019, 29.01: 26-30.

[4] M. Taleai R, Sliuzas, J Flacke. An integrated framework to evaluate the equity of urban public facilities using spatial multi-criteria analysis[J]. Cities, 2014.

[5] Gao Junbo, Han Yong, Wang Yimin, et al. Medical treatment space and planning of urban residents based on individual behavior: a case study of Guangzhou central district[J]. Urban planning, 2017, (10), 46-52.

[6] DuanYaqiong. Research on the mechanism and optimization of land intensive use in Xi'an built-up area under the guidance of low-carbon travel (doctoral dissertation, Chang'an University) [EB/OL]. https://kns.cnki.net/KCMS/detail/detail.aspx?dbname=CDFDLAST2020&filename=1019628151.nh.

[7] Yuan Liang, WuPeixun. Study on urban residents' willingness to choose between online car hailing and taxi hailing and its influencing factors- a logistic analysis based on survey data of Jiangsu Province[J]. Soft science, 2018, 32(04): 120-123.

[8] Chai Y, X Zhang, D Sun. A Study on Life Circle Planning Based on Space Time 12 Behavioural Analysis:

A Case Study of Beijing[J]. Urban Planning Forum, 2015, (3): 61-69.

[9] Cervero R, M Duncan. Which Reduces Vehicle Travel More: Jobs-Housing Balanceor Retail-Housing Mixing[J]. Journal of the American planning association, 2006, 72(4): 475 – 490.

[10] Wang Daixia, Shi Dehao, Wu Yizhou, et al. Classification evaluation and spatial pattern characteristics of regional small town development: a case study of Zhejiang Province[J]. Journal of urban planning, 2018, (02): 89-97.

[11] Han Zhiling, Chen Yanyan, Li Jiaxian, et al. Analysis on Influencing Factors of intercity travel mode choice in snowy weather[J]. Highway Engineering, 2018, (04): 133-139 + 159.

[12] Ran Linna, Li Feng. Analysis of travel characteristics and behavior of bike sharing[J]. Traffic information and safety, 2017, (06): 93-100 + 114

交通强国背景下中小城市综合交通规划的探讨与实践

任彦铭 张 旭

(华设设计集团股份有限公司)

摘 要 在交通强国建设背景下,面对经济社会转型变革的新形势,以及交通行业发展的新趋势,如何更加科学地编制中小城市的综合交通规划成为亟待解决的问题之一。通过分析中小城市综合交通的现状与问题,结合交通强国建设的目标与要求,探讨中小城市综合交通的发展路径。以江苏省灌云县综合交通规划为例,基于对灌云县所处区位战略格局的分析,提出灌云县综合交通发展的定位和规划策略,并阐述了综合交通的规划方案。

关键词 区域交通规划 综合交通网 交通强国 中小城市 国土空间规划

0 引 言

交通运输是国民经济中的基础性、先导性、战略性产业,是重要的服务性行业。党中央、国务院高度重视交通运输的发展,作出了建设交通强国的重大战略部署,印发了《交通强国建设纲要》,对交通强国建设的目标和重大任务进行了系统谋划和全面部署,而编制综合立体交通网规划是推进交通强国建设的基础[1]。在新的国土空间规划框架下,综合交通不是一个独立的封闭系统,在战略层面上需要讨论交通系统与社会、经济、生态等外部环境的相互作用,在具体的技术方案中,需要明确交通系统内部的结构与布局优化[2]。空间规划框架下的区域交通基础设施规划与传统的城市区域交通规划相比,着眼于交通基础设施空间的管控和引导,更加强调交通基础设施规划的落地性,强调公、铁、水、空等多种交通运输方式在空间上的综合立体和区域一体化[3-5]。中小城市是我国城镇体系的重要组成部分,开展中小城市的综合立体交通网规划研究,统筹各种运输方式的规划建设,完善综合立体交通网络,为城市经济社会发展和人民美好生活提供支撑和保障[6]。本文在对中小城市综合立体交通网的现状和问题进行分析的基础上,结合交通强国战略,对中小城市综合立体交通的发展路径进行探讨,为开展综合立体交通网规划提供思路。

1 中小城市综合立体交通网发展的现状与问题

1.1 就交通论交通,简单落实上位规划,对城市发展的引领和支撑不足

传统的中小城市区域综合交通规划以上位规划为编制前提,不能随意突破上位中长期规划的刚性约

束[7]。因此，在实际工作中，往往对上位规划的交通基础设施方案研究不够深入，未能从城市发展的角度出发，讨论城市形态、空间布局、产业发展、生态保护等方面与区域交通基础设施的功能定位和空间布局的关系，仅从交通系统发展的角度出发，简单落实上位规划中的交通系统规划方案，就交通而论交通，缺乏与城市其他系统的互动与协调，对城市发展的引领和支撑不足。

1.2 基建规模偏小，设施建设滞后，综合立体交通网不完整

交通基础设施建设所需的资金投入较大，除上位规划落实的重大交通基础设施有国家和省级的资金扶持，中小城市的其他交通基础设施建设通常依赖其自身的财政状况。受限于自身的财政状况，中小城市在区域交通的投入则需要"精打细算"，导致了区域交通基础设施的建设资金投入不足[8-9]。而建设资金的缺乏，在一定程度上造成了中小城市区域交通基础设施的建设规模偏小、设施建设滞后的情况，综合立体交通网并未完全形成，各交通系统之间的一体化程度不高，"各自为战"。实际工作中，常遇到"十二五"期已经列入建设计划的项目拖至"十三五"期继续建设的情况，有些未得到国家和省扶持的项目甚至要列入"十四五"期的建设计划中，也导致综合立体交通网的规划工作"畏首畏尾"。

1.3 落地冲突，与空间规划协调不够

传统的中小城市综合交通网络规划中，城区与乡镇通常被表述为一个点，规划关注的重点是"点"与"点"之间的公路、铁路、航道，以及在"点"上的机场、火车站、汽车站、港口等枢纽[10]。由于缺乏与空间规划的协调，综合交通网络规划的方案在"落地"时会经常与城市的空间发生冲突[11]。现实中，我们可以看到很多中小城市的空间规划布局结构受制于综合交通网的规划方案，城区被高速公路或者铁路分割，被分割城市用地需要花费很大的代价才能实现沟通，同时还要面对交通组织和交通安全的问题，导致城市的发展空间和功能布局受到限制。

2 中小城市综合立体交通发展战略

2.1 发展原则

（1）服务城市

中小城市的综合立体交通，需要服务乡村振兴和城市的经济社会发展，服务和促进国土空间开发，服务区域一体化发展，服务国家、省的发展战略，使综合立体交通的规划和建设真正起到中小城市发展先行官的作用。

（2）统筹协调

中小城市的综合立体交通，需要统筹考虑区域一体、城乡一体和综合立体[12]。统筹国家、省综合立体交通网规划及上位各交通专项规划，加强与城市相关规划的融合，做好与国土空间规划的融合，处理好与城镇、农业、生态空间的关系，做好与城镇开发边界、生态保护红线、永久基本农田及其他保护线的衔接，从而落实综合立体交通网的空间布局。

（3）人民满意

人民满意是交通强国建设的根本宗旨，坚持以人民为中心的发展导向，围绕满足人民群众高品质的交通需求出发，建设综合立体交通网，提升出行服务水平，提升物流配送水平，推动由"便出行"向"悦出行"转型，由"畅其流"向"优其流"转型，建设人民满意的综合立体交通网[13]。

（4）远近结合

对标国内外先进水平，以交通强国两个阶段的发展目标，展望未来交通运输发展场景，提出面向2035年和2050年远景的规划目标，进而布局综合立体交通网。同时，强化2025年近期建设目标任务，突出中小城市在十四五期的城市发展要求，目标化、项目化、任务化提出近期发展重点，构建并逐步完善综合立体交通网。

（5）创新驱动

创新发展交通运输新业态、新模式，抢抓大数据、互联网、人工智能、区块链、智能制造、新材料、新能

源等前沿科技发展契机,以创新驱动综合立体交通网的建设和运行,使智慧交通从城区向农村延伸,全面提升中小城市的交通信息化水平。

2.2 发展目标

中小城市综合立体交通的发展目标,以交通强国建设的战略部署为重要依据,以"人民满意、保障有力、世界前列"的交通强国建设发展总目标为总体要求,按照2035年和2050年两个阶段,设定反映中小城市交通出行需求和城市发展趋势的具体目标。具体而言,中小城市综合立体交通的发展目标,需要体现其在国家、省发展战略的作用,需要结合其在国家、省综合立体交通网规划中的交通区位,需要反映其市(县)域内人民群众的客货运需求,需要判断适合其发展的交通运输方式。在此基础上,构建安全、便捷、高效、绿色、经济的综合立体交通网,到2035年,基本建成交通强市(县),到2050年,全面建成交通强市(县),与交通强国的发展目标相呼应。

2.3 发展路径

(1)提升在区域一体化发展中的交通作用

区域一体化发展对城市提出了更高的要求,对于中小城市而言,综合立体交通网不完整,无法满足城镇发展的迫切需求,也不能支撑中小城市与周边都市圈的区域交通联系。中小城市作为都市圈联系通道上的节点,需要以"枢纽"的形式承担交通方式转换的功能,积极衔接上位交通规划,提高对外辐射能力,在更广阔的区域范围与其他城市进行交通功能的分工与协作,提升其在区域一体化中的地位,并带动中小城市发展。

(2)加强内外交通体系的联通

加强中小城市内外交通体系联通主要有两个层面,一个是加强综合立体交通网中的对外交通系统与市(县)域内的交通系统的联通,另一个是加强传统的区域交通系统与城市道路交通系统的联通。前者主要解决中小城市对外交通廊道中的综合立体交通骨干线网与在市(县)域内支撑城镇发展的低等级交通线网联系不够紧密的问题,后者则重点解决传统城市对外交通系统与城市道路交通系统存在冲突的问题,从而使不同级别的交通网络真正实现整合,形成综合立体交通网,支撑中小城市发展。

(3)融合交通体系与城乡空间

国土空间规划强化了"多规合一"的原则,在全局上对城市空间资源使用以及各系统对空间使用方案之间相互关系进行统筹安排,实质上形成了综合立体交通规划体系与其他中长期规划协调的政策窗口。充分利用这个政策窗口,中小城市需在国土空间规划平台上对综合立体交通网规划进行必要的调整与优化,争取支撑城市发展的重大交通基础设施的空间资源配置,合理构建综合立体交通网和客货运体系,以综合立体交通骨架网络引导城乡空间发展,以多级和多式交通联运体系适应及引领区域和城乡的产业发展。

3 灌云县综合立体交通网规划的实践

灌云县位于连云港市中南部,是连云港市联系长三角发达地区的必经节点,也是连云港市沟通宿迁、合肥等城市的重要节点。

近年来,灌云县不断完善公路网络、大力发展海河联运、主动推进铁路建设、积极协调机场迁建,综合立体交通网建设取得较大成就。但受限于基础薄弱,灌云县综合立体交通网尚不完整,发展水平相较于苏南发达地区仍有较大差距。同时,由于对交通与城镇发展、土地管控的关系缺乏准确认知,既有的交通基础设施不足以支撑和引领灌云县城镇高质量发展。

3.1 明确战略定位,引领城市发展

江苏省高质量推进"一带一路"交汇点建设,要求连云港市从强调地缘区位的"一带一路交汇点"转变为强调战略功能的"一带一路强支点"。长三角一体化上升为国家战略,促使连云港市加快融入长三角经济圈。此外,沿海开发、淮河生态经济带等战略也为连云港市带来了新机遇、新挑战,要求连云港市

进一步完善对外交通,打造亚欧重要国际交通枢纽,形成集聚优质要素的开放门户。

灌云县作为连云港市向南对接长三角中心城市的第一站,连云港市沿海通道、连宁通道、连宿通道等对外通道的必经节点,应全面融入连云港市对外交通环境改善的进程,打造淮河生态经济带与沿海经济带交汇点的"陆、海、空"三位一体的江苏沿海重要交通枢纽,建成综合交通发展水平位于全国县级区划前列的交通强县,从而助力连云港市"一带一路强支点"建设,与长三角中心城市联动发展。

3.2 以构建区域交通枢纽为抓手,优化综合立体交通网络

灌云县内共有三个区域交通枢纽,分别是:以花果山国际机场为核心的一类客运枢纽、省级货运枢纽,服务对象为连云港市域乃至更大范围;以连淮扬镇铁路灌云站为核心的二类客运枢纽,服务对象为灌云县域;以灌河港区(燕尾港)为核心的地区级货运枢纽,服务对象为连云港腹地。

以花果山国际机场综合交通枢纽建设为抓手,将高速铁路、市域铁路、城市轨道、公路客运、城乡公交、城市公交、出租车、网约车等多种交通方式引入枢纽。以此为契机,结合灌云站综合交通枢纽集疏运需求,大幅度提升灌云县铁路服务水平,完善公路系统。以灌河港区(燕尾港)综合货运枢纽建设为契机,梳理灌云境内内河水系,提升航道等级,形成结构合理、规模适中的内河航道网(图1)。

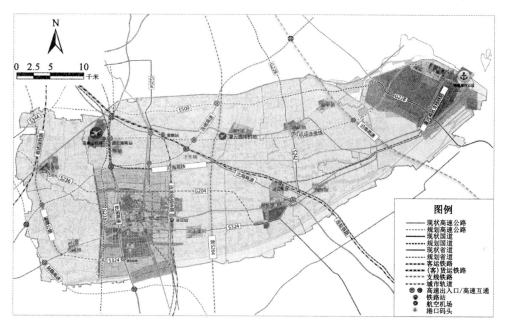

图1 灌云县综合交通规划图

3.3 协调国土空间规划

在比例尺1∶10000的地形图上,协调铁路、公路、机场、航道、港口以及场站、高速出入口等交通基础设施与城镇建设用地、生态保护红线的空间,并结合城镇空间布局及城市和乡镇产业规划,对综合立体交通网的基础设施进行优化调整(图2)。

3.4 强化保障

完善灌云县综合立体交通规划、建设、管理体制机制,推进综合立体交通规划一张图、建设一盘棋、管理一体化。加强与国家、省、市综合立体交通网规划的对接,争取重大项目纳入国家和江苏省的综合立体交通网规划。同时,加强灌云县交通规划相关部门的配合,共同建立项目储备库,并明确分解目标任务,采取考核评价、监督评估等措施,统筹协调推进综合交通运输发展的重大项目、重大工程,保障规划落到实处。

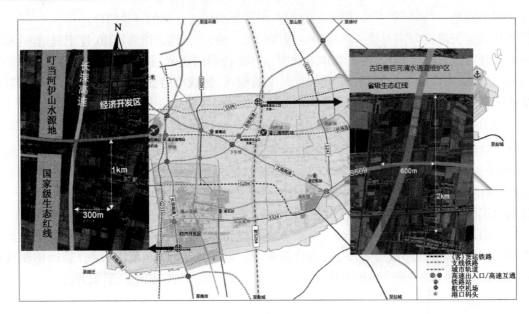

图2 高速公路出入口布局与国土空间协调示意图

4 结　语

当前,我国正处于经济社会发展和社会治理的转型期,在交通强国背景与新的国土空间规划框架下,如何落实一体化、高质量发展理念,促进交通规划有机融入国土空间规划,保障交通基础设施建设空间,是现阶段交通规划需要重视的问题。很多中小城市在推进综合立体交通网规划的编制工作,如何把握交通强国建设战略、科学合理的规划中小城市的综合立体交通网规划。同时,在国土空间规划框架下,如何确定中小城市综合立体交通网相关的规划管控要素,消除上位规划前提条件中的不确定性,处理综合立体交通网规划方案"落地"问题,是实现多规合一不可避免的问题。本文以灌云县的综合立体交通网规划方案为例,提出了以提升中小城市交通功能定位为目标,以枢纽建设为抓手,以国土空间规划为基底,从而确定综合立体交通网的规划方案,是对中小城市综合立体交通网规划的初步尝试,对其他中小城市开展综合立体交通网规划具有一定的借鉴意义。

参考文献

[1] 中华人民共和国中央人民政府. 中共中央 国务院印发《交通强国建设纲要》[EB/OL]. (2019-09-19)[2020-03-01]. http://www.gov.cn/zhengce/2019-09/19/content_5431432.htm.

[2] 中华人民共和国中央人民政府. 国土空间规划"多规合一"将加快实现[EB/OL](2019-09-20)[2020-03-01]. http://www.gov.cn/xinwen/2019-09/20/content_5431771.htm.

[3] 奉鸣,聂向军,何佳媛. 交通运输战略规划体系构建探析[J]. 交通运输,2019,41(4):31-36.

[4] 刘振国,常馨玉,贺明光. 国土空间新形势下综合交通规划的问题与对策[J]. 交通运输研究,2019,5(4):64-68.

[5] 李潭峰,郝媛,姚伟奇. 国土空间规划背景下我国交通规划转型思考[J]. 交通运输研究,2019,5(6):50-60.

[6] 黄勇,邱乾. 中小城市区域交通规划的国家战略响应[J]. 大众科技,2018,20(7):141-145.

[7] 王睿. 基于情景规划的城市总体规划编制方法研究[D]. 武汉:华中科技大学,2007.

[8] 全永燊,潘昭宇. 城市交通供给侧结构性改革研究[J]. 城市交通,2017,15(5):1-7.

[9] 全永燊,刘剑锋. 区域轨道交通规划若干问题与思考[J]. 城市交通,2017,15(1):12-19.

[10] 汪光焘. "多规合一"与城市交通规划变革[J]. 城市规划学刊,2018(5):19-28.

[11] 刘占山,张哲辉,杜丽楠. 改革开放以来交通运输发展战略回顾[J]. 综合运输,2017,39(8):

[12] 荣朝和. 论运输业发展阶段及其新常态和供给侧改革[J]. 综合运输, 2016, 38(12): 5-10, 14.
[13] 张泰, 蔡垚, 张哲辉, 等. 加快完善我国现代综合交通运输体系的分析和思考[J]. 综合运输, 2017, 39(5): 1-5.

响应预约需求的定制公交线路动态规划模型与求解算法

郑 好[1]　王 云[1]　闫学东[1]　李云伟[2]

(1. 北京交通大学交通运输学院; 2. 中国汽车技术研究中心有限公司)

摘要　"定制公交"是一种具有需求响应功能的公交服务模式。现在，已有的定制公交调度模型大多只能基于静态线路进行服务，从而，本文构建了定制公交两阶段规划模型与求解算法，在满足静态预约需求的前提下，对动态预约需求进行响应，并通过算例对模型进行了验证。结果表明，本文所提出的方法可以同时对静态与动态需求进行响应，为定制公交的线路规划提供了依据。

关键词　需求响应　定制公交　线路规划　动态调整

0 引　言

当前，"定制公交"因其能够为各类乘客量身定制出行方案的优势，正在成为常规公交系统的有效补充。对于需求响应式公交系统的理论研究可以分为合乘站点布设、静态线路规划、动态线网优化、乘客需求分析等方向。蔡永旺[1]在对需求点的聚类处理中使用改进的 DBSCAN 算法。刘喜[2]在定制公交站点生成中采用 K-means 算法。胡郁葱等[3]构建了运行模式多样化的静态定制公交线路规划模型，并利用改进的遗传算法进行求解。陈汐等[4]构建了多区域运营的定制公交线路规划模型，构建了多目标优化模型，并使用了两阶段启发式算法获得 Pareto 解。申婵等[5]提出一种基于可靠性最短路的实时线路优化模型，采用禁忌搜索算法进行求解。韩霜等[6]提出了两阶段法定制公交调度模型，并使用遗传算法进行求解。

综上所述，目前对可以同时满足静态预约需求与实时即时响应的定制公交模式研究比较少，且有关即时响应公交系统的研究大多采用实时全盘更新线路实现需求响应；在这种方式下响应前后定制线路变化较大，影响公交系统的稳定运营。

基于此，本文提出了一种两阶段即时响应预约需求的定制公交站线规划方法，将公交站线规划分为满足开始运营前已提交需求的静态线路生成，与发车后提交需求的动态需求插入两个阶段，在已生成的静态线路的基础上进行是否响应动态需求的判断，以及对动态需求的插入位置进行决策，从而在响应即时预约需求的前提下，保证线路的稳定性与乘客的出行体验。

1 响应预约需求的定制公交线路动态规划求解算法

1.1 两阶段求解思路

响应预约需求的定制公交需要同时满足开始运营前产生的静态预约需求，以及对发车后实时产生的新的动态预约需求予以响应，从而，本文将定制公交线路规划问题划分为发车前与发车后两个阶段，分别进行线路优化处理。

基金项目：国家重点研发计划资助(2019YFF0301403)。

1.2 阶段一:初始运营线路规划模型

设 $V = \{1, \cdots, n, n+1, \cdots, 2n, 2n+1, \cdots, 2n+p\}$ 为路网点集,$V = P \cup D \cup DEP$,其中 $P = \{1, \cdots, n\}$ 为上车点点集,$D = \{n+1, \cdots, 2n\}$ 为下车点点集,$DEP = \{2n+1, \cdots, 2n+p\}$ 为场站集合,$A = \{(i,j) | i, j \in V\}$ 为路网弧集,设 $\{i, i+n\}$ 表示乘客由 i 点至 $i+n$ 点的运输需求。初始运营线路规划模型如下所示。

$$\min f(x) = \alpha_1 C_0 + \alpha_2 C_t + \alpha_3 C_{pw} + \alpha_4 C_{vw} + c_1 \beta_1 Q_1 + c_2 \beta_2 Q_2 + c_3 \beta_3 Q_3 \tag{1}$$

s.t.
$$\sum_{p \in M_j} \sum_{j \in V'} x_{ij}^p \leq 1, \forall i \in P' \tag{2}$$

$$\sum_{j \in V'} x_{ij}^p - \sum_{j \in V'} x_{ji}^p = 0, \forall j \in V', p \in M \tag{3}$$

$$\sum_{i \in V'} x_{ij}^p - \sum_{i \in V'} x_{ji}^p = 0, \forall j \in V', p \in M \tag{4}$$

$$\sum_{j \in P'} x_{j,\text{dep}(p)}^p = y^p, \forall p \in M \tag{5}$$

$$\sum_{j \in D'} x_{\text{dep}(p)j}^p = y^p, \forall p \in M \tag{6}$$

$$x_{ij}^p \leq y^p, \forall i, j \in V', p \in M \tag{7}$$

$$Q_j^p \geq q_j + Q_i^p - q^p(1 - x_{ij}^p), \forall i, j \in V', p \in M_k, k \in K \tag{8}$$

$$Q_j^p \leq q_j + Q_i^p + q^p(1 - x_{ij}^p), \forall i, j \in V', p \in M_k, k \in K \tag{9}$$

$$\max\{0, q_i\} \leq Q_i^p \leq \min\{q^p, q^p + q_i\}, \forall i \in V', p \in M_k, k \in K \tag{10}$$

$$A_j^p \geq B_i^p + S_{ti} + t_{ij} - (l_i + S_{ti} + t_{ij})(1 - x_{ij}^p), \forall i, j \in V', p \in M_k, k \in K \tag{11}$$

$$A_j^p \leq B_i^p + S_{ti} + l_{\text{dep}(p)}(1 - x_{ij}^p), \forall i, j \in V', p \in M_k, k \in K \tag{12}$$

$$W_i^p = \max\{B_i^p - A_i^p, 0\}, \forall i \in V', p \in M \tag{13}$$

$$L_i^p = B_{n+i}^p + S_{y,n+i} - B_i^p - S_{ti}, \forall i \in P', p \in M_k, k \in K \tag{14}$$

$$t_{i,i+n} + S_{t,n+i} \leq L_i^p \leq T_i, \forall i \in P' \cup D', p \in M_k, k \in K \tag{15}$$

$$e_i \leq B_i^p \leq l_i, \forall i \in P' \cup D', p \in M_k, k \in K \tag{16}$$

$$0 \leq A_{\text{dep}(p)}^p - B_{\text{dep}(p)}^p \leq T_{\max}, \forall p \in M \tag{17}$$

$$A_i^p, B_i^p, L_i^p, Q_i^p \geq 0, \forall i \in V', p \in M_k, k \in K \tag{18}$$

$$x_{ij}^p \in \{0, 1\}, \forall i, j \in V', p \in M_k, k \in K \tag{19}$$

$$y^p \in \{0, 1\}, p \in M_k, k \in K \tag{20}$$

响应预约需求定制公交站线规划问题涉及的符号及其对应的含义见表1。

表1 符号说明

符号	含义	符号	含义
M	$M = \{1, \cdots, m\}$ 车辆集	B_i^p	p 车在 i 点开始服务的时间,$p \in M$
S	$S = \{1, \cdots, a\}$ 备选站点集($1, \cdots, a$)为备选站点编号,路网节点总数为 a)	L_i^p	需求 i 被 p 车服务的在车时间,$p \in M$
K	车辆类型数目	Q_i^p	p 车离开 i 点的载客量,$p \in M$
M_k	k 类型车辆集($|M| = m_k; k = 1, \cdots, K; M = \sum_{k=1}^{K} M_k$)	W_i^p	p 车在 i 点的等待时间,$p \in M$
$\text{dep}(p)$	p 车所属场站,$p \in M$	x_{ij}^p	如果 $x_{ij}^p = 1$,则 p 车在弧 (i, j) 上运行
q^p	p 车的额定载客量,$p \in M$	y^p	如果 $y^p = 1$,则 p 车被使用
d_{ij}	点 i 至点 j 的最短直达距离	λ_k	使用 k 型车的固定成本
t_{ij}	点 i 至点 j 的最短直达时间	cp_k	k 型车在车乘客等待单位时间的成本
S_{ij}	乘客在 i 的上下车时间	cw_k	k 型车等待单位时间的成本
T_i	乘客最大在车时间(包括在下车点的等待时间)	ct_k	k 型车运行单位时间的成本
$T_{\max}$	车辆最大运行时间	c_i	各服务质量指标单位成本($i = 1, 2, 3$)
q_i	i 点的上下车人数(如果 i 为上车点,则 $q_i > 0$;如果 i 为下车点,则 $q_i < 0; q_i = -q_{n=i}$)	a_i	各相关成本权重系数($i = 1, 2, 3, 4$ 且权重之和为1)
(e_i, l_i)	时间窗范围	β_i	各服务质量指标权重系数($i = 1, 2, 3$ 且权重之和为1)
A_i^p	p 车在 i 点的到达时间,$p \in M$		

本文模型中:

目标函数(1)由以下子函数构成。

i. 车辆固定成本。

$$C_0 = \sum_{k=1}^{K} \sum_{p \in M_k} \lambda_k y^p \tag{21}$$

ii. 车辆运行时间成本。

$$C_t = \sum_{k=1}^{K} \sum_{p \in M_k} ct_k (A_{\text{dep}(p)}^p - B_{\text{dep}(p)}^p) y^p \tag{22}$$

iii. 在车乘客等待时间成本。

$$C_{pw} = \sum_{k=1}^{K} \sum_{p \in M_k} \sum_{i \in V'} \sum_{j \in V'} cp_k x_{ij}^p Q_i^p W_j^p y^p \tag{23}$$

iiii. 车辆等待时间成本。

$$C_{vw} = \sum_{k=1}^{K} \sum_{p \in M_k} \sum_{i \in V'} cw_k W_i^p y^p \tag{24}$$

iiiii. 服务质量指标。

a. 车辆开始服务时间与乘客期望服务时间的偏离程度。

$$Q_1 = \sum_{i \in p'} \sum_{p=1}^{m} \left| \frac{e_i + l_i}{2} - B_i^p \right| y^p \tag{25}$$

b. 车辆服务结束时间与乘客期望到达时间的偏离程度。

$$Q_2 = \sum_{i \in D'} \sum_{p=1}^{m} |e_i - B_i^p| y^p \tag{26}$$

c. 车辆的绕行程度。

$$Q_3 = \sum_{i \in P'} \sum_{p=1}^{m} |L_i^p - t_{i,j+n}| y^p \tag{27}$$

约束(2)表示每个乘客最多只被一辆车服务。
约束(3)表示每个 OD 对被同一辆车执行服务。
约束(4)为流平衡约束。
约束(5)~(7)为车辆使用约束。
约束(8)~(10)为载客量约束。
约束(11)~(12)用于表示车辆到达时间和开始服务时间之间的等量关系。
约束(13)定义了车辆等待时间。
约束(14)~(15)约束了乘客的在车时间及其范围。
约束(16)用于定义定制公交上下车站点的时间窗范围。
约束(17)用于约束车辆驶回场站时间与车辆最大运行时间。
约束(18)~(20)用来定义变量取值范围。

1.3 阶段二:运营线路动态调整模型

$$\min \Delta F = F - F_0 \tag{28}$$

$$x_{di} = \begin{cases} 1 & \text{动态预约需求 } d \text{ 选择备选站点 } i \text{ 为服务站点} \\ 0 & \text{动态预约需求 } d \text{ 未选备选站点 } i \text{ 为服务站点} \end{cases}, i \in S \tag{29}$$

$$x_{di} l_{di} \leq R, i \in S \tag{30}$$

$$\begin{cases} e_i = e_{d_1} + t_0^{d_1 i} \\ l_i = l_{d_1} + t_0^{d_1 i} \end{cases}, i \in S \tag{31}$$

$$\begin{cases} e_i = e_{d_2} - t_0^{d_2 i} \\ l_i = l_{d_2} - t_0^{d_2 i} \end{cases}, i \in S \tag{32}$$

$$e_i \leq B_i^p \leq l_i, i \in S, p \in M \tag{33}$$

$$R_{ij}^p = \begin{cases} 1 & i,j \text{ 为线路 Route}_p \text{ 中相邻两需求点} \\ 0 & \text{需求点 } i,j \text{ 在线路 Route}_p \text{ 中不相邻} \end{cases}, i,j \in \text{Route}_p, 1 \leq p \leq m \quad (34)$$

$$B_m^p \leq B_i^p \leq B_n^p, \exists R_{mn}^p = 1, i \in S, p \in M, m \text{ 与 } n \in \text{Route}_p \quad (35)$$

$$\begin{cases} A_i^p = B_m^p + S_{tm} + t_{mi} \\ A_n^p = B_i^p + S_{ti} + t_{in} \end{cases}, R_{mn}^p = 1, i \in S, p \in M, m \text{ 与 } n \in \text{Route}_p \quad (36)$$

$$\frac{R}{2} + 1 \leq q^p, p \in M \quad (37)$$

式中,l_{di} 表示动态预约需求 d 的预约提交位置与可选备选站点 i 之间的距离;R 为乘客最大走行距离;t_0^{ij} 表示从 i 步行至 j 的走行时间。

目标函数(28)表示动态响应过程目标函数为系统总目标函数值变化最小。

约束(29)~(30)为备选站点范围约束。

式(31)~(32)为时间窗更新规则。

约束(33)为动态预约需求的开始服务时间约束。

式(34)表示线路需求点间的连接情况。

约束(35)~(36)为站点服务时间约束。

约束(37)为载客量约束。

除上述约束外,动态响应阶段同样满足 1.3 节中提到的一系列约束条件。

2 求解算法

本文的求解算法分为两个阶段。第一个阶段是静态线路生成,分为基于 Clarke-Wright 算法的初始解生成与基于禁忌搜索的优化解生成两个子阶段;第二阶段是动态需求响应,将发车后产生的动态预约需求插入当前的线路链中,实现公交系统对动态需求的服务。

2.1 基于禁忌搜索的初始运营线路生成算法

本节使用 Clark-Wright 节约算法的思想,以单次插入成本最低的标准在各条车辆运营线路中插入静态预约需求对,构造可行的初始解。然后,在禁忌算法中引入 Swap 和 2-opt 两种算子生成优化解。

2.1.1 求解算法

算法的具体流程如下:

利用 C-W 算法获得初始可行解 insolution

bestsolution = inisolution , currentsolution = insolution ;

Repeat

    Repeat

    随机选择一种变换算子及两条车辆链组合,随机选取车辆链变换位置,将当前解进行邻域变换并判断生成的邻域解是否满足约束,直至生成可行的邻域解放入邻居候选集中;

    Until

    邻居候选集中邻居数量达到预设值;

    基于禁忌表执行以下循环操作:

    Repeat

        依次判断所得邻居候选集中邻居的禁忌状态:

        If 邻居处于非禁忌状态

            比较处于非禁忌状态的邻域解与当前邻域最优解的目标函数值,将使目标函数值最小的解设置为当前邻域最优解;

        Else

比较处于禁忌状态的邻域解与当前邻域最优解的目标函数,若禁忌解更优,则特赦该解,进而判断该解与最优解的优劣,若特赦解更优,则将其设置为当前邻域最优解;

    End

  Until

    所有生成的邻域解均被判断完毕;

  若当前最优邻域解优于 exsolution,则将该值赋给 bestsolution;

  令 currentsolution = bestsolution,作为下次迭代的当前解;

Until 满足停止条件

2.1.2 评价函数

本算法在求解过程中允许不可行解的存在,因此在确定评价函数时,需要考虑车辆的额定载客量、车辆最大运行时间以及上下车时间窗的惩罚值。本文的评价函数为:

$$f(x) = c(x) + \alpha q(x) + \beta d(x) + \gamma w(x) \tag{38}$$

式中,$f(x)$ 表示解 x 的评价函数;$c(x)$ 表示目标函数;$q(x)$ 表示载客量惩罚值;$d(x)$ 表示车辆最大运行时间惩罚值;$w(x)$ 表示时间窗惩罚值;α、β、γ 为惩罚因子,且 $\alpha > 0$、$\beta > 0$、$\gamma > 0$。在本文中,α、β、γ 均取固定常数。

2.2 基于动态需求插入的线路调整算法

2.2.1 松弛时间定义

在本研究中,车辆链 p 中需求节点 i 的松弛时间的计算如式(39)所示。

$$t_{\text{slack}}^p(i) = \max\{e_i - A_i^p, 0\}, i \in P' \cup D', p \in M_k, k \in K \tag{39}$$

2.2.2 运营线路动态调整算法

Innpt 静态线路生成结果 S_0;令 $S = S_0$;

While($0 \leq t \leq T$ 生)(t 为时刻,运营时段为 $[0, T]$)

  Repeat

  实时采集动态预约需求;

  If t 时刻出现了动态预约需求 i;

    根据当前车辆行驶实际状况,从线路链 S 删除已服务路段,更新 S;

    选择以 i 为圆心的某一范围内的备选站点构成备选集;

    遍历备选集中的站点,依据松弛时间和时间窗范围等约束条件判断该动;

    态需求站点在当前规划线路链 S 中可插入的车辆链和插入位置;

    If 将动态需求 i 按照插入规则插入到 S 中可行

      选择使得目标函数变化最小的备选站点、车辆链和上下车节点插入位置组合,生成新的线路链 S';令 $S = S'$

    Else

      拒绝服务

    End

  Ese(t 时刻未出现动态预约需求 i)

    继续实时采集动态预约需求

  End

  Until

    定制公交结束运营服务。

End

3 案例分析

3.1 基础数据处理

3.1.1 备选站点选取

本算例选取北京市昌平区中心城区实际路网为研究对象,经过路网简化、用地性质分析等筛选出100个定制公交站点,绘制如图1所示的路网拓扑结构图。

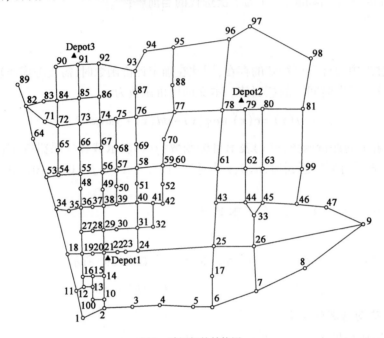

图1 路网拓扑结构图

3.1.2 数据生成

本文随机生成100个静态预约需求订单和10个动态预约需求订单作为测试集。

3.1.3 公交站点的生成

本文首先采用层次聚类法划分需求数据,根据需求点初始提交位置间距离对需求点分类,并通过聚类后类别间的距离直接确定乘客聚类数目,即最佳站点个数。然后,将预约需求初始位置作为输入量,基于聚类中心修正的合乘站点生成方法生成改进后的合乘站点位置。在此之后,基于新的合乘站点位置更新点集和时间窗。最后,采用Floyd算法计算路网节点对之间的最短运行时间及其对应路径,获得车辆在路网上聚类合乘站点间的运行时间。

3.2 算例说明

基于现有定制公交实际运营情况,本文将定制公交系统发车条件设定为订单请求产生T时间或累计产生N条订单请求,两个条件满足其一即可发车。本例中车辆基本信息、分布情况及其他参数取值见表2~表4。

不同车型车辆基本信息 表2

车型编号	额定载客量 q^p (人)	固定成本 λ_k (元)	车辆等待时间成本 cw_k (元/min)	车辆等待时间成本 ct_k (元/min)
1	5	100	2	1.5
2	10	150	3	2
3	15	200	4	2.5

各场站车辆分布情况 表3

场站	车型1(辆)	车型2(辆)	车型3(辆)
Depot 1	2	2	1
Depot 2	2	1	2
Depot 3	1	2	2

其他模型参数取值 表4

参数	含义	取值
T_{max}	车辆最大走形时间	250min
T_i	乘客最大在车时间	$t_{ce}^i - t_{ss}^i$（根据时间窗规定）
cp_k	k 型车在乘客等待时间成本	3元/min
$c_i(i=1,2,3)$	服务质量指标单位成本	10元/min、8元/min、元/min
$\alpha_i(i=1,2,3,4)$	相关成本权重系数	0.15、0.25、0.3、0.3
$\beta_i(i=1,2,3)$	服务质量指标权重系数	0.4、0.4、0.2
$\alpha、\beta、\gamma$	惩罚因子	1000

3.3 求解结果

3.3.1 静态预约需求定制公交线路规划求解结果

本文所提出的算法对静态线路规划问题的求解结果见表5。

静态线路规划求解结果 表5

车辆编号	所属场站	车辆类型	规划线路服务需求编号	停靠站点
1	1	1	[15↑,20↑,43↑,20↓,15↓,43↓,95↑,95↓]	90,63,4,30,98,47,8,86
2	1	1	[30↑,29↑,30↓,60↑,29↓,81↑,60↓,81↓]	58,34,63,25,61,88,98,98
3	2	1	[26↑,25↑,25↓,26↓,46↑,46↓,56↑,56↓,62↑,62↓]	34,58,61,30,61,26,25,98,47,34
4	2	1	[23↑,23↓,22↑,22↓,24↑,24↓]	34,30,30,4,30,61
5	3	1	[2↑,27↑,2↓,64↑,27↓,64↓]	98,86,34,58,47,8
6	1	2	[18↑,21↑,21↓,18↓,34↑,34↓]	88,30,25,8,80,4
7	1	2	[28↑,17↑,28↓,17↓]	63,80,25,30
8	2	2	[16↑,14↑,16↓,39↑,71↑,39↓,71↓,14↓,78↑,78↓]	61,88,47,80,61,88,88,8,61,30
9	3	2	[5↑,5↓]	34,25
10	3	2	[4↑,4↓,7↑,7↓]	30,86,14,88
11	1	3	[11↑,11↓,13↑,13↓]	47,30,25,34
12	2	3	[9↑,9↓,10↑,10↓]	14,90,30,98
13	2	3	[6↑,19↑,6↓,59↑,19↓,59↓]	98,25,90,34,86,68
14	3	3	[8↑,8↓,12↑,12↓]	63,58,47,30
15	3	3	[1↑,3↑,3↓,1↓,53↑,53↓]	90,98,26,80,61,11

3.3.2 动态预约需求定制公交线路响应求解结果

依据本文模型与算法求解,可得数据测试集中第 2、3、8 条订单请求预约成功。线路调整结果见表 6,其中 $i+$ 表示第 i 条动态预约订单的上车需求,$i-$ 表示第 i 条动态预约订单的下车需求。

规划线路调整结果 表 6

车辆编号	调整前经过路网节点编号	调整后经过路网节点编号	调整后服务需求编号	调整后停靠站点
9	91-85-73-66-55-48-36-35-34-18-19-20-21-22-23-24-25-24-31-40-51-58-69-76-87-93-92-91	91-85-86-92-93-94-93-87-76-69-58-57-56-55-48-36-35-34-18-19-20-21-22-23-24-25-17-6-5-6-17-25-24-31-40-51-58-69-76-87-93-92-91	[3+,5↑,5↓,3-]	94,34,25,5
11	21-22-23-24-25-43-44-45-46-47-46-45-44-43-25-24-34-30-31-24-25-24-23-22-21-20-19-18-34-18-19-20-21	21-22-23-24-25-43-61-78-61-43-44-45-46-47-46-45-44-43-25-24-31-30-31-24-25-24-23-22-21-20-19-18-34-18-19-16-12-13-100--10-14-21	[2+,11↑,11↓,13↑,13↓,2-]	78,47,30,25,34,100
12	79-78-61-43-25-24-23-22-21-14-21-20-19-27-36-48-55-54-65-72-84-90-84-72-65-54-55-56-49-38-29-30-31-40-51-58-59-60-61-78-79-80-81-98-81-80-79	79-78-61-60-59-58-57-56-55-54-65-54-55-48-36-27-19-20-21-14-21-20-19-27-36-48-55-54-65-72-84-90-84-72-65-54-55-56-49-38-29-30-31-40-51-58-59-60-61-78-79-80-81-98-81-99-63-62-79	[8+,9↑,9↓,10↑,10↓,8-]	65,14,90,30,98,99

4 结 语

本文考虑车辆路径问题基本约束以及需求响应情况约束,并同时将运营成本与服务质量两方面作为目标函数的考量因素,构建了定制公交线路规划模型。在问题求解的过程中,本文首先采用层次聚类法生成公交站点,再基于聚类中心修正的合乘站点生成方法对站点位置进行修正,然后使用 Clarke-Wright 算法生成初始定制公交运营线路,针对发车前线路规划设计了基于禁忌搜索的定制公交静态线路生成算法,并针对发车后线路规划设计了动态需求插入算法。之后,本文基于实际路网情况设计算例,验证了模型和算法的有效性。

参考文献

[1] 蔡永旺,杨炳儒.适用于公交站点聚类的 DBSCAN 改进算法[J].计算机工程,2008,34(10):190-192. DOI:10.3969/j.issn.1000-3428.2008.10.069.

[2] 刘喜.城市定制公交线路设计研究[D].长沙:长沙理工大学,2015.

[3] 胡郁葱,陈栩,罗嘉陵.多起终点多车型混载的定制公交线路规划模型[J].广西师范大学学报(自然科学版),2018,36(4):1-11. DOI:10.16088/j.issn.1001-6600.2018.04.001.

[4] 陈汐,王印海,刘剑锋,等.多区域通勤定制公交线路规划模型及求解算法[J].交通运输系统工程与信息,2020,20(4):166-172,186. DOI:10.16097/j.cnki.1009-6744.2020.04.024.

[5] 申婵,崔洪军.基于可靠性最短路的实时定制公交线路优化研究[J].交通运输系统工程与信息,2019,19(6):99-104. DOI:10.16097/j.cnki.1009-6744.2019.06.015.

[6] 韩霜,傅惠.即时响应式定制公交调度优化[J].公路交通科技,2020,37(6):120-127,158. DOI:10.3969/j.issn.1002-0268.2020.06.015.

基于熵值法与 DEA 的城市公交线路组合评价方法

王瑄[1] 齐超[2,3,4] 陈学武[2,3,4]

(1. 东南大学苏州联合研究生院；2. 东南大学江苏省城市智能交通重点实验室；
3. 东南大学现代城市交通技术江苏高校协同创新中心；4. 东南大学交通学院)

摘要 以往对于公交运营服务的评价多采用综合评价方法将多个指标加权后得出一个综合评分值，较难发现关键问题，难以实际指导公交服务的优化改善。本文提出了利用多源数据，基于熵值法与 DEA 的城市公交线路组合评价方法，从固有设施、运行水平、车辆运营三个角度选取相应的指标对公交线路进行评价，并基于苏州市地面公交系统多源数据，进行了实例研究。结果显示该方法可有效找出待改进线路及其存在的问题，以便于提出针对性的改善措施，具有较高的应用价值。

关键词 公共交通 运营服务评价方法 熵值法-DEA 组合方法 常规公交 多源数据

0 引言

常规公交作为城市公共交通的重要组成部分，其运营服务水平关系到城市公共交通的吸引力，关系到城市交通问题的改善。因此，有必要对公交线路的运营状况进行深入分析，特别是需要提出一套可操作性强、简单易行、方便直观的公交线路运营评价方法，用于分析公交线路实际运营状况，辅助公交运营管理部门发现问题线路并能够针对性地提出相应的改善措施，从而提升公交运营服务水平，提高城市公交吸引力，发挥城市公共交通的优势。

对于常规公交线路运营服务的评价目前已有一些研究。Hassan 等[1]、Ryus[2]、蒋新[3]等由层次分析法计算得到各评价指标的权重，以得到系统最终的综合评价水平，反映公交运行的综合状况。这类方法为主观评价法，简单易操作，能结合决策者的经验和专业知识，对定性问题尤其适用，但容易造成主观性过强且需要耗费大量时间得到较为一致的结果。Yao 等[4]提出了针对中国 11 个城市的 SE-NDEA 模型。周媛等[5]基于信息熵来确定多指标模糊综合评价中的指标权重，构建城市公交网络的多层次评价模型。朱文铜等[6]运用使用熵值法计算指标的权重，克服了以往公交线网优化中对目标函数取权重时的主观性。这类方法为客观评价法，完全依赖实测数据，不受决策者的主观因素影响，但可能由于实测数据误差导致最终评价结果与实际结果相差较大。总体来说既有研究多用综合评价方法将多个指标加权后得出一个综合评分值，未能反映某一具体指标的状况，仅得出研究对象排名情况，未能反映对象各指标总体表现，且部分指标数据获取较难，求解烦琐。

鉴于此，本文提出基于熵值法和数据包络法(Data Envelopment Analysis,DEA)的组合评价方法，借鉴机器学习中打包(Bagging)的思想，集成两种方法的结果对公交运营服务进行评价。利用公交 IC 卡、AVL、线路信息等多源数据数量大、易获取、准确度高的特点，从固有设施、运行水平、车辆运营三个角度选取相应的指标来获取线路特征。最后以苏州为例，对苏州市公交线路运营服务进行评价，根据评价结果给出具体建议。本文提出的方法可作为国内城市公交线路运营服务评价的参考，促进企业发现问题并针对性地提出改善措施。

1 熵值法

熵值可用于判断某个指标的离散程度，若离散程度越大，该指标对综合评价的影响越大，熵值也越大。因此可利用熵计算出各个指标的权重,为公交线路运营服务多指标综合评价提供依据。应用熵值法进行城市公交线路运营服务评价的评价流程如图 1 所示,所需要使用的数据主要包括公交 IC 卡数据、AVL 数据、公交线路信息。

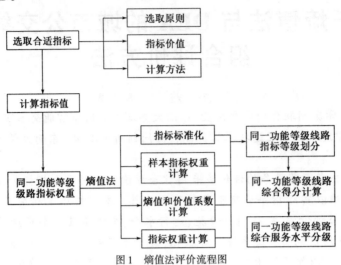

图 1 熵值法评价流程图

1.1 选择指标

对国内外常用标准中出现的公交运营指标总结如表 1 所示。

表 1 常用标准中公交运营指标总结[7,8]

准 则 层	指 标 层
固有设施	线路长度、线路非直线系数、线网密度、线路配车数、万人客位数、站点覆盖率、平均站间距、万人平均配车数
客运水平	站点客流量、线路客流量、断面客流、路段客流不均匀系数、客运周转量
车辆运营	运行速度、公共交通正点率、行车间隔稳定率、行车准点率、发车间隔、发车频率、高峰平峰满载率、车辆人均占有面积、周转率、单程行程时间

基于上述指标,以客观独立、层次清晰、定义明确且有针对性和可比性为基本原则,选取如下能从多源数据(包括 AVL、IC 卡、公交线路信息)中直接计算获取而无须估算的指标:

(1)固有设施方面:

每公里线路配车数

$$n = \frac{N}{L} \tag{1}$$

式中:N——线路配车数,辆;

L——线路长度,km;

n——每公里线路配车数;辆·km^{-1}。

该指标可以直观反映线路的车辆供给状况。指标值越大,表明线路的车辆供给越充足,更能满足乘客出行需求。计算该指标需要公交线路信息、AVL 数据。

(2)客运水平方面:

①发车频率

$$f = \frac{F}{D} \tag{2}$$

式中:F——线路统计时段内发车次数,车次;

D——天数,日;

f——平均日发车频率,车次·日$^{-1}$。

该指标是衡量公交车运行水平的重要指标,对客运能力有直接的影响。指标值越大,表明线路对乘客提供的客运能力越强。计算该指标需要 AVL 数据。

②运行速度

$$v = \frac{L \cdot F}{T} \tag{3}$$

式中：L——线路长度，km；

T——统计时段内各车次单向运行时间之和，h·车次；

F——线路统计时段内发车次数，车次；

v——平均运行速度，km·h^{-1}。

车辆的运行速度一定程度上反映了车辆在道路上的运营效率，以及其在道路上为乘客出行提供运营服务的质量。评价时认为运行速度指标越大，表明运营效率越高，同时乘客感受到的运营服务水平越高。计算该指标需要公交线路信息、AVL 数据。

(3) 车辆运营方面

①车公里客运量

$$PC = \frac{C}{F \cdot L} \tag{4}$$

式中：F——线路统计时段内发车次数，车次；

L——线路长度，km；

C——线路统计时段内刷卡量，人次；

PC——车公里客运量，人次·(车次·km)$^{-1}$。

该指标反映线路在所运营车辆成本投入下的运营效率，车公里客运量越大，表明运营效率越高。计算该指标需要公交线路信息、IC 卡数据。

②线路人均停站时间

$$t = \frac{\text{STime}}{C} \tag{5}$$

式中：STime——线路统计时段内停站时间，s；

C——线路统计时段内刷卡量，人次；

t——线路人均停站时间，s·人次$^{-1}$。

反映了统计时段内线路站点的运行效率，该值越小，反映线路站点运营效率越高，运营服务水平越高。计算该指标需要 AVL 数据、IC 卡数据。

1.2 使用熵值法进行权重计算

利用熵值法为所选取的评价指标计算权重，具体步骤如下[9]：

(1) 指标标准化

先对各项指标进行直线型无量纲化。将各项指标值 x_{ij} 转换为无单位的相对数 x'_{ij}，其数值大小规范在[0,1]内。

(2) 样本指标权重计算

样本指标权重 y_{ij} 指第 i 个样本第 j 项指标占所有样本的该项指标的比重。样本指标权重利用式(6)计算。

$$y_{ij} = \frac{x_{ij}}{\sum_{i=1}^{m} x_{ij}} \tag{6}$$

(3) 熵值 e_j 和价值系数 d_j 计算

利用公式(7)计算指标 x_j 的信息熵值。

$$e_j = -k \sum_{i=1}^{m} (y_{ij} \ln y_{ij}) \tag{7}$$

其中常数 k 和系统的样本数 m 相关联，取 $k = 1/\ln m$。

利用公式(8)计算信息熵价值系数。
$$d_j = 1 - e_j \tag{8}$$
信息熵价值系数 d_j,可以衡量各指标间的差异。熵值 e_j 越小,指标间的差异系数 d_j(即信息熵价值系数)就越大,指标就越重要[9]。

(4)指标权重 w_j 计算

x_j 指标的权重 w_j 可以利用公式(9)进行计算。
$$w_j = \frac{d_j}{\sum_{j=1}^{n} d_j} \tag{9}$$

1.3 使用数理统计方法进行指标等级划分

交通工程中有85%位车速、50%位车速与15%位车速的概念。85%位车速与15%位车速常被用作道路限速的最高限速值与最低限速值。本文参考这一概念,将公交运营指标的85%分位数与15%分位数分别作为公交运营水平优秀与公交运营水平较差的阈值。当公交运营某指标大于其85%分位数时,认为该指标下公交运营水平优秀;当低于其15%分位数时,认为该指标下公交运营水平较差;以50%分位数为界,其两侧认为公交运营水平良好和一般。因此,由公交运营指标值的85%位分位数、50%分位数与15%分位数将公交运营水平从好到差依次被分为了运营优秀、运营良好、运营一般、运营待改进四级,为方便表示,由 A、B、C、D 分别代表。

1.4 线路综合得分计算和分级

$$S(z) = \begin{cases} 25(z - z_{0\%})/(z_{15\%} - z_{0\%}), z \in (z_{0\%}, z_{15\%}] \\ 25 + 25(z - z_{15\%})/(z_{50\%} - z_{15\%}), z \in (z_{15\%}, z_{50\%}] \\ 50 + 25(z - z_{50\%})/(z_{85\%} - z_{50\%}), z \in (z_{50\%}, z_{85\%}] \\ 75 + 25(z - z_{85\%})/(z_{100\%} - z_{85\%}), z \in (z_{85\%}, z_{100\%}] \end{cases} \tag{10}$$

z-指标值 S-某线路指标得分

由公式(10)以百分制确定各线路各指标分值,再通过公式(11)计算线路综合得分。
$$SI = a_1 S_1 + a_2 S_2 + a_3 S_3 + a_4 S_4 + a_5 S_5 \tag{11}$$

式中:S_1——线路每公里配车数得分;

S_2——发车频率得分;

S_3——车公里日客运量得分;

S_4——人均停站时间得分;

S_5——运行速度得分;

a_1——线路每公里配车数权重;

a_2——发车频率权重;

a_3——车公里日客运量权重;

a_4——人均停站时间权重;

a_5——运行速度权重;

SI——线路运营服务综合得分。

最后由线路运营服务综合得分的85%位分位数、50%分位数与15%分位数将公交综合运营水平从好到差依次被分为了运营优秀、运营良好、运营一般、运营待改进四级。

2 DEA 方 法

DEA 方法从运筹学中发展而来,是根据多项投入指标和多项产出指标,利用线性规划对具有可比性的同类型单位进行相对有效性评价的一种数量分析方法。应用 DEA 方法进行城市公交运营服务评价的流程如图2所示,所需要使用的数据、采用的评价指标同熵值法。

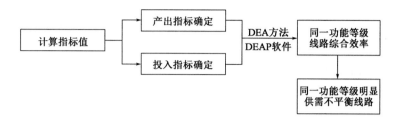

图2 DEA方法评价流程图

2.1 确定投入产出指标

公交线路的综合效率表现为公交线路中的单位资源投入所获得的产品和服务数量与价值的多少。在这个意义上,将上述5个评价指标分为投入指标和产出指标。

将每公里线路配车数、发车频率、人均停站时间3个指标作为投入指标,如表2所示。

投入指标示意图　　　　　　　　　　　　　　表2

投入指标	指标意义
每公里线路配车数	属于线路固有设施的投入成本。为了减少投资和成本,公司对每条公交线路的公交车数量有上限。当该指标值变大时,相应的公交线路上有更多的公交车可用。然而,随着一条公交线路的公交车数量增加,相应的投资也会越来越高[10]
发车频率	属于运营投入成本。公交公司安排的发车次数越多,公司应支付的成本就越高,包括出行时间成本和相应的司机工资和能源消耗
人均停站时间	人均停站时间短意味站点的效率比较高,也可以理解为在每个人的身上投入的时间成本比较少

将车公里客运量、运行速度2个指标作为产出指标,如表3所示。

产出指标示意图　　　　　　　　　　　　　　表3

产出指标	指标意义
车公里客运量	能够反映乘客对线路的需求,车公里客运量越大,表明乘客对线路需求越大
运行速度	一方面,运行速度与乘客的行程时间有一定关联,而使用较短的行程时间到达目的地是乘客的需求;另一方面,停站时间会影响运行速度,且较少的人均停站时间并得到较大的运行速度是公交公司希望的

2.2 计算综合效率

常用的 DEA 模型 C^2R 为[11]:

$$\begin{aligned} &\min \theta \\ s.t. \quad &\sum_{j=1}^{n} A_j \lambda_j + S^- = A_0 \theta \\ &\sum_{j=1}^{n} A_j \lambda_j - S^+ = B_0 B \\ &\lambda_j \geq 0, S^- \geq 0, S^+ \geq 0 \end{aligned} \quad (12)$$

式中,θ 为综合效率值,$A_j = (a_{1j}, a_{2j}, \cdots, a_{kj})$,$j = 1, 2, \cdots, n$;$i = 1, 2, \cdots, m$;$x_{ij}$ 为第 j 个 DMU 的第 i 种投入量,$B_i = (b_{1i}, b_{2i}, \cdots, b_{mi})$,$y_{ij}$ 为第 j 个 DMU 的第 i 种产出量。(A_0, B_0) 为被评价对象。$\lambda_j (j = 1, 2, \cdots, n)$ 为第 j 个 DMU 的组合权重。$S^- = (S_1^-, S_2^-, \cdots, S_m^-)^T$ 与 $S^+ = (S_1^+, S_2^+, \cdots, S_m^+)^T$ 为松弛变量向量。

根据 DEA 有效性判定定理,决策单元综合效率值为1为 DEA 有效,其余决策单元为非 DEA 有效,综合效率值为相对值,可表示在所有决策单元中的效率情况[12]。

3 熵值法与 DEA 组合评价方法

现有研究常采用层次分析法与熵值法结合确定指标权重从而计算得到综合指数值[13-14]。熵值法的优点是可以得到具体分数,反映线路的总体指标表现情况,结果直观,但是对反映运营者较为关心的供需是否平衡的问题反映不够敏感。也有研究使用 DEA 方法对公交线路或企业的绩效、运行管理进行综合评价,通过相对效率进行排名[15][16]。DEA 方法能够较好的找出供需较不平衡的线路,并通过各指标的等级来判断不足的方面为具体分析线路存在的问题并提出改进措施提供依据。但 DEA 效率值是相对的,同时只能反映投入产出情况,而无法从总体表现维度来评价公交线路运营服务。两者各有优缺点,且这两种方法均简单易操作,可以较好的运用到实际应用中,故结合这两种方法对公交运营服务进行评价可以提高判别能力,得到更加客观的评价结果。应用熵值法与 DEA 组合评价方法进行城市公交运营服务评价的流程如图 3 所示。

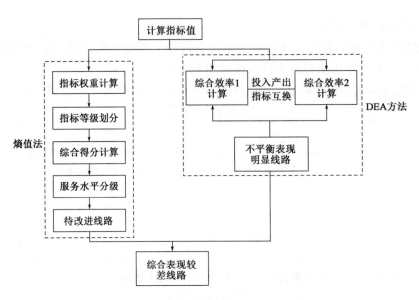

图 3 熵值法与 DEA 组合评价方法流程图

(1)使用 DEA 方法计算线路综合效率

将每公里线路配车数、发车频率、人均停站时间作为投入指标,车公里客运量、运行速度作为产出指标,使用 DEA 方法计算线路综合效率 1 以便于选取出现供给大于需求的问题线路。将投入指标和产出指标互换,再次使用 DEA 方法计算线路综合效率 2 以便于选取出现需求大于供给的问题线路。

(2)基于 DEA 确定不平衡表现明显的线路

将综合效率 1 的上 15% 分位数与综合效率 2 的上 15% 分位数分别作为临界值。以 15% 分位数为界,综合效率 1 低于上 15% 分位数普遍认为投入高于产出较多,综合效率 2 低于上 15% 分位数普遍认为产出高于投入较多,这两类线路大多存在需求和供给不平衡的问题,从中选取出不平衡表现较为明显的线路(指标评价等级相差 2 个等级及以上)定为待改进线路。

(3)结合熵值法和 DEA 选取综合表现较差线路

选取熵值法综合得分在上 15% 百分位以内的线路,DEA 综合效率 1 在上 15% 以内百分位和 DEA 综合效率 2 在上 15% 以内百分位的线路三者的交集作为综合表现较差的线路。

4 实例分析

4.1 研究范围与数据来源

本文研究范围是苏州市辖区,不含其代管的昆山、太仓等县级市。所使用的数据来源于苏州公交公司提供的公交线路信息、公交线路站点信息、2018 年 10 月 12—25 日公交 IC 卡刷卡数据和 AVL 数据。各数据字段及示例数据如表 4~表 6 所示。

苏州市公交线路信息数据字段说明 表4

字段说明	示 例
线路编号	b9434375-db2d-49c0-9561-938fa7b29071
线路名称	1
线路长度(km)	14.1
线路方向	上行
首站	苏州站北广场公交枢纽
首站经度	120.607147216797
首站纬度	31.3341808319092
末站	公交一路新村首末站
末站经度	120.632263183594
末站纬度	31.2570762634277
线路种类	常规线

苏州市公交IC卡刷卡数据字段说明 表5

字段名称	字段说明	示 例
kbh	卡编号	21500000372337
dealrq	刷卡日期	20181112
dealsj	刷卡时间	10:20:11
flname	线路名称	27
flguid	线路编号	c6e8e0b5-c717-4c19-9dd7-60c6ed438d33
fldirection	线路方向	2.5 产业园
flsname	上车站点名称	胜浦首末站
flsguid	站点ID	ec7dddab-5d60-4bc4-bca7-9d3ae04fa404
qcbh	车辆编号	102372

苏州市公交AVL数据字段说明 表6

字段名称	字段说明	示 例
flguid	线路编号	a3b35bb3-ef5c-45c7-b3e4-e89cf24ff0c7
flname	线路名称	502
fldirection	线路方向	苏州站南广场公交枢纽
flsname	站点名称	富士胶片
flsguid	站点编号	76be2dc7-9d51-c9fd-0474-c456ffa74cef
fdintime	进站时刻	2018/11/12 10:30:54
fdouttime	出站时刻	2018/11/12 10:31:26
fdbuscard	车牌号	苏××××××

根据公交线路在运营网络中承担的功能差异,考虑线路的服务范围、需求水平及供应能力,选择线路长度、是否跨越行政区、刷卡量和配车数这四个指标利用聚类的方法可将苏州公交线路划分为骨架网、主体网、支撑网三个层级,对于三个层级的公交线路可以分别建立标准并进行评价。由于篇幅所限,本文仅选取骨架线路共71条作为研究对象,这类线路具有跨区联系,沿主要客流走廊,穿越大型客流集散点,客运量最大,线路最长,配车数最多,提供最快速、最充分的服务,保证通道的畅通性等特征[17]。

4.2 基于熵值法和DEA的城市公交运营服务评价。

利用上文提出的方法对所研究的苏州公交骨架线路运营服务进行评价。

(1)计算线路指标权重,结果如表7所示。

骨架线路指标权重 表7

骨架线路	每公里线路配车数	发车频率	车公里日客运量	人均停站时间	运行速度
权重	0.19	0.13	0.30	0.05	0.34

(2)计算线路等级划分标准,结果如表8所示。

骨架公交线路指标等级划分标准 表8

骨架线路	A	B	C	D
每公里线路配车数(辆/km)	>1.68	1.05<x≤1.68	0.74<x≤1.05	≤0.74
发车频率(车次/日)	>211	156<x≤211	127<x≤156	≤127
车公里客运量(人次/(车次·km))	>2.75	1.80<x≤2.75	1.12<x≤1.80	≤1.12
人均停站时间(s/人次)	≤24	24<x≤32	32<x≤42	>42
运行速度(km/h)	>23	19<x≤23	18<x≤19	≤18

(3) 计算熵值法综合得分、DEA综合效率1和综合效率2,选取熵值法综合得分在15%百分位以内的线路,DEA综合效率1在15%百分位以内和DEA综合效率2在15%百分位以内的线路三者的交集作为综合表现较差的线路。表9和表10列举了熵值法标准下表现较差的11条线路,其中加粗的为综合表现较差的5条线路。

综合表现较差的骨架线路(1) 表9

线路名	产出				投入						综合得分	综合效率1
	车公里客运量(人次/(车次·km))		运行速度(km/h)		每公里线路配车数(辆/km)		发车频率(车次/日)		人均停站时间(s/人次)			
	等级	数值	等级	数值	等级	数值	等级	数值	等级	数值		
69	D	0.888	A	28.08	D	0.43	D	119	D	47	31.77	1
200	C	1.283	D	16.64	B	1.18	A	213	C	33	34.75	0.403
27	C	1.512	C	18.17	C	0.94	C	139	C	38	37.08	0.598
63	D	1.120	A	23.78	D	0.63	D	75	D	50	37.14	1
166	C	1.217	B	19.86	C	0.79	C	135	C	40	38.04	0.617
55	C	1.718	C	18.97	D	0.71	D	110	C	39	38.72	0.755
8	B	1.843	B	20.02	D	0.57	D	83	C	33	38.85	1
622	C	1.254	B	22.96	D	0.64	D	101	C	38	40.25	0.891
106	D	0.847	B	20.99	C	1.00	A	230	C	41	41.18	0.436
43	C	1.116	A	23.62	C	0.82	D	112	D	65	41.29	0.717
6	D	1.072	B	21.92	D	0.66	B	173	C	33	41.90	0.704

综合表现较差的骨架线路(2) 表10

线路名	产出						投入				综合得分	综合效率2
	每公里线路配车数(辆/km)		发车频率(车次/日)		人均停站时间(s/人次)		车公里客运量[人次/(车次·km)]		运行速度(km/h)			
	等级	数值	等级	数值	等级	数值	等级	数值	等级	数值		
69	D	0.43	D	119	D	47	D	0.888	A	28.08	31.77	1
200	B	1.18	A	213	C	33	C	1.283	D	16.64	34.75	0.403
27	C	0.94	C	139	C	38	C	1.512	C	18.17	37.08	0.598
63	D	0.63	D	75	D	50	D	1.120	A	23.78	37.14	1

续上表

线路名	产出						投入				综合得分	综合效率2
	每公里线路配车数 （辆/km）		发车频率 （车次/日）		人均停站时间 （s/人次）		车公里客运量 [人次/(车次·km)]		运行速度 （km/h）			
	等级	数值	等级	数值	等级	数值	等级	数值	等级	数值		
166	C	0.79	C	135	C	40	C	1.217	B	19.86	38.04	0.617
55	D	0.71	D	110	C	39	C	1.718	C	18.97	38.72	0.755
8	D	0.57	D	83	C	33	B	1.843	B	20.02	38.85	1
622	D	0.64	D	101	C	38	C	1.254	B	22.96	40.25	0.891
106	C	1.00	A	230	C	41	D	0.847	B	20.99	41.18	0.436
43	C	0.82	D	112	D	65	D	1.116	A	23.62	41.29	0.717
6	D	0.66	B	173	C	33	D	1.072	B	21.92	41.90	0.704

由表9可以看出，综合表现较差的线路中200路、106路DEA效率值1均小于0.5，由各指标等级来看，车公里客运量相对较低，但每公里配车数、发车频率、人均停站时间相对较高，说明相对于投入的运力和时间成本，吸引的客流较少。

由表10可以看出，69路、63路运行速度都较高，但是主要问题在于人均停站时间较长，这可能是公交车必须出站进站，但是客流量较少，造成时间成本投入较高的现象。8路相对于车公里客运量，其每公里配车数和发车频率较低。

基于上述评价结果，结合苏州实际情况，可提出以下改善措施：①改善客流量较大交通站点附近公交设施和管理，以保障公交的运行速度、运营稳定性和准时性，从而降低投入成本；②调整发车次数，以减少客流量较少时段的发车次数为主要方向，制定更加精细化的措施以减少运力浪费。需要注意的是，不可一味地减少发车次数。对于客流量大的站点，应结合实际调研，考虑开设区间线或社区巴士，满足这些时段居民必要的出行需求，避免发车次数的缩减对居民正常出行产生影响。

5 结 语

本文提出了基于熵值法与DEA的城市公交运营服务组合评价方法，从固有设施、运行水平、车辆运营三个角度选取相应的指标对公交运营服务进行评价。基于苏州市常规公交系统多源数据，应用提出的组合评价方法进行了实例研究，找出了待改进线路及其存在的问题，并提出了相应的改善措施。本方法通用性较强，适合于各种类型的城市，同时指标易计算，操作性强，具有较高的应用价值。

但本文研究也有一定的不足，在此提出以下展望：①本研究中以刷卡量来代替线路客流量，但实际生活中，公交线路不仅有刷卡客流，还有一定比例的投币客流和手机支付客流。若未来有研究得到某城市的公交刷卡比例则可以更好地反映线路客流情况。②后续若能获得更多类型的数据比如线路配置公交车型及座位数等，可以丰富指标类型，从更多的角度来评价公交运营服务。

参考文献

[1] Hassan M N, Hawas Y E, Ahmed K. A multi-dimensional framework for evaluating the transit service performance[J]. Transportation Research, 2013, 50A(Apr.):47-61.

[2] Ryus P. A Summary of TCRP Report 88: A Guidebook for Developing a Transit Performance-Measurement System [J]. TCRP Research Results Digest, 2003, (56).

[3] 蒋新. 基于多源数据的大城市常规公交运行评价研究[D]北京:. 北京交通大学, 2011.

[4] Yao D, Xu L, Li J, et al. Evaluating the Performance of Public Transit Systems: A Case Study of Eleven Cities in China[J]. Sustainability, 2019, 11(13).

[5] 周媛, 邓卫, 胡启洲. 基于信息熵的城市公交网络模糊评价[J]. 交通运输工程与信息学报, 2008,

006(002):79-84.
[6] 朱文铜,卞兆洋,李海鹏.基于信息熵TOPSIS的公交线网优化方案排序[J].交通科学与工程,2013,29(03):72-76.
[7] 魏贺,戴冀峰."公交都市"考核评价指标体系探讨[J].城市交通,2014,12(05):18-25.
[8] Transportation Research Board. Transit Capacity and Quality of Service Manual (Third Edition)[R]. TCPR Report 165. Washington DC: National Academy Press, 2013.
[9] 张慧丽,谭桂菲.基于DEA-熵值法的公路网交通适应性研究[J].公路交通科技:应用技术版,2018,v.14;No.164(08):305-309.
[10] Liu Z, Wu N, Qiao Y, et al. Performance evaluation of public bus transportation by using dea models and Shannon's entropy: An example from a company in a large city of China[J]. IEEE/CAA Journal of Automatica Sinica, 2020.
[11] 张春勤,隽志才,景鹏.公交企业运营绩效的信息熵与SE-DEA组合评价方法[J].工业工程与管理,2015(1):146-153.
[12] 程晓庆.长沙市公共交通系统运行效率评价及仿真研究[D].长沙:湖南大学,2010.
[13] 王梅力.基于可持续发展理论的绿色交通综合评价研究[D].重庆:重庆交通大学,2016.
[14] 董晓.城市绿色交通发展水平评价及对策研究[D].北京:中国矿业大学,2018.
[15] 胡国政.城市常规公交运行管理系统评价指标体系研究[J].交通运输研究,2012(19):103-105.
[16] 吕慎,田锋,王京元.基于DEA的接运公交运营绩效评价[J].公路交通科技,2010,27(8):96-102.
[17] 许威.城市公交线路功能分级指标研究[D].南京:东南大学,2014.

大型高铁枢纽布局及交通组织特征研究

蔡燕飞[1] 刘安迪[2] 戴继锋[1] 罗彦[1]

(1.中国城市规划设计研究院深圳分院;2.北京大学深圳研究生院城市规划与设计学院)

摘要 当前我国大型高铁枢纽的数量及规模正迅速增长,本文通过梳理我国已建成大型高铁枢纽在城市中的空间布局及发展历程,对枢纽的敷设方式、场站规模、接驳设施等方面的特征进行总结,归纳总结出"分方式接驳、全流程管道化、上落客分流"三种典型接驳组织模式,为后续大型高铁枢纽规划设计提供技术参考。

关键词 大型高铁枢纽 选址布局 交通接驳组织 特征分析

1 基本概况

截至2020年初,全国铁路运营里程已达到13.9万km,高速铁路里程达3.5万km,超过世界高铁里程的三分之二。随着人们出行服务需求多样化,大部分高铁站在原有旅客站房功能的基础上叠合了多种城市交通方式的转换功能和城市综合服务功能,是大型的客流集疏运场所[1]。

《铁路旅客车站设计规范》中对"大型"的规模定义为高峰小时发送量大于等于5000人、小于10000人[2],然而这个定义是针对车站的站房规模,存在一定的局限性[3],结合目前我国高铁站运行的实际情况,场站的站台数量往往决定了车站的总体客流规模和相应的设施规模,因此本文讨论的大型高铁枢纽定义为站台数不小于10的、在高速铁路网中为全国性枢纽或节点地位城市的主要高铁站。

经统计,全国已建成大型高铁枢纽共33座(含香港西九龙站)。

我国的大型高铁枢纽最早从京津地区、中部地区开始建设,超过88%布局于省会城市。随着2003年中国第一条高速铁路秦沈客专建成通车,早期建设的普铁车站被逐步改建为集高铁、铁路、地铁、公交等多种交通方式于一体的大型综合枢纽。2009年京广高铁武广段开通运营,中国正式进入高铁时代,在2010—2018年间全国基本实现各区域高铁互联互通,各大型高铁枢纽在此时期内先后建成。

2 枢纽选址

大型高铁枢纽通常分为郊区型和城中心型[4],从发展历程来看,2008年之前建成的客运站如天津站、沈阳站为城中心型客站;2008年以后大型新高铁枢纽都与市中心相距甚远(南京南站、深圳北站等虽然距市中心约8公里,但考虑当时城市规模也可定义为郊区型);2018年西九龙站的建设引起了业界的反思,深圳新规划的西丽枢纽选址于城市中心区核心地带。

高铁枢纽点的布局选择与城市的发展阶段紧密相关,已完成规模扩张的城市将高铁枢纽布局于城市中心区或距离城市中心区较近的地区,可达性更高;仍处于空间扩张时期的城市将枢纽设于郊区可疏解城中心区压力、引导城市空间结构的调整。

各大型高铁枢纽与市中心区距离(经由百度地图测量) 表1

距离市中心区 d (km)	大型高铁枢纽	数量
$d \leq 3$	石家庄站、兰州西站、天津站、沈阳站、西九龙站	5
$3 < d \leq 6$	杭州东站、重庆北站、天津西站、北京南站	4
$6 < d \leq 9$	汉口站、贵阳北站、南京南站、成都东站、徐州东站、合肥南站、南昌西站、深圳北站、北京西站	9
$d \geq 10$	西安北站、郑州东站、上海虹桥站、昆明南站、重庆西站、广州南站、南宁东站、长沙南站、济南东站、沈阳南站、武汉站、佛山西站、太原南站、哈尔滨西站、大连北站	15

3 枢纽布局

3.1 敷设方式

当前79%的大型高铁枢纽为高架敷设,仅西九龙站为地下敷设。地面站多为早期已投入使用的车站,后期建设的高铁站多采用高架敷设方式。地面、高架两种方式都存在城市景观、噪声振动影响等问题;地下站可有效解决因铁路穿越城市中心区带来的噪音干扰、征地拆迁等影响,但也带来了地下人流、车流集散安全风险等问题,因此应谨慎选择。

3.2 场站规模

车站到发线数量与车站台数相关性强,但接发列车数量相关性却不明显(车站接发列车数量受线路列车资源影响较大),当前部分的大型高铁枢纽存在设计规模过大的问题。(图1、图2)

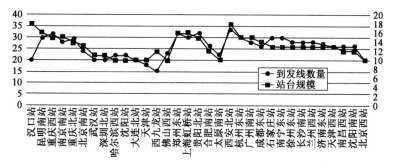

图1 到发线数量与站台规模关系图

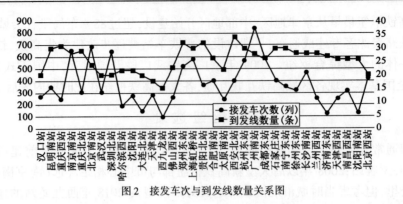

图2 接发车次与到发线数量关系图

3.3 接驳设施

大型高铁枢纽设置地铁、公交、出租车等各类接驳设施,枢纽接发列车数量与地铁、公交线路及停车场规模的相关性呈递增,对于小汽车接驳的依赖度较高;从相关系数的倍数关系来看,公交接驳能力并未得到充分发挥,地铁接驳线路的数量(通常为1~3条)并未对高铁车站停车场规模产生显著影响(图3、表2)。

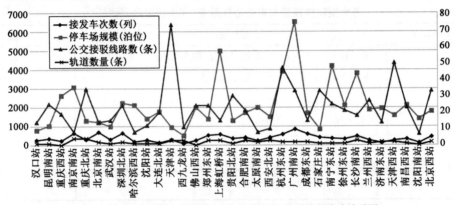

图3 接发车次与停车场规模、公交接驳线路、轨道接驳线路关系图

接发列车次数与接驳设施规模相关性分析表　　　　　　　　　　　　　　　　　　　　表2

	接发车次数(列)	公交接驳线路数(条)	轨道数量(条)	停车场规模(泊位)
接发车次数(列)	1.00			
公交接驳线路数(条)	0.11	1.00		
轨道数量(条)	0.40	0.13	1.00	
停车场规模(泊位)	0.55	0.03	0.12	1.00

停车场规模与枢纽距离市中心的距离也呈现一定关系,郊区型枢纽停车设施规模较大(3000个以上),中心型枢纽停车场规模较小(小于1000个),见表3。

(部分)大型高铁枢纽相关情况数据　　　　　　　　　　　　　　　　　　　　　　　　表3

高铁站	距离市中心区距离(km)	停车场规模	接驳轨道交通条数
上海虹桥站	15	5000	3
广州南站	16	6540	2
南宁东站	10	4200	1
长沙南站	11	3800	3
汉口站	7	800	1
天津站	3	945	3
西九龙站	3	500	3
石家庄站	3	850	1

4 交通组织

4.1 内部组织

目前我国90%以上的大型高铁枢纽均采用线上高架候车,"上进下出"是大型高铁枢纽最为常见的组织模式(达70%);随着地铁接驳客流比重增加,结合地铁敷设方式形成了"下进下出""上进上出"的组织模式;为了满足不同接驳方式到达乘客的便捷性需求,也开始探索多进多出的组织模式,但未广泛应用(表4)。

各大型高铁枢纽敷设方式、客流组织模式　　　　表4

高铁站	枢纽敷设方式	客流组织模式	高铁站	枢纽敷设方式	客流组织模式
汉口站	地面	上进下出	合肥南站	高架	上进下出
昆明南站	高架	上进下出	太原南站	高架	上进下出
重庆西站	高架	上进下出	西安北站	高架	上进下出
南京南站	高架	上下进下出	杭州东站	高架	上进下出
重庆北站	地面	上进下出	广州南站	高架	上下进下出（城际旅客下进下出）
北京南站	高架	上下进下出			
武汉站	高架	上进下出	成都东站	高架	上进下出为主,平进平出为辅
深圳北站	高架	上进上出	石家庄站	地面	上进下出
哈尔滨西站	高架	上进下出	南宁东站	高架	上进下出
沈阳站	地面	上进下出	徐州东站	高架	上进下出
大连北站	高架	上进下出	长沙南站	高架	上进下出
天津站	地面	上下进下出	兰州西站	高架	上进下出
西九龙站	地下	上进下出	济南东站	高架	上进下出
佛山西站	高架	上进下出	天津西站	高架	上进下出
郑州东站	高架	上进下出	南昌西站	高架	上进下出
上海虹桥站	高架	上进下出	沈阳南站	高架	上进下出
贵阳北站	高架	上进下出	北京西站	地面	上进下出

4.2 外部接驳

枢纽接驳面布局分为端部、腰部及四面接驳模式,其中端部和腰部比较普遍。外部交通衔接有三种模式:"分接驳方式"采用不同的专用匝道等将公共汽车、社会车辆等交通引导到不同的空间;"全流程管道"模式采用全流程专用匝道服务,接客车流需经落客区落客后选择至接客平台载客或直接离场;"上落客分流"采用上、下客站分离方式结合到达、出发层车道边分别组织车流(图4~图7)。

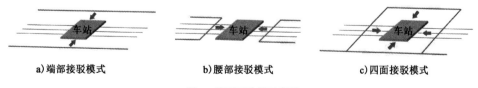

图4　接驳面分类示意图

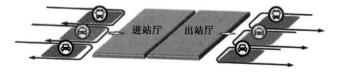

图5　"分接驳方式"流线示意图

图6 "全流程管道"流线示意图

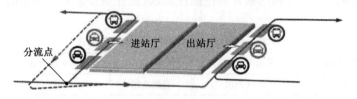

图7 "上落客分流"流线示意图

大型高铁枢纽接驳组织模式情况　　　　　　　　　　　　　　　　　　表5

接驳面	腰部	端部	四面
	13个(40%)	19个(57%)	1个(3%)
外部接驳	分接驳方式	全流程管道	上落客分流
	13(40%)	6(18%)	14(42%)

"分接驳方式"模式为各类公共交通方式配置专用场站与匝道,设施布局相对分散,总体规模大;"全流程管道""上落客分流"模式更注重对车流的定向、分流组织,"全流程管道"落客区瓶颈风险大,"上落客分流"的关键在于对分流点的组织。

5 结　语

我国大型高铁枢纽规划设计工作已积累了丰富的经验:多采用高架敷设方式,形成了"上进下出""上下进下出"的主要人流组织模式;适宜配置1～3条地铁线路进行接驳;小汽车停车场的设置规模应对应枢纽的类型,中心型枢纽停车场泊位宜小于1000个;枢纽外部接驳面以端部、腰部接驳为主,不同的接驳模式具有不同的适应性。结合当前发展形势,建议未来可加强以下方面研究:

(1)增加"即停即走"设施供应:随着旅客出行量的增长及出行模式的转变,出租车、网约车接驳需求大增,应增加"即停即走"设施供应并加强管控。

(2)提升接驳场站设施规模的合理性:应加强社会停车场、公交停车场规模与枢纽客流规模相关性设计,避免出现了利用率较低或资源过饱和的情况。

(3)加强枢纽服务便捷性设计:郊区型高铁站应强化与高快速路网等衔接;城中心型高铁站需同时考虑近、远距离接驳需求,避免"灯下黑"。

参考文献

[1] 唐子涵.综合客运枢纽站流线组织与分析[D].成都:西南交通大学,2010.

[2] 国家铁路局.铁路旅客车站建筑设计规范:TB 10100—2018[S].北京:中国铁道出版社,2018.

[3] 谢雨宏.大型高铁客站站房使用后评价[D].广州:华南理工大学,2019.

[4] 叶嵩.基于乘客出行特征分析的郊区型高铁站选址研究[C]//中国城市规划学会.城乡治理与规划改革——2014中国城市规划年会论文集.北京:中国城市规划学会,2014:831-844.

中小城市公交免费政策下居民出行行为研究
——以济源市为例

李 帅[1]　朱成明[2]　肖新梁[2]

(1.中国建筑第五工程局总承包公司;2.河南理工大学)

摘 要 为研究公交免费政策对居民出行方式决策影响,以济源市为例,通过问卷调查的方式,建立 logistic 模型,分析出行行为的影响因素以及政策实施前后出行方式的变化。结果表明:在公交免费政策下,女性出行者较男性更倾向于选择公交出行,不同年龄的出行者选择免费公交的偏好也不同,年龄越大者越倾向于乘坐免费公交,月收入越高,居民选取公交车出行的概率越低;免费公交政策实施后,选择免费公交出行增长了5%;大部分居民对于济源市免费公交持满意态度。

关键词 公共交通　公交免费　logistic 模型　出行方式选择

1 研究背景

"公交优先"理念的正式提出源于20世纪60年代末的法国。我国免费公交起步较晚,一些城市免费公交的实施之路较为坎坷。2019年2月22日,济源市在财政全额补贴的基础上,城区公交全部实现对市民免费乘坐。

在公交免费的推行过程中,对于"免费公交的影响"及"如何推进免费公交"国内外学者进行了大量的研究。Fujii, S, Garling, T. Kitamura[3]研究快速路封闭情况下,驾驶员对于公交交通的选择和认知,结果表明选择公共交通的可能性更大。Fujii. S[4]通过实验,证明一个月的免费公交票会改变人们的乘车结构。提倡预信号交叉口上游的使用继续提供公交优先,同时尽量减少交通中断。S. Ilgin Guler, Monica Menendez[5]对公交优先通行信号进行研究,提倡一种预信号的实施,可有效降低延迟。Andy Vobora[6]研究了交通区免费服务的财务和运营方面的影响。Astrid De Witte, Cathy Macharis, Olivier Mairesse[7]针对比利时等城市基于第三方支付系统发展的免费公交,提出价格支付应降低公共服务的质量和能力,提高流动性应调整公司政策,以利公共交通。Astrid De Witte, Cathy Macharis, Pierre Lannoy[8]等将布鲁塞尔的学生分成两组,通过对比试验,研究免费公交对于学生旅游行为的影响。谢伟[9]研究了大卖场免费公交乘客行为特性,并制定相应的管理对策。林福成[10]运用博弈论分析了中小城市发展免费公交的可行性,并基于公交满意度建立补贴模型。唐闪闪[11]采用系统动力学构建免费公交影响子系统,从而构建整个免费公交交通模型,并利用实例验证交通模型的可行性。

纵览国内外研究现状,关于出行者出行行为的研究已经相对成熟,而对于免费公交的研究,都倾向于研究公交乘客的变化、公交票价等;而对于免费公交政策前后,居民出行行为的变化的研究较少。虽然部分学者对公交免费后的客流做了预测研究,但是选择公交出行是居民日常出行的一部分,有必要深入研究居民出行方式的选择。

2 问卷调查

2.1 调查问卷

为充分研究公交免费政策下济源市居民的出行方式选择,遵循合理性、客观性、明确性和可实施性等原则,采用SP与RP结合的问卷调查方式[11],设计的济源市免费公交政策下居民出行意愿问卷调查表见图1。

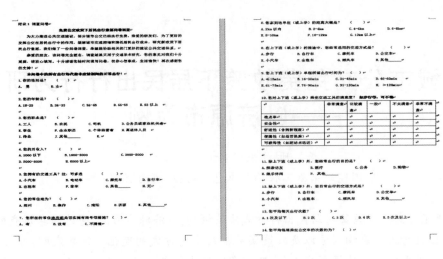

图 1　问卷调查

2.2　数据检验

使用 SPSS 18.0 软件得到公交免费政策下居民出行方式选择的信度统计结果,如表 1 所示。将问卷分为四个部分,分别是个人数据、出行数据、主观性评价与假设场景。第一部分、第二部分、第三部分的 α 值均大于 0.7,虽然第四部分的 α 值略小于 0.7,但是总体 Cronbach's α 值为 0.826,表示问卷整体信度较好。

信度检验表　表1

潜变量	Cronbach's α 值	总体效度
问卷的第一部分	0.87	0.826
问卷的第二部分	0.919	
问卷的第三部分	0.784	
问卷的第四部分	0.673	

效度即是有效程度,是指问卷能够准确测量其题目属性的程度。采用因子分析的方法对问卷的结构效度进行检验。首先要做 KMO 和 Bartlett's 球形检验来判断其能否做因子分析,其值有效范围为 0.5 ~ 1,越接近 1 表示越适合做因子分析,之后进行因子分析[12](表 2)。

各部分因子分析表　表2

变量	KMO	Baetlett 球形度检验			因子载荷
		近似卡方值	df	Sig.	
问卷的第一部分	0.847	186.182	12	0.000	0.870
问卷的第二部分	0.785	147.875	28	0.000	0.854
问卷的第三部分	0.771	154.538	36	0.000	0.830
问卷的第四部分	0.753	242.580	21	0.000	0.797

2.3　问卷调查初步分析

此次调查共获得有效样本 500 份,其中男性占比 59.7%,常住地为济源的占比 85%,上班族占比 11.95%,平均月收入为 2731 元,其中每位受访者对 7 种假设情景中的选项进行选择,因此获得了 854 个假设情景的选择结果。

91.04% 的受访者的年龄介于 18 ~ 25 岁之间,2.99% 的受访者的年龄在 26 ~ 35 岁之间,5.97% 的受访者的年龄在 36 ~ 45 岁之间;受访者多为学生或者上班族,分别占总体的比例为 74.55% 和 11.95%,受访者拥有私家车的比例占 30.91%。

绝大多数是居民对当前济源市公交的态度是满意,占比61.82%,然而数据显示,68.75%的居民认为济源市免费公交的效果一般,或者效果不好。有63.64%的居民对免费公交政策持支持态度,有27.27%的受访者持中立态度。

3 基于 logistic 模型的出行方式影响因素研究

3.1 模型构建

在济源市实施免费公交的政策下,设各个因素(性别、年龄、职业、月收入、交通工具、出行距离、出行目的等)形成前提是指示器,因素的选择方式设定为多因素,对问卷调查得到的数据进行二项 logistic 回归研究。其中样本数量为500条,被选中的样本数493条,接着通过分析,得到初始方程中的变量和初始预测分类结果,因为初始方程模型中没有因素,只有一个常数,结果十分不理想。在初始模型的基础上多次迭代,最终收敛后,得到了公交车出行影响因素的最终分析结果(表3)。

最终分类预测表 表3

已 观 测		已 预 测		
		出行方式		百分比较正
		其他	公交车	
步骤0 出行方式	其他	161	231	42.6
	公交车	175	326	83.1
总计百分比				89.6

注:1. 模型中包括常量。
    2. 切割值为500。

从表3可以得到,在最终模型,由于引入了出行方式、出行距离等影响选择公交车的因素,模型的预测百分比得到改善。非公交出行的数值变化为161,预测百分比变化为42.6%,而公交出行的数值变为326,预测百分比为83.1%,总体预测正确率为89.6%。

因此,按照表3所示二项 Logistic 回归分析研究的结果,选择公交出行的可能性比已知的显著性程度 α(本论文取0.05)小的变量为性别、年龄、月收入、职业、出行距离、出行时长、步行距离、公交费用、小汽车拥有量等,以上变量已经可以确定为对选择公交出行存在显著性作用的因素。由此可得,二项 Logistic 回归分析也表明了所选各个因素之间的相关性矩阵,如表4所示。

出行各变量间的相关性矩阵 表4

	Constant	性别	年龄	月收入	职业	步行距离	出行时长	出行距离	公交费用	小汽车拥有
Constant	1.000	.061	.018	-.366	.093	.252	-.162	-.116	-.522	-.350
性别	0.061	1.000	.126	-.086	.038	-.053	-.003	.002	-.061	-.259
年龄	.018	.126	1.000	-.071	-.010	.061	-.194	-.027	.044	-.041
月收入	-.366	-.086	-.071	1.000	-.040	-.046	.113	-.049	.053	-.072
职业	.093	-.038	-.010	-.040	1.000	.020	-.176	-.032	-.213	-.108
步行距离	-.252	-.053	.061	-.194	.113	1.000	-.012	-.012	.088	.110
出行时长	-.162	-.003	-.194	-.027	-.049	-.032	1.000	-.176	.162	.156
出行距离	-.116	.002	-.027	-.049	-.032	-.011	-.282	1.000	.006	-.232
公交费用	-.522	-.061	.044	.053	-.213	.088	.162	.006	1.000	.201
小汽车拥有	-.350	-.259	-.041	-.072	-.108	110	.156	-.232	-201	1.000

经过以上分析,根据表4,得到公交出行的 Logistic 回归方程:

$$LogitP = 2.181 + 0.061X_1 + 0.18X_2 - 0.366X_3 + 0.093X_4 + 0.252X_5 - 0.162X_6 - 0.116X_7 - 0.522X_8 - 0.350X_9$$

3.2 出行方式变化及原因探析

从表中可以看出评价量(出行方式选择)与公交费用有较强的相关性,其相关系数为 -0.522;出行距离与出行时长和评价量(出行方式选择)的相关性相对较弱,相关系数为 -0.116 和 -0.162;性别、年龄与职业基本与评价量无关,系数分别为 0.062、0.116 和 0.042;月收入、步行距离小汽车拥有则与评价量成弱负相关的关系,系数为 -0.366、-0.252 和 -0.160;由以上变量与评价量之间的 Pearson 相关系数绝对值的大小,可以直接得到各变量对评价量(出行方式选择)的具体影响因素,很明显可以看出公交费用对评价量(出行方式选择)较高,因此,公交费用的定价高低将极大地影响居民出行方式的选择。

在公交免费政策下,女性出行者较男性更倾向于选择公交出行;不同年龄的出行者选择免费公交的偏好也不同,年龄越大者,越倾向于乘坐免费公交,中年人更趋向于其他方式出行,青少年对公交出行较为热衷。上班族、学生选取公交出行的可能性较大;相对于短距离出行,长距离出行选择公交的可能性较小。月收入越高,居民选取公交车出行的概率就越低;乘坐公交车需要步行距离越远、公交乘车时间越长越会减少公交出行的概率。同时,相对于公交收费而言,该样本的被访者对价格不太敏感,从而引起公交免费前后,通勤出行的出行方式结构没有太大变化。

4 公交免费政策效果评价以及中小城市公交发展策略

4.1 公交免费政策效果评价

以上分析研究表明,济源市实施公交免费政策以来,公共交通的吸引力并没有得到明显的改善。随着社会经济的发展,出行方式变得更加多样化,居民的出行需求日益增加。居民个人机动出行对公共交通出行存在排挤影响,机动出行正以快速、舒适等优势与公共交通展开剧烈的竞争。对于中小城市而言,竞争只会更加剧烈。

以济源市为例,实施公交免费政策后,城市公交的客流虽然短期上升幅度较大,可是从长远的角度来看,效果并不理想,公共交通并没有吸引到出行者。因此,对于每个城市而言,是否实施公交免费政策,需要经过详细的研究部署,且实施公交免费政策并非提升公共交通吸引力的唯一途径。

4.2 中小城市公交发展策略分析

对于中小城市而言,实施免费公交政策无法提升公交车吸引力,那相关部门应当立即止损,积极探索,大力发展公共交通,探索多途径增加公共交通的分担率。

一是加大绿色交通出行的宣传,女性、无小汽车人群、中低收入人群等更趋向与选择公交出行,因此在倡导公交出行时,**更要关注此类人群的公交出行体验,加大宣传力度**,促使选择公交出行成为习惯。二是加强基础设施建设;加大城市公交基本设施构建,建立大容量公交体系,合理增加城市公交运营网络。具体而言,合理规划城市公交线路,增设公交车辆数,合理安排公交车站间距等。三是不断提升服务质量;可以利用互联网等智能交通途径,减少乘客缺少零钱而无法乘坐公交。同时,可以开展定期优惠活动。

5 结 语

本文以济源市为例,探索了中小城市公交免费政策下居民出行方式,通过问卷调查,建立了 logistic 模型,分析居民出行方式的影响因素,对济源市公交免费政策进行了简单评价,结果表明济源市免费公交政策实施以来,并没有提高公交吸引力,并浅析了中小城市公共交通发展的道路。

免费公交所涉及的因素较多,是一项庞大的系统工程。由于调查数据等因素的限制,本文研究还存在着许多不足。对于不足,将在以后的工作中持续学习,对论文进行改进,以期完善论文的研究成果。

参考文献

[1] 唐闪闪.基于系统动力学的免费公交交通模型研究[D].西安:长安大学,2016.

[2] Lin D, Allan A, Cui J. The impact of polycentric urban development on commuting behavior in urban China:Evidence from four sub-centres of Beijing[J]. Habitat International,2015,50:195-205.

[3] Fujii S, Garling T, Kitamura R, Changes in driver's perceptions and use of public transport during a freeway closure: effects of temporary structural change on cooperation in a real-life social dilemma[J]. Environment and Behavior, 2001, 33(6): 796-808.

[4] Fujii S, Kitamura R. What does a one-month free bus ticket do to habitual drivers? [J]. Transportation, 2003, 30(1):81-95.

[5] S. Ilgin Guler, Monica Menendez. Pre-signals for bus priority: basic guidelines for implementation[J]. Springer Verlag Berlin Heidelberg, 2015.

[6] Andy Vobora. Fare-Free Service at Lane Transit District: An Overview of Financial and Operational Impacts[J]. Fare-free Services Overview, 2008.

[7] Astrid De Witte, Cathy Macharis, Olivier Mairesse. How persuasive is 'free' public transport? A survey among commuters in the Brussels Capital Region[J]. Transport Policy, 2008(15): 216-224.

[8] Astrid De Witte, Cathy Macharis, Pierre Lannoy, et al. The impact of 'free' public transport: The case of Brussels[J]. Transportation Research Part A, 2006(40): 671-689.

[9] 谢伟.大卖场免费公交乘客行为与设计管理策略研究[D].上海:同济大学,2009.

[10] 林福成.基于博弈论的城市免费公交研究[D].广州:华南理工大学,2011.

[11] 王方.基于SP调查的行为时间价值研究[D].北京:北京工业大学,2005.

[12] 盛骤,谢式千.概率论与数理统计[M].北京:高等教育出版社.1989,264-304.

Exploring the Impacts of Accessibility Measures to Public Transport Equity with Decomposition of Zenga index

Zhigang Yao　Yuhao Fu　Jie Yang

(Department of transportation, College of transportation engineering, Chang'an University)

Abstract　There is relatively little research on how different accessibility measures affect the results of equity evaluation. In this paper, we compared buffer method of accessibility to transit with road-network decay method to evaluate public transport equity of Haining City, China. The buffer method is the most commonly used measure, while the road-network decay method is more in line with the actual. Zenga index and its subgroup decomposition were used to explore the impacts of accessibility measures to the values of Zenga indices between/within rural and urban areas. The decomposition of Zenga index shows that the majority contribution of regional inequality of public transport comes from inequalities of public transport between urban and rural areas. The results indicate that the inequality index of buffer method is higher than that of the road-network decay method, that is an overestimation of inequality with buffer method caused by the factor of population density. This study presents suggestion to choose appropriate accessibility methods for public transport equity evaluation.

Keywords　Public transport equity　accessibility　buffer method　Zenga index

1 Introduction

Measurement of spatial equity to public transport is increasingly concerned as planners and policy makers always pursue public transport equity to all residents in their jurisdiction. Some researches on public transport equity have shown that accessibility can effectively measure social equity and service deprivation, so accessibility is used as an indicator of public transport supply and measure equity[4][8]. Accessibility refers to the ease with which activities at one place may be reached from another via a particular travel model. It is generally be divided into place-based accessibility and people-based accessibility, which various measures have been proposed and implemented. People-based accessibility makes assessment more accurate but requires multiple data, while place-based accessibility is still widely used due to the easily understanding and implement[7]. In the latter method, the buffer method based on the specified Euclidean distance threshold is the most widely used. However, the buffer method has been shown consistently overestimate population within the service area since actual walking distance within the buffer is greater than the Euclidean distance used to generate the buffer Therefore, improvements on the Euclidean distance buffer methods such as the polygon buffer method (buffer generated by network distance)[14], the network ratio method (population distributed evenly along the network)[2] or the distance decay method (population decaying with distance) are also widely used to measure[14] access to transit stops.

Various approaches of transportation equity have been presented in the past few decades. such as, Loerenz curve, Gini coefficient, Thei index and Atkinson index But these measures have defects to draw different conclusions for the evaluation of PT equity. Gini coefficient does not satisfy the additive decomposition properties, and Thei index always seriously overestimate the inequality within subgroups and underestimate the inequality between subgroups even to negative values, The decomposition of Atkinson index is more complex and the aversion parameter setting of its equation is often subjective[1][6][9][11]. Zenga index, received more attention as its excellent advantages[13]. which can measure the inequity at various points of the distribution and reflect each observation's contribution to the overall inequity, and it can also decomposable into two multiplied contributors, additive contributors and sub group contributors[12].

When access the accessibility of public transport, the use of accessibility methods that take different factors into account can result in different accessibilityresults, which can also be used to evaluate the equity of public transport as a level of provision. Therefore, if decision makers choose accessibility as the basis for their equity evaluation, they must know how different the accessibility values obtained by the chosen accessibility calculation method are, and further how much it will affect the regional equity evaluation, and whether it will be different in different regions[8].

This paper takes two commonly used methods to measure accessibility to transit stop: the circular buffer method for straight-line distance and the polygon buffer method for road network distance with a distance-decay function. We use these methods to measure accessibility to transit stop in Haining City, Zhejiang Province. The results of accessibility are used to measure the equity of public transport services, and to compare and analyze how different accessibility methods will affect the equity evaluation.

2 Methods

2.1 Calculating public transport accessibility

In this paper, data such as bus stops, bus routes and traffic analysis zones (TAZ) are used to measure public transport (PT) accessibility. The accessibility to transit stop can be calculated with Equation (1):

$$A_S = \frac{P_S}{P_T} F \tag{1}$$

where, A_S is PT accessibility; P_S is the number of population in the PT station buffer area; P_T is total population; F is the frequency of bus services for each PT station. Here we use two methods: European distance buffer (circular buffer) method and road network distance decay method. The standard walking distances used to delimit service areas in most transit research are 0.25 miles (400 m) for bus stops, here we also use 400m as walking threshold of a buffer area of bus station.

(1) Buffer Method

The buffer method assumes a uniform distribution of population within traffic Analysis Zones (TAZ). This paper applied the transit supply index proposed by Delbosc and Currie (Delbosc & Currie, 2011). The transit accessibility was calculated as Equation (2):

$$A_{Bi} = \sum_{j=1}^{n} \sum_{L \subset L_j} \frac{S_{ij}}{S_i} (f_l t_l) \tag{2}$$

where i is the TAZs number, j is the transit stop access coverage number, l is the transit route number, A_{Bi} is the accessibility index for the TAZs, n is the number of walk access buffers to stops in each TAZs, S_{ij} is the area of buffer j in TAZs i (transit stop can be located outside the TAZs i), S_i is the square kilometer spatial area of the TAZs i, L_j is the transit route passing through the stop access coverage j, f_l is the frequency of transit route l (number of transit per hour), t_l is transit route l operating time (hours).

(2) Road network distance decay method

The network-ratio method assumes that population is evenly distributed along all streets (Biba et al., 2010), based on this we consider the station coverage area to be a polygonal coverage area with a network distance threshold of 400m, within which population density decays along the road network. The calculation formula of the corresponding accessibility index is as Equation (3)-(4):

$$P_{Si} = \sum_k \int_0^{d_k} f(d) \rho_N dd \tag{3}$$

$$A_{NC_i} = \sum_{j=1}^{n} \sum_{l \subset L_j} \frac{P_{Si}}{P_i} (f_l t_l) \tag{4}$$

The only difference is ρ_N, here the ρ_N is population density along the road network, people/km. where A_{NC_i} is accessibility of traffic analysis zone i; d_k is the Euclidean distance from centroid to station, $f(d)$ is distance decay function, km, ρ_N is population density of coverage area, people/km².

The distance decay function here considers the negative exponential form, corresponding to the decay function as Equation (5)-(6), where d_0 is the distance threshold, 400km.

$$f(d) = e^{-\beta d} \tag{5}$$

$$\beta = -\frac{\ln 0.01}{d_0} \tag{6}$$

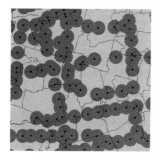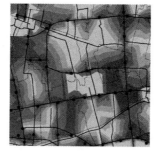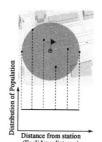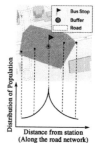

Fig. 1 Two methods to measure accessibility to transit stop

2.2 Zenga Index Decomposition

Based on the ratios between lower and upper arithmetic means, Zenga index is a new approach of inequality. Further, Radaelli and Zenga suggested its decomposition by subgroups (Radaelli, 2010; Zenga, 2007) For the accessibility distribution $\{(NSI_i, p_i): i=1,\cdots,n; 0 \leq NSI_1 < \cdots < NSI_n; \sum p_i = P\}$, P is the total population, P_i is the cumulated p_i. Therefore, the point inequality index I_i is defined as Equation (7)

$$I_i = 1 - \frac{\bar{M}_i}{\overset{+}{M}_i} = 1 - U_i \tag{7}$$

where $\bar{M}_i$ is the lower and $\overset{+}{M}_i$ is the upper means, U_i measures the uniformity between the lower and the upper group, representing the proportion of $\overset{+}{M}_i$ occupied by $\bar{M}_i$. The synthetic inequality measure can be calculated as the weighted arithmetic mean of the point measures I_i. The minimum and maximum value of I is 0 and 1 respectively indicating the case of no inequality and maximum inequality as Equation (8):

$$I = \sum_i \frac{p_i}{P} I_i = 1 - U \tag{8}$$

Define p_{iu} and p_{ir} represent the population of the value NSI_i in urban and rural respectively. The key point of the decomposition allows a comparison both within the same subgroup and between two different subgroups as follows Equation (9)-(10):

$$_{u,r}U_i = \frac{_u\bar{M}_i}{_r\overset{+}{M}_i} \tag{9}$$

$$_{r,u}U_i = \frac{_r\bar{M}_i}{_u\overset{+}{M}_i} \tag{10}$$

Therefore, the overall synthetic uniformity index U can be decomposed into a within and a between components as follows Equation (11):

$$U = \sum_i \left(_{u,u}U_i \frac{_uP_i}{P_i} {_uw_i} \frac{p_i}{P} + {_{r,r}}U_i \frac{_rP_i}{P_i} {_rw_i} \frac{p_i}{P} \right) + \sum_i \left(_{u,r}U_i \frac{_uP_i}{P_i} {_uw_i} \frac{p_i}{P} + {_{r,u}}U_i \frac{_rP_i}{P_i} {_rw_i} \frac{p_i}{P} \right) \tag{11}$$

where the weight $_uw_i$ is the upper group share of urban, $_uP_i$ is the cumulated p_{iu}, similarly, $_rw_i$ is the upper group share of rural, $_rP_i$ is the cumulated p_{ir}.

3 Data

The data in this article are from the public transport system in Haining City, Zhejiang Province. Haining City is located in the southern wing of the Yangtze River Delta, north of Zhejiang, and is under the jurisdiction of Jiaxing City, with a land area of 700.50 km^2 and a resident population of 843600 in 2017, under the jurisdiction of four streets, eight towns, 225 administrative villages (communities). In 2003, Haining City took the lead in the country in carrying out the reform of rural passenger transport, promoting the integrated development of urban and rural public transport, and all rural passenger transport lines in the area under its jurisdiction have achieved bus operation. As of December 2017, Haining City has 104 bus routes (including 37 urban buses, 44 urban-rural buses, 11 intercity buses, and 12 community buses), 1164 stations, and 487 operating vehicles, with a total annual passenger traffic of 34.68 million.

4 Results

4.1 Different methods to measure PT accessibility

With the two methods mentioned above, two sets of accessibility values are obtained. Here we draw box plots of the two sets of accessibility data. The original distribution of the two sets of accessibility values and the normalized value distribution are shown in the box plot as follows. We observed that the data are described by the five-number generalization method, the buffer method most of the values are distributed in the lower value areas (0-50 and 0-25 respectively), and there are more high value outliers determined by the box plot (the maximum is more than 2000, 350 respectively), the box plot is considered more than 1.5 times the IQR (the middle quartile is very different) for the data outliers, the outliers determined from the box plot analysis), indicating that the accessibility values calculated by this methods is concentrated near the lower value, and there are more observations with very high accessibility values.

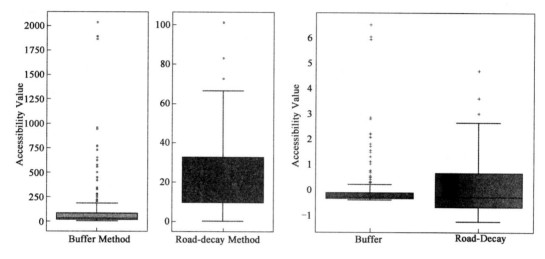

Fig. 2 Raw data & normalized data box plot of two methods

Compared with the buffer method, the accessibility value distribution obtained by the road decay method, shows a larger difference. Significant increase of box indicating that the accessibility value distribution is no longer concentrated in the low value region, but spans about two to three value bands (0-2.5-5-7.5, 0-20-40). It can also be observed that the number of outlier points determined by the box line diagram is significantly reduced compared to the previous two methods, indicating that the number of high outliers of accessibility values is significantly reduced, and most values are more reasonable from the statistical distribution point of view.

Since Haining City contains two types of regions: urban and rural, we plot the histogram with kernel density curves to compare the differences in the distribution of accessibility values when regions are divided into two types. The following figure shows the histogram and kernel density curves of the accessibility by urban and rural areas for both methods.

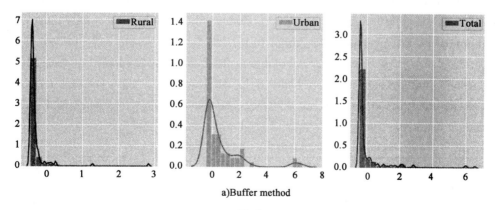

Fig. 3

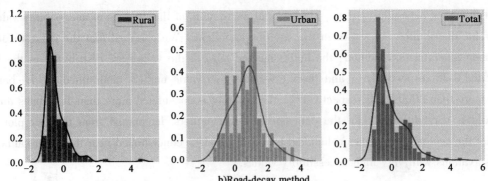

Fig. 3　Histogram with kernel density curves of two methods

It can be seen that the accessibility values from buffer method are generally distributed in the lowest value range (rural: -0.5-1.0, urban: -0.5-2.0). It can be seen that after considering passenger decay, the distribution of accessibility values is richer, showing more variability, which is especially evident in urban areas, with better differentiation for the data itself. This is mainly because the buffer method only takes into account the station coverage and the density of the surrounding population, but not the decreasing effect of the number of people served, which has a large error with the actual situation, in some urban areas with high population density and station coverage there will be extremely high accessibility values, resulting in more normalized data concentrated in the range of low values; and after taking into account the decay of the population served along the road distance of the station, which is more close to actual situation. Some TAZs with high accessibility values for high population density and high coverage areas are also reduced by decay function, so that the normalized accessibility value distribution is more realistic and tends to obey a normal distribution.

Then, we plotted the accessibility values to show how the accessibility values vary depending on the method geographically. Here we employed the Jenks natural discontinuity classification method of software ArcGIS 10.5 to classify accessibility values into six groups.

It can be seen from the figure that the buffer method (left) does not have a clear effect on the accessibility classification of the whole city due to the distribution of accessibility values in the lower value intervals for more TAZ. Haining city as a whole shows a low value accessibility distribution, the rural area only shows a high value distribution in the central and western part of the TAZs, but only one value interval higher than the surrounding area; and the central part of the city shows a very high accessibility value. The figure on the right shows the distribution of accessibility values after considering the decay of the passenger. Compared to the left graph, the accessibility distribution changes significantly, and the overall hierarchical map is more colorful, with significant differences in accessibility values for different TAZs. In urban area, the accessibility is highest in the center and decreasing in the periphery. It can be seen that the accessibility method, after considering decay function allows for a better differentiation of accessibility values between regions, with a more distinct hierarchical coloration, which helps to identify areas with higher or lower accessibility values and to compare the differences.

4.2　Measure PT equity based on Zenga index

The Zenga inequality index (hereinafter referred to as the Z index) was adopted to assess the magnitude of inequity. The value of the Z-index is the area between the curve and the X-axis. For each method, we plot the inequality curves for rural, urban and city as a whole, and calculate the corresponding Z-indexes for each method as follows (Tab. 1).

Zenga index in different regions　　　　　　　　　　　　　　　　Tab. 1

Method	Total Z Index	Rural Z Index	Urban Z Index
Buffer method	0.9390	0.8854	0.9104
Road decay method	0.7684	0.7429	0.7381

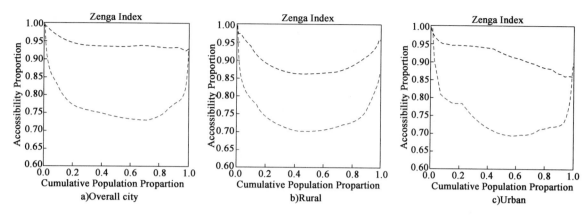

Fig. 4 Zenga index curve in different regions

From the values of Z-index and the relative positions Z-index curves by each method, we find that whether in urban or rural areas or in general, the buffer method yielding higher values of the inequality index (overall: 0.9390, rural: 0.8854, urban: 0.9104), whlie the road decay method is lower (overall: 0.7684, rural: 0.7429, urban: 0.7381). This also indicates that when using the accessibility values obtained by buffer method as a measure of transit equity, which assuming an even distribution of the population served, the resulting inequality index values are high and most inequitable for the regional measurement of transit resource inequality. This is mainly due to the differences in accessibility values between the different methods. When used buffer method, station coverage and population density are the main factors influencing accessibility, which can cause a bias in accessibility values for different population densities and bus coverage in urban and rural areas. This results in some TAZs have very high accessibility, which is an overestimation of the actual accessibility of the error. So this leads to a large gap in accessibility index between areas, and also makes the regional inequality index measurement results are high. The road decay method is more in line with the actual passenger arrivals, which effectively reduces the errors caused by the surrounding population for the accessibility calculation and further reduces the value of the high accessibility region, which also makes the results of the equity measurement more equitable and closer to the actual situation.

In addition, we find that the overall Zenga index of the region is higher than the Zenga index of the urban-rural divide, while the comparison of the size of the Zenga index of the urban-rural divide shows that the relationship is different depending on the method used. The buffer method has Z urban > Z rural, while the road decay method yields Z rural > Z urban. This may be due to the higher density of the road network in the urban, taking the road network into account in some areas of the urban to play a neutralizing role in the value of high accessibility, and the road network as a reference system to attenuate the effect of the attenuation of passengers more obvious, which makes the measurement of the results for the urban more equitable, while for rural areas of the road network density is less obvious for the effect of low density.

5 Discussion

In the previous section we got different accessibility methods for the Z-index for total region, urban and rural areas, but based on the Z-index resuluts we cannot judge which area's transit resource allocation is more inequitable based on the size of the Z-index value alone, because the urban and rural Z-indexes are calculated separately and are not directly related to each other, and for a deeper exploration of the sources of inequality we need to decompose the regional overall Z-index. Here, the total Z index is decomposed into two subgroups, urban and rural, and the results of decomposition are shown in the table below.

Zenga Index Subgroup Decomposition Tab. 2

Method & Zenga Index	Subgroup Decomposition			Total	Contribution rate
	Groups	Rural	Urban		
Buffer method					
Z = 0.9417	Within group	0.1325	0.1551	0.2876	30.54%
	Between group	0.6267	0.0274	0.6541	69.46%
Road decay method					
Z = 0.7639	Within group	0.2209	0.1104	0.3312	43.36%
	Between group	0.3755	0.0572	0.4327	56.64%

By doserving the results of the subgroup decomposition, it can be found that the total Zenga index can be divided into four parts: within rural groups, between rural groups, within urban groups, and between urban groups, and the inequalities can be grouped into two parts through horizontal summing, i. e., inequalities within subgroups and inequalities between subgroups, and the contribution rates obtained by the two methods are different. Among them, the difference between the two contributions obtained by buffer method is larger (30.53% within group and 69.46% between groups), and the difference between the two contributions by road decay method is smaller (46.36% within group and 53.64% between groups), but in general, no matter which method is chosen, there is a contribution of inequality between subgroups that is larger than the contribution of inequality within subgroups, which also indicates that for the overall city, inequality between subgroups, which is unequal access to public transport resources between urban and rural areas, is the main cause of overall city inequality, which is made particularly evident by the use of the buffer method, where the contribution of within group inequality is about 30% ~40% higher than between group inequality, and this gap is reduced but does not disappear after using decay method, and the contribution of within group inequality is still a higher fraction, which also indicate that the chosen different accessibility method causes differences in contribution values, but may not affect the evaluation results.

6 Conclusions

In this paper, two accessibility measures, buffer method and road decay method, were selected to investigate the impacts of accessibility methods on the evaluation of public transport equity. The buffer method assumes that passengers distribute within the buffer area evenly, while the road decay method considers that the distribution of passenger decays along the road network around stations. Zenga index and subgroup decompositions were used to access equity.

Accessibility values to public transport obtained with the two methods are different. Most normalized values obtained with the buffer method distributed in low range. It can be found that when we consider actual distribution of the population and use the decay method, the accessibility values are more heterogeneous and distinguish more clearly among TAZs. Based on the values of accessibility to public transport with the two methods, the Zenga indices of rural, urban and overall region were calculated respectively. Equity indices based on the buffer method may overestimate inequality outcomes. However, the buffer method is still widely used by researchers(Delbosc & Currie, 2011; Gutiérrez & García-Palomares, 2008; Zhao et al., 2003), so we should be cautious when choosing accessibility methods to evaluate equity.

Decomposition of the overall Z-index into two subgroups, rural and urban, we can find that both methods have higher contributions between subgroups than within subgroups. It indicates that the unbalanced public transport service between urban and rural is the majority contribution of the overall inequality. Buffer method makes difference between the two subgroups much greater.

The appropriateness of accessibility measures is closely related to the purpose of accessibility analysis, the purpose of this paper is not to try to clear which accessibility measure is the best in general. Road decay method capture more aspects of transit accessibility, but they are not easy to use in real because of limited data. While buffer method is usually relatively easy to interpret and use. This paper can make recommendations regarding which measure(s) to use in evaluative studies of service delivery and to examine to what extent some accessibility measures overestimate the public transport inequity. For further research, we can use routes and timetable data to evaluate access to destinations via public transit for a more comprehensive measure of the equity of public transport systems.

7 Acknowledgments

This research was sponsored by a grant from the Haining Transportation Bureau.

References

[1] Amir S, Mortazavi H, Akbarzadeh M. A Framework for Measuring the Spatial Equity in the Distribution of Public Transportation Benefits[J]. 2017,20(1).

[2] Biba S, Curtin K M, Manca G.. A new method for determining the population with walking access to transit[J]. International Journal of Geographical Information Science, 24(3), 347-364. https://doi.org/10.1080/13658810802646679.

[3] Carleton P R, Porter J D. A comparative analysis of the challenges in measuring transit equity: definitions, interpretations, and limitations. 2018, 72,64-75.

[4] Delbosc A, Currie G. Using Lorenz curves to assess public transport equity[J]. Journal of Transport Geography, 19(6), 1252 – 1259. https://doi.org/10.1016/j.jtrangeo.2011.02.008

[5] Gutiérrez J, García-Palomares, J C. Distance-measure impacts on the calculation of transport service areas using GIS[J]. Environment and Planning B: Planning and Design, 35(3), 480 – 503. https://doi.org/10.1068/b33043

[6] Hamidi Z, Camporeale R, Caggiani L. Inequalities in access to bike-and-ride opportunities: Findings for the city of Malmö[J]. Transportation Research Part A: Policy and Practice,2019, 130(October), 673-688. https://doi.org/10.1016/j.tra.2019.09.062

[7] Lucas K, Wee B Van, Maat K. A method to evaluate equitable accessibility: combining ethical theories and accessibility-based approaches[EB/OL]. https://doi.org/10.1007/s11116-015-9585-2

[8] Neutens T Schwanen T, Witlox F, et al. Equity of urban service delivery: a comparison of different accessibility measures[EB/OL]. 42. https://doi.org/10.1068/a4230

[9] Radaelli P. On the decomposition by subgroups of the gini index and zenga's uniformity and inequality indexes[J]. International Statistical Review, 2010,78(1), 81 – 101. https://doi.org/10.1111/j.1751-5823.2010.00100.x

[10] Ricciardi A M, Xia J C, Currie G. Exploring public transport equity between separate disadvantaged cohorts: A case study in Perth, Australia[J]. Journal of Transport Geography, 2015,43, 111-122. https://doi.org/10.1016/j.jtrangeo.2015.01.011

[11] Souche S, Mercier A, Ovtracht N. The impacts of urban pricing on social and spatial inequalities: The case study of Lyon (France)[J]. Urban Studies,2016, 53(2), 373 – 399. https://doi.org/10.1177/0042098014563484

[12] Wang C, Guo Y, Shao S, Fan M., et al. Regional carbon imbalance within China: An application of the Kaya-Zenga index[J]. Journal of Environmental Management, 2020,262, 110378. https://doi.org/

[13] Zenga M. Inequality curve and inequality index based on the ratios between lower and upper arithmetic means[J]. InStatistica & Applicazioni：V, 1, 2007. Vitae Pensiero. https：//doi.org/10.1400/209575

[14] Zhao F, Chow L F, Li M T, et al. Forecasting transit walk accessibility：Regression model alternative to buffer method[J]. Transportation Research Record, 1835, 34-41. https：//doi.org/10.3141/1835-05

基于POI数据的公共服务设施步行可达性分析——以上海市为例

余淼[1] 王洋[2]

(1. 中国城市规划设计研究院上海分院；2. 交通运输部公路科学研究院)

摘 要 城市公共服务设施为居民提供生存和发展所需的资源和服务。合理的空间布局有利于保障社会公平和稳定发展。本文基于POI数据,将上海市的公共服务设施分为7类,并使用最近距离法,选择从各街道和乡镇到各类公共服务设施的最短步行时间,作为评估空间可达性水平的指标。结果表明,各类设施的可达性水平具有相似的空间格局：可达性水平较高的街道和乡镇集中在城市的中心,并从中心到外围可达性水平逐渐降低。最后,定量评价各市辖区的设施达标情况,并根据地理位置和人口密度的不同,提出了差异化的公共服务设施配置和可达性改善策略。

关键词 公共交通规划与管理 最近距离法 可达性 公共服务设施 兴趣点 上海市

0 引 言

城市公共服务设施是指为公民提供教育、医疗、体育等公共服务的社会基础设施。城市公共服务是城市居民赖以生存和发展的重要资源和服务,直接决定着城市公共服务的质量。合理的空间分布有利于政府公共服务资源的公平配置,有利于保障社会公平和稳定发展,有利于实现"基本公共服务均等化"目标。

交通可达性可以理解为利用某种特定的交通系统从某一给定区位到达活动地点的便利程度,是城市交通规划的重要依据。可达性可以根据不同的标准进行分类：广义的可达性包括可进入性、可获得性、可接受性、可容纳性和可支付性五个方面,其中可进入性和可获得性主要反映空间信息,称为空间可达性[1]。可达性是衡量城市公共服务设施服务水平的重要指标[2,3]。

从目前涉及居住区或社区层面的公共服务设施配置要求来看,对城市不同的地理区位均采用统一的可达性配置要求。而承担不同功能及有着不同人口集聚程度的城市各区域,公共服务设施的数量和密度都有着明显差异。本文以上海市公共服务设施步行可达性分析为主要研究内容,通过对现状问题的总结,探索不同区位人口密度与公共服务设施配置的关系,提出城市公共服务设施优化与提升策略。

1 方法与数据

1.1 研究数据

本文旨在评估上海市公共服务设施步行可达性,公共服务设施的位置数据需要从互联网地图的POI数据中获取。POI(Point-of-Interest)是指一切可以抽象为点的地理对象,它们与居民生活密切相关,如超市、菜市场、体育馆、餐厅等。网络地图的POI数据具有数据量大、覆盖面广、精度高、更新速度快等优点,其中包括位置和类别属性信息。

1.2 研究方法

国内外学者提出了许多不同的可达性评价方法,如比例法、缓冲区分析法、最短距离法、两步移动搜索法等。近年来,随着地理信息科学技术的飞速发展,城市公共服务设施空间可达性的研究方法和模型得到了迅速的发展。研究对象主要集中在基础教育[4-5]和医疗卫生[6-7]等领域。

本文选取与居民生活需求最密切相关的公共服务设施为研究对象,根据各项设施的功能特点,公共设施分为七大类:餐饮类设施、游憩类设施、交通服务设施、科教文化设施、生活服务设施、体育休闲设施、医疗保健设施。由于本文研究的公共服务设施处于居住区层面,更倾向于保障居民的基本生活需要,居民希望通过最短的距离或时间获得基本的公共服务,因此采用最近距离法。本文选取上海市的214个街道和乡镇内最靠近几何中心的居住小区为抽样点,通过高德地图的路线规划 API 批量计算出居住小区与附近七类公共服务设施的最短步行时间。

2 公共服务设施可达性评价

2.1 公共服务设施可达性空间分布特征

将各街道、乡镇的居住小区至七类公共服务设施的最短步行时间通过 ArcGIS 进行可视化,如图1所示。各街道至各类公共服务设施的最短步行时间越短,可达性越高,街道颜色越深,反之,颜色越浅。可以看出,七类公共服务设施可达性水平由中心城区向外围区域均有呈现可达性水平较低的街道增多、可达性水平较高的街道减少的趋势。

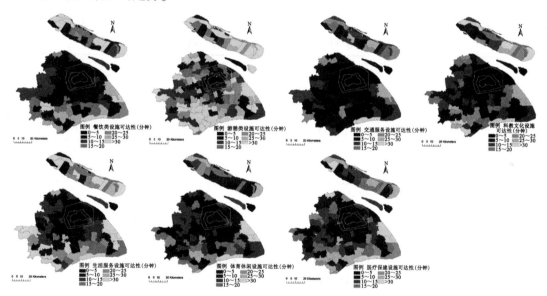

图1 各类公共服务设施步行可达性空间分布

将最短步行时间分组,计算七类公共服务设施的数量和比例。各街道和乡镇至医疗保健设施的最短步行时间在15min以内占比仅67.3%,配置水平较差;各街道和乡镇至餐饮、交通、科教文化、生活服务、体育休闲设施的最短步行时间在15min以内占比均在80%以上,配置水平较高。

2.2 公共服务设施可达性分析

2.2.1 公共服务设施达标率分析

调查表明,人们在出行活动中可以接受15min以内的步行,超过15min大多数人会避免采用步行方式,而采用机动车出行。用"达标率"表征上海市16个县级行政区公共服务设施的达标情况。"达标率"为每个行政区中,步行到各类公共服务设施在15min以内的街道和乡镇,占每类地理区位街道和乡镇总数的比例。统计结果如图2所示。

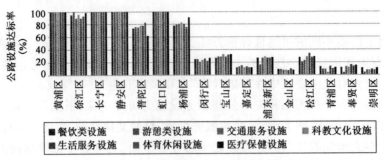

图 2 上海市下辖县级行政区公共设施达标率

不难看出,上海中心城区内的设施达标率普遍较高:黄浦区、徐汇区、长宁区、静安、虹口区的设施达标率均在 80% 以上;郊区的设施达标率水平普遍较低:嘉定区、金山区、青浦区、奉贤区、崇明区的设施达标率均低于 20%;同时,上海市辖区的各类设施达标率水平存在差异:普陀区的体育休闲设施达标率较高达到 83%,而医疗保健设施达标率仅为 62%;杨浦区与普陀区情况相反,医疗保健设施达标率较高为 91%,而体育休闲设施达标率仅为 76%。松江区、浦东新区的游憩类设施达标率与其他设施相比也处于较低水平,嘉定区、闵行区的各类设施达标率水平差异较小。

2.3.2 公共服务设施达标率与人口密度关系分析

为探究公共服务设施的达标率是否与地理区位有关,对不同地理区位的七类公共服务设施达标率与人口密度进行相关性分析,相关性分析结果见表1。可以发现,七类公共服务设施的达标率与人口密度均显著相关,且呈现正相关关系,即居住区所在区位的人口密度越高,公共服务设施可达性的达标率越高。

人口密度与七类公共服务设施达标率相关性　　　　　　　　　　　　表1

	餐饮类设施	游憩类设施	交通服务设施	科教文化设施	生活服务设施	体育休闲设施	医疗保健设施
N	16	16	16	16	16	16	16
均值	50.7%	49.1%	49.9%	51.0%	51.5%	50.9%	51.7%
标准差	0.392	0.417	0.396	0.403	0.387	0.395	0.394
皮尔逊相关系数	0.947**	0.947**	0.953**	0.946**	0.949**	0.951**	0.932**
Sig.	0.000	0.000	0.000	0.000	0.000	0.000	0.000

注:**表示在 99% 置信水平(双侧)上显著相关。

绘制不同地理区位七类公共服务设施达标率与人口密度的分布图(图3),对比来看,主城区内的黄浦区、徐汇区、长宁区、静安区、普陀区、虹口区和杨浦区的七类设施达标率和人口密度均处于较高水平:各类设施达标率均在 62% 以上,人口密度最小为 18120 人/km²。其他地区的设施达标率和人口密度均处于较低水平:各类设施达标率在 0~33% 间浮动,人口密度最大为 7536 人/km²。

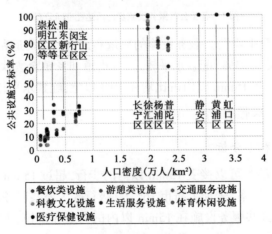

图 3 不同人口密度区位的公共服务设施达标率

3 基于人口密度的公共服务设施步行可达性提升策略

在公共服务设施建设过程中,除了要考虑设施空间布局的数量外,还要考虑区域的人口需求。针对上海不同地理区域人口密度的差异,探讨公共服务设施的配置和提高可达性的策略。一方面,城市规划应充分考虑社会公平性,在发展城市重点地区的同时也要考虑落后地区的状况,通过公共服务设施的规划建设,带动片区发展,适度提高片区的城市更新活力,从而提升城市的整体公平性。与此同时,在"存量规划"的背景下,设施质量的提高远远优于数量的增加,如设施服务水平的提高、服务范围的扩大、缓解公共服务设施的压力和拥挤。另一方面,要注意改善慢性交通系统。在自行车道和人行道的规划和建设中,建设一个连通性强、运行有序、安全、低碳的缓慢移动的生活空间,改善区域居民的生活环境,提高城市居民的生活质量。尤其重视综合商业、文化娱乐、景观功能区慢行系统设置,以新城市主义理念为指导,构建慢行生活圈,引导和满足出行活动需求。

4 结 语

本文利用高德地图 API 获取上海市七类公共服务设施的 POI 数据,计算居住区至最近的公共服务设施的最短步行时间,将其作为各街道乡镇七类公共服务设施的可达性水平,采用达标率指标评价 16 个市辖区七类公共服务设施达标情况。评价结果发现不同地理区位公共服务设施达标率差异明显,其中中心城内达标率最高,外围地区公共服务设施达标率较低(小于 20%)。通过相关性分析,发现人口密度与七类公共服务设施达标率都存在显著的正相关关系,即人口密度越高,七类公共服务设施达标率越高。

参考文献

[1] Penchansky Roy D B A, Thomas J William. The Concept of Access: Definition and Relationship to Consumer Satisfaction [J]. Medical Care, 1981, 19(2): 127-140.
[2] Pooler J A. The Use of Spatial Separation in the Measurement of Transportation Accessibility [J]. Transportation Research, 1995, 29(6): 421-427.
[3] 宋正娜,陈雯,张桂香,等. 公共服务设施空间可达性及其度量方法[J]. 地理科学进展, 2010, 29(10): 1217-1224.
[4] 刘安生,赵义华. 基于可达性分析的常州市乡村地区基本公共服务设施布局均等化研究——以教育设施为例[J]. 江苏城市规划, 2010(6): 6-8.
[5] 孔云峰,李小建,张雪峰. 农村中小学布局调整之空间可达性分析——以河南省巩义市初级中学为例[J]. 遥感学报, 2008, 12(5): 800-809.
[6] 付加森,王利,赵东霞,等. 基于GIS医疗设施空间可达性的研究——以大连市为例[J]. 测绘与空间地理信息, 2015, 38(4): 102-105.
[7] 邓丽,邵景安,郭跃,等. 基于改进的两步移动搜索法的山区医疗服务空间可达性——以重庆市石柱县为例[J]. 地理科学进展, 2015, 34(6): 716-725.

新能源汽车推广政策对消费者购买汽车的效果研究

高 蕾 王碧玲 柳靖钰

(北京交通大学经济管理学院)

摘 要 近年来传统能源带来了严重的环境污染问题,新能源推广政策备受关注。以往学者研究集中于单一政策并预设作用机理,未考虑多种政策综合效果及消费者的真实反应。本文运用焦点小组访谈法,探讨了供需两侧政策效果以及补贴退坡背景下较为可行的互补替代政策。研究发现,消费者认为基础设施建设以及补贴优惠政策较重要。政策通过减少新能源汽车购置成本、提高汽车性能使人们有购车欲望。影响消费者购买新能源汽车的阻碍因素为性能与基础设施建设,激励因素为新技术及社会潮流,消费者对新能源汽车的购买意愿受疫情影响较小。本文提出,政策制定时应考虑消费者购车的原因,从刺激消费者购买欲望的因素出发。制定政策并加大基础设施建设。

关键词 政策分析 焦点小组访谈 新能源汽车购买意愿 作用机制

0 引言

近年来传统燃油汽车带来了严重的大气污染,发展新能源汽车成了世界各国的共同选择[1]。2001年新能源汽车研究项目被列入中国"十五"期间的"863"重大科技课题,但我国新能源汽车产业的发展尚处于不成熟阶段,需要政策来推动。然而,现有政策普遍存在推广度不够、吸引力不足、缺乏创新等问题,未能有效提升消费者对新能源汽车的购车意愿[2-3]。已有研究从区域或国家层面分析了新能源汽车推广政策对消费者购车行为的影响,但是多聚焦单一政策的影响[4],对多种政策的综合作用缺乏深入分析,且未从消费者真实反馈分析政策的作用机制[5-6]。此外,新冠肺炎疫情给新能源汽车带来了新的冲击[7,8],在此背景下消费者购车意愿产生了哪些新的变化,又该如何通过相关政策促进新能源购车需求回升,尚未有文献进行讨论。

本文通过设计、实施焦点小组访谈,收集消费者对多种新能源汽车推广政策的真实评价和反馈,探讨供需两侧政策效果以及补贴退坡背景下较为可行的互补替代政策。本文主要研究的问题有:①消费者对现有不同新能源推广政策的干预效果和互动关系如何评价?②差异化政策对消费者购车意愿的影响机理是什么?③疫情及其他因素对消费者购车有哪些影响?本文的创新主要有以下几点:第一,是从消费者行为视角对多种政策效果进行评价,并研究补贴政策互补替代关系;第二,本文以消费者反馈真实数据信息为基础,分析差异化政策作用机理;第三,分析疫情新背景对新能源汽车购车行为的影响,为疫情背景下刺激新能源汽车推广政策的选取和制定提供实证参考。

本文的框架展开如下:首先介绍焦点小组访谈方法,介绍样本招募和数据收集的过程,之后运用描述性统计对访谈结果进行数据整理,综合各问题访谈的回答和数据分析结果得出结论。

1 焦点小组访谈

1.1 访谈提纲设计

焦点小组访谈法通过对访谈对象表达的内容与观点的分析,深入研究行为的内涵意义,能够找到人们特定思想或行为的准确原因,最终得出或者验证某种结论。其突出优点在于可以真实可靠地获取丰富的信息[9]。本文研究影响消费者对新能源汽车购买意愿的政策及其他因素,由于政策背后作用机理不清晰,无法提前设置,且其他影响因素太多,难以量化分析,所以我们选择焦点小组访谈的方式。

访谈主要包括以下五个部分:
(1)现行政策认识:探究消费者认为最具代表性的新能源汽车推广政策及其效果判断。
(2)购车补贴替代政策:从消费者行为视角探究其他政策对财政补贴的替代效果。
(3)政策影响机制:探究不同推广政策鼓励消费者购买新能源汽车的影响机制。
(4)其他因素影响:挖掘其他非政策因素对消费者购买新能源汽车的促进或者阻碍作用。
(5)疫情对购车意愿影响:探究疫情期间消费者对新能源汽车推广政策的了解程度及作用效果评价。

1.2 样本招募和数据收集

在进行焦点小组访谈之前,我们通过发送短信等方式向80人发送了邀请,最终有20人接受邀请,样本回复率为 25%。访谈最终在 2020 年 8 月至 9 月之间进行(三名学生成对进行),以线上腾讯会议的方式进行焦点小组访谈,访谈分四次完成,每次参与人数为 5 人,持续约 2 小时,所有的采访都被记录。样本基本情况如图 1 所示。

基本信息	类别	选项	频数	频率(%)
个人信息	性别	男	7	35
		女	13	65
	年龄	小于30岁	15	75
		30~40岁	2	10
		40~50岁	3	15
		50岁以上	0	0
	教育程度	高中及以下	0	0
		本科	20	100
		硕士及以上	0	0
	工资收入	小于3000元/月	15	75
		3000~6000元/月	2	10
		6000~9000元/月	3	15
		9000元/月及以上	0	0
	工作状态	全职	5	25
		兼职	0	0
		实习	0	0
		学生	15	75
	户籍	北京户籍	7	35
		北京周边户籍(冀、津)	0	0
		其他户籍	13	65
家庭信息	家庭组成	1人	0	0
		2人	0	0
		3人	11	55
		3人以上	9	45
	孩子	无	15	75
		有——初中及以下	0	0
		有——高中及以上	5	25
	家庭收入来源	1人工作收入	2	10
		2人工作收入	15	75
		3人及以上工作收入	3	15
	家庭机动车保有量	无	0	0
		1辆	7	35
		多于1辆	13	75

图 1 样本基本情况

2 结 果

为了解消费者对于我国现有新能源汽车推广政策的了解程度,我们首先请受访者对政策进行重要性排序,之后询问政策实施效果,最后邀请受访者针对效果一般和比较差的政策提出意见。我们整理出 11 个典型政策为受访者提供参考:①加大基础设施建设政策;②政府补贴、购车优惠政策与税收优惠政策;③免摇号牌照政策;④免通行费政策与停车费免费或优惠政策;⑤限制碳排放政策;⑥旧能源汽车淘汰政策;⑦电池回收政策;⑧购车双重信贷政策。

2.1 现有汽车政策的重要性排序

27% 受访者表示,加大基础设施建设政策是激励消费者最有效的政策,其次为免摇号牌照政策,23% 受访者认为补贴政策最有效,补贴额度决定政策效用。受访者普遍偏好基础设施建设政策、补贴优惠政策与免摇号牌照政策,具体排序情况如图2所示。

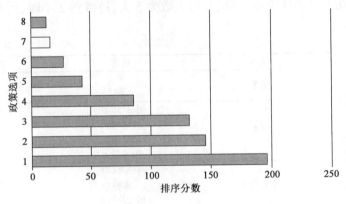

图2 政策重要性排序

2.2 政策补贴的互补替代政策

我们继续探究受访者在现有补贴政策效果衰退现状下,上述政策中哪些可以弥补其补贴效果。

23%的受访者认为涉及减免费用或者优惠政策有较好的替代效果。20%受访者认为加大基础设施建设政策也能起到一定的作用,有较好替代效果。受访者均认可免除相关费用或者给予一定的优惠是政府补贴政策退坡效果的一种弥补政策。

2.3 政策作用的机制

为了对政策作用方式有更深层次的认识,我们进一步向受访者询问政策对消费者个体行为发挥作用的情况。

45%受访者表示加大基础设施建设政策,可提高新能源汽车的使用便利程度,消费者更加愿意购买新能源汽车。14%受访者认为新能源汽车的免摇号政策会增加其购买新能源汽车的想法。36%受访者表示购车优惠和政府补贴,降低了购车成本激,会提高购车欲望。5%受访者认为旧能源汽车淘汰政策会影响其购买意愿。政策从生活便利度、时间及购车成本、社会影响等方面使人们有购车的欲望。

2.4 其他影响因素

通过假设情景,进一步探究其他非政策因素对消费者购车的促进或者阻碍作用。

23%受访者表示相对于新能源汽车,他们仍会选择传统汽车,认为新能源汽车普及程度不高,并且对技术水平和性能存在怀疑。阻碍大家购买新能源汽车的因素主要是性能与基础设施建设。图3总结了影响消费者车购买新能源汽的激励因素与障碍因素。7%受访者认为环保和成本低增加了他们的购车意愿,17%受访者认为环保和未来发展起劣影响其购车意愿。33%受访者没有一定的品牌偏好,汽车的性能、使用成本、技术成熟度等和新能源汽车的优质性能与新技术会促使其购买。17%受访者认为朋友家人会影响其购买新能源汽车的意愿,另外17%受访者表示不会有明显从众心理。

障碍因素	激励因素	障碍因素	激励因素
车辆行驶性能	采用新技术	购车价格	车辆外观内饰
实际出行需求	周围环境包括家人朋友的影响	社会潮流	社会潮流
基础设施不完善	车辆原产国		

图3 影响消费者购买新能源汽车的障碍因素与激励因素

2.5 疫情对购车意愿的影响

为探究新能源汽车推广政策在疫情时期发挥的作用,我们向受访者询问疫情对他们购车及出行心理的改变和影响。在疫情的影响下,20%受访者表示认识到私家车的重要性,会使有购车意愿的消费者直接去购买私家车。13%受访者认为目前没有政策可以使自己改变购车选择,但16%的受访者认为如果购车补贴和购车优惠力度较大就会去选择新能源汽车。4%受访者表示了解在疫情期间政府采取了更大力度的优惠和补贴政策以促进新能源汽车的销售,37%受访者表示未在疫情期间了解过新能源汽车相关的推广政策。

3 结　语

本研究通过焦点小组访谈,研究消费者对新能源汽车政策的干预效果和互补关系的评价、差异化政策对其购车意愿的作用机制、疫情及其他因素对其购车意愿的影响。结果表明,消费者认为基础设施建设政策、政府补贴和购车优惠政策和税收优惠政策以及免摇号政策较重要。政策从节约时间及购车成本、提高生活便利度、社会影响等方面使人们有购车欲望。阻碍购车的因素是新能源汽车性能与基础设施建设。疫情影响下,购车补贴和购车优惠力度较大,消费者更有可能选择新能源汽车。政策制定者应充分考虑新能源汽车推广政策作用的机理,加大基础设施建设政策及补贴优惠政策实施,使政策发挥应有的作用与效果。

参考文献

[1] 陈军,张韵君.基于政策工具视角的新能源汽车发展政策研究[J].经济与管理,2013,27(08):77-83.

[2] Kai Chen, Chaoran Ren, Rong Gu, et al. Exploring Purchase Intentions of New Energy Vehicles: From the Perspective of Frugality and the Concept of "mianzi"[J]. Journal of Cleaner Production, 2019, 230.

[3] Lei Wang, Zhong Lin Fu, Wei Guo, et al. What Influences Sales Market of New energy Vehicles in China? Empirical Study based on Survey of Consumers' Purchase Reasons[J]. Energy Policy, 2020, 142.

[4] 祖明,宫群,杨武.消费者环境价值导向与新能源汽车购买意愿关系研究[J].企业经济,2019(06):21-27.

[5] Jizi Li, Yaoyao Ku, Chunling Liu, et al. Dual Credit Policy: Promoting New Energy Vehicles with Battery Recycling in a Competitive Environment? [J]. Journal of Cleaner Production, 2020, 243.

[6] Qian L, Grisolia J M, Sopramanien D. The Impact of Service and Government-Policy Attributes on Consumer Preferences for Electric Vehicles in China[J]. Transportation Research Part A, 2019, 122.

[7] 吴征,刘金周.疫情期间地方新能源汽车促进消费政策分析[J],汽车文摘,2020(10).

[8] 樊雪梅,卢梦媛.新冠疫情下汽车企业供应链韧性影响因素及评价[J].工业技术经济,2020,23-30.

[9] 邢晓秀.焦点小组作为一种研究工具的优点与缺点探析[J].新闻窗,2016(04):52-53.

[10] Wangsness P B, Proost S, Rdseth K L. Vehicle choices and urban transport externalities. Are Norwegian policy makers getting it right? [J]. Transportation Research Part D, 2020, 86.

[11] Wenchao Zuo, Yueqing Li, Yuhong Wang. Research on the Optimization of New Energy Vehicle Industry Research and Development Subsidy about Generic Technology Based on the Three-Way Decisions[J]. Journal of Cleaner Production, 2019, 212.

[12] Yongqing Xiong, Liuying Wang. Policy Cognition of Potential Consumers of New Energy Vehicles and Its Sensitivity to Purchase Willingness[J]. Journal of Cleaner Production, 2020, 261.

[13] Wenbo Li, Ruyin Long, Hong Chen. Consumers' Evaluation of National New Energy Vehicle Policy in China: An Analysis Based on a Four Paradigm Model[J]. Energy Policy, 2016, 99.

[14] Lixian Qian, Jose M. Grisolia, Didier Soopramanien. The Impact of Service and Government-Policy Attributes on Consumer Preferences for Electric Vehicles in China[J]. Transportation Research Part A, 2019, 122

[15] Jingjing Li, Jianling Jiao, Yunshu Tang. Analysis of the Impact of Policies Intervention on Electric

Vehicles Adoption Considering Information Transmission—Based on Consumer Network Model[J]. Energy Policy,2020,144.

保障高速公路畅通问题的研究

刘德雄

(江西省交通投资集团有限责任公司)

摘要 针对当前高速公路以及相关收费站经常出现拥堵现象,分别从高速公路主线车道容量、特殊情况下相关单位联合处置效率以及出口收费站分流效率等方面分析造成拥堵的原因。本文运用案例研究和对比研究,提出保障高速公路畅通的五项应对措施,对目前实施成功的案例进行梳理,在对比的基础上,总结出:保障高速公路畅通是一个系统性工程,需要从车道设计、高速交警快速处理、清障队伍及时疏通、出口收费站科学处置、制度的细化和落实以及社会的理解和支持等方面共同努力,才能较好地实现这一目标。

关键词 高速公路 畅通 措施 收费站 拥堵

0 引言

2020年1月1日,是中国高速公路拥堵现象发生明显变化的分水岭。在这之前,社会抱怨的拥堵现象经常凸显在主线省界收费站。自2020年1月1日起,全国29个联网省份的487个省界收费站全部取消,从根本上解决了以前省界收费站拥堵现象;在这之后,拥堵现象存在两个特点:一是主线上的拥堵只是在特殊情况(交通事故、施工或者恶劣天气等)下才会发生;二是拥堵现象凸显在收费站,特别是一些相邻省份的最近匝道收费站。据交通运输部新闻发言人孙文剑于2020年8月27日发布新闻称:6月、7月两个月,全国高速公路日均拥堵缓行收费站数量为271个。高速公路拥堵现象的新变化,成为高速公路管理者面临的新课题。

本文以沪昆高速江西省境内的一段(456公桩至530公桩)以及该路段上的玉山收费站为例,剖析拥堵规律,提出应对措施,提供政策参考。

1 拥堵主要原因

在高速公路上,出现拥堵现象的地点一般有两处:一处是高速公路主线路段、另一处是出口收费站。那么,造成高速公路拥堵的主要原因是什么呢?

主要原因有以下三个:

(1)一些高速公路设计车道严重跟不上当地车流增加的步伐。一些主线路段车道少,仅有行车和超车2个车道,同时单位时间内通过路段车辆流量大,导致一旦出现货车侧翻等占据2个车道的事故,就会产生恶劣的大拥堵。以2020年8月19日发生在沪昆高速玉山段K485公桩事故为例,该事故发生时间在14:00左右,在14:00-15:00这一个小时内,通过该卡口车辆共计1196辆。也意味着,在分流前,这1196辆车被堵在高速主线上。这些车辆在两个车道上造成大约6649m的拥堵。

(2)特殊情况下相关单位联合处置效率不高是引发拥堵的另一个主要原因。当发生车辆爆炸、车辆火灾或交通事故时,参与处置事故的相关单位如果效率不高,或者没有进行高效的联合处置,那么处置时间就会延长,从而引发拥堵现象。

(3)出口收费站分流效率低。一个出口收费站,不能及时有效地分流车辆,将会导致车辆拥堵到主线路段。以玉山收费站为例:正常情况下,所有车道都能满足车辆通行,但在分流情况下,车流量1h可以达到1196辆,超过平时流量的9倍,这时,ETC车道还能保持畅通,人工收费车辆仍然较多,有622辆,占总车流量的52%,特殊需要检测车道也很缓慢,这两类车道已经形成严重拥堵了。

2 应对拥堵问题的五项措施

根据引起拥堵的三个主要原因,可以采取以下五项措施。

2.1 增加主线路段车道

增加主线路段车道,是传统的治理措施。如改扩建高速公路,将原来的双向4车道改成6车道,或者8车道,能取得一定的成效,但会增加较多的社会成本。主线路段车道的增加与否？首先需要参考该路段高速公路利用率的高低。根据国家公布数据,高速公路利用率较高的地方有上海市、江苏省和北京市,它们产生的经济效益和社会效益之和分别为每千公里135.4亿元、103.7亿元和100.6亿元;而利用率低的地方有青海省、黑龙江省和宁夏回族自治区,它们产生的经济效益和社会效益之和分别为每千公里7.1亿元、12亿元和17.2亿元,差距是如此之大。作为判定改扩建高速公路主线路段车道的标准,利用率的高低是一个主要参考量。其次,影响改扩建的另外一个参考数据,就是高速公路的持续发展态势,数据显示,只有上海和新疆的高速运营是盈利的,全国共亏损4849亿元,而债务余额还有61535亿元。在建设高速公路和改扩建高速公路时,一定要结合实际经济发展形势来规划设计主线路段车道数,交通发展可以适度超前,但不宜过度超前,这既需要国家政策的扶持,更需要科学和系统性经营管理。

2.2 共享信息和资源,系统性提高处置事故效率

高速公路上,处置事故效率的高低与车辆拥堵严重程度成反比例关系。处置一起发生在高速公路上的交通事故,往往需要几个不同单位通力协作。在处置过程中,既需要各单位提高自身的处置效率,更需要他们共享信息和资源,高效运作,系统性提高处置事故效率。

首先需要各单位加强处置效率,如高速交警要做到早发现,抓紧探索将全国报警电话(包括但不仅限于12122)升级到视频的方法,并及时根据现场情况安排工作。同时对于危险路段要尽早发布预警信息,尽早提醒导航人员调整行驶线路;也要利用主线路段情报板,以及其他先进电子预警设备(如预警小精灵)让行驶在附近范围的司乘人员提前知道相关信息,以便他们早做计划。在及时预警的同时,高速交警还要充分利用无人飞机等先进设备,提高勘测定损等工作的效率,然后,根据交通管制时间和程度以及相关收费站和国省道情况,合理采取分段分流形式预防拥堵。施救和清障单位也要加强处置效率,在接到信息的第一时间,对信息进行正确的研判:何时？何地？从哪个入口入？从哪个出口出？需要什么设备和人员？设备规格是多少？都要具体清楚,在清理障碍的时候,需要科学高效。对于出口收费站,要加强的分流效率,在接到分流通知后,立即启动应急预案,开通所有车道,甚至采取借道或者复式收费等形式,简化查验程序,应急分流车辆,并请求地方交警配合疏通已经驶出高速的分流车辆,最大限度地提高分流效率。

其次,需要参与处置事故的各个单位共享信息和资源,系统性地提高处置事故效率。这需要我们建立有序、有效和科学的信息资源共享和联动系统。首要求信息传递必须有序,有时事故的信息来源不一,还需要进行求证。其次要求信息的有效传递,即信息必须规范和标准。最后,要求信息联动必须具备科学性,现场的信息由哪个单位负责？由谁用哪种设备进行正式传递？传递的顺序是什么？都必须具备科学性,信息依次传递到哪一级,都要有科学安排。

2.3 提高ETC使用率

出口收费站的分流能力与ETC使用率的高低密切相关。目前,ETC使用率并不高,如何提高ETC使用率？需要从以下三个方面着手:一是落实好当前ETC优惠政策,当前,国家政策宣传使用ETC至少优惠5%,但是实际上,在有些省份,行驶ETC车道所缴纳的通行费比行驶普通人工车道所缴纳的通行费更高。经调研,江西省联网中心最新计费调整如下:现金收费为"四舍五入"精确到元;ETC收费为"四舍五入"精确到分,ETC计费公式里存在漏洞,目前,江西省联网中心已根据调查结果对高速费率进行了调整,

据报道,交通运输部也已开始统一部署调整。二是做好 ETC 车辆的后续服务,由于前期 ETC 发行服务机构和合作金融机构数量较多,服务水平参差不一,导致不少车主办理了 ETC,却不能正常使用,经常在出口收费站反馈 ETC 后续服务跟不上,应提升 ETC 后续服务水平。三是做好上高速公路必须使用 ETC 的政策引导,随着 ETC 的优点越来越被大众所理解和接受,应该及时出台相应的制度或者政策,引导人们认识到没有 ETC 就不能上高速公路,让 ETC 技术真正保障高速公路的畅通。

2.4 完善高速公路车辆通行费优惠预约通行服务制度

对于运输鲜活农产品、跨区作业联合收割机(插秧机)的车辆,以及国际标准集装箱运输车辆,在认真落实这些优惠政策制度的过程中,查验工作需要较长时间,碰到有逃费嫌疑的车辆,查验时间就更长,因此对于高速收费站而言,查验工作也是一个负担。同时绿通产品标准模糊,各地方理解不一,执行判断较困难,各省运输集装箱车辆和运输绿通产品车辆的司机为了确保享受优惠政策,经常选择临近省界的收费站,于是,集装箱车辆、绿通车和逃费车的拥堵压力也转移到了临近省界的出口收费站。另外,绿通查验方式不规范,也增加了执行者查验难度:查验不严格,放行速度提高了,但利用假绿通而逃费的现象会层出不穷;查验严格会降低收费站的通行效率,还会因查验工作导致堵道,引发矛盾纠纷。

针对这些需要查验才能享受通行费优惠政策的车辆,需要做好三个方面的工作:一是完善制度,对于集装箱车辆,全国优惠政策要统一,才能避免集装箱车辆在各省临近省界的出口收费站不停上下的现象;二是尽快细化查验车辆的政策,结合用户历史数据,对无不合格查验记录的高频用户,探索实行预约后降低查验频次或免查验的激励措施,对于那些在固定时间出入固定收费站,且长期运输固定绿通产品的车辆,可以采取抽查的方式,避免每次都要查验,同时,对于抽查中发现有作弊行为的车辆,也要出台相应的处罚措施;三是做好查验方式的创新工作,当前的查验方式太原始,大部分以人工为主,科技设备极少,严重影响查验效率,因此不仅要从科技设备上创新查验方式,而且要从绿通产品装载的源头方面创新查验方式,可以像集装箱那样设置与装箱单、封箱号等相似的方式来证明所装载产品为绿通产品,从而减少在收费站查验的频次。

2.5 规范处置逃费车

引起拥堵的另外一种特殊车辆就是逃费车辆,处置这些逃费车,极易引起收费站的拥堵,因为任何一起逃费车的处置,从发现、取证、解释、到处理完毕都要花费大量的人力和物力,重要的是需要花费大量的时间来解释,通常在取证的过程中容易引发收费车道的拥堵。在现行新的政策下,司机把 ETC 作为逃费的新通道。经调研,从 2020 年 5 月 6 日至 2020 年 6 月 4 日,对绑定 OBU 为 3 型的货车进行统计调查,在新干北收费站以 3 型货车 ETC 形式的出口,实际上 6 型的货车竟然达到 66 辆,占到该站同时间段出口所有 3 型车辆总数 1038 辆的 6.3%,少扣的通行费达到 15203.72 元,从 OBU 发行省份来看,涉及浙江、上海、北京、辽宁、山东、安徽、河南和福建。针对这种用牵引车车头去办理普通货车 OBU 而导致少扣通行费的现象,目前采取的措施是要求该车辆到原 OBU 发行省份进行更改。这项工作需要多个相关单位密切配合才能完成,为规范此项工作,至少需要以下五个方面,一是司机具备诚信意识,自己的车辆是属于哪种类型,就应该申办与实际车型一致的 OBU;二是 OBU 发行单位在办理 OBU 时,一定要制订严格的审核流程,并且要有监督机制、考核机制,以及事后追责机制;三是作为高速公路管理单位,加强稽查,发现少扣款现象时,及时核查,并将相关车辆信息反馈给相应单位和个人;四是联网中心要做好软件设计、黑名单设计和处理、预防逃费等协调工作;五是社会要加强宣传逃费是违法行为,提倡合法运输,减少因打击逃费而造成拥堵的现象。

3 结 语

如何避免高速公路经常出现拥堵现象?如何提高高速公路的服务品质?既需要高速公路管理单位根据发展形势不断升级高速公路配套的硬件和软件;也需要高速交警、高速路政、施救清障等单位利用先进技术和管理经验联勤联动,共享信息和资源,系统性地提高处置交通事故的工作效率;还需要收费政策的细化、具体和落实;更需要社会对收费政策(推广ETC以及合法运输等)的理解和支持。只有这样,在全国一盘棋的思路下,才能真正保障高速公路安全畅通,促进经济发展。人们对美好生活的追求永无止境,标准只会越来越高,优质服务将永远是稀缺品,只有解决拥堵现象,才能进一步为民众提供畅通舒适的美好出行优质服务。

参考文献

[1] 刘德雄.如何提高ETC使用率？[J].中国公路,2020(8):60-61.
[2] 唐宽厚,杨少填.大数据破解ETC逃费新方案[J].中国公路,2020(8):56-59.
[3] 吴士尹.优质服务永远是稀缺品[J].中国公路,2019(10):93.
[4] 叶向才,麦华东.多措并举,缓堵破局[J].中国公路,2020,No.578(22):46-47.

浙江省高速公路网合理规模研究

程亚杰　何佳玮　李　乐　戴美伟　陈坤杰

(浙江数智交院科技股份有限公司)

摘　要　高速公路网是综合交通运输体系的重要组成部分,确定合理的高速公路网规模对于区域综合交通可持续发展具有重要意义。在分析浙江省高速公路发展现状的基础上,采用国土系数法、连通度法、类比法等方法,分析高速公路网与经济、人口、面积等因素的关系,预测了2035年浙江省高速公路网的合理规模。

关键词　高速公路网　合理规模　国土系数法　连通度法　类比法

0　引　言

高速公路是社会经济发展的重要战略性基础设施和满足公众出行需求的公益性基础设施,是现代综合交通运输体系的重要组成部分[1]。浙江高速公路经多年发展,已从缓解公路交通瓶颈制约逐步转向促进区域间公路运输交流的纽带角色,对于城镇空间发展、枢纽集疏运体系完善等发挥了重要作用。

在建设交通强国背景下,高速公路的发展对于浙江未来更好地承担国家战略、融入长三角一体化具有举足轻重的作用,因此如何把握全省高速公路的合理规模,使其社会和经济效益得到充分发挥,同时满足资源环境承载能力,是浙江省高速公路网规划需要解决的问题。

1　浙江省高速公路现状

1.1　发展成就

浙江省高速公路发展起步于20世纪九十年代。自1991年建成沪杭甬高速钱江二桥至今,经过近30年快速发展取得了令人瞩目的成绩。截至2018年底,全省高速公路通车总里程4421 km,全省"两纵两横十八连三绕三通道"主骨架已经形成,连通沿海港口的主要港区、机场、铁路等重要枢纽,基本实现"县县通高速",建成17个高速公路省际接口。高速公路成为推动"八八战略"实施、保障浙江经济社会发展的大动脉、主通道。

1.2　适应性分析

浙江省高速公路在推动区域协调发展、引领产业转型升级、提高运输供给等方面发挥了突出作用,但对照高水平交通强省的发展要求,在规模结构、服务能力等方面仍然存在不足。

一是总体规模与经济社会发展水平不适应,浙江作为沿海发达省份,与发达国家、东部省份及中西部部分省份相比规模已明显滞后,路网规模与城镇化、经济增长水平不适应。二是主要通道运输能力不足,6车道以上线路比例低,部分路段技术标准偏低。三是对区域一体化的支撑性不足,规划省际接口仅24个,与周边省份的联络有待加强,省内四大都市区辐射能力、互联互通水平有待提高。四是覆盖不均衡,省内加快发展县,以及重要海岛、山区、景区的线路覆盖率偏低,仍存在10万人以上城镇未通高速公路。五是局部网络布局不完善,主通道内相邻平行线路之间缺乏联络,城市过境线布局不完善,路网存在较多T字形枢纽,区域路网沟通不便捷。

2 浙江高速公路网合理规模分析

高速公路作为浙江推进高水平交通强省建设的重点领域,其网络规模和结构与区域经济发展、土地利用情况、城镇人口分布等因素密切相关[2]。本文统筹考虑经济社会发展和交通运输需求,选取国土系数法、连通度法、类比法等,以期确定合理的高速公路网规模,为浙江省高速公路网规划提供依据。

2.1 国土系数法

根据国土系数理论"道路长度与人口和面积的平方根及其经济指标成正比",采用国土系数法来计算区域内的理论公路长度[3],如式(1)所示。

$$L_i = K_i \times \sqrt{P_i \times A} \tag{1}$$

式中:L_i——第i年公路网长度,km;

K_i——第i年区域高速公路面积人口综合密度,km/(100km²*万人)$^{1/2}$;

P_i——第i年区域人口总量,万人;

A——区域国土面积,100km²,浙江省陆域面积取104302 km²,下文同。

浙江省2002—2018年高速公路通车里程、人口和国内生产总值等历史数据,如表1所示。

浙江省2002-2018年高速公路里程、常住人口、GDP 表1

年份	通车里程/km	人口/万人	GDP/亿元
2002	1307	4536	8003.67
2003	1438	4552	9705.02
2004	1475	4577	11648.7
2005	1866	4602	16417.68
2006	2283	4629	15718.47
2007	2651	4659	18753.73
2008	3073	4688	21462.69
2009	3298	4716	22998.24
2010	3383	5447	27747.65
2011	3500	5463	32363.38
2012	3618	5477	34739.13
2013	3787	5498	37756.58
2014	3884	5508	40173.03
2015	3893	5539	42886.49
2016	4062	5590	47251.36
2017	4154	5657	51768.26
2018	4421	5737	56197.15

经回归拟合,得到浙江省高速公路面积人口综合密度 K 与人均国内生产总值之间关系,如式(2)所示。

$$K = 0.7582\ln(P_{Gn}) + 0.1048 \tag{2}$$

式中:P_{Gn}——人均国内生产总值,万元。

根据浙江省国民经济和社会发展远景目标,2035 年全省人均生产总值力争达到发达经济体水平。对比美欧等国发展水平,预计 2035 年全省人均国内生产总值达 4.5 万~6.5 万美元,合人民币 29 万~42 万元,人口将达到 6000 万~6500 万人(下文同)[4]。代入式(1)和式(2),计算得到 2035 年高速公路合理规模为 6648~7652 km。

2.2 连通度法

连通度法是根据网络几何形状结构和节点连通度的分析来预测未来公路网的合理规模,要求首先确定路网节点、路网变形系数和节点连通度等参数[5],其计算公式如式(3)所示。

$$L = D\xi\sqrt{N100A} \tag{3}$$

式中:L——路网规模,km;

D——路网连通度,D 值为 1.0 时路网布局为树状,各节点之间多为两路连通,节点之间的连接性较差,D 值为 2.0 时路网布局为方格网状,节点多为四路连通,规划路网中节点之间连接性较好,D 值大于 3.0 时,路网呈方格加对角线型,节点多为六路连通,路网布局完善;

ξ——路网变形系数,即节点间公路实际长度与直线距离之比,由地形条件决定;

N——区域内节点数;A 为区域国土面积,100km²。

浙江各地区的区域面积、人口密度、城市空间布局以及地理特征存在较大差异,"七山一水两分田"的特点决定了路网连通形态和规模需求有所不同。本研究按人口密度和地形特征将全省划分为浙北、沿海、浙中、浙西南四个区域,基本上反映了地理自然环境、人口和城镇分布以及经济发展水平等不同特点,据此确定不同地区的路网连通度和变形系数。

结合全省 10 万人口以上城镇高速公路全覆盖原则,本规划确定县(市、区)及县以上的省内节点共 71 个,同时考虑浙江高速公路网与省外的连通,确定周边省市的连通节点共 18 个。通过定性定量分析,运用连通度法测算出 2035 年浙江高速公路网的理论规模,如表 2 所示。

连通度法预测高速公路网规模　　　　表2

区域	国土面积/100km²	节点数/个	变形系数/个	连通度	合理规模/km
浙北	345.87	31	1.1	2.2~2.8	2506~3189
沿海	326.30	34	1.1	1.8~2.2	2086~2549
浙中	109.42	9	1.1	1.6~2.0	552~690
浙西南	261.43	15	1.2	1.0~1.8	751~1353
合计					5895~7781

2.3 类比法

类比分析是基于因素分析法的思路提出来的,由于经济发展水平、人口密度、自然条件等因素与高速公路发展规模之间存在着客观、内在的联系,因此,可以根据国外发达国家的发展轨迹,分析研究公路网规模与影响因素之间的相关关系,并借鉴国外的发展情况,并将之与区域国土面积、人口密度、地理特征、以及未来经济发展水平等实际结合起来,分析确定区域高速公路的合理发展规模[6]。

浙江高速公路网合理规模的确定是一项战略性决策,一方面它与区域人口增长、经济发展、运输强度、区位特点等因素密切相关,另一方面也要借鉴和对比世界发达国家的高速公路发展水平。发达国家的高速公路经过几十年的发展后已进入基本稳定状态,以这种稳定状态下的发展水平作为参考,采用类比法可以大致确定浙江高速公路网的长远发展规模。

本文选取部分发达国家和国内省份为类比对象,相关高速公路网规模数据如表3所示。

发达国家及国内省份高速公路网规模　　　　表3

区　　域	年份/年	里程/km	面积/100km²	人口/万人	面积人口综合密度/[km/(100km²*万人)^{1/2}]
韩国	2015	3776	1000	5022	1.68
英国	2015	3641	2436	6410	0.92
德国	2015	12879	3570	8062	2.40
日本	2015	8100	3780	12734	1.17
意大利	2015	6726	3010	5983	1.58
法国	2015	11465	5440	6603	1.91
浙江	2018	4421	1043	5737	1.81
江苏	2018	4710	1072	8051	1.60
广东	2018	9002	1797	11346	1.99

对比国外,浙江按区位特征和人口面积综合指标衡量,高速公路网的发展水平应该与法国、德国等中等国土面积的国家具有较好的可比性,法、德等国高速公路规模已经趋于稳定,其面积人口综合密度基本保持不变,即1.9~2.5。另外法、德等国除发达的高速公路网外还具有完善的铁路网,与之相比,浙江的铁路发展差距较大。对照国外发展情况,浙江高速公路网络规模还有较大上升空间。

对比国内,江苏、广东的平均经济社会发展水平与我省较为接近,可比性较好。浙江省上一轮高速公路规划里程为5000 km,而江苏、广东高速公路规划至2035年里程分别为6666 km、15000 km,高速公路面积人口综合密度指标约2.1~3.3。

对照发达国家和国内同等发展水平省份,在充分考虑区域社会经济发展水平的基础上,确定2035年浙江高速公路网综合密度为2.0~2.9,则浙江省2035年高速公路里程为5003~7551km。

2.4　结果分析

根据上述各方法预测结果,综合考虑未来经济发展水平、人口增长情况及城镇化水平、区域地理特征条件等因素,并经过专家咨询论证,确定2035年浙江省高速公路网合理规模为6700~7600km,如表4所示。

浙江省高速公路网合理规模预测结果　　　　表4

方　　法	合理规模/km
国土系数法	6648~7652
连通度法	5895~7781
类比法	5003~7551
计算取值	6648~7551
专家推荐	6700~7600

3　结　语

高速公路是综合交通体系的重要基础设施,分析和确定高速公路网合理规模,对于促进经济社会发展、提高高速公路建设的可持续性具有重要作用。

本文结合浙江省未来经济社会发展趋势,考虑交通容量需求平衡,运用多种方法对浙江省高速公路网合理规模进行了预测,确定了浙江省高速公路网的合理规模是6700~7600km。在上述范围内适度开展高速公路建设,有助于更好地支撑经济社会的发展,更好地利用土地资源,提高公路网的运输水平,对于指导全省高速公路规划具有一定的实践和参考价值。

参考文献

[1] 丁金学,樊一江.现代综合交通运输网络框架体系研究[J].综合运输,2018,40(09):66-68.
[2] 孟腾.交通运输与区域产业发展的协同性分析[J].山东交通学院学报,2019,27(01):7-13.
[3] 王富强,谢艳,王敏军.基于国土系数法的江西省普通国省道合理规模测算[J].黑龙江交通科技,2020,43(03):165-167.
[4] 浙江省国民经济和社会发展第十四个五年规划和二〇三五年远景目标纲要[N].浙江日报,2021-02-05(009).
[5] 陆由付,李贻武,施庆利,等.山东省高速公路网合理规模研究[J].交通科技,2015(02):132-135.
[6] 刘雄伟.公路网合理规模预测和评价方法研究[J].山西交通科技,2020(03):44-46+58.

Applicability of Immersive Virtual Reality Platform in Pedestrian Crossing Experiments

Dingyi Ye[1] Yuliang Hong[1] Junfeng Li[1] Guanghua Zhao[1] Wenbo Huang[2]

(1. China Architectural Design and Research Institute; 2. Beijing Keg Laboratory of Traffic Engineering, Beijing University of Technology)

Abstract Intersection is the serious area where pedestrians and vehicles conflict. In order to improve the safety of pedestrian crossing at intersection, the microscopic behavior of pedestrian crossing needs to be explored. In view of the unrepeatable, dangerous and economical problems of real traffic experiments, immersive virtual reality technology is increasingly used in traffic experiments. In this paper, the immersive virtual reality platform were developed based on HTC Vive Head-mounted display device and Unity 3D. The pedestrian crossing experiments were carried out to explore the difference of the behavior between virtual and real scenes, and to verify the adaptability of the platform. Subjective data obtained in the experiments indicates that the pedestrians have a certain physiological response to the virtual reality platform in terms of visual and physical response, and have a strong sense of immersion and high expectation on the platform. Objective data obtained in the experiments indicates that pedestrians have strong motion adaptability in the virtual reality platform. The speed, acceleration and emergency response of pedestrians in the virtual and real scenes are highly consistent. The results show that the immersive virtual reality platform has high applicability in pedestrian crossing experiments. The platform can be used to provide experimental simulation and effect verification for pedestrian control at intersections.

Keywords Traffic engineering Pedestrian crossing Immersive virtual reality platform Real-time 3D interaction

0 Introduction

Scientifically obtaining the micro-behavior and perception experience of pedestrians crossing is the premise for managers to reasonably formulate and implement passenger flow control schemes at intersections, guarantee the safety of intersections and improve traffic efficiency [1-3]. At present, the application of simulation technology in pedestrian behavior research has been relatively mature [4-6]. However, this method is difficult to accurately control the subjective perception and experience of pedestrians, and cannot truly reflect the rationality of the implementation effect of organizational control measures. The investigation in real scene can reflect the real behavior characteristics of pedestrians. However, due to the non-repeatability, traffic safety, economical and other problems of the real scene experiments, they are difficult to be carried out, so that it is difficult to make a detailed comparison of the effectiveness of passenger flow control measures. With the rapid development of computer, communication and VR [7-10] technologies, immersive virtual reality technology has been great developed. The technology can generate realistic virtual scenes based on three-dimensional graphics generation, multi-sensor interaction and high-resolution display technologies. Wearing special helmets, data gloves and other sensing devices, users can enter the virtual space, perceive and operate various objects in the virtual world, so as to achieve the purpose of immersive experience. Compared with other experimental methods, the use of immersive virtual reality technology for pedestrian crossing experiments can accurately obtain the subjective feelings and motion data of participants, which is on the basis of ensuring the repeatability, safety and economy of the experiments. Therefore, immersive virtual reality technology has gradually been applied in the study of pedestrian behavior.

However, the experimental scene generated based on immersive virtual reality may be affected by equipment factors such as picture quality, update speed, wearing comfort, participants' own conditions, and experimental methods, etc.. This may cause the inaccuracy of data collection, especially for participants' subjective feelings. Therefore, the applicability of immersive virtual reality platform in pedestrian crossing experiments becomes the focus of this paper.

1 Literature Review

Virtual reality can be classified into non-immersive VR and immersive VR. The non-immersive VR was first developed rapidly. In 2000, a windowed virtual environment was generated using 3d mapping software by White bread et al. [11]. With the virtual environment, the influence of pedestrian visual search strategy on children's walking development is studied. In 2008, the effectiveness of the application for non-immersive virtual reality in children crossing streets is tested by David c. Schwebel et al. [12]. In 2010, the influence of gender on pedestrian crossing behavior was explored by Holland et al. [13] based on non-immersive virtual reality. In 2015, the danger degree for children in traffic was evaluated by Meir et al. [14] using non-immersive virtual reality, and some suggestions on the protection of children in traffic safety was proposed. However, for this non-immersive virtual reality method, pedestrians can only perceive the virtual world through visual perception, which is quite different from the real world.

With the development of immersive virtual reality technology, pedestrians can be immersed in interactive virtual environment, and feel realistic scenes through visual, auditory and tactile senses. In 2012, an immersive virtual scene with real environment sound was created by Charron et al. [15] to study the movement behavior of children crossing the street. However, the participant could only move using joystick and could not really walk in the virtual scene, which limited the development of their experiments. In 2015, 3D immersive virtual reality was used by Thrash et al. [16] to track and analyze the trajectories of individuals and groups. In this virtual environment, pedestrians could actually walk, and could be controlled by joystick, mouse, keyboard and other hardware devices. After that, immersive virtual reality devices were gradually upgraded and improved. Projective virtual reality technology was also developed. In 2016, a 3D immersive theater was built by Natapov et al. [17], and the virtual environment was created using a screen and HD projector to assess the impact of urban visibility on pedestrian path selection. In the same year, the crosswalk scene was projected with a projector by Jiang et al. [18] With the scene, pedestrians could pass through the crosswalk alone or in groups. However, the projection scope was only about dozens of square meters, which cannot build a large virtual scene.

In the experimental study of pedestrian crossing, the sense of immersion in the virtual world and the sense of participation of individuals are gradually combined. In 2015, in order to explore the relationship between pedestrian crossing and signal timing design, a strong sense of immersion for pedestrians was created by Morrongiello et al.[19] using a head-mounted helmet display with headphones. With the method, the user could be separated from the real world. In 2017, a pedestrian simulator was developed by Shuchisnidha et al.[20] using HTV vive head-mounted display and Unity 3D to study the impact of vehicles on pedestrians crossing. Then In 2018, which characteristics of FAV (fully autonomous vehicle) could affect pedestrian crossing behavior was explored by Shuchisnidha[21].

In this paper, a 3D immersive virtual reality platform was built based on Unity 3D and HTC Vive head-mounted display devices. The subjective and objective data of pedestrian crossing behavior were collected by experiments in virtual and real scenes. The applicability of the immersive virtual reality platform in pedestrian crossing experiments is explored by analyzing the difference of experimental results between the two scenes.

2 Methods

2.1 Participants

In order to avoid the interference on the experimental results by participants' physical and social conditions, participants were strictly screened. In this paper, 15 people were selected to participate in the pedestrian crossing experiments. All participants were between 20 and 30 years old and in good health. All participants had normal or corrected normal vision, no cardiovascular diseases such as hypertension, arrhythmia and congenital heart disease, no infectious diseases, and no skin diseases. In order to ensure the success of the experiments, participants must observe the following before participating in the experiments:

(1) Participants are not allowed to drink alcohol or take medication on the day before experiments. Participants are not allowed to exercise vigorously and stay up late the day before experiments to ensure good health during the experiments.

(2) Participants should keep their hair, scalp and skin which are in contact with the test equipments clean to ensure normal tests for physiological indicators.

2.2 Apparatus

In this paper, the immersive virtual reality platform was built. The hardware of the platform includes HTC Vive (HMD) display, information processor, positioner and operating handles. The working process of the platform is: Firstly, the operating system runs Unity 3D and Steam VR to generate virtual scenes. Then, the VR images and stereo sounds are output to the head-mounted HTC Vive (HMD) device by the stream box. The real walking and the body posture of the participants which are captured by the platform can be mapped to the corresponding physical objects in virtual scene. While the participants interact with the virtual objects using HTC Vive (HMD) devices, the operation signals can be received and handled by the signal processor. The participant's view image, location and environment information can be recorded and output by the processor.

With the platform, 3D virtual scenes consistent with the real scenes are generated, and interact with the objects in virtual scene is allowed, so that the participants can feel that they are in the virtual scene. In the experiments, video acquisition equipment was used to track the trajectories (with the trajectories, the speed and acceleration can be calibrated) for pedestrians, and the cardiac physiology acquisition equipment was used to collect the data about pedestrians' heart rate and blood pressure.

2.3 Questionnaires

In this paper, five types of questionnaires were designed to obtain subjective experimental data from participants. The purpose and contents of these questionnaires are as follows.

The 1st type of questionnaire is about the baseline report. Its main purpose is to get the basic data of participants and serve as a reference for comparing with experimental data. The 2nd type of questionnaire is mainly used to investigate participants' physiological reactions and physical symptoms after using the immersive virtual reality platform. The main contents of the questionnaire are about whether they have physical discomfort such as nausea, head distension and dizziness, etc. and the degree of discomfort. The 3rd type of questionnaire is about the usability survey of the platform. Its main purpose is to investigate the subjective evaluation of the participants on the immersive virtual reality platform. The 4th type of questionnaire is about the survey of the sense of immersion when using the platform. The contents of the survey is about the participants' visual perception, sound realism, and picture coherence. The 5th type of questionnaire is about the subjective perception assessment. Its main purpose is to investigate the subjective factors affecting the reality of the virtual reality platform, and the contents include the participants' emotions, character, time of adaptation, etc.

2.4 Experimental Scenes

In order to accurately obtain the experimental data based on the immersive virtual reality platform, three immersive virtual scenes were built: steam Home scene, non-interfering intersection and signal control intersection, as shown in Fig. 1a).

The Steam Home scene was used for participants to adapt to the immersive VR environment before the experiment, which can eliminate the tension and discomfort brought by the virtual scene in advance. It is convenient for the follow-up experiments.

The non-interfering intersection scene was built based on the real intersection in a university, as shown in Fig. 1b). The crosswalk in this scene is about 7m long and 5m wide. It is located in the left two-lane road at the T-junction. The two sides of the road are the buildings and basketball court. There is fewer vehicles and no signal light control in this scene. So there is no interference from signal and vehicles while a pedestrian crossing, and the scene is used to obtain the basic motion parameters of pedestrian crossing behavior.

The intersection scene with vehicles and signal control built in this paper referred to a Tjunction near a university, as shown in Fig. 1c). The length of crosswalk in the intersection is 9m and its width is 5m. The pedestrian signal timing at this intersection is 60s with green light and 120s with red light, and the traffic flow in the road where the crosswalk located is about 240 pcu/h. Pedestrians are disturbed by vehicles and signal lights while crossing the street at this intersection. In this paper, the impact of non-motor vehicles on pedestrian crossing is not considered. Therefore, the scene is mainly used to explore the reaction and emergency behavior of pedestrians when encountering vehicles. In order to ensure the personal safety of the participants, only the virtual experiments are performed in this scene, but the results obtained in the scene will be compared with existing literatures.

a)Three immersive virtual scenes

Fig. 1

  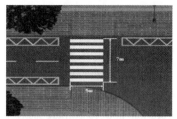

b) Real scene and corresponding virtual scene of the intersection without interference

  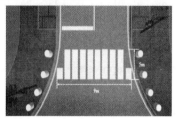

c) Real scene and the corresponding virtual scene of the intersection with vehicles and signal control

Fig. 1 Scenes Design

2.5 Experiments and Data Collection

1) Experimental Procedures

The experimental procedures generally includes screening of participants, experiments in realworld scenes, experiments in immersive virtual scenes, and questionnaire surveys. The details of the procedures are as follows:

Step 1: The participants read and sign the consent form as confirmation that they agree to participate in the experiments.

Step 2: The participants fill in the 1st type questionnaire to record their health status.

Step 3: Screen and select the participants who meet the criteria to participate in the experiments.

Step 4: The participants wear data acquisition devices and participate in the experiments in real scenes. Collect the physiological and motion data of the participants.

Step 5: The participants enter the Steam Home virtual scene to adapt to the immersive virtual environment.

Step 6: The participants fill in the 2nd type of questionnaire.

Step 7: The participants participate in the experiment in the virtual scene of the intersection without interference. The objective motion data of the participants are recorded and output.

Step 8: The participants fill in the 3rd and 4th questionnaires.

Step 9: The participants participate in the experiment in the virtual scene of the intersection with signal control and vehicles.

Step 10: The participants fill in the 5th questionnaire after the virtual experiment.

2) Real Scene Experiments

For the non-interference crosswalk scene, real scene experiments are conducted. The experiments are divided into two stages: experiment preparation and formal experiments.

(1) Preparation

Before the experiments, participants were trained and required to pay attention to traffic safety and obey traffic rules in real scenes. Moreover, each participant was required to imagine a travel purpose, such as going to work, going to school, shopping or playing.

(2) Experiments

Participants completed all the experiments in real scenes, and each kind of experiment was carried out for 10 times to collect relevant experimental data.

Compared with manual method, using video technology to collect trajectory data will get more accurate and comprehensive data. In the experiments, a camera was arranged at a height of 10m from the ground. In order to avoid deviation caused by lens angle, vertical erection method was adopted, as shown in Fig. 2a).

In this paper, the motion parameters of pedestrians were extracted from trajectories with George 2.1 software, as shown in Fig. 2a). In the software, the DLT (Direct Linear Transformation) method is adopted for pedestrian scene calibration and coordinate conversion, and the mean-shift and particle swarm optimization algorithm are used to automatically track pedestrians in video. When the pedestrian enters the camera area, the trajectory of the pedestrian will be marked, and the position, speed and acceleration of the pedestrian will be obtained.

3) Immersive Virtual Scene Experiments

In order to improve the authenticity of each scene simulated by the immersive virtual reality platform, not only the picture quality and wearing comfort were meticulously processed, but also the ambient audio was collected from the real traffic scene and played in the headwear device during the experiment.

The experimental site can provide sufficient space for the participants to move. The participants debugged each wearing device and started the experiment at the specified location. The microscopic motion data of pedestrians were collected, recorded and output in the platform. The experimental scene is shown in Fig. 2b).

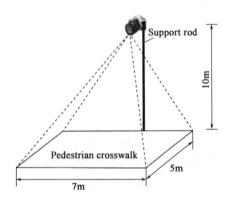 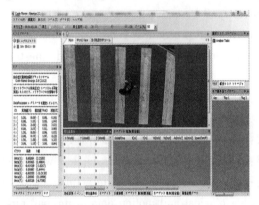

a) Video data acquisition and extraction of recorded data in George 2.1

b) Pedestrian crossing experiments in immersive virtual scene

Fig. 2 Pedestrian Crossing Experiments

3 Results and Discussion

3.1 Analysis of Subjective Survey Data

The influence of the platform on participants' physical symptoms is divided into four levels: no effect, slight, moderate and severe. The main physical symptoms investigated include 18 items such as dizziness, sweating, headache, body fatigue, blurred vision and difficulty in focusing, etc. It is found that 11 of the 15 participants had no adverse reactions, 2 participants felt dizzy and 2 participants had several kinds of mild adverse reactions. And the adverse reactions can be classified into four parts: sound, vision, disorientation and body reaction. The average score of each part obtained is shown in Tab. 1. The score ranges from 0 to 3, and the higher the score, the stronger the adverse reaction. As can be seen, in general, the platform has little effect on participants' physical symptoms, especially on hearing and body reaction.

Physical Symptoms Survey   Tab. 1

Parts of PQ	Item	Mean Score (SD)
Hearing	Tinnitus	0 (1)
Vision	Visual fatigue, squint, blink, inattention, and blurred vision	0.25 (0.43)
Sense of direction	Dizziness, giddiness, and head swelling	0.32 (0.47)
Body reaction	Nausea, vomiting, headache, physical fatigue, snoring, saliva secretion, stomach upset, s Sweating, and confusion	0.05 (0.21)

The average scores of items in usability survey for the platform are shown in Tab. 2. The average score of all the survey items is 3.96, which indicates that participants have high expectations for the platform and the platform has high applicability. We can see that the participants have a strong desire to use the platform, and think that the platform have a high degree of functional integration and easy to use.

Usability Survey of the Immersive VR Platform   Tab. 2

Item	Mean Score (SD)
I want to experience the system again	4.429 (0.904)
I found the system design very well	3.571 (1.050)
I thought the system don't has too many bugs	3.857 (0.350)
I found the various functions in the system well integrated	4.000 (0.756)
I thought the system can be used under the guidance of technicians	4.143 (0.833)
I thought the system don't needs lots of training before it can be used	4.000 (1.069)
I thought the system is easy to use	4.286 (0.700)
I have great confidence in the systematic study of traffic problems	4.143 (0.990)
I think the virtual scene is consistent with the real one	4.000 (1.069)
Virtual reality systems are comfortable to wear	3.143 (0.990)

The survey results of the sense of immersion for the platform is shown in Tab. 3. The average score of all items is 3.86, which shows that all participants have a good sense of immersion in the platform. The number of girls and boys is 7 and 8. As can be seen, the p-values of gender, age, and VR experience are greater than 0.1, compared with boys, girls have a higher sense of immersion for the platform. In addition, compared with other participants, people with VR experience and more than one year of experience in games have a stronger sense of immersion.

Survey Results of the Sense of Immersion for the Platform   Tab. 3

Measure by Demographics [Mean (SD)]		Test Statistics	P Value
gender	male	female	—	
PQ	3.62(0.34)	4.23(0.01)	$F = 3.18$	0.15
age	under 20	over 20	—	
PQ	3.58(0.37)	4.06(0.26)	$F = 1.10$	0.35
VR experience	none	have	—	
PQ	3.78(0.14)	4.11(0.14)	$F = 1.99$	0.20
game experience	over 1 year	under 1 year	—	
PQ	4.25(0.01)	3.55(0.24)	$F = 7.55$	0.03

3.2 Non-interference Pedestrian Crossing

The average time of pedestrian crossing was recorded in real and virtual scenes, and the relationship between crossing time and frequency was counted, as shown in Fig. 3. It can be seen that, in general, the average crossing time in real scene is 7.3s, which is 0.3s shorter than that in virtual scene, but the consistency of the data in the two scenes is more than 92%, which indicates that pedestrians' crossing time in both two scenes is highly consistent.

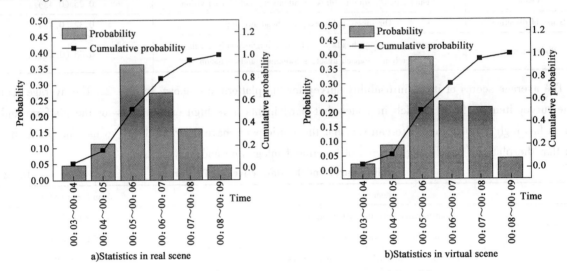

Fig. 3 Statistics of Pedestrian Crossing Time in Real Scene and Virtual Scene

The speed comparison of each participant in real and virtual scenes is shown in Fig. 4a). As can be seen, there is one participant has the roughly same speed in both scenes, and the average speed of the five participants in the real scene is about 0.4 m/s higher than that in virtual scene. Therefore, there is little difference in speed between real scene and virtual scene for pedestrian crossing.

The acceleration comparison of each participant in real and virtual scenes is shown in Fig. 4b). As can be seen, there are four participants has the roughly same acceleration in the two scenes, and the acceleration of two participants in the real scene is slightly higher than that in the virtual scene, indicating that there is little difference in the acceleration between the two scenes for pedestrian crossing.

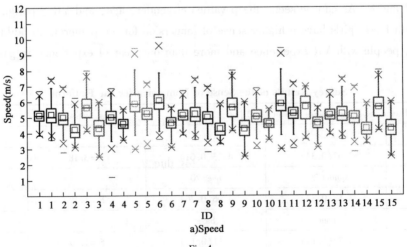

Fig. 4

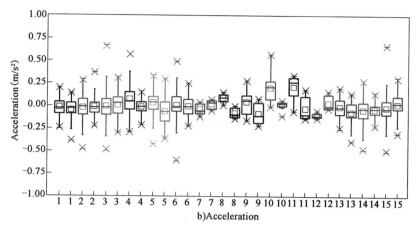

Fig. 4 Comparison of Pedestrian Speed and Acceleration in Real and Virtual World. (A color represents a pedestrian, and for the same color, the left one represents the real scene, and the right one represents the virtual scene.)

3.3 Pedestrian Crossing with Interference

Because pedestrian crossing experiment at intersections with vehicle interference are of high risk, the real-scene experiment on this type of intersection is not conducted in this paper. In order to verify the applicability of the platform for pedestrian crossings at intersections with vehicles and signal lights, the virtual experimental results are compared with relevant references in this paper.

In the virtual scene experiment, the phenomenon of running red lights is serious. Among them, seven participants waited no more than 20 seconds (as seen in Fig. 5), and one participant collided with a vehicle. The average crossing time of pedestrians in violation of regulations is 9 ~ 10s. Compared with no vehicle interference, the crossing time in this case is longer, which is consistent with the results obtained by reference [20-23].

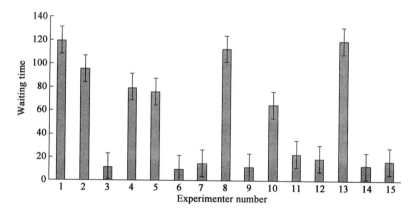

Fig. 5 Waiting Time of Participants Crossing the Crosswalk

The average speed of pedestrians crossing in virtual scene is about 6.3 m/s which is higher than that without interference. Compared with non-interference scene, the average acceleration of pedestrians crossing is larger and has a larger amplitude of change. This is mainly due to the fact that pedestrians are disturbed by vehicles, causing a stoppage phenomenon, resulting in a large amplitude of change, which is consistent with the results in reference [20-23].

The average heart rate and average blood pressure of the participants before and during the experiments are shown in Fig. 6. As can be seen, the oscillation amplitude of participants' average heart rate during the experiment is larger than that before the experiment. The participants' average blood pressure during the experiment is significantly higher than before the experiment.

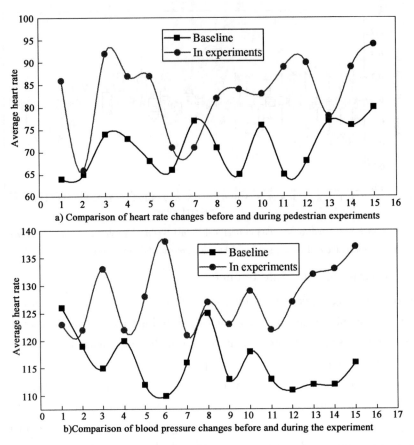

Fig. 6 Pedestrian Heart Physiological Changes in Interfering Intersections

4 Conclusions

In the paper, an immersive virtual reality platform was developed using HTC Vive headmounted display and Unity 3D. The pedestrian crossing experiments are conducted and compared in real and virtual scenes. The analysis of the acquired pedestrian behavior data shows that the speed, acceleration and emergency response for pedestrian crossing in the virtual scene are consistent with that in the real scene, which indicates that the pedestrians has strong motion adaptability in the platform. Based on the platform, experimental studies can be carried out on traffic facilities optimization and pedestrian crossing behavior, and reasonable suggestions can be put forward to reduce pedestrian-vehicle conflicts at intersections and improve traffic safety.

By comparing the experimental data in the immersive virtual scene with that in the real scene, we get some interesting discoveries. Compared with the real scene, the average crossing time in the virtual scene is longer and the average speed is slower for participants. On the one hand, the reason for this result may be due to the fact that the equipment such as the helmet that pedestrians wear during walking has a certain impact on the flexibility of movement. To solve this problem, we can improve the virtual experimental equipment. On the other hand, it may be because pedestrians cannot see the real world environment after entering the virtual scene. In order to avoid obstacles in the real world, the body will consciously acts of avoidance and slows down the speed. To solve this problem, we can consider setting a small window of the real environment in the virtual environment of helmet to avoid participants completely immersed in the virtual scene, eliminating visual impairment. But in general, it can be seen that the platform still has good applicability in pedestrian crossing experiments. The platform can be used for training and simulation of pedestrian experiments, as well as verification of traffic facility optimization effects, especially as a substitute for real scene experiment with high risk and non-economy.

References

[1] King M J, Soole D, Ghafourian A. Illegal Pedestrian Crossing at Signalised Intersections: Incidence and Relative Risk. Accident Analysis & Prevention, 2009, 41(3):485-490.

[2] Marisamynathan, Perumal V. Study on Pedestrian Crossing Behavior at Signalized Intersections. Journal of Traffic & Transportation Engineering, 2014, 1(2):103-110.

[3] Yang X, Abdelaty M A, Huan M, et al. An Accelerated Failure Time Model for Investigating Pedestrian Crossing Behavior and Waiting Times at Signalized Intersections. Accid Anal Prev, 2015, 82:154-162.

[4] L. J. Xu, Wang W. Model of Pedestrians Crossing Time at Signalized Intersection. Journal of Traffic & Transportation Engineering, 2005.

[5] Pu Q, Sun L Y, Gu C. The Microscopic Simulation Based on Conflict of Pedestrian Crossing Street. Applied Mechanics & Materials, 2014, 505-506:1102-1106.

[6] S. S. Li, D. L. Qian, Y. Luo. Microscopic Dynamic Simulation Model for Pedestrian at Signalized intersection. Journal of Central South University, 2012, 19(11):3351-3362.

[7] BIERBAUM, A. VR Juggler. A Virtual Platform for Virtual Reality Application Development[C]// Virtual Reality, IEEE. 2001.

[8] Broll W. Distributed Virtual Reality for Everyonea Framework for Networked VR on the Internet. 1997.

[9] Virvou M, Katsionis G. On the Usability and Like ability of Virtual Reality Games for Education: The Case of VR-ENGAGE. Computers & Education, 2008, 50(1):154-178.

[10] Chaudhry A, Sutton C, Wood J, et al. Learning Rate for Laparoscopic Surgical Skills on MIST VR, A Virtual Reality Simulator: Quality of Human-Computer Interface. Ann R Coll Surg Engl, 1999, 81(4): 281-286.

[11] Whitebread D, Neilson K. The Contribution of Visual Search Strategies to the Development of Pedestrian Skills by 4-11 Year-Old Children. British Journal of Educational Psychology, 2011, 70(4):539-557.

[12] David C, Schwebel, Joanna, et al. Validation of Virtual Reality as A Tool to Understand and Prevent Child Pedestrian Injury. Accident analysis and prevention, 2008, 40(4):1394-400.

[13] Holland C, Hill R. Gender Differences in Factors Predicting Unsafe Crossing Decisions in Adult Pedestrians Across the Lifespan: A Simulation Study. Accident Analysis & Prevention, 2010, 42(4): 1097-1106.

[14] Meir A, Orongilad T, Parmet Y. Can Child-Pedestrians' Hazard Perception Skills Be Enhanced?. Accident Analysis & Prevention, 2015, 83:101-110.

[15] Charron C, Aurélie Festoc, Nicolas Guéguen. Do Child Pedestrians Deliberately Take Risks When They Are in A Hurry? An Experimental Study on A Simulator. Transportation Research Part F Psychology & Behaviour, 2012, 15(6):635-643.

[16] Thrash T, Kapadia M, Moussaid M, et al. Evaluation of Control Interfaces for Desktop Virtual Environments. Presence, 2015, 24(4):322-334.

[17] Natpov A, Fisher-Gewirtzman, D. Visibility of Urban Activities and Pedestrian Routes: An Experiment in A Virtual Environment. Computers Environment & Urban Systems, 2016, 58(July 2016):60-70.

[18] Jiang Y, Rahimian P, O'Neal E E, et al. Acting Together: Joint Pedestrian Road Crossing in An Immersive Virtual Environment[C]// 2016.

[19] Morrongiello B A, Corbett M, Milanovic M, et al. Innovations in Using Virtual Reality to Study How Children Cross Streets in Traffic: Evidence for Evasive Action Skills. Injury Prevention Journal of the International Society for Child & Adolescent Injury Prevention, 2015, 21(4):266.

[20] Deb S, Carruth D W, Sween R, et al. Efficacy of Virtual Reality in Pedestrian Safety Research. Applied Ergonomics, 2017:S0003687017300662.
[21] Shuchisnigdha D, Strawderman L J, Carruth D W. Investigating Pedestrian Suggestions for External Features on Fully Autonomous Vehicles: A Virtual Reality Exeriment. Transportation Research Part F: Traffic Psychology and Behaviour, 2018, 59:135-149.
[22] Bühler, Marco A, Lamontagne, et al. Locomotor Circumvention Strategies in Response to Static Pedestrians in A Virtual and Physical Environment. Gait & Posture.
[23] Lehsing C, Feldstein I. Urban Interaction-Getting Vulnerable Road Users into Driving Simulation. 2018.

国内外机动车驾驶人安全考核与培训分析及比对

徐鑫 刘传攀 袁天宇 马兰婕

(长安大学汽车学院)

摘要 为了促进我国机动车驾驶人的安全考核与培训体系发展，并为健全合理、有效的机动车驾驶人安全培训政策提供建议，本文首先展开了对美国、德国、英国、日本与澳大利亚的机动车驾驶人安全考核与培训制度的分析；同时对我国驾驶人安全考核与培训相关政策法规进行总结；对比了我国与国外在驾驶人安全考核与培训体系中的差异，结果表明：我国更加注重驾驶人安全操作的考核，在培训过程中缺乏对驾驶人安全意识的培养，在未来驾驶人考核与培训制度改革中可借鉴国外经验，加强对驾驶人安全意识的考核及培训中对安全意识的培养。最后，从法律法规、管理制度、技术发展等角度提出促进我国驾驶人安全考核与培训行业发展的对策建议。

关键词 交通安全 驾驶人 安全培训 政策分析

0 引言

我国城市区域内的交通环境日益复杂，这对驾驶人提出了更高的驾驶技能以及更好的安全意识的要求。而在2019年内，我国的交通事故发生起数为24万次，累计伤亡人数为31.8万人，万车事故率远高于发达国家[1]。尽管导致事故率较高的原因较为复杂，涉及"人—车—路"系统内的多方面问题，但驾驶人作为事故的主要参与者，往往是造成事故的主要原因。降低驾驶过程中人为因素导致的错误是减少交通事故的有效手段，而驾驶人安全意识教育将是极为重要的一环。

针对这一系列的道路安全问题，国务院于2012年发布的《关于加强道路交通安全工作的意见》中明确提出以安全第一、预防为主等原则实施道路安全管控工作，严格驾驶人培训考核及管理，强化驾驶人安全文明驾驶意识。2015年，由公安部及交通运输部联合发布的《关于推进机动车驾驶人培训考试制度改革的意见》中指出我国机动车驾照考试中存在的应试化、机械化、模式化的应考问题亟待解决，应随着交通环境的逐渐变化完善驾驶培训考核内容和标准，强化交通安全意识和文明交通理念教育，编制统一的机动车安全文明驾驶操作规范，建立安全文明的驾驶规则体系。由此可见，驾驶人安全培训在驾驶培训中的地位逐步突显，驾驶人安全考核将成为驾照考试中重要的评价指标[2]。

本文结合国外驾驶人安全考核与培训领域的发展经验，分析我国现阶段在该领域的关键问题，通过对比剖析我国现行方案中可能存在的缺陷。最后，提出切实可行的驾驶人安全培训改进建议，为政府在制定相关政策法规方面提供决策依据。

1 国外驾驶人安全考核及培训体系

1.1 美国

美国的驾驶人安全考核与培训体系实行州自治的模式,由国家公路交通安全管理局(NHTSA)给出指导意见,各州再制订各自的培训以及考试政策,各种交通安全相关协会及组织对驾驶人安全培训也颁布了各类指导性文件。考试制度方面,美国主要实行分级驾照制度,在这项制度中,新手驾驶人首先需要通过一项内容主要是交通规则的笔试,随后便可领取到初学者驾照,在获得该驾照后一年内都必须在监护人的陪同下进行驾驶,同时还限制夜间驾驶与载客,以保证他们在安全的条件下驾驶。在完成监督驾驶中要求的培训课程后,则可参与路试,考试对驾驶人安全表现极为重视,如安全意识和安全操作考核不达标,则可能被"一票否决"[3]。

美国驾驶人受到的安全教育与培训一般贯穿于三个阶段之中,分别为预驾照阶段、毕业阶段、后驾照阶段。预驾照阶段是作为公众受到的安全宣传教育,包括学生在学校、社区内受到的驾驶安全教育;毕业阶段是驾驶人为获取驾照而进行的驾驶安全教育,由父母与驾驶培训机构进行教学;后驾照阶段是驾驶人在获得驾照后,由保险、企业、政府等团体组织的安全教育,这一阶段的安全教育既有强制性要求也有非强制性要求[2]。安全教育与培训的内容由高速公路管理局(National Highway Traffic Safety Administration, NHTSA)发布的新手驾驶人教育与培训管理标准进行规范,一共推荐了两套课程标准。其一为美国驾驶人与交通安全协会(American Driver Traffic Safety Education Association, ADTSEA)颁布的新手驾驶人教学课程标准。ADTSEA标准的教学内容主要围绕驾驶安全的主题,结合室内教学与车内教学,内容覆盖车辆基础知识、控制技巧、驾驶路线规划、驾驶风险管理、应急操作等,详细的教学内容安排可见表1。其二为美国驾校协会(Driving School Association of the Americas, DSAA)颁布的新手驾驶人教育与训练课程内容标准。DSAA标准要求了室内教学、实车教学、观察教学三种形式,根据不同教学内容可采取不同教学形式,包括道路交通法规、车辆组成、车辆控制、驾驶人行为、道路分享、驾驶人注意力、感知与风险管理、车辆故障与维护、应急控制与恶劣驾驶环境、文明驾驶、车辆技术系统以及自动驾驶系统等内容。

ADTSEA 新手驾驶人教学课程标准　　　表1

第一部分(*虚线部分为室内教学与车内教学对应)	
室内教学标准	车内教学标准
标准1 驾驶车辆的准备工作	标准1 驾驶车辆前的准备工作
标准2 了解车辆控制	
标准3 交通入口的驾驶技巧	标准2 交通入口和十字路口的汇入技巧
标准4 十字路口、弯道、陡坡的驾驶技术	
标准5 在中等风险环境下的空间管理和车辆控制	标准3:车辆控制任务中的视觉与心理感知
标准6 速度低于55英里①/小时下的交通流发展以及空间管理技巧	
标准7 最高公路车速下的交通流发展以及空间管理技巧	
标准10 其他道路使用者知识	
标准9 恶劣天气条件下的驾驶技巧	标准4 对紧急状况的反应
标准11 对紧急情况以及碰撞事故的反应&了解车辆技术	
标准8 驾驶表现的影响因素	标准5 驾驶人表现评估
标准12 用车过程中的消费选择(导航、车险、生态驾驶等)	——
第二部分	
室内教学标准	车内教学标准(*基于驾驶系统进行)
标准1 心理与风险感知意识	标准1 解释驾驶评估

① 1英里 1.609千米

续上表

第二部分	
标准2 驾驶人适应性任务	标准2 SEE系统训练
标准3 避免碰撞威胁	标准3 解释空间管理评估
—	标准4 高级避撞技巧

1.2 德国

在德国，年满十六岁半的青少年便可参加驾驶培训，首先进入理论教育阶段，在三个月后可参加理论考试，通过理论考试后再过三个月可参加实车考试，十七至十八岁期间处于监督驾驶阶段，在二十一岁后方能够获得无限制驾照。此外，德国还要求在参与驾驶培训前，必须掌握急救知识，若没有则必须完成八节课的急救知识教学[4]。德国在公法上设立了《驾驶人驾驶培训条例》，规定了驾驶培训的目的与原则，并要求驾驶培训必须在正规的驾驶培训机构进行，驾照考试则有驾照管理中心负责，理论考试在统一的考试中心进行[5]。德国对驾驶教练的审核十分严格，驾驶教练有着专门的准入机制，需要进行长期的专业培训与实习并通过资格考核才能够上岗。

德国驾驶教练协会发布的《汽车驾驶员实践训练课程指南》对驾校的培训给出了指导意见，该指南将驾驶培训分为五个阶段。首先进行意识与基础知识教育，为后续训练做准备，其次是在不考虑交通条件下的驾驶操作学习阶段，然后是驾驶人进入交通环境的适应阶段以及开放训练阶段，最后在参与驾驶考核前进行应试训练。一般而言，德国驾校提供理论学习与实车训练的培训内容，理论学习包括12节课，每节课为90分钟，课程内容涉及交通行为规则、交通法规、交通风险因素等。实车训练包括基础训练以及针对性训练。基础训练的内容主要包括车辆技术和检测、车辆控制、车道保持、换道、险情应对等；针对性训练主要内容有倒车、泊车、坡道起步等。实车训练没有固定的时间要求，但必须在乡村公路上训练5小时以上、在高速公路上训练4小时以上以及在夜间训练3小时以上。

1.3 英国

英国的驾驶人培训与考核都由驾驶人与车辆标准局(DVSA)主管。该机构归属于英国交通部，还主管驾驶教练员与考官资格考试以及车辆安全检查等业务。英国的驾驶考核同样分为理论测试与驾驶测试。理论测试包括了多项选择题与危险感知测试，多项选择题涵盖交通规则、车辆基础知识等常规内容，包含了50道题目；危险感知测试是英国较有特色的考核项目，在测试中驾驶人需要观看14个存在潜在危险的交通短片，并在危险发生前要求驾驶人及时地按下反应键。驾驶测试包含六个板块，包括视力测试、车辆问答与演示、一般驾驶技术、调转车辆、倒车入库与靠边停车、独立驾驶[6]。

英国的驾驶人可自由选择培训方式，可以由驾校进行驾驶培训也可由其他专业人士进行培训。尽管英国并没有对驾驶培训机构设置强制的培训与教学标准，但由DVSA公开的《轻型货车与轿车驾驶标准》中给出了对驾驶人的明确要求，并发布了对应的教学大纲作为驾驶人学习与培训的指导文件。DVSA标准中要求驾驶人能够实现6项任务，分别为对车辆与驾驶出行的准备、引导以及控制车辆、按照公路法规使用道路、在交通系统中安全可靠地驾驶、回顾与调整驾驶行为、表现自身驾驶技术与知识理解，标准结构如表2所示。由此可见，英国对于驾驶人驾驶意识的重视程度较高，并要求驾驶人基于自身经验调整合适的驾驶行为。

DVSA轻型货车与轿车驾驶标准结构　　　表2

任务一	对车辆与驾驶出行的准备
1.1	为自己和乘客做好出行准备
1.2	确保车辆能够安全行驶
1.3	做好出行计划

续上表

任务二	引导以及控制车辆
2.1	安全可靠地启动、移动、停车和下车
2.2	安全可靠的驾驶车辆
2.3	驾驶车辆同时拖着拖车或篷车
任务三	按照公路法规使用道路
3.1	正确地通过道路
3.2	遵守各种信号、标志和道路标记
任务四	在交通系统中安全可靠地驾驶
4.1	与其他道路使用者正确互动
4.2	将驾驶风险降到最低
4.3	有效控制事故
任务五	回顾与调整过往驾驶行为
5.1	从经验中学习
5.2	与时俱进的改变
任务六	表现自身驾驶技术与知识的理解
6.1	表现对国家驾驶标准和法规的理解

1.4 日本

日本的驾照一般由所在地政府的公安委员会颁发,全国范围内的机动车驾驶人培训与考核工作由国家警察厅下辖的交管局负责。日本的驾校一般分为"指定驾校"与"非指定驾校"两类。"指定驾校"受到公安委员会认定,对于培训质量与培训规范有着严格的要求。因此,在指定驾校中进行驾驶培训时,其中期测试与结业考试的成绩受到公安委员会认可,驾驶人在"指定驾校"中的培训与考试流程可见图1所示[7]。"非指定驾校"则按是否在公安委员会登记备案分为"备案驾校"与"未备案驾校"。"备案驾校"需接受公安委员会的技术指导,遵循相关规则,与"指定驾校"相比,培训质量较差,但价格相对便宜;"未备案驾校"不受公安委员会的指导与监督,但并不被法律所禁止。驾驶人可根据自身需求选择不同类型的驾校,甚至可在一定条件下通过自学来获取驾照。

日本的驾照考试分为临时驾照考试与正式驾照考试。临时驾照考试主要考试驾驶人是否掌握车辆操纵能力以及能否遵循交通法规进行驾驶,考试内容分为理论考试与驾驶技能考试,通过后可获得临时驾照。正式驾照考试主要考试驾驶人的危险预测能力以及交通事件应对能力,同样包括理论考试与驾驶技能考试,而此时的驾驶技能考试还包括开放路面测试,考官重点考察驾驶人的观察能力、危险预测能力、突发事件应对能力等,通过所有测试后可获得正式驾照。在指定驾校进行培训的驾驶人可在指定驾校的中期测试后获得临时驾照,并在正式驾照考试中,以结业考试代替驾驶技能考试,只参与理论考试[8]。

国家公安委员会以《关于申报汽车培训所进行的培训课程指定规则》来规定指定驾校与备案驾校的教学内容与课时安排。指定驾校中的第一阶段教学包括了14项理论培训内容与23项技能训练内容,第二阶段包括17项理论培训内容与16项技能训练内容。通过指定驾校以外的方式参加驾照考试,在通过正式驾照考试后还必须接受由公安委员会提供的7

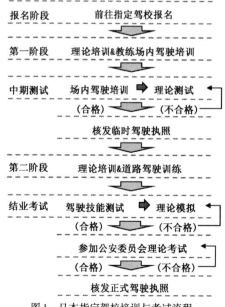

图1 日本指定驾校培训与考试流程

学时安全驾驶知识培训,包括危险预测知识、高速公路安全驾驶知识、急救知识。

1.5 澳大利亚

澳大利亚每个州的驾驶人考试与培训存在着略微的不同,大部分都实行了分级驾照制度(GDL),有初学者驾照、临时驾照 P1、临时驾照 P2、无限制驾照,不同等级的驾照有不同限制与考核要求。驾驶考核内容一般包括交通规则考试、危险感知测试、路试、驾驶人资格考试。交通规则考试以书面形式进行,危险感知测试以机考形式进行,路试一般是在选定区域内进行且路线灵活变动,驾驶人资格考试则综合了交通规则、危险感知的内容[9]。

昆士兰州在 2007 年引入了现行的分级驾照制度,在昆士兰州获得驾照的流程图如图 2 所示。该州规定年满 16 岁即可申请初学者驾照,但至少到 20 岁才能够获得无限制驾照,且在无限制驾照以外的阶段中都对安全驾驶有着要求。虽然获取驾照的流程中并未强制由驾驶培训机构对驾驶人进行培训与教育,但由于路试过程中考核标准较高,除了驾驶操作以外,考官还考察驾驶人的安全意识,因此一般需要专业的驾驶教练进行指导后,才能够通过路试取得临时驾照。获得初学者驾照后,驾驶人会获得一本驾驶日志,需记录在此阶段的驾驶过程,在参与临时驾照 P1 的路试时需提交给考官检查,驾驶日志中一般会记录日期、出发地与目的地、交通流状况、监督人等,若驾驶过程中有驾驶教练指导驾驶,则需驾驶教练签字。驾驶培训的内容主要基于路试内容进行,教练将从安全意识、安全操作等方面进行教学,同时还会协助驾驶人熟悉路试过程,帮助其通过路试。

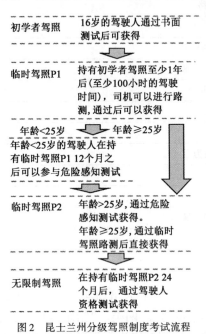

图 2 昆士兰州分级驾照制度考试流程

2 我国驾驶人安全考核及培训体系

我国目前的驾驶人考核与培训管理执行的是"考培分离"模式,在《道路交通安全法》中明确驾驶人申领机动车驾驶证须符合国务院公安部门规定的驾驶许可条件,由公安机关交通管理部门发给相应类别的机动车驾驶证;而执行驾驶人培训的基层单位,即驾驶培训学校或驾驶培训班,则是由各级交通行政主管部门管理,由其所属的各级道路运输管理机构具体执行管理任务。

2.1 我国机动车驾驶人考试中的安全考核

我国现阶段的机动车驾驶人考核体系主要以《机动车驾驶人培训教学与考试大纲》(以下简称《大纲》)指导。《大纲》中规范了我国现行机动车驾驶人考试制度中的科目一为道路交通安全法律、法规和相关知识考核科目;科目二为机动车驾驶人场地驾驶技能考核科目;科目三为机动车驾驶人道路驾驶技能和安全文明驾驶常识考核科目。对驾驶人安全考核涉及安全操作考核、安全意识考核以及安全认知考核。其中,安全操作考核的内容包含各种驾驶装置的安全操作方法、安全设施的使用、车速控制、紧急状况处置、复杂场景下的安全驾驶技术等;安全意识考核的内容包含了安全驾驶意识、文明礼让意识、防御性驾驶意识等;安全认知考核的内容包含了事故案例分析、违法行为判断、各类危险知识、事故急救常识等。

在 GA 1026—2017《机动车驾驶人考试内容和方法》中进一步细化了考试内容,对考试的形式、流程、时长、要求给出了更加具体的标准,其结构如图 3 所示。我国的机动车驾驶人考试包含理论考试环节和实车驾照考试环节,安全操作考核主要在实车驾照考试环节中,分别在科目二、科目三中涉及。而安全意识考核与安全认知考核通常以文字或图片、视频等情景形式表现,题型为判断题、单项选择题或多项选择题。

总体来说,我国目前机动车驾驶人考试相较于过去更加重视驾驶人对驾驶知识技能的实际应用,采取较为多样的驾驶考核方法使驾照考试内容更加贴合于实际驾驶体验,对驾驶人在安全考核方面的要求不仅仅是了解安全知识,更应该熟知并掌握安全知识,要求能够深入理解原理并能综合应用。

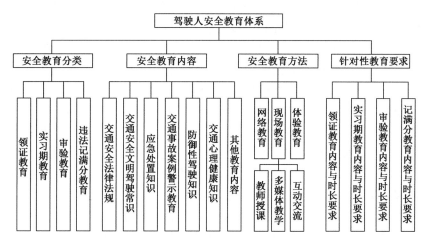

图3　GA1482—2018驾驶人安全教育体系

2.2　我国机动车驾驶人安全培训体系

我国驾驶人培训系统的控制主体包括政府的公安及交通等部门,主要以制订驾驶人培训标准及相关政策等宏观手段或对驾驶人培训市场进行资格审查、实施培训质量考核等监督手段进行干预;而实施主体则是取得驾驶人培训资格的各机构,主要通过设置培训课程以及教练员指导的手段开展对驾驶人的驾驶培训。根据《机动车驾驶员培训管理规定》的要求,培训机构的培训内容应按《大纲》执行,对应着考试中的科目一、科目二、科目三以及安全文明驾驶常识四个部分。

JT/T 915—2014《机动车驾驶员安全驾驶技能培训要求》标准将驾驶人安全驾驶技能扩展为车辆基本操控能力、一般道路条件下的安全驾驶技能、复杂道路条件下的安全驾驶技能、紧急情况处理能力、事故现场处置能力,并且对每一项内容的要求、规范操作进行了详细阐述。JT/T 916—2014《道路运输驾驶员 特殊环境与情境下安全驾驶技能培训与评价方法》则规定了道路运输驾驶员在特定状况下的安全驾驶技能的培训要求,与JT/T 915—2014中提及的一般与复杂道路条件下的安全驾驶技能不同,该标准对特殊环境与情境的定义为对行车安全有影响的特殊天气、特殊路段、特殊场景以及各种潜在危险因素,并且实施培训的设备也被限定为驾驶训练模拟器,因此该标准中所提及培训项目的场景要求、培训内容、评价方法等都基于道路运输驾驶员在使用汽车驾驶培训模拟器进行安全驾驶技能培训的前提。

GA/T 1482—2018《机动车驾驶人安全教育内容和方法》主要规范了公安机关对驾驶人展开的各项安全教育,对驾驶人安全教育类型、内容、方法以及要求做出了规定。驾驶人安全教育分为领证教育、实习期教育、审验教育、违法记满分教育;安全教育内容包括但不限于道路交通法律法规教育、交通安全文明驾驶常识教育、应急处置知识教育、交通事故案例警示教育、防御性驾驶知识以及驾驶心理健康知识。对驾驶人安全教育的形式也允许通过线上或线下的方式进行。

综合各项法律法规及标准分析,我国驾驶人现阶段的安全培训体系大致可分为驾驶人取得驾驶许可证前的培训阶段以及取得驾驶许可证后的再培训阶段,涉及操作以及知识层面的安全培训。培训阶段的安全培训内容由驾驶培训机构根据教学大纲进行设置,主要以驾驶操作与安全知识的教育为主,驾驶教练员是在该阶段进行安全培训的教学主体。再培训阶段内安全教育由公安机关交通管理部门实施,教育的方式主要是以传授安全知识为主,主要对取得驾照后安全表现较差的驾驶人有强制性要求,但对于一般驾驶人仅作推荐要求。

3　国内外机动车驾驶人安全培训与考核比对

不同国家针对自身国情所采取的驾照考试制度不同,不管是否实行分级驾照制度,考核驾驶人安全知识的方式主要通过笔试完成且题目类型以选择题居多,涉及图片场景的分析、交通标志的识别、交通情景的判断、法律法规的理解等内容。而安全意识与安全操作考核的主要方式以路试居多,主要由监考人根据驾驶人在路试过程中的操作,对驾驶人的操作进行主观评价。尽管在考试形式上,我国与其他国家都采取了笔试和路试两种方式,但考试流程和考核要求上有着显著差异。

首先,国外对驾驶人获取驾照的时间线要求严格,驾驶人能够较早地获得驾驶资格,但获取无限制驾照的时间却要相对长得多,在此期间有着诸多的驾驶安全限制,如监督驾驶、禁止夜间驾驶、禁止载客等。而我国在获取驾照的过程中,驾驶人只需要通过驾照科目考试就可取得驾照,所有中间培训内容都由驾驶培训机构负责,驾驶人能够在短期内获得驾照。此外,我国驾照体系只分类而不分级,只有通过了驾照考试获得驾照后,才具有上路驾驶的资格;而国外对于上路驾驶的资格把控相对宽松,设立不同等级的驾照,无须通过所有驾照考试就能够在一定要求下上路驾驶。这就导致了我国驾驶人在获得驾照前缺乏在开放道路驾驶的经验,而国外允许驾驶人在学习期间上路驾驶积攒驾驶经验,等通过所有驾照考试取得无限制驾照后,就能够具备应对开放道路驾驶环境的能力。

其次,英国、澳大利亚以及美国部分州的驾照考试中都纳入危险感知测试作为安全意识考核的一种手段,在日本的考试中也存在危险预知的概念,这项测试能够促进驾驶人在培训中培养危险感知技能,而我国驾照考试体系由于缺乏针对安全意识考核的明确要求,因此在培训过程中缺乏以此为导向的安全培训内容。虽然我国交通部相关管理部门已出台驾驶培训机构的培训教学大纲,对安全知识与安全意识的教学课时制定了标准,但由于在考试过程中,题型单一,且使用抽题模式进行,因此安全知识与安全意识的教学也主要以"刷题"为主,缺乏教练讲解,这种应试模式不利于驾驶人学习安全知识和培养安全意识[10]。

通过与国外的驾驶人培训模式的比对,我国驾驶人安全培训中更多地重视驾驶操作,对驾驶操作的要求较高,但在安全意识层面上的要求较低。除此之外,培训机构无法传递驾驶人实际应用驾驶技能的经验,驾驶人在了解安全知识与安全操作后,无法进一步强化驾驶技能在实际应用中的熟练程度。

4 我国驾驶人安全培训发展对策建议

(1)加强部门间的驾驶人安全管理信息沟通。

由于主管驾照考试与驾驶培训的上级部门不一致,驾驶人安全考核与培训之间难以在政策与标准层面实现有机结合。应通过加深主管部门间的协作,共同指定相关法律法规,编制合理的培训与考试大纲,确定考核与培训重点,使驾驶人的安全培训与考核更加合理。

(2)提高驾驶人培训机构的安全培训要求。

强化对驾驶人培训机构实施驾驶人安全培训课程的监督,在"应考"模式的培训风气盛行的现状下,及时遏制驾驶人培训机构对于安全培训的忽视态度,提高驾驶培训机构对驾驶人安全培训的担当意识,真正落实培养安全文明驾驶人的责任[12]。

(3)建立驾驶人安全培训绩效审查机制。

应由公安交通管理部门对驾驶人事故进行记录,或对驾驶人安全意识、安全知识、安全操作进行抽检从而评价驾驶培训机构的安全培训绩效。或由交通部门主管单位从驾驶培训机构的管理机制、课程设置、教练员考核、学员评价等维度进行考核,对绩效不达标或安全培训不合格的机构实施相应惩罚。

(4)改进安全培训技术手段,提高培训质量。

安全培训的方式方法以及所采用的技术手段对于培训效果有着极大影响,而目前我国主要采用讲授的方式进行安全培训,这种方式对于驾驶人而言,是较为低效的被动学习过程。因此,应改进现有的安全培训技术,可以采用较为先进的教学方法,例如采用驾驶模拟器、VR设备等,使驾驶人对于安全驾驶有更加深层次的体验,从而全方面地提高驾驶人的安全驾驶员能力。

(5)完善驾驶人安全管理要求的法律法规。

驾驶人在渡过驾驶培训期后一般较少能够接受后续的安全培训,长此以往容易忽视安全,并且随着自身驾驶经验的积累,逐渐对驾驶技术产生自信[13]。完善驾驶人安全管理要求法律法规,应主要在后期驾驶人管理中,通过外部手段,施加安全教育或安全培训,维持驾驶人长期的安全意识。

(6)进一步强化多维度、有深度的安全培训。

安全知识、安全操作与安全意识之间有着紧密的联系,安全培训应紧密贴合三个维度将驾驶人打造为储备充足安全知识、具备安全意识并且能够执行安全操作的合格驾驶人。进一步强化我国安全培训体系中驾驶人多维度安全性能的培养,并使培训更具深度,十分重要。

(7)促进驾驶培训行业交流与教学资源共享。

驾驶培训机构是我国驾驶人培训的实施主体,在管理层面上我国各驾驶机构独立,业内交流较浅。促进行业交流,提高业内整体教学水平,同时鼓励教学资源共享,在安全培训相关的教学资源应由有关部门进行制作,并实施行业统一标准,弥补不同驾驶培训机构间的安全培训水平差异。

参考文献

[1] 国家统计局. 2019年中国统计年鉴[M]. 北京:中国统计出版社,2019.
[2] Thomas F D, Blomberg R D, Fisher D L. A Fresh Look at Driver Education in America[R]. Washington, DC: National Highway Traffic Safety Administration, 2012.
[3] 王政. 我国机动车驾驶人培训管理机制研究[D]. 沈阳大学,2015.
[4] National Highway Traffic Safety Administration. Noviceteen driver education and training administrative standards[S]. Washington, DC: National Highway Traffic Safety Administration, 2017.
[5] Genschow J. Novice Driver Preparation-An International Comparison[R]. Bergisch Gladbach: Federal Highway Research institute, 2009.
[6] Department for Transport. Learn to drive a car: step bystep[EB/OL]. https://www.gov.uk/learn-to-drive-a-car.
[7] 孟文戟,曾诚,曹仁磊. 日本机动车驾驶培训与考试综览(上)[J]. 中国道路运输,2016,(04):78-81.
[8] 柴晓军,孟文戟,曾诚等. 日本机动车驾驶培训与考试综览(下)[J]. 中国道路运输,2016,(05):74-76.
[9] Senserrick T M, Williams A F. Summary of Literature of the Effective Components of Graduated Driver Licensing Systems[R]. Sydney: Austroads Ltd, 2015.
[10] Beanland V, Goode N, Salmon P M, et al. Is There a Case for Driver Training? A Review of the Efficacy of Pre- and Post-Licence Driver Training[D]. Safety Science, 2013 51:127-137.
[11] 许可. 新形势下深化新驾驶人培训考试管理的思考——以苏州市为例[D]. 苏州大学,2016.
[12] 刘苗苗. 低驾龄驾驶员交通安全特性及事故预防对策研究[D]. 吉林大学,2012.
[13] O'Neill B. Driver Education: How Effective?[J]. International Journal of Injury Control and Safety Promotion, 2020, 27(1):61-68.

窗口服务人数配置标准的研究

刘德雄

(江西省交通投资集团有限责任公司)

摘 要 针对当前高速公路收费站等窗口服务人数配置标准不科学的现象,以高速公路收费站为例,分别从服务对象的数量和类型确定服务窗口的数量,再根据服务窗口的数量、服务人员的工作量以及服务任务的工作量,利用数字进行量化,精准计算出确保高速公路收费站高质量服务水平所必须配置的窗口服务人数标准。本文运用案例研究,从服务时间的角度,提出保障高速公路收费站等窗口服务单位服务质量的人数配置标准,对目前实施的案例进行梳理剖析,在对比的基础上,总结配置窗口服务人数标准是一个系统性工程,需要从服务对象的数量和类型、服务窗口的数量、服务人员的素质、服务成本效率等方面进行设计,才能制定出一个比较合理的配置标准,从而实现高质量服务社会的目标。

关键词 窗口服务 人员 配置 标准 收费站

0 引 言

日常工作或生活当中,人们经常碰到这样的现象:在一个服务场所,有多个服务窗口,但只有少量服务窗口有人员对外服务,即使这少量服务窗口排起了长长的队伍,碰到有服务人员要上厕所、吃饭、打电话的情况,礼貌的服务员还会摆上一个"暂停服务"的标牌,不礼貌的,则忙他的事务去了,服务对象被晾在一边排队。这种不人性的服务,肯定谈不上好,这种不走心的服务,永远不得人心。造成这种服务质量不高的原因,大多数是由于配置窗口服务人数标准不合理[1]。那么,是否有一个科学的配置窗口服务人数标准呢?本文以沪昆高速江西省境内的上饶西收费站收费广场为例,剖析拥堵规律,提出应对措施,提供参考。

1 概念及名词释义

沪昆高速上饶西收费站。沪昆高速上饶西收费站,隶属于江西省交通投资集团有限责任公司南昌东管理中心,该站2020年11月入口日均4304辆,其中货车日均1033辆,出口车流量日均4450辆,其中绿通车辆日均53辆。该站是沪昆高速沿线车流较多的收费站之一,本文以它作为主要研究对象,具有较为现实的指导意义。

2 现 状

当前,高速公路收费站收费广场服务人员的配置标准一般有三种:一是以设施设备为标准的高配型,这种配置标准以服务设施设备为准则,一般存在实际服务对象和服务工作量少于设计服务总量的情况,所以往往会造成人力资源的浪费;二是以节约人力成本为标准的低配型,这种配置标准以最低成本为准则,一般存在实际服务对象和服务工作量大于设计服务总量的情况,所以往往会造成设施设备的浪费,同时造成服务紧张、拥堵和服务质量下降;三是以主观判断为标准的经验型,这种类型最普遍,当服务场所反映服务人员不够,就增加一些服务人员,当反映服务人员超过所需,就减少一些服务人员,对于机动人员的配置标准,也是根据车流量的多少预估一个数字,这样虽然能维持窗口服务的运行,但是由于没有一个科学的配置窗口服务人数标准,服务质量也不高。那么,如何制定一个科学的配置窗口服务人数标准?

3 标准的建立

要制定一个科学的配置窗口服务人数标准,需要从以下三个方面实施:一是需要知道窗口服务要求,对于一个高速公路收费站收费广场来讲,确保车辆一天24小时随时都能进出,且进出收费站不拥堵,这是收费站这个窗口服务的要求;二是需要知道服务对象的数量和类型,然后根据服务效率计算出服务窗口的数量;三是根据计算出的服务窗口数量和特定服务任务来确定服务人数。

根据国家收费政策规定,在推广ETC缴费方式的同时,仍然保留了人工收费方式,所以最小型的收费站,进出口各有2个车道,分别是1个ETC车道和1个人工车道。也必须按照如下标准来配置服务人数:进出口每个人工车道各需要1人,由于每个收费站出口车道都会有需要查验的特殊车辆(绿通车、联合收割机等),需要查验人员最低1人,同时每个收费班组都需要有人在别人上厕所、吃饭的时间休息在打扫车道卫生、管理等事务,所以最低也需要1人,即每个收费班组必须有4人。根据实行4班3运转的方式确保一天24小时服务,则需要16人,为了确保这16人的班在1年365天都能有人上,还需要计算机动人员。机动人员计算方法为:首先计算出每个人1年最多能上的班数,1人工作8小时为1个班,按照4班3运转的形式,每4个星期就工作21个班,1年52个星期就得工作273个班,而1个员工年平均休年假10个班、病假3个班、事假3个班、正常假(年龄大的可能请丧假,中年的可能请陪考假,年轻的请婚假或者陪护假,还有的请时间更长的探亲假以及参加单位的培训、考试以及各种需要脱岗的活动),减去这19天假,则每位员工1年最多只能上254个班;其次计算出1年当中正常运行需要多少个班数,根据计算一个收费班组最低需要4人,一天24小时分为3个班,1年按照52个星期计算,总共有3·4·52·7＝4368个班,那么需要员工为4368/254＝17.2(人),即18人,减去班组16人,则得出2个机动人员的数据。所以,最小型的收费站最低配置服务人数标准是18人。随着ETC的推广使用,ETC车道的通行能力得到提高,全国绝大部分高速公路收费站正常情况下在进出口分别开通一个ETC车道和一个人工车道即可满足实际需要,所以,绝大多数的收费站服务窗口人数的配置标准就是18人。

当然,随着车流量的增加,当出现车流量超过车道实际服务能力时,就得相应增加开通收费车道和人员;如果该站绿通车辆较多时,还得专门开通一个检验车道;如果ETC车道需要专人值守,那么在班组中又必须增加人数;还有一些入口车道出现较多货车的收费站,为做好入口货车治超工作,也需要增加相应的协助治超人员,不然,入口车道就会经常出现超限车倒车而造成严重拥堵现象。当班组人数达到一定数量的时候,还要增加专门替道的机动人员,因为在一个工班8个小时期间,假设每人上厕所3次,每次来回15分钟,当班组人数超过10人($8*60/45=10.7$)时,仅专门替道上厕所的机动人员就需要增加1人。

除了以上这些正常机动人员外,还必须考虑一些特殊情况,如女员工的保胎假和产假、大病需要长期住院的员工、长期外借的员工等,这些也需要统筹考虑,因为服务窗口人员中女性员工较多,会有需要请产假的女性员工。

依据以上的分析,我们就可以推导一个服务窗口人数的配置公式:

$$Q = x + y$$

$$x = \frac{H}{h} = \frac{a \cdot b \cdot c}{h}$$

$$y = \frac{0.75 \times (b+1)}{8}$$

其中字母含义分别为:Q,需要配置人员数;x,服务窗口人员数,小数点后有数值则加1人;y,机动人员数,当$b<10$时,$y=0$,当$b \geq 10$时,y取整数,小数点后有数值则加1人;H,一年52周364天所有班次和人员总的工作量;h,个人一年52周364天实际能上的班次工作量;a,一天中所含班次,如果8小时一班,24小时轮班,则是3个班次;b,服务窗口人数加上1个替换人数;c,一年52周364天服务天数,固定值。

以沪昆高速上饶西收费站为例,该站2020年11月份日均进出口车流及所需车道,见表1。

不同方式进出车辆耗时以及所需配置人数表 表1

出入口	车道类型	通行时间	理想通行车辆数	日均车流	需要车道	配置人员	备 注
入口	人工	15	5760	1977	1	2	
	ETC	5	17280	2327	1	1	入口货车日均1033辆,为做好治超工作,需要人员在入口协助
出口	ETC	5	17280	2432	1	1	
	人工	50	1728	1965	2	2	
	检验绿通	240	360	53	1	1	

表 1 数据表明:ETC 车道进出口都能满足通行,但车流量都较大,为确保畅通,一般至少要安排 1 人值守 ETC 车道,以便及时处理那些 ETC 黑名单、卡余额不足、未插卡、自行拆卸 ETC 标签失灵、误闯入车辆等异常情况;入口 1 个人工车道也能满足通行,但由于该站入口货车流量达到日均 1033 辆,其中有一定比例的超限车辆,会严重堵塞入口人工车道,所以,实际操作上,一般是开通 2 个入口人工车道,或者安排 1 人到入口处指挥,即入口需要 2 人;出口人工车道车流大于单车道通行,所以至少要开通 2 个人工车道;另外,由于该收费站出口绿通车辆较多,假冒绿通车也多,查验起来很费时间,所以开通 1 个专道。除了以上需要 6 个窗口服务人员之外,还需要一个管理或者机动人员来替道,以便服务人员上厕所、吃饭或处理打扫卫生等事务,即每个班组至少需要 7 人。根据以上公式计算,该站窗口服务总的工作量为: $H = a \cdot b \cdot c = 3 \cdot 7 \cdot 364 = 7644$ 班,平均每人 1 年实际能工作量为: $h = 254$ 个班,所以,服务窗口人数为: $x = \frac{H}{h} = \frac{7644}{254} = 30.09 \approx 31$,由于 $b = 7 < 10$,所以,$y = 0$,结果就是: $Q = x + y = 31 + 0 = 31$,即需要人员 31 人,需要请长假的特殊人员另外增加。

4 结 语

如何确保窗口服务的高质量发展?中国有句老话:己所不欲,勿施于人。放在服务里,要反过来,己所欲,施于人。除了需要服务人员的高素质服务能力,也需要服务流程的改进和服务设施的技术创新,更需要科学地配置窗口服务人员[2],只有从各个方面一点点地微小改善,促进窗口服务质量、安全、效率的提升和成本的节约,才能实现窗口服务高质量发展以及满足人民美好生活的需求。

参考文献

[1] 吴士尹. 优质服务永远是稀缺品[J]. 中国公路,2019,000(010):93.
[2] 吴士尹. 服务说难也不难[J]. 中国公路,2017,06(127):105.

The Role of 5G Enabling Rail Innovations and Applications

Rui Xue　Zhiqiang Ma　Xiaoning Ma　Siqi Sun　Dongsheng Yang
(China Academy of Railway Sciences Corporation Limited Beijing)

Abstract Scientific, operational, and, increasingly, business requirements drive advances in emerging technologies. Despite being introduced at a rapid rate in industries, these data-driven technologies, such as IoT, blockchain, big data, artificial intelligence, virtual reality, and digital twin, still stay far from a widespread deployment in industry and penetrating the market. One major limitation comes from communication. The new capabilities that emerge from 5G are changing the game, and thus directly affect the potential innovations and applications in many industries such as transportation. This paper overviews benefiting technologies impacted by 5G, discusses how 5G enables them in detail and combines scene analysis with these technologies in the rail sector. Considering three service categories of 5G, this paper slices rail scenarios to corresponding three aspects and then details how 5G and other technologies empower rail through three trending rail examples, automatic train operation (ATO), intelligent dispatching, and intelligent maintenance. A new framework was employed in this paper to allow a systematic analysis, and present the general solution to rail innovations and applications in 5G, offering strategical insights to digital transformations for decision-makers in rail sectors.

Keywords 5G enabling Ensemble technologies Rail innovations

0 Introduction

With development for decades, advancements in computing, sensors, and networking have finally placed state-of-art technologies on the cusp of mass-market adoption. However, these technologies are still hard to deploy high-quality systems with mobility and robust user-experience. Enabling massive connectivity and low-latency access to remote computing power, 5G changes the whole situation and pulls technologies such as blockchain, artificial intelligence (AI), digital twin, etc. together from the pages of science fiction into mainstream reality.

Leveraging 5G, more applications will reach passengers once it becomes broadly available on devices in the consumer space. Not just about providing more bandwidth to passengers, 5G is more designed for industrial applications. Presenting an entire generational shift that allows for 1 ms of latency and 1 Gbps download speeds in the 5G era, there will be huge advances in the digital transformation of the rail sector, covering multi-domains such as the power grid, stations, rolling stock, infrastructure, and ticket sales. More than this, the fruition of 5G with other technologies bolsters novel solutions enabling tracking, monitoring, and perceptions of devices, equipment, and asset information for the entire railways, as well as analysis of various systems. Besides, railway operators can model and track almost all the operations from end to end, due to digital techniques. As worldwide demand to travel by rail continues to grow, it is urgent to systematically discuss how 5G with other technologies empowers innovations and applications in rail, which is otherwise seldom quite detailed in the previous paper.

The rest of the paper is organized as follows. The second part overviews the 5G concept, categories, and key techniques. In the third part, we discuss how 5G enables data-driven technologies, including the Internet of Things (IoT), blockchain, big data, AI, etc. In the following part, we further analyse and detail these ensemble technologies applying rail innovations and applications. The final part is the conclusion.

1 5G Concept and Key Techniques

The 5th generation mobile communication, termed as 5G, aims at meeting diverse capacity and quality of service requirements, where one size may not fit all. Compared to previous mobile communication, 5G combines existing and new radio access technologies.

Some technical performance requirements of 5G are listed in Tab. 1. Based on performance on user experienced data rate, area traffic capacity, latency, energy efficiency, and the number of connections, 5G is envisaged to support a diverse variety of usage scenarios in three vital broad categories, enhanced mobile broadband (eMBB), ultra-reliable low latency communications (uRLLC), and massive machine-type communications (mMTC) (Ma et al., 2015). eMBB refers to enhance communication speed based on current mobile bandwidth service, covering a range of cases such as wide-area coverage and hotspots, and thus offering an increasingly seamless user experience. uRLLC, as a typical scene of 5G, indicates data communication with low latency and high reliability to better serve industrial applications. mMTC mainly targets applications involving massive devices or terminals when 5G has a large communication capacity with relatively low energy cost.

Technical Performance Requirements for 5G Tab. 1

KPI	Values	KPI	Values
Peak data rate/Gbps	DL20, UL10	Area traffic capacity (Mbps/m^2)	10
User experienced data rate /Mbps	DL100, UL50	Reliability	0.001% packet loss rate
Bandwidth /MHz	≥100	Latency /ms	1
Connection density (devices/km^2)	1000000	Mobility (km/h)	500

Communication in China railways includes various scenarios and often requires full coverage. Previous research classified railway 5G applications according to location or based on business applications (Ai et al., 2020). However, railways are a collection of multiple disciplines and technologies, many business scenarios cannot simply correspond to one of 5G broad categories. On the contrary, in complex business scenarios, each of these three categories has its emphasis at different levels. To address this issue, this paper abstracts the common features of railway applications and then slices complicated railway scenes into three aspects. After that, we correspond these detailed aspects to 5G broad categories, technical requirements, and corresponding core techniques, as listed in Tab. 2. Regarding requirements from broad categories, key techniques of 5G include millimetre-wave (mm-wave) spectrum, multiple-input and multiple-output (MIMO), nonorthogonal multiaccess (NOMA), device-to-device communication (D2D), ultra-dense networking (UDN), and network slicing (Duan et al., 2020).

Rail Scenario, 5G Categories, and Corresponding Key Technologies Tab. 2

Rail scenarios	Scenario slice	5G categories	Key technologies
Automatic Train Operation Intelligent dispatching Intelligent maintenance	ubiquitous perception	mMTC	NOMA D2D Network slicing
	self-learning intelligence	uRLLC	D2D UDN
	immersive interaction	eMBB	mm-wave MIMO NOMA D2D

2 5G Enable Technologies and Applications

Driven by 5G, many technologies, such as the Internet of Things, blockchain, big data, artificial intelligence, have promising application potential. This section exposes the current limitations of state-of-the-art technologies and then discusses how 5G enables them, so that the use of these technologies will go beyond early adopters to horizontal industry penetration, especially when used in rail.

2.1 Blockchain and IoT

Although blockchain has attracted oodles of enthusiasm from both the academy and industry, its wide use is still at an early stage regarding current technical limitations. For example, transaction capacities of bitcoin and Ethereum are 7TPS and 15TPS, respectively, and even Hyperledger Fabric cannot reach 2000TPS (Zheng et al., 2018), which is much lower compared to the capacity of current databases. 5G helps blockchain to cross this boundary through accelerating transactions and providing a stable network. The communication of 5G with

10Gbits/s speeds up blockchain transactions, thus improving the user experience of various interactions and applications in the blockchain.

Internet of Things (IoT) refers to an intelligent network with access to multiple types of sensors, devices, and systems, sharing information and the Internet through the communication protocol (Atzori et al., 2010). IoT can identify, locate, monitor, and manage massive devices, thus, massive IoT has huge application potential in many industries, such as smart cities, automatic agriculture, and intelligent transportation. However, because of environments and network resources, nodes of IoT in industrial practices are usually less than hundreds, and the collected scalar information is also limited to only a few. Commonly collected information is temperature and humidity. 5G allows rich network resources for massive IoT, and thus breaks barriers in information perception and interaction. Meanwhile, 5G improves load balance, reduces network latency, and expands traffic capacity. In the 5G environment, the wide deployment and application of massive devices can help digital transformations of many industries.

2.2 Edge Computing, Big Data, and Artificial Intelligence

Though edge computing shares task with cloud computing, and thus alleviate the pressure of cloud centre, greatly releasing the occupied bandwidth resources, clients using online data-intensive applications may still bother by long latency and thus poor user experience, when they request data across heterogeneous environments (edge network, WAN, data centre, etc.). These targeted clients are usually massive distributed and time-sensitive. 5G benefits edge computing by dividing computing resources along the cloud-network-edge continuum possible. Moreover, shorter connections between the device and the edge become more efficient owing to ultra-reliable and low-latency capabilities of 5G.

Big data describes enormous information resources with a high increasing rate and various types, which requires new processing and analysing methods for better decisions, profound insights, and optimal strategies (Sagiroglu et al., 2013). Taken big data as a basis, knowledge-driven artificial intelligence has been applied in many industries such as economy, energy, transportation, and manufacture (Russell et al., 2013). However, big data and artificial intelligence encounter novel challenges when electronic devices in the information era are booming. On one hand, the wide use of personal devices such as smartphones, tablets, wearable devices, smart home devices, and drones, becomes a trend. The trend is more obvious with regard to industrial applications. Millions even billions of sensors and devices are generating data, requesting bandwidth resources far beyond what the current network can afford. Lacking sharing, isolated data stored in edge devices would be the waste, and even toxic because biased information may lead to misjudgements. On the other hand, the recent trends to offer user-centred personalized services are a clear indication that the era of real-time responsive recommendation is upon us, where recommendation prosumers will adapt content dynamically to match clients' attention, engagement, and situation. However, trained in the cloud, most of these models are then deployed as other forms in the edge terminals. With requests increasing, the overloading network cannot cope with the massive requirements nor response in time.

5G can be viewed as a solution to these issues. Firstly, 5G offers rich bandwidth resources so that more devices with access to the network and faster communication become available. In this case, 5G puts data in use and thus allows real values of big data. Secondly, beyond rapid communication between devices and base stations, 5G can build a direct connection among devices and clients through the D2D technique. Moreover, 5G will drive the convergence of edge computing, big data, and artificial intelligence. One trend in 5G is shifting the training phase of algorithms from the could centre to the terminals to save traffic time and keep data privacy. Meanwhile, the terminal devices are not only carrying information, but also processing data and analysing them. In addition, 5G also boosts the development of new techniques, especially acritical intelligence, to meet new challenges in 5G applications. Sampled from data sources around edge nodes, data collected and stored in edge devices are low dimensional, sparse, unstructured, and unbalanced. To deal with these data, some AI algorithms, such as transfer learning, meta-learning, and knowledge distillation, have spurred an unprecedented interest, and thus achieved promising developments. Besides, 5G drives federated learning to cover data privacy and safety issue. Federated learning can be interpreted as a shared model constructed through iteratively updating a part of the model after each local training (Yang et al., 2019). In the 5G era, more complex situations regarding a number of objects distributed in multi-layer will inspire novel algorithms and models, thus operating connected devices in the 5G network in coordination.

2.3 Virtual Reality and Digital Twin

Virtual reality is widely used in professional training, design verification, and enhanced experience (Bastug et al., 2017). These applications require the sharing of virtual content between users from different perspectives, and the bandwidth needs are minimal for demonstrating the basic technology. Besides, many of them target remote collaboration or remote assistance with real-time video transmission. Moreover, the bandwidth and latency requirements are much more demanding. Thus, immersive technology demands massive improvements in terms of bandwidth, latency, and reliability. Virtual reality with the help of 5G can carry rich content and facilitate more effective collaboration on the go, allowing much more potential to earn widespread market adoption.

As a multi-physical, multi-scale, and multi-disciplinary technology, digital twin refers to a comprehensive physical and functional description of a component, product, or system together with all available operational data (Tao et al., 2018). Currently, digital twin technology is still far from a full application in the industries, mainly due to the following limitations. First, digital twin involves massive large-scale data with different types from various sources, such as sensor data, simulated data, mixed data, and so on. The existing network would not suffice to afford constantly increasing data and updated models in transmission, use, and computing. Second, digital twin requires real-time feedback and dynamic control, meaning data updating from environments need to be available instantly and at the same time. Finally, digital twin often asks for more interactive and immersive display or dense computation, requiring rich bandwidth resources. Providing abundant network resources, 5G accelerates widespread digital twin applications, empowering industry developments. Conversely, due to its role in the industry, digital twin also promotes industrial IoT, and thus becomes a strong coupling for every device interconnection.

3 Rail Innovations and Applications

5G helps to shape the future of the rail by offering a huge variety of applications. Other than improved services to passengers, 5G with other technologies can turn many impossible innovations in railin to possible as well. In this section, we will delineate how 5G contributes to multi-domain rail scenarios with other technologies and their promising prospects.

3.1 Automatic Train Operation

5G enhances Automatic Train Operation (ATO) from the following three aspects, V2X perception, self-learning decisions, and in-time responses to disruptions. First, 5G allows numerous sensors deployed on-board, trackside and vehicle-to-ground equipment to obtain information such as location, speed, line, and operation plan. Besides, with 5G help, vehicles can exchange information with other vehicles, known as V2V communication, with the roadside infrastructure, with the Internet, and in the same way with any element within the system, and all types of vehicular communication thus expand to vehicle to everything (V2X) (Guevara et al., 2020). Combined with the Internet of Things and blockchain technology, this V2X perception of ATO covering trackside sensors, vehicle-ground, vehicle-vehicle, and intelligent sensing equipment along the line, allows real-time, multi-channel, and full-scene perception of trains and environments. This improved perception also mitigates risks in GoA3 and GoA4 scenarios by correlating detection of noise or shock with the impact of disruptions such as a block of ice. Taking into these scenarios, the main trends for V2X are presented herein, introducing prospects for safety mobility and precise operation control.

ATO emphasis not only auto departure, arrival, and operation between stations, but also automatic door control and linkage control between vehicle and platform. Learning from previous and real-time perceptive data, models adapt the curve optimization and tracking control, leading to smooth operation and precise parking control in ATO. As the core part, self-learning decisions play a vital role in ATO to partially or ideally completely replace the driver even in complex operating scenarios.

Moreover, full coverage and high-performance of information exchange in the 5G era allow in-time responses to disruptions through high-resolution image or video monitoring. Rail experts can intervene and thus handle emergencies without obvious delay to ensure the safety and stability of train operation. Following up the above example, even if the ice detection fails, which barely happens under ubiquitous perception, the monitoring video can still record and identify this risk. And then models will give the solution automatically, or an expert will be introduced to offer guidance if necessary.

3.2 Intelligent Dispatching

A train dispatcher, termed as the rail traffic controller, train controller, or signalman as well, indicates making real-time decisions to command trains based on available data and previous experience (Wen et al., 2019). It needs resilience to avoid risking the subsequent operations once the delay occurs. Train dispatching usually involves relevant data collection, information processing, and knowledge or experience-based decision s. Highly relying on experience, traditional dispatching therefore results in many uncertainties and inconsistencies in the same or similar circumstances. To tackle this drawback, 5G improves intelligent dispatching from three aspects as below, comprehensive awareness, data-driven design, and dynamic adjustment. Owing to a full arrangement of trains and lines, intelligent dispatching requires the real-time perception of transportation resources in change. Besides, it also needs information about lines, on-board and trackside equipment, which covering all majors in rail. Based on this, it has a high requirement of information exchanging and sharing from multi-disciplines. Meeting all the demands above, 5G allows information perception and immediate feedback to accurate and optimal decision-making in the following steps. Shifting from manual experience to data-driven, based on large-scale operation data, intelligent dispatching integrates various data science techniques and advanced AI models to learn knowledge and rules and thus design an overview operation plan in rail. This turns traditional step-by-step iteration design into a data-driven organization regarding vehicles, stations, and crew. On this basis, digital twins, virtual reality with 5G can offer a panoramic presentation of train operation, dynamic timetable design, and real-time train operation adjustment.

3.3 Intelligent Maintenance

Most major types of maintenance, including breakdown maintenance, preventive maintenance, and condition-based maintenance, are defined as passive maintenance (Wang et al., 2015). Different from this "fail and fix" pattern (Lee et al., 2016), intelligent maintenance utilizes predictive algorithms and models to detect faults and prevent failures in advance, based on massive data from various sources. As the key of prognostics and health management (PHM), intelligent maintenance presents huge potential in rail. However, current applications are limited owing to inadequate real-time data collected from the monitoring system. 5G can break limitations and lead to booming prospects through support from three aspects, equipment status perception, predictive maintenance, and remote fault diagnosis. First, 5G allows collecting data from numerous equipment and environment through the large-scale railway Internet of Things. Besides, with the help of 5G, edge devices and equipment within the network can mutually pass, share, and fuse information, and thus achieve comprehensive equipment perception from multiple domains. By taking advantage of real-time equipment perception data, along with historical records, predictive maintenance applies big data and AI techniques to link massive data, find data patterns, and target potential risks. To mitigate these risks, it then publishes the maintenance plan and details to the maintenance scheduling department, aiming to prevent unexpected equipment failures. 5G and edge computing make sure the optimal decisions and efficient response of the whole maintenance system. Though predictive maintenance may detect the majority of potential faults, some failures caused by unknown reasons, or coupled by multiple factors could be issues bothering rail operators. In this case, domain knowledge and expert experience are highly required. Virtual reality and digital twin with 5G support can efficiently deal with failures in complex scenarios by real-time remote fault diagnosis. For example, a remote expert can easily tell the potential hazard from a live video feed from an on-board camera. And then covering long distances with high throughput and low latency for continuous video streaming, the expert can coordinate on-site resources and thus figure out the feasible solution.

4 5G Enabling Framework

Though presented as different descriptions in ATO, intelligent dispatching and intelligent maintenance, three fundamental aspects can be concluded as ubiquitous perception, self-adaptive learning, and immersive interaction, shown in Fig. 1.

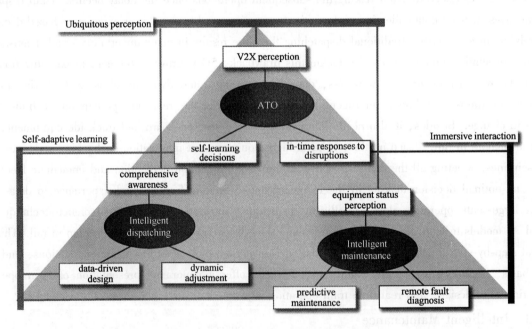

Fig. 1 Three General Aspects in Rail Scenarios

Generally, ubiquitous perception builds the basis for rail in the 5G era, combined with the Internet of Things and blockchain. Driven by data and domain knowledge, self-adaptive learning, with big data and AI techniques, plays a key role in rail intelligence. Finally, presented with virtual reality and digital twin, immersive interaction not only offers client-central services, but also supports the safe and efficient operation of railways, as seen in Fig. 2.

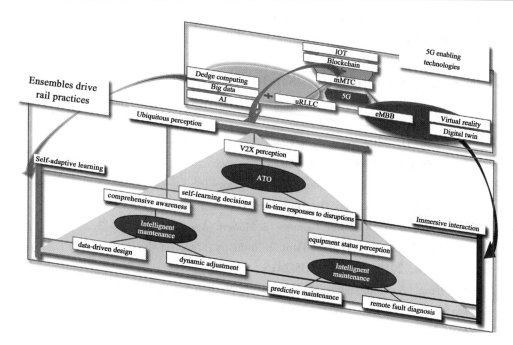

Fig. 2 The Framework of 5G and Ensemble Technologies in Rail Applications

5 Conclusions

This paper focuses on 5G and enabling technologies that are deemed to have a particular impact on the rail sector. It describes the benefits and improvements of ensemble technologies, and how these ensembles can be used in rail scenarios through three detailed examples. It asserts that as communication improves, the perceptive abilities from more devices and data availabilities will increase rapidly. Measurements of uncertainty are better defined with big data and AI models, and thus more and more ways will be found or created to use information profitably, leading to numerous potential advances in digital rail. Finally, the widespread availability of visualization and interaction makes it much easier for all rail participants to display and better communicate information. Thus, the following three aspects, ubiquitous perception, self-adaptive learning, and immersive interaction, connects rail practices with ensemble technologies in the 5G era as a framework. And three examples in rail are detailed to verify this overall framework, pointing out directions to develop digital rail in the future.

References

[1] Ai B, Molisch A F, Rupp M, et al. 5G Key Technologies for Smart Railways[J]. Proceedings of the IEEE, 2020, 108(6):856-893.

[2] Al-Falahy N, Alani O Y. Technologies for 5G Networks: Challenges and Opportunities[J]. It Professional, 2017, 19(1):12-20.

[3] Atzori L. The Internet of Things: ASurvey. Computer Networks[J]. 2010.

[4] Bastug E, Bennis M, Medard M, et al. Toward Interconnected Virtual Reality: Opportunities, Challenges, and Enablers[J]. IEEE Communications Magazine, 2017, 55(6):110-117.

[5] Duan W, JGu, Wen M, et al. Emerging Technologies for 5G-IoV Networks: Applications, Trends and Opportunities[J]. IEEE Network, 2020, PP(99):1-7.

[6] Emery D. Towards Automatic Train Operation for Long Distance Services: State-of-the Art and Challenges [R]. In 17th Swiss transport research conference ,2017.

[7] Guevara L, Cheein F A. The Role of 5G Technologies: Challenges in Smart Cities and Intelligent

Transportation Systems[J]. Sustainability, 2020, 12.
[8] Lee J, Ni J, Djurdjanovic D, et al. Intelligent Prognostics Tools and E-Maintenance[J]. Computers in Industry, 2006,57(6), 476-489.
[9] Ma Z, Zhang Z Q, Ding Z G, et al. Key Techniques for 5G Wireless Communications: Network Architecture, Physical Layer, and MAC Layer Perspectives[J]. Science China, 2015, 58(4): 41301-041301.
[10] Sagiroglu S, Sinanc D. Big data: A review[C]// 2013 International Conference on Collaboration Technologies and Systems (CTS). IEEE, 2013.
[11] Rispoli F. Modern Railways: Connecting Train Control Systems with Mobile and Satcom Telecom Networks[R]. Wit Transactions on The Built Environment, 2020,199, 393-403.
[12] Russell S J, Norvig P. Artificial Intelligence: A Modern Approach[M]. 2003.
[13] Fei T, He Z, Liu A, et al. Digital Twin in Industry: State-of-the-Art[J]. IEEE Transactions on Industrial Informatics, 2019, 15(4):2405-2415.
[14] Qi W, He Z, FDing. A Maintenance Mode Decision Method for Traction Power Supply System of High-Speed Railway[C]// Prognostics & Health Management. IEEE, 2015.
[15] Wang Y, Zhang M, Ma J, et al. Survey on Driverless Train Operation for Urban Rail Transit Systems [J]. Urban Rail Transit, 2016, 2(3-4):1-8.
[16] Wen C, Huang P, Li Z, et al. Train Dispatching Management With Data-Driven Approaches: A Comprehensive Review and Appraisal[J]. IEEE Access, 2019, PP(99):1-1.
[17] Yang Q, Liu Y, Chen T, et al. Federated Machine Learning: Concept and Applications[J]. ACM Transactions on Intelligent Systems and Technology, 2019, 10(2):1-19.
[18] Yin M, Li K, Cheng X. A Review on Artificial Intelligence in High-Speed Rail[J]. Transportation Safety and Environment, 2020.
[19] Zheng Z, Xie S. BlockchainChallenges and Opportunities: A Survey[J]. International Journal of Web and Grid Services,2018, 14(4), 352-375

智慧出行服务新模式的解析和场景应用

殷韬 廖璟琩
（中国城市规划设计研究院）

摘要 近年随着云计算、大数据、物联网等时代前沿技术助力科技创新，传统交通出行服务与新兴技术渗透融合，正逐步向智慧出行服务模式变革。尤其是在当前资源紧约束的大环境下，作为一种革新的交通管理与出行服务相结合的服务新理念——管理和出行相结合的服务模式（TMMaaS）是未来出行服务新模式的重要探索方向。本文在总结国内外出行服务革新的实践基础上，对TMMaaS进行了四要素解析，并在通勤场景下，阐述了TMMaaS的应用。

关键词 智慧交通 出行服务 新模式 TMMaaS

0 引言

近年随着云计算、大数据、物联网等时代前沿技术助力科技创新，传统交通出行服务与新兴技术渗透

基金项目：2019年国家重点研发计划项目"城市智慧出行服务系统技术集成应用"（项目编号2019YFB1600300）资助。

融合,正逐步向智慧出行服务模式变革,为出行者提供多渠道、多方式、可预约、可定制的高品质出行服务,提升大城市交通出行效率。《交通强国建设纲要》提出要推进"出行服务快速化、便捷化",打造"基于移动智能终端技术的服务系统,实现出行即服务"。

Uber、Lyft、滴滴出行等网约车公司通过开启共享出行服务,对传统出行服务市场发起了冲击,之后随着 MaaS(Mobility-as-a-Service)出行即服务这一核心概念的出现与兴起,为智慧出行又赋予了新的内涵,"一站式出行服务"迅速成为当下的热点与发展趋势。

与此同时,交通供给不断增加,供需矛盾不平衡所导致的资源不充分利用、分配不公平、城市生存环境恶化、土地资源紧张等问题也不断凸显。究竟什么才是出行服务模式的变革?什么样的出行新模式可以解决现在城市交通拥堵常态化、出行体验差等痛点?什么样的出行服务新模式是适合中国国情和体制机制的?

本文首先对出行服务革新的国内外探索进行了总结,然后明确了"全要素联动、一站式服务"的未来出行新模式——管理和出行相结合的服务模式(TMMaaS),然后利用"第一性原理"的本质思维角度别从"人、车、路、环境"四要素解析 TMMaaS。最后,以通勤为典型场景,阐述 TMMaaS 的应用。

1 出行服务革新的国内外探索

本文重点总结了利用智慧交通手段,提升出行服务的国内外探索,选取了 MaaS(出行即服务)、预约出行、主动需求管理和 TMaaS(主动需求管理即服务)四个已取得良好效果的实践案例。可以看出国内外在出行服务的技术革新从个体出行服务逐渐转向管理即服务的宏观调控。

1.1 MaaS 定义

MaaS(Mobility-as-a-Service)出行即服务的概念首次提出是在 2014 年赫尔辛基的欧洲 ITS 大会,2015 年在法国波尔多举办的世界 ITS 大会中正式提出定义 MaaS,随之成立欧盟 MaaS 联盟。MaaS 的定义为通过电子交互界面获取和管理交通相关服务[1],以满足消费者的出行要求,实现按需响应的出行自由和提供高效便利的出行服务。

MaaS 将用户、服务、数据、运输、生态系统整合成一个巨大的生态系统。成熟的 MaaS 体系将用户作为出行服务核心,上承政府主管部门,通过服务整合、信息整合有效整合多种不同交通资源,并完成支付体系一体化。按照 MaaS 的发展整合阶段(如图1),国外典型应用案例包括瑞典 UbiGo、芬兰 Whim 等平台已经达到第三级整合水平阶段。国内出行服务应用集中在出行路径规划与交通接驳推荐,多为单一交通服务,仍处于1~2级整合服务水平。

图 1 MaaS 整合阶段

1.2 预约出行

城市交通系统中,在需求短期高度集中,超过系统供给能力,对系统效率产生影响时,通过预约规范供需秩序以保障系统服务能力。利用预约模拟计算推荐出行方案,为用户提前制定出行计划,可避免在路上拥堵,减少约50%的无效等待[3]。出行预约为出行服务变革提供了新思路,突破了多元化交通服务与资源统筹调度的壁垒。平台整合用户预约出行需求,根据交通系统供给状况,进行供需匹配、仿真模拟,实现供需平衡的全局优化。

国内在预约出行服务变革进行了多次实践。北京交通发展研究院在回龙观进行了预约出行的相关实践,结果显示,通过预约调节出发时刻错峰出行,每个用户通过堵点的时长可减少 17~39 分钟,为整个交通系统节约 76~97 分钟的拥堵时耗[3]。深圳针对东部景区,提出了一站式信息服务和一站式出行服务,基于海量数据融合,构建面向用户的信息服务。2018 年"五一"期间,大鹏半岛率先进行通行政策试点。在预约总量方面,预约配额饱和度为 78.5%,交通运行方面,拥堵指数同比下降 40%,走廊车速最高提升 26.8%，景区服务水平平均值高达 3.93。

1.3 主动需求管理

主动需求管理，是指对交通需求、交通流、交通设施的一种动态控制、影响和综合管理。2012 年，美国学者首次提出此概念。相对于传统的交通需求管理，其主要特点是针对需求实施动态智能管理；提供多种选择进行综合调控以及主动管理与有效激励相结合。主动交通需求管理方法和战略主要内容见表 1。

主动需求管理方法和战略　　　　　　　　　　　　表 1

主动需求管理	主动交通管理	主动停车管理
动态共乘	动态车道使用控制	动态定价停车
按需运输	动态限速	动态停车预定
动态定价	排队警告	动态路径查找
预测旅客信息	自适应匝道测控	动态停车容量

美国联邦公路局实施主动交通需求管理以来，取得了良好的交通管理绩效，主要体现在以下四方面：一是整合需求管理、交通管理和停车管理三类交通管理策略，实现对全出行链的综合动态管理；二是对交通系统实行主动管理和动态控制；三是实行有效的激励机制与政策体系；四是建立、加强管理绩效体系和评估体系[6]。

美国马里兰大学也在大华府都市圈落地实施了综合交通主动需求管理，例如动态实时拼车服务、高峰时段错峰出行和出发时间调整诱导、个体化的金钱和非金钱的需求管理激励机制等，达到了综合多模式系统出行管理和系统运营最优。

国内，北京交通绿色出行一体化服务平台（简称"北京 MaaS 平台"）联合高德地图、百度地图，推出绿色出行碳普惠激励措施，累计服务市民绿色出行达 245 万人次，鼓励市民优先采用公交等交通方式，引导人们绿色、高效、安全出行。

1.4 TMaaS 交通管理即服务

TMaaS（Traffic Management-as-a-Service）交通管理即服务是一个革新的交通管理理念，是基于 Mobility Management-as-a-Service（出行管理即服务）系统框架内的，面向中小型城市的出行服务和管理的实践应用。其宗旨在于持续探索可持续发展的、多方式的、绿色集约的出行方式和精明管控手段[7]。

2019 年 ITS 智能交通大会上，比利时根特市发布了首个 TMaaS 移动出行平台。该平台融合了多元利益主体，包括：地方政府（根特市）、两所大学（根特大学和鲁汶大学），两家移动交通服务提供商（BeMobile 和 TomTom）和一家软件开发公司（Waylay）。其主要创新点如下：①建议以用户为中心的多模式交通管理方法；②精准地提供有效信息，提升民众出行体验；③融合多元利益主体，打造伞型螺旋生态圈；④打破交通管控数据壁垒，强化数据间融合共享；⑤不依赖于硬件改造，通过云平台体用服务。

总体来说，从业务服务对象角度，国内外对出行新模式的探索还是以出行端个体为核心，侧重微观个体出行服务，对宏观交通结构优化不足。此外，由于出行新模式的运营端（资源端）都是第三方企业，存在与管理端协同不足等问题。与此同时，针对管理端的系统平台，例如交通大脑和主动需求管理，又很难与以出行端用户为核心的个人出行平台协同，这样就很难维持交通出行的公平性，也很难协同交通供给侧与出行需求侧。比利时根特市的 TMaaS 出行服务平台在积极探索以用户为核心、以数据为驱动的出行服务新模式给了我们很好的启示。但该系统也仅是在数据层面上打通了管理端、出行端和运营端，并不能进行实时的资源调控和全链条的一站式服务。

如何横向贯通数据、应用、服务以及协同管理者、服务者、出行者，实现多方参与、多元互动、协调共治的交通出行新形态，是智慧出行新模式的未来趋势。

2 智慧出行新模式——TMMaaS

中国城镇化已步入下半场，在资源紧约束的大环境下供需矛盾日益凸显，解决交通问题不再是一味地增加基础设施建设,而是增强交通管理水平,从"以供养需"转变为"按供调需"。2019年国务院印发的《交通强国建设纲要》中明确了"大力发展共享交通,打造基于移动智能终端技术的服务系统,实现出行即服务",现代交通已不仅仅是解决交通本身系统的问题,而是重塑一种新的出行服务模式。

在大数据、人工智能、物联网等信息化技术的赋能下,未来交通运输系统将是一个多模式、高品质、融合协同的体系。将MaaS、主动需求管理和TMaaS融合的"管理促服务,出行即服务"的服务模式(TMMaaS)将成为未来出行新模式的重要探索。TMMaaS最明显的转变就是将面向个体的出行服务转变为面向宏观系统调控和个体出行服务相结合的"双服务"模式。用四个字总结管理和出行相结合的服务模式(TMMaaS)的核心特点便是"多快好省":"多"——出行选择多,"快"——出行用时短、速度快,"好"——出行体验感好,"省"——运输成本最小化和出行消费最节省。

2.1 TMMaaS 服务对象(图2)

通过数据赋能,联动管理端、出行端与资源端,实现"三位一体"包含交通出行者、交通管理者、交通工具运营商等之间实时和高效的信息交换;管理端、运营端通过TMMaaS获取出行端实时动态需求,并通过主动交通管理的手段对系统进行宏观调控。同时推送激励措施,对交通个体出行端进行引导,形成系统最优、实时调控和一站式的出行服务组合方案。

基于TMMaaS的出行服务模式理念,管理端可以打通交通局、交警、城管、规划局等各个部门的管理壁垒,实现交通基础数据的部门间共享与统一,感知交通系统的运行状态,支撑对城市路网交通运行状况的精准监测与控制。

运营端通过感知交通系统实时状态数据,汇聚出行端出行需求,提升供给体系(交通工具、交通基础设施)对需求的适配性,形成需求牵引供给、供给引导需求的更高水平动态平衡。

此外,TMMaaS旨在为出行端提供出行一站式服务,通过对出行端个体的历史出行数据进行学习,预测出行需求并给出适宜用户出行习惯及需求的最优出行方案,并推荐优惠换乘、累计折扣等优惠政策,推动出行端由小汽车出行向绿色集约的公交出行的意识和出行方式转移,实现主动需求管理。

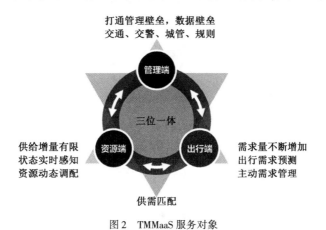

图2 TMMaaS 服务对象

2.2 TMMaaS 结构框架

TMMaaS新模式以"全要素联动、一站式出行"为核心理念,以"出行服务高品质、资源利用高效率"目标,通过智慧出行服务平台,将信号、事故、拥堵状况等交通管控数据与个性化出行服务方案相结合,不仅可以提高城市的交通运行水平,还可以实现出行全过程智能化服务。

出行前,用户通过客户端可以进行预约出行,并享受路径组合的方案推送(图3);出行中,通过前端的感应设施,管理端和运营端可以实时调配交通资源,进行交通管控和诱导,为用户提供行停一体、无缝换乘的出行服务;出行后,用户通过客户端进行一体化支付,若安装推荐路径出行,还可以获得相应的奖励。通过历史出行数据,还可以进行闭环反馈和效果评估,为管理者制定交通政策和规划方案提供数据支撑。

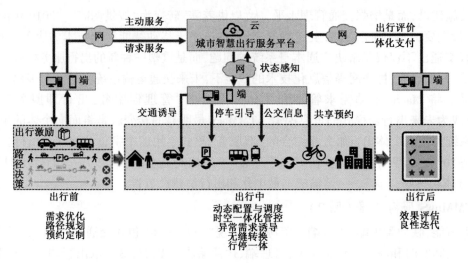

图 3　出行全过程智能化服务

2.3　TMMaaS 四要素解析

第一性原理是一个物理学的专业名称,是指某些硬性规定或者由此推演得出的结论。第一性原理的思维实际是一种"追本溯源"的思考方式,万事都要寻找到根本性问题,也可以叫本质思考法。与之相对的是归纳法思维,就是从诸多的已经出现的出行方式中归纳总结出新模式的定义。我们利用"第一性原理"来解析 TMMaaS,目的并不是将其与当前国内外的各种出行新模式相比较,而是用传统的交通系统四要素"人、车、路、环境"去解析 TMMaaS,探究其本质。

TMMaaS 的本质就是把"人、车、路、环境"四要素统一管理起来(图 4),利用大数据和智能化手段打通各个要素之间的关系,同时也改变各要素之间的关系,实现对微观个体出行服务的优化以及对宏观交通结构的优化,从而为整个交通系统提供更高效和舒适的服务。

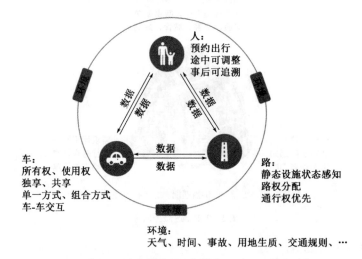

图 4　管理和出行相结合的服务模式(TMMaaS)组成要素

2.3.1　人

"以人为本"是 TMMaaS 的核心所在,交通管理者和决策者不能只关注基础设施的完善和高新技术的应用,却忽略人在交通系统中的角色和地位。TMMaaS 出行新模式将人的出行行为转变为出行服务方案,并为方案消费,主要有以下五个方面的转变(图 5)。

(1)出行服务由单次转变为多次。TMMaaS 为用户提供一站式出行服务,用户只需指定出行起讫点即可得到多方式组合的出行服务,并通过平台一次性支付费用,比起需要多次查看、规划路线并分开支付费用的传统单方式出行服务,TMMaaS 可以更加高效、便捷地实现门到门的服务。

(2)用户角色的可变性。例如顺风车服务,用户乘客的身份向司机身份转变,自己出行的同时也可以为别的用户提供出行服务,提高车辆及道路资源的利用率。

(3)单人出行向多人出行的转变。依据社群经济,TMMaaS 为用户提供拼车合乘的可能。TMMaaS 系统可以依据用户需求及历史数据对用户出行进行个性化的匹配,利用用户出行起讫点及时间等方面的契合程度提供高质量的拼车服务。

(4)一般化服务向个性化服务的转变。不同的出行场景中,如通勤、商务、旅游等,用户会针对性地选择合适的时间、网点和车型等。区别于传统的出行服务,TMMaaS 可以根据用户的特点、偏好等属性,在特定场景下为消费者提供个性化的车型和服务,为用户提供私人定制的差异化出行服务。

(5)单一出行目的向"出行 + 消费"的转变。通过使用 TMMaaS 下的出行服务,系统会为用户推荐目的地周边的兴趣点等,同时用户可以得到一定的积分奖励,形成"交通 + 旅游"的出行模式。

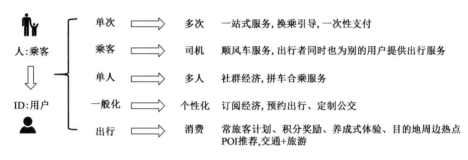

图 5　组成要素"人"

2.3.2　车

从"车"的角度理解 TMMaaS,即将车从交通工具转变为出行商品,贴近人的需求,为人服务,主要有以下三个方面的转变(图 6)。

(1)车辆拥有权向使用权的转变,独享性向共享性的转变。新模式下的出行服务让供给和需求都能实现快速、精准、高效的匹配,为广泛而复杂的共享运营提供了可能,可以极大化地改善供需关系,提高道路资源及交通工具的利用率。

(2)车辆状态由不可知向可监测的转变。通过接入交通动态数据,为乘客提供实时车辆信息,如公交车的实时位置、地铁站点当前的拥挤情况等,从而掌握车辆还有几站以及几分钟到达,避免用户焦急等待,极大地提升出行体验。

(3)出行模式由片段式向组合式的转变。TMMaaS 拓展 MaaS 系统的核心功能,整合各种方式的交通出行服务,为市民提供一站式出行服务。

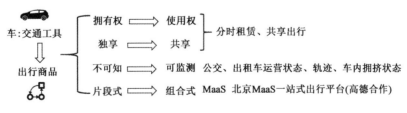

图 6　组成要素"车"

2.3.3　路

"路"是 TMMaaS 的数字底座。通过智能感知设备,静态交通设施转变为动态信息流,更好服务人和车(图 7)。主要包含四个关键信息流:道路、路口、公交站点、枢纽。以道路为例,道路上的数字化、智能化设施设备,可以为交通管理中心提供道路上的实时交通信息,通过分析得到的交通信息,管理中心可以掌握路网运行状态,为道路上的车辆提供精确、准确的诱导信息,保障整个交通系统的运行。再者,通过公交站点的采集设备,系统能得到公交车辆的实时运行状态、站点的候车人数等信息,从而很大程度上提升用户乘坐公共交通的体验。

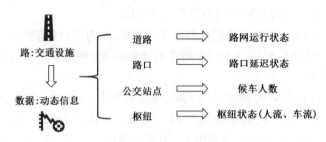

图7 组成要素"路"

2.3.4 环境

"环境"提升TMMaaS服务效率。利用大数据和算法模型,建立环境与出行行为的关系(图8):一方面,通过对环境数据的分析,增加道路安全性。以道路天气传感器为例,该设备能自动检测当前道路的天气状况,如雨水、结冰、积雪等,通过对这些数据的分析演算得到当前路面的摩擦因数并反馈给交通管理中心。交通管理中心则会依据这些数据调整信号配时,为驾驶员提供更安全的出行环境。另一方面,通过在时间尺度上分析用户出行行为,得到用户出行特征与时间的相关性,从而更好地调配资源。以网约车为例,研究发现,对比工作日,非工作日时网约车的需求大于供给,出现了不平衡的状况,因此,可以考虑在非工作日增加供给或引导部分用户乘坐公共交通,以实现交通系统的供需平衡。

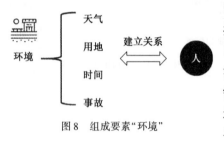

图8 组成要素"环境"

3 TMMaaS通勤应用场景

通勤交通是交通出行的重要组成部分。以北京为例,六环以内的通勤交通出行占到整个出行总量的52%。基于TMMaaS出行新模式,在高强度通勤场景下,可以从供需两侧实时调控,同时对出行者提供"一站式出行服务方案",达到"多快好省"的最优效果。

对于用户来说,出行需求只需在APP端发起,可以预约出行,也可以实时呼叫。和传统出行换乘不一样的是,出行一站式服务方案可以极大减少换乘等候时间,解决了出了地铁找不到共享单车,等候换乘公交时间长等问题。不仅如此,通过推荐实施如换乘优惠、积分奖励等出行激励策略,完成面向出行需求的主动管理,鼓励更多的乘客使用公交方式出行,减少小汽车的使用,达到交通系统的全局最优。

交通资源运营方可以根据需求预测,在早晚高峰,对轨道站点接驳的公交车、公共自行车、共享单车等交通工具进行动态调度,满足乘客换乘需求。

交管部门可以对行人过街红绿灯进行控制,使大规模人群快速疏散。以公交出行优先为目标,在节点进行公交优先的信号管控(图9)。

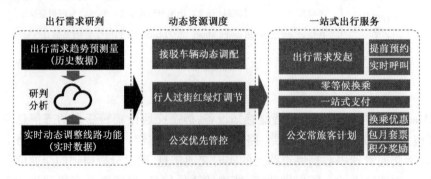

图9 一站式出行服务流程图

4 结 语

中国智能交通协会副理事长兼秘书长关积珍认为,信息技术的变革正在重构交通系统,也在助推智能交通新业态、新模式的形成和产业的提升,智能交通系统已经从1.0时代发展到了3.0时代,主要面向服务,围绕需求,以共享化和协同化为特征。

"管理促服务,出行即服务"的服务新模式(TMMaaS)正符合了3.0时代的智能交通系统的要求。本文对TMMaaS的新模式进行了四要素解析,并详细阐述了在高强度通勤场景下的应用,探索了管理者、运营者和使用者"三位一体"的多方共建共赢的出行新模式,为我国在新时期大中城市交通综合治理和出行服务提供了新思路。

参考文献

[1] 邵源,孙超,严治. MaaS体系构建及应用思考[A]. 中国城市规划学会城市交通规划学术委员会.创新驱动与智慧发展——2018年中国城市交通规划年会论文集[C]. 中国城市规划学会城市交通规划学术委员会:中国城市规划设计研究院城市交通专业研究院,2018:12.

[2] JanaSochor, Hans Arby, Marianne Karlsson, Steven Sarasini. A Topological Approach to Mobility as a Service: A Proposed Tool for Understanding Requirements and Effects, and for Aiding the Integration of Societal Goals[J] Research in Transportation Business and Management 2018 Volume 27: Pages 3-14.

[3] 郭继孚,刁晶晶,王倩,等.预约在城市交通中的应用——北京市回龙观地区的预约出行实践[J].城市交通,2020,18(01):75-82.

[4] 王乐.交通预约通行政策与深圳市实践[J].交通与运输,2019,32(S1):97-102+107.

[5] 尼古拉斯·勒福里奇,赵继宏,安博·米拉德.美国华盛顿州主动交通需求管理的一些新模式[J].上海公安高等专科学校学报,2017,27(01):5-12.

[6] 周永根.美国交通需求管理模式及启示[J].中国社会科学报,2018(007).

[7] IvanaSemanjski, Sidharta Gautama, Suzanne Hendrikse. Traffic Management as a Service[C]// Singapore, In Smart Mobility, Empowering Cities: 26th ITS World Congress, 2019: EU-TP2320.

基于影响非对称分析的旅客空巴联程服务满意度研究

张霁扬[1,2,3] 季钧一[2,3] 杨敏[2,3]

(1. 华设设计集团股份有限公司智能交通研发中心;2. 东南大学交通学院;
3. 东南大学江苏省城市智能交通重点实验室)

摘 要 为研究旅客空巴联程服务整体满意度的影响因素并提出针对性的改善方案,本文基于在南京禄口国际机场开展的旅客调查,创新性地运用梯度提升决策树方法对空巴联程服务满意度感知进行影响非对称分析,充分挖掘关键服务环节对整体满意度的非线性影响。通过预测空巴联程出行全过程中各服务环节提升或降低整体满意度的能力,运用服务满意度评价三因素理论,将服务环节具体分为基础因素、附加因素和无差异因素,结合服务环节重要度和平均满意度的计算分析,提出空巴联程服务改善的六级优先顺序和实施建议。

关键词 出行即服务 旅客满意度研究 影响非对称分析 旅客空巴联程服务 梯度提升决策树方法

0 引言

近年来,我国综合交通运输体系正从多种交通方式独立发展向一体化融合发展转变,这对以综合交通枢纽为载体的旅客联程服务提出了更高的要求。随着社会经济与民航运输业的发展,民航枢纽成为区域重要的旅客集散点,多项国家级政策要求加快推进空铁和空巴等旅客联程出行服务。目前全国的民用机场中仅有少数内设高铁站,实现空铁联运。考虑到将高铁引入机场需要大量的工程建设和资源调整,道路交通在相当长一段时期仍是航空出行的主要接驳方式,而以机场大巴为主形成的"空巴联运"业态,由于其灵活度高、覆盖率广、投入成本低的特点,可满足旅客跨地域、多方式、个性化的出行需求,是民航机场的一种重要且基础性的集疏运手段。

目前联程出行的建设在全国范围内尚处于初级阶段,旅客空巴联程普遍存在转换衔接不顺畅、联运设施不完善、票务支付不连续、信息服务不及时等突出问题。国内外学者分别针对机场长途巴士时刻表优化设计[1]、机场大巴发车时间表优化模型[2]、影响旅客选择空巴联运方式的重要因素及其灵敏度[3]以及旅客选择空巴联运服务的愿意度和支付意愿开展了研究[4]。

综合国内外现有成果,目前尚无聚焦旅客空巴联程出行全过程中各环节满意度的研究。在研究方法上,现有文献较多采用离散选择模型分析用户满意度[5],而离散选择模型的拟合效果和泛化能力相比机器学习算法都有较大的差距。本文基于梯度提升决策树方法对空巴联程旅客整体满意度与出行全过程中各服务环节之间的关系进行影响非对称分析,以南京禄口国际机场的空巴联程客运为实证,有针对性地提出联运服务改善优先级和具体措施。

本文的结构如下:首先介绍南京禄口国际机场空巴联程旅客感知满意度调查的组织和问卷回收情况,随后介绍基于梯度提升决策树方法进行旅客满意度影响非对称分析的过程,最后根据分析结果提出空巴联程服务改善的优先级建议。

1 空巴联程旅客服务满意度数据获取

1.1 问卷设计与调查组织

如图1所示,旅客空巴联程出行的全链条包括机场巴士服务、值机登机服务和机场换乘设施共17个关键环节。设计问卷采集旅客对于现有空巴联程服务的整体满意度以及对于图中出行全过程17个服务环节的满意度,通过Likert 5级量表量化旅客的出行满意程度。

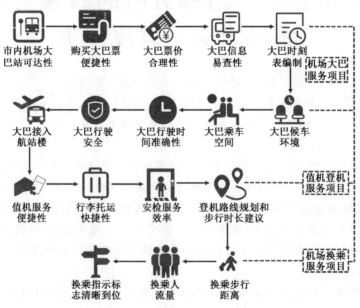

图1 旅客空巴联程出行全过程服务环节图

本文调查组于2020年12月的工作日在南京禄口国际机场T1航站楼候机大厅和机场到达区城际巴士候车室发放问卷,调查进行过程中提前与受访旅客沟通是否使用过空巴联程服务,并遵照每隔1名旅客发放1份问卷的规则,在保证针对性的前提下充分体现受访群体抽样的随机性。

1.2 问卷回收与描述性统计

本次调查,共回收有效问卷773份,经过分析发现,有效受访旅客群体的性别、年龄和工作分布特征都与同时期南京禄口国际机场空巴联程出行旅客人群的构成一致,说明受访旅客具有代表性。

对于回收问卷进行描述性统计,现有空巴联程整体服务以及17个服务关键环节的满意度平均值如表1所示。由表可知,受访旅客对于现在南京禄口国际空巴联程服务整体的平均满意度是3.85分,介于比较满意(4分)和一般(3分)之间,说明空巴联程服务仍有较大提升空间。

现有空巴联程旅客各环节满意度情况　　　　表1

编号	类别	环节名	环节平均满意度	大类平均满意度
		空巴联运整体满意度	3.85	
1	机场大巴服务	市内机场大巴站可达性	3.74	3.83
2		机场大巴票销售	3.88	
3		机场大巴票价	3.91	
4		机场大巴行驶时间准确性	3.87	
5		机场大巴信息查询	3.68	
6		机场大巴时刻表编制	3.61	
7		机场大巴候车环境	3.69	
8		机场大巴乘车空间	3.81	
9		机场大巴行驶安全	3.94	
10		机场大巴接入航站楼	4.11	
11	值机登机服务	值机办理	4.24	4.05
12		行李托运	4.04	
13		登机路线规划	3.96	
14		安检互认	3.97	
15	机场内换乘设施	换乘步行距离	3.83	3.92
16		换乘人流量	3.86	
17		换乘指示标志	4.08	

具体的服务环节上,旅客对于值机办理、大巴接入航站楼和机场内的换乘指示标志的平均满意度高于4分,旅客满意度较高。大巴时刻表编制、大巴信息查询、大巴候车环境、市内机场大巴站可达性、大巴乘车空间以及换乘步行距离的平均满意度低于整体服务平均满意度3.85分,旅客满意度较低。

2 旅客出行满意度研究方法

2.1 影响非对称分析

Kano等人在三因素理论中提出,子服务环节对于整体满意度通常有着非线性影响[6]。由此,服务环节可基于对整体满意度的影响程度而被分为三类:无差异因素、基础因素和附加因素。无差异因素对于整体满意度有近似线性正相关的影响;基础因素在服务水平低时会对整体满意度产生显著的负面影响,而在服务水平较高时对整体的影响很小;附加因素在服务水平高时会显著提升整体满意度,但当服务水平较低时对整体的影响很小。如图2所示,基础因素和附加因素对于整体满意度都有着非线性的影响,区别在于基础因素可被视作"必需"的服务环节,而附加因素可被视作"添彩"的服务环节[7]。

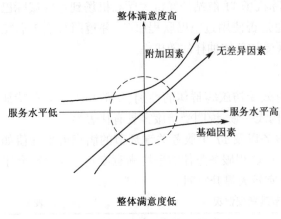

图 2 三因素理论中的服务环节分类

为准确研究关键服务环节提高或降低整体满意度的能力从而找出关键的服务因素,本文运用影响非对称分析量化关键环节满意度对于整体满意度的影响程度,实质是计算关键服务环节满意度变化所引起的整体满意度变化值,从而精细化服务环节分类[8],步骤如下:

第一步:选取基准值对满意度重新编码。将服务水平恰好达到预期的满意度设置为基准,编码为 0;将服务水平低于和高于预期的满意度重新编码为-1 和 1。基于奖惩对比理论[8],任何低于服务预期的环节都会对整体满意度产生负影响,任何高于服务预期的环节都会对整体满意度产生正影响。

第二步:预测每个关键服务环节的奖惩指数。如图 3 所示,当一个关键环节的服务水平从第一步重新编码后的 0 提升到 1 时,所产生的整体满意度变化是该环节的奖励指数 RI(Reward Index,RI);当一个关键环节的服务水平从第一步重新编码后的 0 降低到-1 时,所产生的整体满意度变化是该环节的惩罚指数 PI(Penalty Index,PI)。

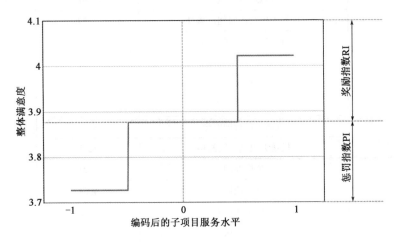

图 3 奖励指数和惩罚指数计算示意图

第三步:度量每个关键服务环节对于整体满意度影响的不对称性。定义关键环节服务水平变化对于整体满意度的影响范围为 RIS,衡量关键环节提高整体满意度能力的指数为 SGP,衡量关键环节降低整体满意度能力的指数为 DGP,关键环节提高与降低整体满意度的能力之差为影响非平衡指数 IA。四个指数的计算方法如式(1)~式(4)所示:

$$RIS = RI + |PI| \tag{1}$$
$$SGP = RI/RIS \tag{2}$$
$$DGP = |PI|/RIS \tag{3}$$
$$IA = SGP - DGP \tag{4}$$

第四步:对关键服务环节进行分类。以影响非平衡指数 IA 值作为服务环节分类的标准,基于现有研究提出的阈值[9],将服务环节分为基础因素、无差异因素和附加因素三类。环节分类的依据如表 2 所示。

关键服务环节分类标准　　　　　　　表 2

IA 值范围	环节类型	环节特征
IA < -0.5	基础因素	服务水平低时会显著降低整体满意度,但在服务水平较高时对整体的影响很小
-0.5≤IA≤0.5	无差异因素	对于整体满意度有近似线性正相关的影响
IA > 0.5	附加因素	服务水平高时会显著提高整体满意度,但在服务水平较低时对整体的影响很小

2.2 梯度提升决策树方法(GBDT)

现有研究中大多基于广义线性回归预测关键服务环节的奖惩指数,然而线性回归在影响非对称分析中存在高维变量空间预测水平低、模型泛化能力弱、数据分布不严格满足假设、变量多重共线性难消除等问题[10]。由此,本文引入梯度提升决策树方法(Gradient Boosting Decision Tree,下文简称 GBDT)对关键环节的奖惩系数进行预测。

GBDT 方法是一种以决策树为基函数的提升方法,基于研究问题的性质决定基础决策树形态。考虑到本文探讨的满意度分析实质是回归问题,故以二叉回归树作为基础决策树[11]。

运用 GBDT 方法进行影响不对称分析的流程如图4所示。考虑到各服务环节的满意度均值分布在4分(比较满意)上下,因此将比较满意编码为基准值0,非常不满意、比较不满意和一般编码为 -1,非常满意编码为1,编码后的0、-1和1分别代表服务水平达到预期、低于预期和高于预期。调整编码后生成的奖励和惩罚数据作为梯度提升决策树预测器的输入、输出关键服务环节对总体满意度的奖惩能力,进而计算各环节的影响非对称指数和重要度。

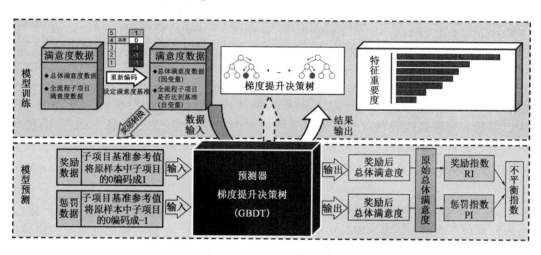

图4 运用梯度提升决策树方法进行影响不对称分析流程图

与广义线性回归算法相比,运用 GBDT 方法进行影响非对称分析的优势主要有四点[12]:首先,GBDT 的预测精度比一般统计回归模型高;其次,GBDT 没有对数据分布的先验要求;第三,GBDT 方法不受变量多重共线性影响;第四,线性回归方法只能判断影响因子是否显著而无法衡量其显著性的大小,而通过 GBDT 方法得到的重要度可以直接量化该服务环节对整体满意度的贡献程度,从而提出更有针对性的服务提升建议。

3 影响非对称分析结果

本文调用 Python 机器学习工具包 Scikit-learn 中的 Gradient Boosting Regressor 回归器运行梯度提升决策树,预测各关键服务环节的奖惩指数[13]。经调试最终确定学习率 $\xi = 0.1$,树的数目为100。所得到的模型对因变量 y 的预测精度 R^2 达到0.58,拟合效果较好。

各服务环节的奖惩指标、重要度以及计算后的 IA 值如表3所示,服务环节依据重要度指标排序,并按照2.1节中介绍的阈值进行分类。

影响非对称分析结果　　　　表3

变量	平均满意度	特征重要度	RI	PI	RIS	IA	环节类型
市内大巴站可达性	3.74	15.43%	0.045	-0.027	0.072	0.242	无差异因素
换乘指示标志	4.08	14.74%	0.048	-0.118	0.166	-0.417	无差异因素
换乘步行距离	3.83	13.92%	0.023	-0.039	0.062	-0.249	无差异因素

续上表

变量	平均满意度	特征重要度	RI	PI	RIS	IA	环节类型
值机办理	4.24	11.79%	0.046	−0.018	0.064	0.428	无差异因素
安检互认	3.97	10.89%	0.02	−0.034	0.054	−0.269	无差异因素
换乘人流量	3.86	8.12%	0.054	−0.055	0.109	−0.01	无差异因素
大巴接入航站楼	4.11	4.98%	0.049	−0.022	0.071	0.375	无差异因素
大巴票销售	3.88	3.37%	0.002	−0.042	0.044	−0.931	基础因素
大巴行驶时间准确性	3.87	3.22%	0.001	−0.005	0.006	−0.593	基础因素
大巴候车环境	3.69	3.18%	0.069	−0.008	0.077	0.803	附加因素
登机路线规划	3.96	3.05%	0.002	−0.056	0.057	−0.946	基础因素
大巴时刻表编制	3.61	3.03%	0.002	−0.019	0.022	−0.783	基础因素
行李托运	4.04	1.96%	0.053	−0.006	0.059	0.802	附加因素
大巴票价	3.91	1.88%	0.005	−0.028	0.033	−0.713	基础因素
大巴乘车空间	3.81	1.80%	0.003	−0.018	0.021	−0.748	基础因素
大巴信息查询	3.68	1.74%	0.016	−0.021	0.037	−0.15	无差异因素
大巴行驶安全	3.94	0.90%	0.019	−0.002	0.02	0.837	附加因素

分析结果可见,在17个调查环节中,大巴时刻表编制、大巴行驶时间准确性、大巴乘车空间、大巴票销售、大巴票价和登机路线规划六个服务环节可被列为基础因素;大巴信息查询、市内机场大巴停靠站可达性、大巴航站楼接入程度、换乘步行距离、换乘人流量、安检互认、换乘设施标志和值机办理八个服务环节可被列为无差异因素;大巴候车环境、大巴行驶安全性和行李托运服务三个环节可被列为附加因素。

关键服务环节对整体满意度的贡献重要度方面,市内机场大巴站点的可达性、换乘指示标志、换乘步行距离、值机办理以及安检互认五个服务环节的重要度均大于10%,对服务整体满意度的影响较大。行李托运服务、大巴票价、大巴乘车空间、大巴信息查询及大巴行驶安全五个服务环节的重要度均低于2%,对于服务整体满意度的影响可以忽略不计[9],故在后续的服务建议中不再讨论。

4 基于旅客满意度分析的服务改善建议

基于旅客服务满意度的影响非对称分析结果,对空巴联程出行全过程中对整体满意度有较显著影响的12个关键服务环节有针对性地改善,提升整体服务满意度。

综合考虑关键服务环节类型、重要度和平均满意度来决定改善服务的优先顺序。依据计算IA值时的满意度基准值将三类服务环节进一步区分为服务水平高于和低于预期的附加因素、非差异因素和基础因素共六类。根据六类环节的满意度特征决定改善环节的类别优先级,再基于每个服务环节的重要度确定环节类别内的服务提升顺序。

基于三类因素的满意度奖惩能力,改善优先级最高的是服务水平低于预期的基础因素,其次是服务水平超过预期的附加因素,下一个关注点在于服务水平低于预期的附加因素,后续再充分关注非差异因素。由于改善服务水平高于预期的基础因素对整体满意度的提升很小,所以无须改善该类服务。

基于影响非对称分析的结果,12个显著关键服务环节的改善顺序建议如图5所示,其中每个关键环节的重要度由圆点大小表征,经影响不平衡指数IA阈值和满意度基准值分割成六个区域内的数字表示改善该类型服务的优先级。

由图5可见,大巴时刻表编制、大巴行驶时间准确性、大巴票购买和登机路线规划属于服务水平低于预期的基础因素,由于四个环节的特征重要度相近,改善优先级均为最高。为提升空巴联程旅客的整体满意度,应充分考虑机场大巴到达时刻和航班起飞时间表的衔接;通过加强机场大巴运行管理、设置专有路权等措施保障机场大巴的行驶时间;拓宽旅客购买机场大巴票的渠道,实行线上线下双轨销售的模式;在航站区内设置智慧查询设施为旅客提供前往登机路线建议,提高旅客在航站区内出行的顺畅性。

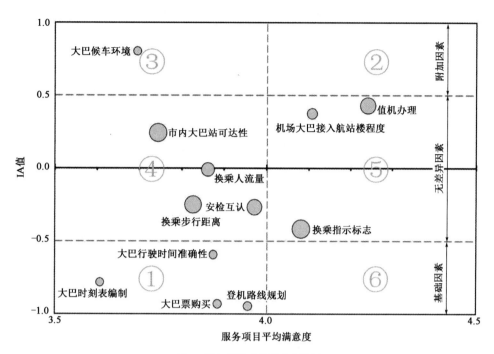

图5　服务环节改善顺序建议图

有效环节中没有服务水平高于预期的附加因素,而机场大巴站候车环境属于服务水平低于预期的附加环节,改善优先级位列第二。应最大限度地改善机场大巴站的候车环境,力求超过旅客预期而对空巴联程整体满意度产生高附加价值。

改善服务水平高于和低于预期的非差异因素对于整体满意度的提升效果相近,为尽可能提高每个环节的服务水平,需优先改善服务水平低于预期的非差异因素。换乘步行距离、换乘人流量、安检互认和市内机场大巴站可达性四个服务环节属于该类,结合各环节的重要度,应首先优化市内机场大巴站的位置。在可达性高、客流量大的区位设置站点;其次改进航站区内换乘通道设计,缩短联程旅客换乘的步行距离;第三,应加强机场与其他交通方式的安检互认,提高旅客的联程出行效率;最后,应实时监测航站区内换乘旅客流量,通过引导分流维持换乘旅客量的动态平衡。换乘指示标志、值机办理以及机场大巴接入航站楼程度三个环节是服务水平高于预期的非差异因素,无须进行服务改善。

5　结　　语

本文基于梯度提升决策树方法对于旅客空巴联程全过程中的17个关键服务环节进行了影响非对称分析,得到各服务环节对联程服务整体满意度的奖惩指数、影响范围、影响不平衡指数以及特征重要度,基于影响不平衡指数将服务分为基础因素、无差异因素和附加因素。在依据服务环节重要度筛选出的12个有效关键服务中,有4个基础因素、7个无差异因素以及1个附加因素。综合考虑服务分类和重要度,本文提出了提高旅客空巴联程整体满意度的服务改进顺序和实施方案。

本文的创新性体现在:

(1)研究角度创新。现有文献中尚无针对旅客空巴联程整体满意度和出行全过程中各服务环节满意度关系的研究。本文创新性地对空巴联程出行中关键服务环节对于整体满意度的影响非对称性进行研究,综合考虑各服务环节的平均满意度和重要度,得到服务环节改善的合理优先级。

(2) 研究方法创新。运用 GBDT 方法进行影响非对称分析,GBDT 方法在预测精度、数据分布要求以及消除变量多重共线性上相比传统的回归模型有着显著优势,且能计算变量重要度,对于提出改善优先级建议有着重要作用。

本文也存在一定的局限性,未来将进行如下更深入的研究:

(1) 缺少针对重点特征群体旅客的影响非对称分析,需要基于联程旅客的个人特征和历史出行进行聚类,对比影响不同群体旅客联程出行整体满意度的服务环节分类情况,进而提出个性化服务改善方案。

(2) 基于影响不对称因子 IA 进行服务环节分类的阈值缺少系统的理论依据。后续研究中应对比更多的分类阈值,选取最优结果。

参考文献

[1] 陆婧,杨忠振,刘瑞菊. 考虑发车间隔与乘客人数关系的机场长途巴士时刻表优化设计[J]. 系统工程理论与实践,2013,33(08):2097-2104.

[2] Lu J, Yang Z, Timmermans H, et al. Optimization of Airport Bus Timetable in Cultivation Period Considering Passenger Dynamic Airport Choice Under Conditions of Uncertainty[J]. Transportation Research Part C: Emerging Technologies, 2016, 67: 15-30.

[3] 周娟. "空巴联运"需求预测模型及收益分配问题研究[D]. 武汉:华中科技大学,2017.

[4] Merkert R, Beck M J. Can A Strategy of Integrated Air-Bus Services Create A Value Proposition for Regional Aviation Management?[J]. Transportation Research Part A: Policy and Practice, 2020, 132: 527-539.

[5] Abenoza R F, Cats O, Susilo Y O. How Does Travel Satisfaction Sum Up? An Exploratory Analysis in Decomposing the Door-to-Door Experience for Multimodal Trips[J]. Transportation, 2019, 46(5): 1615-1642.

[6] Tahanisaz S, Shokuhyar S. Evaluation of Passenger Satisfaction With Service Quality: A Consecutive Method Applied to the Airline Industry[J]. Journal of Air Transport Management, 2020, 83: 101764.

[7] Lee J, Min C. Prioritizing Convention Quality Attributes From the Perspective of Three-Factor Theory: The Case of Academic Association Convention[J]. International Journal of Hospitality Management, 2013, 35: 282-293.

[8] Zhang C, Cao X, Nagpure A, et al. Exploring Rider Satisfaction with Transit Service in Indore, India: An Application of the Three-Factor Theory[J]. Transportation Letters The International Journal of Transportation Research, 2017: 1-9.

[9] Wu X, Jason Cao X, Ding C. Exploring Rider Satisfaction with Arterial BRT: An Application of Impact Asymmetry Analysis[J]. Travel Behaviour and Society, 2020, 19: 82-89.

[10] Ding C, Wu X, Yu G, et al. A Gradient Boosting Logit Model to Investigate Driver's Stop-or-Run Behavior at Signalized Intersections Using High-resolution Traffic Data[J]. Transportation Research Part C: Emerging Technologies, 2016, 72: 225-238.

[11] Ding C, Cao X J, Næss P. Applying Gradient Boosting Decision Trees to Examine Non-Linear Effects of the Built Environment on Driving Distance in Oslo[J]. Transportation Research Part A: Policy and Practice, 2018, 110: 107-117.

[12] Dong W, Cao X, Wu X, et al. Examining Pedestrian Satisfaction in Gated and Open Communities: An Integration of Gradient Boosting Decision Trees and Impact-Asymmetry Analysis[J]. Landscape and Urban Planning, 2019, 185: 246-257.

[13] Pedregosa F, Varoquaux G, Gramfort A, et al. Scikit-learn: Machine Learning in Python[J]. the Journal of machine Learning Research, 2012(12): 2825-2830.

浅析非现场执法在公路治超领域的应用

韩国兴[1]　阿米娜·玉努斯[2]　陈　晖[3]　张柱庭[1]

(1. 交通运输部管理干部学院；2. 新疆维吾尔自治区交通运输综合行政执法局；
3. 交通运输部公路科学研究院)

摘　要　为研究非现场执法在公路治超工作推进过程中出现的问题，明确公路治超非现场执法的政策法规支撑和执法信息化系统流程的构造，本文基于调查和研究，对非现场执法在公路治超领域应用中遇到的检测点布局不完善、执法流程不统一、执法处罚不一致、执法保障不充分等关键问题进行分析，并从地方立法、规划布局、流程设计、执法保障等方面给出了对策建议，以期为行业相关工作实践提供思路。

关键词　公路治超　非现场执法　执法流程　对策建议

0　引　言

到 2019 年末，全国公路总里程 501.25 万 km，公路养护里程 495.31 万 km。四级及以上等级公路里程 469.87 万 km；二级及以上等级公路里程 67.20 万 km；高速公路里程 14.96 万 km；运输装备方面，牵引车 267.89 万辆、挂车 279.63 万辆[1]。随着公路里程增加、道路通行能力提升、运输装备增多，货运市场竞争日趋激烈，导致货运市场出现恶性竞争、部分从业人员驾驶违法超限运输车辆行驶公路，影响道路交通安全。与此同时，由于治超队伍人数增长缓慢、治超手段相对滞后，无法满足全天候巡查、全覆盖流动治超，治超工作任务依然艰巨，生产安全风险隐患长存。因此，传统的路面执法方式已不能完全适应当前治超工作需要，亟需推广适应新形势下的治超工作模式。

治超非现场执法是公路治超从传统方式向现代化、智能化执法的一个有益尝试，是现有治超手段的有效补充，可缓解流动执法的压力。国内多个省份开展治超非现场执法试点工作，深入探索治超非现场执法工作机制，积累了宝贵经验，但也遇到了很多问题。本文将从以下几个方面简要分析治超非现场执法工作存在的问题及相关建议，以期为交通运输行业主管部门提供参考。

1　非现场执法的现状

《道路交通安全违法行为处理程序规定》(公安部 2004 年第 69 号令)将处理道路交通安全违法行为的程序分为"现场处理程序"和"非现场处理程序"，在部门规章中首次出现"非现场"一词。新修订的《道路交通安全违法行为处理程序规定》(公安部 2008 年第 105 号令)中，专门在调查取证章节增加"交通技术监控"，规定"可以利用交通技术监控设备收集、固定违法行为证据"，在现有法律中只能隐约可见"非现场执法"身影[2]。《中华人民共和国行政诉讼法》(2015 年 5 月 1 日实施)关于"电子数据类"的条文规定和《中华人民共和国反恐怖主义法》(2016 年 1 月 1 日施行)第二十二条、二十七条有关规定，不仅为非现场执法奠定法律基础，还将配备、安装技防、物防设备、设施变成了法定义务，从法律法规和政策层面，非现场执法已经具备了可行性，并在国家层面的指导意见下，交通运输非现场执法进入大力推广阶段[3]。

非现场执法是在货物运输主通道、重要桥梁入口处等重要路段和节点设置检测技术监控设备，并根据设备记录的电子信息，经认定违法事实后，根据相关法律法规对违法运输车辆的当事人(包括车辆所有人、驾驶人或者车辆管理人)做出行政处罚决定的治超管理模式[4]。

交通运输行业在公路治超非现场执法领域的探索和试点过程中形成了如图 1 所示的非现场执法检

基金项目：宁夏回族自治区交通运输综合执法监督局综合执法业务规范与业务咨询，交通运输行政执法电子化办案规范流程咨询。

测点布局,并积累了较好的经验。2013年,临安在昌化开展"S208千秋关路段治超非现场执法试点工作"[5],构建了"告知区、监测区、卸载区、拦截区"四区一体治超非现场执法路段的现场布局,布点24h筛查超限运输车辆。2015年,宁波在全市全面实施非现场执法,到2017年,已累计建设公路治超电子检测系统68处,投入使用54处、207个车道,公路货运车辆超限率由2013年的10%下降到2%以内。2019年上线"治超非现场执法系统平台",虽然仅在3条国道省道上设置了3处不停车检测系统,但在2019年9月—2020年10月的一年时间里累计下达行政处罚决定书3768份,取得显著效果。此外,宁波市从2016年11月1日起正式实施《宁波市公路超限运输管理办法》,在浙江全省乃至全国开创先河。通过科技、法规双重保障,实现了公路治超的全路网覆盖和全天候监控,破解了治超难题。

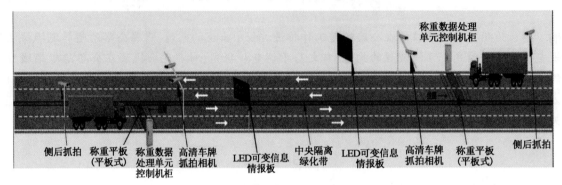

图1 非现场执法检测点示意图

2 非现场执法存在的问题分析

非现场执法在公路治超领域经过多年的探索、试点和区域性推广,取得了比较显著效果,但仍存在不完善、需明确的方面。下一步继续推行非现场执法过程中,需要进一步对当前存在问题加以分析,归纳并提出解决思路。

2.1 非现场执法检测点布局不完善,公路治超整体网络尚未形成

随着基础设施互联互通,高速公路网、普通国省道网、农村公路网"三网"基本完善,为居民出行和物资流通提供强有力的保障。2019年12月16日零时起高速公路入口称重治超工作启动,标志着高速公路网中封闭式路段全面进入治超。超载的货运车辆无法进入高速公路,执法过程中未发现的超载车辆可能绕行至普通国省道网和农村公路网的线路,加剧了这些路网线路的治超工作,带来交通安全隐患。由于公路治超非现场执法各地尚未全面布局,导致治超非现场监测点的布设与其他形式的治超站、流动治超点无法完全互补(图2),形成封闭的监测网络,从而出现超限车辆绕行等情况,需要进一步强化治超的整体布局和非现场执法的网络布局研究。[6]

图2 仁怀市公路网非现场执法检测卡点分布

2.2 非现场执法流程不明确

根据《中华人民共和国行政处罚法》规定了行政处罚的简易程序（图3）、一般程序、听证程序,并没有明确非现场执法程序,因此不能把非现场执法变成行政处罚程序[3]。当前,非现场执法的设计流程普遍将行政处罚法的程序作为系统信息化流程的设计参考,忽略了非现场执法电子证据的调查取证环节,开发设计的系统流程随意性强,不断依靠人工和机器互动确认完成非现场执法的过程,违背了非现场执法设计和信息化建设的初衷,对执法人员的素质提出了更高要求、增加了工作量。

此外,对于路面执法工作,也应有明确的巡查职责机制,明确非现场执法路段的路面执法时间等规则。以免管理部门因为人手或者其他原因,怠于路面执法,影响管理的时效性[7]。

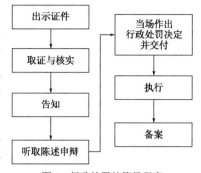

图3 行政处罚的简易程序

2.3 非现场执法与联合执法处罚金额不一致

就目前而言,公路治超领域由于实施处罚的主体不同,处罚依据、监测违法的方式不同,从而导致处罚幅度和处罚内容有所不同[8]。根据交通运输部、工业和信息化部、公安部、工商总局、质检总局联合开展货车非法改装和超限超载治理工作的要求"对经检测确认超限超载的车辆,由公路管理机构监督消除违法行为;公安交通管理部门依据公路管理机构开具的称重和卸载单,依法进行处罚、记分后放行"。但针对非现场执法查处案件,交通运输主管部门依据《中华人民共和国公路法》《超限运输车辆行驶公路管理规定》进行处罚。两种不同的执法情形,产生不同的处罚结果,缴纳的罚款金额也不相一致。

2.4 非现场执法所需保障不充分

公路治超领域试点和推广非现场执法以来,非现场检测设备点位的扩充、违法行为数量的激增,出现了非现场检测设备点建设运维经费不足、执法队伍短缺、技术力量薄弱等现象,执法队伍人员数量和知识结构都难以适应的局面,点位增多势必也会带来更大的案件办理压力。此外,随着非现场执法的深入、数据量的增加,如何协调非现场和现场执法的联合智能调度需统筹考虑。

3 相关建议

3.1 加密非现场执法检测点,完善公路治超网络

公路治超非现场执法监测点位布局应根据公路路网发展和治超业务需求,从全局性、系统性、综合性、前瞻性出发,以高速公路入口和公路超限检测站的布局为路网重要节点,统筹考虑重点货运源头单位的分布情况,优化布局超限检测点、公路治超非现场执法检测点作为次要节点,对公路路网进行超限治理的监控网络布局,对监控网络中不能完全覆盖的线路和当前不宜设置上述情形的站点及设施设备的线路,按相关规定开展流动联合执法,逐步形成传统手段与新型技术相结合、高速公路与普通公路网相衔接、固定检测与流动执法相补充的高速公路入口拒绝进入、超限检测站（点）治超、非现场执法检测点治超、联合执法流动治超与货运源头单位治超"五合一"的全局性、常态化、智慧化、流程化的治超工作布局（图4）。

治理超限超载应当实现全路网管控,其中高速公路已经实现了所有入口货车称重;农村公路中的乡道、村道能够依靠依法设置的限高限宽设施治理,但县道设置限高限宽设施尚无法律依据;国道、省道中重要的省界入口、多条国道或者省道的交汇点、跨省货物运输的主通道等全国性公路网的重要路段和节点,经省级人民政府批准可以设置超限检测站（点）治理超限超载,但尚未设置超限检测站（点）的国道、省道容易成为治超网络中的缺口。从当前各地非现场监管的试点成效看,非现场执法检测点的设置能够起到较好补缺的作用。鉴于此,在上述国道、省道及部分县道布设非现场监管设施,加密非现场执法检测

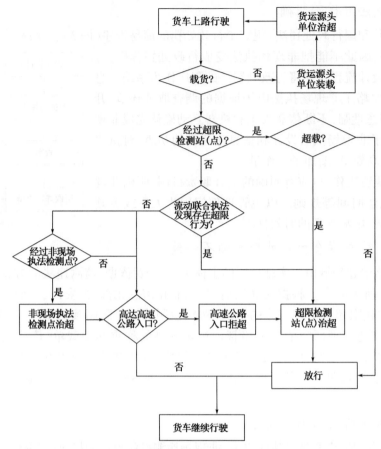

图 4　公路治超的五种模式流程示意图

点,可以促进完善公路治超的整体网络。

3.2　进一步完善非现场监管的信息化流程

根据公路治超的相关规定,图4所示的五种治超模式(图中绿色方框环节)有更为具体详细的治超业务要求和流程,需要按规定实施。关于非现场检测点的非现场监管信息化流程,当前的非现场执法信息系统的业务流程普遍对于非现场监管中调查取证环节缺乏详细设计,更偏重于行政处罚的一般程序。

根据2021年新修订的《中华人民共和国行政处罚法》第四十一条第二款"电子技术监控设备记录违法事实应当真实、清晰、完整、准确。行政机关应当审核记录内容是否符合要求;未经审核或者经审核不符合要求的,不得作为行政处罚的证据",建议非现场监管信息系统设计的重点应当是非现场监管调查取证的证据取得、记录、审查、应用等环节(图5虚线框所示内容),这一环节流程设计好就可以和现行行政处罚法规定的行政处罚简易程序、一般程序、听证程序进行有效衔接。同时应当强化行政处罚简易程序、一般程序、听证程序中电子化的步骤和文书的改进。

3.3　进一步加强执法保障

开展非现场监管以来,运维经费不足,队伍数量和知识结构都难以适应,特别是内设机构几乎是传统执法模式下的架构,不足以支撑非现场监管的技术要求和数量要求。目前暂时靠系统设计和设备供应商提供技术人员进行技术运维,靠法治科负责处理案件,但这终究不是长期办法。建议政府有关部门应当按照中央《深化交通运输综合行政执法改革指导意见》中"大力推进非现场执法和信息化移动执法"的精神,从人员编制、经费保障、内设机构三个方面给予支持。同时,制定相关技术设备和装备标准,从行政执法收集证据设备、设施的产品合格性角度来看,毋庸置疑这些技术设备、装备要按照质量技术监督部门要求,具有检定的合法证明。但从目前实践来看,大量使用的系统平台还缺乏国家标准和行业标准。建议借鉴《道路运输车辆动态兼顾管理办法》的立法经验,规定系统平台、装置、车载终端等技术应当通过有关专业机构的标准符合性技术审查;对通过标准符合性技术审查的系统平台、装置、车载终端等,由主管部门发布公告。

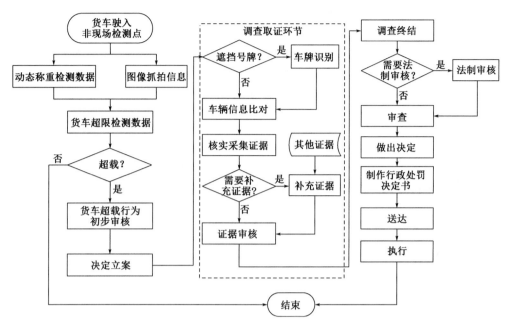

图5 非现场监管的信息化流程图

3.4 进一步加快推进治超立法工作

根据2021年新修订的《中华人民共和国行政处罚法》第二十九条"对当事人的同一个违法行为,不得给予两次以上罚款的行政处罚。同一个违法行为违反多个法律规范应当给予罚款处罚的,按照罚款数额高的规定处罚"和第四十一条"行政机关依照法律、行政法规规定利用电子技术监控设备收集、固定违法事实的,应当经过法制和技术审核,确保电子技术监控设备符合标准、设置合理、标志明显,设置地点应当向社会公布。电子技术监控设备记录违法事实应当真实、清晰、完整、准确。行政机关应当审核记录内容是否符合要求;未经审核或者经审核不符合要求的,不得作为行政处罚的证据。行政机关应当及时告知当事人违法事实,并采取信息化手段或者其他措施,为当事人查询、陈述和申辩提供便利。不得限制或者变相限制当事人享有的陈述权、申辩权",现行的超限超载治理法律法规规定尚未满足上述要求,主要表现为:①交通运输的法律法规中,未明确规定非现场监管;②交通运输的法律法规规章中对于非现场监管的法制和技术审核程序,尚无明确规定;③电子技术监控设备向社会公布的相关制度尚需要进一步明确;④电子技术监控设备收集、固定违法事实的流程尚需要规范和明确;⑤电子技术监控设备收集、固定的证据真实、清晰、完整、准确的技术标准需要进一步补充完善;⑥超限超载行为违反公安和交通运输相关法律法规给予罚款处罚的,处罚主体和处罚标准要做相应调整。

4 结 语

公路治超非现场执法监管的最终目标是提高公立超限的执法效率和科技治理水平,有效治理公路超限违法行为,促进交通运输行业全面协调可持续发展,相信公路超限治理的最有效手段必将是治超非现场技术的广泛应用以及非现场执法监管大力普及。文章对公路治超领域当前存在的非现场执法检测点布局不完善、非现场执法流程不明确、非现场执法与联合处罚金额不一致、非现场执法所需保障不充分四方面主要问题进行简要阐述,并给出了对策、建议,对全面开展非现场执法工作具有理论指导意义,后续的研究工作中将重点对非现场执法流程和推动部门间数据交换以及立法等工作做进一步研究和讨论。

参考文献

[1] 中华人民共和国交通运输部.2019年交通运输行业发展统计公报[EB/OL]. http://xxgk.mot.gov.

cn/2020/jigou/ zhghs/202006/ t20200630_3321335. html.

［2］ 张怀阳. 道路交通安全管理非现场执法研究［D］. 苏州：苏州大学，2009.

［3］ 陈晖，张柱庭. 交通运输非现场执法的若干问题分析［J］. 中国公路，2019.

［4］ 淮水市市场监督管理局. 交通非现场执法 执法规范：DB 3406/T001—2020［S］.

［5］ 马俊. 基于车辆高速精确检测的公路治超非现场执法模式研究［D］. 重庆：西南大学，2014.

［6］ 李轶舜. 公路治超非现场执法业务流程和布局方法［J］. 中国公路，2020(13)：82-83.

［7］ 王志勇，林杨. 宁波交通运输非现场执法建设研究［J］. 宁波经济（三江论坛），2020.

［8］ 王星刚. 治超非现场执法的法制路线图［J］. 中国公路，2016(15).

A Customized Passenger Transport Service Mix Pricing Study Based on CVP Analysis Method and Dynamic Pricing Strategy

Jiawei Gui　Qunqi Wu　Yahong Jiang

（Chang'an University）

Abstract　In recent years, customized buses have developed rapidly in China. Few related works focused on pricing problems or took dynamic pricing strategy into consideration. To explore that, a mix pricing plan is proposed for customized passenger transport enterprises based on CVP analysis method and dynamic pricing strategy. Future directions could be improving the mix plan, measuring fluctuation ranges of passengers' acceptable prices and making empirical researches based on big data.

Keywords　Public Transport　Customized Passenger Transport　Transport Service　Pricing　CVP Analysis Method　Dynamic Pricing Strategy

0　Introduction

In recent years, transportation and economic development has become a global problem and has garnered special importance. And customized passenger transportation has attracted more and more attention from researchers and practitioners. As Liu et al. (2015)[1] pointed out, customized buses have developed rapidly in China. Related works have focused on several potential topics, as follows：

（1）Passenger demands. Zhang et al. (2017)[2] analyzed the passenger demand of customized buses based on demand analysis and network modelling. Li et al. (2019)[3] proposed a commuter mode selection model to explore the influencing factors and the impact on the potential demand of Shanghai customized buses.

（2）Customized bus network. Liu et al. (2016)[4] proposed a customized bus transit system designed by commuting travel mode, which includes advanced, personalized and flexible interactive services on demand. Ma et al. (2017)[5] designed a customized bus network framework based on demand characteristics and operational purposes. Cao et al. (2017)[6] proposed an optimization design for passenger allocation based on customized buses, which ensures the interests of passengers by comprehensively considering factors such as travel time, waiting time, delay and economic costs.

（3）Customized bus scheduling. Qiu et al. (2019)[7] proposed a spatial clustering algorithm based on pair-density to identify the origin and destination distribution of potential passengers' customized buses. Li et al.

(2019)[8] proposed a customized bus passenger flow analysis algorithm and a multi-destination customized bus line capacity scheduling algorithm.

(4) Customized bus route optimization. Tong et al. (2017)[9] proposed a joint optimization model to solve many practical challenges in providing flexible customized bus services. Guo et al. (2019)[10] proposed a mixed-integer programming model with complete space-time constraints for custom bus route optimization problems. Li et al. (2019)[11] proposed a method framework for extracting potential customized bus routes from bus smart card data, which provides a reference for customized bus planners to conduct purposeful and effective investigations.

Furthermore, some studies explored other customized services besides customized buses. Lin et al. (2015)[12] indicated that customized logistics supply chains may choose more effective customized production levels than public logistics supply chains. Crudden et al. (2017)[13] designed, implemented and evaluated customized transportation assistance measures for the visually impaired based on concepts related to customized employment. Fargnoli et al. (2018)[14] proposed a method to analyze customized market needs and customer customized needs based on the quality function deployment method, and to simulate life cycle scenarios through screening life cycle modelling, life cycle assessment and life cycle costing tool support Methods. However, few of them focused on pricing problems. Besides, few of them took dynamic pricing strategy into consideration.

In our previous studies[15-17], we indicated that customized transport service meets the individualized needs of various passengers. And we also indicated that the demand of customized buses had cyclical rhythms influenced by trip, season and date. Furthermore, we also indicated that customized transport service has a bright future in the field of road transportation markets.

In this study, a mix pricing plan is proposed for those enterprises that providing customized passenger transport services based on CVP analysis method and dynamic pricing strategy.

1 CVP Analysis Method

1.1 CVP Principle

Cost-Volume-Profit (CVP) analysis is a method of cost accounting that looks at the impact that varying levels of costs and volume have on operating profit as introduced by Drury (1992)[18]. CVP analysis is also often referred to as the breakeven point (BE) analysis, a costing method that studies the location of breakeven points under different sales volumes and cost structures. This method is often used to assist managers in short-term economic decisions. In recent years, CVP analysis is still applied in the field of passenger transportation.

The variable P represents total profit. The variable I represents total income. The variable C represents total cost. Total profit P can be calculated by Formula (1).

$$P = I - C \tag{1}$$

The variable p represents the selling price. The variable v represents the selling volume. Total income I can be calculated by Formula (2).

$$I = p \times v \tag{2}$$

The variable c_v represents variable cost. The variable c_f represents fixed cost. Total cost C can be calculated by Formula (3).

$$C = c_v \times v + c_f \tag{3}$$

Based on Formulas (2)(3), Formula (1) can be converted into Formula (4).

$$P = (p - c_v) \times v - c_f \tag{4}$$

Based on Formula (4), from the perspective of breakeven, breakeven point BE can be calculated by Formula (5).

$$BE = \frac{c_f}{p-c_v} \tag{5}$$

Different selling volumes result in different situations.

(1) $v < BE$. In this situation, $I < C$ and $P < 0$, which means that total profit is negative.

(2) $v = BE$. In this situation, $I = C$ and $P = 0$, which means that total profit is zero.

(3) $v > BE$. In this situation, $I > C$ and $P > 0$, which means that total profit is positive.

Based on Formula (4), from the perspective of pricing, selling price p can be calculated by Formula (6).

$$p = c_v + \frac{c_f + P}{v} \tag{6}$$

Based on Formula (6), in order to make positive total profit, selling price p can be calculated by Formula (7).

$$p \geqslant c_v + \frac{c_f}{v} \tag{7}$$

Based on Formula (7), taking no account of fixed cost, selling price p can be calculated by Formula (8).

$$p \geqslant c_v \tag{8}$$

Different selling prices result in different situations.

(1) $p < c_v$. In this situation, every sale is unworthy, and enterprise is in danger.

(2) $p = c_v$. In this situation, income covers variable cost only, and enterprise is still in danger.

(3) $c_v < p < c_v + \frac{c_f}{v}$. In this situation, income covers variable cost and makes some profits, and it is feasible for enterprise to earn fixed cost back in the future.

(4) $p = c_v + \frac{c_f}{v}$. In this situation, income covers both variable cost and fixed cost, and it is breakeven point for enterprise to make real profits.

(5) $p > c_v + \frac{c_f}{v}$. In this situation, every sale is worthy, and enterprise is not in danger.

1.2 Fixed Cost Analysis

(1) Costs of operating vehicles, represented by c_{f_1}. Operating vehicles are an indispensable means of transportation for the realization of customized passenger transportation, and their comprehensive cost is also an important part of the fixed cost of the customized passenger transportation business, including vehicle purchase, vehicle parking, vehicle insurance, vehicle maintenance, etc. Obviously, enterprises purchasing vehicles at different prices correspond to their different goals and expectations. The higher the price of operating vehicles, the more comfortable and safer the customized passenger transport service can be, and the happiness and sense of acquisition of passengers. However, at the same time, it is more difficult for enterprises to achieve profitability through providing customized passenger transport services.

(2) Costs of business premises, represented by c_{f_2}. Business premises are necessary places to realize customized passenger transportation, and their costs are also an important part of the fixed costs of customized passenger transportation services, including office buildings, parking lots, temporary passenger pick-up and drop-off points, lease costs, water and electricity costs, security costs, information A series of related costs for maintaining the normal production and operation of the enterprise, such as chemical construction costs.

(3) Costs of enterprise employees, represented by c_{f_3}. Enterprise employees are the necessary human capital to realize customized passenger transportation, and their cost is also an important part of the fixed cost of customized passenger transportation business, including employee wages and benefits. Among them, the driver

of a customized passenger vehicle is a special type of employee. They follow the vehicle and passengers to complete the same time and space displacement. The wages and related rewards of such special employees will be reflected in the variable cost.

1.3 Variable Cost Analysis

(1) Costs of energy consumption, represented by c_{v_1}. Currently, most operating vehicles still use fossil fuels such as gasoline and diesel. Fossil fuel is the energy basis for the realization of custom passenger transport, and fuel consumption costs are also an important part of the variable cost of the custom passenger transport business. In order to reduce fuel consumption costs, some enterprises have set fuel consumption standard indicators for prescribed routes and rewarded fuel-efficient drivers. In addition, with the progress of energy technology and the in-depth reform of the concept of sustainable development, in the future, fossil fuels such as gasoline and diesel may be replaced by chemical raw materials such as urea and ethanol, as well as new-generation energy such as electricity and hydrogen. By then, energy consumption costs are expected to be obtained.

(2) Costs of tolls, represented by c_{v_2}. Tolls include tolls and tolls. Traffic in the urban area is generally not involved, and cross-city passenger transport may incur road and bridge tolls. In addition, airport expressways in some cities require tolls. Therefore, intercity customized passenger transportation often involves road and bridge tolls, and its cost is also an important part of the variable cost of customized passenger transportation business. In actual operation, the collection of road and bridge tolls is often related to the vehicle type, and has nothing to do with the actual number of passengers carried by the operating vehicle.

(3) Costs of drivers, represented by c_{v_3}. The driver is the necessary human capital to realize customized passenger transportation, and its cost is also an important part of the variable cost of customized passenger transportation. 7-seater commercial vehicle drivers need to have a C1 driving license, 14-seater commercial vehicle drivers need to have a B1 driving license, and 19 commercial vehicle drivers need to have an A1 driving license. However, in actual operation, most of the drivers equipped with 14-seater commercial vehicles by transportation enterprises have A1 driver's licenses, and there is a high distribution phenomenon. Obviously, the result of the high allocation is that the enterprise has increased the employment cost of drivers. In addition, in the whole process of customized passenger transport services, drivers often also undertake some tasks other than driving. For example, for passengers boarding outside the passenger terminal, the driver needs to use a hand-held security device to conduct safety inspections on him and his luggage.

(4) Costs of customized services, represented by c_{v_4}. Customized services can meet the customized needs of passengers, but the cost of customized services is often higher than that of traditional services. This is because in the customized passenger transportation mode, the transportation services provided by transportation enterprises to passengers actually include two parts: one is traditional transportation services, which transport passengers from point A to point B by vehicles; the other is value-added services customized by passengers. The cost of customized services refers to the latter. For example, passengers need drivers to help carry luggage, passengers want to get drinking water and snacks on passenger vehicles, passengers want to take a specific route and pick up a companion on the way to the destination, and so on. The provision of the above-mentioned customized value-added services to passengers under the premise of operating in compliance with laws and regulations will increase part of the cost. Transportation enterprises provide passengers with customized services through drivers. Although the driver's contribution will be reflected in their salaries, the essence is the personalized service needs of passengers. Therefore, the costs incurred should be distinguished from the normal passenger transportation costs and classified as customized service costs.

(5) Costs of partners, represented by c_{v_5}. The capabilities of a enterprise are often limited. In the whole process of customizing passenger transportation business, different enterprises have made different contributions: platform enterprises have built information exchange platforms to realize the function of online transactions; passenger stations have created passenger distribution centers, provided places for vehicles, completed passenger security, and ticket checking and other functions; transportation enterprises have undertaken the actual passenger transportation tasks, meeting passenger displacement needs and other value-added needs. Therefore, the income from passengers should be distributed among the enterprises. If a transportation enterprise cooperates with a platform enterprise or a passenger terminal enterprise and collects the full amount from the passengers, then the transportation enterprise should share with the platform enterprise and the passenger terminal enterprise after the event is completed. From the perspective of transportation enterprises, this part can be regarded as the cost of purchasing the corresponding functions of other enterprises.

1.4 Sales Volume Analysis

(1) Personalized travel demands of passengers. In the existing transportation service market, there are already many transportation service providers, including airplanes, trains, ships, buses, taxis, and public bicycles. The production of customized passenger transportation business comes from passengers. Its essence is that in the existing transportation service market, the various transportation service products provided by transportation service providers fail to fully meet the personalized travel needs of passengers, and these unmet needs can be to a certain extent, it is satisfied by customizing passenger transportation. Therefore, before analyzing the sales volume of customized passenger transportation business, the analysis must investigate the passenger's customized passenger transportation business needs.

(2) Competitive advantages of customized passenger transport enterprises. In the urban short-distance field, there are generally urban buses, subways, urban taxis, various platforms for online car-hailing, various platform-sharing bicycles and other legal market supplies; in the inter-city long-distance field, there are generally airplanes, high-speed rails, ships, Supply from various legal markets such as intercity taxis. In addition, there is a special illegal market supply of illegal cars. Passenger travel demand is often divided by the above-mentioned transportation service providers, and the sales volume of the custom passenger transportation business is obviously the result of competition with the above-mentioned transportation service providers. Therefore, when analyzing the sales volume of the custom passenger transport business, we must also consider the competitive advantages between the transportation enterprises that provide custom passenger transport services and other market participants.

(3) Individual choices of passengers. Only when the customized passenger service product launched by the transportation enterprise is selected by the passenger, can it finally be transformed into the actual sales volume of the customized passenger service. The choice of passengers mainly depends on two aspects: first, the competitive advantage between the transportation enterprises that provide customized passenger transportation services and other market participants; second, the individual of the passenger group is better. This result is difficult to accurately measure by formulas, but compared with other market participants, the more significant the competitive advantage of the transportation enterprises that customize passenger transportation services, the higher the sales volume of customized passenger transportation services.

1.5 Selling Price Analysis

Based on Formula (6), combined with those analyses above mentioned, selling price p can be calculated by Formula (9).

$$p = \sum_{i=1}^{5} c_{v_i} + \frac{\sum_{i=1}^{3} c_{f_i} + P}{v} \tag{9}$$

Different selling prices result in different situations.

(1) $p < \sum_{i=1}^{5} c_{v_i}$. In this situation, every sale is unworthy, and enterprise is in danger.

(2) $p = \sum_{i=1}^{5} c_{v_i}$. In this situation, income covers variable cost only, and enterprise is still in danger.

(3) $\sum_{i=1}^{5} c_{v_i} < p < \sum_{i=1}^{5} c_{v_i} + \frac{\sum_{i=1}^{3} c_{f_i}}{v}$. In this situation, income covers variable cost and makes some profits, and it is feasible for enterprise to earn fixed cost back in the future.

(4) $p = \sum_{i=1}^{5} c_{v_i} + \frac{\sum_{i=1}^{3} c_{f_i}}{v}$. In this situation, income covers both variable cost and fixed cost, and it is breakeven point for enterprise to make real profits.

(5) $p > \sum_{i=1}^{5} c_{v_i} + \frac{\sum_{i=1}^{3} c_{f_i}}{v}$. In this situation, every sale is worthy, and enterprise is not in danger.

2 Dynamic Pricing Strategy

There are 4 main assumptions in CVP analysis. First, all costs can be divided into variable costs or fixed costs. Second, all revenues and costs have a significant linear relationship with sales. Third, selling price p, variable cost c_v, and fixed cost c_f are all constants. Fourth, the enterprise's sales mix is always remained unchanged. However, customized passenger transport has the characteristics of flexibility and small batches. In other words, the passengers' demands of customized transportation is random. Moreover, the requirements for customized transportation services proposed by different passengers may also be different. Therefore, the analysis of customized passenger transportation pricing based entirely on the CVP analysis method results in a gap between the actual operation of transportation enterprises. There are 2 dynamic pricing strategies for customized passenger transport service mix pricing.

(1) Based on the cost of customized services. Passengers may put forward various demands, such as requiring the driver to assist in carrying luggage. Passengers may wish to obtain drinking water and snacks on passenger vehicles. Passengers may wish to take a specific route and pick up a companion on the way to the destination. For example, passenger A and passenger B go to the airport together. Passenger A has no special customization requirements. Passenger B has 3 pieces of excess luggage and needs the driver's assistance to carry it into the commercial vehicle from the 3rd floor. And, passenger B is willing to pay the extra cost incurred by customized baggage handling services. When placing an order, passenger B paid extra 10 yuan to the transportation enterprise compared with passenger A. At the end of the month, the transportation enterprise pays 8 yuan to the driver on duty. In this scenario, the cost of customized services generated by passenger B is included in the total price of customized passenger transportation by way of floating up customized passenger motion pricing. With the advancement of technology, in the future, transportation enterprises that provide passenger transportation services can set up various customized scenarios and value-added items for passengers to choose in advance, and charge for additional services requested by passengers based on the principle that "who enjoys, who pays".

(2) Based on supply and demand market. Customized passenger transportation is cyclical and seasonal. As an upgraded version of traditional passenger transport services, the use of dynamic pricing mechanisms for

customized passenger transport services is conducive to better giving play to the market's decisive role in resource allocation. Mainly can be divided into 3 kinds of modes.

First, set the lower limit and float upward. Passenger transport enterprises calculate the variable cost price based on the CVP analysis method, and use this as the lower limit to float upward. Transport enterprises can set up some automatic adjustment mechanisms. For example, the more passengers applying for customized passenger transport services, the higher the price.

Second, set the upper limit and float downward. Based on the CVP analysis method, transportation enterprises set a price ceiling in conjunction with the provisions of the Price Bureau, and this is the ceiling to float downward. Transport enterprises can set up some preferential measures. For example, the earlier passengers book a customized passenger transport service, the lower the price; the closer the departure, the higher the price.

Third, floating up and down dynamically. The transportation enterprise calculates the comprehensive cost price based on the CVP analysis method, and fluctuates up and down based on this. Transport enterprises can set up some automatic adjustment mechanisms and preferential measures at the same time. For example, passengers who have booked customized passenger services on the same route multiple times are promoted to frequent travelers and can enjoy a certain range of preferential policies; in relatively bad weather such as snow and thunderstorms Under the current situation, the charges for customized passenger transport services have been moderately increased.

3 Discussion

Over the course of this research, 3 details had not been contemplated within.

(1) Dynamic pricing strategy has negative impacts. The implementation of a dynamic pricing system for customized passenger transport is conducive to improving the degree of matching between customized passenger transport service charges and actual costs. However, frequent price changes and some unreasonable price changes mechanisms may induce resistance among some passengers, which will reduce the reputation of transportation enterprises. Therefore, before implementing the dynamic pricing scheme of customized passenger transportation, transportation enterprises must conduct adequate market research to come up with a scientific and reasonable price floating mechanism. In addition, in the implementation process, flexible response is required, which requires the support of traffic big data and strict surveys.

(2) Passenger transport enterprises should choose the model of operating vehicles carefully. With the continuous improvement of the national governance system, the country has continuously improved the requirements of passenger vehicles in terms of safety factor and environmental protection. It can be seen that the national motor vehicle pollutant emission standards are getting faster and faster, and they have been shorter than the service life of motor vehicles. For passenger transport enterprises, some passenger vehicles have not exceeded the prescribed service life but have not met the national motor vehicle pollutant emission standards. If they still cannot meet the national standards after repairs and adjustments, they must be scrapped. Therefore, operating vehicles purchased at full price have already formed sunk costs since the date of purchase, and face the risk of being eliminated in the future. Therefore, transportation enterprises should take into consideration the choice of vehicle models when formulating customized passenger transport pricing strategies, and conduct research and judgments appropriately in advance based on the high-end market positioning of customized passenger transport, instead of just focusing on its current price-performance ratio.

(3) Social benefits should also be considered. Traveling is an indispensable need for people. Passenger transport is an important industry that guarantees basic people's livelihood. Passenger transport enterprises bear

certain social responsibilities. With the improvement of the people's quality of life and the people's continuous yearning for a better life, the travel needs of passengers have become increasingly diversified and personalized. In this context, the development of customized passenger transport is the only way for the supply-side reform of the passenger transport industry and the transformation and upgrading of passenger transport enterprises. Although transportation enterprises lose money in the early stages of customizing passenger transportation, this reduces the living space of illegal passenger transportation operators and further improves passenger travel safety. This is the responsibility and mission of a transportation enterprise, and also a reflection of its social value.

To sum up, the results of customized passenger transportation pricing analysis based entirely on Cost-Volume-Profit analysis methods have a certain deviation from actual operations. When finalizing the pricing of customized passenger transport service products, transportation enterprises also need to consider from the perspective of the long-term development of the enterprise and the industry.

4 Conclusions

In this study, we proposed a mix pricing plan for customized passenger transport enterprises based on CVP analysis method and dynamic pricing strategy, which is conducive to improve service quality for passengers and reduce service costs for enterprises. Future directions for research can be in several ways, which are described as follows.

(1) To take more aspects into consideration and improve the mix plan. For instance, taxes are not mentioned in this study. Government might provide tax preference for those customized passenger transport enterprises that suffering deficits. Thus, the mix plan is still worth to be replenished.

(2) To measure fluctuation ranges of passengers' acceptable prices. The wellnesses and acceptability of passengers are quite essential for building dynamic fare customization models. For instance, frequent changes, like one price per day, is not friendly for old people to accept.

(3) To make empirical researches based on big data. For instance, we would make comparisons among several enterprises in the same area and further analyze the differences of customized transport service once we acquire enough data from customized passenger transport enterprises.

References

[1] Cao Y, Wang J. An Optimization Method of Passenger Assignment for Customized Bus. [J]. Mathematical Problems in Engineering, 2017:1-9.

[2] O'Mally, Jamie. A Customized Transportation Intervention for Persons with Visual Impairments. [J]. Journal of Visual Impairment & Blindness, 2017, 111(4):341-353.

[3] Drury C M. Management and Cost Accounting[J]. Springer, 1992, 205-235.

[4] Fargnoli M, Costantino F, Gravio G D, et al. Product Service-Systems Implementation: A Customized Framework to Enhance Sustainability and Customer Satisfaction[J]. Journal of Cleaner Production, 2018, 188, 387-401.

[5] Jiawei, Gui, Qunqi, et al. Relationship Between Road Networks and Regional Economic Developments in China[C]// 2019 世界交通运输大会, 0.

[6] Gui J, Wu Q. Customized Passenger Transport Service Innovation for Intelligent Time: Evidence from Empirical Data in Siping[M]. 2020.

[7] Gui J, Wu Q, Jiang Y. Customized Bus Survey and Data Analysis Based on Round-Trip Data between Changchun and Tonghua[M]. 2020.

[8] Guo R, Wei G, Zhang W, et al. Customized bus routing problem with time window restrictions: model

and case study[J]. Transportmetrica A: Transport Science, 2019, 15(2):1804-1824.

[9] Li D, Ye X, Ma J. Empirical Analysis of Factors Influencing Potential Demand of Customized Buses in Shanghai, China[J]. Journal of Urban Planning and Development, 2019, 145(2):05019006.1-05019006.10.

[10] Li J, Lv Y, Ma J, et al. Methodology for Extracting Potential Customized Bus Routes Based on Bus Smart Card Data[J]. Energies, 2018, 11(9).

[11] Lin X, Ma L, Zheng Z. Customized Transportation, Equity Participation, and Cooperation Performance within Logistics Supply Chains[J]. Mathematical Problems in Engineering, 2015, (2015-1-22), 2015, 2015:9.

[12] Liu T, Ceder A A. Analysis of a New Public-Transport-Service Concept: Customized Bus in China[J]. Transport Policy, 2015, 39(apr.):63-76.

[13] Tao L, Ceder A A, Bologna R, et al. Commuting by Customized Bus: A Comparative Analysis with Private Car and Conventional Public Transport in Two Cities[J]. Journal of Public Transportation, 2016, 19(2):55-74.

[14] Lyu Y, Chow C Y, Lee V, et al. CB-Planner: A Bus Line Planning Framework for Customized Bus Systems[J]. Transportation Research Part C: Emerging Technologies, 2019, 101(APR.):233-253.

[15] Ma J, Yang Y, Guan W, et al. Large-Scale Demand Driven Design of a Customized Bus Network: A Methodological Framework and Beijing Case Study[J]. Journal of Advanced Transportation, 2017, 2017:1-14.

[16] Qiu G, Song R, He S, et al. Clustering Passenger Trip Data for the Potential Passenger Investigation and Line Design of Customized Commuter Bus[J]. IEEE Transactions on Intelligent Transportation Systems, 2018:1-10.

[17] Tong L, Zhou L, Liu J, et al. Customized Bus Service Design for Jointly Optimizing Passenger-to-Vehicle Assignment and Vehicle Routing[J]. Transportation Research Part C Emerging Technologies, 2017, 85(dec.):451-475.

[18] Zhang J, Wang D, Meng M. Analyzing Customized Bus Service on a Multimodal Travel Corridor: An Analytical Modeling Approach[J]. Journal of Transportation Engineering, 2017, 143(11):04017067.1-04017067.12.

公私合营模式下环境可持续的道路收费与养护策略优化方法

赵 宇 陈 笑
（长安大学）

摘 要 近年来，交通基础设施的环境可持续发展已经受到越来越多的关注。随着车辆保有量及人们出行需求的增加，城市的环境压力和政府部门对交通基础设施的建设与维护压力日益增加，现有的基础设施的管理模式已无法满足社会发展的要求。近年来日益兴起的公私合营伙伴关系(PPP)的建设模式，能够有效弥补现有模式的不足。本文基于公私合营伙伴关系提出一种环境可持续发展的道路收费与养护策略优化框架，通过最大化特许期内私营单位利润、最小化系统二氧化碳(CO_2)排放以及车辆运行产生的氮氧化合物(NOx)排放，以满足私营单位对利润、政府对环境以及人们对健康的要求。该优化框架应用于美国佛罗里达州的一个高速公路的PPP项目,研究结果表明:所构建的优化框架能够在考虑不同参与者利益的情况下动态给出特许期内最优收费策略和路面养护规划,能够为决策者提供一种实现目前交通基础设施环境可持续发展的有效方案。

关键词 零排放与可持续交通　通行费定价策略　路面养护策略　CO_2与NO_x排放　公私合营伙伴关系

0 引　言

随着我国社会经济的迅猛发展及人们生活水平的提高,城市机动车保有量和人们出行需求持续增加,对交通基础设施的建设和维护管理提出了新的挑战。同时,由于交通系统中车辆运行及路面养护活动会有大量废气排放,给交通基础设施的环境可持续发展带来很大影响。2019年我国机动车保有量达到3.48亿辆,由机动车产生的NO_x排放量达到635.6万吨,同年我国按照《联合国气候变化框架公约》的相关要求发布的2014年国家温室气体清单显示,交通运输温室气体CO_2排放量达8.2亿吨,占全国温室气体排放总量的6.7%,道路运输是交通运输温室气体排放的主要方式,占84.1%[1]。CO_2是全球变暖的主要推手,而NO_x更会对人类健康和生态环境造成严重影响,是人类呼吸障碍疾病和酸雨、光化学烟雾的主要诱因之一[2],近年来由车辆运行产生的NO_x的比例还在不断上升[3]。此外,由于传统的高速公路项目具有建设运营成本昂贵、回收期长、技术要求高、管理难度大等特点,政府部门在道路建设运营方面巨大的财政压力。最近兴起的PPP道路建设运营模式,通过在特许期内赋予私营单位对交通基础设施投融资、建设维护、收费等权力,吸引私人资本参与交通基础设施的建设与发展,可以有效弥补现有模式的不足。在PPP道路中,设定合理的收费费率和路面养护规划是私营部门实现盈利的关键。同时,政府部门对道路的服务水平及排放要求进行限定,能够充分发挥政府部门和私营单位的优势,对交通基础设施的建设和环境可持续发展具有重要意义。

由于高速公路拥有对道路使用者收取通行费的权利,PPP模式得到了广泛应用。很多研究通过不同的方法对PPP模式下道路收费进行了探讨,如主因子分析法[4]、系统动力法[5-8]、多目标规划[9-10]以及Stacklegerg决策理论方法和模糊规划理论[11]等。此外,柯冬梅[12]结合PPP模式下高速公路定价的主要影响因素,提出了综合考虑项目成本、投资收益、风险因素以及消费者效益的定价模型。Ferrari[13]在优化通行费框架中考虑了私营单位和政府部门建设和养护成本的分配,并充分考虑了政府边际成本和使用者的支付意愿对最优通行费的影响。Chen[14]通过基于仿真的动态交通分配模型对交通路网中收费费率进行优化,以实现系统平均出行时间最短。Rouhani[15]等从社会福利的角度提出公私合作道路的收费优化框架,以最小化系统出行成本和最大化私营单位利润。此外,道路的养护管理是私营单位最关心的问题,对其利润有直接影响。张宏[16]等对PPP高速公路的路面养护与利益相关者之间的动态复杂关系进行了分析,构建了基于系统动力学的路面养护绩效研究模型。董庆庆[17]等对普通公路全寿命周期养护过程中出现的问题进行了分析总结,提出了PPP模式下普通公路养护管理的总体框架设计。袁勇[18]结合实际PPP公路项目,对路面养护管理体系、养护技术、养护时机、养护规划决策等技术的应用进行了探讨。以上研究均是从PPP项目的收费或路面养护的单一角度出发,忽略了二者之间相互影响的关系。

基于以上研究不足,道路的收费与养护策略同时优化便显得非常重要。路面养护能够改善路面性能,吸引更多使用者,使私营单位利润增加;过高的通行费会使出行者选择其他道路而使交通量减少,减少私营单位利润。Wu和Zhang[19]提出PPP模式下考虑特许期内私营单位利润最大化的道路收费定价与养护策略优化框架;Unnikrishnan[20]充分考虑了路面退化和道路性能的双向影响以及对用户路径选择的影响,提出了基于BOT项目的考虑养护决策的最优通行费的多目标优化模型,以最大化私营单位利润和最小化系统出行成本。Li和Sheng[21]提出了双层多周期优化模型对PPP项目中路面养护规划和通行费定价进行优化,以最大化私营单位利润和社会福利。Chu和Tsai[22]将道路的养护成本考虑进拥堵收费的框架中,并基于不同类型车辆对道路的损害程度而提出针对不同类型车辆使用者的道路收费定价模型。以上研究虽然对道路收费与养护策略进行了较为详细的探索,但并没有充分考虑在道路系统中车辆运行和路面养护所造成的环境负担。

全球变暖与环境污染在全球日渐显著。在路网系统中,车辆运行和路面养护活动是产生CO_2和NOx排放最主要的来源。在CO_2排放方面,本文综合考虑了路面养护活动和车辆运行所产生的排放。道路定价与养护策略会对用户的路径选择及系统CO_2的排放产生直接影响。在考虑CO_2排放的道路定价策略方面,Wang[23]等提出双层优化框架对路网收费策略进行优化,充分考虑了用户出行希望出行时间和通行费最小的因素,以实现系统出行时间、车辆总排放量以及对健康的负面影响最小的目标。Sinha[24]等提出路网收费的双层多目标优化框架,充分考虑了出行者和决策部门的利益,以最小化用户出行成本和出行时间,同时实现通行费收入最大以及污染水平最小的目标。Wen和Eglese[25]提出道路定价的双层多目标优化模型,以实现路网CO_2排放和系统出行时间最小。在考虑CO_2排放的路面养护方面,诸多研究表明合理的养护策略和路面材料选择能够有效减缓CO_2的排放压力[26-28]。Lidicker[29]等从CO_2排放和全寿命周期成本最小的角度对路面养护规划进行优化。Shoghli[30]等通过构建路面养护的多目标优化框架,寻找多种理论最优的路面养护技术,以实现最小的养护成本、养护时间及环境影响。Santos[31]等利用遗传算法解决道路养护规划的多目标问题,以最小化用户成本、机构成本及温室气体排放。Torres-Machi[32]等在资金预算约束的条件下对路面养护规划进行优化,以最大化路面养护的长期效能和最小化CO_2排放。Lee和Madanat[33]对单个或多个预算约束条件下路面养护策略进行了优化,以实现CO_2排放最小。另外,本文仅考虑了车辆运行所产生的NOx排放,Fomunung[34]等通过分析大量的测试数据构建了轻负荷汽油汽车NOx的排放预测模型。Nüesch[35]等提出柴油与电力混合动力的设想,通过控制汽车功率和电池荷电状态来最小化汽车实际行驶过程中的NOx排放。Nüesch[36]等提出柴油混合动力汽车的最优管理策略,以平衡车辆燃料消耗、颗粒物排放以及NOx的排放。Lee[37]等量化了标准和非标准车辆操作条件之间NOx排放的差异,并对超过法定排放标准的NOx排放量进行了估算。Barth[38]等采用参数化的物理方法构建了重型柴油汽车的综合模态排放模型,充分考虑了NOx、CO和HC等的排放。许建昌[39]等利用车载排放设备对北京市柴油公交车颗粒物和NOx的排放进行了研究。张金会[40]对北京市柴油公交车进行了实际道路排放数据采集,并对公交车NOx排放与车速、功率、排温等因素之间的关系进行了研究。黄伟[41]等根据重庆市交通干线空气质量检测和车流数据对区域环境内机动车NOx排放和对空气质量的影响进行了研究。根据以上内容可知,虽然国内外对CO_2和NOx有大量研究,但均是从单一角度进行探索,尤其是忽略了道路系统中不同利益相关者之间的相互作用对系统排放的影响。

如上所述,国内外对PPP模式在道路领域的应用开展了大量的研究,以期克服目前交通基础设施发展所面临的资金与运营管理困难。此外,全球变暖日益的加剧与城市居民健康意识的提升,使新的研究需综合考虑多方面的因素,以满足交通基础设施环境可持续发展的新要求。据此,本文构建了PPP模式下环境可持续的道路收费策略与养护规划的优化框架,以最大化私营单位利润、最小化系统CO_2排放及车辆运行产生的NOx的排放。在优化框架中,充分考虑了私营单位和政府之间的相互作用、路面性能的动态衰变以及路面性能和通行费率对用户出行需求的影响,能够动态得到考虑多方面影响因素条件下PPP道路在特许期内最优的收费定价策略与路面养护规划。该框架能够为决策者提供一种解决目前道路基础设施发展困难的有效方案。

1 模型方法

一般而言,公私合营伙伴关系中涉及多个利益相关者,不同利益相关者之间在特许期内的交互关系会十分复杂,甚至彼此的利益会相互冲突。对于公私合营伙伴关系模式下的道路项目来说,私营单位希望在特许期内尽可能降低道路的运营和养护成本,并实现自身利润的最大化。对于政府部门来说,希望在项目的特许期内确保道路对公众的服务水平,同时希望最小化在道路系统中由路面养护活动及车辆运行产生的CO_2排放和车辆运行产生的NOx排放,最大化社会福利。为了解决该问题,本文基于公私合营伙伴关系提出了一种环境可持续发展的道路收费与养护策略优化框架,充分考虑了私营单位和政府部门的相互制约关系和彼此的利益,实现了道路的环境可持续发展,为决策者提供了一种从环境可持续角度解决道路收费与路面养护管理的新方法。

1.1 私营单位利润模型

1.1.1 通行费收入模型

在 PPP 项目中，私营单位的主要目标是实现自身利润的最大化，通行费是私营单位最主要的收入来源，路段 l 在第 n 年的通行费收入可以用如下函数来表达：

$$R_l^n = \delta v_l^n d_l \pi_l^n \tag{1}$$

式中，R_l^n 为路段 l 在第 n 年的通行费收入，v_l^n 为路段 l 在第 n 年的年平均日交通量，d_l 为路段 l 的长度，π_l^n 是私营单位在第 n 年对路段 l 上出行者收取的费率，参数 δ 将路段 l 在第 n 年的年平均日交通量转换为年交通量。

政府部门在合同中会对私营单位收费的范围进行限定，以保护使用者的利益：

$$0 \leq \pi_l^n \leq \phi \tag{2}$$

式中，ϕ 为允许收取通行费费率的范围上限。

1.1.2 成本模型

私营单位合理控制成本是实现盈利的关键要素，其成本模型如下[19]：

$$C_l^n = \begin{cases} cons_l + \beta_0 + \beta_1 \mu_l^n + \beta_2 + \beta_3 \delta v_l^n d_l \pi_l^n, & \mu_l^n \neq 0 \\ cons_l + \beta_2 + \beta_3 \delta v_l^n d_l \pi_l^n, & \mu_l^n = 0 \end{cases} \tag{3}$$

私营单位的成本主要由道路在开放之前的建设成本 $cons_l$、道路的养护成本 $\beta_0 + \beta_1 \mu_l^n$ 以及道路收费系统的运营成本 $\beta_2 + \beta_3 \delta v_l^n d_l \pi_l^n$ 三部分组成。其中，β_0 表示第 n 年养护过程中产生的固定成本，$\beta_1 \mu_l^n$ 为第 n 年对路段 l 进行养护活动所产生的支出，μ_l^n 为第 n 年对路段 l 进行养护的量，本文考虑路面加铺作为路面养护措施。当对路面未采取任何养护措施时，即 $\mu_l^n = 0$ 时，该年该路段的养护成本 $\beta_0 + \beta_1 \mu_l^n$ 变为 0。此外，每年对道路的养护的量是一个非负数，其约束可以表示如下：

$$\mu_l^n \geq 0 \tag{4}$$

1.1.3 需求模型

在实际路网情况中，用户的出行路径选择受到诸多因素的影响，如出行驾驶体验、出行成本、出行时间等。本文采取了线性的需求模型[19]，充分考虑了出行成本和出行驾驶体验对用户路径选择的影响，其表达式如下：

$$v_l^n = \alpha_1 v_l^{n-1} + \frac{\alpha_2 (\pi_l^n - \pi^d)}{\pi^d} + \frac{\alpha_3 (S_l^n - S^d)}{S^d} \tag{5}$$

路段 l 在第 n 年的年平均日交通量主要由其前一年交通量的增长 $\alpha_1 v_l^{n-1}$、通行费定价对交通量的影响 $\alpha_2 (\pi_l^n - \pi^d)/\pi^d$ 以及路面性能对交通量的影响 $\alpha_3 (S_l^n - S^d)/S^d$ 三部分决定。其中，α_1 为出行需求的增长率，α_2 和 α_3 分别表示费率每增加 10% 和路面性能每退化 10% 对交通量的影响，π^d 和 S^d 分别表示最初设定的通行费率和期望的路面性能。

为了保证道路的服务水平，每个路段的交通量不应超过其设计的通行容量：

$$v_l^n / \zeta \leq k_l \tag{6}$$

参数 ζ 将第 n 年对路段 l 的年平均日交通量转换为每小时的交通量，k_l 为路段 l 的设计通行容量。

1.1.4 路面性能衰退模型

路面性能的衰退是一个连续过程，并受到车辆荷载及外界环境因素的影响。本文中用路面粗糙度来表示路面性能，并采取了一个线性的路面性能衰退函数[19]，其具体表达式如下：

$$S_l^{n-} = \gamma_0 + \gamma_1 S_l^{n-1} + \gamma_3 v_l^{n-1} \tag{7}$$

式中，S_l^{n-} 为路段 l 在第 n 年采取养护措施前的路面粗糙度，S_l^{n-1} 为第 $n-1$ 年的路面粗糙度，γ_0、γ_1

和 γ_3 为路面性能衰退系数。

路面的养护活动能够有效改善路面性能,则在第 n 年采取养护措施后路段 l 的路面粗糙度可表示如下:

$$S_l^n = \gamma_0 + \gamma_1 S_l^{n-1} + \gamma_2 \mu_l^{n-1} + \gamma_3 v_l^{n-1} \tag{8}$$

γ_2 表示养护活动对路面性能改善的影响。此外,在特许期内路面粗糙度不能劣于合同中允许最大值:

$$S_l^n \leq u \tag{9}$$

μ 为特许期内允许的路面粗糙度的最大值。

1.2 二氧化碳排放模型

路网系统中车辆运行和路面养护活动是产生 CO_2 的主要来源,路段 l 在第 n 年的总排放 E_{l,CO_2}^n 可以表达如下:

$$E_{l,CO_2}^n = E_{l,CO_2}^{n,V} + E_{l,CO_2}^{n,M} \tag{10}$$

式中,$E_{l,CO_2}^{n,V}$ 为第 n 年在路段 l 上行驶车辆产生的 CO_2 总排放,$E_{l,CO_2}^{n,M}$ 为在第 n 年对路段 l 采取的养护活动产生的 CO_2 总排放。车辆运行产生的 CO_2 排放受到道路上的交通量、出行距离、出行速度、路面性能等因素影响,其具体表达式如下:

$$E_{l,CO_2}^{n,V} = p_1 \delta F_{l,CO_2}^{n,V} v_l^n d_l \tag{11}$$

式中,参数 p_1 为将单位 g 转换为 t 产生的系数,$F_{l,CO_2}^{n,V}$ 为第 n 年在路段 l 上车辆运行产生 CO_2 的排放因子[42],CO_2 排放因子表示如下:

$$F_{l,CO_2}^{n,V} = f_1 + f_2 \vartheta_l^n + f_3 \ln(\vartheta_l^n) \tag{12}$$

其中,f_1、f_2 和 f_3 是 CO_2 排放因子系数,ϑ_l^n 为第 n 年路段 l 上车辆的行驶速度,可以用路段 l 的长度与该路段上车辆出行时间的比值来表示:

$$\vartheta_l^n = \frac{d_l}{T_l^n} \tag{13}$$

第 n 年在路段 l 上车辆的出行时间 T_l^n 如下[43]:

$$T_l^n = t_l^0 \left[1 + a \left(\frac{v_l^n}{\zeta k_l} \right)^b \right] \tag{14}$$

式中,t_l^0 为车辆在路段 l 上自由流时间,a 和 b 是常数。

第 n 年对路段 l 采取养护活动产生的 CO_2 总排放 $E_{l,CO_2}^{n,M}$,与该路段的长度、车道数以及加铺层厚度相关,$E_{l,CO_2}^{n,M}$ 的表达式[44]如下:

$$E_{l,CO_2}^{n,M} = p_2 d_l (e_1 p_3 m_l h_l^n + e_2 m_l) \tag{15}$$

式中,e_1 和 e_2 是路面养护活动产生 CO_2 的系数,m_l 是路段 l 的车道数,h_l^n 表示在第 n 年对路段 l 的路面加铺层厚度,与路段 l 在第 n 年采取养护措施前后的路面性能变化相关,其表达式[45]如下:

$$h_l^n = \frac{\omega_2 + \omega_3 / S_l^{n-}}{\omega_1} (S_l^{n-} - S_l^n) \tag{16}$$

式中,ω_1、ω_2 和 ω_3 为路面加铺层厚度函数的参数。

1.3 氮氧化合物排放模型

车辆运行的尾气排放是空气中 NOx 的主要来源之一。同样,NOx 的排放与出行距离,道路上的交通量以及出行速度等因素相关:

$$E_{l,NO_X}^{n,V} = p_1 \delta F_{l,NO_X}^{n,V} v_l^n d_l \tag{17}$$

$$F_{l,NO_X}^{n,V} = \chi_1 + \chi_2 \vartheta_l^n + \chi_3 (\vartheta_l^n)^2 \tag{18}$$

式中,$F_{l,NO_X}^{n,V}$ 是由车辆运行产生 NOx 的排放因子,χ_1、χ_2 和 χ_3 是 NOx 排放因子的系数[42]。

1.4 道路动态收费与养护策略优化框架的构建

在此优化框架下,充分考虑了在特许期内私营单位的利润、车辆运行及路面养护活动产生的 CO_2 总排放以及车辆运行产生的 NOx 总排放。在目标函数中,CO_2 和 NOx 排放通过其相应的排放价格转换为排放成本,以实现不同目标之间单位的统一,并通过净现值将特许期内现金流转换为初始年的现金价值。目标函数的表达如下:

$$\max J = \sum_{n=1}^{N}\sum_{l\in L}\frac{1}{(1+i_n)^n}\left\{(R_l^n - C_l^n) - P_{CO_2}^n E_{l,CO_2}^n - P_{NO_x}^n E_{l,NO_x}^{n,V}\right\} \quad (19)$$

式中,i_n 为第 n 年折现率,$P_{CO_2}^n$ 和 $P_{NO_x}^n$ 分别为第 n 年每吨 CO_2 和 NOx 排放的碳税和 NOx 税。优化框架从私营单位利润最大化、系统总 CO_2 排放最小化和车辆产生的 NOx 排放最小化的角度,充分考虑了私营单位和政府部门的利益,实现了路网的环境可持续发展。

约束条件总结如下:

$$R_l^n = \delta v_l^n d_l \pi_l^n \quad (20)$$

$$C_l^n = \begin{cases} \text{cons}_l + \beta_0 + \beta_1 \mu_l^n + \beta_2 + \beta_3 \delta v_l^n d_l \pi_l^n & (\mu_l^n \neq 0) \\ \text{cons}_l + \beta_2 + \beta_3 \delta v_l^n d_l \pi_l^n & (\mu_l^n = 0) \end{cases} \quad (21)$$

$$E_{l,CO_2}^n = E_{l,CO_2}^{n,V} + E_{l,CO_2}^{n,M} \quad (22)$$

$$E_{l,CO_2}^{n,V} = p_1 \delta F_{l,CO_2}^{n,V} v_l^n d_l \quad (23)$$

$$F_{l,CO_2}^{n,V} = f_1 + f_2 \vartheta_l^n + f_3 \ln(\vartheta_l^n) \quad (24)$$

$$\vartheta_l^n = \frac{d_l}{T_l^n} \quad (25)$$

$$T_l^n = t_l^0 \left[1 + a\left(\frac{v_l^n}{\zeta k_l}\right)^b\right] \quad (26)$$

$$E_{l,CO_2}^{n,M} = p_2 d_l (e_1 p_3 m_l h_l^n + e_2 m_l) \quad (27)$$

$$h_l^n = \frac{\omega_2 + \omega_3 / S_l^{n-}}{\omega_1}(S_l^{n-} - S_l^n) \quad (28)$$

$$E_{l,NO_x}^{n,V} = p_1 \delta F_{l,NO_x}^{n,V} v_l^n d_l \quad (29)$$

$$F_{l,NO_x}^{n,V} = \chi_1 + \chi_2 \vartheta_l^n + \chi_3 (\vartheta_l^n)^2 \quad (30)$$

$$v_l^n = \alpha_1 v_l^{n-1} + \frac{\alpha_2(\pi_l^n - \pi^d)}{\pi^d} + \frac{\alpha_3(S_l^n - S^d)}{S^d} \quad (31)$$

$$S_l^{n-} = \gamma_0 + \gamma_1 S_l^{n-1} + \gamma_3 v_l^{n-1} \quad (32)$$

$$S_l^n = \gamma_0 + \gamma_1 S_l^{n-1} + \gamma_2 \mu_l^{n-1} + \gamma_3 v_l^{n-1} \quad (33)$$

$$0 \leq \pi_l^n \leq \phi \quad (34)$$

$$\mu_l^n \geq 0 \quad (35)$$

$$v_l^n / \zeta \leq k_l \quad (36)$$

$$S_l^n \leq u \quad (37)$$

此优化框架在目标函数中通过统一单位将三个设计目标转化为单目标优化问题,并在 Matlab 中利用 fmincon 求解器通过内信赖域的方法对该框架进行优化求解。该方法开始优化前需要提供一组可行的初始解,本文通过给定每个 OD 之间初始的出行需求,随机生成区间范围内的通行费率和路面养护的值,通过约束(31)到约束(37)计算得到该组可行的初始点。

2 案例分析

2.1 案例基本情况

本文提出的优化框架将应用于美国佛罗里达州一条高速公路 I-75 的 PPP 项目。I-75 连接盖恩斯维尔市(Gainesville)和奥卡拉市(Ocala),为设计速度为70mph的双向6车道道路。

在此案例中,道路的设计通行容量 k_l 根据实际路况进行计算[46],PPP项目的特许期为30年,假设该PPP道路从2020年开始向社会公众开放,除通行费率外,我们将特许期内所有现金流转换为2020年美元的价值进行计算。

优化框架中的参数设置如下:折现率 i_n 在特许期内取值为6%;碳税 $P^n_{CO_2}$ 取值为15.62美元/t[47];NOx税 $P^n_{NO_X}$ 取值为11128美元/t[48];参数 β_0、β_1、β_2 和 β_3 分别取值为2、3.61、4和0.15[19];a 和 b 分别取值0.15和4[43];α_1 在特许期内为1%;α_2 和 α_3 分别取值为-6000和-3000;p_1、p_2 和 p_3 取值分别为10^{-6}、10^{-3}和10^3;ζ 取值为24;δ 取值为365;系数 f_1、f_2、f_3 分别为1005、4.15和-263[42];χ_1、χ_2 和 χ_3 分别取值1.360、0.0217和$-4\times10^{-5[42]}$;系数 e_1 和 e_2 分别取值225kg-CO_2E(lane-km-mm)-1 和 3375 kg-CO_2E(lane-km)-1[44];系数 γ_0、γ_1、γ_2 和 γ_3 分别取值 -3、1.07、-1 和 $1.1\times10^{-4[19]}$;系数 ω_1、ω_2 和 ω_3 取值为0.66、0.55和18.3[45]。此外,第一年道路交通量取自佛罗里达州交通部数据[49]。

在此应用案例中,我们假定该PPP道路向社会公众开放时路面性能为40QI,并以此为该道路最佳的路面性能,即期望路面性能 S^d,路面的最差状态即路面性能的上限 μ,设定为60QI,私营单位需在特许期内将路面性能控制在此区间内。此外,私营单位最初设定的通行费率 π^d 为0.25美元/英里①,可以向道路使用者收取通行费率的上限 ϕ 设定为0.625美元/英里。其他详细信息可参考之前的研究[19]。

2.2 案例结果分析

求解优化框架的结果见图1,不同下角标表示不同车辆行驶方向,如I-75$_N$表示车辆从奥卡拉市向盖恩斯维尔市方向行驶,I-75$_S$则相反。图1分别为特许期内的路面粗糙度、路面养护的量、费率、年平均日交通量、私营单位每年的利润、私营单位累计利润、每年系统CO_2的总排放量和每年车辆NOx的总排放量。

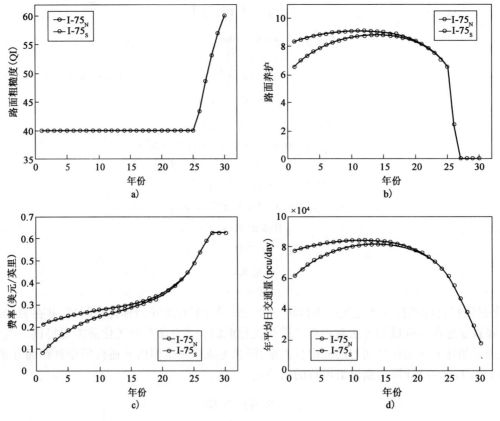

图 1

---

① 1英里 = 1.609km。

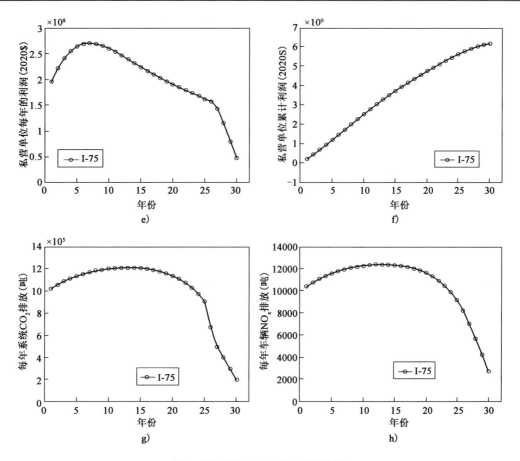

图 1 优化框架应用于研究项目的性能

图 1a)表示特许期内每年路面粗糙度的变化,路面粗糙度在前 25 年一直保持在最佳的状态,从第 26 年开始逐渐退化至上限 60QI;图 1b)为路面养护的量,路面养护量呈现先增加后降低的趋势,在特许期的最后四年,没有对路面采取任何养护措施;图 1c)表示费率的变化,费率在前期维持在较低的水平,以吸引更多的出行者使用该 PPP 道路,之后收费费率逐年上升,在第 28 年时达到费率的上限 0.625 美元/英里;图 1d)表示特许期内年平均日交通量的变化,年平均日交通量呈现先增加后降低的趋势;私营单位每年的利润和累计利润如图 1e)和图 1f)所示,私营单位年利润在第 7 年达到最大值后逐渐下降,由于每年的利润均为正值,所以累计利润一直呈上升趋势;图 1f)和图 1g)分别表示特许期内每年车辆运行和路面养护活动产生的 CO_2 总排放和车辆运行产生的 NOx 的排放,二者趋势相似,均先上升后逐渐降低。

3 结 语

本文提出了一个利于环境可持续发展的动态优化框架,以寻找 PPP 道路项目在特许期内最优的收费定价策略和路面养护规划。优化框架中充分考虑了多方的利益,通过最大化特许期内私营单位的利润,最小化系统 CO_2 排放及车辆产生的 NOx 排放,实现私营单位对利润、政府对环境以及人们对健康的要求。在此框架中,私营单位、政府部门、通行费及路面性能对用户路径选择的影响,车辆行驶速度对排放的影响以及养护活动对排放的影响之间的相互关系得到充分的考虑。案例结果表明,在特许期内,私营单位应在前 25 年内将路面性能保持在最佳状态,来吸引更多的出行者使用该道路,之后减少路面养护活动,以降低养护成本。而通行费率后在一开始设定为较低的值,以吸引更多的出行者使用该 PPP 道路,之后费率逐渐上升,在特许期结束前达到允许收取费率范围的上限,以谋求更多的通行费收入。

本文为决策者制定环境可持续发展的道路收费策略与养护规划提供了一种全新方法,但本文对用户的选择进行了简化,每年的交通量高度依赖前一年的交通量,并不能完全符合现实交通情况,同时,应用案例是项目级的道路,并不能充分分析PPP道路对整个路网的影响。今后将基于路网进行相关研究,并充分考虑用户出行时间、出行成本、驾驶体验对用户路径选择的影响,同时对PPP道路对整个路网性能的影响加以分析。

参考文献

[1] 中华人民共和国生态环境部. 中国移动源环境管理年报[R]. 2020.8.10.

[2] 贺泓,翁端,资新运. 柴油车尾气排放污染控制技术综述[J]. 环境科学, 2007, 28(6): 1169-1177.

[3] Yun Shi, Yinfeng Xia, Bihong Lu, et al. Emission Inventory and Trends of NOx for China, 2000 – 2020 [J]. Journal of Zhejiang University-Science A (Applied Physics & Engineering), 2014, 15 (06): 454-464.

[4] 侯丽,王松江. 基于收费公路PPP项目特许经营权定价影响因素研究[J]. 项目管理技术, 2012 (02): 26-29.

[5] 刘旭. 基于系统动力学的高速公路PPP项目定价研究[D]. 重庆: 重庆交通大学, 2016.

[6] 刘秋林,贾立敏. 基于系统动力学的高速公路PPP项目收益研究——以田林至西林(滇桂界)高速公路为例[J]. 价值工程, 2019 (16): 7.

[7] 邓小鹏,熊伟,袁竞峰,等. 基于各方满意的PPP项目动态调价与补贴模型及实证研究[J]. 东南大学学报(自然科学版), 2009, 39(6): 1252-1257.

[8] 陈欢欢. 基于系统动力学的高速公路PPP项目特许定价模型研究[D]. 兰州: 兰州交通大学, 2014.

[9] 张晓波. PPP模式高速公路特许定价模式研究[D]. 成都: 西南交通大学, 2016.

[10] 朱海波. PPP模式下高速公路项目定价机制研究[D]. 武汉: 武汉工程大学, 2017.

[11] 姚鹏程. 不确定环境下的高速公路PPP项目定价问题研究[D]. 昆明: 昆明理工大学, 2011.

[12] 柯冬梅. PPP模式下高速公路特许经营项目的定价机制研究[D]. 重庆: 重庆交通大学, 2013.

[13] Ferrari P. Road Network Toll Pricing and Social Welfare[J]. Transportation Research Part B: Methodological, 2002, 36(5): 471-483.

[14] Chen X, Zhang L, He X, et al. Surrogate-Based Optimization of Expensive-to-Evaluate Objective for Optimal Highway Toll Charges in Transportation Network[J]. Computer-Aided Civil and Infrastructure Engineering, 2014, 29(5): 359-381.

[15] Rouhani O M, Geddes R R, Gao H O, et al. Social Welfare Analysis of Investment Public-Private Partnership Approaches for Transportation Projects[J]. Transportation Research Part A: Policy and Practice, 2016, 88: 86-103.

[16] 张宏,郑荣贝,乔文珊. 基于路面维护的高速公路PPP项目特许期绩效研究[J]. 系统仿真学报, 2018 (8): 39.

[17] 董庆庆,崔亚雷. 基于PPP融资方式普通公路养护管理模式研究[J]. 交通财会, 2017 (7): 15-18.

[18] 袁勇. 基于公路PPP项目运营期管养技术应用研究[J]. 中国公路学会养护与管理分会第八届学术年会论文集, 2018.

[19] Wu H, Zhang Z. Managing Transportation Facilities in Design-Build-Finance-Operate Partnerships: Toll-Pricing Strategies[J]. Transportation Research Record, 2013, 2345(1): 92-99.

[20] Unnikrishnan A, Valsaraj V, Damnjanovic I, et al. Design and Management Strategies for Mixed Public Private Transportation Networks: A Meta-Heuristic Approach [J]. Computer-Aided Civil and Infrastructure Engineering, 2009, 24(4): 266-279.

[21] Li Z C, Sheng D. Pavement Rehabilitation Scheduling and Toll Pricing Under Different Regulatory Regimes [J]. Annals of Operations Research, 2014, 217(1): 337-355.

[22] Chu C P, Tsai J F. Road Pricing Models with Maintenance Cost[J]. Transportation, 2004, 31(4): 457-477.

[23] Wang J Y T, Ehrgott M, Dirks K N, et al. A Bilevel Multi-Objective Road Pricing Model for Economic, Environmental and Health Sustainability[J]. Transportation Research Procedia, 2014, 3: 393-402.

[24] Sinha A, Malo P, Deb K. Transportation Policy Formulation as a Multi-Objective Bilevel Optimization Problem[C]. 2015 IEEE Congress on Evolutionary Computation (CEC). IEEE, 2015: 1651-1658.

[25] Wen L, Eglese R. Minimizing CO_2e Emissions by Setting a Road Toll[J]. Transportation Research Part D: Transport and Environment, 2016, 44: 1-13.

[26] Santero N J, Masanet E, Horvath A. Life-cycle Assessment of Pavements. Part I: Critical Review[J]. Resources, Conservation and Recycling, 2011, 55(9-10): 801-809.

[27] Giustozzi F, Toraldo E, Crispino M. Recycled Airport Pavements for Achieving Environmental Sustainability: An Italian case study[J]. Resources, conservation and recycling, 2012, 68: 67-75.

[28] Santos J, Flintsch G, Ferreira A. Environmental and Economic Assessment of Pavement Construction and Management Practices for Enhancing Pavement Sustainability[J]. Resources, Conservation and Recycling, 2017, 116: 15-31.

[29] Lidicker J, Sathaye N, Madanat S, et al. Pavement Resurfacing Policy for Minimization of Life-Cycle Costs and Greenhouse Gas Emissions[J]. Journal of Infrastructure Systems, 2013, 19(2): 129-137.

[30] Shoghli O, De La Garza J M. A Multi-Objective Decision-Making Spproach for the Sustainable Maintenance of Roadways[C]. Construction Research Congress 2016. 2016: 1424-1434.

[31] Santos J, Ferreira A, Flintsch G, et al. A Multi-Objective Optimisation Approach for Sustainable Pavement Management[J]. Structure and Infrastructure Engineering, 2018, 14(7): 854-868.

[32] Torres-Machi C, Pellicer E, Yepes V, et al. Towards a Sustainable Optimization of Pavement Maintenance Programs Under Budgetary Restrictions[J]. Journal of cleaner production, 2017, 148: 90-102.

[33] Lee J, Madanat S. Optimal Policies for Greenhouse Gas Emission Minimization Under Multiple Agency Budget Constraints in Pavement Management[J]. Transportation Research Part D: Transport and Environment, 2017, 55: 39-50.

[34] Fomunung I, Washington S, Guensler R. A Statistical Model for Estimating Oxides of Nitrogen Emissions from Light Duty Motor Vehicles[J]. Transportation Research Part D: Transport and Environment, 1999, 4(5): 333-352.

[35] Nüesch T, Cerofolini A, Mancini G, et al. Equivalent Consumption Minimization Strategy for the Control of Real Driving NOx Emissions of a Diesel Hybrid Electric Vehicle[J]. Energies, 2014, 7(5): 3148-3178.

[36] Nüesch T, Wang M, Isenegger P, et al. Optimal Energy Management for a Diesel Hybrid Electric Vehicle Considering Transient PM and Quasi-Static NOx Emissions[J]. Control Engineering Practice, 2014, 29: 266-276.

[37] Lee T, Park J, Kwon S, et al. Variability in Operation-Based NOx Emission Factors with Different Test Routes, and Its Effects on the Real-Driving Emissions of Light Diesel Vehicles[J]. Science of the total environment, 2013, 461: 377-385.

[38] Barth M, Scora G, Younglove T. Modal Emissions Model for Heavy-Duty Diesel Vehicles[J]. Transportation Research Record, 2004, 1880(1): 10-20.

[39] 许建昌,李孟良,秦孔建,等. 北京市柴油公交车辆尾气颗粒物和氮氧化合物排放研究[C]. 中国汽车工程学会燃料与润滑油分会第13届年会论文集.2008:(26). 200-204.

[40] 张金会. 柴油公交车实际道路氮氧化物排放特性研究[D].北京:北京理工大学,2016.

[41] 黄伟,余家燕,鲍雷,等.重庆市交通道路氮氧化物排放简析[J].环境科学导刊,2015,34(02):131-135.

[42] Hickman J, Hassel D, Joumard R, et al. Methodology for Calculating Transport Emissions and Energy Consumption[J]. 1999.

[43] Bureau of Public Roads. Traffic Assignment Manual US Department of Commerce, 1964.

[44] Lee J, Madanat S, Reger D. Pavement Systems Reconstruction and Resurfacing Policies for Minimization of Life-Cycle Costs Under Greenhouse Gas Emissions Constraints[J]. Transportation Research Part B: Methodological, 2016, 93: 618-630.

[45] Lee J, Madanat S. A Joint Bottom-Up Solution Methodology for System-Level Pavement Rehabilitation and Reconstruction[J]. Transportation Research Part B: Methodological, 2015, 78: 106-122.

[46] Margiotta R, Washburn S, 2017. Simplified Highway Capacity Calculation Method for the Highway Performance Monitoring System. Technical Report PL-18-003. Federal Highway Administration.

[47] The World Bank, 2019. Carbon pricing dashboard.

[48] South Coast AQMD. NOx and SOx RTCs Rolling Avg Price CY 2019-20 - Oct 2020.

[49] FDOT, 2017. Florida traffic online.

附录：

参数解释　　　　　　　　　　　　　　　　　　　　　　　　　　　　表1

参　数	解　释
L	研究区域路段集合
N	特许期年限
i_n	第 n 年折现率
R_l^n	第 n 年私营单位在路段 l 的通行费收入
C_l^n	第 n 年私营单位在路段 l 的支出成本
$E_{l,CO_2}^{n,V}$	第 n 年在路段 l 上行驶车辆产生的 CO_2 总排放
$E_{l,CO_2}^{n,M}$	第 n 年对路段 l 采取的养护活动产生的 CO_2 总排放
$F_{l,CO_2}^{n,V}$	第 n 年在路段 l 上车辆产生 CO_2 的排放因子
$F_{l,NO_X}^{n,V}$	第 n 年在路段 l 上车辆运行产生 NOx 的排放因子
$P_{CO_2}^n$	第 n 年每吨 CO_2 排放的碳税
$P_{NO_X}^n$	第 n 年每吨 NOx 排放的 NOx 税
S_l^{n-}	第 n 年路段 l 在采取养护措施前的路面粗糙度
S_l^n	第 n 年路段 l 在采取养护措施后的路面粗糙度
S^d	期望的路面性能
S_l^{n-1}	第 $n-1$ 年路段 l 的路面粗糙度
T_l^n	第 n 年在路段 l 上车辆的出行时间
cons_l	建设成本
ϑ_l^n	第 n 年路段 l 上车辆的行驶速度
v_l^n	第 n 年路段 l 的年平均日交通量
h_l^n	第 n 年对路段 l 的路面加铺层厚度
μ_l^n	第 n 年对路段 l 的养护的量
π_l^n	第 n 年路段 l 的通行费率
π^d	最初设定的道路通行费率
d_l	路段 l 的长度

续上表

参　数	解　　释
t_l^0	车辆在路段 l 上自由流时间
ϕ	通行费费率的上限
μ	特许期内允许的路面粗糙度的最大值
k_l	路段 l 的设计通行能力
m_l	路段 l 的车道数
δ	将第 n 年路段 l 的年平均日交通量转换为年交通量
ζ	将第 n 年对路段 l 的年平均日交通量转换为每小时的交通量
a、b	常数
β_0、β_1、β_2、β_3	道路养护活动和运营成本相关参数
α_1、α_2、α_3	出行需求函数相关参数
γ_0、γ_1、γ_2、γ_3	路面性能衰退系数
f_1、f_2、f_3	CO_2 排放因子系数
χ_1、χ_2、χ_3	NOx 排放因子系数
e_1、e_2	路面养护活动产生 CO_2 的系数
p_1、p_2、p_3	单位转换系数
ω_1、ω_2、ω_3	路面加铺层厚度函数的参数

第六篇 水上运输

三峡河段智能通航框架与评价体系构建

谭志荣[1,2] 王洋[1] 王海滨[3]

(1.武汉理工大学航运学院;2.内河航运技术湖北省重点实验室;3.长江三峡通航管理局)

摘 要 智能通航的概念与内涵还没有明确的定义,暂无评判通航智能化程度与指导智能通航建设的评价指标体系。为服务交通强国试点建设,对三峡河段智能通航进行系统研究,建立系统自主等级评价,提出智能通航系统的定义与总体框架;建立评价指标体系,确定各因素对智能通航影响的权重值。结果表明,影响较大的因素有人船智能识别水平、信息采集水平、航行异常告警效率、智能拍档、船舶协同调度水平。进一步丰富智能通航理论体系,为长江航运高质量发展、实施交通强国建设试点项目及三峡智能通航建设提供技术支撑。

关键词 智能通航 影响因素 层次分析 德尔菲法

0 引 言

三峡船闸在长江航运体系中起到了沟通中上游地区水上运输的作用,是水路运输的关键运输枢纽,因此开展三峡河段智能体系研究可以促进长江水运的高速发展。

现状,国内外有关智能通航的概念还未给出清晰的定义,因此没有相关指标可以对三峡枢纽智能通航程度进行评价。在另一方面,目前,对智能通航的概念与内涵还没有明确的定义,暂无可以用来评判通航智能化程度的评价指标体系。同时,从三峡枢纽未来发展需求的角度出发,收集和整合信息、监测和维护、高科技设备的使用水平等方面还需要进一步发展,以满足三峡枢纽的智能航运建设。

因此,本文拟建立三峡河段智能通航水平评价体系,用于评判目前三峡枢纽智能通航的建设水平。

1 系统自主等级评价

到目前为止,相关学者对于智能通航体系的研究相对较少,其中李定国[1]以三峡枢纽信息化水平为研究对象,从信息整合、应用水平、标准体系的建立等方面进行了研究。郑钧[2]为促进三峡智能调度水平的提升,研究了一套航道水位实时监管系统,用以对水位进行监控并提供了相应的水位信息。

同时,国内外有关学者对于智能通航的评价体系研究相对缺乏,因此本文通过借鉴对于系统自主化水平的评价体系,来对有关的评价体系进行研究。其中,Parasuraman等[3]将某个特定种类及程度自主化水平对个体的影响水平作为设计系统自主化水平的评价依据,并将系统的可靠性以及产生的后果作为次要的评价指标,构建了一个评价自主化程度的评价指标体系,具体如表1所示。

统自主等级评价 表1

	序号	内容
高	10	不受人类干涉,计算机自动决定所有事
	9	仅在计算机决定时告知
	8	仅当人类询问时告知
	7	计算机自动执行方案,在必要时告知人类
	6	人在决策自动执行之前有一段有限的时间来否决
	5	在人类允许的情况下,计算机执行方案

基金项目:国家自然科学基金(项目批准号:51809207)长江航务管理局科技项目(批准号:202010001)作者简介:谭志荣(1978-),男,湖北武汉人,副教授,博士,硕士生导师,从事载运工具运用工程与交通系统安全性评价研究。

续上表

序号	内 容
4	计算机仅提供一种方案
3	计算机缩小决策/行动方案的范围
2	计算机提供一系列完整的决策/行动方案
低　　1	计算机不提供任何帮助,人类需要自主做出决定和行动

2 三峡河段智能通航方案设计

通过研究智能航运的发展趋势,对三峡枢纽的智能通航系统展开远期规划,并根据规划进一步确定三峡河段智能通航的概念、系统的逻辑层次。三峡河段智能河段智能通航的技术框架如图1所示。

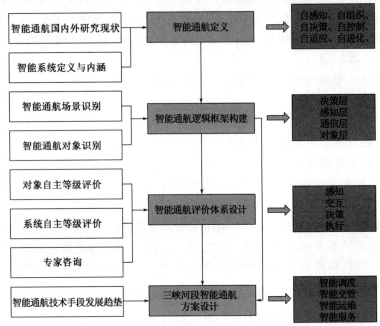

图1 总体技术框架

根据有关研究可知,目前智能系统的特点包含以下几点:自我感知、自我决策、自我控制、自我反馈和自我进化。为了进一步定义三峡河段智能通航系统的逻辑框架,本文通过研究三峡河段通航现状,判断智能通航发生的对象及地点,并以此为基础构建出三峡河段智能通航的体系框架,具体逻辑框架如图2所示。

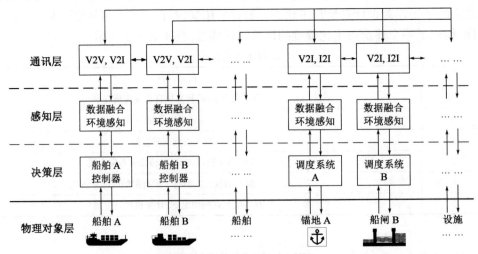

图2 智能通航系统逻辑框架

通过分析环境、船舶及通信网络在物理系统中的自主性,并依据物理对象在感知、交互、决策和控制等层面的自主能力,分析了智能通航系统的自主化程度,并依据智能通航水平评价指标建立于对象的形式,由管理人员实现,并通过智能辅助决策系统支持管理决策。然后依据有关知识,分析了以这些方法和手段为基础建立的智能通航系统的智能化水平,并依据分析结果完善有关的评价指标体系。

3 模型的建立与指标权重计算

3.1 模型的建立

层次模型的建立,需要对各影响指标进行分析,并将有关因素进行分类,每类对应为一个层级,每层对应着目标层、准则层、指标层,并依据三峡河段智能通航体系构建层次模型。同时,通过文献查阅[4-7],对影响三峡智能通航系统的各个指标进行了研究,层次结构模型如表2所示。

三峡河段智能通航影响因素层次结构模型　　　表2

目标因素(目标层)	一级影响因素(准则层)	二级影响因素(指标层)
三峡河段智能通航影响因素 A	智能监管因素 B_1	航行异常告警效率 C_1
		信息采集水平 C_2
		人船智能水别水平 C_3
		油污排放自动水别水平 C_4
	智能管理因素 B_2	智能拍档(艘/小时) C_5
		智能指泊(艘/小时) C_6
		船舶协同调度水平 C_7
		自动发航(艘/小时) C_8
	基础设施因素 B_3	CCTV 视频监控点(个) C_9
		VHF 通信基站(个) C_{10}
		通航指挥中心(个) C_{11}
		雷达站(个) C_{12}
	通航保障因素 B_4	应急设备数量(个) C_{13}
		安检设施数量(个) C_{14}
		安检设施智能化水平 C_{15}
		应急设备智能化水平 C_{16}
		智能浮式系船柱数量 C_{17}

3.2 相关指标权重的计算

3.2.1 判断矩阵的建立

采用层次分析法解决问题的关键步骤在于判断矩阵的建立。判断矩阵是通过分析各影响因素间的关系,并进行定量化处理,通过将各因素间的数量关系以矩阵形式表示,通常可以表示为 $A = (a_{ij})_{n \times n}$。在处理的过程中,通常以问卷调查的形式进行,并将各因素之间的相对程度进行对比分析,以此获得判断矩阵。

3.2.2 判断矩阵单排序与一致性检验

由于问题存在复杂性和认知上存在的局限性的,对客观事物进行分析时,如果是直接将影响因素两两比较,从而得到判断矩阵,但为了减低计算过程中有关指标权重的误差,需要开展判断矩阵一致性检验[9]。

当一致性比率<0.1,可以认为判断矩阵是合理的,即各影响因素权重分配符合要求;相反的,如果一致性比率≥0.1,应对判断矩阵进行修改,以降低判断矩阵的一致性比率。

3.2.3 判断矩阵排序与一致性检验

层次总排序的总权重计算公式如下:即把各层次单排序计算结果合成最高层级因素的相对重要性的排序,总权重计算式为:

$$w'_i = \sum_{j=1}^{n} a_j b_j^i \quad (i=1,2,\ldots n) \tag{1}$$

层次总排序一致性检验,具体计算步骤为:

(1)计算总排序一致性指标:

$$CI' = \sum_{i=1}^{n} W_i CI_i \tag{2}$$

(2)计算总排序平均随机一致性指标:

$$RI' = \sum_{i=1}^{n} W_i RI_i \tag{3}$$

(3)计算总排序一致性比率:

$$CR' = \frac{CI'}{RI'} \tag{4}$$

式中:a_n——权值;

b_n^i——单排序结果;

B_n——本层次的影响因素。

4 结果与分析

4.1 问卷的信度与效度分析

本文主要通过发放调查问卷对三峡通航管理局的管理人员以及相关领域的专家进行咨询,并根据有关的统计结果,来确定各个影响因素的权重,问卷调查的可信度与准确性会显著的影响评价体系,因此在确定各个影响因素权重之前,首先需对调查结果进行分析。

4.1.1 问卷的信度分析

信度分析分析主要用于分析问卷的一致性或者稳定性,就是通过对设计好的问卷进行反复测量,观测所得结果的一致性。在问卷调查中,样本的信度越高,就表示问卷调查的结果越可信。下面通过SPSS21.0对本次问卷调查的结果进行信度分析——即通过评价不同调查结果中的问题测量的是否为同一个概念。

表3为经过SPSS21.0处理后的问卷信度统计表,本次主要是对问卷调查中的17个项目进行信度分析。其中问卷的克朗巴哈α系数为0.923,标准化后的克朗巴哈α系数为0.934,数值均大于0.8(一般来讲:α系数最好在0.8以上,0.7~0.8之间属于可以接受范围,而分量表的α信度系数希望在0.7以上,0.6~0.7之间可以接受。如果α信度系数低于0.6则考虑修改量表。),因此可以认为本次设计的问卷能够有效地对事先想要调查的方向进行收集,调查结果的可信度较高。

调查问卷信度统计量　　　　表3

克朗巴哈α系数	标准化后的克朗巴哈α系数	问卷调查的项目
0.923	0.934	17

从表4可以看出三峡河段智能通航评价体系的各个因素的克朗巴哈α系数均在0.8以上,说明本次针对三峡河段智能通航评价体系所选的各个指标均为有效变量,能够较好评价三峡河段的智能通航建设水平。

调查问卷测量因素的信度统计　　　　表4

	因素删除后的尺度均数	因素删除后的尺度方差	校正因素总相关系数	因素被删除后的克朗巴哈α系数
航行异常告警效率 C_1	54.072	70.003	0.672	0.951

续上表

	因素删除后的尺度均数	因素删除后的尺度方差	校正因素总相关系数	因素被删除后的克朗巴哈 α 系数
信息采集水平 C_2	51.235	72.006	0.695	0.836
人船智能水别水平 C_3	55.669	63.957	0.841	0.892
油污排放自动水别水平 C_4	58.431	62.098	0.693	0.85
智能拍档(艘/小时) C_5	50.592	65.623	0.993	0.897
智能指泊(艘/小时) C_6	56.406	65.059	0.428	0.917
船舶协同调度水平 C_7	60.467	70.662	0.263	0.916
自动发航(艘/小时) C_8	54.154	67.234	0.506	0.839
CCTV 视频监控点(个) C_9	56.723	71.617	0.106	0.931
VHF 通信基站(个) C_{10}	54.268	73.638	0.805	0.809
通航指挥中心(个) C_{11}	58.459	65.393	0.860	0.814
雷达站(个) C_{12}	56.254	67.231	0.499	0.918
应急设备数量(个) C_{13}	59.432	68.222	0.575	0.846
安检设施数量(个) C_{14}	55.241	64.378	0.241	0.932
安检设施智能化水平 C_{15}	59.149	65.023	0.674	0.852
应急设备智能化水平 C_{16}	51.713	69.959	0.492	0.803
智能浮式系船柱数量 C_{17}	59.426	66.712	0.603	0.931

综上所述,本次问卷总体信度高,可靠性好。

4.1.2 问卷的效度分析

效度分析,简单来说就是问卷设计的有效性、准确程度。对于问卷调查数据而言,一般效度高,信度一定高;信度高,效度不一定高。因此问卷调查的效度分析对于确定问卷调查结果的准确与否至关重要。下面再次通过 SPSS21.0 对本次问卷调查的结果进行效度分析。

调查数据的效度分析如表 5 所示。

信 度 统 计 量　　　　　　　表 5

KMO 取样适切性数量		0.869
Bartlett 球形度检验	近视卡方	3435.772
	df	129
	Sig	0

通过调查数据效度检验,发现 KMO 统计量的取值大于 0.8,球形检验 p 值小于 0.05,Sig 为 0,表示所有变量间相关性较强,适合作因子分析,本次问卷调查的数据有效度较高。

4.2 各影响因素权重的确定

本文通过对有关专家学者进行了咨询,并发放了调查问卷,并依据专家对问卷的反馈结果,对各个指标进行加权求值,并依据计算结构建造准则层依据相关指标层的各判断矩阵[10]。

三峡河段智能通航一级影响因素判断矩阵及各因素权重见表 6。基础设施因素、智能监管因素、智能监管因素、通航保障因素的指标判断矩阵及各因素权重见表 7~表 10。

智能通航一级影响因素判断矩阵及各因素权重　　　　　　　表 6

A	B_1	B_2	B_3	B_4	权　重
B_1	1	4	5	6	0.5945
B_2	1/4	1	3	2	0.2065

续上表

A	B_1	B_2	B_3	B_4	权重
B_3	1/5	1/3	1	2	0.1159
B_4	1/6	1/2	1/2	1	0.0831

基础设施因素指标判断矩阵及各因素权重 表7

B_1	C_1	C_2	C_3	C_4	权重
C_1	1	2	1/3	4	0.2469
C_2	1/2	1	2	3	0.2724
C_3	3	2	1	5	0.4186
C_4	1/4	1/3	1/5	1	0.0622

智能监管因素指标判断矩阵及各因素权重 表8

B_2	C_5	C_6	C_7	C_8	权重
C_5	1	3	2	1/2	0.3001
C_6	1/3	1	1/2	1/4	0.0680
C_7	1/2	2	1	5	0.3385
C_8	2	4	1/5	1	0.2934

智能管理因素指标判断矩阵及各因素权重 表9

B_3	C_9	C_{10}	C_{11}	C_{12}	权重
C_9	1	4	1/3	2	0.2916
C_{10}	1/4	1	5	3	0.3178
C_{11}	3	1/5	1	5	0.3188
C_{12}	1/2	1/3	1/5	1	0.0718

通航保障因素指标判断矩阵及各因素权重 表10

B_4	C_{13}	C_{14}	C_{15}	C_{16}	C_{17}	权重
C_{13}	1	1/3	1/5	2	3	0.1543
C_{14}	3	1	3	6	4	0.4105
C_{15}	5	1/3	1	1/5	1/2	0.1652
C_{16}	1/2	1/6	1/5	1	2	0.1742
C_{17}	1/3	1/4	2	1/2	1	0.0959

经验证,对应判断矩阵的一致性比率均小于0.1,因此本文确定的各因素间的权重分配是可以接受的。

4.3 综合权重的确定

依据以上分析,可以获得各个因素的权重值。为方便进行数据分析,需得到全部因素对于总目标的权重排序,并计算出影响智能通航各因素之间的定量化关系。各权重之间的排序汇总情况,如表11。

各指影响标综合权重 表11

层次	B_1	B_2	B_3	B_4	综合权重
C_1	0.2469				0.1468
C_2	0.2724				0.1620
C_3	0.4186				0.2489
C_4	0.0622				0.0370

续上表

层　　次	B_1	B_2	B_3	B_4	综 合 权 重
C_5		0.3001			0.0620
C_6		0.0680			0.0140
C_7		0.3385			0.0700
C_8		0.2934			0.0606
C_9			0.2916		0.0338
C_{10}			0.3178		0.0369
C_{11}			0.3188		0.0370
C_{12}			0.0718		0.0083
C_{13}				0.1543	0.0129
C_{14}				0.4105	0.0341
C_{15}				0.1652	0.0137
C_{16}				0.1742	0.0144
C_{17}				0.0959	0.0080

4.4　各影响因素重要性比较

根据上述计算结果,可得各因素对三峡河段智能通航影响的相对重要程度。一级和二级影响因素对船闸通过能力影响的相对重要程度见图3。

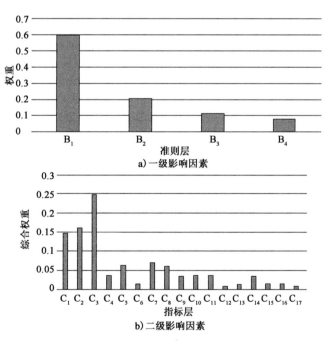

图3　智能通航系统影响因素权重

从图3a)知,在一级影响指标中,智能监管因素对于智能通航系统的影响最大,而通航保障因素对智能通航系统的影响较小;图3b)显示,在二级影响指标中,二级影响因素中,人船智能识别水平(C_1)、信息采集水平(C_2)、航行异常告警效率(C_3)对三峡河段智能通航影响较大,而其他因素对智能通航体系的建立影响相对较小。

依据上文对各指标的比较可知,智能监管对三峡河段智能通航的影响水平相对较大,因此可以从智能监管的角度提升三峡河段智能通航水平,并在智能通航水平评价指标体系中,加强对智能监控因素的权重。

5 结　语

（1）本文基于监管、管理、基础设施和通航保障等方面搭建了三峡河段智能通航影响指标层次结构模型，并依据各因素的判断矩阵，确定了各个指标对智能通航的影响程度。分析结果表明，评价指标具有一定的主观意识，而评价结构是否可靠依赖于各个指标权重的排序和综合指标的权重值。

（2）依据各指标的权重排序，可以确定各指标对智能通航体系的影响程度，为三峡河段智能通航体系的完善、发展提供理论依据。

参考文献

[1] 李定国,陈学文.信息化"顶层设计"助力数字三峡智能通航——浅析三峡坝区通航管理综合信息系统工程建设成效[J].中国水运,2014(02):40-41.

[2] 郑钧,陈东,姜冲,等.通航水位智能监测与预警应用[J].水利科技与经济,2016,22(08):117-120.

[3] Parasuraman, R., T. B. Sheridan, C. D. Wickens. A model for types and levels of human interaction with automation. IEEE Transactions on Systems, Man, and Cybernetics-Part A: Systems and Humans, 2000. 30(3):286-297.

[4] Patraiko D, Wake P, Weintrit A, et al. e-Navigation and the Human Element[J]. Mar. Navig. Saf. Sea Transp, 2009, 4: 29.

[5] 胡适军,等.船舶排闸的遗传算法设计与仿真.中国航海,2015.38(02):38-42+73.

[6] 肖恒辉.三峡—葛洲坝联合通航调度问题的研究.2008,华中科技大学.

[7] 商剑平,吴澎,唐颖.基于计算机仿真的船闸联合调度方案研究.水运工程,2011(09):199-204.

[8] 王莲芬,许树柏.层次分析法引论[M].北京:中国人民大学出版社.

[9] 吴祈宗,李有文.层次分析法中矩阵的判断一致性研究[J].北京理工大学学报,1999,19(4):502-505.

[10] 冯俊文.模糊德尔菲层次分析法及其应用[J].数学的实践与认识,2006(09):44-48.

世界一流港口集疏运网络建设

刘万锋　周嘉男

（浙江省交通规划设计研究院）

摘　要　交通运输部等九部委印发的《关于建设世界一流港口的指导意见》，提出到2035年，全国港口发展水平整体跃升，主要港口总体达到世界一流水平，若干个枢纽港建成世界一流港口，引领全球港口绿色发展、智慧发展。过去十年我国沿海港口一直呈现快速发展态势，全国乃至全球争相建设区域枢纽港的同时，港口的规模化扩张、集群化发展，给港口集疏运带来新一轮挑战，集疏运体系成为制约世界一流强港建设的关键因素，本文将探索基于世界一流港口视角下的港口集疏运体系建设。

关键词　水运运输　世界一流港口　港口网络　集疏运体系

0　引　言

（1）世界级枢纽港"集群化"格局明显。过去十年我国沿海港口一直呈现快速发展态势，在全球港口大型化发展进程中表现亮眼，全球吞吐量十大港口中国占据7个席位，中国港口已发展成为全球名副其实的大港，呈现大型化建设、规模化扩张、集群化发展、专业化提升的特点。大型化港口码头在中国沿海地区快速增长，对以枢纽港为中心的高度国际集聚化的港口集群主要特征，20～40万吨级油品、铁矿石、专用煤炭散货码头、2万 TEU 以上的集装箱码头等投入使用,沿海港口吞吐量呈现快速扩张。

(2)多种运输方式高效衔接融合更为充分。多种运输方式融合发展是一流港口建设集疏运重要特征,以满足客户多样化进出港需求。对应港口大型化发展,要求强化港口枢纽性港区疏港铁路、高等级公路等的高标准接入,做好与城市交通的协调,建设畅通、可靠的集疏运体系。以铁水联运、江海联运、江海直达等为重点,大力发展以港口为枢纽、"一单制"为核心的多式联运。规划至2025年,集装箱、干散货重要港区铁路进港率达到60%以上,矿石、煤炭等大宗货物主要由铁路或水路集疏运;到2035年,重要港区基本实现铁路进港全覆盖,港口集装箱铁水联运比例显著提升。

(3)船舶大型化、全球港口能力扩张对集疏运新挑战。船舶大型化和船公司的全世界范围的联盟趋势,导致船舶企业大量在亚欧等国际航线上投入20000标箱以上的集装箱船,要求更高的码头装卸效率,速度和安全性。超大型集装箱船到港意味着货物的集中抵港带来货物快速卸下后,如何能够将数以万计的货物从码头前沿疏散至港区后方堆场并快速移送到腹地的难题。新加坡大士港,计划用30年时间建设一批超大型集装箱深水泊位,总吞吐能力达6000万标箱以上,世界集装箱港口规模正逐步增大,从初期的千万箱级,逐步上升到5000万箱以上级别,港口能力的扩大对枢纽港规模增大带来持续挑战。

(4)国际碳排放标准对集疏运能源使用的挑战。港口城市由于船舶到港、装卸运输设备和集疏运需要消耗大量的能源,其产生的污染物要比非港口城市增加20%左右。绿色低碳是一流港口建设的重要内容,选择低碳运输方式,合理使用清洁能源,降低碳排放对大型枢纽港将是新的挑战。交通运输部发布了珠三角、长三角、环渤海水域船舶排放控制区实施方案,设立了水域船舶排放控制区,确定了排放控制区内的核心港口区域,并对硫氧化物的排放控制做出了规定,未来港口集疏运必将走绿色、智慧、生态之路。

1 国内外枢纽港集疏运网络理论基础

1.1 国外枢纽港集疏运网络建设经验借鉴

借鉴国内外相关研究基础和系统网络研究方法,世界一流港口建设中枢纽港规模化是重要限定条件,集疏运网络体系构建是重要内容,其中铁路、水运等是主要中转表现形式。相较国内而言,国外枢纽港更加注重水水中转、海铁联运等集疏运形式。鹿特丹港、安特卫普港集装箱水水中转比例约40%和45%,温哥华港、鲁伯特王子港和汉堡港集装箱海铁联运比例已达到约75%、83%和46%,而我国同类腹地型宁波舟山港集装箱水水中转和海铁联运比例仅为26%和3%,主要依靠公路集散,对港口周边环境和交通系统造成较大压力。部分国外枢纽港开展疏港铁路改造以降低货运线路对城市环境的影响,例如洛杉矶-长滩港打造横穿市区的Alameda快速疏港铁路地堑式货运通道,消除港口集疏运列车与城市其他交通方式的干扰。智能化集疏运系统在日益得到重视,例如汉堡港为集卡司机配备随身终端设备并生成移动端最优路线,缓解由于船舶改期而造成集卡大量无效集结,增强用户体验等。综上而言,我国在一流港口集疏运建设过程中,在打造多式联运网络、提升物流组织能力等方面尚未形成综合集疏运系统,有较大提升空间。

1.2 世界一流港口集疏运网络理论

目前国内外已有权威机构对一流港口集疏运建设做出理论指导,但针对各港口腹地、集疏运条件不同,无统一集疏运网络体系建设要求。交通运输部等九部委发布的《关于建设世界一流港口的指导意见》中指出,建设一流港口,需注重港口集疏运形式的多样性,注重铁路、水路、管道集疏运比重,注重港口集疏运体系的完备性建设,以反映港口集疏运体系通过结构化减排实现绿色发展的水平、反映港口对所在城市及内陆腹地辐射和服务保障能力。研究借鉴新华·波罗的海国际航运中心发展指数评价指标体系,将物流绩效指数作为评价港口综合环境的重要指标,该指标关注运输质量相关基础设施的质量、安排价格具有竞争力的货运的难易度、物流服务的质量、追踪查询货物的能力以及货物在预定时间内到达收货人的频率,受港口集疏运发展水平影响较大。

2 世界一流港口专业化集疏运网络建设

2.1 建立世界级港口群体系,以应对船舶大型化、班轮联盟化的集疏运需求

在我国港口区域港口一体化整合基础上,形成"枢纽港+支线港+喂给港、无水港"的世界级港口群体系,形成以 2~3 个枢纽港为中心世界级高度集聚港口集群。以超大型的港口集群体系分工,来应对 24000TEU 集装箱船、40 万吨级原油和 40 万吨级铁矿石等超大型船舶集中到港的冲击,同时应对国际班轮联盟所形成的对港口的压力,以达到货物规模化集聚和快速疏运的需求。以长三角世界级港口群为例,形成以上海港、宁波舟山港为核心,南京、杭州、苏州、温州等港口为骨干,其他港口共同发展的格局,形成稳定管理体制和利益共享机制。统一各区域港口规划,形成一体化合理和资源利用计划;以资本为纽带,形成港口集群运营的利益共享、风险共担机制,统筹港口集群集疏运体系建设。

2.2 建立跨区域多式联运网络,促进江海、海河、海铁、海管等联运方式高效融合

依托单一运输无法满足超大型世界级港口集疏运效率和个性化需求,全国港口规模水平在"十四五"期间仍将整体跃升,至 2035 年规模仍将维持高位,上海港集装箱吞吐量将超 5000 万 TEU,形成国际第一的超大型集装箱的集散枢纽,目前集装箱海铁联运占比不到 2%。从铁路、内河、管道等基础设施规划来看,长三角世界级港口集群多式联运仍围绕着区域单个港口展开。在世界一流港口集疏运体系网络体系下,做大做强多式联运,提升枢纽辐射能力,提升都是联运比例是未来工作方向重点。高品质推进舟山江海联运中心建设,加强安徽、江苏沿江港口江海直达、江海联运相关码头技术改造和锚地建设,有序整合芜湖、马鞍山港口资源,大力发展以港口为枢纽、"一单制"为核心的多式联运,构建辐射北部沿海、中部沿江、西南部腹地的综合集疏运大通道。

2.3 建设集装箱、大宗散货等专业货种全球运输体系,构建全球海运网络枢纽

加快长三角区域各港区功能布局优化调整,完善主要货类运输体系,融入全球集装箱、大宗散货运输网络,在"一带一路"等全球重要海运网络节点上发挥枢纽作用。集装箱海运网络构建是一流港口建设竞争力的重要标志,重点推进以上海小洋山、外高桥宁波舟山梅山、穿山和江苏沿江港口为重点的集装箱运输体系,建设小洋山、大洋山、穿山、梅山、北仑、金塘、苏州等千万标箱级集装箱港区,发挥世界级集装箱港区合力,打造亚太地区超大型集装箱港区集聚中心。建设集装箱国际中转服务区,建设集装箱江海联运服务区。以宁波舟山港 30~40 万吨级油品、铁矿石等大宗散货码头储运集聚资源为重点,积极拓展通州湾港口开发,发展国际油品、矿石和煤炭储运加工交易基地。依托长江南京以下 12.5m 深水航道,优化整合长江南京以下江海联运港区布局和功能,有序推动南通通州湾港区江海联运发展,构建分工协作、运转高效的干散货江海联运系统和集装箱、干散货江海直达系统。

2.4 提升现代化港口群枢纽辐射能级,构建国际对内对外辐射大通道

统筹优化干线铁路、高速公路、长江黄金水道等内河航道、港口、机场布局,实现与国际、国内其他经济板块高效联通,加快构建长三角地区多向立体、内联外通的综合运输辐射通道,以长三角为中心,构建南北向沿海、西向沿长江、西北向、西南向等辐射大通道,高效对接"一带一路"、京津冀地区、长江经济带和粤港澳大湾区。重点构筑以沿海、近洋水路集疏运为重点的海上通道,增强长三角世界级港口集群在全球海运运输网络的中心地位后,通过对东部沿海区域、日韩、东南亚等区域近洋航线辐射能力,构建海上疏运辐射大通道;在现有长江水运通道基础上,依托重庆、武汉、芜湖、南京、太仓等长江沿线港口,以及沿江铁路运输大通道,构筑长江经济带国内东西向辐射大通道,提升对沿线"九省一市"集疏运辐射带动能力;依托义新欧、甬新欧等"中欧"班列运输路线,打通沿海港口、内陆腹地至欧洲市场的国际铁路集疏运大通道,提升通道运输的整体通过能力,构建沿海港口陆向对外辐射的大通道。

2.5 建设国际一流港集疏运配套的物流组织能力

积极拓展"一带一路"海上丝路航线网络,以上海港、宁波轴上港口为重点完善长三角港口至全球航

线网络,在巩固中欧、中美航线基础上,重点增加至印度尼西亚、马来西亚等东盟国家和南亚、中东、非洲等国家的集装箱航线,以物流促进贸易往来和产能合作。在长三角规模以上枢纽性港区为节点,优化区域货运通道,以海铁联运、江海联运等为重点,加快推进多式联运发展,提升全程物流服务水平,构建高效便捷的物流体系。转变港口战略功能,从运输方式的交换点、集散中心,向运输、信息、工业、现代物流的集散中心,全程运输中心的贸易后勤基地,实现资金流、信息流与物流的同步发展,随着国际市场更加开放,海洋运输体系将提高到更加重要的位置。

2.6 提升全球化大宗商品资源配置能力,拓展世界一流港口的金融贸易、产业配置属性

以上海金融贸易中心为依托、宁波舟山港国际大宗物质储运中心为依托,加快建设自由贸易港加工交易中心,建设国际油气储运、加工、交易全产业链基地,以石油商业储备为核心,推进完善小洋山、舟山中北部、宁波镇海大榭区域等油品国际化石油基地,积极推进舟山绿色石化基地基础设施建设;创新油品储备体制机制,赋予自贸试验区符合条件的油品加工企业原油进口资质,给予原油进口配额,形成国储商储并重、国内海外连通、储备交割联动的国际油品全产业链服务基地。加快建设铁矿石亚太分销中心,统筹长三角区域矿石码头规划、生产、运营,统筹管控江海联运高效服务,持续深化与巴西淡水河谷、澳大利亚必和必拓等铁矿石巨头的混配矿合作,积极探索海关特殊监管区域内矿石保税仓储、加工、出口业务,推进完善铁矿石全程物流方案定制化服务。加快建成以长三角为标准的全球一流的国际性大宗商品综合交易、结算和定价中心,积极发挥大宗商品交易中心作用,推进油品交易政策创新,推动人民币国际化进程,以拓展世界一流港口的金融贸易、产业配置属性。

垃圾重量不确定环境下船舶收集海洋垃圾路径优化

陈晓惠 段 刚 范 涛 魏越娇 陶 玲

(兰州交通大学交通运输学院)

摘 要 海洋垃圾问题日益严重,清理海洋垃圾的花费巨大,并且在使用船舶收集海洋垃圾的过程中,会造成温室气体排放。本文通过物流网络方法对海洋垃圾进行收集。建立了一个以海洋垃圾收集总成本最小为目标,海洋垃圾重量不确定的随机机会约束规划模型,并在模型中引入了碳税成本,使用大规模邻域搜索算法求解。以中国东海上海港附近的垃圾收集为例,验证模型有效性。结果表明,海洋垃圾收集总成本和海洋垃圾与港口平均距离数据为高度正相关关系。碳税成本和平均距离数据为高度正相关关系。对比最坏情况,选择最佳时间收集海洋垃圾的总成本节约22.38%,碳税成本节约23.21%。海洋垃圾重量服从不同分布对结果没有影响。灵敏度分析表明目标对碳税价格同样不敏感。

关键词 水路运输 机会约束 船舶路径规划 大规模邻域搜索算法 海洋垃圾回收 碳税

0 引 言

从20世纪70年代,人们就开始关注海洋垃圾[1,2]。每年有480万吨到1 270万吨垃圾进入海洋[3]。目前有关船舶收集海洋垃圾路径优化的研究较少。Shah等人[4]建立了一个考虑废弃物价值不确定的随机优化模型,量化了回收行动对环境和社会的影响。Akhtar等人[5]利用改进的回溯搜索算法(BSA)对垃圾收集路径进行优化,使距离节约36.80%,燃油消耗降低50%,CO_2排放降低44.68%。

海洋垃圾收集与陆地垃圾收集有所不同。由于受到洋流、风向等影响,海洋垃圾点位置不断移动。

Duan 等人[6]提出的三阶段海洋垃圾收集框架:首先利用遥感等技术对海洋垃圾初始定位,再使用 GNOME(General NOAA Operational Modeling Environment)等软件来预测海洋垃圾的移动轨迹,最后建立船舶路径优化模型并求解。

1 问题描述及模型建立

1.1 问题描述及假设

①本文使用混合坐标海洋模型(HYCOM)构建海洋流场,美国国家环境预报中心全球天气预报系统(NCEP-GFS)导出风场数据,导入 GNOME 的诊断模式,预测不同时刻海洋垃圾的位置。②在海洋中垃圾的位置不断变化,所以本文设定海洋垃圾移动的距离小于 5 海里的时间为该海洋垃圾点的时间窗。③本文使用物流网络方法对海洋垃圾进行收集,建立随机机会约束模型,通过分布函数转化方法,将无法准确计算的垃圾重量,转化成确定性等价,并使用 LNS 算法求解。④本文以节能环保为立足点,考虑燃油消耗和碳排放。

问题假设条件如下:①同质船队,载重量、油箱容量和船速相同的船;②本文收集在海洋中的漂浮垃圾;③船到达每个垃圾点的时间要满足时间窗约束;④每个垃圾点位置都需要被服务仅一次;⑤每个海洋垃圾点的垃圾重量分别服从某一分布,并且相互独立。

1.2 模型建立

设船舶路径图 $G=(L,A)$,其中 $L=\{0\}\cup L_1\cup\{n+1\}$ 是所有顶点的集合,其中 0 和 $n+1$ 分别是同一个港口作为起点和终点时的符号;$L_1=\{1,2,\cdots,n\}$ 是垃圾位置点的集合;$A=A_1\cup A_2\cup A_3$ 是所有路径的集合,$A_1=\{(i,j)\mid i=0,j\in L_1\}$ 表示从港口到垃圾位置点路径的集合;$A_2=\{(i,j)\mid i\in L_1,j\in L_1,i\neq j\}$ 表示两个不同垃圾位置点间路径的集合;$A_3=\{(i,j)\mid i\in L_1,j=n+1\}$ 表示从垃圾位置点回到港口路径的集合;S 表示船的集合。c_i 为在垃圾位置点 i 的收集时间,$i\in L_1$;ξ_i 为在垃圾位置点 i 的垃圾重量,随机变量 $\xi_i:\Phi(\xi_i),i\in L_1$;$[t_i^e,t_i^l]$ 为顶点 i 的时间窗,$i\in L$;d_{ij} 为从顶点 i 到顶点 j 的距离,$(i,j)\in A$;v 是实际船速;v_{max} 是最大设计船速;b_1 是单位油耗系数;b_2 是单位油耗排放因子;f^{fix} 是单位船舶固定成本;f^{fuel} 是单位船舶航行油耗成本;f^c 是碳税率;P^w 是载重量;P^f 是油箱容量。$x_{ijs}=1$,当船舶 s 从顶点 i 到顶点 j;$x_{ijs}=0$,其他 $(i,j)\in A,s\in S$;t_{is} 表示船舶 s 到达顶点 i 的时间,$i\in L,s\in S$;Q_{is} 表示船舶 s 到达顶点 i 前累积的垃圾重量,$i\in L,s\in S$。

垃圾重量不确定的海洋垃圾收集随机机会约束模型(M_1)。

$$\min F=\sum_{j\in L_1}\sum_{s\in S}f^{fix}x_{0js}+\sum_{(i,j)\in A}\sum_{s\in S}\frac{f^{fuel}b_1(d_{ij}v^2+c_i)}{v_{max}^3}x_{ijs}+\sum_{(i,j)\in A}\sum_{s\in S}\frac{f^c b_1 b_2(d_{ij}v^2+c_i)}{v_{max}^3}x_{ijs} \tag{1}$$

$$\sum_{j\in L_1}x_{0js}=\sum_{j\in L_1}x_{j,n+1,s} \quad s\in S \tag{2}$$

$$\sum_{i\in\{0\}\cup L_1}x_{ijs}=\sum_{i\in L_1\cup\{n+1\}}x_{jis} \quad j\in L_1,s\in S \tag{3}$$

$$\sum_{j\in L_1\cup\{n+1\}}\sum_{s\in S}x_{ijs}=1 \quad i\in L_1 \tag{4}$$

$$t_{is}+\frac{d_{ij}}{v}+c_i\leq t_{js}+M(1-x_{ijs}) \quad (i,j)\in A,s\in S \tag{5}$$

$$t_j^e\leq t_{js}\leq t_j^l \quad j\in L,s\in S \tag{6}$$

$$\sum_{(i,j)\in A}\frac{b_1(d_{ij}v^2+c_i)}{v_{max}^3}x_{ijs}\leq P^f \quad s\in S \tag{7}$$

$$Pr\{\sum_{i\in L_1}\sum_{j\in L_1}x_{ijs}\cdot\xi_j\leq P^w\}\geq\alpha \quad s\in S \tag{8}$$

$$Q_{0s} = 0 \quad s \in S \tag{9}$$

$$x_{ijs} \in \{0,1\} \quad (i,j) \in A, s \in S \tag{10}$$

$$t_{is}, Q_{is} \geq 0 \quad i \in L, s \in S \tag{11}$$

目标函数公式(1)旨在最小化回收作业总成本。第一项表示固定成本，包括船的租金，人工成本，保险费用和港口装卸费用。第二项是燃料成本，包括船舶在航行，等待和收集作业过程中消耗的燃油费用。第三项是碳税成本。约束(2)~(3)表示船舶流量平衡。约束(2)保证从港口出发的船舶数量等于回到港口的。约束(3)保证进入垃圾点位置的垃圾船数量和离开的相等。约束(4)使每个垃圾点位置都会被一艘垃圾船服务仅一次。约束(5)追踪了每艘垃圾船到达每个垃圾点的时间，其中 M 表示一个极大的数。垃圾船到每个垃圾点位置要满足时间窗约束在约束(6)体现。约束(7)计算了油箱容量。约束(8)表示每艘垃圾船满足的随机容量机会约束，保证垃圾随机重量之和不超过船舶载重量 P^w 的概率大于置信度水平 α。每艘船累计垃圾重量被初始化在公式(9)。公式(10)和公式(11)是变量声明。将随机机会约束(8)通过分布函数转化方法[7]转化为确定性等价约束(12)，如下所示：

$$\sum_{(i,j) \in A} E[\xi_j] x_{ijs} \leq \bar{Q} \tag{12}$$

其中 $\bar{Q} = (2P^w + \tau^2 - \sqrt{\tau^4 + 4P^w \cdot \tau^2})/2$，$\tau = \Phi^{-1}(\alpha)$，$\Phi(\cdot)$ 为垃圾重量 ξ_i 的分布函数，$\xi_i \sim \Phi(\xi_i)$，$\Phi^{-1}(\cdot)$ 为 $\Phi(\cdot)$ 的逆函数。

转化后得到确定性模型(M^2)：

目标函数：公式(1)

约束条件：约束(2)~(7)；

约束(9)~(11)；

约束(12)。

2 求解方法

本文使用基于 VB（Visual Basic）的 LNS 算法[8]求解海洋垃圾回收的船舶路径规划问题。在 LNS 算法中使用了三个局部搜索算子：EXCHANGE，1-OPT，2-OPT。EXCHANGE operator 搜索目前解中所有的客户对，并交换它们的顺序。1-OPT operator 在目前解中随机移除一个客户点。2-OPT operator 在目前解中随机移除两个弧。采用了两种启发式方法：贪婪插入和最大后悔插入。贪婪插入是将客户插入产生成本最小的位置。最大后悔插入是基于选择插入产生成本最小位置与产生成本第二小位置之间差值最大的位置。两种启发式的选择概率相同。

3 实例分析

3.1 数据描述

在带有 IntelCorei5-4260U、1.40GHz 处理器和 4.0GB 安装内存(RAM)的计算机上计算，运行时间 2 分钟。上海港位置为 121.50°E，31.38°N。$b_1 = 0.42t$(柴油)/小时，$b_2 = 3.85t(CO_2)/t$(柴油)。$f^{fix} = 6400$ 元/条，$f^{fuel} = 6000$ 元/t，$f^c = 15$ 元/t(CO_2)，$P^w = 50t$，$P^f = 38t$，$v_{max} = 50km/h$，$v = 50km/h$，收集时间 0.5 小时，$\mu = 2$，$\sigma^2 = 1.33$，$\alpha = 0.9$。垃圾重量 ξ_i 服从正态分布 $N(2, 1.33)$，$\tau = 3.48$，$\bar{Q}^* = 30.71$，公式(12)化为：

$$\sum_{(i,j) \in A} E[\xi_j] \cdot x_{ijs} \leq 30.71 \tag{13}$$

设定当垃圾点位置移动距离小于 5 海里的时间范围为时间窗约束，$[t_i^e, t_i^l] = [8:00, 20:00]$，$i \in L$。

3.2 实验结果

3.2.1 海洋垃圾最佳收集时间

由于漂浮在海洋上的垃圾位置在不断变化,选择收集海洋垃圾的时间是至关重要的。海洋垃圾距离港口越远,越分散,需要派出的船舶就越多,总成本越高,反之亦然。

从图1和图2中可以看出,总成本、碳税成本和距离港口的平均距离变化趋势基本一致。标准差变化范围为-6.71%~7.60%,变化较小。对比最坏情况,选择第7天收集海洋垃圾的总成本节约22.38%,节约27 433.58元,碳税成本节约23.21%,节约200.52元。通过数值计算,总成本和平均距离数据的相关系数为0.98,相关系数大于0.8[9],总成本和平均距离为高度正相关关系。碳税成本和平均距离数据的相关系数为0.98,碳税成本和平均距离为高度正相关关系。

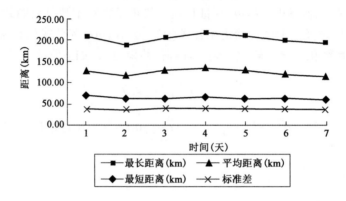

图1 海洋垃圾点位置到港口的距离

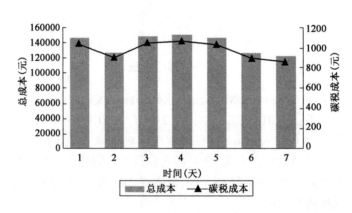

图2 总成本和碳税成本

3.2.2 海洋垃圾的重量服从不同分布函数的影响

在本文中,对海洋垃圾重量进行灵敏度分析。选择第7天的垃圾点位置进行规划安排,其他参数同3.1节。垃圾重量 ξ_i 分别服从正态分布 $N(2,1.33)$,泊松分布 $P(2)$,均匀分布 $U(0,4)$,指数分布 $E(2)$ 时,Q 分别等于30.71,28.61,30.21,26.36。海洋垃圾收集总成本均等于122 604.82元,碳税成本均等于863.76元。解结果相同,如表1所示,均使用5条船,平均每条船的时间饱和度为93.17%。分布函数选择通过期望和方差计算得到。时间饱和度计算公式如下:

$$时间饱和度 = \frac{每条船总工作时间}{最长工作时间} \times 100\% \tag{14}$$

所以,海洋垃圾重量服从不同分布,虽然对随机容量机会约束产生影响,但对路径优化,收集成本和碳税成本没有影响。表1中,解中0表示出发和到达的港口。

船舶路径 表1

船	解	总工作时间	时间饱和度
1	0-28-14-10-18-15-19-16-0	11:55	99.31%
2	0-25-38-3-37-11-36-2-8-0	8:43	72.76%
3	0-22-9-39-12-40-27-1-7-0	11:54	99.29%
4	0-23-33-32-5-29-6-21-20-26-0	11:40	97.23%
5	0-13-24-4-17-35-31-30-34-0	11:40	97.26%

3.2.3 碳税价格的灵敏度分析

根据国际货币基金组织的工作报告[10]，在2017年中国预计每吨二氧化碳征税15元。并且出于对环境、财政、经济和健康等方面考虑，本节对进行碳税价格进行的灵敏度分析，选择第7天的垃圾点位置，碳税价格将逐渐上升，其他参数同3.1节。

从图3中，可以看出碳税价格每增长100%，总成本增加0.70%，总成本的变化幅度较小，船舶路径不产生变化。因此，如果适当提高碳税价格，有可能一方面没有过度增加企业负担，另一方面可以增加税收，促进节能减排，减轻空气污染，达到保护环境的目的。

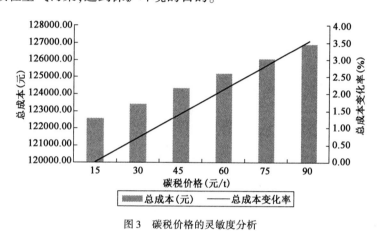

图3 碳税价格的灵敏度分析

4 结 语

海洋垃圾遍布四大洋，他们正在持续不断地伤害着人类、海洋生物和环境。甚少有研究关注船舶收集海洋垃圾的路径优化。本文使用物流网络的方法对海洋垃圾进行收集，以中国东海上海港附近的海洋垃圾收集问题为例，得到以下结果，对比最坏情况，选择最佳时间收集海洋垃圾的总成本节约22.38%，碳税成本节约23.21%。分布函数不同和碳税价格增加对总成本的影响不明显。所以，管理部门可以考虑适当增加碳税价格，可以增加税收，促进节能减排，达到保护环境的目的。

虽然本文考虑了海洋垃圾重量不确定的情况，但在海洋中，不确定的情况还有很多，在未来的研究中，可以考虑海洋垃圾点位置不确定的情况。其次本文假设船舶匀速前进，在未来的研究中，可以在模型中引入速度变量，考察它与总成本和碳排放间的关系。

参考文献

[1] Carpenter E J, Smith K L. Plastics on the Sargasso Sea Surface[J]. Science, 1972, 175(4027): 1240-1241.

[2] Venrick E L, Backman T W, Bartram W C, et al. Man-made objects on the surface of the central North Pacific Ocean[J]. Nature, 1973, 241: 271.

[3] Jambeck J R, Geyer R, Wilcox C, et al. Plastic waste inputs from land into the ocean[J]. Science, 2015, 347(6223): 768-771.

[4] Shah P J, Anagnostopoulos T, Zaslaysky A, et al. A stochastic optimization framework for planning of waste collection and value recovery operations in smart and sustainable cities[J]. Waste Management, 2018, 78:104-114.

[5] Akhtar M, Hannan M A, Begum R A, et al. Backtracking search algorithm in cvrp models for efficient solid waste collection and route optimization[J]. Waste Management, 2017, 61:117-128.

[6] Duan G, Nur F, Alizadeh M, et al. Vessel routing and optimization for marine debris collection with consideration of carbon cap[J]. Journal of Cleaner Production, 2020, 263.

[7] 李阳. 需求不确定的车辆路径问题模型与算法研究[D]. 大连:大连海事大学, 2018. LI Y. Optimization models and algorithms of vehicle routing problem under uncertain demands[D]. Dalian: Dalian Maritime University, 2018. (in Chinese)

[8] Erdogan G. An open source spreadsheet solver for vehicle routing problems[J]. Computers & Operations Research, 2017, 84: 62-72.

[9] Ganti A. Correlation Coefficient[EB/OL]. (2020.2.19)[2020.12.16] https://www.investopedia.com/terms/c/correlationcoefficient.asp.

[10] Parry I, Shang B, Wingender P, et al. Climate mitigation in China: Which policies are most effective [C]. IMF Working Papers, 2016, 16(148):1.

Risk Evolution Simulation on Process Safety of LNG-Fueled Vessel Traffic with STAMP Model and Genetic Algorithm

Wenjing Li　Shenping Hu　Shaoyong Xuan　Jinxian Weng

(Merchant Marine College, Shanghai Maritime University)

Abstract　In order to explore the law of risk evolution of LNG-fueled vessels during traffic process, the evolution of risk performance of LNG-fueled vessels during traffic process is simulated based on genetic algorithm (GA), and introduced by systems-theoretic accident modeling and processes (STAMP) methods. At first, on that basis of clarifying the risk performance, a STAMP model is constructed for the LNG-fueled vessel's traffic process, and the components of the vessel subsystem, LNG fuel subsystem are proposed, and external environmental factors are identified. Secondly, established genetic law, STAMP-GA coupling simulation was conducted on the vessel, LNG fuel subsystem and the overall system to build the LNG-fueled vessel process, then we analysed the risk evolution of the fuel supplying process of the LNG-fueled vessel during traffic process, so that to obtain the overall risk trend of the system. Finally, combined with the traffic process scenarios of LNG-fueled vessels from a certain anchorage on the Yangtze River to the designated berth, the risk evolution of the fuel supplying process of LNG-fueled ships during traffic process is simulated. The simulation results show that the risk evolution of LNG-fueled vessels during traffic process is a "U-shaped curve" law. The fusion of STAMP and genetic algorithm can solve the coupling and mutation of risk factors in risk evolution.

Keywords　LNG-fueled vessel　STAMP　Process safety　Genetic algorithm　Risk evolution

0　Introduction

In the field of maritime risk, there are many kinds of probability measurement and result quantification. On the one hand, the probability can be directly measured with the help of mature algorithm tools; on the other hand, a mathematical model can be established for risk indirect measurement, analyzing and quantifying risk factors in the process of simulating accidents.

In the following parts of this study, simulation demonstrations will be conducted around the risk evolution of LNG-fueled ships during navigation. Section 2 define risk and risk performance, expound STAMP principles and GA algorithms, cloud models are presented to process initial state data and build STAMP-GA models, then describe a set scenario of ship entering the port and obtain relevant information data. Section 3 simulate the scenarios with STAMP-GA models, the results of the risk evolution of the LNG-fueled ship's navigation process can be obtained, and the sensitivity of the model is verified. Section 4 discusses separately risk evolution based on STAMP, risk simulation based on genetic law and evolution of risk performance of LNG-fueled vessels. Section 5 provides the conclusions of this research effort.

1 Method and Data

1.1 Problem Description

1.1.1 Risk and Risk Performance

Risk is defined as the existence of a foreseeable event that may threaten the safety of human, loss of property, and reduced efficiency during traffic process. It is usually a combination of the probability and result of accidents. With the development of research, the focus of research began to turn to the research on the causes of risk, that is, risk is the degree of uncertainty in the occurrence of unexpected events, and the overall risk can be reflected through the relationship and status of its factors.

When the system has already changed, the performance of risk and the state it is presenting is the risk performance at the system structure level. In the process of traffic process, the characterization of each moment in the operating state of the system will have a corresponding impact on the overall risk, and affected by the current situation, the system risk at the next moment will show a composite state of the past and the present. When the risk is inside the system, the risk will show the life cycle and process evolution, which is the concept of risk performance in the time dimension.

We believe that there is a certain regularity and control ability in the dynamic change of the nature of risk, the change can interact the operating mode and development direction of the system to which it is attached. According to the system status that affects each other, the risk performance can be divided into four levels:

$$S = \{s_1, s_2, s_3, s_4\} \quad (1)$$

The distribution of the corresponding golden section ratios of risk performance levels in the interval $[0,1]$ is as follows (Tab. 1).

risk performance Tab. 1

A	B	C	D
Safe	Single failure	Part failure	Full failure
$[0, 0.375]$	$[0.375, 0.606]$	$[0.606, 0.752]$	$[0.752, 1]$

1.1.2 Evolution of Process Risk

Risk depends on its system, the development and operation of the system must also be completed in the time dimension. The study of process risk is the study of the accumulation method and evolution trend of system risk in the time dimension. In the time dimension, risk presents no aftereffect of Markov chain, risk can only be generated but cannot disappear, and the risk at each moment depends only on the risk state of the previous moment.

During the navigating process of a vessel, the independent variable of risk evolution is the accumulation of time, the risk performance of each component under the dimension is characterized as the result of the coupling between the system operation process and the risk factors of the completed traffic process. It can be displayed as:

$$S_t = \{P_{1t}, P_{2t} \cdots P_{nt}, S_{t-1}\} \qquad (2)$$

S_t is the risk status of the system at time t.

$P_{1t}, P_{2t} \cdots P_{nt}$ is the risk status of the n components (subsystems) of the system at time t.

S_{t-1} is the risk status of the system at time $t-1$.

1.1.3 Evolution of Process Risk of LNG-Fueled Vessel

We divide the LNG power vessel system into two subsystems: vessel subsystems and LNG fuel subsystems. Each subsystem involves the circulation of information, and both subsystems will be disturbed by the external environment.

Like the overall system, there is also the flow of information inside the subsystem. The information flow of the subsystem can be further described as control commands and feedback: the control commands are issued by a1 to a2, and the status information of a2 is fed back to a1, based on the feedback information, a1 will re-evaluate the control command, then choose whether to adjust the command and reissue it. The feedback between a1 and a2 will not cause the feedback transmission between the next group of nodes in the feedback direction. The relationship diagram between the nodes is shown in Fig. 1.

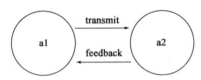

Fig. 1 Information interaction inter system

The subsystem is placed on the time axis of the entire traffic process of the LNG-fueled vessel for analysis. Because the time dimension itself has the characteristics of "irreversibility" and "feedback without aftereffect", it can also be explained by genetic theory. During the traffic process, both the system as a whole and the subsystems are completing their own evolution and development. In this paper, nine sampling points, T1-T9, are set in the traffic process. The risk status of the system at each sample is the inheritance and development of the completed traffic process sample. The expression of the Risk performance of each stage in equation 2.3 can be regarded as a piece of equation 2.1:

$$S_t = \{S_1, S_2 \cdots S_{t-1}\} \qquad (3)$$

1.2 Analysis Method on Risk Evolution

The first step of the description of the process risk mechanism is to clarify and restore the process. From the two dimensions of system and time, this part we explore the way of risk accumulation and the transmission chain, and simulate the process of risk evolution by establishing a suitable model.

1.2.1 Stamp

The operation diagram of the LNG fueled vessel system is shown in Fig. 2. The control command transmission chain of the vessel subsystem is described as: the information of vessel deck facilities is displayed through the information interaction component (Transducer), and the transducer transmits the current state and position to the controller (Deck manager), and then the deck manager notify the processor (Deck crew) of the required operations based on the current information and component status, then the deck crew operate according to the management leadership orders and the deck conditions; The control command transmission chain of LNG fuel subsystem can be described the same way. The expression of equation 2.3 for the Risk performance of system components at each information chain node can be regarded as a split of one of the dimensions of equation 2.1:

$$S_t = \{P_{1t}, P_{2t} \cdots P_{nt}\} \tag{4}$$

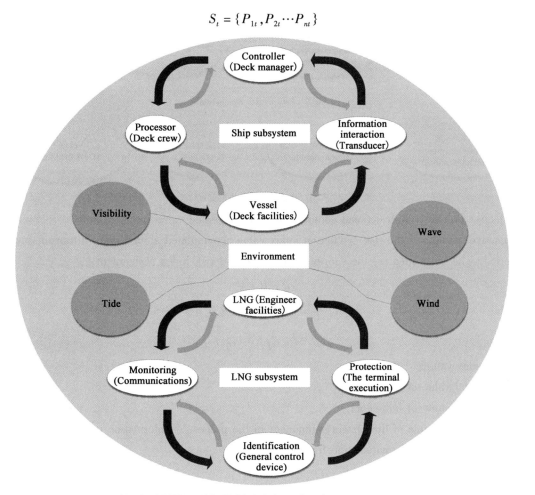

Fig. 2 STAMP model of LNG-fueled vessel in the operation process

1.2.2 Principal of Genetic Algorithm

(1) What is the meaning of offspring DNA?

The four information transmission chains are organized as follows:

Chain 1: Starting from the controller, ending with the sensor via the control loop.

Fig. 3 Path in risk conduction

Chain 2: Start from the actuator and terminate through the control loop to the controller.

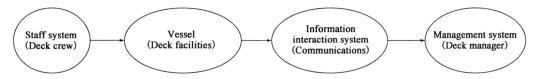

Fig. 4 Path in risk conduction

Chain 3: Take the controlled object as the starting point, and terminate through the control loop to the actuator.

Chain 4: Starting from the sensor, it ends through the control loop to the controlled object.

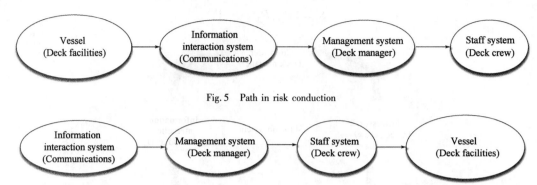

Fig. 5 Path in risk conduction

Fig. 6 Path in risk conduction

(2) Objective function: Bidirectional comparison of accumulated value

The objective function is the risk evaluation index value accumulated along different transmission chains in a certain period. The basic idea is: the sum of basic value and risk index assignment:

$$R = B + V \tag{5}$$

$$B_{S[i,j]} = \max\{R_{S[i,j]}, R_{S[m,j]}\}$$
$$R_{S[i,j]} = B_{S[i,j]} + V(i,j) \tag{6}$$

Where: R ——Index value;

B ——Initial value of indicator;

$m \times n$ ——Initial value of indicator;

i ——the code name of the system component in the process of information transmission;

j ——the previous information transfer node;

$R_{S[i,j]}$ ——the value of index $S[i,j]$;

$B_{S[i,j]}$ ——the initial value of index $S[i,j]$;

$V(i,j)$ ——the assignment of index $S[i,j]$.

When the system information is transmitted in the components, each component corresponds to the risk evaluation index and its risk assignment. The risk value is accumulated during the working process of the system. It is also analyzed from the perspective of system structure and time dimension. The accumulation methods are as follows Two kinds:

①Information flows along the transmission chain, and the accumulation of risks in the time dimension is the accumulation of risks in different components of the transmission chain.

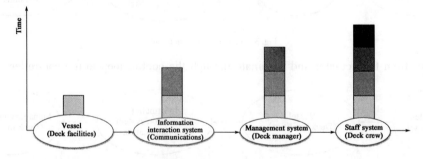

Fig. 7 Information flows along the transmission chain

②The feedback of information between the two components: When the risk flows to the feedback object component, the transmission stops. The accumulation of time dimension is the risk accumulation of the object component.

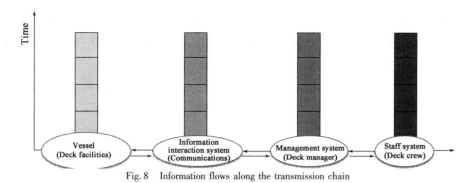

Fig. 8　Information flows along the transmission chain

1.2.3　Cloud Model

The randomly generated data within the proportional interval corresponding to each risk performance level is used as the cloud model input data. After the mean, variance, and super entropy are calculated inside the model, the cloud diagram corresponding to each behavior level is generated as shown in Fig. 9.

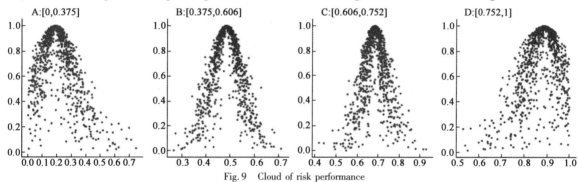

Fig. 9　Cloud of risk performance

1.3　Model Simulation

1.3.1　Simulation Process

(1) Generation of offspring DNA

DNA is an $m \times n$ two-dimensional array: an information transmission chain formed by the orderly arrangement of m system component codes. The number of transmission chains is n, that is, the number of Risk performance evaluation indicators that the system components may encounter.

(2) Objective function and fitness function

In each assessment, a selection of the risk accumulation method described in 2.2.1 is required. The specific work is as follows: the path corresponds to the index, and each process stage is differentiated. In each process, the path is selected firstly then the system starts to run. There are two dimensions of path and index sequence during operation.

1.3.2　Multiple Dimensional Simulations

(1) Time dimension simulation

We divide the traffic process into nine stages. From T1 to T9, the simulation process in 2.4.2 is carried out in sequence. At the level of the simulation algorithm, it is embodied as follows: on the premise that the objective risk evaluation index formulated before the simulation remains unchanged, starting from T1 (not included), the evaluation index involved in the simulation model of the voyage stage t will be randomly inserted into the risk value of stage t-1, then it will be normalized with the original indicator assignment, and participates in the genetic algorithm cycle as a new indicator assignment. Equation 2 can be referenced.

(2) the Simulation in system structure dimension and time dimension

In this step, the subsystems described above need to be reintegrated, after the integration, in the STAMP-based In the GA model, the Risk performance ratio between the vessel system, the LNG fuel system, and the external environmental disturbance is 4:3:2:1. Equation 2 and Equation 3 can be referenced.

The simulation flowchart in 2.3.1 and 2.2.2 above is shown in Fig. 10.

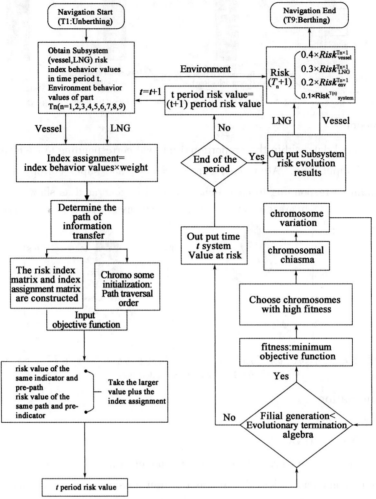

Fig. 10 Simulation work-flow chart

1.4 Scenario Description and Data Acquisition

1.4.1 Scenario Description

Basic information of the LNG-fueled vessel "X vessel": bulk carrier; dual fuel; gross tonnage 23493t, net tonnage 13247t, length 72m, width 13m. On April 17, 2020, the Yangtze River sailed into the port, and sailed from the anchorage to the berth to berth at Waigaoqiao.

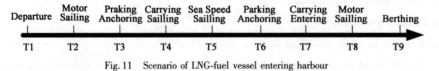

Fig. 11 Scenario of LNG-fuel vessel entering harbour

1.4.2 Data Collection and Processing

(1) Empirical assessment of Risk performance of factors

We divide ten experts and scholars into two groups, each with five people. Tab. 2 and Tab. 3 shows the results of the risk performance level of which the indicators corresponding to the nine voyage stages. Then, we limit the risk value to the interval [0,1] according to the severity, and hand it over to the second group of experts for scoring.

Inital data of ship sub-system components   Tab. 2

Evaluation index of ship system components	T1	T2	T3	T4	T5	T6	T7	T8	T9
Detection of radar	A	A	A	A	A	A	A	A	A
Communication equipment	C	C	B	A	A	B	C	B	C
Working condition of ship	D	D	C	B	A	D	C	C	D
Emergency equipment	A	B	A	A	A	B	A	B	A
Situational Awareness	C	C	C	B	A	C	C	C	C
Emergency response efficiency	D	D	C	B	A	D	C	B	D
Safety awareness (current situation)	C	C	C	C	C	C	C	C	C
Operation specification	C	C	B	A	A	B	B	A	C
Leak monitoring system	D	D	D	D	D	D	D	D	D
Fire protection system	C	C	C	C	C	C	C	C	C

Inital data of environment sub-system components   Tab. 3

DxtDrnal DnvironmDntal intDrfDrDnBD Dvaluation inCDx	T1	T2	T3	T4	T5	T6	T7	T8	T9
storm	D	D	C	B	A	/	C	/	D
winC CirDBtion	D	C	B	A	A	D	A	C	D
visiAility	C	D	C	C	A	C	/	D	C
High tiCD	A	B	A	A	A	A	A	A	A
Bity(BurrDnt) Bross flow	D	D	B	A	A	A	A	A	D
BhannDl BurvaturD	A	B	A	/	/	/	/	/	/
BhannDl wiCth	B	C	B	/	/	/	/	/	/
BhannDl CDpth	A	B	A	/	/	/	/	/	/
Ship CDnsity	B	D	C	B	A	D	D	C	B

According to the traffic process environment and weather conditions in the simulation scenario, the environmental disturbance evaluation during traffic process is shown in Tab. 4.

Inital data of LNG fuel sub-system components   Tab. 4

Evaluation index of LNG system components	T1	T2	T3	T4	T5	T6	T7	T8	T9
Gas supply pressureGas supply pressure	D	D	C	B	A	D	C	C	D
Fuel tank layout and safe distance	C	C	B	A	A	A	B	A	C
Fuel system operating conditions	D	D	C	B	A	D	C	C	D
Fuel piping operating conditions	D	D	C	B	A	D	C	C	D
LNG subsurface pump operating monitoring operation	D	D	C	B	A	D	C	C	D
Monitoring fuel supply assurance system	B	B	A	A	A	B	A	A	B
Fuel supply assurance system	D	D	C	B	A	D	C	C	D
Ventilation system	B	B	B	B	B	B	B	B	B
Operation specification	C	C	B	A	A	B	B	A	C

(2) Quantification ratio of risk performance

The obtained risk performance assessment result is a vague qualitative description, which cannot be used as quantitative data to be input into the subsequent model. Therefore, it is necessary to quantitatively map the uncertain language description in the cloud model so that the level of Risk performance corresponds to the data set. This paper selects the concept of "golden section method" in the image field as the mathematical basis for the division of proportions, and applies the aesthetic and scientific theory of the image field to the data distribution work.

2 Result

2.1 Path Dependency in Risk Evolution

The simulation work is carried out in three levels. The overall mechanism of risk evolution is analyzed, and the three levels of simulation results are as follows.

In the system model, the Gantt chart based on the risk performance evaluation of the information transmission chain and risk indicators is shown in Fig. 12. The figure shows the operation of the objective function when the genetic algorithm in the model reaches the last generation. Fig. 12 respectively show the

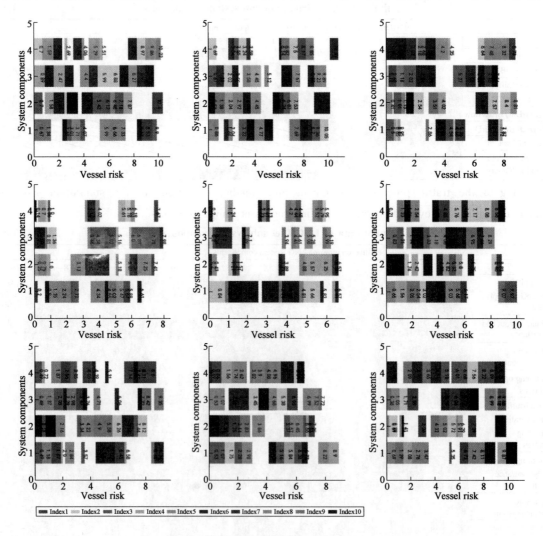

Fig. 12 Simulation with GA for vessel sub-system

accumulation of risk indicators for the vessel subsystem.

The data in the figure shows that: Changes in the circulation risk performance can be regarded as the assignment of risk indicators. For example, the accumulation process of risk in the information transmission chain is truncated 16 times, and the longest accumulation process is the maximum value of the assignment matrix, when the value of accumulation on the information transmission chain is truncated, and the accumulation of system risk has not stopped.

2.2 Risk Evolution of Traffic Process Safety

We perform 10 simulations on vessel system, LNG system and the overall traffic process changes of the system with external environmental disturbances. The simulation results and environmental disturbances at each stage of the subsystem are input to the simulation model as the overall risk index value of the system. The overall risk evolution of subsystems and systems is shown in Fig. 13.

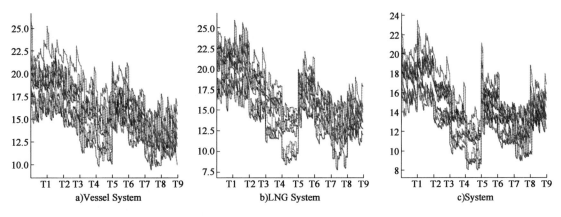

Fig. 13 simulation results

From the above risk evolution simulation results, we can see: The overall floating width of the ship subsystem is wide, that is the risk index values of multiple simulations are quite different, but the trend is relatively the same, that is, there is a jump in the risk value at the departure stage, and the risk value reaches the lowest value at anchorage. Compared with the ship subsystem, the LNG subsystem has a small floating width, and the difference between multiple simulations is small. The fluctuation range of the risk curve of external environmental conditions is relatively small, and the trend is more gradual than other subsystems.

3 Discussion

This article puts the traditional static indicators in the space-time dimension, restores the spread mode of risk in time and space during traffic process, and then analyzes the mechanism of risk evolution.

In the case of external environmental disturbance, the two sub-systems in the entire traffic process evolve their own risk performances. The evolution process has both common and individuality, commonality is the Markov chain genetic attributes that both the subsystem and the system have, their own development is irreversible, and the mutual influence only exists between the offspring and the parent.

The simulation in this article includes three models. The three models are mutually integrated and assisted with each other in the simulation structure: the genetic model is the framework of the entire simulation, which is equivalent to a stable time axis, and the internal objective function of the genetic algorithm is based on the calculation relationship between the system components established by the model and the risk performance evaluation index of STAMP model.

4 Conclusion

(1) Use the STAMP model based on system theory to simulate the ship subsystem and fuel (LNG) subsystem of the fuel supplying process of the LNG-fueled vessel during traffic process, and use the STPA method for analysis, which overcomes the drawback of traditional safety analysis method for the subsystem. The correlation and coupling between the two and the insufficient consideration of human factors have fully restored the information transmission path of each component of the LNG-fueled vessel during operation.

(2) The genetic algorithm is used to perform coupling simulation analysis on the subsystems, combined with the steps of the fuel supplying process, and the genetic algorithm is used to calculate the index matrix to obtain the risk evolution mechanism of the LNG-fueled vessel during traffic process, which proves the interaction between the risk factors.

(3) Based on the STAMP model, the risk evolution simulation of the whole process from anchoring to berthing of the LNG-fueled vessel under the set scene conditions is carried out. The data shows that the risk evolution simulation diagram conforms to the "U-shaped curve" rule, and the fuel system has the greatest impact on the overall risk.

Reference

[1] Allison C K, Revell K M, Sears R, et al. Systems Theoretic Accident Model and Process (STAMP) Safety Modelling Applied to An Aircraft Rapid Decompression Event[J]. Safety science, 2017, 98: 159-166.

[2] Baksh, Al-Amin, R Abbassi, V Garaniya, Faisal Khan. Marine Transportation Risk Assessment Using Bayesian Network: Application to Arctic Waters[J]. Ocean Engineering, 2018, 159.

[3] Cabello JM, Cejudo JM, Luque M, et al. Optimization of the size of a solar thermal electricity plant by means of genetic algorithms, 36, 11.

[4] Fu S, Yan X, Zhang Di, et al. Framework for The Quantitative Assessment of the Risk of Leakage From LNG-Fueled Vessels By an Event Tree-CFD[J]. Journal of loss prevention in the process industries, 2016, 43: 42-52.

[5] Fernandes R F, Braunschweig F, Loureno R. Neves. Combining Operational Models and Data into A Dynamic Vessel Risk Assessment Tool for Coastal Regions[J]. Ocean Science Discussions, 2015, 12(4).

[6] Faghih-Roohi, Xie M, KM Ng. Accident Risk Assessment in Marine Transportation Via Markov Modelling and Markov Chain Monte Carlo Simulation[J]. Ocean Engineering, 2014, 91.

[7] Hu S, Huang C, Deng H, et al. Markov Chain Model for the Dynamic Simulation of Process Risk in Ship Pilotage at Harbor[J]. Journal of Harbin Engineering University, 2017, 38(9): 1391-1398.

[8] Hu S, LI Zhuang, XI Y, et al. Path Analysis of Causal Factors Influencing Marine Traffic Accident Via Structural Equation Numerical Modeling[J]. Journal of Marine Science And Engineering, 2019, 7(4): 96.

[9] International Marine Committee. Technical Circular No. 53, International Code of Safety for Ships Using Gases or Other Low-Flashpoint Fuels[S]. 2017.

[10] Irani Rasoul, Nasimi Reza. (2013). Evolving Neural Network Using Real Coded Genetic Algorithm for Permeability Estimation of the Reservoir, 40, 11

[11] Jeong B, Lee, Byungsuk, Zhou P, Ha S. Evaluation of Safety Exclusion Zone for LNG Bunkering Station on LNG-Fuelled Ships[J]. Journal of Marine Engineering & Technology, 2017, 16(3): 121-144.

[12] Khan B, Khan F, Veitch B, Yang M. An operational Risk Analysis Tool to Analyze Marine

Transportation in Arctic Waters[J]. Reliability Engineering and System Safety,2018,169.

[13] Kim T E, Nazir S, ØVERGÅRD K I. A STAMP-Based Causal Analysis of the Korean Sewol Ferry Accident[J]. Safety Science, 2016, 83: 93-101.

[14] Kujala P, Haenninen M, Arola T, Ylitalo J. Analysis of the Marine Traffic Safety in the Gulf of Finland [J]. Reliability Engineering and System Safety,2009,94(8).

[15] Kwak D H, Heo J H, Park S H, et al. Energy-Efficient Design and Optimization of Boil-Off Gas (BOG) re-LiquefaCtion Process for Liquefied Natural Gas (LNG)-Fuelled Ship [J]. Energy, 2018, 148: 915-929.

[16] Lei, Wab Qla C, Sd A, Cgs B. Guedes Soares. EffectiVeness Assessment of Ship Navigation Safety Countermeasures Using Fuzzy Cognitive Maps[J]. Safety Science,2019,117.

[17] Leveson N, Samost A, Dekker S, S Finkelstein, J Raman. A Systems Approach to Analyzing and Preventing Hospital Adverse Events[J]. Journal of Patient Safety, 2020, 16(2): 162-167.

[18] Leveson N. A New Accident Model for Engineering Safer Systems[J]. Safety Science, 2004, 42(4): 237-270.

[19] Leveson N. A Systems Approach to Risk Management Through Leading Safety Indicators[J]. Reliability Engineering & System Safety, 2015,136: 17-34.

[20] Li Bo. Navigation Risk Assessment Scheme Based on Fuzzy Dempster-Shafer Evidence Theory [J]. International Journal of Advanced Robotic Systems,2018,15(5).

[21] Li J, Huang Z. Fire and Explosion Risk Analysis and Evaluation for LNG Ships [J]. Procedia engineering, 2012,45: 70-76.

[22] Min O, Hong L, Yu MH, Qi F. STAMP-Based Analysis on the Railway Accident and Accident Spreading: Taking the China-Jiaoji Railway Accident for Example[J]. Safety science, 2010, 48(5): 544-555.

[23] NK Im. Potential Risk Ship Domain as a Danger Criterion for Real-Time Ship Collision Risk Evaluation [J]. Ocean Engineering,2019,194.

[24] PAD Dr, E Fort. LNG as a marine fuel: Likelihood of LNG releases[J]. Journal of Marine Engineering & Technology, 2013, 12(3): 3-10.

[25] Shanghai Jiao Tong University. Sustainability Research; Reports From Shanghai Jiao Tong University Describe Recent Advances in Sustainability Research (Risk Assessment and Decision Support for Sustainable Traffic Safety in Hong Kong Waters)[J]. Energy & Ecology,2020.

[26] Sui Z, Wen Y, Huang Y, Zhou C, Xiao C, Chen H. Empirical Analysis of Complex Network for Marine Traffic Situation[J]. Ocean Engineering,2020,214.

[27] Thomson H, Corbett JJ, Winebrake JJ. (2015). Natural Gas as a Marine Fuel[J]. Energy policy, 87: 153-167.

[28] Wan C, Yan X, Z Di, Fu S. (2013) Reliability Analysis of a Marine LNG-Diesel Dual Fuel Engine [J]. Chemical Engineering Transactions, 33: 811-816.

[29] Wen Y, Huang Y, Zhou C, Yang J, Xiao C, Wu X. Modelling of Marine Traffic Flow Complexity[J]. Ocean Engineering,2015,104.

[30] Wu J, Hu S, Jin Y, et al. Performance Simulation of the Transportation Process Risk of Bauxite Carriers Based on the Markov Chain and Cloud Model[J]. Journal of Marine Science and Engineering, 2019, 7(4): 108.

[31] Xuan S, Hu S, Li Z, et al. Dynamics Simulation for Process Risk Evolution on the Bunker Operation of an LNG-Fueled Vessel with Catastrophe Mathematical Models [J]. Journal of Marine Science and

Engineering, 2019, 7(9): 299.
[32] Xue J, P H A J M. Gelder Van, Reniers G, E Papadimitriou, C Wu. Multi-Attribute Decision-Making Method for Prioritizing Maritime Traffic Safety Influencing Factors of Autonomous ships' Maneuvering Decisions Using Grey and Fuzzy Theories[J]. Safety Science,2019,120.
[33] Yang Z, Wang J, Yan X, Zhang Di, Jin fen. Use of Fuzzy rule-Based Evidential Reasoning Approach in the Navigational Risk Assessment of Inland Waterway Transportation Systems[J]. Safety Science, 2016,82.
[34] Yu Q, Liu K, Chang C, Yang Z. Realising Advanced Risk Assessment of Vessel Traffic Flows Near Offshore Wind Farms[J]. Reliability Engineering and System Safety,2020,203.
[35] Zhang S, Jing Z, Li W, Wang L, Liu D, Wang T. Navigation Risk Assessment Method Based on Flow Conditions: A Case Study of the River Reach Between the Three Gorges Dam and the Gezhouba Dam [J]. Ocean Engineering,2019,175.
[36] Zhen R, Riveiro M, Jin Y. (2017) A Novel Analytic Framework of Real-Time Multi-Vessel Collision Risk Assessment for Maritime Traffic Surveillance[J]. Ocean Engineering,2017,145.

珠江口水域航标灯塔桩设计与施工刍议

袁靖周[1] 岳志伟[2]

(1. 交通运输部南海航海保障中心广州航标处；2. 交通运输部南海航海保障中心三沙航标处)

摘　要　本文根据广州航标处辖区航标灯塔桩建设情况，结合笔者建设管理经验，对常用的几类航标灯塔桩材质特性、结构设计、基础设计及施工等进行了总结分析，并提出了一些设计与施工管理方面建议。

关键词　航标　灯塔桩　设计　施工

0　引　言

灯塔、灯桩是一种常见的水上交通类航标设施，为航行船舶提供导助航、定位等服务。随着社会发展及水运经济日益发达，灯塔、灯桩建设也得到了快速发展。一方面，随着水上航标配布结构的完善，灯塔、灯桩布设数量逐年增加。另一方面，灯塔、灯桩材质、外观形式等越来越多样化。如近20年来广州航标处在珠江口逐步布设了玻璃钢、超高分子聚乙烯、铝合金等新材质灯塔桩，造型也变化多样，如图1～图10所示。特别在外观形式上，近年来建设的灯塔桩相对20世纪90年代之前建设的灯塔桩在造型上更富特色。

究其原因，其一是由于随着航运经济逐步复苏，陆岛交通日益频繁，水上航线、船舶种类及数量等逐年增加，对导助航及定位等服务需求增多，对灯塔桩建设的要求也越来越高。其二是随着越来越多的海岛旅游开发，灯塔在保证正常导助航功能同时，也为海岛开发建设增加了亮点，甚或成为当地小地标。如图2荷包岛灯塔即是在珠海旅游开发岛-荷包岛建设的一座大型灯塔。图3所示为在深圳某景区岬角设置的一座小型灯桩。其三是灯塔往往建于沿海岬角、礁石上，施工十分困难，开发一些新材质的灯塔建筑材料更便于施工和节省成本。

为此，笔者结合在广州航标处辖区建设灯塔桩的实践经验，对灯塔桩建设的材质、结构形式、基础设计及施工进行了归纳总结，并提出了相关建议，以期在航标灯塔桩建设上取得进一步发展。

图1 牛利角灯桩(钢筋混凝土结构,建于1989年)

图2 荷包岛灯塔(钢筋混凝土结构,建于2019年)

1 灯塔桩材质及结构设计

20世纪90年代之前,灯塔桩设计基本采用钢筋混凝土结构、砖砌体结构、钢结构这三种结构形式。90年代后,逐步开始引入玻璃钢材质灯塔桩,目前在珠江口水域仍存在大量玻璃钢灯塔桩且保存较完好,如图3所示广州港内一座玻璃钢灯塔桩已建有21年,外观及结构仍保持完好。2010年左右,超高分子聚乙烯材料被引入制作灯塔桩,如广州航标处于2013—2017年在辖区水域分批建设了多座超高分子聚乙烯灯塔桩。近年来,铝合金材质灯桩,因其造型可自主设计、耐腐蚀性强,又可在工厂加工完成后在现场安装,逐步被引入,如图4所示。特别是在海南西南沙海域,其环境条件恶劣,腐蚀性极强,运输材料成本及人工成本高,因此受到青睐。以下分别对常用的几类灯塔桩结构设计情况予以概述。

图3 广州港海心岗灯桩(玻璃钢材质,建于1999年)

图4 深圳背仔角灯桩(铝合金结构,建于2017年)

1.1 玻璃钢灯塔桩

玻璃钢学名玻璃纤维增强塑料,简称GFRP(Glass Fiber Reinforced Plastics),即纤维增强复合塑料。它是以玻璃纤维及其制品(玻璃布、带、毡、纱等)作为增强材料,以合成树脂作基体材料的一种复合材料,外观上类似塑胶制品,如图4所示。

玻璃钢具有质轻而硬、不导电、性能稳定、机械强度高、耐腐蚀等特性,可以代替钢材制造机械零件、汽车图船舶外壳等。相对密度在1.5~2.0之间,只有碳钢的1/4~1/5,可拉伸强度接近。玻璃钢灯桩可按照设计样式制作相应的模具,采用手糊法、喷射法、模压法、树脂传递模塑等方法生产成型。

广州航标处于20世纪90年代使用的一批玻璃钢灯桩,造型相对简单,分节制作成型圆柱形、锥形玻璃钢,每节桩体之间、上部护栏与桩体、门与桩体、桩体与基础之间通过螺栓连接固定,如图3所示。

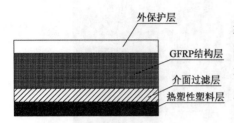

图5　玻璃钢材质截面图

如图3所示,该玻璃钢灯桩已使用长达21年,外观颜色仍比较鲜明,材料本身基本完好。当然,玻璃钢材质也存在缺点,一是弹性模量低,从而易变形;二是长期耐温性差,一般的GFRP不能在高温中长期使用;三是老化现象,在紫外线、风沙雨雪、化学介质、机械应力等作用下性能下降;四是剪切强度低。

根据广州航标处使用玻璃钢材质灯桩的经验,玻璃钢灯桩老化现象不明显,依所处环境恶劣程度区别不大,刚度也基本满足使用要求。出现损坏的地方往往位于暴露在外的金属合页与玻璃钢连接处。总体来说,玻璃钢材质灯桩质量较好,抗腐蚀性好,维护需注意的是每节之间螺栓防腐蚀处理。

1.2　超高分子聚乙烯灯塔桩

超高分子聚乙烯英文全称为UHMW-PE(Ultra-high molecular weight polyethylene),是一种耐冲击、耐磨损、自润滑性能好以及低温性能优异的工程塑料,是由乙烯、丁二烯单体在催化剂的作用下,聚合而成的平均分子量大于200万的热塑性工程塑料。一般意义上把粘均分子量在200万以上的线形结构聚乙烯称为UHMW-PE。最早由德国赫斯特(Hoechst)公司于1958年开发研制成功,并实现工业化生产。美国赫尔克勒斯(Hercules)公司,日本三井石油化学工业株式会社,荷兰DSM公司等相继实现较大规模的工业化生产。

超高分子聚乙烯的特性:①耐磨特性,耐磨性高于一般的钢管4~7倍,是不锈钢的27.3倍。年磨损率平均值0.58mm,提高了使用寿命。②耐冲击性,在现有的工程塑料中超高分子量聚乙烯的冲击韧性值最高,其抗冲击强度常温下是PE100的10倍以上。③耐腐蚀性能,能耐绝大多数腐蚀性介质和有机溶剂的侵蚀,可以在浓度小于80%的浓盐酸中应用,在浓度小于75%的硫酸、浓度小于20%的硝酸中性能相当稳定。④自润性,自身滑动性能优于用油润滑的钢或黄铜。在环境恶劣、粉尘、泥沙多的地方,超高分子量聚乙烯管自身干润滑性能更好。⑤无毒性,超高分子量聚乙烯材料是国家已认证的环保材料,无毒无味。中国许多城市的主供排水道管都改用超高分子量聚乙烯管。⑥耐低温性、抗老化,可长期在-269℃到80℃的温度下工作,由于分子链中不饱和分子团很少、分子量大、稳定性高,老化速度特别缓慢,使用寿命加长。⑦表面非附着性、不结垢,超高分子量聚乙烯管由于摩擦系数小和无极性,具有表面非附着性。⑧抗开裂性最优,超高分子量聚乙烯管通过拉伸试验证明,它具有100%~300%的延伸率。

在超高分子聚乙烯材料应用于航标灯塔桩之前,该工程塑料通常用于管道制作或其他工业品。正是基于超高分子聚乙烯材质有着耐腐蚀、自润性好、耐老化、表面不结垢等优点,且可在工厂制作完成后于现场安装。广州航标处于2010年开始引入试用,如图6所示。整个灯塔桩也是分节制作后通过螺栓拼接而成,桩体中心设置钢柱作为内部支撑。众所周知,航标灯塔桩一般设置于沿海海岛或礁石等风浪力较大的位置,珠江口经常出现大台风,根据广州航标处这些年试用情况来看,抗风能力较强(理论值可抗17级(60m/s)),尚未出现折断或倾覆情况。

图6　超高分子聚乙烯灯桩

广州航标处在珠江口水域实际应用的超高分子聚乙烯材质灯桩也还有其他几种形式,如图7、图8所示。图7所示是在灯桩内部设置钢结构骨架,将超高分子聚乙烯材料外壳通过螺栓与内部钢结构固接。图8所示灯桩,是通过螺栓将使用超高分子聚乙烯材质制作的小型部件组装成一种抗风能力强的结构形式。这两种灯桩在抗风、防腐蚀、现场安装便利性等几方面有明显的优势。特别是图8所示灯桩,每个零部件最重不超过15kg,这对于设置在礁石、孤石或施工不便利位置处的灯桩来说,工人在现场施工安装非常便利,提高了效率和安全性。

图7 超高分子聚乙烯灯桩(内含钢结构,建于2018年)

图8 超高分子聚乙烯灯桩(建于2018年)

1.3 铝合金灯塔桩

铝合金是一种以铝为主要成分的合金材料,用作灯桩桩身时,常用标号为5A05的工业铝合金,它是一种Al-Mg系防锈型铝合金,成分为硅Si:0.50、铁Fe:0.50、铜Cu:0.10、锰Mn:0.30~0.6、镁Mg:4.8~5.5、锌Zn:0.20、铝Al:余量,通常用于制造要求工艺塑性高、耐蚀性好、承受中等载荷的焊接管道、焊制油箱和其他液体容器,以及其他零件。如图4、图9所示即为在广州航标处辖区建设的铝合金灯塔桩。

工业铝合金,其密度仅为钢的1/3,约2.7g/cm³。屈服强度在100~170MPa之间,抗拉强度达225MPa以上,与钢筋混凝土结构抗拉强度相当。其次,它对水、雾、光氧化、盐雾酸雨均有很好的防腐性,特别是在盐水、石油化学等恶劣环境下具有优良的抗腐蚀性。它已广泛应用于船舶、舰艇、汽车和飞机板焊接件、需严格防火的压力容器、致冷装置、电视塔、钻探设备、交通运输设备、导弹元件、装甲等等领域。

工厂制造成品一般按照放样下料→卷板成型→法兰制作钻孔→拼装焊接→矫正打磨→预组装→钝化→清洗→铬铬→清洗→烘干→喷漆→烘烤固化等流程实施,工业化程度较高,无需开模,所以品种、规格非常齐全。每个灯桩都可制作成不同外观。表面涂料采用氟碳烤漆,漆膜强度高,不易划伤和磨损,有自清洁功能,表面有脏污物可通过水洗清洁,维护便捷性较好。

图9 工业铝合金灯桩

铝合金灯桩一般按照设计图,在工厂分节制作,每节之间通过螺栓连接,运至现场安装。不得不提的是,铝合金灯桩密度虽然较钢材低很多,但因为考虑到设计效果,每节灯桩仍然重量达100kg,现场安装也相较超高分子聚乙烯材料灯桩更为吃力。

1.4 钢筋混凝土结构灯塔桩

钢筋混凝土结构通常认为发明于1848年。1872年,世界第一座钢筋混凝土结构的建筑在美国纽约落成,人类建筑史上一个崭新的纪元从此开始,钢筋混凝土结构在1900年之后在工程界方得到了大规模的使用,目前被广泛应用于建筑结构中。顾名思义,钢筋混凝土结构,就是由钢筋和水泥混合而成的结构形式。混凝土是水泥(通常硅酸盐水泥)与集料(砂、石)的混合物,在混凝土中加入钢筋与之共同工作,由钢筋承担其中的拉力,混凝土承担压应力部分,即为钢筋混凝土结构。

钢筋混凝土灯塔桩是传统的灯塔桩形式,特别是在新形式结构灯桩(即上述所提玻璃钢、超高分子聚乙烯、铝合金等)出现之前基本都是采用这种形式。

该种结构整体强度高,刚度大,变形小,稳定性好。一般在外表面黏贴瓷砖,抗腐蚀性好,广州航标处辖区的20世纪80年代建成的都保持完好,如图1所示。通过设计,可以设计出许多精美造型的灯塔桩,如图2所示。其次,该结构使用年限长,按照建筑物重要性设计年限可达50年以上。最后,该结构相较于超高分子、玻璃钢、铝合金、钢结构等形式,更具有厚重感。在观赏性、标志性、象征性方面能很好地体现出灯塔桩的文化意义、历史意义。

但是,若要建设钢筋混凝土结构灯桩,也有以下几点需加以考虑。第一,所需要的钢筋、沙、石、淡水等材料海上运输困难,且运输过程易受海水盐分侵蚀,造成施工质量问题。第二,施工过程需要模板支护、钢筋绑扎、浇筑混凝土、模板拆除等流程,施工较为复杂,且在海岛、礁石等施工条件恶劣的情况下施工稍有不慎,容易产生质量问题。第三,由于钢筋混凝土结构的初凝、终凝施工规范都有严格的时间要求,即使使用早强剂、速凝剂等,也需要达到施工规范要求的强度才可以进行下一步施工,所以导致施工工期较长,施工期间遇到恶劣天气、海况的概率更大。第四,因涉及材料、人工、运输、工艺等问题,整体造价很高。

1.5 钢结构灯塔桩

钢结构主要是由钢制材料组成的结构,是主要的建筑结构类型之一。结构主要由型钢和钢板等制成的钢梁、钢柱、钢桁架等构件组成,各构件或部件之间通常采用焊缝、螺栓或铆钉连接。用于灯塔桩桩身是常用钢管和钢桁架两种结构,如图10、图11所示。

图10 钢结构灯桩

图11 钢结构导标

钢结构强度高、自重轻、整体刚性好、变形能力强,材料匀质性和各向同性好,属理想弹性体,最符合一般工程力学的基本假定;材料塑性、韧性好,可有较大变形,能很好地承受动力荷载;抗风及抗冲击性好。钢结构灯塔桩一般按照设计图纸,在工厂加工制造,成品运至现场后可采用螺栓装配。钢结构也可设计出漂亮造型(如埃菲尔铁塔),但从目前使用或保存的钢结构灯塔桩来看,大部分都比较单调,有待提升。需要注意的是,钢结构灯桩表层油漆日后维护过程基本每年都需要重新现场涂刷油漆。因此,钢结构灯塔桩日常维护给基层增加了工作量,受欢迎度不高。

总体来说,钢结构与上述4种结构在综合性能上有以下可取之处。第一,在设计高度上,钢结构可设计出高度较高的灯塔桩或导标,而玻璃钢、超高分子及工业铝合金灯塔桩设计高度基本控制在15m内。第二,钢结构灯塔桩也可以像玻璃钢、超高分子、铝合金灯塔桩一样现场安装,现场施工时间较短,而钢筋混凝土结构现场施工复杂、工期长。第三,一般来说,造价上低于钢筋混凝土。

1.6 其他结构类型灯塔桩

除上述玻璃钢、超高分子聚乙烯、铝合金、钢筋混凝土、钢结构几类常用的结构外,也还包括少量的砖砌体结构及新型材料结构,如聚脲材料等,在此不叙。

2 灯塔桩基础设计

基础是连接上部结构与地基之间的过渡结构,起承上启下作用,一般而言,基础形式可分为浅基础和深基础两类。根据《建筑地基基础设计规范》,目前常见的基础形式有无筋扩展基础、扩展基础、柱下条形基础、高层建筑筏板基础、桩基础、岩石锚杆基础。在灯塔桩建设中,小型灯塔桩上部结构简单,除风荷载、检修荷载需考虑外,无其他外部作用。珠江口灯塔桩建设位置大部分处于沿海礁石、沙滩及海岛硬岩,故灯塔桩基础多采用岩石锚杆基础、钢筋混凝土独立基础及桩基础,如图12～图14所示。

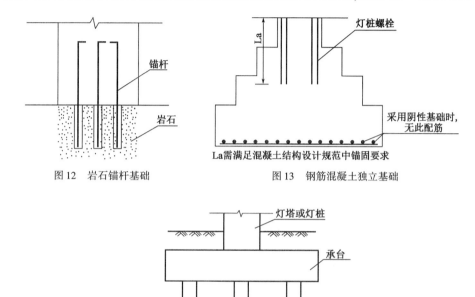

图12 岩石锚杆基础　　图13 钢筋混凝土独立基础

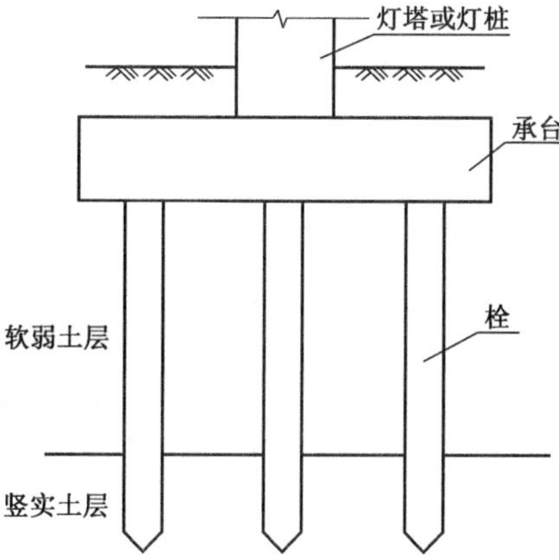

图14 桩基础

对于大型的灯塔桩,基础形式多采用桩基础,其原因一是桩基础形式在建筑行业比较成熟,积累了很多工程经验;二是根据各类基础横向比较,桩基础受力性能是相对安全可靠。对于沿海大型灯塔如华阳灯塔、赤瓜灯塔等,均采用桩基础。

但笔者想提出的是,基于灯塔桩重点考虑风荷载的特点,无其他外部荷载,在基础设计时可以考虑参照《烟囱设计规范》中的基础形式(烟囱基础设计还需考虑烟气温度作用、烟气压力作用及积灰荷载等,而一般航标灯塔桩基本无须考虑其他任何外荷载)。与桩基础相比,图15～图17基础形式的造价成本将比桩基础大大减小,施工难度降低,施工时间及效率提升。而这三类基础在抗倾覆能力方面较强,这对于灯塔桩建设来说非常实用。通过查阅现有灯塔桩建设资料,大型灯塔桩多采用桩基且偏于保守,而采用环形基础、圆形基础及壳体基础的甚少。

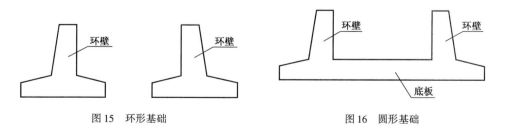

图15 环形基础　　图16 圆形基础

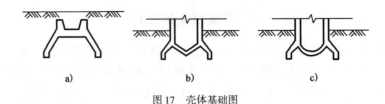

图 17　壳体基础图

3　灯塔桩施工

因灯塔桩建设地点一般位于沿海岛礁、岬角等处,故灯塔桩施工比陆地上的工程建设要困难很多。主要表现在:

(1)施工条件差。一般海岛施工无淡水、无市电、无道路,场地崎岖,可以说是"三不通,一不平"。因此,施工所需的淡水及饮用水全部靠从陆地海运,电源靠柴油发电机,道路需新开辟且大多都岩石或微风化岩石。其次,施工工人的生活住宿、材料工具堆放须要搭建工棚,而某些礁石上搭建施工工棚非常困难,如图18、图19所示。再次,工棚一般都是较简易的,施工期存在台风侵袭可能,而岛礁风力很强,因此,在海岛礁石作业时施工安全、施工时间都是必须要认真考虑。

图 18　珠海长咀灯桩

图 19　珠海凤尾咀灯桩

(2)运输问题。所有材料、设备、工具、物品都需海运及二次搬运,有些建设地点在海岛山顶,若无平整道路,机械工具无法使用,人工二次搬运工作量很大,有时甚至动用最原始省钱的畜力搬运。基于以往灯塔建设经验,采用驴运输材料比较节约成本,供同行参考。其次,建设点需找好靠泊位置,注意潮汐,满足船舶靠泊要求。

(3)基于以上条件,并考虑安全风险及各项损耗等,在海岛建设灯塔桩造价比陆地高出好几倍。

根据笔者经验,灯塔桩施工还需注意以下几点:

(1)制定合理施工方案。除前已述及的靠泊点的选择、材料搬运方法,施工时间也必须合理安排。如图20所示,长嘴灯桩位于东南角,该处涌浪极大,东北风时船舶很难靠泊,可密切关注天气选择西南风时施工。对于混凝土结构的施工工法,因较成熟,在此不详叙。

(2)施工质量控制。除对材料质量、工艺工法等常规程序把关外,海岛施工质量尤其需注意防腐措施。特别是钢筋、脚手架等堆放在海岛一段时间极易发生锈蚀,必须涂刷防腐料。如图21所示,在珠海高栏荷包岛灯塔基础中使用的钢筋就是涂刷有环氧树脂的钢筋。另外,在运输过程中,组成钢筋混凝土的钢筋、沙石、淡水等材料海上运输困难,且运输过程易收海水盐分腐蚀,这些都是需注意的。

(3)台风预案。海岛施工经常面临台风侵袭,如2017—2018年遭遇"山竹""天鸽"等强台风,对工程建设造成极大损失。因此,必须做好台风预案,做好保护措施,保证成品质量和人员安全等。

(4)成本控制。前已述及,因海岛施工比陆地施工困难很多,造成造价成本比陆地建筑高出几倍。

成本控制主要在:第一,合理安排施工组织方案,缩短工期。第二,从设计源头上处理,优化设计方案。第三,利用当地条件,因地制宜。如看可否寻找淡水源,利用机械工具等提升施工效率。

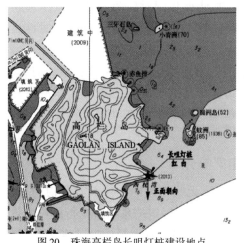

图20 珠海高栏岛长咀灯桩建设地点

图21 荷包岛灯塔基础钢筋

(5)工人管理。具体施工人员文化素质不高,因方言等沟通不便,因此,技术交底首先要把工艺工法等落实。其次,安全意识教育要每天做,安全措施要落实。第三,若在海岛施工,工期较长,应适当安排好一些活动或专人做好心理健康咨询与辅导工作。

4 结　语

航标灯塔等构筑物属于航标领域的一类重要目视航标,在21世纪前发挥很重要作用。随着电子导航技术发展,航标灯塔的作用逐步弱化,但它目前仍属于不可或缺的一类助航标志。灯塔建设不同于陆地构筑物建设,海岛施工条件差,效率低,关注度不高,设计及施工从业人员不多,本文旨在通过总结广州航标处在珠江口建设的一些灯塔桩,并根据实际工作经验提出一些粗浅建议,供同行参考商讨。

参考文献

[1] 袁靖周,岳志伟,李凤山. 浅析沿海航标灯塔桩基础选型[J]. 珠江水运,2017,6.

[2] 袁靖周. 三种高分子材料灯桩的对比与应用建议[J]. 珠江水运,2018,4.

[3] 徐文华,岳志伟,袁靖周. 目前业内五种主流灯桩材质之横向比较及选型建议[J]. 航测技术,2018,6.

[4] 袁靖周. 大型航标灯塔设计要点探讨[J]. 航测技术,2019,12.

基于无线自组网的多媒体应急通信保障系统

谭志荣[1]　陈　维[1]　冒　欣[1]　王海滨[2]

(1.武汉理工大学航运学院;2.长江三峡通航管理局)

摘　要　为了保障社会突发事件后的基本通信,需要快速建立有效的通信网络以保护受灾人员的生命和财产。首先介绍了我国应急通信保障的技术现况及应用,进而结合无线自组网的特点在通信方面的优势,探讨无线自组网技术在三峡库区应急通信保障中的应用,设计基于无线自组网的多媒体应急通信保障系统,为海事、航道、公安在处置应对库区干线水域紧急突发事件提供可靠的应急通信网络保障。

关键词　应急　通信保障　无线自组网　三峡库区

0 引言

近些年来,自然灾害频发,而由此引发的一系列问题,使得我国对应急通信保障体系的建设更为重视。而我国由于相关研究起步较晚,目前的通信保障系统普遍存在着传送速率低、延时性高以及互联互通性差的问题。

为紧急突发事件提供快速、畅通、有效的应急通信网络,实现紧急突发事件的现场和指挥中心之间数据、视频、语音信息的实时传输,亟须开发一套基于无线自组网的多媒体应急通信保障系统用于应急现场,并将此套系统切实用到三峡库区应急保障通讯,为海事、航道、公安在处置应对库区干线水域紧急突发事件提供可靠应急通信网络保障。

1 无线自组网简介

无线自组网络(MANET),是一种自组织、无中心网络。无线自组网——不需要物理基地站,各主机相互连通,主机即可充当服务器。传统的无线网络技术需要一个固定的基站来执行用户的接入和对用户的数据进行转发。在人口相对来说比较密集的地方,一般来说都有着大量的基站来供给我们进行通信,而在偏远的地区或者进行紧急救援大范围移动的时候,由于没有基站的覆盖,就会导致通信困难,在空间上限制了信息的传播,为了应对这种情况,无线自组网应运而生。

无线自组网不依赖于特定的服务器,是一个相对独立的网络系统,该系统能短时间内部署到位,建立起一套完整、强大、高抗干扰的网络通信系统,提供有效的数据和多媒体通信服务。作为一种新型的网络模式,无线自组网可以和传统网络相互补充,相辅相成。

2 无线自组网适在应急保障中应性分析

2.1 无线自组网网络结构

当地震、洪水、泥石流等自然灾害发生时,短期内会造成通信设备损毁,灾区往往面临着大面积通讯中断、电力中断、道路受阻的情况,极端情况下还可能导致大面积通信网络中断,导致无法正常通讯。在面对这些极端情况下,可以设计一种混合无线 Ad Hoc 网络技术来解决这种情况。该技术 MT 移动终端的操作可以自由选择自组织模式或蜂窝模式。蜂窝网络直接通过基站 BS 发送数据,而自组织网络则通过节点逐层发送数据。当遇到紧急情况时,蜂窝网络无法直接将数据传输到基站,Ad Hoc 网络将自动启动,并根据不同的程序算法,构造一条可以将数据传输到基站的路由,以解决网络瘫痪的问题。

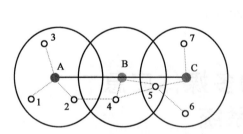
图1 Ad Hoc 网络和蜂窝多跳混合通信网络结构

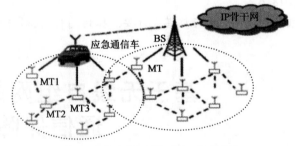
图2 混合式应急通信网络工作示意图

2.2 基于安全预警和监控的无线传感技术

除了确保紧急情况发生后网络的畅通之外,紧急情况通信网络还必须对紧急情况发生地区进行有效而全面的监控,以防止风险并进行现场管理。无线传感器网络技术与现有的异构网络通信系统具有很好的兼容性,并且远程数据传输的可靠性。例如,为了提高无线传感器网络的容错性、安全性和生存性,将使用基于集群的多层网络系统来使整个传感器网络系统执行基本的操作,例如测试、调整、维护并自行恢复。这样可以避免因部署多节点传感器网络而带来的巨大成本,可以提高无线传感器网络技术的信息收集和服务交付的可靠性。

2.3 建立在可移动基站上的便携式通信网络

自身带有移动基站的便携式移动通信网络可以根据环境需要构建陆路运输、海上运输和空中运输的网络通信平台，而无须预设的基础设施。该通信网络可以支持本地通信，并且几乎不需要额外的人工干预就可以灵活地调整网络设置。该便携式移动通信网络可用于公共基础设施通信设施覆盖范围有限，河流中心的运营商网络信号不稳定，并且难以在短时间内恢复基本通信的各种灾区中使用。救援人员可以使用便携式移动通信网络可以非常方便地实现通信网络的建立。

3 三峡库区应急通信网络保障

3.1 三峡库区应急通信网络存在的问题

（1）灾害往往发生突然，所以存在时间、地点和准备周期短的特征，应急救援人员在通信网络保障准备工作上难度较大，通信设备运输困难收拢难度较大，一些大型通信装备只能通过人力搬运至现场，且一些通讯装备对于使用人员的专业技能要求非常严格，不能在第一时间建立临时通信网络。

（2）库区水域地理环境复杂，公共基础通信设施覆盖范围极为有限；运营商网络在江中心水域的信号也不稳定，有的水域信号差甚至无信号。

（3）库区虽然有卫星覆盖，但其传输能力有限，大部分区域山势险峻，岸壁陡峭。

3.2 设计思路

由于有些库区及江中心运营商网络信号不稳定，难以满足日常通讯，且灾难发生后，通过使用有效的通信手段完成重大灾害和事故的救援指挥和现场汇报，并迅速建立并形成有效的应急通信网络，这不仅是减少灾害造成的损失程度的决定性因素，也是消防通信保障的主要任务。要求，基于此有机结合有线与无线等多种通信技术手段，有效的解决紧急突发事件中的应急通信保障问题，充分发挥自组网多媒体应急通信平台快速响应、高灵活性的技术优势。主要目标：

（1）搭建稳定可靠的通信网络，提供网络数据传输通道。

（2）搭建现场视频会议系统，实现现场调度指挥。

（3）搭建高清视频系统，实时传输现场视频画面。

3.3 一体化应急系统综合平台视频会议终端的设计

3.3.1 主要组成部分。

（1）无人机等高清视频信号的接入。

在保证现场指挥部与各级指挥中心基本语音通信需求的基础上，实现音视频通话和多媒体信息交互，从而完成一人远程指挥一线人员救援的任务，由于固定摄像机不能进行近距离动态跟踪与拍摄画面，本设计中无人机高清视频信号的接入，实现目标画面的近距离动态跟踪与画面拍摄，准确传送灾区画面，可实现快速部署，出现突发事件时能够快速反应。

（2）Mesh组网的应用。

Mesh组网是一种容量大、速率高、覆盖范围广的无线网络系统，在无线传输行业中具有智能快捷自动组网、安装方便、结构灵活、稳定性好、高带宽的优势、可同时接入多个AP及音视频。

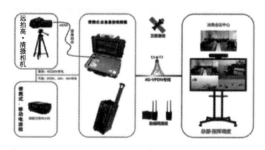

图3 一体化应急系统综合平台

3.3.2 一体化应急系统综合平台视频会议终端。

(1)将各类分散部件及线路整合为拉杆箱一体式设计,方便携带。
(2)取随用、操作连接简单,只需要接通电源与网络即可进行连接使用。
(3)多接口数据交换设计,组网接入更方便,灵活性更强。

4 结语

一旦有突发的紧急事件发生,应急通信保障功能就显得尤为重要。通过第一时间建立起较为完善的应急通信保障系统,可以在灾难发生地建立一个简易通信站,使其与外界恢复联系,救援人员及时抵达救援现场且第一时间上报现场具体信息,为指挥部正确指挥提供参考依据。将突发灾害造成的损失降到最小。

本文提出的基于无线自组网技术的一体化应急综合平台视频会议终端用能够应用于地理环境复杂的库区水域,公共基础通信设施覆盖范围有限地区;而且在灾难发生时,现有网络瘫痪的情况下,也可以应用无线自组网迅速建立应急网络,发挥出巨大的技术优势。电源和视频箱也采用便携式设备可以有效解决以往灾难发生时通信设备搬运难、收拢难度较大的问题。在救援过程中,迅速建立起有效的通信网络,指挥部门利用视频应急通信系统及时了解与掌握灾害事故现场实际受困情况,针对问题给出正确指挥命令,尽可能地保障受灾人民群众的生命财产安全。

参考文献

[1] 张胤龙.应急通信保障指挥平台的研究与实践[J].电脑知识与技术,2018,14(24):36-37.
[2] 贾群峰.论我国应急通信保障面临的问题和对策分析[J].网络安全技术与应用,2018(01):105,109.
[3] 李崇鞅.基于无线自组网技术的应急通信网络设计及应用[J].电子世界,2016(17):128,159.
[4] 刘琴.PHS网络在高话务冲击下的应急保障[J].信息通信,2009,22(02):70-72.
[5] Arwa M J Jwaifel, Ibrahim Ghareeb, Samir Shaltaf. Impact of Co-Channel Interference on Performance of Dual-Hop Wireless ad Hoc Networks Over α-μ Fading Channels [J]. International Journal of Communication Systems,2020,33(14).

模袋混凝土在码头前沿护底工程中的应用

封有德[1] 陶然[2] 黄睿奕[1]
(1.中交第二航务工程局有限公司;2.中国港湾工程有限责任公司)

摘 要 本文依托某港口工程的建设,根据国际航运协会(PIANC)的指导手册通过数值模拟分析运输船舶的螺旋桨推动器靠泊时所产生的射流对直立式码头前沿的冲刷作用,通过对传统的抛石护底和模袋混凝土两种结构进行对比研究,得出了模袋混凝土更适用于逐步大型化的码头前沿护底结构的结论,并介绍其配合比设计要点和主要水下充填施工工艺,具有推广价值。

关键词 码头前沿护底工程 水下现浇自密实模袋混凝土 对比分析 配合比设计

0 引言

随着国民经济的快速发展,沿海港口吞吐量大幅增长并逐步开始向深水水域发展,运输船舶也随之不断向大型化发展。根据相关资料,一些大型运输船舶的推动器全速运转时产生的射流流速可达10m/s左右,远远高于的潮流流速。高速的射流极易对码头前沿的海床或基床造成冲刷、淘蚀作用,严重的将导致码头结构产生较大位移甚至倾覆失稳。但目前在国内规范中,对直立式码头的前沿护底设计中通常仅考虑波浪潮流的冲刷影响,而尚未对于船舶运动引起的冲刷有明确的规定。

本文结合某港口工程建设中板桩码头前沿模袋混凝土护底的建设案例,为类似工程的设计施工提供借鉴参考。

1 工程概况

某港口工程新建码头岸线全长800m,最大设计船型为18270标箱的马士基3E级集装箱船,码头结构采用H+AZ组合板装形式,前沿设计底高程为-17.3m,防冲刷护底采用30cm厚的模袋混凝土(如图1所示)。

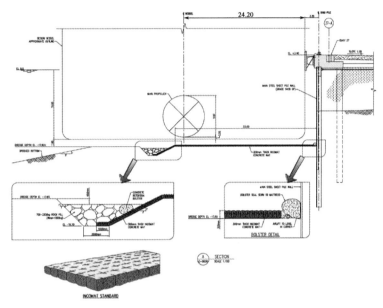

图1 工程典型断面示意图

2 护底设计

2.1 螺旋桨推进器的射场分布规律研究

目前,国际上主流的大型运输船舶均采用的螺旋桨式推动器,螺旋桨通过旋转产生的高速水流提供推动力,根据国外学者的相关研究结果可知,螺旋桨尾流的流场通常呈现为锥形扩张式分布,且分为两个发展阶段(图2)。

(1)起始段:在尾流起始段,低速核心形成于尾流会中心处,其轴向流速分布曲线呈双峰状;

(2)主体段:随着尾流向下游发展,低速核心四周的高速水流逐渐向内外扩散,使得其轴向流速分布曲线的双峰逐渐平缓,直至一定距离后呈单峰状,此时尾流进入主体段。

图2 螺旋桨推进器尾射流流场分布数值模型示意图

2.2 初始射流速度计算

根据国际航运协会(PIANC)的指导手册中关于船舶螺旋桨和推动器对直立式码头前沿冲刷流速的

计算方法，基于 Albertson 提出的孔口射流理论和试验数据，假设螺旋桨射流场分布呈现为从出口向无限水体中喷射的自由射流过程，螺旋桨推动器的初始射流速度可按如下经验公式计算：

$$V_0 = C \left(\frac{f_p \cdot P_D}{\rho_w \cdot D_p} \right)^{0.33}$$

式中：P_D——最大推动器装机功率；

ρ_w——海水密度；

D_p——螺旋桨直径；

C——计算系数，无管道自由螺旋桨取 1.48、有管道螺旋桨取 1.17；

f_p——推动器功率利用率，主推动器通常取 5%～15%。

以马士基 3E 级集装箱船为例，其主推动器最大装机功率 P_D 为 29,680kW、螺旋桨直径 D_p 为 9.8m，取推动器功率利用率 f_p 为 0.15、计算系数 C 为 1.48，计算可得推动器的初始射流速度为 5.198m/s。根据工程所在地相关水文监测资料显示，潮流流速在全年 90% 的时间里低于 0.35m/s，且最大潮流流速不超过 1m/s。因此，对于码头前沿海床的冲刷作用主要是由船舶的螺旋桨和推动器产生的射流造成。

2.3 海床冲刷流速计算

根据国际航运协会（PIANC）的指导手册中推荐的经验公式，采用下式计算主推动器对海床的冲刷流速：

$$V_{b,\max} = (0.2 \sim 0.3) V_0 \frac{D_p}{h_p}$$

式中：h_p——螺旋桨轴线与海床面的距离。

以马士基 3E 级集装箱船为例，取螺旋桨轴线与海床面的距离 h_p 为 7m，计算可得其螺旋桨对海床的最大冲刷流速为 2.184m/s。

2.4 防冲刷措施设计

2.4.1 抛石护底

抛石护底包括抛石、石笼、袋装砂等，是码头前沿防冲刷最常采用的工程方案，具有施工工艺简单等特点，根据国际航运协会（PIANC）的指导手册，可采用 Pilarczyk 公式计算满足稳定要求的块石尺寸：

$$\Delta D = \phi \frac{0.035}{\psi_{cr}} k_h k_{sl}^{-1} \frac{k_t^2 V_{b,\max}^2}{2g}$$

式中：Δ——相对密度，可按 $(\rho_s - \rho_w)/\rho_w$ 计算，其中 ρ_s 为块石密度，取 2,650kg/m³；

ϕ——稳定系数，采用块石护底时通常取 0.75～1.0；

ψ_{cr}——临界 Shields 系数，采用块石护底时通常取 0.035；

k_{sl}——坡度系数，海床面水平时取 1.0；

k_t^2——湍流系数，对螺旋桨射流 PIANC 建议取 5.2～6.0；

k_h——深度/速度分布系数，可取 1.0；$D = D_{n50} \cong 0.84 D_{50}$。

取 ϕ 为 0.9，k_t^2 为 5.2，计算得块石的稳定粒径 $D_{50} = 0.86$m。

2.4.2 模袋混凝土

随着国际航运的运输船舶逐渐大型化发展，船舶所配备的推动器功率越来越大，相应的其产生的水流流速也越来越大，传统的防冲刷措施成本越来越高，因此越来越多的工程项目开始采用水下模袋混凝土、预制混凝土连锁块等防冲刷措施。

通过在模袋中高压泵灌入混凝土或水泥砂浆，当其固结后形成具有一定强度的模袋混凝土整体结构，可广泛应用于堤坝护坡、护岸、港湾、码头等防护工程，尤其适用于大面积护坡和护底工程。模袋混凝土的厚度可通过模袋内的吊筋进行约束来控制，由于通常采用一次喷灌成型，因此具有整体性好、施工简便的有点,此外还可以适应各种复杂的地形特征,尤其是对于水深较大区域的护岸及护底工程,可以无需填筑围堰,就可以直接进行模袋混凝土的水下灌注施工。

模袋混凝土护坡技术最早被用于20世纪50年代日本伊势湾的围堰修复工程,随着1966年美国采用模袋混凝土进行水利工程的岸坡防护实验取得成果,模袋混凝土逐步在美国、日本、欧洲等国家和地区得到了广泛的推广和使用。自从1983年模袋混凝土技术引入国内,随着国内对模袋混凝土护坡的不断应用,对该技术的研究也逐渐增多,并在设计参数优化、施工工艺和质量控制方面积累了不少经验。

模袋混凝土护底的厚度可通过计算抵抗水流上举起力来确定,根据国际航运协会(PIANC)的指导手册,螺旋桨推进器射流所产生的上举力可近似满足伯努利方程:

$$\Delta\left(z + \frac{P}{\rho_w \times g} + \frac{V^2}{2 \times g}\right) = 0$$

式中:z——距离海床面的计算高度;

P——水流产生的上举压力;

V——水流流速。

对于模袋混凝土护底,计算时水流流速采用海床面水流流速,即$z = 0$。为保持稳定,模袋混凝土所受的上举力需小于其水下自重,则满足稳定的模袋混凝土最小厚度为:

$$D \geq \frac{C_L}{2 \times \Delta \times g} \times V_{b,max}^2$$

式中:C_L——上举力系数,对于连续铺设的模袋混凝土可取0.5。

此外考虑1.5的安全系数,计算可得模袋混凝土的最小稳定厚度为0.116m,远小于护底块石的稳定粒径,因此当设计冲刷流速较大时,相比传统的抛石护底,采用模袋混凝土护底可以有效减少护底结构厚度(图3)。

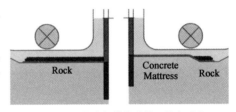

图3 抛石护底与模袋混凝土护底对比

3 施工工艺

模袋混凝土的施工工艺可分为两种,分别是"先铺后灌法"和"先灌后铺法"。"先铺后灌法"的施工操作相对简单,但受环境影响较大,尤其受制于水质对潜水员水下的能见度的制约,而且需要通过混凝土将模袋内的水挤出,因此导致水下混凝土充填的速度比较缓慢,而且对混凝土的强度和密实度控制难度也比较大。"先灌后铺法",是近年在国内兴起的施工工艺,又称"滑道法"。其工艺流程是首先在滑道上完成模袋混凝土充填密实,然后通过滑道将模袋混凝土缓慢拖放至水中,使得混凝土的强度和密实度都能得到较好的保证,而且充填速度快。相比"先铺后灌法",虽然"先灌后铺法"在充填施工效率、模袋充填质量等方面有明显的优势,但是由于需要是一次性投入的设备较多,因此"先灌后铺法"不适用于水深较大且工程量不大的护底工程。

本项目模袋混凝土共计190块,混凝土用量约9550m³,因此综合技术经济考虑,采用"先铺后灌法",即预先将模袋平铺于海底,然后再浇灌混凝土。

3.1 配合比设计

模袋混凝土采用高流动性的自密实混凝土,采用化学外加剂分散作用代替了机械振捣作用。充填一块模袋大约需要6~7h,因此混凝土的配合比设计中需要考虑缓凝时间。此外由于模袋中布设有吊筋带,吊筋带的布设会对混凝土的自流平产生一定影响。

此外,还需要综合考虑混凝土的流动性和和易性。如果混凝土集料在重力作用下产生的剪应力超过其屈服应力,则会从水泥浆中离析出来,而且由于粗集料与砂浆的流变特性不同,也会导致混凝土在流动过程中流动性差的集料与相对流动性好的砂浆之间产生的剪应力超过混凝土的屈服应力,也会造成粗集料的离析。

因此,配置模袋混凝土需要在保证强度的前提下,通过合理的配合比设计,实现混凝土高流动性的同时又不出现离析泌水,具体体现在以下几方面:

(1)水泥浆用量大。由于泵送和填充模袋的要求,需要混凝土拌和物流动性大且不产生泌水和离析,因此模袋混凝土的水泥浆量要大,一般占混凝土总量的30%左右。

(2)砂率大。模袋混凝土的砂率不仅要满足泵送的要求,还要满足填充模袋的要求,一般控制在50%左右。

(3)石子粒径小。石子的最大粒径需要根据模袋混凝土的厚度来确定,一般15～25cm厚的模袋混凝土,石子的最大粒径不超过20mm。

(4)掺入粉煤灰。模袋混凝土的拌和物需要较多的胶凝材料,掺入粉煤灰,既可以增加流动性,还可以替代一部分水泥,节约工程成本,通常采用超量取代法。

(5)掺入减水剂或泵送剂。外加剂的掺入可以减少用水量、节约部分水泥,同时增加混凝土的和易性。

3.2 工艺流程

模袋混凝土施工的关键工序为坡底平整度、模袋的分块、模袋的铺设、布料孔的布置、浇筑顺序、浇筑速度等。其施工工艺流程(图4)。

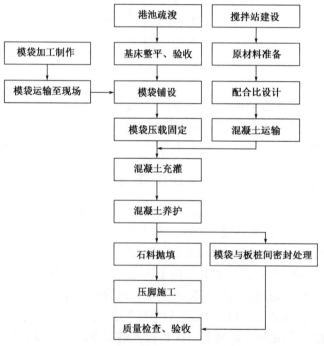

图4 模袋混凝土施工工艺流程图

3.2.1 模袋铺设

首先将成卷模袋平行码头前沿下放至指定位置,在将模袋端头套袋中的钢管固定在板桩上,在安装后续模袋时,同样将模袋的钢管排成一列,首尾连接以便于在宽度方向上进行控制。在水下将成卷的模袋展开前,先将相邻两块模袋的上下拉链起始端连接,模袋展开的同时对两块模袋进行拉链连接,模袋完全展开后在拉链末端用绑扎带将拉锁绑扎固定。

最后检查展开的模袋是否在指定位置,两块模袋是否完全连接上及模袋是否平整。在第一阶段、第二阶段模袋施工时,充填混凝土之前保证后面有一块多余的模袋。各个模袋的位置在模袋安装过程需要进行不断的检查,以监测安装过程偏位尺寸。

3.2.2 模袋固定

第一块模袋铺设时可采用导缆绳定位,以便为后续的模袋铺设提供基准。模袋面板由潜水员向侧边拉至平整展开,并对未充填的模袋可以使用沙袋压载固定。

3.2.3 模袋连接

模袋间的拉链连接由潜水员在水下从靠近板桩墙的一端开始连接。模袋充填混凝土之后,由于拉链太紧导致无法连接,因此水下施工过程中必须有一块未充填的模袋留在水中(图5)。

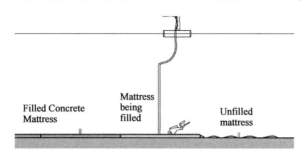

图5 模袋混凝土水下施工示意图

3.2.4 模袋混凝土填充

每个标准模袋的混凝土充填量约为 $55\sim60m^3$,充填速度为 $15\sim25m^3/h$。为了防止充填过程因泵送压力过大造成破坏,需要控制整体有效充填速率不超过 $25m^3/h$。为了防止混凝土泵送过程发生堵管问题,在开始泵送前,将混凝土循环泵送 5mins。混凝土搅拌运输车到达现场后,需要对混凝土的流动性进行检查。此外,在泵车料斗上加装网口约为 3cm 的钢筋网片过滤掉搅拌运输车中因未能充分搅拌形成的水泥硬块,防止施工中发生堵管。

混凝土泵车停靠在码头前沿,输送管沿着浮筏布置,为了方便施工,在满足施工要求的前提下尽量缩短泵送管的使用长度。

充填过程需潜水员对模袋形态不断的进行检查,当模袋顶面形成模袋内部连接线拉紧即达到模袋全厚度。充填过程需要对两块模袋连接处间断进行检查,查看拉链套窝结合处的形成状况(图6)。

图6 模袋达到全厚度时表面形状及内部状况

模袋面板充填完成后移除模袋与板桩墙连接的永磁体,继续充填板桩墙和模空隙间的压袋,最后对板桩间空隙进行充填至压带标高。

3.2.5 填充控制

充填过程中,需要控制模袋中混凝土的流体压差不超过 2.6m,需要潜水员注意检查和监测随混凝土的充填模袋外观形态的变化。

模袋表面鼓包通常发生在充填模袋袖口附近,因为充填袖口附近压力最大,此外基床的起伏不平也容易导致模袋鼓包或开裂,因此在进行充填时潜水员需要对这些部位重点监测。

4 结 语

综上所述,模袋混凝土护坡技术具有应用效果好、适应能力强、施工便捷等特点,在港航整治工程的

参考文献

[1] 陆澄. 直立式码头在船舶推动器射流作用下的防冲刷设计[J]. 中国水运(下半月),2020,20(03):147-148,151.

[2] 张伟. 模袋混凝土护坡施工技术在港口航道整治中的运用研究[J]. 中国水运,2019(09):89-90.

[3] 乐砾,吴遵奇,陶然. 强浪条件下深水板桩码头成套施工技术[J]. 水运工程,2017(12):240-244.

[4] 陈俊. 船闸引航道模袋混凝土护坡设计优化及试验研究[D]. 南京:东南大学,2016.

[5] 刘晔. 20000TEU超大型集装箱船舶时代与港口面临的挑战[J]. 港工技术,2015,52(02):9-13.

[6] 张志满. 模袋混凝土施工工艺[J]. 水运工程,2008(02):109-113.

[7] 张升光. 铰链式模袋混凝土沉排结构在黄河防洪工程中的研究与应用[D]. 济南:山东大学,2007.

[8] 陈学良,张景明. 土工织物在长江口深水航道治理工程中的应用[J]. 水运工程,2000(12):48-52.

[9] 王瑞海,孙卫平. 模袋混凝土充灌施工工艺[J]. 水运工程,2000(12):70-72.

[10] 黄国兴. 模袋混凝土护坡及其病害调查[C]. 第五届全国混凝土耐久性学术交流会,2000(10).

LNG码头前沿冲突水域风险可视化研究

谭志荣[1,2] 屈文鹏[1] 王洋[1] 叶晓庆[1]

(1. 武汉理工大学航运学院;2. 内河航运技术湖北省重点实验室)

摘要 选取了50000余个连续观测的船舶AIS数据,通过轨迹提取和数据聚类对武汉白浒山待建LNG码头前沿水域的船舶流行为特征进行了数据挖掘。首先,规范要求内河LNG码头停泊水域距离航道边界不小于50m,以白浒山2018—2019年观测数据,对临近码头的上行航路的船舶轨迹进行聚类分析,得出了该河段上行航道的船舶分布密度。进而,以基准点外延30m、60m、90m、120m为Near Miss值提取了船舶AIS的分布和船舶流行为特征,运用matlab求解了洪枯水期的船舶流分布函数。最后,运用AIS虚拟航标技术建立了武汉白浒山LNG码头停船安全自适应警戒区域,该方法可以实现内河LNG码头前沿水域交通冲突的定量分析。

关键词 交通冲突 数据挖掘 船舶轨迹 聚类分析 Near Miss

0 引言

伴随长江经济带的发展,长江船舶交通量日益增多,内河LNG船舶的停泊安全形势正日益严峻,内河船舶领域正成为一个研究的热点。风泽[1]等通过考虑航道条件、船舶类型、船舶行为以及操作人员的技能等条件提出了船舶动态领域模型,该模型可显著的提高内河船舶通航安全;范贤华[2]分析不同水流条件下,对船舶领域的影响,提出一种基于水流条件下的内河船舶领域模型;谭志荣等[3]分析船舶的时空特性后,结合水上交通会遇及交通冲突的概念,提出了基于船舶领域的Near Miss模型,将交通冲突风险可视化;文元桥[4]提出了一种基于船舶碰撞事故概率和事故发生后的可接受标准的LNG船舶停泊安全区定量计算模型;徐言民等[5]运用网格化理论和模糊综合评价方法提出了船舶碰撞黑点的评判方法;Jinpeng Xie等[6]提出了基于船舶操纵性的交通冲突建模方法;Zikun Feng等[7]基于船舶领域判断交通冲突,提出了船舶交通冲突可视化方法。

LNG码头停泊区域的相关研究较少,相关安全标准也比较匮乏。武汉白浒山码头作为具有代表性的内河LNG接收站具有较大的研究意义。随着AIS和VTS的普及,使得通过船舶交通大数据挖掘,研究船舶航行风险,进而基于船舶领域分析交通冲突区域,以此来建立更加适合的停泊水域范围。

1 LNG 停泊安全区域的确定

1.1 LNG 停泊区的设计标准

根据《液化天然气码头设计规范》可知河港液化天然气码头前沿停泊水域不得占用主航道,水流平缓河段码头前沿停泊水域宽度可取 2 倍设计船宽,水流较急河段可取 2.5 倍设计船宽。由表 1 取停泊船舶的型宽为 30m,因此停泊水域宽度至少应为 60m。

研究船型尺度(单位:m)   表1

研究船型	总长	型宽	型深	满载吃水
2 万 m³LNG 船	169	30	15.8	5.5
2 万 m³LNG 船	152	26	12	5.6

1.2 交通冲突区

交通冲突源自公路领域,在水路交通中指两艘及以上的船舶在同一时间,同一空间上相互接近时,一方面采取非正常的驾驶方式(转向、变速、停车等),另一方则必须采取相应的避险措施否则就会有相撞的危险。而停泊中的 LNG 船舶与附近航行的船舶可能会存在一个区域,当航行船舶进入这个区域时不可避免地会发生事故,因此可以将这一区域称为船舶停泊的交通冲突区域。

1.3 基于风险的 LNG 码头交通冲突区

由图 1 可见码头距航道边界线为 80m,规范中停泊水域范围侵入主航道水域 10m,此安全范围对水域正常航行的船舶影响较大。因此通过对航道边界线不同距离航行船舶的数量、航行时间、航行速度进行统计分析,确定距离航道水域 10m 范围内是否为交通冲突区域,进而确定该码头停泊水域范围。

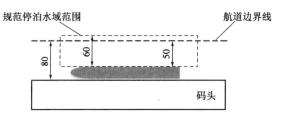

图 1 LNG 船舶停泊示意图(尺寸单位:m)

结合研究水域的水文条件和过往船舶确定此地 LNG 船舶停泊水域的合适宽度,过往船舶参数见表 2。

过往船舶参数(单位:m)   表2

船 型	总长	型宽	型深	满载吃水
5000 吨级散货船	115	18.8	9.0	7.0
15000 吨散货船	135	25	11.8	5.5

2 AIS 数据处理

2.1 AIS 数据的提取

由于本文研究水域航行船舶较多,但研究区域仅为上行航道,所以对上行航道 AIS 数据进行相应的处理。

处理流程:①提取、解析 AIS 数据,建立数据库,数据预处理;②使用相应算法获取航向或航速的特征点,进行轨迹划分[8];③进行轨迹相似度聚类,获得运动轨迹[9]。

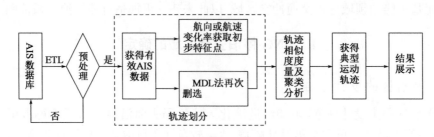

图 2 AIS 数据处理流程

2.2 船舶轨迹分析

利用提取的 AIS 数据,将其导入到 matlab 中并画出相应上行航道船舶轨迹图,如图 3 所示。

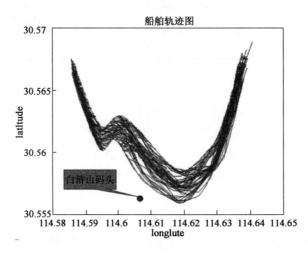

图 3 船舶轨迹拟合图

从图 3 可以看到 9 月份白浒山码头附近的船舶较多,对码头区域停泊的 LNG 船舶的安全构成了较大的威胁。因此有必要对码头停泊安全区域附近船舶的动态进行深入的研究,以确定交通冲突区域。

3 数理分析交通冲突区

3.1 航道的划分

船舶在追越或会遇时,由于存在兴波,两船之间会存在一个船吸效应[10],会危害到航行船舶的安全,且与航航速、船舶间距有关。

一般认为船舶在内河航道行驶时,船舶两侧各自保持一倍船宽的距离即可。船舶在会遇时,船舶尺寸越大,所需的安全距离也越大,见表 3。

表 3 船舶尺寸与安全会遇距离(单位:m)

船舶尺度 L	安全会遇距离 z	船舶尺度 L	安全会遇距离 z
50	23	150	111
75	39	175	142
100	59	200	176
125	83		

由于本文主要研究过往船舶对白浒山码头停泊的 LNG 船舶的影响来确定停泊水域的范围。因此主要根据距离航道不同距离范围过往船舶的数量、航行时间、航行速度综合考量,来判断交通冲突区。综上,将航道边界线作为基准点,对白浒山码头水域上行航道进行 30m 等分,统计 9 月份(洪水期)和 1 月

份枯水期经过相应航道区域的船舶数量，并以此评价过往船舶对停泊水域LNG船舶的影响。

3.2 数量统计分析

主要的停泊船型为2万m^3的LNG运输船，船舶宽度为30m。码头距航道边界线为80m，表示当船舶靠泊码头时，与航道边界线距离不足规范停泊水域距离。过往船舶可能对停泊的船安全造成影响，因此有必要对相应的船舶信息进行统计分析。

对白浒山码头船舶AIS轨迹信息提取，统计了2018年9月（洪水期）和2018年1月（枯水期）经过相应水域的船舶数量，如图所示。

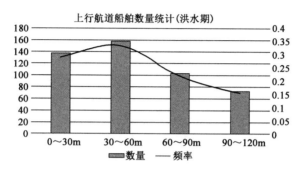

图4 上行航道船舶频率分布直方图（洪水期）

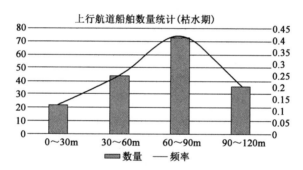

图5 上行航道船舶频率分布直方图（枯水期）

可以看出在不同的时间和空间范围内分布的船舶数量有显著性的差异。在洪水期时，多数船舶倾向于贴近航道边界线行驶，而在枯水期由于水位的降低，大部分船舶开始远离航道两侧。从表4可以看出洪水期船舶的各项统计数据明显小于枯水区，表明航行船舶在洪水期时更易对LNG船舶的停泊安全造成威胁。

上行航道船舶距离数值统计表（单位：m） 表4

	平均值	中位数	众数	标准差
洪水期	50.49	55	47	30.59
枯水期	70.73	64	62	29.18

3.3 速度统计分析

为了研究船舶在进出码头前沿区域时速度的分布特征，将相应的航道区分为三段：①驶入码头警戒区的航段；②在码头警戒区域行驶的航段；③驶离码头警戒区的航段。并依据AIS提取的数据进行数据处理，得出相应航道区域的船舶航行速度，取其平均值。表5可看出不同航道区域船舶航行速度有显著差异。距离航道边界线越近，船舶航行的速度也就越小；同样的，船舶在进出码头警戒区域时，船舶航行的速度也存在显著性的差异，由表5可知船舶在驶入码头停泊警戒区域时，其速度存在一个明显的下降，这表明LNG停泊码头对过往船舶的航行存在一定影响。

上行航道船舶平均速度表　　　　　　　　　　　　　　　　　表5

外延	0~30m	30~60m	60~90m	90~120m
驶入警戒区速度(km/h)	8.77	9.77	12.24	13.22
警戒区航行速度(km/h)	6.25	6.89	10.56	11.22
驶离警戒区速度(km/h)	7.78	8.36	11.42	12.99

3.4 安全性分析

为了分析航行船舶对停泊的LNG船舶风险的大小,取船舶转向点进行研究。通过对船舶在转向点速度的分解,分析相应船舶在转向点驶向警戒区域的时间(见表6)。

行驶时间(单位:h)　　　　　　　　　　　　　　　　　　表6

外延	0~30m	30~60m	60~90m	90~120m
时间	0.5157	0.4606	0.3676	0.3409

距离航道边界线越近,船舶航行的时间反而大,这表明船舶虽然离警戒区更近,但由于本身船速低,因此有充足的时间改变航向、航速,交通冲突区域范围可适当减小。

4 虚拟航标

在停泊船舶周围设置非实物的虚拟AIS警戒区,能够较好标识LNG码头前沿水上冲突水域。

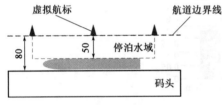

图6　虚拟航标位置示意图(尺寸单位:m)

(1)利用虚拟航标技术在交通冲突区边界设置无实体虚拟航标,该警戒区域包含3个虚拟航标。

(2)综合距离航道边界线不同距离的船舶数量、航行速度及安全性定量分析,停泊水域的设置可依据交通冲突区域为距离航道边界线0m。

停泊水域设置见图6。

5 结　语

本文将距码头50m范围内的区域定为交通冲突区。当附近航行船舶进入这一区域内时,由于船吸效应的影响,航行船舶和停泊船舶会有碰撞的可能性,这会严重危害到附近船舶和人员的安全。因此结合《液化天然气码头设计规范》的相关规定及白浒山LNG码头实际情况,将交通冲突区域设置为船舶停泊水域范围,并设立虚拟航标。

参考文献

[1] Liu J, Zhou F, Li Z, et al. Dynamic Ship Domain Models for Capacity Analysis of Restricted Water Channels[J]. Journal of Navigation, 2016, 69(03):481-503.

[2] 范贤华,张庆年,周锋,等.水流条件下内河船舶领域模型[J].大连海事大学学报,2013,39(1):46-48.

[3] 谭志荣,张球林,王伟,范中洲.基于Near Miss的成山头水域交通冲突风险可视化[J].中国航海,2016,39(4):43-46

[4] 文元桥,王乐,杨雪.LNG船舶停泊安全区宽度计算建模[J].中国安全科学学报,2014,24(5):73-78

[5] 徐言民,唐成港,许鹏,刘钊,刘敬贤.基于网格化理论的船舶碰撞事故黑点研究[J].中国航海,2013,36(4):72-75,151.

[6] Jinpeng Xie, Zhao Liu, Yanmin Xu, Zheng Chang. Research on Ship Traffic Conflict in Crossing Situation

[7] Zikun Feng, Haojie Yang, Xinyi Li, Yan Li, Zhao Liu, Ryan Wen Liu. Real-Time Vessel Trajectory Data-Based Collison Risk Assessment in Crowded Inland Waterways [C]. The 4th International Conference on Big Data Analytics (ICBDA 2019), Chengdu, China, 12-15 April, 2019.

[8] 王伊冰,阮林林,陈琼冰,蔡敏,周中华,万祥.基于AIS数据的船舶航行轨迹估计研究[A].中国卫星导航系统管理办公室学术交流中心.第九届中国卫星导航学术年会论文集——SO_2导航与位置服务[C].中国卫星导航系统管理办公室学术交流中心:中科北斗汇(北京)科技有限公司,2018:4.

[9] 谢萍,马社祥等.星载AIS信号的提取仿真研究[J].计算机仿真,2016,33(8):168-171.

[10] 甘浪雄.船舶在桥区安全航行可靠性分析[J].武汉理工大学学报(交通科学与工程版),2003,27(4):455-458.

船舶号灯可见度评价模型

阎际驰　朱金善　李春男　李志荣

(大连海事大学)

摘　要　为了更好地评价夜航船舶号灯的可见度以保障船舶的夜航安全,提出了一种评价船舶号灯可见度的计算模型。基于光度学原理对船舶号灯在复杂背景灯光下的可见度进行推算,并利用色度学原理将号灯的光色视觉转化为等效亮度视觉,最终确定船舶号灯的可见度计算模型。以天津港水域背景灯光的实地测量数据为基础,将《1972年国际海上避碰规则》中号灯的技术数据代入模型进行计算,同时对该港区的船舶驾驶人员进行问卷调查,通过调查结果验证了计算模型的可行性,可为船舶的夜航安全性评价提供一定的借鉴与参考。

关键词　安全船舶夜航光环境　船舶夜航安全性　船舶号灯　亮度可见度

0　引　言

避碰是保障船舶夜航安全的重要手段,通过识别号灯,船舶驾驶人员可以获得他船尺度以及航行动态等信息,并利用这些信息对两船是否构成碰撞危险,两船处于何种会遇局面做出判断。随着灯光捕鱼技术的兴起以及各海滨城市修建了许多民生照明亮化工程,船舶夜航避碰环境已经发生了实质性的变化,导致船舶号灯的可识别性受到了严重的影响。

随着海上光污染影响船舶夜航避碰的问题日益严重,人们开始重视这一客观存在的现象,目前的研究多为海上光污染对船舶号灯可识别性影响的机理分析,但是对于船舶号灯可识别性定量的研究较为鲜见。文献[1]利用光学、色度学原理,分析并验证了海上光污染对船舶夜航安全的影响,从技术与法律两个层面提出了防治海上光污染的措施。文献[2-5]利用BP神经网络对船舶号灯的可识别性进行了深入研究,以[0,1]的区间值代表号灯可识别性程度的高低,0表示能识别,1表示不能识别,该方法很好地解决了号灯可识别性过程中的多参数复杂性及高度非线性等问题,但需要多组样本进行计算分析。文献[6-7]设计了一种新型的半导体激光船舶号灯,并对该号灯的颜色、光强以及光弧进行了研究,提高了船舶号灯在复杂光环境下的可识别性,但该新型号灯的推广仍需一定的时间,无法定量地确定船舶号灯的可见度。船舶号灯的识别性可认为是小物标的可见度,其在船舶驾驶行为的作用是不可忽视的[8],号灯的可见度是评价船舶驾驶人员视觉可靠性的主要指标[9]。

为进一步对船舶号灯可识别性进行定量研究,解决现有研究存在的样本量大,推广困难等问题,本文以国内外相关研究成果为基础,拟利用光度学、色度学原理推导船舶号灯的亮度可见度计算模型,对天津港的背景灯光进行实测计算,同时发放问卷以验证该模型的合理性,力求建立一种简单有效,并具有实际应用价值和推广价值的号灯可见度计算模型,为船舶的夜航安全性评价提供一定的参考。

1 船舶号灯的亮度可见度计算模型

可见度是指人眼在一定条件下辨别目标存在或轮廓的难易程度,是人眼主观感知目标清晰程度的物理量[11],如汽车前照灯会影响道路的可见度[12,13]。船舶夜航时,船舶号灯能否被驾驶人员清晰的识别,不仅与船舶号灯的亮度和色度等技术参数有关,还需要使船舶号灯亮度和水域背景亮度的差别高于一个特定的数值。光学中常用可见度水平来表示可见度的大小,其表示为目标与背景的亮度差大于可见阈值的倍数[14],如式(1):

$$VL = \frac{\Delta L}{\Delta L_0} = \frac{L_t - L_b}{L_{t0} - L_b} \tag{1}$$

式中:L_t——目标亮度;
L_b——背景亮度;
L_{t0}——在特定背景亮度下能被识别出的最小目标亮度。

从上式可知,驾驶人员能否在复杂的背景灯光中辨识出船舶号灯,取决于可见度水平的高低,其影响因素主要有船舶号灯的亮度值、背景灯光的亮度值以及亮度差阈值。亮度差阈值的确定又受观察者视力、年龄以及目标物出现的时间等因素影响,由于海上交通运输的特殊性,船舶驾驶人员的视力都在0.5以上;年龄多处于20~45之间;除紧急情况,船舶号灯在规定情况下是连续显示的,因此,航海上将亮度差阈值规定为0.5。

色度作为船舶号灯的重要显示部分,同样会影响船舶号灯的可见度。国际照明委员会(CIE)建立了一个在2°明视觉条件下的等效亮度经验公式[15],如式(2):

$$L_{eq} = 10^{c(x,y)} L \tag{2}$$

式中:L——亮度计实测的目标亮度;
$c(x,y)$——目标的色品坐标,可由式(3)确定:

$$c(x,y) = 0.256 - 0.184y - 2.527xy + 4.656x^3y + 4.657xy^4 \tag{3}$$

因此,结合式(1)~(3),可推导出船舶号灯可见度的计算模型,如式(4):

$$VL = \frac{L_{teq} - L_{beq}}{0.5} \tag{4}$$

式中:L_{teq},L_{beq}——号灯亮度和背景亮度在2°明视觉条件下的等效亮度。

而物标对比度分8个等级(如表1),等级为1的物标是最容易被辨别的[16]。按德国眼科协会(DOG)建议的对比度等级2车辆驾驶员夜间驾驶最低要求为[17]。

物标对比度等级 表1

等 级	比率(L_0:L_b)	对比度 c	等 级	比率(L_0:L_b)	对比度 c
1	1:23	0.96	5	1:1.67	0.4
2	1:5	0.8	6	1:1.47	0.32
3	1:2.7	0.63	7	1:1.25	0.2
4	1:2	0.5	8	1:1.14	0.12

根据表1将各号灯的可见度等级分为Ⅰ~Ⅴ五个等级,分别对应"影响严重""影响较大""影响一般""影响轻微"和"影响可忽略"这五个评价结果,由此得出号灯可见度的评价等级的如下表2所示。

船舶号灯可见度等级表 表2

号灯类型	可见度等级				
	Ⅰ	Ⅱ	Ⅲ	Ⅳ	Ⅴ
左舷灯	(0,1.3]	(1.3,2.7]	(2.7,5]	(5,10]	[10,23)
右舷灯	(0,1.3]	(1.3,2.7]	(2.7,5]	(5,10]	[10,23)
桅灯	(0,1.3]	(1.3,2.7]	(2.7,5]	(5,10]	[10,23)
尾灯	(0,1.3]	(1.3,2.7]	(2.7,5]	(5,10]	[10,23)
拖带灯	(0,1.3]	(1.3,2.7]	(2.7,5]	(5,10]	[10,23)

2 船舶号灯技术参数

号灯对于船舶夜航安全的重要性不言而喻,《1972 国际海上避碰规则》(简称《规则》)针对船舶号灯的技术细节作了特别的规定,包括号灯的颜色、光弧范围、显示要求及基本位置等。

2.1 船舶号灯的基本参数

船舶号灯的基本参数主要包括灯色、光弧、显示要求以及安装位置等参数,《规则》规定了主要船舶号灯的基本参数,见表3。

《规则》对部分号灯的规定 表3

类型	颜色	水平光弧(°)	照明要求	安装位置
桅灯	白	225	从船的正前方到每一舷正横后22.5°,不间断显示灯光	首尾中心线
左舷灯	红	112.5	从船的正前方到左舷正横后22.5°,不间断显示灯光	左舷
右舷灯	绿	112.5	从船的正前方到右舷正横后22.5°,不间断显示灯光	右舷
尾灯	白	135	从船的正后方到每一舷67.5°,显示不间断光	尽可能接近船尾
拖带灯	黄	135	从船的正后方到每一舷67.5°,显示不间断光	尽可能接近船尾

2.2 船舶号灯的发光强度

《规则》中"号灯和号型的位置和技术细节"第8条"号灯的发光强度"规定,船舶号灯的最低发光强度可用式(5)进行计算[18]:

$$I = 3.43 \times 10^6 \times T \times D^2 \times K^{-D} \tag{5}$$

式中:I——船舶号灯的发光强度;

T——临阈系数,取 2×10^{-7} 勒克司;

D——号灯的照明距离;

K——大气透射率。

对于规定的号灯,K 值应是0.8,相当于约13n mile 的气象能见度。

如表4所示,利用公式(5)对不同能见距离的号灯发光强度进行计算。

船舶号灯在不同能见距离下的光强 表4

号灯类型(L/船长)	能见距离(n mile)	号灯光强(cd)	备注
$L<12$m 舷灯	1	0.9	注:航海号灯的最大发光强度应予限制,以防止过度的光耀,但不应该使用发光强度可变控制的办法
$12 \leq L<50$m 舷灯、尾灯	2	4.3	
$L \geq 50$m 舷灯、尾灯,$12 \leq L<20$m 桅灯	3	12	
$20 \leq L<50$m 桅灯	5	52	
$L \geq 50$m 桅灯	6	94	

2.3 船舶号灯的色度信息

《规则》对船舶号灯光色的区域进行了划分,规定了各区域边界点的坐标,也就确定了光色的区域范围,为更好地表述上述区域,利用 CIE1931-xy 色品图对区域进行绘制,如图 1 所示,图中外围曲线为光谱色色品轨迹,E 点为白光参考点。

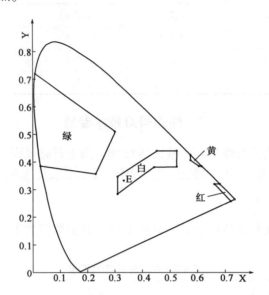

图 1　CIE1931 色品图(2°视场)中《规则》为每种颜色的号灯规定的区域

对于船舶号灯的色度信息,本文取《规则》中对号灯技术范围区间的中心坐标值,因此,在获取船舶号灯的亮度和色度数据后转化为等效亮度来计算船舶号灯的可见度。

3　实例验证

为了验证船舶号灯可见度计算模型的合理性,通过电话、网络等途径了相关船员和港口管理人员关于我国主要港口的船舶夜航光环境现状,最终,选取了天津港南疆港区 4#码头水域的船舶夜航光环境(图 2)。

图 2　天津港南疆港区 4 号码头的船舶夜航光环境

本节为了获取天津港南疆港区 4 号码头的背景亮度和色度数据,利用 CS-100 色彩亮度计对该水域的船舶夜航光环境进行了多次测量,再求平均值,得出该光环境的背景亮度、色度(Y,x,y)为(6.32,0.473,0.435)。将所得光环境数据和船舶号灯的标准值带入公式(2)～公式(4)计算对应的船舶号灯可见度,结合表 2 的号灯可见度等级划分,得出该水域号灯的可见度,见表 5。

船舶号灯在天津港南疆港区 4#码头水域的可见度　　表5

亮度、色度(Y,x,y)	船舶号灯类型 (船长 $L \geq 50m$)	色度中心坐标	可见度	可见度
$(6.32,0.473,0.435)$	桅灯	$(0.419,0.363)$	15.47	V
	左舷灯	$(0.697,0.287)$	2.37	II
	右舷灯	$(0.163,0.538)$	1.71	II
	尾灯	$(0.419,0.363)$	1.13	I
	拖带灯	$(0.589,0.410)$	1.39	II

为了验证船舶号灯可见度计算模型的合理性,在对天津港南疆港区水域光环境进行实地测量的同时,随机给该水域航行的船舶驾驶人员发放问卷120份,剔除回答重复和缺少项数过多等无效问卷,共回收98份有效问卷,并通过SPSS软件分析其数据得出其信度系数0.976,大于0.85,效度KMO值0.806,大于0.7,因此,该问卷的信度和效度良好。另外,为了便于计算,问卷答案的统计形式为1~5分,依次为"同意""比较同意""拿不准""不太同意""不同意",并与表2的可见度等级分别对应为应"影响严重""影响较大""影响一般""影响轻微"和"影响可忽略"。问卷调查统计如表6。

天津港水域船舶夜航光环境问卷统计　　表6

指标因素	影响评价				
	同意	比较同意	拿不准	不太同意	不同意
影响桅灯的识别	0	2	1	17	78
影响左舷灯的识别	30	45	16	3	4
影响右舷灯的识别	26	61	7	4	0
影响尾灯的识别	65	26	3	3	1
影响拖带灯的识别	35	55	5	1	2

根据有效问卷的数据,运用加权平均法对数据进行统计分析,并结合表2关于号灯的可见度等级划分,统计结果如表7。

天津港水域夜航光环境号灯识别的影响程度评价　　表7

类别	影响程度评价	可见度等级
影响桅灯的识别	4.745	V
影响左舷灯的识别	2.041	II
影响右舷灯的识别	1.887	II
影响尾灯的识别	1.459	I
影响拖带灯的识别	1.776	II

通过表5和表7所得出的所在水域船舶号灯可见度可知,天津港水域船舶夜航光环境中:尾灯可见度等级为I(影响严重);舷灯的可见度等级为II(影响较大);桅灯的可见度等级为V(影响可忽略),因此,本文所提出的船舶号灯可见度计算模型所得出的可见度等级与问卷调查所得出的结果一致,验证了该计算模型的有效性。

将计算结果与水域光环境进行对比,计算结果与该水域夜航光环境的实际情况有较好的一致性。该水域的夜间照明的灯光较多、亮度较大且逸散光较大,易影响夜航船舶驾驶人员的视觉工效,从而导致号灯的可见度较低,使得船舶驾驶人员无法判断他船的类型、尺度以及航行动态等信息,且会导致对船舶间的会遇局面以及是否存在碰撞危险的无法判别。建议天津港相关部门控制背景灯光亮度以及照射角度,从而减少对船舶号灯识别的影响,以及航行在该水域的夜航船舶驾驶人员要加强对他船号灯的瞭望,从而减少船舶间紧迫局面的出现,保障船舶的夜航安全。

与现有的其他方法相比,本文所提出的船舶号灯可见度计算模型不需要大量样本数据,船员和港口管理人员只需利用色彩亮度计等仪器设备即可获得待测水域的光环境数据,并通过该模型进行计算,应用方便,实际应用价值高,具有较强的推广性。通过该模型的使用,可以有效地对港口附近水域光环境进行量化,进而有效减少船舶夜航安全评价中的人为主观性,港口相关部门也可以推广和利用该模型以对港口周围的光环境进行控制,以保障船舶夜航安全。

4 结 语

本文利用光度学原理,推导出船舶号灯在复杂背景灯光下的可见度计算模型,在考虑色度的基础上将号灯的光色视觉转化为等效亮度视觉,然后确定了船舶号灯的可见度计算模型。另外,根据《1972年国际海上避碰规则》中关于号灯的色度和发光强度数据得出桅灯、左右舷灯、尾灯以及拖带灯在所选的船舶夜航光环境背景下的可见度,同时对号灯的可见度进行了问卷调查,结果发现计算结果和问卷结果一致,验证了该模型计算船舶号灯可见度是可行的。后续可以开发以本模型为后端的应用软件,以方便船员利用该模型对号灯进行识别。本文建立计算模型有一定的实用价值,不仅为船舶夜航光环境中的号灯的可见度计算提供一种计算方法,也为评价船舶驾驶人员的视觉工效提供一定参考价值,并具有一定的实用价值。

参考文献

[1] 朱金善.海上光污染对船舶夜航安全的影响与对策研究[D].大连:大连海事大学,2015.

[2] 黄成,朱金善.海上光污染对船舶驾驶员视觉绩效影响的研究[J].灯与照明,2017,41(03):41-43+54.

[3] 朱金善,孙立成,尹建川,等.基于BP神经网络的船舶号灯识别模型与仿真[J].应用基础与工程科学学报,2012,20(03):455-463.

[4] 熊蕾,金欢.利用BP神经网络进行船舶号灯识别[J].舰船科学技术,2017,39(04):175-177.

[5] 刘娜.BP神经网络在治理海上光污染中的应用[J].舰船科学技术,2016,38(18):163-165.

[6] 朱金善,孙立成,胡江强,等.基于克隆优化的船舶号灯神经网络识别模型[J].大连海事大学学报,2015,41(02):41-45.

[7] 吴同飞,朱金善,孙立成,等.半导体激光船舶号灯颜色属性的设计与仿真[J].应用光学,2015,36(02):321-326.

[8] 朱金善,吴同飞,孙立成,等.半导体激光号灯光强及光弧范围的设计与仿真[J].中国航海,2015,38(03):5-8+40.

[9] AnaisMayeur, Roland Bremond, J. M. Christian Bastien. The effect of the driving activity on target detection as a function of the visibility level: Implications for road lighting[J]. Transportation Research Part F: Traffic Psychology and Behavior,2010(2):115-128.

[10] Lewis I. Lumen effectiveness multipliers for outdoor lighting design[J]. Journal of the Illuminating Engineering Society,2001(2):40-52.

[11] 梁波,凌超,李翔,等.汽车前照灯对隧道路面照明质量影响研究[J].重庆交通大学学报(自然科学版),2018,37(03):14-21.

[12] SatoshiHirakawa, Yoshinori Karasawa, Tsuyoshi Funaki. Visibility evaluation of expressway-tunnel lighting in consideration of vehicle headlights[J]. Electrical Engineering in Japan,2015,193(2):1-9.

[13] Ekrias Aleksanteri, Eloholma Marjukka, Halonen Liisa. Effects of vehicle headlights on target contra-st in road lighting environments[J]. Journal of Light Visual Environment,2008,32(3):302-314.

[14] 翁季,何荣,黄珂.道路照明阈限亮度差简化计算模型[J].土木建筑与环境工程,2010,32(03):88-93.

[15] H WBodmann. Elements of photometry, brightness and visibility[J]. Lighting Research and Technology,1992,24(1):29-42.

[16] 季卓莺,邵红,林燕丹.暗适应时间、背景亮度和眩光对人眼对比度阈值影响的探讨[J].照明工程学报,2006(04):1-4+15.

[17] María C. Puell, Catalina Palomo, Celia Sánchez-Ramos, et al. Mesopic contrast sensitivity in the presence or absence of glare in a large driver population [J]. Graefe's Archive for Clinical and Experimental Ophthalmology,2004,242(9):755-761.

[18] 吴兆麟,赵月林.船舶避碰与值班[M].大连:大连海事大学出版社,2015:354-356.

基于 MNL 模型的中国邮轮消费选择行为研究

吴鋆杰[1]　余　尧[2]　肖军华[1]

(1.同济大学交通运输工程学院;2.上海海事大学交通运输学院)

摘　要　改革开放40年来,人民生活水平不断提高,对旅游的重视程度逐年上升,尤其是对20世纪80年代在中国兴起的邮轮旅游产生了极大兴趣,使我国邮轮行业成为全球最具潜力的邮轮市场。为了吸引更多的邮轮游客,促进我国邮轮产业的健康发展,很有必要研究潜在邮轮游客的消费行为,为此本文开展了基于MNL模型的中国邮轮消费选择行为研究。首先设计了问卷调查表,将受访人群分为无意向邮轮旅游者、潜在邮轮旅游者和既成邮轮旅游者三类,研究了受访者基本信息、邮轮旅游的限制因素、旅游者的消费偏好和消费行为等四类问题,发现了旅游者对目前邮轮旅游各个方面的选择倾向。其次,采用二元logit模型对旅游者是否会再次乘坐邮轮选择行为进行建模。最后,使用MNL模型对旅游者在邮轮上的付费服务进行选择行为研究,并且进行讨论分析。研究表明,游客对挂靠港旅游、特色餐厅、免税店和户外场所的消费概率相对比较高,对影视剧院、室内健身的消费概率相对比较低。

关键词　邮轮旅游　消费行为预测　问卷调查　MNL模型

0　引　言

改革开放40多年来,中国经济社会建设取得了巨大成就,人民生活水平不断提高,人们对旅游的重视程度逐年上升,尤其是对20世纪80年代在中国兴起的邮轮旅游产生了极大兴趣。这促进了我国邮轮行业迅速发展,使我国邮轮行业成为全球最具潜力的邮轮市场。目前我国的邮轮旅游行业还处于发展初期,市场规模较小,增长较快,发展潜力巨大[1,2]。如何吸引更多的游客来乘坐邮轮、引导游客在邮轮上消费是目前我国邮轮旅游业发展急需破解的问题[3]。国内外专家在这些方面有了一些研究。James F. Petrick[4]认为价格敏感度较低的游客更容易花更多的钱,而价格敏感度较高的游客更容易对自己的旅行过程感到满意。叶欣梁、孙瑞红[5]认为邮轮游客登岸后最主要的活动项目是观光游览和购物。刘永涓、孟世文[6]采用SPSS统计分析软件和EXCEL统计软件研究分析认为,收入是细分邮轮旅游市场的重要依据;价格是邮轮旅游出行的关键因素。王迎[7]利用活动理论以及出行链理论,对城市居民的出行活动进行了分析,并将其应用于城市居民出行方式选择模型。目前虽然已有一些有关我国邮轮旅游行业如何发展研究,也给出了一些建议和意见,但是,总体而言还不够全面、针对性还不够强。为此,我们从邮轮消费者的年龄、职业、收入、受教育程度等人口结构层面研究乘坐邮轮的目的、邮轮线路、邮轮娱乐、品尝美食、进行购物、价格因素等消费行为,开展了基于MNL模型的中国邮轮消费选择行为研究。通过设计问卷调查表和社会调查,研究受访者基本信息、邮轮旅游的限制因素、旅游者的消费偏好和消费行为等四类问题,发现旅游者对目前邮轮旅游各个方面的选择倾向;采用二元logit模型对旅游者是否会再次乘坐邮轮选择行为建模。最后,使用MNL模型对旅游者在邮轮上的付费服务进行选择行为研究。研究结果表明游客对挂靠港旅游、特色餐厅、免税店和户外场所的消费概率相对比较高,对影视剧院、室内健身的消费概率相对比较低。这些研究结果,可以为我国邮轮旅游行业设计更有吸引力的线路、提供更好更多更有针对性的服务产品提供数据支持,也有助于推进我国邮轮旅游业的健康快速发展。

1 问卷设计与数据统计分析

本研究在广泛的文献调研综合分析基础上设计了问卷调查表,在受访者个人基本信息、不愿意乘坐邮轮原因、参加邮轮的动机、邮轮上的消费情况等四个方面对受访者提出了26个问题,在两周的时间内回收了211份调查表。通过统计分析收回的调查问卷表,将受访人群分为无意向邮轮旅游者、潜在邮轮旅游者和既成邮轮旅游者三类,发现填写调查表的受访者中有能力负担邮轮消费的中高收入人群占比高,超过了3/4,其回答结果对本文的研究有很大的参考价值;研究了受访者基本信息、邮轮旅游的限制因素、旅游者的消费偏好和消费行为等问题,揭示了旅游者对目前邮轮旅游各方面的选择倾向。

2 邮轮消费行为分析

2.1 无意向旅游者邮轮消费行为分析

对于无意向邮轮旅游者来说,"航行时间长"和"船上环境局促狭窄"是最制约旅游者选择邮轮旅游的因素;"船上活动有限"和"目的地有限"是两个争议性较大的因素;"不了解邮轮"和"不安全"是两个最弱的限制因素。邮轮运营者需要根据这些问题来作出运营调整,比如开辟一些短期航线;增加邮轮的挂靠港以解决目的地有限的问题;邮轮船厂在设计邮轮时也要更多考虑旅客空间舒适性。

2.2 潜在旅游者邮轮消费行为分析

对于潜在的邮轮旅游者来说,他们比较倾向于亲友互相抱团参加邮轮旅游,相比于小长假,他们更希望在长假或者带薪休假中进行邮轮旅行。绝大多数潜在旅游者会选择一周及以内的短期航线,他们大多数愿意为整个邮轮旅游提供的日均预算低于1万元。

潜在邮轮旅游者分为两类,一类将邮轮视为交通工具,另一类将邮轮视为一个消费场所。尽管两类消费者对邮轮态度不一样,但他们目的都趋向于"陪伴家人情侣体验邮轮"和"观看海景",得分分别为4.13、4.19和3.89、4.29;"购买免税商品""商务社交"的目的性都低,分别为2.13、2.52和1.8、2.54。他们间较大区别在于"体验邮轮上的娱乐设施和服务""品尝邮轮上的各国美食"和"挂靠港城市旅游"。将邮轮视为交通工具的旅游者比较看重风景和挂靠港的旅游;将邮轮视为消费场所的旅游者会更加看重体验邮轮上的娱乐设施和特色餐厅。在当前新冠疫情影响下,大部分潜在邮轮旅游者不会放弃自己的邮轮旅游计划。

2.3 既成旅游者邮轮消费行为分析

对于既成邮轮旅游者来说,他们已经有了乘坐邮轮的经历。他们大多数会选择10天及以内的中短期航线。在邮轮消费行为方面,既成旅游者在特色餐厅、免税店和挂靠港旅游上消费较多;在电信服务、电影剧场和室内健身房消费较少。此外,他们在邮轮上的消费金额与他们的消费倾向分布相一致。

据所得到的既成邮轮旅行者每日的消费分成两类,邮轮上日均消费5000元人民币及以下的为保守型消费者,5000元以上的为主动型消费者,共有22位主动型消费者和19名保守型消费者,建立二元logit回归模型研究邮轮旅游者是保守型消费者还是主动性消费者的概率[8]。建模计算结果表明,娱乐倾向、养生倾向、影视倾向和饮食倾向对消费者的消费有积极影响;观光倾向和购买倾向对消费者的消费有消极影响。

同样建立二元logit回归模型研究邮轮旅游者对不同服务的满意度与再次乘坐邮轮的概率。模型采用的影响因素有总体印象、基本服务、高档餐厅、娱乐设施,免税商店和挂靠港旅游。

建模计算结果表明对基本服务和挂靠港旅游的满意度对再次乘坐邮轮的概率有积极影响,对高档餐厅、娱乐设施和免税商店的满意度对再次乘坐邮轮的概率有消极影响。

3 邮轮不同付费服务选择模型

邮轮游客选择付费服务的行为可以描述为以下过程:游客由于自身对不同邮轮付费的倾向程度,结合自身的各种条件,对付费服务进行选择。这些条件包含但不限于:游客的社会经济条件、家庭背景、预算和对邮轮的概念。建立各种付费服务的效用,结合自身的偏好,最后选择消费最多的邮轮付费服务。假设游客在选择服务时候有良好的辨识能力,可以自由选择消费内容,并且将效用由各个付费服务的消费金额占比表示。付费服务选择模型整体结构如图 1 所示,付费服务选择的 MNL 模型变量如表 1 所示。

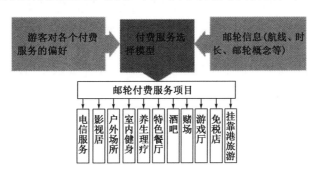

图 1　付费服务选择模型

付费服务选择的模型变量　　　　　　　　表 1

服务编号	付费服务	效用变量名称	影 响 因 素			
1	电信服务	V_1	航线时长	邮轮概念(邮轮是否视为消费场所)	可接受的日均消费(支付意愿)	对 1 偏好程度
2	影视剧	V_2				对 2 偏好程度
3	户外场景	V_3				对 3 偏好程度
4	室内健身	V_4				对 4 偏好程度
5	养生护理	V_5				对 5 偏好程度
6	特色餐厅	V_6				对 6 偏好程度
7	酒吧	V_7				对 7 偏好程度
8	赌场	V_8				对 8 偏好程度
9	游戏厅	V_9				对 9 偏好程度
10	免税店	V_{10}				对 10 偏好程度
11	挂靠港旅游	V_{11}				对 11 偏好程度

建立 MNL 模型,即多元 logit 回归模型。只要估算出各个付费服务的效益 V_i 和系数 $[\theta_i]$,就能计算出概率 P_{in}。[9]

$$P_{in} = \frac{\exp(V_{in})}{\sum_{j \in A_n} \exp(V_{jn})} \tag{1}$$

式中:i——付费活动序号($i \in [1,11]$);

P_{in}——游客 n 选择付费活动 i 概率;

V_{in}——游客 n 效用函数;

A_n——游客 n 选择活动范围集合;

j——集合 A_n 中的元素。

其中,效用函数为:

$$V_{in} = \theta_1 X_{i1n} + \theta_2 X_{i2n} + \cdots + \theta_K X_{iKn} = \sum_{k=1}^{K} \theta_k X_{ikn} \tag{2}$$

式中:　　　　X_{iKn}——游客 n 选择活动 i 的第 k 个特性变量;

K——特性变量个数；

$X_{in} = [X_{i1n}, X_{i2n}, \cdots, X_{iKn}]^T$——游客 n 选择活动 i 的特性向量；

θ_K——第 k 个特性变量的未知参数；

$[\theta_1, \theta_2, \cdots, \theta_K]^T$——未知参数向量。

由此，可以得到概率的函数：

$$P_{in} = \frac{\exp(V_{in})}{\sum_{j \in A_n} \exp(V_{jn})} = \frac{1}{\sum_{j \in A_n} \exp\left[\sum_{k=1}^{K} \theta_k (X_{jkn} - X_{ikn})\right]} \quad (3)$$

通过 41 个样本进行参数估计得到了各个特性变量的系数，再通过 11 个效用函数进行每个游客对 11 个付费服务选择枝的选择概率的计算，最终对每个付费服务选择枝的 41 个概率数值进行算术平均，得到了受访的既成旅游者选择各付费服务的平均概率。模型计算结果如表 2 所示，表中 P_1 到 P_{11} 对应着表 4 中服务编号 1 到 11 的付费服务概率。

游客选择各付费服务概率　　　　　　表 2

P_1	P_2	P_3	P_4	P_5	P_6	P_7	P_8	P_9	P_{10}	P_{11}
8.83%	8.76%	9.11%	8.75%	8.88%	9.48%	8.90%	8.81%	8.97%	9.45%	10.07%

对付费服务选择模型的研究表明，邮轮吸引游客的主要项目分别为挂靠港旅游、特色餐厅、免税店和邮轮户外场景，其中概率最高的是挂靠港旅游，为 10.07%，特色餐厅、免税店和户外场景的消费概率分别为 9.48%、9.45% 和 9.11%。其次是电信服务、养生护理、酒吧、赌场和游戏厅的概率分别为 8.83%，8.88%，8.90%，8.81% 和 8.97%。影视剧院、室内健身等消费概率相对比较低，分别为 8.76% 和 8.75%。将计算得到的付费服务选择概率与既成旅游者实际的消费金额进行比较发现，本研究采用 MNL 模型预测的旅游者对于不同付费服务的选择概率与其实际消费金额趋势相一致。对比结果如图 2 所示，图中蓝色柱状表示采用 MNL 模型计算的服务概率结果，橙色曲线是实际消费的金额情况，两者趋势一致。

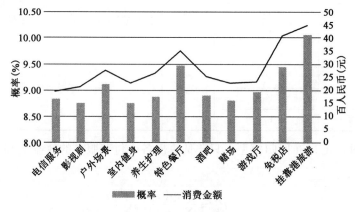

图 2　游客选择各付费服务概率与消费金额

4　结　语

本研究虽然在问卷调查表的设计、分发人群、模型参数选择等方面还不够完善，还存在一些不足，但是，总体而言调查问卷结果还是比较符合实际情况的，对本文的研究具有很好的参考价值，而且理论建模预测的结果与实际邮轮旅行者消费情况基本一致，也从一个方面证明了本研究结果的可靠性。因此，本论文的研究结果可以为我国邮轮旅游行业更好地了解邮轮游客的消费需求、消费行为、消费心理提供数据支持，促进他们设计出更有吸引力的线路，提供更好、更多、更有针对性的特色服务产品，推进我国邮轮旅游业的健康、快速发展。

参考文献

[1] 汪泓. 邮轮绿皮书：中国邮轮产业发展报告(2019)[R]. 北京：社会科学文献出版社，2019：1-68，87-111，219-231.
[2] 汪泓. 邮轮绿皮书：中国邮轮产业发展报告(2018)[R]. 北京：社会科学文献出版社，2018：35-69.
[3] 刘利娜，孔洁. 中国邮轮旅游产业发展研究[J]. 武汉职业技术学院学报，2014，13(03)：101-104.
[4] James F. Petrick. Segmenting cruise passengers with price sensitivity[J]. Elsevier Ltd, 2005, 26(5).
[5] 叶欣梁，孙瑞红. 基于顾客需求的上海邮轮旅游市场开发研究[J]. 华东经济管理，2007(03)：110-115.
[6] 刘永涓，孟世文. 厦门邮轮旅游市场消费行为调查研究[J]. 福建师大福清分校学报，2017，(2)：89-96.
[7] 王迎. 基于活动的城市居民出行方式选择模型研究[D]. 长安大学，2007.
[8] 潘驰，赵胜川. 基于Logit模型的大连市居民通勤出行行为研究[J]. 交通信息与安全，2012，030(003)：25-28，51.
[9] 金安. LOGIT模型参数估计方法研究[J]. 交通运输系统工程与信息，2004(01)：71-75.

海洋强国建设背景下我国船员流失问题与对策

刘嘉琪[1] 葛颖恩[2]

(1. 广东海洋大学海运学院；2. 上海海事大学交通运输学院)

摘 要 2019年以来，我国船员流失问题日益严峻，对航运业可持续发展、交通强国国家战略落实和海洋强国建设均带来负面影响。解读《2019年中国船员发展报告》的数据得知我国船员流失主要集中于从事沿海航行和国际航行的三副与三管轮。在访谈和问卷调查的基础上，通过定量和定性相结合的研究方法，从更宏观的视角分析三副与三管轮流失原因。结果表明，海陆收入差异减小、社会地位偏低、晋升困难、英语能力不足等原因是船员流失的主因。在此基础上，本文从政府和主管机关以及海事类院校两方面提出相应改进措施，旨在减缓船员流失状况。

关键词 水上运输 船员流失原因 访谈与问卷调查 船员

0 引 言

我国是交通大国、海洋大国、船员大国[1]。交通运输部在2020年6月发布了最新的《2019年中国船员发展报告》(以下简称《报告》)，《报告》显示，截至2019年底，全国注册船员总数1659188人，同比增长5.3%。在各类别注册船员中，国际航行海船船员占比34.7%，沿海航行海船船员占比12.6%，而内河航行船舶船员所占比例在一半以上，高达52.7%[2]。

2019年，我国持有国际航行海船适任证书的船员同比增长3.8%，然而，三副持证人数与活跃人数分别同比下降18.0%和20.7%，三管轮持证人数与活跃人数分别同比下降19.0%和23.3%[2]。持有沿海航行海船适任证书的船员同比增长8.0%，而三副持证人数与活跃人数同比下降13.8%和14.1%，三管轮持证人数和活跃人数同比下降14.4%和15.0%[2]。

国际航行船舶船员与沿海航行船舶船员均有所增加，但持证和活跃的三副和三管轮均明显减少；而内河航行船员数量整体稳定，不存在明显减少。

1 船员流失原因

沿海和国际航行三副和三管轮流失可分为显性流失和隐性流失两类,显性流失指已持证并有一定工作经验的三副和三管轮"弃海从陆",隐性流失指航海类院校培养出来的学生并未参加三副和三管轮适任证书考试或未通过该考试而最终未上船工作,可理解为预备三副和三管轮的流失。

1.1 持证三副和三管轮流失原因

为了解持证三副和三管轮流失原因,对20位某国企航运公司三副和三管轮进行访谈。综合访谈结果得知,海陆工作待遇差异逐渐缩小、长期远离亲人朋友、缺乏职业自豪感使三副和三管轮失去继续留船工作的动力。报告对持有证书船员的年龄进行数据统计,2019年,国际航行三副和三管轮平均年龄均为29岁,而沿海航行海船的三副和三管轮平均年龄分别为32岁和31岁。"三十而立"的思想在中国人心中根深蒂固,而海上工作性质对他们的婚恋会造成影响;相对而言,二副和二管轮及以上的高级船员工资待遇更高,年龄更大,工资待遇更有吸引力、家庭也更稳定,因此流失率较低。

在访谈基础上,通过问卷调查进一步了解不同因素对持证三副和三管轮流失的影响程度。调查问卷的对象为各大航运企业中从事沿海航行和国际航行的三副和三管轮,发放问卷800份,回收有效问卷738份,问卷回收率达92.3%。问卷调查对象对问卷中涉及的各类导致船员流失因素进行打分,结果如表1所示。通过对影响船员流失的七大因素进行排名,船员社会地位偏低及薪酬待遇不理想成为持证三副和三管轮流失的主要原因,而晋升困难的现实以及语言和文化方面的差异也使其留船工作的信心进一步动摇。

持证三副和三管轮对船员流失因素的评价及排序 表1

导致船员流失因素	严重程度分值	排 名
船员职业社会地位偏低	61.7	1
海陆收入差异缩小	59.7	2
晋升困难	56	3
语言与文化差异大	53.7	4
工作性质艰苦	50.5	5
婚恋受影响	48	6
身心压力过大	47.8	7

注:以100表示最严重。分值=调查问卷结果的算术平均值。

1.2 预备三副和三管轮流失原因

海事类本科和专科院校培养的航海类学生成为报考国际航行三副、三管轮证书的主力军,为扩大我国在国际船员中的比例,国家持续增加航海类学生的招生规模和数量。2019年,全国航海类专业全年共招生18864人,同比增长11.0%[2]。然而,招生数量的增加并未能有效提升持证船员或者活跃船员数量,参见报告中表3-3可知,2017年至2019年十个主要航海类院校毕业生中,只有约三分之一选择上船工作,这无疑是对教育资源的极大浪费。

为进一步了解航海类学生不愿上船原因,对广东海洋大学17级航海技术和轮机工程专业学生进行访谈。结果显示,航海类专业在高考填报志愿时属于提前批招录,部分学生在被提前批录取时对该专业所涉及的内容和未来就业方向尚缺乏了解,导致对专业缺乏认可度和忠诚度。此外,随着生活水平的不断提高,学生更不倾向选择航海类的艰苦行业,海陆工资待遇差异的缩小进一步降低了他们上船工作的信念。另外,英语能力偏低也是制约学生上船工作的重要因素,使得部分原本有上船打算的学生不得不放弃自己的理想。

在访谈基础上,通过问卷调查方式进一步了解影响预备三副和三管轮职业选择的因素及影响程度。调查问卷对象为各大航海类本科及专科院校2021届应届毕业生,发放问卷800份,回收有效问卷752

份,问卷回收率达94%。问卷调查对象对问卷中涉及的各类影响其选择上船工作的因素进行打分,结果如表2所示。排名在前两位的因素分别为认为海上工作性质艰苦以及对所学专业的不认可和缺乏兴趣。英语能力偏低也成了阻碍学生选择上船工作的另一重要因素。值得注意的是,在学生看来,相比成为海员,做公务员或者考研究生能给他们带来更多的尊严和自豪感。

预备三副和三管轮对影响其选择上船工作因素的评价及排序   表2

不愿上船工作影响因素	严重程度分值	排名
海上工作性质艰苦	56.2	1
对所学专业缺乏认可度和兴趣	55.6	2
英语能力不足	52.1	3
受师兄师姐择业观影响	49.7	4
更倾向于考公考研等	45.2	5
海陆收入差异缩小	44.7	6
远离家人朋友	44.3	7

注:以100表示最严重。分值=调查问卷结果的算术平均值。

2　改善船员流失问题对策分析

长期以来,社会地位偏低、薪酬待遇缺乏优势、英语语言能力薄弱都进一步加速了船员流失,也降低了我国船员队伍在国际上的竞争力。因此,希望政府、主管机关和海事类院校在相关方面加以改善,确保"建设海洋强国、交通强国"战略的航运人才队伍可持续发展。

2.1　政府和主管机关方面

提升船员职业的社会认可度。建议政府和主管机关加大对海员职业的宣传,如疫情期间海员的艰辛付出以及不可替代的重要作用应通过网络与媒体让广大民众了解,树立海员的积极形象,以提升他们的社会地位和社会认可度。使船员热爱航海并为自己的职业感到骄傲才能有效激发其潜能。

优化船员薪酬体系。建议政府和主管机关能根据社会和经济的发展水平,结合船员工作的特殊性质,考虑到船员在全球供应链中的重要地位,对他们的薪酬进行合理化调整。另外,船上也可以建立绩效奖励机制,对作出突出贡献以及工作上有突出表现的船员,通过绩效奖励机制进一步促进其工作积极性,同时也将有助于建立业务更加精湛、工作热情更高的船员队伍。

建立健全船员晋升机制。主管机关应监督船公司建立健全合理的考核、评价、奖惩机制,以此提振三副和三管轮的工作热情,使其能够按照各自的晋升目标积极努力,从而减少船员流失情况。另外,借助"互联网+教育"的便利,建立线上英语学习平台,使船员能够利用业余时间不断提升自己的英语能力,为晋升打下坚实基础。

2.2　海事类院校方面

注入蓝色基因。航海类学生初入校园时对未来工作缺乏了解与认知,充满航海和海洋元素的校园文化有助于加强学生的专业认同感、亲切感和自豪感。人类的认知规律是从感性认识过渡到理性认识,在校园、走廊、教室等位置设置航海文化内容可潜移默化提升学生对航海的感性认识,并进一步强化学生的专业认可度。内容可包括航海相关历史介绍、知名船公司介绍、航海绳结图片、各类船用设备和仪器图片,海员精神的介绍,航海类专业有成就的前辈介绍等,特别是在社会上和行业内对优秀船长和船员的宣传,逐步提高他们在社会上的认可度和从事该行业的荣誉感。

重视职业规划引导。如今船上工作环境和条件已得到有效改善,从饮食到娱乐设施都能满足船员要求,院校辅导员或教师应积极将此类正能量的信息传递给学生;此外,应使学生意识到,船员将来航行到世界各地,代表的不仅是个人更是国家,学生要对自己的职业充满自豪感和荣誉感,具备民族意识;同时,可邀请优秀毕业生回校为师弟师妹分享真实的船上工作生活,通过此类互动使学生对船上工作有更深刻的理解。

加强海事英语教育改革。我国的英语教育普遍存在重读写轻听说的现象,但船员的工作更多涉及听说能力,因此有必要在海事英语教学中提升听说训练,通过设定真实工作情景等教学方法鼓励和培养学生进行英语口语输出练习。此外,语言和文化密不可分,语言的教学不可脱离文化渗透,从事国际航行的船员会接触到来自世界各地拥有不同文化背景的人,缺乏对多种文化的了解和认识难免会导致沟通上的障碍。因此,海事英语的教育有必要加大对各国文化介绍,这样才能培养出符合国际航行需要的复合型航海人才。

3 结　语

通过《2019年中国船员发展报告》的数据厘清目前我国船员队伍的整体现状,发现流失船员主要包括从事沿海航行和国际航行的三副与三管轮,并结合数据分析导致我国船员梯队"断链"的主要原因。分别从持证三副和三管轮"弃海从陆"的显性流失以及航海类院校培养的预备三副和三管轮的隐形流失两方面进行原因分析,并在此基础上提出相应对策。建议政府和主管机关出台相关政策和措施提升船员职业的社会认可度,优化船员薪酬体系,以及建立健全船员晋升机制,而航海类院校需在校园文化中注入蓝色基因,重视对学生职业规划的引导、加强对优秀船员的宣传,同时进一步做好海事英语教育改革。

本文从更宏观的角度探讨我国船员流失的根本原因并提出对策建议,为相关部门决策提供有益参考。然而,本文对持证三副和三管轮的访谈样本数量和区域的代表性尚显不足,今后的研究将进一步做好样本采集,持续研究我国船员流失的原因并提出有效建议。

参考文献

[1] 张天赦.为海洋强国战略目标提供人才保障——交通运输部海事局局长许如清解读《中国船员发展规划(2016-2020年)》[J].中国水运,2016,37(11):10-12.

Liner Shipping Route and Schedule Optimization with Uncertain Sailing Time: Application to the Northern Sea Route

Jiaxuan Ding　Chi Xie

(School of Transportation Engineering, Tongji University)

Abstract　The Northern Sea Route (NSR) is expected to serve as a new commercial shipping route facilitating international trade. Compared to the traditional shipping route via the Suez Canal, the NSR has a significant edge on short maritime mileage. The sailing time, however, is heavily subject to the seasonal variation of sailing conditions along this route. Any participating shipping company must think this changeling situation over, say how to manage the risk caused by uncertain sailing time. The purpose of this article is to strike a balance between return brought by a tight schedule and risk caused by an unexpected delay. In order to maximize profit over all possible shipping environment scenarios, this paper proposes a two-stage stochastic nonlinear integer programming model for liner ship routing and scheduling with uncertain sailing time and cost, the nonlinearity of which arises from the coexistence of schedule-sensitive shipping demand and uncertain delay time in the objective function. By introducing a set of nominal delay variables, the model is converted into an equivalent linear integer programming counterpart and then solved by Benders decomposition. Numerical experiments are performed to validate the effectiveness of the model, the results of which come up with several managerial insights that can be used to guide liner shipping under uncertain sailing conditions.

Keywords　Liner ship routing and scheduling　Shipping uncertainty　Northern sea route　Two-stage stochastic programming　Linear integer programming

0　Introduction

As a transit corridor connecting the Atlantic Ocean and the Pacific Ocean through the Arctic Ocean, the Northern Sea Route (NSR) provides an alternative transportation shortcut between East Asia and Europe. Currently, global warming give rise to the dramatic shrinkage of the ice thickness and extent in the Arctic Ocean and make it possible for liner ship seasonal sailing through the NSR during summer. Liner shipping companies usually publish the shipping schedule 3 to 4 months ahead of the scheduled departure times. However, the sailing time in the NSR is heavily subject to sea ice conditions. Sailing speed may vary from 9 kn/day to 14 kn/day in terms of different sailing circumstances (Pierre and Pierre, 2015), which leads to a situation that shipping companies have to come up with the final routing and scheduling plan in uncertain sailing conditions. Previous studies, however, mainly focused on economic viability (Verny and Grigentin, 2009; Tseng and Cullinane, 2018; Theocharis et al., 2019; Ding et al., 2020) and sailing feasibility (Ho, 2010; Li and Kim, 2015; Aksenov et al., 2017; Meng et al., 2017) of the NSR, the research on planning and management of vessels along this potential shipping line is very limited, not to mention considering uncertain sailing conditions.

Uncertainties in shipping demand accounted for a large proportion of uncertain studies in liner shipping (Wang et al., 2012, 2013; Meng et al., 2012, 2015; Dong et al., 2015; Liu et al., 2020; Meng and Wang, 2010). While uncertainties in shipping service, though prevalent and usually resulting in low schedule reliability, received much less attention in existing studies. To model these uncertain factors, uncertainties at sea and uncertainties at ports, commonly, are translated into random port times and random sailing times, respectively. Under the framework of stochastic programming, Wang and Meng (2012) addressed the liner ship scheduling problem with uncertainties at sea and at ports, where port times were random variables and sea contingency times were proportional to the sailing distance. Qing and Song (2012) made the attempt to minimize the fuel consumption costs and developed a simulation-based method to find an optimal schedule while taking weekly service into account, in which port times in every port followed a known distribution. To optimize the sailing speed considering uncertain port times and time windows, Aydin et al. (2017) put forward a dynamic programming model aimed at minimizing the fuel consumption cost and imposed waiting cost and delay penalty to strike a balance between the service level and the sailing cost. By using chance-constrained programming to require different service levels in different ports, Gürel and Shadmand (2019) managed to figure out the optimal shipping schedule for the heterogeneous fleet considering uncertain waiting and handling times.

Besides, the majority of the studies on shipping schedule design problems are to design the optimal shipping schedule via a predetermined shipping route. (Meng and Wang, 2014; Aydin et al., 2017; Dulebenets, 2018; Mulder and Dekker, 2019). Very few studies have considered ship routing and scheduling decisions simultaneously, expect Wang and Meng (2011) and Kevin et al. (2018).

This article comes up with a two-stage stochastic programming model to address the single liner ship routing and scheduling problem under uncertain sailing time in the NSR. To devise an optimal shipping schedule, the ship routing decisions and scheduling decisions are simultaneously optimized. Moreover, delay penalty and elastic shipping demand are introduced to find a balance between the return brought by a tight schedule and risk caused by an unexpected delay. The remainder of the paper is organized in the following order. A two-stage stochastic model is constructed in section 1. Section 2 states the linearization technique and a solution algorithm. While Section 3 presents a real-life case study. Finally, Section 4 provides noteworthy conclusions.

1 Model Development

The shipping network in this article is constructed as a loop structure with predetermined origination and destination, as shown in Fig. 1. We further define that a round trip includes both the outbound trip and the inbound trip. While the trip from the origin port to the destination port denotes the outbound trip and the trip from the destination port back to the origin port is defined as the inbound trip.

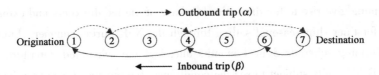

Fig. 1 The Network of Ports and Shipping Links

To construct a tractable model, we make the following modeling assumptions in this paper.

(1) Cargolay time and waiting time at ports are excluded in this paper.

(2) The number of cargos is measured in real numbers.

(3) Sailing speed is predetermined according to different sea ice conditions and remains the same in the duration of sailing on a segment.

(4) The probability distribution of actual sailing times in the NSR can be deduced from historical Arctic sea ice data.

For reading convenience, the notation of sets, parameters, and variables used in this paper, and their explanations are listed as follows.

Sets

N Set of all candidate ports, where $N = \{1, 2, \cdots, n\}$

S Set of all possible sailing scenarios in a round trip

Parameters

n Total number of candidate ports in the network, where $n = |N|$

c^f_{ij} Fixed sailing cost (in \$) on segment (i,j)

c^v_{ij} Fuel consumption cost (in \$/day) on segment (i,j)

c^d_i Delay penalty (in \$/TEU/day) at port i

r_{pq} Revenue (in \$/TEU) charged per unit of goods from origin port p to destination port q

a_{ij} Ship capacity (in TEU) on the segment (i,j)

D_{pq} Base cargo demand (in TEU) from origin port p to destination port q

se_{pq} Demand sensitivity parameter (in TEU/day) for the cargo demand from origin port p to destination port q

t_{ij} Nominal sailing time (in days) on the segment (i,j)

$\tilde{t}^l_{ij}$ Actual sailing time (in days) on the segment (i,j) under sailing scenario $l, (l \in S)$

p^l_{ij} Probability of the occurrence of actual sailing time $\tilde{t}^l_{ij}$

$\tilde{T}^\alpha_{i,l} (\tilde{T}^\beta_{i,l})$ Actual arrival time (in days) at port i under sailing scenario $l, (l \in S)$ for the outbound (or inbound) trip

$P^\alpha_{i,l} (P^\beta_{i,l})$ Probability of the occurrence for actual arrival time $\tilde{T}^\alpha_{i,l} (\tilde{T}^\beta_{i,l})$ for the outbound (or inbound) trip

 M A very large number

 Variables

 x_{ij} 0-1 binary variables: If the shipping route contains segment (i,j), $x_{ij}=1$; otherwise, $x_{ij}=0$

 y_{pq} Continues variables denote served cargo demand (in TEU) from port p to port q

 $T^{\alpha}_{i}(T^{\beta}_{i})$ Continues variables represent announced arrival time (in days) at port i for the outbound (or inbound) trip

The two-stage stochastic model reads:

$$\max \sum_{p \in N}\sum_{q \in N} r_{pq} y_{pq} - \sum_{i \in N}\sum_{j \in N} c^{f}_{ij} x_{ij} - \sum_{i \in N}\sum_{j \in N}\sum_{l \in S} c^{v}_{ij} p^{l}_{ij} \tilde{t}^{l}_{ij} x_{ij} -$$

$$\sum_{i=2}^{n} c^{d}_{i}(\tilde{T}^{\alpha}_{i,l} - T^{\alpha}_{i}) + \sum_{p=1}^{i-1} y_{pi} - \sum_{i=n-1}^{1} c^{d}_{i}(\tilde{T}^{\beta}_{i,l} - T^{\beta}_{i}) + \sum_{p=i+1}^{n} y_{pi} \tag{1}$$

subject to

$$\sum_{p=1}^{i}\sum_{q=j}^{n} y_{pq} \leq a_{ij} + M(1-x_{ij}) \quad \forall i=1,\cdots,n-1; j=i+1,\cdots,n \tag{2a}$$

$$\sum_{p=1}^{n}\sum_{q=1}^{j} y_{pq} \leq a_{ij} + M(1-x_{ij}) \quad \forall i=2,\cdots,n; j=1,\cdots,i-1 \tag{2b}$$

$$y_{pq} \leq M \sum_{i=p}^{q-1} x_{iq} \quad \forall p=1,\cdots,n-1; q=p+1,\cdots n \tag{3a}$$

$$y_{pq} \leq M \sum_{i=q+1}^{p} x_{iq} \quad \forall p=2,\cdots,n; q=1,\cdots p-1 \tag{3b}$$

$$y_{pq} \leq M \sum_{j=q+1}^{q} x_{iq} \quad \forall p=1,\cdots,n-1; q=p+1,\cdots n \tag{4a}$$

$$y_{pq} \leq M \sum_{j=q}^{p-1} x_{iq} \quad \forall p=2,\cdots,n; q=1,\cdots p-1 \tag{4b}$$

$$\sum_{j=2}^{n} x_{1j} = 1 \tag{5a}$$

$$\sum_{j=1}^{n-1} x_{nj} = 1 \tag{5b}$$

$$\sum_{i=1}^{p-1} x_{ip} - \sum_{j=p+1}^{n} x_{pj} = 0 \quad \forall p=2,\cdots,n-1 \tag{5c}$$

$$\sum_{i=p+1}^{n} x_{ip} - \sum_{j=1}^{p-1} x_{pj} = 0 \quad \forall p=2,\cdots,n-1 \tag{5d}$$

$$\sum_{i=2}^{n} x_{i1} = 1 \tag{5e}$$

$$\sum_{i=1}^{n-1} x_{in} = 1 \tag{5f}$$

$$y_{pq} \leq D_{pq} - s^{e}_{pq}(T^{\alpha}_{p} - T^{\alpha}_{q}) \quad \forall p=1,\cdots,n-1; q=p+1,\cdots,n \tag{6a}$$

$$y_{pq} \leq D_{pq} - s^{e}_{pq}(T^{\beta}_{p} - T^{\beta}_{q}) \quad \forall p=2,\cdots,n-1; q=1,\cdots,p-1 \tag{6b}$$

$$T^{\alpha}_{n} = T^{\beta}_{n} \tag{7}$$

$$T^{\alpha}_{1} = 0 \tag{8}$$

$$T^{\alpha}_{j} - T^{\alpha}_{i} \geq t_{ij} x_{ij} \quad \forall i=1,\cdots,n-1; j=i+1,\cdots,n \tag{9a}$$

$$T^{\beta}_{j} - T^{\beta}_{i} \geq t_{ij} x_{ij} \quad \forall i=2,\cdots,n; j=1,\cdots,i-1 \tag{9b}$$

$$x_{ij} \in \{0,1\} \quad \forall i \in N, j \in N \tag{10a}$$

$$y_{pq} \geq 0 \quad \forall p \in N, q \in N \tag{10b}$$

$$T^{\alpha}_i, T^{\beta}_i \geq 0 \quad \forall i \in N \tag{10c}$$

The objective function ① maximizes the profit of planning a single ship in a round trip. The first term represents the total revenue charged by serving shipping demand between ports; the second item denotes the fixed sailing cost; the third item states the fuel consumption cost; the remaining items are delay penalties. Constraints ② ensure that the carrier would never overload a liner ship on any sailing segment (i,j). Arrival constraints ③ and departure constraints ④ are coupling constraints, guaranteeing only if port p and port q are connected can cargo be shipped between port p and port q. Constraints ⑤ denote that the shipping network is constructed as a loop structure, in which the first port and the last port must be visited no matter in the outbound trip or the inbound trip. Demand constraints ⑥ state that the actual shipped cargo volume between port p and port q is no more than the induced demand rate. Constraint ⑦ represents that the arrival time at the last port in the outbound trip is equal to the departure time in the inbound trip. Constraint ⑧ sets the announced departure time from the first port to zero. Constraints ⑨ serve as a lower bound on the sailing time on any sailing segment (i,j). Constraints ⑩ are variable bound constraints.

2 Solution Method

2.1 Linearization of The Objective Function

The delay penalty items in the objective function result in the nonlinearity within the problem structure. Thus, we introduce some new constraints, sets, and variables to linearize the model.

Sets

D_i Set of all possible integer delay times (in days) at port i

Variables

$\phi^{\alpha}_{i,l,u}$ ($\phi^{\beta}_{i,l,u}$) 0-1 binary variables: for the outbound trip, if the delay time (in days) at port i in scenario $l(l \in S)$ equals $u(u \in D_i)$ days, then $\phi^{\alpha}_{i,l,u} = 1$; otherwise $\phi^{\alpha}_{i,k,u} = 0$

$\psi^{\alpha}_{i,l,u}$ ($\psi^{\beta}_{i,l,u}$) Continuous variables: for the outbound trip, if the delay time (in days) at port i under scenario $l(l \in S)$ equals $u(u \in D_i)$ days, then $\psi^{\alpha}_{i,l,u}$ is equal to the delay time multiplied by the number of delay cargos; otherwise $\psi^{\alpha}_{i,l,u} = 0$

With the help of these nominal variables, we can linearize the objective function using the following constraints.

$$\widetilde{T}^{\alpha}_{i,l} - T^{\alpha}_i \leq \sum_{u \in D_i} u \, \phi^{\alpha}_{i,l,u} \quad \forall i \in N; l \in S \tag{11a}$$

$$\widetilde{T}^{\beta}_{i,l} - T^{\beta}_i \leq \sum_{u \in D_i} u \, \phi^{\beta}_{i,l,u} \quad \forall i \in N; l \in S \tag{11b}$$

$$\sum_{u \in D_i} \phi^{\alpha}_{i,l,u} = 1 \quad \forall i \in N; l \in S \tag{12a}$$

$$\sum_{u \in D_i} \phi^{\beta}_{i,l,u} = 1 \quad \forall i \in N; l \in S \tag{12b}$$

$$\psi^{\alpha}_{i,l,u} \geq u \sum_{p=1}^{i-1} y_{pi} + M(\phi^{\alpha}_{i,l,u} - 1) \quad \forall i \in N \setminus \{1\}; l \in S; u \in D_i \tag{13a}$$

$$\psi^{\beta}_{i,l,u} \geq u \sum_{p=i+1}^{n} y_{pi} + M(\phi^{\beta}_{i,l,u} - 1) \quad \forall i \in N \setminus \{n\}; l \in S; u \in D_i \tag{13b}$$

$$\phi^{\alpha}_{i,l,u}, \phi^{\beta}_{i,l,u} \in \{0,1\} \quad \forall i \in N; l \in S; u \in D_i \tag{14a}$$

$$\psi^{\alpha}_{i,l,u}, \psi^{\beta}_{i,l,u} \geq 0 \quad \forall i \in N; l \in S; u \in D_i \tag{14b}$$

Constraints (11)-(14) denote a new continuous variable $\psi^{\alpha}_{i,l,u}$ can replace the product of the delay time multiplied by the volume of delay cargos in the objective function. Specifically, when the delay time at port i under scenario l equals u days ($\sum_{u \in D_i} \phi^{\alpha}_{i,l,u} = 1$), $\psi^{\alpha}_{i,l,u}$ equals the delay time multiplied by the volume of delay cargos ($\psi^{\alpha}_{i,l,u} = u \sum_{p=1}^{i-1} y_{pi}$); otherwise $\psi^{\alpha}_{i,l,u} = 0$ (namely, $\psi^{\alpha}_{i,l,u} = 0$, when $\sum_{u \in D_i} \phi^{\alpha}_{i,l,u} = 0$). After which, the mixed linear integer programming model is as follows:

$$\max \sum_{p \in N} \sum_{q \in N} r_{pq} y_{pq} - \sum_{i \in N} \sum_{j \in N} c^f_{ij} x_{ij} - \sum_{i \in N} \sum_{j \in N} \sum_{l \in S} c^v_{ij} pl_{ij} \tilde{t}l_{ij} x_{ij}$$
$$- \sum_{i=2}^{n} c^d_i \sum_{l \in Su} \sum_{\in D_i} \psi^\alpha_{i,l,u} P^\alpha_{i,l} - \sum_{i=n-1}^{1} c^d_i \sum_{l \in Su} \sum_{\in D_i} \psi^\beta_{i,l,u} P^\beta_{i,l} \tag{15}$$

subject to constraints (2)-(10), (11)-(14)

2.2 Benders Decomposition

Benders decomposition is commonly used to solve large-scale mixed linear integer programming problems, especially for those with complicating variables that, when temporarily fixed, render the rest problem more tractable (Benders, 1962). A MIP programming model can be decomposed into one master problem containing all binary variables (complicating variables) and one subproblem including only continuous variables. In each iteration, the master problem is firstly solved, then a subproblem is determined given the values of complicating variables. If current solutions are not optimum, then some new cuts are added to the master problem, which is then resolved, until the solution gap is sufficiently small. A more detailed description of the above Benders decomposition procedure can be referred to in Ding and Xie (2021).

3 Case Study

3.1 Data collection

We construct a China-Europe liner shipping network along the NSR containing 7 candidate ports: Shanghai, Provideniya, Pevek, Dikson Island, Archangel, Murmansk and Rotterdam. The shipping revenue, base demand volume, and demand sensitivity parameter are presented in Tab. 1 (Liu and Kronbak, 2010; Schøyen and Bråthen, 2011; Furuichi and Otsuka, 2015) and estimated sailing time and its probability distribution are shown in Tab. 2. Different uncertainty levels refer to different sailing conditions. Moreover, to facilitate the construction of sailing scenarios and reduce the total number of sailing scenarios, we assume that sailing times on different sailing segments are independent, except sailing segments (Shanghai-Provideniya) and (Provideniya-Pevek). Thus, we can calculate the sailing time and its probability on independent sailing segments based on the equations (25).

$$\tilde{t}^l_{i,j} = \tilde{t}^l_{i,j-1} + \tilde{t}^l_{j-1,j} \quad \forall l \in S; i=1,\cdots,n-2; j=i+2,\cdots,n \tag{16a}$$

$$p^l_{i,j} = p^l_{i,j-1} p^l_{j-1,j} \quad \forall l \in S; i=1,\cdots,n-2; j=i+2,\cdots,n \tag{16b}$$

$$\tilde{t}^l_{i,j} = \tilde{t}^l_{i,j+1} + \tilde{t}^l_{j+1,j} \quad \forall l \in S; i=3,\cdots,n; q=1,\cdots j-2 \tag{16c}$$

$$p^l_{i,j} = p^l_{i,j+1} p^l_{j+1,j} \quad \forall l \in S; i=3,\cdots,n; q=1,\cdots j-2 \tag{16d}$$

Tab. 1 Nominal Sailing Time, Revenue, Shipping Demand Sensitivity and Base Shipping Demand between Ports

		1	2	3	4	5	6	7
		Shanghai	Provideniya	Pevek	Dikson Island	Archangel	Murmansk	Rotterdam
1 Shanghai	Nominal sailing time (days)	—	10	12	17	20	20	24
	Revenue ($/TEU)	—	900	1,200	1,700	1,800	2,000	2,160
	Base shipping demand (TEU)	—	1,600	1,600	2,000	2,000	1,600	1,600
	Demand sensitivity parameter	—	30	20	30	20	30	20
2 Provideniya	Nominal sailing time (days)	10	—	2	7	10	10	14
	Revenue ($/TEU)	900	—	180	630	840	900	1120
	Base shipping demand (TEU)	1,600	—	1,200	1,600	1,600	1,200	1,200
	Demand sensitivity parameter	30	—	30	50	30	50	30

continue

		1	2	3	4	5	6	7
		Shanghai	Provideniya	Pevek	Dikson Island	Archangel	Murmansk	Rotterdam
3 Pevek	Nominal sailing time (days)	12	2	—	5	8	8	12
	Revenue ($/TEU)	1,200	180	—	500	720	800	1,080
	Base shipping demand (TEU)	1,600	—	1,200	1,600	1,600	1,200	1,200
	Demand sensitivity parameter	20	30	—	30	20	30	20
4 Dikson Island	Nominal sailing time (days)	17	7	5	—	3	3	7
	Revenue ($/TEU)	1,700	630	500	—	270	300	630
	Base shipping demand (TEU)	2,000	1,600	1,600	—	2,000	1,600	1,600
	Demand sensitivity parameter	30	50	30	—	30	50	30
5 Archangel	Nominal sailing time (days)	20	10	8	3	—	1	5
	Revenue ($/TEU)	1,800	840	720	270	—	90	400
	Base shipping demand (TEU)	2,000	1,600	1,600	2,000	—	1,600	1,600
	Demand sensitivity parameter	20	30	20	30	—	30	20
6 Murmansk	Nominal sailing time (days)	20	10	8	3	1	—	5
	Revenue ($/TEU)	2000	900	800	300	90	—	450
	Base shipping demand (TEU)	1,600	1,200	1,200	1,600	1,600	—	1,200
	Demand sensitivity parameter	30	50	30	50	30	—	20
7 Rotterdam	Nominal sailing time (days)	24	14	12	7	5	5	—
	Revenue ($/TEU)	2,160	1,120	1,080	630	400	450	—
	Base shipping demand (TEU)	1,600	1,200	1,200	1,600	1,600	1,200	—
	Demand sensitivity parameter	20	30	20	30	20	20	—

Tab. 2 Actual Sailing Time and Probability between Neighbouring Ports under Different Uncertainty Levels of Sailing Conditions

(a) The low uncertain sailing condition

	1	2	3	4	5	6	7
	Shanghai	Provideniya	Pevek	Dikson Island	Archangel	Murmansk	Rotterdam
1 Shanghai	-	11 (0.5) 12 (0.3) 14 (0.2)	14 (0.5) 16 (0.3) 19 (0.2)				
2 Provideniya	11 (0.5) 12 (0.3) 14 (0.2)	-	3 (0.2) 4 (0.6) 5 (0.2)				
3 Pevek	14 (0.5) 16 (0.3) 19 (0.2)	3 (0.2) 4 (0.6) 5 (0.2)	-	5 (0.4) 6 (0.5) 7 (0.1)			
4 Dikson Island			5 (0.4) 6 (0.5) 7 (0.1)	-	3 (0.2) 4 (0.7) 5 (0.1)		

continue

(a) The low uncertain sailing condition

	1	2	3	4	5	6	7
	Shanghai	Provideniya	Pevek	Dikson Island	Archangel	Murmansk	Rotterdam
5 Archangel				3 (0.2) 4 (0.7) 5 (0.1)	-	1 (1)	
6 Murmansk					1 (1)	-	5 (1)
7 Rotterdam						5 (1)	-

(b) The high uncertain sailing condition

	1	2	3	4	5	6	7
	Shanghai	Provideniya	Pevek	Dikson Island	Archangel	Murmansk	Rotterdam
1 Shanghai	-	11 (0.3) 14 (0.5) 18 (0.2)	13 (0.3) 17 (0.5) 23 (0.2)				
2 Provideniya	11 (0.3) 14 (0.5) 18 (0.2)	-	2 (0.3) 3 (0.3) 5 (0.4)				
3 Pevek	13 (0.3) 17 (0.5) 23 (0.2)	2 (0.3) 3 (0.3) 5 (0.4)	-	6 (0.4) 7 (0.4) 9 (0.2)			
4 Dikson Island			6 (0.4) 7 (0.4) 9 (0.2)		4 (0.3) 5 (0.4) 6 (0.3)		
5 Archangel				4 (0.3) 5 (0.4) 6 (0.3)	-	1 (1)	
6 Murmansk					1 (1)	-	5 (1)
7 Rotterdam						5 (1)	-

Moreover, the ship capacity is estimated at 4,000 TEUs; the fixed sailing cost c^f_{ij} on each segment approximates \$20,000; the fuel consumption cost c^v_{ij} on each segment is set as \$30,000/day; the unit delay penalty c^d_i is estimated as \$30/TEU/day.

Benders decomposition is coded using Python and Gurobi 9.0.3 and runs in an Intel Core i5-8250U CPU, 8 GB RAM personal computer. Benders decomposition can find the optimal solution with a 1.3% optimality gap within 1,978 CPU seconds.

3.2 Result Discussions

To validate the effectiveness of the proposed stochastic model, we compared the performance of the stochastic model and its deterministic counterpart under different uncertainty levels. Note that the sailing time on any segment follows the discrete distribution in the stochastic model but takes its expected value in the deterministic model. Schedule reliability at each port is equal to the ratio of the number of non-delay arriving scenarios to the number of total possible arriving scenarios. While the schedule reliability for a round trip equals the expected value of the schedule reliability at all visited ports.

As shown in Fig. 2, the stochastic model holds a competitive edge on the deterministic one, in terms of both expected profit and schedule reliability. Moreover, as the uncertainty level increases, the advantage of the stochastic model are even more obvious. Besides, the stochastic model can guarantee a relatively high level of schedule reliability under different sailing conditions.

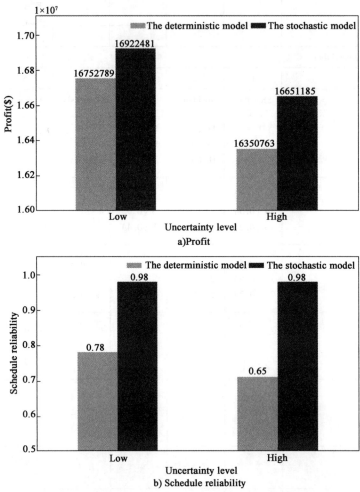

Fig. 2 Profit and Schedule Reliability Made by the Deterministic Model and Stochastic Model under Different Uncertainty Levels of Sailing Conditions

And we can find that the routing decision from the stochastic model can provide more adaptive routing and scheduling plans according to various sailing conditions. To spread the risk of delay, for routing decisions, the stochastic model tends to increase the number of ports in the final shipping route; for shipping schedule decisions, it tends to prolong the announced sailing time in some key sailing segments. These strategic adjustments are consistent with the risk reduction strategy in risk management, meaning that companies take action to reduce the severity and the likelihood of the eventuality.

4 Conclusions

This article attempts to answer the question of how to search for the optimal ship route and shipping schedule considering the uncertain sailing time. This problem is critical but challenging for commercial liner shipping in some shipping cases. In this study, the uncertainty arises from the unpredictable sea ice conditions in the NSR. Therefore, we take uncertain sailing time as stochastic parameters recorded in available probability distributions and develop a stochastic programming model, which may provide a modeling framework for liner ship routing and scheduling under uncertainties. Especially, we consider the delay penalty and schedule-sensitive demand to find a good trade-off between the return from a tight schedule and the risk caused by an unexpected delay. Moreover, linearization techniques and Benders decomposition are applied to solve the stochastic problem.

The case study is based on a real-life China-Europe shipping line via the NSR, where we can find that compared to the deterministic model, the stochastic model can ensure higher expected profit and higher on-time arrival rate in any uncertainty level and prove to be a more valuable tool for enacting liner shipping routes and schedules under uncertain conditions.

5 Acknowledgements

This research is sponsored by National Natural Science Foundation of China (Grant No. 71771150, 71890970, 72021002) and National Key Research and Development Program of China (Contract No. 2018YFB1600900).

References

[1] Agarwal R., and Ergun O. (2008). Ship scheduling and network design for cargo routing in liner shipping. Transportation Science, 42(2), 175-196.

[2] Aksenov Y., Popova E. E., Yool A., Nurser A. G., Williams T. D., Bertino L., and Bergh J. (2017). On the future navigability of Arctic sea routes: High-resolution projections of the Arctic Ocean and sea ice. Marine Policy, 75, 300-317.

[3] Aydin, N., Lee H., and Mansouri. S. A. (2017). Speed optimization and bunkering in liner shipping in the presence of uncertain service times and time windows at ports. European Journal of Operational Research, 259(1), 143-154.

[4] Benders J. F. (1962). Partitioning procedures for solving mixed-variables programming problems. Numerische Mathematik, 4(1), 238-252.

[5] Bialystocki N., Konovessis D. (2016). On the estimation of ship's fuel consumption and speed curve: a statistical approach. Journal of Ocean Engineering and Science, 1(2), 157-166.

[6] Ding W., Wang Y., Dai L., and Hu H. (2020). Does a carbon tax affect the feasibility of Arctic shipping? Transportation Research Part D, 80, 102257.

[7] Ding J. and Xie C. (2021). Stochastic programming for liner ship routing and scheduling under uncertain sea ice conditions in the Northern Sea Route. Transportation Research Record. (In press)

[8] Dong J. X., Lee C. Y., and Song D. P. (2015). Joint service capacity planning and dynamic container routing in shipping network with uncertain demands. Transportation Research Part B, 78, 404-421.

[9] Dulebenets M. A. (2018). The vessel scheduling problem in a liner shipping route with heterogeneous fleet. International Journal of Civil Engineering, 16(1), 1-14.

[10] Furuichi M. and Otsuka N. (2015). Proposing a common platform of shipping cost analysis of the Northern Sea Route and the Suez Canal Route. Maritime Economics and Logistics, 17(1), 9-31.

[11] Gürel, S. and Shadmand A. (2019). A heterogeneous fleet liner ship scheduling problem with port time uncertainty. Central European Journal of Operations Research, 27, 1153-1175.

[12] Ho J. (2010). The implications of Arctic sea ice decline on shipping. Marine Policy, 34(3), 713-715.

[13] Kevin T., Fabian E. J., Melissa C. A., and Müller D. (2018). Liner shipping single service design problem with arrival time service levels. Flexible Services and Manufacturing Journal, 31, 620-652.

[14] Lee T. and Kim H. J. (2015). Barriers of voyaging on the Northern Sea Route: A perspective from shipping Companies. Marine Policy, 62, 264-270.

[15] Liu M. andKronbak J. (2010). The potential economic viability of using the Northern Sea Route as an alternative route between Asia and Europe. Journal of Transport Geography, 18(3), 434-444.

[16] Liu M., Liu X., Chu F., Zhu M., and Zheng F. (2020). Liner ship bunkering and sailing speed planning with uncertain demand. Computational and Applied Mathematics, 39(1), 1-23.

[17] Meng Q. and Wang T. (2010). A chance constrained programming model for short-term liner ship fleet planning problems. Maritime Policy and Management, 37(4), 329-346.

[18] Meng Q., Wang T., and Wang S. (2012). Short-term liner ship fleet planning with container transshipment and uncertain demand. European Journal of Operational Research, 223(1), 96-105.

[19] Meng Q., Wang T., and Wang S. (2015). Multi-period liner ship fleet planning with dependent uncertain container shipment demand. Maritime Policy and Management, 42(1), 43-67.

[20] Meng Q., Wang S., Andersson H., and Thun K. (2014). Containership routing and scheduling in liner shipping: Overview and future research directions. International Journal of Control, 48(2), 265-280.

[21] Meng Q., Zhang Y., and Xu M. (2017). Viability of transarctic shipping routes: a literature review from the navigational and commercial perspectives. Maritime Policy and Management, 44(1), 16-41.

[22] Mulder J. and Dekker R. (2019). Designing robust liner shipping schedules: Optimizing recovery actions and buffer times. European Journal of Operational Research, 272(1), 132-146.

[23] Nam J. H., Park I., Lee H. J., Kwon M. O., Choi K., andSeo Y. K. (2013). Simulation of optimal arctic routes using a numerical sea ice model based on an ice-coupled ocean circulation method. International Journal of Naval Architecture and Ocean Engineering, 5(2), 210-226.

[24] Pierre C. and Olivier F. (2015). Relevance of the Northern Sea Route (NSR) for bulk shipping. Transportation Research Part A, 78, 337-346.

[25] Qi X. and Song D. (2012). Minimizing fuel emissions by optimizing vessel schedules in liner shipping with uncertain port times. Transportation Research Part E, 48(4), 863-880.

[26] Schøyen H. and Bråthen S. (2011). The Northern Sea Route versus the Suez Canal: Cases from bulk shipping. Journal of Transport Geography, 19(4), 977-983.

[27] Shou J. and Feng Y. (2015). Potential for container transport through the Arctic Northern Sea Route. Chinese Journal of Polar Research, 1, 65-73.

[28] Theocharis D., Rodrigues V. S., Pettit S., and Haider J. (2019). Feasibility of the Northern Sea Route: The role of distance, fuel prices, ice breaking fees and ship size for the product tanker market. Transportation Research Part E, 129, 111-135.

[29] Tseng P. H., and Cullinane K. (2018). Key criteria influencing the choice of Arctic shipping: a fuzzy analytic hierarchy process model. Maritime Policy and Management, 45(4), 422-438.

[30] Verny J. and Grigentin C. (2009). Container shipping on the Northern Sea Route. International Journal of Production Economics, 122(1), 107-117.

[31] Wang H., Zhang Y., and Meng Q. (2018). How will the opening of the Northern Sea Route influence the Suez Canal Route? An empirical analysis with discrete choice models. Transportation Research Part A, 107, 75-89.

[32] Wang S. and Meng Q. (2011). Schedule design and container routing in liner shipping. Transportation Research Record, 2222, 25-33.

[33] Wang S. and Meng Q. (2012). Liner ship route schedule design with sea contingency time and port

time uncertainty. Transportation Research Part B, 46(5), 615-633.

[34] Wang T., Meng Q., and Wang S. (2012). Robust optimization model for liner ship fleet planning with container transshipment and uncertain demand. Transportation Research Record, 2273(1), 18-28.

[35] Wang T., Meng Q., Wang S., and Tan Z. (2013). Risk management in liner ship fleet deployment: A joint chance constrained programming model. Transportation Research Part E, 60, 1-12.

Research and Application of Multifunctional Light Buoy in Guangdong-Hong Kong-Macao Greater Bay Area

Hong Chen　Jingzhou Yuan

(Aids to navigation department of Guangzhou)

Abstract　Introduce a new type of light buoy. The light buoy is mainly equipped with hydrological and meteorological equipment and video surveillance to provide diversified navigation information for vessels sailing in Guangdong-Hong Kong-Macao Great Bay Area.

Keywords　Multifunctional light buoy　E-Navigation　Diversified navigation information　Aids to navigation

0　Introduction

In recent years, with the rapid development of science and technology, new technologies, new materials and new energy sources for aids to navigation have been continuously developed and utilized. The maintenance quality, efficiency and the service capacity of aids to navigation are also getting better which provides a more comprehensive, reliable, convenient and efficient service guarantee for ship navigation safety and various activities at sea. At the same time, the extensive application of new technologies in the field of aids to navigation has profoundly changed the service functions, quality and management mode of traditional aids to navigation. In particular, the role of radio buoy is becoming increasingly prominent, which has a huge impact on traditional buoy. It is foreseeable that this influence will continue to intensify in the future, especially the development of E-Navigation and the concept of intelligent shipping, which indicates that the development of aids to navigation has entered a new era of digitalization, information and intelligence. Against the background of the ever-increasing demand for maritime support and the rapid development of new technologies in aids to navigation, the development of aids to navigation in multi-function, digitalization and intelligence will become an inevitable trend.

We design and add a variety of equipment and develop corresponding software and hardware through the buoy body, so as to develop a new multi-functional buoy. The multi-functional buoy can not only meet the navigation aid function of the traditional buoy, but also realize the real-time monitoring of the hydrological and meteorological data of the buoy position and the return of surrounding video data. The multi-functional buoy adopts a modular design, which involves the separation of the traditional buoy and the energy system and the module for collecting hydrological, meteorological and video data to ensure basic functions. The material of the buoy body is polyethylene polymer, which is more environmentally friendly than the traditional steel buoy, has a long service life and is convenient for later maintenance. The proposal of multi-functional buoy provides a new idea for the transformation and upgrading of aids to navigation, which is beneficial to the upgrade, intelligence and multi-functional buoy of the Guangdong-Hong Kong-Macao Great Bay Area, thereby better serving the construction of water traffic safety in the Guangdong-Hong Kong-Macao Great Bay Area.

This article will introduce the preliminary research results and actual trial situation of the Guangzhou Aids to navigation Department in multi-functional buoy.

1 Multifunctional Light Buoy System and Function Design

1.1 Technical Solution

The functional design of the multi-functional buoy must first meet the requirements of buoy (preserving the four elements of the original light buoy: accurate position, normal light quality, bright colors, and good structure.). On this basis, we consider energy consumption and Communication, and design the frame of multi-functional buoy.

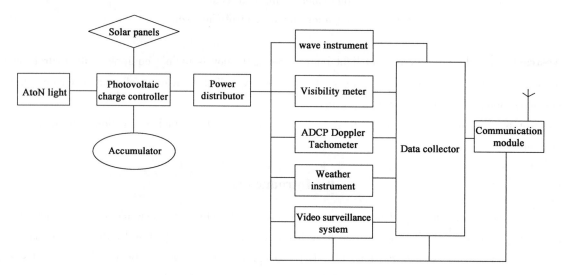

Fig. 1 Frame of the multi-functional buoy system

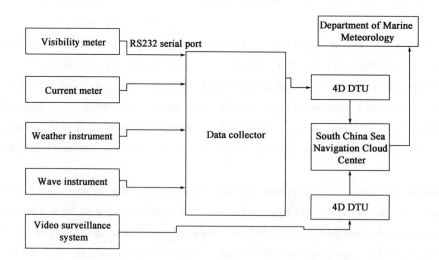

Fig. 2 Frame of data transmission system and devices in multifunctional buoy

1.2 Each Device on The Multifunctional Buoy Can Realize The Following Functions

(1) The visibility meter collects visibility information near the monitoring platform;

(2) The meteorological instrument collects wind speed, wind direction, temperature, humidity, air pressure, and rainfall information;

(3) Doppler flow meter collects information such as water temperature, flow rate and flow direction of ocean;

(4) The wave instrument collects wave height, wave direction and other data;

(5) Beidou positioning collects buoy latitude and longitude information, calculates the buoy offset direction and offset distance according to the original throwing position. And it generates an alarm if the offset distance is exceeded.

(6) The electronic compass collect sbuoy status information such as tilt angle, pitch angle and roll angle;

(7) The accelerometer collects the acceleration of the three axes of XYZ and calculates the collision alarm according to the mathematical model.

(8) The control box system collects the temperature and humidity in the control box, and collect sthe status of opening and closing the door through the door controller to generate an alarm for illegal opening of the door.

(9) Video surveillance will record and take photos in time for collision alarm and cabin door alarm.

(10) The power supply system includes solar panels, batteries, and BMS modules. It is responsible for providing power protection for the entire system.

(11) Equipped with AIS (auto identification system), lights, anchor equipment, etc.

(12) The data acquisition control system mainly completes sensor communication, information acquisition, data processing, data storage and control data transmission. It ensures that data is stably transmitted to the designated server through different communication methods.

(13) The communication module transmits the information message of the data acquisition control system back to the data receiving end of the shore-based system.

2 Standard Material Selection and Design

2.1 Body Selection

The material of the buoy body is usually steel, polyethylene, polyurea, glass fiber reinforced plastic, etc. After comparison, the material of the multifunctional buoy should be high molecular polyethylene.

Polyethylene is a high-molecular organic compound with corrosion resistance and good insulation properties. It has the characteristics of rigidity, hardness and mechanical strength. Moreover, it is insoluble in water and has little water absorption.

Since the buoy carries more equipment and is placed on the side of the channel, it needs to have certain anti-collision performance. In addition, considering the protection of the marine environment, marine buoys should pay attention to the use of environmentally friendly materials. 98% of the buoys currently used in China's waters are steel buoys. They need to be moved back to shore regularly for maintenance, such as removing sea creatures, anti-corrosion paint, high maintenance costs, and polluting the environment. The International Navigation Marks Association (IALA) and the China Maritime Safety Administration have repeatedly emphasized that buoys that are environmentally friendly, long-lived, and low-maintenance are required. Foreign countries have gradually replaced them with non-steel buoys. In summary, the standard material is high molecular polyethylene with good anti-collision performance, with a diameter of 3m.

2.2 Device Installation

As shown in Fig. 3, for the visibility meter, weather meter, wave meter, video surveillance and other equipment on the upper part of the buoy body, the bottom flange of the equipment is fixed and rigidly connected.

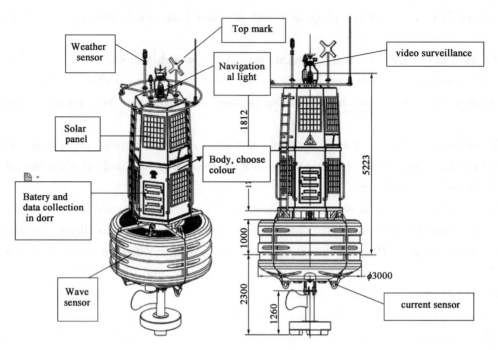

Fig. 3 Multi-functional light buoy

The equipment power supply system, data acquisition equipment, and communication equipment are all installed in the box under the light stand, and the wall-through cables are all waterproof connectors.

The sea current meter is installed in a round well type. A round open well is reserved on the buoy body. When the sea current meter is installed, it is first fixed on the mounting bracket, and then the bracket is inserted from the upper part of the well, and the upper part is fixed by a butt flange. The disassembly and assembly are simple. It is convenient for equipment maintenance in the later stage.

3 Data Acquisition System

The data acquisition control system is mainly responsible for sensor communication, information acquisition, data processing, data storage and control data transmission. It ensures that data can be stably transmitted to the designated server through different communication methods.

Details as follows:

(1) Power up each functional module and communication equipment according to the predetermined time sequence (settable), and close it after the collection is completed.

(2) Under normal conditions, the hydrological and meteorological elements are automatically collected and processed at a predetermined frequency; under severe sea conditions, the observation frequency can be increased according to the internally set threshold, and the normal observation can be automatically controlled after the end of the severe sea conditions.

(3) Perform preliminary quality control on the collected data, including: removing gross errors; checking the upper and lower limits of the measured value, etc.

(4) Automatically compile messages and use the communication transmission system to send the data to the

shore-based system.

(5) Large-capacity solid-state data storage is used to save the collected raw data.

4 Communication Transmission

Common wireless data communication methods include: radio communication, mobile network communication, Wi-Fi communication, microwave communication, satellite communication and so on.

The waters where the multi-functionallight buoys are deployed are covered by mobile network signals. Taking into account the economic and technical feasibility, 4G communication is used for data transmission. The specific functions are as follows:

(1) Data communicationuses wireless communication network connection to ensure that the effective data reception rate is not less than 95%.

(2) Transmit the information message of the data acquisition control system back to the data receiving end of the shore-based system for receiving and processing.

(3) It can remotely detect and initialize the observation equipment, and can perform fault diagnosis and fault alarm for each component.

(4) The memory data of the information acquisition control module can be read remotely.

5 Power Supply Design

Principles of multifunctional buoy power supply system:

(1) The data acquisition system, sensor system, hydrological and meteorological equipment and the power supply system of the navigation lights are independent of each other.

(2) The power supply system of the data acquisition system, sensor system and hydrological and meteorological equipment must be able to work normally under 20 consecutive days of cloudy and rainy weather. The power supply system of the beacon light must be able to work normally under 30 consecutive days of cloudy and rainy days.

5.1 Calculation of Battery Capacity and Solar Panel Power Generation

5.1.1 Battery Capacity Calculation

The capacity of the battery is very important to ensure continuous power supply. The electricity generated by solar energy must be stored in storage batteries for equipment consumption, and continuous rainy weather should also be considered.

The calculation formula of battery capacity BC is:
$$BC = A \times QL \times NL \times TO / CC \tag{1}$$

In the formula: A is the safety factor, which is between 1.1 and 1.4.

QL is the daily average power consumption of the load, which is the working current multiplied by the daily working hours;

NL is the longest number of consecutive rainy days;

TO is the temperature correction coefficient, generallyit sets 1, if it is above 0℃; it sets 1.1, if it is above -10℃; and it sets 1.2, if it is below -10℃;

CC is the depth of discharge of the battery, generallyit sets 0.8 for the battery.

5.1.2 Solar Panel Calculation Method

According to the above-mentioned distribution table of China's solar energy resources, combined with relevant meteorological data of the water area, the average annual total sunshine hours in the waters of the Pearl River Estuary is about $T = 2600h$, that is, the daily solar sunshine time is:

$$H = 2600/365 = 7.12 \text{ (h/d)} \tag{2}$$

Daily power generation of a single solar panel = power × sunshine time × comprehensive charging efficiency.

5.2 Energy Allocation Calculation

According to the sensor equipment loaded, calculate the total power consumption of the sensor equipment, and then configure the battery and solar panel according to the total power consumption (the actual power consumption of each device = power consumption * duty cycle * number).

Device power consumption   Tab. 1

Number	Required equipment	Power consumption	Sampling interval (min)	Sampling time (min)	Duty cycle
1	Visibility meter	3.0W	—	—	1
2	Weather meter	0.2W	—	—	1
3	Current meter	1.0W	—	—	1
4	Wave meter	1.0W	30	18	3/5
5	Video surveillance system	10.0W	24Hours	14Hours	7/12
6	4G data transmission module	2.0W	—	—	1
7	Data collector	2.0W	—	—	1

6 Multi-Functional Buoy Inspection and Maintenance

6.1 Daily Management

The data server is placed in the Navigation Guarantee Centre of South China Sea, and daily management is managed by the aids to navigation Department of Guangzhou. The manager check the technical parameters of the multi-functional buoy every day, and maintain it in time if any abnormality is found.

6.2 Site Maintenance

(1) Inspect and maintain solar panels, charge controllers and maintenance-free batteries. Check and maintain and clean the appearance of solar panels and other equipment. Check the working status of each equipment, if there is any fault or damage, repair or replace the failed parts in time;

(2) Check and maintain the appearance and working status of communication equipment such as antennas and data terminals. If there is a fault or damage, repair or replace the failed parts in time;

(3) Check and maintain the sensor system, including visibility meter, weather meter, ocean current meter, wave meter, and video monitoring system. If there is any fault or damage, repair or replace the failed parts in time;

(4) Check and maintain measuring equipment. Inspection and maintenance include regular cleaning and inspection of the appearance of the equipment, and checking the working status of the equipment. If there is a fault or damage, repair or replace the failed parts in time;

(5) Affected by natural disasters and human factors, when the equipment is damaged, the manager must repair and replace the equipment to ensure the normal operation of the multifunctional buoy.

7 Applications

7.1 Multi-functional Buoy Release Principle

(1) Principle of adaptability. The waters of the Pearl River Estuary are characterized by rapid water flow, large traffic flow, complex flow, and frequent ship activities. In order to enhance the navigation aid capability of navigation services and meet the ever-increasing demand for navigation services, multi-functional buoy should be placed in important locations such as entry and exit ports, channel junctions, and bridge waters.

(2) The principle of complementary. According to the construction of the environmental monitoring system of the Pearl River Estuary Hydrological Station and the configured functions, the functions of each multifunctional buoy are comprehensively considered.

7.2 Instance

As shown in the figure below, the green dots are the hydrological and meteorological monitoring points that have been built at the Pearl River Estuary, and the red dots are the locations of the proposed multi-functional buoys. From top to bottom, they are buoys in the south of Humen Bridge, the No. G3 of Ling-ding Bridge East, and Hong Kong-Zhuhai-Macao Bridge Police No. 7.

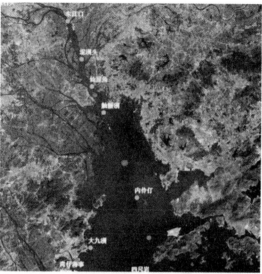

Fig. 4　position of multifunctional buoy (red dots)

The situation of the multifunctional buoys that has been put on the south of Hu-men Bridge is introduced as follows:

7.2.1 Placement analysis

Buoy in south of Humen Bridge is located at the junction of the inner and outer harbors of the Pearl River Estuary. It is located in the Chuan-bi Waterway, connected to the Da-hu Waterway and down to the Ling-ding Waterway, and the Pearl River Power Waterway crosses and converges. The location is very important, the navigation environment is extremely complicated, and the waters are windy and waves. The various elements of the flow have changed greatly, and the demand for various navigation information of past ships has been increasing, which is of great practical significance to the position monitoring.

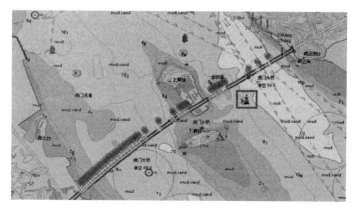

Fig. 5　The position of multifunctional buoy in south of Hu-men Bridge

In addition, the Hu-men Bridge water area has a large flow of ships and complicated hydrology and weather, which are not conducive to ship manipulation and are prone to collisions. The Xian-wu-jiao Hydrological Station within 2 miles from Hu-men Bridge has collected tide level, visibility, wind speed and direction. However, it lacks real-time and effective hydrological and meteorological information in the bridge area. At the same time, in order to strengthen the monitoring and management of buoys in the water area, multifunctional buoy equipped with weather meters, current meters, wave meters and video monitoring systems are set up at this point.

Fig. 6 multifunctional buoy in South of Hu-men Bridge

Top mark of the buoy is an isolated dangerous object mark. It will take the initiative to avoid this mark when the ship passes a bridge next to the main channel. The possibility of this buoy being hit by the ship is low, which can ensure long-term and stable data collection and transmission. The buoy and various equipments are more safer.

7.2.2 Power supply calculation

According to the aforementioned power supply design method, the capacity of the power supply battery for the buoy is calculated as follows:

$$BC = 1.1 \times 220.8 \times 20 \times 1/0.8 = 6072$$

Therefore, 5 pieces of 12V ~ 100Ah batteries are required.

For 12V, 100W solar panels,

The daily power generation capacity of a single solar panel = $100W \times 7.12h \times 0.6 = 427.2Wh$

8 pieces of solar panels generating electricity continuously for 2 days can meet the power required by the South of Humen Bridge buoy to work continuously for 20 days.

Energy consumption of South of Hu-men Bridge buoy   Tab. 2

Name of buoy	Equipped equipment	Actual power consumption (W/h)	Daily power consumption (WH)	Total power consumption WH(20days)	Single battery capacity	Number of batteries	Monocrystalline solar panel capacity	Number of solar panels
Buoy in South of Hu-men Bridge	Weather meter	0.20	220.8	4416	12V-100AH	5	100W	8

continue

Name of buoy	Equipped equipment	Actual power consumption (W/h)	Daily power consumption (WH)	Total power consumption WH(20days)	Single battery capacity	Number of batteries	Monocrystalline solar panel capacity	Number of solar panels
Buoy in South of Hu-men Bridge	Current meter	1.00	220.8	4416	12V-100AH	5	100W	8
	Wave meter	0.60						
	Video surveillance system	5.83						
	4G data transmission module	2.00						
	Data collector	2.00						

7.2.3 Instance for Data Acquisition System

Fig. 7 Data acquisition system in south of Hu-men brige buoy

8 Conclusions

Next, we will continue to optimize the research of multi-functional buoy, summarize experience based on the current actual use, and do the following tasks. The first is observing and calibrating the accuracy of hydrological and meteorological equipment. The second is to verify the stability of the system and the high reliability of information data return. The third is to contact and visit the meteorological department and the hydrological department to improve data utilization through data sharing. At present, data collection is placed on the cloud intranet of the Navigation guarantee center of south china sea. We will continue to conduct App and iPad application research. When the time is right, it will be linked to E-Navigation System of the Navigation guarantee center of south china sea to serve marine users.

References

[1] Liao Rong. et al. Fundamentals of Computer Information Technology[M]. Beijing: Tsinghua University Press. 2002.

[2] Zhang Dan, Ding Xiao-feng, Zeng Jian-ming. Microcomputer and Its Interface Technology[M]. Beijing: China Water Conservancy and Hydropower Press, 2010.

[3] Wang Zhi ying, Aids to Navigation[M]. Dalian: Dalian Maritime University Press, 1997.

[4] Maritime buoyage system (GB4696-2016) [S]. Beijing: China General Administration of Quality Supervision and Quarantine, 2016.

[5] Code of hydrology for habour and Waterways (JTS145-2015) [S]. Ministry of Transport of the People's Republic of China, 2015.

[6] Specification for Hydrological data auto-acquisiton and Tansmission System (SL61-2015) [S]. Ministry of Water Resources of the People's Republic of China, 2015.

[7] Design Code of Environmental Protection for Port Engineering (JTS149-1-2007) [S]. Ministry of Transport of the People's Republic of China, 2007.

第七篇 轨道交通

基于社会力模型的地铁站行人流组织优化研究

詹 郡 李昕光

(青岛理工大学机械及汽车工程学院)

摘 要 为了提升地铁站客运效率,应用社会力模型建立了青岛市井冈山路地铁站行人流仿真模型,识别其拥堵瓶颈点及敏感性位置,并对形成原因进行分析。以有效疏解拥堵点、平衡设施设备使用率为目标,基于以行人路径优化为主,以设施设备布局优化为辅的优化理念,提出了地铁站客流组织优化方法。优化仿真结果表明,设施设备使用率明显更为均衡,以安检区为代表的严重拥堵点疏解效果明显,提出的客流组合优化方案能够提高地铁站的客流组织效率。

关键词 城市轨道交通 行人流组织优化 社会力模型

0 引 言

作为地铁网络重要节点的地铁站,其客流的动态性与随机性容易导致客流量与客运效率的不平衡[1],在大客流环境下,极易引发区域内局部拥堵、排队过长等问题。国外研究多以行人路径优化为主,国内研究以实例研究为主,通过调研行人步速等属性,以及设施设备运行效率对实例进行研究[2-3],且多侧重于设施设备的角度,通过改变服务设施的数量、大小、位置,以及楼梯、扶梯、直梯等连接性服务设施的通行宽度实现优化目的,为解决实际问题起到明显效用[4-5],但在基于行人个体感知与心理因素对设施设备通过性影响方面的研究仍有不足。同时,由于地铁站内大多数布局具有可变更性弱的特点,更宜基于包括乘客与工作人员的行人流特点,从行人流组织优化角度出发,优化行人路径网络,进而实现优化目的。因此本文基于社会力模型,依据设施设备为主的空间布局、行人流线、站内行人行为等分析,以提高乘客出行的效率、便捷度及舒适性为目的,构建地铁站三维仿真模型,找到地铁站拥堵瓶颈点及敏感性位置,提出行人流组织优化方案。

1 地铁站流线分析

社会力模型是应用较为广泛的一种行人微观仿真模型,其主要是以受力的形式来解释行人在一定空间内的微观交通行为,并借助牛顿第二定律推导出行人的运动状态。MassMotion 软件基于社会力模型,以最小成本的行人逻辑为原则,可以从乘客感知和心理因素角度量化乘客在枢纽内设施选择的效用损失,体现排队长度、进站延迟时间、出入口单向使用、出入口优先使用权、通道宽度等因素以及各因素对行人路径选择的影响实现三维模型空间的仿真模拟。

地铁站一般分为站厅层、站台层两层。站厅层由非付费区与付费区两个区域构成,非付费区包括自动售票区、服务与信息咨询区、安检区、检票区。非付费区与付费区由护栏隔开。按照行人行为方向与行为目的,地铁流线可以分为进站流线、出站流线、中转流线、循环游走流线等。

2 地铁站行人流模型构建

基于空间与流线分析以及客流分析,地铁站模型主要由自动售票、自动检票、安检、站台、行人上下楼

基金项目:山东省自然科学基金面上项目(ZR2020MG017)。

等主要情景,及相应服务设施构成。通过设置半径、速度参数,区分结伴行人、携带行李行人、中老年行人、工作人员个人属性。其中,行人半径参数对行人流密度变化有重要影响作用。行人速度呈现正态分布。参数设置如表1所示。

行人个体属性参数 表1

行人类型	参数					
	半径(m)			速度(m/s)		
	最小值	最大值	平均值	最小值	最大值	平均值
标准行人	0.125	0.375	0.25	0.65	2.05	1.35
结伴行人	0.35	0.44	0.39	1	1.9	1.37
中老年行人	0.12	0.29	0.22	0.4	1.2	0.8
携带小行李行人	0.125	0.29	0.22	1.1	1.9	1.53
携带大行李行人	0.24	0.36	0.3	0.65	2.05	1.53

3 实例分析

3.1 青岛井冈山路地铁站三维仿真模型

井冈山路地铁站是目前青岛地铁13号线的端点站,也是未来青岛地铁网络的重要中转站。井冈山路地铁站整体呈狭长形,包含站厅层、站台层两层地下区域,以及出入口2个。地铁站配备的服务设施包括自动售票机9台、安检机2台、进出闸机28台、直梯组2组,自动扶梯与楼梯组4组。井冈山路地铁站三维仿真模型如图1所示。

图1 井冈山路地铁站三维仿真模型

3.2 拥堵瓶颈点及敏感性位置分析

结合仿真分析结果,可分析识别得到拥堵瓶颈点及敏感性位置。当客流量达到阈值后继续上升时,瓶颈点实际通行能力将逐渐下降,进而造成拥堵。

(1)行人最大密度分析

基于Fruin和IATA(国际航空运输协会)提出的服务水平,可以确定不同服务设施对应的拥堵瓶颈的密度最大值与空间最小值。A-F分别表示不同拥堵程度下对应的服务水平。当服务水平达到F等级时,即达到严重拥堵水平的阈值,可设定为拥堵瓶颈点参考值,如表2所示。

拥堵瓶颈点参考值 表2

服务设施参数	通道	楼梯	站台
密度(人/m²)	2.174	2.702	5.263
空间(m²/人)	0.46	0.37	0.19

分别以站厅层、站台层为观察对象,行人密度地图如图2、图3所示。红色区域即为服务水平达到F等级。

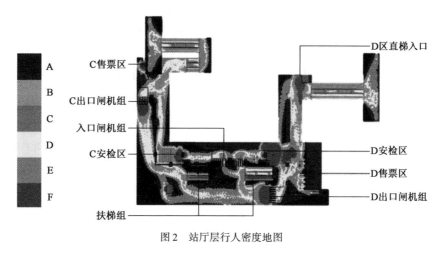

图2 站厅层行人密度地图

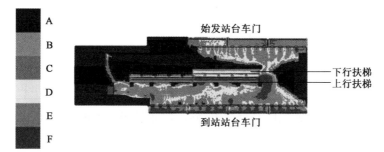

图3 站台层行人密度地图

由图中观察可知,站厅层C安检区与D安检区入口处拥堵最为严重;站厅层D区直梯入口、C售票区、站台层两扶梯入口处、出口闸机组出现明显拥堵;站厅层入口闸机组、下行扶梯、始发站各车门的使用率明显不均。

(2)行人流线分析

通过生成行人个体路线地图可以对行人流流线进行分析,得到行人流与区域间的关系,进而直观反应不同类型的行人在区域内的活动范围。井冈山路地铁站的站厅层与站台层的行人个体路线地图如图4所示。

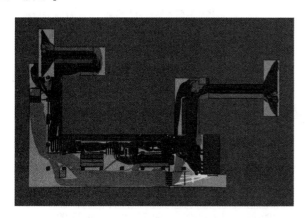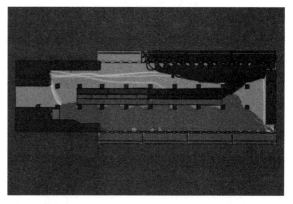

图4 站厅层(左)与站台层(右)个体路线地图

其中,蓝色流线代表进站流线,红色流线代表出站流线,黄色流线代表工作人员循环游走流线。通过行人流线交织情况,可观察到D区直梯入口、安检区入口、售票区处的出站与进站客流交织复杂,工作人员循环游走流线也经过此区域。结合最大密度地图可以判断出客流交织是该拥堵点或敏感性位置的主要成因。此外,经过观察发现,由于两扶梯组均为由西向东走向,进站行人选择自动检票机时,观察到一侧扶梯组入口较远,时间成本较高,因此基于最小成本原则,偏向于选择距离较近的扶梯组入口,进而造成多数人选择邻近车厢乘车,造成车门使用率严重不均衡,易产生拥堵现象。

(3)拥堵瓶颈点与敏感性位置及成因分析

基于仿真分析结果,可提取主要拥堵瓶颈点及敏感性位置,并分析其成因,如表3所示。

拥堵瓶颈点与敏感性位置及成因分析　　　　　　　　表3

	位　置	成　因　分　析
瓶颈点	C、D安检区入口	安检流程较慢,时间较长。尤其D安检入口处,进站客流与出站客流交织严重,拥堵现象严重
	出口自动检票机	自动检票机服务能力与输入客流不匹配,导致客流拥堵
	D区直梯入口	直梯与扶梯、楼梯的行走距离相近,且时间成本更低;直梯入口处在较为狭窄的直角区域,进站客流与出站客流严重交织
敏感性位置	上行扶梯	站内楼梯较长,选择楼梯上行的行走成本更高
	下行扶梯	两组扶梯运行方向相同,因此下行成本不同,造成使用率不平衡
	D2、D4售票机	处于售票机组靠近区域边界,行走距离较短,同时由于售票机间距较大,排队区域较宽阔,舒适度更高
	站台层始发站台	扶梯方向造成客流集中于站台东侧,进而导致车门使用率严重不平衡

站厅层安检区C和D的入口处拥堵最为严重;站厅层非付费区直梯入口、C售票机、站台层两扶梯入口处出现明显拥堵;站厅层入口闸机组、下行扶梯、始发站各车门的使用率明显不均衡。

3.3 客流组织优化

地铁站客流组织优化不仅需适应新地铁站的规划设计和设施设备布局优化,还应结合实际,考虑由于已建成设施设备的尺寸大小、所在位置等参数较为固定所产生的局限性。如井冈山路地铁站等已建成地铁站,更适于采用外界引导行人选择适当路径的客流组织优化方式。

(1)安检区人流量

安检区是站厅层严重拥堵瓶颈点,解决人流密集与设施设备使用率不均衡问题是该区域客流组织优化的主要目标。图5为优化前后安检区累积人流量对比图。由图5可知,相同时间段内,优化后C、D区安检区累积人流量总和提升、行人通行速率提高,设施设备使用率平衡性较优化前大幅提高。

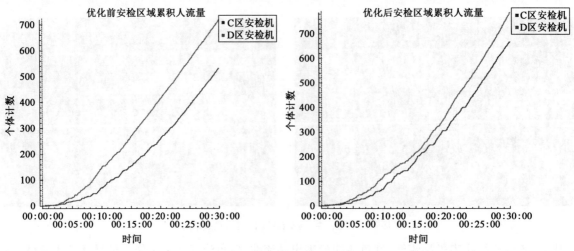

图5　优化前后安检机累积人流量对比

(2)行人密度

以行人密度为指标,观察整体优化效果,图6为站厅层优化前后的最大行人密度对比图,通过优化结果观察到,拥堵瓶颈点获得有效疏解,车门、安检机、自动扶梯等主要设施设备的使用率与平衡性明显提高。

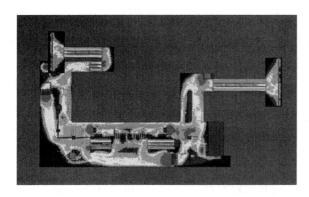
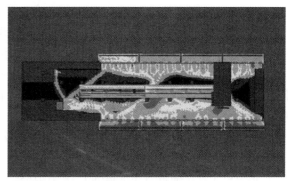

图6 优化后站厅层(左)与站台层(右)最大行人密度地图

4 结 语

本文应用社会力模型,以井冈山路地铁站为实例,在对地铁站设施调查和行人流分析的基础上,应用社会力模型进行了客流仿真分析,从行人密度、行人流线、排队线角度综合分析了拥堵瓶颈点与敏感性位置,并从行人路径优化与设施设备布局优化相结合的角度制定了合理的客流组织方案。本文为相似新站点的布局设计、已有站点的客流组织优化提供参考方法,同时也为后续井冈山路地铁站向中转、换乘站转型提供研究基础。

参考文献

[1] 邓紫欢,胡华,胥旋.考虑时空特性的地铁车站大客流预警方法研究[J].中国安全生产科学技术,2020(16):24-28.

[2] 王雨佳.城市轨道交通车站站台行人跟随行为仿真模型研究[D].北京:北京交通大学,2019.

[3] 张达奇.基于MassMotion的城市轨道交通换乘枢纽客流组织方案评估[D].深圳:深圳大学,2019.

[4] 王存秋,李超辉.基于Anylogic的北九水站客流组织仿真研究[J].交通科技与经济,2020,22(121):34-36.

[5] 姜彦璘.基于社会力模型的城市轨道交通换乘站客流组织仿真与优化研究[D].西安:长安大学,2018.

既有线运用27t轴重货车经济效益研究

宋文波

(中国铁路成都局集团有限公司)

摘 要 在分析27t轴重货车的适车货流和运输组织模式的基础上,以获得的收益最大化为目标,基于0-1整数规划方法构建经济效益模型,并设计模拟退火求解算法。以哈尔滨局和沈阳局为对象进行案例分析,运用设计的算法求解,结果表明:哈尔滨局和沈阳局运用27t轴重货车采用装车地直达模式时,

---

基金项目:中国铁路总公司科技研究开发计划(2014X002-B)。

获得的收益为7.44亿元,需要改造的线路里程数为6926km,并给出相应的线路改造方案。所构建模型为定量分析27t轴重货车运用的效益提供依据。

关键词 铁路运输 27t轴重 0-1整数规划 经济效益 改造方案

0 引言

提高货车轴重是重载运输发展的方向,在既有线上运用大轴重货车是实现扩能的主要途径。既有线运用27t轴重货车能有效提高列车牵引质量,增加运能、满足货运需求、提高运输效率。

对于重载运输问题,许多学者已经进行了深入研究[1-7]。文献[1]研究了中国铁路货物列车编组计划问题。文献[2-4]研究了既有线发展重载运输的技术经济及效益问题。文献[5-7]研究了27t轴重货车运用模式及技术经济问题。既有研究主要集中在重载运输对运输组织模式和设备设施的要求,对27t轴重货车在实践推广运用中的经济效益问题研究较少,并且对既有线采用重载运输进程中线路改造方案的研究较少。

本文给出了27t轴重货车实际推广运用中经济效益问题的定量研究方法,在对既有线运用27t轴重货车的经济效益定量分析的基础上,以收益最大化为目标建立模型,设计模拟退火求解算法,并给出既有线运用27t轴重货车的线路改造方案。

1 问题分析

只有充分利用27t轴重货车的载重能力,才能达到既有线扩能效果。由于27t轴重货车有其特殊性,因此在对运用27t轴重货车效益定量研究时,必须分析适应27t轴重货车的货物品类和运输组织模式。

1.1 适应27t轴重货车的货物分析

铁路货车装载能力利用率取决于重量和容积。密度较大的货物品类受轴重的限制,存在亏容;密度较小的货物受货车体积及机车车辆限界的限制,存在亏重。以比重较大的敞车为例,不同类型敞车在满载满容条件下货物品类合理密度值如表1所示。

各类型敞车参数及满载满容状态下的货物合理密度值　　表1

参　　数	C64(通用)	C70(通用)	C80(大秦线专用)	27t轴重通用敞车
标记载重(t)	61	70	80	80
轴重(t)	21	23	25	27
自重(t)	≤23	24	20	26.5
容积(m³)	73.3	80.8	87	92
比体积(t/m³)	1.20	1.15	1.09	1.15
满载满容状态下合理密度(t/m³)	0.832	0.866	0.920	0.870

表1中,27t轴重通用敞车装载货物的最佳密度值为0.870t/m³,考虑到该类货车高度距机车车辆限界较近,无法采用起脊装载等措施,因此最佳密度值下调空间较小。与铁路通用货车C70相比,密度小于0.712t/m³的货物,满容状态下实际轴重小于23t,装载货物吨数为65.5t,利用27t轴重货车扩能效果不如采取扩容措施的C70。由于27t轴重通用敞车自重较大,与C70比较,考虑到C70货车采用起脊装载等措施,密度大于0.761t/m³的货物采用27t轴重通用敞车扩能效果明显。

1.2 既有线运用27t轴重货车运输组织模式分析

由于27t轴重货车的特殊性,在既有线上运用27t轴重货车要受线路条件、桥隧涵条件、驼峰条件、列车编组条件影响。因此在不同技术条件和货车生产数量限制下,需制定与技术条件相适应的运输组织模式,如表2所示[5]。

既有线应用 27t 轴重货车在不同条件下的运输组织模式   表 2

对应的条件	运输组织模式			
	全通用模式	装车地直达模式	技术站直达模式	限制区域模式
线路通过条件	所有线路满足	主要径路线路满足	主要径路线路满足	区域内线路满足
驼峰解体条件	所有驼峰满足	不满足	不满足	区域内所有驼峰满足
桥隧涵条件	所有桥隧涵满足	装卸站之间满足	技术站之间满足	区域满足
列车混编条件	满足	不限	不限	满足
27t 轴重货车数量	大	小	较小	按区域确定
运输需求	不限	集中、稳定	集中、稳定	不限

2 经济效益模型的构建

为了加快货物送达、减少铁路运营支出和充分利用铁路运输能力,车流应沿经济、合理的径路输送,本文假设车流以最短径路输送。在计算既有线运用 27t 轴重货车的收益时,应考虑收入效益及成本费用。由于影响 27t 轴重货车运用收入和成本的因素比较复杂,难以清算,本文以运用 27t 轴重货车增加的直接运输收益和线路改造费用两个指标来衡量其经济效益,确定在特定的运输组织模式下,根据现有货运需求,决定线路改造方案。

假设研究的铁路路网图为 $G=(V,A)$,其由各铁路站点集合 V 和各站点间的路段 a 组成, $a=1 \cdots n$;各站点间的距离为 L_a;既有线运用 27t 轴重货车可以采用的运输组织模式为 k, $k \in K$; F_{ijk} 为从 i 站到 j 站采用运输组织模式 k 时的货流量大小,其中 $i,j \in V$; ρ_{ij} 表示从 i 站到 j 站运送的货物品类的密度; r_{ij} 表示从 i 站运送货物到 j 站的最短径路; $A(r_{ij})$ 表示 i 站到 j 站间最短径路 r_{ij} 上的路段集合; $L(r_{ij})$ 表示 i 站到 j 站间最短径路 r_{ij} 的距离; C 表示改造每公里线路所花费的成本; R 表示增加单位货物周转量所获得的收益,根据现行的货物运价率计算; x_a 为决策变量,表示所经由的路段是否需要被改造,如需要改造,则 $x_a=1$,否则 $x_a=0$;定义 0-1 变量 $\delta_a^{i,j}$,其表示路段 a 是否位于 i 站到 j 站间最短路径 r_{ij} 上,若 $a \in A(r_{ij})$,则 $\delta_a^{i,j}=1$,否则 $\delta_a^{i,j}=0$;定义 0-1 变量 r_{ij}^c,表示 i 站到 j 站间最短路径 r_{ij} 是否改造,若 $\sum_{a=1}^{n} \delta_a^{i,j} \cdot x_a = 1$,则 $r_{ij}^c = 1$;否则 $r_{ij}^c = 0$。

目标函数为特定区域运用 27t 轴重货车所获得的收益最大化:

$$\max f = \sum_{a=1}^{n} \sum_{k \in K} \sum_{i,j \in V} [F_{i,j,k} \cdot L(r_{ij}) \cdot x_a \cdot r_{ij}^c \cdot R - L_a \cdot x_a \cdot C] \tag{1}$$

约束条件如下:

(1)采用运输组织模式 k 时,两站间的货流需求大小应满足运输组织模式 k 对日均发送货车数的要求:

$$F_{ijk} \geq F_k \tag{2}$$

F_k 表示运输组织模式 k 对两站间日均发送货车数的最小要求;

(2)采用运输组织模式 k 组织货物运输时,两站间最短径路上的各路段牵引定数大小必须满足运输组织模式 k 对线路区段牵引定数的要求:

$$\sum_{i,j \in V} \sum_{a=1}^{n} \delta_a^{i,j} \cdot \alpha_a \geq \alpha_k \tag{3}$$

α_a 表示路段 a 的牵引定数大小, α_k 表示既有线运用 27t 轴重货车采用运输组织模式 k 组织货物运输时,按列车满重或满长编组条件下对线路区段牵引定数大小的最低要求。其中,按列车编组的空重车数比例不同,区段牵引定数大小的最低要求取值也相应不同。

(3) 所运送货物的密度必须满足27t轴重货车对货物密度值的要求。

$$\rho_{ij} \geq \rho \tag{4}$$

ρ 表示运用27t轴重货车对货物品类密度值的最小要求。

式(1)~式(4)构成了既有线运用27t轴重货车经济效益模型。

3 求解算法

由于模型是0-1非线性整数规划问题,对于一个路网来说,路段的数量较多,导致决策变量较多,而当改造某些路段时,所改造的路段可能构不成最短径路,这样的解并不是可行解,并且会导致运算效率降低。为了提高运算效率、减少变量的数量,因此在设计算法时,先确定改造的最短径路,再确定改造的路段。针对模型特点,本文设计模拟退火算法求解,得出相应结论。

目标函数计算方法:用 A_1 表示需要改造的路段的集合。若 $r_{ij}^c=1$,路段 $a \in A(r_{ij})$ 且 $a \notin A_1$,则 $A_1 = A_1 \cup a$。用 F_1 表示最短径路改造后可以开行的货流的集合,F_{gmk} 表示采用运输组织模式 k 组织货物运输时,g 站到 m 站之间的货流量大小,若 $r_{ij}^c=1$,$A(r_{gm}) \subset A(r_{ij})$ 且 $F_{gmk} \notin F_1$,则 $F_1 = F_1 \cup F_{gmk}$。根据得到的集合 A_1 计算改造成本 C,根据集合 F_1 计算总收益 R,则目标函数 $f = R - C$。模拟退火算法的步骤如下:

(1) 指定算法参数,初始温度 T_0,降温参数 α,并设 $p=1, q=0$;

(2) 读取基本数据,即从数据文件中读取运用27t轴重货车后,各站之间适应27t轴重货车的货物增加的货运量和各路段牵引定数数据;

(3) 根据运输组织模式 k 对货流量大小的要求,对货流筛选;

(4) 根据筛选后的数据文件,利用Floyd算法,计算各站之间的最短径路的距离 $L(r_{ij})$ 及各站之间最短径路的路段集合 $A(r_{ij})$;

(5) 计算各站之间的最短径路 r_{ij} 的数量 N,随机产生 N 个 $0-1$ 整数,作为初始解 S_0,r_{ij}^c 为1表示最短径路进行了改造,否则 r_{ij}^c 为0;计算 $f' = f(S_0)$,令 $S_1 = S_0$;

(6) 随机产生一个 $0 \sim N$ 之间的整数 h,若 $S_1(h)=1$,则 $S_1(h)=0$,否则 $S_1(h)=1$,则产生新解 $S_2 = S_1$;

(7) 根据产生的新解,判断各路段的牵引定数是否满足第 k 种运输组织模式对区段牵引定数的要求。若满足,则 $\overline{f'} = f(S_2)$,计算 $\Delta f = \overline{f'} - f'$,并转向下一步;否则,返回步骤6;

(8) 根据Metroplis准则判断是否接受新解,具体如下,当 $\Delta f > 0$ 时,令 $S_1 = S_2$;$f' = \overline{f'}$;当 $\Delta f < 0$ 时,产生一个 $[0,1]$ 之间的随机数 ξ,如果 $\exp(\Delta f/T) > \xi$,则令 $S_1 = S_2$;$f' = \overline{f'}$,进入下一步;否则,不接受新解,转步骤6;

(9) 内循环 $q = q+1$,转步骤6;

(10) 给定数值 Num,当迭代 Num 次解不发生变化时,终止计算;

(11) 温度下降,执行 $T_{p+1} = T_p \times \alpha$。

4 案例分析

4.1 基础数据

沈阳局和哈尔滨局是装车地直达运输比较集中的路局,非常适合应用27t轴重货车。因此本文将哈尔滨局和沈阳局作为整体,以采用装车地直达模式为例,利用上述模型和算法对其进行优化,确定收益最大情况下的沈阳局和哈尔滨局的线路改造方案,路网如图1所示。

线路改造项目的投资回收期对线路改造的规模有很大的影响。投资回收期短,每年的线路改造费较大,根据现有货运需求,线路改造规模较小;反之,线路改造的规模较大。在实际计算线路改造方案过程中,应对改造项目的投资回收期进行具体研究,得出每年合理的线路改造费用。根据文献[7],本文以投资回收期 10 年为例,则哈尔滨局和沈阳局每年的线路改造费用为 3.6 万元/km,给出收益最大情况下的线路改造方案。

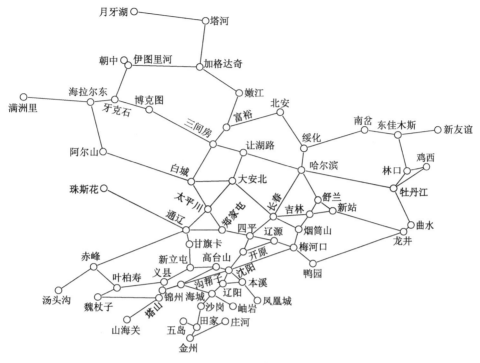

图 1 沈阳局和哈尔滨局路网图

4.2 模拟退火算法求解结果

利用 MATLAB 进行编程,取 $T_0 = 1000, \alpha = 0.9, Num = 15$,得到的优化迭代过程如图 2 所示,线路改造方案如图 3 所示。图 3 中虚线是需要改造的路段,沈阳局和哈尔滨局利用 27t 轴重货车,采用装车地直达方案时获得的收益为 7.44 亿元,需要改造的线路里程数为 6926km。

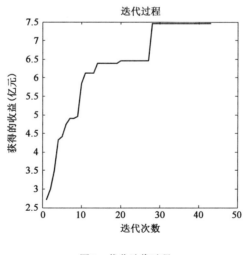

图 2 优化迭代过程

4.3 结果分析

根据图 3 的线路改造方案,沈阳局和哈尔滨局利用 27t 轴重货车可以开行的装车地直达车流如表 3 所示。

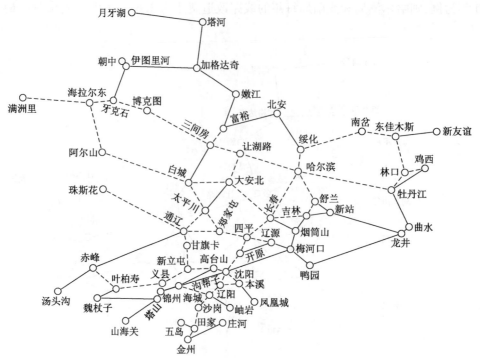

图 3 线路改造方案

运用 27t 轴重货车开行的装车地直达流　　　　　　　　　　　　表 3

装车站	卸车站	装车站	卸车站	装车站	卸车站
金州	本溪	满洲里	南岔	辽阳	沙岗
金州	沟帮子	鸡西	东佳木斯	珠斯花	沈阳
锦州	赤峰	海拉尔东	吉林	赤峰	锦州
珠斯花	金州	鸡西	本溪	珠斯花	锦州
珠斯花	吉林	富裕	让湖路	叶柏寿	锦州
吉林	金州	林口	海城	沙岗	珠斯花
珠斯花	开原	海拉尔东	长春	开原	金州
珠斯花	辽源	东佳木斯	海城	海城	金州
珠斯花	塔山	东佳木斯	吉林	本溪	金州
珠斯花	白城	本溪	沙岗	沙岗	吉林
海拉尔东	东佳木斯	开原	沙岗	辽阳	海城
让湖路	金州	吉林	沙岗	沙岗	海城
海拉尔东	牡丹江	海城	沙岗	开原	海城
珠斯花	高台山	珠斯花	郑家屯	金州	海城
珠斯花	长春	珠斯花	通辽	义县	叶柏寿
金州	沈阳	沙岗	本溪	珠斯花	四平
海拉尔东	哈尔滨	沈阳	本溪	哈尔滨	让湖路
牡丹江	哈尔滨	牙克石	三间房	满洲里	海城
海拉尔东	三间房	海拉尔东	绥化	满洲里	沙岗
海拉尔东	让湖路	海拉尔东	白城	本溪	沈阳

5 结 语

(1)针对既有线运用27t轴重货车经济效益问题,构建了经济效益模型对问题进行定量分析,并以哈尔滨局和沈阳局为例进行计算,得出运用装车地直达模式可获得的收益及其需要改造的线路和车流组织方案。

(2)在构建模型时对27t轴重货车的收益及其成本问题进行了简化处理,没有考虑车流的特定径路和线路改造项目的投资回收期问题,因此考虑这些因素更加切合实际的模型构建问题将是今后研究的方向。

参考文献

[1] Lin B L, Wang Z M, Ji L J, et al. Optimizing the Freight Train Connection Service Network of a Large-scale Rail System[J]. Transportation Research Part B, 2012(46):649-667.
[2] 杜旭生. 铁路既有线发展重载运输的模式研究[J]. 铁道货运, 2013, 10:1-11.
[3] 王东, 闫平, 乔延洪, 等. 铁路重载运输效益评价研究[J]. 中国铁路, 2008, 10:13-16.
[4] 范振平, 魏玉光, 林柏梁. 重载运输扩能的效益分析[J]. 物流技术, 2007, 26(4):47-49.
[5] 宋文波, 赵鹏. 既有线运用27t轴重货车运输组织模式研究[J]. 综合运输, 2015, 37(10):87-92.
[6] 朱小军. 既有线应用27t轴重货车运输组织问题研究[D]. 北京:北京交通大学, 2013.
[7] 西南交通大学. 既有线运用27t轴重货车技术经济论证[R]. 成都:西南交通大学, 2013.

对东北地区高铁运输组织管理的观察与思考

程显平

(京沈客专辽宁公司(哈大客专公司))

摘 要 本文简要介绍了当前中国高铁建设和运营的新成就,客观分析了东北地区高铁运输组织管理中存在的一些问题,从运输组织原则和车站设置等方面探寻问题的根源,提出改进建议和具体措施,并以此为切入点,重点阐述在高铁运输管理理念方面的新思考,为推进全国高铁网络运输管理的综合现代化水平提供新思路。

关键词 中国高铁 运输组织 存在问题 改进措施

0 引 言

中国高铁建设成就举世瞩目,每年都有新的亮点和发展,国家"十二五"计划的"四纵四横"高铁网络已全部建设完成,在此基础上列入"十三五"规划的"八纵八横"高铁网络正在建设中。2018年设计速度400km/h的"复兴号"新型高速动车组正式上线运行,标志着中国在高速动车组设计制造技术上已经处于世界领先地位。中国高铁不但在线路建设和设备制造上取得了伟大的成就,在高铁运营管理和运输组织方面,也是成果丰硕,高铁路网运营规模、高铁动车组开行数量和旅客发送量均高居世界首位。目前,全国高铁运营里程已超过2.9万公里,日均开行动车组列车5000余趟,为广大旅客提供了更加安全优质、快捷、舒适的出行服务,社会效益十分显著;从铁路企业自身来看,高铁客运收入也成为运输收入不可或缺的重要组成部分,成为铁路企业经济效益新的重要增长点。

与法日德等老牌高铁强国相比,中国高铁从无到有,从起步到赶超,在短短20年间实现跨越式发展,成绩卓著,全国人民为之振奋和自豪,但我们在看到成绩的同时,还要客观地理性地思考和看待当前我国高铁建设和运营管理中存在的问题,并积极探讨和研究改进措施及管理方法,挖掘运输潜力、提高运输效率、节约运输成本,实现高铁运营领域的改革创新,不断进步。

笔者作为高铁运营领域的财务管理人员,结合工作实际,用了一年左右的时间深入沈、哈两局集团公司调查研究,走访了东北地区的哈大、京沈等主要高铁沿线车站,乘坐各类动车组列车,研究列车运行图和客运组织相关文件电报等资料,分析大量统计数据,从中发现了很多问题,并针对这些问题进行深入思考,提出了一些解决方案与措施,下面从问题与不足、问题原因、改进方案与措施三个方面进行研究探讨和分析认证。

1 东北地区高铁运输管理上存在的问题和不足

1.1 运能运力分布不合理,调整不及时

铁路旅客运输的方向性、季节性、时段性比较突出,有些区段或时段"一票难求",而多数区段和时段又运力过剩。我们通过跟踪调研发现,东北地区进京和一些直达列车座位利用率较高外,大部分车次都是有些区段不足有些区段过剩,例如从承德南到大连北的G3727次列车,朝阳至沈阳间一直客流很大,到沈阳后又经常性的有沈阳-辽阳间短途客流加入其中,而辽阳站过后客流则明显下降,区段客流密度差异十分显著。特别是核心城市圈的周边客流密度明显高于其他区段,客流密度比较大的区段是沈阳-辽阳间,沈阳-本溪间、沈阳-阜新间,而辽阳、本溪、阜新以外的客流密度并不是很大,客座利用率不是很高,说明我们的运行图安排还是和客流特点有些脱节,客观上造成一些区段满足不了旅客的需要,而另一些区段又出现运力过剩。铁路旅客运输的固有特征要求运输服务的供给方必须根据客流的不同特点合理调整运力,最大限度地实现动力的供需平衡。

1.2 部分中间站的旅客需求没有得到满足

哈大高铁于2012年12月1日正式开通运营,几年来各高铁站间还存在着一些运输"死角",个别中间站之间互不通车,通过多次调整列车运行图,目前状况虽已有很大改观,但还是不能完全满足旅客的需要。部分车站列车间隔太长,首车太晚末车太早;或者只有本线列车停靠,缺少长途跨线列车,增加换乘频次等问题,目前看,比较突出的问题有两个方面,一是一些中间站的需求得不到满足,比如海城西站有很多西柳大集的服装上货旅客,遍布东北的一些中小城市,高铁动车还不能完全满足这些旅客的需求,二是沈阳周边城市圈的短途旅客需求比较大,在车次安排上,还不能完全满足旅客的需求,例如沈阳晚上回阜新和朝阳的动车,除了六点左右的一趟外,就是晚上九点的了,中间再没动车了,旅客普遍反映中间应该加一趟动车。

1.3 三大省会城市之间交流不畅

哈大高铁自开通运营以来,本线开行的跨局列车绝大多数是哈尔滨-大连间的长交路列车,由于受到维修"天窗"时间的限制,哈尔滨到大连的最后一趟列车发车较早,以现行列车运行图为例,哈尔滨-大连间最后一趟G728次列车哈尔滨西站始发时间是18:32,终到大连北站的时间是22:53,此后当日再无大连方向列车,哈尔滨到长春、沈阳及沿线各站的旅客除G728次别无选择。同样的原因,途经长春第一班到达哈尔滨的动车是大连北站始发的G701次,长春西站9:11发车,时间有些晚;东北四大城市除大连外,其他三个省会城市沈阳、长春和哈尔滨之间的高铁列车早晨发车晚、夜间收车早,使得拥有几千万人口的三大省会城市这一东北地区最大的客流市场潜力没有充分挖掘,旅客出行选择受到限制,影响了三大省会城市之间的沟通和交流,说明高铁运输供给还不完全到位,服务质量还有待于进一步提高,铁路企业的运输收入和经济效益也受到了一定程度的影响。

1.4 高峰时段的运输能力依然不足

现行列车运行图已经考虑到了高峰客流的需要,除日常运行线以外,还铺画了周末线和高峰线,但还是不能满足早晚通勤高峰和周末高峰的运输需求。一是开行能力有限,有时确实不能在局部区段开行更多的列车,二是受到长交路列车折返时间限制,很多区段顾及不到早晚短途旅客的出行需求。总体来看,日均运力能够满足主要车站旅客发送量的需要,但是在时间安排上确实无法完全满足所有车站旅客出行的需求,导致部分旅客流失。

1.5 普铁列车挤占部分高铁客流

沈阳局集团公司2018年全年发送旅客24,261万人,其中:普铁发送13,474万人,占比55.54%,高铁发送10,787万人,占比44.46%,与全路高铁发送人数占总发送人数60%的比率相比明显偏低。沈阳局集团公司管内高铁营业里程2909km,占管内营业里程13834km的21%,与全路22%的占比相当,说明东北地区的高铁利用率与全路相比还存在较大差距。而普铁发送人数中,硬座11,020万人,占普铁旅客的81.78%。这就直接导致了高铁客运收入率偏低,整体效益受到较大影响。我们对辽阳站列车到发及客流情况进行了重点调查分析:辽阳站是高铁和普铁混合站,每天到发普铁列车20对左右,高铁动车组列车30对左右,2018年全年发送旅客370万人,其中普铁195.5万人,占比52.79%,高铁174.8万人,占比47.21%,而普铁中硬座人数为179.4万人,占比91.79%,假如这部分硬座客流中50%目的地是沈阳,硬座与高铁二等座客票差价是17元,如果这些旅客改乘高铁,每年将增收1500万元以上,可见,高铁和普铁对铁路企业增收增效的影响还是很大的,在客观条件允许的情况下,大城市之间应该优先安排高铁运输。

2 高铁运输组织存在问题的原因分析

2.1 现行的高铁客运组织原则存在问题

哈大高铁的客运组织原则是"以长带短",跨局列车大部分实行长交路,哈大线动车始发、终到站基本都是哈尔滨西站和大连北站。本线列车如此,一些跨线动车也是这个原则。局管内动车也基本是在沈阳—大连间和沈阳—长春(吉林)间往返开行,除沈阳—本溪间安排有短途列车外,沈阳—辽阳间无始发终到列车,而沈阳—辽阳间是整个哈大线客流密度最大的区段,类似的区段还有一些,开行对数和客流密度不相符合,原因首先在于客运组织原则。"以长带短"的运输组织原则初衷没有错,这样的组织原则有利于合理安排客运、车辆和机务乘务交路,有利于动车组的夜间整备,也有利于运输调度指挥。

按传统习惯,我们在考虑安排列车运行线时一般都是优先考虑客座率,而对区段客流密度则难以兼顾,二者比较而言,客流密度能更加准确地反映旅客需求。根据沈阳局集团公司统计部门2018年的客流密度统计(客报四),我们对比沈(阳)—大(连)和沈(阳)—丹(东)两个区段的客流密度数据,考虑到高铁和普铁并行,包括普铁和高铁的上下行平均密度,不难发现客流密度的差异:沈阳—本溪间为70,205百人/km,本溪—丹东间为49,794百人/km,后者仅占前者的70%;沈阳—海城段客流密度为207,074百人/km,瓦房店—大连段为159,803百人/km,后者也仅是前者的77%;区段客流密度统计没有沈阳—辽阳间,如果单独统计这一段,密度应该高于沈阳—本溪间。可见区段客流密度差异还是很大的,而现行运行图却很少安排区段短途列车,按照以长带短的原则基本都是全线开行。

"以长带短"的列车开行原则造成的另外一个弊端,就是在时间上满足不了每个区段的旅客出行需求,特别是上下行动车的后半程基本都错过了早晚高峰时间段,既不能有效满足旅客的需求,也客观上造成了部分旅客的流失。

2.2 以路局集团公司所在地为中心的辐射模式存在弊端

路局集团公司所在地都是省会城市,即是动车段(所)所在地,也是客运段及旅服机构所在地,还是几条高铁线路的交汇点,作为客运中心枢纽向周边辐射是必然的,但是,客流的走向却是多样性的,有多点目的地,有些中间站所在的中小城市依托商业集散中心或者重点旅游景点,也成了客流集中点,比如海城西站因为西柳镇是东北的服装加工集散中心,辐射整个东北地区,黑龙江和吉林两省的客流也不小,同时海城西站又处于沈大高速和盘营高铁交汇的枢纽位置,很有必要作为客运分中心安排一定数量到达牡丹江、佳木斯和吉林等东北重要城市的始发终到列车;和海城类似的城市还有鲅鱼圈、本溪、阜新、承德等,都有不少的客流,也具备办理一定数量动车到发作业的条件,完全可以成为客运分中心,满足旅客出行的多目的需求,缓解路局集团公司所在城市客运中心枢纽的压力。

2.3 高铁车站现状对客运组织有很大的制约

(1)高铁站设置较远影响了高铁客流

高铁站的设置地点对客流的影响很大,同样都是地级市,辽阳和铁岭由于高铁站距离市中心的远近不同,客流的差异十分巨大。辽阳站由于是旧站改造,位置处于市中心,老百姓往返沈阳就像坐公交车一样,每天客流爆满,早晚高峰时间段有时一票难求,很多旅客被迫改乘普铁列车或公路长途客车,这一部分旅客随即流失。而铁岭高铁站铁岭西站远离市区和开发区,从市中心乘坐公交到高铁站的时间与在铁岭站乘坐普铁列车直接到达沈阳站的时间总体相当,高铁时间优势无法发挥,高票价的弊端却完全暴露,沈阳—铁岭间的短途旅客极少选择高铁出行。辽阳、铁岭西两个高铁车站地位相当,发送人数却相差一倍左右,既浪费了高铁运力资源,又满足不了旅客的出行需求;像铁岭西这样的高铁车站还有瓦房店西、开原西、营口东等,由于客流少又导致了停靠的动车减少,形成了不良循环,长此以往,部分车站的运力大量闲置,高铁优质资源得不到充分利用,铁路经济效益也必将受到影响。在其他的高铁线路上,这种情况也普遍存在,例如哈尔滨局集团公司管内的是哈(尔滨)—牡(丹江)客专(高铁)线,中间站基本都远离主城区,加之沿线原有普铁线路分享客流,高铁对沿线百姓的吸引力不大,绝大部分客流都是在始发和终到站乘降,哈牡客专实际上仅仅发挥了哈尔滨—牡丹江间城际铁路的作用。

(2)枢纽站能力不足制约了动车开行

高铁主要枢纽站的能力不足不是体现在传统的站房面积问题上,而是指站场接发车能力不足。高铁多数中间站基本都是两台两线或三台四道线布置,办理列车短时站停作业不存在问题,但如果办理列车始发终到作业则能力紧张,一些客流较大的中间站都存在类似问题。而作为中心枢纽的主要车站问题最为突出,比如沈阳站和沈阳北站是几条高铁线路交汇的枢纽站,哈大、京沈和沈丹三条高铁在此交汇,现在每条高铁线路开行动车能力占用率基本也就是设计能力的三分之一,但枢纽站能力已经趋于饱和,成了制约高铁运能的"瓶颈"。

3 对于改进当前一些问题的思考及措施建议

3.1 改变观念,调整客运组织原则

从东北地区的情况来看,除哈大高铁沿线的哈尔滨、长春、沈阳和大连四个大城市外,黑龙江、吉林、辽宁三个省的客流情况不尽相同:黑龙江省主要是哈尔滨与齐齐哈尔、大庆、佳木斯、牡丹江四个城市之间的客流;吉林主要是长春与吉林、白城等城市之间的客流;而辽宁省除沈大沿线客流外,其他大部分客流则主要集中在沈阳周边的城市圈,沈阳与辽阳、抚顺、本溪、铁岭组成了一个人口密集、经济发达的城市圈,在这个城市圈内,铁岭市因为高铁站距离市区太远而流失了大部分旅客,辽阳和本溪的客流密度都比较大。省内客流的特点非常值得重视,运输供给企业应该根据这一实际情况,改变服务理念,具体体现就是在编制列车运行图时应该对传统的"以长带短"原则进行适当调整,要结合城市圈区域客流特点,重点安排开行城际动车组列车、区段短途动车组列车以及早晚高峰时段的通勤列车,即将现行的"以长带短"运输组织原则调整优化为"以长带短、区段加密"的原则。短途车密度加大后,长途车可适时减少站停次数,增加一站直达的动车比例,让高铁更加充分地发挥出速度优势,而短途车宜根据客流情况增加停站频次,长短途列车各自分担主要客流,分别满足长、短途旅客的不同出行需求,特别是要最大限度地满足早晚高峰期通勤客流和周末、节假日突发客流的密集出行需求。变"以长带短"运输组织原则为"以长带短、区段加密"原则,对铁路运输企业来说,一方面能够提高高铁的运输收入,另一方面又能减少低密度区段的动车运力过剩,节约运营成本,是铁路企业增收节支、节能创效的一个有效途径;从旅客需求方面看,"长途快捷、短途便利"的运输供给服务会更加贴心,更加适合旅客的出行密度和出行时间需求,最大限度地体现出高铁运输的社会效益。

3.2 公交化开行,满足城市圈的需求

核心城市圈内提高列车开行密度,实行公交化开行,这里重点强调"公交化"的概念,即首、末班车制

度。有些规模较小的高铁站接近中午时分才有去往大城市的列车,相反下午从大城市返回的可乘坐车次又很少,限制了旅客的出行选择。有效的解决措施之一是实行首、末班车制度,即在大城市周边实行早晚站站停车,为早晚出行的"准通勤"旅客提供可靠保证,用高铁的深度服务,拓宽百姓生活的空间和时间,同时,这也是铁路运输企业最大限度地争取客流和增加客运收入的一个有效手段。

3.3 打破局间限制,统筹东北地区的运力安排

沈阳、哈尔滨两个铁路局集团公司之间应该加强沟通和协作,统一考虑和安排东北地区高铁网的运能运力,在"全国一张网、全路一盘棋"的前提下,系统做好东北局域网的统一筹划,扩大视野和战略布局,改变目前以沈阳和哈尔滨两个路局集团公司所在地为中心、以主干线为重点的传统格局,实现更加密布和交织复杂、覆盖面更广的高铁列车运行图,在保证主干线运输能力,确保主干线畅通的同时,尽最大可能满足其他各个地区的局部需要,吸引更多的高铁客流,以高铁优势资源推动中国东北老工业基地区域性协调发展。

3.4 统筹安排,提高枢纽站的发送能力

枢纽站能力饱和,成为高铁运能的制约瓶颈,虽是一个不争的事实,但还是可以采取一些可行办法适当分流,缓解枢纽站能力紧张的现状,以下是笔者一些不成熟的建议:

(1)沈丹客专非重点时段的"D"字头列车宜逐渐改在沈阳南站始发、终到,同时最大限度地压缩在沈阳站折返时间,释放沈阳站的部分接发车能力。

(2)取消部分长途列车在中间枢纽站的客运业务和站停作业,比如由哈尔滨西站、长春站、吉林站和丹东站始发终到北京、大连等地的"D"字头列车近半数具备在沈阳枢纽通过的条件,不必所有列车都在沈阳站或沈阳北站停靠办理客运业务。

(3)高峰时段尽量开行重连动车组列车,减少对高铁线路尤其是枢纽站的能力占用。根据客流市场变化情况,对于客流比较大的车次都应该考虑采用重连编组,一方面能够提高运输效率,另一方面也会大大降低运营成本,按照国铁集团清算原则,开行一列重连动车组的线路使用费仅相当于开行两列单组列车的75%左右。

(4)增加枢纽以外中间站的始发终到车次,今年哈尔滨局集团公司开行了哈尔滨西—鲅鱼圈的G4036/5次列车,既能满足夏季哈尔滨游客去鲅鱼圈旅游的需要,又不占用大连枢纽的运输能力,类似这样的车具备条件的应考虑多开,而且可以考虑在沈阳枢纽通过。除鲅鱼圈外,本溪、辽阳、阜新、四平东等车站都可以作为始发终到站,沈阳枢纽的压力将得到有效释放。

(5)适应短途列车实行公交化开行的需要,对部分车站站区进行更新改造,考虑为公交化列车单独开设"绿色通道",接入普速场或另建简易站台和进出口,不挤占沈阳站高速场的到发线能力。从城市布局和远期发展来看,沈阳站的客车整备库外迁,对于改善周边环境状况非常有利,也可以考虑延伸利用原西站、东站和南站等周边车站。

(6)尽快打通京哈直通线。笔者认为原来设计预留的京哈直通线是比较科学的,一旦京沈高铁全线贯通,沈阳枢纽的压力将会进一步增大,从当前情况年看,以哈尔滨为首的东北北部地区几个大城市进京的动车始发直达客流上座率历来很高,多数车次没有必要在沈阳枢纽停靠。所以打通京哈直通线,部分列车经由京哈直通线运行,不经沈阳北站,既能大大缓解沈阳枢纽的运输压力,又能提高北部地区几个大城市进京列车的运行速度,这是解决沈阳站、沈阳北站运力紧张问题的根本措施。虽然目前不具备在沈北建设高铁站的条件,但打通京哈直通线却很有必要,从六王屯线路所直接接轨到沈阳西站,投资不大但效益却十分显著,应该抓紧时间立项审批,争取与京沈全线同步开通运营,为争取地方投资也可以考虑在沈北地区预留高铁站站址。

3.5 采取措施,弥补中间站设置偏远的不足

哈大高铁沿线除了辽阳站等少数由既有站改造而成的高铁车站外,大部分新建中间站都离主城区较远,旅客乘车很不方便,对于有普铁列车经过的中小县城或乡镇,高铁的吸引力就更加弱化,如何采取措

施提高旅客出行的便捷度,是解决问题的主要途径之一。当前部分地区已经提出了"无轨高铁站"尝试,考虑普遍性地为远离城区的高铁站提供免费大巴车服务理应成为可能。高铁车站可以在市内或者周边城镇设置高铁售票接送服务中心延伸高铁服务,让更多的旅客有乘坐高铁的体验,使他们成为高铁长期性旅客,这也是一种客运营销手段,客观上虽然会增加一些人力物力投入和费用,但投入有限,收益无限,社会效益亦将得到彰显。

3.6 合理配置普铁与高铁运力资源,提高整体收益

在高铁飞速发展的同时,开好普铁慢车仍很有必要,这不但能够展现出"人民铁路为人民"的服务宗旨,更是铁路落实精准扶贫的具体措施。因此,合理做好高普分工,满足不同层次旅客的出行需求,也是一个值得深入研究的课题。在主要铁路干线,高铁应该是白天开行的主力,普铁应该是夜间和长途开行的主力;在售票限制上,普铁应该更远一些,满足长途出行旅客的需求;在边远和贫困地区的支线铁路,普铁不但要多开,还要开成公益性的扶贫列车,满足偏远和贫困地区广大人民的出行需求。另外,如何把高铁和普铁有效连接起来也是一个值得研究的课题,高铁毕竟不能覆盖所有的区域,这就需要把普铁和高铁的衔接做得更好,把两张网合并成一张网,才能更方便为所有旅客提供更加快速便捷的出行条件。最后,就是要考虑研究如何消化已有的大量普铁车体问题,比如可以考虑利用这些富余资源开行更多的旅游列车。目前看仅仅依靠铁路旅行社的力量是远远不够的,要眼光向外,加强与地方旅行服务机构的合作,特别是要加强与全国性及外地旅行服务机构的合作,适度增加投入和付出,最大限度地开发利用好旅游列车。

3.7 适应市场、实行更加灵活的票价政策

票价政策看似和客运运输组织没有直接关系,但实际影响很大,运输服务的基本原则是按客流开行列车,但并不是完全被动的开车,开好车能满足客流需要,同时也能主动地吸引调节客流,调节客流的有效手段之一就是票价,那些对时间要求不是很高的中低收入群体对票价的敏感性普遍高于对时间的关注度,而且这部分人群人数众多,通过票价浮动完全可以实现有效地调节客流。首先就是要解决高峰时段客流过度集中的矛盾,缓解峰谷之间的客流差距,这对于缓解高峰时段枢纽站的压力是十分必要的,也是十分有效的。我们目前实行的是单一票价,而以法国为首的欧洲国家则实行的是多种票价,比如18:00前后高峰时段巴黎—里昂高铁票价比其他时间段的同等列车高约30%,差额票价的强迫分流作用十分明显。其次要合理调整普铁与高铁、"D"字头与"G"字头、直达与慢车等不同等级列车之间的比价关系,也是缓解各种矛盾的有效手段。另外,通过对淡季或平峰列车实行降价也是让利于民的有效手段。虽然目前由于国家之前特价政策的限制,实行浮动票价的可操作空间十分有限,但越是受政策限制而不是受硬件条件限制,这个手段未来的发展前景就越广阔,是一个很有学问和值得深入研究的领域,应该投入更多的精力去研究和探讨。

4 结 语

高铁旅客运输组织是一项专业性很强的技术管理工作,特别是运输调度指挥系统,更是十分严密的技术管理体系,作为铁路运输企业管理的重要组成部分,高铁系统经营管理不论是内涵还是外延都要比普铁系统更专业、范围更大,从路网的规划建设开始,一直到营销策略和票价政策,涵盖的范围广、跨度大,是一个关系多学科的交叉体系,目前需要完善和改进的地方还很多;特别是在当前"交通强国、铁路先行"战略方针和国企新一轮改革大潮引导下,国铁企业将逐步由运输生产任务型向市场经营效益型转变。高铁及其相关领域正处于国铁企业改革发展的核心位置,不但需要在理论方面深入研究探讨,而且需要在实际工作中发动相关专业人员和管理人员广泛参与。本文提出来的两个主要观点:一是优化调整当前高铁的客运组织原则,变"以长带短"为"以长带短与区段加密相结合"的原则;二是改变单纯以几个核心大城市为旅客到发中心的单一模式,增加区域性分中心为高铁列车始发终到作业站,进而形成多交路的分散型列车运行图。这两个观点的核心都是为了更大限度地满足不同层次旅客的出行需求,更进一步强

化高铁运输组织管理的市场化和效益化需求。一己之见,抛砖引玉,希望能够引起专家学者和铁路运输企业管理者的重视,进一步改善和优化高铁运输组织管理,不断满足广大旅客的出行需求,提高高速铁路旅客运输的经济效益和社会效益,推动我国高铁事业持续健康地发展。

地铁短期客流预测模型研究综述

张 源 郝亚睿 张 鹏 李佳晨 温 岩

(西安建筑科技大学)

摘 要 本文梳理了地铁短期客流预测模型近年来的发展状况,总结了地铁短期客流预测的三类预测方法的优缺点以及适用情况,并讨论未来研究的方向。研究结果表明:随着机器学习和神经网络的深入研究,其对环境变化具有较强的自适应学习能力和抗干扰能力,并且能对历史数据进行归纳,总结出数据的内在规律。因此可以根据客流特征,进一步研究基于神经网络的组合模型,优势互补,提高预测的精度以及对突发情况的适用性。

关键词 轨道交通 客流预测模型 神经网络 短期客流

0 引 言

地铁的大客流问题近年来受到广泛关注,为了保证人们出行的安全和舒适度,准确的短期客流量预测已成为地铁科学合理的运营管理面临的一项重大挑战[1,2]。地铁短期的客流预测主要就是对下一周内或一个月内的客流量进行预测[3]。其中,最主要的就是预测模型的选用。所以需要对短期客流预测模型进行分类总结,根据情况选择合适的预测模型,准确的预测出地铁短时间的客流量变化情况[4]。

1 统计学的预测方法

1.1 加权历史平均自回归模型

加权历史平均自回归在客流时空特征分析和历史客流数据收集的基础上,构造加权历史平均自回归模型,即:

$$\hat{Q}_1(t) = \omega_t Q(t-1) + (1-\omega_t) Q_{hist}(t) \tag{1}$$

式中:$\hat{Q}_1(t)$——t 时段的客流量预测值;

$Q(t-1)$——$t-1$ 时段的实际客流量值;

ω_t——t 时段的预测权重系数;

$Q_{hist}(t)$——历史同期 t 时段的实际客流量值。

1.2 时间序列模型

时间序列模型是根据历史客流数据的规律,建立相应的时间序列模型。

自回归滑动平均模型表达式为:

$$Y_t = \Phi_1 Y_{t-1} + \Phi_2 Y_{t-2} + \cdots + \Phi_p Y_{t-p} + \varepsilon_t - \theta_1 \varepsilon_{t-1} - \theta_2 \varepsilon_{t-2} - \cdots - \theta_q \varepsilon_{t-q} \tag{2}$$

式中:Y_t——t 时段的客流量预测值;

p——自回归模型的阶数;

q——滑动平均模型的阶数;

ε_t——t 时段的误差。

移动平均自回归模型表达式为：

$$Y_t = \theta_0 + \varphi_1 Y_{t-1} + \cdots + \varphi_p Y_{t-p} + \varepsilon_t - \theta_1 \varepsilon_{t-1} - \cdots - \theta_q \varepsilon_{t-q} \tag{3}$$

式中：φ_i、θ_j——参数，$i = 1, 2, \cdots, p, j = 1, 2, \cdots, q$。

在时间序列模型中，自回归分析法的精度较高，但计算量大且复杂。因此建立季节ARIMA模型，引入客流平稳性的概念，得出在历史数据充足的条件下具有较高的预测精度。但是，对历史客流存在一定的依赖性。当其他因素的变化较大时，存在较大误差[5-11]。

1.3 卡尔曼滤波模型

卡尔曼滤波模型由状态方程和观测方程组成，利用观测方程和卡尔曼滤波来预测客流量。

首先，确定状态变量$Q(t)$：

$$Q(t) = Q(t-1) + W(t) \tag{4}$$

式中：$W(t)$——t时段的误差。

观测方程为：

$$H(t) = \omega \cdot Q(t) + e(t) \tag{5}$$

式中：$H(t)$——t时段地铁的历史平均客流量；

$e(t)$——高斯白噪声序列。

卡尔曼滤波预测结果误差较小，且适用性较广。但是，卡尔曼滤波属于线性模型，在环境复杂时，预测结果的精度差，不宜采用[12-15]。

2 非线性的预测方法

2.1 非参数回归模型

非参数回归预测，不需要对原始数据进行处理，只需要尽量完备的历史数据，就可以满足预测的精度要求。

文献[16-18]对非参数回归模型进行修正，构建K近邻非参数回归模型，从而对地铁短时的进出站客流量进行预测，并对预测结果进行验证，表明此方法具有良好的预测精度，并且随着客流数据不断增加，能够为非参数回归提供数据支持。非参数回归比较适用于短期的进出站客流量预测。

2.2 灰色理论模型

灰色理论模型是通过少量的、不完全的历史数据，建立微分预测模型，从而预测客流量。灰色理论仅从复杂的数据中找出规律，并拟合客流发展规律，不考虑地铁影响客流的复杂因素，可以将复杂的客流数据拟合为曲线：

$$\hat{y}(k) = \hat{x}^{(0)}_{k+1} = Ae^{bk} \tag{6}$$

灰色理论模型利用处理后的数据进行建模，容易找出数据的规律，建模所需的信息较少，运算方便，预测结果具有较高的精度，但对历史客流数据波动大的序列的预测精度不是很高[19,20]。

2.3 小波理论模型

地铁短期客流受天气、时间段等众多因素的影响，因此短期的客流复杂且波动性较大，而小波理论能够获取时间、空间以及频域上的信息。构建小波理论模型：

$$\psi_{a,b}(t) = \frac{1}{\sqrt{|a|}} \psi\left(\frac{t-b}{a}\right) \tag{7}$$

式中：a——尺度因子；

b——平移因子。

小波理论模型具有很好的自学习、适应性等，很适合对短时客流进行预测[21]。但是，小波理论模型对权值和小波因子的初值敏感，容易导致预测结果不稳定。

2.4 SVM模型

SVM模型主要针对小样本情况,在历史数据不足的时,依然能够保证短期客流预测的精度。并且不会存在神经网络面临的局部最优解的问题。SVM模型能够与径向基函数等现有学习算法相结合,从而处理非线性的问题。

通过SVM模型,预测正常和突发状况下的短期交通量,能够将历史客流的空间和时间特征同时考虑在内,并且在少量历史数据的条件下具有较高的精度,但是核函数的选择对预测精度影响较大[22]。

3 神经网络的预测方法

3.1 BP神经网络模型

BP神经网络对历史数据的内在因素和外在影响因素归纳总结,从而预测未来短时间的客流量[23,24]。

这种方法在网络模型中比较简单,容易编程仿真,但是也存在一些难点,如:隐含层节点个数的选取、网络结构的确定,这些都只能靠经验进行选取[25,26]。通过这种方法对短期客流进行预测,发现这种模型的适用性强,并且预测的精度较高,但是容易陷入局部最优解的问题[27-29]。

3.2 RBF神经网络模型

RBF网络规模较大,属于局部逼近网络,且仅有三层网络,因此学习速度快,短时间便可找出历史样本中的规律。

文献[30-38]通过RBF神经网络对地铁短期的客流量进行预测,并且对预测结果进行修正,从而提高预测的精度。但该方法完全基于数据驱动,具有一定的局限性,并且在训练过程中,容易陷入过度拟合。

3.3 模糊神经网络模型

模糊神经网络的结构更加复杂。在结构方面,相同的是均有输入层和输出层,不同的是没有中间的隐含层,而是变为模糊化层以及模糊规则层。

通过对数据进行模糊化处理,构建输入与输出变量的映射关系,建立模糊神经网络模型。模糊神经网络的适应能力强,鲁棒性好,具有较好的预测精度[39-42]。

4 结 语

统计学的方法理论简单,预测因子选择灵活,预测精度较高,但大部分模型都基于线性基础,且在每次计算时都要进行权值的调整,因此适用于变化不大的客流预测。非线性的方法能够满足预测客流的实时性、非线性特点,适用于随机性较大,环境情况复杂,甚至突发状况下的客流预测。神经网络对外界因素具有较强的适应性和抗干扰能力,能对已有的数据自动进行归纳,获取数据的内在规律。但是各种神经网络均有其缺陷存在,所以应进一步研究神经网络的组合模型。

参考文献

[1] 顾保南,杨照,徐雷,等.1997—2017年中国地铁发展统计分析[J].地铁研究,2018(5):85-89.
[2] 中国地铁协会.地铁2017年度统计和分析报告[J].地铁,2018(4):8-27.
[3] 段金肖,丁川,鹿应荣,等.考虑动态波动性的轨道交通站点短时客流预测方法[J].交通信息与安全,2017(5):68-75.
[4] Duan Y,Lv Y,Wang F Y. Performance evaluation of the deep learning approach for traffic flow prediction at different times. IEEE,2016:223-227.
[5] 郝勇,朱海燕.基于客流n日均量的地铁客流量的时间序列分析[J].铁道运输与经济,2009,31(10):42-46.
[6] 张伯敏.沪宁城际铁路客流短期预测研究[J].中国铁路,2014(9):29-33.
[7] 四兵锋,何九冉,任华玲,等.基于时序特征的地铁客流预测[J].北京交通大学学报,2014,38(3):

1-6.
[8] 谢辉,董德存,欧冬秀,等.轨道交通短期客流预测方法及其算法研究[J].现代地铁,2011(3):96-99.
[9] Shitan M,Karmokar P K,Ierd N Y. Time Series Modeling and Forecasting of An Bang Line Passenger Ridership in Malaysia[J]. Pakistan Journal of Statistics. 2014. 30(3):411-428.
[10] 赵鹏.基于ARIMA模型的地铁进站量预测研究[J].重庆交通大学学报,2020,1.
[11] 王进,史其信.短期时交通流预测模型综述[J].中国公共安全(学术版),2005,92-98.
[12] 杭明升,杨晓光,彭国雄.基于卡尔曼滤波的高速道路行程时间动态预测[J].同济大学学报(自然科学版),2002,1(9):1068-1072.
[13] 刘美琪,焦朋朋,孙拓.地铁进站客流量短时预测模型研究[J],地铁研究,2015(11):13-17.
[14] Liu L,Chen R C. A Novel Passenger Flow Prediction Model Using Deep Learning Methods[J]. Transportation Research Part C:Emerging Technologies,2017,84:74-91.
[15] 杨军.地铁客流短期预测及客流疏散模拟研究[D].北京:北京交通大学,2013.
[16] Li Y,Wang X,Sun S,et al. Forecasting Short-term Subway Passenger Flow Under Special Events Scenarios Using Multiscale Radial Basis Function Networks[J]. Transportation Research Part C:Emerging Technologies,2017,77:306-328.
[17] 谢俏,李斌斌,何建涛,等.基于非参数回归的城轨实时进出站客流预测[J].都市快轨交通,2017,30(2):32-36.
[18] 姚恩建,周文华,张永生,等.地铁新站开通初期实时进出站客流预测[J].中国铁道科学,2018,39(2):32-36.
[19] Sun Y,Leng B,Guan W. A Novel Wavelet-SVM Short-time Passenger Flow Prediction in Beijing Subway System[J]. Neurocomputing,2015,166:109-121.
[20] Ni M,He Q,Gao J. Forecasting the Subway Passenger Flow Under Event Occurrences with Social Media[J]. IEEE Transactions on Intelligent Transportation Systems,2016,18(6):1623-1632.
[21] 李丽辉,朱建生,强丽霞,等.基于随机森林回归算法的高速铁路短期客流预测研究[J].铁道运输与经济,2017,39(9):12-16.
[22] Castro-Neto M,Jeong Y S,Jeong M K,et al. Online-SVR for Short-term Traffic Flow Prediction Under Typical and Atypical Traffic Conditions[J]. Expert Systems with Applications,2009,36(3-part-P2):6164-6173.
[23] Guo J,Xie Z,Qin Y,et al. Short-term Abnormal Passenger Flow Prediction Based on the Fusion of SVR and LSTM[J]. IEEE Access,2019,7:42946-42955.
[24] 王宏杰,林良明,徐大渣.基于改进BP网交通流动态时序预测算法的研究[J].交通与计算机,2001.19(99):13-14.
[25] 周春光,梁艳春.计算智能人工神经网络.模糊系统.进化计算[M].长春:吉林大学出版社,2001.
[26] 谭国真,丁浩.广义神经网络的研究及其在交通流预测中的应用[J].控制与决策,2002(增刊):776-779.
[27] Tsung-Hsieen Tsai. Neural Network Based Temporal Feature Models for Short-term Railway Passenger Demand Forecasting[J]. Expert Systems with Applications. 2009(36):3728-3736.
[28] Ke J,Yang H,Zheng H,et al. Hexagon-based Convolutional Neural Network for Supply-demand Forecasting of Ride-sourcing Services[J]. IEEE Transactions on Intelligent Transportation Systems,2018,20(11):4160-4173.
[29] Zhang K,Liu Z,Zheng L. Short-term Prediction of Passenger Demand in Multi-zone Level:Temporal Convolutional Neural Network with Multi-task Learning[J]. IEEE Transactions on Intelligent Transportation

Systems,2019,21(4):1480-1490.

[30] 陈平.一种改进的RBF神经网络及其在短期交通量预测中的应用[J].智能自动化,2003,25(1):36-38.

[31] 侯晓云,邵丽萍,等.基于深度学习的地铁短时客流起讫点预测[J].东南大学硕士学位论文,2004.

[32] 王树盛.都市圈轨道交通客流预测方法理论及方法研究[D].南京:东南大学硕士学位论文,2004.

[33] 丁涛,周惠成.基于径向基函数神经网络的预测方法研究[J].哈尔滨工业大学学报,2005,37(2):272-275.

[34] 屠小娥.基于神经网络的非线性预测控制研究[D].兰州:兰州理工大学,2007.

[35] 韩雪.铁路客票发售数据抽取及短时客流预测研究[D].北京:北京交通大学,2008.

[36] 杨冉.地铁客流预测及运营调度方法研究[D].北京:北京交通大学,2010.

[37] 李晓俊,吕晓艳,刘军.基于径向基神经网络的铁路短期客流预测[J].铁道运输与经济,2011.33(6):86-89.

[38] Li H,Wang Y,Xu X,et al. Short-term Passenger Flow Prediction Under Passenger Flow Control Using a Dynamic Radial Basis Function Network[J]. Applied Soft Computing,2019,83:105620.

[39] 李春晓,李海鹰,蒋熙,等.基于广义动态模糊神经网络的短时车站进站客流量预测[J].都市快轨交通,2015,28(4):57-61.

[40] 崔洪涛,陈晓旭,杨超,等.基于深度长短期记忆网络的地铁进站客流预测[J].地铁研究,2019(9):41.

[41] Zhang J,Chen F,Cui Z,et al. Deep Learning Architecture for Short-term Passenger Flow Forecasting in Urban Rail Transit[J]. IEEE Transactions on Intelligent Transportation Systems,2020.

[42] Zhang J,Chen F,Shen Q. Cluster-based LSTM Network for Short-term Passenger Flow Forecasting in Urban Rail Transit[J]. IEEE Access,2019,7:147653-147671.

列车网络控制系统CCU安全冗余设计

张 凯　梁海泉　胡景泰

(同济大学铁道与城市轨道交通研究院)

摘　要　为提高基于工业以太网的列车网络控制系统的安全性,使中央控制单元(CCU)符合欧洲EN50129安全标准,本文提出了新的CCU冗余机制。设计了基于二乘二取二安全冗余的CCU硬件架构,并对CCU输入输出板卡和电源做了冗余设计。相比于传统双机热备的安全机制,二乘二取二拥有更高的安全性,对进一步提升列车安全运行具有重要意义。

关键词　交通安全　列车安全性　二乘二取二　CCU　列车网络

0　引　言

网络控制系统是列车关键系统之一,通过协调各子系统有序工作从而保证列车安全运行[1]。中央控制单元(CCU)是列车网络控制系统的通信指挥中心,列车网络通信在CCU的调度下有序进行,CCU的安全性是影响列车网络控制系统安全性的主要因素。MVB总线网络是构成列车网络控制系统的重要部分,其传输速率最高为1.5Mbit/s。随着高速列车智能化程度的提高,接入列车网络的微型计算机控制器数

基金项目:动车组和机车牵引与控制国家重点实验室开放课题基金(2019YJ201);上海市磁浮与轨道交通协同创新中心资助。

量和所需传输的数据量越来越多,使得由传统 MVB 总线转向以太网寻求带宽和速率的提升成为列车网络发展的主要方向[2,3]。传统列车网络 CCU 采取双机热备的冗余方式,对基于工业以太网的列车网络则需要安全性更高的冗余架构。

本文将拥有更高安全性的二乘二取二冗余机制运用于 CCU 设计,国内外研究者对二乘二取二做了大量的研究。陈光武等[4]将二乘二取二用于铁路车站全电子连锁系统,该系统在应用中运行稳定。韩安平等[5]提出了二乘二取二信号控制平台的安全设计方法,并对其可靠性进行了分析。张永贤等[6]提出了一种二乘二取二安全系统降级使用的故障运行策略。陈峰等[7]分析比较了双机热备和二乘二取二架构的自律机的安全性,得出二乘二取二冗余能够很大程度提高安全性的结论。

1 二乘二取二冗余 CCU 整体架构

二乘二取二冗余 CCU 的系统架构如图 1 所示,两个二取二子系统相互独立,功能相同,都可以独自承担网络控制系统的控制任务。系统内两个逻辑单元工作步调一致,其计算结果经由表决单元比较,若一致才视为二取二子系统工作正常。两个子系统通过系间同步通信实现任务级同步,要求在主系统处于不可使用状态时,系统能够无缝切换,由备系统继续执行功能。

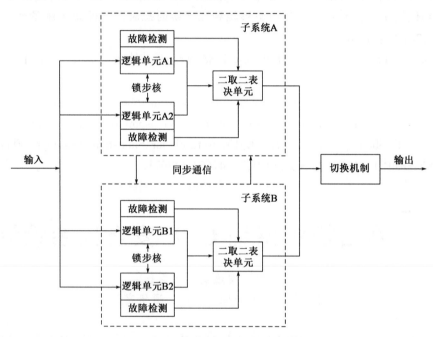

图 1 二乘二取二冗余 CCU 系统架构

1.1 安全机制

传统的双机热备冗余结构也有两个相同的子系统,但是子系统内部仅包含一个逻辑单元,故障检测单元检测到故障时,系统启动切换机制。然而检测单元的故障覆盖率是无法达到 100% 的,且单纯提高检测单元故障覆盖率是有上限的,在安全性要求较高的系统中往往难以满足需求。二乘二取二结构系内包含两个逻辑单元,除自身的故障检测之外,还通过表决单元比较计算结果,可以有效检出部分故障检测单元未能检测到的错误,有效提高了整个系统的故障诊断覆盖率。

1.2 二取二实现策略

二取二系统内部两个逻辑单元需要在极小的时间粒度上实现同步运行,若采用时钟同步的方式则需要精准的时钟同步算法,且表决单元设计也会比较困难。锁步核(lock-step)是实现高诊断覆盖度的一种传统方法,CPU 内部的两个处理核执行相同的程序,周期性比较两核输出的结果。Lock-step 技术在实现功能安全的处理器平台很常见,在硬件上能够实现两核时钟的精准同步,比较机制固化在芯片设计当中,具有不可调整性,不受软件执行的影响,在微控制器领域已经过多年的成功验证。采用锁步核实现二取二系统的冗余功能,能够可靠地提升系统故障诊断的能力。

1.3 设计要素

二乘二取二架构的两子系统需要保持独立,其中一个系统发生任意单点故障不能影响另一系统正常工作。各子系统采用独立电源供电,配置独立的输入输出接口、外扩存储单元、故障诊断模块、时钟、网络端口等。子系统之间的同步通信连接以及硬线连接须经隔离,防止电磁耦合等引起干扰。

单个逻辑单元的诊断覆盖率对整个二乘二取二系统的安全性影响较大[8],提高逻辑单元诊断覆盖率可以有效提高整个系统的安全性。对电源、输入、输出等设计专门的检测电路,实时监测异常状态。对时钟、存储单元、程序运行状态,设置自诊断程序实时监测相关寄存器状态,重要参数和运行结果进行数据校核以及故障诊断。

列车网络控制系统任务处理需要具有实时性,中央控制单元采用实时嵌入式操作系统,对网络其他系统设备在确定时间内作出响应。切换机制作用的时间和状态与 CCU 主任务线程协调,CCU 拥有多达 200 个线程,且任务周期也不尽相同,切换机制基于任务周期发挥作用,不打断正常周期任务,切换后也不重复上一周期的输出结果。软件需要互锁机制,避免在切换过程的短时间内两系统同时作为主系统工作,保证除停机状态外有一系统作为主系统输出控制指令。

1.4 可行性论述

二乘二取二等安全冗余系统目前已用于多种轨道交通信号系统,表现出超高的安全性。本文设计所遵循的安全完整性标准,其主动策略的功能安全拥有更高的实用价值也在国际上被普遍认同。拥有复杂冗余架构的 CCU,设计遵从安全完整性理论,将对列车网络的整体安全性的提高提供一个可以在理论上证实安全的平台。本设计已采用马尔可夫分析理论,根据本文提出的冗余架构,结合具体的硬件参数,对 CCU 的安全性和可靠性进行了精确分析,从结果来看,二乘二取二冗余的 CCU 表现出远高于传统双机热备架构的安全性。此外,传输速率更高的以太网替代 MVB 网络,提高了通信效率,能够留出更多时间以及 CCU 的处理能力的裕度,用于故障诊断和功能安全的维护。综上,本文 CCU 冗余安全设计将满足新一代列车网络系统安全需求。

2 系统关键技术实现

2.1 系间同步

CCU 冗余的两个子系统执行相同的线程任务,若不加干涉,随着时间累积两系统必定会出现任务不同步现象,带来的主要问题之一就是两系统可能给出互斥的诊断结果,干扰网络系统的正常运行。同步通信可以解决这一问题,本文在冗余子系统之间建立起高速同步信道,主系统 CCU 周期性地发送同步信息给备系统,备系统 CCU 接收同步信息,调整自身运行状态,与主系统保持一致,使得 CCU 在高性能运转的同时,两系统能够始终对列车网络的调度处于相同的相位。同步通信采用嵌入式以太网协议 LWIP,使用百兆传输速率,为减少传输延迟,通信不经由交换机,而是使用交叉网线直连的方式,同时采用全双工传输介质避免传输冲突。同步时序逻辑如图 2 所示,每个周期内主系统与备系统在特定的时间内完成同步传输,备系统在任务周期层面跟随主系统状态。

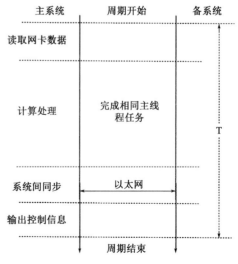

图 2 系统间同步时序

2.2 实时以太网

相比 MVB 总线网络,以太网能够提供更快速的传输和更方便的组网功能,但是标准以太网传输延迟的不确定性在工业控制领域是不可接受的。TSN 网络在保持标准以太网分布式架构的基础上,能够解决工业通信的实时性问题。将 TSN 网络应用于列车网络取代传统 MVB 总线,需要考虑 MVB 与 TSN 通信调度的不同,为了不改变 CCU 应用层的软件设计,需要在 TSN 网络协议的应用层保留 MVB 的调度策略。TSN 网络可以根据接入设备的重要性分配固定带宽和周期时间片,这一功能也在 CCU 的通信设计中实现,对于关键系统,CCU 分配给足够的带宽,保障其数据传输的实时性和确定性。

2.3 通信安全机制

根据国标 GB/T 24339.2,铁路信号安全通信协议定义安全通信的威胁/防御矩阵如表 1 所示。为全面覆盖安全威胁,系统采取序列号、时间戳、双重校验三种手段保障数据传输安全正确。TCP/IP 协议包含序列号与时间戳功能选项,由协议添加在报文帧头部,报文尾包含 32 位校验数据,其覆盖整个报文帧的校验。报文尾的校验由数据链路层完成,为了达到双重校验的要求,在应用层对数据区单独校验,将校验码附在数据尾部,接收方应用层接收完成后校验应用数据。CCU 的通信模块包括 TSN 应用以太网通信、系统间同步通信、调试诊断以及处理器内部通过内存的数据传输。其中调试诊断通信没有过高的安全需求,只采用常规安全策略,其他各通信功能均遵守安全标准,采取相应的安全校验措施覆盖所有危险情形。

铁路信号安全通信协议威胁/防御矩阵　　　　表 1

危险情形	序列号与时间戳	时间戳	超时	源标识	反馈报文	双重校验
重复	√					
丢失	√					
插入	√			√	√	
错序	√					
错码						√
延迟	√	√	√			

3　结　语

本文将二乘二取二冗余架构应用于列车网络控制系统 CCU 设计,根据 CCU 工况制定了硬件设计,对系统设计要素和关键技术环节制定了具体的策略。相比传统的双机热备冗余机制,二乘二取二能够大幅提高 CCU 的功能安全性。对冗余架构而言,共因失效是影响系统安全性的一个重要因素,在本文研究的基础上还需进一步探究相同硬件故障引起的两点失效对行车安全的威胁。

参考文献

[1] 高杰,李文正.新型轨道车辆网络控制系统设计与应用[J].铁道机车车辆,2019,39(01):118-122.

[2] 靳建宇,等.列车通信网络并行冗余方法与协议的研究[J].铁道学报,2017,39(12):76-85.

[3] 简捷,等.基于以太网的列车通信网络冗余结构可靠性分析[J].北京交通大学学报,2018,42(2):76-83.

[4] 陈光武,等.基于二乘二取二的全电子计算机联锁系统[J].中国铁道科学,2010,31(04):138-144.

[5] 韩安平,段武.二乘二取二硬件安全冗余信号控制平台关键部件的安全设计和可靠性研究[J].铁路技术创新,2015(2):99-102.

[6] 张永贤,等.二乘二取二系统的一种新降级策略研究[J].华东交通大学学报,2017,34(5):99-105.

[7] 陈峰,等.高速铁路智能 CTC 自律机系统的可靠性与安全性评估[J].自动化学报,2020,46(3):463-470.

[8] 魏臻,许崇,胡庆新.计算机联锁系统二乘二取二结构的可靠性和安全性分析[J].铁道通信信号,2019,55(12):1-5.

基于改进决策树 SVM 多分类算法的 GSM-R 系统干扰识别研究

张志满 马 征

(西南交通大学信息科学与技术学院)

摘 要 为提升 GSM-R 系统识别未知来源干扰信号类型的性能,本文利用改进决策树 SVM 多分类算法建立 GSM-R 系统干扰识别模型。该模型选用最大值、平均值和峭度等 7 种特征,完成对单音干扰、多音干扰和脉冲干扰等 9 种干扰信号类型的识别,识别准确率达到 99.34%。该模型相对于其他基于 SVM 多分类算法的模型,识别准确率最高,识别速度提升明显。其中与最常用的——区分法相比,识别时间降低 77.27%。试验结果表明,本文建立的模型在 GSM-R 干扰识别方面具有显著优势。

关键词 GSM-R 干扰识别 决策树 SVM 特征提取

0 引 言

在 GSM-R 系统中,列车与基站之间通过无线的方式进行通信,其通信质量不可避免地会受到干扰。在铁路沿线存在大量电信运营商的无线通信系统,若沿线附近的公共无线通信系统占用 GSM-R 频点、发射功率过大或带外杂散辐射过高,都会给 GSM-R 系统带来干扰。除此之外,沿线的其他专用无线通信系统甚至一些非法的无线通信系统,也会给 GSM-R 系统带来干扰[1]。这些干扰会对 GSM-R 系统的运行产生严重影响,对铁路运输造成安全隐患。因此,及时准确地检测并识别干扰,对后续排除干扰,保证 GSM-R 系统稳定可靠运行至关重要。

传统的 GSM-R 系统干扰识别方式主要通过频谱仪和扫频仪完成。文献[2-3]分别介绍了通过频谱仪和扫频仪完成干扰识别的实际案例。但这些方式均需要人工分析,并且均依赖于检测列车,不能完成对持续时间较短的干扰进行识别。

近年来,机器学习在 GSM-R 系统干扰识别方面得到广泛研究。文献[3-5]均利用决策树算法完成对多种类型干扰的识别,但都无法识别未知来源干扰的信号类型。

在目前关于 GSM-R 系统干扰识别的研究中,主要利用决策树算法完成对干扰的识别,但由于决策树算法本身的缺陷,其识别准确率和适应能力要低于 SVM(Support Vector Machine,支持向量机)等其他机器学习算法[6]。此外,目前的相关研究均未能识别未知来源干扰的信号类型,这对后续干扰排查以及抗干扰措施的实施造成不良影响。为解决这两个问题,本文利用 SVM 算法对识别 GSM-R 系统未知干扰的信号类型进行研究,并通过改进决策树 SVM 多分类算法降低识别时间。

1 频谱数据处理与特征提取

1.1 数据来源

本文数据来源于成灌快速铁路沿线的小型固定站,该固定站能够实现对成灌快速铁路 GSM-R 系统的持续检测。本文利用该固定站完成对 GSM-R 下行频段的采样,采样点为 201 个。

为提升模型的适应性,本文利用 USRP 模拟多种类型的干扰信号,扩充干扰来源。共有无干扰、单音干扰、多音干扰、脉冲干扰、噪声调制干扰、阻塞干扰、杂散干扰、移动占用 GSM-R 频点的干扰和联通占用 GSM-R 频点的干扰 9 种类型,具体的干扰信号类型的频谱图如图 1 所示。

本文获取的频谱数据共有 2443 组,各种类型干扰的数量如表 1 所示。

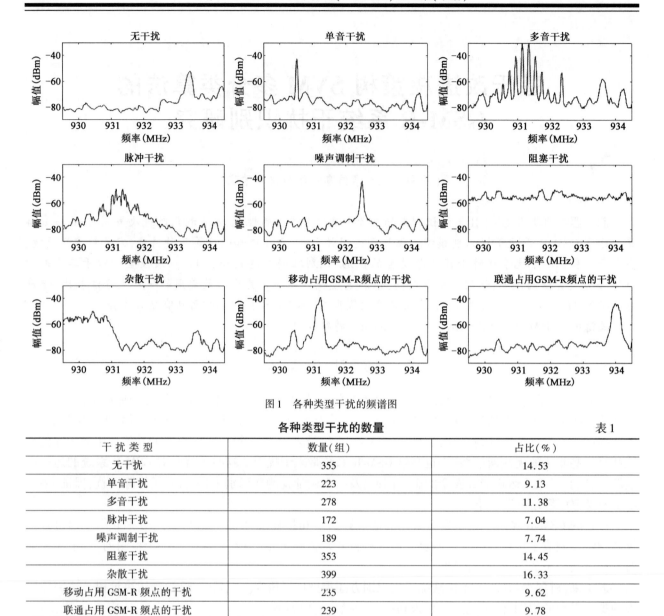

图 1 各种类型干扰的频谱图

各种类型干扰的数量 表1

干扰类型	数量(组)	占比(%)
无干扰	355	14.53
单音干扰	223	9.13
多音干扰	278	11.38
脉冲干扰	172	7.04
噪声调制干扰	189	7.74
阻塞干扰	353	14.45
杂散干扰	399	16.33
移动占用 GSM-R 频点的干扰	235	9.62
联通占用 GSM-R 频点的干扰	239	9.78

1.2 特征提取

由于获取的数据的维数较高,直接进行机器学习将会影响学习效果,因此需要通过特征提取实现降维。对于特征的选取,参考文献[6-8]的研究,本文选择了以下7种特征。

(1)最大值

该特征能够反映数据的上限,公式如式(1)所示。

$$X_{\max} = \max_{i=1,2,\cdots,N}(x_i) \tag{1}$$

式中:x_i——第 i 个样本数据;
　　N——该样本数据的总量。

(2)平均值

该特征能够反映数据的集中趋势,公式如式(2)所示。

$$\mu_x = \frac{1}{N}\sum_{i=1}^{N}x_i \tag{2}$$

(3)标准差

该特征能够反映数据集离散程度,公式如式(3)所示。

$$\sigma_x = \sqrt{\frac{1}{N}\sum_{i=1}^{N}(x_i - \mu_x)^2} \tag{3}$$

(4)峭度

该特征能够反映数据变化平缓程度,公式如式(4)所示。

$$K_x = E\left[\left(\frac{X - \mu_x}{\sigma_x}\right)^4\right] = \frac{\sum_{i=1}^{N}(x_i - \mu_x)^4}{N\sigma_x^4} \tag{4}$$

式中:X——全体样本数据。

(5)偏度

该特征能够用于描述数据的分布,公式如式(5)所示。

$$S_x = E\left[\left(\frac{X - \mu_x}{\sigma_x}\right)^3\right] = \frac{\sum_{i=1}^{N}(x_i - \mu_x)^3}{N\sigma_x^3} \tag{5}$$

(6)波形因子

该特征能够反映数据的波动性,公式如式(6)所示。

$$W_x = \frac{\sqrt{\frac{1}{N}\sum_{i=1}^{N}x_i^2}}{\frac{1}{N}\sum_{i=1}^{N}|x_i|} \tag{6}$$

(7)GSM 信号类型

由于在采样频段内的 GSM 信号可能来自 GSM-R、移动和联通,为区分这三类 GSM 信号,本文规定若频段内没有 GSM 信号,则 $T_{GSM} = 0$;若 GSM 信号来自移动,则 $T_{GSM} = 1$;若来自联通,则 $T_{GSM} = 2$;若来自 GSM-R,则 $T_{GSM} = 3$。如公式(7)所示。

$$T_{GSM} \in \{0,1,2,3\} \tag{7}$$

上述 7 种特征的效果如图 2 所示,除 GSM 信号类型这一特征外,其余六个特征均能较明显地区分各种类型干扰,但该特征对于区分移动和联通占用 GSM-R 频点的干扰这两种类型干扰至关重要,故保留该特征。

2 基于改进决策树 SVM 多分类算法的模型建立

由于 SVM 是一个二分类器,当其用于解决多分类问题时,需要对其进行改进[9]。常用的方式为——区分法(OVO SVM,one-versus-one SVM)、逐一鉴别法(OVR SVM,one-versus-rest SVM)和基于决策树的 SVM 多分类算法(DT SVM,Decision Tree SVM)。

为了降低识别时间,本文选取基于决策树的 SVM 多分类算法完成对 GSM-R 干扰识别模型的建立。传统的基于决策树的 SVM 多分类算法使用各类中心点之间欧式距离作为决策树构建顺序的依据[10],这种构造方式未考虑各类样本数据的离散程度的影响。本文将各类中心点之间欧式距离和各类样本数据的离散程度作为决策树构建顺序的依据,其中离散程度使用同类样本点到该类中心点平均欧氏距离衡量。本文利用考虑离散程度的欧氏距离(Euclidean Distance Considering Dispersion,EDCD),对传统的基于决策树的 SVM 多分类算法进行改进。具体计算方式如下所示。

对于 N 分类问题,每个类中心点 $c_i(i=1,2,\cdots,N)$ 的计算方式如式(8)所示。

$$c_i = \frac{1}{N_i}\sum_{x \in X_i}x \tag{8}$$

式中:X_i——第 i 类中所有的样本数据;

x——X_i 的一个样本数据;

N_i——第 i 类样本数据总数。

第 i 类与第 $j(j=1,2,\cdots,N,j \neq i)$ 类的欧氏距离的计算方式如式(9)所示。

$$ED_{ij} = \|c_i - c_j\| \tag{9}$$

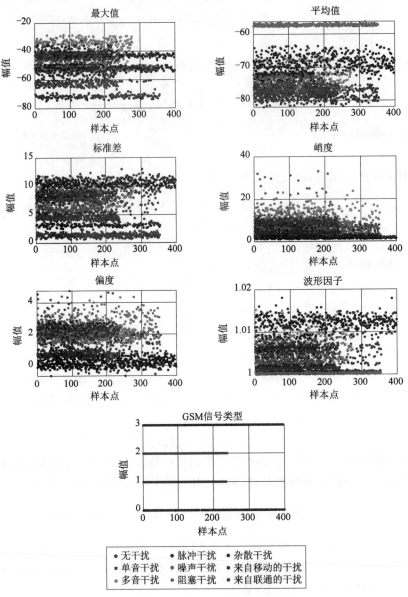

图 2 特征提取效果

第 i 类样本数据到该类中心点平均欧氏距离的计算方式如式(10)所示。

$$ED_i = \frac{1}{N_i}\sum_{x \in X_i} \| c_i - x \| \tag{10}$$

则第 i 类与第 j 类考虑离散程度的欧氏距离的计算方式如式(11)所示。

$$EDCD_{ij} = \frac{ED_{ij}}{ED_i + ED_j} \tag{11}$$

定义第 i 类的构建顺序的度量值如式(12)所示。

$$d_i = \min_{j=1,2,\cdots,N, j \neq i} EDCD_{ij} \tag{12}$$

用 S 表示该问题全部的类别标签的集合,基于改进决策树的 SVM 多分类算法的训练算法的步骤如图 3 所示。

在测试时,将测试数据按照构建的决策树顺序依次对二分类器进行测试。如果测试结果大于 0,则该结果就为测试数据的类别;否则使用下一个二分类器进行测试,直到测试结果大于 0。

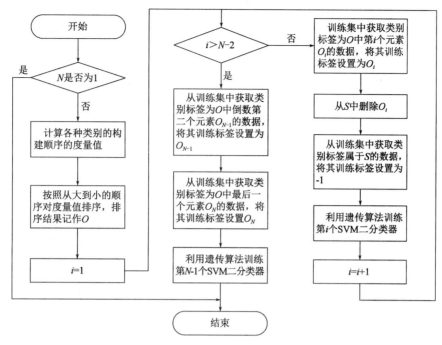

图 3　基于改进决策树的 SVM 多分类算法流程图

3　结果与分析

对于获取的 2443 组频谱数据,选取 1833 组作为训练样本,其余的 610 组作为测试样本。使用基于改进决策树的 SVM 多分类算法构建干扰识别模型,得到的最优决策树结构如图 4 所示。对测试数据进行识别,得到的混淆矩阵如表 2 所示。

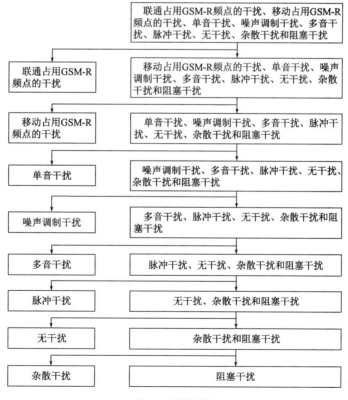

图 4　最优决策树

测试结果的混淆矩阵　　　　　　　　　　　　　　　　　　　　　　　表2

测试结果		实际结果								
		无干扰	单音干扰	多音干扰	脉冲干扰	噪声调制干扰	阻塞干扰	杂散干扰	移动干扰	联通干扰
	无干扰	97.74%	1.78%	0	0	0	0	0	0	0
	单音干扰	1.13%	96.44%	0	0	0	0	0	0	0
	多音干扰	1.13%	0	100%	0	0	0	0	0	0
	脉冲干扰	0	0	0	100%	0	0	0	0	0
	噪声调制干扰	0	1.78%	0	0	100%	0	0	0	0
	阻塞干扰	0	0	0	0	0	100%	0	0	0
	杂散干扰	0	0	0	0	0	0	100%	0	0
	移动干扰	0	0	0	0	0	0	0	100%	0
	联通干扰	0	0	0	0	0	0	0	0	100%

从结果中可以看出，本文的模型对于后7种干扰的识别准确率均能达到100%，对于无干扰和单音干扰的识别准确率也都在96%以上。对于这9种类型的干扰均取得较高的识别效果。

为进一步证明本文模型在GSM-R干扰识别方面的优势，将本文模型与基于决策树、OVO SVM、OVR SVM和传统DT SVM建立的识别模型进行对比。各个模型对各种类型干扰的识别准确率对比如图5所示。

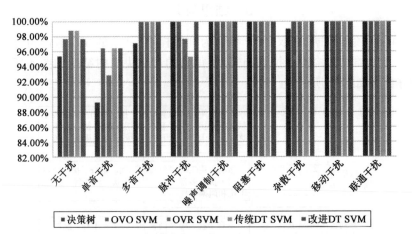

图5　各个模型对各种类型干扰的识别准确率对比

各模型整体识别准确率及识别时间如表3所示。

各个模型整体识别准确率及识别时间　　　　　　　　　　　　　　　　　　　表3

算法	决策树	OVO SVM	OVR SVM	传统 DT SVM	改进 DT SVM
识别准确率(%)	97.87	99.34	99.02	99.18	99.34
识别时间(s)	0.0027	0.088	0.064	0.029	0.020

根据上述结果，本文模型相对于其他多分类SVM模型，在保持最高整体识别准确率的情况下，在识别速度上提升明显，相对于一一区分法，识别时间降低了77.27%，相对于传统决策树SVM，识别时间降低了31.03%。试验结果表明，本文的模型在GSM-R干扰识别方面具有显著优势。

4　结　　语

本文对来源于成灌快速铁路沿线的小型固定站的频谱数据，提取最大值、平均值和峭度等7种特征，利用改进决策树SVM多分类算法建立GSM-R系统干扰识别模型。该模型能够对7种干扰类型进行识别,对于多音干扰、脉冲干扰、噪声调制干扰、阻塞干扰、杂散干扰、移动占用GSM-R频点的干扰和联通占用GSM-R频点的干扰的识别准确率均能达到100%,对于无干扰和单音干扰的识别准确率也都在96%以上。该模型相对于基于决策树算法的模型识别准确率提升明显。

本模型相对于其他基于SVM多分类算法的模型,整体识别准确率最高,识别速度提升明显。其中与最常用的一一区分法相比,识别时间降低77.27%;与传统决策树SVM相比,识别时间降低31.03%。试验结果表明,本文的模型在GSM-R干扰识别方面具有显著优势。

本文算法的缺点是构建的决策树是偏二叉树,该类型的二叉树会存在误差累积的问题,后续会构建基于完全二叉树的SVM多分类算法,进行性能的分析对比。此外,本文主要针对单一干扰类型的识别问题进行研究,后续会对同时存在多种干扰类型的识别问题进行研究。本文的数据主要来源于成灌快速铁路沿线,为分析本文构建模型的扩展性,后续会对其他铁路场景进行实验。

参考文献

[1] H Wang,H Chen,L Gao,et al. China Railway Radio Interference and Protection[C],2014 XXXIth URSI General Assembly and Scientific Symposium (URSI GASS),Beijing,2014:1-4.
[2] 代赛.GSM-R系统在线干扰监测技术研究[D].北京:北京交通大学,2013.
[3] 马良德.GSM-R网络干扰检测及数据分析技术研究[D].北京:中国铁道科学研究院,2015.
[4] 张瑞霞.GSM-R系统干扰问题及优化方法研究[D].兰州:兰州交通大学,2015.
[5] Z Ma,X Chen,M Xiao,et al. Karagiannidis and P. Fan. Interference Control for Railway Wireless Communication Systems:Techniques,Challenges,and Trends[J]. IEEE Vehicular Technology Magazine,2020.
[6] 徐国进.典型通信干扰信号识别技术研究[D].成都:电子科技大学,2018.
[7] 付玉龙.基于功率信号的多特征值刀具磨损监控系统研究及开发[D].成都:西南交通大学,2018.
[8] 冯博,裴峥,伊良忠,等.基于支持向量机的C波段无线电异常信号识别[J].中国无线电,2013(01):60-62+69.
[9] 周志华.机器学习[M].北京:清华大学出版社,2016:10-16.
[10] 王正海,方臣,何凤萍,等.基于决策树多分类支持向量机岩性波谱分类[J].中山大学学报(自然科学版),2014,53(06):93-96.

基于车—车通信的新型CBTC系统运力分析

张启鹤[1] 王海峰[2] 叶晨雨[1]

(1. 北京交通大学电子信息工程学院;
2. 北京交通大学轨道交通运行控制系统国家工程研究中心)

摘 要 基于车—车通信的新型CBTC系统架构应用于铁路运输时,需要对其系统能力进行分析和评估,以确保其满足运力需求。为此,本文首先介绍了基于车—车通信的新型CBTC系统组成和特点;然后从列车运行追踪间隔计算的角度,给出了不同作业场景下的理论追踪间隔计算方法,进而给出运力评估方法;之后引入了虚拟连挂等新的运行控制理念分析了不同系统结构和作业模式对运力的影响;最后给出了仿真结果对比。研究结果表明,基于车—车通信的新型CBTC系统由于不涉及列车运行控制和追踪的本质性变化,对运输能力的影响有限,车站区域和折返区域追踪间隔分别缩短4.3%和4%,换算成运输能力每小时可增加1到2列列车。而在车站区域采用新的追踪方式时,移动闭塞模式下每小时分别可以增加11列列车,虚拟连挂模式下每小时可增加30列列车。本文的研究,从理论角度给出了新型

CBTC系统运力评估方法,对系统的进一步完善和优化具有借鉴意义。

关键词 车—车通信 精简CBTC 运输能力 追踪间隔

0 引 言

随着城市轨道交通运输需求的增大,对运输效率和安全性提出了更严苛的要求。现有的基于通信的列车控制系统(Communication Based Train Control System,CBTC)由于其系统结构复杂,轨旁设备的数量庞大,存在系统造价高昂、维护困难等问题;同时车—地—车的通信方式造成系统较高的通信延时,对运行效率造成一定影响,已不能满足未来轨道交通的需求[1]。为了追求更好的运输能力和更精简的系统结构,基于车—车通信的列车运行控制系统等新型列车运行控制架构受到越来越多的关注。

基于车—车通信的CBTC系统(Train-to-train Communication Based Train Control System,以下简称T-CBTC)引入"以列车为核心"的设计理念,将传统CBTC系统中的联锁和ZC功能"移植"到车载设备上,从而减少轨旁设备、优化系统结构[2]。由于其潜在的优势,国内外相关机构进行了很多研究。法国阿尔斯通提出了一种精简的CBTC解决方案——UrbalisFluence系统,并将其应用到法国里尔地铁1号线改造项目中,该系统将传统列控系统中的联锁功能整合到车载设备和轨旁目标控制器中,遵循以"资源管理"为核心和以列车为中心的管理原则,能够有效减少地面设备,同时将列车间的追踪间隔缩短至1min左右[3]。美国通用电气公司研发了增强的列车控制系统(Incremental Train Control System,ITSC),由车载设备负责处理所有列控数据并对列车运行进行安全控制[4]。欧洲Shift2Rail计划也将基于车—车通信的列控系统作为主要的创新项目之一,开发一种新的控制系统,在减少基础设施投入的同时,提升系统运行效率[5,6]。东日本铁路公司也计划研发一套新的列控系统,整合地面多套逻辑控制设备,并由车载设备承担更多的列车运行控制功能[7]。国内相关学者和企业也开展了相关研究,提出了不同的基于车—车通信的新型CBTC系统结构[8]。

本文将T-CBTC作为研究对象,首先分析了简化后的系统结构及功能特点;然后从系统运输能力的角度给出了系统分析方法;并将多种新型系统结构和列车运行控制方法进行了对比;最后进行了仿真计算。通过全面的对比分析,给出T-CBTC系统对现有系统运输能力的影响,多种结构和控制方式对比,也给出了T-CBTC系统进一步提升运输能力的可行方向。

1 T-CBTC系统组成

为了精简CBTC系统结构、减少轨旁设备,同时追求更高的系统运输能力,国内外学者都在构思一种基于车—车通信的列车运行控制系统。由于没有统一的系统架构和设计依据,本文以阿尔斯通精简的CBTC解决方案——UrbalisFluence为参考[3],给出了一种典型的T-CBTC系统组成,并作为后续分析验证的依据。

T-CBTC系统以车—车通信为基础,采用一体化设计思想,通过优化系统结构并进行功能重分配,车载设备将承担更多的系统功能。如图1所示,系统中,取消区域控制器(ZC)和地面联锁(CBI),其联锁功能由车载设备承担;使用卫星定位等高精度的自主定位技术取代计轴设备;同时为了尽可能地减少地面设备,不再部署信号机和有源应答器。系统由骨干传输网络(DCS)、列车自动监控(ATS)、车载子系统(VOBC)、地面对象控制单元(OCU)及轨旁设备构成。

ATS负责向列车发送运行计划,实现全线列车的运营监督,通过骨干网络与列车通信,并获取地面OCU提供的轨旁资源状态信息。OCU负责向列车提供轨旁设备的状态并接收车载发来的控制道岔、屏蔽门等指令,同时与中央ATS服务器进行信息交互。车载子系统实现列车安全路径规划、移动授权和速度曲线的计算以及辅助驾驶等功能,通过无线通信与OCU进行信息交互。DCS负责提供可靠的车—车和车—地通信通道。

T-CBTC系统具有三个显著的特点:

(1)精简的系统结构:取消了CBI和ZC,使用车载设备和OCU进行轨旁资源控制。

(2) 以列车为中心：自主化的列车运行，车载设备承担更多的控制功能。

(3) 车—车直接通信。

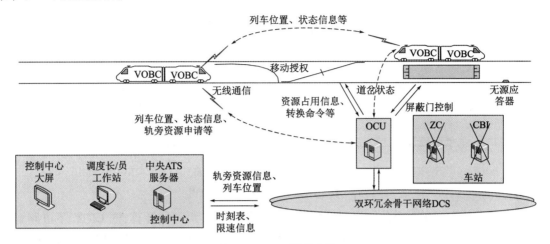

图 1　T-CBTC 系统结构图

针对 T-CBTC 系统提出的目的，结合系统特点，有必要对 T-CBTC 系统进行全面的系统分析，需要验证下面两个问题：

(1) 精简的系统结构能否在保证安全和实现系统功能的前提下，完成地面设备的简化。

(2) 新的系统结构改变了传统轨旁资源（如道岔）的控制方式，车—车的直接通信和以列车为中心的控制改变了传统控制数据的传输方式，这些改变是否有助于提高系统运输能力。

本文的工作主要针对第二个问题，研究新的 T-CBTC 系统结构对于运输能力的影响。运输能力与列车运行追踪间隔直接相关，下面首先通过计算系统在典型作业场景下运行间隔，最终可以计算出新型系统的理论运输能力。

2　T-CBTC 系统运输能力评估方法

T-CBTC 系统提出的一个重要的目的是应对日益提高的对铁路运输能力的需求，期望通过新型列控系统的设计，达到提升既有线路运输能力的目的。因此，对新型 T-CBTC 系统进行运输能力评估具有重要意义。为了验证系统结构、控制方式、通信方式的改变对系统运输能力的影响，本节借鉴 UIC406 方法，基于 T-CBTC 列车运行控制原理，结合典型作业场景，通过计算与运输能力直接相关的列车运行追踪间隔，最终给出了系统运输能力评估方法。

2.1　进站追踪间隔计算

列车追踪间隔是指前行列车不影响后续列车运行的情况下，他们连续通过同一点的时间间隔[9]。列车在区间连续运行时，T-CBTC 系统与传统 CBTC 的追踪方式没有本质区别，追踪间隔由列车当前位置最不利情况的制动距离、前行列车的位置不确定性、列车运行速度和列车长度等因素决定[10]，仅改变控制系统结构不会造成列车在区间追踪间隔的明显差异，因此本文主要分析车站和折返区域的追踪间隔计算。

T-CBTC 系统中列车进站过程如图 2 所示，当 A 车在站内停车时，A 车将自己的状态信息告知 B 车，B 车根据 A 车传来的信息，将自己的移动授权终点设置为道岔 9 位置。只有当 A 车告知 B 车，自己能够安全驶离站台时，B 车才允许进行进站作业。列车进站时采用匀减速方式使列车停在规定的停车点上。基于上述设定，B 车距离站台规定停车点的距离应为 $S_0 = L_0 + L_1$。其中 L_0 表示站台规定停车点到道岔 9 的距离，L_1 为道岔控制触发距离。

L_1 为道岔触发距离，与 CBTC 系统中进路触发区段对应，是指在 T-CBTC 系统中，在列车要越过某个道岔之前，车载设备必须先同该道岔的所有相关的 OCU 设备建立连接，并向所有相关 OCU 发送列车当前信息及道岔位置请求,以此申请"资源锁"。OCU 根据列车发送的信息和道岔位置请求,决定是否给列车发放"资源锁"。若列车获得了 OCU 发放的"资源锁",则列车取得控制道岔的权限。通过列车及 OCU 间的相互配合,来控制道岔锁闭在正确位置,从而确保列车安全通过。道岔控制触发距离,即列车何时开始控制道岔,影响着系统运行效率,是一个关键指标,下面结合列车安全制动模型,考虑通信延时、道岔转换时间等因素,对合理的道岔控制触发距离进行计算。

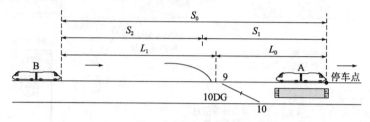

图 2 T-CBTC 系统进站追踪间隔示意图

根据车—车通信下列车对道岔的控制过程分析道岔控制触发距离的计算,同 CBTC 下进路触发区段计算原理类似,在道岔前增加 D_1 安全余量, D_2 制动距离,并考虑 ATC 层面延时和 OCU 层面延时期间的走行距离 D_3 和 D_4 ,如图 3 所示。

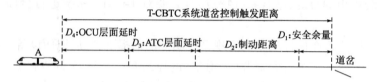

图 3 T-CBTC 系统道岔控制触发距离示意图

车—车通信下道岔控制触发距离可由公式(1)计算。

$$S_{SW} = D_1 + D_2 + D_3 + D_4 \tag{1}$$

其中 D_4 为 OCU 子系统延时期间(包括列车同 OCU 间的通信延时和道岔的转动到位所需的时间)列车行走距离的总和。可由公式(2)计算。

$$D_4 = v \cdot t_{OCU} \tag{2}$$

v 表示列车在当前线路实际运行速度。

D_3 表示触发制动后,列车在制动开始前走行的距离。根据列车安全制动模型[11],可由公式(3)计算:

$$D_3 = v \cdot t_{delay} + \frac{a_{max} \cdot t_{delay}^2}{2} + v_{max} \cdot t_{coast}$$

$$v_{max} = v + a_{max} \cdot t_{delay} \tag{3}$$

其中, t_{delay} 是车辆牵引系统的反应延迟时间, a_{max} 是车辆的最大加速度, v_{max} 是列车结束失控加速阶段后的速度, t_{coast} 是列车在紧急制动力尚未达到标称值前的惰行时间。

D_2 表示列车由制动开始直到完全停止时走过的距离,可由公式(4)进行计算:

$$D_2 = \frac{v_{max}^2}{2 \cdot a_{eb}} \tag{4}$$

其中, a_{eb} 为列车最不利情况下的紧急制动率。

D_1 为道岔前方预留的安全余量,根据列车当前速度和线路实际情况确定,可由公式(5)计算。

$$D_1 = k_0 + k_1 v + k_2 v^2 \tag{5}$$

其中 k_0, k_1, k_2 ,根据线路和车辆的实际情况设置。至此只要确定列车参数和系统各类延时时间等,就可以对 T-CBTC 系统道岔控制触发距离进行计算。

进一步假设,列车在线路上的按照限速 v_0 运行,然后在某一点以加速度 a_0 开始匀减速运动,正好能够停在规定的停车点上,则制动距离 S_1 可由公式(6)计算:

$$S_1 = \frac{v_0^2}{2 \cdot a_0} \tag{6}$$

同传统 CBTC 系统进站理论间隔时间类似，T-CBTC 系统中列车进站的理论间隔时间 T_1 由三部分组成，见公式(7)：

$$T_1 = t_{stay} + t_{decelerate} + t_{uniform} \tag{7}$$

其中，制动过程用时 $t_{decelerate} = v_0/a_0$；匀速行驶距离里为 S_2，用时 $t_{uniform} = (S_0 - S_1)/v_0$；另外 A 车停站时间为 t_{stay}。

2.2 折返追踪间隔计算

在 T-CBTC 系统中，以站前单渡线折返作业为例，过程如图 4 所示。

A 车连接 9-10 道岔的 OCU（T-CBTC 中，道岔 9 和道岔 10 可独立操作），获取道岔 9 的"资源锁"并将道岔 9 控制到定位；之后 B 车连接 9-10 道岔的 OCU，只能获得 9、10 道岔中道岔 10 的"资源锁"，B 车将道岔 10 锁闭在反位，但由于无法控制道岔 9，B 车被禁止侧向通过 9-10 道岔。A 车越过道岔 9 后，OCU 释放道岔 9 的"资源锁"。B 车即刻获取道岔 9 的"资源锁"，将道岔 9 转动到反位。B 车确认 A 车驶入安全区域后（确保 A 车和 B 车不会侧向冲突的位置），即可开始侧向通过 9-10 道岔。而 CBTC 系统中，A 车离开道岔区段后，联锁系统才能够控制道岔，排列进路，待进路排列完成后，B 车才能侧向通过道岔。因此在 T-CBTC 系统中下，列车能够更早地对道岔进行控制。

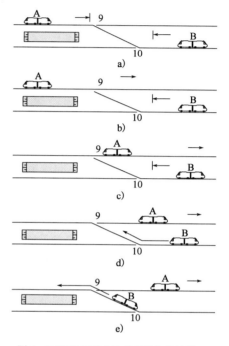

图 4 T-CBTC 系统中站前折返作业过程

从 A 车完全释放道岔 9 的资源开始计时，列车释放道岔 9 资源后，B 车申请道岔 9 的资源锁，接着 B 车经过道岔 9 运行至站台并停站办理乘客上下车业务。之后列车 B 从站台发车至释放道岔 9 资源锁，计时结束，这个时间即为折返触发间隔 T_2。计算公式如下：

$$T_2 = T_{switch} + T_{reaction} + T_{in} + T_{stay} + T_{out} \tag{8}$$

其中，T_{switch} 为列车申请并占用道岔资源锁及道岔位置转换锁闭时间；$T_{reaction}$ 为车载设备反应时间；T_{in} 为列车进站时间；T_{stay} 为列车停站时间；T_{out} 为列车从站台驶出至释放道岔 9 的资源锁的时间。

2.3 运输能力计算

通过上文对 T-CBTC 系统列车控制原理和不同场景下的追踪间隔的分析计算，可以进一步对 T-CBTC 系统的运输能力进行评估。参考 UIC406 方法[12]，将运输能力定义为"在一个规定的时间窗口内，可办理的列车运行线总数目"。若只选取折返区域和车站区域进行分析，则计算方法如下：

$$N = \frac{T}{t_{block}} \tag{9}$$

其中 N 为列车运行线总数，T 为选取的时间窗口长度，t_{block} 为追踪间隔时间，由于列车在运行过程中可能受到多种因素的干扰，因此列车实际追踪间隔比理论间隔长，根据 UIC406 的相关规定，额外增加一个附加时间，此时间是最小运行间隔的 8% ~ 13%。

3 不同模式下的车站区域能力计算

前文介绍了 T-CBTC 系统中传统模式下的车站区域及折返区域能力计算方法，为了验证不同系统结构及不同运行模式对运输能力的影响，寻求提升铁路系统运输能力的关键环节，本节介绍了不同系统结构下和不同运行模式下的运力计算方法。引入了目前新提出的虚拟连挂（Virtual Coupling，VC）列车运行控制的概念。既有CBTC系统中传统进站模式的计算参考文献[13]，本节另外分析了四种模式，包括CBTC下的MB(移动闭塞,Moving Block)进站模式、T-CBTC下的MB进站模式、CBTC下的VC进站模式、T-CBTC下的VC进站模式。

3.1 MB进站模式

本节的MB进站模式包括CBTC系统和T-CBTC系统。

CBTC系统下后车B不考虑前车A所处状态，始终以A车的车尾作为移动授权的终点的进站方式，如图5所示。

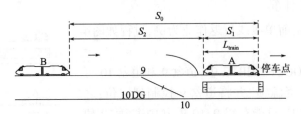

图5 CBTC系统MB进站模式

同样列车进站时采用匀减速的方式使列车停在规定的停车点上。那么可以预见，最理想的情况应该是，B车在与停车点距离为S_1某个位置上开始做匀减速运动，恰好停在站台规定停车点，并且此时，A车恰好已安全经驶离站台，S_2同样为匀速行驶距离。

设A车正常启动的时间为t'_1，A车的制动距离S_1和时间的关系可由公式(10)计算：

$$S_1 = \frac{a_1 \cdot t_1'^2}{2} \tag{10}$$

B车的走行距离S_0和时间的关系可由公式(11)计算：

$$S_0 = v_0 \cdot t'_1 - \frac{a_0 \cdot t_1'^2}{2} \tag{11}$$

为确保A车和B车之间安全，S_0和S_1的关系需满足公式(12)，其中L_{train}为列车长度。

$$S_0 - S_1 > L_{train} \tag{12}$$

此时列车进站的理论间隔时间T_1可由公式(13)计算：

$$T_1 = t_{stay} + \frac{v_0}{a_0} + \frac{S_0 - S_1}{v_0} \tag{13}$$

进而利用2.3节中的公式即可计算运输能力。

T-CBTC系统与传统CBTC系统MB模式下车站区域的计算过程不存在明显差异。

3.2 VC模式进站

虚拟连挂(Virtual Coupling,VC)技术是为了提升铁路系统运输能力而提出的新型列车运行控制技术，采用车—车无线通信取代物理车钩，使两列甚至多列列车通过虚拟连挂作为一个整体在轨道上运行[14,15]。

VC运营场景还没有统一的认识和规范，因此本文选取最具代表性的一种VC运营场景——两列车通过虚拟连挂作为一个整体进站[16]（前提为站台长度足够两列车停靠）。

CBTC系统中，一个Train set作为一个整体，依然遵循传统的进站模式，如图6所示。

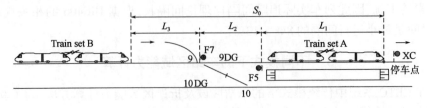

图6 CBTC系统VC进站模式

图中 L_1 为传统 CBTC 进路触发区段长度，L_2 为道岔区段 9DG 的长度，L_3 为 VC 列车组长度及防护距离，S_0 为 L_1、L_2、L_3 的总长度。此时的列车理论追踪间隔 T_1 为：

$$T_1 = t_{\text{stay}} + \frac{v_0}{a_0} + \frac{\left(S_0 - \frac{v_0^2}{2 \cdot a_0}\right)}{v_0} \tag{14}$$

此时由于列车为两两编组，实际的列车数和运输能力为公式(9)的 2 倍，即 2N。

T-CBTC 系统中的 VC 模式与传统 CBTC 系统的差别在于计算中使用道岔触发控制距离代替进路触发区段长度 L_1，其他计算过程均相同。

4 仿真分析

4.1 进站追踪间隔结果对比

第 2 节中，推导出了 T-CBTC 系统中进路触发距离和理论列车间隔时间等指标的计算过程。利用上述结果，采用 Matlab 仿真工具对进路触发长度进行求解并定性和定量进行分析，进而给出进站和折返作业的列车理论间隔时间。

根据 IEEE 1474[11]，获得城市轨道交通系统各参数值如表 1 所示。

城市轨道交通系统参数取值　　　　表1

参　数	含　义	取　值
$a_{\max}$	列车最大加速度	1.058 m/s²
a_{eb}	列车紧急制动加速度	0.85 m/s²
t_{delay}	施加制动力的延迟时间	1.8s
t_{coast}	惰行时间	2s
t_{ATS}	ATS 层面延时	0.55s
t_{CBI}	CBI 层面延时	4.55s
t_{ZC}	ZC 层面延时	0.55s
t_{OCU}	OCU 层面延时	4.55s
k_0 k_1 k_2	与线路和车辆实际情况相关参数	1 0.1 0.01

使用表 1 中的参数取值，在 Matlab 中对公式(1)进行仿真计算，同时计算传统 CBTC 系统进路触发区段长度。之后将计算出的触发距离作为输入，结合进站作业场景，分析不同系统中的列车追踪间隔。其中车站作业参数取值如表 2 所示。

进站作业中参数取值　　　　表2

参　数	含　义	取　值
L_0	停车点到道岔 9 距离	215m
L_1	停车点与 JZ21 距离	150m
L_2	9DG 长度	129m
$L_{\text{train-set}}$	VC 停车点与 JZ21 距离	320m
	线路限速	70km/h
	匀减速减速度	0.7m/s²
	停站时间	40s

区段触发长度如图 7a)所示，T-CBTC 系统的道岔控制触发距离要小于 CBTC 系统中进路触发区段的长度，并且随着列车运行速度的增加，二者间的差值递增。这有助于提高车辆通过轨道区段时的效率。

不同作业模式下进站作业理论时间如图7b)所示,在列车允许最大运行速度为70km/h时,同样进站作业模式下,CBTC系统理论时间为92s,T-CBTC系统理论时间为88s,T-CBTC系统由于不涉及缩短进站间隔的本质影响因素,效率的提升仅停留在缩短触发距离等影响较小的方面,时间提升约为4.3%,优势并不明显。而总是以前车车尾作为移动授权终点的MB进站方式,理论进站时间可缩短至为70s,效率提升约为23.9%,对效率的提升显著。另外CBTC+VC和T-CBTC+VC对应的时间间隔分别为96s和94s,是由于列车组长度更长造成的时间增加。由图中可以看出进站间隔只能在一定范围内随速度的提升而缩短,之后速度超过一定范围,进站间隔反而呈增加趋势。

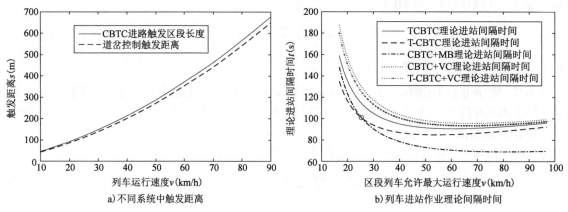

图7 触发距离及进站时间仿真结果

4.2 折返追踪间隔结果对比

对于折返作业,结合前文计算的进站时间,在CBTC系统和T-CBTC系统中各单项作业的作业时间如表3所示。

折返作业各单项作业时间标准　　　　　表3

CBTC作业项目	作业时间(s)	T-CBTC作业项目	作业时间(s)
列车进站时间 t_{in}	52	列车进站时间 t_{in}	48
站台停站时间 t_{stay}	40	站台停站时间 t_{stay}	40
列车出站时间 t_{out}	52	列车出站时间 t_{out}	48
设备反应延迟时间 $t_{reaction}$	5	设备反应延迟时间 $t_{reaction}$	5
驾驶员换端时间	50	驾驶员换端时间	50
办理接车进路时间	14	道岔资源占用及锁闭时间	12
办理发车进路时间	14	—	—

由于T-CBTC系统中申请并占用道岔资源时可以单独占用单个道岔,且不需要通过地面CI和ZC,仅有列车和OCU的直接通信即可完成,因此将作业时间设置为12s,小于CBTC系统中的接发车进路办理时间。另外在T-CBTC系统中以车为核心的列车运行控制理论上不需要驾驶员参与,但是为应对各种复杂的环境,分析中依然计算了折返过程的驾驶员换端时间。可以通过公式(8)计算站前单渡线折返的折返时间,同时与CBTC系统对比如图8所示。

可以看出在站前单渡线折返过程中,T-CBTC系统与传统CBTC系统相比的优势在于缩短了进路办理时间和进出站时间,单个道岔的控制方式,整体折返间隔大约可以由98s缩短至94s,对折返能力有一定提升,但并不明显。

4.3 运输能力对比

为对比T-CBTC与传统CBTC运输能力的差异,选取时间窗口$N=1h$,分别对车站区域和折返区域进行计算,实际阻塞时间t_{block}按如下公式计算。

$$t_{block} = (1 + \Delta)t_{headway}, \Delta \in (8\% \sim 13\%) \tag{15}$$

式中：$t_{headway}$——前文计算的追踪间隔时间。

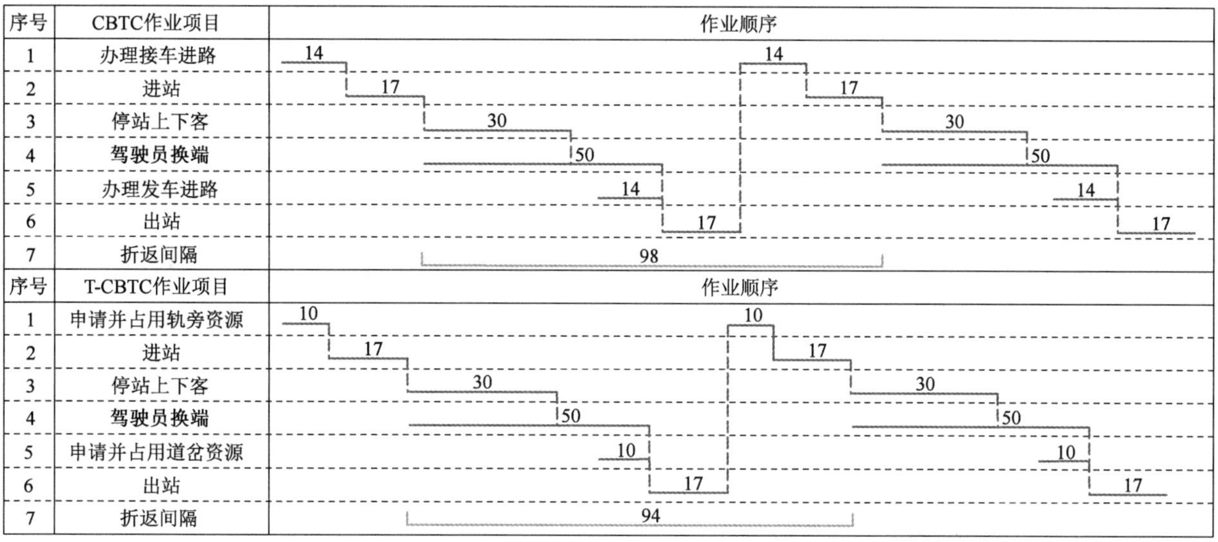

序号	CBTC作业项目	作业顺序
1	办理接车进路	14 ... 14
2	进站	17 ... 17
3	停站上下客	30 ... 30
4	驾驶员换端	50 ... 50
5	办理发车进路	14 ... 14
6	出站	17 ... 17
7	折返间隔	98

序号	T-CBTC作业项目	作业顺序
1	申请并占用轨旁资源	10 ... 10
2	进站	17 ... 17
3	停站上下客	30 ... 30
4	驾驶员换端	50 ... 50
5	申请并占用道岔资源	10 ... 10
6	出站	17 ... 17
7	折返间隔	94

图 8　站前单渡线折返时间示意图

车站区域结果见表 4，相比于 CBTC 系统，T-CBTC 系统架构下，每小时能够对规划 1~2 列列车，对系统运输能力的提升与 4.1 节进站追踪间隔的提升效果一致。CBTC 系统进站区域结合 MB 模式，能够增加约 11 列列车效果提升明显。仿真结果也表明，VC 等新的列车运行控制理念可以实现更高的运力提升。

一小时内进站作业列车数目　　表 4

列车进站模式	列车总数目（列）
CBTC	34~36
T-CBTC	36~37
CBTC + MB	45~47
CBTC + VC	66~69
T-CBTC + VC	67~70

折返区域的提升效果如表 5 所示，仅改变系统结构和轨旁资源控制方式，能增加 1 到 2 列列车。

一小时内折返作业列车数目　　表 5

列车运行模式	列车总数目（列）
CBTC	32~34
T-CBTC	33~35

5　结　语

本文分析了基于车—车通信的列车运行控制系统新型系统结构和特点，并结合列车运行控制原理，提出了 T-CBTC 系统典型作业区域运输能力评估方法，并给出了不同模式下仿真对比结果。论文主要成果有：

（1）本文从追踪间隔的角度出发的 T-CBTC 系统运输能力评估方法，能够准确量化 T-CBTC 系统在不同运营场景下的运输能力。

（2）T-CBTC 系统的引入，从理论上为能够将进站追踪间隔缩短 4.3%，折返追踪间隔缩短 4%，换算为每小时增加的列车数为 1~2 列，从运力角度来说提升效果有限。

(3)以列车为中心的系统架构为新型列控模式,如虚拟连挂等,提供可能。采用虚拟连挂运行模式的 T-CBTC 系统,理论上能够将每小时运行列车数提升 1 倍。

本文的 T-CBTC 系统运输能力评估方法能够实现 T-CBTC 系统不同场景下的运力分析,对 T-CBTC 系统的实施和改进具有借鉴意义。

参考文献

[1] 宁滨,刘朝英. 中国轨道交通列车运行控制技术及应用[J]. 铁道学报,2017,39(2):1-7.

[2] He L N. Research on Train Control System Based on Communications[J]. Applied Mechanics & Materials,2013,253-255:1427-1430.

[3] Briginshaw D. Alstom's simplified CBTC technology to debut in Lille[J]. International Railway Journal,2013(6):29.

[4] Hann,G. Incremental Train Control System[J]. IEEE Vehicular Technology Magazine,2010,5(4):50-55.

[5] European Commission within the Seven Framework Programme,Next generation of train control systems project[R],2013,WEB:http://www.NGTC.eu.

[6] M. Haltuf. Shift2Rail JU from Member State's Point of View[J]. Transportation Research Procedia,2016,14:1819-1828.

[7] Nakamura,Yasuyuki. Overview of the Next-generation Railway Operation System in the Tokyo Metropolitan Area[J]. jr east technical review,2011.

[8] 陈坦. 以列车为核心的 CBTC 系统安全防护方法研究[D]. 北京:北京交通大学,2019.

[9] 陈荣武,诸昌铃,刘莉. CBTC 系统列车追踪间隔计算及优化[J]. 西南交通大学学报,2011(4):579-585.

[10] 田长海,张守帅,张岳松,等. 高速铁路列车追踪间隔时间研究[J]. 铁道学报,2015,37(10):1-6.

[11] Rail Transit Vehicle Interface Standards Committee of the IEEE Vehicular Technology Society. IEEE Std 1474.1-2004. IEEE Standard for Communications-Based Train Control (CBTC) Performance and Functional Requirements. USA:The Institute of Electrical and Electronics Engineers,2005:1,16.

[12] Leaflet UIC406-Capacity[M]. International Union of railway(UIC),Paris,2006.

[13] Wang H,Zhao N,Chen L. An integrated capacity evaluation method for CBTC-system-equipped urban rail lines[J]. Proceedings of the Institution of Mechanical Engineers,Part F:Journal of Rail and Rapid Transit,2013.

[14] Meo C D,Vaio M D,Nardone R,et al. ERTMS/ETCS Virtual Coupling:Proof of Concept and Numerical Analysis[J]. IEEE Transactions on Intelligent Transportation Systems,2019.

[15] ERTMS level 4. Train Convoys or Virtual Coupling[J]. IRSE News,2016,219:14-15.

[16] T Schumann. Increase of Capacity on The Shinkansen High-speed Line Using Virtual Coupling[J]. International Journal of Transport Development and Integration,2017,4(1):666-676.

基于 PSO-RF-SVR 组合模型的城市轨道短时客流预测研究

徐金华　鲁文博

(长安大学运输工程学院)

摘　要　对城市轨道客流进行准确预测是智能交通系统中非常关键的一步,而城市轨道短时客流呈现出非线性的特征。基于此,提出一种基于粒子群算法(PSO)优化的随机森林(RF)与支持向量回归(SVR)组合预测方法。利用改进粒子群算法对 RF 和 SVR 关键参数及组合权重进行优化,构建 PSO-RF-SVR 组合模型,并与 RF 及 SVR 模型作对比分析,以西安市轨道交通 2 号线客流预测为例进行实例分析。结果表明,PSO-RF-SVR 组合模型预测的平均相对误差为 1.15%,精度高于 RF 和 SVR 这 2 种模型。PSO-RF-SVR 模型具有较高的预测精度,可为城市轨道短时客流预测提供参考。

关键词 轨道交通 客流预测 组合模型 随机森林 支持向量机

0 引　言

城市轨道交通已成为城市内部公共交通系统中重要的组成部分。为了降低城市轨道交通的运营成本,提高运输效率,需要依据未来一段时间内客流波动情况来动态调整列车运行组织方案,而城市轨道短时客流预测是核心部分。较为精准地预测未来一段时间内城市轨道交通的客流量,可以为列车运行组织提供客观依据,有利于城市轨道运行管理部门做出科学的管理与控制措施。

目前,国内外在短时客流预测上较为常用的方法有 ARIMA 模型[1]、神经网络[2]、最近邻法[3]、支持向量机[4]、贝叶斯模型[5]等。然而,上述各方法均有其优势和不足之处,仅仅利用单一的方法对城市轨道交通客流进行预测常常难以取得较高的预测精度。随机森林(Random Forest,RF)模型是 Leo 提出的一种机器学习模型,其可以处理分类和回归问题[6]。随机森林(RF)是基于决策树分类器的融合算法,可以有效地避免"过拟合"和"欠拟合"的情况。支持向量机(Support Vector Machines,SVM)是 Vapni 等依据统计学理论提出的机器学习方法。支持向量机(SVM)中用于解决回归问题的模型为支持向量回归(Support Vector Regression,SVR)。支持向量回归模型(SVR)在解决非线性回归问题时将其转换为高维空间中的线性问题,具有较好的泛化能力,这也使其成为客流预测领域中较为流行的一种方法[7]。随机森林中决策树数量 t 和分裂个数 m 以及 SVR 中的惩罚因子 C、核函数参数 σ、不敏感系数 ε 参数是决定预测精度的关键参数[8]。当前常用的方法为网格搜索(grid search)和随机搜索(randomize search)结合交叉验证(cross validation)来确定参数,但结果往往不太理想。

为有效地提高城市轨道交通客流预测精度,本文提出了一种基于改进粒子群算法(Particle swarm optimization,PSO)优化的 RF-SVR 组合模型,利用粒子群算法对 RF 和 SVR 的关键参数及组合权重进行优化,建立 PSO-RF-SVR 组合模型,并构建以网格搜索法确定关键参数的 RF 和 SVR 模型作对比分析。以西安市 2 号线地铁客流为例进行实例分析,验证了 PSO-RF-SVR 组合模型在提高客流预测精度上的有效性。

1 PSO-RF-SVR 组合模型

1.1 粒子群算法

粒子群优化算法(Particle swarm optimization,PSO)是 Eberhart 等人首先提出[9],是一种群智能优化算法。它模拟了鸟群觅食行为:假设某区域仅有一处有食物,鸟群不知道食物所在位置,鸟群的任务是搜索食物。它们能相互传递彼此的信息,将自身的位置信息传播出去,由此判断谁距食物最近,进而得出最佳方案,再将此最优方案传递给整个鸟群。粒子群优化算法将鸟看作是搜索空间中的粒子,每个粒子都有自身的位置和速度信息以及一个适应值,每个粒子通过追踪个体极值和全局极值来不断地更新自身,并最终使得整个粒子群收敛到最优解。

设 D 表示搜索空间的维度,$x_i = (x_{i1}, x_{i2}, \cdots, x_{iD})T$ 表示粒子 i 当前位置,$p_i = (p_{i1}, p_{i2}, \cdots, p_{iD})T$ 表示粒子 i 曾经到达的最好位置,最优粒子序号为 g,$v_i = (v_{i1}, v_{i2}, \cdots, v_{iD})T$ 是粒子 i 的速度,每个粒子依据式(1)和式(2)更新自身的速度与位置:

$$v_{id}(t+1) = \omega v_{id}(t) + c_1 r_1 [p_{id}(t) - x_{id}(t)] + c_2 r_2 [p_{gd}(t) - x_{gd}(t)] \quad (1)$$

$$x_{id}(t+1) = x_{id}(t) + v_{id}(t) \quad (2)$$

式中:t——算法迭代次数;

c_1,c_2——学习因子,本文取$c_1=1,c_2=1$;

r_1,r_2——[0,1]间的随机数;

ω——惯性权重系数。

1.2 随机森林模型

随机森林模型建立了一个森林,这个森林是由若干个决策树组成,而且每颗决策树之间没有关联。利用 Bootstrap 方法从原始数据集中随机抽取k个训练样本集,并将每个训练集生成对应的决策树;其次,从T个输入变量中随机选择$m(m<T)$个变量进行训练,m在训练过程中保持不变;训练结束后,当输入测试集时,每颗决策树均会对测试样本进行预测,并采用平均加权得到最终的回归结果。

假设对于一个测试样本x,第l颗决策树的输出为$xf_{\text{tree},l}(x)=i,i=1,2,3\cdots,c,l=1,2,\cdots,L,L$为RF决策数棵数,则RF的输出为:

$$f_{\text{RF}}(x) = \arg\max\{I[f_{\text{tree},l}(x) = i]\}, i = 1,2,\cdots,c \tag{3}$$

式中:$I(\cdot)$——满足括号中表达式的样本个数。

1.3 支持向量回归模型

支持向量回归(SVR)将传统线性方程中的线性项替换成核函数,在高维空间中建立线性决策函数,从而进行预测。SVR 使用了ε不敏感损失函数。SVR 目前被认为是解决机器学习回归问题的有效模型。

对于给定的训练样本:

$$D = \{(x_1,y_1),(x_2,y_2),\cdots,(x_n,y_n)\}, y \in R \tag{4}$$

对于非线性回归问题,使用非线性函数将训练数据映射到高维特征空间,在该高维特征空间中进行线性回归。训练样本x_i满足下列条件:

$$y_i(x_i * w + b) - 1 + \delta_i \geq 0 \tag{5}$$

式中:δ_i——松弛变量,满足$\delta_i \geq 0, i=1,2,3,\cdots,n$;

w——权向量;

b——偏置。

定义ε不敏感损失函数如下:

$$l_\varepsilon(z) = \begin{cases} 0, & if|z| \leq \varepsilon \\ |z| - \varepsilon, & \text{otherwise} \end{cases} \tag{6}$$

式中:ε——不敏感系数,表示对于偏差小于的项不进行惩罚。

求最大化支持向量回归边界等价于如下问题:

$$\begin{cases} \min \frac{1}{2}\|\omega\|^2 + c\sum_{i=1}^{n}\delta_i \\ \text{s.t.} y_i(x_i \cdot w + b) - 1 + \delta_i \geq 0 \end{cases} \tag{7}$$

式中:δ_i——$\delta_i \geq 0, i=1,2,3,\cdots,n$;

c——惩罚参数,其作用是调节优化松弛变量。

通过上述推导,得到SVR函数:

$$f(x) = \sum_{i=1}^{n}(a'_i - a_i)k(x,x_i) + b \tag{8}$$

其中,$k(x,x_i)$是满足 Mercer 条件的核函数,a'_i和a_i为对应的拉格朗日乘子。本文选取高斯径向基核函数,和其他核函数比而言参数较少,其表达式如下:

$$k(x,x_i) = e^{-\frac{\|x-x_i\|^2}{2\sigma^2}} \tag{9}$$

式中:σ——核宽度,代表了训练样本的分布特性,从而确定局部领域的宽度。

1.4 PSO-RF-SVR 组合模型实施步骤

本文预测模型基本思路为:基于 PSO 优化算法及 RF 和 SVR 模型,构建 PSO-RF-SVR 组合模型,确定组合模型待优化的适应度函数、模型参数和组合权重的搜索范围,利用 PSO 算法对 RF-SVR 组合模型决策树个数 t、分裂属性个数 m 以及 SVR 模型的惩罚因子 C、核函数参数 σ、不敏感系数 ε 和组合模型权重 ω_{SVR} 的搜索范围。以样本平均误差绝对值之和作为组合模型的适应度函数 f,如下所示:

$$f = (1 - \omega_{SVR})f_{RF} + \omega_{SVR}f_{SVR} = (1 - \omega_{SVR})\sum_{i=1}^{n}\frac{|y_i - \hat{y}|}{y_i} + \omega_{SVR}\sum_{i=1}^{n}\frac{|y_i - \hat{y}|}{y_i} \tag{10}$$

式中:y_i——第 i 个样本的真实值;

$\hat{y}$——第 i 个样本的预测值;

ω_{SVR}——SVR 模型的权重系数。

组合模型 PSO-RF-SVR 的参数优化步骤如下:

(1)确定粒子群规模数量 M,初始化粒子群$(t,m,C,\sigma,\varepsilon)$,设定最大迭代次数 t_{end},给定算法的惯性权值。将各粒子个体极值 p_{besti} 设置为当前位置,用适值函数计算每个粒子的适应度取适应度最好的粒子对应的个体极值作为初始全局极值 g_{best}。

(2)根据式子(1)和式子(2)更新粒子速度和位置。

(3)评价每个粒子的适应度。若每个粒子的适应值优于其 p_{besti} 对应的值,则更新 p_{besti},否则保留原始 p_{besti} 值。

(4)如果更新后每个粒子的 p_{besti} 值优于全局极值 g_{best},则更新 g_{best},否则保留原始 g_{best} 值。

(5)如果达到最大迭代次数或所得解不再变化,则停止迭代,输出最优解。否则,返回(3)。

2 案例分析

2.1 数据来源与参数优化

实例数据为西安市地铁 2 号线 2017 年 10 月 1 日至 2017 年 12 月 28 日日客运量,数据如图 1 所示。2017 年 10 月 1 日至 2017 年 12 月 14 日的客流数据作为训练集来标定模型参数,2017 年 12 月 15 日至 2017 年 12 月 28 日客流数据作为预测集来检验模型预测效果。

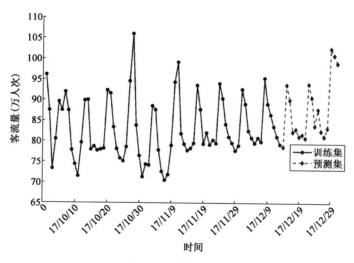

图 1 实例数据折线图

为加快计算收敛,将数据作区间规范化处理,根据数据的区间边界值将数值归一到[0,1]区间内,计算如式(11)所示。

$$x'_i = \frac{x_i - A_{\min}}{A_{\max} - A_{\min}} \quad (11)$$

式中：$A_{\min}$、$A_{\max}$——数据中的最小值和最大值；
x_i——数据原始值；
x'_i——规范化后的值。

PSO 算法最大迭代次数 $t=200$。PSO-RF-SVR 模型待优化参数搜索空间为：决策树数量 $t\in[1,1000]$，分裂个数 $m\in[1,40]$，惩罚因子 $C\in[10^{-10},10^{-10}]$，核函数参数 $\sigma\in[10^{-10},10^{-10}]$，不敏感系数 $\varepsilon\in[10^{-10},10^{-10}]$，权重系数 $\omega_{SVR}\in[0,1]$，交叉验证参数 $V=10$。利用 PSO 算法优化 RF 和 SVR 模型的参数搜索空间与 PSO-RF-SVR 模型相同。

利用 PSO 算法对 RF-SVR 模型的参数及权重优化结果为：决策树数量 $t=20$，分裂个数 $m=4$，惩罚因子 $C=3.35982$，核函数参数 $\sigma=0.29763$，不敏感系数 $\varepsilon=0.18264$，权重系数 $\omega_{SVR}=0.7397$。

2.2 预测结果与分析

经过 PSO 优化后的 RF-SVR 模型预测结果及其与 RF 模型和 SVR 模型对 2017 年 12 月 15 日至 2017 年 12 月 28 日的客流量进行预测，结果如图 2 所示。

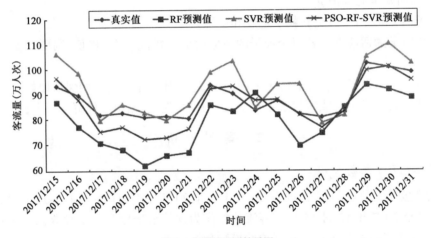

图 2　各模型预测结果图

采用 MRE 和 RMSE 指标来评估模型的准确率及稳定性。MRE 和 RMSE 表示了真实值与预测值之间的偏差，其值越小表示预测效果越好，计算公式如下：

$$\mathrm{MRE} = \frac{100\%}{n}\sum_{i=1}^{n}\frac{|A_i - F_i|}{A_i} \quad (12)$$

$$\mathrm{RMSE} = \sqrt{\frac{1}{n}\sum_{i=1}^{n}(A_i - F_i)^2} \quad (13)$$

式中：A_i——客流真实值；
F_i——客流预测值。

PSO-RF-SVR 模型及 RF 模型和 SVR 模型的预测误差指标结果如表 1 所示。从表 1 可以看出，PSO-RF-SVR 模型对预测样本的 MRE 为 4.1%，精度高于 RF 模型和 SVR 模型，这表明本文提出的 PSO-RF-SVR 模型具有更高的预测精度与泛化能力，可以作为城市轨道客流预测的有效方式。从 PSO 算法优化 RF-SVR 模型的权重系数 $\omega_{SVR}=0.7397$ 来看，SVR 模型在组合模型中占主导地位。但从 PSO-RF-SVR 模型的预测效果来看，RF 模型和 SVR 模型具有较好的互补性，组合模型可以有效地综合 RF 模型和 SVR 模型的优点。从 RMAE 指标来看，PSO-RF-SVR 模型对预测样本 RMSE 为 4.3，优于其他两种模型，再次验证了 PSO-RF-SVR 模型具有较好的预测效果。

各模型预测误差指标结果表			表1
模 型	MRE		RMSE
RF	11.5%		17.6
SVR	6.1%		10.4
PSO-RF-SVR	4.1%		4.3

3 结 语

本文基于粒子群算法(PSO)、随机森林(RF)和支持向量机(SVR)三者的优点,提出了PSO-RF-SVR组合预测模型模型。以西安市城市轨道交通2号线客流预测为例,对PSO-RF-SVR模型进行了验证,并与RF模型和SVR模型进行对比。结果表明,PSO-RF-SVR模型具有较好的精度和泛化能力,其用于城市轨道交通客流预测,结果是可信的,方案是可行的。

参考文献

[1] WILLIAMS B M, Hoel L A. Modeling and forecasting vehicular traffic flow as a seasonal ARIMA process: theoretical basis and empirical results[J]. Journal of transportation engineering,2003,129(6):664-672.

[2] Vlahogianni E I, Karlaftis M G, Golias J C. Optimized and meta-optimized neural networks for short-term traffic flow prediction:a genetic approach. Transp. Res. Part C,2005,13(3):211-234.

[3] Smith B L, Williams B M, Oswald R K. Comparison of parametric and nonparametric models for traffic flow forecasting[J]. Transportation Research Part C (Emerging Technologies),2002,10(4):303-321.

[4] ZHANG Y, XIE Y. Forecasting of short-term freeway volume with v-support vector machines[J]. Journal of the transportation research record,2007,2024(1):92-99.

[5] Khan A M. Bayesian predictive travel time methodology for advanced traveller information system[J]. Journal of Advanced Transportation,2012,46(1):67-79.

[6] 温博文,董文瀚,解武杰,等.基于改进网格搜索算法的随机森林参数优化[J].计算机工程与应用,2018,54(10):154-157.

[7] 胡昌军.基于改进相空间重构原理的支持向量机月径流模拟[J].水资源与水工程学报,2013(04):213-219.

[8] 崔东文.多重组合神经网络模型在年径流预测中的应用[J].水利水电科技进展,2014(02):63-67.

[9] 董颖,唐加福,许宝栋,等.一种求解非线性规划问题的混合粒子群优化算法[J].东北大学学报(自然科学版)(12):21-24.

基于SVDD的滚动轴承健康状态评估

巫忠书 杜红梅 杨 阳 李夫忠 李凤林

(成都运达科技股份有限公司)

摘 要 针对故障样本少的情况下对滚动轴承的健康状态进行分类与评估的问题,提出了基于支持向量数据描述的轴承健康状态评估方法。首先,基于总体经验模态分解(EEMD)对采集到的振动信号进行分解;其次,对信号进行特征提取,计算出有效值,峰值等关键特征;然后,将关键特征输入训练完成的SVDD模型进行分类,识别出故障数据;最后,根据文中提出的指标进行滚动轴承的健康状态评估。通过分析轴箱轴承实测振动信号,证明了该方法的可行性和有效性。

关键词 轨道交通 健康状态评估 支持向量数据描述(SVDD) 滚动轴承

0 引言

近年来我国轨道交通发展迅速,但安全始终是车辆运行中最重要的因素。滚动轴承作为走行部的关键部件之一,运行环境复杂,受到周期性载荷冲击,容易出现磨损或疲劳剥落等现象,从而影响正常工作,甚至引发严重事故。在实际应用中,轴承的性能劣化是一个渐变的过程,因此识别出轴承的当前健康状态是一个关键的问题。同时轴承健康状态的识别也具有重要的工程应用价值。

目前,通过采集振动加速度信号进行轴承故障识别及其性能退化评估是较成熟的方法,而较多的国内外学者也在不断对其优化改进。有学者[1]提出了基于Gath-Geva模糊聚类进行轴承状态划分的方法,能实现对轴承不同退化阶段的模式识别;有学者[2]提出了基于LMD和SVDD的轴承健康状态评估方法,并通过实验数据验证了该方法的有效性;有学者[3]提出了基于卷积神经网络(CNN)的轴承故障诊断方法,并采用能够自适应学习效率的Adam算法对其进行优化;有学者[4]提出了基于流形空间主曲线相似度的状态评估方法,对滚动轴承性能退化程度进行评估。

在实际应用中,轴承发生故障的频率很低,故障样本数据对比正常数据要少很多。针对这种样本分布不均衡的数据集,多采用单值分类方法。鉴于以上情况,本文提出了一种基于支持向量数据描述(SVDD)的轴承故障识别及健康状态评估方法,通过对振动加速度信号的分析与处理,对轴承的健康状态进行评估。

本文综合考虑了信号处理流程及单值分类算法特点,以总体经验模态分解(EEMD)对信号进行预处理,对降噪后的信号提取特征参数,再将特征值输入SVDD模型求解出最小超球体及支持向量,通过样本点是否落在球内区分故障数据与正常数据,最后提出了一种轴承性能退化程度的评估方式,分析结果表明了本文所提方法的有效性和可行性。

1 基于EEMD的信号处理及特征提取

1.1 总体经验模态分解理论(EEMD)

总体经验模态分解(Ensemble Empirical Mode Decomposition,EEMD),由N.E.Huang等人在EMD[5,6]的基础上提出的添加辅助噪声的信号分解方法,利用白噪声频谱均匀分布的特性,改善EMD分解时出现的模态混叠现象[7]。

EEMD算法的具体步骤如下:

(1)在原信号$x(n)$中多次加入相同幅值的白噪声:

$$y_i(t) = x(t) + an_i(t) \tag{1}$$

式中:a——白噪声幅值;

$n_i(t)$——白噪声$(i=1,2,3,\cdots,N)$;

N——对原信号加噪的次数。

(2)分别对加噪声的多组信号进行EMD分解,得到对应的IMF:

$$y_i(t) = \sum_{j=1}^{m} \text{IMF}_{ij}(t) + r_i(t) \tag{2}$$

式中:$\text{IMF}_{ij}(t)$——第i次加噪信号的第j个IMF分量;

m——IMF分量个数;

$r_i(t)$——第i次加噪信号的分解残差。

(3)对多组IMF进行平均,得到最终的IMF分量:

$$\text{IMF}_j(t) = \frac{\sum_{i=1}^{N} \text{IMF}_{ij}(t)}{N} \tag{3}$$

上述过程中,EEMD通过对原始信号添加噪声,改善原始信号中间歇性噪声或脉冲导致的信号不连续,最后对多组IMF做集成平均以抑制白噪声带来的干扰。所以EEMD既能消除模态混叠,又能提高信号分析的精度。

1.2 信号特征提取

轴承的故障形式主要包括压痕、电腐蚀、磨损、断裂等,在其发生故障后会使得振动明显加剧且异常,此时对运行过程中轴承振动信号进行采集和处理,即可实现实时故障监测与诊断[1,8]。

通过分析振动加速度信号时域特征,提取了若干能够反映轴承健康状态的特征参数。

其中,主要时域参数包括信号峰值、有效值和峭度指标,如式(4)~式(7)所示。

$$\text{MEAN} = \frac{\sum_i x(n)}{N} \tag{4}$$

$$\text{PPV} = \max[x(n)] - \min[x(n)] \tag{5}$$

$$\text{RMS} = \sqrt{\frac{\sum_{n=1}^{N} x(n)^2}{N}} \tag{6}$$

$$\text{KUR} = \frac{\frac{1}{N} \times \sum_{n=1}^{N} [x(n) - x_{\text{MEAN}}]}{x_{\text{RMS}}^4} \tag{7}$$

2 基于 SVDD 的轴承故障诊断及健康状态评估

2.1 SVDD 原理

支持向量数据描述(Support Vector Data Description,SVDD),是由 Tax 和 Duin 提出的一种单值分类方法,近年来被广泛应用在故障诊断、医学成像、语音识别等领域[9]。其基本思想[10]是:首先,通过非线性映射将原始训练样本 x,映射到高维的特征空间;然后,在特征空间中寻找一个包含全部或大部分被映射到特征空间的训练样本且体积最小的超球体;最后,通过非线性映射,如果新样本点落入最优超球体内,则该样本被视为一个正常点;否则,如果新样本落入到最优超球体外,则该新样本被视为一个异常点。最优超球体由其球心和半径决定。

SVDD 算法的基本原理如下。

设训练样本集 $X = \{x_i | x_i \in R_d, i = 1,2,3,\cdots,n\}$($d$ 为数据维数),a 和 R 分别表示包含所有数据的超球体的球心与半径,则可通过求解以下优化问题在特征空间上建立超球体:

$$\min F(a, R, \xi_i) = R^2 + C \sum_i \xi_i \tag{8}$$

$$\text{s.t.} \ \|x_i - a\|^2 \leq R^2 + \xi_i \tag{9}$$

式中:a——超球体球心;

R——超球体半径;

ξ_i——松弛因子;

C——某个常数,用来平衡错分误差和球体体积。

为了求解以上的二次优化问题,引入拉格朗日乘子将其转化为拉格朗日极值问题:

$$L(R, a, \xi, \alpha, \gamma) = R^2 + C \sum_i \xi_i - \sum_i \alpha_i [R^2 + \xi_i - \|x_i - a\|^2] - \sum_i \gamma_i \xi_i \tag{10}$$

式中:α_i、γ_i——拉格朗日乘子,$\alpha_i \geq 0$,$\gamma_i \geq 0$。

对上式中各自变量求偏导,令其全部等于零,可得:

$$\begin{cases} \sum_i \alpha_i = 1 \\ a = \sum_i \alpha_i x_i \\ \gamma_i = C - \alpha_i \end{cases} \tag{11}$$

将上式代入式中,可得优化后的拉格朗日目标函数:

$$L(R, a, \xi, \alpha, \gamma) = \sum_i \alpha_i (x_i \cdot x_i) - \sum_{i,j} \alpha_i \alpha_j (x_i \cdot x_j) \tag{12}$$

SVDD算法在工程应用中的表现通常与其选择的核函数性能密切相关。常用的核函数包括线性核函数、多项式核函数、高斯核函数等，本文采用的是高斯核函数，表示为如下形式：

$$K(x,y) = \exp\left(-\frac{\|x-y\|^2}{\sigma^2}\right) \quad (13)$$

式中：σ——高斯核函数宽度。

2.2 健康状态评估方法

SVDD模型通过特征空间中样本点是否落在超球体内来判断该样本点代表的状态是健康或是故障。在此基础上，我们还期望能够将故障状态进一步划分，使其能表征出轴承性能退化的各阶段[11]。本文在详细分析了SVDD分类结果与各样本点在空间的分布的基础上，提出一个能够表征轴承健康状态的指标P，如下式所示。

$$P = \frac{d}{R} + K(x,a) + dv \quad (14)$$

$$dv = \frac{\|x-a\|^2}{\|x\|^2 + \|a\|^2} \quad (15)$$

式中：d——SVDD模型输出用于分类的结果；
$K(x,a)$——高斯核函数计算结果。

由上式可知，当样本点落在球内时P值趋于零；当样本点逐渐远离球心，P值也逐渐增大。

3 试验验证

本文采用某型机车实测数据进行验证，列车最大运营速度为80km/h，车轮名义滚动圆直径1250mm。通过轴箱位置的加速度传感器监测轴箱轴承的振动情况，传感器安装位置如图1所示。本文选取轴承全生命周期数据，从正常状态到故障发展最后到拆解，其拆解结果如图2所示。

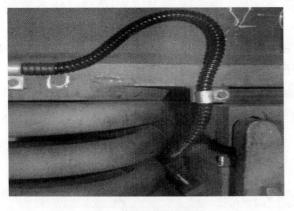

图1 传感器现场安装图

图2 轴承外环故障拆解图

对轴承全生命周期数据进行分析处理，首先，对振动信号样本数据进行EEMD分解，提取包含主要信息的IMF分量，本文选取前3个IMF分量得到重构信号；然后，对上述信号计算特征值，包括峰值、有效值和峭度等。

试验过程中，选取正常状态的滚动轴承特征向量作为训练数据。使用训练得到的SVDD模型对测试数据进行分类。测试数据选取上述故障轴承的全生命周期数据，适当抽取后的识别结果如图3所示。

如图3所示，SVDD模型可以对轴承的故障状态进行识别，识别准确率为100%。

由2.2节健康状态评估计算方式可得测试数据全生命周期的健康状态曲线如图4所示。

如图4所示，基于SVDD模型分类结果及其相对距离，可以对轴承的健康状态进行评估。当轴承处在健康状态时其指标值较低，当轴承出现故障并逐渐发展时，指标值也逐渐增大，其健康状态趋势基本符合轴承性能劣化的演变情况[12]。因此，基于SVDD模型的轴承健康状态评估有较好的可用性及可解释性。

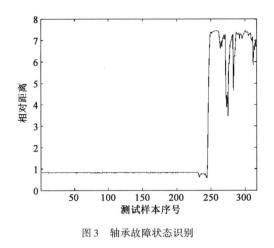

图3 轴承故障状态识别

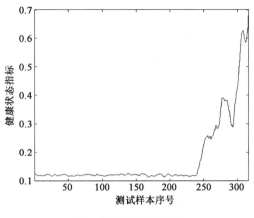

图4 轴承健康状态曲线

4 结 语

根据实测轴箱轴承数据进行滚动轴承健康状态评估方法的验证。(1)采用EEMD方法对滚动轴承信号进行分解,选取前3个IMF分量重构信号,并作特征提取;(2)将正常状态数据的特征向量作为训练数据,输入SVDD模型,得到最优超球体的球心与半径;(3)对测试数据依据其到球心的距离进行故障判别;(4)根据轴承全生命周期数据得出其健康状态变化趋势。试验结果表明,该方法能准确识别出轴承的故障及健康状态,验证了该模型的有效性。

本文对轴承故障的识别及其健康状态的评估方法作了初步探究,还有能够进一步完善的地方:基于振动信号的特征提取是评估模型能够准确工作的前提,因此还可以对信号分解及特征提取技术做进一步研究,以便能够更好地表征部件的运行状态。

参考文献

[1] 方博.滚动轴承健康状态评估方法研究[D].哈尔滨:哈尔滨工业大学,2019.
[2] 杨艳君,魏永合,王晶晶,等.基于LMD和SVDD的滚动轴承健康状态评估[J].机械设计与制造,2019(05):163-166+170.
[3] 刘布宇.基于深度学习的滚动轴承故障诊断研究[D].杭州:杭州电子科技大学,2019.
[4] 尹爱军,梁子晓,张波,等.基于主曲线相似度的轴承健康状态评估方法[J].振动.测试与诊断,2019,39(03):625-630+676.
[5] Huang N E. Review of Empirical Mode Decomposition[J]. Proceedings of Spie—wavelet Applications VIII,2001,4391:71-80.
[6] 陈东月.基于改进的CEEMD及IMF价值评价的高速列车齿轮箱故障诊断研究[D].成都:西南交通大学,2018.
[7] Zhaohua Wu,Norden E. Huang. Ensemble Empirical Mode Decomposition:A Noise-assisted Data Analysis Method[J]. Advances in Adaptive Data Analysis,2009,1(1).
[8] 刘亚.数据驱动的滚动轴承故障诊断与健康状态评估[D].济南:山东大学,2019.
[9] 冉一然.基于PCA-SVDD的故障检测研究与应用[D].重庆:西南大学,2020.
[10] 杨晨.基于SVDD的分类方法研究[D].太原:山西大学,2020.
[11] 赵丽琴,刘昶,邓丞君.样本不均衡条件下设备健康度评估方法[J].计算机测量与控制,2020,28(09):272-275+281.
[12] 周裕华.滚动轴承的性能退化评估与剩余使用寿命预测方法的研究[D].广州:华南理工大学,2018.

铁路电务大数据平台框架体系研究

陈建译[1,2]

(1.西南交通大学信息科学与技术学院;2.中国铁路广州局集团公司)

摘　要　本文提出了一种铁路电务大数据平台框架体系,包括数据平台架构、数据源接口规范、数据采集归一化设计以及数据服务策略等四个方面。本文所提出的体系架构涵盖了系统数据分析、挖掘及融合应用的全过程,为实现数据共享交互、数据综合利用提供了有力支撑和参考。

关键词　大数据技术　电务运维系统　接口规范　归一化采集　服务策略

0　引　言

伴随铁路通信信号技术发展数字化,各实时监测系统产生并存储了海量数据,急需运用大数据技术对累积的数据进行关联分析,挖掘数据价值,及时掌握电务设备运用状态,预防设备隐患,优化检修模式,提升作业水平,降低设备故障,有效确保铁路安全生产[1]。然而目前,电务专业相关监测、监控系统多采用分级部署模式,数据较为分散,集成整合困难;各系统设备厂家数据产生及储存执行的标准差异,数据的可移植性、可用性难以保证[2];数据分析缺乏有效手段,深入挖潜关联性数据难以实现,造成大量可用数据流失[3-5]。针对上述问题,结合电务系统现状,提出一种电务大数据智能运维平台技术体系架构,建立统一的技术框架和标准,为大数据分析技术在电务运维的深入运用提供基础的技术框架和应用平台。

1　数据平台架构

数据平台架构基于既有通信信号系统,在不改动各个子系统和通信传输网络的前提下,实现数据的采集和融合。在硬件系统方面,建立电务数据采集归一化平台,通过安全隔离措施采集各子系统的数据,并完成对电务各子系统数据的清洗、筛选和归一化处理,为电务大数据应用开发奠定统一的数据基础。基于大数据分析的电务智能运维平台整体架构如图1所示。

铁路大数据智能运维平台的软件结构如图2所示,数据平台共分采用数据集成、数据服务和分析应用三级架构,由源数据、存储数据、计算数据、分析业务和呈现数据五个层次组成[6]。

1.1　数据集成

数据集成通过电务各系统数据的归一化处理,实现数据的标准化、规范化、插件化和可替换。通过对通信信号专业监控、监测、检测子系统数据进行归类,包括各信号子系统监测数据、履历信息、生产数据,各通信子系统性能指标、资源数据、告警报警消息,及所有人员管控类数据,接入归一化平台中,在源数据层中采用归一化模块手段对各类通信信号系统数据完成采集和解析[7]。

1.2　数据服务

数据服务包含数据存储和数据计算两层:数据存储层采取混搭架构,充分考虑数据的差异性,兼容管理图形数据、音频影像数据、报表等非结构化数据,提供多种存储形式以解决不同类型数据差异,提高数据快速访问能力及数据存储形式扩展兼容性。数据计算层,采用先进的数据计算处理技术(如流计算、内存计算、分布式计量),并具备数据库存储与查询功能,有效实现差异性数据计算及实时数据计算需求。

基金项目:电务大数据平台运维智能化关键技术研究与应用(K2018G053)。

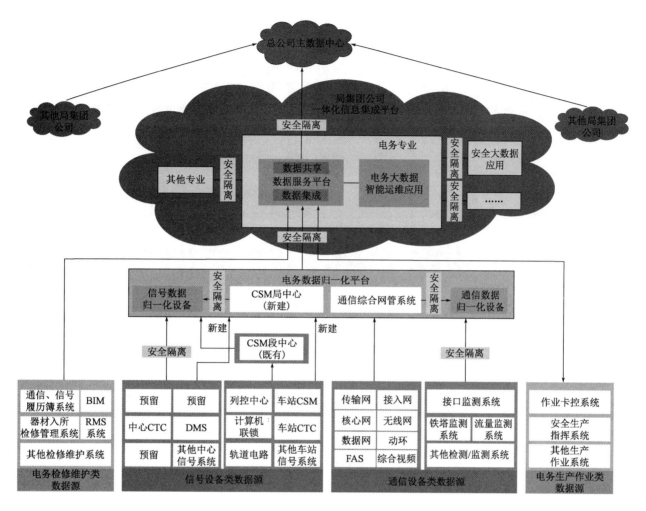

图1　电务大数据智能运维平台系统

1.3　数据应用

数据应用是指对经过数据服务处理后的数据，分要素和用户需求进行选择性提取并进行挖掘运用的过程。数据应用包含业务分析和数据呈现两部分：业务分析部分根据具体需要实现设备分析功能，如电务全生命周期管理、健康管理与故障预测、应急指挥、作业盯控、车地闭环分析、电务一体化分析等。数据呈现部分是一个人机交互窗口，如实现融合展示、位置展示、关联展示、三维展示及可视化图纸，通过地理信息、网络图谱结构、流程引擎和自动报表等实现可视化的呈现方式。

2　数据源接口规范

数据源接口规范是电务大数据智能分析应用的基础。电务子系统较多且多为独立运作，子系统间接口分散，产生源数据难以关联，因此，本文对各子系统数据源进行分类并规范接口方式，大体可分为三类源数据：公共数据源接口、通信数据源接口、信号数据源接口。

2.1　公共数据源接口

电务公共大数据应用主要数据源接口包括电务安全生产指挥系统、作业卡控系统、地理信息接口，接口数据源信息，如表1所示。

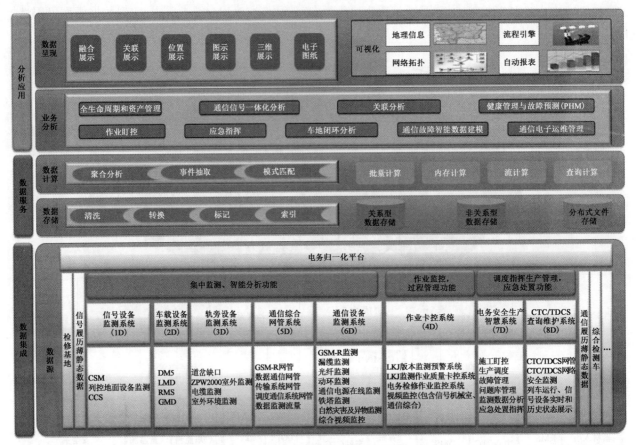

图 2 电务大数据智能运维平台软件结构

公共数据源接口表　　　　　　　　　　　　　　　　　　　　　　表1

接口分类	交互系统	接口方式	接口数据源
作业卡控信息	检测作业质量卡控系统	socket	报警信息
	检修作业监控系统	socket	报警信息、作业信息、工器具信息、视频信息
	机械室门禁	socket	报警信息
	视频监控(含信号机械室、通信综合、移动单兵)	socket	视频、报警信息
生产作业信息	电务安全生产指挥信息	数据库表	施工信息、天窗信息、故障信息、设备信息
地理信息	GIS 平台	WebService	设备地理信息图层、服务等

2.2 通信数据源接口

铁路通信大数据应用主要数据源接口包括通信履历系统、各子系统网管系统、动态检测车系统、视频监控系统、车载无线通信设备运用维护系统以及其他相关信息系统的信息接口。

2.3 信号数据源接口

铁路信号大数据应用主要数据源接口包括信号履历系统、信号设备监测系统、车载设备监测系统、轨旁设备监测系统、CTC/TDCS 查询维护系统以及其他相关信息系统的信息接口。

3 数据采集归一化设计

数据采集归一化处于承上启下的核心地位,为北向应用提供全方位的外部访问协议支持和外部统一标准的访问接口。通过归一化平台框架实现数据采集可适配规范化、标准化、置换化和插件化。运用采集管控方式实现设备影响可知,增强数据采集可靠性,确保数据按照用户需求采集,实现数据模型可用性和实用性。归一化平台如图3所示。

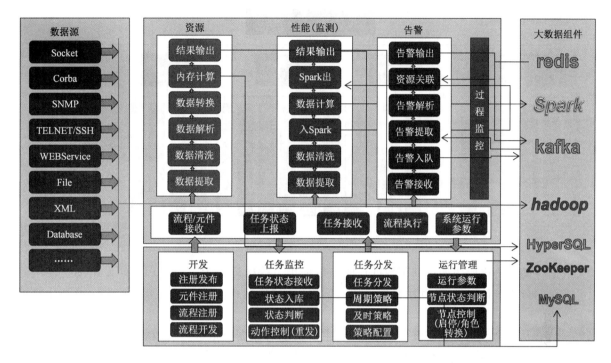

图3 归一化平台示意图

数据源:归一化平台从信号集中监测系统、轨旁监测系统、车载设备监测系统、CTC查询系统、通信网管系统、通信监测监控系统等采集电务设备动态数据信息,支持Socket、Corba、WebService等多种标准接口协议。

数据处理:归一化平台对采集的设备动态数据信息分资源、性能、告警分别进行清洗、解析、汇总输出。对采集到的不规则的原始数据进行词法分析,数据格式标准化,根据处理规则将采集到的原始数据转换成相应的信息模型数据。根据业务需要,提供对数据进行业务的抽取、清洗等能力。

管理控制:界面化管理数据归一化任务,通过页面可实现对采集源、采集机、采集任务的配置、任务执行情况、数据质量报表进行管理、分析的能力。对数据完整性、及时性、合理性进行监控,生成分析报表,从采集和厂家多维度关联分析,方便问题定位,并提供详细信息。

4 数据服务策略

数据服务策略主要用于将归一化平台中已经处理完成的数据通过数据集成实现数据的抽取、转换和导入,并根据数据类型选择操作型数据存储和非结构化数据存储,对于分析类数据可以在数据仓库中构建数据集市,同时为电务大数据应用提供数据支持。

数据服务包括基础数据管理、数据集成、数据共享、大数据存储与分析、数据治理、系统管理六部分,如图4所示。

基础数据管理模块主要提供主数据管理、地理信息管理及数据服务平台所涉及的元数据信息管理功能,满足基础数据集中统一管理和服务提供的需求。

数据集成模块是针对各类数据提供结构化、非结构化、实时流等集成功能,完成用户需求数据采集。

数据共享模块实现了结构化、半结构化、非结构化等全类型数据的规模存储、快速读取及可靠查询功能。采用高效低成本的大数据计算存储技术与传统数据库存储技术相结合的创新运用,用以实现各类结构化、半结构化、非结构化数据的存储;采用云技术实现数据申请、授权、管理、计算和共享,并针对不同用户需求定向产生不同的数据共享策略,控制精度可达字段级。

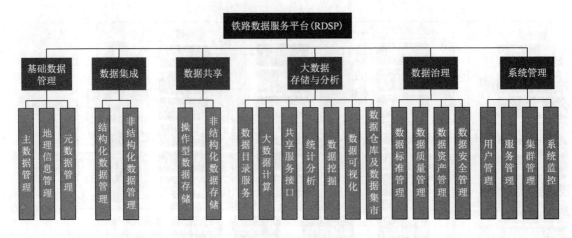

图4 数据服务策略

大数据存储与分析模块通过利用数据仓库和数据集市等构建面为平台管理者研发出易于使用的模块化可视化的分析统计组件,并利用组件强化数据深入挖掘,具有人机交互简洁、易封装、可视化效果好等优点。

数据治理是一个数据质量监督和回馈模块,主要实现对数据质量进行有效管理。数据质量管理,是指对数据全生命周期(产生、获取、存储、共享、应用、维护、消亡)的每个阶段可能存在的各类数据正确及安全问题,进行识别、捕捉、监控、预警、修正等一系列管理活动,并通过优化组织、改善措施、有效管理等正向反馈控制机制,修正数据偏差,提高数据质量。

系统管理模块通过提供用户管理、集群管理、各数据组件状态及服务监控、平台审计等方式,实现数据治理、用户授权等交互功能[8]。

5 结　　语

铁路电务大数据平台框架体系研究,分别从数据平台架构、数据源接口规范、数据采集归一化设计、数据服务策略等环节进行阐述,介绍了数据平台设计层次架构、分类并规范数据源接口、创造性实现各类数据归一化采集并提出了数据服务策略,为实现电务系统数据共享交互、数据综合利用提供支撑和参考。

参考文献

[1] 刘俊,王普,吴艳华,等.智能铁路大数据分析平台研究.第十一届中国智能交通年会大会论文集[C].

[2] 蒋敏建,李国兴.铁路电务智能运维系统技术浅谈[J].电子信息,2019.

[3] 王同军.中国铁路大数据应用顶层设计研究与实践[J].中国铁路,2017(1):8-16.

[4] 中国铁路总公司.铁总信息[2017]155号.中国铁路总公司关于印发铁路大数据应用实施方案的通知[R].2017.

[5] 黄靖茹,钟章队,李斌,等.智能电务研究与探索[J].中国铁路,2018(12):73.

[6] 陈建译.电务大数据智能运维平台研究与应用[J].铁道通信信号,2019,55:162-166.

[7] 朱超平,白雪.基于大数据的电务智能运维平台方案研究[J].铁道通信信号,2017(4):74-78.

[8] 中国铁道科学研究院集团有限公司.铁路数据服务平台[J].铁路计算机应用,2018(027):010.

基于多目标跟踪的地铁车厢客流检测方法

郭 宁[1,2]　胡小晨[1,2]　董德存[1]

(1. 同济大学道路与交通工程教育部重点实验室；
2. 同济大学上海市轨道交通结构耐久与系统安全重点实验室)

摘 要　为了从监控视频中获取地铁车厢内乘客数量，本文在基于深度学习的多目标跟踪方法(Deepsort算法)基础上，引入时空模型，提出了基于Deepsort的多帧融合的客流检测方法，提高了检测精度。经试验比较，逐帧检测方法的平均精度为66.7%，本文方法的平均准确率为78.5%，提高了17.7%。本方法获得的地铁车厢内客流数据可以为铁路运营管理、乘客出行引导、应急救援管理等提供帮助。

关键词　地铁客流检测　Deepsort　多帧融合　时空模型

0 引 言

随着城市化进程的加快，城市人口飞速增长，地铁因其具有线路封闭、运行准时、不易受天气影响等特点，迅速发展成为城市公共交通的重要组成部分，客流量逐年递增。人群过度拥挤极易引发情绪焦虑、碰撞踩踏等安全事故，地铁的安全有序运营与乘客日益增长的出行需求间的矛盾日益突出，如何在有限的运营能力基础上实现对乘客的合理引导越来越重要。这促使地铁管理模式向科学化、精细化方向发展，并且需要准确和丰富的交通信息作为支撑，如地铁系统的行人数量。

对车厢内的乘客数量、客流密度和拥挤程度进行自动监测并实时发布，可以方便乘客选择候车区域及班次，优化出行计划，避免客流集中，提高乘车舒适度。同时，为地铁运营部门提供数据支持，方便进行运力的动态调度、突发危险情况的下的客流疏散引导。

就研究的空间区域而言，地铁客流量的检测主要集中在地铁车站区域和进出站闸机及安检区域，而对地铁列车车厢客流量的检测研究较少。

就检测手段而言，当前使用的检测技术主要有主动红外检测技术[1]、被动红外检测技术[2]、手机信号检测技术、压力检测技术[3]、视频检测技术等。其中红外检测技术在人流密集时，无法对同时通过的乘客分别计数；手机信号检测技术在地铁站及车厢内则存在信号干扰等问题，精度不高；压力检测技术在道路公交客流统计中有一定应用，在地铁车厢的应用体现为车辆称重技术，但不能获得客流量的精确结果；而基于视频图像的客流检测技术近些年迅速发展，可依托现有视频监控设备，对道路公交、地铁车站等区域的客流量进行较为精准的统计。

文献[4]根据运动目标的光流信息提取特征并结合支持向量机实现目标检测。文献[5]根据运动目标的时空和运动矢量信息表征其特征。文献[6]依据经验值划分单个目标像素面积，以判断前景目标的面积中包含多少个体。文献[7]通过贝叶斯函数构建人体姿态模型，并使用图像似然函数对目标图像进行分割。

近年来，有关深度学习的相关研究已经广泛展开，与传统的人工设计的特征提取不同，深度学习架构可以自动提取特征。文献[8]采用卷积神经网络进行特征提取，将支持向量机作为分类器，以检测教室中的人数。文献[9]利用Faster R-CNN进行头部检测。文献[10]采用Mask R-CNN对地铁车厢内乘客进行检测。

可以看到，现有研究多适用于车站站内区域的客流检测，对地铁车厢内客流检测研究较少。对于少数的车厢内客流检测研究[10]，只采用目标检测方法，不能很好地利用历史信息，存在将单个目标识别为多个或将非检测目标识别为检测目标的情况，此外不能很好地处理目标遮挡这一情况。

针对于此,本文采用基于 Deepsort 的多目标跟踪算法,使用 YOLOv4 作为目标检测器,引入跟踪算法以利用历史信息、减小误检率、减少短期遮挡带来的检测影响,从地铁车厢监控视频中检测乘客数量,结合建立的车厢内乘客数量的时空模型,依据乘客数量波动情况,对检测结果进行融合处理,以求提高检测效果。

1 基于 Deepsort 的客流检测方法

1.1 Deepsort 目标跟踪算法

Deepsort[11]是对 Sort 算法[12]的改进。Sort 是一种简单的在线多目标跟踪算法,它以每个检测框与现有目标的所有预测边界框间的交并比(IoU)作为前后帧之间目标匹配关系的度量指标,采用卡尔曼滤波器预测目标位置,通过匈牙利算法关联目标与检测框,使用 Faster R-CNN 作为目标检测器,该方法对目标遮挡未进行处理,致使目标 ID 切换次数较高。Deepsort 算法(图1)引入了在行人重识别数据集上离线训练得到的模型,提取目标的外观特征进行匹配,这样有效改善遮挡情况下的目标跟踪效果,而其目标检测器可以有多种选择,如 YOLO 等。本文采用 YOLOv4 作为其目标检测器。

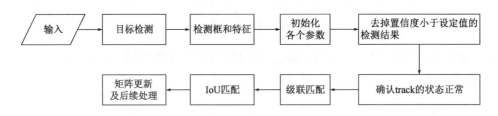

图 1 Deepsort 算法的整体流程

1.2 YOLOv4 目标检测算法

YOLO(You Only Look Once)[13]是一种端到端的检测算法,将物体检测任务直接当作回归问题(regression problem)来处理,将候选区和检测两个阶段合二为一。它采用卷积网络来提取特征,然后使用全连接层来得到预测值,网络结构借鉴 GooLeNet 模型,包含 24 个卷积层和 2 个全连接层。YOLOv4[14]是在 YOLO 基础上不断改进得到的,主要以 CSPDarknet53 网络为基础,利用残差网络来进行深层特征的提取,最终经过多尺寸的特征层得到目标的类别和位置,其结构如图2所示。

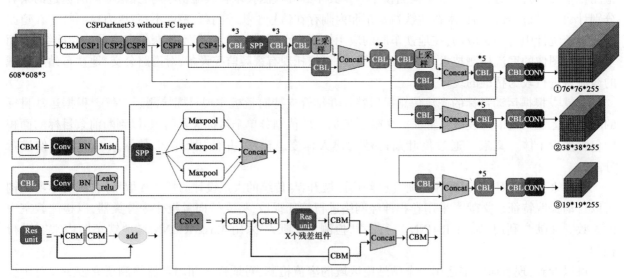

图 2 YOLOv4 结构图

2 基于 Deepsort 的多帧融合的客流检测方法

2.1 时空模型

地铁车厢内大致分为两个区域:座位区、站立区,列车门一般均匀对称的间隔分布于列车两侧。当列车到站时,一侧车门打开,乘客进出列车,行驶时车门关闭。这里,将一扇车门到相邻另一扇车门间的空间定义为 S_i,其包含两个座位区和一个站立区(图3)。

图3 车厢空间模型图

列车到站时,乘客上下车,车厢内人数出现较大波动,而行驶时,乘客基本不在相邻 S 区域内移动,车厢人数波动较小。这里将列车到站与离站之间的时间间隔定义为 T_d,将列车站间行驶时间定义为 T_s (图4)。

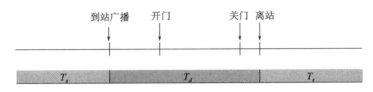

图4 时间分割模型图

2.2 多帧融合处理

若视频数据 1s 有 f 帧,在第 i 帧,时间 t_i 为:

$$t_i = \frac{i}{f} \tag{1}$$

车厢内区域 S_j 检测到的人数为 $D(t_i,S_j)$,实际人数为 $N(t_i,S_j)$,则误差 $E(t_i,S_j)$ 为:

$$E(t_i,s_j) = D(t_i,s_j) - N(t_i,s_j) \tag{2}$$

误差 E 来自两方面:误检、漏检,误检即非目标检测为目标以及一个目标检测为多个,漏检即未检测出该目标。由于采用跟踪算法,这里误检可忽略,误差 E 主要来自漏检。漏检主要原因为检测器性能与目标遮挡。对于检测器性能带来的误差,可通过扩充样本进行重新训练进行减小,而对于目标遮挡引起的误差,可采用融合多帧检测结果进行减小。

这里设置阈值 d,检测到的相邻两帧的人数差 ΔD 为:

$$\Delta D = |D(t_i,S_j) - D(t_i - 1,S_j)| \tag{3}$$

若 $\Delta D \geq d$,则判断其处于 T_d 阶段,即 $t_i \in T_d$,这里取 1s 为最小检测周期,将 1s 内检测数据融合(取极大值),则第 m 秒检测值 $D'(m,S_j)$ 为:

$$D'(m,S_j) = \max \begin{pmatrix} D(t_i,S_j) \\ D(t_{i+1},S_j) \\ \dots \\ D(t_{i+f},S_j) \end{pmatrix} \tag{4}$$

若 $\Delta D < d$,则判断其处于 T_s 阶段,即 $t_i \in T_s$,将 1s 内检测数据融合(取众数),则第 m 秒检测值 $D'(m,S_j)$ 为:

$$D'(m,S_j) = \text{mode}\begin{pmatrix} D(t_i,S_j) \\ D(t_i+1,S_j) \\ \ldots \\ D(t_{i+f},S_j) \end{pmatrix} \quad (5)$$

2.3 基于 Deepsort 的多帧融合的客流检测方法

对于获取到的地铁车厢内监控视频,使用 Deepsort 多目标跟踪算法(YOLOv4 为检测器)进行客流检测,获取逐帧乘客数量,然后根据帧间乘客数量差值 ΔD,即乘客数量波动情况,判断其所处时间段(到达区间、行驶区间),采用不同方式融合 1s 内检测到的乘客数据,获得最终地铁车厢内乘客数量(图5)。

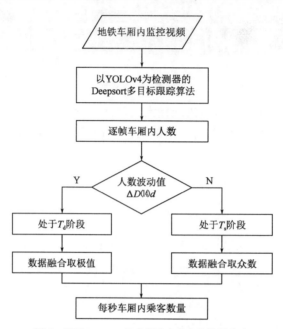

图5 基于 Deepsort 的多帧融合的客流检测方法

3 实验结果及分析

本文实验数据来自上海地铁 10 号线某节车厢的真实视频监控系统,视频帧速度 25 帧/秒(图6),逐帧检测结果如图 7 所示。

图6 车厢视频单帧图片示例

图8 是在非出行高峰期时地铁车厢客流检测的结果,该段视频包含行驶与到站两种情况。地铁行驶时,检测误差主要来自长期遮挡以及乘客靠近鱼眼摄像头时产生较大的形变。地铁到站时,乘客走动带来的短期遮挡使单帧检测结果出现较大波动,此外乘客的姿态以及与摄像头间远近距离产生的形变也使单视频帧中对乘客的检测出现误差。对于融合处理前的逐帧检测结果,其平均精度为 84.5%,经过多帧融合处理后,平均精度提升为 88.4%,减小了逐帧检测结果的波动带来的影响。

图9 是在出行高峰期时地铁车厢客流的检测结果,该视频片段包含列车即将到站与到站上下客的情况。列车到站前车厢内人数相对较少,存在乘客移动至车门准备下车的情形,此时融合处理前后的检测结果均表现不错。当列车到站后,众多乘客涌入,检测结果不甚理想,融合处理后的检测结果的精度最低达到了 52%,而逐帧检测结果最低达到了 24%,这是由于乘客大量走动导致遮挡、形变,使得未检测跟踪到目标,因而在乘

客站稳及停止移动后,检测精度出现回升。总体来看,对于融合处理前的逐帧检测结果,其平均精度为65.1%,经过多帧融合处理后,平均精度提升为77.7%,提升效果明显。

图 7　检测结果示例

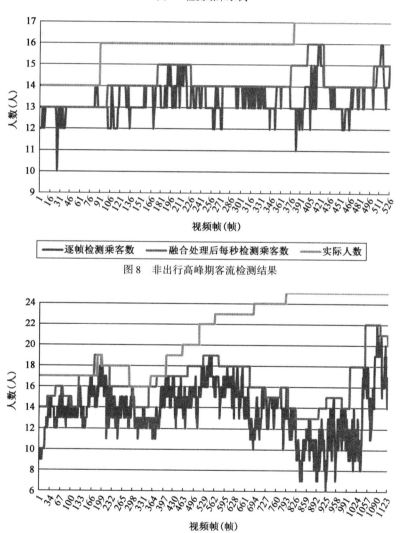

图 8　非出行高峰期客流检测结果

图 9　出行高峰期到站时期客流检测结果

图 10 是在出行高峰期时地铁车厢客流的检测结果,该视频片段包含列车到站上下客即将完成、车门关闭、列车行驶等情况。此视频片段中到站时主要为下客,在到站阶段检测结果依旧不甚理想,但相对逐帧检测,多帧融合后的检测结果精度较好。在列车行驶阶段,由于处于出行高峰期,车厢内乘客数量较

多,长期遮挡带来的影响更大。总体来看,逐帧检测结果的平均精度为57.8%,经过多帧融合处理后,平均精度提升为73.3%,提高了27%,提升效果明显。

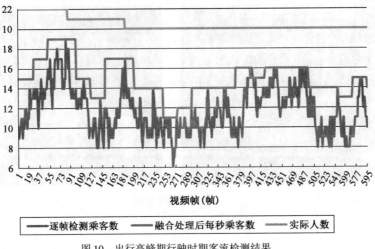

图10 出行高峰期行驶时期客流检测结果

4 结　语

将基于Deepsort的多目标跟踪算法与多帧信息融合相结合,通过对车厢内监控视频进行处理,可以有效地检测车厢内乘客数量,为精细化、智慧化运营服务管理提供信息支持。此外,在建立的时空模型上进行分析处理,将逐帧检测得到的结果进行多帧融合,可以有效减少检测误差,在本文的实验中,逐帧检测的平均准确率为66.7%,通过对多帧检测结果进行融合,平均准确率变为78.5%。在本文的研究中,误差出现的最大原因是长期遮挡,引入身体节点检测,对遮挡下露出的部分肢体进行检测,能一定程度上解决该问题。此外,基于Deepsort的多目标跟踪算法的检测效果十分依赖检测器的性能,使用效果更好的检测器或将提高其检测性能。

参考文献

[1] Niu Q,Wu H,Gao C,et al. Laser-Based Bidirectional Pedestrian Counting via Height Map Guided Regression and Voting[J]. Signal,Image and Video Processing,2017,11(5):897-904.

[2] 余燕.基于红外CCD与激光测距仪融合的行人检测技术研究[D].长春:吉林大学,2008.

[3] 王连震,王晖,罗孟德.基于压力传感器的出租车客流检测系统[J].交通科技与经济,2018,20(5):29-31.

[4] Sidenbladh H,Black M J. Learning image statistics for Bayesian tracking[C]//Proceedings Eighth IEEE International Conference on Computer Vision. Vancouver:IEEE,2001:709-716.

[5] Babu R V,Ramakrishnan K R. Recognition of human actions using motion history information extracted from the compressed video[J]. Image and Vision computing,2004,22(8):597-607.

[6] Chen T H,Chen T Y,Chen Z X. An intelligent people-flow counting method for passing through a gate[C]//2006 IEEE Conference on Robotics,Automation and Mechatronics. IEEE,2006:1-6.

[7] Rauschert I,Collins R T. A generative model for simultaneous estimation of human body shape and pixel-level segmentation[C]//European Conference on Computer Vision. Springer,Berlin,Heidelberg,2012:704-717.

[8] Gao C,Li P,Zhang Y,et al. People counting based on head detection combining Adaboost and CNN in crowded surveillance environment[J]. Neurocomputing,2016,208:108-116.

[9] Song D,Qiao Y,Corbetta A. Depth driven people counting using deep region proposal network[C]//2017 IEEE International Conference on Information and Automation (ICIA). IEEE,2017:416-421.

[10] Shen G,Jamshidi F,Dong D,et al. Metro Pedestrian Detection Based on Mask R-CNN and Spatial-tempo-

ral Feature[C]//2020 IEEE 3rd International Conference on Information Communication and Signal Processing (ICICSP). IEEE,2020:173-178.
[11] Wojke N,Bewley A,Paulus D. Simple online and realtime tracking with a deep association metric[C]//2017 IEEE international conference on image processing (ICIP). IEEE,2017:3645-3649.
[12] Bewley A,Ge Z,Ott L,et al. Simple online and realtime tracking[C]//2016 IEEE International Conference on Image Processing (ICIP). IEEE,2016:3464-3468.
[13] Redmon J,Divvala S,Girshick R,et al. You only look once:Unified,real-time object detection[C]//Proceedings of the IEEE conference on computer vision and pattern recognition. 2016:779-788.
[14] Bochkovskiy A,Wang C Y,Liao H Y M. YOLOv4:Optimal speed and accuracy of object detection. arXiv 2020[J]. arXiv preprint arXiv:2004.10934,2020:1-17.

季节性冻土挡墙综合检测与安全风险评估

张 棋[1] 牛乐乐[2] 苏 谦[1]

(1.西南交通大学土木工程学院;2.中铁第四勘察设计院集团有限公司)

摘 要 季节性冻土地区的挡墙将因墙后填料冻胀效应而出现结构前倾、强度破坏等问题,威胁铁路安全运行,而目前直接针对季节性冻土挡墙的有效检测及安全风险评估相关研究尚不多见。针对现有研究存在的不足,本文首先结合地质雷达法与高密度电法,提出了适用于季节性冻土挡墙的综合检测方法。然后在总结现有挡墙安全风险评估体系的基础上,给出了适用于季节性冻土挡墙的安全风险评估体系。最后以朔黄铁路原平段的某处季节性冻土挡墙工点为例,来验证本文所述综合检测方法及安全风险评估体系的有效性。研究结果表明:综合检测方法可实现对季节性冻土挡墙的准确、经济检测,安全风险评估体系能定量评估季节性冻土挡墙的风险等级。

关键词 路基土工结构 风险评估 综合检测 挡墙 季冻区 朔黄铁路

0 引 言

挡墙指用以抵抗边坡土体侧向压力、支撑路基边坡填土并防止边坡失稳的构筑物,沿线挡墙的安全状况对保障线路运输安全具有重要意义。

季节性冻土具有显著的冻胀效应。受冻胀效应影响,季节性冻土填料将产生冻胀力,致使挡墙结构出现前倾变形或局部强度破坏,威胁铁路行车安全[1]。为更好地掌握季节性冻土挡墙的安全状况,有必要针对季节性冻土挡墙的安全状况开展相关检测与安全风险评估工作。

目前,针对挡墙检测的主要方法有地质雷达法与高密度电法两种。其中,地质雷达法是通过分析其发射的电磁波在被测结构中不同介质交界面产生的反射信号,来判识挡墙的墙体结构特征及其墙后填土情况[2]。高密度电法则是以介质电性差异为基础,通过分析在人工施加电场的作用下电流传导的变化特征,来反映挡墙结构及其墙后填土情况[3]。对于季节性冻土,在冻结指数恒定的条件下,其含水率的变化与土体的冻胀率正相关,且是产生冻胀力的前提[4]。雨水及地下水的入渗富集将显著增大季节性冻土挡墙墙后填料的含水率,并在受墙体约束的情况下产生水平冻胀力[5],故需对挡墙墙后填土的含水情况进行检测。使用地质雷达虽然可以对挡墙墙后填土积水区域进行快速识别,但由于其检测精度不高,致使

基金项目:国家重点研发计划(NO.2016YFC0802203-2,NO.2016YFC802203-3)。

不能准确获取积水区域的位置及大小[6]。使用高密度电法虽可以对积水区域进行精确检测,但需布设大量测线,存在工作量大、工程造价高的缺陷[7]。因此,采用单一的检测方法,难以实现对季节性冻土挡墙墙后填土积水进行高效、准确与经济的检测。

在安全风险评估方面,近年来有不少学者从挡墙的表观状态、材质状况、受力状况三方面着手开展了挡墙安全风险评估的相关研究,并取得了一定成果[8,9]。但由于现有的挡墙安全风险评估指标未充分考虑墙后填土积水因素,因而无法有效评估冻胀效应对挡墙安全性能的影响程度,致使现有评估体系无法直接适用于季节性冻土挡墙。因此,有必要提出适用于季节性冻土挡墙的安全风险评估体系。

综上所述,本文针对季节性冻土挡墙,首先通过将地质雷达法和高密度电法技术优势结合应用,实现了对季节性冻土挡墙墙后填土积水区域准确、经济的检测。然后通过引入填土积水等因素作为评估指标,提出适用于季节性冻土挡墙的安全风险评估体系,从而为季节性冻土挡墙的检测与安全风险评估工作提供相关依据。

1 研究工点概况

朔黄铁路位于季节性冻土区[10]。本文研究工点位于朔黄铁路原平段龙宫站附近,其结构为采用浆砌片石砌筑的重力式挡墙,如图1所示。挡墙墙高 $h_2 = 5$ m,墙顶宽 $d_2 = 1.59$ m,墙趾台阶 $b_1 = 0.22$ m,墙趾台阶 $h_1 = 0.55$ m,底部摩擦因数 $f = 0.5$。勘测资料显示,墙后粉质黏土填料重度 $\gamma_1 = 17.2$ kN/m³,综合内摩擦角度 $\varphi = 39°$,墙背与墙后土体摩擦角 $\varphi_1 = 19.7°$。

现场勘察发现该工点存在以下病害,如图2所示:挡墙表面出现多条长约5 m、宽5 mm左右的裂缝;挡墙勾缝严重脱落,单处脱落长度约10 cm;排水沟淤积现象严重,淤塞比大于70%;约80%的泄水孔已被淤积,基本丧失排水功能;截水沟多处出现开裂,单条裂缝长约6 m、宽3 mm。现场地勘资料显示,工点边坡土层分布主要为粉质黏土,层厚4~20 m。

图1 挡墙结构尺寸图

2 综合检测方法概述

挡墙检测需同时满足快速与精确的要求。地质雷达可实现快速但相对粗略的检测,高密度电法可实现精确但相对较慢的检测。因此,对于季节性冻土挡墙,可先用地质雷达检测图像快速判识出挡墙墙后填土积水的位置,然后在这些位置使用高密度电法对该区域进行详细检测,进一步精确获取积水区域的详细位置参数与分布情况,从而对季节性冻土挡墙墙后积水分布情况实现既准确又经济的检测。该检测流程如图3所示。

 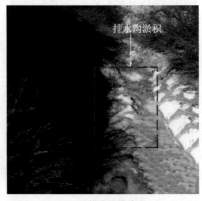

a) 挡墙表面病害　　　　　　　　b) 排水设施病害

图2 工点现场图

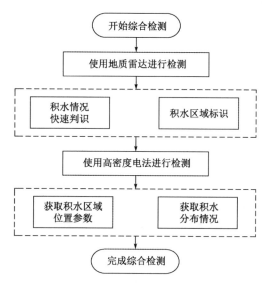

图 3　综合检测实施图

3　现场检测结果

3.1　现场检测方案

通过查阅工点留存的技术资料,墙后积水区域可能位于挡墙中部附近,因此地质雷达的测线沿挡墙中部进行布设,布设数量为 1 条。高密度电法的测试方法采用单边三极的装置形式,其电极极距为 1 m;其测线自挡墙面顶部开始,通过钻孔的形式布设安装于墙面,测线布设数量为 2 条且分列于积水区域起终点所处的剖面。现场实施如图 4 所示。

3.2　现场检测结果分析

地质雷达检测结果如图 5 所示。图中的虚线为挡墙与填土的接触面。从图中可以看出,在里程 K 57 + 535 到 K 57 + 530 区域内,接触面附近存在多组强反射信号,电磁波能量快速衰减且能量团分布不均,多条反射波同相轴上下起伏。根

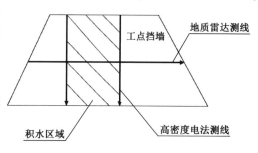

图 4　现场工点检测实施示意图

据文献[11]中的地质雷达图像含水判识方法,可判断该区域内存在墙后积水。因此,需要在该区域使用高密度电法进行进一步精确的检测判断。

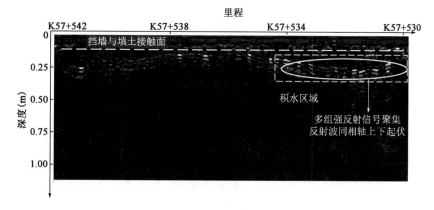

图 5　雷达检测结果

高密度电法的测线布设在 K57+530 和 K57+535 这两处,检测结果如图 6 与图 7 所示。

由图 6 可知,在测线长度 14~15m、深度 0.20~0.60 m 的区域内,土层电阻率值域为 1.76~4.03Ω·m,显著低于正常土层的正常电阻率(约为 21.2Ω·m),可知该处土层积水。类似地,由图 7 可知,位于测线长度 6~7m、深度 0.5~0.8m 附近范围内的土层处也存在积水。根据粉质黏土电阻率同土体含水率之间的负相关关系[12,13],可知,K57+530 处的体积含水率超出 K57+535 处,积水区域内的体积含水率沿线路行进方向递减。

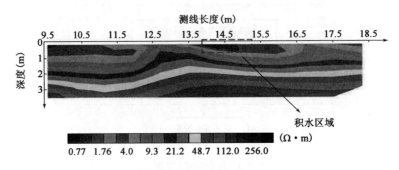

图 6　K57+530 剖面电阻率分布图

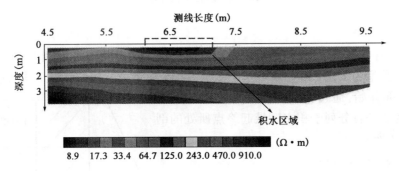

图 7　K57+535 剖面电阻率分布图

结合上述结果可以发现,该工点积水区域的详细分布情况为:其在挡墙平面内的 4 个投影点分列于 K57+530 与 K57+535 的两条测线处,其中位于 K57+530 处的两投影点距该处挡墙顶部距离分别为 14m 与 15m,位于 K57+535 处的两投影点距该处挡墙顶部距离则分别为 6m 与 7m;积水区域在填土内的分布深度约为 0.20~0.80m;积水区域内体积含水率沿线路行进方向总体呈现递减趋势。

4　安全风险评估

4.1　安全风险评估指标

本节主要从挡墙结构受损和挡墙稳定性两方面来建立季节性冻土挡墙的安全风险评估指标。

4.1.1　挡墙结构受损风险评估指标

因含水情况、土质条件与温度均为墙后填料冻胀诱发的主要影响因素[14],为对季节性冻土挡墙结构受损程度进行风险评估,本文在参考相关文献[15,16]的挡墙评估指标基础上,添加积水体积含量、填料类型与填料温度作为新的评价指标,以反映冻胀效应对挡墙的影响,建立的挡墙结构受损风险评估指标体系如图 8 所示。其中,土温为墙顶以下 20cm 处填料的温度值,积水体积含量为积水区域体积在以被测挡墙平面区域为底、高密度电法检测最大深度值为高所形成的立体区域内占比。同时,为方便对季节性冻土挡墙结构受损风险进行定量评估,参考文献[16-19],给出具体的指标标准,如表 1 所示。

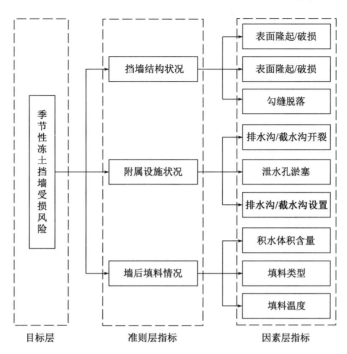

图 8　季节性冻土挡墙结构受损风险评估指标体系

季节性冻土挡墙结构受损风险评估指标标准　　　　　　　　　　　　　　　　表 1

指　　标		受损风险等级			
		低	中	高	极高
挡墙结构状况	表面隆起/破损	无明显隆起/破损病害	隆起/破损面积小于 2 m²	隆起/破损面积为 2~3 m²	隆起/破损面积大于 3 m²
	表面开裂	无开裂	单条裂缝长度低于 0.5 m	单条裂缝长度为 0.5~1.5 m	单条裂缝长度超过 1.5 m
	勾缝脱落	完整无脱落	单处脱落长度低于 0.5 m	单处脱落长度为 0.5~0.8 m	单处脱落长度大于 0.8 m
附属设施状况	排水沟/截水沟开裂	无开裂	单条裂缝长度低于 0.5 m	单条裂缝长度为 0.5~0.8 m	单条裂缝长度大于 0.8 m
	泄水孔淤塞	无淤塞	淤塞比低于 30%	淤塞比为 30%~65%	淤塞比大于 65%
	排水沟/截水沟设置	设施合理充分	设施缺失数量少于 5 处	设施缺失数量为 5~8 处	设施缺失数量大于 8 处
墙后填料情况	积水体积含量	0.5~1	0.35~0.5	0.2~0.35	0~0.2
	填料类型	碎石土	砂土	粉土	黏土
	填料温度	0℃~-4.8℃	-4.8℃~-14.2℃	-14.2℃~-25.4℃	<-25.4℃

4.1.2　挡墙稳定性风险评估指标

参考文献[15-20],构建季节性冻土挡墙稳定性风险评估指标体系,具体的指标类型及评估标准如表 2 所示。

季节性冻土挡墙稳定性风险评估标准　　　　表2

评估指标	稳定性风险等级		
	高	中	低
抗滑稳定性	$K_c \geq 1.3$	$1.0 \leq K_c < 1.3$	$K_c < 1.0$
抗倾覆稳定性	$K_0 \geq 1.6$	$1.0 \leq K_0 < 1.6$	$K_0 < 1.0$

4.2 安全风险评估实施

挡墙的安全状况由其受损程度与稳定性综合评估而来。由此,需要先计算评估挡墙的受损程度,再计算评估挡墙的稳定性,最后计算评估挡墙的安全状况等级。

4.2.1 挡墙受损风险评估实施

为评估季节性冻土挡墙的受损风险等级,使用综合评估算式法[21]对挡墙受损程度进行了打分评价,其计算式如下所示:

$$f_1 = 100 - \frac{\sum R_i W_n}{3} \tag{1}$$

式中:f_1——挡墙受损风险等级对应的得分;

R_i——表2中低、中、高、极高四个等级对应的分数值,分别为0、1、2、3。

W_n——表2中各指标的权重,其值在充分采纳各专家评价结果的基础上通过层次分析法求得,计算过程可参照文献[22]执行。挡墙受损风险评估指标权重结果如图9所示。

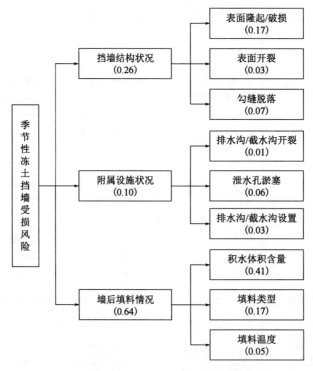

图9　季节性冻土挡墙结构受损风险评估指标权重

参考相关文献[8,21]的分级标准,并根据式(1)中得到的f_1的大小的不同,可将季节性冻土挡墙的受损程度风险划分为三个等级:当$f_1 \geq 80$时,可认为挡墙的受损风险等级为低风险;当$80 > f_1 \geq 60$时,可认为挡墙的受损风险等级为中风险;当$f_1 < 60$时,可认为挡墙的受损风险等级为高风险。

4.2.2 挡墙稳定性风险评估指标

为评估挡墙稳定性的风险等级,同样使用综合评估算式法[21]对挡墙稳定性进行了打分评价。

$$f_2 = 100 - \frac{\sum T_n N_i}{2} \tag{2}$$

式中：f_2——挡墙稳定性风险等级对应的得分；

N_i——表 3 中低、中、高三个等级对应的分数值，分别为 0、1、2；

T_n——表 3 中各指标的权重，其计算过程同样可参照文献[22]执行。挡墙稳定性风险评估指标的权重计算结果如表 3 所示。

季节性冻土挡墙稳定性风险评估指标权重值　　表 3

指　标	权　重　值
抗滑稳定性	0.5
抗倾覆稳定性	0.5

参考相关文献[15,16]的分级标准，并根据式(2)中得到的 f_2 的大小的不同，可将季节性冻土挡墙的稳定性风险等级划分为三个等级：当 $f_1 \geqslant 80$ 时，可认为挡墙稳定性风险等级为低风险；当 $80 > f_1 \geqslant 60$ 时，可认为挡墙稳定性风险等级为中风险；当 $f_1 < 60$ 时，可认为挡墙稳定性风险等级为高风险。

4.2.3 挡墙安全风险评估实施

挡墙的安全风险由其受损风险与稳定性风险综合评估而来。为避免因上述两项指标各自权重取值的主观性而影响最终评估结果的客观公正性，因此采用客观性较强的动态加权综合方法来评估挡墙的安全风险。

基于动态加权综合法的挡墙安全风险评估步骤如下[23]。

(1) 数据标准化

通过倒数变换 $x'_i = 1/x_i$，对前述两小节计算得到的挡墙结构受损风险得分与稳定性风险得分 $x_i (i=1,2)$ 作极小化处理，然后再作极差变化将其标准化以得到 $x''_i (i=1,2)$。

(2) 确定动态加权函数

因上述两项指标对综合评估结果的影响进程表现为先缓慢增加、再快速变化、后趋于平稳的趋势，且符合正态分布特征，故将偏大型正态分布函数作为动态加权函数，即

$$w_i(x) = \begin{cases} 0, & \text{当} x \leqslant \alpha_i \\ 1 - e^{-\left(\frac{x-\alpha_i}{\sigma_i}\right)^2}, & \text{当} x > \alpha_i \end{cases} \quad (3)$$

式中：α_i —— x_i 第一等级区间的中值，即 $\alpha_i = (b_1^i - a_1^i)/2$，$\sigma_i$ 由 $w_i(a_3^{(i)}) = 0.9 (i=1,2)$ 确定。

(3) 确定综合评估函数模型

基于标准化后的 x''_i 与相应的动态加权函数 $w_i(x) (i=1,2,3,\cdots m)$，建立挡墙安全评估的函数模型，即

$$X = \sum_{i=1}^{m} w_i(x''_i) \cdot x''_i \quad (4)$$

式中：X——挡墙安全风险的评估结果。经分析与计算，可得出挡墙安全风险评估的分级标准，如表 4 所示。

季节性冻土挡墙安全风险评估标准　　表 4

状况等级	高风险	中风险	低风险
评估结果	(100, ∞)	(75, 100)	(60, 75)

4.3 安全风险评估结果

根据本文所述的安全评估体系，对工点的安全风险状况进行了评估。同时为论证所述安全评估体系的有效性，采用文献[15]所述的安全评估方法针对同一工点进行了对比评估。

基于本文所述安全评估体系的评价结果如下：结合工点现场勘察与综合检测情况，根据式(1)可求得该结构受损风险相应的得分为 50.63 分，结构受损风险等级为高风险；基于工点现场情况，可计算求得工点的抗滑稳定性系数 K_c 为 0.808，抗倾覆稳定系数 K_0 为 1.850，根据表 3、表 5 与式(2)可求得该结构稳定性风险得分为 50.00，稳定性风险等级为高风险；基于结构受损程度与稳定性评估结果，通过使用动

态加权综合评价方法求得结果为100.22,根据表6可判定该工点安全风险等级为高风险,与现场情况相符。

而根据文献[15]的方法,在未考虑墙后填土积水的情况下,得分为170,对应的安全风险等级为低风险,这与现场情况严重不符。通过对比两种方法的评估结果,从而验证了本文所述安全体系针对季节性冻土挡墙风险评估的有效性。

5 结 语

本文提出了一种适用于季节性冻土挡墙的综合检测方法,并在总结现有挡墙安全评估体系的基础上,提出了适用于季节性冻土挡墙的安全风险评估体系。本文主要取得了以下成果:

(1)通过先应用地质雷达对墙后填土积水进行快速判识,再使用高密度电法对已判识的积水区域进行详细检测,从而实现对季节性冻土挡墙墙后填土积水区域的位置参数与含水率变化情况的准确与经济检测。

(2)考虑到季节性冻土冻融效应的危害与诱因,在现有挡墙安全评估体系的基础上,增加了积水体积含量等作为新的评价指标,从而可对季节性冻土挡墙的安全风险进行定量评估。并以朔黄铁路原平段内的一处季节性冻土挡墙工点为例,验证了本文所述安全风险评估体系的有效性。

本文是针对朔黄铁路龙宫站沿线的季冻区挡墙开展的综合检测与安全风险评估研究,研究范围及成果具有一定局限性,接下来拟对朔黄铁路全线的季冻区挡墙开展相应研究,以期获得更具普适性的研究结论。

参考文献

[1] 王建州,刘书幸,周国庆,等.深季节冻土地区基坑工程水平冻胀力试验研究[J].中国矿业大学学报,2018,47(4):815-821.

[2] 李尧,李术才,徐磊,等.隧道衬砌病害地质雷达探测正演模拟与应用[J].岩土力学,2016,37(12):3627-3634.

[3] 周冬冬,刘建刚,蒋甫玉.高密度电法在挡墙测量中的应用[J].长江科学院院报,2015(2):68-71.

[4] 张子白.L型挡土墙墙背水平冻胀力特性研究[D].北京:北京交通大学,2014.

[5] 汪恩良,钟华,孙景路,等.加筋土挡墙冻融试验研究[J].岩土工程学报,2010,32(02):265-270.

[6] Thitimakorn T, Kampananon N, Jongjaiwanichkit N, et al. Subsurface void detection under the road surface using ground penetrating radar (GPR), a case study in the Bangkok metropolitan area, Thailand[J]. International Journal of Geo-Engineering, 2016,7(1). DOI:10.1186/s40703-016-0017-8.

[7] 闫亚景,闫永帅,赵贵章,等.基于高密度电法的天然边坡水分运移规律研究[J].岩土力学,2019,40(07):2807-2814.

[8] 雷华阳,周骏,贺彩峰.既有线重力式挡土墙综合安全评估方法研究[J].工程地质学报,2015,23(04):700-705.

[9] Damians I P, Bathurst R J, Adroguer E G, et al. Sustainability assessment of earth-retaining wall structures[J]. Environmental Geotechnics, 2018,5(4):187-203. DOI:10.1680/jenge.16.00004.

[10] 李彦龙,汪自力.考虑水分迁移影响的浅层膨胀土抗剪强度冻融劣化特征[J].岩石力学与工程学报,2019,38(06):1261-1269.

[11] Cheung B W Y, Lai W W L. Field validation of water-pipe leakage detection through spatial and time-lapse analysis of GPR wave velocity[J]. Near Surface Geophysics, 2019, 17(3-GPR in Civil and Environmental Engineering: Recent Methodological Advances):231-246.

[12] 冯怀平,马德良,王志鹏,等.基于范德堡法的非饱和土电阻率测试方法[J].岩土工程学报,2017,39(04):690-696.

[13] 查甫生,刘松玉,杜延军,等.基于电阻率的非饱和土基质吸力预测[J].岩土力学,2010,31(03):1003-1008.

[14] 刘炳宇,孟上九,王淼. 季冻区路基冻胀影响因素分析及权重判别[J]. 自然灾害学报,2018,27(02):68-73.
[15] 张宁波. 铁路既有线路堑地段重力式挡土墙安全评估与加固技术研究[D].成都:西南交通大学,2012.
[16] Gabr M A, Rasdorf W, Findley D J, et al. Comparison of Three Retaining Wall Condition Assessment Rating Systems[J]. Journal of Infrastructure Systems, 2018, 24(1): 04017037.
[17] 钟敏辉,王少斌. 季节性冻土路基冻胀性分析及治理措施[J]. 铁道建筑,2009(04):96-98.
[18] 尹传军. 季冻区路基土冻胀特性及评价指标体系研究[D].哈尔滨:东北林业大学,2014.
[19] 严健. 高海拔寒区特长公路隧道冻胀特性及防冻研究[D].成都:西南交通大学,2019.
[20] 国家铁路局.铁路路基支挡结构设计规范:TB 10075—2019[S]. 北京:中国铁道出版社,2019.
[21] 刘红森. 既有重力式挡土墙安全评估技术探讨[D].成都:西南交通大学,2012.
[22] 汪益敏,郭继幸,李林生,等. 基于层次分析法的公路运营期路基状况评价[J]. 华南理工大学学报(自然科学版),2017,45(06):37-43+51.
[23] 王顺达,何云乾,付郁. 对长江流域水质的综合评价——基于层次分析法和动态加权法[J]. 环境保护科学,2014,40(03):88-92.

Statistical Analysis and Prediction Model for Maintenance Management in Urban Railway System

Yixin Shen   Chi Kwong Wong   Siu Ming Lo

(Department of Architecture and Civil Engineering, City University of Hong Kong)

Abstract A reliable checking plan in a railway system can prevent unexpected defects or severe failures from causing long delays and financial losses. Statistical analysis methods can be used to investigate the relationships between the actions being taken and the observed situations and influential factors in a railway system. In this study, railway track defects and characteristics and their relevant maintenance actions were investigated based on 579 assumed track investigation records. Several regression-type models were calibrated and developed using the R statistical package to predict the required maintenance actions. Historical minimum actions in terms of relevant action codes were set as the dependent variable. Railway track characteristics and maintenance histories were modeled as predictors in various regression-type models. Logistic regression, ordinal logistic regression, multinomial logistic regression, Poisson regression and negative binomial regression models were tested to establish statistical relationships between various predictors and action codes. By comparing their accuracies and pseudo R-square, it was found that the predicted minimum action codes as calculated by the multinomial logistics regression model best matched the observed action codes that were used during the maintenance of the railway system. Statistically significant predictors for the action codes were track identification, defect type, recheck period and number of previous checks. Overall model prediction accuracy for replicating the observed action codes was approximately 88.95%, and the corresponding effective safety rate was 92.23%. Accuracy would be improved by adopting a conservative maintenance action—i.e., shortening the recheck period by increasing the maintenance actions (code) by one level from the predicted results.

Shorter recheck periods—will enhance the effective safety rate. It was found that the Poisson and negative binomial regression models performed best, revealing effective safety rates of up to 97.58%.

Keywords Railway track defects   Railway system maintenance and management   Multinomial logistic regression   Poisson regression   Negative binomial regression

0 Introduction

In most metropolitan cities in the world, underground metro systems are a key transportation mode, carrying the largest proportions of trips with respect to the total travel demand. Such underground railway systems are considered the most effective transportation mode for alleviating traffic congestion. With high utilization rates, any minor failure affecting service in the railway system would lead to severe congestion on other road transportation modes. Although the on-time arrival records of the MTR system reached 99.9% in 2017 (MTR, 2018), delays remain unavoidable in metro systems due to unexpected and uncommon incidences. While, delays result in millions of commuters being late for work, and stations with large crowds of waiting passengers are at a high risk of stampede accidents (Ma et al., 2013; Wang et al., 2015; Zhang et al., 2016). Thus, more attention should be paid to the performance of metro systems, and reliable maintenance practices should be developed to minimize unexpected railway track failures and errors.

In railway system, vehicle, track and signalling equipment are the three main sections of railway maintenance management (Ghofrani et al., 2018). Railway track is the foundation of metro system, thus, track failures and defects usually result in losses and accidents. Because of the importance of railway tracks, a minimum action code was applied in maintaining a railway system to denote the seriousness of a railway track defect and describe the necessary repair action to be taken. Such repairs are made immediately if there expects a high probability of failure. However, each defect has its own minimum action code to ensure a timely response. A summary of the minimum action codes is shown in Tab. 1.

Summary of minimum action code   Tab. 1

Minimum action code	Minimum action taken	Maximum functional time of rail	Probability of rail failure	Number of assumed value (used in regression model)
NA	No action	Unknown	N/A	0
H, N	Normal checking	Unknown	N/A	1
G, L	Changing rail or checking within 3 months	3 months	Probability of rail failure (being occurred within 3 months)	2
D	Changing rail within 4 weeks	4 weeks	Probability of rail failure (being occurred within 4 weeks)	3
E	Changing rail within 2 weeks	2 weeks	Probability of rail failure (being occurred within 2 weeks)	4
C	Changing rail within 7 days	7 days	Probability of rail failure (being occurred within a week)	5
B, M	Immediate changing rail or repair work	0 day	Probability of rail failure (being occurred next day)	6

To prevent failures and errors and to improve the reliability and stability of the metro system, it is necessary to conduct a comprehensive analysis of railway track defects and develop a predictive model to assist the scientific decision-making process involved in scheduling maintenance. Notably, compared with the number of studies of track defects in railway systems, the studies on scheduling maintenance in a metro system are limited. However, it is important to determine the characteristics of railway track defects from historical data, and thereby to establish a regression model to identify the optimal minimum action-coding system for use in scheduling maintenance.

Due to the rule that a metro system must run without interruption during operational period (Zoeteman, 2001), the required inspection and maintenance have to be carried out in skylight time during non-operational period. Thus, a preventive maintenance plan should be devised to ensure the normal operation of metro systems (Nappi, 2014). However, infrequent maintenance or excessive maintenance problems occur in railway systems that use interval-based maintenance strategies (Liu & Huang, 2019). It is nevertheless clear that corrective maintenance is very expensive in terms of the cost of emergency repairs or renewal work and the cost of recovery or losses caused by accidents (Ghofrani, 2018; Liu et al., 2013). Thus, reasonable planning can prevent too-frequent maintenance and thus eliminate waste (Liu et al., 2014), and can efficiently prevents delays and accidents caused by inadequate maintenance (Sadeghi & Akbari, 2006).

Utilizing historical failure data in data-driven models is a way to capture the characteristics of maintenance (Morant et al., 2016). Historical detector data, such as failure data, maintenance action data, inspection schedule data and train type are used to determine the rules of failure (Li et al., 2014). In addition to historical data, real-time monitoring data are used in BP neural networks to predict the service states of railway systems, thereby ensuring timely checking and (re)scheduling of maintenance plans (Liu & Huang, 2019).

Numerous factors have been examined to estimate their influence on the performance of railway track, including temperature (Liu & Huang, 2019), rail speed, weight and curvature (Xu et al., 2011), axle load, track construction, weather and environment (Jidayi, 2015). In addition, railway track is subject to rail wear, fatigue, corrugation, abrasion, defects and damage, which decrease its lifetime (Guler, 2012). The growth of cracks (Jamshidi et al., 2017) and related deterioration mechanisms (Guler, 2014; Jamshidi et al. 2018) also affect the probability of railway failure, and the relationship between cumulative load and deterioration phases indicates the maintenance limit (Zhang, 2013).

Overall, current research shows that corrective (failure-driven) maintenance leads to delays in metro systems and thus should be avoided, while preventative (time-based) maintenance is an inaccurate approach because it can lead to insufficient or excessive maintenance and subsequent system failure or wastage. Accordingly, we studied integrated (on life-cycle) maintenance based on optimization theory to determine the optimal way to manage infrastructure, equipment and the whole railway system. The aim of this study was to analyse the relationship between maintenance action codes and the characteristics of railway track, and to use the resulting data to build a predictive model to generate a reasonable maintenance strategy for railway track. Such a model would be an invaluable aid for managers in timetabling maintenance and preventing defect formation on or failure of railway track.

The rest of this paper is organized as follows: In section 2, we introduce a regression model for the categorical variables and count data. In section 3, maintenance action code and characteristics parameters are detailed. The accuracy and effective safety rate of the regression model are discussed in section 4. In the final section, we state our conclusions.

1 Methodology

In this section, the statistics model related to categorical variables and count data is introduced and used to build a regression model to predict maintenance action codes. The purpose of a statistical method is to determine how a set of factors (independent variables) quantitatively affects certain phenomena (the dependent variables). In general, linear regression is utilized to study the relationship between continuous dependent variables and independent variables, but it is difficult to predict the value of categorical variables. Thus, we need to solve such problems with other regression models, such as logistic regression models or Poisson regression models, as outlined below.

1.1 Logistic Regression

Logistic regression describes the relationship between a binary dependent variable and one or more independent variables, where these can be nominal, ordinal, interval or ratio-level variables. A logistic regression model estimates the probability that an event occurs based on a randomly selected observation versus the probability that the event does not occur, and thus it predicts the effect of a series of variables on a binary response variable.

In the present study, we use a logistic regression model to predict the probability of the minimum action code being recorded, and minimum action code with the highest probability is the predicted result. For the minimum action code, it represents the seriousness of a rail defect and defines the maximum functioning time of the railway track, and how this depends on the value of a set of categorical or numerical independent variables.

The equation of the logistic regression is:

$$\log it(P_{ac}) = \ln[p_{ac}/(1-p_{ac})] = \beta_0 + \beta_1 x_1 + \cdots + \beta_j x_j + \cdots + \beta_J x_J \tag{1}$$

$$odds_{ac} = p(happen)/p(not\ happen) = \frac{p_{ac}}{(1-p_{ac})} \tag{2}$$

$$p_{ac} = n_{ac}/N_{total} \tag{3}$$

The constant part β_0 in Eqs. (1) is the logarithm of odds, where odds equals to the probability when a value of the minimum action code comes out divided by the probability it does not take place as shown in Eqs. (2). While, n_{ac} denotes the number of specific minimum action code and N_{total} is the total number of action code in record. β_j indicates the variation of the logarithm of odds when independent variables j change one unit. According to Eqs. (1), the probability when specific action code occurred and not occurred is shown in Eqs. (4) and (5):

$$p_{ac} = \exp(\beta_0 + \beta_1 x_1 + \cdots + \beta_J x_J)/[1 + \exp(\beta_0 + \beta_1 x_1 + \ldots + \beta_J x_J)] \tag{4}$$

$$1 - p_{ac} = 1/[1 + \exp(\beta_0 + \beta_1 x_1 + \cdots + \beta_J x_J)] \tag{5}$$

In addition to problems based on binary variable, there are others in which the dependent variable is categorical in nature, meaning that it can have more than two possible values. Such multiple categorical variables are classified as nominal variables or ordinal variables. Problems containing multiple categorical variables cannot be solved by binary logistic regression models and instead require the use of multinomial logistic regression models or Ordinal regression models.

1.2 Multinomial Logistic Regression

When the dependent variable of a problem is a nominal variable, the number of classifications is greater than two and there is no rank (order) relationship, we use a multinomial logistic regression model, as described by the following equation

$$\begin{cases} \log it(p_{ac\ 1}/p_{ac\ n}) = \ln[p(Y=1)/p(Y=n)] \\ \qquad = \beta_{0,ac\ 1} + \beta_{1,ac\ 1}x_1 + \cdots + \beta_{j,ac\ 1}x_j + \cdots + \beta_{J,ac\ 1}x_J = g_{ac\ 1}(x) \\ \log it(p_{ac\ 2}/p_{ac\ n}) = \ln[p(Y=2)/p(Y=n)] \\ \qquad = \beta_{0,ac\ 2} + \beta_{1,ac\ 2}x_1 + \cdots + \beta_{j,ac\ 2}x_j + \cdots + \beta_{J,ac\ 2}x_J = g_{ac\ 2}(x) \\ \qquad \cdots \\ \log it(p_{ac\ n-1}/p_{ac\ n}) = \ln[p(Y=n-1)/p(Y=n)] \\ \qquad = \beta_{0,ac\ n-1} + \beta_{1,ac\ n-1}x_1 + \cdots + \beta_{j,ac\ n-1}x_j + \cdots + \beta_{J,ac\ n-1}x_J = g_{ac\ n-1}(x) \end{cases} \tag{6}$$

For all possible value of the minimum action code, minimum action code $ac\ n$ is selected as reference action code. For the left part of the formula in Eqs. (6), $p_{ac\ i}/p_{ac\ n}$ in the bracket present that the model describes the ration of the probability of two minimum action codes, action code $ac\ i$ and the reference action code $ac\ n$. The regression coefficient $\beta_{j,ac\ i}$ corresponding to the independent variable x_j and action code $ac\ i$, it describes the logarithm variation of ration of the probability of $ac\ i$ and reference action code $ac\ n$ when independent variable x_j change one unit and other independent variables remain unchanged. For example, when $\beta_{j,ac\ i} > 0$, the action code is more likely to be $ac\ i$ when x_j increasing, but more likely to be $ac\ n$ when x_j increasing while $\beta_{j,type\ i} < 0$.

For any data, if we have the value of all independent variable x_j, the probability of corresponding action code can be computed by the following Eqs. (7) and (8):

$$\begin{cases} p_{ac\ 1}/p_{ac\ n} = e^{g_{ac\ 1}(x)} \\ p_{ac\ 2}/p_{ac\ n} = e^{g_{ac\ 2}(x)} \\ \cdots \\ p_{ac\ n-1}/p_{ac\ n} = e^{g_{ac\ n-1}(x)} \end{cases} \tag{7}$$

$$p_{ac\ 1} + p_{ac\ 2} + \cdots + p_{ac\ n} = P\{Y=1\} + P\{Y=1\} + P\{Y=2\} + \cdots + P\{Y=n\} = 1 \tag{8}$$

The corresponding probability of the action code:

$$\begin{cases} p_{ac\ 1} = P\{Y=1\} = e^{g_1(x)}/[1 + e^{g_{ac\ 1}(x)} + e^{g_{ac\ 2}(x)} + \cdots + e^{g_{ac\ n-1}(x)}] \\ p_{ac\ 2} = P\{Y=2\} = e^{g_2(x)}/[1 + e^{g_{ac\ 1}(x)} + e^{g_{ac\ 2}(x)} + \cdots + e^{g_{ac\ n-1}(x)}] \\ \cdots \\ p_{ac\ n-1} = P\{Y=n-1\} = e^{g_{n-1}(x)}/[1 + e^{g_{ac\ 1}(x)} + e^{g_{ac\ 2}(x)} + \cdots + e^{g_{ac\ n-1}(x)}] \\ p_{ac\ n} = P\{Y=n\} = 1/[1 + e^{g_{ac\ 1}(x)} + e^{g_{ac\ 2}(x)} + \cdots + e^{g_{ac\ n-1}(x)}] \end{cases} \tag{9}$$

1.3 Ordinal Logistic Regression

Ordinal variable is another type of categorical variables, when two or more categories with hierarchical relationship exists in dependent variable, ordinal logistic regression model is employed to solve such problem. Ordinal logistic regression is derived from logistic regression, and due to the hierarchical relationship of the dependent variable, it is set as a cumulative logistic regression model. The equation of ordinal logistic regression is as shown in Eqs. (10).

In ordinal logistic regression model, the dependent variable is discrete, ordered and categorical, and the independent variable can be any action code. In this study, the values of the dependent variable include seven minimum action codes: 0, 1, 2, 3, 4, 5 or 6, and corresponding action taken are shown in table 1. Eqs. (10) is based on the same formula of binary logistic regression as in Eqs. (1), but the difference between them is the type of dependent variable, as they use a categorical hierarchical variable and a binary variable, respectively. In ordinal logistic regression, the independent variables have the same tendency to influence the different categorical values of the dependent variable.

$$\begin{aligned} \log \text{it}(P\{Y \leq 1\}/[1 - P\{Y \leq 1\}]) &= \log \text{it}[p_1/(p_2 + p_3 + \ldots + p_n)] \\ &= \beta_{0,ac\ 1} - \beta_1 x_1 - \cdots \beta_j x_j - \cdots - \beta_J x_J \\ \log \text{it}(P\{Y \leq 2\}/[1 - P\{Y \leq 2\}]) &= \log \text{it}[(p_1 + p_2)/(p_3 + p_4 + \cdots + p_n)] \\ &= \beta_{0,ac\ 2} - \beta_1 x_1 - \cdots - \beta_j x_j - \cdots - \beta_J x_J \\ &\cdots \\ \log \text{it}(P\{Y \leq n-1\}/[1 - P\{Y \leq n-1\}]) &= \log \text{it}[(p_1 + p_2 + \cdots + p_{n-1})/p_n] \\ &= \beta_{0,ac\ n-1} - \beta_1 x_1 - \cdots - \beta_j x_j - \cdots - \beta_J x_J \end{aligned} \tag{10}$$

Based on Eqs. (10), the probability value of each result in the dependent variable are:

$$p_1 = P\{Y=1\} = P\{Y \leq 1\} = \{\exp(\beta_{0,ac\ 1} - \beta_1 x_1 - \cdots - \beta_J x_J)/[1 + \exp(\beta_{0,ac\ 1} - \beta_1 x_1 - \cdots - \beta_J x_J)]\}$$

$$p_2 = P\{Y=2\} = P\{Y \leq 2\} - P\{Y \leq 1\} = \exp(\beta_{0,ac\ 2} - \beta_1 x_1 - \cdots - \beta_J x_J)/[1 + \exp(\beta_{0,ac\ 2} - \beta_1 x_1 - \cdots - \beta_J x_J)] - p_1$$

$$p_n = P\{Y = n\} = P\{Y \leq n\} - P\{Y \leq n-1\} = 1 - p_1 - p_2 - \cdots - p_{n-1} \tag{11}$$

When the dependent variable of the problem is categorical and the level of the categorical variables is hierarchical, we use an ordinal logistic regression model to analyse the relationships between the dependent and independent variables.

1.4 Poisson Regression

Count variable is another variable that used to characterize the variable occurred repeatedly. When the dependent variable is count variable, Poisson regression model is employed. In this study, it is assumed that the dependent variable follows Poisson distribution, and we use counts per monitoring time as the rate. The probability mass function of Poisson distribution is: $Y \sim \text{Poisson}(\lambda)$ if

$$p(Y = y) = e^{-\lambda}\lambda^y/y!, \quad y = 0,1,2,\cdots \tag{12}$$

Where, y is the count of specific dependent variable, λ is the average number of occurrence of specific action code in a specified time. One important feature of Poisson distribution is the mean of the Poisson distribution $E[Y]$ equals to its variance $Var[Y]$, that $E[Y] = Var[Y] = \lambda$. Thus, when dependent variable is count variable and follows the Poisson distribution, Poisson regression model is employed, the equations are:

$$\log it(\lambda) = \ln(\lambda) = \beta_0 + \beta_1 x_1 + \cdots + \beta_j x_j + \cdots + \beta_J x_J \tag{13}$$

$$\lambda = \frac{1}{n}\sum_{i=1}^{n} y_i \tag{14}$$

Different from logistic regression, the left part in Eqs. (13) is the logarithm of the mean of all count variables (Eqs. (14)), while the left part in logistic regression is related to the logarithm of probability of dependent variable, and the p in Eqs. (1) is the expected value of dependent variable. However, the left part of the logistic regression model, multinomial logistic regression model, and ordinal logistic regression model related to the logarithm of expected value of dependent variable.

According to Eqs. (13), we have the following equation about λ.

$$\lambda = e^{\beta_0 + \beta_1 x_1 + \cdots + \beta_j x_j + \cdots + \beta_J x_J} \tag{15}$$

In Eqs. (15), β_0 is the influence on the expected of Y when all independent variables equal to zero, and β_j indicates the influence of every unit increase in x_j. If $\beta_j = 0$, it means that Y and X are not related, and $\lambda = E[Y] = e^{\beta_0}$; and if $\beta_j > 0$, it means $\lambda = E[Y]$ is e^{β_j} times larger than expected value of Y when $x_j = 0$; when $\beta_j < 0$, it means $\lambda = E[Y]$ is e^{β_j} times smaller than the mean of Y when $x_j = 0$.

1.5 Negative Binomial Regression

Negative binomial regression is an extension of Poisson regression model, it adds an ancillary parameter that allows over dispersion, and the ancillary parameter approaches 0 when negative binomial becomes closer to Poisson. The probability mass function of negative binomial distribution is: $Y \sim NB(\alpha, p)$ if

$$p(Y) = \frac{\Gamma(Y + \alpha^{-1})}{\Gamma(Y+1)\Gamma(\alpha^{-1})}\left(\frac{\alpha^{-1}}{\alpha^{-1}+\mu}\right)^{\alpha^{-1}}\left(\frac{\mu}{\alpha^{-1}+\mu}\right)^{Y}, \quad \mu > 0, \alpha \geq 0 \tag{16}$$

where α is the ancillary parameter, and the mean μ is the product of r, which is the rate of the events occurs, and sampling exposure t according to

$$E(Y) = \mu = rt \tag{17}$$

$$Var(Y) = \mu + \alpha\mu^2 \tag{18}$$

In negative binomial regression, the mean of Y is determined by the exposure time t and a set of J regressor variables. The expression relating these quantities is

$$\mu = e^{[\ln(t) + \beta_1 X_1 + \beta_2 X_2 + \cdots + \beta_J X_J]} \tag{19}$$

Thus, with expression in Eqs. (19) and Eqs. (16), the probability when dependent variable equals to Y with the mean of μ and ancillary parameter α is detailed.

2 Case Study: Predicting Maintenance Action

This section describes a case study in predicting maintenance action in a railway system, relationship between maintenance action and railway track characteristics was detailed. In railway system, maintenance staff checks the characteristics of railway track and judges if it needs maintenance service to ensure a normal and safe operation. In this case, we assumed a database containing 579 rail defect records of a railway system and the data were consolidated and corrected. From the dataset, maintenance action code was set as dependent variable and the characteristics of railway track as predictors to diagnose the defects. The summary of the observations is shown in Fig. 1.

As shown in Fig. 1a), minimum action code is the dependent variable in the study and "no action" dominates the track-defect record, that means the most railway track defects were not serious defects, while the second-and third-most frequent minimum action codes were "normal checking" and "change rail with 4 weeks". While in independent variables, categorical variables including track, rail identification, defect type, defect nature, joint type and detection method are summarized in Fig. 1b)-g). In Fig. 1b), track (T) refers to the direction of the railway, "DT" and "UT" represent the ways of downtown and uptown direction, while "DT" dominates 77.03% in railway track defects. The condition of rail identification (RI) is shown in Fig. 1c), it refers to the specific part, 13 types are listed, while most of the defect happens in "RHRR" part, and "LHRR" donates the second place. For defect type (DT) in Fig. 1d), it is the detailed section of crossing and "Turnout" is the most frequent part that failure detected and "Plain rail" donates 44.73% in second place. Defect nature (DN) is the type of rail failure and most failure occurred in "Shelling" with 33.68%, and "Hair crack" contributes 29.53% in second place. Rail joint (JT) is an important component in railway track, there are total 6 types of joint recorded in the dataset, while "Termite weld" occurred the most frequently in the records and 35.75% maintenance recorded on "Others". Detection method (DM) is the way to inspect the presence of the defect, while "MS inspection" found 43.01% defects which is the most in record, and "NDT" detect 41.28% of records. Apart from these categorical variable, numerical variables "Maximum defect size" (MDS), "Recheck period" (RP) and "Number of checking before" (NCB) are included in the independent variable to help predict the minimum action code for railway track.

To achieve high accuracy and efficiency in regression model, correlation analysis of predictors is calculated by R (R Core Team, 2018), and the result is shown in Fig. 2. It is found that the detection method and number of check before gets the maximum correlation coefficient of 0.43. However, it proves that they are weak related, and we regard all predictors as independent variables.

Thus, all predictors will be accounted in the initial state of model generation. While, to reveal unnecessary predictors, stepwise regression is employed and predictors in the model with the minimum Akaike information criterion (AIC) (Akaike, 1974) are selected. After determining the proper predictors in each model, pseudo R-squared is calculated to check the effectiveness of the model and a higher R-squared value indicates better model performance, which follows:

$$R^2 = \left(\frac{1 - (\sum_{i=1}^{N}(y_i - \hat{y}_i)^2)}{\sum_{i=1}^{N}(y_i - \bar{y})^2} \right) \times 100\% \tag{20}$$

Where N is the number of observations in the model, y is the dependent variable, $\bar{y}$ is the mean of the y values, and $\hat{y}$ is the value predicted by the model.

Apart from AIC and pseudo R-squared, accuracy is defined to evaluate the goodness of the regression model:

$$accuracy = \frac{n_{predict = record}}{n_{total}} \times 100\% \quad (21)$$

Where $n_{predict = record}$ count the number of same predicted outcome and record minimum action code, which calculated by regression model with same predictors. While n_{total} is the number of total collected data, which is 579 in the case study. However, according to the value of the minimum action code in Tab. 1, larger value of minimum action code indicates serious defect on a railway track. Whereas track with higher minimum action code needs more frequent checking or to be changed and ensure the normal operation. Conversely, it makes serious mistake if the railway track needs to be changed immediately but the result of regression model tells longer changing period. Such mistakes must be avoided in railway maintenance management. Thus, we define effective safety rate:

$$effective\ safety\ rate = \frac{n_{predict \geq record}}{n_{total}} \times 100\% \quad (22)$$

where $n_{predict \geq record}$ is the number of predict minimum action code when it is larger than that in the record. Whereas higher value of effective safety rate indicates more effective maintenance plan but may be more cost on maintenance.

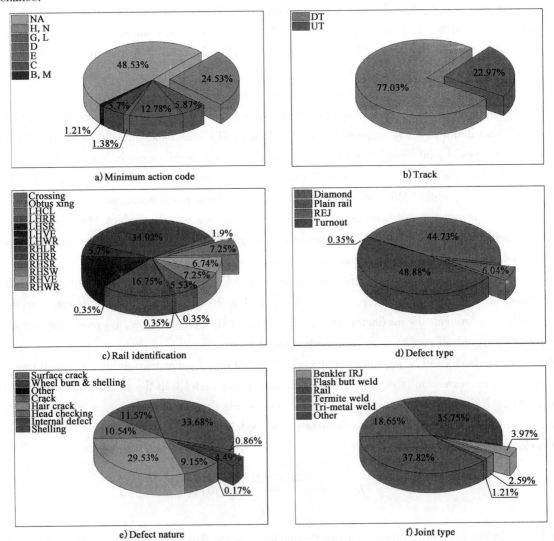

Fig. 1

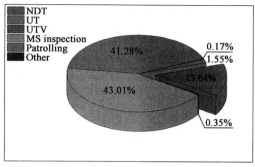

g) Detection method

Fig. 1 Summary of minimum action code and characteristics of railway track

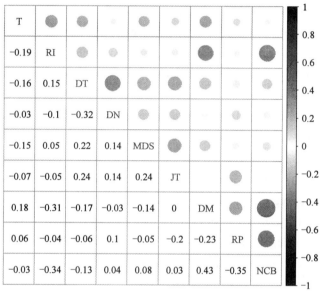

Fig. 2 Result of correlation coefficient of predictors. (T for track, RI for rail identification, DT for defect type, DN for defect nature, MDS for maximum defect size, JT for the joint type, DM for detection method, RP for recheck period, NCB for the number of check before)

After model generation and calculation of AIC and accuracy, proper predictors for each model were selected, the results are shown in the following Tab. 2.

Summary of regression results　　Tab. 2

Models	Best combination factors	AIC (compare within the model)	Pseudo R-squared	Accuracy	Effective safety rate
Logistic regression (minimum action code are 0 and 1)	RI, JT, MDS, DM, NCB	48	0.68	100%	100%
Logistic regression (minimum action code are 0 and 2)	T, DT, MDS, RP	14	0.25	100%	100%
Logistic regression (minimum action code are 0 and 3)	R, NCB	41.53	0.18	88.26%	88.26%
Logistic regression (minimum action code are 0 and 4)	T, RP	9.74	0.10	98.62%	98.62%
Logistic regression (minimum action code are 0 and 5)	DT, DN, DM, MDS, RP, NCB	51.53	0.16	92.75%	94.99%
Logistic regression (minimum action code are 0 and 6)	MDS	25.88	0.03	99.14%	99.14%
Multinomial logistic regression	RI, DT, RP, NCB	252.79	0.85	88.95%	92.23%

Models	Best combination factors	AIC (compare within the model)	Pseudo R-squared	Accuracy	Effective safety rate
Ordinal logistic regression	T, JT, DM, RP	181.22	0.42	58.38%	69.43%
Poisson regression	T, RI, DN, MDS, JT, RP	186.61	0.78	66.15%	81.69%
Negative binomial regression	T, RI, DN, MDS, JT, RP	188.61	0.65	66.15%	81.69%
Ordinal logistic regression	T, JT, DM, RP	181.22	0.42	58.38%	69.43%

Because of the predictor is binary variable in logistic regression, six sub-models were generated in case study. The results showed that the logistic regression model was most accurate when predicting certain minimum action codes, such as 0 and 1, and 0 and 2, but it was difficult to discern which two minimum action codes should be considered as dependent variables. Thus, logistic regression was not suitable for solving problems in which the dependent variable had more than two possible categorical values. For the other models generated in this section, we found that the multinomial logistic regression model had the highest accuracy (88.95%) among all regression models, and the best combination of factors were rail identification, defect type, recheck period and number of previous checks. The accuracy of the Poisson regression and the negative binomial regression was the same (66.15%), while the ordinal logistic regression model performed the worst, with an accuracy of 58.38%.

The comparison of the records and predicted results calculated by multinomial logistic regression model is listed in Tab. 3. In this table, the numbers on the diagonal represent the count of results with same value in predict and observed result, and the off-diagonal numbers are the number of wrong results. The effective safety rate of the multinomial logistic regression model was 92.23%, which indicated that 3.25% of the predicted outcomes were overestimated (shown in the lower triangular area in Tab. 3). Thus, conducting checking based on this result shortens the checking interval but improves the safety level of the railway track.

Comparison of the records and predicted results (Multinomial logistic regression) Tab. 3

Predict	Record						
	0	1	2	3	4	5	6
0	275	9	0	14	0	7	0
1	17	132	0	0	0	0	0
2	0	0	34	0	0	0	0
3	2	0	0	54	0	11	4
4	0	0	0	0	8	0	0
5	0	0	0	0	0	11	0
6	0	0	0	0	0	0	1

With the result of multinomial logistic regression, it is found that the chance of getting "normal checking" will increase tremendously when track match the characteristics RI4, RI6, RI12, DT4 compared with "no action". While, the occurrence of RI3, RI4, RI5, RI6, RI7, RI9, RI10, RI12, DT2, DT3 will increase the chance of getting "changing rail or checking within 3 months" compared with "no action". For the code "changing rail within 4 weeks", RI2, RI3, RI5, RI6, RI7, RI8, RI12, DT2 will increase the probability of getting it compared with "no action". When the track matches part of RI3, RI4, RI5, RI7, RI8, RI9, RI10, DT2, DT3, DT4, it is more likely to "changing rail within 2 weeks" compared with "no action". The probability of "changing rail within 7 days" will increase with the track that matches some of RI9, RI10, DT2, and the increment in RP has positive effect on the probability. However, only DT4 has positive effect on code "immediate changing rail or repair work".

As mentioned above, accuracy can be determined by strictly comparing the results predicted by the regression model with records. Thus, we propose to evaluate regression model with effective safety rate. To further increase the effective safety rate of regression model and improve the safety level of metro systems, we set one level up the minimum action code which predicted by the regression model. While, the effective safety rate of this advanced result was superior to the original effective safety rate. For example, the predicted minimum action code for a given set of input characteristics of "changing rail within 4 weeks" became "changing rail within 2 weeks" after applying this advanced strategy. The results of the advanced strategy are shown in Fig. 3 and detailed data are in Tab. 4.

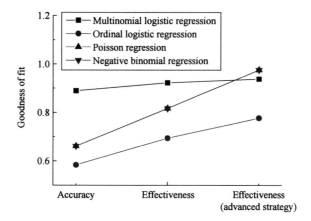

Fig. 3   Comparison of predicted results and advanced strategy

Summary of regression results   Tab. 4

Models	Best combination factors	Accuracy	Effective safety rate	Effective safety rate (advanced strategy)
Multinomial logistic regression	RI, DT, RP, NCB	88.95%	92.23%	93.78%
Ordinal logistic regression	T, JT, DM, RP	58.38%	69.43%	77.72%
Poisson regression	T, RI, DN, MDS, JT, RP	66.15%	81.69%	97.58%
Negative binomial regression	T, RI, DN, MDS, JT, RP	66.15%	81.69%	97.58%
Ordinal logistic regression	RI, DT, RP, NCB	88.95%	92.23%	93.78%

Binomial logistic regression model is not employed in this part due to the characteristics of the predictors. Thus, other regression models are employed and it is found that the effective safety rates for all regression models are improved by utilization of the advanced strategy. Specifically, the effective safety rate with the advanced strategy is 1.55% greater than the original one, the accuracy of the multinomial logistic regression model is improved by 4.83%, while the ordinal logistic regression model is improved by 8.29% in terms of the safety rate and 19.33% in terms of accuracy. The greatest improvement is found with Poisson regression model and the negative binomial regression model, which improves 15.89% in effective safety rates and 31.43% in accuracies. The effective safety rate 97.58% of the Poisson regression model and the negative binomial regression are the highest among all regressions processed with advanced strategy. By comparing observed and predicted results, 92 predicted results are one level lower than the observed minimum action code, as shown in the grey cells in Tab. 5. This indicates that the effective safety rate improved tremendously with the application of our advanced strategy.

Comparison of records and predicted results (Multinomial logistic regression)   Tab. 5

Predict	Record						
	0	1	2	3	4	5	6
0	258	21	0	2	0	0	0
1	20	91	14	0	0	0	0

continue

Predict	Record						
	0	1	2	3	4	5	6
2	16	29	20	49	0	0	0
3	0	0	0	3	8	7	0
4	0	0	0	14	0	0	5
5	0	0	0	0	0	11	0
6	0	0	0	0	0	11	0

3 Conclusions

Continuous monitoring of rail networks is an insufficiently effective and passive part of daily rail inspection and maintenance. To address this problem, we built predictive models based on logistic regression, multinomial logistic regression, ordinal logistic regression, Poisson regression and negative binomial regression to determine the minimum action code required for optimal maintenance management. We used 579 railway crack records from an assumed database in the case study, and 7 predictors were accounted for in the model: track, rail identification, defect type, defect nature, maximum defect size, joint type, detection method, recheck period and number of previous checks. The dependent variable of the prediction model was the minimum action code, which indicates the maintenance schedule of a railway track.

By stepwise and trial actions, the optimized model was developed according to the AIC and the accuracy of the model. We obtained an accuracy of 88.95% and an effective safety rate of 92.23% in the prediction, and the predicted minimum action code that best fitted the records was calculated by multinomial logistic regression. The best combination of factors in the model was found to be rail identification, defect type, recheck period and number of previous checks.

To further improve the effective safety rate of the regression model, the levels of all the predicted minimum action codes were increased by one in what we term an advanced strategy. This increased the effective safety rate of all regression models except the binomial logistic regression model. Specifically, the Poisson regression and negative binomial regression model had the highest effective safety rate, 97.58%, after the application of this advanced strategy, which was 15.89% and 31.34% higher than their respective original effective safety rates. This showed that our advanced strategy was tremendously effective for improving the prediction model, but as the cost of maintenance is also an important consideration in maintenance management, it is necessary to find a balance between maintenance and expenditure. Because of the dearth of data on the cost of maintenance, future work should investigate the optimum maintenance strategy for a metro system in terms of both maintenance costs and safety levels.

4 Acknowledgements

The research was fully supported by the Research Grant under the TBRS Hong Kong Research Grant Council No. T32-101/15-R.

References

[1] Akaike H. A new look at the statistical model identification[J]. IEEE transactions on automatic control, 1974, 19(6), 716-723.

[2] Ghofrani F, He Q, Goverde R M., et al. Recent applications of big data analytics in railway transportation systems: A survey[J]. Transportation Research Part C: Emerging Technologies, 2018, 90, 226-246.

[3] Guler H. Decision support system for railway track maintenance and renewal management[J]. Journal of

Computing in Civil Engineering,2012,27(3), 292-306.
[4] Guler H. Prediction of railway track geometry deterioration using artificial neural networks: a case study for Turkish state railways[J]. Structure and Infrastructure Engineering,2014,10(5), 614-626.
[5] Jamshidi A, Faghih-Roohi S, Hajizadeh S,. A big data analysis approach for rail failure risk assessment [J]. Risk analysis,2017,37(8), 1495-1507.
[6] Jamshidi A, Hajizadeh S, Su Z,et al. ,A decision support approach for condition-based maintenance of rails based on big data analysis[J]. Transportation Research Part C: Emerging Technologies,2018,95, 185-206.
[7] Jidayi Y M. Reliability improvement of railway infrastructure (Doctoral dissertation, Stellenbosch University)[J].2105.
[8] Li H, Parikh D, He Q,et al. Improving rail network velocity: A machine learning approach to predictive maintenance[J]. Transportation Research Part C: Emerging Technologies,2014,45, 17-26.
[9] Liu D, Huang X. Condition monitoring preventive maintenance of ballastless track systems for high-speed railways[J]. China mechanical engineering, 2019,30(3), 349-353.
[10] Liu X, Lovett A, Dick T,et al. Optimization of ultrasonic rail-defect inspection for improving railway transportation safety and efficiency[J]. Journal of Transportation Engineering,2014,140(10), 04014048.
[11] Liu X,Saat M R, Qin X,et al. Analysis of US freight-train derailment severity using zero-truncated negative binomial regression and quantile regression[J]. Accident Analysis & Prevention,2013,59, 87-93.
[12] Ma J, Lo S, Song W,et al. Modeling pedestrian space in complex building for efficient pedestrian traffic simulation[J]. Automation In Construction,2013, 30, 25-36.
[13] Morant A, Larsson-Kråik P O, Kumar U. Data-driven model for maintenance decision support: A case study of railway signalling systems. [J] Proceedings of the Institution of Mechanical Engineers, Part F: Journal of Rail and Rapid Transit,2016,230(1), 220-234.
[14] MTR. MTR Sustainability Report 2017[R]. Hong Kong: MTR. Retrieved from http://www.mtr.com.hk/sustainability/2017rpt/ch/corporate/sustainability/2017rpt/pdf/MTR_Full2017_Chi.pdf.
[15] Nappi R. Integrated maintenance: analysis and perspective of innovation in railway sector. arXiv preprint arXiv:1404.7560.
[16] R Core Team. R: A language and environment for statistical computing. R Foundation for Statistical Computing, Vienna, Austria. URL https://www.R-project.org/.
[17] Sadeghi J, Akbari B. Field investigation on effects of railway track geometric parameters on rail wear. Journal of Zhejiang University-SCIENCE A, 7(11), 1846-1855.
[18] Wang W, Lo S, Liu S,et al. On the Use of a Pedestrian Simulation Model with Natural Behavior Representation in Metro Stations. Procedia Computer Science, 52, 137-144.
[19] Xu P, Sun Q, Liu R,et al. A short-range prediction model for track quality index. Proceedings of the Institution of Mechanical Engineers, Part F: Journal of Rail and Rapid Transit, 225(3), 277-285.
[20] Zhang, L., Liu, M., Wu, X.,et al. Simulation-based route planning for pedestrian evacuation in metro stations: A case study. Automation In Construction, 71, 430-442.
[21] Zhang Z. Prediction of high-speed railway track maintenance cycle based on track quality state (graduate). BeijingJiaotong University.
[22] Zoeteman A,Braaksma E. An approach to improving the performance of rail systems in a design phase. In World Conference on Railway Research,2001,1-9.

四轮转向车辆转向中心位置后移研究

杨更生 杨蔡进 张卫华

（西南交通大学）

摘 要 本文研究目的是明确车辆四轮转向中心位置的选取对车辆动态行驶的影响；主要研究在高速公路行驶时车辆四轮转向中心后移距离与车辆动力学姿态的关系。本文主要采用动力学理论和方法，从车辆动力学建模入手，考虑车体、车轮均为刚性。车辆在平滑进入圆周曲线时，求解车辆因受到斜坡激励作用而引发的动力学响应。主要分析车辆行驶速度、横向转向半径、转向中心后移距离对车辆俯仰角度、侧倾角度以及合成加速度的影响。结论是车辆在其他条件相同的情况下，合理地设置转向中心后移距离可有效减低车辆在转向时的侧倾角以及合成加速度等，从而提升车辆在通过弯道时的乘坐舒适性。

关键词 交通运输 转向中心后移 动力学建模 四轮转向

0 引 言

我国汽车工业起步较晚，对四轮转向技术的研究也比较晚，吉林工业大学提出了一种新型的车载模型控制方法[1]，北京理工大学、东南大学等也进行了四轮转向相关研究。

四轮独立转向与传统的前轮转向相比，具有突出的优势。表现为在低速时具有相当的灵活性[2]，在高速时具有良好的稳定性；此外，四轮转向响应速度更快、转向精度更高、可降低车辆侧倾和摆尾[3]。

本文将以四轮转向为研究中心，重点研究四轮转向车辆的转向中心位置，分析四轮转向车辆行驶速度、横向转向半径以及转向中心后移距离对车辆动态行驶姿态的影响。

1 车辆动力学模型

通过分析可知，当四轮转向车辆在低速工况下行驶时，其最佳的转向中心在车身几何中心的水平延长线上；而四轮转向车辆为了增加其高速公路行驶稳定性，其转向中心往往会后移，通过增加车辆的虚拟轴长来提升行驶稳定性。

为了衡量车辆行驶稳定性，此处引入动力学模型，通过动力学分析指标来评判转向中心的选取。建立车辆动力学模型，将车体和车轮均视为刚体，其质心位于车体几何中心处，距离地面高度为 h；K、C 分别表示 A、B、M、N 车轮处的弹簧刚度和阻尼系数；$F_{xM/N/A/B}$、$F_{yM/N/A/B}$、$F_{zM/N/A/B}$ 分别表示各车轮在横向、纵向、垂向的受力；α、β、θ 分别表示绕 x、y、z 轴旋转的角度，如图1、图2、图3所示。

车辆在高速转向时会受到侧倾力矩 M_c 和俯仰力矩 M_f 的作用，使得 A、B、M、N 车轮的垂向受力 F_{zA}、F_{zB}、F_{zM}、F_{zN} 大小各不相同，从而引起 A、B、M、N 车轮在转向时的侧向摩擦力 f_A、f_B、f_M、f_N 不同，因此产生使得车体旋转的转向力矩 M_t，如图4所示。

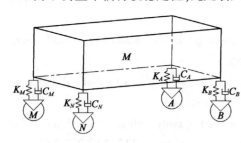

图1 车辆动力学模型

图4是车辆在曲线工况行驶时各个车轮的受力情况分析图，主要目的是明确 A、B、M、N 车轮处驱动力 $F_{qA/B/M/N}$、行驶阻力 $f_{sA/B/M/N}$、侧向摩擦力 $f_{A/B/M/N}$ 的大小关系。

根据已知，假设1：$f_s \propto v$，定义车辆在转向时其几何中心速度为 v，故 A、B、M、N 车轮的速度、质心速度与速度瞬心的距离成比例，即：

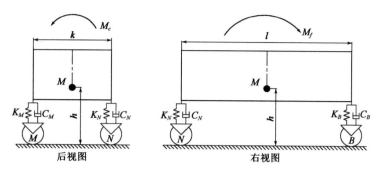

图 2　车辆模型平面视图

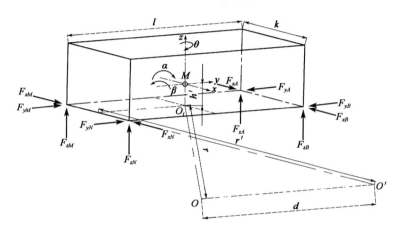

图 3　车体受力模型

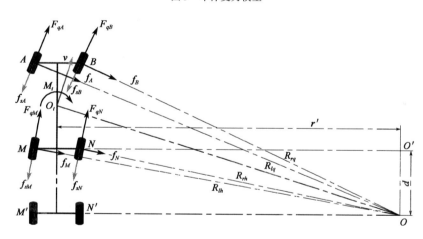

图 4　车辆曲线行驶四轮受力图

$$\frac{v_A}{R_{lq}} = \frac{v_B}{R_{rq}} = \frac{v_M}{R_{lh}} = \frac{v_N}{R_{rh}} = \frac{v}{r} \Rightarrow \frac{f_{sA}}{R_{lq}} = \frac{f_{sB}}{R_{rq}} = \frac{f_{sM}}{R_{lh}} = \frac{f_{sN}}{R_{rh}} = \frac{f'_s}{r} \tag{1}$$

其中，将几何中心处的等效行驶阻力 f'_s 作近似平均处理，即 $f'_s = \frac{1}{4} f_s$，即：

$$\begin{bmatrix} f_{sA} \\ f_{sB} \\ f_{sM} \\ f_{sN} \end{bmatrix} = \frac{P}{4rv} \begin{bmatrix} R_{lq} \\ R_{rq} \\ R_{lh} \\ R_{rh} \end{bmatrix} \tag{2}$$

$$r = \sqrt{r'^2 + \left(\frac{1}{2}l + d\right)^2}, \; p = r' + \frac{1}{2}k, \; q = r' - \frac{1}{2}k, \; s = l + d \tag{3}$$

$$\begin{bmatrix} R_{lq} \\ R_{rq} \\ R_{lh} \\ R_{rh} \end{bmatrix} = \begin{bmatrix} \sqrt{p^2+s^2} \\ \sqrt{q^2+s^2} \\ \sqrt{p^2+d^2} \\ \sqrt{q^2+d^2} \end{bmatrix}, \begin{bmatrix} \alpha_{lk} \\ \alpha_{rk} \\ \theta_{lk} \\ \theta_{rk} \end{bmatrix} = \arctan \begin{bmatrix} s/p \\ s/q \\ d/p \\ d/q \end{bmatrix} \qquad (4)$$

假设2：为了尽可能避免出现转向不足的问题，将前后轴驱动力进行60：40分配，左右轮驱动力50：50分配，即：$F_{qA} = F_{qB} = 0.3F_q$，$F_{qM} = F_{qN} = 0.2F_q$，$F_q = \dfrac{P}{v}$。

俯仰力矩 M_f 与侧倾力矩 M_c 由离心力 F_r 产生，即：

$$F_r = M\frac{v^2}{r}, \quad \tan\gamma = \frac{\frac{1}{2}l + d}{r'}, \quad \begin{bmatrix} M_f \\ M_c \end{bmatrix} = F_r \begin{bmatrix} \sin\gamma \\ \cos\gamma \end{bmatrix} \times h \qquad (5)$$

建立俯仰力矩 M_f 与侧倾力矩 M_c 的动力学模型，如图5所示。

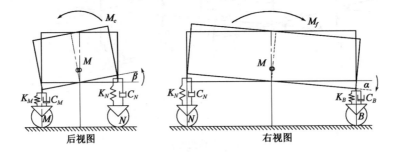

图5 车辆模型侧倾、俯仰受力图

$$\begin{bmatrix} F_{Ax} \\ F_{Bx} \\ F_{Mx} \\ F_{Nx} \end{bmatrix} = \begin{bmatrix} K_A \\ K_B \\ -K_M \\ -K_N \end{bmatrix} \times \frac{l\alpha}{2} + \begin{bmatrix} C_A \\ C_B \\ -C_M \\ -C_N \end{bmatrix} \times \frac{l\dot{\alpha}}{2} \qquad (6)$$

$$\begin{bmatrix} F_{Ay} \\ F_{By} \\ F_{My} \\ F_{Ny} \end{bmatrix} = \begin{bmatrix} K_A \\ -K_B \\ K_M \\ -K_N \end{bmatrix} \times \frac{k\beta}{2} + \begin{bmatrix} C_A \\ -C_B \\ C_M \\ -C_N \end{bmatrix} \times \frac{k\dot{\beta}}{2} \qquad (7)$$

$$\begin{bmatrix} F_A \\ F_B \\ F_M \\ F_N \end{bmatrix} = \begin{bmatrix} F_{Ax} \\ F_{Bx} \\ F_{Mx} \\ F_{Nx} \end{bmatrix} + \begin{bmatrix} F_{Ay} \\ F_{By} \\ F_{My} \\ F_{Ny} \end{bmatrix} \qquad (8)$$

$$\sum M'_f = \begin{bmatrix} F_A \\ F_B \\ -F_M \\ -F_N \end{bmatrix} \times \frac{1}{2}l - M_f, \quad \sum M'_c = \begin{bmatrix} F_A \\ -F_B \\ F_M \\ -F_N \end{bmatrix} \times \frac{1}{2}k - M_c \qquad (9)$$

车辆在转向时存在由离心力 F_r 引起的俯仰和侧倾作用，导致车体发生轴荷转移，使得A、B、M、N车轮处的垂向力大小各不相同，即：

$$\begin{bmatrix} F_{zA} \\ F_{zB} \\ F_{zM} \\ F_{zN} \end{bmatrix} = \frac{Mg}{4} + \frac{\frac{1}{4}(M_f - I_x\ddot{\alpha})}{\frac{l}{2}} \times \begin{bmatrix} 1 \\ 1 \\ -1 \\ -1 \end{bmatrix} + \frac{\frac{1}{4}(M_c - I_y\ddot{\beta})}{\frac{k}{2}} \times \begin{bmatrix} 1 \\ -1 \\ 1 \\ -1 \end{bmatrix} \tag{10}$$

令 A、B、M、N 车轮处受到的侧向滑动摩擦力系数为 μ，即各车轮处可提供的最大侧向滑动摩擦力分别为 $f_{A/B/M/N\max} = \mu F_{zA/zB/zM/zN}$，且 $f_{A/B/M/N} < f_{A/B/M/N\max}$。

侧向摩擦力合力 $\sum f = F_r$，且 $f_{A/B/M/N} \propto F_{zA/zB/zM/zN}$，即：$f_{A/B/M/N} = \lambda F_{zA/zB/zM/zN}$。

其中：

$$\lambda = \frac{F_r}{\sum F_z} \tag{11}$$

即当 $\lambda < \mu$ 时，车辆各车轮均不会发生侧滑。

根据对上述 A、B、M、N 车轮处驱动力 F_q、行驶阻力 f_s、侧向摩擦力 f 的分解，可以求得各个车轮处的横向力和纵向力。令：

$$A = [\cos\alpha_{lk} \ \cos\alpha_{rk} \ \cos\theta_{lk} \ \cos\theta_{rk}] \tag{12}$$

$$B = [\sin\alpha_{lk} \ \sin\alpha_{rk} \ \sin\theta_{lk} \ \sin\theta_{rk}] \tag{13}$$

$$\begin{bmatrix} F_{xA} \\ F_{xB} \\ F_{xM} \\ F_{xN} \end{bmatrix} = \begin{bmatrix} f_A \\ f_B \\ f_M \\ f_N \end{bmatrix} \times A + \begin{bmatrix} F_{qA} \\ F_{qB} \\ F_{qM} \\ F_{qN} \end{bmatrix} \times B - \begin{bmatrix} f_{sA} \\ f_{sB} \\ f_{sM} \\ f_{sN} \end{bmatrix} \times B \tag{14}$$

$$\begin{bmatrix} F_{yA} \\ F_{yB} \\ F_{yM} \\ F_{yN} \end{bmatrix} = - \begin{bmatrix} f_A \\ f_B \\ f_M \\ f_N \end{bmatrix} \times B + \begin{bmatrix} F_{qA} \\ F_{qB} \\ F_{qM} \\ F_{qN} \end{bmatrix} \times A - \begin{bmatrix} f_{sA} \\ f_{sB} \\ f_{sM} \\ f_{sN} \end{bmatrix} \times A \tag{15}$$

建立动力学方程如下：

$$\begin{cases} M\ddot{x} = \sum F_x \\ M\ddot{y} = \sum F_y \\ I_z\ddot{\theta} = \sum M'_t \\ I_x\ddot{\alpha} + \sum M'_f = 0 \\ I_y\ddot{\beta} + \sum M'_c = 0 \end{cases}, \sum M'_t = \begin{bmatrix} F_{xA} \\ F_{xB} \\ -F_{xM} \\ -F_{xN} \end{bmatrix} \times \frac{1}{2}l + \begin{bmatrix} F_{yA} \\ -F_{yB} \\ F_{yM} \\ -F_{yN} \end{bmatrix} \times \frac{1}{2}k \tag{16}$$

求解上述动力学方程组，为了简化计算，令：

$$K_A = K_B = K_M = K_N = K; C_A = C_B = C_M = C_N = C \tag{17}$$

$$S = \begin{bmatrix} 1 & 1 & 1 & 1 \\ 1 & 1 & -1 & -1 \\ -1 & -1 & 1 & 1 \\ -1 & -1 & -1 & -1 \end{bmatrix}, T = \begin{bmatrix} \frac{l\alpha}{2}K & \frac{l\dot{\alpha}}{2}C & \frac{k\beta}{2}K & \frac{k\dot{\beta}}{2}C \end{bmatrix}^T \tag{18}$$

$$\sum M'_f = S \times T \times \frac{1}{2}l - M_f, \quad \sum M'_c = S \times T \times \frac{1}{2}k - M_c \tag{19}$$

$$I_x\ddot{\alpha} + Cl^2\dot{\alpha} + Kl^2\alpha - M_f = 0, \quad I_y\ddot{\beta} + Ck^2\dot{\beta} + Kk^2\beta - M_c = 0 \tag{20}$$

2 车辆通过圆周曲线

当四轮转向车辆稳态通过半径恒定的圆周曲线时,此时车辆的转向半径 r,仅与横向转向半径 r' 和转向中心后移距离 d 有关;M_f 和 M_c 均为定值。考虑到实际情况下车辆均为平稳入弯,设置合理的过渡曲线,使得 M_f 和 M_c 是以斜坡激励的方式介入,经过 t_1 时间后逐渐达到最大值并保持不变,最终使得车辆在圆周曲线上稳态行驶,如图6所示。在此工况下,求解上述方程组。此时,激励为斜坡激励和阶跃激励的组合,如图7a)所示。

此时相当于求解方程:

$$I_x\ddot{\alpha} + Cl^2\dot{\alpha} + Kl^2\alpha = at, \quad 0 \leq t \leq t_1 \tag{21}$$

$$I_x\ddot{\alpha} + Cl^2\dot{\alpha} + Kl^2\alpha = M_f, \quad t > t_1 \tag{22}$$

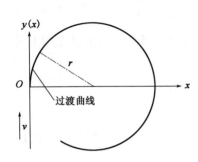

图6 行驶路径

假设 $t_1 = 1s$,其中:

$$\frac{Kl^2}{I_x} = \omega^2, \frac{Cl^2}{I_x} = 2\zeta\omega, \omega' = \sqrt{1-\zeta^2}\omega, a = \frac{M_f}{t_1} \tag{23}$$

式(21)的通解为:

$$\alpha_1 = e^{-\zeta\omega t}(D_1\cos\omega't + D_2\sin\omega't) + \frac{at}{Kl^2} - \frac{Cl^2 a}{(Kl^2)^2} \tag{24}$$

已知 $t = 0$ 时,$\alpha(0) = \dot{\alpha}(0) = 0$,则积分常数为:

$$D_1 = \frac{Cl^2 a}{(Kl^2)^2}, D_2 = \frac{a}{Kl^2\omega}(2\zeta^2 - 1) \tag{25}$$

式(22)的通解为:

$$\alpha_2 = e^{-\zeta\omega t}(C\cos\omega't + D\sin\omega't) + M_f/(Kl^2) \tag{26}$$

当 $t = t_1$ 时,此时 $\alpha(t_1)$、$\dot{\alpha}(t_1)$ 作为初始条件易求得,但积分常数 C, D 不能直接得出。故将激励输入方式理解为两个斜坡激励的叠加,如图7b)所示。

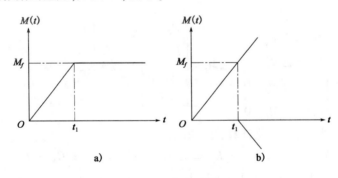

图7 力矩激励输入

由式(21)的通解式(24)可得出,激励叠加后的俯仰角度总响应为:

$$\alpha = \alpha_1(t) - \alpha_1(t - t_1) \tag{27}$$

同理,激励叠加后的俯仰角度总响应为:

$$\beta = \beta_1(t) - \beta_1(t - t_1) \tag{28}$$

车辆基本参数如表1所示。

车 辆 参 数 表　　　　　　　　　　表1

名　称	符　号	数　值	单　位
轴距	l	3.024	m
轮心距	k	1.641	m
重心高度	h	0.5	m
摩擦因数	μ	0.78	—
车辆总质量	M	1800	kg
绕x轴转动惯量	I_x	4044	kg·m²
绕y轴转动惯量	I_y	835.5	kg·m²
绕z轴转动惯量	I_z	4291.5	kg·m²
弹簧刚度	C	2000	N/(m/s)
阻尼系数	K	40	kN/m

根据表1参数信息,代入模型可得到车辆在速度v下的入弯动态特性。

令$v=10$m/s, $r'=50$m, $d=5$m,可得到车辆的俯仰角响应曲线、侧倾角响应曲线,如图8a)所示;横摆角加速度响应曲线、横向加速度响应曲线、纵向加速度响应曲线、合成加速度响应曲线,如图8b)所示。

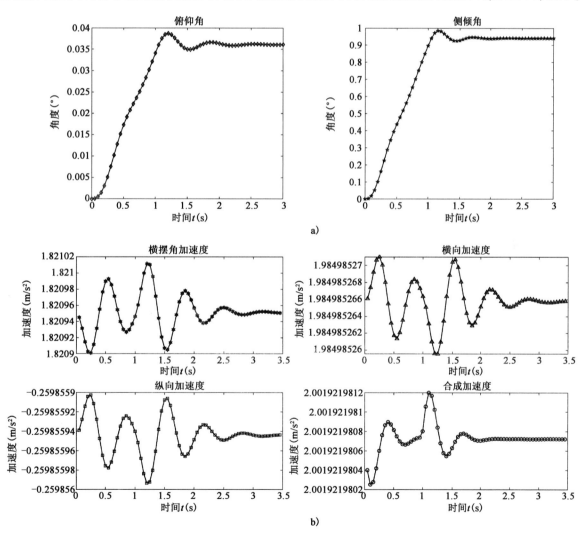

图8　动态响应曲线

在 $0 \sim t_1$ 时刻的过程中($t_1 = 1s$),车辆按照斜坡激励进行动态响应;而在 t_1 时刻后,激励变为定值,以阶跃力矩的方式存在,车辆发生阶跃激励的动态响应。车辆在入弯时,因受到 F_r 的作用产生 M_f 和 M_c,使得车辆发生俯仰运动和侧倾运动。而当激励逐渐达到最大值,车辆运动姿态达到稳态,最终车辆以匀速在半径恒定的圆周曲线上稳态运行。可以看出,侧倾角度在 $t = 2s$ 左右达到稳态;俯仰角度和合成加速度在 $t = 2.5s$ 左右达到稳态,而横摆角加速度、横向加速度和纵向加速度在 $t = 3s$ 左右达到稳态。

取稳态值作为车辆在定半径圆周曲线上的行驶评价指标。指标规定,车辆在以一定的速度 v 入弯,绕横向转向半径为 r' 的圆周曲线行驶时,其车辆转向中心后移距离为 d(其中 $d \ll r'$)时,车辆拥有最优的动力学性能,即最小的侧倾角度、最小的俯仰角度、最小的转向角加速度、最小的横向和纵向加速度(即合成加速度)等。并规定车辆在转向时,各车轮均不能悬空。

车辆发生侧翻的条件:

当 N 轮与地面的正压力为零时,认为此时车辆会发生侧翻,即:

$$F_N = \frac{1}{4}Mg - \frac{1}{4}M_f \Big/ \frac{l}{2} - \frac{1}{4}M_c \Big/ \frac{k}{2} = 0 \tag{29}$$

综上所述,取最具代表性的最小侧倾角 β 和最小合成加速度 a_{xy} 作为评判指标,得到车速 v、横向转向半径 r'、转向中心后移距离 d 三者的关系,并绘制相应曲线。

由于 d 的存在,使得车辆在高速区随着 d 的增大,安全区域减小,侧翻区域增大;在低速区随着 d 的增大使得侧翻区域减小,而安全区域增大。由此表明,为了避免车辆发生侧翻,应合理设置 d,即在低速区应适当增加 d,在高速区尽可能减小 d,由此可有助于车辆的稳定,不易侧翻,如图9所示。

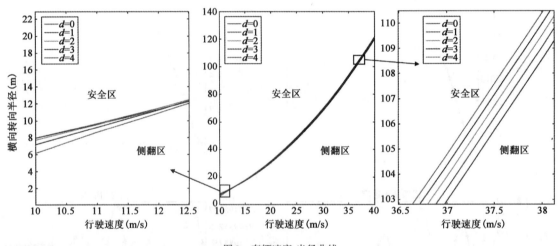

图9 车辆速度-半径曲线

考虑车辆速度对车辆侧倾角的影响,过大的车辆侧倾角会使得乘坐舒适性急剧降低。假设车辆在高速转向时车辆侧倾角不得大于3°,其次合成加速度尽可能小。

下面以速度 $v = 10m/s$ 为例,分析俯仰角度 α、侧倾角度 β 与横向转向半径 r'、转向中心后移距离 d 的关系。

在 $v = 10m/s$ 的条件下,α 随着 d 的增加而增大,且 r' 越小,α 增加越快。β 随着 d 的增加而减小,且 r' 越小,β 减小越快,如图10所示。α 与 r' 的关系、β 与 r' 的关系,如图11所示。

在相同的 r' 的情况下,α、β 都随着 v 的增大而增大;在相同的 α 或相同的 β 时,v 越大对应的 r' 就越大,如图12所示。在最大侧倾角 $\beta = 3°$ 时,各速度条件下合成加速度的最大值不超过 $5.25m/s^2$,且随着 r' 的增加,合成加速度 a_{xy} 逐渐减小,速度 v 越小,合成加速度 a_{xy} 减小越快;在相同的 r' 条件下,速度 v 越大,合成加速度 a_{xy} 越大,如图13所示。在相同 β 时,r' 越大,此时对应的 v 也越大;随着 β 的增加,对应的 v 也增加较快,如图14所示。

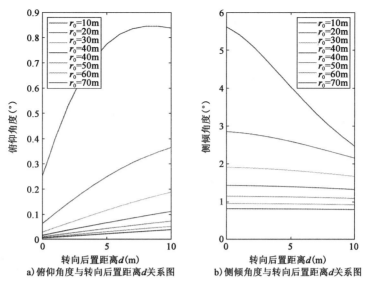

图 10 俯仰、侧倾角度与转向中心后移距离曲线

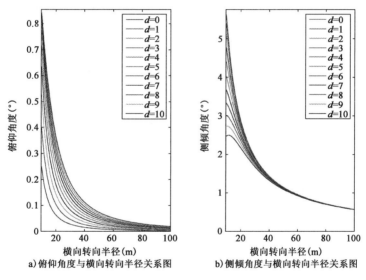

图 11 俯仰、侧倾角度与横向转向半径曲线

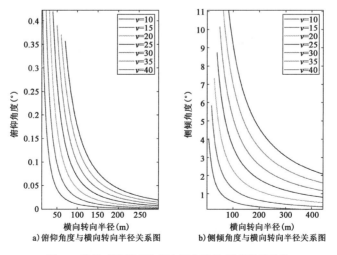

图 12 俯仰、侧倾角度与横向转向半径、速度关系曲线

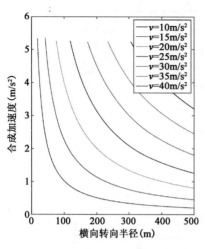

图13 横向转向半径与合成加速度关系曲线

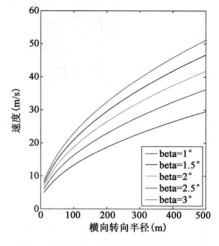

图14 横向转向半径与舒适速度关系曲线

3 结语

本文主要研究车辆在高速公路情况下转向中心位置选取对车辆动态行为的影响。建立了四轮转向车辆动力学模型来分析车辆在进入曲线时的动力学响应,明确车辆的侧倾作用和俯仰作用带来的影响,探寻侧倾角的大小与车辆曲线通过安全性的关系。通过分析车辆转向中心的位置,确定车辆评价指标,为评判四轮转向车辆对乘坐舒适性的影响提供了条件。

本文对四轮转向车辆转向中心位置进行了研究,取得了初步成果,但研究内容和理论方法还有待深入,应继续展开相关研究,采用更严谨科学的方法来探寻多种因素对四轮转向车辆的影响,后续将继续努力,对四轮转向展开更加深入的研究。

参考文献

[1] 高越,高振海,李向瑜,等.基于自适应Kalman滤波的汽车横摆角速度软测量算法[J].江苏大学学报(自然科学版),2005,26(1):24-27.

[2] 姬晓,李刚,曹天琳.四轮独立驱动与转向电动汽车四轮转向研究综述[J].新能源汽车,2020,17:5-7.

[3] 武楠.电动车四轮转向系统的运动仿真研究[D].广州:华南理工大学,2015.

城市轨道交通车辆内置消毒装置的设计及应用研究

涂 杰 吴 娟 梁同天 黄小庆 袁 满
(西南交通大学希望学院)

摘 要 受新冠肺炎疫情影响,为加强疫情防控,解决交通车辆快速及时的消毒问题,本文打破传统的人工消毒模式,设计出一种车辆内置消毒装置,建立数学模型,计算出每节车厢喷洒消毒的有效消毒范围,实现联动性自动消毒,有针对性地对人员密集、流动性大的列车进行实时消毒,将人工消毒转化到设备自动消毒。以成都地铁为例对其可行性进行分析验证,在保证疫情防控的同时提高消毒作业效率。

关键词 城市轨道交通车辆 内置消毒装置 自动化消毒 疫情防控

0 引　言

公共交通运输工具是传播各种疾病的重要途径。特别是在公共汽车、火车车厢内,由于空间狭小,乘坐的人数较多,乘坐人员的来路、去向复杂,因此,很容易通过接触以及呼吸使病菌、病毒得以迅速传播,尤其是当发生重大的传染病疫情时,地铁车厢相对密闭,人流量大,容易造成各种污染物累积而导致空气质量恶化,进而影响人体健康[1]。而刚爆发的新冠肺炎疫情防控工作更是给我们的一大启示,全社会需要大力加强公共卫生以及传染病防治领域的供给侧改革,也应建设完善的公共卫生与防疫基础设施[2]。

近年来,许多城市、地区为提高公共交通的舒适度,开设了空调公共车辆、火车空调车厢,使乘客享受到舒适的环境温度,但所付出的代价则是车厢内的空气质量恶化。出于保持温度的原因,车厢处于封闭状态,虽然许多车辆在制冷或制热中采用吸入外界新风的方式,但是,由于风量太小,车内空气的流动性太差,无法解决疾病传播的问题。特别是因为地铁属于公共设施中人群最为密集、流动性最大、健康和非健康个体特别混杂的公共设施,在这些特点的基础上它会存在一定的卫生问题。这些卫生问题的产生主要包括以下几个方面:①人流量大,传染疾病易发作;②车厢内环境潮湿,相对密闭,空气不流通;③车内公共设施未消毒,多人接触;④车内消毒彻底时间较长,暂无迅速便捷的消毒方式。

目前,对车厢进行消毒的方式是在车辆停运时,由车辆运行工作人员或专业消毒单位对车厢内进行通风、清洗、喷洒消毒制剂操作。这种方式虽然对车厢内的清洁卫生有较大的益处,但在随后的再次投入运行中,乘客携带进入车厢的病菌、病毒对车厢内的空气将造成再次污染,因此,解决车厢内,特别是空调车厢内空气的流动问题[3]是减少乘客之间互相感染,传播疾病的有效途径,是目前公共交通行业急待解决的问题。

1　车辆内置消毒装置设计

1.1　设计思路

该装置设计克服现有技术采用人工方式对地铁车厢进行消毒对人力造成浪费并且消毒液会对人体造成伤害的不足,提供了一种车厢内置消毒装置,通过喷头对消毒液的喷洒,对车厢内进行消毒的同时对工作人员进行了有效的保护。

1.2　装置结构介绍

车辆内置消毒喷洒装置,包括位于座椅下方的储液箱,储液箱侧面的连接管,连接管的一端与储液箱固定,其另一端连接输液管,输液管的下端是与连接管固定,其上端固定有降液槽,所述降液槽位于地铁车厢的顶部并延伸布满整个地铁车厢的顶板,在降液槽的下表面均匀地分布有若干个顶部喷头,所述顶部喷头与降液槽固定,降液槽、顶部喷头、输液管、连接管和储液箱的内部连通,构成一个完整的地铁车内自动消毒装置。

在接到联动装置的讯息时,触发自动消毒装置的开启,通过新型喷头喷洒消毒的方式对地铁车厢的内部进行消毒。

1.2.1　装置结构图

本研究通过结构示意图展示装置的各个细节点,更加直观的展示解决方案。本实施例涉及一种车厢内置消毒装置,包括地铁车厢,在地铁车厢内设有车窗2和车门7,所述车窗2均匀分布于车门7的两侧,在车窗2的下方设有座椅,还包括位于座椅下方的储液箱6,储液箱6与地铁车厢固定,在储液箱6的侧面设有连接管5,连接管5的一端与储液箱6固定,其另一端设有输液管4,输液管4的下端与连接管5固定,其上端固定有降液槽1,所述降液槽1位于地铁车厢的顶部并延伸布满整个地铁车厢的顶板,在降液槽1的下表面均匀地分布有若干个顶部喷头8,所述顶部喷头8与降液槽1固定,在地铁车厢的两端分布有若干个盲区喷头3,所述盲区喷头3与降液槽1固定,所述盲区喷头3、降液槽1、顶部喷头8、输液管4、连接管5和储液箱6的内部连通[4]。结构如图1所示。

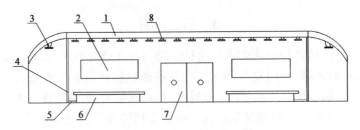

图1 车辆内置消毒装置的结构示意图

1.2.2 盲区喷头结构

盲区喷头3包括喷头外壳31,喷头外壳31的内部中空,在喷头外壳31的侧面上开有若干均匀分布的环形侧孔32,在喷头外壳31的底面开有若干均匀分布的底部开孔33,所述喷头外壳31的上方设有液体通道35,液体通道35的上端与降液槽1固定,其下端与喷头外壳31固定,在液体通道35内设有叶轮34,叶轮34与液体通道35通过电机固定,叶轮34的转动方向与液体的流动方向相同。结构如图2所示。

1.2.3 储液箱结构

储液箱6包括箱体外壳61,在箱体外壳61内设有液体传输组件62,所述液体传输组件62与箱体外壳61的内壁固定,并且液体传输组件62与所述连接管5连通,在液体传输组件62远离连接管5的侧面设有防涡流组件63,所述防涡流组件63与液体传输组件62固定,在储液箱6的侧面设有加液口64,所述加液口64靠近储液箱6的顶部,在加液口64内设有止回组件65,止回组件65与加液口64固定。结构如图3所示。

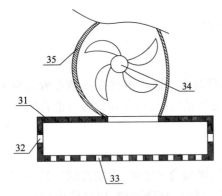

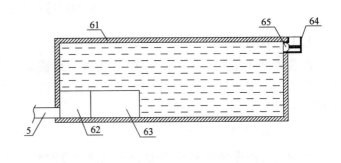

图2 盲区喷头结构示意图　　　　　图3 储液箱结构示意图

1.2.4 液体传输组件结构

液体传输组件62包括传输外壳623,在传输外壳623上设有进液口621,所述进液口621与所述连接管5以传输外壳623的中间线为基准对称设置,在传输外壳623内设有能够将传输外壳623内分为上下独立两部分的薄膜622,所述进液口621与连接管5位于薄膜622的同侧部分,薄膜622的另一侧部分内设有伸缩杆624,所述伸缩杆624的一端与传输外壳623固定,其另一端与薄膜622固定。结构如图4所示。

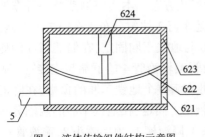

图4 液体传输组件结构示意图

1.2.5 防涡流组件结构

防涡流组件63包括进液外壳631,在进液外壳631的顶部开设有顶部液口633,在进液外壳631的侧面开设有排液口634,所述排液口634与所述液体传输组件62的内部连通,在进液外壳631的顶部液口633处设有能够防止液体产生涡流的涡流板632,涡流板632与传输外壳623的顶板固定;所述涡流板632包括圆板6321,在原版上设有若干支柱6323,支柱6323的下端与圆板6321固定,其上端与所述进液外壳631固定,在圆板6321的上表面设有互相垂直的垂交板6322和横交板6324,所述垂交板6322和横交板6324与圆板6321固定。结构如图5和图6所示。

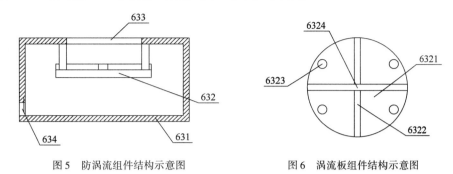

图5　防涡流组件结构示意图　　　　图6　涡流板组件结构示意图

2　车辆内置消毒装置模型

2.1　模型原理

喷洒消毒效果与喷头自身特性以及喷洒压力、流量密切相关。为了有效地喷洒、消毒,关于喷头的喷洒特性已经有了大量研究,喷洒特性一般包括喷洒速度、液滴大小、运行轨迹和水流分布等。喷洒速度是一个关键参量,它决定着喷头的保护半径及消毒的有效范围。曾有人对液滴初始速度进行过分析。近来对液滴大小进行了研究,得到了平均粒径大小与喷头直径、喷洒压力之间的关系。而后通过求解液滴动量方程,得到液滴运动速度以及喷洒有效保护半径的理论模型。经调查发现,我国目前所用的喷头一般为ZXTP15,压力一般为0.1Pa时,液滴的初速度考虑为4.2m/s。喷头喷出的液滴可分为水平方向及竖直方向,水平方向液滴喷出后在短时内保持水平速度不变。据此特性,假设喷头喷出的液滴运动轨迹在一定高度空间上为圆锥。即可考虑在车厢宽度范围内,液滴在三维空间的运动轨迹总体为圆锥。在圆锥以下部分,喷洒区域可考虑为长方体。以此求出每个喷头的有效消毒范围,而后求出每个车厢有效消毒范围[5]。

2.2　模型假设

为确保模型的模拟环境具有广泛的适用性,做出如下假设:
①列车停靠时,在地铁车厢内部,空气流动强度低,假设液滴下落时空气阻力忽略不计;
②研究地铁车型为A型车;
③雾化喷头喷出的液滴初速度相同;
④假设雾化喷头喷出的液滴运动轨迹在一定高度空间上为圆锥。

2.3　符号及定义

字母符号及意义　　　　表1

字母表示	符号意义
V_0	喷头小孔喷出的液滴初速度
L_C	地铁A型车厢的车厢长度
L_K	地铁A型车厢的车厢宽度
L_G	地铁A型车厢的车厢高度
V_d	单个雾化喷头有效消毒体积
V_c	单节车厢有效消毒体积
V	单节车厢体积
R	圆锥底面半径
a	重力加速度,取9.8(m/s)

续上表

字母表示	符号意义
X	雾化喷头高度
T	液滴的空间运动轨迹为圆锥时的下落时间
h	液滴的空间运动轨迹为圆锥时的下落高度
η	单节车厢有效消毒效率
V_1	有效消毒区域上半部分
V_2	有效消毒区域下半部分

2.4 模型建立

2.4.1 确定雾化喷头高度

在最低成本控制的原则下,有假设条件为"假设喷头喷出的液滴运动轨迹在一定高度空间上为圆锥"。即可考虑在车厢宽度范围内,液滴在三维空间的运动轨迹总体为圆锥。由图7可知,在圆锥以下部分,喷洒区域可考虑为长方体。我国目前所用的喷头一般为ZXTP15,压力一般为0.1Pa,液滴的初速度为$4.2 m/s^{[6]}$。

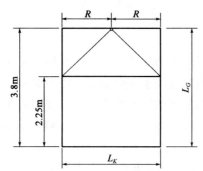

图7 地铁车厢消毒区域纵断面图

$$R = \frac{1}{2}L_K$$
$$T = \frac{R}{V_0}$$
$$h = V_0 T$$

代入$R = 1.5m$,$V_0 = 4.2 m/s^2$,可得到$h = 1.5m$。

已知地铁A型车厢高度为3.8m,经过计算可知圆锥高度为1.5m。因为在地铁车厢中,重点消毒区域为乘客活动的区域,结合实际可取重点消毒区域为2.25m。综上所述可得出雾化喷头高度为0.05m。

2.4.2 确定喷头间距

在计算雾化喷头高度的过程中,假设圆锥半径为R。且圆锥半径为地铁车厢宽度的一半。

消毒区域上半部分考虑为圆锥,因此可以由圆锥地面圆半径确定间距,如图8所示,设置喷头间距为3m。

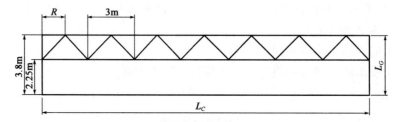

图8 地铁车厢消毒区域侧面图

2.4.3 确定单节车厢喷头数量

因车厢上半部分不是消毒重点区域,结合成本最低原则,设置车厢内喷头数量。

由$L_C = 22m$,$R = 1.5m$,$R = \frac{1}{2}L_K$,$14R < L_C < 15R$

可计算出喷头数$N = \frac{L_C}{L_K}$

即每节车厢设置7个喷头。

2.4.4 计算单节车厢有效消毒效率

车厢长度为22m,宽度为3m,高度为3.8m。一般车厢人工消毒区域高度在2.8m。即假设车厢上部

1m，在人工消毒时难以消毒。喷洒装置消毒上半部分区域考虑为圆锥，圆锥底面圆半径 R 为 1.5m，高度为 1.5m。消毒下半部分考虑为长方体，长方体长为 22m，宽为 3m，高为 2.25m。（车厢连接处面积较小，计算当中忽略不计）

$$V_1 = \frac{7}{3}\pi R^2 h$$

$$V_2 = L_C L_K (L_G - 0.05 - 1.5)$$

$$V_d = V_1 + V_2$$

$$V = L_C L_K (L_G - 1)$$

$$\eta = \frac{V_d}{V}$$

经过计算得到：$V_1 = 24.74m^3$，$V_2 = 148.5m^3$，$V_d = 173.24m^3$，$V = 184.8m^3$

$\eta = 93.74\%$

得到单节车厢有效消毒效率为 93.74%。

3 车辆内置消毒装置的应用研究——以成都地铁为例

3.1 成都地铁各线路客流量现状

疫情防控时期，地铁车厢消毒也成为人们关注的重点。根据相关资料显示，成都地铁日均客运量大于 400 万人次，如表 2 所示；客流量高强度，如表 3 所示；客流量大增幅，如表 4 所示，经汇总发现，这些数据都要求成都的地铁车厢消毒要及时、有效且消毒剂量要兼顾早高峰与晚高峰的大客流。相较于目前使用的人工消毒方法，需要耗费大量人工对车厢座椅、扶手、拉环等地方进行人工擦拭，抹布重复使用消毒效果不理想，清洗抹布的水重复利用，在一定程度上减少了防控力度。为此，以成都市为例，初步探讨由成都市客流量密度来制定车厢内自动喷洒消毒方案。

成都地铁客流量强度 表 2

线 路	昨日客流量（万乘次）	运营里程（公里）	客流强度（万/公里）	站数（个）	客流强度（万/站）
1 号线	81.11	41.00	1.98	35	2.32
2 号线	72.73	42.30	1.72	32	2.27
3 号线	68.30	49.89	1.37	37	1.85
4 号线	59.46	43.30	1.37	30	1.98
5 号线	47.79	49.01	0.98	41	1.17
6 号线	36.77	68.76	0.53	56	0.66
7 号线	72.57	38.61	1.88	31	2.34
8 号线	22.49	29.10	0.77	25	0.90
9 号线	19.52	22.21	0.88	13	1.50

成都地铁日均客流量及累计客流量(万乘次) 表 3

线 路	年日均	1 月日均	年度累计	1 月累计
1 号线	62.69	62.69	501.54	501.54
2 号线	61.02	61.02	488.15	488.15
3 号线	59.23	59.23	473.87	473.87
4 号线	50.46	50.46	403.66	403.66
5 号线	39.43	39.43	315.44	315.44
6 号线	30.71	30.71	245.65	245.65
7 号线	59.91	59.91	479.25	479.25
8 号线	18.41	18.41	147.30	147.30
9 号线	15.74	15.74	125.95	125.95

2020年1月成都地铁客流量及增幅　　　　表4

线　路	昨日客流量（万乘次）	前一天客流量（万乘次）	增量（万乘次）	增幅（%）
1号线	81.11	38.35	42.76	111.5
2号线	72.73	54.31	18.42	33.92
3号线	68.30	55.49	12.81	23.09
4号线	59.46	44.33	15.13	34.13
5号线	47.79	30.54	17.25	56.48
6号线	36.77	28.26	8.51	30.11
7号线	72.57	48.85	23.72	48.56
8号线	22.49	15.69	6.80	43.34
9号线	19.52	12.02	7.50	62.40

3.2 依据客流密度制定消毒方案

3.2.1 定量消毒

以成都地铁为例，将4号线、5号线、6号线、7号线、8号线、9号线、10号线、17号线、18号线的A型车辆，设置规格为每节车厢7个喷头，根据计算得出，如此定量设置，则空间有效消毒率为93.74%

3.2.2 不定时消毒

经过收集大量的数据资料，汇总整理出成都市1号线、2号线、3号线、4号线、5号线、6号线、7号线、8号线、9号线的首班车时间、末班车时间、早高峰、晚高峰以及发车间隔，如表5所示。

成都市各线路发车信息数据　　　　表5

线　路	方　　向	首班车	末班车	早高峰	晚高峰	发车间隔(min)
1号线	韦家碾—科学城	6:10	22:50	7:50-9:20	17:30-19:30	5
	科学城—韦家碾	6:35	23:57	7:50-9:20	17:30-19:30	5
	韦家碾—五根松	6:15	23:00	7:50-9:20	17:30-19:30	5
	五根松—韦家碾	6:35	23:47	7:50-9:20	17:30-19:30	5
2号线	犀浦—龙泉驿	6:10	23:00	7:50-9:20	17:30-19:30	5
	龙泉驿—犀浦	6:48	0:10	7:50-9:20	17:30-19:30	5
3号线	双流西站—成都医学院	6:59	0:10	7:50-9:00	17:30-19:30	5
	成都医学院—双流西站	6:10	22:50	7:50-9:00	17:30-19:31	5
4号线	万盛—西河	6:10	23:00	7:50-9:00	17:30-19:30	5
	西河—万盛	6:57	0:08	7:50-9:00	17:30-19:30	5
5号线	回龙—华桂路	7:07	0:17	7:50-9:00	17:30-19:30	5
	华桂路—回龙	6:10	22:50	7:50-9:00	17:30-19:30	5
6号线	望丛祠—兰家沟	7:07	0:17	8:00-9:00	17:30-19:30	5
	兰家沟—望丛祠	6:10	22:50	8:00-9:00	17:30-19:30	5
7号线	外环—内环	6:15	23:05	7:50-9:30	17:30-19:30	5
	内环—外环	6:34	23:05	7:50-9:30	17:30-19:30	5
8号线	莲花—十里店	6:57	23:48	8:00-9:00	17:30-19:00	5
	十里店—莲花	6:10	23:00	8:00-9:00	17:30-19:00	5

续上表

线　路	方　　向	首班车	末班车	早高峰	晚高峰	发车间隔(min)
9号线	黄田坝—金融城东	6:35	23:25	8:00-9:00	17:30-19:00	5
	金融城东—黄田坝	6:10	23:00	8:00-9:00	17:30-19:00	5

由以上数据,得知成都市1、2、3、4、5、6、7、8、9号线,共9条线日客流量达到480.74万人次,全线网237座车站,每日共300次停靠。

经过大量数据调查,成都市目前单个车站单次消毒时间平均为2h,平均每日消毒9次。12条线,每日共计300次停靠,每日累计消毒次数为2700次,每日累计消毒时间为5400小时,工作量非常大,需要大量人力资源。

因此使用车内自动消毒喷淋装置,减少人工擦拭过程,在各线路列车发车前5min进行一次消毒,并且针对各线路的早晚高峰期发车前进行二次消毒。

针对客流量较多的车次根据现实情况增大剂量即可。

4　车辆内置消毒装置应用前景

4.1　装置的影响

4.1.1　对公共场合环境的影响

对地铁公共卫生而言,车厢内空气中的飞沫及尘埃是呼吸道感染的重要传播途径。以前段时间疫情防控为例,疫情期间地铁公司专业消毒人员对地铁进行人工消毒来达到减少病毒传播的效果。现有的人工消毒方式,对车厢进行消毒的主要操作是在车辆停运时,由车辆清洁工作人员或专业消毒单位对车厢内进行通风、清洗、喷洒消毒制剂操作。这种方式十分浪费人力资源,并且在消毒时容易对工作人员造成安全卫生威胁,并且在随后的再次投入运行中,乘客携带进入车厢的病菌、病毒对车厢内的空气将造成再次污染。

以上是我们装置对公共场合环境所能进行极大改善的地方,我们装置作为内部喷洒消毒装置,采用无人工自动喷洒。

对公共环境而言,不仅通过在地铁运营过程中定时定量的喷洒消毒,有效减少呼吸道类病毒的传播,还能有效保护清洁人员以及地铁消毒人员的安全,并且在极大程度上杜绝病毒的二次传播。在喷洒消毒的过程中,形成的气雾滴能黏附空气中的颗粒,引起沉降,从而起到清洁空气的作用,使旅客在周围环境消毒的同时还能呼吸到新鲜空气,降低可吸入颗粒物对人呼吸道的刺激和损伤,在不危害健康的情况下再次避免诱发呼吸道疾病的发生。

4.1.2　对智慧型交通系统的影响

本装置属于智慧型交通设施,旨在加快城市交通出行智能化发展,建设完善城市公共轨道交通智能化应用系统。对于未来而言发展智慧交通是对现有的大量人力物力的节约,对于本装置而言,则是进一步增进了装置所带来的消毒效率,完善了智慧交通的相关结构,节约了成本。

智慧交通综合管理服务平台指挥中心近几年广泛应用在了以计算机处理为中心的相关智能交通设备中。回顾装置,若采用智能机车联动系统实现地铁车辆与智慧交通综合管理服务平台指挥中心的联动控制,未来的地铁消毒装置将会趋向无人工的自动化发展。

设想本装置在使用过程中趋于自动化,在计算机自动进行客流分析、流行病毒集中预测的同时反馈相关数据给指挥中心,再由指挥中心发出经过评定后的智能命令,就可以在装置普通定时消毒的前提下实现智能控制。如此经由计算机监测的地铁内置消毒喷洒装置才是真正作用于未来的智能交通装置。

本装置的智能自动功能是人工消毒所不具备的,消毒功能是以往普通智能联动装置所没有的。与智慧交通设备结合,不仅完善未来的智慧型交通结构,还能提升装置的有效利用率,节约控制成本,对装置的发展也是双赢。

4.2 装置的前景

本文主要阐述单一装置,具有一定的局限性。本文将自动喷洒装置的作业过程设置为定时定量工作,而定时定量喷洒消毒的前提则是现有大数据通过数学分析得出。装置预计将在未来得到不断完善,加入相关机车联动装置,以有效仪器直接对车内环境进行监控监测,后通过联动装置进行后台测评分析,如此便可科学地达到智能消毒。

预计未来在机车联动的同时进一步加入大数据分析,达到环保便捷高效的消毒愿景。

本装置所采用的自动化则是对人工的极大改进,结合疫情背景实现装置理想工作后,可提升消毒人员的安全保障,在运行过程中自动喷洒消毒也可以节约时间和人力资源。同时,也降低了旅客在乘坐过程中被感染的风险。

5 结 语

本文旨在优化地铁消毒方法,研究新型车内自动消毒系统。在疫情防控,减少病毒传播的大背景条件下,以高效率、高标准、低投入、少人力为目标,优化原有的人工消毒方案,利用计算机检测车内的空气质量实现联动一体化,触发自动消毒装置开启,对车内进行消毒,通过对喷洒系统的喷洒液滴的数学假设预算,求得在有效条件下(针对成都地铁车型)在每节列车安防7个喷头时,列车空间有效消毒率高达93.74%。计算结论认为,消毒范围覆盖面较大能够有效地改善空气质量和公共卫生环境。

环保,便捷,高效是未来交通发展必不可缺的前提,本装置一改以往的人工消毒,有效避免耗时耗力,损害消毒人员身体的弊病。但装置的检修,装置的老化等一系列随之而来的安全隐患是目前需要进一步研究的问题,在未来工作中,我们将根据装置存在的弊病入手,努力减少此类问题的发生,做到该装置的优势超过劣势,做到能够将本研究运用到实际生活当中,为智慧型交通添砖加瓦,为疫情防控做出贡献。

参考文献

[1] 杨颖华,王凯,张霞,等.某市轨道交通列车车厢可吸入颗粒物浓度调查[J].环境与职业医学,2020,37(6):599-602.

[2] 孙章.新冠肺炎疫情防控与新型城市轨道交通系统开发[J].城市轨道交通研究,2020,23(03):200.

[3] 薛宇,叶蔚,张旭,等.地铁车厢内病原体佩戴口罩对飞沫病毒传播抑制效果的模拟研究[J].建筑科学,2020,36(10):115-118.

[4] 肖玉京.基于情境构建的地铁车内关键功能件设计研究[D].四川:西南交通大学设计研究院,2019.

[5] 李思成,阳东,李开元.喷淋液滴运动轨迹及有效控制半径的理论模型研究[J].中国科学技术大学学报,2018,38(12):1462-1463.

[6] 温学雷,张广勋.基于Fluent灭火用气泡雾化喷头设计仿真[J].液压与气动,2015(11):47-49.

[7] 杨蓉,宋敏华.新型冠状病毒肺炎疫情下城市轨道交通企业的应对策略[J].百家论坛,2020,(11):1-5.

Study on Wheel Flat-Induced Impact Force Considering the Flexibility of Wheelset

Wei Wang　Qiyuan Peng

(Southwest Jiaotong University, School of Transportation and Logistics)

Abstract　A coupled vehicle/track dynamic model integrating with the flexible wheelset was developed to investigate the effects of wheel flats, in terms of the wheel/rail impact forces, the vertical acceleration of axle box and the dynamic stress of wheelset axle. The Multi-body dynamic model of vehicle is a typical high-speed train, in which the wheelset is considered as the flexible wheelset using the modal method to compute the flexible vibration of wheelset. The slab track model consisting of the rails and the track slab is adopted in the coupled vehicle/track dynamic model. Based on the model, the comparison between the rigid wheelset and flexible wheelset, and the effects of wheel flats sizes and vehicle speeds were discussed. Results indicated that the flexible wheelset model can effectively reflect the flexible vibration induced by the wheel flats. The length of wheel flats and vehicle speeds significantly affect the fluctuations of wheel/rail normal forces and the dynamic stress of wheelset axle.

Keywords Wheel flat Flexible wheelset Remove criteria of wheel flat

0 Introduction

Railways have been considered as the most efficient mode of public as well as freight transportation since it began to operate. The growing demands for enhanced operational efficiency via high-speed and heavy-haul railway systems, there have been increasing concerns related to their safety dynamics. The essential character of the railway vehicles is the wheel/rail contact that directly affects operational efficiency as well as the dynamic safety. The gradual wear of the wheels and the rail tends to alter geometric profiles of wheels and the rail and thereby the wheel-rail contact. The wear-induced surface defects in the wheels and the rail are known to pose greater derailment risks, especially with higher axle loads and high-speed, apart from the higher stresses in the infrastructure and railway system components[1].

The wheel flat is a typical defect induced by the sliding of the wheel under braking when the braking force is larger than the wheel/rail friction or when the brake system poorly adjusted or defective[2, 3]. Because of sliding the local temperature of contact patch rises significantly, and then cools down rapidly due to the wheel rotation. This process would cause the material phase transformations (formation of martensite) and residual stresses beneath the surface of wheel [4]. Such wheel/rail defects can cause impact loads to the track, rolling stock and the infrastructure (including railway bridges), which substantially deteriorate the operational safety limits of railway vehicles [5]. Therefore, a vast number of investigations have been devoted to study the influences of wheel flats on the dynamics impact loads between the wheel and rail [5-9]. Moreover, several wheel removal criteria have been established to maintain the wheel tread based on the flat size and the impact load generated by the wheel flat [1].

To describe the wheel flats in the dynamic model, the geometry of wheel flat is commonly simplified to two typical types, which are respectively the chord type flat and cosine type flat. The chord type flat is adopted to describe the newly formed flat with sharp edges[10]. Due to the wheel/rail wear the shape edge of wheel flats would become more rounded during the operation, which is well known as the cosine type flat or the haversine flat [6, 11]. Using the simplified geometry of wheel flat a large number of studies have been conducted in terms of the dynamic impact forces and noise generated by the wheel flats.

In the 1950's and 1970's the experiments were respectively performed by researchers at the ARR and British Rail[5, 6] to investigate the dynamic impacts induced by wheel flats. Newton and Clark [12] conducted the experiment to study the effects of wheel flats on railway vehicles and validated three theoretical models in the presence of wheel flats. It suggested that the beam on elastic foundation model adequately describes the mechanism for low frequencies, but over-estimates impact effects at high frequencies. Moreover, the discrete support model should be employed in the simulation investigation, because it can present the track more realistically.

It is evident that the high magnitude of impact loads would be caused by the wheel flats[5], which is bound to excite the flexible vibration of the vehicle and track components. Therefore, in the past decades the flexible track models were developed rapidly and widely employed in the investigation of the wheel/rail defects and wheel/rail interaction. As the published results[8] indicated that the discrete supported track model with the sleepers can effectively reflect the dynamic features of track in the frequency range from 50 to 1500 Hz. Whereas, in most of investigations the rigid wheelset model without consideration of the flexible vibration of wheelset is still adopted to study the effects of wheel/rail defects, which may cause the errors in the estimation of influence of wheel/rail defects on railway vehicles.

Consequently, a comprehensively vehicle/track dynamic model that comprises of the vehicle dynamic model, flexible wheelset model and track model was established to study the dynamic response of railway vehicles in the presence of wheel flats.

Following contents of this paper can be divided into four sections. A comprehensive coupled vehicle/track dynamic model integrating the flexible wheelset model is proposed firstly in Section 1. Section 2 shows the geometries of wheel flat involved in this study. The effects of wheel flat on the dynamic behaviors of railway vehicle is presented in Section 3. Finally, a remove criteria of wheel flats is suggested Section 4.

1 Model Description

The model is comprised of the vehicle dynamic model, the slab track model and the flexible wheelset model. The vehicle dynamic model and the flexible wheelset model were developed by Simpack, and the slab track model was established by Simulink. The SIMAT[13] is used to communicate between the Simulink model and Simpack model in each integration step. The wheel/rail force is estimated by the Simpack, and then transferred to the Simulink by the SIMAT. Using the outputs of Simpack, the Simulink calculates the motions of track and inputs feedbacks into the Simpack, as shown in Fig. 1.

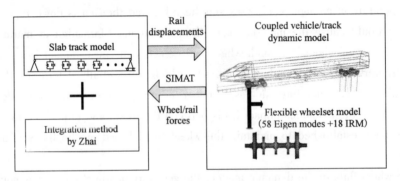

Fig. 1 Coupled Vehicle/Track Dynamic Model

In the model, the vehicle is a typical High-speed train operating on the High speed railway of China, in which it consists of a car body and two bogies, the bogie contains two wheelset and a bogie frame. The car body rests on two bogies through secondary suspension, and the wheelsets are connected to the bogie frame by the primary suspension in the vertical direction and the axle box by the rubber element in the longitudinal direction. The primary and secondary suspension are modelled as linear springs in parallel with linear dampers acting in all three directions.

To consider the flexible vibration and dynamic stress of wheelset induced by wheel flats, the flexible wheelset model was considered in the Multi-body dynamic model of vehicle using the modal synthesis method[14], as shown in Fig. 2. In the model the highest frequency of Eigen mode reaches 2533 Hz. Moreover, 18 IRMs (inertial relief mode) at the interface position of wheelset is taken into account, which considers the deformation of flexible component due to external loads[14].

In the slab track model the rail is described by the Timoshenko beam, the slab is established by the 3D solid element, and the modal superposition method is adopted to solve the motions of track, as shown in Fig. 3.

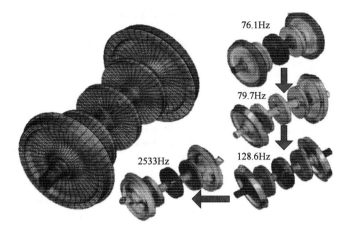

Fig. 2　FE Model of the Flexible Wheelset

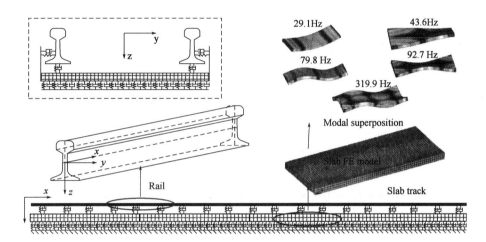

Fig. 3　Slab Track Model

The wheel flat can be classified into the new formed wheel flat and the haversine wheel flat[10]. The new formed wheel flat is equipped with sharp edges that would be more round as the wheel continues to be service due to wear and deformation under impact loads, and then transfers to the haversine wheel flat. Consequently, the haversine wheel flat is employed to describe the wheel flat, as shown in Fig. 4.

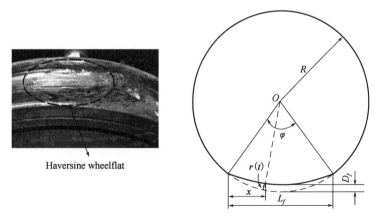

Fig. 4　Haversine Wheel Flat

The variations of the radius in the contact point $r(t)$ an be expressed as:

$$r(t) = \frac{1}{2}D_f[1 - \cos(2\pi x/L_f)] \quad (1)$$

Where D_f is the flat depth that relates to the wheel radius R, and can be given as:

$$D_f = \frac{L_f^2}{(16R)} \quad (2)$$

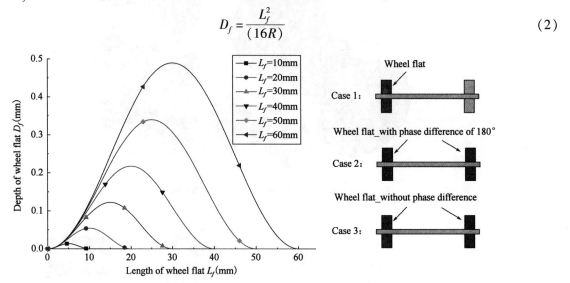

Fig. 5 Geometries of Wheel Flat

In this study, the length of wheel flat ranges from 10 mm to 60 mm are taken into account to study the effects of the length of wheel flat on the performance of railway vehicles, as shown in Fig. 5. Furthermore, three Cases are formulated to contain the possible conditions of wheel flat existing in the wheelset, as shown in Fig. 5. In Case 1 the left wheel of wheelset has the wheel flat. In Case 2 the wheel flats on the both wheels have the phase difference of 180°. But, for the Case 3 the wheel flats are generated on both wheels of wheelset without any phase difference.

2 Comparison of the Flexible Wheelset and Rigid Wheelset in the Presence of Wheel Flat

It is evident that the wheel flat can cause considerable impact loads between the wheel and rail[5,6,9,10], which may result in the flexible vibration of wheelset. But, in the existing researches the rigid wheelset is still widely adopted to investigate the effects of wheel flat. Hence, a comparison of the flexible wheelset and rigid wheelset in the presence of wheel flat is conducted in terms of wheel/rail normal forces and vertical acceleration of axle box, as shown in Fig. 6 and Fig. 7. In this case the wheel flats with length of 40 mm are generated in both wheels of wheelset without any phase difference. Fig. 6a) and Fig. 6b) indicated the maximum wheel/rail normal forces induced by wheel flats at different speeds for two wheelset model. As the comparison indicates that both wheelset models express the same trend and amplitude in the maximum wheel/rail normal force induced by wheel flats with increasing of vehicle speeds, which means that the flexible vibration of wheelset has little influence on the evaluation of the wheel/rail normal force induced by wheel flats.

Fig. 7 illustrates the comparison of vertical acceleration of axle box for two wheelset models. Fig. 7b) and Fig. 7c) show that the maximum vertical acceleration of axle box caused by wheel flats for the flexible wheelset is significant higher than the rigid wheelset. It implies that the flexible vibration can be induced by the wheel flats, and the flexible wheelset model should be employed in the investigation of effects of wheel flats.

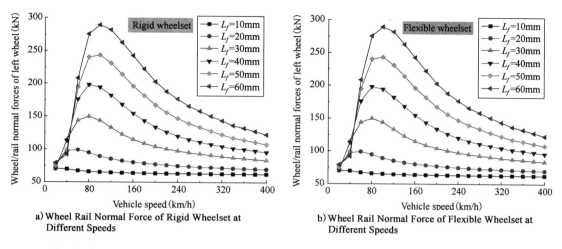

Fig. 6 Comparison of the Flexible Wheelset And Rigid Wheelset in Term of The Wheel/Rail Normal Forces

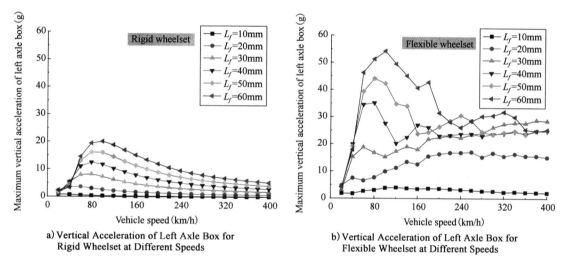

Fig. 7 Comparison of the Flexible Wheelset And Rigid Wheelset in Term of Vertical Acceleration of Axle Box

3 Dynamic Behavior of Railway Vehicle in the Presence of Wheel flats

In order to identify the dynamic behaviors of railway vehicle in the presence of wheel flats in different cases, a large quantity of calculations were performed for different wheel flat sizes and vehicle speeds. The results in the wheel/rail normal force and vertical acceleration of axle box for 3 Cases are given in Fig. 8-Fig. 10. As can be seen from the results that the normal force of wheel/rail increases considerably as the vehicle speed rises, and then decreases gradually after the normal forces reaches the maximum of wheel/rail normal forces, which is caused by the critical speed of the wheel flat[6]. When the vehicle speed is smaller than the critical speed of wheel flat, the impact loads induced by wheel rises rapidly with the increasing of velocity. However, the impact loads drop gradually when the speed exceeds the critical speed of the wheel flat [6]. In addition, the vertical acceleration of axle box follows the similar patterns of the wheel/rail normal forces, in which it increases with the increasing of vehicle speeds and the wheel flat size.

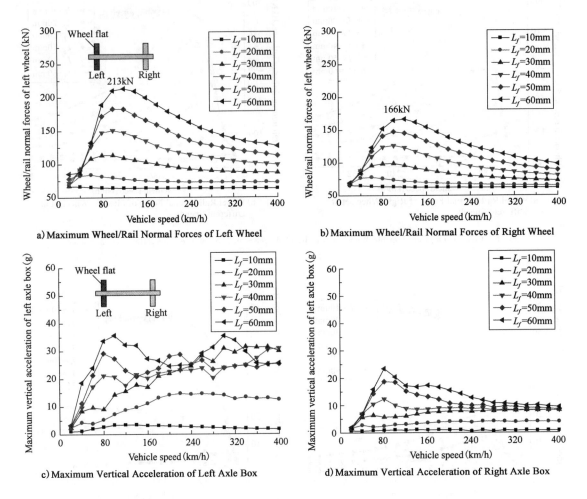

Fig. 8 Normal Forces And Vertical Acceleration of Axle Box for the Case 1

In the Case 1, although the wheel flat is only in the left wheel, the right wheel also expresses the fluctuation of wheel/rail normal forces due to the wheel flat on the left wheel, as shown in Fig. 8b). As the comparison analysis between the left and right wheel indicates that due to the wheel flat on the left wheel the wheel/rail normal force of left wheel and vertical acceleration of left axle box are apparently larger than the right wheel. It can be seen from Fig. 8 that for the case of $L_f = 60$ mm the maximum wheel/rail normal force for the left and right wheel reach the peak of 213 kN and 166 kN at the speed of 120 km/h, respectively.

Fig. 9 illustrates the wheel/rail normal forces and vertical acceleration of axle box induced by the wheel flats for the Case 2. In this case the wheel flats are generated in both wheels of wheelset with a phase difference of 180°. As the Fig. 9a), b) depicts that the amplitudes of wheel/rail normal forces for the left and right wheel express the similar trend with the variation of the velocity and wheel flat size. Moreover, the wheel/rail normal force of the Case 2 comes to a great agreement with the wheel/rail normal force of left wheel for the Case 1 in terms of the amplitude and fluctuation. It means that the wheel flats in both wheels of wheelset with the phase difference would not increase the effects of the wheel flats. The reason is that after one impact generated by the wheel flat the fluctuation of the wheel/rail normal force would decay rapidly as shown in Fig. 6.

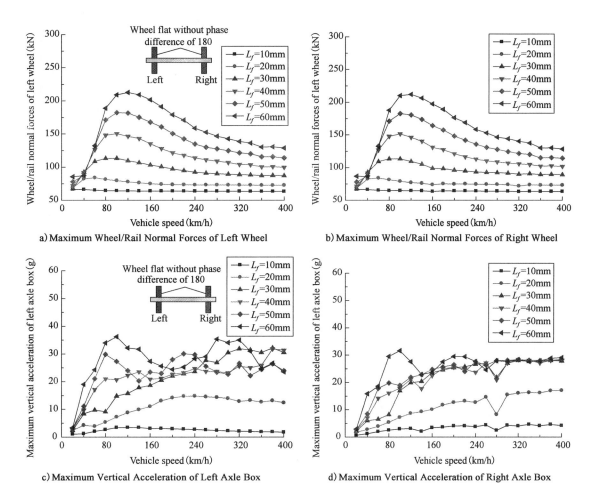

Fig. 9 Normal Forces And Vertical Acceleration of Axle Box for The Case 2

When the phase difference of the wheel flats in both wheels decreases to zero, it becomes the Case 3 showed in Fig. 10. It can be observed in Fig. 10a), b) that the variation of the wheel/rail normal force for the left and right wheel show the similar trend since there is no phase difference for the wheel flat between the left and right wheels. Whereas, the vertical acceleration of left and right axle box express different variations, especially in the range of critical speed of wheel flat, which could be caused by the different flexible vibrations of wheelset axle at the position of axle box showed in Fig. 10c), d). In addition, the amplitude of wheel/rail normal force for the Case 3 is obviously larger than the Case 1, which means that the wheel flat at the same position of both wheels of wheelset would amplify the effects of the wheel flats. In the case of Lf = 60 mm the maximum wheel/rail normal force for the left and right wheel reach the peak of about 289 kN. Therefore, it is necessary to maintain the wheel profile regularly to avoid the wheel flats appearing in the same position of both wheels of wheelset.

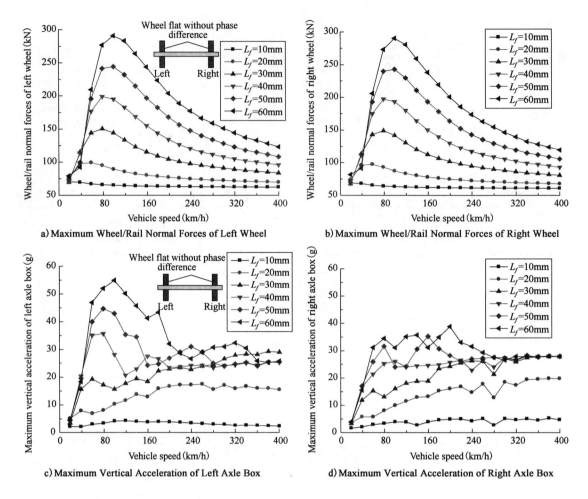

Fig. 10 Normal Forces And Vertical Acceleration of Axle Box for the Case 3

4 Discussion on the Remove Criteria of Wheel Flats

In the past decades several remove criteria of wheel flats have been defined according to the operation experience. The ARR[15] indicates that a wheel with 50.8mm long single flat or 38.1 mm long two adjoining flats cannot continue to be service. The ARR also states the threshold value of wheel/rail impact loads due to a single flat. According to [16], the wheel should be replaced if the peak impacts force due to single flat approaches in the 222.41 to 266.89 kN range. In the Swedish, a wheel with a flat length of 40 mm and flat depth of 0.35 mm should be replaced[17]. Transport Canada safety regulations states that a rail vehicle may not continue to be in service if the wheel has a flat that is more than 63.5mm in length or two adjoining flat each of which is more than 50.8 mm. According to UK Rail safety and standard board, freight vehicle with axle load equal to or over 17.5 tones a wheel with flat length exceeding 70mm must be taken out of service.

According to the design specification of High speed train in China, the wheel/rail normal force should not exceed the limitation of 170kN. Fig. 11 indicates the maximum impact loads induced by wheel flats. The maximum impact loads increase monotonously with the increasing of the length of wheel flats. Furthermore, the maximum impact load of Case 3 reaches 170kN when the length of wheel flat is about 34 mm. For the Case 1 and Case 2, when the length of wheel flat is about 46 mm, the maximum impact load reaches 170 kN.

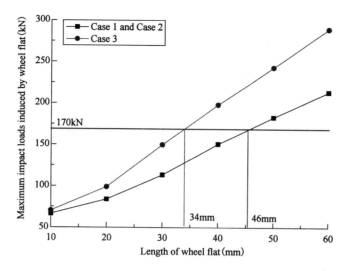

Fig. 11 Stress Increment Ratio for Case 3

Consequently, based on the investigations of impact loads induced by the wheel flats, the limitation of 40 mm for the length of wheel flat should be adopted in the remove criteria of wheel flat.

5 Conclusions

In this study, a comprehensive vehicle/track dynamic mode integrating with the flexible wheelset model was developed. The comparison between the rigid wheelset and flexible wheelset in the simulation of effects of wheel flats was performed firstly, then the effects of wheel flats on the wheel/rail normal force and axle box acceleration were investigated. Based on the above investigation, the conclusions can be drawn as follows:

(1) The comparison analysis of the rigid wheelset and flexible wheelset shows that the flexible wheelset have little influence on the evaluation of wheel/rail normal force, but the significant difference exists in the estimation of vertical acceleration of axle box. Thus, the flexible wheelset model is suggested to be adopted in the presence of wheel flats or other types of high level of wheel/rail impact situations.

(2) The case of wheel flats on the one wheel of wheelset shows the similar trend of wheel/rail normal force with the case of wheel flats on the different position of both wheels of wheelset. The wheel flats on the both wheels of wheelset with the same phase would amplify the effects of wheel flats on railway vehicle.

(3) Finally, based on the investigations of impact loads induced by the wheel flats, a suggested remove criteria of wheel flat for High speed train that the length of wheel flat should not exceed 40 mm is presented.

References

[1] Nielsen J C O, Johansson A. Out-of-round railway wheels-a literature survey[J]. Proceedings of the Institution of Mechanical Engineers Part F Journal of Rail & Rapid Transit,2000,214(2), 79-91.

[2] Wu T X, Thompson D J. The effects of track non-linearity on wheel/rail impact[J]. Proceedings of the Institution of Mechanical Engineers Part F Journal of Rail & Rapid Transit,2004,218(1), 1-15.

[3] Thompson D J, Wu T X. Armstrong T D. Wheel / Rail Rolling Noise-the Effects of Non-Linearities in the Contact Zone[J]. Econometric Theory,2003,23(5), 1022-1032.

[4] Jergeus J. Railway Wheel Flats. Martensite Formation, Residual Stresses, and Crack Propagation[M]. Chalmers University of Technology:1998.

[5] Dong, R. Vertical dynamics of railway vehicle-track system[D]. Concordia University:1994.

[6] Dukkipati R V, Dong R. Impact Loads due to Wheel Flats and Shells[J]. Vehicle System Dynamics, 1999,31(1),1-22.

[7] Cai Z, Raymond G. Theoretical Model for Dynamic Wheel/Rail and Track Interaction[M].
[8] S, L, Grassie, et al. The Dynamic Response of Railway Track to High Frequency Vertical Excitation[J]. Journal of Mechanical Engineering Science, 1982.
[9] Zhai W M, Wang Q C, Lu Z W, et al. Dynamic effects of vehicles on tracks in the case of raising train speeds[J]. Proceedings of the Institution of Mechanical Engineers Part F Journal of Rail & Rapid Transit, 2001, 215(2), 125-135.
[10] Hou K, Kalousek J, Dong R. A dynamic model for an asymmetrical vehicle/track system[J]. Journal of Sound & Vibration, 2003, 267(3), 591-604.
[11] D, L. The calculation of track forces due to dipped rail joints, wheel flats and rail welds[D]. 1972.
[12] Newton S G, Clark R A. An investigation into the dynamic effects on the track of wheelflats on railway vehicles[J]. ARCHIVE Journal of Mechanical Engineering Science 1959-1982, 1719, 21(4), 287-297.
[13] www.simpack.com.
[14] Craig R R, Kurdila A J. Fundamentals of Structural Dynamics[M]. John Wiley, 2006.
[15] Lonsdale, C S D A, J Pilch. Effects of increased gross rail load on 36-inch diameter freight car wheels [J]. Railway wheel manufacture's engineering committee: 2001, 12-18.
[16] Tajaddini A, Kalay S F. TIME TO REVISE WHEEL-REMOVAL RULES[M]. Railway Age, 1995.
[17] Bizindavyi, L F Z G. Parametric study of dynamic response of resilient track for transit system[R]. 4th structural specialty conference of the Canadian society for civil enginerring, montreal, Quebec, Canada, June 5-8, 2002.

基于最优航向索引算法的门式虚拟轨道列车循迹控制策略

孙泽良　冷　涵

(同济大学铁道与城市轨道交通研究院)

摘　要　针对多铰接、全轮转向门式虚拟轨道列车路径跟随问题,文章提出了一种基于几何学模型的循迹控制策略。其中,第一轴的控制输入采用Stanley算法,后轴采用基于最优航向索引算法。建立了门式虚拟轨道列车的五自由度简化横向动力学模型,通过仿真分析,验证了循迹控制算法的性能。结果表明:该控制算法能够提高门式虚拟轨道列车的轨迹跟随性能与转弯通过性。

关键词　新型轨道交通　循迹控制　几何学模型　门式虚拟轨道列车

0　引　言

虚拟轨道列车作为一种新型轨道交通系统,既具备传统轨道交通运量大的特点,又缓解了轨道交通基础设施成本高、周期长等问题[1]。但是,其全轮转向、多铰接的特点导致其动力学性能复杂,运行过程中可能出现偏离车道等现象,严重影响行驶安全[2]。Zhituo Ni[3,4]等针对重型多挂式铰接车辆提出了一种基于LQR的主动转向系统,车辆的机动性和横向稳定性得到增强。Yoshitaka Marumo[5]利用后轮主动转向来补偿前方铰接处速度矢量与拖车行驶方向的差角,降低了车辆的横向偏移。严永俊[6]等利用随动转向的方式对智轨电车轨迹跟踪控制进行了研究,实现了一定的轨迹跟踪效果。张建全[7]等提出了一种以引领点的侧偏角和横摆角为目标,控制跟随点的侧偏角和横摆角的超级大巴跟随控制,提高了其横向稳定性,降低了失稳现象的发生。冷涵[8]提出了一种新型门式虚拟轨道列车架构和循迹控制方案,实现了列车低速转向过程中的路径跟随。以上方法均能提高车辆的曲线通过性和稳定性，但是大多存在模型复杂，难于工程实现等问题。

本文以门式虚拟轨道列车为研究对象，建立了五自由度横向动力学模型，提出了一种基于几何学模型的循迹控制策略，提高了门式虚拟轨道列车的轨迹跟随性与转弯通过性。

1 门式虚拟轨道列车横向动力学模型建立

1.1 门式虚拟轨道列车架构形式

门式虚拟轨道列车由端部车体模块 ECM、中间车体模块 ICM、端部悬架模块 ESM、中间悬架模块 ISM 和门式车间连接模块 GCM 等单元组成，可根据需要采用不同的编组形式。车体模块与 GCM 之间通过铰接连接，中间设有锁闭机构，用来约束门式车间连接模块与其前位车体的 6 向自由度。所有悬架均为具有主动转向功能的非独立悬架，转向形式为基于四连杆机构的轮转形式，各悬架均配有转向作动器[8]。如图 1 所示，本文以四模块五悬架的编组形式为研究对象。

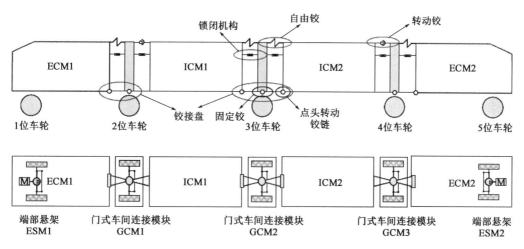

图 1 四模块编组门式虚拟轨道列车架构示意图

1.2 门式虚拟轨道列车横向动力学模型

1.2.1 模型假设

为便于对虚拟轨道列车横向动力学进行分析研究，合理简化了车辆模型，做出以下假设：
(1) 整车简化为"bicycle"模型，即每轴上的两个车轮简化为车轴中间的一个车轮；
(2) 仅考虑车辆的横移、横摆运动，忽略空气阻力的影响；
(3) 车辆每个车轮的侧偏刚度为常数；
(4) 车体间的铰接角度较小。

1.2.2 五自由度横向动力学模型

如图 2 所示，经过简化后的门式虚拟轨道列车拥有五个自由度，分别为：第一节车体的侧向速度 v_1，各个车体的横摆角速度 $r_i (i=1,2,3,4)$。

图 2 中，V_i 为第 i 节车体质心处的横向速度；ψ_i 为第 i 节车体的横摆角；r_i 为第 i 节车体的横摆角速度；a_i 为第 i 节车体质心至前轴（前方铰接点）的距离；b_i 为第 i 节车体质心至后轴（后方铰接点）的距离；θ_i 为第 i 节车体与第 $i+1$ 节车体间的铰接角，$\dot{\theta}_i$ 为其角速度；α_i 为 i 位车轮的轮胎侧偏角；δ_i 为 i 位车轮的轮胎转角。

门式虚拟轨道列车的受力分析如图 3 所示。

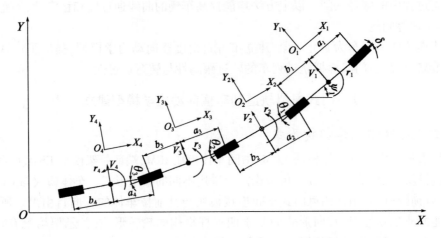

图 2　门式虚拟轨道列车五自由度"bicycle"模型

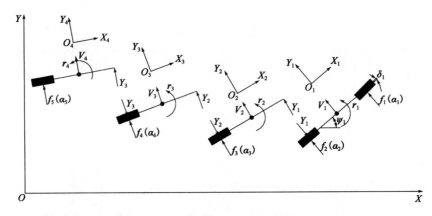

图 3　门式虚拟轨道列车受力分析图

根据牛顿第二定律可以得到每节车的动力学方程。第 1 节车的动力学方程为：

$$m_1(\dot{V}_1 + Ur_1) = f_1(\alpha_1) + f_2(\alpha_2) - Y_1 \tag{1}$$

$$I_1\dot{r}_1 = a_1 f_1(\alpha_1) - b_1 f_2(\alpha_2) + b_1 Y_1 \tag{2}$$

第 2 节车的动力学方程为：

$$m_2(\dot{V}_2 + Ur_2) = f_3(\alpha_3) + Y_1 - Y_2 \tag{3}$$

$$I_2\dot{r}_2 = a_2 Y_1 - b_2 f_3(\alpha_3) + b_2 Y_2 \tag{4}$$

第 3 节车的动力学方程为：

$$m_3(\dot{V}_3 + Ur_3) = f_4(\alpha_4) + Y_2 - Y_3 \tag{5}$$

$$I_3\dot{r}_3 = a_3 Y_2 - b_3 f_4(\alpha_4) + b_3 Y_3 \tag{6}$$

第 4 节车的动力学方程为：

$$m_4(\dot{V}_4 + Ur_4) = f_5(\alpha_5) + Y_3 \tag{7}$$

$$I_4\dot{r}_4 = a_4 Y_3 - b_4 f_5(\alpha_5) \tag{8}$$

各轴轮胎侧偏角为：

$$\alpha_1 = \frac{V_1 + a_1 r_1}{U} - \delta_1 \tag{9}$$

$$\alpha_2 = \frac{V_1 - b_1 r_1}{U} - \delta_2 \tag{10}$$

$$\alpha_3 = \frac{V_2 - b_2 r_2}{U} - \delta_3 \tag{11}$$

$$\alpha_4 = \frac{V_3 - b_3 r_3}{U} - \delta_4 \tag{12}$$

$$\alpha_5 = \frac{V_4 - b_4 r_4}{U} - \delta_5 \tag{13}$$

相邻两节车体通过铰接连接起来,因此前后车体在铰接处的速度需要匹配,第 i 个铰接处($i=1,2,3$)的速度可由以下方程得出:

$$V_{i+1} + a_{i+1} r_{i+1} = V_i - b_i r_i + U(\psi_i - \psi_{i+1}) \tag{14}$$

对其求导可得到:

$$\dot{V}_4 + a_4 \dot{r}_4 = \dot{V}_3 - b_3 \dot{r}_3 + U(r_3 - r_4) \tag{15}$$

式中 U 为列车的前进速度; Y_i 为第 i 节车体与第 $i+1$ 节车体间的铰接处的横向力; $f_i(\alpha_i)$ 为第 i 轴车轮所产生的侧偏力,可由式(16)得到,式中 C_i 为第 i 轴的侧偏刚度。

$$f_i(\alpha_i) = C_i \times \alpha_i \tag{16}$$

联立式(1)-(16),由第4节车的动力学方程,可以得出第3节与第4节车间铰接的横向力与第4节车状态的关系,并将其带入第3节车的动力学方程,以此类推,消除动力学模型中铰接处的横向力,得到门式虚拟轨道列车的横向动力学模型,其可写作状态空间方程如式(17)

$$\dot{x} = Ax + Bu \tag{17}$$

式中 $x = [V_1 \quad \psi_1 \quad \psi_2 \quad \psi_3 \quad \psi_4]^T$, $u = [\delta_1 \quad \delta_2 \quad \delta_3 \quad \delta_4 \quad \delta_5]^T$。

2 循迹控制策略

虚拟轨道的循迹控制是指通过控制算法对第2-5轴进行转向控制,使得虚拟轨道列车在运行过程中后轴中点的轨迹尽可能与前轴中点的轨迹相同,达到近似拥有"轨道"的运动效果。通过循迹控制,车辆的操纵性能将得到一定程度的提升,列车通过曲线时的通道宽度将大大降低。

第一轴的控制输入采用Stanley算法。通过测量得到第一轴中心点与参考路径的横向偏差 y_e 与航向偏差 φ_e,利用式(18)得到第一轴车轮转角控制率。

$$\delta_1 = \varphi_e + \arctan\frac{ky_e}{v} \tag{18}$$

式中: k ——增益系数;

v ——车速。

欲使车辆后轴能够沿着前轴的轨迹行驶,则后轴车轮的方向应与前轴轨迹切线的方向相同,即不同车轮在通过相同位置时,相对于大地坐标系下的角度 $\varphi+\delta$ 相同。据此对第2-5轴进行循迹控制,控制方法如下:

(1)在第1节车体上安装横摆角速度传感器和三向加速度传感器,分别用以获取第1节车体的横摆角速度与纵向加速度;

(2)在每个铰接处安装角位移传感器,用以获取各个车体之间的铰接角度;

(3)据此可求得某时刻第1节车体的横摆角 $\varphi = \int_0^t r dt$,纵向速度 $v_x = \int_0^t a_x dt$,列车行驶的距离 $S = \int_0^t v_x dt$;

(4)设定控制器采样步长为 Δt,每次采样后将列车行驶距离 S、第1节车体的横摆角 φ 以及第1轴的车轮转角 δ_1 记录至ECU控制器的寄存器中,用于后轴理论车轮转角的索引;

(5)根据列车轴距对第2轴的车轮转角进行索引,得到第2轴车轮此刻相对于大地的理论角度,减去此刻车体的横摆角即得到此刻第 2 轴车轮的理论转角；

(6) 第 3-5 轴采用相同的控制方法跟随第 1 轴控制。

如图 4 所示，当 $t = t_0$ 时第 1 轴车轮相对于大地坐标系下的转角为 $\delta_{1(t0)} + \varphi_{1(t0)}$，经过 Δt 后，第 2 轴车轮运动至第 1 轴车轮轨迹处，此时第 2 轴车轮转角应当与第 1 轴车轮在 $t = t_0$ 时刻相同，即第 2 轴车轮的理论转角为：

$$\delta_{2(t0+\Delta t)} = \delta_{1(t0)} + \varphi_{1(t0)} - \varphi_{1(t0+\Delta t)}$$

第 3-5 轴车轮的理论转角计算方法与第 2 轴相同。

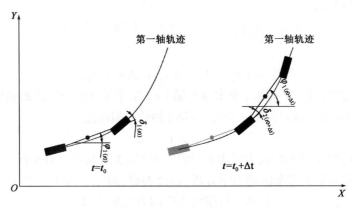

图 4　循迹控制策略示意图

3　仿真分析

本文对门式虚拟轨道列车进行了单移线及圆曲线工况仿真分析，分别对比了有无循迹控制时列车各轴轨迹以及横向偏差，验证了循迹控制算法。

图 5 为仿真分析流程图，首先获取第 1 轴的位置信息，计算其与参考位置的偏差，利用 Stanley 算法求得列车第 1 轴车轮转角；将列车第 1 轴车轮转角、第 1 节车体的横摆角度以及各铰接的角度等信息输入循迹控制器，利用基于最优航向索引算法的循迹控制策略，计算得到第 2-5 轴车轮转角，输入至车辆动力学模型。

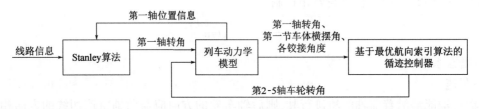

图 5　仿真分析流程图

3.1　单移线运动分析

本节对列车单移线工况进行了仿真分析。城市道路宽度通常为 3.5～3.75 m，因此设置线路为车辆在 30 m 完成 3.5 m 宽度的车道转换，仿真速度为 18km/h。

图 6 为列车单移线工况的跟踪效果，利用各个车轴中心点的轨迹来描述列车的整体轨迹。图 7 为列车在单移线工况下各轴的横向偏差。从图 6，图 7 可以看出，在无循迹时列车各轴的轨迹与参考轨迹偏差较大，且越后轴的偏差越大，最大横向偏差为 0.62 m 左右；具有循迹控制时，各轴的轨迹几乎与参考轨迹相同，最大横向偏差减小至 0.10 m 左右。

3.2　圆曲线运动分析

本节对虚拟轨道列车通过圆曲线工况进行了仿真分析，设置线路为 90°半径的 30m 圆曲线，仿真速度为 5km/h。

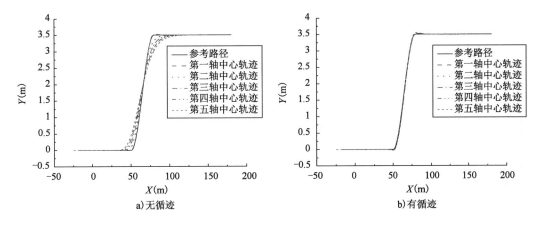

图6 单移线工况跟踪效果

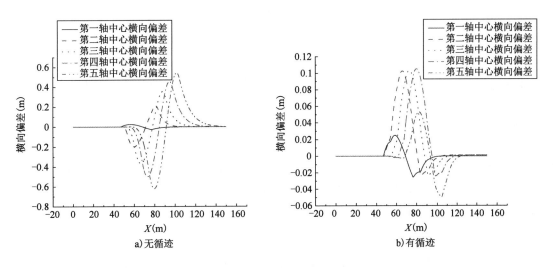

图7 单移线工况下横向偏差

图8为列车圆曲线工况的跟踪效果。图9为列车在圆曲线工况下各轴的横向偏差。从图8,图9可以看出,其横向偏差的变化规律与单移线工况相同,最大横向偏差由2.39m减小至0.05m左右。无循迹控制时,只有第一轴具有转向功能,其他轴由于不能转向,导致其轨迹内偏,且存在"放大效应",即越后轴产生的偏差越大;有循迹控制时,初始与无循迹控制相同,产生轨迹内偏,此时控制系统工作,轨迹偏移量降低,由于超调作用,使得后轴轨迹产生了一定的外偏,因此具有循迹控制时横向偏差出现了先内偏后外偏的现象。

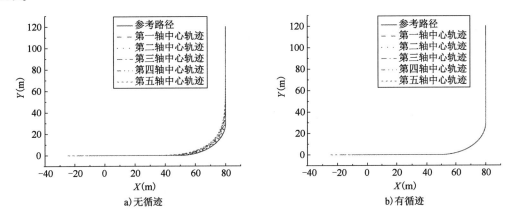

图8 圆曲线工况跟踪效果

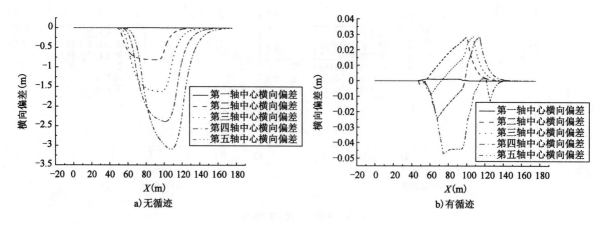

图9 圆曲线工况下横向偏差

4 结 语

本文建立了门式虚拟轨道列车五自由度横向动力学模型,设计了一种基于几何的循迹控制算法,对单移线、圆曲线两个工况进行了仿真分析。结果表明具有循迹控制时,列车的运行轨迹几乎与参考轨迹重合,达到了良好的循迹效果。此循迹控制算法,能够提高列车的轨迹跟随能力,提升其转弯通过性。

但是,由于循迹控制算法是基于几何的循迹控制算法,忽略了列车动力学特性与作动器的力学特性,当运行速度较大时,其循迹性将会下降。为此,我们将更加深入地研究其动力学性能,设计基于动力学的循迹控制算法,以提高循迹控制对速度的适应性以及列车的横向稳定性。

参考文献

[1] 冯江华. 轨道交通装备技术演进与智能化发展[J]. 控制与信息技术,2019(01):1-6.
[2] 贾梦泽. 多节铰接汽车列车挂车主动转向控制研究[D]. 厦门:厦门理工学院,2019.
[3] NI Z, HE Y. Design and validation of a robust active trailer steering system for multi-trailer articulated heavy vehicles[J]. Vehicle system dynamics, 2018,57(10):1545-1571.
[4] NI Z. Design and Validation of High Speed Active Trailer Steering System for Articulated Heavy Vehicle[Z]. ProQuest Dissertations Publishing, 2016.
[5] MARUMO Y, YOKOTA T, AOKI A. Improving stability and lane-keeping performance for multi-articulated vehicles using vector follower control[J]. Vehicle system dynamics, 2020, 58(12):1859-1872.
[6] 严永俊,王金湘,胡云卿,等. 智轨电车横向运动预测控制研究[J]. 控制与信息技术,2020(02):25-30.
[7] 张建全,沈龙江,陶功安,等. 超级大巴轨迹控制技术与动力学性能研究[J]. 电力机车与城轨车辆,2020,43(05):7-12.
[8] 冷涵. 门式虚拟轨道列车及循迹控制策略研究[D]. 上海:同济大学,2020.

磁悬浮列车基础梁的柔性对悬浮稳定性的影响

李 钦 沈 钢

(同济大学铁道与城市轨道交通研究院)

摘 要 本文从理论上解释了基础梁刚度和阻尼、质量对磁悬浮车辆系统稳定性的影响。为了解决磁悬浮列车的车轨耦合问题,降低目前磁悬浮车辆对于基础轨道过高的质量、刚度要求,提出了一种考虑轨道弹性振动的悬浮控制策略方案。通过在基础梁上添加弹性的轨道板,并使用考虑轨道弹性振动的悬浮控制算法来解决车轨耦合振动问题,降低磁悬浮列车对轨道基础要求过高的问题,理论上可以降低磁悬浮列车线路的建设成本。使用新提出的控制方案进行仿真实验计算,同时与传统的控制方案进行比较,仿真结果较好的说明了通过悬浮控制方案的改进,可以使得磁悬浮车辆系统在更小的基础梁刚度质量阻尼条件下保持稳定。

关键词 基础梁 磁悬浮列车 悬浮控制 耦合振动

0 引 言

目前的磁悬浮列车系统中,为了保证悬浮系统垂向的整体稳定,对轨道基础梁有着很高的要求[1]。其刚度和质量、阻尼等参数需足够大,这样系统的稳定性才能够保证。一旦梁的参数不够好,整个系统便容易出现耦合振动并可能失稳。在工程中已经出现有磁悬浮车辆在维修基地全钢梁静悬浮出现失稳的情况[2]。本文希望通过控制方案的提升,解决目前磁悬浮系统对轨道基础要求过高的问题。传统的磁悬浮控制算法一般基于轨道梁全为刚性物体且没有自由度的假设。这样就造成了为了保证悬浮稳定,梁和轨道板的质量要足够大。越接近理想中的刚性状况,整个系统就越为稳定。如果可以在设计控制算法时对电磁铁下的轨道基础的振动加以考虑,那么理论上讲车轨耦合振动则会从理论上得到控制,同时轨道基础也可以相应的降低标准。

本文进行了新的考虑轨道振动状态的控制器的设计以及仿真验证。同时也对传统悬浮控制算法下轨道基础参数的变化对稳定性的影响进行了分析,解释了为何传统控制算法控制下悬浮系统在轻梁上较易失稳。结果证明通过控制方案的提升,磁悬浮列车车辆与车轨基础的耦合振动可以得到抑制。从理论上讲,新的控制方法可以降低磁悬浮系统对轨道的高要求,降低磁悬浮系统建设的成本。

1 数学建模

将磁悬浮车轨耦合系统简化为上述系统,X_b代表基础梁的位移,X_t代表轨道板的位移,X_v为电磁铁的位移。传统的磁悬浮控制器一般假设电磁铁之上的基础梁和轨道板皆没有位移,即其皆为绝对的刚体,X_b和X_t皆为定值,系统示意图如图1所示。所以控制器为此假设下的较为简单地对气隙进行反馈控制的控制器。现实中为了保证此假设下的控制器使得整个系统稳定,往往需要使得基础梁的刚度、质量足够的大,使其振动的位移足够的小,可以近似为实际中的没有自由度的刚体,才可以确保系统稳定。此种假设下的控制器反馈矩阵设为K_{ft}。

而如果将电磁铁之上的结构自由度纳入控制器的考量,建立考虑电磁铁之上轨道振动的控制器,那么理论上可以通过控制抑制轨道的振动,提高整个系统的稳定性,如图2所示。此种假设下的控制器反馈矩阵设为K_{fn}。

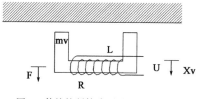

图1 传统控制策略下磁悬浮系统简化结构图

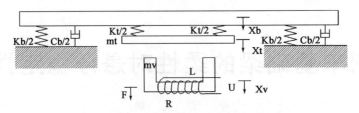

图 2 考虑轨道基础振动的磁悬浮系统简化结构图

使用状态方程描述磁悬浮耦合振动系统。

$$\dot{X} = AX + BU \tag{1}$$

其中[3]:

$$A = \begin{bmatrix} 0 & 0 & 0 & 1 & 0 \\ 0 & 0 & 0 & 0 & 1 \\ -\dfrac{P_S R}{m_v L} & -\dfrac{\eta P_S}{m_v} & \dfrac{P_S R}{m_v L} & \dfrac{\eta P_S}{m_v} & -\dfrac{R}{L} \\ 0 & 1 & 0 & 0 & 0 \\ -\dfrac{k_b}{m_b} & 0 & 0 & 0 & -\dfrac{m_v}{m_b} \end{bmatrix}, B = \begin{bmatrix} 0 \\ 0 \\ -\dfrac{P_I}{m_v L} \\ 0 \\ 0 \end{bmatrix}$$

传统假设下的系统矩阵降阶为的三阶矩阵。按照该状态方程,定义最优控制的加权函数后,求解黎卡提方程组[4]:

$$U = -KX = -RB^{\mathrm{T}}PX \tag{2}$$

$$-PA - A^{\mathrm{T}}P + PBR^{-1}B^{\mathrm{T}}P - Q = 0 \tag{3}$$

即可求出两种假设下的控制反馈矩阵 K_{ft} 和 K_{fn}。

2 仿真计算分析

本研究建立了磁悬浮系统的车轨耦合振动 Matlab/Simulink 模型(图 3),分析了不同轨道基础等效刚度、质量、阻尼对悬浮稳定性的影响。

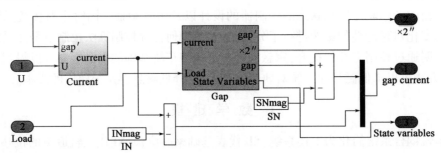

图 3 磁悬浮系统 Matlab/Simulink 图

2.1 基础梁等效刚度和等效阻尼对稳定性的影响

逐渐减小基础梁等效刚度和等效阻尼,进行悬浮系统响应的仿真计算。图 4 中 X 和 Y 轴分别为等效刚度和阻尼。Z 轴为定义的描述振动强度的振动强度函数。图 4 中上面的曲面为刚性控制下系统的响应,图 5 曲面为柔性控制下系统的响应。

可以看到,随着等效刚度和阻尼的变小,刚性控制下的曲面向上扬起,振动强度函数的值变大。说明整个系统的稳定性变差。两者小到一定程度时,整个系统失稳。振动强度函数在值等于 790 时电磁铁的位移响应如图 6 所示,已成发散趋势。可认为振动强度函数继续增大则意味着系统失稳。

而柔性控制的响应曲面整体在刚性的曲面之下。说明整体来看每一个质量刚度参数组合情况下,柔性控制下的系统的振动都更小,稳定性都更好。其曲面随质量刚度的变化而变化的趋势相对来说也更小。

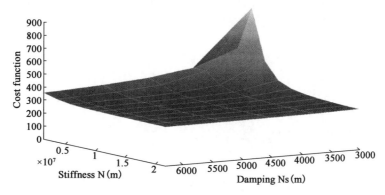

图 4　刚性假设控制算法下基础梁的等效刚度和阻尼对稳定性影响图

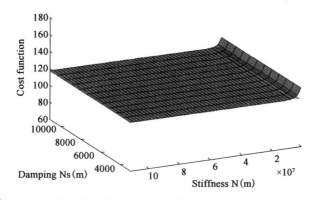

图 5　考虑轨道振动控制算法下基础梁的等效刚度和阻尼对稳定性影响图

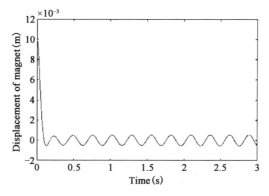

图 6　临近失稳状态时电磁铁位移响应

将刚性控制下的曲面在 XY 平面上投影，X 和 Y 轴分别为等效刚度和阻尼（图 7）。可以更清晰地看出，整个系统越往左下角方向越不稳定。即等效刚度和等效质量越小，越不稳定。可以印证和解释在工程实际中出现的磁悬浮列车在维修基地中的全钢梁状态下难以悬浮的情况。

2.2　基础梁等效质量对稳定性的影响

以 X 和 Y 轴分别为等效质量和刚度。Z 轴仍为我们定义的描述振动强度的目标函数。图 8 为刚性控制下系统的响应，图 9 曲面为柔性控制下系统的响应。仍旧可以看到柔性控制下曲面整体数值偏小，说明振动更小，稳定性更好。

刚性控制下的曲面可以看出，随着等效刚度的减小，等效质量的减小，整个系统的稳定性变差，振动变大，曲面向上卷起（图 10）。

将平面投影在 XY 平面。同样可以看到，在平面的左下方，也就是等效质量、等效刚度变小的方向，系统变得不稳定，振动变大。以上结论证明了对于传统控制方案下的磁悬浮系统，基础梁的刚度、质量和阻尼变小都会对稳定性有着负面影响。而采用考虑梁振动的控制算法则可以改善稳定性，降低磁悬浮系统对基础梁的过高的要求，理论上可以降低磁悬浮线路的建设成本。

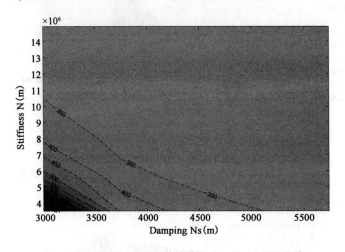

图 7　磁悬浮系统在基础梁等效质量-阻尼平面上的稳定域

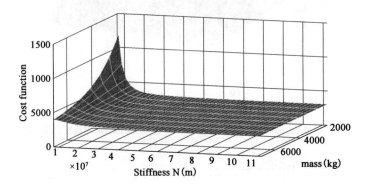

图 8　刚性假设控制算法下基础梁的等效刚度和质量对稳定性影响图

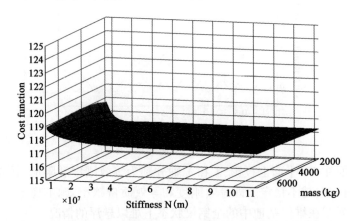

图 9　考虑轨道振动控制算法下基础梁的等效刚度和质量对稳定性影响图

3　结　语

本文中的计算和仿真结果表明，随着基础梁的等效质量、等效刚度、等效阻尼的减小，整个磁悬浮系统的稳定性会变差。工程实际中出现的磁悬浮列车在维修基地中的全钢梁中难以悬浮的情况可以由此得到解释。通过仿真计算结果可以看出，采用柔性的控制策略，使用在轨道桥梁基础上添加弹性的轨道板，并采用考虑轨道振动的悬浮控制算法的策略下，磁悬浮系统可以在较低的基础梁刚度、质量和阻尼情况下依旧稳定悬浮。理论上可以降低磁悬浮系统对基础梁的过高的要求。

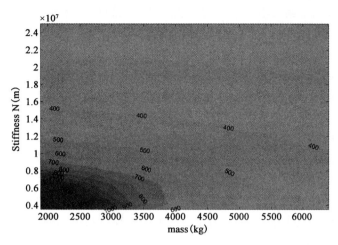

图10 磁悬浮系统在基础梁等效质量-刚度平面上的稳定域

参考文献

[1] 孙玉玲. 磁悬浮轨道交通国际研发态势分析[M]. 北京:电子工业出版社,2020.

[2] 汪科任,罗世辉,张继业. 磁悬浮控制器设计及静悬浮稳定性分析[J]. 西南交通大学学报,2017,52(01):118-126.

[3] Hui Wang, Gang Shen, Lin Li, et al. Study on the Maglev vehicle-guideway coupling vibration system[J]. Proceedings of the Institution of Mechanical Engineers, Part F: Journal of Rail and Rapid Transit,2015, Vol. 229:507-517.

[4] 刘豹. 现代控制理论[M]. 北京:机械工业出版社,2006.

轨道交通用直线电机的电磁力对比分析

张树鑫 黄苏丹 曹广忠 吴超

(深圳大学广东省电磁控制与智能机器人重点实验室)

摘 要 直线电机牵引系统是一种非黏着直接驱动的新型交通方式,在轻轨、地铁、磁浮列车中得到日渐广泛的应用。与传统轮轨式列车相比,直线电机牵引列车具有爬坡能力强、转弯半径小、建设成本较低等优点。直线电机电磁力特性直接决定直线电机牵引系统的牵引性能,因此,本文提出研究轨道交通用直线感应电机、直线永磁同步电机与直线开关磁阻电机的电磁力特性。给出了三类直线电机的结构和电磁力解析模型,设计了轨道交通用三类直线电机的结构,采用有限元分析方法,建立了三类直线电机的电磁有限元模型,改进了设计的电机结构,得到了电机的电磁力特性,并对三类直线电机的电磁力特性进行了比较分析。

关键词 轨道交通 直线感应电机 直线永磁同步电机 直线开关磁阻电机

0 引 言

随着城市的快速发展,城镇之间的联系不断加强,各区域需要更加快速、安全、舒适的互联互通,而这

资助项目:国家自然科学基金项目(编号:51907128,U1813212,51677120);广东省自然科学基金项目面上项目(编号:2021A1515011704,2021A1515011685);深圳市自然科学基金基础研究面上项目(编号:JCYJ20190808142211388);深圳市基础研究自由探索项目(编号:JCYJ20180305124348603)。

也对城市轨道交通领域提出了新要求。传统的轮轨式列车受到黏着与弓网的限制,在速度方面很难进一步提升,逐渐无法适应社会的发展,而应用直线电机的城轨车辆,相比较于传统的轮轨式列车具有更好的爬坡能力、更小的转向半径、更优良的性能和更低的建设成本,更加适合城市这种多建筑的环境,线路规划更加灵活。因此,在更高的运行速度、更安全更舒适的旅行环境的要求下,直线感应电机具有明显的优势。

直线感应电机主要应用于城市轨道交通中的中低速场合,比如直线电机轮轨车辆和中低速磁悬浮列车。虽然直线感应电机可以看成是旋转电机剖开伸展而成,但是直线感应电机存在着纵向、横向的边缘效应和次级的集肤效应的影响[1],用旋转电机的计算方法来计算会有较大的误差。因此现在的研究者多聚焦在如何减小这些效应的影响,以及如何在牵引力产生脉动的情况下更好的控制电机。直线永磁同步电机因其效率和推力密度较高,可控性好等优点适用于高速场合。随着稀土材料钕铁硼的出现,由于其具有高剩磁密度、高矫顽力和高磁能积等优良特性,直线永磁同步电机得到快速发展[2]。然而,在快速发展过程中存在的挑战有:直线永磁同步电机的宽运行范围的控制要求和弱磁控制策略[3]。现在的研究者着重研究如何在逆变器电压输出能力内进行稳定与快速的电机运行控制[4]。而直线开关磁阻电机因其具有很多优点,且在高精度直线往复运动中也有良好的表现[5],越来越受研究者的关注。近年来,直线开关磁阻电机系统也开始被研究用在城市轨道交通,升降平台和无人机电磁弹射装置等方面。

本文通过有限元分析大气隙的直线感应电机,直线永磁同步电机和直线开关磁阻电机的电磁力,研究不同电流幅值,频率以及不同位置下的受力情况,对三种电机的性能进行比较。

1 直线电机的电磁力对比分析

对直线感应电机、直线永磁同步电机和直线开关磁阻电机电磁力进行有限元分析。

1.1 直线感应电机的电磁力分析

直线感应电机的尺寸参数和仿真模型分别如表1和图1所示,仿真模型中不同零件的材料参数设定如表2所示。

直线感应电机尺寸参数 表1

参　数	数　值	参　数	数　值
初级长度(mm)	2476	初级齿宽(mm)	11.2
初级宽度(mm)	400	初级槽宽(mm)	20
初级高度(mm)	107	初级槽深(mm)	77
极数	8	气隙(mm)	10
总槽数	79	极距(mm)	280.8
相数	3	次级铝板厚度(mm)	8
每极每粗槽数	3	次级钢板厚度(mm)	32

图1 直线感应电机仿真模型

不同零件材料参数 表2

零　件	材　料	参　数
初级铁芯	D23.50	B-H curve 电导率 $\sigma=0$
初级绕组	铜	相对磁导率 $\mu=0.999991\mathrm{H/m}$,电导率 $\sigma=5.8\times10^8\mathrm{S/m}$
气隙	空气	相对磁导率 $\mu=1.000004\mathrm{H/m}$,电导率 $\sigma=0$
铝板	铝	相对磁导率 $\mu=1.000002\mathrm{H/m}$,电导率 $\sigma=3.8\times10^7\mathrm{S/m}$
钢板	10号钢	B-H Curve,电导率 $\sigma=3.53\times10^6\mathrm{S/m}$

当初级电流幅值为200A,频率为20Hz时,不同位置的推力、法向力和推力密度变化情况如表3和图2所示。

不同位置的推力、法向力和推力密度　　　　　表3

位置(mm)	稳定后推力(N)	稳定后法向力(N)	推力密度(N/m³)
0	4198	8333	45630
20	4165	8294	45272
40	4224	8267	45913
60	4310	8219	46848
80	4352	8158	47304
100	4356	8313	47348
120	4393	8338	47750
140	4404	8340	47870
160	4423	8321	48076
180	4380	8318	47609
200	4347	8440	47250
220	4281	8279	46533

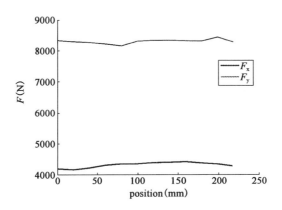

图2　不同位置下稳定后的推力和法向力变化情况

初级电流频率固定为20Hz,位置不变,改变初级电流幅值后推力、法向力和推力密度变化情况如表4和图3所示。

不同初级电流幅值的推力、法向力和推力密度　　　　　表4

初级电流幅值(A)	稳定后推力(N)	稳定后法向力(N)	推力密度(N/m³)
100	997	1066	10837
150	2136	3823	23217
200	4198	8366	45630
250	5616	13520	61043
300	8962	18056	97413
350	10638	27441	115630
400	15490	31796	168370

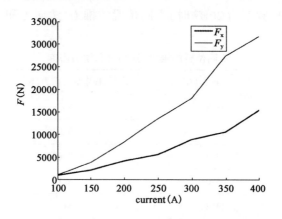

图3 通入不同电流稳定后的推力和法向力变化情况

位置不变,初级电流幅值固定为200A,改变初级电流频率后的推力、法向力和推力密度变化情况如表5和图4所示。

不同初级电流频率下稳定以后的推力、法向力和推力密度 表5

初级电流频率(Hz)	稳定后推力(N)	稳定后法向力(N)	推力密度(N/m³)
10	8202	7019	89152
15	5640	7569	61304
20	4138	8063	44978
25	3203	8159	34815
30	2299	8286	24989
35	1636	8202	17783
40	1489	8119	16185

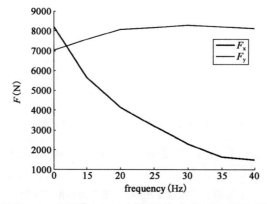

图4 通入电流频率不同时稳定后的推力和法向力变化情况

由实验结果可知:

①直线感应电机在不同位置的推力略有波动,但是相对稳定。

②当初级电流幅值增大时,推力和法向力也会大幅增大,法向力和推力的比值随之增大。

③当初级电流频率增大时,推力大幅度减小,法向力只是略微增大,法向力和推力的比值大幅增大。

因此,在选择初级电流频率和幅值时,需要综合考虑二者对推力和法向力的影响,从而提高推力密度。

1.2 直线永磁同步电机的电磁力分析

直线永磁同步电机的尺寸参数和仿真模型分别如表6和图5所示,仿真模型中不同零件的材料参数设定如表7所示。

直线永磁同步电机的尺寸参数　　　　　　　　　　　　　　　　　　　　　　　表6

参　数	数　值	参　数	数　值
电机长度(mm)	2450	定子齿宽(mm)	50
初级宽度(mm)	600	定子槽宽(mm)	50
初级高度(mm)	107	定子槽深(mm)	50
永磁体横向宽度(mm)	600	气隙(mm)	50
永磁体相对磁导率	1	极距(mm)	300
永磁体矫顽力(A/m)	890000	永磁体长度(mm)	300
永磁体极数	4	永磁体高度(mm)	240

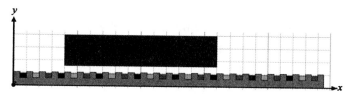

图5　直线永磁同步电机仿真模型

直线永磁同步电机材料参数　　　　　　　　　　　　　　　　　　　　　　　表7

零　件	材　料	参　数
永磁体	钕铁硼 N35M	相对磁导率 $\mu=1\mathrm{H/m}$，电导率 $\sigma=6.25\times10^5\mathrm{S/m}$
定子绕组	铜	相对磁导率 $\mu=0.999991\mathrm{H/m}$，电导率 $\sigma=5.8\times10^8\mathrm{S/m}$
气隙	空气	相对磁导率 $\mu=1.000004\mathrm{H/m}$，电导率 $\sigma=0$
定子	铝	相对磁导率 $\mu=1.000002\mathrm{H/m}$，电导率 $\sigma=3.8\times10^7\mathrm{S/m}$

直线永磁同步电机改变绕组的电流频率并不改变推力的大小,当绕组电流为200A时,不同位置下的最大推力、法向力和推力密度的变化情况如表8和图6所示。

不同位置下的最大推力、法向力和推力密度　　　　　　　　　　　　　　　　表8

位置(mm)	法向力(N)	推力(N)	推力密度(N/m³)
0	5824	3513	23736
20	5856	5025	33953
40	5856	4184	28270
60	7227	4119	27831
80	6247	4020	27162
100	6918	3581	24196
120	6089	3757	25385
140	6108	3598	24311
160	6834	3092	20892
180	6181	3547	23966
200	6964	3185	21520
220	6117	3535	23885

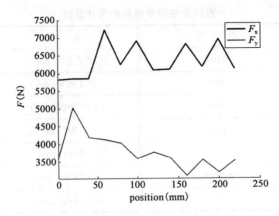

图6 不同位置下的最大推力和法向力变化情况

位置不变时,不同电流下的最大推力、法向力和推力密度的变化情况如表9和图7所示。

不同电流下的最大推力、法向力和推力密度 表9

电流(A)	推力(N)	法向力(N)	推力密度(N/m³)
100	3246	4131	21932
150	4133	4993	27926
200	5021	5849	33926
250	5915	6719	39966
300	6805	7582	45980
350	7688	8445	51946
400	8585	9308	58007

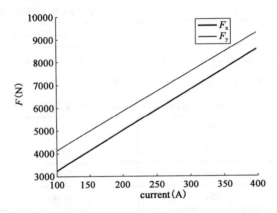

图7 通入不同电流下的最大推力和法向力变化情况

由实验结果可知:

①直线永磁同步电机的推力密度比直线感应电机小很多,原因在于直线永磁同步电机的气隙较大,当气隙增大时电机的推力会大幅度减小。用在轨道交通上的直线感应电机的气隙一般为10mm左右,而用在轨道交通上的直线永磁同步电机由于一般用于高速场合,因此需要更大的气隙来保证安全性。在本次实验中直线永磁同步电机的气隙高达50mm,仍可提供与直线感应电机在10mm气隙下接近的推力,因此可知直线永磁同步电机在相同情况下效率和推力密度较高。

②在不同位置的推力和法向力变化较大,而增大电流幅值时,推力和法向力也会按比例增大,因此直线永磁同步电机可以通过增大电流来获得更大的推力。

1.3 直线开关磁阻电机的电磁力分析

用在高精度运动中的开关磁阻电机的气隙很小,一般小于1mm,且齿宽、齿距也很小,当齿宽太小时,通入电流很容易导致磁通饱和,此时继续增大电流对于电机推力的作用减小,因此,这种小齿宽的直线开关磁阻电机的推力较小。本文设计的大齿宽的直线开关磁阻电机能够提供更大的推力和减小法向吸力,电机的尺寸参数如表10所示。设计的开关磁阻电机的长度是直线感应电机和直线永磁同步电机的两倍,搭建的仿真模型如图8所示,仿真模型中不同零件的材料设定如表11所示。

直线开关磁阻电机尺寸参数 表10

参　数	数　值	参　数	数　值
定子长度(mm)	5173.2	每相绕组匝数	16
上、下齿宽(mm)	10.8	动子高度(mm)	108
上、下槽深(mm)	10.8	动子轭部厚度(mm)	32.4
定子高度(mm)	50	气隙(mm)	1
动子块间距(mm)	18	定子宽度(mm)	200

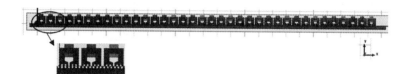

图8　直线开关磁阻电机仿真模型

直线开关磁阻电机的材料参数 表11

零　件	材　料	参　数
动子绕组	铜	相对磁导率$\mu=0.999991$H/m,电导率$\sigma=5.8\times10^8$S/m
气隙	空气	相对磁导率$\mu=1.000004$H/m,电导率$\sigma=0$
动子块和定子	DW360_50	B-H Curve,电导率$\sigma=0$

直线开关磁阻电机的工作原理是利用磁阻最小原理,因此各相绕组依次通入电流,且电流没有方向之分,可以直接依次通入直流电。首先研究当电流幅值固定在200A,在不同气隙下电机的最大推力、法向力和推力密度的变化情况如表12和图9所示。

不同气隙下的最大推力、法向力和推力密度 表12

气隙(mm)	推力(N)	法向力(N)	推力密度(N/m³)
1	10248	28615	120225
1.5	7844	24976	92023
2	5811	21225	68172
2.5	4078	17247	47841
3	2989	14626	35066
3.5	2190	12488	25692
4	1619	10751	18993
4.5	1210	9352	14195
5	912	8192	10699
10	76	3026	892

当气隙固定为3mm,通入不同的电流时电机的最大推力、法向力和推力密度的变化情况如表13和图10所示。

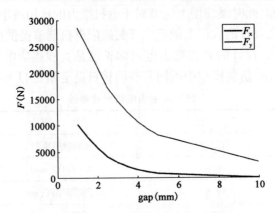

图9 不同气隙下的最大推力和法向力变化情况

不同电流下的最大推力、法向力和推力密度　　　　　　　　　　表13

电流(A)	推力(N)	法向力(N)	推力密度(N/m³)
100	770	3759	9033
150	1727	8455	20260
200	2986	14606	35031
250	3959	19376	46445
300	4630	22661	54317
350	5073	24915	59514
400	5365	26586	62940

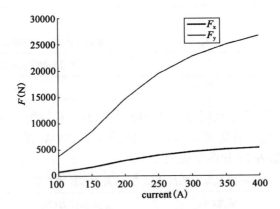

图10 通入不同电流时的最大推力和法向力变化情况

由实验结果可知：

①开关磁阻电机在小气隙的推力密度很大，而且法向力和推力的比值比较合适，但是当气隙增大时，推力快速减小，法向力和推力的比值增大。

②当气隙为10mm时，电机产生的推力非常小，只有76N，完全无法满足轨道交通的需求。

③增大电流，当电流产生的磁场未达到饱和时，推力将成比例增大；当电流产生的磁场达到接近饱和时，推力随电流增大的幅度将很小。

2 结　语

本文对直线感应电机、直线永磁同步电机和直线开关磁阻电机进行了有限元分析，由分析结果可知：①一般情况下，增大气隙虽然会导致电机推力减小，但直线永磁同步电机在通入200A电流时产生的推力仍比直线感应电机的大，而直线永磁同步电机的气隙是直线感应电机的5倍，说明直线永磁同步电机的电磁力性能更好，更加适合应用在高速领域这种需要气隙大而且推力大的情况。②直线感应电机推力在不同位置的波动小，更加稳定，推力也能达到列车的需求，而且可以通过改变初级电流频率和幅值来增大推力,推力密度较大,因此适合用在中低速这种气隙要求不大而推力密度要求大的场合。③直线开关磁阻电机并不适合应用在高速领域,因为高速领域需要电机有较大的气隙以保证安全性。在相同电流情况下,直线开关磁阻电机气隙才达到直线永磁同步电机气隙的3/20时,推力密度就已经接近了,而当气隙相同时,直线开关磁阻电机的推力过小以至于无法满足轨道交通的要求。因此,可以考虑把直线开关磁阻电机应用于不需要气隙很大的场合,通过合理设计电机结构和控制电流,结合直线开关磁阻电机的诸多优点,有望使直线开关磁阻电机在轨道交通中有更好的表现。

参考文献

[1] Lv Gang, Zhou Tong, Zeng Di-hui. Influence of the ladder-slit secondary on reducing the edge effect and transverse forces in the linear induction motor[J]. IEEE Transactions on Industrial Electronics, 2018, 65(9): 7516-7525.

[2] 李崇坚. 交流同步电机调速系统[M]. 北京:科学出版社,2006.

[3] Hoopengardner R, Thompson M. FTA low-speed urban maglev research program: updated lessons learned[R]. Federal Transit Administration, 2012.

[4] 张梓绥. 轨道交通中永磁同步电机控制关键技术研究[D]. 北京:北京交通大学,2019.

[5] 黄苏丹. 平面开关磁阻电机的高精度运动机理及其控制方法[D]. 成都:西南交通大学,2016.

时速400公里高速铁路接触网弹性吊索结构优化研究

陈 可 鲁小兵 杨 洋 杨成吉

(中铁二院工程集团有限责任公司)

摘 要 电气化铁路接触网负责为列车提供持续电能,通常采用施加弹性吊索的方式降低接触网的弹性不均匀度,提升受流质量。但是,弹性吊索的参数配置一直是工程设计中的难点。针对该问题,本文以我国成渝高速铁路弹性链形悬挂接触网为研究对象,采用空间梁单元构建接触网非线性模型。分别以弹性吊索张力、弹性吊索长度、弹性吊弦位置为变量,分析了弹性吊索的多种参数组合方式对弓网受流质量的影响。研究结果表明,弹性吊索几何参数的配置方式对弓网受流质量有较大影响;接触网的弹性分布曲线较好地解释了弹性吊索参数对弓网受流质量的影响机理;并针对我国成渝高铁弹性链形悬挂接触网提出了弹性吊索参数的建议配置方案。

关键词 接触网 受电弓 接触力 弹性吊索 高速铁路

0 引 言

电气化铁路接触网是架设在铁路沿线的悬索状结构系统,负责为高速运行的列车提供持续的电能。通常,接触网通过与高速滑行的受电弓相互滑动接触的方式为列车供电(图1)。因此,通常将接触网和受电弓系统称为弓网系统,它既是一个电能传输设备,又是一个机械设备。需要同时保证电气和力学的良好特性[1]。

近年来,我国陆续开通了成渝、京沪、沪昆、京张等高速客运专线,高速列车的运行速度不断提高。接触网在高速运行的受电弓的冲击下,会发生剧烈的振动,从而造成弓网间接触力的剧烈波动,导致引起弓网受流质量的严重恶化,具体表现在两方面。其一,接触力峰值的增大会引起接触线和受电弓滑板的更多磨损和疲劳破坏,降低弓网系统的服役寿命。其二,过小的接触力会引起弓网发生分离的风险,导致滑板与接触线之间产生电弧,引起材料烧蚀和熔融。严重的还会导致供电中断,影响行车安全。

图 1 电气化铁路接触网示意图

因此,为了提升弓网的受流质量,众多学者对这一领域进行了研究。文献[2]构建了接触网的运动微分方程,并考虑重力因素进行了修正;文献[3]求解了接触网的初始形态,为研究接触网动态特性提供了条件;文献[4]构建了多体动力学受电弓模型,分析了弓网的动态特性;文献[5]以提升受流质量为目标,对受电弓参数进行了优化;文献[6]考虑双弓运行的特殊工况,分析了双弓运行时的弓网受流质量;文献[7]基于简化载荷谱和雨流计数法,评估了接触网的疲劳寿命;文献[8]基于欧拉伯努利梁单元构建了接触网的运动微分方程,分析了不同张力等级下的弓网电能传输特性;文献[9]通过构建弓网和车网联合仿真模型,分析了车速对弓网接触电阻的影响;文献[10]基于 GO-FLOW 法,对高速铁路接触网的系统可靠性进行了分析;文献[11]采用销盘式高速载流设备,研究了弓网高速滑动时电接触摩擦力特性;文献[12]引入空气动力的影响,修正了弓网运动微分方程,评估了环境风对弓网受流特性的影响。

在以往研究中,针对接触网结构优化的研究主要集中在提升接触网的张力等级。然而,受材料极限的影响,接触网张力不可能无限制增大。因此,在实际高速铁路工程中,一般采用在接触网支持处布置弹性吊索,以降低接触网的弹性不均匀系数。然而,针对弹性吊索布置方案的研究工作开展较少,本文将致力于解决这一问题,寻求弹性链形悬挂中接触网弹性吊索的最佳配置方案。

本文的研究思路如下:首先,通过求解欧拉梁单元的偏微分方程,获得张力梁的有限元矩阵,施加适当的边界条件,构建接触网的运动微分方程。其次,以多体动力学为基础,构建受电弓的框架模型,实现弓网的动态交互仿真;接着,通过改变弹性吊索的张力,研究弹性吊索张力对弓网受流质量的影响;然后,通过改变弹性吊索长度,研究弹性吊索长度对受流质量的影响;最后,提出弹性吊索的最佳布置方案。

1 电气化铁路接触网三维力学建模

据虚功和虚位移原理,空间欧拉伯努利梁单元的几何非线性静力学方程可以写为:

$$([K_0^{(e)}] + [K_L^{(e)}] + [K_\sigma^{(e)}])\{\Delta d_e\} = \{F_e\} - \{Q_e^{\{P\}}\} \tag{1}$$

式中,$[K_0^{(e)}]$ 是单元的线性刚度矩阵,$[K_L^{(e)}]$ 是大位移刚度矩阵,$[K_\sigma^{(e)}]$ 是初应力刚度矩阵,$\{\Delta d_e\}$ 是节点位移增量向量,$\{F_e\}$ 是等效节点载荷向量,$\{Q_e^{\{P\}}\}$ 是节点不平衡力向量。$[K_0^{(e)}]$、$[K_L^{(e)}]$、$[K_\sigma^{(e)}]$ 可由固体力学中增量虚功方程导出:

$$\int_{t_V}^{\delta} \delta\Delta E^T S d^t V = \int_{t_V}^{\delta} \delta\Delta d_s^T({}^t p_0 + \Delta p_0) d^t V + \int_{t_A} \delta\Delta d_s^T({}^t q_0 + \Delta q_0) d^t A \tag{2}$$

式中,δ 表示变分,ΔE 为 Green 应变增量,S 为 t 时刻的 Euler 应力 ${}^t\sigma$ 与增量应力 VS 之和,${}^t p_0 + \Delta p_0$ 和 ${}^t q_0 + \Delta q_0$ 分别为体积力矢量和面积力矢量。Δd_s 为梁单元任意点的位移,可由梁的端点位移表示。梁单元任意点的位移 Δd_s 可由其两端节点位移和位移插值函数矩阵 N 表示:

$$\Delta d_s = N\Delta d_e \tag{3}$$

式中,位移插值函数矩阵 N 具有如下形式:

$$N = [N_l, N_r] \tag{4}$$

式中,

$$N_l = \begin{bmatrix} N_1 & & & & \\ & N_3 & & & N_4 \\ & & N_3 & -N_4 & \\ & & & & N_1 \end{bmatrix}$$

$$N_r = \begin{bmatrix} N_2 & & & & \\ & N_5 & & & N_6 \\ & & N_5 & -N_6 & \\ & & & & N_2 \end{bmatrix}$$

式中,$N_1 = 1 - \xi, N_2 = \xi, N_3 = 1 - 3\xi^2 + 2\xi^3, N_4 = (\xi - 2\xi^2 + \xi^3)/l, N_5 = 3\xi^2 - 2\xi^3, N_6 = (-\xi^2 + \xi^3)/l, \xi = x/l$。

空间梁单元的刚度矩阵的具体推导过程参考文献[12]。根据该假设,接触线、承力索、弹性吊索等可离散为两节点 5 自由度的三维梁单元。因此,梁单元的线性刚度矩阵$[K_0^{(e)}]$和初应力刚度矩阵$[K_\sigma^{(e)}]$的具体形式如下:

$$[K_0^{(e)}] = \begin{bmatrix} K_{0\,lu}^{(e)} & \\ K_{0\,lb}^{(e)} & K_{0\,rb}^{(e)} \end{bmatrix} \tag{5}$$

$$[K_\sigma^{(e)}] = \begin{bmatrix} K_{\sigma\,lu}^{(e)} & \\ K_{\sigma\,lb}^{(e)} & K_{\sigma\,rb}^{(e)} \end{bmatrix} \tag{6}$$

式中,$[K_{0\,lu}^{(e)}] = \begin{bmatrix} \dfrac{EA}{l} & & & & \\ 0 & \dfrac{12EI}{l^3} & & & \\ 0 & 0 & \dfrac{12EI}{l^3} & & \\ 0 & 0 & -\dfrac{6EI}{l^2} & \dfrac{4EI}{l^3} & \\ 0 & \dfrac{6EI}{l^2} & 0 & 0 & \dfrac{4EI}{l^3} \end{bmatrix}$

$$[K_{0\,lb}^{(e)}] = \begin{bmatrix} -\dfrac{EA}{l} & 0 & 0 & 0 & 0 \\ 0 & -\dfrac{12EI}{l^3} & 0 & 0 & -\dfrac{6EI}{l^2} \\ 0 & 0 & \dfrac{12EI}{l^3} & \dfrac{6EI}{l^2} & 0 \\ 0 & 0 & -\dfrac{6EI}{l^2} & \dfrac{2EI}{l} & 0 \\ 0 & \dfrac{6EI}{l^2} & 0 & 0 & \dfrac{2EI}{l} \end{bmatrix}$$

$$[K_{0\,rb}^{(e)}] = \begin{bmatrix} \frac{EA}{l} & & & & \\ 0 & \frac{12EI}{l^3} & & & \\ 0 & 0 & \frac{12EI}{l^3} & & \\ 0 & 0 & \frac{6EI}{l^2} & \frac{4EI}{l^3} & \\ 0 & -\frac{6EI}{l^2} & 0 & 0 & \frac{4EI}{l^3} \end{bmatrix}$$

$$[K_{\sigma\,lu}^{(e)}] = \begin{bmatrix} 0 & & & & \\ 0 & \frac{6}{5l} & & & \\ 0 & 0 & \frac{6}{5l} & & \\ 0 & 0 & -\frac{1}{10} & \frac{4l}{30} & \\ 0 & \frac{1}{10} & 0 & 0 & \frac{4l}{30} \end{bmatrix}$$

$$[K_{\sigma\,lb}^{(e)}] = \begin{bmatrix} 0 & 0 & 0 & 0 & 0 \\ 0 & -\frac{6}{5l} & 0 & 0 & \frac{1}{10} \\ 0 & 0 & -\frac{6}{5l} & \frac{1}{10} & 0 \\ 0 & 0 & -\frac{1}{10} & -\frac{l}{30} & 0 \\ 0 & \frac{1}{10} & 0 & 0 & -\frac{l}{30} \end{bmatrix}$$

$$[K_{\sigma\,rb}^{(e)}] = \begin{bmatrix} 0 & & & & \\ 0 & \frac{6}{5l} & & & \\ 0 & 0 & \frac{6}{5l} & & \\ 0 & 0 & \frac{1}{10} & \frac{4l}{30} & \\ 0 & -\frac{1}{10} & 0 & 0 & \frac{4l}{30} \end{bmatrix}$$

其中，E 为杨氏模量，$I = I_z = I_y$，I_z 和 I_y 分别为绕 z、y 轴旋转的惯性矩，A 为横截面积，T 为张力。

根据有限元方法，将刚度矩阵按照接触网拓扑结构组装成整体刚度矩阵。结合集中质量矩阵，从而构建接触网动力学方程：

$$M\ddot{U} + C\dot{U} + KU = F \tag{7}$$

其中，M、C 和 K 分别为接触网的整体质量、阻尼和刚度矩阵。$\ddot{U}$、$\dot{U}$ 和 U 分别为接触网的整体加速度、速度和位移向量。接触网的初始形态对其动态性能的影响至关重要，本文采用文献[12]中所提出的动坐标法对接触网的初始形态进行求解。

2 受电弓模型

本文将受电弓简化为集中质量模型,如图2所示。其动力学方程可以写为:

$$M_P \ddot{U}_P + C_P \dot{U}_P + K_P U_P = F_P \quad (8)$$

式中,

$$M_P = \begin{bmatrix} m_1 & & \\ & m_2 & \\ & & m_3 \end{bmatrix} \quad (9)$$

$$C_P = \begin{bmatrix} c_1 & -c_1 & \\ -c_1 & c_1+c_2 & -c_3 \\ & -c_3 & c_2+c_3 \end{bmatrix} \quad (10)$$

$$K_P = \begin{bmatrix} k_1 & -k_1 & \\ -k_1 & k_1+k_2 & -k_3 \\ & -k_3 & k_2+k_3 \end{bmatrix} \quad (11)$$

$$U_P = [y_1 \quad y_2 \quad y_3]^T \quad (12)$$

$$F_P = [f_c \quad 0 \quad f_p]^T \quad (13)$$

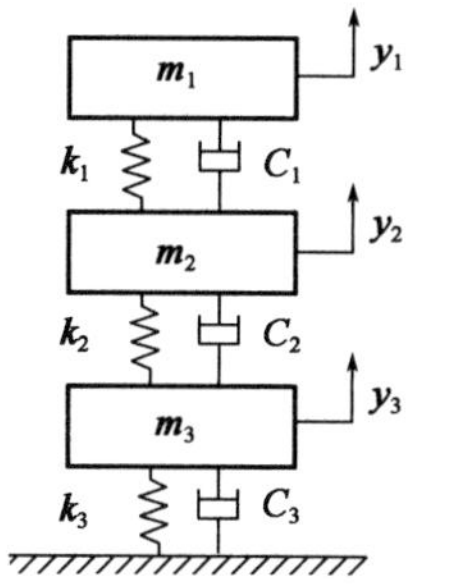

图2 受电弓集中质量模型

受电弓仿真参数选取为 DSA380 型高速受电弓。

3 弹性吊索优化布置方案

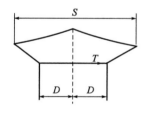

图3 弹性吊索主要优化参数

弹性链形悬挂接触网的结构参数选取我国成渝高铁标准跨接触网。弹性吊索参数主要考虑弹性吊索张力 T、弹性吊弦位置 D,和弹性吊索长度 S,具体物理意义如图3所示。

根据图3的弹性吊索参数,给出如表1中的22种组合,用于分析弹性吊索对弓网动态性能的影响。仿真车速选取为250km/h,运行条件为双弓受流。根据欧标 EN 50367 规定[18],评估受流质量最重要的两个指标为统计最小值和接触力标准差。

弹性吊索优化仿真组合方案   表1

吊弦距定位点位置 D (m)	弹性吊索长度 S (m)	弹性吊索张力 T (N)	方案编号
4	14	2.8	1
		3.5	2
	18	2.8	3
		3.5	4
	22	2.8	5
		3.5	6
5	14	2.8	7
		3.5	8
	18	2.8	9
		3.5	10
	22	2.8	11
		3.5	12

续上表

吊弦距定位点位置 D (m)	弹性吊索长度 S (m)	弹性吊索张力 T (N)	方案编号
6	14	2.8	13
		3.5	14
	18	2.8	15
		3.5	16
	22	2.8	17
		3.5	18
7	18	2.8	19
		3.5	20
	22	2.8	21
		3.5	22

图4分别给出了前后弓在不同组合下接触力的统计最小值和标准差。可以看出,弹性吊索参数组合对前后弓受流质量的影响规律基本一致。组合方案5的接触力标准差达到峰值,其接触力最小值出现负值,在实际工程设计中影响严格避免。相反,在组合方案7、8、13下,前后弓表现出较好的受流质量。

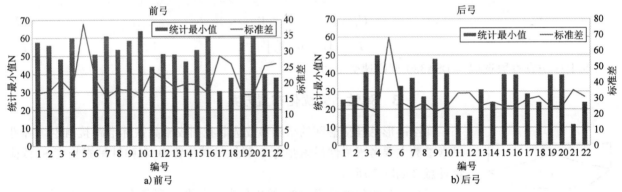

图4 接触力的统计最小值和标准差

为了进一步揭示弹性吊索参数对弓网受流质量的影响机理,通过在接触线不同位置施加垂向 $F = 100N$ 的静态载荷,计算接触线各点静态抬升,从而计算出接触网的静态弹性曲线:

$$k = \frac{l_{st}}{F} \tag{14}$$

图5给出了7、8组合方案下的接触网等效刚度曲线,可以看出,接触网弹性吊索长度会对接触网等效刚度曲线产生较大影响。为了量化这种影响,引入接触网弹性不均匀度 u 进行评判:

$$u = \frac{\eta_{max} - \eta_{min}}{\eta_{max} + \eta_{min}} \tag{15}$$

其中,η_{max} 和 η_{min} 分别为接触网等效弹性的最大和最小值。接触网弹性不均匀度直接反映了接触网在受电弓移动载荷下的动力学特性。

图6a)和b)分别给出了不同组合方案下前后弓的接触力标准差和接触网弹性不均匀系数的计算结果。可以看出,前后弓标准差和接触网弹性不均匀系数呈现出较好的对应关系。接触网的弹性不均匀度较好地解释了弹性吊索参数对弓网受流质量的影响机理。在组合方案5下,接触网弹性不均匀系数达到了最大值,相应的前后弓标准差分别上升到37 N和68 N,体现了接触力较大的波动现象,严重恶化受流质量。相反,在组合方案7、8和13下,前后弓的标准差达到了最小值,此时的接触网弹性不均匀系数也为各种组合方案下的相对最小值。为该弹性链形悬挂接触网的建议优化方案。

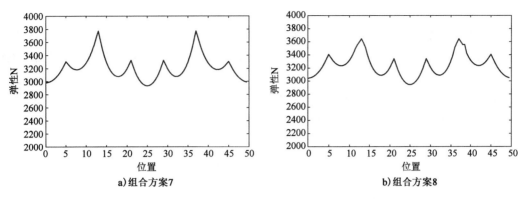

图 5 接触网等效弹性曲线

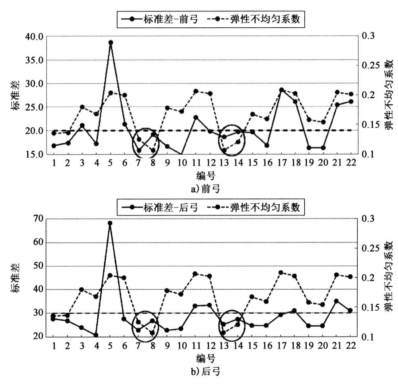

图 6 弹性吊索综合优化指标

4 结 语

本文针对成渝高速铁路弹性链形悬挂接触网的弹性吊索布置方式进行优化，寻找弹性吊索参数的最佳配置方案。首先，基于非线性有限元理论，采用空间梁单元构建了接触网模型；其次，采用集中参数模型描述了受电弓的动态特性；接着，以接触力标准差、统计最小值和接触网弹性不均匀度为指标，评估了不同参数组合下的弹性链形悬挂接触网的动态特性；最后，给出了成渝高铁接触网弹性吊索参数的最佳配置方案。研究结果表明，弹性吊索的几何参数对弓网受流质量有较大影响，具体表现在接触力波动和统计最小值的升降；前后弓受流质量和接触网弹性不均匀系数呈现出较好的对应关系，接触网的弹性不均匀度较好地解释了弹性吊索参数对弓网受流质量的影响机理。针对本文研究的接触网，在组合方案 5 下，接触网弹性不均匀系数达到了最大值，在工程设计中应严格避免。相反，在组合方案 7、8 和 13 下，前后弓的标准差达到了最小值，接触网弹性不均匀系数也为各种组合方案下的相对最优值。为该弹性链形悬挂接触网的建议优化方案。

参考文献

[1] 关金发,吴积钦,李岚.弓网动态仿真技术的现状及展望[J].铁道学报,2015(10):35-41.
[2] 李丰良,粟谦,孙焰.接触网的力学模型及运动微分方程[J].铁道科学与工程学报,1996(2):90-93.
[3] 李刚,梅桂明.简单链形悬挂接触网静态形态计算新方法[J].电气化铁道,2011(1):7-9.
[4] 赵晨,周宁,邹栋,等.基于非线性多刚体受电弓模型的弓网仿真分析[J].高速铁路技术,2016,7(3):1-6.
[5] 马果垒,马君,苏安社,等.基于多体系统动力学的受电弓参数优化[J].大连交通大学学报,2010,31(4):33-37.
[6] 王晖,张忠林,毕继红.双弓作用下锚段关节处弓网耦合系统受流分析[J].铁道标准设计,2011(11):104-107.
[7] 毕继红,陈花丽,任洪鹏.基于简化载荷谱法与雨流计数法的接触网疲劳寿命对比分析[J].铁道标准设计,2012(4):116-119.
[8] 刘方林.不同张力等级下电气化铁路弓网电能传输特性研究[J].电气技术,2017,18(12):86-89.
[9] 刘方林.电气化铁路动态弓网接触电阻研究[J].电气技术,2018,10:36-39.
[10] 赵峰,梁丽,王思华.基于GO-FLOW法的高速铁路接触网系统可靠性分析[J].电工技术学报,2015,30(12):351-356.
[11] 郭凤仪,陈明阳,陈忠华,等.弓网滑动电接触摩擦力特性与建模研究[J].电工技术学报,2018,33(13):2982-2990.
[12] 宋洋,刘志刚,鲁小兵,等.计及接触网空气动力的高速弓网动态受流特性研究[J].铁道学报,2016,38(3):48-58.
[13] 刘光栋,王解君,何放龙.空间梁单元的几何非线性刚度矩阵的分解形式[J].湖南大学学报(自科版),1992,19(1):60-71.
[14] 李东阳,吴积钦,关金发.DSA250型受电弓振动特性仿真与测试[J].电气化铁道,2012,23(4):7-10.
[15] 郭雅婕.欧洲弓网系统标准体系特征研究[D].成都:西南交通大学,2013.

第八篇 航空运输

基于时空图卷积网络的机场流量和航线流量预测

姚远 卞磊 刘宇 唐红武 王殿胜
(中航信移动科技有限公司)

摘要 本文基于时空图卷积网络,提出了用于预测机场进/出港客流量和航线客流量的模型。在构建图网络的过程中,对处于不同空间尺度上的机场采用了多图融合的方式,深度挖掘中国国内机场地域空间上的相关性特征,结合航班客流在时间上的周期性,设计了时空卷积网络模型,最终得到未来机场进/出港客流和航线客流的预测结果。模型对全国235个民航机场2年的进/出港客流量数据和航线数据进行对比测试,结果显示了该模型的准确性和稳定性。同时,该模型在基于时间输入探索时空结构方面具有巨大潜力,具有更快的训练速度和更少的参数,并具有灵活性和可伸缩性。这些特点对于具有时空特性的交通预测相关学术研究和行业部署都有很高的应用价值。

关键词 客流预测 航线预测 机场 深度学习

0 引言

随着我国民航业的飞速发展,机场的客流量和航线数量也呈逐年递增的趋势。准确预测机场进/出港客流量情况可以帮助机场已经机场配套交通设施提前合理化安排资源,缓解由于客流突然增长或减少所带来的公共设施和地面交通资源不足和浪费的情况;而预测未来航线客流量情况则可以帮助航空公司提前安排航班计划,从而避免机组和飞机资源的不足和低效利用问题。

机场客流预测和航线客流预测属于交通流量预测问题,近年来,越来越多的研究开始使用具有处理多维特征数据和非线性数据能力的深度学习模型来解决交通流量预测问题。深度信任网络(DBN)[1]和堆叠式自动编码器模型[2-3]首先被应用来学习交通流量的特征。但是这些模型每次只处理一个区域,而实际上来自附近甚至远处区域的交通量测量具有空间和时间的相关性,因此仅基于本地区域的信息来预测未来的交通数据还远远不够。卷积神经网络(CNN)作为一种典型的深度神经网络,在计算机视觉领域取得许多突破[4]。由于CNN可以通过卷积运算自动分层捕获空间结构信息[5],因此研也可将其应用于交通数据预测。Zhang等[6]提出了一个ST-ResNet,解决人群流量预测问题,它由卷积层和残差单元组成,用来模拟城市范围内的空间依赖性。至于时间特征,ST-ResNet只是将相邻时间间隔中的信息视为多个通道,因此,在第一个卷积层之后,ST-ResNet会丢失输入的时间信息。循环神经网络(RNN)作为深度神经网络的另一种经典类型,擅长对时间信息进行建模。但是,RNN在模型训练中会发生梯度消失的问题,这使得RNN难以记住长时间的信息。为了学习长时间范围内的时间依赖性,Ma等[7]和Zhao等[8]提出了长期短期记忆神经网络(LSTM)[9]和门控递归单元网络(GRU),来预测短期交通速度和交通流量。但是这些模型无法自动捕获空间特征,必须将空间信息手动编码为输入。为了解决时空序列预测问题,提出了新颖的卷积LSTM网络(ConvLSTM)[10]。但是,其体系结构十分复杂,当网络深度增加时,训练成本会大幅增加,这限制了网络的深度和捕获大范围时空相关性的能力。另外,这些基于LSTM的网络无法有效捕获远程时间相关性,例如交通数据中的周期性和趋势模式,这些在长期预测中都极为重要。

综上所述,交通流量预测需要同时考虑交通数据的时空相关性,而且交通数据的相关性在时间和空间上是异质的。因此,在交通数据建模中,正确识别和量化时空的相关性是必要的。但是,大部分现有的研究中都忽略了时空相关性,为了克服这些不足,本文引入了几种策略,来有效模拟交通流的时间动态和空间依赖性:首先,为了充分利用空间信息,通过一般图形对交通网络建模而不是单独处理(例如网格或线段)。其次,为了处理递归网络在训练中的固有缺陷,本文在时间轴上采用了完全卷积的结构。更重要的是,本文采取了一种新颖的深度学习架构,即时空图卷积网络,用于客流预测。该架构包括几个时空卷积块,它们是图卷积层[11]和卷积序列学习层[12]的组合,以建模空间和时间相关性。据我们所知,这是第一次在空中交通研究中应用卷积结构同时从图结构时间序列中提取时空特征。通过真实的民航数据集上评估本文提出的模型,实验表明,在具有多个预设的预测长度和网络规模的机场流量预测和航线流量预测任务中,该模型均展示出其准确性和稳定性。

1 时空图卷积网络预测模型

本节将详细介绍时空图卷积网络(STGCN)的网络结构。STGCN 是由若干个时空卷积块(ST-Conv Block)组成,如图1所示。每个时空卷积块具有3层结构,该3层结构由两个门控时序卷积层和夹在两个门控时序卷积层中间的空间图卷积层构成。这两个时序卷积层可以实现从图卷积到时间卷积的快速空间状态传播。这种3层结构还可以帮助网络充分利用瓶颈策略,通过在图卷积层上缩小和放大通道 C 来实现比例压缩和特征压缩。

序列 $v_{t-M+1}, \cdots, v_t$ 按顺序输 ST-Conv 块中,来提取序列中的空间和时间相关性信息。输出层结合了时空卷积后提取的全部时间和空间的相关特征,生成最终预测 $\hat{v}$。每个 ST-Conv 块内都利用层归一化,来防止过度拟合。1.1~1.3 节按顺序详细介绍时空图卷积网络(STGCN)中时空卷积块负责提取空间特征的图卷积网络和负责提醒时间特征的门控图卷积网络。

1.1 门控图卷积网络(Temporal Gated Convolution),提取时间特征

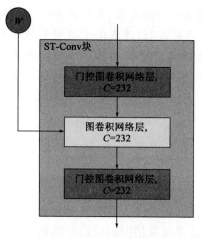

图1 ST-Conv Block 时空卷积块结构

目前,RNNs 以及基于 RNNs 演变来的 LSTM 模型是构建处理时间序列最为广泛使用的模型,但是 RNNs 类的模型含有复杂的门控机制,模型训练需要较高的运算能力和较长的计算时间,而且 RNNs 模型对于时间序列之中的动态变化反馈也较为缓慢。相比之下,CNNs 模型结构简单,不依赖前序输入的状态,训练速度也比 RNNs 更快。为了利用 CNNs 模型进行航班客流这样的时空数据预测,本文根据 Gehring 等人 2017 提出的方法[16],采用整个卷积结构来捕捉时间轴上客流量的动态变化,同时设计允许通过多层卷积结构,使得模型以分层的形式并行训练。

如图2所示,时间卷积层包含一维因果卷积(1-D Convolution),其卷积核的宽度为 K_t,连接的是非线性的门控线性单元(GLU)。对于图网络 G 中的每个节点,由于时间卷积每次探索输入元素的 K_t 个邻居没有填充,而导致每次卷积后序列长度缩短为 K_t-1。因此,为了保证卷积序列长度不变,图网络 G 中每个节点的时间卷积的输入可以看作通道 C_i 中长度为 M 的时间序列,其中 $Y \in \mathbb{R}^{M \times C_i}$,卷积核 $\Gamma \in \mathbb{R}^{K_t \times C_i \times 2C}$ 将把输入 Y 映射到单个输出元素 $[PQ] \in \mathbb{R}^{(M-K_t+1) \times (2C)}$($P,Q$ 被拆分为一半的频道大小)。因此,时间门控卷积可以定义为:

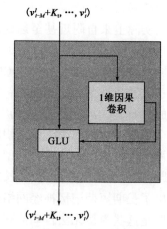

图2 门控图卷积网络结构

$$\Gamma *_T Y = P \odot \sigma(Q) \in \mathbb{R}^{(M-K_t+1) \times C_0} \quad (1)$$

式中: P,Q——GLU 中的门的输入;

$\odot$——Hadamard 元素乘积。

Sigmoid 型激活门 $\sigma(Q)$ 控制当前状态输入 P 与时间序列中哪些部分和动态变化有关。

因此,GLU 非线性门可以通过堆叠的时间层来填充完整的输入。此外,在堆叠的时间卷积层之间还可以实现残余连接。与之类似,通过对图网络 G 中的每个节点 $Y_i \in \mathbb{R}^{M \times C_i}$(每个机场)采用相同的卷积核 Γ,可将时间卷积泛化为 3 维变量。

1.2 图卷积网络(Spatial Graph Convolution),提取空间特征

空中交通网络通常以图结构(航线、场站)形式来刻画。因此,用数学方法将空中交通建模为图网络的模型是十分合理的。但是,先前的大部分研究只考虑了交通网络中的时间维度的特征而忽略了空间特征信息。即使考虑了空间特征,也大多是将网络分为多个网段或网格,因此忽略了网络的连通性和全局性。而且在网格上进行二维卷积,也只能捕获空间局部性。因此,针对以上提到的不足,在本文的模型中,考虑并使用图结构化数据进行图卷积,用来提取空间域中重要程度高的特征。本节将首先介绍用于构建图网络特征的邻接矩阵构造方法,其次介绍进行图卷积时为了降低图卷积计算成本而使用的两种近似策略。

(1)图卷积网络计算

如式(1)所示,进行图卷积的卷积核,是以图傅立叶为基础的基于频谱图卷积,本文引入了图卷积算符"$*g$"的概念,即信号 $x \in \mathbf{R}n$ 与核 Θ 的乘积:

$$\Theta * gx = \Theta(L)x = \Theta(U\Lambda U^T)x = U\Theta(\Lambda)U^T x \tag{2}$$

其中,图傅立叶基 $U \in \mathbf{R}^{n \times n}$ 是归一化后的图拉普拉斯算子本征向量的矩阵 $L = I_n - D^{-\frac{1}{2}}WD^{-\frac{1}{2}} = U\Lambda U^T \in \mathbf{R}^{n \times n}$($I_n$ 是单位矩阵,$D \in \mathbf{R}^{n \times n}$ 是对角度矩阵,其中对角线元素 $D_{ii} = \sum_j W_{ij}$);$\Lambda \in \mathbf{R}^{n \times n}$ 是 L 的特征值所构成的对角矩阵,滤波器 $U\Theta(\Lambda)$ 也是对角矩阵。基于以上描述,信号 x 通过内核 Θ(内核 Θ 和图傅立叶变换 $U^T x$ 相乘)完成滤波变换[19]。但是基于这种卷积核的网络计算时间复杂度为 $\Theta(n^2)$。为降低计算成本,可使用以下两种近似策略。

①Chebyshev 多项式。通过切比雪夫多项式的近似拟合卷积核,可以降低卷积核的维度,降低计算复杂度。在切比雪夫多项式中,可将内核 Θ 限制为 Λ 的多项式,因为 $\Theta(\Lambda) = \sum_{k=0}^{k-1} \theta_k \Lambda^k$,其中 $\theta \in \mathbf{R}^k$ 是多项式系数的向量。K 为卷积核的大小,它确定了从中心节点开始的卷积的最大半径。利用 Chebyshev 多项式代替卷积核[13],可以得到下式:

$$\Theta(\Lambda) = \sum_{k=0}^{k-1} \theta_k T_k(\widetilde{\Lambda}) \tag{3}$$

式中:T_k——k 阶的 Chebyshev 多项式;

θ_k——对应的系数,即训练中迭代更新的参数。

$$\widetilde{\Lambda} = \frac{2\Lambda}{\lambda_{max}} - I_n \tag{4}$$

式中:$\widetilde{\Lambda}$——重整化的特征值对角矩阵。λ_{max} 是最大特征值[21]。

综上所述,图卷积公式可以重新写为:

$$\Theta * gx = \Theta(L)x \approx \sum_{k=0}^{k-1} \theta_k T_k(\widetilde{L})x \tag{5}$$

其中,$T_k(\widetilde{L}) \in \mathbf{R}^{n \times n}$ 是在按比例的拉普拉斯算子 $\widetilde{L} = \frac{2\Lambda}{\lambda_{max}} - I_n$ 上求值的阶 k 的切比雪夫多项式。通过多项式逼近递归计算 K-localized 局部卷积,可将式(1)中计算图卷积的计算复杂度降低到式(5)中的 $\Theta(K|\varepsilon)$[14]。

②一阶近似。根据 Kipf 和 Welling 在 2016 年提出的方法[20],可以将多个局部图卷积层与图拉普拉斯的一阶逼近叠加来定义分层线性公式[15]。通过此方式,可以构建更深的模型架构来获取更深层次的空间信息,而不仅限于多项式给出的显式参数化。由于神经网络对特征的缩放和归一化,可以进一步假设 $\lambda_{max} \approx 2$,因此卷积公式(5)可以进一步简化为:

$$\Theta * gx \approx \theta_0 x + \theta_1 \left(\frac{2}{\lambda_{max}} L - I_n \right) x \\ \approx \theta_0 x + \theta_1 \left(D - \frac{1}{2} W D^{-\frac{1}{2}} \right) x \tag{6}$$

其中,θ_0、θ_1 是卷积核的两个共享参数。为了限制参数并稳定计算的性能,可以用单个参数 θ 代替 θ_0 和 θ_1,并且让 $\theta = \theta_0 = -\theta_1$。W 和 D 分别通过 $W = W + I_n$ 和 $\widetilde{D}_{ii} = \sum_j \widetilde{W}_{ij}$ 重新归一化。由此,图卷积可以表示为:

$$\Theta * gx = \theta \left(I_n + D - \frac{1}{2} W D^{-\frac{1}{2}} \right) x \\ = \theta \left(\widetilde{D}^{-\frac{1}{2}} \widetilde{W} \widetilde{D}^{-\frac{1}{2}} \right) x \tag{7}$$

因此利用中心节点的 $(K-1)$ 阶邻域中进行一阶近似的图卷积,可达到与水平局部卷积相似的效果。在这种情况下,K 就是模型中连续过滤操作或卷积层的数量,而且由于近似图的阶次被限制为 1,这种分层的线性结构可以有效减少大型图网络的参数。本文后续的模型与试验均采用了一阶近似的方法,来降低图卷积网络的计算成本。

(2)空间特征构建

为了抽取航线图网络中的空间特征,本文选择了使用邻接矩阵的方式。而对于构造邻接矩阵,则采用了多图融合的方式,分别为距离图(Distance Graph)、相互作用图(Interaction Graph)、卷积图(Correlation Graph)[18]。

图 3 示出了航线图网络的邻接矩阵构造方法。

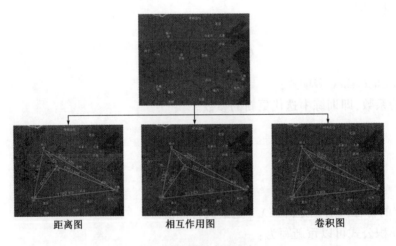

图 3 多图融合邻接矩阵

本文以西安、成都、银川和上海 4 座机场为例,来说明 Distance Graph、Interaction Graph 及 Correlation Graph 的计算方式。

Distance Graph 邻接矩阵的计算是根据机场之间的距离来构造,将距离(km)取倒数,就可以得到 4 座机场基于距离的邻接矩阵 A_1:

$$A_1 = \begin{bmatrix} 0 & \dfrac{1}{\text{dist}_{0,1}} & \dfrac{1}{\text{dist}_{0,2}} & \cdots & \dfrac{1}{\text{dist}_{0,N-1}} \\ \dfrac{1}{\text{dist}_{1,0}} & 0 & \cdots & \cdots & \dfrac{1}{\text{dist}_{1,N-1}} \\ \dfrac{1}{\text{dist}_{2,0}} & \dfrac{1}{\text{dist}_{2,1}} & 0 & \cdots & \dfrac{1}{\text{dist}_{2,N-1}} \\ \vdots & \vdots & \vdots & \ddots & \vdots \\ \dfrac{1}{\text{dist}_{N-1,0}} & \cdots & \cdots & \cdots & 0 \end{bmatrix}$$

$$A_1 = \begin{bmatrix} 0 & \dfrac{1}{1207} & \dfrac{1}{606} & \dfrac{1}{1782} \\ \dfrac{1}{1207} & 0 & \dfrac{1}{508} & \dfrac{1}{2047} \\ \dfrac{1}{606} & \dfrac{1}{508} & 0 & \dfrac{1}{1250} \\ \dfrac{1}{1782} & \dfrac{1}{2047} & \dfrac{1}{1250} & 0 \end{bmatrix}$$

Interaction Graph 邻接矩阵根据机场之间的日历史平均客流量计算得到：

$$A_2 = \begin{bmatrix} d_{0,0} & d_{0,1} & d_{0,2} & \cdots & d_{0,N-1} \\ d_{1,0} & d_{1,1} & d_{1,2} & \cdots & d_{1,N-1} \\ d_{2,0} & d_{2,1} & d_{2,2} & \cdots & d_{2,N-1} \\ \vdots & \vdots & \vdots & \ddots & \vdots \\ d_{N-1,0} & \cdots & \cdots & \cdots & d_{N-1,N-1} \end{bmatrix}$$

$$A_2 = \begin{bmatrix} 0 & 2132 & 1804 & 15743 \\ 2132 & 0 & 2439 & 2903 \\ 1804 & 2439 & 0 & 10313 \\ 15743 & 2903 & 10313 & 0 \end{bmatrix}$$

Correlation Graph 邻接矩阵的计算是结合机场所在城市的人口数、地区生产总值、历史航线数量等特征，计算相关性邻接矩阵 A_3：

$$A_3 = \begin{bmatrix} 0 & r_{0,1} & r_{0,2} & \cdots & r_{0,N-1} \\ r_{1,1} & 0 & r_{1,2} & \cdots & r_{1,N-1} \\ r_{2,0} & r_{2,1}0 & 0 & \cdots & r_{2,N-1} \\ \vdots & \vdots & \vdots & \ddots & \vdots \\ r_{N-1,0} & \cdots & \cdots & \cdots & 0 \end{bmatrix}$$

$$A_3 = \begin{bmatrix} 0 & 0.51 & 0.91 & 0.89 \\ 2132 & 0 & 2439 & 2903 \\ 1804 & 2439 & 0 & 10313 \\ 15743 & 2903 & 10313 & 0 \end{bmatrix}$$

得到 3 个邻接矩阵后，3 个不同的图将合并为一个融合图。通过加权求和的方式来融合不同的图。由于不同图的邻接矩阵的值可能相差很大，因此首先对每个图的邻接矩阵 A 进行归一化：

$$A' = D^{-1}A + I \tag{8}$$

$$D = \begin{bmatrix} \sum_{j=0}^{N-1}A_{0,j} & 0 & \cdots & 0 \\ 0 & \sum_{j=0}^{N-1}A_{1,j} & \cdots & 0 \\ \vdots & \vdots & \vdots & \ddots \\ 0 & 0 & \cdots & \sum_{j=0}^{N-1}A_{N-1,j} \end{bmatrix}$$

如式(8)所示，A'是具有自环的归一化邻接矩阵。自环可以在卷积部分保持目标站本身的信息，这是图卷积神经网络中必需的设计策略。为了使融合结果通过加权和运算归一化，本文还向权重矩阵添加了一个最大运算。假设有 N 个图混合在一起，可以将图融合过程表示为：

$$W'_1, W'_2, \cdots, W'_N = \mathrm{softmax}(W_1, W_2, \cdots, W_N)$$
$$A'_i = D_i^{-1}A_i + I, 1 \leq i \leq N$$
$$F = \sum_{i=1}^{N} W'_i \circ A'_i \tag{9}$$

并通过 Soft-max 激活函数得到 3 个邻接矩阵的权重，∘是按元素乘积，F 是将在图卷积部分中使用的图融合结果。这种方法计算得出的邻接矩阵可以很好反映不同机场空间上的相关性。

1.3 时空卷积块

1.1 节和 1.2 节说明了为了融合来自时间和空间的特征，构造了时空卷积块(ST-Conv block)，来共同处理具有图网络空间结构的时间序列。而时空卷积块本身可以根据不同模型的规模和复杂性进行堆叠或扩展，通过堆叠，构成了最终的空图卷积网络(STGCN)，如图 4 所示。

时空卷积块的输入和输出都是三维向量。对于卷积块 l，输入 $v^l \in \mathbf{R}^{M \times n \times C^l}$ 和输出 $v^{l+1} \in \mathbf{R}^{(M-2(K_t-1)) \times n \times C^{l+1}}$ 由下面的公式计算获得：

$$v^{l+1} = \Gamma^l_1 *_T \mathrm{ReLU}[\Theta^l * g(\Gamma^l_0 *_T v^l)] \tag{10}$$

式中：Γ^l_0 和 Γ^l_1——第一个 ST-Conv Block 内的上、下时间卷积核；
Θ^l——图卷积的谱核；
$\mathrm{ReLU}(\cdot)$——线性单位激活函数。

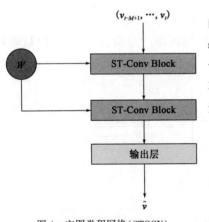

图 4 空图卷积网络(STGCN)

再堆叠两个 ST-Conv block 之后，再添加一个全连接层作为最后的输出层。时间卷积层将最后一个 ST-Conv 块的输出映射到 single-step 预测，然后可以从模型中获得最终输出 $Z \in \mathbf{R}^{n \times c}$，最终通过在 c 个通道上应用 $\hat{v} = Z\omega + b$ 的线性变换，来获得 n 个节点的客流预测。本文使用 L2 Loss 来衡量模型的性能。因此，STGCN 的预测损失函数可以写为：

$$L(\hat{v}; W_\theta) = \sum_t \| \hat{v}(v_{t-M+1}, \cdots, v_t, W_\theta) - v_{t+1} \|2 \tag{11}$$

式中：W_θ——模型中所有可训练的参数；
v_{t+1}——真实值；
$\hat{v}(\cdot)$——模型的预测值。

综上所述，可以将 STGCN 模型的主要特征的总结如下：

①STGCN 的时空结构决定了它可以作为处理结构化时间序列的通用框架。它不仅可以解决交通网络建模和预测问题，而且可以应用于更一般的时空序列学习任务。

②ST-Conv 块结合了图卷积网络(GCN)和门控时间卷积网络(GTCN)，可以有效提取最有用的空间特征并连续捕获时间特征。

③与传统构建时间序列的RNN网络相比,该模型完全由卷积结构组成,因此可以以较少的参数和更快的训练速度实现输入的并行化。更重要的是,这种经济架构允许模型以更高的效率处理大规模网络。

2 模型训练与测试

2.1 数据集

图5展示了基于全国机场航线可视化出的航线网络图。

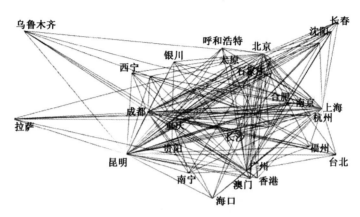

图5 全国主要机场航线可视化图

由于235个机场全部的航线太过复杂、密集,为了便于展示,这里仅绘制了全国省会机场及吞吐量较大的135个机场间的航线网络图。

本文使用了全国235个机场从2018年1月1日到2019年12月31日两年之中每天的进出港量数据来测试模型。数据集大小为2.1GB,其中包含机场的名称、日期、进港人数及出港人数。

2.2 数据预处理

由于本文的预测分为机场流量预测和航线流量预测两部分,因此对于数据进行了不同方式的处理。对于机场流量预测问题,将进港流量和出港流量分开进行计算和预测,因此每个机场每天会统计生成进港总人数和出港总人数。对于航线流量预测问题,每个场站每天会有232个数据点(包含自己),因此最终每天的数据是一个232×232的矩阵。对于缺失值,则采用了linear interpolation的方式[17],数据标准化则采用了Z-Score方法。除此之外,对于上海、北京和贵州茅台镇3个城市拥有两个机场的情况,则对两个机场进行了合并,使得航路图中的每个点是一个城市,这样也便于与空间信息特征进行融合。

2.3 试验验证

使用一套Linux系统环境的集群[CPU:Intel(R) Xeon(R) Gold 5118 CPU @ 2.30GHz]来进行全部模型的训练和测试。本文分别设置了使用10d、12d、14d、16d($M=10、12、14、16$)的时间窗数据来进行训练,并且使用时间窗后紧接着的2d、4d、6d、8d($H=2、4、6、8$)的数据进行测试。

机场客流预测和航线客流预测训练结果如图6所示。

表1和表2分别展示了机场客流预测结果和航线客流量预测结果。

机场客流量预测结果 表1

时间窗	MAE ($H=2$)	MAPE ($H=2$)	RMSE ($H=2$)
10	777.1	54.4	1157.5
12	658.3	49.9	965.1
14	609.2	47.8	892.3
16	546.9	44.7	818.9

注:MAE-平均绝对误差(人);MAPE-平均绝对百分误差;RMSE-均方根误差;H-测试天数。

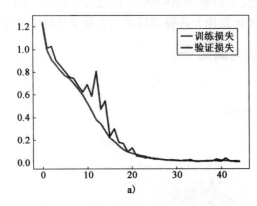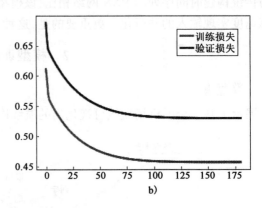

图6　机场客流预测(左)和航线客流预测(右)结果

航线客流量预测结果　　　　　　　　　　　　　　　　　　表2

时间窗	MAE	MAPE	RMSE
10	12.4/12.7/13.3/14.4	0.32/0.35/0.40/0.43	26.3/28.6/30.4/33.9
12	11.6/12.2/13.1/13.9	0.29/0.35/0.37/0.41	25.8/27.9/29.2/32.7
14	11.3/11.6/12.7/13.7	0.27/0.33/0.36/0.38	25.1/27.5/28.7/31.5
16	10.6/11.2/11.7/12.1	0.23/0.26/0.27/0.31	24.5/26.7/28.1/30.3

注:MAE-平均绝对误差(人);MAPE-平均绝对百分误差;RMSE-均方根误差;H-测试天数。

在机场客流量预测测试中,分别设置了使用10d、12d、14d、16d($M=10、12、14、16$)的时间窗数据来进行训练,并且使用时间窗后紧接着的2d、4d、6d、8d($H=2、4、6、8$)的数据进行测试。由于表格空间有限,本文仅将$H=2$的结果进行展示,从结果中可以看到,对未来两天机场客流量预测的平均绝对误差在546.9~777.1人之间,这对于日进出港客流在几万人的枢纽机场来说,预测结果是十分精准的。

对于航线客流量预测测试,同样分别设置了使用10d、12d、14d、16d($M=10、12、14、16$)的时间窗数据来进行训练,并且使用时间窗后紧接着的2d、4d、6d、8d($H=2、4、6、8$)的数据进行测试,从结果中可以看到,根据不同的训练时间窗和测试天数,航线上客流量预测的平均绝对误差在10.6~14.4人之间。

3　结　语

在本文中,提出了一种使用新型深度学习架构STGCN来预测机场进/出港客流量和航线客流量的模型。它通过时空卷积块集成了图卷积和门控时间卷积。在构建图网络的过程中,对处于不同空间纬度上的机场,本文采用了多图融合的方式,深度挖掘中国国内机场地域空间上的相关性特征,结合航班客流在时间上的周期性,通过时空卷积网络最终得到机场进/出港客流和航线客流的预测结果。在使用全国235个民航机场2年的进/出港客流量数据和航线数据进行对比测试后,表明在机场客流预测和航线客流预测问题上,该模型均展示出其准确性和稳定性。同时,该模型在基于时间输入探索时空结构方面具有巨大潜力,具有更快的训练速度,更容易收敛,使用更少的参数,并具有灵活性和可伸缩性。这些方面对于具有时空属性的交通预测相关学术研究和行业部署都有很高的应用价值。

参考文献

[1] W Huang, G Song, H Hong, et al. Deep architecture for traffic flow prediction：Deep belief networks with multitask learning[J]. IEEE Trans. Intell. Transp. Syst,2014,15(5):2191-2201.

[2] Y Lv, Y Duan, W Kang, et al. Traffic flow prediction with big data：A deep learning approach[J]. IEEE Trans. Intell. Transp. Syst,2015,16(2):865-873.

[3] H F Yang, T S Dillon, Y P P Chen. Optimized structure of the traffic flow forecasting model with a deep learning approach[J]. IEEE Trans. Neural Netw. Learn. Syst,2017,28(10):2371-2381.

[4] Y Le Cun, Y Bengio, G Hinton. Deep learning[J]. Nature,2015,521:436-444.

[5] Y Le Cun. L Bottou, Y Bengio, et al. Gradient-based learning applied to document recognition[J]. Proc. IEEE, 1998.86(11):2278-2324.

[6] J Zhang, Y Zheng, D Qi. Deep spatio-temporal residual networks for citywide crowd flows prediction [C]. //in Proc. 31st AAAI Conf. Artif. Intell, Feb,2017,1655-1661.

[7] X Ma, Z Tao, Y Wang, et al. Long short-term memory neural network for traffic speed prediction using remote microwave sensor data[J]. Transp. Res. C, Emerg. Technol. ,2015,54:187-197.

[8] Z Zhao, W Chen, X Wu, et al. LSTM network: A deep learning approach for short-term traffic forecast [J]. IET Intell. Transp. Syst,2017,11(2):68-75.

[9] S Hochreiter, J. Schmidhuber. Long short-term memory[J]. Neural Comput,1997,9(8):1735-1780.

[10] S H I. Xingjian, Z Chen, H Wang, et al. Convolutional LSTM network: A machine learning approach for precipitation nowcasting[C]//in Proc. Adv. Neural Inf. Process. Syst, 2015, 802-810.

[11] T Cheng, J Haworth, J. Wang. Spatio-temporal autocorrelation of road network data[J]. J. Geograph. Syst,2012,14(4):389-413.

[12] Bing Yu, Haoteng Yin, Zhanxing Zhu. Spatio-Temporal Graph Convolutional Networks: A Deep Learning Framework for Traffic Forecasting[D]. Beijing:Peking University,2018.

[13] David K Hammond, Pierre Vandergheynst, R'emi Gribonval. Wavelets on graphs via spectral graph theory[J]. Applied and Computational Harmonic Analysis, 30(2):129-150, 2011.

[14] Michaël Defferrard, Xavier Bresson, Pierre Vandergheynst. Convolutional neural networks on graphs with fast localized spectral filtering[C]. // In NIPS,2016,3844-3852.

[15] Thomas N Kipf, Max Welling. Semi-supervised classification with graph convolutional networks [EB/OL]. arXiv preprint arXiv:2016.1609.02907.

[16] Jonas Gehring, Michael Auli, David Grangier, et al. Convolutional sequence to sequence learning[EB/OL]. arXiv preprint arXiv:1705.03122, 2017.

[17] Peres, Pedro L D, Bonatti. The linear interpolation method: a sampling theorem approach[J]. Sba: Controle & Automação Sociedade Brasileira de Automatica,2003,14(4), 439-444.

[18] Di Chai, Leye Wang, Qiang Yang. Bike Flow Prediction with Multi-Graph Convolutional Networks[D]. Hong Kong:Hong Kong University,2018.

[19] David I Shuman, Sunil K Narang, Pascal Frossard, et al. The emerging field of signal processing on graphs: Extending high-dimensional data analysis to networks and other irregular domains[J]. IEEE Signal Processing Magazine, 2013,30(3):83-98.

[20] Thomas N Kipf, Max Welling. Semi-supervised classification with graph convolutional networks [EB/OL]. arXiv preprint arXiv:1609.02907, 2016.

[21] David K Hammond, Pierre Vandergheynst, R'emi Gribonval. Wavelets on graphs via spectral graph theory[J]. Applied and Computational Harmonic Analysis, 2011,30(2):129-150.

飞行态势—管制相依网络的脆弱性分析

林福根[1] 温祥西[1,2] 吴明功[1,2] 王泽坤[3] 杨文达[1]

(1. 空军工程大学空管领航学院;2. 空军工程大学国家空管防相撞技术重点实验室;
3. 中国人民解放军32211部队)

摘 要 为了保证飞行安全,航空器在空域中发生飞行冲突时,会采取相应管制手段使冲突解除。为了让管制员更好地对存在飞行冲突的航空器进行调配,本文对管制网络、飞行态势网络两个层网络构建了飞行态势—管制相依网络模型,提出了该相依网络脆弱性的度量方法。在对两个层网络进行随机攻击和蓄意攻击的不同失效模式下删除一定比例节点,通过定义聚集系数、管制效率系数指标,分析网络链路脆弱性;创建相依效用率、效用下降比指标,剖析网络效用脆弱性。结果表明,蓄意攻击对相依网络的影响更大,管制网络的脆弱性更强,节点删除引起的级联失效以及大度值节点周围的冗余是脆弱性显著的根源。

关键词 飞行安全 相依网络 管制网络 脆弱性

0 引 言

航空系统由一个庞大的复杂系统构成,在这个系统中可分为多个复杂网络。例如,机场网络、飞行态势网络、航路网络以及管制网络等,这些复杂网络互相影响,相互依存,若某个环节出现问题,都有可能危及整个系统。问题的产生往往是由于复杂网络之间组成的相依网络具有一定的脆弱性。通过探究相依网络脆弱性,发现复杂网络间的脆弱源及其规律,对飞行安全具有重要意义。

在复杂网络体系逐步建立和不断完善的过程中,兴起的相依网络是当下研究的一个热点。根据国内外现有学者的研究,2010年,Buldyrev等[1]在Nature上发表了关于相依网络级联失效机理的文章,提出了全相依的相依网络模型。Parshani等[2]利用渗流模型,探究了网络间的耦合强度对相依网络鲁棒性的影响。蒋文君等[3]通过对国内外学者研究的整理,对多层网络级联失效的预防和恢复做了详细阐述。吴佳键等[4]提出了基于相连边的择优恢复算法,并且利用渗流理论的随机故障模型,使相依网络遭受随机故障时,恢复能力得到了极大提升。李从东等[5]考虑了节点负荷过载、相依节点失效和节点连接损失这些因素,构建基于介数耦合的相依网络级联故障模型,探究了相依网络的鲁棒性规律。Bernstein等[6]探究了电力网络在断电时荷载转移的过程中,电力网络的脆弱性。

复杂网络在交通领域的应用也有一定的研究。王灵丽等[7]提出以节点介数、节点交通量和PageRank值作为节点重要性评价指标,利用K-Means算法和随机森林加权的改进FCM算法,对复杂交通网络节点的重要性进行评价。Belkoura等[8]从航空网络的结构、动力学特征等出发,对航空复杂网络的拓扑结构提出了优化方法。曾小舟等[9]运用复杂网络理论,从度值、簇系数、介数等特征值进行实证分析,发现中国航空网络出现了以度值大的节点为中心的中心集群现象。Lordan等[10]组建了欧洲航空的多层网络,对这些网络的鲁棒性及结构进行探究,并且发现了两者之间所存在的规律。Oriol[11]等对三大航空联盟的复杂航空网络效率进行了对比分析。王兴隆等[12-17]应用华北航空网络的实例,构建了机场—航路—管制扇区三层相依网络,对其进行了相关的鲁棒性、脆弱性、拥堵性及弹性分析,形成了一套成体系的理论。Han等将导航台视为节点连接成一个复杂网络,并且对其进行脆弱性分析。

综合现有学者的研究,大多数都是倾向于机场、航路、管制扇区的复杂网络研究,鲜有对飞行态势与

基金项目:国家自然科学基金项目(71801221)。

管制网络之间的关系作出相关的论证。航空器与航空器之间的冲突关系,管制员与管制员的移交关系以及管制员对航空器的指挥关系本身就形成了一个复杂系统。对飞行态势冲突网络的脆弱性分析,有助于更好调配存在冲突的航空器;对管制网络的脆弱性分析,能够更高效分配管制席位。为此,本文构建了飞行态势—管制相依网络模型,在随机攻击及蓄意攻击两种策略下,对该网络的链路脆弱性及效用脆弱性进分析,探究其内部之间的关系。

1 飞行态势—管制相依网络模型

飞行态势网络中,小于安全距离的航空器之间存在一定的冲突关系。管制网络中,管制员与管制员之间相邻的扇区存在移交关系。

若网络与网络之间存在相依性,则该多层网络之间可以构成相依网络,构建相依网络有3个要素:组成相依网络的子网络、子网络间的相依连边及子网络的组合方式。子网络内部的连边称为相连边,子网络间的连边称为相依边,连接类型有连接边(Connectivity Links)、依赖边(Dependency Links)两种[18]。根据飞行态势网络及管制网络的现实意义,连接边适用于层网络内的节点连边,它可以表示为航空器与航空器、管制员与管制员之间的协同工作关系;依赖边适用于层网络间的节点连边,它能够表示为航空器节点依赖于管制员调配的关系。

1.1 飞行态势网络

构建相依网络,首先需要构建飞行冲突态势网络。本文利用原始映射法及复杂网络理论,将航空网络抽象成拓扑结构。根据国际民航组织8168号文件[19]规定,空中防撞系统(Airborne Collision Avoidance System,ACAS)询问其他装备应答机飞机的范围为26 km,以26km半径圆作为航空器之间的安全距离(也称为保护区),航空器个体为节点,若航空器之间的半径圆出现交叠现象,则以此作为航空器之间的影响构成冲突边。如图1所示 $v_1 \sim v_6$ 分别表示6架航空器,其中 $v_1 \sim v_5$ 半径圆有交叠现象发生,因此构成冲突边 $\{e_1,e_2,e_3,e_4,e_5\}$。因航空器 v_6 与其他半径圆没有发生交叠现象,所以不构成冲突边,由此构成了第一层网络 G_1。G_1 中的连边均为无向边,连边的权重设定为两两航空器之间距离越近权重越大,反之亦然。

1.2 管制网络

管制网络主要由管制扇区中的管制员构成,将每个扇区内的管制员抽象成节点,如图2所示,有1~4四个扇区,扇区内有节点 $\mu_1 \sim \mu_4$ 代表不同的管制员,它们之间存在管制移交关系,该关系构成连边 $\sigma_1 \sim \sigma_4$,由此构成层网络 G_2。G_2 中的连边均为无向边。该连边的权重表示为管制员的负荷强度,用点强表示,管制员的负荷强度越大,点强的数值也越大;反之亦然。当某个扇区内的节点发生异常情况或需要管制移交时,该节点可以向相邻扇区的管制员节点进行交付。

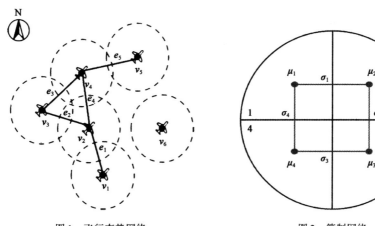

图1 飞行态势网络　　　　图2 管制网络

1.3 相依网络

依据《民用航空空中交通管理规则》(CCAR-93-R5)的管制要求,建立层网络 G_1、G_2 间的相依关系。在管制网络 G_2 中,各扇区的管制员不仅要对其所在扇区上方的航空器进行管制,还应对其相邻扇区的航空器进行监控,以防止潜在的安全隐患。因此,构建双层网络的相依连边时,管制网络中的每个节点不仅与本扇区上方航空器节点相连接,还应与相邻扇区上方的航空器节点相连接,以达到管制的目的。

如图3所示,上层为上文所构建的飞行状态网络 G_1,下层为管制网络 G_2,层网络内部关系有内部边相连,G_1 中的连边体现各航空器之间的冲突关系,G_2 中的连边为各扇区之间管制员的移交关系,在图中均用黑边相连表示;层网络与层网络之间有相依边相连(耦合边)表示管制员对航空器的指挥与调配,在图中用虚线相连表示。航空器的正常飞行依赖与管制网络的正常工作。

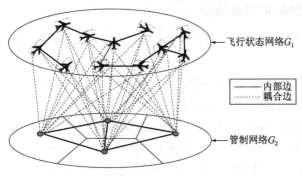

图3 相依网络示意图[20]

为了更好体现层网络与层网络之间的关系,图中虚线的相依边设置为加权、无向连接,权重用来表示管制员对航空器的管制难度。管制员对本扇区上空的航空器具有监控和指挥作用,而对相邻扇区上空的航空器通常只具备监控作用,相邻扇区的航空器越接近管制员所在扇区时,管制员的管制难度也随之上升。因此,为了更好量化它们之间的关系,现规定:

当管制员只管制本扇区上方的航空器时:

$$T'_{uv} = q_v \tag{1}$$

式中:T'_{uv}——管制难度;
u——管制员;
v——航空器。

管制员管制相邻扇区的航空器时:

$$T''_{uv} = \ln\left(\frac{1}{1-d}\right) \cdot q_v \tag{2}$$

式中:d——相邻扇区航空器接近管制员所在扇区的程度,d 的取值为 $(0,1)$,航空器与相邻扇区的距离越近 d 的取值越大。

2 相依网络的脆弱性分析

飞行—管制相依网络的自身存在一定的薄弱环节,层网络任何一个节点受到干扰,都有可能导致网络功能的失效,从而对整个网络产生影响。除此以外,失效的节点也会随着网络的特征进行传播、扩散,致使更大规模的节点失效。若网络的脆弱性是由于网络内部拓扑结构所产生的,称其为网络链路脆弱性;若网络的脆弱性是由于运行态势被随意或蓄意扰动所产生的,称其为网络效用脆弱性。本文将扰动分为随机攻击(调配)和蓄意攻击(调配),随机攻击是对目标网络随意挑选进行扰动,蓄意攻击是对目标网络按一定指令进行扰动。

2.1 网络链路脆弱性探究

2.1.1 网络链路脆弱性评价指标

定义1 聚集系数:该系数用于反映上层飞行态势网络节点邻居间的链路连接紧密程度,可表示为任意两个相邻节点间相互连接的概率。飞行态势网络中度的节点 i,若 i 的 c_i 个邻居节点之间两两相连,则节点 i 周边最多的连边数为 $c_i(c_i-1)/2$。从上文飞行态势网络的定义可知,若两架航空器之间大于安全距离则不构成连边。因此,对于度为 c_i 的节点 i,若 i 的相邻连边数为 e_i,则该节点的聚集系数为:

$$L = \frac{\sum_{i=1}^{n} e_i}{c_i(c_i-1)/2} \tag{3}$$

式中:$\sum_{i=1}^{n} e_i$——节点 i 相邻节点连边的总数,若节点 i 无连边,则该系数为零。

L 的取值在 $(0,1)$ 之间。

定义2 管制效率系数:网络的节点受到蓄意或者随机攻击后(管制员的调配或者自然演化后),可能造成某些节点孤立,这些孤立的节点会被剔除,也就是部分冲突节点的解除。此时,网络图中用1减去最大子图相连的节点数与节点总数的比值就是管制效率系数 f,即:

$$f = 1 - \frac{N_c}{n} \tag{4}$$

式中:f——管制效率系数;

N_c——在管制员进行管制(调配)后除孤立节点外还两两相连的节点数。

利用管制效率系数的大小,可以简易看出节点删除一定比例后的管制效果,根据网络层在不同攻击模式下的管制效率系数上升率进行分析,在相同比例节点失效的情况下,上升越快,则管制、调配效果越显著。

2.1.2 网络链路脆弱性分析方法

由所构建的相依网络模型之间的关系,现将其层网络节点失效机理表示如下:

①管制网络的节点失效后,所对应飞行态势冲突节点也失效。

②飞行态势网络中的节点失效后,并不会引起管制节点的失效。

③无论是上层还是下层网络的节点失效,都会导致相依网络的相依边失效。

在随机攻击与蓄意攻击两种模式下,计算当一定比例节点失效后的网络聚集系数及管制效率系数的变化情况。节点的删除比例达到60%(依据管制员的负荷压力计算模型,节点删除达60%时,管制员负荷较小)或层网络彻底失效后停止计算。网络链路脆弱性算法的具体过程如图4所示。

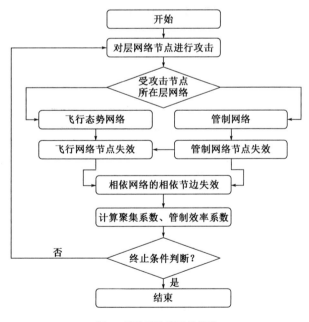

图4 网络链路脆弱性算法

2.2 网络效用脆弱性探究

2.2.1 网络效用脆弱性评价指标

定义3 相依效用率:为了考察删除节点后对相依边的影响,构建该指标可以用于评价该相依边的效用强弱,移除网络中相应的节点时,由于网络的整体权重发生改变,这些节点所对应的相依边权重随之变化,进而使得相依网络的效用受到改变。该相依效用率用下式表示:

$$\sigma = \frac{1}{\varphi_{G_1} + \varphi_{G_2}} \left(\lambda_{ij} - \sum_{\substack{i \in G_1 \\ j \in G_2}} \sigma_{ij} \right) \tag{5}$$

式中:φ_{G_1}、φ_{G_2}——上下层网络权重;

λ_{ij}——原始相依边总权重;

σ_{ij}——删除节点后上下层节点相连边的权重。

定义4 效用下降比:通过删除上下层一定比例随机或特定的网络节点,可以达到模拟网络遭受攻击的仿真效果;建立该网格受攻击前后的关系,计算该网络的效用下降比例,能够量化该网络效用变化。该效用下降比表示为下式:

$$\eta = 1 - \frac{\sigma}{\sigma_0} \tag{6}$$

式中:σ——删除节点后的相依效用率;

σ_0——最初的相依效用率。

η在$(0,1)$取值,取值越大,说明该网络效用变得越差。

2.2.2 网络效用脆弱性分析方法

分析相依网络的效用时,应分别探究上下层网络受到攻击后相依边的变化情况,由所构建的网络效用指标来量化层网络之间的关系。现将其层网络间节点失效机理表示如下:

①管制网络的节点失效后,其所对应飞行态势冲突节点发生转移,应分配到就近的管制员,负荷小的管制员节点分担更多,反之亦然。

②飞行态势网络中的节点失效后,与之相对应的管制节点的连边失效,管制员负荷减小。

③管制网络节点失效后,若转移过程中相邻管制员的负荷都已经饱和,则该网络彻底失效。

在随机攻击与蓄意攻击两种模式下,计算当一定比例节点失效后的网络相依效用率及效用下降比的变化情况。节点的删除比例达到60%或层网络彻底失效后停止计算。该算法的具体过程如图5所示。

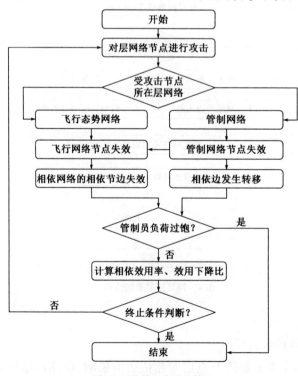

图5 网络效用脆弱性算法

3 算例仿真

为了较为真实地模拟空中情况,本文利用 Matlab 软件进行仿真,在 400km × 400km 的空域内随机生成了 80 架航空器,设置了 16 个扇区,每两架航空器小于安全距离时便会连接成边,距离越近该边的权重越大。如图 6 所示,4 号扇区内右下角的航空器与 8 号扇区右上角的航空器构成连边(图中画圈所示),这种跨扇区的连边,对管制员的指挥或监视都构成了较大的负荷强度。

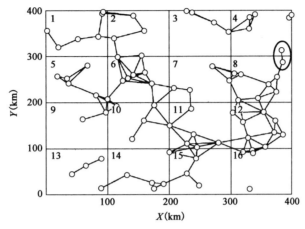

图 6 网络效用脆弱性算法

对所设定的仿真场景进行随机攻击和蓄意攻击。其中,随机攻击时对层网络所有的点随意选取进行扰动,蓄意攻击时,上层网络 G_1 按照度值的大小顺序依次进行攻击,下层网络 G_2 按照管制员负荷强度点强的大小顺序进行攻击,当有两个以上节点度值或点强相同时,任意选取其中一个进行攻击。对网络进行攻击后,计算相依网络的聚集系数和管制效率系数的数值,以便于探究其网络链路脆弱源的产生和变化趋势(攻击、干扰、失效分别代表解脱冲突、预解脱冲突、脱离高度层解脱)。

图 7、图 8 中,A 表示随机攻击,D 表示蓄意攻击,聚集系数 L、管制效率系数 f、相依效用率 σ、效用下降比 η 分别用序号 1~4 表示,A_1 表示随机攻击网络时聚集系数的数值,D_1 表示蓄意攻击网络时聚集系数的数值,以此类推。

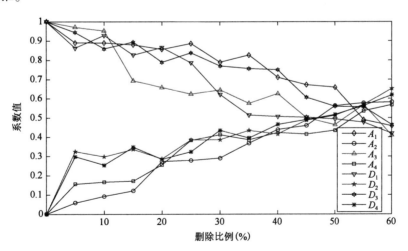

图 7 扰动上层网络时系数值的变化

若聚集系数维持在一个较高的水平上,则表示该网络的链路脆弱性没有被触发,聚集系数会随着节点删除比例的增大而平稳减小;若聚集系数在某段节点删除比例变化后发生震荡,则表明该网络链路脆弱性显著。管制效率系数会随着节点删除比例的增加而逐渐增加,若出现剧烈震荡或者减小的情况,则表明触发了网络链路的脆弱性。相依效用率随着节点删除比例的增加而减小,若出现不减反增的现象,则说明该相依网络效用脆弱性明显。效用下降比在一个稳定的网络中会随着节点删除比例的增加而增加,若在一区间段出现剧烈震荡或不增反降的现象,则说明其网络效用的脆弱性明显。

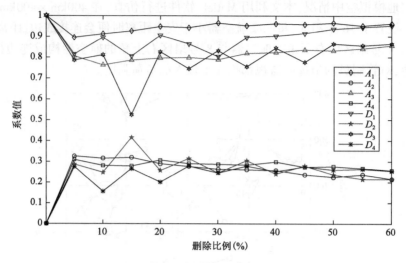

图 8 扰动下层网络时系数值的变化

如图 6 为随机扰动、蓄意扰动 G_1 时,相关定义值的变化情况。两种攻击模式下聚集系数和相依效用率的最终值都处于 0.4~0.5 之间,总体呈现下降趋势;随机攻击时除个别间隔内出现较大的浮动外,走势均较为平稳,而蓄意攻击时两值都呈现震荡下行的现象,具有显著的脆弱性。管制效率系数、效用下降比最终的值处于 0.55~0.7 之间,在随机攻击的情况下两值稳定增长;而在蓄意攻击下,前期两值大幅增长,脆弱性显著,中期缓慢增长,最终值均超过随机攻击下的系数值。

分析系数值变化的过程中,出现大幅波动或震荡的情况,一是因为删除了某些节点引起的级联失效,使得失效节点的积累而导致系数大范围的大范围波动;二是因为删除度值较大的节点时,其周围存在较多的冗余会引起数值的震荡。

如图 8 为随机扰动、蓄意扰动 G_2 时系数值的变化情况。聚集系数和相依效用率的最终取值在 0.8~1 之间,整个过程都维持在较高的值平稳波动,与之对应的 D_1、D_3 在过程中震荡较为明显,表现出较强的脆弱性,并且在 10%~20% 区间段有一个明显下降的点,是其删除了点强较大的点引起的。管制效率系数、效用下降比的值洛在 0.2~0.3 之间,并且出现系数值不增反而缓慢下降的一个过程,在蓄意攻击的过程中震荡较随机攻击较为明显。

综合图 7 与图 8 的分析可知,在两种攻击模式下,蓄意攻击网络会使得网络具有较强的脆弱性。因此,在对调配飞行冲突及分配管制员的过程中应特别注意其度值和点强较大的关键节点;在飞行—管制相依网络的脆弱性分析中,探究上层网络的脆弱性有利于更好地寻找关键节点,解决飞行冲突问题,探究下层层网络的脆弱性可以更好地分配管制员工作,对于负荷较大的管制员应给予特别的关注;管制网络与飞行网络相比,具有更强脆弱性,应给予更多的关注,保障飞行安全。

4 结 语

(1)依据管制员与航空器之间的关系,客观建立了飞行态势—管制相依网络,表达了其相互之间的耦合关系,以便于分析其网络特征。

(2)利用随机攻击和蓄意攻击两种模式删除节点,充分考虑了节点删除后权重分配的情况,定义了聚集系数、管制效率系数、相依效用率、效用下降比 4 个指标队伍网络的链路结构和效用,并进行分析。结果显示,对飞行—管制相依网络蓄意攻击时网络的脆弱性显著,并且在两层网络中,下层管制网络的脆弱性更明显。

(3)节点删除时引起的级联失效以及管制节点一对多的特点,是引起飞行—管制相依网络脆弱性的主要原因。

(4)对飞行—管制相依网络的脆弱性探究,有助于为管制员的分配提供更加有效的策略,并且能够提高管制员调配效率。

根据本文的结论可知,分析飞行—管制相依网络的脆弱性,不仅可以提高管制员的管制效率,还能够保障飞行安全。因此,根据脆弱性的产生源,深入探究相依网络的级联失效,是接下来需要进一步研究的方向。

参考文献

[1] Buldyrev S V, Parshani R, Paul G, et al. Catastrophic cascade of failures in interdependent networks[J]. Nature,2010,464(7291):1025-1028.

[2] Parshani R, Buldyrev S V, Havlin S. Interdependent networks: reducing the coupling strength leads to a change from a first to second order percolation transition[J]. Physical Review Letters (S0031-9007), 2010, 105(4): 048701.

[3] 蒋文君,刘润然,范天龙,等.多层网络级联失效的预防和恢复策略概述[J].物理学报,2020,69(08):81-91.

[4] 吴佳键,龚凯,王聪,等.相依网络上基于相连边的择优恢复算法[J].物理学报,2018,67(08):296-307.

[5] 李从东,李文博,曹策俊,等.面向级联故障的相依网络鲁棒性分析[J].系统仿真学报,2019,31(03):538-548.

[6] Bernstein A, Bienstock D, Hay D, et al. Power grid vulnerability to geographically correlated failures-Analysis and control implications[J]. IEEE INFOCOM,2014,22(4):54-67.

[7] 王灵丽,黄敏,高亮.基于聚类算法的交通网络节点重要性评价方法研究[J].交通信息与安全,2020,38(02):80-88.

[8] Belkouras, Cook A, Pena J M, et al. On the multi-dimensionality and sampling of air transport net-works [J]. Transportation Research Part E,2016,94:95-109.

[9] 曾小舟,唐笑笑,江可申.基于复杂网络理论的中国航空网络结构实证研究[J].交通运输系统工程与信息,2011,11(06):175-181.

[10] Lordan O, Sallan J M. Analyzing the multilevel structure of the European airsport network[J]. Chinese Journal of Aeronautics,2017,30(2):554-560.

[11] Oriol L, Jose M S, Pep S, et al. Robustness of the air transport net-work[J]. Transportation Research Part E,2014,68: 155-163.

[12] 王兴隆,潘维煌,赵末.空中交通相依网络的脆弱性研究[J].航空学报,2018,39(12):275-284.

[13] 王兴隆,潘维煌,赵末.华北航空相依网络统计特征与鲁棒性分析[J].科学技术与工程,2018,18(13):180-185.

[14] 王兴隆,潘维煌,赵末.航空相依网络故障传播机理研究[J].武汉理工大学学报,2018,40(06):41-46.

[15] 王兴隆,朱丽纳,石宗北.多层航线聚合网络建模及相关性分析[J].科学技术与工程2020,20(03):1243-1249.

[16] 王兴隆,潘维煌,赵末.航空相依网络的鲁棒性与拥堵性分析[J].中国安全科学学报.2018,28(02):110-115.

[17] 王兴隆,刘洋.航空多层网络弹性测度与分析[J].复杂系统与复杂性学,2020,17(02):31-38.

[18] 老松杨,王竣德,白亮.相依网络研究综述[J].国防科技大学学报,2016,38(1):122-128.

[19] ICAO. Aircraft Operation (8168)[M]. Montreal, Canada, 2018: 337-338.

[20] 李昂,聂党民,温祥西,等.管制—飞行状态相依网络模型及特性分析[J].北京航空航天大学学报,2020,46(06):1204-1213.

基于航迹预测的随机化飞行冲突探测方法

徐鑫宇　万路军　蔡　明　高志周

（空军工程大学空管领航学院）

摘　要　随机化方法是一种经典的概率型飞行冲突探测方法,但因实时性差难以应用于空中交通流量密集型空域。首先,详细分析随机化方法的数学原理,该方法在预测时间范围内按均匀分布随机抽样,并比较出最大瞬时冲突概率作为总的冲突概率,因此存在因抽取不到最大瞬时冲突概率时刻而导致准确性低,以及运算量大导致实时性差的不足。其次,提出了一种改进型随机化方法,即通过计算最小预测间距时刻,并以该时刻的瞬时冲突概率代替原随机化方法的结果。最后在仿真试验中,验证了改进型随机化方法提高了稳定性和实时性,拓展了其适用范围。

关键词　空中交通管制　飞行冲突探测　随机化方法　最小预测间距时刻　航迹预推

0　引　言

随着民用航空的飞速发展,空中交通流量日益增长,使得航空器之间发生飞行冲突的可能性大幅增加[1-2],使得飞行冲突探测变得越来越重要。对潜在的飞行冲突进行及时探测,能够为后续的飞行冲突消解奠定基础[3-4]。因此,及时高效的冲突探测对于保证飞行安全意义重大。

飞行冲突探测按照探测结果的不同可分为几何型飞行冲突探测和概率型飞行冲突探测两种[5-6]。其中,几何型飞行冲突探测只能探测航空器之间是否会发生飞行冲突,无法得到飞行冲突发生的概率。概率型飞行冲突探测能够计算出航空器之间发生飞行冲突的概率,在此基础上可以设置不同的门限值,空中交通管理系统依据不同的门限值设置不同的告警级别,管制员可以根据不同的告警级别有针对性地采用不同的飞行冲突消解手段,能够更加及时高效地化解飞行冲突风险。概率型飞行冲突探测根据冲突概率的不同计算方式,又可分为解析估计法[7]和随机化方法两种。随机化方法[8-9]在计算冲突概率的过程中使用随机函数以及随机抽样的方法,以冲突探测时间范围内的最大瞬时冲突概率作为航空器之间的冲突概率。此方法虽然能够适用于多航段航路,但其运算量大,算法实时性和准确性较差,限制了其工程应用。

本文针对随机化方法的上述缺点,通过计算航空器之间的最小预测间距以及到达最小预测间距的时刻,以该时刻的冲突概率作为最大瞬时冲突概率,提高了算法的实时性和准确性。

1　随机化方法

1.1　经典位置误差预测模型

进行飞行冲突探测,首先根据航空器航迹信息、飞行计划及高空风外界因素影响,建立航空器位置预测模型;然后根据预测位置计算航空器之间的间距是否满足安全间隔规定,以此进行冲突判定;最后输出计算结果。由于飞机在飞行过程中受到高空风、雷达量测误差、导航和飞行控制误差等多种不确定因素的影响,使得完全按照飞行计划对飞机未来航迹进行预测是不准确的,在大量空管数据分析的基础上,Paielli 和 Erzberger 提出一种经典的飞机位置预测误差模型[10],在机体坐标系下,飞机的纵向和横向位置预测误差服从零均值的高斯分布。Prandini 和 Hu[9]在该模型的基础上进行了修正,指出纵向误差的方差 $\sigma_a^2(t)$ 与时间 t 的二次方正相关,横向误差的方差 $\sigma_c^2(t)$ 与航程 $s(t)$ 的二次方正相关,直至达到一个最大值,即

基金项目:空军工程大学校长基金(XZJ2020080)。

$$\sigma_a^2(t) \sim \gamma_a^2 t^2$$
$$\sigma_c^2(t) \sim \min\{\gamma_c^2 s^2(t), \overline{\sigma}_c^2\} \tag{1}$$

基于对大量空管数据的分析,文献[9]对3个参数的估计值予以明确:$\gamma_a = 0.25$ 海里/min,$\gamma_c = 1/57$,$\overline{\sigma}_c^2 = 1$ 海里。由于航路飞行的航空器大多是等气压面高度飞行,因此本文将两航空器的运动看作水平二维平面运动,三维运动情况只需在二维基础上直接拓展。

由经典的航空器位置预测误差模型可知,航空器的预测位置是一个服从均值为 $m(t)$,协方差为 $V(t)$ 的二维高斯随机变量。均值 $m(t)$ 在不考虑高空风等不确定因素情况下根据飞行速度和时间计算出的航空器位置,可表示为

$$m(t) = x^0 + \mathbf{R}(\theta)\begin{bmatrix} vt \\ 0 \end{bmatrix} \tag{2}$$

式中:x^0——航空器初始位置;

$\mathbf{R}(\theta)$——由机体坐标系到惯性坐标系的旋转矩阵。

$$\mathbf{R}(\theta) = \begin{bmatrix} \cos\theta & -\sin\theta \\ \sin\theta & \cos\theta \end{bmatrix} \tag{3}$$

惯性坐标系下,协方差 $Q(t)$ 可表示为

$$V(t) = \mathbf{R}(\theta)\begin{bmatrix} \sigma_a^2(t) & 0 \\ 0 & \sigma_c^2(t) \end{bmatrix}\mathbf{R}(\theta)^{\mathrm{T}} \tag{4}$$

1.2 冲突概率的计算

在惯性坐标系下,两架航空器 Ⅰ 和 Ⅱ,t 时刻位置分别为 $x_1(t)$ 和 $x_2(t)$,相对位置间距为 $x_{12}(t) = |x_1(t) - x_2(t)|$。如果该间距小于水平安全间隔,则判定为存在飞行冲突;否则,不存在飞行冲突。航路区水平安全间隔为 5 海里[11]。

假设 $x_1(t)$ 和 $x_2(t)$ 是不相关的,则 $x_{12}(t)$ 服从二维高斯分布,即 $x_{12}(t) \sim N(u(t), Q(t))$,其中 $u(t)$ 为不考虑误差因素的两航空器理论间距,$Q(t)$ 为两架航空器之间间距的协方差,分别表示为:

$$\begin{cases} u(t) = m_1(t) - m_1(t) \\ Q(t) = V_1(t) + V_2(t) \end{cases} \tag{5}$$

因此,t 时刻两航空器的相对位置间距的概率分布函数为:

$$f(x_{12}(t)) = \frac{1}{2\pi\sqrt{\det[Q(t)]}}\exp\left\{-\frac{1}{2}[x_{12}(t) - u(t)]^{\mathrm{T}}Q^{-1}[t(x_{12}(t) - u(t))]\right\} \tag{6}$$

两架航空器在 t 时刻的瞬时冲突概率为:

$$P_c(t) = \int_{x_{12}(t) \leq 5} f[x_{12}(t)]\mathrm{d}x_{12}(t) \tag{7}$$

随机化方法以冲突探测时间范围 T 内最大瞬时冲突概率作为两航空器的冲突概率。T 的典型值为 20min[5],因此需要计算 1200 个时刻的瞬时冲突概率并比较出最大值,这个过程需要耗费大量时间。为提高算法的运算效率,应用随机化方法根据抽样原理,在时间 $[0, T]$ 内,按照均匀分布随机抽取 N 个秒时刻,计算 N 个秒时刻的瞬时冲突概率,来代替原来需要计算 1200 个秒时刻的瞬时冲突概率。N 的表达式为:

$$N = \left\lceil \frac{\ln\left(\frac{\delta}{2}\right)}{\ln(1-\tau)} \right\rceil \tag{8}$$

此结果能达到置信水平为 $1-\delta$,显著水平为 τ,δ、τ 的取值分别为 0.05、0.025[10]。

对于每个抽样时刻的瞬时冲突概率,利用式(7)不能直接求解,随机化方法为此设计了一种方法,以解决此难题。因为协方差矩阵 $Q(t)$ 为实对称正定矩阵,因此可以对 $Q(t)$ 进行 Cholesky 分解:

$$Q(t) = L(t)L(t)^{\mathrm{T}} \tag{9}$$

令 $\omega = L(t)^{-1}[x_{12}(t) - u(t)]$，则 ω 服从标准正态分布，用变量 ω 替换瞬时冲突概率 $P_c(t)$ 中的积分变量 $x_{12}(t)$。随机抽取 M 个 ω，即计算 t 时刻的瞬时冲突概率需要进行 M 次相对位置抽样，这样概率分布函数 $f(x_{12}(t))$ 变成 $f(\omega)$。此时计算 t 时刻两航空器的瞬时冲突概率就变为对变量 ω 在 Et 范围内求标准正态分布的积分：

$$P_c(t) = \int_{Et} \frac{1}{2\pi} e^{-\frac{1}{2}\omega^T \omega} d\omega \tag{10}$$

其中 $Et = \{\omega \in R^2 | L(t)\omega + u(t) \leq 5\}$。该方法关键在于 M 的取值，即抽取多少个 ω，使得结果可信。一般取

$$M = \left[\frac{1}{2\varepsilon^2}\ln\frac{4N}{\delta}\right] \tag{11}$$

式中：ε——参数精度，ε 取 $0.1^{[5]}$。

2 到达最小预测间距时刻 T_0 求解

本文对于随机化方法的改进在于，不再按均匀分布随机抽样 N 个时刻，而是通过相遇几何计算求得 T_0，以 T_0 时刻的瞬时冲突概率作为最大瞬时概率。改进型随机化方法使运算量大幅减少，并能够克服原随机化方法可能抽取不到最大冲突概率时刻导致计算结果不稳定的缺点，提高了算法的稳定性和实时性。为分析方便，以真北方向为 y 轴正向，以正东方向为 x 轴正向建立惯性坐标系。在惯性坐标系下，两架航空器 I 和 II 沿着各自航路飞行，飞行速度分别为 v_1 和 v_2，航向分别 C_1 和 C_2，两架航空器的初始位置分别 x_1^0 和 x_2^0。假设两航空器航向和航速均保持不变，经过时间 t 之后，航空器 I 的位置为：

$$\begin{cases} x_1(t) = x_1^0 + v_1 t\cos\alpha_1 \\ y_1(t) = y_1^0 + v_1 t\sin\alpha_1 \end{cases} \tag{12}$$

同理可得航空器 II 的位置为：

$$\begin{cases} x_2(t) = x_2^0 + v_2 t\cos\alpha_2 \\ y_2(t) = y_2^0 + v_2 t\sin\alpha_2 \end{cases} \tag{13}$$

其中，α_1、α_2 分别为航向 C_1、C_2 与 x 轴正向的夹角，由航向和坐标轴的定义可知：

$$\alpha_i = \begin{cases} 90° - C_i, & 0 \leq C_i \leq 270° \\ 450° - C_i, & 270° < C_i < 360° \end{cases}, i = 1, 2 \tag{14}$$

由式(12)、式(13)可计算经过时间 t 后，两航空器的水平间隔为：

$$\begin{aligned} D^2(t) &= [x_1(t) - x_2(t)]^2 + [y_1(t) - y_2(t)]^2 \\ &= (v_1 t\cos\alpha_1 - v_2 t\cos\alpha_2)^2 t^2 + (v_1 t\sin\alpha_1 - v_2 t\sin\alpha_2)^2 t^2 + \\ &\quad 2(x_1^0 - x_2^0)(v_1 t\cos\alpha_1 - v_2 t\cos\alpha_2)t + 2(y_1^0 - y_2^0)(v_1 t\sin\alpha_1 - v_2 t\sin\alpha_2)t + \\ &\quad (x_1^0 - x_2^0)^2 + (y_1^0 - y_2^0)^2 \end{aligned} \tag{15}$$

令

$$\begin{cases} \Delta x = x_1^0 - x_2^0 \\ \Delta y = y_1^0 - y_2^0 \\ D_0^2 = (\Delta x)^2 + (\Delta y)^2 \\ \Delta v_x = v_1 t\cos\alpha_1 - v_2 t\cos\alpha_2 \\ \Delta v_y = v_1 t\sin\alpha_1 - v_2 t\sin\alpha_2 \end{cases} \tag{16}$$

则式(15)可化简为：

$$D^2(t) = [(\Delta v_x)^2 + (\Delta v_y)^2]t^2 + 2(\Delta x \Delta v_x + \Delta y \Delta v_y)t + D_0^2 \tag{17}$$

若$(\Delta v_x)^2 + (\Delta v_y)^2 \neq 0$,则式(17)为一抛物线,且$(\Delta v_x)^2 + (\Delta v_y)^2 > 0$。此时,若$\Delta x \Delta v_x + \Delta y \Delta v_y \geq 0$,则两航空器的水平间距不断增加;若$\Delta x \Delta v_x + \Delta y \Delta v_y < 0$,则两航空器的水平间距存在一个最小值,即最小预测间距$D_{\min}$。如果$D_{\min}$小于5n mile,则两航空器存在飞行冲突[12-13]。式(17)对t进行求导,得:

$$\frac{dD^2(t)}{dt} = 2[(\Delta v_x)^2 + (\Delta v_y)^2]t + 2(\Delta x \Delta v_x + \Delta y \Delta v_y) \tag{18}$$

令式(18)等于0,解得达到最小预测间隔时刻T_0为:

$$T_0 = -\frac{\Delta x \Delta v_x + \Delta y \Delta v_y}{(\Delta v_x)^2 + (\Delta v_y)^2} \tag{19}$$

将式(19)代入式(17),解得最小预测间距$D_{\min}$为:

$$D_{\min} = \sqrt{\frac{(\Delta x \Delta v_y - \Delta y \Delta v_x)^2}{(\Delta v_x)^2 + (\Delta v_y)^2}} \tag{20}$$

3 改进型随机化方法仿真实验

为验证改进型随机化方法相比原方法在稳定性和实时性方面的优势,针对不同的相遇几何情形,设计仿真试验。设两航空器在同一高度层飞行,航速分别为480海里/h和500海里/h。实验采用的硬件环境为Inter i5-4460处理器,3.2GHz,8GB内存,Windows64位操作系统。软件平台为node.js,用JavaScript语言编写。将利用蒙特卡洛方法(Monte-Carlo Method)得到的结果作为参考,检验改进型随机化方法是否提高了稳定性与实时性。仿真试验的设计思路如下。

步骤1:对于给定了飞行计划的两航空器,分别利用与飞行冲突检测方法无关的航迹模拟方法模拟出未来20min内的航迹。

步骤2:反复利用步骤1生成上述两航空器在未来20min内的多组模拟航迹对,模拟出受航迹误差影响,两航空器在同一组飞行计划下冲突概率。在试验中,为了使蒙特卡洛方法具有统计规律性,对于每一组飞行计划,模拟出2000组模拟航迹对。在每一组模拟航迹中,若两航空器最小预测间距小于安全间隔即认为存在飞行冲突。统计出2000组模拟航迹中发生飞行冲突的组数为numbers_conflict。numbers_conflict/2000,即为蒙特卡洛方法得到的参考冲突概率值。

步骤3:一组飞行计划代表了两航空器间的一种相遇几何。在多种典型相遇几何情况下,将改进的随机化方法、原随机化方法结果与蒙特卡洛方法计算得到的冲突概率值进行对比,并比较运算时间。

试验1:两航空器航向交叉角为90°,最小预测间距为5n mile,到达最小预测间距时刻的仿真步长为0.5min,变化区间[3min,18min]。上述3种方法在此相遇几何变化范围内的仿真结果如图1所示。

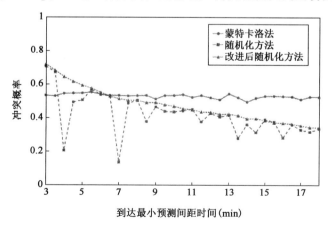

图1 3种方法在试验1中的结果对比

试验 2：两航空器航向交叉角为 90°，到达最小预测间距的时刻为 8min，仿真设置的最小预测间距步长为 0.5n mile，变化区间[0n mile,8n mile]。上述 3 种方法在此相遇几何变化范围内的仿真结果如图 2 所示。

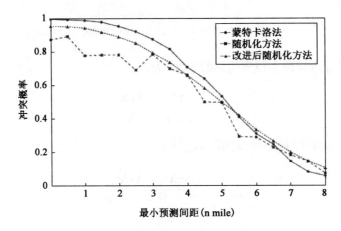

图 2 3 种方法在试验 2 中的结果对比

试验 3：两航空器最小预测间距为 5n mile，到达最小预测间隔的时刻为 8min，航向交叉角变化步长为 5°，变化区间[0°,180°]。上述 3 种方法在此相遇几何变化范围内的仿真结果如图 3 所示。

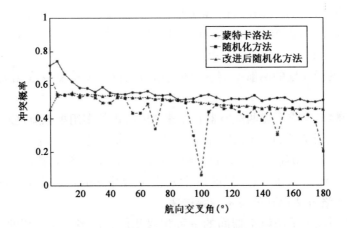

图 3 3 种方法在试验 3 中的结果对比

试验 4：两航空器航向交叉角为 130°，到达最小预测间距时刻为 6min，最小预测间距的仿真步长为 0.5n mile，变化区间[0n mile,8n mile]。上述 3 种方法在此相遇几何变化范围内的探测结果如图 4 所示。

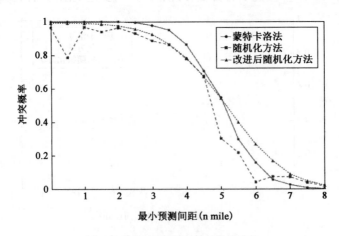

图 4 3 种方法在试验 4 中的结果对比

3 种方法在上述 4 个仿真试验中的运算耗时(单位为 s)对比如表 1 所示。

表 1　3 种方法运算耗时(s)对比

试验号	蒙特卡洛法	随机化方法	改进的随机化方法
1	1.6716	0.0836	0.0015
2	1.3879	0.0843	0.0014
3	1.4807	0.0832	0.0015
4	1.2686	0.0828	0.0015

从上述 4 个不同相遇几何变化范围的仿真试验结果，分析出改进型随机化方法得到的概率曲线，消除了原随机化方法因抽取不到最大冲突概率时刻而导致的冲突概率值不应有的突变，并且更符合蒙特卡洛方法概率曲线的变化趋势，使得计算得到的冲突概率更加稳定、准确。从表 1 可以看出，蒙特卡洛方法运算时间太长，运算效率低，而改进的随机化方法相比原方法，计算效率大大提高，算法的实时性更强。

4　结　语

本文提出了一种基于航迹预推的改进型随机化飞行冲突探测方法。分析原随机化方法的不足；针对其稳定性低，实时性差的缺点，在不考虑位置误差的前提下，通过航迹预推计算出最小预测间距及到达最小预测间距的时刻，以该时刻的冲突概率作为总的冲突概率，使得计算量大大减小，并克服了原随机化方法因可能抽取不到冲突概率最大时刻导致计算结果出现突变误差，提高了冲突探测的稳定性与实时性。通过仿真试验，验证了改进型随机化方法在稳定性与实时性方面的优势，能够满足飞行流量密集地区对飞行冲突探测功能的需求。

参考文献

［1］Tang J. Conflict Detection and Resolution for Civil Aviation：A Literature Survey［J］. IEEE Aerospace and Electronic Systems Magazine，2019，34(10)：20-35.

［2］Ayhan S，Costas P，Samet H. Prescriptive Analytics System for Long-range Aircraft Conflict Detection and Resolution［C］// Proceedings of the 26th ACM SIGSPATIAL International Conference on Advances in Geographic Information Systems. 2018：239-248.

［3］JIANG Xu-rui，WEN Xiang-xi，WU Ming-gong，et al. A SVM Approach of Aircraft Conflict Detection in Free Flight［J］. Journal of Advanced Transportation，2018：1-9.

［4］ZHANG Yi-fan，ZHANG Ming，YU Jue. Real-time Flight Conflict Detection and Release Based on Multi-Agent System［J］. IOP Conference Series：Earth and Environmental Science，2018，108：032053.

［5］孙梦圆，田勇，叶博嘉，等. 飞行冲突探测与解脱方法研究综述［J］. 航空计算技术，2019，49(05)：125-128.

［6］石磊. 空中交通管理中概率型飞行冲突探测算法研究［D］. 天津：天津大学，2014.

［7］Paielli R A，Erzberger H. Conflict Probability Estimation for Free Flight［J］. Journal of Guidance，Control，and Dynamics，1997，20(3)：588-596.

［8］Prandini M，Lygeros J，Nilim A，et al. Randomized Algorithms for Probabilistic Aircraft Conflict Detection［C］. // In Proceedings of the 38th IEEE Conference on Decision and Control，1999，3：2444-2449.

［9］Prandini M，Hu J，Lygeros J，et al. A Probabilistic Approach to Aircraft Conflict Detection［J］. IEEE Transactions on Intelligent Transportation Systems，2000，1(4)：199-220.

［10］Erzberger H，Paielli R A，Isaacson D R，et al. Conflict Detection and Resolution in the Presence of Prediction Error［C］. // In 1st USA/Europe Air Traffic Management R&D Seminar，Saclay，France. 1997：17-20.

[11] International Civil Aviation Organization. Procedures for Air Navigation Services-air Traffic Management [S]. 2007.
[12] 尹成义,谭安胜. 基于航空器航迹预推的飞行冲突探测模型[J]. 电光与控制, 2015, 22(12): 20-23.
[13] 张宏宏, 甘旭升, 李昂, 等. 基于速度障碍法的无人机避障与航迹恢复策略[J]. 系统工程与电子技术, 2020, 42(08): 1759-1767.

世界繁忙机场空管运行分析框架研究

许健武[1] 许超前[2] 唐奇志[2] 和平[2] 李文峰[2]

(1. 中国民航管理干部学院; 2. 中国民用航空局华北空管局)

摘 要 繁忙机场是航空运输系统的重要组成,对提升我国空管运行效率、改善航班正常率、增强国际竞争力等具有重大影响和重要作用。本文尝试综合宏观与微观两个研究视角,从新视角对世界繁忙机场空管运行进行研究,构建繁忙机场空管运行的分析框架。首先,基于2006—2016年的实际运行指标,建立统一的研究数据集,分析世界范围的繁忙机场历史演化、发展趋势,筛选出典型的世界繁忙机场作为进一步的研究对象。进而,从候机楼构型、跑道构型、机场容量、运行效率和飞行程序等5个主要影响因素,进行相关性分析,开展世界繁忙机场的比较研究。本文通过实证研究结果,为我国繁忙机场空管运行研究提供借鉴,为空管运行单位提供决策依据。

关键词 繁忙机场 空管运行 分析框架 相关性分析 比较研究

0 引 言

繁忙机场是指旅客运输量、货邮运输量或飞机起降架次达到一定规模的机场,是航空运输系统的重要组成。2019年,北京首都国际机场、上海浦东国际机场、上海虹桥国际机场、广州白云国际机场四大繁忙机场的旅客吞吐量、货邮吞吐量、飞机起降架次分别占全国237个民用航空机场的21.8%、46.4%和16.0%。而且,北京首都国际机场在旅客吞吐量排名世界第2位,上海浦东国际机场、广州白云国际机场等也已经入围前20位,在世界繁忙机场中占据重要地位。此外,从2006—2018年的空中交通管理(以下简称"空管")运行来看,2015年全国航班正常率最低降至68.33%,上述四大繁忙机场问题尤其突出,均排名全国放行正常率最低的20名,而平均航班到达延误均超过20min。因此,繁忙机场对提升我国空管运行效率、改善航班正常率、增强国际竞争力等具有重大影响和重要作用。

繁忙机场空管运行受到了世界航空运输领域的广泛关注。2012年,国际民航组织全球航行计划(Doc 9750)、组块升级计划[5-6]中将"机场运行——全面的进场、离场和场面管理"作为关键改进领域。欧洲单一天空计划的总体发展计划和美国新一代航空运输系统[7-8]的最新实施路线图,均将繁忙机场空管运行作为关键领域,提出"高密度进场/离场运行、等效目视运行""一体化的机场运行、新的间隔模式"等。中国民用航空局空中交通管理局2016年发布了《中国民航空管现代化战略》,2019年发布了实施路线图,繁忙机场运行是空管现代化战略的八大运行概念之一。研究界对繁忙机场空管运行的具体研究工作,可以分为"宏观"和"微观"两个视角。国际机场协会(Airports Council International, ACI)从宏观视角,通过系统研究旅客运输量、货邮运输量或飞机起降架次等指标,每年发布世界繁忙机场排名、研究报告。此外,研究者从微观视角分析了影响繁忙机场空管运行的主要因素,例如,候机楼设计、跑滑系统设计、管制员工作负荷、飞行程序设计、终端区空域、扇区结构等。然而,宏观视角的研究侧重评估机场整体状况、运营服务质量,缺少从空管运行角度的深入比较分析,难以为空管运行单位提供直接参考。微观视角的研究对单个机场、单个因素进行空管运行的定量分析,缺少多个因素的联动、多个机场的比较,尚未勾勒出繁忙机场空管运行的"整体图景"。

因此,本文尝试从新视角开展研究,综合宏观与微观两个研究视角,系统构建繁忙机场空管运行的研究框架。首先,分析世界范围的繁忙机场历史演化、发展趋势,通过系统采集2006—2016年期间国际机场协会、欧洲、亚洲、美国等繁忙机场的运行数据、航行资料汇编等,建立统一的研究数据集,进而筛选出典型的世界繁忙机场作为进一步的研究对象。其次,本文从候机楼构型、跑道构型、机场容量、运行效率和飞行程序等5个维度,开展世界繁忙机场的比较研究,通过旅客运输量、货邮运输量或飞机起降架次等指标的相关性分析、比较研究,建立世界繁忙机场空管运行分析框架。

本文立足世界繁忙机场的宏观角度,旨在为我国繁忙机场空管运行研究提供借鉴,为空管运行单位提供决策依据。本文第1章建立统一的研究数据集,筛选出典型世界繁忙机场作为进一步的研究对象。第2章提出繁忙机场空管运行的分析框架,并从候机楼构型、跑道构型、机场容量、运行效率和飞行程序等进行量化研究。第3章给出结论。

1 世界繁忙机场的历史演化和发展趋势

通过系统采集2006—2016年期间国际机场协会、欧洲、亚洲、美国等繁忙机场的运行数据、航行资料汇编等数据,建立统一的研究数据集,筛选出29个世界繁忙机场作为进一步的研究对象。图1给出了世界繁忙机场列表(以"城市名—机场三字码"表示),考虑旅客运输量、货邮运输量和起降架次等国际机场协会指标中,任意单项指标排名至少1次进入世界前10名的机场。可以看出,世界繁忙机场中,美国共14个、亚洲共10个、欧洲共5个。进一步考虑任意单项指标排名至少1次进入世界前5名的世界繁忙机场,美国共8个、亚洲共7个、欧洲共2个。反映出世界繁忙机场的地理、国别分布情况,可以看出美国繁忙机场的综合指标占有主导地位,亚洲繁忙机场的综合指标在规模上具有一定优势(7个入围机场排名前5),欧洲繁忙机场总体数量较少,其他地区尚无排名进入前10位的繁忙机场。从历史演化维度分析,如图2所示,美国繁忙机场数量呈下降趋势(下降23.5%),亚洲繁忙机场数量明显上升趋势(增长42.9%),欧洲繁忙机场数量基本持平。

序号	前1名	前2名	前3名	前4名	前5名	前6名	前7名	前8名	前9名	前10名
1	亚特兰大	亚特兰大	亚特兰大	亚特兰大	亚特兰大	亚特兰大	亚特兰大	亚特兰大	亚特兰大	亚特兰大
2	香港	香港	香港	香港	香港	香港	香港	香港	香港	香港
3	孟菲斯	孟菲斯	孟菲斯	孟菲斯	孟菲斯	孟菲斯	孟菲斯	孟菲斯	孟菲斯	孟菲斯
4	芝加哥	芝加哥	芝加哥	芝加哥	芝加哥	芝加哥	芝加哥	芝加哥	芝加哥	芝加哥
5		北京	北京	北京	北京	北京	北京	北京	北京	北京
6		伦敦	伦敦	伦敦	伦敦	伦敦	伦敦	伦敦	伦敦	伦敦
7			迪拜	迪拜	迪拜	迪拜	迪拜	迪拜	迪拜	迪拜
8			安克拉治	安克拉治	安克拉治	安克拉治	安克拉治	安克拉治	安克拉治	安克拉治
9			上海	上海	上海	上海	上海	上海	上海	上海
10			达拉斯	达拉斯	达拉斯	达拉斯	达拉斯	达拉斯	达拉斯	达拉斯
11			洛杉矶	洛杉矶	洛杉矶	洛杉矶	洛杉矶	洛杉矶	洛杉矶	洛杉矶
12				东京	东京	东京	东京	东京	东京	东京
13				仁川	仁川	仁川	仁川	仁川	仁川	仁川
14					巴黎	巴黎	巴黎	巴黎	巴黎	巴黎
15					拉斯维加斯	拉斯维加斯	拉斯维加斯	拉斯维加斯	拉斯维加斯	拉斯维加斯
16					东京	东京	东京	东京	东京	东京
17					丹佛	丹佛	丹佛	丹佛	丹佛	丹佛
18						休斯顿	休斯顿	休斯顿	休斯顿	休斯顿
19						夏洛特	夏洛特	夏洛特	夏洛特	夏洛特
20							法兰克福	法兰克福	法兰克福	法兰克福
21							路易斯维尔	路易斯维尔	路易斯维尔	路易斯维尔
22								菲尼克斯	菲尼克斯	菲尼克斯
23								阿姆斯特丹	阿姆斯特丹	阿姆斯特丹
24									雅加达	雅加达
25										马德里
26										新加坡
27										迈阿密
28										台北
29										费城

注:根据ACI统计数据
2006—2016年,综合指标(旅客运输量、货物运输量、或起降架次)进入世界前10名的机场共29个,其中,美国14个,亚洲10个,欧洲5个;
2006—2016年,综合指标(旅客运输量、货物运输量、或起降架次)进入世界前5名的机场共17个,其中,美国8个,亚洲7个,欧洲2个。

图1 按综合指标排名的世界繁忙机场(2006—2016年)

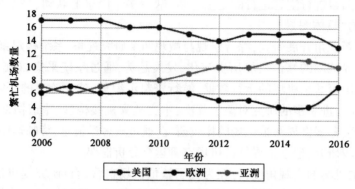

图2 世界繁忙机场历史演化(2006—2016年)

图3、图4、图5分别从旅客运输量、货邮运输量和起降架次等指标,分析了世界繁忙机场的发展特征。从旅客运输量来看,在2006—2016年期间共有14个机场排名至少1次进入世界前10名,其中,美国共5个、亚洲共5个、欧洲共4个,亚洲繁忙机场数量与美国繁忙机场数量持平,多于欧洲繁忙机场数量,表明了亚洲繁忙机场旅客运输量方面的优势和潜力。从货邮运输量来看,在2006—2016年期间共有13个机场排名至少1次进入世界前10名,其中,美国机场4个、亚洲机场7个、欧洲机场2个,可以看出亚洲繁忙机场在货邮运输量方面的优势。从起降架次来看,在2006—2016年期间共有15个机场排名至少1次进入世界前10名,其中,美国机场10个、欧洲机场3个亚洲机场2个。可以看出美国繁忙机场在起降架次方面的明显优势。

序号	前1名	前2名	前3名	前4名	前5名	前6名	前7名	前8名	前9名	前10名
1	亚特兰大	亚特兰大	亚特兰大	亚特兰大	亚特兰大	亚特兰大	亚特兰大	亚特兰大	亚特兰大	亚特兰大
2		芝加哥	芝加哥	芝加哥	芝加哥	芝加哥	芝加哥	芝加哥	芝加哥	芝加哥
3			伦敦	伦敦	伦敦	伦敦	伦敦	伦敦	伦敦	伦敦
4				北京	北京	北京	北京	北京	北京	北京
5					迪拜	迪拜	迪拜	迪拜	迪拜	迪拜
6						东京	东京	东京	东京	东京
7							洛杉矶	洛杉矶	洛杉矶	洛杉矶
8							巴黎	巴黎	巴黎	巴黎
9							达拉斯	达拉斯	达拉斯	达拉斯
10								法兰克福	法兰克福	法兰克福
11								香港	香港	香港
12	注:根据ACI统计数据							雅加达	雅加达	雅加达
13	2006—2016年,旅客运输量进入世界前10名的机场共14个,其中,美国5个、亚洲5个,欧洲4个;									丹佛
14	2006—2016年,旅客运输量进入世界前5名的机场共8个,其中,美国3个、亚洲3个,欧洲2个。									马德里

图3 按旅客运输量指标排名的世界繁忙机场(2006—2016年)

序号	前1名	前2名	前3名	前4名	前5名	前6名	前7名	前8名	前9名	前10名
1	香港	香港	香港	香港	香港	香港	香港	香港	香港	香港
2	孟菲斯	孟菲斯	孟菲斯	孟菲斯	孟菲斯	孟菲斯	孟菲斯	孟菲斯	孟菲斯	孟菲斯
3			安克拉治	安克拉治	安克拉治	安克拉治	安克拉治	安克拉治	安克拉治	安克拉治
4			上海	上海	上海	上海	上海	上海	上海	上海
5				仁川	仁川	仁川	仁川	仁川	仁川	仁川
6						东京	东京	东京	东京	东京
7						巴黎	巴黎	巴黎	巴黎	巴黎
8						迪拜	迪拜	迪拜	迪拜	迪拜
9								法兰克福	法兰克福	法兰克福
10								路易斯维尔	路易斯维尔	路易斯维尔
11	注:根据ACI统计数据									新加坡
12	2006—2016年,货物运输量进入世界前10名的机场13个,其中,亚洲7个,美国4个,欧洲2个;									迈阿密
13	2006—2016年,货物运输量进入世界前5名的机场共8个,其中,亚洲5个,美国2个,欧洲1个。									台北

图4 按货邮运输量指标排名的世界繁忙机场(2006—2016年)

序号	前1名	前2名	前3名	前4名	前5名	前6名	前7名	前8名	前9名	前10名
1	亚特兰大	亚特兰大	亚特兰大	亚特兰大	亚特兰大	亚特兰大	亚特兰大	亚特兰大	亚特兰大	亚特兰大
2	芝加哥	芝加哥	芝加哥	芝加哥	芝加哥	芝加哥	芝加哥	芝加哥	芝加哥	芝加哥
3			达拉斯	达拉斯	达拉斯	达拉斯	达拉斯	达拉斯	达拉斯	达拉斯
4			洛杉矶	洛杉矶	洛杉矶	洛杉矶	洛杉矶	洛杉矶	洛杉矶	洛杉矶
5					拉斯维加斯	拉斯维加斯	拉斯维加斯	拉斯维加斯	拉斯维加斯	拉斯维加斯
6					丹佛	丹佛	丹佛	丹佛	丹佛	丹佛
7					北京	北京	北京	北京	北京	北京
8						休斯顿	休斯顿	休斯顿	休斯顿	休斯顿
9						夏洛特	夏洛特	夏洛特	夏洛特	夏洛特
10							巴黎	巴黎	巴黎	巴黎
11								菲尼克斯	菲尼克斯	菲尼克斯
12								阿姆斯特丹	阿姆斯特丹	阿姆斯特丹
13									上海	上海
14										费城
15										伦敦

注：根据ACI统计数据
2006—2016年，起降架次进入世界前10名的机场共15个，其中，美国10个，欧洲3个，亚洲2个；
2006—2016年，起降架次进入世界前5名的机场共7个，其中，美国6个，亚洲1个。

图5 按起降架次指标排名的世界繁忙机场(2006—2016年)

2 世界繁忙机场空管运行分析框架

2.1 分析框架

从候机楼构型、跑道构型、机场容量、运行效率和飞行程序等维度，构建世界繁忙机场空管运行分析框架。其中，候机楼构型包括线型(L型)、中置型(C型)、指廊型(P型)和卫星型(S型)等，跑道构型包括平行跑道、交叉跑道、V型跑道、混合跑道等，对29个繁忙机场的主要指标(旅客运输量、货邮运输量或飞机起降架次)的相关性进行量化分析，讨论航站楼构型、跑道构型对繁忙机场空管运行的影响。进一步针对机场容量、运行效率进行研究。这里采用美国联邦航空局提供的机场跑道容量(极值)，选择10个典型的繁忙机场，根据起降架次与机场容量的比值，比较繁忙机场空管运行的总体运行效率和运行饱和程度。此外，通过机场进港点数量、离港点数量、飞行程序的加权平均距离等指标，比较机场对之间的飞行程序，并采用北京机场与亚特兰大机场实际航行资料汇编数据，进行实证研究。基于以上5个维度，具体比较繁忙机场空管运行受基础设施、空域结构、容量效率等方面的影响。

2.2 候机楼构型相关性分析

表1给出了29个繁忙机场的候机楼构型。可以看出，繁忙机场主要采用C型、L型、P型等构型，较少采用S型。这里，若机场只包括一种候机楼构型，例如，香港机场为P型候机楼。若机场包括多种不同候机楼构型，则标示出主要航站楼构型，例如，亚特兰大机场，以C型候机楼为主。

世界繁忙机场候机楼和跑道构型特征 表1

序号	繁忙机场	候机楼数量	候机楼构型	跑道数量	跑道构型
1	亚特兰大	7	C型	5	平行
2	香港	2	P型	2	平行
3	孟菲斯	1	P型	4	混合
4	芝加哥	4	L型	8	混合
5	北京	3	S型	3	平行
6	伦敦	4	P型	2	平行
7	迪拜	3	L型	2	平行
8	安克拉治	2	L型	3	交叉
9	上海	2	C型	4	平行
10	达拉斯	5	L型	7	混合
11	洛杉矶	9	P型	4	平行
12	东京	3	C型	4	混合
13	仁川	2	C型	3	平行

续上表

序号	繁忙机场	候机楼数量	候机楼构型	跑道数量	跑道构型
14	巴黎	3	L型	4	平行
15	拉斯维加斯	2	S型	4	混合
16	东京	2	P型	2	平行
17	丹佛	1	C型	6	混合
18	休斯敦	4	S型	5	混合
19	夏洛特	1	S型	4	混合
20	法兰克福	2	P型	4	V型
21	路易斯维尔	1	S型	3	交叉
22	菲尼克斯	2	P型	3	平行
23	阿姆斯特丹	1	P型	6	混合
24	雅加达	3	L型	2	平行
25	马德里	4	L型	4	V型
26	新加坡	3	P型	3	平行
27	迈阿密	3	P型	4	混合
28	台北	2	L型	2	平行
29	费城	7	S型	3	混合

从图6可以看出,2006—2016年期间,不同候机楼构型条件下,繁忙机场旅客运输量、货邮运输量、起降架次平均值随时间变化的曲线分别如图6a)、b)、c)所示。可以看出,C型候机楼构型条件下,旅客运输量平均值最高,而S型候机楼构型条件下,旅客运输量平均值最低,说明C型候机楼机场更适合大规模旅客运输。P型候机楼构型条件下,货邮运输量平均值最高,而S型候机楼构型条件下,货邮运输量平均值最低,说明P型候机楼机场更适合大规模货邮运输。C型候机楼构型条件下,起降架次平均值最高,而S型候机楼构型条件下,起降架次平均值最低,但4种构型差异较小,而且近年来差异在减小,说明C型候机楼机场较为适合大规模起降架次。

2.3 跑道构型相关性分析

表1给出了29个繁忙机场的跑道构型。在2006—2016年期间,不同跑道构型条件下,繁忙机场旅客运输量、货邮运输量、起降架次平均值随时间变化的曲线分别如图7a)、b)、c)所示。可以看出,平行跑道构型条件下,旅客运输量平均值最高,而V型跑道构型条件下,旅客运输量平均值最低,说明平行跑道机场更适合大规模旅客运输。混合跑道构型条件下,货邮运输量平均值最高,而V型跑道构型条件下,货邮运输量平均值最低。平行跑道构型条件下,单跑道货邮运输量平均值最高,而V型跑道构型条件下,单跑道货邮运输量平均值最低。因此可以看出,混合跑道、平行跑道在繁忙机场货邮运输中具有相对明显的优势。

2.4 机场容量与运行效率比较

表2给出了10个典型繁忙机场在目视规则、仪表规则下的小时跑道容量估计值,以及2014年机场年起降架次统计数据。其中,亚特兰大、芝加哥、洛杉矶、达拉斯、丹佛、夏洛特等美国采用美国联邦航空局提供的评估数据[15-16]。北京按2条窄距(760m)1条宽距(1036m)平行跑道,目视规则下146~184架次/h,仪表规则下111~120架次/h,进行容量估计。阿姆斯特丹按4条V型跑道,2条平行跑道760m间隔,目视规则下129~158架次/h,仪表规则下56~60架次/h,进行容量估计。上海、巴黎均按2条窄距平行跑道(760m间隔),目视规则下94~121架次/h,仪表规则下56~60架次/h,进行容量估计。

可以看出,北京、亚特兰大、芝加哥、洛杉矶等机场的年起降架次—跑道容量比最高,反映了这些繁忙机场空管运行在较高饱和度条件下,仍保持了高效率运行。

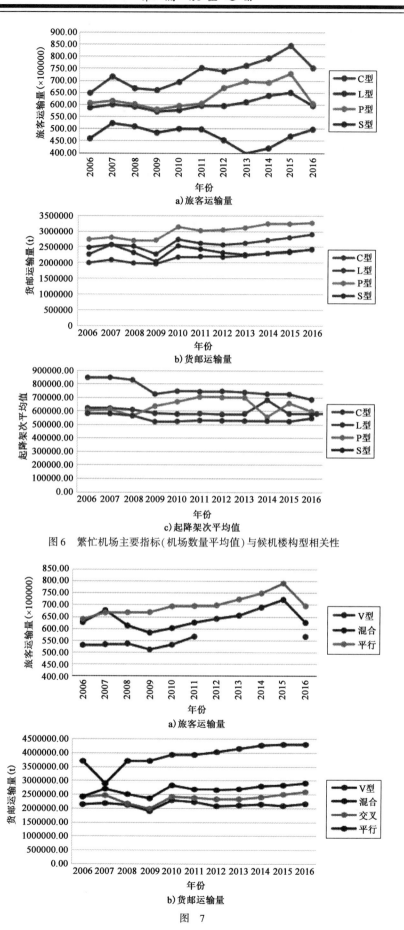

图6 繁忙机场主要指标(机场数量平均值)与候机楼构型相关性

图 7

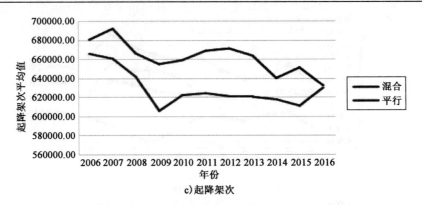

c) 起降架次

图7 繁忙机场主要指标(机场数量平均值)与跑道构型相关性

典型繁忙机场的年起降架次—跑道容量比(2014年)　　表2

序号	繁忙机场	小时跑道容量估计值（目视规则）	年起降架次	年起降架次—跑道容量比（目视—仪表）
1	亚特兰大	216～226	868359	67.28%～83.07%
2	芝加哥	214～225	881933	68.80%～87.29%
3	洛杉矶	167～176	636706	63.57%～79.00%
4	达拉斯	226～264	679820	47.51%～68.48%
5	北京	146～184	581773	60.37%～86.25%
6	丹佛	262～298	565525	34.58%～41.47%
7	夏洛特	176～182	545178	52.15%～65.51%
8	阿姆斯特丹	202～243	439549	33.83%～45.34%
9	上海	189～242	401861	31.93%～59.07%
10	巴黎	189～242	469026	37.27%～68.94%

2.5 飞行程序比较

根据北京与亚特兰大的航行资料汇编数据进行比较,统计北京与亚特兰大的进港点数量、离港点数量、飞行程序的加权平均距离等指标(表3)。可以看出,亚特兰大的进港程序中,共7个进港点、34个跑道方向,与北京6个进港点、33个跑道方向非常接近。然而,亚特兰大的离港程序中,共33个离港点、268个跑道方向,远多于北京8个离港点、85个跑道方向,说明相比北京,亚特兰大具有更好的空域环境、更少的空域限制。亚特兰大7个进港程序的加权平均距离为57.5km,仅为北京6个进港程序的加权平均距离128.4km的44.8%。而亚特兰大33个离港程序的加权平均距离为81.4km,为北京8个离港程序的加权平均距离96.6km的84.3%,说明相比北京,亚特兰大具有更短距离的进离港飞行程序,空管运行的复杂度较小。

北京与亚特兰大飞行程序比较　　表3

繁忙机场	进港程序		离港程序	
	进港点数量/跑道方向数量	加权平均距离(km)	离港点数量/跑道方向数量	加权平均距离(km)
亚特兰大	7/34	57.5	33/268	79.17
北京	6/33	128.4	8/85	96.6

3 结语

本文围绕世界繁忙机场空管运行分析框架开展研究,分析世界范围的繁忙机场历史演化、发展趋势,通过系统采集2006—2016年期间国际机场协会、欧洲、亚洲、美国等繁忙机场的运行数据、航行资料汇编等,建立了统一的研究数据集,进而筛选出29个典型繁忙机场作为进一步的研究对象。本文从候机楼构型、跑道构型、机场容量、运行效率和飞行程序等5个维度,开展世界繁忙机场的比较研究,通过旅客运输量、货邮运输量或飞机起降架次等指标的相关性分析、比较研究,建立了世界繁忙机场空管运行分析框架。本文通过量化分析、比较研究,为我国繁忙机场空管运行研究提供借鉴,为空管运行单位提供决策依据。

参考文献

[1] 中国民用航空局. 2019年民航机场生产统计公报[EB/OL]. 2020, http://www.caac.gov.cn/XXGK/XXGK/TJSJ/202003/t20200309_201358.html.

[2] 中国民用航空局. 2015年民航机场生产统计公报[EB/OL]. 2016, http://www.caac.gov.cn/XXGK/XXGK/TJSJ/201603/t20160331_30105.html.

[3] 中国民用航空局. 中国民航航空系统组块升级(ASBU)发展与实施策略[EB/OL]. 2015, http://www.ccaonline.cn/wp-content/uploads/2018/01/9e8ac68e1871179614f3.pdf.

[4] 李欣, 成辉, 赵元超. 枢纽机场航站楼构型分析模式研究[J]. 工业建筑, 2016(9):56-61.

[5] 张洪海, 范围, 廖志华, 等. 平行跑道运行模式对终端区交通流特性的影响研究[J]. 交通运输系统工程与信息, 2017(3):198-204.

[6] 徐肖豪, 于跃, 黄宝军, 等. 不同运行模式的近距平行跑道容量分析[J]. 中国民航大学学报, 2012, 30(6):34-39.

[7] 韩松臣, 胡明华, 蒋兵, 等. 扇区容量与管制员工作负荷的关系研究[J]. 空中交通管理, 2000, (6):42-45.

[8] 王超. 飞行程序运行评估的理论方法及仿真应用研究[D]. 南京:南京航空航天大学, 2012.

不同温度和湍流强度下尾涡演化规律的大涡模拟研究

潘卫军　罗玉明　韩　帅　王靖开

(中国民用航空飞行学院)

摘　要　随着中国民航快速发展,如今的尾流间隔已成为制约航班量增长和机场运行效率的关键因素。为了能够缩短尾流间隔,针对航空器尾流演化机理的研究逐渐成为民航研究重点之一。鉴于此,本文通过大涡模拟方法,计算航空器在不同的温度和湍流强度下尾流的耗散情况,通过计算分析得到了不同条件下尾流的耗散机理,并得到航空器尾流的涡量、Q准则等量化参数随时间的变化关系,最终得到以下结论:温度越高尾流耗散速度越快,在20℃时尾流强度在5s内可以减少70%;湍流强度越大,尾流耗散速度越快,10%的湍流强度下尾流强度在5s左右同样减少70%。

关键词　空管运行安全与效能　尾流演化机理　计算流体力学　航空器尾流　尾流间隔

0　引　言

中国经过十几年发展已经成为航班吞吐量的大国,然而随着吞吐量的不断增长,枢纽机场也将迎来容量上限。因此如何科学合理的增加航班量并保障机场运行效率,成为民航业亟待解决的问题。尾流间

基金项目:国家自然科学基金(U1733203),民航专业项目(TM2019-16-1/3)。

隔是影响机场容量和运行效率的一个关键因素,为了确保飞行安全我国往往采用最严格的尾流间隔,这导致两架飞机之间的水平间隔比较大,制约了航班量的增长。因此通过对不同环境条件下尾流耗散机理进行研究,掌握尾流演化机理,以此判断现有的尾流间隔是否有缩减的空间,对于提高机场容量和运行效率具有非常重要的意义。

国内外许多学者都对飞机尾流的产生、发展和耗散机理进行了研究。国外的Crow[1]首先研究了一对涡在相互诱导作用下的最佳失稳模式,指出了尾涡的长波不稳定性是尾涡快速衰减的机制之一。Greene[2]首次提出了尾涡估计模型,假定了尾流单位长度脉冲与黏性阻力、浮力及湍流耗散等有关,进而确定尾流的环量、速度及垂向位置等。此后,Corjon与Poinsot[3]通过增加考虑近地面及侧向风的影响,对Greene的模型进行了完善。Sarpkaya[4]排除了Greene所提出的模型中性阻力这一因素,并利用涡流耗散率代替湍流动能的方法给出了湍流耗散的经验公式。国内学者张宇轩等[5]针对近区尾涡的演化耗散过程以及其对气动力的影响进行了探讨。崔桂香等[6]提出了升力面尾涡生成方法,用于对飞机尾涡在大气中的演化特性进行研究,并以此构建了尾流快速预测系统。

国外对于尾流机理的研究比较深入,尤其是美国和欧洲都开发了自己的尾流预测系统,国内对于尾流的研究尚处于起步阶段,研究内容比较单一、不够系统,往往考虑的是单一因素比如地效和侧风对尾流的影响。

本文将通过研究尾流在不同大气参数下的演化情况,较为系统地揭示环境参数对于尾流演化规律的影响[7-8],同时采用 WALE-LES 湍流模型精确捕捉小尺度的尾涡,最终选择对尾涡强度描述更准确的Q准则,来衡量尾流强度的变化情况。

1 前处理工作

1.1 控制方程

CFD 计算的方法一般分为3种:直接数值模拟(DNS)、雷诺平均方程(RANS)、大涡模拟(LES)。其中 DNS 最为精确,但是现如今的计算资源无法满足;RANS 所需计算资源最小,但是对于尾涡的数值模拟来说计算精度不够;LES 精度较高而且所需计算资源介于 DNS 和 RANS 之间,因此本文采取湍流模型(WALE-LES)进行计算,模型方程见式(1)~式(5):

$$\frac{\partial \rho}{\partial t} + \frac{\partial}{\partial x_i}(\rho \overline{u_i}) = 0 \tag{1}$$

$$\frac{\partial}{\partial t}(\rho \overline{u_i}) + \frac{\partial}{\partial x_i}(\rho \overline{u_i}\,\overline{u_j}) = \frac{\partial}{\partial x_j}\left\{\left[\mu\left(\frac{\partial \overline{u_i}}{\partial x_j}+\frac{\partial \overline{u_j}}{\partial x_i}\right)\right] - \frac{2}{3}\mu\frac{\partial \overline{u_l}}{\partial x_l}\delta_{ij}\right\} - \frac{\partial \overline{p}}{\partial x_i} - \frac{\partial \tau_{ij}}{\partial x_j} \tag{2}$$

$$\frac{\partial \rho\,\overline{h_s}}{\partial t} + \frac{\partial \rho\,\overline{u_i}\,\overline{h_s}}{\partial x_i} - \frac{\partial \overline{p}}{\partial t} - \overline{u_j}\frac{\partial \overline{p}}{\partial x_i} - \frac{\partial}{\partial x_i}\left(\lambda\frac{\partial \overline{T}}{\partial x_i}\right) = -\frac{\partial}{\partial x_j}\left(-\frac{\mu_{SGS}C_p}{Pr_{SGS}}\frac{\partial \overline{T}}{\partial x_j}\frac{1}{sef}\right) \tag{3}$$

式中:ρ——流体密度;

t——时间;

u_i——计算域中 x_i 方向的速度;

u_j——计算域中 x_j 方向的速度;

p——流体压力;

μ——流体黏性系数;

τ_{ij}——亚格子 Reynolds 应力;

h_s——流体显热函;

λ——流体导热系数;

T——流体温度;

μ_{SGS}——亚格子黏度;

Pr_{SGS}——亚格子普朗特数,等于0.85;

C_p——流体恒压比热。

$$\tau_{ij} - \frac{1}{3}\tau_{kk}\delta_{ij} = -\mu_t\left(\frac{\partial \overline{u_i}}{\partial x_j} + \frac{\partial \overline{u_j}}{\partial x_i}\right) \tag{4}$$

式中:τ_{kk}——亚格子应力的各向同性部分;

μ_t——亚格子湍流黏度。

$$\mu_t = \rho L_s^2 \frac{(S_{ij}^d S_{ij}^d)^{3/2}}{(\overline{S}_{ij}\overline{S}_{ij})^{5/2} + (S_{ij}^d S_{ij}^d)^{5/4}} \tag{5}$$

式中:L_s——亚格子混合长度;

S_{ij}——应变率张量。

1.2 流体域

1.2.1 物理模型

本文采用的是长方体计算域,如图1a)、b)、c)所示。计算域长(飞机飞行方向)600m,宽(飞机左右方向)200m,高(飞机上下方向)200m,使用Ansys DM模块进行模型几何处理和流场域划分。

a)左视图

b)俯视图

c)正视图

图1 计算域图

1.2.2 网格模型

本文在Ansys ICEM CFD中进行网格划分,采用结构化网格,在飞机后部尾流区进行局部加密,网格总量为4800万,全局网格质量在0.23以上。图2a)、b)为网格局部截图,图2c为网格质量图。

1.3 参数设置

本文研究的是大气参数变化对尾流演化的影响,因此流体参数的设置是重点。计算域边界条件采用的是压力远场的设置,飞机为无滑移壁面。本文流体材料选择的是理想气体,通过改变气体的温度和湍流强度实现不同大气参数情况的计算。此外压力速度耦合算法采用Coupled,空间离散中的梯度采用基于最小二乘法格式,动量、湍动能等采用二阶迎风格式。

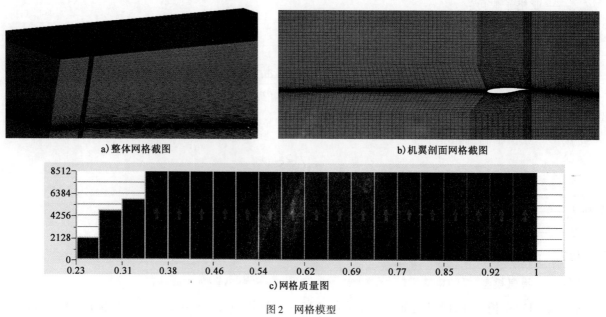

a) 整体网格截图   b) 机翼剖面网格截图

c) 网格质量图

图2　网格模型

2　后处理工作

2.1　不同大气参数时的涡量变化

本文给出了不同大气温度（T）和湍流强度（I）下的尾涡涡量随时间变化的计算结果，如图3a）、b）所示。

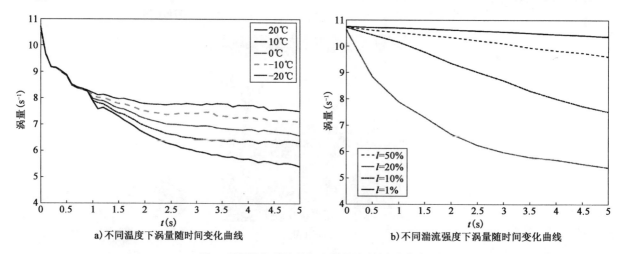

a) 不同温度下涡量随时间变化曲线   b) 不同湍流强度下涡量随时间变化曲线

图3　不同温度、湍流强度下，涡量随时间变化曲线

根据飞机实际飞行情况，本文选择了20℃、10℃、0℃、-10℃、-20℃四个典型温度。从图3a）可以看出，温度对尾涡耗散的影响呈正相关，温度越高尾涡耗散越快，而且在尾涡生成的前几秒钟耗散速度最快。同时从图中还可以看出在尾涡生成后的1s内，不同的温度仍具有相同的耗散规律，这是因为在尾涡初始生成阶段温度对尾涡耗散并不起主导作用，而且本文在计算不同温度情况时设置的湍流强度比较大，最终产生以上结果。

根据以往研究，大气湍流对尾涡的耗散有着重要的作用。本文通过设定不同的大气湍流强度来研究大气湍流对尾涡耗散规律的影响。从图3b）可以看出，湍流强度与尾涡耗散速度同样呈正相关，湍流强度越大尾涡耗散越快。图中湍流强度在10%以下时，尾流的耗散速度都比较慢，而飞机在高空飞行时湍流强度一般比较小，因此在不受其他条件影响时尾流会在飞机后方存在比较长的时间。

2.2 不同大气参数时的Q准则变化

以往的尾流研究中,尾涡强度的衡量往往采用涡量,但是受限于涡量自身的定义,其对漩涡的描述并不够准确,因此本文采用了Q准则这一更加精确的物理量,来描述不同大气参数时尾涡的变化情况,结果如图4a)、b)所示。

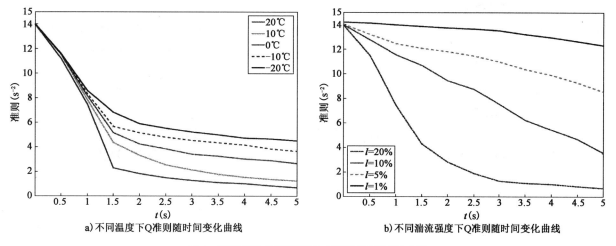

图4 不同温度、湍流强度下,Q准则随时间变化曲线

如图4a)为不同温度时尾涡Q准则变化情况。和涡量相似的是,不同温度下尾涡的耗散规律还是温度越高耗散速度越快,和涡量不同的是,在本文计算的5s内,温度20℃时Q准则显示尾涡的强度有着70%左右的耗散,而相同情况下涡量显示尾涡强度耗散了50%。由此可见Q准则对于尾涡强度的衡量时更为准确的。

如图4b)所示,尾涡在不同湍流强度下的Q准则变化和图3b)显示的涡量变化规律基本是相同的,均说明湍流强度越大尾涡耗散越快。但是和不同温度下的结果类似的是,湍流强度20%时,Q准则在本文计算的5s内减少了90%而涡量减少了50%。由此可见,采用Q准则量化尾涡在不同大气参数下的变化规律更加准确。

3 结 语

本文采用计算流体力学方法研究了航空器尾流在不同大气温度和大气湍流下的耗散规律,建立了航空器和流体域的数学模型、物理模型、网格模型等,采用计算精度更高的WALE-LES模型,完成了航空器尾流场的精确计算。同时,在后处理分析中还采用了更准确的衡量尾涡强度的物理量Q准则,得到了尾流在不同温度和湍流强度下定性和定量的规律。本文得到的主要结论如下:

(1) 温度的升高对尾流耗散有积极的影响,温度越大尾流耗散越快。20℃时,在5s内也就是飞机后方500~800m时,尾流强度会减少70%左右,温度降低减少量也会降低。

(2) 湍流强度的增大对尾流耗散也有着积极作用,湍流强度越大,尾流耗散越快。湍流强度10%时,尾流强度会在5s内减少70%左右。

(3) 在衡量尾流强度时,Q准则比涡量更加准确,因为涡量包含了流体的旋转剪切,在湍流比较大的情况下涡量就会比较大,而Q准则筛掉了剪切流的影响,其对尾涡这种旋转流体强度的衡量更加准确。

本文虽然基本实现了对不同温度和湍流强度下尾涡演化规律的计算研究,但是由于篇幅所限,没有对计算变量进行足够的控制。例如,在进行不同温度的计算时,应该同时考虑湍流强度的变化,本文的温度计算都是在湍流强度2.2%的情况下进行的,而进行不同湍流强度计算式也应该考虑温度的变化,本文湍流强度的计算都是在温度20℃情况下进行的。因此在后续工作中应进行更多更详细的计算,从而实现更为系统的研究。

参考文献

[1] Crow S C. Stability Theory for a Pair of Trailing Vortices[J]. AIAA Journal, 1969, 88(12):2162-2179.
[2] Greene G C. An Approximate Model of Vortex Decay in the Atmosphere[J]. 1985, 23(7).
[3] Corjon A, Poinsot T. Vortex Model to Define Safe Aircraft Separation Distances[J]. Journal of Aircraft, 2015, 33(3):547-553.
[4] Sarpkaya T. New Model for Vortex Decay in the Atmosphere[J]. Journal of Aircraft, 2000, 37(1):53-61.
[5] 张宇轩,王福新. 翼尖涡多阶段演化过程及其对气动力的影响[J]. 科学技术与工程, 2016, 16(19):11-19.
[6] 林孟达,崔桂香,张兆顺,等. 飞机尾涡演变及快速发展动态预测的大涡模拟研究[J]. 力学学报, 2017, 49(06):1185-1200.
[7] 栾天. 大气风场影响飞机尾涡的数值模拟研究[D]. 广汉:中国民用航空飞行学院, 2019, 53-71.
[8] 潘卫军,栾天,康贤彪,等. 飞机尾流观测研究进展[J]. 空气动力学学报, 2019,37(04):511-521.

A New Metric for the Psychomotor Vigilance Test Based on Standard Deviation

Sun Ruishan Han Shaohua Zhang Yao

(Research Institute of Civil Aviation Safety, Flight Technology College, Civil Aviation University of China)

Abstract The Psychomotor Vigilance Test (PVT) is a performance-based vigilance testing method that is widely used in related research associated with sleep loss, cognition, and fatigue, but most of the existing PVT metrics are based on the response time(RT) mean or number of lapses (usually defined as the response time greater than 500 ms). These metrics may reflect the average level of vigilance within a certain period time, rather than reflect the stability of vigilance. Therefore, we proposed a new evaluation metric based on the standard deviation of response time(SDRT). By analyzing the formula of SDRT, we verified that the new metric could well reflect the stability of vigilance and could be better applied to different PVT test equipment. Later, we used PVT experimental data to verify the sensitivity of new metric. We selected 6 participants and completed the PVT experiment in 2 consecutive days, and compared the output results of the traditional PVT metrics with the new metric. We tested the correlation coefficients between each of the metrics and performed paired t tests on each metrics to compare their vigilance sensitivity. Our analysis showed that the new metric was significantly related to most traditional PVT metrics at the 0.05 level, as well as its effect size was 0.617 and at a high level among all metrics. Based on these findings and the fact that the new metric provides extra information on RT stability, we concluded that new metric offered a number of potential advantages over traditional PVT metrics.

Keywords Psychomotor vigilance test(PVT) Vigilance Standard deviation of response time(SDRT) Effect size

0 Introduction

Vigilance refers to the ability of a person to maintain attention for a long time when performing a task or to maintain vigilance and awareness of random signals(Qin 2012). Excessive workload or insufficient sleep can lead to decreasing vigilance and cognitive impairment, and then affect work efficiency and operational accuracy

(Dinges 1995, Philip and Akerstedt 2006). In civil aviation and related fields, flight accidents and incidents caused by reduced fatigue due to staff fatigue are common. In July 2015, when a China Eastern Airlines flight MU2528 communicated with the tower during the approach phase of Wuhan Tianhe International Airport, the tower controller on duty fell asleep and no one answered. As a result, the flight had to be suspended.

Because the change of human vigilance is such a critical factor in the field of safety, an objective and quantitative assessment method is needed to detect possible fatigue problems, especially the existing studies have shown that the fatigue self-assessment scale widely used by airlines currently is not reliable (Frey, Badia and Wright 2004, VAN Dongen, Baynard, Maislin and Dinges 2004). In this case, the study of an vigilance assessment method which is objective, effective, scalable, easy to use, sensitive to vigilance, and can be reused in actual operation management with little time is of great significance.

PVT is a fatigue detection technology based on visual response time. It is widely used in related research on sleep loss, cognition, and fatigue (Palikhe, Kim and Park 2011). The standard PVT test (ie, 10-minute duration, inter-stimulus intervals (ISI) 2—10 seconds) was proposed by Dinges and Powell in 1985 (Dinges and Powell 1985) and has been shown to be very sensitive to changes in vigilance of total and partial sleep deprivation (Basner and Dinges 2011). When human vigilance decreases, reaction time (RT), number of lapses (usually defined as RT $\geq$ 500 ms) increase significantly and false start (RT $\leq$ 100 ms) increase slightly in the PVT (Doran, Van Dongen and Dinges 2001). The advantage of PVT over other cognitive testing methods is that PVT is almost immune to learning effects (Dinges, et al. 1997), which means that PVT performance does not improve due to repeated testing.

The standard 10-minute PVT is the most commonly used, although longer (Anderson, Wales and Horne 2010) or shorter (Loh, Lamond, Dorrian, Roach and Dawson 2004) duration versions have been evaluated, and depending on the evaluation metrics, their ability to distinguish vigilance or fatigue may be only slightly lower (Sometimes slightly higher) than the standard PVT (Basner, et al. 2011). Therefore, for some metrics, the optimal test duration may be less than 10 minutes. According to previous studies (Loh, et al. 2004, Basner, et al. 2011, Arsintescu, et al. 2019), 5-min PVT has been validated in both laboratory and field studies investigating sleep deprivation and fatigue. The main advantage of the 5-min PVT was that it could be easily used in the field due to its short duration time. However, it has been verified that the 2-minute and 90-second PVT is not sensitive enough to changes in vigilance (Loh, et al. 2004), and cannot be used as an effective tool for detecting the effects of fatigue. Therefore, we chose 5-min PVT to consider both test accuracy and efficiency.

Existing PVT evaluation indicators are mainly used to evaluate vigilance by testing changes in the average of response time and the number of lapses, but it is difficult to form a unified standard in the evaluation of diverse crowd, RT average will be affected by individual ability difference, only by the RT mean cannot completely represent the real vigilance level of different individuals. That is, there is a case where the RT mean of the test subjects is larger because they are slower to react, not because they are less alert. The number of lapses varies from person to person too. In addition, the test results include the response time of the test equipment. Therefore, it is necessary to study the evaluation metrics that have uniform standards, identify the changes in vigilance of different individuals more accurately, and can reflect the stability of vigilance.

The objective of this paper is twofold: ①to propose a new PVT metric that eliminates errors in test equipment and reflects alert stability and ②to compare the performance difference between the new metric and the existing PVT metrics.

1 A New Pvt Metric

In the standard 10-min PVT, the RT mean and the number of lapses are the most common evaluation metrics, which have been verified by scholars in various countries as gold indicators to reflect sleep loss and circadian rhythm imbalance (Belenky, et al. 2003, VAN Dongen, Maislin, Mullington and Dinges 2003). It is generally believed that in a PVT test, the larger RT or number of lapses is, the lower subject's vigilance is, and the more prone to fatigue performance such as lack of concentration, slow reaction, and decreased work accuracy. Also, there are variables such as 1/RT (called the reciprocal of reaction time or reaction speed) and the fastest 10% RT. These metrics can better reflect the change in vigilance, but they mainly reflect information related to the RT size and ignore the key information of the RT stability. The "state instability hypothesis" about sleep states that in the case of sleep deprivation, human performance (such as reaction time) is in an unstable state and fluctuates within a few seconds, which cannot be described as complete awake or sleep, especially in tasks that require constant attention, this unstable state is more likely to occur (Doran, et al. 2001). In conclusion the RT stability is closely related to the vigilance, and we proposed a new PVT metric based on the SDRT, which can provide information on the RT stability and make up for the lack of existing PVT evaluation metrics.

Statistics defines data stability as an index to measure data volatility and dispersion. The smaller the data fluctuation is, the smaller the dispersion degree is, and the higher the stability is. The standard deviation is the square root of the arithmetic mean from the square deviation, which can reflect the RT stability well. In addition, when using RT mean as the evaluation variable, it will also be affected by the delay of the test equipment, and the standard deviation can reduce these effects, making the evaluation result more accurate.

At present, RT mean is used to evaluate vigilance in PVT, and RT mean is calculated as follows:

$$\overline{RT} = \frac{1}{n}\left(\sum_{i=1}^{n} RT_i\right) = \frac{1}{n}\sum_{i=1}^{n}(RT_{pi} + \Delta T) = \frac{1}{n}\sum_{i=1}^{n} RT_{pi} + \Delta T = \overline{RT}_p + \Delta T \tag{1}$$

Where, $\overline{RT}$ is the mean of all single reaction time, n is the total number of samples, RT_i is the single reaction time, RT_{pi} is the actual reaction time of the subject, ΔT is the delay time of the test equipment, and $\overline{RT}_p$ is the mean of all actual reaction time.

When the PVT is implemented on different equipment, due to the performance differences, the delay time ΔT (ms) of different terminals is not the same, which will cause large errors in the calculation of existing evaluation metrics (e.g. the RT mean of the subjects), and may lead to different levels of vigilance when the same subject tested under the same condition at different equipment. Using SDRT as the evaluation metric can eliminate the interference of the terminal delay time. The specific arguments are as follows:

The formula for the standard deviation is:

$$\sigma = \sqrt{\frac{1}{n}\sum_{i=1}^{n}(RT_i - \overline{RT})^2} \tag{2}$$

$$\overline{RT} = \frac{1}{n}\left(\sum_{i=1}^{n} RT_i\right) \tag{3}$$

The derivation process of standard deviation is as follows:

$$\sigma = \sqrt{\frac{1}{n}\sum_{i=1}^{n}(RT_i - \overline{RT})^2} = \sqrt{\frac{1}{n}\sum_{i=1}^{n}\left[RT_{pi} + \Delta T - \left(\frac{1}{n}\sum_{i=1}^{n} RT_{pi} + \Delta T\right)\right]^2}$$

$$= \sqrt{\frac{1}{n}\sum_{i=1}^{n}\left(RT_{pi} - \frac{1}{n}\sum_{i=1}^{n} RT_{pi}\right)^2} = \sqrt{\frac{1}{n}\sum_{i=1}^{n}(RT_{pi} - \overline{RT}_p)^2} \tag{4}$$

Where, $\overline{RT}_p$ is the mean of all the actual reaction time of subjects, and σ is the standard deviation of all single reaction time.

From the formula of the standard deviation, it can be seen that the delay time of the test equipment will not affect the result of this variable, and it is more suitable for PVT evaluation metrics of different terminals. However, metrics such as RT mean and number of lapses are based on the reaction time, which is easily disturbed by equipment delays, their ability to assess changes in vigilance may be affected.

2　Data and Methods

2.1　Subject

The data come from a study of the relationship between circadian rhythms and fatigue in air traffic controllers. In the experiment, 6 college students (3 males and 3 females) majoring in air traffic control from a certain university in China were selected as the subjects. Their age ranged from 23 to 26 years old (average 25.2). The subjects had similar and regular work and rest in the week before the experiment, and had no bad habits such as excessive smoking and drinking. Subjects were healthy, with normal visual acuity or corrected visual acuity, and not dependent on psychotropic drugs. All subjects expressed willingness to participate in the experiment and understood the procedure and requirements of the experiment.

2.2　Environment

The experiment was conducted in a laboratory conform to the environment in practical engineering application. The light in the laboratory was held constant at less than 50 lux during the experiment. The ambient temperature was maintained between 22°-25°C and sound was maintained below 50 dB. The laboratory was provided with comfortable desks and chairs. All subjects used the same equipment during the experiment to keep all parameters consistent.

2.3　Tools

PVT-192 is a handheld test that widely used in laboratory studies. And is regarded as the authority of the PVT(Thorne, et al. 2005, Honn, Riedy and Grant 2015, Arsintescu, Mulligan and Flynn-Evans 2017, Arsintescu, et al. 2019). According to PT-192, we developed a PVT to be used on touchscreen devices. This self-designed PVT software installed on a certain brand of android mobile phone. We used the 5minute duration, 2-10 seconds ISI as the experimental PVT version, and this version has been verified to have comparable testing performance and results with the standard 10minute PVT(Honn, et al. 2015). The test software records the time interval between each visual stimulus and each screen hit during the duration of the experiment.

2.4　Process

The experiment was conducted for two consecutive days. During the test, subjects were required to come to the laboratory before 8:00 am every day and fill in the sleep quantity and sleep quality scale of the previous night. During the experiment, no refreshing items such as coffee were allowed, and no vigorous exercises or nap were allowed to eliminate the resulting vigilance error. From 8:00 am to 10:00 pm, the subjects performed PVT every two hours. Between neurobehavioral test bouts, subjects were asked to complete a certain amount of work (simulate air traffic control) in a laboratory. Meals were provided at regular times (7:00 am - 8:00 am; 12:00 am - 1:00 pm; 6:00 pm - 7:00 pm). The subjects were not allowed to return to their dormitories to sleep until the end of the last PVT test of the day, at 10:30 pm usually. The whole experiment was monitored by the relevant staff to ensure that the subjects strictly followed the experimental procedure. The subjects used the same PVT tool in turn to complete the PVT test. During the test, one subject was tested in a laboratory under the supervision of employees, while the rest of the subjects stayed in another room.

2.5 Data analysis method

Experiments obtain a total of 96 sets of data. Firstly preprocess the experimental data, we remove the invalid data that the software does not respond after clicking the screen. In addition, we consider RT <= 100 ms as an error start, that is, the subjects clicked the screen before the visual stimulus signal appeared, and it was not included in the subsequent Statistical analysis, test data at 8 am was removed to avoid the effects of sleep inertia, and finally 82 sets of valid data remained. Based on relevant studies at home and abroad(Basner, Mollicone and Dinges 2011, Basner, Mcguire, Goel, Rao and Dinges 2015, Honn, et al. 2015, Arsintescu, et al. 2017, Arsintescu, et al. 2019), the following variables were selected as the analysis objects: ①number of lapses, ②RT mean, ③SDRT, ④1/RT (also called reciprocal response time or response speed), ⑤fastest 10% RT, ⑥slowest 10% 1/RT. According to research Basner(Basner, et al. 2011), number of lapses and 1/RT in the standard 10 minutes PVT is the most sensitive metrics to total sleep deprivation, and also kept high sensitivity under the condition of partial sleep deprivation, moreover Dinges study(Dinges, Kribbs and Monk 1991) also prove number of lapses is an effective metric to evaluate the fatigue level of subjects, representing decrease of vigilance. In the PVT with 5 minutes duration, number of lapses is also widely used. Therefore, we believe that number of lapses is an effective metric to identify changes in vigilance and serve as the main benchmark indicator in this paper.

Because the test equipment we use has certain delay, that is, the response time of the equipment from testers click screen to test device record this click, response time obtained in the experiment will increase correspondingly compared with the actual response time of the subjects, and the sensitivity of the lapses (RT > 500 ms) may be affected. Therefore we counted the lapses of RT > 500 ms and RT > 600 ms and compared their sensitivity to vigilance.

In order to analyze the difference of each metric in the evaluation of vigilance, we intend to select test data at two moments, which represent the vigilance state and fatigue state, and compare the similarities and differences of vigilance evaluation results of different metrics in the two sets of data. We used paired t test to detect the difference of PVT metrics. The paired t test is used to test whether there is a significant difference between non-SD and SD conditions.

We selected the effect size to describe the ability of the PVT parameter to distinguish vigilance from fatigue. The effect size is an improvement on the statistical method of hypothesis significance test and provides some statistical information different from the results of the hypothesis test. Cohen defines the effect size as "the extent to which a phenomenon exists in the population", specifically in the hypothesis significance test (such as the t test), that is, "the extent to which null hypothesis H_0 is wrong(Cohen 1988)". The effect size can be divided into standard deviation differences type and strength of association type(Lu, Tang and Zeng 2011). Standard variation refers to the measurement of the total effect size by standardized difference units, and strength of association type represents the covariation relationship between two or more variables. The effect size not only solved the sensitivity problem of PVT, but also was used as a verification standard by other scholars(Basner, et al. 2011). According to the study of National Aeronautics and Space Administration (NASA)(Basner, et al. 2011), we chose Cohen's d value in effect size variable to measure the sensitivity of PVT metrics to changes in vigilance. The specific formula is as follows:

$$d = (\overline{x1} - \overline{x2})/\sigma_{pooled} \tag{5}$$

$$\sigma_{pooled} = \left[\frac{(n_1-1)s_1^2 + (n_2-1)s_2^2}{n_1+n_2}\right]^{1/2} \tag{6}$$

Where, n_1, n_2 represents the sample capacity of each group, x_1, x_2 represents the mean of each group of samples, s_1, s_2 are the standard deviation of each group of samples, and the denominator σpooled is called the pooled standard deviation.

3 Result

3.1 Normal Inspection

According to the trend figure to the change of RT and SDRT with test time (Fig. 1, Fig. 2), it could be seen that, due to the influence of human circadian biological rhythm, RT mean and SDRT showed similar fluctuation trends at different times. At 10:00 am, both the RT mean and SDRT were at low levels, which indicated that the subjects were more alert, and at 2:00 pm, the RT mean and SDRT were at the top in the test, indicating that the subjects had the lowest vigilance. Therefore, the 10:00 am sample and the 2:00 pm sample were selected as controls, the 10:00 am sample was regarded as the alert state, and the 2:00 pm sample was regarded as the fatigue state.

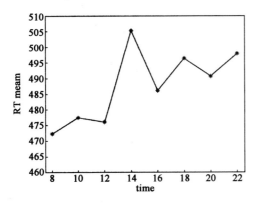
Fig. 1 Trend analysis of reaction time mean

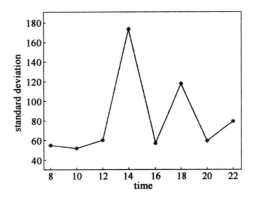
Fig. 2 Trend analysis of SDRT

We analyzed differences in PVT metrics between the two groups. First, all the effective response times of 6 subjects at 10:00 am and 2:00 pm were selected, among which the number of valid test samples was 634 at 10:00 am and was 648 at 2:00 pm. PVT metric (number of lapses, RT mean, SDRT, 1/RT, fastest 10% RT, slowest 10% 1/RT) of different subjects in the two groups of data were calculated respectively, and these metrics were performed Shapiro-Wilk test to analyze whether they conformed to the normal distribution. The test results (Tab. 1) showed that the SDRT (both group alert and group fatigue) did not conform to the normal distribution, and the other variables conformed to the normal distribution basically. Therefore, the SDRT was converted by $\sqrt{\ln x}$, and the converted value was detected to conform to the normal distribution and could be used for subsequent data analysis.

Shapiro-Wilk test result value   Tab. 1

SDRT	RT mean	1/RT	Lapses 500	Lapses 600	Fastest 10% RT	Slowest 10% 1/RT	SDRT
Sig(group alert)	0.480	0.231	0.346	0.133	0.035	0.099	0.004
Sig(group fatigue)	0.088	0.296	0.299	0.043	0.504	0.743	0

3.2 Association Strength Analysis

Association strength analysis is mainly used to judge the statistical association between two or more variables. If there is an association, the association strength and direction are further analyzed. We use Pearson correlation analysis to study the strength of the correlation between the metrics. Since Pearson correlation analysis requires variables to be normally distributed, converted SDRT data were selected. The correlation test results were shown in Tab. 2.

Pearson correlation analysis results showed that compared with standard PVT lapses (RT > 500 ms), corrected lapses (RT > 600 ms) was stronger and significantly correlated with RT mean, SDRT, and the slowest 10% 1/RT. Although the correlation with the 1/RT was weakened, it was still significantly correlated at the 0.01 level, and the correlation with the fastest 10% RT was weaker, but the correlation between the fastest 10% RT and other metrics was almost at a low level. The corrected lapses was statistically more correlated with most metrics and was more suitable as a benchmark indicator in this paper.

In addition, the correlation coefficient r between the SDRT and the number of corrected lapses was 0.694 (Tab. 2), which mean a high positive correlation. The correlation with other metrics (except the fastest 10% RT) was also significantly correlated at the 0.05 level (|r| value range is 0.569-0.883). This showed that the existing metrics also affected by the stability of RT.

Pearson correlation analysis results Tab. 2

Metrics	RT mean	1/RT	Lapses 500	Lapses 600	Fastest 10% RT	Slowest 10% 1/RT	SDRT
RT mean	1	−0.778	0.662	0.784	0.328	−0.922	0.883
1/RT	−0.778	1	0.909	−0.761	−0.651	0.861	−0.569
Lapses 500	0.662	−0.909	1	0.737	0.379	−0.765	0.458
Lapses 600	0.784	−0.761	0.737	1	0.215	−0.873	0.694
Fastest 10% RT	0.328	−0.651	0.379	0.215	1	0.346	0.081
Slowest 10% 1/RT	−0.922	0.861	−0.765	−0.873	−0.346	1	−0.880
SDRT	0.883	−0.569	0.458	0.694	0.081	−0.880	1

3.3 Analysis of differences between groups

In addition to analyzing the relationship between the correlation strength of the metrics, we also studied the differences in the evaluation results of the two groups of data by each indicator. Paired t-test was performed on two groups of PVT evaluation metrics, and the test results were shown in Tab. 3. From the results of the t-test, it could be seen that there was no statistically significant difference between all the evaluation indicators for the two groups of samples ($p < 0.05$). Then, the d value of each PVT metric was calculated by formula 5, as a result the RT mean, the number of corrected lapses had the largest effect size; followed by SDRT, the number of lapses, and the slowest 10% 1/RT. It could be seen that the number of corrected lapses and the RT mean had the highest sensitivity to changes in vigilance, followed by the SDRT and the slowest 10% 1/RT. Compared with the most sensitive index RT mean, the effect size of SDRT had decreased by 5.22%, but considering the advantages provided by the SDRT, we believed that the decrease in the effect size was acceptable. The effect size of PVT metrics is show in Fig. 3

Paired t-test results Tab. 3

Metrics	t Value	Sig(two-sided)	95% Confidence Interval	
			Lower Limit	Upper Limit
RT mean	−1.671	0.123	−64.513	8.823
1/RT	1.031	0.325	−0.040	0.110
Lapses 500	−1.909	0.083	−12.020	0.853
Lapses 600	−1.706	0.116	−3.054	0.387
Fastest 10% RT	0.908	0.383	−8.215	19.748
Slowest 10% 1/RT	1.860	0.090	−0.025	0.296
SDRT	−1.438	0.178	−308.286	64.626

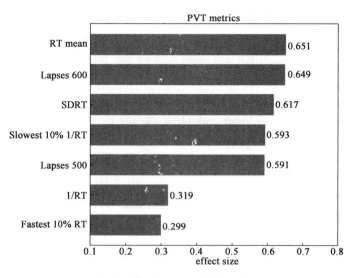

Fig. 3 The effect size of PVT metrics

4 Discussion and Conclusions

4.1 Discussion

Aiming at the deficiency of the existing PVT metrics, we proposed a new evaluation metric, SDRT, to measure the change of subjects' vigilance in PVT. Although some scholars had calculated the SDRT in PVT studies before, it was not analyzed as an independent PVT indicator, but as a statistical supplement. This is the first time that the SDRT is used as the main metric of PVT evaluation, and the difference of evaluation results between it and the traditional PVT metrics is compared. The new metric has two important advantages, the first SDRT reflects the RT stability of subjects during the PVT, which is such critical information and has close relations with vigilance, while the existing PVT metrics are based on the RT and its conversion, though the fastest 10% RT, the slowest 10% 1/RT also can reflect the RT stability partially, but only focus on the extreme value of RT, there will be a large error in the actual evaluation, and the information it reflects is not comprehensive enough; Secondly, SDRT eliminates the delay of PVT test equipment and can be used as a unified metric of test data among different implements. Mobile terminal-based PVT testing is low-cost, easy to carry, simple and easy to implement, but the touch delay of the device will have a great impact on the response time result, especially considering the interference factors such as differences between devices, the use environment, and the life period of device, existing indicators such as RT mean and number of lapses may not be reliable, while SDRT, can eliminate the error caused equipment delay, make evaluation result of PVT tools based on mobile terminal more scientific and accurate.

In addition, the new evaluation metric should remain sensitive to changes in vigilance, that is, it has a better ability to distinguish between vigilance and non-vigilance. Through experimental data of circadian rhythm, we verified that SDRT had better sensitivity to changes in vigilance. With reference to domestic and foreign research, we chose the number of lapses as the benchmark variable of this article, that is, the main reference object for metric comparison. Due to the delay of the test equipment, we revised the threshold of lapses (increased from 500ms to 600ms) and studied the difference between the metric before and after the correction. Based on the changes in RT and SDRT at each moment, we selected the two moments with the greatest difference in vigilance as a comparison, where 10:00 am represents the alert state and 2:00 pm represents the fatigue state, and analyzed the differences in the evaluation results of the two groups of data by each PVT metrics.

According to Pearson correlation analysis, the correlation strength between the number of corrected lapses and most metrics was larger, which means the number of corrected lapses was more suitable as the benchmark metric in this paper. The SDRT and most metrics were significantly correlated at the level of 0.01, and the correlation coefficient with the number of lapses had reached 0.694. It was worth noting that the correlation between the fastest 10% RT and various other metrics was not ideal, and the value of the alert group was greater than the fatigue group, which was not in line with expectations. After analyzing the data, it was found that the average response time of a subject was obvious Lower than others, and his vigilance difference between the two groups of moments was not obvious, so the fastest 10% RT was likely to be affected by individual differences. Except for the fastest 10% RT, there was a good correlation between the SDRT and other PVT metrics, which proved that it could be used as an evaluation metric of vigilance.

We used paired t-test and Cohen's d value to measure the differences among different groups of metrics. The results showed that the sensitivity of the SDRT to changes in vigilance was second only to the RT mean and the number of corrected lapses (RT > 600 ms), and SDRT was effective as a new PVT evaluation metric. Compared with the RT mean which had the largest effect size, the effect size of the SDRT decreased by 5.22%, but it was still at a good level (d = 0.617), with a similar sensitivity to the slowest 10% 1/RT.

4.2 Conclusions

We develop a novel PVT metric, the SDRT, which reflects the change of vigilance based on the stability of reaction time compared with the existing evaluation metric. By comparing the mathematical formulas of RT mean and SDRT, we prove that the new metric is not affected by the delay of different PVT test equipment, which reduces the evaluation error and makes up the deficiency of the existing metrics. Moreover, we analyzed the performance difference between the new metric and the existing PVT metrics, especially the main and most sensitive PVT metric (number of lapses) in the past research. Analysis results show that the SDRT associated with most of the existing metrics significantly at 0.05 level, and the sensitivity to the change in vigilance of SDRT is only 5.22% lower than the number of lapses, which is sufficiently sensitive in the 5-minute PVT.

4.3 Future Research Directions

The future research directions are as follows: ①We only selected healthy young college students as subjects, the conclusion may not be generalized to larger age distribution or some unhealthy population. The next step is to study the performance difference of the new metric for subjects at different ages; ②Our conclusion is based on the PVT with 5 minutes duration. Since the SDRT is based on the stability of response time, in a longer duration PVT, it may show more superior performance. This is also a direction for subsequent research; ③In the future the relationship between the metrics can be studied in-depth, and the advantages of the indicators can be synthesized to finally form a quantitative result of the vigilance assessment.

References

[1] Anderson C, Wales A W, Horne J A. PVT Lapses Differ According to Eyes Open, Closed, Or Looking Away[J]. SLEEP, 2010, 33(2): 197-204.

[2] Arsintescu L, et al. Validation of a Touchscreen Psychomotor Vigilance Task[J]. Accident Analysis & Prevention, 2019, 126: 173-176.

[3] Arsintescu L, Mulligan J B, Flynn-Evans E E. Evaluation of a Psychomotor Vigilance Task for Touch Screen Devices[J]. Human Factors: The Journal of the Human Factors and Ergonomics Society, 2017, 59: 661-670.

[4] Basner M, Mcguire S, Goel N, et al. A New Likelihood Ratio Metric for the Psychomotor Vigilance Test and its Sensitivity to Sleep Loss[J]. Journal of Sleep Researchm,2015,24: 702-713.

[5] Basner M, Mollicone D,Dinges D F. Validity and Sensitivity of a Brief Psychomotor Vigilance Test (PVT-B) to Total and Partial Sleep Deprivation[J]. Acta Astronautica,2011,69: 949-959.

[6] Basner M,Dinges D F. Maximizing Sensitivity of the Psychomotor Vigilance Test (PVT) to Sleep Loss[J]. SLEEP,2011,34: 581-591.

[7] Belenky G, et al. Patterns of Performance Degradation and Restoration During Sleep Restriction and Subsequent Recovery: A Sleep Dose-Response Study[J]. Journal of Sleep Research,2003,12: 1-12.

[8] Cohen 1988. Statistical Power Analysis for the Behavioral Sciences, Hillsdale, NJ: Lawrence Erlbaum Associates,Pub.

[9] Dinges D F. An Overview of Sleepiness and Accidents[J]. Journal of Sleep Research,1995,4: 4-14.

[10] Dinges D F, et al. Cumulative Sleepiness, Mood Disturbance, and Psychomotor Vigilance Performance Decrements During a Week of Sleep Restricted to 4-5 Hours Per Night[J]. Sleep,1997,20: 267-277.

[11] Dinges D F,Powell J W. Microcomputer Analyses of Performance On a Portable, Simple Visual RT Task During Sustained Operations [J]. Behavior Research Methods, Instruments, & Computers, 1985, 17: 652-655.

[12] Dinges D, Kribbs N B,Monk T H. Performing while Sleepy: Effects of Experimentally Induced Sleepiness [M]. Chichester, London: John Wiley & Sons,1991.

[13] Doran S M, Van Dongen H, Dinges D F. Sustained Attention Performance During Sleep Deprivation: Evidence of State Instability[J]. Archives Italiennes de Biologie,2001,139: 253-267.

[14] Frey D J, Badia P,Wright K J. Inter-and Intra-Individual Variability in Performance Near the Circadian Nadir During Sleep Deprivation[J]. Journal of Sleep Research,2004,13: 305-315.

[15] Honn K A, Riedy S M,Grant D A. Validation of a Portable, Touch-Screen Psychomotor Vigilance Test [J]. Aerospace Medicine and Human Performance,2015,86: 428-434.

[16] Loh S, Lamond N, Dorrian J,et al. The Validity of Psychomotor Vigilance Tasks of Less than 10-Minute Duration[J]. Behav Res Methods Instrum Comput,2004,36: 339-346.

[17] Palikhe N S, Kim J H,Park H S. Biomarkers Predicting Isocyanate-Induced Asthma[J]. Allergy Asthma Immunol Res,2001,3: 21-26.

[18] Philip P, Akerstedt T. Transport and Industrial Safety, How are they Affected by Sleepiness and Sleep Restriction? [J]. Sleep Medicne Reviews,2006,10: 347-356.

[19] Thorne D R, et al. The Walter Reed Palm-Held Psychomotor Vigilance Test[J]. Behavior Research Methods,2005,37: 111-118.

[20] Van Dongen H P, Baynard M D, Maislin G,et al. Systematic Interindividual Differences in Neurobehavioral Impairment From Sleep Loss: Evidence of Trait-Like Differential Vulnerability [J]. SLEEP, 2004, 27: 423-433.

[21] Van Dongen H P, Maislin G, Mullington J M,et al. The Cumulative Cost of Additional Wakefulness: Dose-Response Effects On Neurobehavioral Functions and Sleep Physiology From Chronic Sleep Restriction and Total Sleep Deprivation[J]. SLEEP,2003,26: 117-126.

[22] Lu X F, Tang Y H, Zeng F M. Effect size: estimation, report and explanation [J]. Psychological Exploration,2011,31: 260-264(in Chinese).

[23] Qin Y G. Alert Attention Characteristics of Visual Stimulus Detection [D]. ChongQing: Southwest University(in Chinese).

基于改进STAMP模型的应急响应系统设计与情报体系构建分析
——以航空器特情事件为例

岳仁田 李君尉

(中国民航大学空中交通管理学院)

摘要 虽然我国目前航空事故发生率较低,但各类与航空器运行有关的特情事件依然时有发生。本文首先基于系统理论事故建模与过程(Systems-Theoretic Accident Modeling and Process,STAMP)模型的原理,通过改进STAMP模型,构建了应急协同联动响应系统,分析了应急响应的控制与反馈过程,选取起落架故障特情事件,分析了该类型事件的应急响应处置的实际运用;其次以改进STAMP模型的应急协同联动响应系统为基础,结合数据全生命周期理论,构建应急决策快速响应情报体系,并论述了情报体系在特情事件的应急响应中发挥的7个作用。研究结果表明,基于改进STAMP模型设计的应急响应系统开拓了应急响应研究的思路,且据此所构建的应急决策快速响应情报体系,能提高应急响应处理水平。

关键词 STAMP模型 情报体系 应急响应 应急决策

0 引言

运行环境复杂多变,航班运行之间交互复杂,航空运输系统是一个对安全性要求极高的运行系统。虽然目前航空运输安全水平总体较高,但特情事件依然频发,例如川航3U8633航班挡风玻璃破裂紧急备降双流机场事件,国航CA983航班货舱遭遇火警备降俄罗斯阿纳德尔机场事件等。假若航空器特情无法得到有效应急处置,那么特情事件可能会进一步恶化为严重事故症候,甚至是航空事故,进而导致重大人员伤亡与财产损失。

目前,航空器特情的应急管理相关研究较少,如王莉莉等[1]分析了在同时仪表进近模式下的4种航空器特情的碰撞风险模型;王浙军[2]构建了空管协同应急总体模型,设计了应急响应与应急处置的工作流程。同时,我国民航系统应急管理主要有民航局颁布的一些管理规则与应急预案,如《中国民用航空局应对突发事件总体预案》《中国民用航空应急管理规定》(CCAR-397)。这些应急管理规范,可作为各组织单位制定应急管理措施的依据。然而,应急管理的实用工具与技术并未有较好的发展,且各组织单位(机场、管制单位、航空公司)各自制定应急预案、应急处置程序等,导致应急管理缺乏系统性。而航空器特情事件应急处置则需要多方互相配合,才能达到多方协同应急响应与应急处置的目的。

STAMP模型是Leveson教授提出的一个可用于复杂非线性系统安全性分析的事故模型。该模型是从系统论的角度来分析事故发生过程,识别出系统存在的不安全控制行为,对系统安全进行分析。目前,STAMP模型已广泛应用于化工生产、交通运输、施工建筑等领域的事故致因研究或系统安全分析,如:祝楷[3]基于STAMP模型剖析了一起煤矿事故,识别出技术、组织机构与工人等关键事故致因;郑磊等[4]采用STAMP模型,分析得到飞机降落过程中的机轮制动系统的不安全控制行为的关键因素;王瑛等[5]利用STAMP模型识别军机飞行训练中的风险,通过仿真得到不同条件下的飞行参数,定量描述军机飞行训练

基金项目:国家自然科学基金民航联合基金(U1533112)。

状态。牛丰等[6]构建了地铁施工安全事故STAMP模型,分析了事故的致因因素以及演化过程。除此之外,STAMP模型也开始应用于应急联动系统的设计,如王起全[7]等基于STAMP模型的原理,设计了应对地铁拥挤踩踏的应急联动系统,用于监测人流密度与紧急疏散。

航空器特情具有突发性、复杂性及危害性等特征,为避免特情事件恶化而导致事故发生,本文基于STAMP模型的控制反馈原理,通过改进STAMP模型,构建航空器特情事件的应急协同联动响应系统,研究其闭环运作机制;并据此结合数据全生命周期理论,构建应急决策快速响应情报体系,分析情报体系在特情事件处置中发挥的作用,为航空器特情事件应急响应及决策提供新的研究思路。

1 基于改进STAMP模型的应急协同联动响应系统的构建

1.1 STAMP模型

STAMP模型从系统的角度,对事故致因进行分析及通过一些安全约束实现安全属性,目前STAMP模型的运用集中于对已发生事故过程的建模及剖析,识别系统的控制缺陷。其原理是将安全问题转化为控制问题,如图1所示。

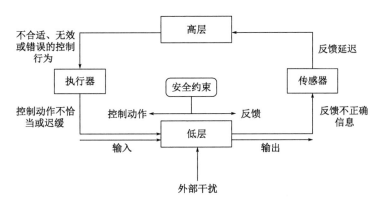

图1 STAMP模型的原理

若将应急响应系统作为一个复杂系统,其应急决策、响应措施则可干预控制突发事件的进一步恶化,防止事故的发生。突发事件的应急响应措施本质上是系统的控制与反馈过程,利用STAMP模型的分层安全控制结构,识别各层的不安全行为,通过干预控制措施,阻止不安全行为的发展。因此,通过STAMP模型由上而下的分层安全控制结构,及时应急响应与决策,完成相应的控制过程,并通过情报的及时反馈,形成闭环运作机制,指导突发事件的应急响应与处置工作。

1.2 应急协同联动响应系统分层结构

航空器特情属于事故类突发事件,对突发事件的快速响应与处置一直是公共安全应急管理的研究重点,其中应急情报体系可对突发事件进行监控、判断、决策与处置。目前突发事件应急管理体系建设将全面纳入"十四五"规划中,同时以构建情报体系为导向的相关研究更是近年来的研究热点[8-13]。无论是从航空器特情事件,还是公共安全的突发事件来说,应急决策体系都需要多部门、多层次、多环节等多方协调。而横向的多组织的协调、整合、互动能够使复杂系统的组织绩效提高[14],可见多方的协同决策与联动能够将突发事件发生时的应急处置有效性发挥到最大。因此,引入协同联动机制具有必要性[15-18]。

综上所述,有必要:"事前"对民航事故致因进行监测、识别及预警;"事中"在航空器特情发生时,及时通过干预控制措施的应急处置来阻止事态的进一步恶化;"事后"通过对事件本身起因与应急响应处置等的反馈与评价,进行预防改正工作。这表明,需要采取快速响应与有效的应急措施,为事前的预警、事中的干预以及事后的防控,提供强有力的保障与支持。而借助应急情报体系能够为突发事件的发生及演化提供监测、识别、预警、决策及干预控制提供支撑,同时也为应对危机的各参与主体提供情报服务,达到提升突发事件应急处置能力的目的。

基于上述的STAMP模型的控制反馈原理,可知系统要达到由上而下的分层控制约束,需要以应急情报体系作为支撑,通过情报流的动态循环,指导应急响应工作。因此,本文结合应急情报体系以及民航运输运行的特点对STAMP模型进行改进,从情报的收集监控、判别告警、分析决策、控制策略及情报评价反馈出发,构建一个具有闭环更新机制的应急协同联动响应系统分层结构,如图2所示。

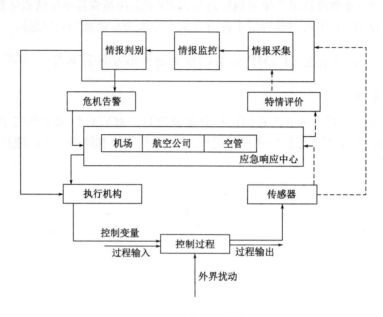

图2 应急协同联动响应系统分层结构

改进后的STAMP模型,事故分析或系统安全性分析的STAMP模型相比,更侧重于研究避免事态恶化的应急处置流程运作,具有事前、事中及事后的闭环运作的指导作用,并非用于具体分析事后(事故)的致因及机理。与STAMP模型类似,在基于改进STAMP模型设计的应急协同联动系统中,将防止事故进一步恶化的措施作为安全约束条件,经过情报采集、情报监控、情报判别等处理过程后,当所采集得到的数据大于系统所设定的阈值时,应急响应中心则会根据情报分析得到的告警等级与特情状况,协同决策应急处置方案,并发出对应的控制指令给执行机构与参与方的应急保障部门,共同做好应急响应的保障工作。当特情事件结束后,对事件进行评价与反馈,并搜集特情信息,录入情报库后更新情报,为后续的应急响应工作做储备。

1.3 应急协同联动响应系统控制过程

控制过程主要包括了各类特情事件征兆的识别、监控、判别以及告警后的应急响应处置。其中事件危机征兆的识别与监控也是情报工作的日常。应急协同联动响应系统控制过程,如图3所示。所收集的大量航班运行的相关数据,经过标准化与精简化处理后,主要用于对实时数据的监控与监测。将收集后的数据存储于数据采集库、事件案例库、知识库等,为应急决策起辅助作用。

判别环节的目的是对特情事件预警与告警,该环节是将数据采集库所采集的当前数据与预警系统中所设置的对应数据的安全阈值予以对比:若采集得到数据的当前值大于系统设定的安全阈值,则会立即发出告警信号传至应急响应中心;若采集得到数据的当前值小于系统设定的安全阈值,则无需采取行动。判别系统的建立,可以通过收集航空公司安全评价指标、机场运行安全评价指标与空管运行安全评价指标,以及各类特情事件案例、航空不安全事件报告与航空事故调查报告等,构建预警指标体系并赋予指标权重,采取合适的评价方法并设定安全阈值。

当预警系统判别当前的数据具有危机征兆时,则会立刻向应急响应中心告警,此时特情事件已发生,同时情报工作进入关键的应急状态。应急响应中心立刻对特情事件的相关数据进行情报分析,具体的表现形式包括特情事件类别判断、飞机运行状态评估、机上人员情况了解、就近机场的着陆条件、事态发展的趋势等,据此进行下一步的应急决策。

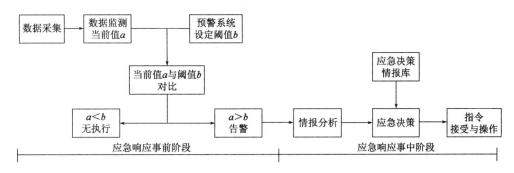

图 3 应急协同联动响应系统控制过程

控制过程的情报输出主要为应急处置方案,借助与应急决策相关的情报库与应急响应指挥小组(专家组),制定可执行的应急方案,并将此控制指令传递给相应的执行机构,例如机组人员、机场、消防、医疗等。

1.4 应急协同联动响应系统反馈过程

反馈过程是指应急处置方案的执行指令已传达到执行机构并予以执行后,传达到应急响应中心,进行应急处置后的情报分析、评价与反馈,如图 4 所示。

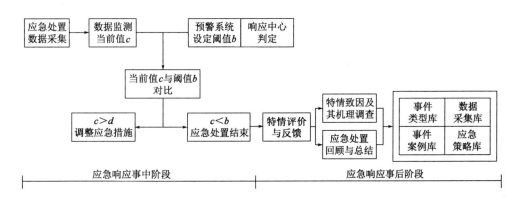

图 4 应急协同联动响应系统反馈过程

将运行安全的相关数据与预警系统设定的安全阈值对比,或者由应急响应中心决定处置后的情况是否需要调整应急处置工作,若处置后的数据值大于阈值,或者响应中心认为有必要对应急处置工作进行调整,则由应急响应中心调整应急决策方案后,再次向执行机构传达指令,开展新的应急处置工作,直至特情事件结束。当特情事件结束后,还需要对特情事件的处置工作进行评价与反馈,及时更新情报,重新输入至相关的情报存储库中,开展下一次的事前、事中以及事后的情报服务,形成一个闭环的更新机制,应对特情事件。

因此,该阶段的情报工作主要包括 3 个方面:是对本次特情事件应急响应过程的回顾与分析,分析事件所造成的人员伤亡与财产损失情况,评估处置工作的效率与取得的效果,总结应急响应的经验教训;二是调查特情事件的起因,分析特情事件的致因因素及其发生机理,对相关单位提出相应的安全整改意见与预防措施;三是将此次特情事件所涉及的数据资料等,输入到特情事件的情报存储库,如事件类型库、数据采集库、事件案例库、应急策略库,丰富所构建的应急响应情报体系。

2 起落架故障特情事件的应急协同联动响应系统

根据我国对航空器特情事件的相关规定,本文将其分为 25 类。当航空器在飞行途中遇到直接或间接威胁飞行安全的情况时,为防止事件恶化,应立即采取有效应急处置措施,避免特情向事故发展。起落架故障是常见的航空器特情事件类型之一,且起落架是航空器的关键部件。当航空器在飞行途中发生起落架放不下或起落架告警的情况时,应立即采取应急处置措施,否则将导致冲偏出跑道严重事故症候或者事故的发生。因此,基于改进STAMP模型的分层结构,构建起落架故障特情事件的应急协同联动响应系统,如图5所示。

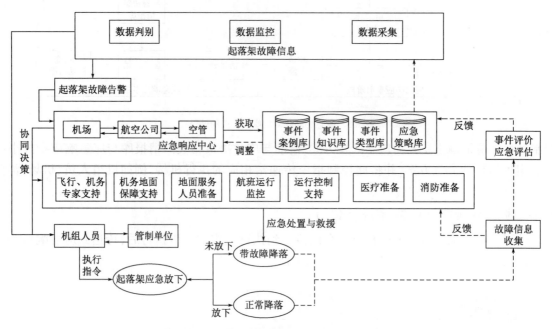

图5 起落架故障特情事件的应急协同联动响应系统

当发生起落架故障特情时,应由空管单位、航空公司与机场组成应急响应中心,通过监控设备、机组报告等方式进一步获取起落架故障的情况,并结合事件案例库、事件知识库、数据采集库等,评估此次事件的严重程度,预计造成的损失等。同时应急决策者根据当前的应急决策存储库综合研判分析,决定应急处置方案后,立即把指令发出给执行机构,向机组人员建议采用大坡度转弯、下降拉升等应急处置方式,将起落架放下,并要求管制单位及时指挥其他航空器避让,留有足够的空域计机组进行大坡度的转弯或紧急迫降等操作。若采取应急措施后,起落架可放下,此时管制单位应予以确认;若无法放下起落架,则应立即通知航空器在就近且满足降落条件的机场迫降,并询问机组有关飞机重量情况是否满足降落标准等,联动航空公司运控中心提供气象条件支持,机务提供航空器机械设备仪表检查判断支持,联动机场地面保障人员紧急就位,通知消防医疗等应急救援队伍,做好可能发生冲偏出跑道、机身起火等事故的救援准备,机组人员按快速检查单(QRH)手册执行着陆程序[19]。

3 特情事件应急决策快速响应情报体系构建

基于改进STAMP模型构建的应急协同联动系统的控制与反馈过程的情报流分析,结合航空器特情事件的特征,可知航空器特情事件的应急响应要做到决策响应时间短,应有信息数据作支撑、协同联动多个参与主体作保障以及先进技术作辅助。情报体系的建立不仅能实时监测潜在的危险信息,而且能分析特情状况,评估危害与预测事态发展。因此,可通过以数据全生命周期理论为基础[20],借助其数据流动过程,构建特情事件应急决策快速响应情报体系(图6),用以分析应急响应情报流及运行机理。探讨围绕大数据时代、协同联动机制与先进技术下的航空器特情应急响应情报工作及功能[10]。

以情报流为基础,分析情报体系的功能,具体如下:

(1)情报收集是情报工作的开始,情报的输入为情报源,其表现形式为各类信息源与数据源,广泛收集多类型的数据与信息是完成情报采集工作的基础,应保证情报的广度与精度。民航运输的情报源主要包括气象数据、通信导航监视设备记录的数据、飞机运行状态数据、航行情报、航线航路数据、地理空域环境数据,以及涉及保障飞行安全相关人员的行为数据。

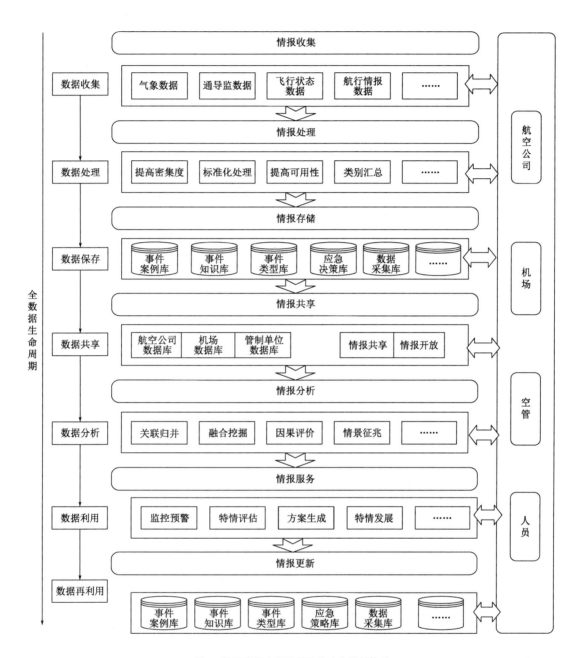

图6 特情事件应急决策快速响应情报体系

(2) 情报处理工作目的是将数量大及类型多的民航运输数据,进行密集度的提高与可用性的处理,并按照统一的数据处理标准进行标准化处理,以方便建立各航空器特情事件的统一规范的数据库,为预警系统和应急决策者获得精准的特征数据,便于数据库之间的交互与共享。

(3) 情报储存是将数据与信息转换成为情报,提供应急决策快速响应所使用的真正有用数据与信息。因此,要求云存储具备不同的功能类型,辅助决策者作出快速响应与决策。云存储库包括:事件案例库,用于存储历史发生的事件案例库;事件知识库,主要分为特情事件的基本信息与可参考的事件主体背景知识、规章制度等资源信息;事件类型库,按照航空器特情的不同类型进行存储;应急策略库,存储应对特情事件的综合性文件,例如应急政策、应急行动程序等;数据采集库,存储实时采集得到的数据,用于判别预警、辅助决策。

（4）情报共享是协同联动应急决策的基础，目的在于化解跨地域、多部门配合等难题。民航运输主要有航空公司、机场、空管三个参与方。将三方的数据与信息共享，以信息数据为基础，设计包括数据整合、应急传输等功能的通信系统，构建数据与信息在各参与方的流向关系，实现各参与方的信息数据共享、实时情报交互，并将应急决策快速响应的优势最大化。

（5）情报分析是应急决策快速响应的关键。考虑到航空器特情事件的复杂性、突发性、多样性，会出现不同类型的特情事件融合的现象，此时需要通过以数学模型为基础的技术手段，分析不同类型特情事件融合后生成的量变或质变的新型航空器特情事件，及其所造成的预计损失、事态发展趋势等[21]。其中利用先进的技术手段，包括关联分析、因果评价以及情景征兆等。通过抽取不同情景下的事件特征数据，进行相互关联分析，事件因果关系评价，预测未来发展的态势等；利用隐马尔可夫模型、时间序列、灰色异构数据预测等数学模型，结合实时监测的数据或信息，研判相关数据是否突破安全阈值，发出危机告警。

各类型航空器特情事件融合框架如图7所示。

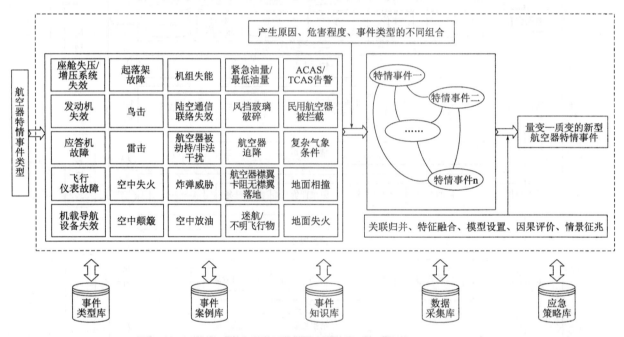

图7 各类型航空器特情事件融合框架

（6）情报服务是情报分析的结果，基于上述的改进STAMP模型的应急协同联动响应系统的控制与反馈过程，情报服务主要包括实时数据的监控与预警、特情事件的等级评估、预估事件发展及造成损失、辅助生成应急决策方案等。其中，应急决策是航空器特情事件应急响应的核心，为应急处置措施提供有效指导。情报服务应急决策辅助流程，如图8所示。

航空器特情事件经过情报分析，能够实现特情等级评估、特征数据提取、事态发展预估。基于此，通过案例推理、语义搜索及数据关联等技术手段，实现相关存储库的提取工作，具体表现为：借助事件案例库所提取的与本特情事件相似的案例；搜寻事件知识库所提取的航空运输与安全科学等领域的专业概念术语及行为规则；参照应急策略库所提取的民航相关的管理规则与应急预案，最终制定多个应急处置方案。对于多个方案决策的模糊性与不确定性，专家组可以借助云模型、模糊数学思想、多目标规划等方式，选择最优的应急处置方案[22-24]。

（7）情报更新是指情报随着特情事件的发展，情报实时更新，动态调整应急响应工作。根据改进STAMP模型的反馈过程与闭环管理理论，情报更新体现在两个方面，一是当特情事件尚未结束，及时反馈给应急响应中心,用以调整下一步的应急处置工作;二是特情事件结束后,完成对特情的调查分析以及应急响应工作的评价,用以补充事件案例库、事件知识库等,为以后同类型的事件的应急响应工作提供更精准的情报支撑。

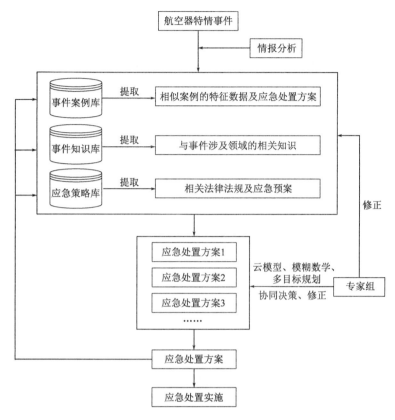

图8 情报服务应急决策辅助流程图

4 结　语

航空器特情事件的应急处置是避免严重事故征候或事故的有效干预控制手段。通过建立有效的航空器特情应急协同联动响应系统与完善的情报体系,能够在特情处置时发挥重要的作用。STAMP模型是利用安全约束将安全问题转化为控制问题来实现安全属性的复杂安全系统模型。该模型为应急响应系统的构建提供了新的思路,为分析应急响应情报体系提供新的视野。

因此,基于STAMP模型的控制与反馈原理,本文通过改进STAMP模型,构建了航空器特情事件的应急协同联动响应系统,该模型能够全面分析应急响应的控制与反馈过程中各个环节与因素之间的关系。以起落架故障特情为例,分析了航空器特情事件发生时应急协同联动响应系统的运作过程,能够为特情事件的应急处置工作提供理论基础。

以改进STAMP模型的应急协同联动响应系统为基础,借鉴全数据生命周期原理,构建了应急决策快速响应情报体系,该情报体系能够系统地、全面地分析情报体系在应对特情事件所发挥的作用。分析表明,该情报体系不仅具有危机监控与告警、应急决策辅助、事后反馈与评价等功能,而且能结合特情事件的复杂性与多样性,提供动态的事件变化趋势等,为应急决策者提供个性化情报服务。

参考文献

[1] 王莉莉,位放.基于同时仪表进近的航空器在特情下的碰撞风险模型研究[J].安全与环境学报,2018,18(01):5-11.

[2] 王浙军.空管协同应急管理机制研究及系统实现[D].广汉:中国民用航空飞行学院,2016.

[3] 祝楷.基于系统论的STAMP模型在煤矿事故分析中的应用[J].系统工程理论与实践,2018,38(04):1069-1081.
[4] 郑磊,胡剑波.基于STAMP/STPA的机轮刹车系统安全性分析[J].航空学报,2017,38(01):246-256.
[5] 王瑛,孙赟,李超,等.基于STAMP模型的军机飞行训练安全性分析[J].中国安全科学学报,2018,28(09):68-73.
[6] 牛丰,王昱,周诚.基于STAMP模型的地铁施工安全事故致因分析[J].土木工程与管理学报,2016,33(01):73-78.
[7] 王起全,吴嘉鑫.基于STAMP模型的地铁拥挤踩踏应急联动系统设计[J].中国安全科学学报,2016,26(12):158-162.
[8] 朱晓峰,冯雪艳,王东波.面向突发事件的情报体系研究[J].情报理论与实践,2014,37(04):77-80,97.
[9] 徐绪堪,钟宇翀,魏建香,等.基于组织-流程-信息的突发事件情报分析框架构建[J].情报理论与实践,2015,38(04):70-73.
[10] 郭春侠,张静.突发事件应急决策的快速响应情报体系构建研究[J].情报理论与实践,2016,39(05):53-57,68.
[11] 苏新宁,朱晓峰,崔露方.基于生命周期的应急情报体系理论模型构建[J].情报学报,2017,36(10):989-997.
[12] 刘浏,苏新宁.突发事件应急响应情报体系案例解析——以自然灾害事件为例[J].科技情报研究,2020,2(02):94-102.
[13] 谷俊,苏新宁.情报系统在事故类突发事件中的作用解析[J].科技情报研究,2020,2(02):67-75.
[14] Park H,Bellamy M A,Basole R C. Structural Anatomy and Evolution of Supply Chain Alliance Networks: A Multi-method Approach[J]. Journal of Operations Management,2018,63(2):79-96.
[15] 何水.从政府危机管理走向危机协同治理——兼论中国危机治理范式革新[J].江南社会学院学报,2008(02):23-26.
[16] 吴国斌,张凯.多主体应急协同效率影响因素实证研究——以湖北省高速公路为例[J].工程研究跨学科视野中的工程,2011,3(02):164-173.
[17] 樊博,刘若玄.应急情报联动的协同管理理论研究[J].信息资源管理学报,2019,9(04):10-17.
[18] 杨巧云,姚乐野.协同联动应急决策情报体系:内涵与路径[J].情报科学,2016,34(02):27-31.
[19] 石彪.应急预案管理中的若干问题研究[D].合肥:中国科学技术大学,2012.
[20] 储节旺,夏莉.嵌入生命周期理论的科学数据管理体系构建研究——牛津大学为例[J].现代情报,2020,40(10):34-42.
[21] 徐绪堪,蒋勋,苏新宁.突发事件驱动的应急情报分析框架构建[J].情报学报,2017,36(10):981-988.
[22] 刘仁涛,姜继平,史斌,等.突发水污染应急处置技术方案动态生成模型及决策支持软件系统[J].环境科学学报,2017,37(02):763-770.
[23] 魏建香,王静,朱云霞.面向药品突发事件应急决策的知识库模型构建研究[J].情报科学,2018,36(07):66-70+90.
[24] 郑霞忠,邵波,陈玲,等.水电厂突发事件应急救援方案云决策模型研究[J].中国安全科学学报,2015,25(04):157-163.

未来空域下无人机通信性能指标研究

周 强 卫永安 刘广才 王龙杰
(北京航空航天大学电子信息工程学院)

摘 要 未来航空系统的发展方向基于空域融合,重点为构建一个囊括无人机和有人机等航空器在内的新型空中交通管理系统。无人机通信为空中交通管理服务提供重要的技术支持,因此有必要对未来空域下的无人机通信技术进行研究以使其满足性能指标要求。本文从无人机通信性能指标要求入手,首先介绍无人机通信性能指标的基本概念和确定方式。并介绍了相关国家和组织的研究现状,之后通过分析未来空域下无人机的运行特点,总结了无人机通信技术的未来发展方向。

关键词 无人机管控 通信性能 指标分析 C2链路 未来空域

0 引 言

随着无人机技术的迅速发展,越来越多的行业都开始应用无人机解决特定场景下的问题。为了对未来空域下无人机进行更为便捷有效的管理,国际民航组织和各国相关机构积极推动无人机融入现有空域系统,实现统一管理。针对无人机进行通信性能分析既是无人机安全应用的重要基础,也是无人机空管的研究热点之一。本文从无人机通信性能指标要求入手,首先介绍无人机通信性能指标的基本概念和确定方式,然后通过分析未来空域下无人机的运行特点,总结了无人机通信技术的未来发展方向。

1 无人机与未来空域

无人机(Unmanned Aircraft Vehicle,UAV)指的是那些不是由机上飞行员操控,而是由其他的控制单元进行操作管理(包括远程操控或依照机上程序自主飞行)的航空器。无人机系统(Unmanned Aircraft System,UAS)指的是包含无人机本身以及支持其进行活动的其他部分所构成的整体系统,包括无人机本身、远程操作单位、通信链路、任务载荷等。

空域指的是航空器运行的空间。随着无人机数量的增加,其在空域内运行时与有人机、其他无人机乃至地面物体之间的冲突风险愈发显著。为了使无人机能够有效安全地进行飞行作业,未来空域这一概念得以诞生。未来空域具备以下特点:

(1)所有航空器融入国家空域统一管理,根据任务的具体要求,飞行在不同空域的无人机应当遵循该空域下的安全管理要求,并和有人机具有等同性能[1]。

(2)对于不同空域下的安全管理要求,采用指标代替传统的技术要求,即满足某些规定的指标就可以认为该飞行器都可以满足安全飞行要求[2]。

目前,各国和有关组织都在进行无人机融入空域的研究,如表1所示。

针对无人机系统融入空域的不同研究路线 表1

国家和组织	研究路线
国际民航组织	视距外无人机的安全监管相关标准与推荐措施
欧盟 SESAR	U-space 新型空域管理
美国 FAA 与 NASA	NextGen 下针对无人机融入国家空域的模拟测试环境搭建和应用

2 无人机的通信性能指标

2.1 所需通信性能的含义

所需通信性能(Required Communication Performance, RCP)指的是能够支持特定空中交通服务运行的通信性能要求。ICAO在官方文件中规定了四种类别的参数来描述所需通信性能指标要求[3],分别是传输时间、连续性、可用性和完好性。

对于无人机系统而言,UTM和ATM的通信基础设施和空域描述大部分是相同的,更多的是两者通信链路的逻辑结构不同以及在超低空等运行环境迥异的空域内存在差别化应用,因此,可以借用所需通信性能这一概念对未来空域下的无人机系统进行要求。

2.2 所需通信性能中指标的确定方法

根据所需通信性能的含义,可以明确的是所需通信性能这一概念与其所支持的空中交通服务功能相关。因此有两种方式确定所需通信性能规定的各项指标:一种是间接的建模推导方法;另一种是直接的统计测算方法。

2.2.1 基于ATS其他影响因素的间接方法

所需通信性能属于空中交通管理服务性能的表述,受到多种因素的综合决定,包括最小间距的要求、空域条件和航路条件、安全等级目标、航路流量表现等,并通过复杂的分析运算得到基于上述因素下特定条件的空域规划方法,根据这一方法再去计算理论上满足安全性要求的空中交通服务性能。

2.2.2 基于分解ATS通信过程的直接统计方法

为了保证空中交通管理下的分离要求,RCP传输时间需要考虑支持分离保证的通信和管制人员干预过程中的事务时间之和t:

$$t = A + U + P + T \tag{1}$$

其中,管制员根据ADS报告发现潜在冲突并给出ATS分离方法的时间,定义为A;向飞行员传达指令的时间,定义为U;飞行员作出反应的时间,定义为P;向管制员返回确认接收指令所用的时间,定义为T。

对于不同链路结构的无人机而言,A时间是一致的,U、P、T则会受到链路拓扑结构的影响。

2.3 无人机的所需通信性能指标研究

根据无人机的运行空域和链路功能,可以把无人机的通信链路划分为如图1所示的种类。根据所需通信性能是基于操作事务的这一特点,无人机的RCP相关指标应当针对指控数据链路(Command and Control, C2)进行讨论。C2链路是一种逻辑上的连接,不局限于实现方式,其作用为支持操作者对无人机进行任务之外的操作干预。

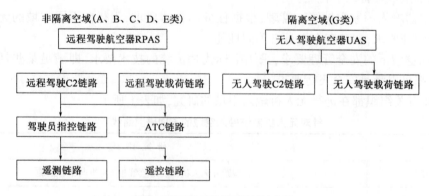

图1 无人机系统的通信链路分类

对于RPAS C2链路而言,在相同外部条件下,无人机所对应的指标要求应该比有人机更严苛。目前无人机系统规则制定联合体JARUS提供了一种射频条件下的RPAS C2链路的所需通信性能指标要求

(Required RPAS C2 Link Performance，RLP)，如表 2 所示[4]。JARUS 提供的性能规定仅限于远程操作者在接收到管制单元信息后对无人机进行操作这一段过程。

JARUS 推荐的一种 RPAS C2 链路通信性能要求[4] 表 2

RCP 参数	RCP A	RCP B	其他
传输时间(s)	3	5	15
连续性(概率)	0.95/0.999	0.95/0.999	0.95/0.999
可用性(概率)	0.9999	0.999	0.999
完好性(概率/h)	10^{-5}	10^{-4}	10^{-4}

对于 UAS C2 而言，由于隔离空域内的无人机数量众多、应用广泛，采用传统地面中心人工监管的方式难以提供完备的空中交通服务功能[5]。FAA 设计了一种基于无人机云平台的 UAS 空中交通管理方式，通过将无人机即时接入蜂窝移动网络或提前进行备案等方式，进行实时的态势监测[6]。该方法需要依托于蜂窝移动网络进行实时的交通管制服务[7]，同时借助于视距内飞行等条件的限制，提高飞手操作无人机的反应能力，从而提升安全性。对于网联无人机，中国民航局发布了其相关性能规范的征求意见稿，里面涉及了 UAS C2 链路的部分性能要求[8]。

2.4 所需通信性能在无人机系统中的应用

所需通信性能不仅可以用来为整个 UTM 服务的通信过程提供指标依据，还可以通过将通信过程分解为不同的子过程，确定其对应的指标规定，以便帮助空管单位和驾驶员及时判断问题所在并采取针对性措施，并为其他服务的指标确定提供参考。此外，所需通信性能还可以帮助新技术演进，以此来维持更高的安全性。

3 无人机通信性能指标研究的发展方向

无人机通信性能指标的研究具有两个方面的重要作用：(1)提升非隔离空域下无人机的安全性能，使其满足相同水平下有人机的安全性能要求；(2)使隔离空域下无人机达到实操与监管的要求，从而满足在低空复杂空域下的安全运行条件，为未来通用航空的发展提供保障。

3.1 新型空域下的空管系统

根据不同类型空域的管理差别，无人机融入国家空域后的空中交通管理系统可以分为两部分，一部分针对管制空域，运行在这一部分空域的无人机应当遵循 CNS/ATM 的管理要求，至少满足相应的通信导航监视性能指标[9]；另一部分是针对非管制空域，运行在这一部分空域的无人机需要通过报备审批或接入无人机云系统等方式进行安全监管[10]。

3.2 未来空域模拟环境测试平台搭建

未来空域是一个复杂的空中环境，对其进行仿真会涉及多种模型和参数，但成功搭建模拟测试平台也有助于对未来空域的性能进行分析，减少实际测试的需要，为新技术和新空管手段提供高效安全的验证平台。未来空域的模拟环境测试平台应当具备以下几方面的特征：一是真实性，仿真平台应该囊括实际空域和航空器系统的特性；二是实时性，仿真平台能够根据输入操作尽可能即时地反馈结果；三是扩展性，仿真平台能够支持新技术和新管理措施的设定。

3.3 C2 链路的融合与改进

需要研究更合适的通信技术，并将其应用在无人机系统当中。

对于非隔离空域的融合，措施如下：通过与有人机目前应用的 C 波段、L 波段等航空频谱进行共享；实施所需通信性能指标的统一化要求，共同应用 ICAO 此前为民航规定的 RCP 指标要求；研究基于共享航空频谱的 C2 数据链路技术(如德国的 C 波段数字航空通信系统 CDACS 等)，提升无人机 C2 链路的实时性与可靠性。

对于隔离空域,措施如下:无人机应该满足实时通信与干预的特性,从而保证在复杂空域下满足安全性能要求。可以考虑采用5G蜂窝移动通信技术为无人机提供通信服务,通过软件定义无线电设计无人机天线,利用蜂窝移动通信组建无人机联网等。

4 结　语

面向无人机融入国家空域的需求,本文总结了无人机通信性能指标确定方式与应用手段,并对未来无人机通信性能研究的方向进行展望,包括新空域下的空管系统搭建、配套的模拟环境测试平台搭建以及无人机指控数据链路的优化与融合等。通过使无人机在未来空域中具备更优秀的通信性能,从而提升航空效率与保障空域安全。

参考文献

[1] 陈志杰. 未来空中交通管制系统发展面临的技术挑战[J]. 指挥信息系统与技术, 2016, 7(06):1-5.

[2] Konstantions Dalamagkidis, Kimon P Valavanis, Les A Piegl. On Integrating Unmanned Aircraft Systems into the National Airspace System (Second Edition) [M]. Springer Science + Business Media, 2015.

[3] Federal Aviation Administration (FAA). Unmanned aircraft operations in the national airspace system [R]. Docket No. FAA-2006-25714, 2007.

[4] Jont Authorities for Rulemaking of Unmanned Systems (JARUS). WG 5. RPAS C2 link Required Communication Performance (C2 link RCP) concept[S]. 2014.

[5] D'souza S, Ishihara A, Nikaido B, et al. Feasibility of Varying Geo-Fence Around an Unmanned Aircraft Operation Based on Vehicle Performance and Wind[C]. 2016 IEEE/AIAA 35th Digital Avionics Systems Conference (DASC). Sacramento, 2016.

[6] 中国民用航空局. 无人机云系统接口数据规范:MHT/T 2009—2017[S]. 2019.

[7] 中国民用航空局. 低空飞行服务保障体系建设总体方案[Z]. 2019.

[8] 中国民用航空局, IB-FS-2018-011. 低空联网无人机安全飞行测试报告[R]. 北京, 2018.

[9] 陈志杰. 空域管理理论与方法[M]. 北京:科学出版社, 2012.

[10] Aweiss A S, Owens B D, Rios J, et al. Unmanned Aircraft Systems (UAS) Traffic Management (UTM) National Campaign II[C]. 2018 AIAA Information Systems-AIAA Infotech@ Aerospace. Florida:AIAA, 2018:1727.

基于人工势场法的无人机路径规划

梁卜文[1]　张晋通[2]

(1. 天津大学;2. 北京航空航天大学)

摘　要　随着无人机在社会生产中的广泛应用,可靠的路径规划成为无人机安全自主飞行的前提。然而,在低空飞行环境下,威胁要素繁多且相互耦合,目前的大多数规划算法不能有效提取和利用环境信息以规划合理的路径。针对这一问题,提出一种基于人工势场法的无人机路径规划方法,该方法将低空威胁要素分为静态威胁、动态威胁和气象威胁,并分别为其构建态势评估模型,使低空威胁要素解耦;将态势评估的结果与人工势场法中的势场构建部分结合,进行路径规划。仿真结果表明,该方法可以在多种低空威胁共存的复杂低空环境下,保障无人机飞行的安全性。

关键词　低空威胁　态势评估　人工势场法　路径规划

0 引 言

在执行不同的任务之前,无人机需要事先规划路径,考虑多种因素,比如,环境动态变化时,算法应具备良好的实时性,快速求出路径以应对突如其来的环境威胁。在复杂低空环境下,路径规划的难度进一步加大,低空场景威胁要素繁多,多变的地形地貌以及气象条件等环境要素都给飞行安全造成挑战。现有路径规划算法依赖原始数据,且缺乏对数据进一步处理分析,无法合理规划有效路径。

为解决上述难点,本文将低空威胁要素分类与解耦,构建低空威胁态势评估的模型,将评估结果与人工势场法中势场的构建相结合,提出一种基于人工势场法的无人机路径规划方法,提高路径规划的安全性与可达性。

1 低空威胁态势评估模型的建立

无人机在低空环境下所受到的静态威胁、动态威胁与气象威胁分别用 P_s、P_d、P_m 表示。

1.1 模型假设

在对低空威胁进行态势评估时共有两条假设:
(1)无人机对自己当前所在位置、目标点及环境因素的定位上不存在误差。
(2)无人机传感器所感知到的信息是理想的,不存在感知受限、受干扰的情况

1.2 静态威胁

在进行态势评估时,静态威胁 P_s 可以表示为如下数学形式,见式(1)。

$$P_s = \begin{cases} \sigma, d(x, \text{obstacle}) \leq \beta \\ 0, d(x, \text{obstacle}) > \beta \end{cases} \tag{1}$$

式中:$d(x, \text{obstacle})$——无人机当前位置与静态障碍物中心的距离;

β——静态威胁范围的作用半径;

σ——常数,表示静态威胁程度。

可以看出在威胁范围外,静态威胁为0,在威胁范围内,静态威胁是恒定的值,与距离变化无关。

1.3 动态威胁

本文引入动态障碍物恶意飞行的假设,利用扇形构建威胁范围,其中轴始终朝向无人机当前位置,动态威胁范围如图1所示。

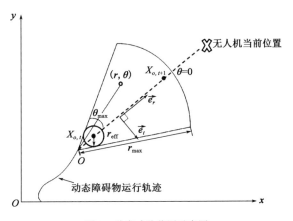

图1 动态威胁范围示意图

如图1所示,本文规定了一个威胁包络,r_{eff} 表示动态障碍物附近圆形威胁包络的半径,$\vec{e}_r$ 和 $\vec{e}_t$ 均是表明方向的单位向量。在时刻 t,动态障碍物位置为 $X_{o,t}$,下一时刻预计运动到的位置为 $X_{o,t+1}$。$X_{o,t}$ 与 $X_{o,t+1}$ 的关系见式(2)。

$$X_{o,t+1} = X_{o,t} + \vec{v}\Delta t \tag{2}$$

在式(2)中,动态障碍物速度$\vec{v}$的方向朝向无人机当前位置。径向速度分量$v_r = v_{max}$,v_{max}表示无人机能提供的最大速率;垂直速度分量$v_t = 0$。Δt表示两时刻间的持续时间。当垂直速度分量$v_t = v_{tmax}$时,径向速度分量$v_r = \sqrt{(v^2 - v_{tmax}^2)}$。此时,$\theta_{max} = \arcsin(\frac{v_t}{v})$,$r_{max}$有如下数学形式,见式(3):

$$r_{max} = ||\overrightarrow{X_{o,t}X_{o,t+1}}|| + r_{eff} + \frac{r_{eff}}{\sin(\theta_{max})} \tag{3}$$

式中:$||X_{o,t}X_{o,t+1}||$——从时刻t到时刻$t+1$,动态障碍物移动的距离;
r_{eff}——动态障碍物的威胁作用半径。

在中轴上动态威胁$P_d(r,0)$有如下数学形式,见式(4):

$$P_d(r,0) = \begin{cases} a_1(r-b_1)(r-r_1)^2 & r_1 \leq r \leq r_2 \\ a_2(r-b_2)(r-r_3)^2 & r_2 \leq r \leq r_3 \\ 0 & \end{cases} \tag{4}$$

在式(4)中,$a_1 = \frac{k_0}{(r_2-b_1)(r_2-r_1)^2}$;$b_1 = \frac{3r_2-r_1}{2}$;$a_2 = \frac{k}{(r_2-b_2)(r_2-r_3)^2}$;$b_2 = \frac{3r_2-r_3}{2}$;$r_1 = r_2 - r_{eff}$;$r_2 = \frac{r_{eff}}{\sin(\theta_{max})}$;$r_3 = r_{max}$,$k_0$为常数,表示中轴上威胁程度的最大值。

在威胁范围上任意一点的威胁程度$P_d(r,\theta)$有如下数学形式,见式(5):

$$P_d(r,\theta) = \begin{cases} \frac{P_d(r,0)}{\theta_{end}^4}(\theta^2 - \theta_{end}^2)^2 & r_1 \leq r \leq r_3 \\ 0 & \text{elsewhere} \end{cases} \tag{5}$$

在式(5)中,$\theta_{end} = \begin{cases} \frac{\pi}{2} - \tan^{-1}(\frac{y_{int}}{x_{int}}) & r1 \leq r \leq r' \\ \theta_{max} & r' \leq r \leq r_3 \end{cases}$;$r' = \frac{r_{eff}}{\tan\theta}$;$y_{int} = \frac{r_2^2 + r^2 - r_{eff}^2}{2r_2}$;$x_{int} = \sqrt{(r^2 - y_{int}^2)}$。

1.4 气象威胁

在进行态势评估时,气象威胁P_m有威胁程度均匀、非均匀两种。对于威胁程度均匀的情况,气象威胁P_m的数学表示形式见式(6):

$$P_m = \begin{cases} \rho & d(x, \text{obstacle}) \leq \gamma \\ 0 & d(x, \text{obstacle}) > \gamma \end{cases} \tag{6}$$

在式(6)中,ρ是常数,表示气象威胁的威胁程度;$d(x, \text{obstacle})$表示无人机当前位置与气象中心之间的距离;γ表示气象因素威胁范围的半径。

对于威胁程度非均匀的情况,气象威胁P_m有如下数学表示形式,见式(7):

$$P_m = \begin{cases} \frac{\rho}{d(x, \text{obstacle})} & d(x, \text{obstacle}) \leq \gamma \\ 0 & d(x, \text{obstacle}) > \gamma \end{cases} \tag{7}$$

在式(7)中,各符号的含义同式(6)。可以看出,在威胁范围外,气象威胁为0;在威胁范围内,无人机所受到的气象威胁随着无人机与气象中心间距离的减小而增强。

2 态势信息引导的路径规划方法

2.1 人工势场法介绍

人工势场法的基本思想是将智能体在周围环境中的运动,抽象为在人造势能场中的运动。通过对势能场求导得到力场,用力场控制智能体的运动。其中,目标点对移动的智能体产生引力,障碍物等有威胁处对移动的智能体产生斥力,通过求合力来指导智能体从起始点移动到目标点。电势场示意图如图2所示。

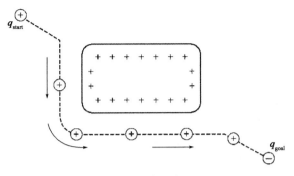

图2 电势场示意图

将移动空间比作一个电势场平面,智能体的位置比作空间中一点。令智能体、智能体的起点q_{start}和障碍物带正电荷,终点q_{goal}带负电荷。智能体将会在势力场的作用下沿着某条路径向终点移动,并避开带正电荷的障碍物。

构建势场时,某一点q上的总势能包括引力势U_{attr}和斥力势U_{repu}两部分。引力势函数表达见式(8):

$$U_{attr}(q) = \frac{1}{2}\eta \, d^2(q, q_{goal}) \tag{8}$$

在式(8)中,η为常数,表示引力增益;$d(q, q_{goal})$表示当前点q到目标点q_{goal}的距离。

斥力势函数见式(9):

$$U_{repu}(q) = \begin{cases} \frac{1}{2}\zeta \left[\frac{1}{D(q)} - \frac{1}{Q^*}\right]^2 & D(q) \leqslant Q^* \\ 0, D(q) > Q^* \end{cases} \tag{9}$$

式中:$D(q)$——点q位置与静态或者动态障碍物的距离;

ζ——常数,表示斥力增益;

Q^*——障碍物的作用距离阈值。

在构建出势场之后,智能体参照势场高低,从势能高的位置向势能低的位置移动。在移动的过程中求负梯度,得到力场即可控制智能体向目标点移动的同时远离障碍物。

2.2 规划算法设计

人工势场法在实现的过程中可以划分为以下两个主要步骤:

（1）在当前环境的基础上构建势场；

（2）智能体参照势场进行移动。

本文的算法在人工势场法基础上进行改进,构建的势场由引力势U_{attr}与斥力势U_{repu}两部分组成。其中,引力势表征目标点对无人机的吸引,控制智能体在整体大方向上朝目标点移动。数学表达形式见式(10):

$$U_{attr} = \frac{1}{2}\eta \, d^2(x, goal) \tag{10}$$

式中:η——常数;

$d(x, goal)$——无人机当前位置到目标点的距离。

在人工势场法中,风险高的位置斥力势大于其他位置,这个特性与低空威胁态势评估的结果相吻合。因此,本文算法中的斥力势U_{repu}表示为如下形式,见式(11):

$$U_{repu} = P_s + P_d + P_m \tag{11}$$

式中:P_s、P_d、P_m——低空威胁态势评估模型中的静态威胁、动态威胁和气象威胁。

从整体上看,环境中某点 q 处的势函数 $U(q)$ 可以表示为该点上引力势 $U_{attr}(q)$ 与斥力势 $U_{repu}(q)$ 之和,见式(12):

$$U(q) = U_{attr}(q) + U_{repu}(q) \tag{12}$$

构建完势场以后,智能体参照势场进行移动。取势场上该位置的负梯度作为力向量,指导智能体的移动决策,在 q 点处智能体的受力可以由式(13)求出:

$$F(q) = -\nabla U(q) = -\left[\frac{\partial U}{\partial q_1}(q), \cdots, \frac{\partial U}{\partial q_m}(q)\right]^T \tag{13}$$

由式(13)中可以看出,某点 q 处负梯度的方向就是势函数 $U(q)$ 衰减最快的方向,说明智能体在移动过程中从势能高的位置向势能低的位置移动。

在示意图3中,暖色调、冷色调的区域分别表示势能高与势能低的区域。

在势场的构建上,起点势能高,引力势大;终点附近势能低,引力势小,且周围没有相近的威胁。低空威胁区域斥力势大,区域势能很高。于是智能体参照势场从高势能向低势能方向移动,就能在趋近目标点的同时,规避环境中存在的风险。

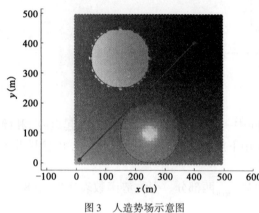

图3 人造势场示意图

3 仿真试验结果与分析

3.1 试验部分总体介绍

试验场景中动态障碍物与静态障碍物相结合,用算法一表示人工势场法,算法二表示本研究的算法。如果在试验结果上算法二优于算法一,那么就说明本文算法能够优化无人机的路径规划。对比试验具有以下性能指标。

冲突次数:动态障碍物移动到无人机冲突范围内的次数。

碰撞次数:无人机与动态障碍物发生碰撞的次数。

超时次数:每次试验中,无人机从起点目标点的步数限制为100步,超出步数限制仍未到达目标点,则视为超时。

成功次数:在100次重复实验内无人机成功规划出路径的次数。

平均步数:无人机在成功规划的实验中的平均移动步数。

3.2 动静结合对比试验

如图4所示,左下角与右上角的"x"分别表示起点与终点。黑色的"x"表示无人机当前位置,红色、黑色圆圈分别表示无人机的探测、冲突范围。黄色标注的方块和圆圈表示静态障碍物,在这个场景下动态障碍物随机运动。试验重复100次,试验结果见表1。

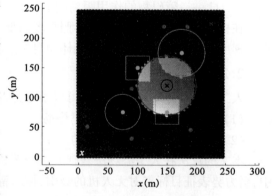

图4 动静结合时的试验场景图

动静结合时的试验结果　　　　　　　　　表1

方　　法	冲突次数	碰撞次数	超时次数	成功次数	平均步数
算法一	7	0	39	61	78
算法二	1	0	12	88	69

从表1的试验结果中可以发现,在两种算法都没有碰撞的情况下,本文算法的规划成功率较高,并且能够以更少的步数到达目标点。

3.3 对比试验结果分析

由对比仿真试验看出,与人工势场法路径规划相比,本文算法具有更优性能。

如图 5 所示,将动态威胁态势评估模型与斥力势场构建相结合以后,得到一个扇形的威胁范围,始终朝向无人机当前位置。

如图 6 所示,传统势场构建方法的斥力势场的威胁从中心向外衰减,朝全方向扩散。

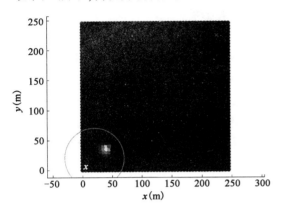
图 5 本研究算法中的动态斥力势场

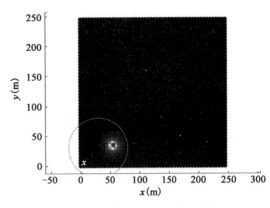
图 6 人工势场法中的动态斥力势场

构建势场差异导致了试验结果的不同,原因在于以下两个方面:

首先是安全性。传统方法设定的威胁是全方向的,而本文在刻画威胁时,假设动态障碍物恶意飞行,朝着无人机当前位置移动,于是能指导无人机避开最危险的方向,减少碰撞次数。

其次,本文将动态威胁精确化,动态障碍物的威胁范围由圆形变为扇形,有效减小了冗余的影响面积,无人机的自由空间变大。当环境复杂,动态障碍物密集时,更容易找到捷径,减少超时次数,提高成功率。

4 结 语

为保证无人机在低空环境下安全飞行,本文先是对低空威胁要素进行机理上的分析,然后将威胁要素分类并分别建立态势评估模型。根据人工势场法具有局部路径规划能力的特点,将其构建势场的环节与态势评估模型相结合,将评估的结果数量化,提出了一种基于人工势场法的无人机路径规划方法。最后通过仿真对比试验,发现本文算法有效提升了无人机路线规划的安全性与应对低空环境下不同种类威胁的能力。

本文所研究内容仍存在一些不足,只考虑了低空环境下周围环境因素的影响,未考虑无人机自身的关键因素。在未来的研究中,会将无人机自身的运动约束考虑进来,更好地进行安全层面上的态势评估,进而指导无人机在低空环境下高效且安全飞行。

参考文献

[1] Dijkstra, Edsger W. A note on two problems in connexion with graphs[J]. Numerische mathematik, 1959, 269-271.

[2] Atramentov A, LaValle S M. Efficient nearest neighbor searching for motion planning[C].//Proceedings 2002 IEEE International Conference on Robotics and Automation (Cat. No. 02CH37292). IEEE, 2002, 632-637.

[3] Kavraki, Lydia E, et al. Probabilistic roadmaps for path planning in high-dimensional configuration spaces [J]. IEEE transactions on Robotics and Automation 1996, 12(4): 566-580.

[4] LaValle, Steven M. Rapidly-exploring random trees: A new tool for path planning[A]. Lowa State University Ames USA, 1998.

[5] Karaman, Sertac, Emilio Frazzoli. Sampling-based algorithms for optimal motion planning[J]. The international journal of robotics research, 2011, 30(7): 846-894.

无人机运行风险分析研究

周强 张杰玮 刘广才

(北京航空航天大学电子信息工程学院)

摘要 随着无人机制造业的快速发展,无人机应用范围日益广泛,然而无人机事故频发,威胁着国家空域安全和人民生命财产安全,因此无人机的运行管理显得尤为重要,而无人机运行风险评估正是其中的关键环节。本文首先介绍当前小型低空无人机的发展情况以及有关低空无人机运行管理的相关政策法规,对无人机运行风险的定义以及无人机运行风险管理框架进行总结,然后对低空无人机风险分析方法的研究现状进行总结,阐述无人机地面风险模型量化分析方法。并对各类风险建模分析方法进行比较,分析了现有方法适用场景和局限性,最后提出了未来无人机运行风险分析的发展方向。

关键词 无人机 空域安全 运行风险 量化建模 地面风险

0 引言

无人机是一种依靠操作员进行无线电遥控控制或者依靠自身自动驾驶程序来执行特定飞行任务的无人驾驶航空器。无人机应用范围日益广泛,然而无人机事故频发,威胁着国家空域安全和人民生命财产安全,因此无人机的运行管理显得尤为重要。无人机与有人机的固有差异和无人机运行环境的多样性问题,急需针对无人机制定相应的监管规则和安全有效的安全监管体系。无人机运行风险评估正是其中的关键环节。本文明确了无人机运行风险的定义,分析了无人机运行风险管理框架,开展了各类无人机运行风险分析方法的比较研究,通过分析现有方法的适用场景和局限性,提出了未来无人机运行风险分析方法的发展方向。

1 无人机运行风险

1.1 无人机运行风险定义

首先,明确风险的定义。不载人这一属性是无人机与有人机相比最显著的特征,所以无人机运行风险指的是无人机在一定空域内飞行过程中因系统失效或者外部原因导致坠机,进而对地面人员生命、地面财产和空域内其他航空器造成威胁的风险。

其次是无人机风险评估中关于危险、风险和事故之间的关系。Ericson 针对三者的关系建立了如图1所示的危险、风险、灾害模型[1]。

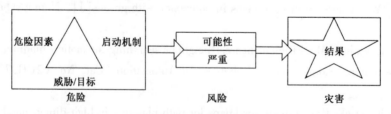

图1 危险、风险、灾害模型[1]

危险是系统的状态或一组条件,与系统环境中的其他条件一起可能导致事故。危险包括危险因素、危险启动机制和目标/威胁,三者构成了危险的来源。

KayWackwitz 等人将危险和风险区分开,认为在通常情况下危险具有相似性,当无人机某项操作发生时,这些存在危险的情况就会转化为风险,如图2所示[2]。

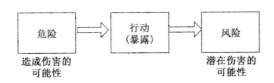

图 2 危险、风险模型[2]

1.2 无人机分类

目前,各国和有关组织根据自身情况制定各自指南和法规进行无人机分类。但对于无人机分类的国际统一标准尚未形成。

2017 年,中国民航局发布了《民用无人驾驶航空器实名制登记管理规定》[3],依照空机重量和起飞重量对无人机进行了分类,如表 1 所示。

无人机分类表[3]　　　　表 1

分 类	空机重量	起飞重量
Ⅰ	0 < W ≤ 1.5	
Ⅱ	1.5 < W ≤ 4	1.5 < W ≤ 7
Ⅲ	4 < W ≤ 15	7 < W ≤ 25
Ⅳ	15 < W ≤ 116	25 < W ≤ 150
Ⅴ	植保类无人机	
Ⅵ	无人飞艇	
Ⅶ	超视距运行的 Ⅰ、Ⅱ 类无人机	
Ⅺ	116 < W ≤ 5700	150 < W ≤ 5700
Ⅻ	W > 5700	

EASA 在立法通告 A-NPA-2015-10[4]中提出了基于风险的无人机分类办法,分为低运行风险开放类无人机、中等运行风险特定类无人机、高运行风险认证类无人机。

1.3 无人机运行风险评估管理

无人机适航安全性可被定义为:一是在特定空域运行时,不会对地面财产和人员造成损失和构成危害;二是不能对其他正在进行航空活动的飞行器的飞行安全造成影响。对此,各国采用基于运行风险的方法制定无人机安全监管框架,并且制定和出台了基于运行风险的无人机系统安全法规。

Reece Clothier[5]等人对 ISO(2009)指南[6]中提出的 SRMP 流程进行了更高层次的解读,并给出了关于无人机运行风险管理流程的 SRMP 流程图,如图 3 所示。

SRMP 流程主要包括以下几步骤:环境建立、风险识别、风险分析、风险评估、风险处理、监控和审查、沟通和协商环节。

JARUS 于 2017 年 6 月首次发布特殊类运行风险评估管理方法(SORA)。SORA 是一套基于地面风险和空中风险评估,为局方等相关方提供评估无人机能否按照经过风险评估后的置信水平实施安全运行的方法。SORA 运行风险评估管理方法流程架构如图 4 所示。

KayWackwitz[2]等人认为 UAS 安全风险评估基于从安全风险识别到风险管理的系统方法,提供了 UAS 安全风险评估的四阶段模型包含安全隐患识别、安全风险评估、安全风险缓解、安全文档,如图 5 所示。

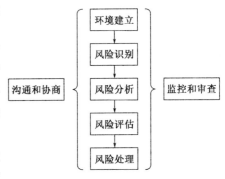

图 3 SRMP 流程图[5]

无人机运行风险分析属于无人机风险管理中的一部分,该过程旨在确保将无人机系统运行风险处理到可接受的水平。通过采取一些决策框架将分析子过程得到的风险值与高级安全标准相比较,以决定是接受该风险值,还是需要采取一定措施来缓解风险。

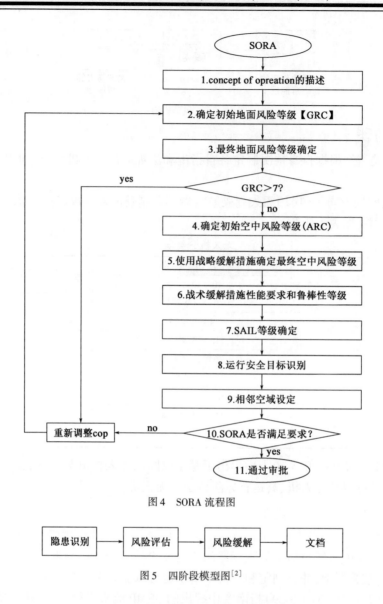

图 4 SORA 流程图

图 5 四阶段模型图[2]

2 无人机运行风险模型量化方法

无人机运行风险模型量化方法不依赖于评估人员的经验和分析角度,也不需要进行系统层面分析。只用聚焦于无人机的运行过程,对无人机运行过程中各个环节进行建模,并进行量化评估,具备很高的客观性和准确性。无人机运行风险模型量化方法的核心就是通过聚焦无人机的运行过程,将风险过程细化到环节进行建模,主要模型如下。

2.1 无人机失效模型

无人机失效模型,描述了无人机故障模式发生的不确定性。通过不同的假设和基本模型的建立,可以得到不同于无人机失效相关的概率数据。

R. Clothier 等人定义了与无人机地面撞击危险相关的四种高级别无人机故障模式,包括失控下降场景、失控故障、进入危险地形、飞行无人机部件掉落[7]。D. A Bruke 等人提出了考虑两种失效模式的模型:失控下降场景 UDS 和负载下飞控系统失效 LOC,根据几何形状和人口密度计算,利用无人机的系统/功能级别细分将较低级别的故障与系统级故障模式联系起来[8]。

无人机失效模型的建立是确定无人机运行风险的一个重要因素,直接对地面碰撞位置和受影响区域造成影响。对于低空轻型无人机来说进行简单的失效模型建立可以基本满足评估分析的要求,而大型高空无人机的运行风险分析评估就需要更加复杂的失效模型来确保分析结果的准确性。

2.2 地面碰撞模型

无人机地面碰撞模型主要分为两类:第一类是假定某一地面特定点,得到无人机对于该确定点的撞击影响;第二类则是通过模拟特定无人机坠落轨迹,得到无人机地面碰撞的撞击位置和受影响区。

C.W. Lum 等人提出无人机对地滑翔撞击模型,根据下降类型建立了无人机在空中碰撞后地面人员和财产的危险区域模型[9]。但在模型中没有区分无人机失事类型,并假定坠毁飞行器只是无人机。Natasha Bradley 等对 6DoF 模型中撞击位置投影的计算方式进行了总结,并引入了直升机模型得到了应用于无人机的直升机坠机模型[10]。Chim Washington、Anders la Cour-Harbo 等对无人机失效导致的几种典型下降类型进行了细分,结合飞行参数和运动学公式,加入对于环境不确定性参数的考虑,建立了无人机对地可能碰撞位置的概率分布模型[11-12]。

2.3 地面暴露模型

地面暴露模型主要用于描绘人口密度或者地面建筑物等财产的分布,而风险分析的目的就是得到单位时间无人机对地面人员和财产的风险值,地面暴露模型的建立是无人机运行风险分析评估中最重要的环节之一。

Anders laCour-Harbo 主要针对地面人员密度进行了建模,根据不同的下降类型导致影响区域的不用调整人口密度的分辨率来进行人口风险图的建模[12]。Uluhan Cem Kaya 等使用 PREM 概念对风险分布进行了建模,通过使用取自地理信息系统(GIS)数据库的特定区域的建筑物轮廓线,对风险分布进行建模[13]。Dalamagkidis 等采用智能分区密度制图法,按照土地利用分区将数据重新分配到人口统计单元和土地利用分区的重叠区域,以此得到高分辨率的人口密度地图[14]。

总之,现有的地面暴露模型都需要进行地理地图的整合,同时人员密集区人口的流动性和聚集性也对地面人口暴露模型的建立带来了困难。

2.4 伤害模型

无人机失效事件将决定具体需要使用哪一类伤害机制来进行建模。同时地面人员的属性也会对伤害模型的建立造成影响。

A.V. Shelley 基于对历史实验数据的收集和研究,动能建立描述无人机对一般男性的条件伤害概率模型[15]。Shakiba-herfeh M 同样也使用动能来建立无人机伤害模型,考虑了地面人员因有遮挡物而免受无人机直接撞击的程度[6]。Magister 认为小型无人驾驶飞机伤害模型与人体接触的部分的冲击动能和特征直接相关。使用钝化标准将撞击的动能与身体承受冲击能量的能力联系起来,同时提出为了尽量减少伤害,小型无人驾驶飞机的基本操作和物理设计的标准[17]。

3 结 语

随着我国低空空域的逐步开放以及无人机产业的发展和无人机管理体系的进一步建立,无人机运行风险分析在未来的无人机运行管理中将会扮演更加重要的角色。

通过对风险分析结果的量化输出无人机运行风险模型量化方法,使得分析评估过程更加直观,分析评估结果更加准确和客观。利用模型量化的运行风险分析方法只能聚焦针对运行任务中某一环节进行风险评估,应当考虑采用将无人机运行风险评估管理流程与量化模型评估方法结合的方式更全面、系统地进行风险评估。

综上所述,相关法律法规的制定是低空空域开放和无人机适航认证的基础,无人机运行风险评估管理架构在考虑严谨性和全面性的同时,还应考虑具体实施过程中的可操作性。在无人机运行风险量化模型方法中,无人机数据和地面数据的处理和整合是保证无人机运行风险分析结果准确的必要条件。

参考文献

[1] Ericson Clifton A. Hazard Analysis Techniques for System Safety[M]. John Wiley & Sons, 2005.

[2] Wackwitz K, Boedecker H. Safety Risk Assessment for UAVOperation[J]. Drone Industry Insights, Safe Airspace Integration Project, Part One, Hamburg, Germany, 2015.
[3] 中国民用航空局. 民用无人驾驶航空器实名制登记管理规定[Z]. 2017.
[4] Clothier R, Walker R. Determination and Evaluation of UAV Safety Objectives[C]//Proceedings of the 21st International Conference on Unmanned Air Vehicle Systems. University of Bristol, 2006: 18.1-18.16.
[5] Clothier R A, Walker R A. Safety Risk Management of Unmanned Aircraft Systems[M]. Springer Netherlands, 2015.
[6] International Organization for Standardization (ISO), Switzerland. Risk Management-Principles and guidelines[S]. 2009.
[7] Clothier R A, Williams B P, Hayhurst K J. Modelling the Risks Remotely Piloted Aircraft Pose to People on the Ground[J]. Safety Science, 2018, (101): 33-47.
[8] D. A. Burke, C. E. Hall, S. P. Cook. System-level Airworthiness Tool[J]. Aircr., 2011, 48(3): 777-785.
[9] Lum C, Waggoner B. A Risk Based Paradigm and Model for Unmanned Aerial Systems in the National Airspace[M]//Infotech@ Aerospace 2011. 2011: 1424.
[10] Bradley N, Burke D. Potential Crash Location (PCL) Model[R]. Naval Air Warfare Center Aircraft DIV Patuxent River MD, 2012.
[11] Washington A, Clothier R A, Silva J. A review of unmanned aircraft system ground risk models[J]. Progress in Aerospace Sciences, 2017, 95: 24-44.
[12] la Cour-Harbo Anders. Quantifying Risk of Ground Impact Fatalities for Small Unmanned Aircraft[J]. Journal of Intelligent and Robotic Systems: Theory and Applications, Journal of Intelligent & Robotic Systems, 2019, 93(1-2): 367-384.
[13] Kaya U C, Dogan A, Huber M. A probabilistic risk assessment framework for the path planning of safe task-aware UAS operations[C]//AIAA Scitech 2019 Forum. 2019: 2079.
[14] Dalamagkidis K, Valavanis K P, Piegl L A. Evaluating the Risk of Unmanned Aircraft Ground Impacts[J]. 2008 Mediterranean Conference on Control and Automation-Conference Proceedings, MED'08, IEEE, 2008: 709-716.
[15] Shelley A V. A Model of Human Harm from a Falling Unmanned Aircraft: Implications for UAS regulation[J]. International Journal of Aviation, Aeronautics, and Aerospace, 2016, 3(3): 1.
[16] Shakiba-Herfeh M. Modeling and Nonlinear Control of a 6-DOF Hypersonic Vehicle[D]. Columbus: The Ohio State University, 2015.
[17] Magister T. The Small Unmanned Aircraft Blunt Criterion Based Injury Potential Estimation[J]. Safety Science, 2010, 48(10): 1313-1320.

多目标决策下快速出口滑行道位置的计算方法

黄学林　王观虎　耿昊　雷继超　王伟

(空军工程大学航空工程学院)

摘　要　为了研究机场快速出口滑行道的位置并使其达到快速出动的目的,提出了快速出动率的概念,建立了综合利用率、综合快速出动率和加权跑道占有时间的多目标优化模型。通过实例分析,得到在混合机型作战训练下,X机场的快速出口位置与综合利用率、综合快速出动率和加权跑道占有时间的关系,最终求得快速出口滑行道的位置于1850m处,取得最优值,此时综合利用率为96.8%,快速出动率为90.8%,跑道占有时间为67s。

关键词 快速出口滑行道 快速出动率 多目标优化模型

0 引言

随着国际形势日趋严峻,军用机场承担的任务越来越重要,多机型保障的机场是未来的发展目标。按照新时代强军思想和"能打仗、打胜仗"强军目标总要求,为着重发展备战打仗能力,首先就必须提高机场的保障能力,提高飞机的出动效率,使飞机在空中夺取优势。

快速出口滑行道可以缩短飞机在跑道上的滑行时间,提高跑道容量与运行效率。王维以最小加权跑道占用时间为目标函数,基于时间的多项式动态规划算法进行求解,并对飞机利用快速出口起飞进行了理论分析。种小雷等从机场利用率的角度出发对快速出口位置进行了优化,并提出了多机型的综合利用率概念。陆松等从可靠性的角度研究了机场中间联络道的位置,分析飞机着陆滑跑过程,建立了中间联络道位置优化模型,并运用蒙特卡洛法进行仿真模拟,确定出不同机型组合,不同角度的中间联络道位置。李明捷等提出了通过增设快速出口滑行道的方法,并利用改进三阶段法,对快速出口道的位置与数量进行了优化。Antoine G. Hobeika开发出跑道出口设计交互模型,该模型可以描述飞机着陆动力学特性,以飞机加权平均跑道占用时间最小为目标函数,运用时间动态规划算法,确定出快速出口道的最优位置。Peng Cheng、Xiang Zou等提出了跑道出口可用性的概念,为每架飞机分配可用的跑道出口,进而建立机场滑行系统的时空网络。

大多数学者都是从跑道占用时间、快速出口利用率、可靠性等方面进行研究,并采用一定的计算方法进行求解,但是对于军用机场,如何保障飞机的快速出动相关的研究较少。本文提出了快速出动率的概念,并以综合利用率、综合快速出动率和跑道占有时间为求解目标,建立了多目标决策的快速出口位置计算模型,并采用逐步法和优选法对其进行求解,最后结合实例分析得到混合机型下某机场的快速出口位置。

1 多目标决策分析

1.1 基于利用率的计算模型

为确定最优快速出口滑行道的位置,以跑道端部中点O为原点,沿跑道方向向东为x轴方向,跑道向北为y轴方向,则快速出口道位置示意图如图1所示。

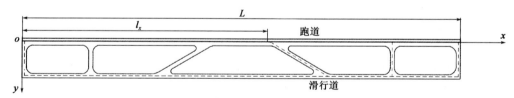

图1 快速出口道位置示意图

由文献[8]可知,着陆滑跑距离的概率分布密度函数与着陆距离的概率分布函数为:

$$f(x) = \frac{1}{\sqrt{2\pi}\sigma} e^{\left[-\frac{1}{2}\left(\frac{x-\mu}{\sigma}\right)^2\right]} \quad 0 < x < +\infty \tag{1}$$

$$F(x) = \int_{-\infty}^{x} f(t)dt \quad 0 < x < +\infty \tag{2}$$

依据军用飞机使用快速出口离开跑道的实际需求,以快速出口利用率γ为指标,表示飞机能够利用快速出口离开跑道的概率,可得利用率γ概率分布函数表达式为:

$$= P\{x \leq l_x\} = \int_{-\infty}^{x} f(t)dt \tag{3}$$

式中：l_x——快速出口滑行道的位置。

假设某机场保障 n 种机型，各机型的架次比例为 ω_i，则：

$$\sum_{i=1}^{n} \omega_i = 1 \tag{4}$$

当多架飞机共用一条快速出口滑行道时，采用综合利用率来保证快速出口道有较高的运行效率。假设 n 种机型使用同一个快速出口道，各机型的快速出口利用率为 γ_i，则定义多种机型使用快速出口滑行道综合利用率 α 为：

$$\alpha = \sum_{i=1}^{n} \omega_i \gamma_i = \omega_1 \gamma_1 + \omega_2 \gamma_2 + \cdots + \omega_n \gamma_n \tag{5}$$

1.2 基于快速出动的计算模型

对于军用机场，飞机快速地滑入跑道并进行起飞也是极其重要的，国内外也有民用飞机利用快速出口滑行道或者中间联络道进入跑道的例子。假设专门为飞机设置一个快速入口，则会造成工程量增加，并且滑入跑道的速度也得不到大幅度提高，所以本文利用跑道快速出口来作为飞机进入跑道的快速入口。

利用快速出口进行起飞时，设计快速出口的位置距跑道另一端的距离能满足大部分机型的起飞长度，才能起到快速出动的目的。假设不同飞机所需要的起飞滑跑距离为 S_{q_i}，跑道端安全区长度为 200m，飞机 i 利用快速出口起飞的可行性为 β_i，借鉴快速出口利用率的思想，将 β_i 定义为某型飞机的快速出动率，则飞机 i 可以利用快速出口进行起飞需要满足：

$$S_{qi} < l_x - 200 \tag{6}$$

假设飞机可以利用快速出口进行起飞的综合快速出动率为 δ，则：

$$\delta = \sum_{i=1}^{n} \omega_i \beta_i \tag{7}$$

$$\beta = P\{x \leq l_x\} = \int_{-\infty}^{x} f(t) \, dt \tag{8}$$

1.3 基于跑道占有时间的计算模型

由图 1 可知，随着快速出口位置向右移动，越来越多的飞机可以利用快速出口滑出跑道，但是随之而来的问题就是一些着陆滑跑距离较短的飞机，则需要在跑道上滑行较长的时间。

当 $l_x \geq S_k$ 时，飞机的具体跑道占用时间可以表示为：

$$T_1 = \frac{v_2 - v_1}{a_1} + \frac{l_x - \bar{l} - S_{q1}}{v_2} + \frac{v_3 - v_2}{a_2} + 6 \tag{9}$$

式中：v_1——接地速度；

v_2——平滑阶段速度；

v_3——转出速度；

a_1、a_2——相应阶段的加速度；

S_{q1}——从接地减速至平滑阶段的距离。

当 $l_x < S_k$ 时，飞机在滑跑过程中的跑道占有时间可以表示为：

$$T_2 = \frac{v_2 - v_1}{a_1} + \frac{L - \frac{1}{5}L - \bar{l} - S_{q1}}{v_2} + \frac{v_4 - v_2}{a_2} + 6 \tag{10}$$

式中：v_4——驶出中间联络道的速度。

综合跑道占有时间优化模型如下：

$$\min T = \sum_{i=1}^{n} \omega_i T_i \tag{11}$$

式中：T——综合跑道占用时间；

T_i——飞机的跑道占用时间；

n——机型种类数量。

2 多目标决策下快速出口计算模型

2.1 模型的建立

对于多机型保障的机场,建立快速出口的目标是使得出口利用率最大化,快速出动率最大化,跑道占有时间最小化,因此建立如下目标函数模型:

$$\begin{cases} \max\alpha = \sum_{i=1}^{n} \omega_i \gamma_i \\ \max T = \sum_{i=1}^{n} \omega_i T_i \\ \max\delta = \sum_{i=1}^{n} \omega_i \beta_i \end{cases} \quad (12)$$

2.2 求解方法

通过建立综合利用率、综合快速出动率、跑道占有时间与快速出口道位置的关系,将综合利用率与综合快速出动率作为主要目标函数,在利用率和快速出动率达到决策者要求后,使得跑道占有时间尽可能地小,以快速出口道的不同位置进行一步一步地迭代计算,直到目标函数达到决策者满意的结果为止。

3 实例分析

机场 X 具有重要的国防战略意义,是一个多机种保障的机场,机场跑道长度 3600m,端联络道距离跑道端 600m,目前具有飞行任务的机型有 A 型、B 型、C 型、D 型,其他机型的飞机进行飞行训练量很少,可以忽略不计。根据近几年机场飞行任务的统计,A 型、B 型、C 型、D 型飞机的架次比为 2∶5∶2∶1。

3.1 利用率分析

根据蒙特卡洛仿真[9],得到各型飞机的着陆滑跑距离分布函数,进而得到在不同快速出口滑行道位置下 A 型、B 型、C 型、D 型飞机和混合机型的快速出口利用率的关系。本文只画出混合机型的快速出口滑行道位置与综合利用率的关系,如图 2 所示。

由图 2 可知,混合机型在 1600m 附近时,利用率达到 80% 以上;在 1750m 附近时,利用率达到 90% 以上。

3.2 快速出动率分析

快速出动率的计算主要依据利用率,同理可得在不同快速出口滑行道位置下 A 型、B 型、C 型、D 型飞机和混合机型的快速出动率的关系,本文只画出混合机型的快速出口滑行道位置与综合快速出动率的关系,如图 3 所示。

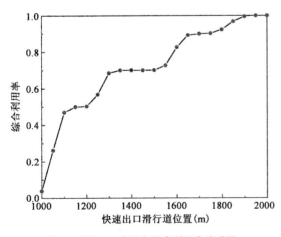

图 2 快速出口位置与综合利用率关系图

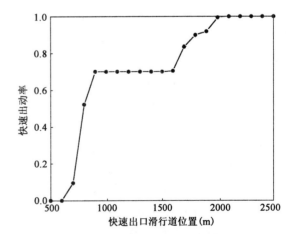

图 3 快速出口位置与综合快速出动率关系图

由图 3 可知,混合机型在 1650m 附近时,出动率达到 80% 以上;在 1850m 附近时,出动率达到 90% 以上。

3.3 跑道占有时间分析

本文利用逐步法进行迭代求解,以1000~2000m为区间,以50m为计算步长,计算不同快速出口位置时,混合机型的加权跑道占有时间,最终得到混合机型的加权跑道占用时间与快速出口滑行道位置的关系,如图4所示。

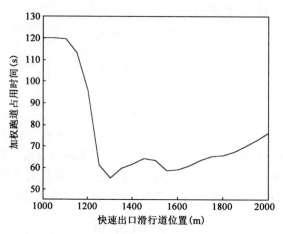

图4 加权跑道占用时间变化规律图

由图4可知,混合机型共用同一条快速出口道时,在1300m和1550m处,加权跑道占用时间出现两个低峰值,跑道占有时间分别是54.91s和58.40s。

3.4 综合分析

通过一步步地迭代计算快速出口滑行道在不同位置时的综合利用率、快速出动率和加权跑道占有时间,使得综合利用率和综合快速出动率达到理想情况下时跑道占有时间尽可能小,得到当快速出口滑行道的位置在1850m时,综合利用率为96.8%,综合快速出动率为90.8%,跑道占有时间为67s,此时得到相对最优解。

4 结 语

结合未来作战情况,提出了快速出动率的概念,并建立了综合利用率、快速出动率和加权跑道占有时间的数学模型和多目标优化模型,并采用逐步法和优选法对其进行求解。通过实例分析,得到当快速出口道的位置在1850m时,综合利用率为96.8%,快速出动率为90.8%,跑道占有时间为67s,达到了理想的优化目标,可以满足多数飞机快速出动。接下来还将考虑飞机滑入跑道占用时间、跑道容量及道面厚度设计作为其中的目标进行决策,并对快速出口的平面布局进行改进,达到飞机快速起飞的目的。

参考文献

[1] 王维,邓松武.跑道快速出口优化模型及仿真分析[J].中国民航学院学报,2006(04):27-31.
[2] 种小雷,许金良,蔡良才,王观虎.现有机场改建快速出口的可行性分析[J].交通运输系统工程与信息,2010,10(05):117-122.
[3] 王维,曹子路.民用机场快速出口滑行道位置优化[J].中国民航大学报,2012,30(01):18-22.
[4] 王维.飞机利用快速出口滑行道起飞的探讨[J].中国民航大学报,2015,33(03):36-40.
[5] 种小雷,蔡宛彤,王克春,等.基于利用率的机场快速出口位置优化分析[J].空军工程大学学报(自然科学版),2013,14(03):6-9.
[6] 陆松,岑国平,林可心,等.基于可靠性理论的机场中间联络道位置优化模型[J].中外公路,2014,34(04):86-90.
[7] 李明捷,王汝昕.基于改进三阶段法的快速出口滑行道转出位置的确定方法研究[J].科学技术与工程,2014,14(36):234-237.

[8] Peng Cheng, Xiang Zou, Wenda Liu. Airport Surface Trajectory Optimization Considering Runway Exit Selection[C].//Proceedings of 17th International IEEE Conference on Intelligent Transportation Systems. Ed , 2014, 611-617.

航空器推出翼尖运动学轨迹模型分析研究

潘卫军　张启阳　朱新平

(中国民用航空飞行学院空中交通管理学院)

摘　要　随着机场吞吐量逐年提高,飞机推出作为在机位附近的重要运动行为,其对于机场运行效率和安全起着重要的作用;本文基于飞机轮式系统运动特征,通过将不可积的非完整运动学约束转化为链式系统实现飞机推出轨迹模型的仿真。本文在传统的只考虑飞机前后轮中心几何关系的基础上,加入翼尖净距轨迹安全线的模型算法,通过该算法可以实现翼尖轨迹与安全净距线的二维轨迹可视化。本文的轨迹模型可应用于CAD二次开发以及机位推出安全测评。最后,本文通过对仿真结果的进一步研究分析得出飞机在推出时,其前轮转向角与机翼之间存在较强线性关系,这一结论对于机坪飞机推出引导系统的开发具有理论指导意义。

关键词　飞机推出轨迹仿真　非完整运动学　标准链式模型　前轮转向角

0　引　言

当前,大型机场机坪内机位滑行通道及进出位滑行线划设日益复杂,尤其是新建大型机场多采取U型机坪设计方式,导致机坪内航空器的进出位管理难度增加,极易引发航空器机位擦刮事件。鉴于此,对航空器进出位过程展开精细化仿真论证,有助于科学设计重点机位的进出模式、合理安排航空器进出机位的管控策略,从而提升机坪运行安全水平。本文将重点构建航空器机位顶推运动学仿真模型。

对飞机地面运动行为的研究方法主要包含动力学模型和运动学模型。其中,动力学模型基于对轮式系统的运动力学分析,可以提供一个精度较高的飞行运动仿真视景,但其数学模型常包含有大量非线性约束。Coetzee, Rankin, Krauskopf等[1-3]利用非线性理论和分歧理论进行分析,得到轮胎中心位置的纵向变化对轮胎性能的影响,考虑飞机胎压的力矩因素建立飞机地面运行的动力学模型;周宇生、文相容则通过基于动态跟踪目标为轮式移动结构设计合适的鲁棒速度跟踪控制器作为动力学的应用[4]。动力学模型对于力学参数的要求较高(例如温度对于飞机气动力影响,实时胎压数据等),考虑到参数本身获取难度较大且仿真难度高,一般用于飞行模拟器和飞机设计过程。

本文结合现行飞行区技术标准[12]建立飞机推出运动学算法,加入翼尖净距线动态安全轨迹算法,实现飞机6点位推出轨迹仿真,满足飞机之间的净距要求以及机坪安全线推出标准程序,可应用于飞机机位推出安全测评及飞机推出停止线设计。

1　航空器轮式结构基本特征分析

航空器在地面滑行过程可以分为直线运动和曲线运动两部分。具体到航空器的进出机位方式主要有拖挂式[13-14]和自动力式[15]。对于廊桥机位而言,飞机从此类机位的推出过程是飞机关闭动力系统,由拖车挂住飞机前轮推出对应的推出停止位置。此类机位的飞机推出过程,可视作直线运动和曲线运动的组合。

基金项目:面向多用户协同的民航应急救援虚拟演练关键技术研究;国家自然科学基金民航联合基金项目(U1733105);四川省中央引导地方科技发展专项项目(2020ZYD094);四川省科技计划项目(2020YFS0541)。

严格来说,飞机在地面的曲线运动,为保证主轮与道面边缘的间距在弯道内侧会有'增补面',如图1所示。

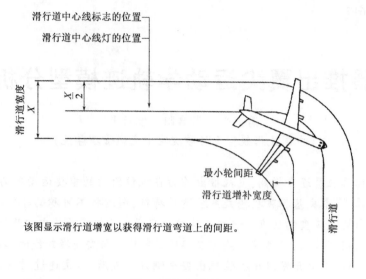

图1 滑行道'增补面'

飞机地面活动过程通常有"PF在线"和"主轮跨线"两种方式。其中,"PF在线"是指飞机活动过程中,飞机前轮始终保持在滑行道中线;"主轮跨线"是指飞机活动过程中,飞机左右侧主轮分别位于滑行道中线两侧,并保持主轮中心在滑行道中线上。通过机场实地调研,了解到'主轮跨线'是当前飞机从机位顶推时采用的方式。本文结合飞机轮式结构及机位推出过程的内在规律特点,开展具体的飞机顶推轨迹运动学仿真模型设计。

2 机位推出的运动学模型建立

2.1 航空器运行假设条件

假设1:视飞机为刚体,前起落架所有轮子的接触点合并为一个接触点P_1,主齿轮的每个轮子的触点合并到一个固定的接触点P_2。

假设2:在飞机推出运动过程中不考虑扭转力矩对飞机形变的影响。

假设3:飞机推出过程采用"主轮跨线"运行方式。

假设4:飞机前轮的线速度与转向角速度保持不变。

假设5:飞机运动过程中不会发生侧滑,且不考虑惯性作用。

2.2 航空器推出几何关系分析

根据飞机几何关系与假设条件,可得飞机推出的运动学约束方程(显含速度)为:

$$\begin{cases} \dot{x}_2\sin\theta - \dot{y}_2\cos\theta = 0 \\ \dot{x}_1\sin(\theta+\delta) + \dot{y}_1\cos(\theta+\delta) = 0 \end{cases} \quad (1)$$

式中:x_1和y_1——前轮中心位置的笛卡尔坐标;

x_2和y_2——主起落架中心位置的笛卡尔坐标;

θ——机身纵轴与x轴的夹角;

δ——飞机主轮的转向角。前后轮坐标关系(不含速度)有:

$$\begin{cases} x_1 = x_2 - l\cos\theta \\ y_1 = y_2 - l\sin\theta \end{cases} \quad (2)$$

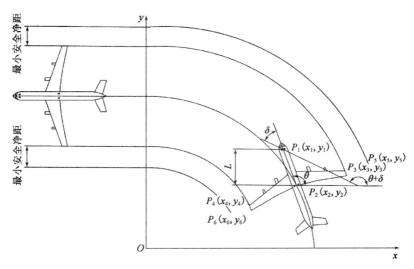

图 2 飞机推出几何关系图

式中，l 代表前轮中心到主起落架中心之间的距离。设 span 为飞机翼展，翼尖坐标 $x_3 y_3$ 和 $x_4 y_4$ 的几何位置关系为：

$$\begin{cases} x_3 = x_2 + \left(\dfrac{\text{span}}{2}\right)\cos\left(\theta - \dfrac{\pi}{2}\right) \\ y_3 = y_2 + \left(\dfrac{\text{span}}{2}\right)\sin\left(\theta - \dfrac{\pi}{2}\right) \\ x_4 = x_2 - \left(\dfrac{\text{span}}{2}\right)\cos\left(\theta - \dfrac{\pi}{2}\right) \\ y_4 = x_2 - \left(\dfrac{\text{span}}{2}\right)\sin\left(\theta - \dfrac{\pi}{2}\right) \end{cases} \quad (3)$$

飞机的运动学约束可以表示为：

$$\begin{cases} \dot{x}_2 = v_1 \cos\theta \\ \dot{y}_2 = v_1 \sin\theta \\ \dot{\theta} = v_1 \tan\delta \\ \dot{\delta} = v_2 \end{cases} \quad (4)$$

转弯半径 R 与机位构型相关，可通过机位数据直接获取，而前轮转向角 δ 需要通过飞机前后轴距换算，因此将 δ 函数转化为 R 的函数，公式为：

$$\begin{cases} \tan\delta = \dfrac{l}{R} \\ \delta = \arctan\left(\dfrac{l}{R}\right) \\ \dot{\theta} = v_1\left(\dfrac{l}{R}\right) \end{cases} \quad (5)$$

根据上述转化，将 δ 转化为 l 与 R 的关系式，更符合应用场景。

3 翼尖安全轨迹模型构建

基于假设 3，首先考虑飞机'主轮中心'沿出位滑行线滑行，因此将飞机主轮中心坐标对 t 进行微分，结合飞机几何约束可直接得到以下显含速度非完整运行学约束。

$$\begin{cases} \dot{x}_2 = v_1\cos\theta \rightarrow x_{t+dt} = x_t + v_1\cos\theta * \mathrm{d}t \\ \dot{y}_2 = v_1\sin\theta \rightarrow y_{t+dt} = y_t + v_1\sin\theta * \mathrm{d}t \\ \dot{\theta} = \omega \rightarrow \theta_{t+dt} = \theta_t + v_1 * R * \mathrm{d}t \end{cases} \quad (6)$$

式(6)中的非完整运动学约束[16-18]为不可积约束,无法直接建立计算机模型求解,因此本文采用标准链式模型[19-21]进行转化,该链式模型可以将不可积约束进行线性处理转化为可积分约束,公式如下:

$$\begin{cases} \dot{\zeta}_1 = u_1 \\ \dot{\zeta}_2 = u_2 \\ \dot{\zeta}_3 = \zeta_2 u_1 \\ \vdots \\ \dot{\zeta}_n = \zeta_{n-1} u_1 \end{cases} \quad (7)$$

将非完整运动学拓展到 n 维空间,从而得到式(8)的链式表示模型:

$$\begin{cases} v_1 = \dfrac{u_1}{\cos\theta} \\ v_2 = \dfrac{-u_1 3\sin\theta \sin^2\left[\arctan\left(\dfrac{l}{R}\right)\right]}{l\cos^2\theta} + u_2 l\cos^3\theta \cos^2\left[\arctan\left(\dfrac{l}{R}\right)\right] \end{cases} \quad (8)$$

$$\begin{cases} \zeta_1 = x_2 \\ \zeta_2 = \left(\dfrac{1}{R}\right)\sec^3\theta \\ \zeta_3 = \tan\theta \\ \zeta_4 = y_2 \end{cases} \quad (9)$$

根据图1给出的飞机推出运动行为与假设3,得到飞机推出的链式表示模型为:

$$\begin{cases} \dot{\zeta}_1 = u_1 \\ \dot{\zeta}_2 = u_2 \\ \dot{\zeta}_3 = \zeta_2 u_1 \\ \dot{\zeta}_4 = \zeta_3 u_1 \end{cases} \quad (10)$$

式(10)满足式(7)链式表示模型。针对图2所给出的飞机几何运动关系,按照假设条件3,设飞机主轮中心在 t 时刻的位置为 $x_2(t)$ 和 $y_2(t)$,可以得到如下链式表示模型:由此得求解模型:

$$\begin{cases} \zeta_1(t) = x_2(t) \\ \zeta_2(t) = \dfrac{\ddot{y}_2(t)\dot{x}_2(t) - \dot{y}_2(t)\ddot{x}_2(t)}{\dot{x}_2^3(t)} \\ \zeta_3(t) = \dfrac{\dot{y}_2(t)}{\dot{x}_2(t)} \\ \zeta_4(t) = y_2(t) \end{cases} \quad (11)$$

$$\begin{cases} u_1(t) = x_2(t) \\ u_2(t) = \dfrac{\dddot{y}_2(t)\dot{x}_2^2(t) - \dddot{x}_2(t)\dot{y}_2(t)\dot{x}_2(t) - 3\ddot{y}_2(t)\ddot{x}_2(t)\dot{x}_2(t) + 3\dot{y}_2(t)\ddot{x}_2(t)}{\dot{x}_2^4(t)} \end{cases} \quad (12)$$

由此可以得到飞机主轮中心位置的运动参数$(x_2, y_2, v_1, v_2, \theta, \delta)$，按照开环思想建立基于时间的前后轮飞机推出轨迹动态仿真模型：

$$\begin{pmatrix} x_1(t+\mathrm{d}t) \\ y_1(t+\mathrm{d}t) \\ x_2(t+\mathrm{d}t) \\ y_2(t+\mathrm{d}t) \end{pmatrix} = \begin{pmatrix} x_1(t) + v_1(t)\cos\left[\theta(t) + \arctan\left(\dfrac{l}{R}\right)\right]\mathrm{d}t \Big/ \cos\left[\arctan\left(\dfrac{l}{R}\right)\right] \\ y_1(t) + v_1(t)\sin\left[\theta(t) + \arctan\left(\dfrac{l}{R}\right)\right]\mathrm{d}t \Big/ \cos\left[\arctan\left(\dfrac{l}{R}\right)\right] \\ x_2(t) + v_1(t)\cos\theta(t)\mathrm{d}t \\ y_2(t) + v_1(t)\sin\theta(t)\mathrm{d}t \end{pmatrix} \quad (13)$$

式中：$x_1(t)$和$y_1(t)$——飞机前轮在t时刻的位置横纵坐标值；

$x_2(t)$和$y_2(t)$——飞机主轮中心在t时刻的位置横纵坐标值。

基于飞机前后轮与飞机翼尖及安全净距的几何位置关系构建翼尖安全轨迹计算机求解模型：

$$\begin{pmatrix} x_3(t) \\ y_3(t) \\ x_4(t) \\ y_4(t) \end{pmatrix} = \begin{cases} x_2(t) + \left(\dfrac{\mathrm{span}}{2}\right)\cos\left[\theta(t) - \dfrac{\pi}{2}\right] \\ y_2(t) + \left(\dfrac{\mathrm{span}}{2}\right)\sin\left[\theta(t) - \dfrac{\pi}{2}\right] \\ x_2(t) - \left(\dfrac{\mathrm{span}}{2}\right)\cos\left[\theta(t) - \dfrac{\pi}{2}\right] \\ y_2(t) - \left(\dfrac{\mathrm{span}}{2}\right)\sin\left[\theta(t) - \dfrac{\pi}{2}\right] \end{cases} \quad (14)$$

式中：$x_3(t)$和$y_3(t)$——以飞机右翼尖t时刻坐标；

$x_4(t)$和$y_4(t)$——以飞机左翼尖t时刻坐标。

同理，得到安全净距线推出轨迹模型：

$$\begin{pmatrix} x_5(t) \\ y_5(t) \\ x_6(t) \\ y_6(t) \end{pmatrix} = \begin{cases} x_2(t) + \left(\dfrac{\mathrm{span}}{2} + \mathrm{sd}\right)\cos\left[\theta(t) - \dfrac{\pi}{2}\right] \\ y_2(t) + \left(\dfrac{\mathrm{span}}{2} + \mathrm{sd}\right)\sin\left[\theta(t) - \dfrac{\pi}{2}\right] \\ x_2(t) - \left(\dfrac{\mathrm{span}}{2} + \mathrm{sd}\right)\cos\left[\theta(t) - \dfrac{\pi}{2}\right] \\ y_2(t) - \left(\dfrac{\mathrm{span}}{2} + \mathrm{sd}\right)\sin\left[\theta(t) - \dfrac{\pi}{2}\right] \end{cases} \quad (15)$$

式中：$x_5(t)$和$y_5(t)$——以飞机右翼尖t时刻坐标；

$x_6(t)$和$y_6(t)$——以飞机左翼尖t时刻坐标；

sd——依据飞行区技术标准所确定的翼尖安全净距。

4 仿真与分析

选取A330-300和A321-200两种机型，分别对其机位顶推过程的开展翼尖轨迹仿真。仿真使用的基本机型参数如下：(1) A330-300机型，机长63.7m，翼展60.3m，前后轴距24.6m；(2) A321-200机型，机长 44.51m,翼展 34.1m,前后轴距 16.78m。飞机顶推推出设置恒定速率 $v=4\text{m/s}$。

图3为两飞机推出轨迹及相对位置关系。点划线为前轮推出轨迹,细实线为主轮推出轨迹,宽条带代表翼尖到安全净距的包络动态范围,浅蓝色为机坪安全线,按照黄线标识,自左向右依次为:服务车道线、翼尖净距线和推出滑行道。同一机位可以从两个方向推出,取决于飞机推出至滑行线后的运行方向,因此两架飞机一共存在4种可能的推出情况。

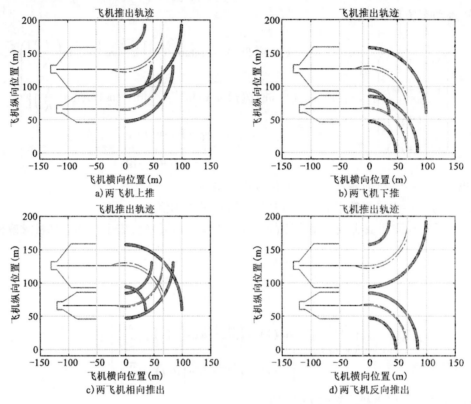

图3 两飞机动态推出轨迹仿真及相对位置关系图

5 结 语

本文提出的运动学模型是较为可靠的推出轨迹研究仿真方法,对于其他特殊机位推出的研究提供理论基础,总结如下:

(1)本文通过飞机推出运行学模型对航空器机位推出轨迹进行仿真,同时对双流机场机坪运行进行实地调研,对现行的推出标准进行核实,证实模型在理论上符合真实的地面运行场景,具备有效性和正确性。

(2)本文的运动学仿真方法适用于当前塔台管制视景仿真对于实时性的要求,相较于动力学模型具有时效性强、简单、参数易获取且调节方便、计算量小的特点,同时满足当前塔台视景仿真精度和显示性能要求。

(3)本文仅考虑飞机推出按照标准的90°圆弧推出方式,而实际场景中机位构型存在更为复杂推出角度,因此在之后的研究中应加强对与近机位附近的复杂机位推出运行的分析;同时本文基于的假设为推车司机严格按照主轮中心压线的方式推出,但实际运行场景中,司机的操作会有随机性和偶然性,对于之后的研究应考虑到操作误差修正的分析。

参考文献

[1] Rankin J, Coetzee E, Krauskopf B, et al. Bifurcation and Stability Analysis of Aircraft Turning on the Ground[J]. Journal of Guidance, Control, and Dynamics, 2009, 32(2): 500-511.

[2] Coetzee E B, Krauskopf B, Lowenberg M H. Nonlinear Aircraft Ground Dynamics[C]. Intornetional Conferece on Problems in Aviation and Aerospace, 2006.

[3] Rankin J. Bifurcation Analysis of Nonlinear Ground Handling of Aircraft[D]. Bristor: University of Bristol, 2010.

[4] 王越超, 景兴建. 非完整约束轮式移动机器人人工场导向控制研究[J]. 自动化学报, 2002, 28(5): 777-783.

[5] 常江. 非完整轮式移动机器人的运动控制方法研究[D]. 哈尔滨:哈尔滨工程大学, 2011.

[6] 周宇生, 文相容, 王在华. 论轮式移动结构的非完整约束及其运动控制[J]. 力学学报, 2020, (4): 1143-1156.

[7] Li Z, Canny J. Motion of Two Rigid Bodies with Rolling Constraint[J]. IEEE Transactions on Robotics and Automation, 1990, 6(1): 62-72.

[8] Li Z, Montgomery R. Dynamics and Optimal Control of a Legged Robot in Flight Phase[C].//Proceedings, IEEE International Conference on Robotics and Automation. IEEE, 1990: 1816-1821.

[9] Montgomery R. Isoholonomic Problems and Some Applications[J]. Communications in Mathematical Physics, 1990, 128(3): 565-592.

[10] Laumond J P. Feasible Trajectories for Mobile Robots with Kinematic and Environment Constraints[C].// Proc. International Conference on Intelligent Autonomous Systems. 1986: 346-354.

[11] Laumond J P. Finding Collision-Free Smooth Trajectories for a Non-Holonomic Mobile Robot[C].// IJCAI. 1987, 87: 1120-1123.

[12] 中国民用航空局. 民用机场飞行区技术标准:MH/T 5001—2020[S]. 北京:中国民航出版社, 2020.

[13] Laumond J P, Siméon T. Motion Planning for a Two Degrees of Freedom Mobile Robot With Towing[R]. Technical Report LAAS/CNRS, 1989.

[14] Fossum T V, Lewis G N. A Mathematical Model for Trailer-Truck Jackknifing[J]. SIAM Review, 1981, 23(1): 95-99.

[15] Coetzee E. Modelling and Nonlinear Analysis of Aircraft Ground Manoeuvres[D]. Bristor:University of Bristol, 2011.

[16] Michałek M. Tracking Control Strategy for the Standard N-trailer Mobile Robot-A Geometrically Motivated Approach[M].//Robot Motion and Control 2011. Springer, London, 2012: 39-51.

[17] Lee J H, Woojin C, Kim M, et al. A Passive Multiple Trailer System with Off-axle Hitching[J]. International Journal of Control, Automation, and Systems, 2004, 2(3): 289-297.

[18] Jean F. The Car with n Trailers: Characterization of the Singular Configurations[J]. ESAIM: Control, Optimisation and Calculus of Variations, 1996, 1: 241-266.

[19] Bullo F, Murray R M. Experimental Comparison of Trajectory Trackers for a Car with Trailers[J]. IFAC Proceedings Volumes, 1996, 29(1): 2804-2809.

[20] Murray R M, Sastry S S. Steering Nonholonomic Systems in Chained Form[J]. 1991.

[21] Duleba I, Khefifi W. A Lie Algebraic Method of Motion Planning for Driftless Nonholonomic Systems [C].//Proceedings of the Fifth International Workshop on Robot Motion and Control, 2005.

[22] RoMoCo'05. IEEE, 2005: 79-84.

[23] Gu Y L. An Exploration of Orientation Representation by Lie Algebra for Robotic Applications[J]. IEEE Transactions on Systems, Man, and Cybernetics, 1990, 20(1): 243-248.

昆明长水国际机场到达层出租车上客区改善研究

马书欣[1] 李晓东[2] 陈兴[2]

(1.长安大学;2.云南机场集团昆明长水国际机场场区管理部)

摘 要 为了提升昆明长水国际机场到达层车道边出租车上客区的通行能力,并为其他机场到达层改建或新建的出租车上客区设计及运营提供参考与借鉴,本文通过实地调查获得该区域的交通运行参数,并结合排队论与工程经验,对出租车上客区域进行改造;最终通过 VISSIM 的仿真试验,对比排队长度、等待时间、运输能力等,对比结果表明,改善方案的运力与现方案相比提升了 47%,可以满足一定的未来年旅客疏散需求。

关键词 出租车上客区 通行能力 组织管理 昆明长水国际机场 VISSIM

0 引 言

随着社会经济的发展,城市间往来交通量与日俱增,而机场作为航空运输的重要场所,需要承担日益增加的运输量,出租车作为乘客进出机场的重要交通方式之一,起着至关重要的作用。

朱亮等[1]建立出租车上客区通行能力计算模型,并通过模型计算得到双通道出租车上客区在不同泊位数量、不同组织措施情况下的通行能力;吴娇蓉等[2]抽象出 3 种典型的上客点出租车管理模式,并用微观仿真模型对 3 种出租车上客点管理模式进行比较分析,得出不同模式的适用条件;汤震[3]针对常见的平行并发式与斜列式两种出租车到达车道边布置方式,研究不同形式下的到达车道边通行能力及服务水平,并提出确定到达车道边合理规模的方法;耿中波等[4]针对机场航站楼进行出租车上客区方案比选的问题,建立了基于 VISSIM 微观交通仿真的比选方法;胡程[5]提出了并列式立体化出租车排队待客系统;黄岩等[6]通过对交通参数进行调查分析,结合实际运营中存在的一些问题,围绕如何提高既有交通设施通行能力,对出租车上客点的组织管理方式进行研究;魏中华等[7]对枢纽内出租车上客区的布局形式进行了分类,基于排队论利用费用决策模型,对北京站多点并列式出租车排队服务系统的服务台数进行了数量优化;郭淑霞等[8]研究不同类型上客区车道边泊位数的阈值,确定了合理的泊位数和其通行能力。

昆明长水国际机场的出租车上客区在改造前运输能力有限,小时运力约为 300 辆车,供需能力不匹配,在高峰时段到港的旅客欲乘坐出租车离开时需排队等待较长时间。本文通过对问题进行实地调查,得出解决问题所需的参数,结合排队论与工程实践的经验,对现状方案进行改造。

1 出租车上客区现状

昆明长水国际机场的航站楼到达层车道边的出租车上客区正对到达层 3 号门,设置 4×2 个矩阵式出租车上客点,与相邻的贵宾(VIP)车道之间有护栏隔离,见图 1。

由于上客区的进出口都是单车道,靠近行人排队区域的一列 4 个停车位中在高峰时段的运力不如靠近 VIP 车道的一列停车位。通过现场调查,在一定时间段内,低运力的一列停车位驶离的出租车约为高运力的一列停车位驶离出租车数量的一半,为了简化计算,在后续的计算过程中将低运力停车位的数量记为 2 个,这 2 个停车位与高运力车道上的 4 个停车位的交通参数相同,见图 2。现场有 1~2 名引导人员为旅客(拿行李、推车)及司机(指引停车点)提供帮助。

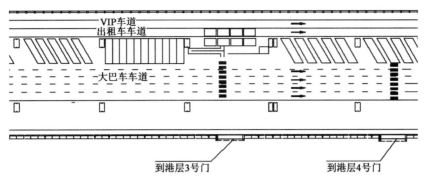

图 1　昆明长水国际机场出租车上客区示意图

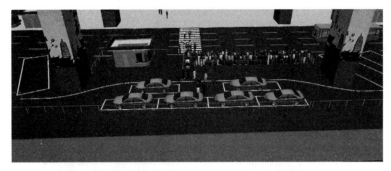

图 2　昆明长水国际机场出租车上客区 VISSIM 仿真效果图

2　交通参数调查

2.1　调查对象

出租车上客区的各种交通运行参数,如一定时间段内从上客区完成上客并驶离的出租车数量的调查;出租车驶入、驶出上客区及上客等步骤所花费的时间,每辆车上去的乘客数等指标的调查。

2.2　调查方法

调查方法主要是现场调研法。调研时间取 2019 年 5 月 5 日 23:00—5 月 6 日 1:00,这是 2019 年出租车停车场驶出车辆的高峰日。通过实地观测和统计监控视频相结合的方法获取实际信息。

2.3　调查结果

经过调查得到的各种参数见表 1。

交通调查结果　　　　　　　　　　表1

调查内容	样本数量	调查结果(取平均值)
每分钟驶离的出租车	30	5辆
出租车驶入上客区停在停车位的时间	100	3.5s
乘客上车时间	100	24s
出租车由停车位驶离上客区的时间	100	4.5s
进入每辆出租车的乘客数	129	1.6人

3　方案改善

3.1　改善方案介绍

新方案取消现有的出租车车道,大巴车停车位向航站楼外侧平移 3.5m。对航站楼由近及远的车道组成分别是出租车车道、大巴车车道、大巴车停车位和 VIP 车道。出租车上客区靠近到港层 4 号门。为了给大巴车提供更多的行车空间,出租车行车道在上客区之前是一条车道,经过上客区之后是两条车道。

出租车上客区改善方案见图3。

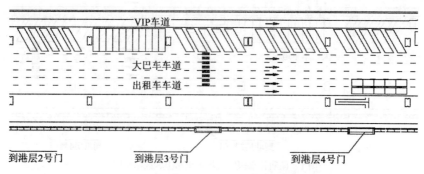

图3　出租车上客区改善方案示意图

该方案与原方案相比,出租车乘客乘车时没有了与大巴车行车路线的冲突,出到港层大门可以直接进入乘客排队区域,更加安全便捷;且4号门距离到达层的出口最近,乘客上车后即可很快离开到达层。出租车上客区改善方案VISSIM仿真效果图见图4。

图4　出租车上客区改善方案VISSIM效果图

3.2　方案对比

出租车运力分析可以采用以下简化上客步骤:①一批出租车按顺序停在上客区;②乘客上车;③出租车驶离。至此,一批车完成上客、驶离,下一批车继续按照上述流程。

现状的出租车运力:在现有交通组织方案下,通过观察监控视频统计得出,出租车按顺序停在停车位平均3.5s/辆;每辆车的乘客上客时间平均为24(s);上完客驶离平均4.5s/辆。一批车(6辆),共需要 $21+24+27=72s$ 完成整个接客驶离程序;平均到每辆车为 $72\div6=12(s)$,则1h可通过300辆出租车,按照平均每车载客量为1.6人计算,1h最多运送480人。

在改善方案中,出租车停车区可设两排,每排5个停车位,假设出租车停车时间、旅客上车时间与出租车驶离时间与现状相同,一批车(10辆)完成整个上客驶离过程总共需要的时间为 $3.5\times10+24+4.5\times5$(每排5辆车)$=81.5s$。平均每辆车8.15s,则一小时可通过441辆出租车,按照平均每车载客量为1.6人计算,1h最多运送705人,相比现状,运力提高了47%。以上是按上客区每排5个停车位计算,如果有需要,还可以增加上客区停车位,以进一步提高出租车的运力。现状与改善方案对比见表2。

方案对比　　　　　　　　表2

比较对象	车道数	上客区车位数	计算运力（人/h）	计算通行能力（辆/h）	VISSIM仿真通行能力（辆/h）	增加停车位
现状	1	6	480	300	297	不可以
改善方案	1进2出	10	705	441	452	可以

3.3 高峰时段新方案排队系统计算

根据机场统计预测出的旅客增长率,机场的未来年出租车上客区高峰小时流量预测见表3。

未来年出租车上客区高峰小时流量预测　　　　表3

年　份	到达率(人/min)	年　份	到达率(人/min)
2020	10.84	2023	12.92
2021	11.49	2024	13.69
2022	12.18	2025	14.51

通过观察监控视频,出租车上客区的旅客到达高峰在晚上,持续时间一般不超过1h。表4排队长度以高峰时间为1h计,且假设高峰小时开始前排队长度为0。

出租车上客区排队系统情况　　　　表4

年份	服务能力 (人/min)	服务强度 (旅客到达率/服务能力)	平均排队长度 (人)	平均排队时间 (min)
2020	11.75	0.92	10.58	1.1
2023	11.75	1.10	平均每分钟增加1.17人,高峰小时后最长为70.2人	最长排队时间为6分钟,平均排队时间为3min
2025	11.75	1.23	平均每分钟增加2.76人,高峰小时后最长为165.6人	最长排队时间为14.1分钟,平均排队时间为7.05min

平均到达率为 λ,平均服务率为 μ,$\rho = \lambda/\mu$ 为服务强度,平均排队人数:$q = \dfrac{\rho^2}{1-\rho}$,平均延误时间(等待时间)$d = \dfrac{1}{\mu - \lambda}$。

2025年改善方案的排队区最长排队时间为14.1min,可以满足乘客的乘车需求,且在远期昆明长水国际机场有新建航站楼的规划,该方案可以满足近期未来年的乘客需求。

4　结　语

本文通过在2019年5月5日、5月6日对昆明长水国际机场出租车上客区进行实地调查,得到出租车车均载客人数、上客点的通行能力。通过分析调查结果并结合实际经验,提出了出租车上客区的改善方案,并通过VISSIM仿真软件得到证实,可以解决该机场当前方案运力不足、高峰时段乘客等候时间过长的问题,也为其他机场新建或改建出租车上客区提供了借鉴与参考。

参考文献

[1] 朱亮,杨旭,王相平.铁路客运站出租车上客区通行能力配置与优化[J].铁道运输与经济,2010,32(07):43-46.

[2] 吴娇蓉,李铭,梁丽娟.综合客运枢纽出租车上客点管理模式和效率分析[J].交通信息与安全,2012,30(004):18-23.

[3] 汤霞.交通枢纽出租车到达车道边通行能力分析[J].中国市政工程,2012(04):1-3.

[4] 耿中波,宋国华,赵琦等.基于VISSIM的首都机场出租车上客方案比选研究[J].中国民航大学学报,2013,31(06):55-59.

[5] 胡程.并列式立体化出租车排队系统研究[J].城市道桥与防洪,2014(7):19-21.

[6] 黄岩,王光裕.虹桥机场T2航站楼出租车上客系统组织管理优化探讨[J].城市道桥与防洪,2014

(12):7-9,35-36.
[7] 魏中华,王琳,邱实.基于排队论的枢纽内出租车上客区服务台优化[J].公路交通科技(应用技术版)2017(10):298-300.
[8] 郭淑霞,吴海俊,陶涛,等.枢纽上客区车道边泊位设置与通行能力研究[J].交通工程,2020,20(01):46-51.

城市群背景下面向机场群协同发展的交通韧性评价研究

徐佳君 陆化普 陈明玉

(清华大学土木工程系交通研究所)

摘　要　城市群背景下机场群协同发展对于降低航空运输系统风险,提高交通韧性具有重要作用。本文通过构建城市群背景下的机场群系统韧性评价指标体系,利用层次分析法对京津冀、长三角和粤港澳三大城市群的机场群交通韧性进行了综合测算实证研究,评价机场群系统韧性总体情况。结果显示,长三角机场群系统交通韧性较好,粤港澳机场群交通韧性较差。根据测算结果,为实现城市群背景下机场群协同的发展目标,针对交通韧性提出了有关建议。

关键词　交通韧性　机场群系统　层次分析法　城市群

0 引　言

根据国际民航组织统计,2018年共有43亿人次乘坐商业航空出行[1],根据国际机场协会对未来的航空市场所做出的预测报告,中国将会成为旅客运输全球占有率第一的国家[2]。

Neufville认为多机场系统是在一地区提供商业运输服务的一系列重要机场的组合,不考虑各机场的所有权或者行政隶属关系[3]。

韧性的概念来自Holling等人,即系统可塑性[4],现今韧性的概念应用到不同领域的研究中[5]。朱金鹤等[6]讨论城市韧性影响因素。傅超琦等[7]研究航空网络的自愈特性。

本文构建城市群背景下面向机场群协同发展的交通韧性评价体系,探讨我国城市群背景下机场群协同发展发展对策和构建韧性交通系统的实施路径。

1 城市群背景下机场群协同发展与交通韧性

1.1 国内城市群背景下机场群发展现状

我国在2018年发布的《新时代民航强国建设行动纲要》中提出推动京津冀、长三角、粤港澳大湾区、成渝等世界级机场群建设。根据中国民用航空局和国际机场协会的统计数据整理,并依照中国民用航空局《民用运输机场建设"十三五"规划》国家综合机场体系分类标准,我国四大机场群主要组成机场与功能属性见表1。

我国四大机场群主要组成机场与功能属性　　　　表1

机场群	机场	2019年旅客(人次)	机场功能属性
京津冀机场群	北京首都	100013642	国际性枢纽
	天津滨海	23813318	区域性枢纽
	石家庄正定	11922801	地区性枢纽

续上表

机场群	机场	2019年旅客（人次）	机场功能属性
长三角机场群	上海浦东	76153455	国际性枢纽
	上海虹桥	45637882	区域性枢纽
	杭州萧山	40108405	区域性枢纽
	南京禄口	30581685	区域性枢纽
	宁波栎社	12414007	地区性枢纽
	合肥新桥	12282384	地区性枢纽
粤港澳大湾区机场群	香港机场	71286633	国际性枢纽
	广州白云	73378475	国际性枢纽
	深圳宝安	52931925	区域性枢纽
	珠海金湾	12282982	地区性枢纽
成渝机场群	成都双流	55858552	区域性枢纽
	重庆江北	44786722	区域性枢纽
	绵阳南郊	4159370	地区性枢纽

从图1可以明显看到，国内四大机场群均由城市群中一到两个国际核心枢纽机场为主要组成部分，机场群内区域性机场和地区性机场则是核心枢纽机场的辅助与支撑，与国外的机场功能属性组成与发展进程相似，如图2所示。

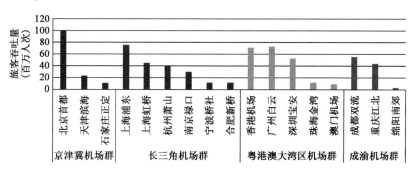

图1　2019年我国四大机场群主要组成机场旅客吞吐量

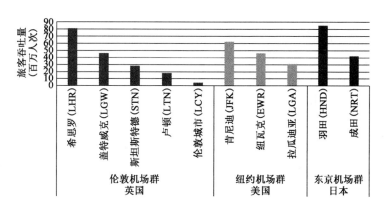

图2　2019年世界三大机场群主要组成机场旅客吞吐量

1.2　城市群和机场群协同发展模式

根据已有文献[8]与实际案例调研，城市群和机场群的发展模式如图3所示。城市群通过机场群的交通衔接以及空间演化，为城市群发展注入新能量；机场群通过机场群内的协同分工以及城市群的优化，达成城市群与机场群可持续发展的发展目标。

图3 城市群、多机场系统及机场群系统发展模式

2 指标体系构建

本文借鉴交通强国战略研究中交通强国战略目标与评价指标体系研究和航空发展战略研究的指标体系[9]和张明斗等建立的城市韧性评价指标体系[10]，构建城市群支撑下机场群系统韧性评价指标体系。

2.1 研究方法

本文主要采用层次分析法对我国三大机场群的韧性进行综合测算，每一个单项指标都从不同角度反映城市群背景下机场群的韧性情况，然后对指标进行综合量化。因此，城市群背景下机场群的韧性采用多目标加权函数计算。

$$R = \sum_{j=1}^{n} \left(\sum_{i=1}^{m} a_i \cdot w_i \right) \cdot W_j$$

式中：R——城市群背景下机场群系统韧性评价指数；

n——准则层数量；

W_j——准则层j的权重；

m——指标层数量；

w_i——指标层第i个指标的权重；

a_i——指标层第i个指标的指标值。

2.2 指标体系构建

在城市群的支撑背景下，讨论机场群系统的交通韧性将涉及城市群和机场群两个系统的韧性评估，必须考虑多个维度并评判指标的选取与意义。机场群系统的韧性发展和演进与机场群本身管理运营的水平有关，同时也涉及城市群中城市综合交通枢纽一体化水平、城市群经济水平以及城市群基础设施水平，因此从以上四个维度作为准则层展开指标体系。

遵从评价指标体系的完整完备性、可行性、可操作性和代表性的原则前提下，选取具有重要意义的指标，指标体系设计分为目标层、准则层、指标层三个层次，并采用德尔菲法为各组成因子赋予权重。

在机场群管理运营水平准则层中，参考交通强国战略研究中航空发展战略研究的指标体系，以及考虑数据可获取的完整性，考虑机场群中的机场密度、机场群系统客运量、机场群系统货运量以及机场群系统运营智能化水平得分，表示机场群系统乘载的吞吐量情况及运营情况；在城市综合交通枢纽一体化准则层中，考虑两个指标，即综合交通枢纽轨道交通换乘站点个数和综合交通枢纽平均换乘距离，这两个指标说明城市群系统内交通在各环节功能性的连接情况；在考虑城市群经济水平中，将人均生产总值与财政收入作为衡量城市群经济水平韧性程度的两个指标，作为衡量城市群经济水平韧性韧性程度，说明城市群系统为各系统提供经济支撑与保障的情况；基础设施是保障城市群系统运转的重要枢纽，在考虑城市群基础设施水平中，将每万人拥有公共汽车量、人均道路面积与国际互联网用户数作为衡量城市群基础设施水平的三个指标，使用人均道路面积与每万人拥有公共汽车量评估城市群内交通出行的保障程度，考虑国际互联网用户数表示网络覆盖使用率影响市群系统内居民接受信息的难易程度。

利用德尔菲法建立指标体系权重的过程中，首先根据文献参考，确定以上具有重要意义的指标，并请相关专业学者根据影响城市群支撑下机场群系统韧性的重要程度,给予准则层和指标层打分。对专家的打分进行整理,归纳统计,去除极端值,再次征求专家意见,反复进行,直至得到专家一致的意见,换算数值为权重,得出本次城市群支撑下机场群系统韧性评价指标体系各指标的权重,本项工作进行了三次循环,权重如表2所示。

城市群支撑下机场群系统韧性评价指标体系　　　　　　　　　　　　　　　　　　　　　　　　　　　　表2

目标层	准则层	权重	指标层	权重
城市群背景下机场群韧性	机场群管理运营水平	0.3596	机场密度(个/万km)	0.0909
			客运量(万人次)	0.0892
			货运量(万t)	0.0838
			机场群运营智能化水平(得分)	0.0957
	城市综合交通枢纽一体化水平	0.1928	综合交通枢纽轨道交通换乘站点(个)	0.0982
			综合交通枢纽平均换乘距离(m)	0.0946
	城市群经济水平	0.1836	人均生产总值(万元/万人)	0.0934
			财政收入(万元)	0.0902
	城市群基础设施水平	0.2640	每万人拥有公共汽车量(辆)	0.0922
			人均道路面积(m²)	0.0876
			国际互联网用户数(户)	0.0842

3 城市群支撑下机场群系统韧性评价分析

采用上述多目标加权函数模型对三大机场群进行计算,本文所使用的数据主要来源于国家统计局、财政部和《中国城市统计年鉴》[11],根据可获取的数据完整性以及代表性,选择京津冀、长三角和粤港澳大湾区三大城市群的机场群作为本次测算主体,通过上文建立的多目标加权函数对数据的综合测算数值,进行多目标加权函数的计算,得到2010—2019年十年间我国三大城市群的机场群系统交通韧性的基本水平,如表3所示。

三大城市群的机场群系统交通韧性综合测算结果　　　　　　　　　　　　　　　　　　　　　　　　　表3

机场群	2010	2011	2012	2013	2014	2015	2016	2017	2018	2019	均值	平均增长率
京津冀	0.5373	0.5429	0.5466	0.5513	0.5528	0.5557	0.5583	0.5623	0.5651	0.5701	0.55424	0.00661
长三角	0.5463	0.5509	0.5539	0.5571	0.5611	0.5632	0.5686	0.5697	0.5721	0.5743	0.56172	0.00557
粤港澳	0.5191	0.5172	0.5199	0.5224	0.5292	0.5369	0.5415	0.5481	0.5478	0.5529	0.5335	0.00703

如图4所示,从2010—2019年,我国三大城市群的机场群系统交通韧性呈稳定上升的状态,表明三大城市群的机场群系统发展的整体态势良好。

从数值计算结果层面来看,综合测算结果绝对数值相对偏小,可以推论我国三大城市群的机场群系统在交通韧性上以及机场群系统与城市群的协同发展程度还有提高的空间。

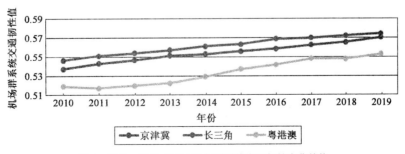

图4 2010—2019年三大机场群系统交通韧性变化趋势

根据测算过程中的数值数值以及测算结果,可以看到我国三大城市群与机场群的发展态势,在城市群的经济以及基础设施的支撑下,提升了城市综合交通一体化水平以及机场群运营服务水平,交通运营效率提升所带来的效益,反哺加速了城市群在经济方面的提升,城市群经济成长提供基础设施建设、完善与投资的经济来源,如此形成城市群以及机场群协同发展的可持续发展模式;而在城市群发展的背景下,机场群管理运营水平、城市综合交通枢纽一体化水平、城市群经济水平以及城市群基础设施水平不断的提高,提升了城市群发展背景下的机场群系统韧性程度,更加保障在城市群发展背景下的机场群在遭遇不可抗力的突发事件时,其系统韧性能够使系统的损失降至最低,加快系统恢复的过程。

4 结 语

通过对城市群背景下机场群系统交通韧性的综合测度可以得知,十年间我国三大城市群的机场群系统韧性呈现稳定上升的状态,在我国城市群逐渐发展成熟的情况下,随着城市群与机场群的发展,城市群背景下的机场群协同发展提高了交通韧性。

在规划方面应评估城市群与机场群发展现状,提出对未来发展的需求预测,合理布局城市群协同发展的机场群规划,明确城市群与机场群边界,确定不同功能的机场指标,机场群与城市群社会经济发展应紧密结合,提高城市群和机场群的交通韧性,对于城市群和机场群提供更加稳定的发展环境,并提高城市群和机场群面对突发事件的应变能力,降低突发事件所造成的损失。我国可利用后发优势,借鉴美国、英国与日本等成熟的发展经验,根据国内发展,内化为适合我国的发展模式。

参考文献

[1] International Civil Aviation Organization(ICAO). Presentation of 2018 Air Transport statistical results. [EB/OL].

[2] Annual World Airport Traffic Forecasts 2018—2040[Z]. Airport Council International(ACI), 2017.

[3] De Neufville R, Odoni A R. Airport Systems: Planning Design, and Management[M]. New York: McGraw-Hill, 2003.

[4] Holling C S. Resilience and Stability of Ecological Systems[J]. Annual Review of Ecology and Systematics, 1973, 4(1): 1-23.

[5] Xu Y Y, Li G, Cui S H, et al. Review and Perspective on Resilience Science: From Ecological Theory to Urban Practice. Acta Ecologica Sinica, 2018, 38(15): 5297-5304.

[6] Zhu Jin-he, Sun Hong-xue. Research on Spatial-temporal Evolution and Influencing Factors of Urban Resilience of China's Three Metropolitan Agglomerations[J]. Soft Science, 2020, v.34;No.242(02):76-83.

[7] Fu Chaoqi, Y Wang, Li Chao, et al. Sun Self-healing characteristics of aviation network under different growth mechanisms[J]. Journal of Beijing University of Aeronautics and Astronautics, 2018, v.44;No.304(06):108-116.

[8] Zhang Jingjing. Research on synergetic development mechanism of airport cluster and urban Agglomeration[D]. Tianjin: Civil Aviation University of China, 2020.

[9] Fu Zhihuan. Strategic research on transportation power[M]. China Communications Press Co., Ltd., 2019.

[10] Zhang Mingdou, Feng Xiaoqing. The resilience of cities in China[J]. Urban Problems, 2018, 000(010):27-36.

[11] National Bureau of statistics. China city statistical yearbook[R]. 2010—2019.

第九篇 交叉学科

基于图注意力卷积网络的短时交通流预测

潘卫鹏 郭唐仪 唐 坤 何 流

(南京理工大学自动化学院)

摘 要 为了深度挖掘城市路网复杂的拓扑结构和交通流数据的动态时空特征,本文提出一种基于图注意力卷积网络(GACN)的短时交通流预测模型。该模型将路网拓扑结构看作为图,考虑节点间的距离,使用图卷积获取交通流时序数据的空间相关性;引入注意力机制计算邻域内节点间的关联度,对节点进行有区别的信息聚合,并调整网络输出;在真实世界数据集 PeMS 上对算法效果进行验证。结果表明,采用提出的 GACN 模型能够有效捕获交通数据的动态时空依赖性,相较于基线模型,GACN 模型具有更好的预测效果。

关键词 智能交通 短时交通流预测 图卷积网络 城市路网 深度学习

0 引 言

短时交通流预测是智能交通领域研究的热点,预测的结果可以为交通管理部门提供科学的交通诱导依据[1]。这对缓解城市交通拥堵、提高行驶效率和安全、减轻交通环境负荷具有极其重要的意义。传统的交通流预测方法依赖数据驱动,仅考虑流量数据的时序特征,忽略了路网拓扑结构,割裂了交通数据的时间相关性与空间相关性,难以提取数据的动态时空特征,并且模型的现实可解释性较差,预测能力有限。

近年来,由于图在众多领域(如社交网络、引文网络等)强大的表现力[2],图神经网络(Graph Neural Network,GNN)[3-4]受到越来越多的关注。将卷积操作扩展到图结构数据中,Kipf 等[5]提出了图卷积神经网络(Graph Convolutional Network,GCN),并在半监督学习任务中取得了较好的效果。Yu 等[6]提出了一种基于图卷积神经网络(GCN)的道路交通速度预测模型,该模型能够区分相邻道路的连接权重,有效地捕获区域交通数据之间的时空依赖关系。Cui 等[7]提出了一种交通图卷积长短期记忆神经网络(TGC-LSTM),以捕获交通网络中道路之间的耦合关系和长时间序列数据的相关性,对路网交通状态进行预测。Guo 等[8]为挖掘交通数据的高度非线性和复杂的时空关系,提出一种带注意力机制的图卷积神经网络(ASTGCN)对交通流动态时空关系建模。鉴于此,本文设计了一种融合注意力机制与图卷积网络的短时交通流预测方法,能够分配邻居节点的注意力权重,有效提取数据的动态时空特征,提升网络预测能力。

1 融合注意力机制的图卷积交通流预测模型

1.1 问题定义

交通流预测的目的是根据历史交通数据和路网拓扑结构来预测未来的交通流量。短时交通流预测问题可描述为,根据传感器历史时刻数据 $[X_{t-T}, X_{t-T+1}, \cdots, X_{t-1}]$ (T 为滑动窗口大小,即历史数据的数量),以及路网拓扑结构 G,来预测下一时间段 t 的流量 X_t,即:

$$[X_{t-T}, X_{t-T+1}, \cdots, X_{t-1}; G] \xrightarrow{F(\cdot)} [X_t] \tag{1}$$

式中,X_t 为交通流特征向量,$X_t \in R^{n \times c}$,其中 n 是节点数,c 是通道数(可代表流量、速度、拥堵指数等,本文仅对流量数据进行预测,因此 $c = 1$);G 为路网拓扑的图结构,$G = (V, E)$,V 为节点,E 为节点间的边;$F(\cdot)$ 为待学习的模型。

交通数据的节点可以由传感器点位、平面交叉口或者一个区域来代表。路网中流量传感器的空间分布属于非欧氏结构,因此流量数据嵌入在不规则的图上。路网中交通数据的时空结构如图 1 所示。

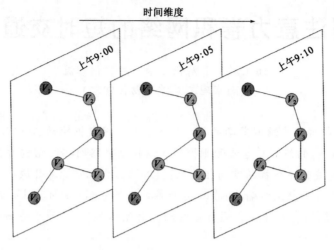

图 1　交通数据的时空结构

1.2　图卷积神经网络

图卷积网络(Graph Convolutional Network,GCN)是一种将卷积操作拓展到图结构的深度神经网络。传统的卷积神经网络(CNN)只能处理栅格图结构的数据[9],无法处理具有拓扑图结构的数据。在实际交通系统中,考虑到道路的方向性,路网被视为一张有向图 $G = (q, V, A)$。路网中的每个传感器被视为 1 个节点 $v_i \in V$,其取值 $q \in R$ 是 1 个标量。$V \in R^N$,N 为传感器数目。节点间的流量关系由邻接矩阵 $A \in R^N \times R^N$ 表示,邻接矩阵的元素 A_{ij} 表示节点 v_i 到 v_j 的连接关系。基于谱域的图卷积中,为分析图的拓扑属性,将图由对应的拉普拉斯矩阵 L 表示为:

$$L = D - A \tag{2}$$

规范化形式为:

$$L = I_N - D^{-\frac{1}{2}} A D^{-\frac{1}{2}} = U \Lambda U^T \in R^{N \times N} \tag{3}$$

式中,I_N 为单位矩阵,度矩阵 D 定义为 $D_{ii} = \sum_j A_{ij}$。将 L 进行特征值分解得 $L = U \Lambda U^T$,Λ 为由 L 的特征值组成的对角矩阵。$U = \{u_1, u_2, \cdots, u_N\}$ 由 L 的特征向量组成,对应 R^N 空间下的一组正交基。

根据图的谱卷积理论,时域中输入信号 x 和卷积核 g 的卷积操作可转换为频域的内积形式,即:

$$x *_G g = F^{-1}[F(x) \cdot F(g)] = U(U^T x \cdot U^T g) \tag{4}$$

式中,F 为傅里叶变换,$\cdot$ 为哈达玛积,$*_G$ 为图卷积运算。

令 $g_\theta = diag(U^T g)$,公式(4)等价转化为:

$$x *_G g_\theta = U g_\theta U^T x \tag{5}$$

由于 $g_\theta(\Lambda)$ 的计算复杂度较高,考虑用一阶切比雪夫多项[10]近似计算,即 $g_\theta(\Lambda) \approx \sum_{k=0}^{1} \beta_k T_k(\Lambda)$。那么,

$$\begin{aligned} x *_G g_\theta &= \sum_{k=0}^{K} \beta_k T_k(\hat{L}) x \approx \sum_{k=0}^{1} \beta_k T_k(\hat{L}) x \\ &= \beta_0 T_0(\hat{L}) x + \beta_1 T_1(\hat{L}) x \\ &= (\beta_0 + \beta_1 \hat{L}) x \\ &= [\beta_0 + \beta_1 (L - I_N)] x \\ &= [\beta_0 - \beta_1 (D^{-1/2} A D^{-1/2})] x \end{aligned} \tag{6}$$

进一步简化,令 $\beta_0 = -\beta_1 = \theta$,则 $x *_G g_\theta = \theta(I_N + D^{-1/2} A D^{-1/2}) x$。

为避免梯度爆炸或梯度消失,存在 $\tilde{D}^{-1/2}\tilde{A}\tilde{D}^{-1/2} = I_N + D^{-1/2}AD^{-1/2}$,其中 $\tilde{A} = I_N + A$ 且 $\tilde{D}_{ii} = \sum_j \tilde{A}_{ij}$。因此,得到最终公式:

$$x *_G g_\theta = \theta(\tilde{D}^{-1/2}\tilde{A}\tilde{D}^{-1/2})x \tag{7}$$

1.3 注意力机制

注意力模型(Attention Model,AM)最初被应用于机器翻译[11],近几年已经成为深度学习领域中的重要概念。每个传感器与周围相连接的传感器形成一个邻域,邻域内的每个邻居节点与中心节点的关联度不同,本文引入注意力机制来计算邻域内节点间的关联度[12]。假设中心节点 i 与邻居节点 j 之间的关联度为:

$$e_{ij} = \alpha(\vec{\mathbf{W}}h_i, \vec{\mathbf{W}}h_j) = \vec{a}^T[\vec{\mathbf{W}}h_i || \vec{\mathbf{W}}h_j] \tag{8}$$

其中,h_i 为节点 i 的特征,h_j 为……$\mathbf{W}$ 为线性变换参数,$\alpha(\cdot)$ 为注意力机制,$\vec{a}^T$ 为学习的参数,e_{ij} 为注意力系数。

使用 softmax 函数对每个节点的注意力系数进行归一化,得到节点间的注意力系数 α_{ij},即:

$$\alpha_{ij} = \text{softmax}(e_{ij}) = \frac{\exp(e_{ij})}{\sum_k \exp(e_{ik})} \tag{9}$$

然后,利用注意力系数对邻域内节点进行有区别的信息聚合,加权求和以输出最终的节点特征。本文引入的注意力机制局部结构如图 2 所示。

1.4 图注意力卷积网络模型

本文融合注意力机制与图卷积神经网络,提出一种基于图注意力卷积网络(GACN)的路网短时交通流预测模型。模型框架如图 3 所示,由多层 GCN 和注意力机制组成。首先,将路网拓扑结构和历史流量数据输入到两层 GCN,提取交通流时序数据的空间相关性。输出 n 个节点特征 $h_i(i=1,2,\cdots,n)$,然后将其输入到注意力机制,计算邻域内节点间的关联度,得到节点间的注意力系数。利用注意力系数对邻域内节点进行有区别的信息聚合,并调整网络输出模型的最终结果,即流量的预测值。

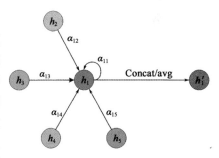

图 2 注意力机制局部结构

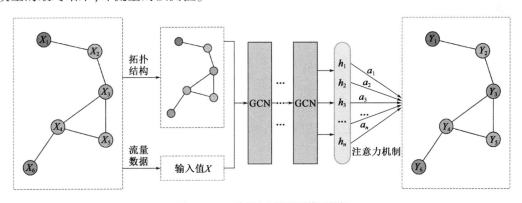

图 3 GACN 路网交通流预测模型框架

2 实 验 过 程

2.1 数据处理与模型训练

本文采用美国加利福尼亚州 PeMS 系统中第 4 区 307 个传感器所采集的交通数据进行试验,包括传感器间距离和交通流量数据。实验数据集 2018 年 1 月 1 日 ~ 2 月 28 日,时间间隔 5 分钟的共 16992 个样本。定义滑动窗口的大小为7,前6个时序数据为输入值x,最后1个时序数据为标签y,即组成了一个训练样本。数据处理与模型训练过程的伪代码如表1所示。

数据处理与模型训练过程　　　　　　　　表1

步骤	内容
输入	传感器间距离 Distance,节点数 N,流量数据 X,时间序列窗口 T

第1步	读入邻接矩阵 A
	　if $distance_{ij}=0$:
	　　$A_{ij}=0$
	　else:
	　　$A_{ij}=1/distance_{ij}$
	　return A

第2步	读入流量数据,将流量值归一化到[0,1],构建数据集 D。按照7∶3的比例划分数据集 D,得到训练集 D_1 和测试集 D_2
第3步	从 D_1 中随机选取 Batch 大小的数据送入模型训练
第4步	以 MSE 为损失函数,用 Adam 算法更新模型参数
第5步	until 满足训练停止条件
输出	训练完成的模型

2.2　模型性能评估指标

为评估模型的有效性,实验采用3种误差函数作为评价模型预测效果的指标:平均绝对误差(Mean Absolute Error,MAE)、平均绝对百分比误差(Mean Absolute Percentage Error,MAPE)和均方根误差(Root Mean Square Error,RMSE)。3项评估指标分别定义为:

$$\text{MAE}=\frac{1}{n}\sum_{i=1}^{n}|y_i-\hat{y}_i| \tag{10}$$

$$\text{MAPE}=\frac{1}{n}\sum_{i=1}^{n}\left|\frac{y_i-\hat{y}_i}{y_i}\right|\times100\% \tag{11}$$

$$\text{RMSE}=\sqrt{\frac{1}{n}\sum_{i=1}^{n}(y_i-\hat{y}_i)^2} \tag{12}$$

式中,n 为测试集的样本数目;y_i 为实际值;$\hat{y}_i$ 为预测值。

3项指标的范围为[0,+∞),值越小表示模型的精确度越高。

2.3　基线模型设置

采用长短期记忆网络(Long short-term memory,LSTM)[13]和图卷积网络(GCN)作为基线模型。所有模型运用 Pytorch 深度神经网络框架搭建,设置均方误差(MSE)作为损失函数,选择 Adam 算法作为参数优化器。实验在 Intel(R) Xeon(R) CPU E5-2660 v2 处理器和 NVIDIA GeForce GTX Titan X 显卡上进行。

3　实验结果与分析

将 GACN 模型在 PeMS04 数据集上进行训练,并与基线模型进行比较,得到模型性能如表2所示。从表中可以看出,GACN 模型在3种性能评估指标下效果提升明显,分别比 LSTM 模型提升15.58%、21.79%和13.24%,比 GCN 模型提升5.04%、6.69%和3.46%。

不同模型在数据集上的性能指标 表2

模型	MAE	MAPE	RMSE
LSTM	22.33	17.30%	32.85
GCN	19.85	14.50%	29.52
GACN（ours）	18.85	13.53%	28.50

模型在测试集上的预测值与真实值对比结果如图4所示。横轴表示时间,以5 min为刻度,纵轴表示每5 min的交通流量值。从图中可以看出,LSTM模型未考虑交通数据的空间特征,预测精确度较差。GCN模型考虑了路网拓扑结构,预测效果比LSTM模型有较大提升。GACN模型在一天中的预测结果与数据真实值最为接近,说明GACN模型通过训练获得了最佳的预测性能。

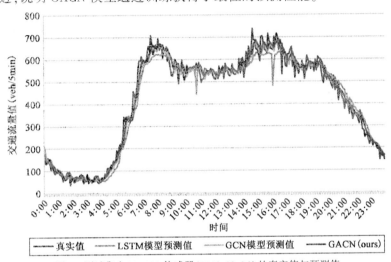

图4 测试集中No.120传感器(2018-02-26)的真实值与预测值

4 结 语

本文针对城市路网短时交通流预测问题,提出了一种基于图注意力卷积网络(GACN)的短时交通流预测模型,在真实世界数据集PEMS上进行实验和验证。GACN模型考虑了城市路网复杂的拓扑结构和交通流数据的动态时空特征,使用图卷积获取交通流时序数据的空间相关性,引入注意力机制对节点进行有区别的信息聚合,并调整网络输出。结果表明,相较于基线模型,GACN模型在MAE、MAPE和RMSE指标下,分别比LSTM模型提升15.58%、21.79%和13.24%,比GCN模型提升5.04%、6.69%和3.46%。本文设计的模型仍有改进之处,一方面对模型的组成和结构进一步优化,另一方面天气、节假日、交通事故等外部因素也会对交通流产生影响,后续研究将进一步提升模型的预测准确性。

参考文献

[1] 陆化普,孙智源,屈闻聪. 大数据及其在城市智能交通系统中的应用综述[J]. 交通运输系统工程与信息, 2015, 15(05): 45-52.

[2] 徐冰冰,岑科廷,黄俊杰,等. 图卷积神经网络综述[J]. 计算机学报, 2020, 43(05): 755-780.

[3] Scarselli F, Gori M, Tsoi A, et al. The Graph Neural Network Model[J]. IEEE Transactions on Neural Networks, 2009, 20(1): 61.

[4] Zhou J, Cui G, Zhang Z, et al. Graph Neural Networks: A Review of Methods and Applications[J]. 2018.

[5] Kipf T N, Welling M. Semi-Supervised Classification with Graph Convolutional Networks[J]. arXiv preprint arXiv:2016.1609.02907.

[6] Yu B, Lee Y, Sohn K. Forecasting Road Traffic Speeds by Considering Area-Wide Spatio-Temporal

Dependencies Based on A Graph Convolutional Neural Network (GCN)[J]. Transportation Research Part C: Emerging Technologies, Elsevier, 2020, 114(January): 189-204.

[7] Cui Z, Henrickson K, Ke R, et al. High-Order Graph Convolutional Recurrent Neural Network: A Deep Learning Framework for Network-Scale Traffic Learning and Forecasting[J]. IEEE Transactions on Intelligent Transportation Systems, PP(99): 1-12.

[8] Guo S, Lin Y, Feng N, et al. Attention Based Spatial-Temporal Graph Convolutional Networks for Traffic Flow Forecasting[J]. Proceedings of the AAAI Conference on Artificial Intelligence, 2019, 33: 922-929.

[9] Zhang J, Zheng Y, Qi D. Deep Spatio-Temporal Residual Networks for Citywide Crowd Flows Prediction [J]. 31st AAAI Conference on Artificial Intelligence, AAAI 2017, 2017: 1655-1661.

[10] Defferrard M, Bresson X, Vandergheynst P, et al. Convolutional Neural Networks on Graphs with Fast Localized Spectral Filtering[J]. Neural Information Processing Systems, 2016: 3844-3852.

[11] Bahdanau D, Cho K H, Bengio Y. NeuralMachine Translation by Jointly Learning to Align and Translate [J]. 3rd International Conference on Learning Representations, ICLR 2015-Conference Track Proceedings, 2015: 1-15.

[12] Velickovic P, Cucurull G, Casanova A, et al. Graph Attention Networks[C].//Procedings of the International Conference on Learning Representations. Vancouver, Canada, 2018.

[13] Tian Y, Zhang K, Li J, et al. LSTM-based Traffic Flow Prediction with Missing Data[J]. Neurocomputing, 2018, 318(NOV.27): 297-305.

基于BiGRU-LAN的航空器适航命名实体识别方法

衡红军 胡刚
(中国民航大学)

摘要 适航领域命名实体识别是航空器适航审定知识图谱自动构建和提高适航审定能力的基础。针对适航领域命名实体识别中英文、数字、特殊字符形式共存问题,提出了基于双向门控循环单元-标签注意力网络(BiGRU-LAN)的航空器适航命名实体识别方法。该方法将适航语料嵌入为字符分布式向量,采用双层BiGRU网络提取双向字符序列特征和建模标签间的相互关系,使用LAN网络计算标签注意力权重并调整标签嵌入向量,最后根据注意力权重得到标签结果。在所构建的适航命名实体识别数据集上F_1值达到了81.68%,该方法无需任何特征模板和NLP工具,能够有效识别适航领域的命名实体,并且训练推理比传统的识别方法更加高效。

关键词 命名实体识别 门控循环单元 标签注意力网络 航空器适航

0 引言

随着我国民用航空产业的飞速发展,航空器适航审定需求正在不断增大。新研发的民用航空产品需要取得相应的适航证件或者适航标签才能生产和使用[1]。通过构建航空器适航审定知识图谱,为适航领域智能化工具软件的研发提供基础,提高信息查询效率以及取证效率,对提高我国适航审定能力具有重要意义。

命名实体识别(Named Entity Recognition, NER)是知识抽取的关键技术之一,是关系抽取的基础,可分为基于规则字典、基于统计机器学习和基于深度学习的方法。基于深度学习的识别方法无需依赖人工构建规则、模板和词典,并且取得了比较好的识别效果,成为研究的热点[2]。Hochreiter 等人[3]提出了一种结合门控机制的长短期记忆网络(Long-Short Term Memory,LSTM)提取长距离依赖关系;Huang 等人[4]发现采用 CRF 推理层的模型在多个数据集上取得了最好的效果;Lample 等人[5]进一步通过实验证明了双向 LSTM-CRF 模型在 NER 任务上的有效性。研究[6]发现,采用 Softmax 或 CRF 为推理层的模型效果差距不大,甚至在个别任务上 Softmax 表现略好;Cui 等人[7]设计了一种标签注意力网络(Label Attention Network,LAN),在序列标注任务的实验结果表明 LAN 推理层和 CRF 的效果相当,但效率高于 CRF。在民航领域,王红等人[8]对民航突发事件实体识别进行了研究。目前,大多数识别模型采用了 CRF 推理层。

适航领域命名实体识别主要有以下难点:(1)存在大量专业术语和审定机构名称,领域性强,且有许多英文缩写简写实体,例如 STC。(2)命名实体以中英文、数字、特殊符号或三者组合的形式存在,使得英文句子分词困难。(3)以字符形式分割语料导致输入序列长度较长,传统的 BiGRU-CRF 模型训练推理效率低。基于此,本文将 BiGRU 与 LAN 相结合为 BiGRU-LAN 网络,形成层级化的 BiGRU-LAN 网络结构,提出基于 BiGRU-LAN 的航空器适航命名实体识别方法,为航空器适航关系抽取和智能问答提供技术支撑。

1 数据获取与处理

本文数据获取和处理等流程示意图如图 1 所示。利用爬虫爬取中国民用航空局官网公开的民航法律和适航规章收集文本,并进行滤除噪声等预处理后构成本文的适航语料。航空器适航命名实体识别需要从文本中确定出该领域命名实体的起始结束位置并分类。结合中国民用航空局官网的分类结构和重要适航术语,同时将实体属性的抽取转变为实体抽取的形式,定义了法律规章、证书标签和组织机构等 12 种实体类型和职位、日期时间和数值 3 种属性类型(后文均统称为实体)。

在本研究中,采用 BIO(Begin,Inside,Outside)的标注策略,将航空器适航领域命名实体识别任务转换为序列标注任务。其中 B 代表实体的起始字符;I 代表实体内部的字符;O 代表实体外部字符;BI 标签后紧跟命名实体的类型。"型号合格证"的标注形式如表 1 所示。根据所定义的命名实体类型和标注策略对适航语料进行命名实体标注,并切分为数据集训练评估模型,同时反馈识别结果纠正标注标签。

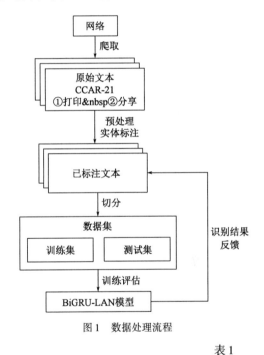

图 1 数据处理流程

标注实例 表1

字符	型	号	合	格	证
标签	B_证书标签	I_证书标签	I_证书标签	I_证书标签	I_证书标签

2 BiGRU-LAN 模型

2.1 模型框架

BiGRU-LAN 模型框架如图 2 所示,其中 ⊕ 表示向量的拼接,箭头为数据的流动方向,文本从底部输入,顶部为标签结果。文本通过随机初始化字符向量表嵌入为字符向量 x_1,输入神经网络模型;同时随机初始化标签嵌入向量表 E_1,两个嵌入向量表同模型一起联合训练。

中间层 BiGRU-LAN 网络使用双层 BiGRU 单元从字符向量序列中提取双向序列特征,得到 Dropout 后的隐藏特征向量 h;LAN 网络对标签嵌入向量 E_1 与隐藏特征向量 h 通过注意力机制求出注意力分布权重,并根据权重调整标签嵌入向量E_l,进而求出备选标签嵌入向量E_l^*;备选标签向量E_l^*和隐藏特征向量h通过残差结构拼接为联合特征向量H^j输入输出层BiGRU-LAN网络。

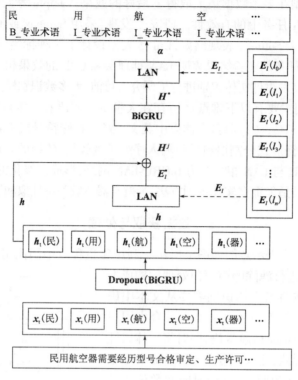

图2 BiGRU-LAN模型结构

输出层BiGRU-LAN网络提取联合特征向量H^j的序列特征,建模标签间的相互关系,输出新的隐藏特征向量H^*,对标签嵌入向量E_l与H^*再次通过注意力机制求出标签的注意力分布向量α,最终根据注意力权重分类标签。

2.2 BiGRU层

门控循环单元(Gated Recurrent Unit,GRU)是Junyoung等人[9]在2014年提出的一种循环神经网络模型,由重置门、更新门和记忆单元构成。GRU单元一个时间步长内的数据更新过程如图3所示。

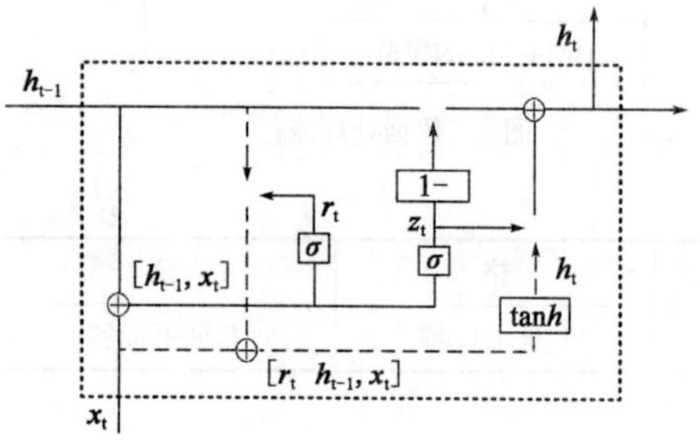

图3 GRU单元结构图

以字符位置t为例,GRU单元具体计算公式为:

$$r_t = \sigma(W_r[h_{t-1}, x_t] + b_r) \quad (1)$$

$$z_t = \sigma(W_z[h_{t-1}, x_t] + b_z) \quad (2)$$

$$\tilde{h}_t = \tanh(W_{\tilde{h}}[r_t \cdot h_{t-1}, x_t] + b_{\tilde{h}}) \quad (3)$$

$$h_t = (1 - z_t) \cdot h_{t-1} + z_t \cdot \tilde{h}_t \quad (4)$$

式中: $\oplus$——向量的拼接;

$\cdot$——Hadamard乘积;

σ——sigmoid函数;

r_t——重置门;

z_t——为更新门;

x_t、h_{t-1}、$\tilde{h}_t$和h_t——当前输入、前一隐状态、当前候选隐状态和当前隐状态;

W——权重参数;

b——为偏置参数。

BiGRU即在输入序列数据的两个方向上提取特征,最终的隐藏特征向量由两个方向的特征向量拼接得到。

2.3 LAN 网络

LAN 网络将隐藏特征向量作为查询向量,标签嵌入向量作为键值向量,经过缩放点积注意力运算求得标签注意力分布,并得到注意力加权的标签嵌入向量。计算公式为:

$$\boldsymbol{\alpha}_t = \text{soft}_{\max}\left(\frac{\boldsymbol{Q}_t \boldsymbol{K}_t^T}{\sqrt{d_h}}\right) \tag{5}$$

$$\boldsymbol{H}_t^l = \boldsymbol{\alpha}_t \boldsymbol{V}_t \tag{6}$$

$$\hat{y}_t = \arg\max(\boldsymbol{\alpha}_t) \tag{7}$$

式中:t——字符位置;

d_h——模型隐藏层维度;

$\boldsymbol{Q}_t$——隐藏特征向量;

$\boldsymbol{K}_t = \boldsymbol{V}_t$——标签嵌入向量;

$\boldsymbol{K}_t^T$——$\boldsymbol{K}_t$ 的转置;

$\boldsymbol{\alpha}_t$——注意力分布权重向量;

$\boldsymbol{H}_t^l$——注意力权重加权的标签嵌入向量,备选标签向量;

$\hat{y}_t$——预测的标签。

在推理时,LAN 网络使用注意力权重最大的标签类别。

3 实验结果及分析

3.1 实验语料和评价指标

实验语料库一共有 17419 个样本,随机取出 75% 的样本构成训练集,剩余样本作为测试集,数据集统计信息和实体分布情况分别如表 2 和表 3 所示。

语料数据集统计信息 表2

	训 练 集	测 试 集
样本数	13064	4355
平均序列长度	58.69	58.06

适航命名实体分布情况 表3

实体类型	训练集	测试集	总 数
专业术语	29246	9575	38821
组织机构	7556	2390	9946
人物	5834	1844	7678
条款章节	3314	1136	4450
证书标签	2582	842	3424
法律规章	2389	793	3182
数值	2218	753	2971
文件	2139	717	2856
日期时间	2038	638	2676
地理位置	916	274	1190
飞行运行类型	650	259	909
飞行阶段	703	241	944
飞行器	555	201	756
职位	411	111	522
标准	349	99	448

使用精确率(Precision,P)、召回率(Recall,R)和F_1值对识别结果进行评估。当实体起始、结束位置和分类同时正确预测时,才视为一个实体的正确识别。以c类实体为例,计算公式为:

$$P_c = \frac{Right_c}{Predicted_c} \tag{8}$$

$$P_c = \frac{Right_c}{Total_c} \tag{9}$$

$$F_{1c} = \frac{2 \times P_c \times R_c}{P_c + R_c} \tag{10}$$

式中:$Right$——实体识别正确的个数;
$Predicted$——模型识别的所有实体个数;
$Total$——测试集中所有实体个数。

模型整体评估采用Micro-P、Micro-R和Micro-F_1指标。精确率与召回率分别从预测精确性和全面性评价;F_1值综合了P和R两个指标,评价更全面。

3.2 模型参数与实验环境

每层BiGRU-LAN均使用了双层BiGRU网络,模型和训练相关的具体参数如表4所示。实验在操作系统为Deepin Linux 15.1的服务器上进行,服务器配置了AMD Ryzen 5 1600处理器,使用了Pytorch 1.2.0深度学习框架,并使用了GTX 1060加速模型的训练。

模型及训练参数　　　表4

参　　数	取　　值
字典字符个数	8081
字符嵌入维度	312
标签嵌入维度	400
隐藏层维度	400
标签分类	31
BiGRU-LAN层数	2
Batch Size	32
Dropout	0.5
损失函数	Cross Entropy
优化算法	Adam
学习率	0.001

3.3 实验结果

使用航空器适航命名实体识别数据集对BiGRU-LAN模型进行训练并评估,得到的各类命名实体识别结果和整体评估结果如表5所示。

识别结果　　　表5

实体类型	$P(\%)$	$R(\%)$	$F_1(\%)$
条款章节	96.22	96.30	96.26
法律规章	92.60	89.91	91.23
日期时间	91.71	90.13	90.91
人物	87.24	86.01	86.62
组织机构	85.75	85.86	85.80

续上表

实体类型	P(%)	R(%)	F_1(%)
数值	85.98	85.52	85.75
证书标签	85.89	84.56	85.22
飞行器	85.43	84.58	85.00
标准	85.87	79.80	82.72
飞行运行类型	80.50	80.50	80.50
地理位置	79.70	78.83	79.27
飞行阶段	82.98	75.29	78.95
职位	78.90	77.48	78.18
文件	79.82	75.59	77.65
专业术语	75.88	76.98	76.43
整体指标	81.78	81.42	81.68

实验结果表明，大部分类型的命名实体均被有效识别，其 F_1 值超过了80%。通过分析识别结果，发现 F_1 值超过90.00%的实体具有固定的形式，如条款章节实体具有"第 xx 条"的形式。文件与专业术语命名实体的嵌套情况非常严重，同时影响两个类别的 F_1 值。例如"试飞项目检查单"文件实体，嵌套了"试飞项目"专业术语实体。

3.4 模型对比

对 BiGRU-LAN 与 BiGRU-CRF 两个模型的训练推理效率进行了对比，结果如表6所示：两个模型取得的 F_1 值相差不大，但训练推理速度差异明显。主要原因是输入文本序列分割为字符，平均长度达到了58.38；而 LAN 推理层与 CRF 推理层的推理渐进时间复杂度分别为 $O(|L|n)$ 和 $O(|L|^2 n)$，其中 $|L|$ 为标签分类数，n 为序列长度，较长的序列长度增大了时间复杂度。

训练推理速度比较结果　　表6

模　型	训练速度 sentence·s^{-1}	推理速度 sentence·s^{-1}	F_1(%)
BiGRU-CRF	46.74	760.40	81.62
BiGRU-LAN	331.98	1101.67	81.68

4　结　语

针对航空器适航命名实体形式复杂的问题，本文提出了一种基于 BiGRU-LAN 的航空器适航命名实体识别方法，该方法不需要任何的特征模板以及 NLP 工具，在适航命名实体识别数据集上 F_1 值达到了81.68%；对比实验表明，相比传统的 BiGRU-CRF 识别方法，本方法训练推理更加高效。

目前还需要进一步标注新的语料，提高适航语料文本的规模，可尝试应用本方法提高领域命名实体的标注效率和标注质量；未来可考虑使用领域语料预训练字符嵌入向量，引入部分先验知识，提高模型识别效果和泛化能力。

参考文献

[1] 白杰,冯振宇.航空器适航审定概论[M].北京:中国民航出版社,2018.
[2] 刘浏,王东波.命名实体识别研究综述[J].情报学报,2018,37(03):329-340.
[3] Hochreiter S, Schmidhuber J. Long Short-Term Memory[J]. Neural Computation, 1997, 9(8):1735-1780.
[4] Huang Z, Wei, X Kai Y. Bidirectional LSTM-CRF Models for Sequence Tagging[J]. arXiv preprint arXiv: Computation and Language, 2015.

[5] Lample G, Ballesteros M, Subramanian S, et al. Neural architectures for Named Entity Recognition[C]. North American Chapter of the Association for Computational Linguistics, 2016: 260-270.
[6] Chung J, Gulcehre C, Cho K, et al. Empirical Evaluation of Gated Recurrent Neural Networks on Sequence Modeling[J]. arXiv preprint arXiv: Neural and Evolutionary Computing, 2014.
[7] Reimers N, Gurevych I. Optimal Hyperparameters for deep LSTM-Networks for Sequence Labeling Tasks[J]. arXiv preprint arXiv: Computation and Language, 2017.
[8] Cui L, Zhang Y. Hierarchically-Refined Label Attention Network for Sequence Labeling[C]. International Joint Conference on Natural Language Processing, 2019: 4113-4126.
[9] 王红,李浩飞,邱帅. 民航突发事件实体识别方法研究[J]. 计算机应用与软件,2020,37(03):166-172.

我国智慧交通应用体验和未来建设

盛一凡　陈宽民

(长安大学运输工程学院)

摘　要　为探究我国智慧交通应用现阶段实情,从用户角度对此进行调查分析,并提出相关建议。通过统计交通运输高水平期刊中的相关文献,以及交通运输部、交通运输行业管理部门公开发布的同"智慧交通"相关的政策文件,结合计划行为理论、技术模型理论,采用问卷分析手段得到相应结论,提出建议措施。感知有用和易用性及主观规范等用户因素对智慧交通应用意向会产生不同程度的影响。通过数据分析结果,可采取改进智慧交通应用产品的操作难度、大力宣传相关的产品等方法促进智慧交通乃至智慧城市的构建。

关键词　智慧城市　应用使用意向　数据分析　智慧交通应用　影响因素

0 引　言

相对于国外来说,我国的智慧交通起步较晚,在一定层面上尚且属于新的应用产品。在20世纪60年代,美国提出"智能交通系统"创想,并历经多年的发展形成了美日欧三大智能交通系统研究开发工程基地。2010年IBM公司提出的关于智慧城市的概念在全球激起了一轮浪潮[1]。2012年,我国发布了关于国家智慧城市的系列通知,拉开智慧城市试点工作建设的大幕。当前我国同"智慧交通"有关的服务提供和设施搭建水平相较于之前有所增加,不过受到发展时间和技术等水平所限,还存在一定的问题,且相关的研究并未构成相应的规模,需要进一步的研究和深化[2]。在这样的社会背景之下,结合当前我国智慧交通的应用情况,通过梳理交通运输期刊中的文献以及交通运输相关部门出台的文件,以技术模型等相关理论为基础,通过实际的数据调研分析,从感知有用和易用性、主观规范等用户因素出发,围绕我国民众对智慧交通应用的使用情况,针对性地提出有参考性的建议,试图为智慧交通乃至智慧城市的构建贡献绵薄之力。

1 相关概念

IBM公司(国际商业机器公司)率先于2008年提出"智慧"这一词汇,它最早来自于该公司对"智慧地球"的论述,自2010年之后,这一词汇被覆盖至"智慧城市"的论述中。在知网上搜索"智慧交通"且定位于"工程科技"类目专业之下,共找到1976条文献条目[3],选中"中文文献"类别,显示一共1010条文献,由此可见,在这方面的研究中,外文文献占了总文献条目将近一半的数量。所搜集到的中文文献显示,最早关于"智慧交通"的文献发表在 2011 年,并且当时的文献多是对我国未来智慧交通的建设和方向进行祈愿和联想,外文文献最早涉及智慧交通的研究时间可以追溯到 1993 年,可见国外对于这方面的研究之早。纵观国内外文献和政策文件,可以对智慧交通的概念做出分析。

国外学者 Gregory、Andrea 等对"智慧交通"的定义,认为智慧交通是利用网络新技术为交通提供服务,打造安全、绿色并且高效率、可以分享的具备广泛性和稳定性的管理手段,从而减少拥挤和事故发生,Yovanof[4] 在其文中对智慧交通的应用范围做了扩大,提出除了单点监测控制之外,智慧交通可对整体或者单个路段,比如高危路线进行检测。

我国对"智慧交通"的内容划分,同样是源自于《国家智慧城市(区、镇)试点指标体系(试行)》,其中对智慧城市的定义做了阐述,提出智慧城市是在水、能源、教育、交通等多个方面,运用现代技术整合相关资源综合规划治理、加强建设管理。由此,从国内的众多学者如钱小鸿、蔡翠[5] 等在相关著述当中对"智慧城市"的定义出发,结合"智慧交通"的特点,可以将"智慧交通"表述为:在智慧城市的基础上,基于智能交通手段,运用物联网、人工智能、云计算等新一代科技手段,对交通活动中包括人、车、路等各要素进行全方位的监控服务的高效方便的交通运输体系[6]。

2 理论依据

由上文可知,智慧交通涉及多个方面,在实际应用当中,具体可以划分为为达到交通配置或者运行的最优化采用的新技术,比如在交通系统中使用摄像头、超声波、交通 APP 等等,这些对交通管理者、出行群众有不可替代的辅助作用。划分智慧交通所涉及的层面,可以大致分为感知层、平台层、应用层、展现层等层次,其所包含的内容如图 1 所示。

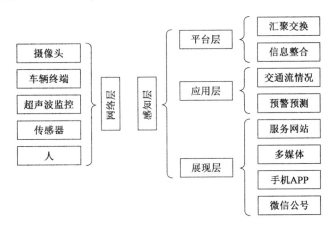

图 1 智慧交通层次图

国内外文献大多基于智慧交通的地位、模式、机制、运输能力等多方面进行研究分析[7],从用户的角度进行分析,甚至采用调查及数据研究的文献颇为少见,然而研究用户的体验对智慧交通的应用发展非常重要,智慧交通的最终目标也是提升社会的便捷性、提高用户的使用感受、方便群众出行。因此从智慧交通所包含的展现层面出发,从公众的角度对智慧交通使用情况进行调查分析,有助于弥补相关研究的空白,同时在实践层面上有助于促进智慧交通应用的进一步完善。

为使问卷设计充分体现研究目的,在问卷的设计中采用以下理论依据。

2.1 计划行为理论

20 世纪 80 年代末,国外学者 Icek Ajzen[8] 提出了影响深远的计划行为理论(Theory of Planned Behavior,TPB),在理性行为概念的基础上,除了考虑了人的能动性原因之外,还加入了控制变量——感知行为,其所描述的模型如图 2 所示。

2.2 技术接受模型

技术接受模型(Technology Acceptance Model,TAM)基于上述所说的计划行为理论,针对用户使用信息的意向与接收情况提出。技术接受模型的两个主要决定因素是个人使用某个工具或者手段是否会对其工作有所帮助的感知有用性,以及使用该工具容易或困难的感知易用性。对技术接受模型的描述可通过图3所得。

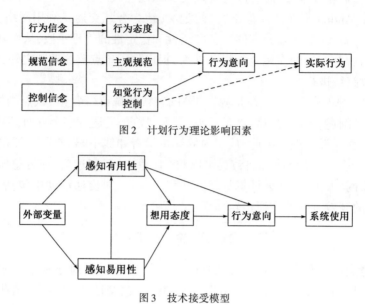

图2 计划行为理论影响因素

图3 技术接受模型

3 问卷构建及数据搜集

3.1 问卷构建

通过对国内外关于智慧交通应用和理论分析的文献的梳理[9],结合我国智慧交通实际情况,选择理论中所提出的适合研究的因自变量,从而构建本文研究问卷框架。基于上述分析,本文选择感知有用性和易用性、主观规范、使用智慧交通应用的行为态度等,将这些因素作为影响使用意向的自变量进行研究。

结合相关的文献[10]以及智慧交通的概念,可对模型所涉及的变量进行具体分析,"使用意愿"即使用者对智慧交通应用使用的意愿程度、"使用态度"即使用者对智慧交通应用的使用是支持或反对、"感知有用性"即使用者在使用智慧交通应用之时是否提升了其效率、"感知易用性"即使用者在使用智慧交通应用之时是否感受到简易方便、"主观规范"即使用者在使用智慧交通应用之时是否受到他人的影响。问卷设计的题目只有基于正确的理论框架才能使获得的结论具有可靠性和借鉴价值。基于上述分析可将变量的设计内容具体化,如表1所示。

问卷变量及其具体内容　　　　　表1

变　量	具　体　内　容
感知有用性	通过智慧交通的应用,使我的生活方便了许多 通过智慧交通的应用,我能够更快地解决麻烦 通过智慧交通的应用,我的工作效能提升了 智慧交通应用对我来说是很有用的
感知易用性	智慧交通应用不会花费过多时间、精力、成本 使用智慧交通应用操作方便 智慧交通应用对我来说是容易使用和操作的
主观规范	我身边的人都有在使用智慧交通应用 对我有重要影响的人认为并且奉劝我使用智慧交通应用 我所在的群体较为认同智慧交通应用 身边越来越多的人使用智慧交通应用

续上表

变 量	具 体 内 容
使用态度	我觉得使用智慧交通应用是很有价值的事情 我觉得值得花费一点儿时间去使用智慧交通应用 我觉得使用智慧交通应用是很好的 我对使用智慧交通应用保持肯定的态度
使用意向	当需要完成某些工作之时我会继续使用智慧交通应用 我会向我的朋友们或者家人们推荐智慧交通应用 今后我会更为高频率地使用智慧交通应用

在问卷的基础问题上对所填写者的性别、地域进行选择填写，对未使用过智慧交通应用的用户进行了"不用填写以下问题"的选项进行筛除，从而符合本研究的主题。在问卷的主题部分，对感知有用性和易用性、主观规范、使用态度和意向的设计中，采用李克特五级量表法，设置为完全同意与否、同意与否和不确定五个选项。

3.2 问卷数据

采用网上电子问卷的形式，通过多平台分享确保随机和广泛覆盖。本次问卷发放数量共计 200 份，总共收集到的问卷共计 188 份，其中被删除的无效问卷 23 份，回收率达到 94%，且此次问卷发放中，有效率达到了 82.5%。

4 问卷数据分析

本次回收问卷 188 份，在回收到的问卷样本之中男生 102 人、占比 54.26%；女生 86 人占比 45.74%。被调查者中位于北京、上海、广州的人占大多数。

为了探究问卷设计中问卷的选项同其相对应的变量因素之间是否符合理论基础，采用验证性因子进行分析，通过分析可知，感知易用性的三个详细内容的提法、使用意向的三个详细内容的提法等的数值都大于 0.8，说明了各个变量的题项设置都能很好地反映其内涵，设置安排是适当的。

信效度分析是除了验证性因子分析之外必不可少的一环。信度分析数据的可靠程度，通常都采用 Cronbach α 系数来进行验证。对感知有用性和易用性、主观规范、使用意向进行 Alph 系数的分析，所得数值皆大于 0.7，说明了调查所得数据较为可靠。信度分析上划分为内容效度和结构效度，内容效度是测量变量同其题目设定题项之间是否符合，而结构效度是测量各个变量之间的结构是否能够互相清晰区分且符合各自指标所需。内容效度的测量显示各变量的平均方差提取值(AVE)均大于 0.5，说明本问卷有较好的内容收敛效度。同时问卷在区分效度的检测上也有较好的效度测试结果。

此外，在相关性分析之中，感知有用性和易用性、主观规范、使用态度和意向这几个变量之间，相关性系数都大于 0.6 的指数，显著性数值皆显示是 0.001，由此可见问卷所选取的变量之间相关关系颇为显著。

对各因素进行了分析之后，对智能交通应用的关系可应用回归分析法进行统计学方面的解释。在整体模型之上显著性 P 值显示为 $0.001 < 0.05$ 可以推断整体模型很显著。而用智慧交通应用的感知有用性、易用性、主观规范为自变量，用使用意向作为因变量进行回归分析，得出以下的结论：

使用态度的显著值小于 0.01 并且感知易用性的显著值小于 0.05，从而说明这两者显著影响人们对于智慧交通应用的使用意向，另一方面，主观规范、感知有用性则呈现不显著的状态。其关系可如图 4 所示。

对"使用态度"变量进行分析较为关键，因为它是影响智慧交通应用使用意向最为直接和关键的因素。通过验证得出，使用态度系数是正值，显著值小于 0.05，由此可以得出使用态度对智慧交通应用的使用意向,呈现出正向的显著影响特征。"感知易用性"系数呈现正相关,显著值小于0.05,同样呈现出显著正向影响特质。而感知有用性是使用者在使用智慧交通应用之时对其工作等的辅助程度,在验证这一因素之中显示其同使用意向之间呈现正相关的关系即系数为正值,然而相关性却不是很显著,对"主观规范"的系数研究验证所得也呈现上述"感知有用性"中表明的结果。

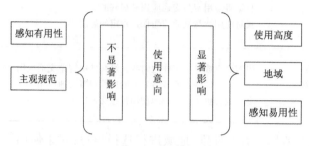

图4 使用意向影响因素图

5 结　语

文中从用户的角度,结合相关的理论对智慧交通应用进行分析研究,在前人的研究基础之上构建了智慧交通应用的使用意向影响因子,并构建了相应的问卷分析调研验证,可以得出这样的结论[11]:

(1)技术模型之中的两大关键变量感知有用和易用性经过论证之后显示对使用者关于智慧交通应用的使用意向有正相关的关系,只不过呈现出的影响显著程度有区分,感知易用性影响相较于感知有用性来说更为显著,如若操作简单、花费时间精力较少,那么人们会增加对其的使用意向。针对有用性显示显著程度较弱这一点,在调查中也发现,部分民众认为智慧交通的应用指的是移动手机APP软件的使用,对"智慧交通"的定义和具体内容所指并未有明确的了解,比如并不知道电子汽车等的使用皆属于智慧交通应用之中[12]。

(2)主观规范作为计划行为理论中的核心要素,对这一应用的使用受到相关人物的影响,也呈现出正向的关系影响,但是通过研究得出主观规范对人们使用意向的影响较为薄弱。

(3)使用者的个人属性在某些角度上也会对智慧交通应用的使用意向进行影响,例如在调查研究中,可得出北京、上海等地域的人使用智慧交通应用的比例较大。

通过上述关于研究框架和问卷的分析可知,影响人们对于智慧交通的使用因素有哪些且相关性的强弱,对相关的研究者、从业者和管理人员等都有参考价值。通过上述的分析,可以得出如下的建议:

(1)使用者的感知易用性对智慧交通应用的使用意向影响显著,相关的应用开发者在对软件进行设计之时可以考虑各种技术手段简化操作步骤、完善功能设置,可使使用者对智慧交通应用使用起来得心应手,从而增加人们的使用意向。多从用户的角度出发设计符合市场需要的产品,有利于我国智慧交通蓝图的构建[13]。

(2)扩大关于智慧交通应用的宣传范围和程度,从而加深民众的了解程度。在一些智慧交通应用较为广泛之地,整体性地采取相应的公共政策措施[14],从而进一步推动智慧交通乃至智慧城市的构建,为其他城市的发展提供参考[15],促进我国城市化建设发展。

(3)增加智慧城市应用的反馈路径,多吸取用户的意见,改善产品的服务水平和质量,从而提高人们对于智慧交通应用的使用意愿。

综上,本文针对民众使用智慧交通应用涉及的一些因素进行了分析,并为我国智慧交通的未来建设和智慧城市的更好构建提出了一些建议。

参考文献

[1] 张盈盈,陈燕凌,关积珍,等.智慧交通的定义、内涵与外延[C].北京:中国智能交通协会.2014第九届中国智能交通年会大会论文集.中国智能交通协会:中国智能交通协会,2014:584-588.

[2] 马洪晶.智慧交通应用使用意向的影响因素研究[D].武汉:华中科技大学,2019.
[3] 金世斌,吴国玖,黄莉.智慧城市建设的国际经验与趋势展望[J].上海城市管理,2016,25(02):12-17.
[4] Yovanof G S, Hazapis G N. An Architectural Framework and Enabling Wireless Technologies for Digital Cities & Intelligent Urban Environments[J]. Wireless Personal Communications, 2009, 49(3): 445-463.
[5] 蔡翠.我国智慧交通发展的现状分析与建议[J].公路交通科技(应用技术版),2013,9(06):224-227.
[6] 王伟.人工智能技术在智慧交通领域的应用研究[J].智能建筑与智慧城市,2020(06):88-89.
[7] 韩直,陈成,贺姣姣,等.智慧交通的起源、文化与发展[J].中国交通信息化,2018(12):27-29.
[8] Martin Fishbein & Icek Ajzen. Belief, Attitude, Intention, and Behavior: an Introduction to Theory and Research,: Addison-Wesley Publishing Company, 1975:53.
[9] 邓玉勇,李璨,刘洋.我国城市智慧交通体系发展研究[J].城市,2015(11):68-73.
[10] 汪晨.共享经济平台用户使用意向研究[D].北京:北京邮电大学,2018.
[11] 时钰涵.大数据背景下智慧交通治理模式研究[D].郑州:郑州大学,2019.
[12] 茹艳,樊阿娇,潘俊方,等.智慧交通在构建智慧城市中的重要作用[J].无线互联科技,2015(20):145-146.
[13] 马靖霖.智慧交通大数据应用中的问题与对策[J].中国公路,2017(05):102-103.
[14] 李琳琳,侯卫真,刘静,等.我国公路水路"智慧交通"发展对策研究[J].中国管理信息化,2020,23(05):160-162.
[15] 夏昊翔,王众托.从系统视角对智慧城市的若干思考[J].中国软科学,2017(07):66-80.

柴油车油耗测量方法及测量不确定度的对比

蔡盼盼　景　峥　李向红　张春化

(长安大学)

摘　要　在《道路运输车辆燃料消耗量检测评价方法》(GB/T 18566—2011)中,利用碳平衡法进行油耗测量时没有考虑柴油车尾气中的碳质成分排放,因此本文进行了碳平衡法的碳质修正研究,并进行了质量法、碳平衡法和碳质修正法三种油耗测量方法的不确定度评定。基于质量法、碳平衡法和碳质修正法的油耗试验在底盘测功机上展开。实验表明碳平衡法相比于质量法,百公里油耗数值稍低,经过碳质修正,计算值接近质量法测量值。考虑到油耗测量过程中存在不确定度,对以上三种方法进行了测量不确定度评定,研究表明基于碳平衡法的碳质修正法可以保证测量结果的可信程度,并能提高测量结果的精度和重复性。

关键词　交通运输　碳质修正法　质量法　碳平衡法　油耗测量　不确定度

0　引　言

能源短缺和环境污染的日益加剧促使人们追求更低的油耗和更清洁的排放。燃油消耗量不仅可以评价汽车的燃油经济性,还与汽车排放紧密相关。因此,精确测量燃油消耗量对节约石油资源和保护环境有着重要意义。

油耗检测技术主要分为直接测量和间接测量[1],直接测量主要为质量法和容积法,间接测量主要为碳平衡法。目前在汽车燃料消耗量的测试方法中,应用较为广泛的主要是碳平衡法和容积法[2]。质量法或容积法:通过测量特定时间内燃油的质量或容积消耗量,也可以测量特定容积的燃油使用时间从而计算汽车的油耗。碳质量平衡法,简称碳平衡法,是根据燃油在发动机中燃烧后,排气中碳质总量与燃烧前的碳质量总和相等的质量守恒定律测算出汽车燃料消耗量的一种方法[3]。与质量法或容积法相比,基于碳平衡法测量燃油消耗量,既可实现汽车不解体又能保证快速测量[4],因此应用前景广阔,研究价值重大。

在基于碳平衡法进行柴油车油耗检测过程中,柴油机的后期燃烧方式为扩散燃烧,易产生"火包油"现象,从而形成包含碳质成分的碳烟Soot和有机可溶成分SOF。然而,目前采用的碳平衡法油耗计算模型并未考虑排气微粒中碳质成分的影响,会产生计算误差。因此,对现行碳平衡法模型进行碳质成分修正是必要的,即所谓的碳质修正。为了全面评价基于上述三种模型的油耗测量结果,还需要合理地赋予测量油耗值的分散性,以期提供相应的测量不确定度。

1 实验设备

1.1 实验设备组成

基于上述三种油耗计算方法的测试试验按照《道路运输车辆燃料消耗量检测评价方法》(GBT18566—2011)要求进行,在底盘测功机上模拟车辆在道路上行驶,设备组成如图1所示。

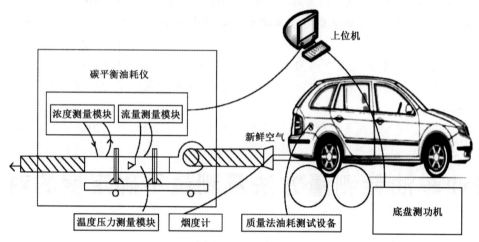

图1 三种油耗测试设备组成

1.2 实验主要测量仪器

油耗测试实验在成都成保 DPCG-10 型底盘测功机上展开,油耗测试车辆为陕汽-德龙 F2000,搭载发动机为潍柴 WP10.270,质量法测量油耗天平型号为沈阳龙腾 ES100K×1,碳平衡法油耗仪为浙大鸣泉 MQL-8201,修正模型中的碳质成分烟度计为 AVL 的 Di Smoke 4000。

1.3 测量仪器主要参数

本次测试所用仪器的主要性能参数如表1~表5所示。

质量法油耗测量中仪器主要技术参数	表1
名称	分辨力
沈阳龙腾 ES100K×1	±1g

气体浓度测量装置主要技术参数			表2
气体	测量量程	分辨力	相对误差
CO_2	0~5%Vol	0.01%Vol	±2%
CO	0~2%Vol	0.001%Vol	±2%
HC	0~100ppmVol	1ppmVol	±3%

流量测量装置主要技术参数　　　　　　　　　　　　　　　　表3

名　　称	参　　数
测量范围	4.00～25.00(30.00) m³/min
分辨力	0.01m³/min
示值误差	±1%
重复性	±0.5%

烟度测量装置主要技术参数　　　　　　　　　　　　　　　　表4

名　　称	测量范围	分辨力
不透光度 N	0～100%	±0.1%
消光系数 K	0～99.99 m⁻¹	0.01 m⁻¹

烟度计装置主要技术参数　　　　　　　　　　　　　　　　表5

名　　称	误　　差
光通路有效长度	±0.002m

2 百公里油耗计算模型

2.1 质量法油耗计算模型

基于质量法进行油耗测量过程中，柴油车百公里油耗的计算公式如式(1)所示：

$$FC_m = \frac{M_s \times 60 \times 100}{d_F \times V_{车} \times 1000} \tag{1}$$

式中：FC_m——柴油车百公里油耗(L/100km)；

　　　M_s——燃油消耗速率(g/min)；

　　　d_F——15℃时柴油的密度(0.838kg/L)；

　　　$V_{车}$——试验车车速(km/h)。

2.2 碳平衡法油耗计算模型

基于碳平衡法进行油耗测量过程中，柴油车每秒燃油消耗量及百公里油耗的计算公式分别如式(2)和式(3)所示：

$$FC_S = \frac{1.155}{d_F} \times [(0.8658 \times M_{HC}) + (0.429 \times M_{CO}) + (0.273 \times M_{CO_2})] \tag{2}$$

$$FC = \frac{100}{S} \times \sum FC_S \tag{3}$$

式中：FC_S——汽车每秒燃油消耗量(mL/s)；

　　　M_{HC}——汽车每秒排放的HC质量(g/s)；

　　　M_{CO}——汽车每秒排放的CO质量(g/s)；

　　　M_{CO_2}——汽车每秒排放的CO_2质量(g/s)；

　　　FC——汽车百公里燃油消耗量(L/100km)；

　　　S——60s内汽车的行驶距离(m)。

2.3 碳质修正法原理及油耗计算模型

2.3.1 排气中碳质成分及稀释系数修正

柴油机排气微粒PM主要包含两部分：一部分是有机不可溶成分碳烟Soot；另一部分是有机可溶成分SOF，主要有各种未燃的HC、含氧有机物和多环芳烃PAH[5]。本次实验的工况为低负荷稳定转速工况，排气温度较低，导致生成的PM中SOF会较多。但Soot中的大部分碳质成分和SOF中的微量碳质成分对油耗计算会产生一定影响,所以需要将 PM 中的碳质成分考虑到油耗计算中去。特别地,若对模型进行微粒中的碳质成分修正,则必须对稀释系数 DF 进行重新计算,因为稀释系数 DF 既会影响稀释排气中 CO_2 浓度的校正,还会影响稀释前的排气流量 Q 的计算。

经过碳质修正之后,稀释系数计算公式如式(4)和式(5)所示:

$$DF = \frac{F_s}{C_{CO2} + C_{CO} + C_{HC} \times 10^{-4} + N} \quad (4)$$

$$N = (1 - e^{-KL}) \quad (5)$$

式中:DF——稀释系数;
  N——不透光度(%);
  K——绝对光吸收系数(mg/m³);
  L——光通道有效长度(m)。

2.3.2 碳质修正法油耗计算模型

基于碳质修正法进行油耗测量的过程中,柴油车每秒的颗粒物排放量转化为每秒燃油消耗量及修正后百公里油耗的计算公式分别见式(6)和式(7)所示:

$$PM_s = \frac{1550 \times Z}{3600 \times d_F} \times \frac{\sum Q}{S} \times (1 - e^{-KL1}) \times \frac{K + 0.01641}{0.0061} \times V_{车} \quad (6)$$

$$FC_{corr} = \frac{100}{S} \times (\sum FC_S + \sum PM_S) \quad (7)$$

式中:PM_s——汽车每秒的颗粒物排放量转化为每秒燃油消耗量,mL/s;
  Z——排气颗粒物中,碳成分占颗粒物质量的20%~40%,计算时一般取中间值30%[6];
  $\sum Q$——60s 内汽车排气总流量,m³。

2.4 百公里油耗计算结果

根据实验数据,对每个等速工况下5次实验数据的百公里油耗计算结果取平均值,得出三种方法的油耗计算结果随车速的变化关系,如图2所示。由图可得:质量法百公里油耗值最高,近似实际值,碳平衡法相比于质量法百公里油耗低6.2%。究其原因可能有以下三个方面:(1)流量测量单元和气体浓度测量单元的检测误差;(2)尾气中碳质成分没有考虑;(3)汽车运行过程中燃油密度发生改变。碳质修正法对比于碳平衡法所得到的百公里油耗值有所提升,相比于质量法低5.35%。进一步探究原因,利用MATLAB 对碳平衡法和碳质修正法计算出的百公里油耗差值与不透光度 N 进行插值拟合,求出两者近似关系式的的 $\Delta FC = 0.0136 \times e^{17.33N}$,即二者近似呈指数分布。差值分布及拟合关系如图3所示。当颗粒物排放浓度大时,即不透光度 N 大,基于碳平衡法进行碳烟修正是有显著效果的。因此,对碳平衡法进行碳质修正可以提高百公里油耗检测值,使计算结果更加精确合理。

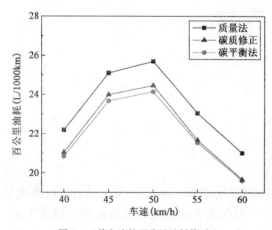

图2 三种方法的百公里油耗值对比

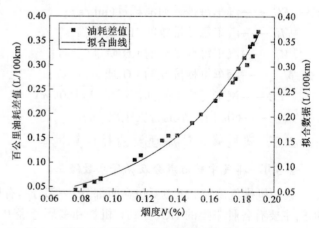

图3 碳质修正和碳平衡法百公里油耗的差值与烟度的关系

3 不确定度分析

3.1 测量不确定度理论

测量不确定度,是测量结果中隐含的一个数值,可以表示被测量数值的分散性。评定过程中,不考虑人为操作误差,忽略质量法、碳平衡法和碳质修正法的方法误差及常数项引来的误差,只分析油耗测量过程中测量仪器引入的误差,从而获得不确定度的函数,对油耗测量不确定度进行分析和计算。

对上述三种油耗测量方法的测量不确定度分析和评定按照《测量不确定度评定与表示》(JJF 1059.1—2012)进行。

3.2 质量法油耗测量的不确定度来源及评定

在质量法油耗实验中,百公里燃油消耗量的测量不确定度主要来源包括天平测量重复性、天平分辨力和车速测量重复性、其中天平分辨力引入的不确定度按B类不确定度进行评定,符合均匀分布,区间半宽为1g,不可靠程度通常取10%[7];天平测量重复性和车速测量重复性归为A类评定方法,计算方法为:在相同实验条件下,进行10次重复测量,按照贝塞尔方法计算。其中,质量法的标准不确定度和自由度的计算结果如表6所示。合成不确定度和扩展不确定度的计算结果如表7所示,灵敏度系数计算结果如图4所示。从表6看出,相对于天平和车速的测量重复性的标准不确定度,天平分辨力标准不确定度较大。这说明测量过程中不会引入太多的不确定度,仪器设备的分辨力对测量结果影响较大。从表7看出,随着车速的增加,合成不确定度和扩展不确定度逐渐减小。车速增加,油耗增加,引入的油耗相对测量误差会降低。灵敏度系数反映了自变量变化程度对因变量的影响程度。从图4看出,相对于燃油消耗率对质量法测量的影响,车速变化对质量法中百公里油耗测量结果影响更大,但随着车速的增加,影响程度逐渐减小。综上所述,选择分辨力好的天平和在较高车速下进行质量法油耗测量可以提高测量结果的精度和重复性。

质量法的标准不确定度和自由度计算结果 表6

不确定度来源	标准不确定度	自 由 度
天平测量重复性	0.32945 g	9
天平分辨力	0.57735 g	50
车速测量重复性	0.13151 km/h	9

质量法的合成不确定度和扩展不确定度计算结果 表7

车速(km/h)	合成不确定度(L/100km)	扩展不确定度(L/100km)
40	0.12693	0.25387
45	0.11752	0.23505
50	0.10666	0.21333
55	0.09516	0.19033
60	0.08563	0.17127

3.3 碳平衡法油耗测量不确定度来源及评定

在碳平衡法油耗测量实验中,每秒燃油消耗量的不确定度来源主要有稀释排气压力、含碳气体浓度、稀释排气流量和稀释排气温度。每个不确定度分量如图5所示。

碳平衡法油耗实验中,百公里燃油消耗量的测量不确定度来源主要有四项,每一项的标准不确定度计算结果如表8所示,合成标准不确定度和扩展标准不确定度如表9所示,灵敏度系数计算结果见图6。从表8可以看出,相对于CO和HC的每秒稀释浓度的测量不确定度,CO_2的标准不确定度较大,稀释排气流量、稀释排气温度和稀释排气压力的标准不确定度较小。从表9可以看出,随着车速增加,碳平衡法的合成不确定度和扩展不确定度先增加后减少,这可能是因为碳质成分(CO、HC 和 CO_2)的生成和排放过程受变化车速影响,较高车速下的测量不确定度更小。从图6可以看出,测量过程中CO和CO_2测量浓度对百公里油耗(基于碳平衡法)测量结果具有更大的影响。综上所述,测量过程中CO和CO_2测量精度对结果影响更大,车速越高,测量结果越精确。

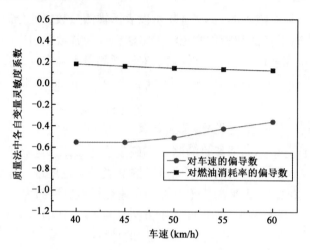

图4　质量法中各自变量的灵敏度系数

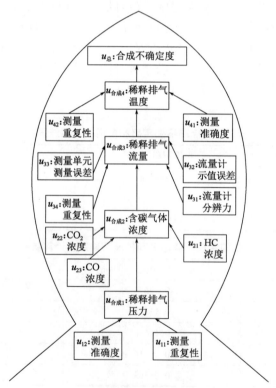

图5　碳平衡法油耗测量结果不确定度来源

碳平衡法的不确定度　　　　　表8

物理量	标准不确定度	自由度
稀释排气流量 Q_g	0.204 m^3/min	39
CO每秒稀释浓度 C_{CO}	0.018% Vol	123
CO_2每秒稀释浓度 C_{CO_2}	0.041% Vol	100
HC每秒稀释浓度 C_{HC}	1.259 ppmVol	111
稀释排气温度 T_g	0.877 K	52
稀释排气压力 P_g	0.232 kPa	51

碳平衡法的合成标准不确定度和扩展标准不确定度　　　　表9

车速(km/h)	合成不确定度(L/100km)	扩展不确定度(L/100km)
40	0.23813	0.47626
45	0.27787	0.55574
50	0.31156	0.62312
55	0.24635	0.49271
60	0.21181	0.42362

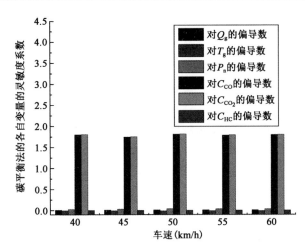

图6　碳平衡法中各自变量的灵敏度系数

3.4 碳质修正法油耗测量不确定度来源及评定

碳质修正法油耗测量实验中,百公里燃油消耗量的测量不确定度的来源除了上述碳平衡法中引入的不确定度分量以外,还包含烟度计测试重复性、烟度计测试分辨力和光通路测量误差。其中烟度计分辨力引入的不确定度按 B 类不确定度进行评定,符合均匀分布,区间半宽为0.01%,不可靠程度通常取 10%[7];烟度计测量重复性归为 A 类评定方法,计算方法为:在相同实验条件下,进行10次重复测量。不确定度和自由度的计算结果如表10所示,碳质修正法的合成不确定度和扩展不确定度如表11所示。灵敏度系数计算结果见图7。烟度计分辨力引入的标准不确定度对百公里油耗(碳质修正法)影响最大。从表11可以看出,随着车速的增加,合成不确定度和扩展不确定度先增加后减少。从图7可以看出,不透光度 N 对百公里油耗(碳质修正法)影响比光通路有效程度 L 的影响较大。影响程度都是随着车速的增加,先增加再减少。综上所述,选择分辨力更小的烟度计和在更高的车速下测量百公里油耗对提高修正精度有较好的效果。

碳质修正法的不确定度　　　　表10

不确定度来源	标准不确定度	自由度
烟度计测量重复性	0.00359%	9
烟度计分辨力	0.05774%	50
光通路测量误差	0.00115m	—

碳质修正法的合成不确定度和扩展不确定度　　　　表11

车速(km/h)	合成不确定度(L/100km)	扩展不确定度(L/100km)
40	0.26661	0.53322
45	0.309935	0.61987
50	0.34004	0.68008
55	0.271185	0.54237
60	0.23498	0.46996

综上所述,从三种方法的不确定度和扩展不确定可以看出,碳质修正法引入的不确定度最大,碳平衡法次之,质量法最小。碳质修正法相对于碳平衡法可以提高百公里油耗检测结果,虽然碳质修正法会引入一部分不确定度分量,但引入的不确定度值在碳平衡法引入的不确定度基础上增加量不超过12%,可以保证测量精度和测量重复性。

从质量法的敏感性系数可以看出,汽车车速的测量对于百公里油耗计算的绝对误差影响最大;从碳平衡法的敏感性系数可以看出,CO_2和CO浓度的测量结果对于百公里油耗计算的绝对误差影响最大;从碳质修正法的敏感性系数可以看出,烟度测量对百公里油耗计算的绝对误差影响最大,光通路有效长度次之。针对敏感性系数计算出来的结果可以给实验测量提供一定的指导意义。

3.5 不确定度结果对比

带不确定度的质量法,碳平衡法和碳质修正法的百公里油耗值如图8所示。

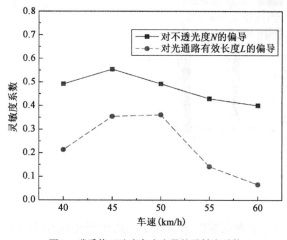

图7 碳质修正法中各自变量的灵敏度系数　　图8 三种带不确定度的方法的百公里油耗值

从上图可以看出,在百公里油耗测量中,质量法测量油耗最高,碳平衡法最低,碳质修正法相对于碳平衡法略有提高,两者差别不是很大,在颗粒物排放多的工况修正量会增加,进行修正可以提高百公里油耗测量精确度和重复性。

4　结　语

(1)分析三种方法各自的测量不确定度,质量法测量不确定度最低,碳质修正法最高,碳平衡法相对于碳质修正法略低,两者差别可以忽略,即碳质修正相对于碳平衡法可以提高百公里油耗计算值,但引入的额外不确定度可以忽略不计。

(2)由三种方法的敏感性系数可知,对于百公里油耗的计算,质量法的绝对误差影响最大;在碳质修正法中,烟度测量对百公里油耗计算的绝对误差影响最大。

(3)在百公里油耗测量中,碳质修正法相对于碳平衡法略有提高,在一定工况下,碳质修正法可以提高百公里油耗的测量精确度。

参考文献

[1] 杨甜.基于碳平衡法的柴油车燃油消耗量修正模型的研究[D].长春:吉林大学,2015.

[2] 董超,张国振,张远军,等.基于碳平衡法的甲醇汽车燃料消耗量计算模型[J].汽车科技,2020,(04):92-97.

[3] 张守明.碳质量平衡法测算燃油消耗量的相关问题探讨[J].计量与测试技术,2020,47(08):57-59+63.

[4] 李大灿.基于碳平衡法的油耗检测方法简析[J].科技风,2020,(11):5.

[5] 张彬.柴油机微粒捕集器性能劣化辨析与优化研究[D].长沙:湖南大学,2017.

[6] 李彦睿,彭育辉,黄育鹏. 基于碳平衡法计算柴油机燃油消耗量的研究[J]. 车辆与动力技术, 2018 (04): 6-10+16.
[7] 孙宇婷. 基于碳平衡法的柴油车燃油消耗量的检测及修正[D]. 西安:长安大学, 2018.

Optimised Decision Making of Transportation Infrastructure Asset Management

Jiarong Li

(Chang'an University, Department of Traffic Engineering)

Abstract After more than 30 years of rapid development and construction, the transportation infrastructure achievements in China have attracted worldwide attention. On the other hand, the demand for Transportation Infrastructure Asset Management (TIAM) is growing quickly and strongly, and the rapid, safe and high-density traffic development trends have placed new demands on transportation infrastructure construction and management. During the durable period of the pavement, it is still necessary to continue investing a large amount of funds to maintain and rebuild the pavement to keep their good performance, but the funds are not always available, so how to allocate the maintenance funds reasonably and keep the pavement in a good condition at the same time has become a hotpot, there are many decision-making methods to deal with it, but all of them have some deficiencies, this paper utilizes the inherent parallel mechanism and the characteristics of global optimization of Genetic Algorithm (GA), proposes a multi-objective genetic algorithm (MOGA) to simulate the problem of TIAM as a biological evolution problem, and by comparing the fitness of each generation of individuals to generate a new generation, in subsequent iterations, the generation is constantly replaced with a high fitness alternative to a low fitness value, so that after several generations, the best can be found. The optimization result of a case study shows that the application of this algorithm in TIAM is successful and effective.

Keywords Transportation infrastructure asset management Optimised decision-making Multi-objective genetic algorithm Large scale road network

0 Introduction

Transportation Infrastructure Asset Management (TIAM) is used to better maintain the public infrastructure of the entire society in a good situation, to preserve its added value, to better serve the public, to decrease the cost and to extend the service life of pavement. The purpose of TIAM is to enable the pavement management department to effectively utilize resources and maintain the pavements with sufficient level of service within the predetermined service period.

Multi-objective optimization problems occupy a large proportion in TIAM. Generally speaking, there is no quasi-optimal solution for a multi-objective optimization problem, and multiple objectives in a multi-objective optimization problem cannot be optimized at the same time. Different decision makers have different preferences for different goals, and they will get different optimal solutions, these possible optimal solutions are called non-dominated solutions or Pareto optimal solutions in multi-objective optimization problems. Obviously, the Pareto solution is a solution set of the multi-objective optimization problem, and there is generally only one of the Pareto solutions can be obtained at a time if using traditional optimization techniques to solve the problem, while more Pareto solutions can be obtained if the genetic algorithm is used to process multi-objective optimization problems.

Due to the multi-objective nature and large amount of data of the TIAM problem, it is difficult to solve such problems by using traditional planning methods. Genetic algorithm has been considered to be a suitable method for multi-objective optimization, the ability to deal with complex problems such as the discontinuity and multimodality of the objective function enhances the potential effectiveness of genetic algorithms in multi-objective search and optimization problems, so genetic algorithm is an effective method to solve multi-objective optimization problems.

This paper introduces Multi-Objective Genetic Algorithms (MOGA) into the optimization of TIAM, and utilizes the inherent parallel mechanism and the characteristics of global optimization of genetic algorithms, and proposes a method for optimal allocation of pavement maintenance budget to realize the best user benefit based on multi-objective genetic algorithms. The problem of optimal allocation of pavement maintenance budget of large-scale pavement network is solved.

1 Multi-Objective Genetic Algorithm

Genetic Algorithm is a kind of random searching algorithm that draws on the natural selection of the biological community and the natural genetic mechanism, and the first time that the algorithm is proposed by Professor Holland (1975), De Jong (1975) also published his thesis "An analysis of behaviour of a class of genetic adaptive system" in the same year, which together with Professor Holland's "Adaptation in Natural and Artificial System" is recognized as a basis of genetic algorithms. In 1993, Fonseca and Fleming proposed Multi-objective Optimization Genetic Algorithms (Fonseca and Fleming, 1993; Fonseca and Fleming, 1995; Fonseca and Fleming, 1996), Different from traditional optimization algorithms, GA is a group-based algorithm. Each individual in the population evolves in parallel, and the final solution is included in the last generation of individuals.

As the mainadvantage of GA is its ability of large-scale computing and parallel searching, it can perform evolutionary operations on the entire population and focus on the set of individuals. Since many practical engineering problems are multi-objective optimization problems, and multiple objectives may compete with each other, multi-objective optimization problems usually require overall optimization, rather than optimising one objective only, so a set of optional solutions is required. Such a set of solutions is a non-dominated solution set, called the Pareto solution set, and GA is an effective method to solve this kind of set, a set of Pareto solutions can be generated in one optimization process if GA is introduced into multi-objective optimization problems, and then the best solution can be found. Applying genetic algorithm to solve multi-objectives problem can maintain the characteristics of multi-directional and global search between the previous generation and the next generation to maintain the population of potential solutions and search for multiple solutions (Neumann et al, 1994; Kuhn et al., 1991).

1.1 Initialization of Population

Initialization of population is a basic step of GA, which is encoded in binary. In order to ensure the feasibility and diversity of individuals in the group, in a general way, initial individuals are randomly generated according to constraint conditions, so that the initial population is feasible.

1.2 Determination of Fitness

The concept of fitness is used in GA to measure the degree to which individual in a population are likely to achieve an optimal solution in an optimization process, individuals with higher fitness have a higher probability of inheriting to the next generation, vice versa. A function that measures individual fitness is called a fitness function, which is evolved from objective function. GA basically does not use external information, it only uses the fitness function as the basis and uses the fitness value of each individual in the population to search for optimal solution (Goldberg, 1989).

Generally speaking, single-objective optimization problems can be solved by comparing the value of fitness, while multi-objective optimization problems are much more difficult to deal with. Traditional multi-objective optimization methods are mainly integrated methods, such as weighting method, which transform multi-objective problems into single-objective problems, and then use mature single-objective optimization algorithms to solve them (Gao et al., 2000).

However, there might be contradiction between objectives, for example, the objectives are highest user benefit and lowest cost, and they are apparently against each other, so they need to be normalized sometimes.

1.3 Genetic Operation

The evolution of the population depends on some genetic operations acting on the current population and generating a new generation of population. Common genetic operations include selection, crossover and mutation. These genetic operations play a decisive role in the performance of the algorithm.

1.4 Optimal Preservation Strategy

The idea of the optimal preservation strategy is to keep the excellent individuals in the parent generation and make them directly into the next generation, that is, the best individuals in the current generation don't perform crossover and mutation operations, but replace the individual with the least fitness after genetic operations such as mutation and crossover in the current generation population.

However, this paper utilizes another way to preserve the optimal strategy, the parent generation and the next generation are put together in the first place, and then rank them, and make the top of them the new parent individual. This method can avoid the situation that the worst individual of next generation are replaced by best individual of parent individual even though the worst individual of next generation is better than the best individual of parent individual.

2 Application of MOGA in TIAM

2.1 Determination of Objective Function

There are various influencing factors in the TIAM problems, and they might be mutually restricted. Therefore, the optimization problem of the TIAM is a multi-objective problem, and the pavement is divided into several segments for convenience, every strategy for every segment include the specific maintenance method, maintenance time and unit price etc.

(1) Social objective: the maximum user benefit. Transforming the benefits of pavement users directly into costs is not a comprehensive reflection of the benefits of pavement users due to improved pavement performance. Therefore, this paper uses effectiveness to represent user benefit, the effectiveness is proposed by Canada Al in the Road Management System (RIPPS) of the province of Berda, it believes that the performance of the pavement is improved through the maintenance and rehabilitation, which will benefit the pavement users. Therefore, the pavement performance can be improved as an indirect indicator of user benefit. For example, the change in area under the pavement performance degradation curve can be used as a map of user benefits (Kong et al., 1998). The specific equation is as follow:

$$\max\{E\} = \sum_{i=1}^{n} \sum_{j=1}^{A_i} X_{ij} [(PPI_{ij} - PPI_{\min})] \times AADT_t \times L_i \tag{1}$$

Where E is the effectiveness, X_{ij} is 1 if segment i selects j-th strategy, otherwise 0, A_i is the number of strategies of segment i; PPI is the Pavement Performance Index, PPI_{ij} is the value of PPI if segment i taking maintenance method j, PPI_{min} is the value of allowable minimum PPI; $AADT_t$ is the value of AADT in time X_{ij} is implemented, t is the year X_{ij} is done; L_i is length of segment i;

(2) Economy objective: minimum annual average present value cost.

$$\min\{C\} = \sum_{j=1}^{A_j}\sum_{i=1}^{n} c_{ij} X_{ij} L_i \qquad (2)$$

Where C is annual average present value cost, c_{ij} is the unit present value cost of maintenance strategy X_{ij}.

2.2 Constraints

(1) Economy constraint. The specific equation is:

$$\sum_{j=1}^{A_i}\sum_{i=1}^{n} c_{ij} X_{ij} \leq B \qquad (3)$$

Where c_{ij} is the unit price of strategy X_{ij}, B is the value of budget.

(2) Strategy constraints. There must be one strategy for every segment, doing nothing is also one kind of strategy.

$$\sum_{j=1}^{A_i} X_{ij} = 1 (\text{for } i \in [1, n]) \qquad (4)$$

2.3 Specific Implementation of MOGA

The MOGA simulates the problem of TIAM as a biological evolution problem, takes the strategy that every segment selects as a decision variable, encodes the decision variable and forms a feasible solution set, and judges the satisfaction degree of each individual, survival of the fittest, resulting in a new generation of feasible solution sets, and iteratively to complete the optimal choice of maintenance strategy.

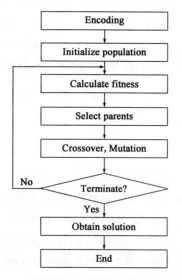

Fig. 1 Flow Chart of Genetic Algorithm

The optimization process of the MOGA is as Fig. 1: generate initial generations first, and then use the established optimization model to perform genetic operations, and select some relatively optimal solutions from the initial generation as the initial generations for the next optimization. Repeat the above optimization process until a set of optimal solutions is found. The process of genetic operation is a process of survival of the fittest.

1) Gene encoding

The basic formation of the encoding is like $[x_1, x_2, x_3, \cdots, x_k]$, the location of each gene means the segment number, and the x_k means that x_k strategy is selected on k-th segment of the whole pavement. For example, [2, 3, 4, 5] means that the first segment selects the 2th strategy, the second segment selects the 3rd strategy etc.

2) Fitness function

It is a multi-objective problem, which means the fitness function includes two objectives, the two objectives are maximum user benefit and minimum cost. However, they are against each other, so the balance between them is needed, and the form of fitness function of multi-objective problem needs to be determined.

This paper chooses the weight coefficient transformation method. However, there exists too much difference between the value of user benefit and the value of cost, so they need to be normalized.

The normalization equation of user benefit is:

$$E^* = \frac{E - \min}{\max - \min} \qquad (5)$$

Max is the maximum value of the user benefit; min is the minimum value of the user benefit.

The less the cost is, the better the result is, so the normalization equation of cost is:

$$C^* = \frac{\max - C}{\max - \min} \tag{6}$$

The final fitness function is:

$$f(x) = w_1 \times E^* + w_2 \times C^* \tag{7}$$

$$w_1 + w_2 = 1 \tag{8}$$

3) Crossover and mutation

The operation of crossover and mutation is very important in the GA, this paper carries out crossover and mutation by defining the probability of crossover and probability of mutation. First generate a random number in a range of {0,1}, then compare the random number with the probability, if the random number is less than the probability, then do the operation.

The method of crossover is the multi-point crossover, every gene of the chromosome has the probability (crossover probability) to do the crossover operation, the gene at the same location of two chromosome can crossover with each other, the gene of chromosome 1 can crossover with the gene of chromosome 2 that is at the same location with gene of chromosome 1, and in a similar way, the gene of chromosome 2 can crossover with the gene of chromosome 3 that is at the same location with gene 2 of chromosome 3, the rest can be done in the same manner, but the last one just can crossover with the one before it, not with the first one.

4) Penalty function

The constraint is the budget, in general, all the strategies combination whose cost exceed the budget have to be rejected, however, if rejecting all the strategy combinations that exceed the budget, the total number of the pop in the pop size will decrease a lot and then it even can't meet the quantity requirement of the pop size, which will cause the algorithm can't keep operating, so this paper chooses the penalty method to deal with this problem.

The penalty is done if the cost exceeds budget, and the equation is:

$$p(x) = \begin{cases} f(x), C \leq B \\ f(x) \times \left(1 - \frac{C}{B}\right), C > B \end{cases} \tag{9}$$

Where $f(x)$ is the fitness function, $p(x)$ is the fitness function after penalty.

3 Case Study

The above model is used to calculate the optimal strategy selection plan for the pavement network in Brampton of Southern Ontario. Under the conditions of meeting the social usage in the area, with the purpose of reducing the maintenance cost, the reasonable allocation of maintenance strategy and maintenance cost in the area can be achieved to meet the needs of growing traffic demand.

3.1 Background of the Case Study

Brampton is a city in the Canadian province of Ontario, situated in Southern Ontario. The city has a population of 593,638 as of the Canada 2016 Census. The pavement of this case includes the total segments of 3640, which includes the effective segments of 1822, and all of them have total 64,188 strategies can be selected. The maintenance strategy is for 20 years.

The coding tool used in this paper is Python, and an accelerator is applied because of the large amount of data. Importing numba to accelerate the speed of algorithm operation, numba is a compiler for compiling Python arrays and numeric calculation functions, it can greatly improve the operation speed of functions written directly in Python.

3.2 Process of Implementing the Algorithm

1) Criteria selection

The economy factor is always important in the TIAM problems, so this paper first selects the minimum cost as the decision-making criteria, and the level of service is also important in Brampton, so the maximum user benefit is selected as another criteria. The limit condition is the budget.

2) Data accessing

Accessing database into SQLite3 database by the software SQLite Expert Professional, SQLite3 is already a standard module of Python3. The process of using python to operate SQLite3 database is as Fig.2.

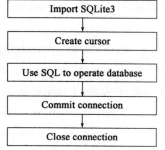

Fig. 2　Flow Chart of Database Accessing

3) Proposition of Multi-objective optimization problem

This is a problem of large-scale pavement network optimization, the optimal solution should be found among 64188 strategies for 1822 segments. The calculation parameter is: pop size = 300, length of chromosome = 1822, number of iterations = 500, mutation probability = 0.2, crossover probability = 0.8, the acceptable PPI = 5.5, budget = 10million dollars per year.

Considering the diversity of the maintenance strategies, the encoding method used in this example is as mentioned before, the encode is determined according to their segment number and strategy number, the location means the segment number, the algebra number means the selected strategy. The mutation method is the uniform mutation, every gene has probability to become other gene if only they are at the same location in their chromosome respectively.

Operate the algorithm, obtain the final pops, and get the annual cost of the total 20 years, but the value of fitness is always minus no matter the fitness of best pop or the average fitness because of the penalty function, it is because there are about 1 in 6th strategy in the database belong to the last year, which cause the high probability of the strategy belong to last year, and it will result in the high cost of the last year, that is the reason the fitness of every pop is minus.

Therefore, using the final pops as the initial pops, and operate the algorithm with 500 iterations again, the results get a little improvement, but not enough, the distribution of annual average cost is as you can see in the Fig. 3.

As you can see from the Fig. 3, the total cost is less than 200 million which meets the total budget requirement, but the cost of last 6 years exceed the annual budget (red line) hardly, which makes the solution infeasible. Save the final population as the final pops 2.

So decreasing the cost might be very difficult for the algorithm, so it should be reversed, initial pops have about 90% segments whose strategy is "do nothing", which means the cost is very low, and as the iteration goes, the cost will increase but not exceeds the annual budget because of the penalty function, and after 500 iterations, the annual cost of the last few years is close to the annual budget, but the cost of first few years is far below the budget line because of the database problem. Save the final population as the final pops 3.

According to the situation of the last two trials, it is obviously that the two generation of final pops is complementary, so combine them together, use the final pops 2 and final pops 3 as the initial pops, and increase the pop size so the final pop 2 has probability to be selected and increase the cost and user benefit of the final results, and the probability of mutation needs to be decreased in case the cost increases too much and then exceeds the budget, in addition, the mutation method is changed, the mutation method used here is the non-uniform mutation, the gene whose strategy is "do nothing" only has the probability to become other strategy that is not "do nothing", and the gene who has specific strategy only has probability to become "do nothing".

After another 500 iterations, obtain the fitness trend and cost trend figure as you can see in the Fig. 4.

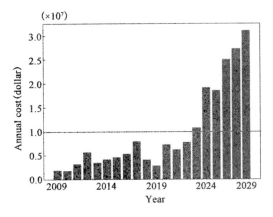

Fig. 3　Annual Cost 1

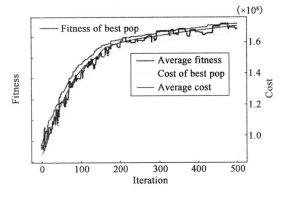

Fig. 4　Fitness and Cost Trend

In Fig. 4, the red line is the fitness trend of the best pop, the blue line is the average fitness of the whole population, the yellow line is the cost trend of the best pop, the green line is the average cost of the population. The curve is getting flatter as the iteration goes, and finally stay stable.

Obtain all the solutions and plot them in the Fig. 5.

As you can see from the Fig. 5, these solutions are not non-dominated solutions, so obtain the non-dominated solutions as shown in the Fig. 6.

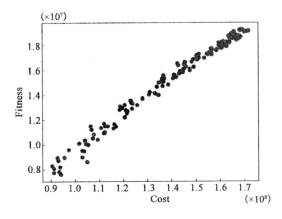

Fig. 5　Solutions Distribution

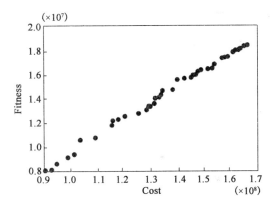

Fig. 6　Non-Dominated Optimal Solutions

4) Selection of the best solution

There are total 40 pareto optimal solutions, they are basically in a line, technically speaking, there is no superior or worse among them, so the selection of the best solution has to according to other standards. According to their distribution of annual cost, improvement of average PPI and the incremental benefit cost ratio, the best solution is selected. It costs $164 677 812 for 20 years, and its user benefit is 18,898,540, the distribution of the annual cost of 20 years is as shown in the Fig. 7.

As you can see from the Fig. 7, the distribution of annual cost is uniform, and close to the budget limitation, too.

Its average PPI compare with "do nothing" is shown as the Fig. 8, the red line represents the condition of "do

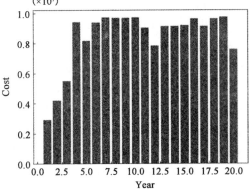

Fig. 7　Annual Cost of the Best Solution

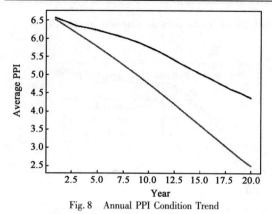

Fig. 8 Annual PPI Condition Trend

nothing", the green line represents the average condition of the best strategy combination.

The red line is decreased rapidly, but after the pavement management, the green line is obviously decreased slower, and the area between the red line and green line is the specific increase of the PPI condition, there are 788 road segments maintained out of total 1822 effective segments during the analysis period of the best solution.

4 Conclusions

Optimal allocation of maintenance budget is an important issue of TIAM problems. Due to the multi-objective nature of the TIAM problems, it is difficult to solve this problem using traditional planning methods. This paper presents the application of multi-objective genetic algorithm in the field of TIAM, and carries out a case study. It can be seen that multi-objective genetic algorithms have good development prospects, but the algorithm itself still needs to be improved in order to adapt it to complex systems. For example, for the problem of TIAM, due to its complex system, especially the problem with many constraints, how to deal with the constraints and so on.

It can be seen from this paper that the optimization decision-making of pavement maintenance is the core part of the road management system. When establishing a pavement management system, it is necessary to implement a maintenance plan that aims to achieve the maximum user benefit of pavement performance in the case of shortage of maintenance funds. The problem that needs to be solved is: what kind of maintenance plan can be adopted to maximize the user benefits of the entire road network when the budget is limited. The research in this paper focuses on how to use the limited funds to develop the most ideal maintenance decision-making plan, so that the user benefit is at its best. There are some conclusions:

(1) This paper takes the whole road network as the research object, first divides the whole road network into several road sections, then conducts specific analysis for each road section, determines the strategy used by each road section and their corresponding cost, and then accumulates the funds needed of every road section.

(2) The multi-objective optimization problem is proposed. The optimization of pavement maintenance decision-making is a multi-objective optimization. When establishing the optimization objectives, the author selects two optimization objectives. The reason for adopting two goals for optimization is the following considerations: The maintenance management of the pavement is actually the problem of investment and benefit, that is, how to get the maximum user benefit with minimum cost. This is obviously a multi-objective problem of how to balance between input and benefit; the so-called income fact is the service state of pavement performance, thus selecting the user benefit of comprehensive evaluation index; The benefits of noise reduction, traffic accident reduction, and reduction of vehicle exhaust emissions are difficult to measure by cost, therefore, in the establishment of the maintenance decision-making model, author uses the form of effectiveness to express user benefits. It should also be pointed out here that when researching multi-objective optimization problems, the more targets are used, the better the optimization effect is. Therefore, this paper regards the minimum cost required for maintenance as a constraint and becomes a problem that is constrained in cost.

(3) In the process of solving the multi-objective optimization problem, the genetic algorithm was adopted, and the superiority of the genetic algorithm was used to optimize the multi-objective pavement maintenance decision-making model. The optimal maintenance plan was obtained, and the algorithm was proved effective.

(4) This paper improves the optimal preservation of best strategy by combining the parent pops and offspring pops together and make top of them the new parent pops, which will be theoretically more effective.

However, there are only two objectives considered in the paper, if more objectives are considered, the result will be closer to actual situation. The factors involved in the pavement maintenance management decision-making optimization model and the related index parameters are numerous, which will directly affect the solution of the model and the formulation of the optimal maintenance plan. From a mathematical point of view, there is still a lack of very effective algorithms for large-scale decision-making problems. From the practical needs of pavement maintenance decision-making, the gradual expansion of the scale of the road network has also brought about the study of the problem and the solution of the model great difficulty. Therefore, in the future, research and improvement on the requirements of algorithms for solving large-scale decision-making problems can not only meet the needs of practical decision-making problems, but also ensure the validity and feasibility of the algorithm.

References

[1] DeJong A. K. An Analysis of the Behavior of a Class of Genetic Adaptive Systems [D]. University of Michigan, 1975.

[2] Fonseca C. M, Fleming P. J. Genetic Algorithms for Multi-objective Optimization: Formulation, Discussion and Generalization[A]. In: Proceeding of the Fifth International Conference on Genetic Algorithms, S. Forrest, Ed. San Mateo, CA: Morgan Kauffman, 1993, 416-423.

[3] Fonseca C. M, Fleming P. J. An overview of Evolutionary Algorithms in Multi-Objective Optimization[J]. Evolutionary Computation, 1995, 3(1): 1-16.

[4] Fonseca C. M, Fleming P. J. Nonlinear System Identification with Multi-objective Genetic Algorithms[A]. In: Proceeding of the 13th World Congress of IFAC, 1996, 187-192.

[5] Goldberg D E. Genetic Algorithms in Search Optimization and Machine Learning [M]. Reading, MA: Addison Wesley, 1989.

[6] Holland J. Adaptation in Natural and Artificial Systems[M]. University of Michigan Press, Ann Arbor, MI: MIT Press, Cambridge, MA, 1975.

[7] H. W. Kuhn, A. w. Tueker. Nonlinear Programming, in "Proceeding of the Second Barley Symposium on Mathematical Statistics and Probability[M]. California: University of California Press, 1991:481-492.

[8] J. Von Neumann, Morgenstern. The Theory of Games and Economics Behaviors[M]. New Jersey: Princeton University Press, 1994:89-90.

[9] Kong Yongjian, Tadashi Fukuda. Modeling of the Network Level Pavement Repair Management System Using Dynamic Programming[C]. // Proceedings of International Conference for Pavement and Bridge Management Systems, 1998.

[10] Ying Gao, Lei Shi Pingjing Yao. Study on Multi-Objective Genetic Algorithm [C]. Proceedings of the 3th World Congress on Intelligent Control and Automation, 2000.

基于收费数据的高速公路可达性特征分析

李起辉 胡爱辉 向宏杨

(长安大学运输工程学院)

摘 要 为了研究高速公路可达性的分布特征差异,利用高速公路收费大数据,利用考虑节点吸引量的基于加权平均出行时间模型和潜能模型的可达性评价模型，并以贵州省为例，从客车和货车的角度分别分析了贵州省各个市的可达性的演化、空间分布特征以及季节性特征。结果表明，贵州省中南部地区可达性较高，其中安顺市的平均出行时间最小，而贵阳市的发展潜力最大。贵州省西部和北部潜力较小城市的发展潜力增速快，而中南部和东部地区的城市潜力增速慢。在时间维度上，各个季度的城市之间的平均出行时间并无较大差异和明显变化规律，但第三季度的城市客运潜能普遍高于其他季度。

关键词 高速公路 可达性 发展潜能 季节特征

0 引言

新时代下的中国经济水平显著提升，现代化工业建设的步伐加快，社会性的交流和经济增长促使了高速公路的快速发展，以满足不断上升的高速、高质量的陆地交通运输需求。据交通运输部统计，自1988年中国建成第一条高速公路以来，截至2018年年末，收费高速公路的总里程在20年间增长到了14.26万km，里程规模居世界首位。高速公路的建设与发展，影响着城市之间的经济联系、空间布局与城市区位。因此，分析高速公路的可达性对于城市发展的影响是至关重要的。

收费公路系统每天可以收集海量的出行数据，而这些数据中蕴含着丰富的信息，但由于噪声数据多、整合多源数据分析困难等原因，并没有得到有效的利用。通过分析高速公路收费数据，分析交通与城市发展的特征，提取对于研究交通、城市发展规划所需的重要信息，可以明确高速公路网的发展对于区域可达性所产生的影响，为投资方、公路运营管理者和城市规划人员的决策提供信息支撑。

1 高速公路可达性

可达性最早由Hansen于1959年正式提出，他将可达性理解为网络中各个节点产生相互作用的机会[1]。但随着可达性这一概念在交通领域的发展，对可达性的理解演化为利用一种特定的交通系统从某一特定区位到达活动地点的便利程度[2]。可达性可以分为个人可达性和地方可达性[3]，对于高速公路可达性的研究主要关注的是地方可达性。Adelheid Holl利用高速公路网络的可达性和市场潜力的可达性指标，对1980年至2000年间的高速公路建设项目的可达性影响进行了空间数据分析。结果显示，高速公路可达性明显上升，外围地区市场潜力增长较快，交通投资对于区域发展具有重要意义[4]。Kotavaara等分析了1970年至2007年之间芬兰公路网和铁路网可达性与人口的变化关系，通过潜在的可达性分析和网络可达性测量，对建成区的单元和城市层面的可达性进行评价。结果显示出芬兰人大多集中在以高速公路为基础的潜在可达区域，并在大力投资长途运输之后，铁路网络的可达性对地区人口变化产生了影响[5]。关于评价路网的可达性方法研究，Stepniak等提出了结合可达性水平、地区凝聚力和空间溢出效应的三重分析方法，并通过波兰两条高速高公路的案例验证了方法的有效性[6]。

国内对高速公路可达性的研究主要包括高速公路网的建设对节点内部及节点之间联系可达性格局的影响，以及分析节点总体可达性格局随高速公路项目建设所发生的变动[7-9]。除此之外，高速公路网可达性与城市区位、城市社会经济指标之间的关系也是研究的热点[10-11]。然而，对不同车型、不同季节的可达性的差异研究较少。因此，本研究将对节点之间不同车型、不同季节的可达性的差异进行分析，并总结高速公路可达性的分布特征。

2 可达性评价方法

2.1 可达性模型

常用的可达性包括空间阻隔模型（距离模型）、累积机会模型、空间相互作用模型（潜能模型）、效用模型和时空约束模型，除此之外，还可以将多种可达性模型进行组合，构成混合模型[12]。各类模型都有自己的特点与适用范围。

2.1.1 空间阻隔模型

空间阻隔模型也称距离模型,其本质就是利用通过实体的距离来度量可达性,是最常用的方法之一[13]。该模型经过众多学者的研究以及修正,模型如公式(1)所示。该模型简单明了,应用广泛。

$$A_i = \frac{\sum_{j=1}^{n}(T_{ij} \times M_j)}{\sum_{j=1}^{n} M_j} \tag{1}$$

式中,A_i 表示的是节点 i 可达性;T_{ij} 是节点 j 到达节点 i 所需要的最短出行时间;M_j 为节点 j 的权重,可以理解为节点 j 的人口,经济等。

2.1.2 潜能模型

潜能模型也称重力模型,该方法最常用的形式由 Hansent 提出[1],如公式(2)所示。该模型同样考虑了吸引点的土地利用状况和土地利用随距离衰减的特征,但是不同节点的衰减速率是不一样的,因此,需要在使用前对距离阻抗影响程度系数进行标定。

$$A_i = \sum_{j=1}^{n} \frac{M_j}{c_{ij}^{a}} \tag{2}$$

式中,A_i 表示的是节点 i 可达性;M_j 为节点 j 的人口、就业机会等;c_{ij}^{a} 为节点 i 至 j 的交通成本;a 为距离阻抗影响程度系数。

2.2 基于收费数据的可达性模型

2.2.1 高速公路收费数据

高速收费数据中蕴含丰富的信息,包含高速公路出行的起讫点、出行时间、车型等。可以从起讫点信息中得到高速公路出行 OD 表、城市的发生和吸引量,根据入口时间、出口时间确定出行的行程时间。车型可以用于分析客车、货车之间的出行差异性。

本研究将利用空间阻隔模型中的加权平均出行时间模型和潜能模型来评价可达性。数据来源为高速公路收费数据。高速公路收费数据中蕴含了大量的信息,如出行时间、起讫点、车型等。城市中包含了多个高速公路收费站,在评价两个城市的可达性时,选取两个城市中收费站之间的加权平均出行时间作为两个城市的平均出行时间,权重为收费站之间的 OD 量。本研究将利用 Python 对高速公路收费数据进行分析与统计。

2.2.2 模型构建

基于加权平均出行时间模型与收费数据的可达性指标计算公式如公式(3)、公式(4)所示,基于加权潜能模型与收费数据的可达性指标计算公式如公式(5)所示。

$$A_i^c = \frac{\sum_{j}^{q} T_{ij}^c \cdot OD_{ij}^c}{\sum_{j}^{q} OD_{ij}} \tag{3}$$

$$T_{ij}^c = \frac{\sum_{k}^{n} \sum_{p}^{m} t_{pk}^c \cdot OD_{pk}^c}{\sum_{k}^{n} \sum_{p}^{m} OD_{pk}^c} \tag{4}$$

式中,A_i^c 表示的是节点 i 中车型 C 可达性,C 为车型集合 $C = \{$客车:c,货车:$f\}$;T_{ij}^c 是节点 i 到节点 j 所需要的加权平均出行时间;t_{pk}^c 是车型 C 在节点 i 中的收费站 k 到达节点 j 中的收费站 p 所需要的平均出行时间;同理,OD_{pk}^c 是车型 C 在节点 i 中的收费站 k 到达节点 j 中的收费站 p 的 OD 量,作为计算出行加权平均时间的权重;OD_{ij}^c 是车型 C 节点 i 到节点 j 的 OD 量(万辆),作为计算可达性的权重;m,n 和 q 分别表示节点 j 中的收费站数量、节点 i 中的收费站数量和节点的数量。

$$A_i^C = \sum_{j=1}^{q} \frac{D_{ij}^c}{T_{ij}^c} \tag{5}$$

式中,A_i 表示的是节点 i 可达性;D_{ij}^c 为节点 j 对节点 i 中 C 型车的吸引量(万辆);T_{ij}^c 为节点 i 至节至 j 的交通成本。

3 案例分析

贵州省一共包含9个市,分别为安顺市、毕节市、贵阳市、六盘水市、黔东南州、黔南州、黔西南州、铜仁市和遵义市。在2015年至2018年间,贵州省高速公路总里程由5128公里增长至6453公里,高速公路出行次数由1.66亿次增长至2.98亿次。高速公路的发展对于各个城市的发展具有促进意义。

本文对2015年至2018年贵州省各个市的可达性变化进行分析,以及不同车型(客车和或者)、不同季度各个城市的可达性差异。本文考虑的出行成本为加权平均出行时间,由于各个季度的交通量、天气因素等影响,会导致各个季度的出行成本发成微小变化。除此之外,由于客车的限速与货车的限速不同导致出行时间成本的不同,因此对客车与货车的可达性分别进行评价。

3.1 可达性评价

通过加权平均出行时间和潜能法度量的2015年至2018年各市的客车、货车可达性如表1所示。从表1中可以了解到,对于客车,安顺市、毕节市、贵阳市、铜仁市和遵义市的出行时间在3年内的变化少于10%。而六盘水市和黔西南市的出行时间分别下降了22%和14%,反映出连接六盘水市和黔西南市与其他节点城市的高速公路基础设施的完善,使得这两个市与其他节点的沟通增强。而黔东南州和黔南州到其他节点的平均出行时间分别增加了47%和29%,考虑为节点内部的高速公路建设连通了节点内部偏远地区,导致了这两个节点与其他节点的出行时间增加。对于货运出行,出行时间的变化趋势与客运出行相似,变化较大的有:六盘水市的出行时间减少了19%,黔东南州和黔南州的出行时间增加了45%和15%。

2015年至2018年贵州省各市客车加权平均出行时间　　　　表1

城市	客车出行时间(h)				货车出行时间(h)			
	2015年	2018年	差值		2015年	2018年	差值	
安顺	1.35	1.32	−0.02	−2%	1.95	1.86	−0.09	−5%
毕节	1.97	1.81	−0.16	−8%	2.39	2.47	0.08	3%
贵阳	1.65	1.64	−0.01	−1%	2.34	2.24	−0.10	−4%
六盘水	2.78	2.18	−0.60	−22%	6.50	5.24	−1.26	−19%
黔东南	1.63	2.40	0.77	47%	1.78	2.58	0.80	45%
黔南	1.10	1.41	0.31	29%	2.10	2.42	0.32	15%
黔西南	2.48	2.14	−0.34	−14%	2.81	2.62	−0.19	−7%
铜仁	2.85	2.88	0.03	1%	5.60	5.47	−0.12	−2%
遵义	2.45	2.32	−0.13	−5%	3.49	3.20	−0.30	−8%

对比各个城市2018年的客车出行时间可得,安顺市到达其他市的出行时间为1.32h,其可达性最优。黔南州、贵阳市的可达性也相对较好,这反映出贵州省出行的中心区域位于贵州省的中南部。铜仁市的可达性最差,出行时间为2.88h。各市的货车可达性与客车可达性类似,但出行时间货车比客车更大。

当使用城市发展潜能作为可达性评价指标时,潜能值越大,说明城市的经济发展水平和可达性越高。如表2所示的是贵州省城市发展潜力以及城市潜能增幅。2015年,贵阳市、安顺市和黔南州具有较大的城市发展潜能。其中贵阳市发展潜能最大为3.19。至2018年,贵阳市的客运发展潜能增长至5.43,仍然位居第一,并且远超其他城市。由于城市发展潜能由高速公路出行量来度量,而高速公路客车交通量远大于货车交通量,因此无法直接将客运潜能与货运潜能直接对比。于是,可以采用发展潜能增幅来衡量客运和货运的发展。

2015年至2018年间,客运和货运都取得了较大幅度的增长,其中毕节市的增幅最大,客运潜能增幅达361%,货运潜能增幅达388%。六盘水市和黔西南市也同样大幅增长,分别为客运潜能增长了180%和185%,货运潜能增长了110%和91%。目前城市发展潜能较大的地区集中在贵州省的中南部,而中南部的发展潜能增长较小,反映出中南部地区的高速公路建设进程已逐渐区域饱和,高速公路出行需求增长也逐渐放缓。相比之下,城市发展潜能较小的西部和北部地区,由于4年的高速公路建设,刺激了高速公路出行需求,使得城市发展潜能迅速增长。

2015年至2018年贵州省各市发展潜能 表2

城 市	客运发展潜能				货运发展潜能			
	2015年	2018年	增幅		2015年	2018年	增幅	
安顺	1.28	1.99	0.71	56%	0.23	0.36	0.13	57%
毕节	0.37	1.71	1.34	361%	0.07	0.32	0.25	388%
贵阳	3.80	5.43	1.64	43%	0.63	0.97	0.35	55%
六盘水	0.30	0.83	0.53	180%	0.10	0.22	0.11	110%
黔东南	0.74	0.90	0.16	21%	0.21	0.24	0.03	15%
黔南	2.19	2.59	0.40	18%	0.39	0.58	0.19	49%
黔西南	0.17	0.48	0.31	185%	0.06	0.11	0.05	91%
铜仁	0.41	0.62	0.21	51%	0.15	0.20	0.05	33%
遵义	0.73	1.31	0.59	80%	0.15	0.25	0.10	68%

3.2 可达性的季节性特征

表3和表4展示的是2015年和2018年各个季度客车和货车的加权平均出行时间。从表中可以了解到,无论是客车还是货车,对于各城市各季度之间的出行时间并无明显变化规律。因此,贵州省各市的加权平均出行时间在同一年内是相对较稳定的。

贵州省各季度客车加权平均出行时间(单位:h) 表3

城 市	2015年各季度				2018年各季度			
	1	2	3	4	1	2	3	4
安顺	1.28	1.36	1.44	1.30	1.29	1.35	1.44	1.20
毕节	2.21	1.86	1.93	1.87	1.77	1.81	1.90	1.74
贵阳	1.63	1.64	1.68	1.65	1.65	1.60	1.66	1.65
六盘水	2.92	2.79	2.8	2.62	2.27	2.11	2.18	2.17
黔东南	1.55	1.74	1.71	1.52	2.89	2.08	2.41	2.20
黔南	1.00	1.06	1.19	1.13	1.43	1.36	1.48	1.36
黔西南	2.44	2.52	2.53	2.43	2.09	2.17	2.13	2.17
铜仁	2.83	2.91	2.90	2.77	3.09	2.66	2.91	2.86
遵义	2.41	2.38	2.50	2.50	2.25	2.20	2.38	2.43

2015年至2018年贵州省各季度货车加权平均出行时间(单位:h) 表4

城 市	2015年各季度				2018年各季度			
	1	2	3	4	1	2	3	4
安顺	1.96	2.03	1.88	1.91	1.85	1.98	1.85	1.74
毕节	2.65	2.32	2.23	2.36	2.4	2.59	2.57	2.31
贵阳	2.38	2.43	2.24	2.30	2.27	2.30	2.18	2.22
六盘水	6.53	8.00	5.98	5.47	5.43	6.19	4.55	4.77
黔东南	1.76	1.89	1.78	1.69	2.56	2.50	2.55	2.72
黔南	2.04	2.18	1.95	2.21	2.38	2.49	2.37	2.42
黔西南	2.59	3.20	2.75	2.71	2.60	2.71	2.47	2.70

续上表

城市	2015年各季度				2018年各季度			
	1	2	3	4	1	2	3	4
铜仁	5.70	6.01	5.37	5.30	5.77	5.53	5.22	5.37
遵义	3.68	3.61	3.23	3.45	3.29	3.21	3.13	3.16

对于高速公路的客运发展潜能而言,贵州省各市展现出较为明显的季节性特征。几乎所有城市第三季度的潜能都要大于其他季度,这说明了第三季度贵州省各个城市间的出行量较大,且出行的交通环境较好。而对于货运发展潜能,这一特征就不太显著。2015年至2018年贵州省各市客货运发展潜能如表5和表6所示。

2015年至2018年贵州省各市客运发展潜能　　表5

城市	2015年各季度				2018年各季度			
	1	2	3	4	1	2	3	4
安顺	1.32	1.2	1.52	1.07	1.81	1.78	2.37	2.00
毕节	0.17	0.38	0.53	0.4	1.59	1.56	1.94	1.74
贵阳	3.91	3.78	4.42	3.08	5.42	5.12	6.38	4.81
六盘水	0.29	0.27	0.37	0.25	0.83	0.76	1.02	0.69
黔东南	0.75	0.67	0.90	0.65	0.79	0.90	1.15	0.76
黔南	2.51	2.30	2.33	1.61	2.52	2.51	3.01	2.31
黔西南	0.17	0.15	0.20	0.15	0.49	0.43	0.58	0.41
铜仁	0.43	0.37	0.50	0.34	0.62	0.58	0.78	0.49
遵义	0.72	0.68	0.91	0.60	1.37	1.24	1.61	1.03

2015年至2018年贵州省各市货运发展潜能　　表6

城市	2015年各季度				2018年各季度			
	1	2	3	4	1	2	3	4
安顺	0.23	0.22	0.24	0.23	0.33	0.33	0.36	0.42
毕节	0.03	0.07	0.08	0.08	0.25	0.31	0.32	0.39
贵阳	0.62	0.62	0.66	0.60	0.91	0.98	1.04	0.95
六盘水	0.11	0.11	0.10	0.09	0.2	0.22	0.24	0.20
黔东南	0.21	0.2	0.22	0.21	0.23	0.25	0.25	0.24
黔南	0.43	0.38	0.39	0.34	0.53	0.58	0.61	0.58
黔西南	0.07	0.05	0.05	0.05	0.10	0.11	0.11	0.10
铜仁	0.16	0.15	0.14	0.15	0.18	0.22	0.20	0.20
遵义	0.15	0.15	0.15	0.14	0.22	0.26	0.25	0.26

4　结　语

本研究对现有的可达性评价方法进行了分析,针对高速公路特性,基于高速公路收费大数据,选择了适用于高速公路的可达性评价的加权平均出行时间模型和潜能模型。在模型中,充分考虑了各个地区的交通吸引量。在此基础上对贵州省各个城市的可达性空间分布特征、可达性变化情况以及发展潜力进行了分析。结果表明,贵州省中南部地区可达性较高,其中安顺市的平均出行时间最小,而贵阳市的发展潜力最大。贵州省西部和北部潜力较小城市的发展潜力增速快,而中南部和东部地区的城市潜力增速慢。除此之外,本文还对可达性的季度特征进行了探索,发现各个季度的城市之间的平均出行时间并无较大差异和明显变化规律,但第三季度的城市客运潜能普遍高于其他季度。高速公路可达性评价结果对于高速公路运营管理人员、决策者进行高速公路项目建设具有参考价值。

参考文献

[1] Hansen W G. How Accessibility Shapes Land Use [J]. Journal of the American Institute of planners, 1959, 25(2):73-76.

[2] 马书红,王元庆,戴学臻.交通运输经济与决策[M].北京:人民交通出版社股份有限公司,2018.

[3] Kwan M P, Murray A T, O'Kelly M E, et al. Recent Advances in Accessibility Research: Representation, Methodology and Applications [J]. Journal of Geographical Systems, 2003, 5(1):129-138.

[4] Holl A. Twenty Years of Accessibility Improvements. The Case of the Spanish Motorway Building Programme [J]. Journal of Transport Geography, 2007, 15(4):286-297.

[5] Kotavaara O, Antikainen H, Rusanen J. Population Change and Accessibility by Road and Rail Networks: GIS and statistical approach to Finland 1970-2007 [J]. Journal of Transport Geography, 2011, 19(4):926-935.

[6] Stepniak M, Rosik P. Accessibility Improvement, Territorial Cohesion and Spillovers: A Multidimensional Evaluation of Two Motorway Sections in Poland [J]. Journal of Transport Geography, 2013, 31:154-163.

[7] 孟德友,陈文峰,王宏科.高速公路网络构建对河南城市可达性的影响分析[J].南阳师范学院学报, 2014,013(003):25-28.

[8] 吴威,曹有挥,曹卫东,等.区域高速公路网络构建对可达性空间格局的影响——以安徽沿江地区为实证[J].长江流域资源与环境,2007,016(006):726-731.

[9] 王成金,程佳佳.中国高速公路网的可达性格局及演化[J].地理科学,2016,36(006):803-812.

[10] 程钰,刘雷,任建兰,等.县域综合交通可达性与经济发展水平测度及空间格局研究——对山东省91个县域的定量分析[J].地理科学,2013,33(9).

[11] 卢茜.长三角地区高速公路网可达性变化与城市区位分析[D].上海:上海师范大学.

[12] 陆化普,王继峰,张永波.城市交通规划中交通可达性模型及其应用[J].清华大学学报:自然科学版,2009(6):781-785.

[13] 杨家文,周一星.通达性:概念,度量及应用[J].地理与地理信息科学,1999,000(002):61-66.

Analysis of Factors Affecting Passenger Boarding Comfort Based on a Cabin Environmental Stress Model

Lina Ma   Yong Tian   Can Xu

(Nanjing University of Aeronautics and Astronautics)

Abstract With the increasingly intense competition in civil aviation, paying attention to and improving passengers' perception is an important way for airlines to gain competitive advantage as well as business profits. Focusing on the key phase of boarding, this research explores the formation mechanism of passenger comfort. Considreing human factors, it develops a cabin environmental stress model, based on which the critical cabin environmental factors that affect passenger comfort are identified, and then are weighed using analytical hierarchy process (AHP) with the questionnaire data of 312 volunteers. Results show that the weight of human factors in cabin environment is significantly higher than that of physical scenes, and it is necessary to implement targeted improvements for specific passenger groups in terms of boarding comfort.

Keywords　Air transportation　Passenger boarding comfort　Cabin environmental stress　Factor analysis　AHP

0　Introduction

In recent years, the air transport industry has been under vigorous development with the increasing improvement of global economic growth and the change of people's travel intention. At the same time, passengers' consciousness of service consumption is gradually awakening and the connotation of comfort is constantly expanding, making the service competition more refined and intensified. Statistics show that 35% of passengers make choices based on their comfort evaluation, past flight experience, and the possibility of delay (Koklic, et al., 2017). Thus, passenger comfort becomes another important issue to be considered in addition to cost, safety and environmental protection during flight operation. Paying attention to and enhancing passenger comfort help airlines to differentiate themselves and obtain profits in an increasingly competitive market especially under the external shock of Covid-19.

Passenger comfort in aircraft cabin refers to the holistic and subjective experience of passengers in an airplane (Liu, et al., 2017), and there are a lot of measuring and evaluating methods for it developed by scholars. The SERVQUAL scale was used by Chou, et al. (2011) to measure the perceived quality of cabin service within five distinct dimensions including reliability, assurance, tangibles, empathy and responsiveness. Ahmadpour, et al. (2014) summarized eight themes in the comfort framework, comprising peace of mind, physical well-being, proxemics, satisfaction, pleasure, social, aesthetics and association, to evaluate the inducing effect of various factors on passenger comfort or discomfort. It has been proved that the cabin environment will greatly affect passengers' comfort (Ahmadpour, et al., 2014). But how does the cabin environment exert this influence and then change passengers' perception? In terms of that, vibration is the most easily perceived factor for passengers during flights (Šika, et al., 2011). Seat parameters are those that scholars pay much attention to. A semantic difference method was employed by Chu, et al. (2020) to study the influence of seat color and material on passengers' psychological comfort; Chen, et al. studied the effect of the space during seat rows and the length of different cabin classes from the perspective of ergonomic requirements. Other factors related to space features such as air temperature and velocity (Gao et al., 2019), noise (Huang & Jiang, 2017), air quality and light (Winzen & Marggraf-Micheel, 2013) have also been discussed in terms of their impact on passenger comfort.

Although there are many studies exploring passenger comfort, they are mostly conducted for the whole flight while not refined according to the operation phase. Additionally, passengers in the cabin must share space with others, so human factors play important parts in passengers' perception, but the current researches on influencing factors to passenger comfort in the cabin are usually limited to the physical aspect, and few offer a quantitative and visualized display from the holistic perspective. This paper aims to explore how cabin environment affects passenger comfort in the boarding phase. The reminder of this paper is organized as follows: Section 2 introduces the evolution of the concept of passenger cabin comfort. Section 3 proposes a cabin environmental stress model and expands the scope of cabin environment, based on which an evaluation index system for passenger boarding comfort is developed. In Section 4, the method of AHP is employed to weigh and analyse the influence of different factors on the comfort level in different types of passengers. Finally, the conclusions are given in Section 5.

Supported by the National Nature Science Foundation of China (Grant number 6167123); and the Graduate Open Foundation of Nanjing University of Aeronautics and Astronautics (Grant number kfjj20200735).

1 Passenger Cabin Comfort

As a key phase of the flight operation, boarding is the demarcation between airport experience and airline experience for passengers. Passengers' perception during this process plays an important role in their whole evaluation of the service quality. The boarding phase described in this paper is defined as the period from the moment when the first passenger enters the aircraft door until all passengers have found their seats correctly and are seated after packing luggage. It means that the studied passenger boarding comfort is a part of cabin comfort.

Since Richard and Jacobson (1975) first proposed the term passenger cabin comfort and carried out the questionnaire studies about it, the exploration of the connotation of cabin comfort has never stopped. With the continuous development of the service theory, passengers have continuously proposed higher requirements for comfort. Consequently, the connotation of cabin comfort has been gradually expanded (Wang, et al.,2019) from the single comfort related to aircraft vibration and turbulence, to the multiple comfort, including physical, sensory, human, management and other factors. Fig. 1 shows the evolution stages that cabin comfort has gone through.

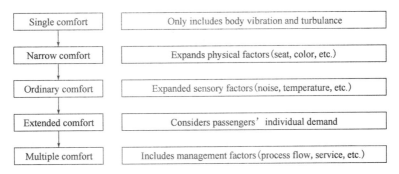

Fig. 1 Evolution of Passenger Cabin Comfort

2 Factor identification Based on Environmental Stress

To further explore the formation mechanism of passenger comfort, a cabin environmental stress model of passenger comfort is proposed in this section, based on which cabin environmental scope is expanded and an evaluation index system of passenger boarding comfort is constructed.

2.1 Cabin Environmental Stress Model of Passenger Comfort

According to the theory in environmental psychology, the environment is not only the place where humans live and produce, but also a huge stressor that causes physiological and psychological effects on personal perception. Combined with the concept of multiple cabin comfort, this paper proposes a cabin environmental stress model of passenger comfort as shown in Fig. 2. Firstly, the cabin environment contains situations or events which function as stressors and stimulate passengers; secondly, against the stressors' stimulation, there are a series of defensive, adaptive, and emotional stress processes developed in passengers involving physical, psychological, and physiological aspects. Additionally, physical and physiological stress can further result in psychological stress, which is manifested as an internal state of tension or arousal; finally, passengers respond to the comprehensive stress process, reflected as their formation or adjustment of perceived comfort.

Therefore, the mechanism in which the cabin environment affects passenger comfort can be summarized as follows: the various cabin environmental elements act as stressors, and exert physical, physiological and psychological influences on passengers during the boarding process, thereby affecting passengers' comprehensive perception.

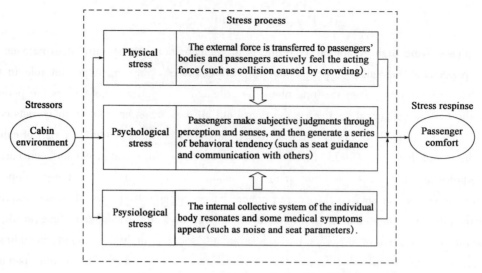

Fig. 2 Cabin Environmental Stress Model of Passenger Comfort

2.2 Generalized Cabin Environment System

In the era of experience economy, the cabin environmental factors that affect passengers' experience not only include the tangible entities or their features that impact on physical and physiological comfort, human factors related to social activities must also be taken into account. In this regard, this article expands the scope of the concept and firstly defines the generalized cabin environment based on the exploration of both tangible entities and intangible forms in cabin environment as well as their interrelationships. As Fig. 3 illustrates, the generalized cabin environment is an interactive system with passengers as the core, and it consists of 4 subjects including physical space, different passenger individuals, cabin attendants, and operational rules, with any two of which having a bidirectional relationship.

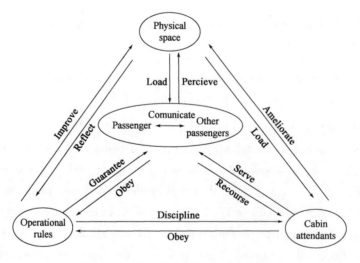

Fig. 3 Generalized Cabin Environment System

Specifically, passengers lie in the center of the interaction, including other passengers who share the space and communicate with the individual during boarding; the physical space refers to the place where all passengers and cabin attendants exist and take activities, it usually affects the first perception of passengers and is also what scholars pay most attention to in previous studies; the subjects of cabin attendants and operational rules are constructed from the perspective of human factors: the cabin attendants are those who directly provide service and contact customers on behalf of airlines, and their image, attitude and tone greatly affect the passenger's comfort; the operational rules refer to the cabin attendants' compliance with the prescriptive regulations or procedure specifications, and their spontaneous behavior in operation, along with the results that generated.

2.3 Evaluation Index System of Passenger Boarding Comfort

According to the cabin environmental stress model and the generalized scope of the cabin environment, the passenger boarding comfort in a cabin is essentially the comprehensive effect in their physical, physiological and psychological perception caused by other passengers, cabin attendants, physical spaces and operational rules. In order to comprehensively identify the specific key factors that affect passenger boarding comfort in the generalized cabin environment, the scenario storyboard (Van der Voet, et al., 2012) shown in Fig. 4 is used to explore the cabin environmental elements that have interaction with passengers when boarding, so as to further build an evaluation index system of passenger boarding comfort.

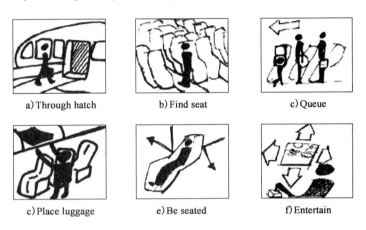

Fig. 4 Scenario Storyboard of Passengers' Boarding Process

From the boarding scenarios presented in the storyboard, the tangible environmental elements on which passengers depend to complete actions or perform activities when boarding, named interacting elements, can be explored and listed in Tab. 1. Based on the stress process of the cabin environmental stress model, and with the comprehensive consideration of all subjects in the generalized cabin environment, the interacting elements are further expanded as listed in Tab. 1.

Expanded Cabin Environmental Elements Interacting with Boarding Passengers   Tab. 1

Scenario	Interacting elements	Stress process	Involved subjects in the generalized cabin environment	Expanded interacting elements
(a)	Cabin hatch	Receive the greetings from cabin crews	Cabin attendants	Personnel image, and attitude
(b)	Aisles, guidance signs, seats	See the physical scene in the cabin, look over the guidance signs, receive guidance from Cabin attendants	Physical space, cabin attendants, rules	Space features, guidance signs, location guidance of seats
(c)	Aisles	Disturbed by other passengers, wait in line	Physical space, cabin attendants, rules	Boarding strategy, congestion solution
(d)	Luggage racks	Place luggage, ask for help	Physical space, cabin attendants, rules	Luggage rack height, proactive assistance
(e)	Seats	Be seated	Physical space	Seat parameters
(f)	Seats, Recreational facilities	Watch out, read, listen, communicate with others	Other passengers	Seat parameters, recreational facilities communication

By classifying the expanded environmental interaction elements according to their physical or social attributes, a three-layer evaluation index system of passenger boarding comfort is constructed and shown in Fig. 5. Including 2 dimensions of physical scenes and human factors, there are 17 indicators of 4 criteria in the index system: the criteria of space features and physical facilities are related to the factors belonging to the subject of physical space in the generalized cabin environment. The personnel characteristics mainly refer to the characteristics of cabin attendants who are in direct contact with passengers. The criterion of interactive behaviors is established based on the subject of operational rules. It mainly includes the consideration of whether the cabin attendants take the initiative to provide seat guidance and luggage assistance to passengers during boarding, whether congestions can be solved in time and effectively by them, and whether they can naturally communicate with passengers in a friendly way to create a pleasant and relaxing atmosphere.

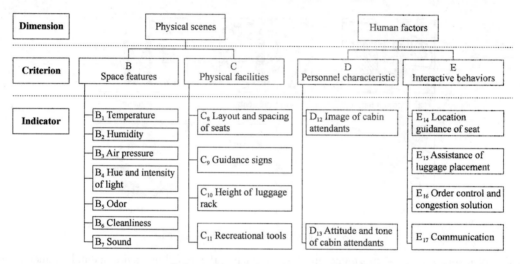

Fig. 5 Evaluation Index System of Passenger Boarding Comfort

3 Indicator Weighing and Analysis Using AHP

In this section, the analytic hierarchy process (AHP) method combined with a questionnaire survey is employed to weigh each indicator in the evaluation index system, namely the critical factors affecting passenger boarding comfort in the generalized cabin environment.

3.1 Research Design and Data Acquisition

AHP combines qualitative and quantitative analysis and has feasibility and applicability to analyze multicriteria decision-making problem (Abdel-Basset, et al., 2020). It uses pair comparisons and matrix algebra to weigh the factors, by which to carefully base decisions (Kaya & Dagdeviren, 2016). Due to the factor analysis involved in this research aims to provide air carriers with decision-making reference for improving the environment and enhancing passengers' experience, what matters more is exploring the relative influence weight of the factors, rather than explaining the correlation structure among them. That contributes to the motivation of employing AHP to weigh the factors in this paper. Additionally, a questionnaire survey was organized to obtain the raw data from people of an expanded scope, contributing to a further reliability improvement of AHP results.

Two topics were included in the questionnaires. One was for the relative comparison in importance and the other involved a satisfaction survey of 17 indicators. Furtherly, there were two parts in the topic of importance comparison, one was the comparison between 4 criteria, and the other was for specific indicators within each criterion respectively. According to the advice from 15 respondents in a preparatory trial, the 1~7 conversion scale was selected for participants to mark the relative importance of the criteria and indicators in the hierarchy, based on which the pairwise comparison matrices required in AHP process were subsequently created. 17 indicators were all scored in the range of 1 ~ 5 by participants according to their perceived satisfaction in the second topic.

The questionnaires were distributed online during two weeks and a field survey was also organized in Tianjin Binhai International Airport. 345 people with historical flight experience took part in the investigation and after filtration, 189 valid online questionnaires (among the total of 208) were obtained and 123 valid paper ones (among the total of 137) were acquired. The respondents providing valid samples included 173 men and 139 women and their average age was 35 years (in the range of 17 ~ 58 years). This roughly matches the distribution information of global air passenger provided by the International Air Transport Association (Li, et al., 2019).

3.2 Weight Calculation and Comparation

Based on the valid questionnaire results, the weights of criteria and indicators were obtained through data processing in Matlab 2016b through the following steps.

Step1: the pairwise comparison matrices for different layers of each participant were constructed individually, and each matrix was formed as follows:

$$A = [a_{xy}] = \begin{bmatrix} 1 & a_{12} & \cdots & a_{1n} \\ a_{21} & 1 & \cdots & a_{2n} \\ \vdots & \vdots & \ddots & \vdots \\ a_{n1} & a_{n2} & \cdots & 1 \end{bmatrix} = \begin{bmatrix} 1 & a_{12} & \cdots & a_{1n} \\ \frac{1}{a_{12}} & 1 & \cdots & a_{2n} \\ \vdots & \vdots & \ddots & \vdots \\ \frac{1}{a_{1n}} & \frac{1}{a_{2n}} & \cdots & 1 \end{bmatrix} \quad (1)$$

where: a_{xy}——the judgement value that a participant compares the criterion or indicator of x with y;

n——the matrix order, namely the number of criteria or indicators.

Step 2: the largest eigenvalue and the corresponding eigenvector of each comparison matrix were obtained by Eq. (2):

$$A \cdot w = \lambda_{max} \cdot w \quad (2)$$

where: λ_{max}——the largest eigenvalue;

w——the corresponding eigenvector.

Step 3: the consistency index (CI) and consistency ratio (CR) were calculated for an examination of the reliability of judgements in the pairwise comparison. If CR was less than 0.1, there was acceptable reliability and the weight vector for criteria or indicators was obtained by normalizing w. CI and CR were defined in Eq. (3) and Eq. (4) respectively.

$$CI = \frac{\lambda_{max} - n}{n - 1} \quad (3)$$

$$CR = \frac{CI}{RI} \quad (4)$$

where: RI——the given random index (Yuan, et al., 2015).

Step 4: by geometrically averaging the results of all samples that pass the consistency examinations, the detailed weight values of criteria or indicators were finally obtained. Tab. 2 shows the specific weight results and their ranks.

Average Values and Ranks of Indicator Weight for the Total Sample　　Tab. 2

Dimension	Criterion	Weight of criterion	Rank of criterion	Indicator	Within-criterion weight	Within-criterion rank	Overall weight	Overall rank
Physical scenes	B	0.1874	4	B_1	0.1089	7	0.0204	17
				B_2	0.1313	4	0.0246	14
				B_3	0.1926	1	0.0361	11
				B_4	0.1115	6	0.0209	16
				B_5	0.1406	3	0.0263	13
				B_6	0.1878	2	0.0352	12
				B_7	0.1275	5	0.0239	15
	C	0.2005	3	C_8	0.2524	3	0.0506	9
				C_9	0.1887	4	0.0378	10
				C_{10}	0.2763	2	0.0554	8
				C_{11}	0.2823	1	0.0566	7
Human factors	D	0.2780	2	D_{12}	0.3097	2	0.0861	4
				D_{13}	0.6093	1	0.1919	1
	E	0.3341	1	E_{14}	0.1821	4	0.0608	6
				E_{15}	0.2302	3	0.0769	5
				E_{16}	0.3007	1	0.1004	2
				E_{17}	0.2870	2	0.0959	3

Form the weight ranks of the 4 criteria in the index system, the volunteered passengers weigh the human factors more compared with the physical scenes. In terms of the specific indicators in the dimension of human factors, for the criteria of personnel characteristics, the cabin attendants' attitude is of significant importance than their external image; for the criteria of interaction behaviors, the cabin attendants' ability to keep order, ease congestion and passenger's communication with others when boarding weigh more than seat guidance and luggage placement assistance. It can be inferred that passengers have less demand for seat guidance and luggage placement assistance, which may be the consequence of the clear identification signs of seat and the luggage allowance in cabin.

Next to the growth in the number of air passengers, there is also an increasement in the diversity of air passengers (Suzanne, et al., 2017). The passengers' judgements about influence weights of cabin environmental factors are affected by their own experiences and attributes (Li, et al., 2019). In order to analyse the differences between various types of passengers, the participants were categorized according to their flight frequency in recent two years and their main purpose of flight respectively, as shown in Tab. 3, and the sample proportion of various types using two classification standards is also presented.

Proportion of Different Types of Passengers Using Two Classification Standards　　Tab. 3

Classification standards	Passenger types	Tags	Numbers	Percentage
Flight frequency in recent two years	Those with 1 – 3 historical flights	Type 1	122	56%
	Those with 4 or 5 historical flights	Type 2	71	32%
	Those with over 5 historical flights	Type 3	27	12%
Main purpose of flight	Those mainly for leisure	Type 4	83	27%
	Those mainly for going to or back from school	Type 5	55	18%
	Those mainly for business	Type 6	106	34%
	Those mainly for visiting relatives and friends	Type 7	64	20%
	Those for other purposes	Type 8	4	1%

Not including Type 8 for the small sample size and insufficient representativeness, the within-criterion weights of each indicator for other 7 types of passengers were calculated and presented in Fig. 6.

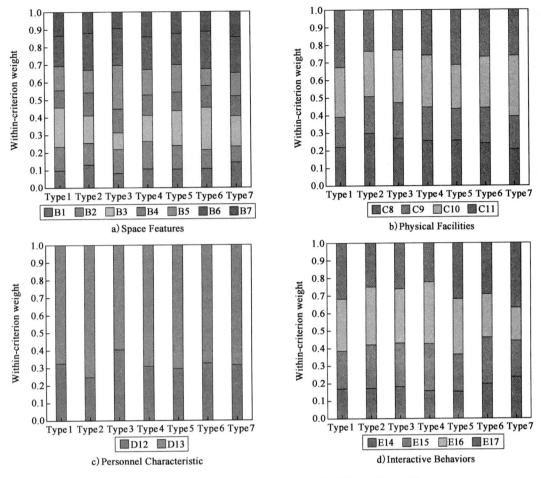

Fig. 6　The Within-criterion Weights of Each Indicator for Different Types of Passengers

A thermodynamic chart as Fig. 7 was further drawn to clearly show the indicator comparation for different passenger groups in weights' overall ranks. For all types of passengers, human factors are more important than physical scenes and the indicator of D_{13}, namely the cabin attendants' attitude and tone, are all at high level in rank as is illustrated in Figure 7. That is consistent with the weight results of the total sample showed in Table 2. However, for the passengers of Type 4, the colour of E_{17} is darker than D_{13}, indicating the passengers for leisure place more weight on communication rather than cabin attendants' attitude. Leisure passengers usually travel in groups, making communication with companions the primary factor that affects their boarding comfort. For the passengers of Type 3 which have more than 5 historical flight experiences in recent two years, and the passengers of Type 7 that travel for visiting relatives and friends, the colour of E_{14} and E_{17} are relatively light compared with other passenger groups, they pay less attention to communication and seat guidance, but value seat parameters and luggage rack height more. In addition, the passengers of Type 1 that have travelled 1~3 times by air in recent two years consider the air pressure in cabin important to their comfort, that may be caused by their tension and anxiety for inexperienced flight.

3.3　Comprehensive Evaluation and Discussion

The satisfactory results for each indicator are taken into consideration to conduct comprehensive analysis in this paper. In order to eliminate the influence of individual preference when scoring, the gray correlation values, which reflect the relative satisfaction level of the individuals with the indicators, were calculated through Eq. (5) taking the respective maximum score among all indicators of each individual as the reference.

$$\zeta_j = \frac{1}{n} \sum_{i=1}^{n} \frac{p_i(j)}{\max P_i} \qquad (5)$$

Where: ζ_j —— the gray correlation value of passengers' average satisfaction with indicator j;

n —— the total number of samples;

P_i —— the satisfaction score vector for 17 indicators of sample i;

$p_i(j)$ —— the specific satisfaction value that the sample i scores for the indicator j.

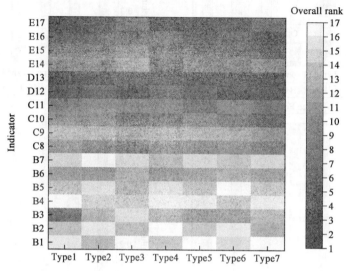

Fig. 7 Indicator Ranks for Different Types of Passengers in Terms of Overall Weights

Fig. 8 shows the calculated gray correlation values of each indicator.

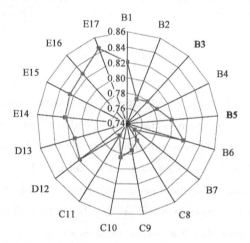

Fig. 8 Gray Correlation Values of Passengers' Satisfaction of 17 Indicators

It can be obviously concluded that passengers' satisfaction with physical scenes is significantly lower than that with human factors. Referring to the effective decision-making tool of Boston Consulting Group (BCG) matrix, a matrix graph reflecting influence weight and relative satisfaction of each indicator simultaneously was developed to conduct quadrant analysis. As shown in Fig. 9, the axes of the matrix cross at the median values.

It can be summarized from quadrant analysis, that seat comfort, luggage rack height, and recreational tools weigh a lot in affecting passenger boarding comfort while perform relatively worse in passengers' satisfaction. They are the factors that airlines must give priority to optimize to improve passenger boarding experience and reduce their complaints effectively. The image of cabin attendants and interactive behaviors in cabin are at high level in terms of both influence weight and satisfaction, contributing to the current competitive advantages of civil aviation, compared with other alternative transportation modes. Airlines need to obtain and maintain these advantages to enhance passenger loyalty and ensure desirable profits; Although sound in cabin has relatively minor impact on passenger boarding comfort, the severity of this factor is reflected in its significantly low value in satisfaction, and it will easily cause passengers discomfort and dissatisfaction if not improved. Therefore, attention needs also to be paid to the factors of this type. As for the temperature, odor, cleanliness in cabin and other similar indicators with high satisfaction and low influence, they should be strictly monitored to prevent deterioration.

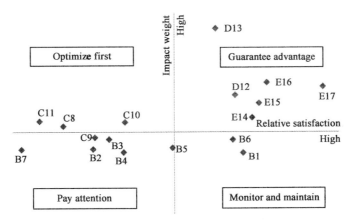

Fig. 9 The Weight VS. Satisfaction Matrix Graph for 17 Indicators

4 Conclusions

This paper focuses on identifying and weighing the factors affecting passenger boarding comfort in the cabin environment. The main contributions are as follows: (1) the cabin environmental stress model of passenger comfort is proposed, and the generalized cabin environment is defined for the first time; (2) an evaluation index system of passenger boarding comfort considering both physical scenes and human factors is constructed, meaning a more comprehensive identification of critical factors in cabin environment that affect passenger boarding comfort; (3) the impact of various indicators on different types of passengers are quantitatively weighed and comparativelyanalyzed. It is found that the influence of human factors is significantly higher than that of physical scenes, and there are obvious differences in the weight ranks of indicators between different passenger groups.

This study not only provides reference for airlines to improve their cabin environmental design and passenger boarding comfort, but also offers theoretical support for the research on passenger experience in other flight phases. The comparative results and analysis of classified passengers are helpful for airlines to perform targeted management according to the specific markets. In the future, targeted studies and in-depth analysis can be conducted considering more information such as the flight attributes, aircraft types, and passengers' travel preference in terms of airline selection. Additionally, the influence of airlines' operation scale and marketing positioning on the results is also worthy further exploration.

References

[1] Abdel-Basset M, Mohamed R, Elhoseny M, et al. Evaluation Framework for Smart Disaster Response Systems in Uncertainty Environment[J]. Mechanical Systems and Signal Processing, 2020, 145.

[2] Ahmadpour N, Lindgaard G, Robert J, et al. The Thematic Structure of Passenger Comfort Experience and Its Relationship to the Context Features in the Aircraft Cabin[J]. Ergonomics, 2014, 57(6):801-815.

[3] Chen H, Pang L P, Wanyan X R, et al. Quantitative Design Model of Civil Aircraft Cabin Layout for Ergonomics[J]. Journal of Beijing University of Aeronautics and Astronautics, 2020, 1-11.

[4] Chou C C, Liu L J, Huang S F, et al. An Evaluation of Airline Service Quality Using the Fuzzy Weighted SERVQUAL Method[J]. Applied Soft Computing, 2011, 11, 2117-2128.

[5] Chu J J, Zhang M X, Wang L, et al. Research on Color and Material Design of Aircraft Cabin Seat Based on Kansei Image[J]. Journal of Machine Design, 37, 2020, 126-130.

[6] Gao F F, Yao B, Liang Y H. Numerical Simulation and Comfort Evaluation of Flow Field in Aircraft Cabin [J]. Aeronautical Computing Technique, 2019, 49, 20-23.

[7] Huang Y. Jiang W K. The Effect of Exposure Duration on the Subjective Discomfort of Aircraft Cabin Noise [J]. Ergonomics, 60, 2017, 18-25.

[8] Kaya B Y, Dagdeviren M. Selecting Occupational Safety Equipment by MCDM Approach Considering Universal Design Principles[J]. Human Factors and Ergonomics in Manufacturing and Service Industries, 2016, 26, 224-242.

[9] Koklic M K, Kukar-Kinney M, Vegelj S. A Investigation of Customer Satisfaction with Low-cost and Full-service Airline Companies[J]. Journal of Business Research, 2017, 80, 188-196.

[10] Li W H, Chu J J, Gou B C, et al. An Investigation of Key Factors Influencing Aircraft Comfort Experience [J]. Advances in Intelligent Systems and Computing, 2019, 794, 222-232.

[11] Liu J, Yu, S H, Chu J J, et al. Identifying and Analyzing Critical Factors Impacting on Passenger Comfort Employing a Hybrid Model[J]. Human Factors and Ergonomics in Manufacturing and Service Industries, 2017, 27, 289-305.

[12] Richards L G, Jacobson I D. Ride Quality Evaluation. Questionnaire Studies of Airline Passenger Comfort [J]. Ergonomics, 1975, 18, 129-150.

[13] Šika Z, Valášek M, Vampola T, et al. Dynamic Model of Aircraft Passenger Seats for Vibration Comfort Evaluation and Control[J]. In Springer Proceedings in Physic, 139, 2011, 217-223.

[14] Van derVoet, Z, Geuskens FJJMM, Ahmed T J, et al. Configuration of the Multi-bubble Pressure Cabin in Blended Wing Body Aircraft[J]. Journal of Aircraft, 2012, 49, 991-1007.

[15] Wang J, Zhi J Y, Chen J P, et al. Review and Outlook of Cabin Comfort of Civil Aircraft[J]. Journal of Machine Design, 2019, 36, 121-126.

[16] Winzen J, Marggraf-Micheel C. Climate Preferences and Expectations and their Influence on Comfort Evaluations in an Aircraft Cabin[J]. Building and Environment, 2013, 64, 146-151.

[17] Yuan B J C, Chang H F, Tzeng G H. Evaluation of Service Quality Continuous Improvement in Coffee Shops[J]. Human Factors and Ergonomics in Manufacturing and Service Industries, 2015, 25, 1-11.

Design of a New Cooperative Vehicle-Infrastructure System Based on Multi-Access Edge Computing Devices

Jinjue Li[1] Ziliang He[1] Yuxuan Sun[1] Ruochen Hao[2] Wanjing Ma[1]

(1. Tongji University, College of Transportation Enginering;
2. Zhaobian Multi-access Edge Computing Limited Liability Company)

Abstract The development of Cooperative Vehicle-Infrastructure System (CVIS) technology has brought more possibilities to reduce traffic delays, improve traffic safety and environmental protection. Since the low connected vehicle (CV) penetration, the existing CVIS applications which only serve to CVs are hard to be useful. As a result, although vehicle-infrastructure collaboration technology develops quickly, it is still difficult to apply on a larger scale. Multi perception device and control device can be introduced to CVIS to communicate regular vehicle (RV) and infrastructure. Then the problem can be solved. Under this situation, a multi-access edge computing device (MEC) is needed. Since RVs are also considered in this new system, the application demand is considered again in this paper. Then the whole CVIS structure is designed by considering perception devices, control devices, and MEC. Both information flow and algorithm positions are designed. The structure of MEC for CVIS is also proposed. CVIS applications can be realized through five approaches: vehicle-vehicle, cloud-vehicle, MEC-vehicle, road-MEC-vehicle, and cloud-MEC-vehicle. All of them are designed in this paper. The proposed new CVIS can support existing applications and extend them to RVs to ensure traffic safety and improve traffic efficiency.

Keywords Cooperative vehicle-infrastructure system　Multi-access edge computing device　Regular vehicles　Connected vehicles　Structure design

0　Introduction

Cooperative Vehicle-Infrastructure System (CVIS) is a safe, efficient, and green traffic system (Lee et al., 2020; Wang et al., 2020; Kopelias et al., 2020). Using advanced technologies, including wireless communication technology, new generation internet technology, etc., CVIS can omnidirectionally realize dynamic real-time information interaction between vehicles and between vehicles and roads (Wang et al., 2018). Based on overall temporal and spatial dynamic traffic information collection and fusion, the system carries on vehicle coordination safety and road coordination control so that the effective coordination among people, vehicles, and roads is realized to ensure traffic safety and improve traffic efficiency.

With the number of motor vehicles increasing, traffic demand growth is higher than the speed of traffic infrastructure construction. The traffic is faced with congestion, accidents, pollution, and other challenges (Albalate and Fageda, 2019). Additionally, the improvement of the economy and technology makes people put forward a higher safety, comfort, and service requirement. There is no doubt that Intelligent Transportation Systems (ITS) are ideal for solving these problems (Lian et al., 2020). The technology of CVIS is an integral part of ITS.

The development of CVIS has gone through a long journey, which can be roughly divided into three main stages.

1) Primary Stage

The development of CVIS began in the 1960s, guided by Japan and the US.

In the 1960s, the US Department of Transportation (DOT) began to research Electronic Route Guidance Systems (ERGS). At the same time, Japan started to research communication between vehicles.

In 1973, Japan developed the Comprehensive Automobile (traffic) Control System (CACS), which was in the lead of the world (Zhang et al., 2003).

In the 1980s, Japan took the lead in the development of the Road Automotive Communication System (RACS), and then it was upgraded to Advanced Road Transportation Systems (ARTS). Besides, Japan developed the Advanced Mobile Traffic Information & Communication System (AMTICS) (Zhang et al., 2003).

In the 1990s, the Japanese government organized Police Agency, Economy and Industry Ministry, Transport Ministry, Post Ministry, and Construction Ministry to be respectively responsible for traffic safety, electronic industry, vehicles, communication, and roads. They developed and operated Vehicle Information &

Communication System (VICS) based on RACS and AMTICS(Zhang et al.,2003).

2) Intermediate Stage

In the 2000s, many countries worldwide started many projects about CVIS to carry on research and experiment.

In 2001, Europe started the CarTalk 2000 project. In 2004, the US began the Vehicle Infrastructure Integration (VII) project and developed it into the IntellDrive project in 2009. In 2006, Europe started Cooperative Vehicle-Infrastructure System (CVIS) project. In 2009, China Intelligent Cooperative Vehicle-Infrastructure Systems 863 Project was started by Tsinghua University.

In 2006, to solve the traffic safety problem, DOT of the US, combined with some vehicle manufacturers, developed and tested the original V2V safety application program and proposed the property of an onboard safety system about adaptive control.

In the same year, Japan showed the Smart Way Public Experiment Demo for the first time. Smart Way project used VICS and Electronic Toll Collection (ETC) system to improve traffic safety and realize other functions. The key to the project is to build an effective platform, such as OBU.

In 2007, the Car2Car communication alliance was composed of BMW, DaimlerChrysler, Volkswagen, and three other vehicle manufacturers in Europe. They aim to build a European public standard for the Car2Car communication system. Besides, the PATH laboratory in the US, using communication between vehicles, made fifteen vehicles run by the platoon.

3) Advanced Stage

Since 2010, countries have gradually entered the application stage of CVIS.

In 2010, DOT of the US put forward ITS Strategic Research Plan (2010-2014). The US proposed developing interconnection technology and automobile application vigorously at the national strategy level for the first time. The aim is to build a nationwide multi-modal transportation system using wireless communication to form a traffic environment connected to vehicles, road infrastructure, and passengers' portable devices.

In the same year, the China Vehicle Information Service Industry Alliance, guided by the Ministry of Industry and Information Technology (MIIT), was founded officially. The alliance aims to enhance the multiple cooperation on the industry chain of CVIS and promote the Chinese Vehicle Information System development. The State Council presented research on intelligent vehicles and CVIS and researched key technology of area traffic coordinated signal control in big cities.

In 2011, Japan introduced Site ITS on the highway, which provided mass information and images for vehicle navigation systems quickly and quickly. The traffic congestion was relieved efficiently, and the driving environment was improved. The US's DOT changed the IntellDrive project's name to Connected Vehicle Research (CVR).

In 2012, the Chinese major special project, "Research and Application of Key Technologies for Urban Intelligent Transportation based on the Internet of Things" was officially started by Guangzhou Traffic Information Investment Limited Company.

In 2014, DOT of the US put forward "ITS Strategic Research Plan, 2015-2019", in which the US ITS strategy was upgraded from simple vehicle interconnection to the dual development strategy of automobile interconnection and auto control intellectualization. The plan would focus the research on the connected vehicle's six main fields, automatic driving, novel function, enterprise data, coordination, and industry expansion.

In 2016, China approved several demonstration bases for intelligent and connected vehicles in Shanghai, Chongqing, Wuhan, Guangzhou, etc. As an initiator, Huawei founded 5G Automobile Alliance (5GAA) and AUDI, BMW, and other companies. Approved by the Ministry of Education (MOE), MOE-CMCC Cooperative

Laboratory, in which CMCC invested 20 million, was constructed by Tsinghua University and Chang'an University.

In the same year, DOT of the US published "Federal Motor Vehicle Safety Standard (FMVSS)", which forced all light vehicles to install Vehicle to Vehicle (V2V) communicationdevices to ensure vehicles can send and receive essential safety information. V2V devices used DSCR as the expected standard of communication among vehicles.

In 2017, the Ministry of Transportation published the 2017—2020 Smart Transportation Program, which proposed to promote the application of ETC. The Telecommunication Institute of MIIT published White Paper on CVIS (2017), presenting the definition and development direction of CVIS. National Development and Reform Commission (NDRC) started Intelligent Vehicle Innovative Development Strategy, focusing on four aspects of building an innovation platform, researching key technologies, improving institutions and regulations, creating conditions to promote the application.

Although the technology of CVIS develops rapidly, it is still difficult to be applied on a large scale. Because of the low proportion of connected vehicles, it isn't easy to realize the information interaction between vehicles and roads. On the one hand, roads can perceive little vehicle information, so roads can't provide valid vehicle information. On the other hand, the information perceived by vehicles is limited, so it's challenging to build an effective connection between vehicles. On account of the low proportion of connected vehicles, the application services make no sense in improving traffic systems.

In order to solve the problem, we increase the perception devices and control devices to break the barrier of information interaction between vehicles and roads. Although the Multi-access Edge Computing device (MEC) can enhance the roadside perception, the current MEC is based on Perception Fusion, lacking algorithms about traffic engineering. Therefore, We develop a MEC for urban roads and highways, which is oriented to many fields, including safety, efficiency, information service, traffic management, intelligent driving, etc., and make systemic design and development.

In this paper, the MEC, combined with the perception device, realizes the fusion process of data detected by millimeter-wave radar, high definition camera, laser radar, etc. In this way, the MEC realizes incident prediction, license plate recognition, and precise vehicle data extraction to complete traffic perception, control, and evaluation. Advanced MEC can realize the interconnection of an area.

The paper's structure and contents are as follows. The first section introduces the definition and development of CVIS and points out the current problem and our solution. The second section analyses the demand for a new environment and presents the function of the system. The third section designs the system architecture, including physical architecture and data flow diagram. The fourth section designs the key device (MEC) and the procedure of algorithms. The fifth section concludes the whole paper and proposes the prospect of MEC.

1 Demand Analysis

1.1 Demand Analysis

Now, there is not CVIS deployed on highways or roads. Regarding information services' data, information collection devices are installed on the highways and roads, including coil detection, vehicle detection camera, and others, to realize traffic flow data collection. But the devices lack vehicle information collection and don't have syndrome information distribution function, so CVIS is needed to cover the blank.

Global information perception is the base of intelligent highway constructions and road constructions, which can entirely control the highways and the roads and deal with the traffic incidents more precisely. On the one hand, the devices of CVIS undertake the function of individuation information perception and uploading. On the other hand, they take part in the decision and the distribution of control instruction. Due to the integration of RV into the service system through sensing equipment and control equipment, demand analysis is oriented towards all vehicles.

On the aspect of scene application, there are two main demands of CVIS. One of the demands is to realize the control foundation scene based on vehicles with the combination of CVIS and automatic driving so that the object of traffic management and control would change from traffic flow to traffic individuals. The other is to realize the scene oriented design of the function module by connected with control infrastructure so that the application of CVIS could possess practical value.

1.2 Functional Design

Functional requirements can be divided into twenty-one categories to improve management and operation effect in all aspects. The realization of these functions needs communication between vehicles and other devices, including vehicle-vehicle, cloud-vehicle, MEC-vehicle, road-MEC-vehicle, cloud-road-MEC-vehicle. The specific functional application design is shown in Tab. 1.

Tab. 1 Function Demand Module

Function Module	Functions and Requirements	Realize
Intelligent driving support broadcast	Provide basic auxiliary information for intelligent driving	road-MEC-vehicle
Roadside payment	Realize the charging function	road-MEC-vehicle
Smart Ramp Control	Coordinated control of ramp signal lights and vehicles	MEC-vehicle
Intelligent road management	Coordinated optimization of lane selection and vehicle speed	MEC-vehicle
Roadside recognition analysis algorithm	Carriage-speed optimization control is carried out for trunk line vehicles	MEC-vehicle
Roadside incident recognition and notification	Identify roadside traffic incidents and send the incident information to the connected vehicles	MEC-vehicle
Roadside incident recognition and broadcast	Identify roadside traffic events, detect and send the traffic events to the connected vehicles related to the events	MEC-vehicle
Roadside incident identification and reporting	identify traffic incidents and report incident information to the cloud platform	cloud-road-MEC-vehicle
Special location broadcast	Broadcast messages in specific sections	cloud-road-MEC-vehicle
Connect detector information, special location broadcast	The detector is installed to sense the occupancy of parking Spaces in gas stations and service areas for message broadcasting	MEC-vehicle
The center transmits the event to the roadside equipment and starts broadcasting	According to the information instruction given by the center, broadcast the message	cloud-road-MEC-vehicle
Basic function module	Realize the synchronization and upgrade of time and space information of the center, roadside equipment, and vehicle equipment	cloud-vehicle
Social Vehicle Service Module	According to the request made by the vehicle, the center conducts information processing and plan formulation and give vehicle feedback	cloud-vehicle
Public travel management	Realize smart dispatch of public vehicles	cloud-vehicle
Emergency Rescue	According to the information reported by the roadside equipment, realize the rapid disposal of emergency rescue	cloud-vehicle
Roadside data reporting	Combine the information in the database and the information reported by the roadside equipment to perform special vehicle trajectory inspection	cloud-road-MEC-vehicle

continue

Function Module	Functions and Requirements	Realize
Payment module	Formulate a reasonable payment plan based on the traffic status reported by the roadside equipment	cloud-road-MEC-vehicle
Vehicle control and event warning	According to the vehicle status along with the information reminder and control	vehicle-vehicle
Active safety control module	Remind by vehicle-to-vehicle communication after discovering the danger	vehicle-vehicle
Information response	According to events, control the vehicle and remind information	vehicle-vehicle/ MEC-vehicle
Cooperative control	Realize collaborative control between vehicles through vehicle-vehicle communication	vehicle-vehicle

2 Architecture Design

2.1 Physical Architecture Design

The physical architecture of CVIS involves the cloud center, management and control facilities, MEC, and terminal equipment. Among them, control facilities include signals controller, variable message board, and so on. The terminal equipment includes onboard equipment, roadside equipment, roadside sensing equipment, etc. Roadside sensing equipment and vehicle terminals report the sensing information to the MEC. The MEC performs full-segment traffic situation awareness and vehicle information matching. Then, MEC reports the sensing results to the cloud platform. The cloud platform will make macro-level control command decisions and cooperates with MEC to formulate control instructions in micro-scenarios. The detailed physical architecture of CVIS is shown in Fig. 1.

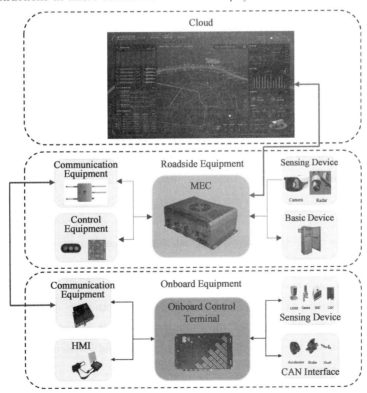

Fig. 1 The Physical Architecture of CVIS

2.2 Data Flow Diagram Design

The detailed data flow diagram of CVIS is shown in Fig. 2. The roadside sensing device and the vehicle terminal report the sensing information to the MEC. MEC carries out full-section traffic situational awareness and vehicle information matching. MEC will report the fused perception information to the cloud center. The cloud center collects the information provided by the external information cloud and the MEC's traffic status. The cloud center, which makes macro-level control command decisions, will give some instructions to the MEC and broadcasts the information that can be broadcast directly to the vehicles. MEC makes detailed control instructions based on its algorithm or combined with cloud initial control instructions, divided into conventional control instructions and connected vehicle control instructions. Conventional control instructions are issued to the roadside control equipment and conveyed to the driver. The connected vehicles' control instructions are transmitted to the OBU through the RSU, conveyed to the driver or the vehicle controller, forming a perception-decision-control closed-loop.

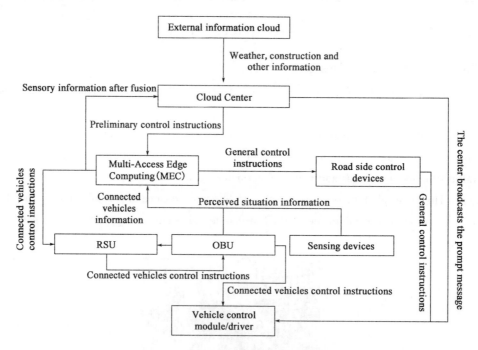

Fig.2 Data Flow Diagram of CVIS

Based on its core algorithm, MEC can solve the traffic problems of urban roads and freeways. MEC's core algorithms reconstruct vehicle trajectory data in urban roads first, including trajectory data repair and map matching. The reconstructed vehicle trajectory serves to solve urban traffic problems because of the connected vehicles' low penetration rate and rough trajectory data. Furthermore, the core algorithms include optimizing a single point, arterial traffic signal optimization, regional traffic signal optimization, and non-signal control intersection, considering buses and cars.

In terms of the freeway solutions, the core algorithm of MEC is firstly multi-source data fusion. MEC integrates radar and high definition video data to enrich the data information and improve data accuracy. The MEC's core algorithm includes flexible lanes and the variable speed limit (VSL) for conventional road segments. For unconventional road segments, to improve weaving areas' safety and efficiency, the core algorithms include vehicle trajectory control and ramp metering (RM) for bottleneck segments with lane reduction, such as the construction area. As for the new control strategy, the bionics-based vehicle control strategy solves the problem that traditional control methods are difficult to adapt to the connected vehicles.

3 Design of MEC

3.1 Software Architecture

The MEC equipment we developed is oriented to safety, efficiency, information services, traffic management, advanced intelligent driving, etc., and can be applied to cooperative vehicle-infrastructure based application scenarios on urban roads and highways. MEC can combine sensing equipment to realize the fusion of detection data such as millimeter-wave radar, high-definition camera, and lidar. It can then realize rapid event warning, license plate recognition, and accurate vehicle data extraction to complete the perception, control, and evaluation of road traffic. MEC's software architecture includes five parts: data processing, data interface, service application, message sending, and local control, as shown in Fig. 3.

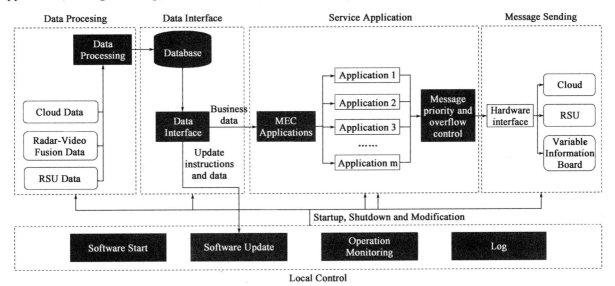

Fig. 3 The Software Architecture of MEC

3.2 Function Realization

The specific realization of the mentioned functions can be divided into five implementation routes: vehicle-vehicle, cloud-vehicle, MEC-vehicle, road-MEC-vehicle, and cloud-MEC-vehicle.

3.2.1 Vehicle-Vehicle

The implementation path of vehicle-vehicle application is to carry out information interaction and information processing between vehicles. The algorithms are mainly completed on the onboard unit, such as the front collision warning, as shown in Fig. 4.

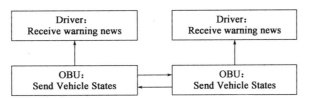

Fig. 4 Flow Chart of Vehicle-Vehicle Application Implementation

3.2.2 Cloud-Vehicle

The cloud-vehicle application is implemented as Fig. 5: The cloud directly communicates with vehicles according to the needs of vehicles, combining the information carried on the roadside and the weather information obtained from the external data cloud, such as vehicle path planning and weather information warning.

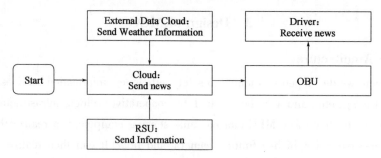

Fig. 5　Flow Chart of Cloud-Vehicle Application Implementation

3.2.3　MEC-Vehicle

MEC-vehicle applications refer to applications that directly exchange information between MEC and vehicles. Most of these applications are passive broadcast applications, such as corner speed limit warnings triggered on fixed road sections, as shown in Fig. 6.

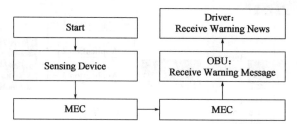

Fig. 6　Flow Chart of MEC-Vehicle Application Implementation

3.2.4　Road-MEC-Vehicle

The road-MEC-vehicle application is implemented as follows: the MEC integrates the roadside sensing device's information. Then it recognizes the event and sends out reminders to vehicles if necessary. For example, active safety applications assisted by roadside facilities such as front-vehicle collision warning can significantly improve the practical control effect of connected vehicles and improve safety when the penetration rate of connected vehicles is low. The specific implementation path is shown in Fig. 7.

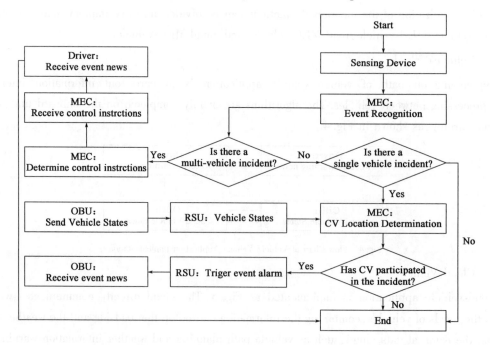

Fig. 7　Flow Chart of Road-MEC-Vehicle Application Implementation

3.2.5 Cloud-Road-MEC-Vehicle Applications

Cloud-road-MEC-vehicle applications evolved from road-MEC-vehicle applications. Their characteristics are mainly reflected in the formulation of primary control instructions. That is, roadside decision-making is transformed into cloud and roadside two-level decision-making. Its implementation path is shown in Fig. 8.

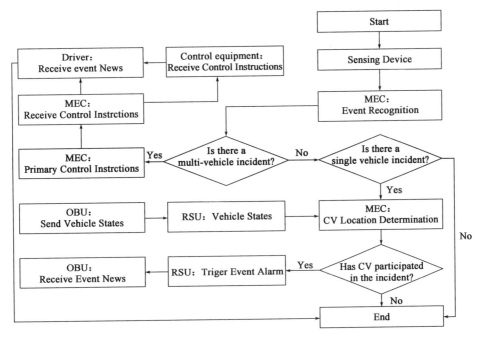

Fig. 8　Flow Chart of Cloud-Road-MEC-Vehicle Application Implementation

4　Conclusions

This study introduced the concept of CVIS, sorts out the development of cooperative vehicle-infrastructure technology, and summarizes the construction requirements and scene requirements of CVIS. CVIS is an essential part of the construction of smart highways and smart cities. The scene application of cooperative vehicle-infrastructure technology can also guarantee roads' serviceability, improve road safety, and control initiative. Since the low connected vehicle (CV) penetration, existing CVIS applications are hard to be useful. Multi perception devices and control devices can be introduced to CVIS to communicate regular vehicle (RV) and infrastructure. Then the problem can be solved. Under this situation, a multi-access edge computing device (MEC) is needed. MEC realizes the design and development of function modules oriented by scenes rather than functions and combines with the basic control facilities so that the application of CVIS can have real practical value.

In this paper, we designed the function of MEC. To realize the solution of urban road and freeway, the MEC's functional requirements can be divided into twenty-one categories. The realization of these functions needs communication between vehicles and other devices, including vehicle-vehicle, cloud-vehicle, MEC-vehicle, road-MEC-vehicle, cloud-road-MEC-vehicle.

The physical architecture and the data flow diagram of the CVIS are designed, too. Meanwhile, the transmission messages between MEC, RSU, OBU, sensing devices, and control facilities are determined. The MEC will report the fused perception information to the cloud and make detailed control instructions based on its algorithms or combined with the cloud's initial control instructions. The algorithms are divided into urban road and freeway schemes, which realize multi-source data perception fusion and improve urban roads and highways' efficiency and safety.

MEC's software architecture and module functions were designed, including data processing, data interface, service application, message sending, and local control. The specific realization of the functions can be divided into five implementation routes, i. e., vehicle-vehicle, cloud-vehicle, MEC-vehicle, road-MEC-vehicle, cloud-MEC-vehicle.

At present, there is relatively little research on the MEC of the CVIS, so the research and discussion of MEC in this study may not be comprehensive enough. With the rapid development of CVIS, autonomous vehicles, and intelligent transportation technology, more and more attention and research will be paid to MEC in the future, which will be conducive to accelerating the implementation of CVIS.

References

[1] Albalate D, Fageda X. Congestion, Road Safety, and the Effectiveness of Public Policies in Urban Areas [J]. Sustainability, 2019, 11.

[2] Chen C, Zhiyong L U, Shanshan F U, et al. Overview of the Development in Cooperative Vehicle-Infrastructure System Home and Abroad[J]. Journal of Transport Information and Safety, 2011.

[3] Kopelias P, Elissaret D, Vogiatzis K, et al. Connected & Autonomous Vehicles-Environmental Impacts-A review. Science of The Total Environment, 2019, 712:135237.

[4] Lee J, Park B. Development and Evaluation of a Cooperative Vehicle intersection Control Algorithm Under the Connected Vehicles Environment[J]. IEEE Transactions on Intelligent Transportation Systems, 2012, 13(1):81-90.

[5] Lian Y, Zhang G, Lee J, et al. Review on Big Data Applications in Safety Research of Intelligent Transportation Systems and Connected/Automated Vehicles[J]. Accident; Analysis and Prevention, 2020, 146(6):105711.

[6] Zhang Y, Peng G, Yang X. The Present Situation and Trend of ITS Development in Japan[J]. China Transportation Review, 2003, 01:58-59.

[7] Wang L, Zhong H, Ma W, et al. How Many Crashes Can Connected Vehicle and Automated Vehicle Technologies Prevent: A meta-analysis. Accident Analysis Prevention, 2020, 136:105299.

[8] Wang Y, Lu G, Yu H. Traffic Engineering Considering Cooperative Vehicle Infrastructure System. Strategic Study of Chinese Academy of Engineering, 2018, 20(2):106-110.

Analysis on the Relationship between the Coordinated Development of Transportation and Tourism

Juan Wu   Jie Tu   Yajun Yu   Simeng Guo   Jia Peng

(Department of Hope College of Southwest Jiaotong University)

Abstract Based on the data of tourism and Transportation in Sichuan Province from 2011 to 2019, this paper studies the relationship between the coordinated development of transportation and tourism, and uses principal component analysis to screen and evaluate the indexes, this paper analyzes the coordination degree of Tourism and transportation, calculates the contribution degree of transportation to the development of tourism, the coupling coordination degree of tourism and transportation, and puts forward some suggestions to realize the win-win cooperation between transportation and tourism.

Keywords   Traffic and Tourism   Collaborative development   Principal component analysis

Coordination measurement

0 Introduction

With the development of economy and the improvement of people's living standard, people's demand for tourism is more universal and diversified, and transportation is an indispensable part in the development of tourism. The development of transportation and tourism can be divided into two kinds of relations: first, because the natural conditions of a place are good and it has been developed into a tourist attraction, the transportation of the place has also been developed, which is tourism-driven transportation development; second, because the transportation of a place is convenient, therefore, people travel to the destination concentrated here, the development of tourism in the region, which is the development of tourism driven by transportation, such a relationship belongs to synergy. The so-called Synergy, that is, the coherence ability between elements, shows that elements in the overall development and operation of the nature of coordination and cooperation. Therefore, synergetic development helps to promote the traffic and tourism. Taking Sichuan Province as an example, this paper collects the index data of Tourism and transportation, and explores the relationship between them by mathematical modeling.

In the process of tourism, the traffic condition is the main factor in the evaluation of tourists' satisfaction degree. The quality of the accessibility, comfort and quality of the traffic have a great influence on the evaluation of the overall quality of tourism, this paper studies the synergy between transportation and tourism can promote the development of tourism and improve the transportation system.

At present, many cities in Guangxi, Guizhou and Yunnan are important tourist destinations because of their rich and varied tourism resources, long history and culture, and unique climatic conditions, how to present the beautiful tourism resources to the tourists in the whole country and all over the world needs the support and promotion of good traffic conditions. Therefore, the coordination between transportation and tourism becomes more important.

1 Current Situation Analysis

1.1 Analysis of Tourism Development Status

According to incomplete statistics, the consumption brought by tourism has the fastest growth in the residential consumption area[2], and it is still increasing year by year. According to the data compiled by China Commercial Industry Research Institute, in 2019, China's tourism economy continues to maintain a faster growth rate than GDP. The domestic tourism market and the outbound tourism market are growing steadily, and the inbound tourism market is on a more solid basis. The number of inbound and outbound tourists reached 300 million, up 3.1% year on year., the realization of tourism revenue totaled 6.63 trillion yuan, up 11% tourism comprehensive contribution to GDP is 10.94 trillion yuan, accounting for 11.05% of the total GDP travel direct employment of 28.25 million people, travel direct and indirect employment of 79.87 million people, accounting for 10.31% of the national employment population tourism industry comprehensive strength Correlation between big long industrial chain, has broken through the traditional scope of tourism, widely involved and penetrating into many related industries, and in industry According to statistics, tourism industry 1 yuan per income, can drive the related industrial increase to $4.3 In developed countries, tourism consumption spending an additional unit of industrial output can be 2.71 times the national income to expand 1.36 times, 0.25 times investment to expand the tourism industry can affect and promote the development of 110 industry associated with it, increase employment, according to the study, every increase 1 person, tourism practitioners can increase 4.2 related industry employment opportunities; In addition to promoting other industries, it can expand the depth of economic and cultural exchanges between China and foreign countries, and strengthen international exchanges and cooperation.

In the future, with the further improvement of people's living standards and the change of consumer subjects and consumption concepts, the demand for tourism will continue to increase, and the development prospect of tourism is broad and considerable. Therefore, it is forecasted that by 2025, the number of domestic tourists will exceed 8.3 billion yuan and the tourism income will be close to 10 trillion yuan.

1.2 Current Situation of Transportation Development

The investment in fixed assets of transportation in the whole year was 3.245.1 billion yuan, an increase of 3.1% over the previous year. In addition, the proportion of investment in various modes of transportation in the transportation industry can be simply analyzed in Fig. 1.

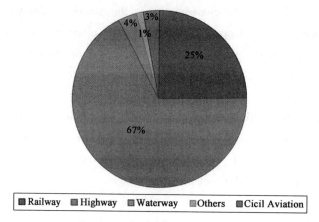

Fig. 1 The Proportion of Investment of Each Mode of Transportation

1) Railway

A total of 802.9 billion yuan was invested in the fixed assets of railways.

2) Highway and waterways

(1) Highways: The investment in highway construction was 2.189.5 billion yuan, an increase of 2.6% over the previous year. Of this, 1.150.4 trillion yuan was invested in highway construction, up 15.4 percent; The investment in provincial road construction was 492.4 billion yuan, down 10.3 percent; A total of 466.3 billion yuan was invested in rural road construction, down 6.5 percent.

(2) Waterways: The investment in waterways construction was 113.7 billion yuan, down 4.4% from the previous year. Among them, inland river construction completed investment of 61.4 billion yuan, down 2.3%; The investment in coastal construction was 52.4 billion yuan, down 6.8%.

(3) Others: A total of 42 billion yuan was invested in highway and waterway support systems and other projects.

3) Civil Aviation

the investment in fixed assets in civil aviation construction was 96.94 billion yuan, up 13.0% over the previous year.

In summary, it can be seen that the transportation industry is more inclined to investment; In addition, as the Internet big data and the integration of the whole society, the development of transportation industry is in the direction of high speed toward the facilitation of light-duty and high-tech development, so the whole appear the phenomenon of living beyond its means, and tourism income after tax by the state in all manage door company to arrange part of the investment for transportation, this is the transportation and tourism on the economic coordination.

2 Index Selection

2.1 Principle of Index Selection

Traffic system and tourism system are two complexes, has certain dynamic[3], or more influenced by external factors, and combining with the principle of building index system, the selection of the indicators should follow the following principles:

(1) a concise scientific principle: the selection of indicators should be scientific, can objectively reflect the transportation and tourism development characteristics and conditions of the two systems, reflect the true relationship, indicators should be relatively typical, cannot overlap phenomenon such as missing, and the calculation method should be simple and clear;

(2) operational quantifiable principles: on the selection of indicators, the overall range to maintain consistency, the index system is established to study comprehensive development level of transportation and tourism, in the index on the measurement and calculation method of also should maintain consistency, also want to consider when choosing the index is easy to do quantitative processing, for calculation and analysis;

(3) Systematic principle: indicators in the transportation and tourism system should not only reflect the state of the system, but also reflect the internal connection and independence among all indicators. At the same time, they should also be interrelated to form an organic system, which should have a certain level, from top to bottom, and step by step.

2.2 Index Selection and System Construction

The link between tourism and transportation Interact with each other According to the traffic and tourism industry development, and combining with index selection is scientific Operational quantifiable systemic principle, selection in the transportation of civil aviation passenger traffic highway passenger railway passenger traffic volume of railway passenger turnover road mileage of expressway mileage railway mileage to eight indexes; In the tourism industry, seven indicators are selected, including the number of domestic tourists, the number of domestic tourists, the number of inbound tourists, the number of star hotels, the number of tourism practitioners, the number of travel agencies. Therefore, the evaluation index system of the synergistic development relationship between tourism and transportation industry is shown in Tab. 1.

Evaluation Index System of the Tourism and Transportation   Tab. 1

Evaluation Objectives	First-level	Secondary index
The coordinated development of tourism and transportation industry relations	Tourism development level	Domestic tourist arrivals (100million) X_1
		Domestic tourism revenue (100 million yuan) X_2
		Inbound tourists (10000) X_3
		Inbound tourism revenue ($) X_4
		Number of the hotel X_5
		Number of Tourism Employed Persons (10000) X_6
		The travel agency quantity X_7
	Transportation industry development level	Civil Air Passenger Capacity (10000) Y_1
		Highway passenger volume (ten thousand) Y_2
		Railway passenger volume (ten thousand) Y_3
		Road passenger turnover (100 million person-km) Y_4
		Railway passenger turnover (100 million person-km) Y_5

Evaluation Objectives	First-level	Secondary index
The coordinated development of tourism and transportation industry relations	Transportation industry development level	Highway mileage (km) Y_6
		The highway mileage (km) Y_7
		Railway mileage (km) Y_8

3 Indicator System and Coordination Degree Analysis

3.1 Principal Component Analysis

According to the evaluation index system of Sichuan province in the statistical yearbook and each big web site to check the related indicators of statistics in 2011—2019, first to no classes of quantitative data, then using SPSS to Sichuan tourism and transportation two parts is the principal component analysis, it is concluded that the traffic and tourism the main component of variance contribution ratio of the two systems and the factors affecting the coefficient, the detailed results are shown in Tab. 2.

PCA's Results Tab. 2

Tourism	Component	Traffic	Component
Principal	87.937%	Principal	85.351%
1	0.995	1	0.985
2	0.983	2	0.985
3	0.972	3	0.977
4	0.953	4	0.972
5	0.915	5	0.928
6	0.666	6	−0.885
7	−0.54	7	−0.871
	0.995	8	0.724

(1) According to Tab. 2, the linear combination of principal components of tourism development level is as follows:

$$Z = 0.995X_2 + 0.983X_1 + 0.972X_3 + 0.953X_4 + 0.915X_7 + 0.666X_6 - 0.55X_5 \quad (1)$$

Extract a principal component, the whole system consists of seven indicators: domestic tourism income, attendances, inbound tourism, domestic tourism, inbound tourism revenue, number of travel agencies, the five indicators of impression coefficients above 0.7 plays a larger role in promoting tourism, and tourism practitioners (mainly catering accommodation), the number of star-rated hotels are less than 0.7, promote tourism is lesser, comprehensively reflect the reliability of 87.937%.

(2) According to Tab. 2, the linear combination of principal components of transportation development level is:

$$Q = 0.985Y_6 + 0.985Y_1 + 0.977Y_8 + 0.972Y_7 + 0.928Y_5 + 0.724Y_3 - 0.885Y_4 - 0.871Y_2 \quad (2)$$

Extracted a principal component, the transportation is the system composed of seven indicators: the development level of highway mileage, civil aviation passenger traffic, railway mileage, the highway mileage, railway passenger turnover, the five indicators of influence coefficients above 0.7, bigger role on the traffic, the highway passenger turnover, highway passenger traffic, railway passenger traffic is less than 0.7, promote small, comprehensively reflect the reliability of 85.351%.

3.2 Development Level

After the principal component analysis of each system, the principle of cumulative contribution of more than 85% was adopted to select the corresponding principal component variance contribution rate as the weight of the metadata, and the score of each year was calculated according to the comprehensive score of each factor, with the formula as follows[3]:

$$S = \sum_{i=1}^{2} \alpha_i d_i \quad (3)$$

where: α_i ——contribution rate of variance of each principal component;

d_i ——the scores of each principal component;

S ——The comprehensive score of each system reflects the level of development.

It is calculated in Tab. 3.

Comprehensive Development Index Tab. 3

Year	2011	2012	2013	2014	2015	2016	2017	2018	2019
Tourism	-1.15	-1.01	-0.79	-0.43	-0.19	0.13	0.45	0.87	1.07
Sequential growth		0.12	0.22	0.46	0.56	1.68	2.46	0.93	0.23
Traffic	-1.25	-1.11	-0.84	-0.37	0.09	0.78	0.93	1.17	1.36
Sequential growth		0.11	0.24	0.56	1.24	7.67	0.19	0.26	0.16

As can be seen from Tab. 3, tourism and traffic systems showed a gradual growth trend from 2011 to 2019, and the growth rate of traffic decreased in 2017.

3.3 Coordination Degree Analysis

The coupling coordination degree model is used to analyze the coordination development level of things. Coupling degree refers to the interaction between two or more systems to realize the dynamic connection of coordinated development, which can reflect the degree of mutual dependence and restriction between systems. The degree of coordination refers to the degree of benign coupling in the coupling interaction relationship, which can reflect the state of coordination between systems.

The coupling coordination degree model involves the calculation of three indexes, which are C value of coupling degree, T value of coordination index and D value of coupling coordination degree. According to the D value of coupling coordination degree, the coordination level is divided into 10 levels. The division criteria are shown in Tab. 4.

Standard for Grading Coupling Coordination Degree Tab. 4

Coupling coordination degree D	Coordination level	Degree of coupling coordination
(0.0~0.1)	1	Extreme disorder
[0.1~0.2)	2	Severe disorder
[0.2~0.3)	3	Moderate disorder
[0.3~0.4)	4	Mild disorder
[0.4~0.5)	5	Near disorder
[0.5~0.6)	6	Barely coordination
[0.6~0.7)	7	Primary coordination
[0.7~0.8)	8	Intermediate coordination
[0.8~0.9)	9	Good coordination
[0.9~1.0)	10	Quality coordination

Finally, the coupling coordination degree between tourism and transportation in Sichuan Province from 2011 to 2019 is finally obtained by using SPSSAU and combining with the D value of coupling coordination degree and coordination grade classification standard, as shown in Tab. 5.

Coupling Coordination Degree Calculation Results   Tab. 5

Term	Coupling	T value	Coupling coordination	Coordination	Degree of coupling
Item 1	0.044	0.154	0.082	1	Extreme disorder
Item 2	0.427	0.179	0.277	3	Moderate disorder
Item 3	0.419	0.130	0.233	3	Moderate disorder
Item 4	0.917	0.336	0.555	6	Barely coordination
Item 5	0.972	0.566	0.742	8	Intermediate coordination
Item 6	0.976	0.677	0.813	9	Good coordination
Item 7	0.000	0.635	0.000	1	Extreme disorder
Item 8	0.924	0.741	0.828	9	Good coordination
Item 9	0.961	0.878	0.918	10	Quality coordination

According to the above two tables, the following conclusions can be drawn: the degree of coordination between the two systems is gradually optimized, but it appeared extreme maladjustment in 2011, moderate maladjustment in 2012—2013, and extreme maladjustment again in 2017.

4 Conclusions and Suggested Countermeasures

1) Conclusion

(1) During 2011—2019, for the coordinated development of tourism and transportation, the contribution of the development level of transportation industry is higher than that of the development level of tourism, and the highest contribution of the development level of transportation industry is the index of civil aviation passenger volume, and the highest contribution of the tourism development level is the index of domestic tourist number.

(2) During the period from 2011 to 2019, the comprehensive development level of tourism and transportation industry in Sichuan Province is on the rise. The annual gradual increase in the comprehensive development level indicates that tourism and transportation industry have carried out effective coordinated development and further improved the economic level.

(3) In 2011—2012, the degree of coupling coordination increased from extremely maladjusted to moderate maladjusted, which shows that tourism and transportation have developed effectively in coordination. The degree of coupling coordination is on the rise, which shows that the coordinated development of tourism and transportation in Sichuan Province has reached the level of high-quality coordination under the development of the present era and the support of national government policy. The sharp decline in coordination in 2017 is due to the extreme mismatch between the level of transport and tourism development.

2) Suggested Countermeasures

(1) To focus on the development of tourism routes and transportation routes suitable for their respective cities in different regions, with emphasis on the connection of various modes of transportation with tourist attractions, and to increase regional cooperation in tourism and transportation; For example, tourist areas facilitate the local production and operation of Civil Aviation Passenger Transport, and civil aviation passenger transport provides preferential tickets in time to stimulate travel. At the same time, we should actively promote the tourism industry to attract more foreign tourists and increase consumption on the basis of consolidating

domestic tourists, so as to promote the development of tourism.

(2) With the development of transportation and tourism, improving the degree of satisfaction of tourists in tourism transportation can make further improvement and development of all kinds of travel modes. Sichuan Province should also set up Sichuan Tourism Promotion Exhibition Hall in Every Transportation Station (high-speed railway station, airport, etc.). On the one hand, it will enrich the time for passengers to wait for the train; on the other hand, it will make people better understand Sichuan and make propaganda for Sichuan tourism.

(3) To strengthen the relationship between the coordinated development of transportation and tourism. Based on the analysis of coupling coordination degree, the coupling coordination degree between transportation and tourism in Sichuan Province from 2011 to 2019 basically presents the trend of good and stable development. Therefore, in the development of tourism and transportation, we should pay more attention to the relationship between the two, pay more attention to the relevant state policies, and make the national transportation facilities and equipment match with the tourism and cultural industries. Only the relationship between the two is highly coordinated, to promote the economic development and social construction of Sichuan Province.

References

[1] Liu Zhu yun. Research on Cooperative Optimization Model of Tourism Resources and Highway Network [D]. Harbin Institute of Technology, 2015.

[2] Tian Bei. A Study on the Coupling Relationship Between Regional Tourism Flow and Transportation Network in Five Provinces of Northwest China [D]. Xi'an: Chang'an University. 2017.

[3] ChengRui fang, Lu Xiaoping. Analysis on the Relationship Between the Coordinated Development of Tourism, Tourism Transportation and Regional Economy in Hebei Province [J]. Journal of Hebei University of Economics and Business: Comprehensive Report, 2015(2)83-86.

基于累积前景理论的旅游交通方式研究综述

路社非 孙小慧 左志
(新疆大学建筑工程学院)

摘 要 交通系统的不确定性使得出行者的出行行为呈现有限理性的特征。本文在对随机效用理论和前景理论简单介绍的基础上,对运用累积前景理论的研究成果从行为决策、出行时间和路径选择三方面进行梳理和总结,同时对旅游交通出行研究进行分析汇总,以期探索累积前景理论适用于旅游交通领域的可能性。通过总结发现:累积前景理论出行模型研究中参考点的设置方式有待进一步突破,少有人探讨城际之间基于累积前景理论的交通出行选择研究,且旅游交通领域多以旅游交通行为和旅游交通规划为研究目标,而对旅游交通方式选择研究偏少,旅游交通研究中少有人运用累积前景理论进行分析。本文的结论可以为未来学者了解研究进展提供参考。

关键词 随机效用理论 前景理论 累积前景理论 旅游交通

0 引 言

交通方式的发达与否标志着一个国家的现代化发展的进程。社会进步科学的创新,使得交通方式的种类不断增多,交通出行研究越来越被学者们重视。交通出行是交通系统规划中最重要的内容之一,以往国内外学者在交通出行研究领域中主要以随机效用理论为基础。McFacdden[1]等人于1974年在期望效用理论的假设上改进为随机效用理论(Random Utility Theory,RUT)。然而,通过许多实验发现了随机效用理论的假设违背了现实中决策者的决策行为,因为实际中的个体在进行决策时呈现出的是有限理性的特征,所以在进行建模的过程中应把决策者设成有限理性。

1979年Kahneman和Tversky[2]应用经济学和心理学原理提出的用于描述不确定条件下人们的实际决策行为的前景理论(Prospect Theory,PT)。在PT中,假设在一个有风险的情况下,决策者选择了前景价值最高的方案,使用加权函数和价值函数,根据参考点对前景值进行评估,该理论认为,每个远景的收益或损失是通过与参考点的比较来评估的。PT下的权重函数是单一的不能研究多个选择结果的实验,因此在1992年Tversky and Kahneman[3]对PT进行了改进形成了累积前景理论(Cumulative Prospect Theory,CPT),累积前景理论适合用于实验结果数量较多的情况下。Rasouli(2014)[4]、Sierra(2015)[5]、Wu(2013)[6]和Avineri(2004)[7]等学者通过实证数据对比分析,发现累积前景理论在不确定条件下交通出行选择的情况上更具有优势。本文对国内外学者在基于累积前景理论的交通出行研究和旅游交通研究的相关成果进行梳理和总结,方便以后的学者进行此类研究时了解目前的研究进展和方向。

1 传统的交通方式研究模型

传统的交通出行研究理论是随机效用理论,即出行者对出行场景有着完美的了解,且在做出选择决策时是绝对理性的。随机效用理论里的非集计模型以个体决策者为研究对象,以个体特性、出行方式特性和社会经济特性定量分析决策者对备选方案选择概率的影响程度,以确定效用最大化的备选方案。具有以下特点:①成本低,非集计模型需要的调查数据比较少,可节约调查成本;②建模方便简单,非集计模型数学结构较简单,建模方便;③可同时包含多种变量,非集计模型能够用比较少的数据包含较多的变量;④可移植性高,只要社会经济属性相同,模型就可移植,可以节省建模的社会成本[8]。关宏志(2004)[9]运用非集计模型对个体出行行为进行模拟分析,测算出行者出行方式的多样性。刘崭(2010)[10]基于MNL模型可以准确预测西安市居民地铁和常规公交出行选择的比例,可为城市公交规划提供决策依据,以期城市公交体系的建设更加合理化。

但是非集计模型的选择依据是效用最大化的交通方式,导致随机效用理论的研究对象假设成"完全理性"的状态,即研究对象对将要选择的方案情况都是完全已知的,而这正是该理论的缺陷所在,违背了交通方式选择的实际情况[11]。

2 基于前景理论的交通方式研究模型

Kahneman和Tversky提出前景理论可以更加真实地反映出行者的行为决策,前景理论模型的建立分为编辑阶段和评价阶段。编辑阶段是对各备选方案进行分析然后进行参考点的选择、价值函数和权重函数的编辑。评价阶段是实验者进行备选方案前景值计算以及比较的过程,根据前景值最大的原则选取适合个体的出行方案[12]。Bogers(2002)[13]和褚耀程(2017)[14]研究发现在路径选择研究中,出行者对备选方案的风险态度与前景理论一致。

1992年,Kahneman和Tversky以累积决策权重代替前景理论中的单个决策权重的方式提出累积前景理论。累积前景理论可以更好地解决多个选择结果的问题研究,扩展了前景理论使用范围。Sagi(2006)[15]、Sepehr(2019)[16]等学者运用累积前景理论来解释决策者面对风险态度时发现:决策者面临小概率收益时是风险追求态度,面临小概率损失时是风险回避态度。基于有限理性的前景理论和累积前景理论被大量地运用到交通出行研究中。

3 国内外交通方式研究综述

3.1 基于累积前景理论的交通出行研究综述

目前,基于累积前景理论的交通出行研究得到了很多国内外专家学者的探索。本文通过对国内外专家学者的研究成果梳理总结,可分为出行者行为决策、出行者出行时间、出行者路径选择行为三方面的影响研究。

3.1.1 出行者行为决策方面

国外研究中,Simon(1955)[17]的研究证明不确定交通方式选择条件下的决策者的决策行为呈有限理性的特征。Xu(2011)[18]和Yang(2014)[19]使用累积前景理论改进了以出行时间设置参考点的方法。基于累积前景理论随机用户均衡模型描述的路径选择行为更接近实际决策。

国内研究中,田丽君(2016)[20]运用累积前景理论和期望效用理论对比发现,期望效用理论下的出行者出行方式选择不受出行场景的变化而变化,而基于累积前景理论下的旅行者的出行个体受到参考点的影响。赵丽娜(2017)[21]从乌鲁木齐市普遍存在的交通问题视角出发,建立了城市居民出行方式选择的模型。研究得出基于前景理论的出行决策结果更为准确地描述出行者的实际出行行为。徐爱庆(2018)[22]等人研究了机场旅客出行决策行为,针对不同出行需求的旅客,基于累积前景理论模型框架综合时间价值和票价动态设置旅客出行参考点,研究发现商务旅客对计划延误时间和在途时间更为敏感,而休闲旅客不太在乎计划延误时间,但更关心票价。

3.1.2 出行者出行时间方面

S. Alger(2003)[23]研究了瑞典居民长途旅行的出行方式和目的地的综合选择模型时,发现该综合模式的影响因素是出行者的出行时间、出行成本和社会经济属性。Chang(2004)[24]基于前景理论研究出行者出行方式选择,得出出行时间是重要的影响因素,且验证了设置参照点的适应性和必要性。Chao(2017)[25]研究了出行者在出行时间变异性下的动态模式选择行为,实验证明出行者更喜欢有一定风险但同时可能带来收益的出行方式,随着出行时间的可变性增加,出行者则会倾向于选择风险较小的出行方式。

张波(2011)[26]等人以出行时间预算为参考点,用累计前景值替换Logit模型里的效用值,在交通流连续分布状态下建立了一个随机用户均衡模型。研究发现网络均衡态具有显著的参照点依赖效应。殷蒙蒙(2018)[27]基于累积前景理论建立了通勤者出发时间选择行为模型,探索在不同拥堵且收费情况下的通勤者出发时间选择行为,以此提出缓解道路拥堵的合理对策和建议。宗刚(2020)[28]等人发现当出行者认为在预期时间内不会迟到,表现为风险规避,当出行者认为不能按时到达工作区而迟到,由于通勤出行者对损失更为敏感,表现为风险追求。

3.1.3 出行者路径选择方面

Katsikopoulos(2002)[29]在居民路径选择实验中发现,实际出行时间或感知出行时间的平均值小于理想预计出行时间时,出行者做出路径选择的决策为"收益"时呈现风险规避状态,为"损失"时呈现风险寻求状态。Jon(2008)[30]发现出行者在选择出行路径和起始出发时间时,做出的选择结果依赖于自身的参照点,参照点不同选择的结果大不相同。Xu(2011)[31]研究证明在路线选择行为上出行者选择出行方式时,面对收益前景时的风险厌恶要高得多,在面对损失前景时的风险寻求程度高得多。Zhang(2014)[32]根据实验研究提出了一种旅行者动态路线选择方法,通过实例分析得出,旅行者在遇到拥堵时往往会改变路线,有时会因为时间的紧迫而选择风险路线,这与实际情况是一致的。刘玉印(2010)[33]通过期望效用理论和累积前景理论对比实验者在路径选择行为上的差异,发现累积前景理论在实验中考虑了人有限理性的特点,对出行效用的度量比期望效用理论更加贴近实际。甘佐贤(2014)[34]等人发现出行者不仅要考虑途中时间成本,还要考虑到达目的地的到达时间感知价值,途中时间成本以出行时间为参考点。

3.2 旅游交通研究综述

旅游交通方式作为交通方式研究的一个分支,逐渐地被学者重视,因为旅游已经变成人们休闲散心的一个重要减压方式。由于旅游交通方式的研究在近几年才火起来,所以本文暂且将综述分为旅游交通行为和旅游交通规划两方面的研究。

3.2.1 旅游交通行为研究

Cheng(2019)[35]等人利用南京旅游调查数据进行研究,采用两步聚类方法研究发现居住区位对老年人(60岁以上)和年轻人(18~59岁)出行行为的影响存在显著差异。Zhu(2019)[36]等人通过提供个性化的激励来修改个人的旅游行为,运用随机效用理论对出行者的选择行为进行建模,发现个人出发时间选择的改变将导致总旅行时间减少48%。Wong(2020)[37]等人研究了生成机器学习方法用于分析多个离散-连续(MDC)旅行行为,研究证明生成机器学习法可被用于建模大型多维旅行信息数据集。

孟轶婷(2020)[38]通过对旅游者的抽样调查获取了旅行者的行为特征,建立了引力预测模型预测客流量。王希良(2020)[39]运用结构工程模型通过问卷调查数据分析发现:旅行者较为关注旅游出行时长;旅行者个体属性中,收入属性是主要影响因素;旅游交通网络中,服务水平的影响更为明显;旅游交通行为中,旅游交通费用成为主导因素。

3.2.2 旅游交通规划研究

Zhou(2017)[40]等人针对旅游者主观印象选择城市景点的情况,建立了基于神经网络缓冲分析模型的旅游路线决策模型,验证了该模型的可行性。Uwaisy M(2019)[41]等人通过研究提出了一种解决旅行商业问题(TSP)的方法。采用随机搜索方法对旅游者进行系统调度和搜索,使旅游者能够根据旅游时间、景点运营时间和每天的访问时间限制来寻找最优解。Han(2020)[42]等人设计并开展了一项揭示性偏好和陈述性偏好调查,建立了目的地和发车时间联合选择的嵌套 Logit(NL)模型,研究发现游客的年龄、受教育程度、到访次数和门票销售比例对目的地和出发时间选择有显著影响。

黄莉苹(2015)[43]利用 SWOT 分析法,对京津冀旅游交通一体化建设的发展目标、区域一体化旅游交通集散体系和旅游立体交通方式的系统架构进行了科学规划和理论研讨。王兆峰(2015)[44]引入旅游交通响应强度的概念,从静态和动态两个方面分析了张家界旅游交通响应强度的影响机制,构建了张家界交通运输响应模型,研究发现区域经济发展水平、交通建设基础、旅游产业地位和旅游资源开发的空间结构4个主要因素影响着交通运输对旅游业的发展。郭建科(2016)[45]构建了可达性模型和修正引力模型,分析哈大高铁开通后对东北各城市旅游交通网络可达性变化和旅游经济联系的影响,研究得出,哈大高铁的开通对东北旅游经济联系呈现时空压缩效应,有利于推动沿线旅游业经济带的形成。

4 结 语

国内外学者对交通方式的研究已有多年。本文通过对文献的梳理总结发现:累积前景理论的参考点多以时间价值和货币价值作为参考点,随着人民生活水平的提高,出行方式的安全性、舒适性、便捷性等因素应被重视起来。已有的交通方式研究多数把累积前景理论运用在城市内部的出行方式研究上,城际之间的交通方式很少有人研究,且城际之间的旅游交通方式研究更少。所以今后学者可以对上述问题进行深层次挖掘,希望本文的结论可以给未来学者了解研究进展提供参考。

参考文献

[1] McFadden D. Conitional Logit Analysis of Qualitative Choice Behavior [M]. In Zarembka(ed), Frontiers in Econometrics. New York:Academic Press,1974:105-142.

[2] D. Kahneman, A Tversky. Prospect Theory: An Analysis of Decision Under Risk. Econometrica. 1979, 47(2):263-291.

[3] D. Kahneman, A Tversky. 1992. Advances in Prospect Theory: Cumulative Representation of Uncertainty. Journal of Risk and Uncertatinty, 297-323.

[4] Rasouli, Soora, Timmermans, Harry. Applications of Theories and Models of Choice and Decision-Making Under Conditions of Uncertainty in Travel Behavior Research[J]. Travel Behaviour and Society, 2014, 1(3):79-90.

[5] Sierra M. G., Bergh J. C. J. M., Guasch C. M. Behavioural Economics, Travel Behavior and Environmental-Transport Policy[J]. Transportation Research Part D, 2015, 41:288-305.

[6] Wu J. J., et al. Bounded-Rationality Based Day-to-Day Evolution Model for Travel Behavior Analysis of

Urban Railway Network[J]. Transportation Research Part C,2013,31:73-82.
[7] Avineri E. A Cumulative Prosperc Theory Approach to Passengers Behavior Modeling: Waiting Time Paradox Revisited[J]. Journal of Intelligent Transportation System,2004,8(4):195-204.
[8] Abane A. Mode Choice for the Journey to Work Among Formal Sector Employee in Accra Ghana[J]. Journal of Fransport Geography,1993,1(4):219-229.
[9] 关宏志.非集计模型—交通行为分析的工具[M].北京:人民交通出版社,2004.
[10] 刘蓟,高璇.基于非集计模型的公交出行选择预测模型[J].公路,2010,5:136-139.
[11] 龚勃文.交通方式划分的非计模型及应用研究[D].长春:吉林大学,2007.
[12] Katsikopoulos K V,Fisher D L,Duse-Anthony Y,et al. Risk Attitude Reversals in Drivers' Route Choice When Range of Travel Time is Provided[J]. Human Factor,2002,44(3):466-473.
[13] Boger E A I,Zuylen H J. The Importance of Reliability in Route Choice in Freight Transport for Various Actors on Various Levels[C].//Strasbourg,France:Proceedings European Transport Conference,2004.
[14] 褚耀程.前景理论下路径选择行为参考点选取问题研究[D].成都:西南交通大学,2017.
[15] Sagi J S. Anchored Preference Relations[J]. Journal of Economic Theory,2006,130(1):283-295.
[16] Sepehr Ghader,Aref Darzi. Modeling Effects of Travel Time Reliability on Mode Choice Using Cumulative Prospect Theory[J]. Transportation Research Part C,2019,108:245-254.
[17] Simon H A. Behavioral Model of Rational Choice[J]. Quarterly Journal of Economics,1955,69(1):99-118.
[18] Xu Hongli,Lou Yingyan,Yin Yafeng. et al. A Prospect-Based User Equilibrium Model with Endogenous Reference Point and is Application in Congestion Pricing[J]. Transportation Research:Part B,2011,45(2):311-328.
[19] Jufen Yang, Guiyan Jiang. Development of an Enhanced Route Choice Model Based on Cumulative Prospect Theory[J]. Transportation Research Part C,2014,47:168-178.
[20] 田丽君,杨茜.基于累积前景理论的出行方式选择模型及实证[J].系统工程理论与实践,2016,36(7):1778-1785.
[21] 赵丽娜.考虑交通信息影响基于前景理论的居民出行选择行为研究[D].乌鲁木齐:新疆大学,2017.
[22] 徐爱庆,陈欣.基于累积前景理论的机场旅客出行决策行为分析[J].交通运输系统工程与信息,2018,18(6):14-21.
[23] S. Alger. Intrgrated Structure of Long-Distance Travel Behavior Models in Sweden[J]. Transportion Research Record:Journal of the Transportion Research Board,2003(1413):141-149.
[24] Rong Chang,J,Ryuichi. Commuter Departure Time Choice:A Reference-Point Approach[DB/OL].2004.
[25] Chao Yang, Binbin Liu. An Experimental Study on Cumulative Prospect Theory Learning Model of Travelers' Dynamic Mode Choice Under Uncertainty[J]. International Journal of Transportation Science and Technology,2017(6):143-158.
[26] 张波,林徐勋.基于累积前景理论的随机用户均衡交通分配模型[J].西南交通大学学报,2011,46(5):868-874.
[27] 殷蒙蒙.拥堵收费情境下通勤者出发时间选择行为研究[D].北京:北京交通大学,2018.
[28] 宗刚,曾庆华.基于时间价值的交通出行方式选择行为研究[J].管理工程学报,2020.34(3):142-150.
[29] Katsikopoulos,Fisher D. Risk Attitude Reversals in Drivers' Rouute Choice When Range of Travel Time is Provide[J]. Human Factors,2002,44(3):466-473.
[30] Jon RC. Dynamic Commmuter Departure Time Choice Under Uncertainty[J]. Transportation Research Part A,2008,42(5):774-783.

[31] HongliXu. A Decision-Making Rule for Modeling Travelers' Route Choice Behavior Based on Cumulative Prospect Theory[J]. Transportation Research Part C,2011,19:218-228.

[32] Wei Zhang, Ruichun He. Dynamic Route Choice Based on Prospect Theory[J]. Procedia-Social and Behavioral Sciences,2014,138:159-167.

[33] 刘玉印,刘伟铭.基于累积前景理论的出行者路径选择模型[J].华南理工大学学报,2010,38(7):84-89.

[34] 甘佐贤,陈红.基于累积前景理论的出行风险分析[J].武汉理工大学学报,2014,38(4):909-913.

[35] Long Cheng, Jonas De Vos. et al. Do Residential Location Effects on Travel Behavior Differ Between the Elder and Younger Adults[J]. Transportation Research Part D,2019,73,367-380.

[36] Xi Zhu, Feilong Wang. et al. Personalized Lncentives for Promoting Sustainable Travel Behaviors[J]. Transportation Research Part C,2019.

[37] Melvin Wong, Bilal Faroop. A Bi-Partite Generative Model Framework for Analyzing and Simulating Large Scale Multiple Discrete-Continuous Travel Behaviour Data[J]. Transportation Research Part C,2020, 110,247-268.

[38] 孟轶婷.陕西省旅游轨道模式的交通需求预测研究[J].经营与管理,2003,(3):114-117.

[39] 王希良,李芳,廉梦柯.基于结构方程模型的京津翼区域旅游交通行为分析[J].综合运输,2020,42(11):64-69.

[40] Zhou Xian, Li Sen. et al. Tourism Route Decision Support Based on Neural Net Buffer Analysis[J]. Procedia Computer Science,2017,107:243-247.

[41] Anranur Uwaisy M, Z. K. A. Baizal, Yusza Reditya M. Recommendation of Scheduling Tourism Routes using Tabu Search Method (Case Study Bandung)[J]. Procedia Computer Science,2019,157:150-159.

[42] Yan Han, Tiantian Zhang, Meng Wang. Holiday Travel Behavior Analysis and Empirical Study with Integrated Travel Reservation Information Usage[J]. Transportation Research Part A,2020,134:130-151.

[43] 黄莉苹,侯学钢.京津冀旅游交通一体化的协同发展刍议[J].城市发展研究,2015,22(1):11-15.

[44] 王兆峰,罗瑶.旅游驱动下的张家界交通运输响应机制分析[J].地理科学,2015,35(11):1397-1403.

[45] 郭建科,王绍博.哈大高铁对东北城市旅游经济联系的空间影响[J].地理科学,2016,36(4):521-529.

铁路路堑区域风吹雪作用下防雪栅对积雪重分布影响及相关因素分析

李鹏翔[1] 白明洲[2]

(1.北京交通大学土木建筑工程学院;2.北京市轨道工程重点实验室)

摘 要 在风吹雪易发区域,减少路堑内沉积雪量对维护交通安全运营具有重要意义。为了研究防雪栅不同形式对铁路路堑区域积雪重分布的影响,采用硅砂模拟雪颗粒进行了风洞试验,得到铁路路堑在防雪栅作用下雪粒重分布特征,并通过数值模拟得到了路基内外和轨道结构区域的积雪分布曲线,最后在现场布置并试验相同形式的三种栅栏,将试验结果与现场实测雪深进行对比。结果表明,3m深路堑

基金项目:国家自然科学基金面上项目(No. 41672339)。

的边坡顶部存在约20m长的侵蚀区域,防雪栅可以使雪粒沉积在栅栏两侧并减弱对路堑边坡顶部的侵蚀作用。相同初始风雪场条件下,防雪栅作用范围内雪量越多,路堑内及轨道结构区域雪量较少,双排3m高栅栏作用下所致的沉积雪量较单排高度3m和单排高度5m的栅栏可增多约50%和20%,多排栅栏作用下其两侧沉积雪量顺风向递减。路堑内产生积雪时会优先向着背风侧积雪平台堆积,在背风侧积雪平台达到承载上限后轨道结构处雪量会迅速增加。

关键词 铁路路堑 风吹雪 风洞试验 数值模拟 积雪重分布 沉积雪量

0 引 言

修建铁路路基会改变自然环境的地形地貌,其中路堑为较易产生积雪堆积的路基结构形式,形成的积雪会影响路基结构并影响交通运营安全。目前交通行业中对风吹雪作用的研究主要集中于公路区域,但公路与铁路路基形式存在较大不同,针对防雪栅作用下铁路路堑内积雪重分布和相关影响因素的研究较少。铁路路堑区域的风吹雪灾害已成为亟待研究和解决的重要科学和工程问题。

常用的风吹雪研究方法中,现场监测可以直接有效地获得风速、风向和积雪分布,但是现场监测难以控制风雪场条件,使得结果具有较大随机性。风洞试验可以有效控制风速、风向及雪量,在理想条件下对风吹雪作用导致的积雪重分布进行分析。Kind[1]、Owen[2]、Iversen and Aerodynamics[3]、Anno and Technology[4]、Isyumov、Mikitiuk and Aerodynamics[5]、Sato, Kosugi and Sato[6]等人对阈值风速、输雪率、跃移层等方面的研究为风吹雪风洞试验的理论奠定了基础,风洞试验所考虑的相似准则也主要与以上研究相关。现阶段风洞试验较多地针对风吹雪对特定结构物的影响,包括阶梯屋面[7,8]、大跨度平面荷载不均、建筑物风雪绕流[9]等。Flaga[10]从风雪场的初始条件、结构物的几何形式、积雪的重分布形态与影响因素、目标受力荷载分析等方面开展研究。但由于风洞试验花费高,对风雪场的测量手段有限,相似准则、模拟材料的选择与风荷载条件很大限度上影响了试验的结果。目前对路基内积雪分布及其防治措施研究的风洞试验目前也相对较少。

平坦区域下孔隙率在50%左右时防雪栅可发挥最大效益[11],而对于防雪栅与作用目标间的最优布置距离由于研究对象、栅栏形式、作用条件等因素的不同尚无统一定论。Tabler and Furnish[12]将应用在俄亥俄州公路旁防雪栅的作用分为四阶段,其中前三阶段下风侧沉积距离在10-20H,栅后雪深超过栅高后为第四阶段,距离为35H。

本文采用风洞试验与CFD相结合的方法研究了不同型式,防雪栅作用下铁路路堑区域的积雪分布,考虑铁路特有的道砟层、钢轨、轨枕组成的轨道结构区域,对影响流场和积雪重分布的因素进行研究。为分析防雪栅结构形式与初始计算条件的不同引起的积雪重分布特征。本文忽略地形因素的影响,所有试验均在平地模型上进行,并只考虑风向垂直于栅栏和路基线路方向的情况。

1 风洞试验

本文风洞试验在北京交通大学常温风洞室进行,该风洞为全钢直流风洞,风洞尺寸1.2m(宽)×1.5m(高)×10.0m(长),最大风速20m/s,试验流场的参考风速采用皮托管和微压计测量与监控。

为了保证风洞试验中流场为完全湍流,试验首先需要满足式(1):

$$\frac{u_{*t}^3}{2gv} > 30 \tag{1}$$

风洞试验过程必须遵循相似理论,风吹雪试验中相似准则主要包括颗粒的起动条件、运动过程与堆积形式三个方面,模型与原型之间的相似性主要在几何尺寸、速度、颗粒物理属性、试验时间方面。

目前相关风洞试验证明了忽略几何相似这一参数不会带来明显影响;速度相似是必须要满足的条件之一,由于阈值风速难以测量,在颗粒阈值摩擦速度和颗粒起动速度相似之间选择满足后者。

试验中颗粒的物理属性主要包括质量、密度和休止角,由于原型与模型颗粒几何尺寸相似,所以原型与模型颗粒的物理性质要尽量保证接近。

由于雪粒间存在黏力,且主要在风场的剪切作用下开始运动,所以本文选择考虑雷诺数而忽略弗劳德数。同时为了保证沉积状态的相似,时间比相似的准则也要满足。

试验选择粒径0.2mm的硅砂作为雪颗粒替代材料,细硅砂性质稳定,已在较多的风吹雪试验中得到运用和验证。

试验模型几何比例为1/30,路基与栅栏模型采用木板打造。路堑模型原型深3m,路基顶面宽8m,边坡坡度1:1.5,风吹雪区域铁路路堑特有的积雪平台宽5m;栅栏模型为10cm和16.6cm两种(对应原型高3m和5m),如图1所示。

图1 插板式防雪栅栏

2 数值模拟

2.1 模型的建立

采用基于欧拉方程的多相流数值模型表示流场与雪粒的运动[13],运动过程中雪粒表面的侵蚀与堆积采用 Naaim、Naaim-Bouvet、Martinez[14] 以及 Beyers、Sundsb、Harms、Aerodynamics[15] 提出的模型。湍流模型采用 RNG $k-\varepsilon$ 模型,其中 k 为湍流动能,ε 为湍流耗散率。

计算域内模型主要包括路堑与栅栏模型,模型尺寸与风洞试验中模型的原型一致。根据单线铁路轨道结构标准建立轨道模型,主要包括道砟层、轨枕、钢轨等结构。图2为数值模拟计算域。

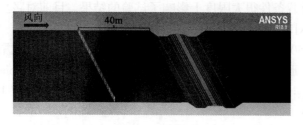

图2 计算域示意图

计算域内X轴为流场方向,为保证入流与出流风场的稳定发展,长度为栅栏与路基间最大距离80m的10倍,即800m,;Y轴是高度方向,为各工况下最高模型高度的10倍,50m;Z轴为线路方向长度,长100m。计算域边界条件采用速度入口、自由流出口,计算域顶面与侧面为对称条件,地面、栅栏与路堑模型为wall。

2.2 试验参数

首先计算定常流场,再加入雪颗粒计算非定常风雪场。定常流场的计算以残差小于1.0×10^{-6}为目标终止计算,大部分工况在经历3000~4000次左右的迭代即可达到收敛;非定常计算时间步长0.05s,总吹风时长1200s与风洞吹风时长相同。求解器采用基于压力修正的Simple算法,对流项的离散化采用二阶迎风格式。

非定常计算前在模型域内平铺体积分数为1的雪粒,其中雪粒密度139kg/m³,沉落速度0.2m/s[17],阈值摩擦速度0.2m/s[17],粒径200um[18]。

2.3 试验工况

在考虑现场雪量和栅栏占地面积的条件上,本文选定三种类型的防雪栅,孔隙率均为50%的插板式底部无空隙栅栏,三种栅栏下风侧沉积距离均处于Tabler四阶段分解中的前三阶段。栅栏参数如表1所示。

三种栅栏规格参数			表1
排数	与路基距离(m)	高度(m)	备注
1	40(13.3H)	3	以下简称"单-3"
1	80(16H)	5	以下简称"单-5"
2	40.80	3	以下简称"双-3"

本文采用控制变量法对研究目标进行分析,所有计算中路基形式保持不变,根据计算需求改变防雪栅结构形式参数。

3 试验分析与结果

图3为三种不同栅栏形式和无防雪栅作用下路堑内外横断面的归一化平均雪量系数。由图3可以看出,各工况下雪量在靠近入流处基本相等,雪深均处于阈值摩擦速度对应的高度。栅栏上风侧的影响范围约为20m,但影响范围内雪量变化存在差异。单-5栅栏上风侧雪量极值为0.784,双-3(第一排)、双-3(第二排)和单-3对应的栅栏上风侧雪量极值分别为0.695、0.610和0.720。同位置处高栅栏比低栅栏栅前产生更多积雪,多排栅栏对积雪的重分布作用顺着来流风向逐渐减弱,而同样型式的栅栏距入流面越远,栅前雪粒堆积越多。

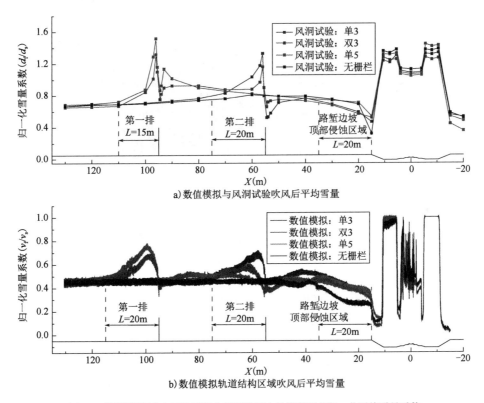

图3 不同栅栏形式和无防雪栅作用下路堑内外横断面的归一化平均雪量系数

以路堑外120m到路基边坡顶部之间的距离计算路堑外平均雪量,风洞试验中,单-3、单-5、双-3三种工况下路堑外雪量系数为0.883、0.953和0.919,较无防雪栅的雪量系数0.771增加14.52%、23.6%和19.7%,在数值模拟中三种工况路堑外雪量系数较无防雪栅工况增加12.9%、18.5%和15.9%。风洞试验和数值模拟中双-3作用所致的沉积雪量约是单-3和单-5的1.5倍和1.2倍,单-5作用所致的沉积雪量约是单-3的1.3倍。

由于钢轨与轨枕对雪粒运动直接的阻碍,雪粒会较多地堆积在钢轨与轨枕的迎风一侧,在路堑外无栅栏区域的平均雪量系数为0.45,轨道结构区域平均雪量系数0.514,即大于路堑外雪量14.22%以上。

单-3、单-5、双-3三种栅栏对应的轨道结构区域平均雪量系数分别为0.493、0.480、0.473,也是路堑外沉积雪量越多,路堑内与轨道结构区域的雪量越少。

4 实例分析

4.1 工程背景

为了验证三种栅栏形式下的积雪分布,以实际铁路路堑风吹雪易发区域为例,在前期自建气象站获得气象数据后,选定主风向与线路垂直的区域,布置三种形式的防雪栅平行于路堑,栅栏孔隙率、高度均与前述实验相同,三种栅栏共长500m。

4.2 现场积雪分布

对该区域的雪深测量在2018年12月一次降雪后,将降雪后测得平均雪深23cm作为初始雪量,并在3日后测量吹风后区域内雪深。

采用精度为0.1mm的钢板尺对现场雪深进行测量,测量范围顺主风向从路堑上风侧120m至下风侧50m,沿线路方向长度500m。以初始雪量为标准将实测雪深归一化后得到图4。为减小地形影响,忽略实际雪深测量中剧烈突变及明显不连续的雪深数据。

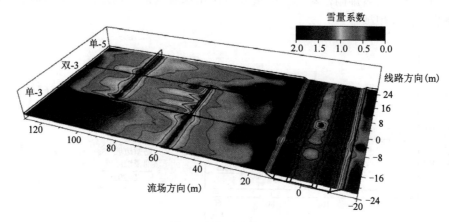

图4 现场雪量等高线图

路堑内外主要的沉积与侵蚀区域的分布与试验保持一致,在栅栏上风侧,不同栅栏区域雪深均从栅前15~20m的范围内开始逐渐向着防雪栅增多,在路堑边坡顶部边缘处出现侵蚀作用。三种栅栏栅前最大雪量系数由大到小依次为1.785(单-5)、1.585(单-3)、1.545(双-3,第一排)、1.379(双-3,第二排),排列顺序与室内试验一致。

在路堑内,无防雪栅区域路基顶面平均雪量系数为1.305,单-3、单-5和双-3三种栅栏对应的路基顶面平均雪量系数分别为1.233、1.193、1.185,分别减少了风吹雪所致的积雪量23.61%、36.72%、39.34%。室内试验时仅考虑了地面堆积雪粒向路堑内的运动,所以室内试验双排栅栏对路基顶面的雪量减少效果明显优于单排高栅栏,而实际环境中高栅栏对空中飘向路堑的雪粒有更明显的阻碍作用,所以双排低栅栏与单排高栅栏对路基顶面雪量的减少效果总体较为接近,但都明显多于单排低栅栏。

5 结 语

(1)多排栅栏作用下可使雪粒较多地沉积于路堑外,但顺风向下各排防雪栅作用效果递减。相同初始雪量条件下防雪栅作用范围内沉积雪量越大,路堑内雪量越少。可以按照栅栏高度与布置距离的相关性混合使用高低栅栏,使路堑外雪量沉积达到最大化。

(2)钢轨与轨枕的迎风侧易产生积雪堆积,轨道结构区域雪量在吹风后通常较路堑外平均雪量增大14.22%以上。

(3)实际防雪栅作用下,雪量大风速小的区域内多排栅栏对地面吹雪有较好的阻挡效果,而雪量小风速大的区域内高度较大的防雪栅对空中飘雪有较好的阻挡效果。

参考文献

[1] Kind R J. A Critical Examination of the Requirements for Model Simulation of Wind-Induced Erosion/Deposition Phenomena such as Snow Drifting [J]. Atmospheric Environment (1967), 1976, 10(3): 219-27.

[2] Owen. Saltation of Uniform Grains in Air [J]. Journal of Fluid Mechics, 1964, 20(02): 225.

[3] Iversen J D J J O W E, Aerodynamics I. Comparison of Wind-Tunnel Model and Full-Scale Snow Fence Drifts [J]. 1981, 8(3): 231-49.

[4] Anno Y J C R S, Technology. Applications of Anno's Modeling Conditions to Outdoor Modeling of Snowdrifts [J]. 1984, 9(2): 179-81.

[5] Isyumov N, Mikitiuk M J J O W E, Aerodynamics I. Wind Tunnel Model Tests of Snow Drifting on a Two-Level Flat Roof [J]. 1990, 36(1-3): 893-904.

[6] Sato T, Kosugi K, Sato A J A O G. Saltation-Layer Structure of Drifting Snow Observed in Wind Tunnel [J]. 2001, 32(1): 203-8.

[7] Tsuchiya M, Tomabechi T, Hongo T, et al. Wind Effects on Snowdrift on Stepped Flat Roofs [J]. 2002, 90(12): 1881-92.

[8] Zhou X, Hu J, Gu M J N H. Wind Tunnel Test of Snow Loads on a Stepped Flat Roof Using Different Granular Materials [J]. 2014, 74(3): 1629-48.

[9] Flaga A, Flaga L J C R S, Technology. Wind Tunnel Tests and Analysis of Snow Load Distribution on Three Different Large Size Stadium Roofs [J]. 2019, 160(APR.): 163-75.

[10] Delpech P, Palier P, Gandemer J J J O W E, et al. Snowdrifting Simulation Around Antarctic Buildings [J]. 1998, 74(98): 567-76.

[11] Bouvet F N, Naaim M, Michaux J L J N H, et al. Snow Fences on Slopes at high Wind Speed: Physical Modelling in the CSTB Cold Wind Tunnel [J]. 2002, 2(3/4).

[12] Tabler R D, Furnish R P. Benefits and Costs of Snow Fences on Wyoming Interstate 80 [M]. 1982.

[13] Tominaga Y, Mochida A, Okaze T, et al. Development of a System for Predicting Snow Distribution in Built-up Environments: Combining a Mesoscale Meteorological Model and a CFD Model [J]. 2011, 99(4): 460-8.

[14] Naaim M, Naaim-Bouvet F, Martinez H J A O G. Numerical Simulation of Drifting Snow: Erosion and Deposition Models [J]. 1998, 26: 191-196.

[15] Beyers J H M, Sundsb P A, Harms T M J J O W E, et al. Numerical Simulation of Three-Dimensional, Transient Snow Drifting Around A Cube [J]. 2004, 92(9): 725-47.

Deformation and Monitoring Analysis of Soil Rock Composite Foundation Pit under Moving Load

Tengfei Jiang[1]　Annan Jiang[1]　Mengfei Xu[1]　Xingsheng Li[2]

(1. Collage of Transportation Engineering, Dalian Maritime University;
2. China Railway First Bureau Group Second Engineering Co., Ltd)

Abstract　In order to explore the deformation law of soil rock composite foundation pit under moving load, this paper takes the soil element composite deep foundation pit project of suoyuwan South Station of Dalian Metro Line 5 as the research object, and based on the field monitoring data, analyzes the lateral deformation, vertical deformation and surrounding surface settlement of soil element composite deep foundation pit retaining structure during gantry crane moving load operation. The results show that: the deformation of the retaining structure and the surrounding ground settlement under the moving load of the gantry crane have obvious dynamic response, but they are all within a reasonable range, and the supporting system of the suspended foot pile is suitable for the soil rock composite foundation pit under the moving load. The research results can provide certain reference significance and reference value for similar deep foundation pit support design.

Keywords Foundation pit Soil rock combination Moving load Retaining structure Suspended pile Monitoring

0 Introduction

With the continuous increase of the scale of foundation pit construction, the soil rock composite foundation pit with the upper part of soil layer and the lower part of rock layer also increases. Due to the great difference between the overlying soil layer and the underlying rock layer in the properties of rock and soil, the form of foundation pit support and calculation model are not the same. The characteristics of deep foundation pit in soil rock dual structure stratum are significantly different from those of soil or rock foundation pit, which are mainly reflected in the following aspects: first, the foundation pit stratum is composed of rock mass and soil mass, and the physical and mechanical properties of the two media are quite different, so it is difficult to use a calculation model to analyze; second, the deformation of foundation pit is not only affected by the upper soil layer, but also the shape of the interface with soil and rock In addition, the deformation characteristics inside and outside the foundation pit do not have a lot of mature experience and rules to follow; third, the failure forms of foundation pit are diverse, which can be caused by the failure of the overlying soil layer, or by the failure of rock mass; fourth, the support types are more complex, and there are many problems Slope, pile anchor, diaphragm wall, anchor rib beam and so on, sometimes the bedrock surface fluctuates greatly, the stratum structure is changeable, and the support type in the same foundation pit often has the characteristics of diversification[1-3]. Therefore, for the foundation pit in composite stratum, the lower stratum is relatively hard, and the retaining pile is difficult to be embedded in the foundation. In order to ensure its economy and rationality, scholars at home and abroad have carried out corresponding research. Bai Xiaoyu et al.[4] carried out field monitoring analysis and Numerical Simulation Research on soil rock composite foundation pit under different steel support system and excavation depth by means of field monitoring and PLAXIS finite element simulation. Liu Hongjun et al.[5] analyzed the influence of the parameters of suspended foot pile on the deformation of foundation pit through numerical simulation. Hu ruigeng[6] analyzed the deformation of soil rock composite foundation pit supporting structure of adjacent buildings, and proposed a reasonable supporting system according to the requirements of horizontal deformation of surrounding environment of foundation pit. Li Tao[7] regarded the supporting structure as a spring member, analyzed the deformation of piles in soil rock composite stratum, and obtained the calculation method of deformation of retaining piles in soil rock composite foundation pit. Cai Jianjun[8] used the finite difference software to analyze the variation laws of the pile deflection displacement, the horizontal displacement and the vertical displacement of the pile top of the deep foundation pit retaining pile with different supporting structures, and obtained the best supporting method for the soil rock composite stratum.

In the construction of subway open cut foundation pit, the gantry crane is usually used as the lifting equipment and erection support, and the track of the gantry crane is usually set near the top of the row of piles, which has the advantages of small floor area, walking with load, and the gantry crane track is laid on the top of the pile crown beam in the back row of the foundation pit support, which is close to the foundation pit, Affect the safety of foundation pit, easy to affect the pile stress and deformation[9-10]. Shang Dayong [11] used a three-dimensional numerical model for the long and narrow subway station to analyze the related laws of the lateral deformation of the retaining pile and the surface settlement. Yang Xiaohua [12] analyzed the change trend of construction data under the load of gantry crane through on-site monitoring data, and obtained the rationality of foundation pit construction method. Yu Tao [13] analyzed the stress and deformation law of diaphragm wall and steel brace under short-term load. Kang Li [14] analyzed the deformation law of foundation pit under traffic load. Wang Zhijie [15] studied the deformation and mechanical problems caused by foundation pit unloading. Therefore, the influence of gantry crane moving load on the excavation construction of soil rock composite foundation pit is very important.

Combined with the field conditions and monitoring data of suoyuwan South Station of Dalian Metro Line 5, this paper analyzes the characteristics of soil settlement, lateral displacement of retaining pile and pile settlement around the soil rock composite foundation pit during gantry crane operation, and explores the deformation law of retaining structure of soil rock composite foundation pit under moving load, so as to provide the basis for the design and construction of soil rock composite foundation pit.

1 Project Overview and Excavation Scheme

The total length of the main structure of the foundation pit project is 150m, the width of the standard section is 25m, and the excavation depth is 27m. The station is a side station with three underground floors, and the width of one side platform is 7m. The main structure of the station adopts double column and three span frame structure, and the main structure and auxiliary structure of the station adopt open cut construction method. The retaining structure adopts the suspended foot pile + internal support system, and the standard section pile enters into the weathered rock at the bottom of the pit for about 3m. The foundation pit earthwork is excavated by the method of " longitudinal segmentation, vertical stratification, middle groove, slope on both sides". The rock stratum is constructed by blasting method, the excavator is used to dump the soil, and the dump truck is used to cooperate with the excavation. The main structure construction is longitudinally divided into 25m sections, and each section is constructed by flow process.

From top to bottom, the bored piles of the retaining structure of the station mainly pass through the following strata: miscellaneous fill, muddy silty clay, silty clay, strongly weathered dolomite and moderately weathered dolomite, with the thickness of 3m、6m、5m、6m and 7m respectively. The bottom plate is in moderately weathered dolomite.

In the construction of foundation pit, the gantry crane is used to transport the equipment across the foundation pit. The load of the gantry crane is 30t and the rated load is 10t. considering the most unfavorable lifting state of the gantry crane, that is, the state of eccentric compression on one side.

The foundation pit adopts 1000mm thick diaphragm wall as enclosure structure and steel support as internal support, as shown in Fig. 1. A total of three internal supports are arranged, with section size of 700×1200mm and spacing of 4m. The excavation of the foundation pit adopts the layered excavation scheme, and the excavation is supported at the same time. The excavation depth of each layer is determined according to the support height difference, and the bottom of the support elevation is taken as the excavation boundary of each layer. The specific excavation process is divided into five stages: ①in the first stage, the excavation is conducted to 3m below the ground, and the first internal support is constructed; ②In the second stage, excavation is 10m below the ground, and the second internal support is constructed; ③In the third stage, the excavation is carried out to 15m below the ground, and the third internal support is constructed; ④In the fourth stage, it is excavated to 21m below the ground level; ⑤In the fifth stage, the excavation is carried out to the design elevation of the bottom of the foundation pit (27m below the ground). In order to effectively ensure the safety of the overall construction of the foundation pit, timely understand the impact of foundation pit construction on the surrounding environment, implement the whole process monitoring in the whole process of construction, and dynamically adjust the overall construction scheme according to the monitoring warning value.

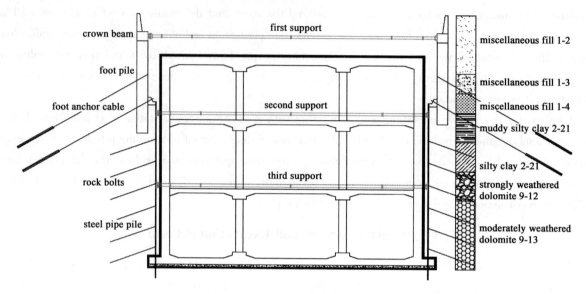

Fig. 1 Section of Retaining Structure for Foundation Pit Excavation

2 Monitoring Scheme

Three monitoring points CX1、CX2、CX3 and CX4、CX5、CX6 are set in the long side and short side of the foundation pit from the middle to the corner brace of the foundation pit. The length of the inclinometer pipe is 27m, and the inclinometer data is extracted every meter in the vertical direction. Three monitoring points ZD1、ZD2、ZD3 and ZD4、ZD5、ZD6 are arranged from the long side and short side of the foundation pit to the corner brace of the foundation pit. Surface subsidence monitoring points DB1、DB2……DB9 is arranged above the long side of the foundation pit, 5m、10m、15m、20m、25m、30m、40m、50m and 60m away from the foundation pit. The layout of monitoring points is shown in Fig. 2.

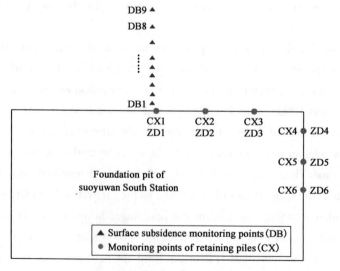

Fig. 2 Layout Plan of Monitoring Points

3 Monitoring Data Analysis

3.1 Lateral Deformation Analysis of Retaining Structure

Under the moving load of gantry crane, the lateral deformation of retaining structure of soil rock composite foundation pit in different excavation stages is shown in Fig. 3. It can be seen that when the foundation pit is excavated in the shallow soil, the lateral deformation of the retaining structure of the foundation pit is similar to that of the cantilever beam, and the lateral deformation of the upper part near the surface is the largest, while the direction finding deformation of the lower part is smaller due to the embedded effect of the rock and soil.

There are obvious differences in the deformation behavior of the long side and short side of the foundation pit in different excavation stages. Taking the first excavation as an example, the maximum deformation of CX1 in the middle of the long side of the foundation pit is 6.21mm, while the deformation of CX4 in the middle of the short side of the foundation pit is only 2.8mm. When the excavation reaches the bottom of the first support of the foundation pit, the first steel support has not yet played its role. At this time, the lateral deformation difference above the retaining structure of the foundation pit is completely determined by the longitudinal, that is, the horizontal relative stiffness of the retaining structure. The horizontal distance from the midpoint of the long side of the foundation pit to the corner of the foundation pit is 75m, while the horizontal distance from the midpoint of the short side of the foundation pit to the corner of the foundation pit is 12.5m, the former is 6 times of the latter, and the longitudinal stiffness of the retaining structure of the long side of the foundation pit is obviously weaker than that of the short side. The results show that the lateral deformation of the retaining structure is related to the relative restraint of the retaining structure along the length of the wall (horizontal direction). The longer the length of the wall is, the closer the deformation behavior of the retaining structure is to the plane strain state. In the subsequent excavation stage of foundation pit, the depth of the maximum direction finding deformation point of the wall gradually develops from the top of the wall to the deep soil, that is, the maximum lateral deformation point of the wall gradually moves down. After the excavation to the bottom of the pit, the maximum lateral deformation of the mid point retaining structure on the long side of the foundation pit is 17.89mm, and the maximum lateral deformation of the mid point retaining structure on the short side of the foundation pit is 12.02mm.

After the excavation of foundation pit, comparing the deformation values of the measured points of the retaining structure, it can be seen that the lateral deformation of the retaining structure of foundation pit has obvious three-dimensional space effect. The deformation near the center symmetry plane of the foundation pit is large, while the deformation near the corner of the foundation pit is small. This is due to the arch effect of the soil and the strong mutual support effect of the retaining structure in the two directions of the corner of the foundation pit The effect limits the lateral deformation of the retaining structure at the corner of the foundation pit.

3.2 Vertical Deformation Analysis of Retaining Structure

Under the action of moving load, the vertical displacement and deformation of monitoring points of foundation pit retaining structure at different excavation depths are shown in Fig.4.

It can be seen from Fig. 4 that when the excavation depth is less than 12m, the retaining structure will sink; when the excavation depth is greater than 12m, the retaining pile will be lifted up, so 12m can be regarded as the critical excavation depth of retaining pile sinking and lifting. This is because when the excavation depth of foundation pit is shallow, the lateral unloading effect of soil is obviously stronger than the vertical unloading effect, and the side wall friction of soil to retaining pile will be weakened due to the lateral unloading, so the retaining structure will sink under its own weight; with the increase of excavation depth, the vertical unloading effect of soil in the pit is more and more obvious, which leads to the rebound effect of soil in the pit After excavation to the bottom of the pit, the monitoring point ZD1 on the long side of the foundation pit is raised by 4.67mm, and the midpoint ZD4 on the short side of the foundation pit is raised by about 3.58mm.

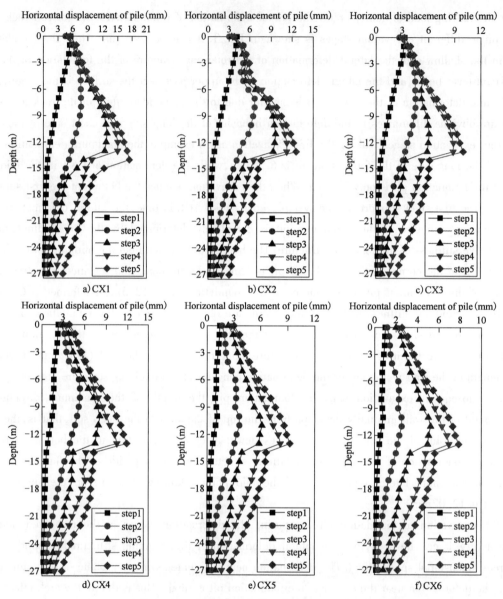

Fig. 3 Horizontal Displacement of Piles at Different Excavation Stages

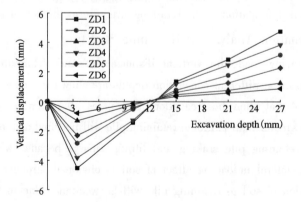

Fig. 4 Vertical Displacement of Retaining Pile

In addition, the vertical deformation of retaining pile also has spatial effect, and the vertical deformation of the long side of the foundation pit is significantly larger than the vertical uplift deformation of the short side of the foundation pit. Because of the large overall stiffness of the retaining pile, the vertical deformation of the same section of the retaining structure along the depth direction is less different.

3.3 Analysis of Surface Subsidence

The change of surface settlement of foundation pit in different excavation stages under the influence of gantry crane moving load is shown in Fig. 5.

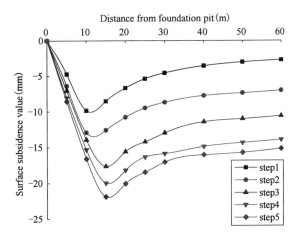

Fig. 5 Variation of Surface Settlement at Different Excavation Stages

After excavation to the bottom of the pit, the maximum settlement of the foundation pit is 22.1 mm; with the increasing of the soil excavation depth, the maximum ground settlement position is gradually away from the retaining structure. When the soil excavation depth is 15m, the position of the maximum ground settlement point does not change, and the influence range of ground settlement tends to a certain value with the increase of the distance from the edge of the foundation pit.

4 Conclusions

By analyzing the field deformation monitoring data of the foundation pit of suoyuwan South Station of Dalian Metro Line 5 under moving load, the variation rules of the lateral displacement, vertical displacement of the retaining structure and the surface settlement of the adjacent soil with the excavation of the foundation pit are obtained

(1) Under the action of gantry moving load, the lateral displacement of the pile in the soil layer changes significantly, while the horizontal displacement at the rock socketed place decreases sharply due to the self stability of the rock layer.

(2) With the increase of the excavation depth, the lateral deformation of the middle part of the retaining pile is larger after the excavation to the bottom of the pit due to the moving load, and the surface settlement is the largest at 15m away from the edge of the foundation pit.

(3) Under the action of gantry crane moving load, the monitoring data of lateral displacement, vertical displacement and surrounding surface settlement of soil rock composite foundation pit pile are in a reasonable range, which indicates that the supporting method of foot pile is reasonable and effective.

(4) In the construction of soil rock composite foundation pit, the additional displacement caused by gantry crane moving load should be considered, and grouting and other measures should be taken to assist

reinforcement, so as to ensure the smooth progress of the project.

References

[1] Dayong Shang. Deformation and Stability of the Deep Foundation Pit in Metro Station in Geotechnical Composite Stratum [J]. Journal of Beijing Jiaotong University, 2020, 44(06):25-33+43.

[2] Cheng Chen, Honglin Yang. Study on the Calculation Method of Preloading Axial Force of Anchor Bolt in the Support System of "Composite Foundation Pit" of Soil and Rock [J]. Tunnel construction (Chinese and English), 2020, 40(10):1441-1447.

[3] Zhiying Lu, Xiaohuan Sun. Design of Support Structure of Deep Foundation Pit in Composite Stratum [A]. Beijing Mechanical Society. Proceedings of 26th Academic Annual Meeting of Beijing Mechanical Society [C]. Beijing Mechanical Society: Beijing Mechanical Society, 2020:5.

[4] Xiaoyu Bai, Mingyi Zhang, Yang Yuan. Deformation Analysis of the Footed Pile of the Foundation Pit Under the Action of Moving Load [J]. Geotechnical Mechanics, 2015, 36(04):1167-1173, 1181.

[5] Honghong Liu, Guilin Zhai, Jianguo Zheng. Numerical Analysis of Foundation Pit Supporting Structure with Anchor and Double Row Piles in Geotechnical Composite Stratum [J]. Journal of Geotechnical Engineering, 2012, 34(S1):103-107.

[6] Ruigeng Hu, Hong Liuhong, Zhaoyao Wang, et al. Deformation Analysis of the Support Structure of the Combined Foundation Pit of Coastal Soil and Rock Near the Building [J]. Journal of engineering geology, 2020, 28(06):1368-1377.

[7] Tao Li, Wen Shao, Liming Zheng, et al. Calculation Method of Deformation of Deep Foundation Pit Supporting Pile in Rock Soil Composite Stratum [J]. Journal of China University of Mining, 2019, 48(03):511-519.

[8] Jianjun Cai, Yan Xie, Shuchen Li, et al. Multi Layer Support Method and Numerical Simulation Research of Deep Foundation Pit Under Complex Conditions [J]. Engineering Mechanics, 2018, 35(02):188-194.

[9] Jinghui Wang, Lian Tang, Menglong Shan. Research on the Effect of External Load on Foundation Pit Slope Support Based on Rationality[J]. Hans Journal of Civil Engineering, 2020, 09(05).

[10] Junsheng Chen, Chen Lin, Shuzhuo Liu, et al. Study on Supporting Structure Performance of Deep Soft Soil Foundation Pit near Sea under Waves, Tides, Vibration, and Unbalanced Loads[J]. Advances in Civil Engineering, 2020.

[11] Dayon Shang. Influence of Gantry Crane Moving Load on Deformation of Deep Foundation Pit of Subway Station[J]. Journal of Safety and environment, 2021, 21(01):172-179.

[12] Xiaohua Yang. Deformation Monitoring and Analysis of Foundation Pit in Soil Rock Composite Stratum Under Gantry Crane Moving Load [J]. Railway Architecture, 2018, 58(09):84-87.

[13] Tao Yu, Yan Liu, Shiqi Zhu, et al. Analysis of the Influence of Short-Time Load on Deep Foundation Pit [J]. IOP Conference Series: Earth and Environmental Science, 2021, 634(1).

[14] Li Kang, Yanwei Wang, Jianhao Cao, et al. Optimization Design of Deep Foundation Pit Support Scheme under Traffic Dynamic Load[J]. IOP Conference Series: Earth and Environmental Science, 2021, 632(2).

[15] Zhijie Wang, feicong Zhou, Ping Zhou, et al. Theoretical Study on Deformation of Existing Station Based on Unilateral Excavation and Unloading of Large Foundation Pit with Strong Proximity [J]. Journal of Rock Mechanics and Engineering, 2020, 39(10):2131-2147.